The Best of
PARIS

Edited by
André Gayot

Also available

The Best of France
The Best of Germany

Adaptation and Translation: Sheila Mooney; *With the contribution of:* Pauline Ridel;
Coordination: Sophie Gayot

Published by RAC Publishing, RAC House, P O Box 100, South Croydon, CR2 6XW

© Gault Millau, Inc. 1993

This book is sold subject to the condition that it shall not, by way of trade or otherwise, be lent, resold, hired out or otherwise circulated without the publisher's prior consent in any form of binding or cover other than that in which it is published.

All rights reserved. No parts of this work may be reproduced, stored in a retrieval system or transmitted by any means without permission. Whilst every effort has been made to ensure that the information contained in this publication is accurate and up-to-date, the publisher does not accept responsibility for error, omission or misrepresentation. All liability for loss, disappointment, negligence or other damage caused by reliance on the information contained in this guide, or in the event of bankruptcy, or liquidation, or cessation of trade of any company, individual or firm mentioned, is hereby excluded.

A CIP catalogue record for this book
is available from the British Library

ISBN 0-86211-241-9

International Advertisement Managers: P. M. C., 5bis avenue Foch, 94160 Saint-Mandé, France, tel.: (33-1) 43 28 20 20, fax: (33-1) 43 28 27 27

Printed and bound in France by Aubin Imprimeur

CONTENTS

■ INTRODUCTION 5

■ RESTAURANTS 9

Gault Millau's penchant for observing everything that's good (and bad) about food and the dining experience is what made these guides so popular in the first place. Here you'll find candid, penetrating and often amusing reviews of the very, very best, the undiscovered and the undeserving. Listed by arrondissement of the city, including a section on the suburbs. Includes the Toque Tally.

■ HOTELS 99

A hotel guide to suit every taste. Where to spend a few days treated as royalty. Where to get the most for your money. Where to find the finest service, the most charm, the best location.

■ CAFES & QUICK BITES 131

Paris's palate may be found in its restaurants, but its heart and soul are found in its many cafés, wine bars and *salons de thé*. Where to hang out with a coffee and a copy of *Libération*, where to refresh yourself with a snack or a glass of wine.

■ NIGHTLIFE 153

A tour of some of the city's most amusing and exciting bars and nightspots, with discerning commentary on what goes on in Paris after dark. Where to go and where to avoid.

■ SHOPS 163

Discover in these pages why Paris is a shopper's dream. Where to buy anything and everything.

■ ARTS & LEISURE 281

Where to discover the lively arts in Paris, from avant-garde galleries to internationally acclaimed museums. How to enjoy your leisure time, indoors and out.

■ OUT OF PARIS 309

Everything you need to know to set off for a wonderful day (or three) in the country. Includes restaurants, hotels and sights in Paris's environs.

■ BASICS 329

Everything you need to know about getting around and about like a Parisian.

■ MÉTRO MAP 340

■ INDEX 342

INTRODUCTION

PARIS

CITY OF LIGHT

Paris is alive in the collective fantasies of the Western world. From the crêpe-stand–studded rue Saint-André-des-Arts, which snakes through the Latin Quarter, to the silk-wrapped glamour and classic chic of the avenue Montaigne, to the Marché d'Aligre, which looks as if it was lifted from downtown Algiers, Paris is one of those throbbing capitals that churns out legends—and spawns myths—as if they were going out of fashion. New clubs, shops, restaurants and even museums are opening up all the time. Hence the need for a guide such as this. With more than 11 million inhabitants tearing along underpasses on the Périphérique, winging into busy airports and commuting to ultramodern, futuristic satellite business centres, Paris is among the world's most up-to-date cities, yet nothing *seems* to have changed in decades, perhaps centuries. The familiar face of central Paris changes slowly, indeed almost imperceptibly. The bustling *grands boulevards* are still lined with giant sycamores that spread over crowded cafés. *Bouquinistes* go on hawking their books along the Seine's noisy *quais*. The open-air markets and speciality food shops in practically every *quartier* disgorge their wares on teeming pavements. And gardens lifted from Impressionist paintings, like the Luxembourg or Parc Monceau, continue to fill daily with armies of au pairs pushing babies in coach-built prams down carefully raked gravel lanes. No wonder Paris is the world's most popular short city break and is visited by the British more often than anywhere else outside the UK. Its artistic wonders are the envy of much of the world but a visit to Paris should not be about taking off as many sights and museums as possible. There are great museums all over the world but nowhere else can you absorb simple Parisian pleasures such as sitting at a pavement café or strolling by the Seine.

Since Day One, about 5,000 years ago, Parisian life has flowed along the Seine. Paris's twenty arrondissements spiral outward clockwise from the Ile de la Cité, its geographical and historical hub. The Cité, where Notre-Dame rears its Gothic bell towers, was the fortified capital of the Parisii, a Gallic tribe overthrown by Julius Caesar circa 52 B.C. Then came the Gallo-Roman period, which lasted several centuries. Although this period left practically no monuments (save the baths at Cluny and the Arena, both in the Latin Quarter), the city was laid out once and for all. In 508 Clovis made Paris the capital of his empire. Later still Hugues Capet, the founding father of the

INTRODUCTION

Capetian dynasty, made Paris (i.e., the Ile de la Cité) his capital. And here we are, 1,000 years later, and the Cité is still an island, detached in every sense from the life of the Left and Right Banks and from the nearby Ile Saint-Louis, famous nowadays as much for its ice cream as for its seventeenth-century architecture. Only place Dauphine, with its lovely triangular garden, antiques shops and brasseries, affords a backward glance of old Paris.

As long ago as 1208, the cathedral schools of Paris were united into a single university on the Left Bank and as you might expect, students flooded into the neighbourhood. They have remained there ever since. From Jussieu in the fifth arrondissement to Saint-Germain-de-Prés in the sixth—commonly though inaccurately known as the *Quartier Latin*—the narrow, twisting streets are thronged by a decidedly young, casual crowd. So the concentration of late-night cafés, clubs, art galleries and bistros comes as no surprise. To many, the Latin Quarter is synonymous with The Real Paris: Saint-Michel, Saint-Germain, Odéon.

The Latin Quarter's sometimes snooty neighbour—still part of the Left Bank but altogether a different world—is the fashionable seventh arrondissement. The key words here are: Eiffel Tower, Invalides, Ecole Militaire and Palais Bourbon, plus at least a dozen ministries (don't get flustered when cabinet ministers and visiting dignitaries descend with their bullet-proof retinues). Some of Paris's finest restaurants, shops and hotels line the seventh's wide, handsome avenues.

At about the time the Latin Quarter was sprouting around the *civitas philosophorum*, the less-than-humble *Ville* on the Right Bank was lifting its patrician nose. Starting in the Middle Ages, merchants and the middle classes settled into the *bourgs* around the villas and palaces of the nobility. Over time, the Louvre, the Tuileries, the Palais-Royal, place Louis-XV (now place de la Concorde), place Vendôme and place des Victoires became the landmarks that set the tone of the Right Bank. In the eighteenth and nineteenth centuries the well-bred and better-heeled built their major theatres there: the Opéra-Comique and Comédie-Française, the Palais Garnier Opéra and many others. They were soon flanked by the Grand Palais and Petit Palais. Napoléon's Arc de Triomphe crowns this ensemble. Now, as then, the Champs-Elysées and surrounding grand avenues and boulevards of the first, eighth and sixteenth arrondissements are the best place to take a stroll in your finest attire or shop for diamonds before dining at the legendary Maxim's or Lucas-Carton, to name but two. However, in this area tennis shoes are equally at home. The Champs-Elysées—on every tourist itinerary—has also become the haunt of the *banlieusards*. These youngsters from the suburbs take the RER express subway to Etoile and spend hours at the Virgin mega-music store, or at the dozens of franchise *restos* and multiscreen cinemas strung along the avenue.

But many a Right Bank devotee will steer you off the thoroughfares and into the maze of nineteenth-century *passages*—passage des Panoramas or Galerie Vivienne, for example—scattered around the second, ninth and tenth arrondissements. Chock-a-block with boutiques, restaurants, food and wine shops and even hotels, these covered emporium-passageways are buzzing with life all year round, not just during a rainstorm. The soulful, industrious *faubourgs*—former working-class neighbourhoods lying beyond the seventeenth-century city gates, now central Paris—whose higgledy-piggledy buildings snake out from the grand boulevards, are all too often overlooked. Likewise the rag-trade area in the second and third arrondissements. A cross between Bangkok and lower Manhattan, it is a colourful hive of incessant activity and a great place to buy ready-to-wear and casual clothing direct from the factory.

The nearby Marais district, from the Centre Pompidou to the Musée Picasso and east to the place de la Bastille, used to be up-and-coming. Now it's up, up and away, a Parisian showcase of gentrification with a sky-high boutique-per-block ratio. Such venerable giants as the Brasserie Bofinger—the oldest and one of the handsomest in town—stand firm in the ebb and flow of new (and often excellent) restaurants and tea rooms. The Musée Carnavalet and Hôtel de Sully have been scrubbed and buttressed. The harmonious place des Vosges (1605) has been trimmed and returfed, its newly plumbed fountains splashing to the great delight of locals and tourists alike. The Marais is also home to France's distinguished and ancient Jewish population. Take a walk down the rue des Rosiers and discover any number of delicatessens and kosher food emporiums.

On the other side of the place de la Bastille, big bucks and revolutionary zeal (funnelled in for the 1989 Bicentenary bash) have worked their magic on the neighbourhood. The new Opéra de la Bastille is the turbo-charged motor that is transforming the faubourg Saint-Antoine, rue de la Roquette, rue de Lappe and rue de Charonne into the latest haven for trendies, artists and restaurateurs with a flair for the profitably offbeat. High rents are becoming the rule in this former working-class neighbourhood.

Above all, Paris is a city for walking, and this may be your best way to see Montmartre, although the newly refurbished funicular will carry those with sore feet to the top. Nowadays young night hawks haunt the notoriously naughty place Pigalle, where strip joints and porno shops are daily giving way to late-night bars and discos. Speaking of dancing, the old Moulin Rouge still stands at the foot of Montmartre, a beacon for the nostalgic for whom the cancan remains the essence of Parisian nightlife. But just a little farther up the hill, the steep steps and winding byways of Montmartre keep a village atmosphere alive in this most sophisticated of cities. Don't despise the droves of sightseers and would-be Picassos packed onto place du Tertre, a traditional stronghold of artists. Instead, duck into that wedding cake of a church, Sacré-Cœur, and most of all admire the stupendous view of Paris laid out at your feet.

Ernest Hemingway called this sprawling metropolis "a moveable feast". Food—both spiritual and material—is indeed paramount here, from snails and scallops served with a cool Sancerre to duck breast in a green-peppercorn sauce washed down with a robust Bordeaux. George Orwell was down and

INTRODUCTION

out in Paris, dreaming of a rare *steack frites*, while Henry Miller was discovering the tropics in brasseries around the seamy place Clichy. A gourmand at heart, Lawrence Durrell loved Paris because here he felt "on a par with a good cheese or a bad one". Gault Millau, a household word in France and respected internationally, has joined forces with the RAC, one of Europe's leading motoring organisations, to provide you with this comprehensive and authoritative guide to the Best of Paris. Crammed with vivid insights and thorough, honest evaluations written in a witty, entertaining style, it will open the doors for you to the infinite variety of pleasures and treasures in Paris. Armed with this inside information you will join the select ranks of chose "in the know". We hope the pages that follow will inspire you to seek—and help you to find—the best Paris has to offer.

The Publisher

RESTAURANTS

INTRODUCTION	10
ABOUT THE REVIEWS	11
TOQUE TALLY	13
FIRST ARRONDISSEMENT	14
SECOND ARRONDISSEMENT	18
THIRD ARRONDISSEMENT	20
FOURTH ARRONDISSEMENT	21
FIFTH ARRONDISSEMENT	23
SIXTH ARRONDISSEMENT	26
SEVENTH ARRONDISSEMENT	31
EIGHTH ARRONDISSEMENT	35
NINTH ARRONDISSEMENT	46
TENTH ARRONDISSEMENT	48
ELEVENTH ARRONDISSEMENT	49
TWELFTH ARRONDISSEMENT	51
THIRTEENTH ARRONDISSEMENT	53
FOURTEENTH ARRONDISSEMENT	53
FIFTEENTH ARRONDISSEMENT	57
SIXTEENTH ARRONDISSEMENT	62
SEVENTEENTH ARRONDISSEMENT	68
EIGHTEENTH ARRONDISSEMENT	76
NINETEENTH ARRONDISSEMENT	78
TWENTIETH ARRONDISSEMENT	79
THE SUBURBS	79

INTRODUCTION

A MANY-SPLENDOURED EXPERIENCE

For food-lovers, the lure of Paris's *haute cuisine* is at least as powerful as the temptations of *haute couture* for followers of fashion, or *haute culture* for the high-minded. In fact, we know of one lady who planned her entire trip abroad around a dinner reservation (made months in advance, of course) *chez* top chef Joël Robuchon, so compelling was her craving for his langoustines aux morilles. Nor is it rare for people who have never even set foot in the French capital to know the names and specialities of many of the city's fashionable chefs. Dining out in Paris is a many-splendoured experience. Elegance reigns here to a degree not often attained in the restaurants of other cities; Le Grand Véfour, Maxim's and Lucas-Carton, for instance, are classified as historic buildings, with interiors of unparalleled beauty. These and the city's other top establishments also offer distinguished service: from the maître d'hôtel and the sommelier to the lowliest waiter, the staff are stylish and professional, a real *corps d'élite*. And the food, on a night when a chef like Alain Senderens is particularly inspired, can be memorable, even thrilling, a joy to the eye and a feast for the palate.

If your tastes (or finances) lead you to prefer less exalted establishments, we urge you to study our reviews of Paris's many marvellous bistros, brasseries and more down-to-earth restaurants, where prices are—usually—far lower than in *grands restaurants* and where the atmosphere veers more towards relaxed informality. Parisians are fiercely loyal to their local bistros where they regularly tuck into familiar, traditional dishes with pronounced regional accents (Gascon, Alsatian, Provençal)—if you go in for local colour, those are the places to try. Brasseries are perfect when you want to eat just a single dish rather than a multicourse meal (but don't try ordering only a salad at Lipp!). Brasseries tend to stay open late, and generally do not require reservations.

RESTAURANT ETIQUETTE

• At top Parisian restaurants, you must **reserve a table** far in advance—at least three weeks, sometimes two or three months for such places as Robuchon and Taillevent. Reservation requests from abroad are taken much more seriously if they are accompanied by a deposit of, say, 300 francs (about £40). Tables at less celebrated spots can be reserved one or two days ahead, or even on the morning of the day you wish to dine. If you cannot honour your reservation, don't forget to call the restaurant and cancel.

• **Men should wear** a jacket and tie in any Parisian restaurant of some standing. **Women are well advised to dress up**, wearing trouser suits only if they are the high fashion variety. Luxury restaurants do not take the question of dress lightly, so be forewarned. At more modest spots, more casual wear is perfectly acceptable (but it's best to avoid tracksuits or running shorts and skimpy tops).

• When you go to a top restaurant, let the **head waiter** suggest some possibilities from the menu (you'll find that they quite often speak English, though they always appreciate an attempt on the customer's part to speak French). Likewise, the **sommelier**'s job is to give expert advice on the choice of a suitable wine—regardless of price. Don't be afraid to seek his opinion, or to tell him your budget.

• **Dinner service** begins around 8 p.m. in most Paris restaurants. People start appearing in the finer restaurants about 9 p.m. **Luncheon is served** between 12:30 p.m. and 2 p.m. In addition to the standard carte, or **à la carte** menu, you will frequently be offered a choice of all-inclusive fixed-price meals called **menus**, which are generally very good value. Also common in finer restaurants is the many-course sampling menu, or **menu dégustation**, a good (though not always economical) way to get an overview of a restaurant's specialities. Dishes that change daily, known as **plats du jour**, are usually reliable, inexpensive and prepared with fresh ingredients (whatever the chef found at the market that morning).

• French law stipulates that the **service charge**, usually 15 per cent, must always be included in the menu prices. You are not obliged to leave an additional tip, but it is good form to leave a little more if the service was satisfactory.

• The **opening** and **closing times** we've quoted are always subject to change, particularly during holiday periods, so be sure to phone first.

• Many chefs have the bad habit of **changing restaurants frequently**, which means a restaurant can become mediocre or even bad in the space of a few days. Chef-owned restaurants tend to be more stable, but even they can decline: a successful owner may be tempted to accept too many customers, which can result in a drop in quality. Should this be your experience, please don't hold us responsible.

ABOUT THE REVIEWS

RATINGS & TOQUES

Gault Millau ranks restaurants in the same manner as French schools mark their pupils: on a scale of zero to 20, 20 representing unattainable perfection. The rankings reflect *only* the quality of the cooking; décor, service, reception and atmosphere do not influence the rating, though they are explicitly commented on in the reviews. Restaurants that score 13 points and above are distinguished with toques (chef's hats), according to the following table:

RESTAURANTS – INTRODUCTION

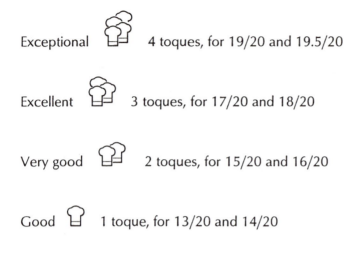

Exceptional — 4 toques, for 19/20 and 19.5/20

Excellent — 3 toques, for 17/20 and 18/20

Very good — 2 toques, for 15/20 and 16/20

Good — 1 toque, for 13/20 and 14/20

Toques in red denote restaurants serving modern, inventive cuisine; toques in white denote restaurants serving classic or traditional food.

Keep in mind that these ratings are *relative*. One toque for 13/20 is not a very good rating for a highly reputed (and very expensive) temple of fine dining, but it is quite complimentary for a small, unpretentious restaurant.

PRICES

At the end of each restaurant review, prices are given—either **A la carte** or **Menus** (fixed-price meals) or both. A la carte prices are those of an average meal (a first course, main course, dessert and coffee) for one person, including service and a half bottle of a relatively modest wine. Lovers of the great Bordeaux, Burgundies and Champagnes will, of course, have higher bills to pay. The menu prices quoted are for a complete multicourse meal for one person, including service but excluding wine, unless otherwise noted. These fixed-price menus often give customers on a budget the chance to sample the cuisine of a restaurant they could not otherwise afford to visit.

> The prices in this guide reflect what establishments were charging at the time of going to press.

TOQUE TALLY

Red toques: Modern cuisine
White toques: Traditional cuisine

The numbers following each restaurant refer to its arrondissement or suburban town.

Four Toques (19.5/20)

Lucas-Carton (Senderens), *Paris 8th*
Robuchon, *Paris 16th*

Four Toques (19/20)

L'Ambroisie, *Paris 4th*
Arpège (Alain Passard), *Paris 7th*
Taillevent, *Paris 8th*
Michel Rostang, *Paris 17th*
Guy Savoy, *Paris 17th*
Vivarois, *Paris 16th*

Three Toques (18/20)

Apicius, *Paris 17th*
Le Bourdonnais, *Paris 7th*
Jacques Cagna, *Paris 6th*
Carré des Feuillants, *Paris 1st*
Le Duc, *Paris 14th*
Faugeron, *Paris 16th*
Le Divellec, *Paris 7th*
Les Trois Marches, *Versailles*

Three Toques (18/20)

La Tour d'Argent, *Paris 5th*
La Vieille Fontaine, *Maisons-Laffite*

Three Toques (17/20)

Les Ambassadeurs, *Paris 8th*
Amphyclès, *Paris 17th*
A. Beauvilliers, *Paris 18th*
Chiberta, *Paris 8th*
Clos Longchamp, *Paris 17th*
Drouant, *Paris 2nd*
Duc d'Enghien, *Enghien*
Jean-Claude Ferrero, *Paris 16th*
Le Manoir de Paris, *Paris 17th*
Morot-Gaudry, *Paris 15th*
Au Petit Montmorency, *Paris 8th*
Le Pré Catelan, *Paris 16th*
Sormani, *Paris 17th*

Three Toques (17/20)

Gérard Besson, *Paris 1st*
Lasserre, *Paris 8th*

1st arrondissement

10/20 Joe Allen
30, rue P.-Lescot
42 36 70 13

Open daily until 1 a.m. Bar: until 2 a.m. Terrace dining. Air cond.

This small Franco-American club is a fine place to sink a few beers and chat up a tall, dark, handsome stranger. Try the chef's salad, chili burger, barbecued spare ribs and apple pie.

A la carte: 150 F.

Armand au Palais-Royal
6, rue de Beaujolais
42 60 05 11

Closed Sat. lunch, Sun. & Aug. 15-30. Open until 11:30 p.m. Air cond.

Chefs Jean-Pierre Ferron and Bruno Roupie cook in an intelligent, sometimes even ingenious style that draws stockbrokers (at lunchtime) and theatre-goers (in the evening) to these handsomely renovated former stables (which once belonged to the maréchal-duc de Richelieu) facing the gardens of the Palais-Royal. Try the sweetcorn crêpe with warm foie gras, skate with cabbage or a plump Bresse chicken, and follow with one of the delicate chocolate desserts. The cellar holds some notable Bordeaux.

A la carte: 320-530 F. Menus: 170 F (lunch only, except holidays), 240 F (dinner only), 290 F (weekdays dinner, Sat. and holidays).

Gérard Besson
5, rue Coq-Héron
42 33 14 74

Closed Sat. & Sun. Open until 10:30 p.m. Air cond.

Gérard Besson may not make front-page news like some other chefs, probably because he is too busy turning out masterpieces of classic cuisine. A disciple of Chapel, Garin and Jamin, Besson has brought his talent for elegant simplicity to such dishes as oyster flan with saffron-mussel cream, brioche of scrambled eggs with prawns, and warm rabbit pâté in flaky pastry. What might be a pompous exercise in style in less skilled hands here becomes light, flavourful and modern.

With his feet thus solidly set in tradition, Gérard Besson makes successful sorties into brave new territory: divinely moist sea bream baked in a crust of coarse salt with fresh herbs and topped with a red pepper coulis; a fragrant fumet de coquilles Saint-Jacques dotted with plump pasta dumplings; fabulous sweet-and-sour pigeon (in a reduced sauce with a hint of quince and cardamom); or sweetbread ragoût in a walnut-bread croûte.

The décor is dignified, despite some coy touches: bleached-wood furnishings, antique paintings, and vitrines filled with silver-plated carafes. Excellent desserts (chocolate sorbet, blancmange with strawberry coulis and almond milk). The service is less stiff now that Alain Delaveyne supervises the staff. The wine cellar boasts some 50,000 bottles, all of them costly.

A la carte: 600-750 F. Menu: 270 F (lunch only).

12/20 Brasserie Munichoise
5, rue D.-Casanova
42 61 47 16

Closed Sat. lunch, Sun., Dec. 24-Jan. 30 & Aug. Open until 12:30 a.m. Private room: 20.

A cosy little brasserie that serves good grilled veal sausages and one of the best choucroutes in Paris. Excellent Hacker-Pschorr beer on tap.

A la carte: 200-300 F.

Carré des Feuillants
Alain Dutournier
14, rue de Castiglione
42 86 82 82,
fax 42 86 07 71

Closed Sat. lunch (and dinner in July), Sun. & Aug. Open until 10:30 p.m. Private room: 14. Air cond.

You can take Alain Dutournier out of his native Landes but you cannot take the *Landais* out of Dutournier. Together with his wife Nicole, Dutournier regularly nips down to his birthplace in south-west France to sniff the cèpes and stimulate his appetite. Paris? The restaurant's sophisticated setting of stone and pale *trompe-l'œil* woodwork might as well be in Gascony.

Here you spread the terrine of foie gras on a slice of warm cornmeal bread and savour vigorous yet elegant specialities such as warm pâté de cèpes enhanced by a fresh-tasting parsley jus, garbure (an earthy cabbage soup) with goose confit, free-range capon with a galette de cèpes, and a venison and foie gras terrine with cranberry jelly. Desserts include an exceptionally fine vanilla ice cream which is made to order, and an ethereal feuillantine sablée garnished with hazelnuts and glazed chestnuts.

Jean-Guy Loustau, the able wine waiter, dispenses in equal measure smiles, good counsel and marvellous bottles (with a marked preference for vintages from the Pays d'Oc). Alas, as one might expect, there is nothing rustic about the prices.

A la carte: 600-800 F. Menus: 250 F (lunch only, except holidays), 550 F (except holidays).

Red toques signify modern cuisine; white toques signify traditional cuisine.

1st arrondissement – RESTAURANTS

Les Cartes Postales
7, rue Gomboust
42 61 02 93

Closed Sat. lunch, Sun., Dec. 23-Jan. 6 & July 31-Aug. 22. Open until 10:15 p.m. Air cond.

Blow-ups of photographs hang on the beige-and-white walls of this small, pretty, flower-filled restaurant. Yoshimasa Watanabe, disciple of the great Robuchon, creates outstanding cuisine with just the right pinch of the exotic. Since his arrival several years ago the restaurant has counted success upon success. Try his deliciously caramelised crab cake with grapefruit vinaigrette, spiced foie gras with broccoli, or the extraordinary Robuchon-style crème brûlée with vanilla and cinnamon. The cellar is improving, but still has some way to go.

A la carte: 350-400 F. Menus: 145 F (weekdays lunch), 345 F (wine incl.), 295 F.

12/20 Le Caveau du Palais
17-19, pl. Dauphine
43 26 04 28

Closed Sat. (except June-Sept.), Sun. & last 2 wks. of Dec. Open until 10:30 p.m. Terrace dining.

The good, solid cooking (grilled andouillette, shin of veal with basil) is served in a charming place Dauphine cellar divided down the centre by a wine bar.

A la carte: 275-350 F.

Bernard Chirent
28, rue du Mont-Thabor
42 86 80 05

Closed Sat. lunch & Sun. Open until 10:30 p.m. Private room: 15. Air cond.

A few years back, chef Bernard Chirent moved from that high-society haunt, Castel, to open his own restaurant here on the ground floor of the Hôtel du Continent. The sober décor is brightened by a touch of pinkish beige. Famous for his sauces and his peerless prawns in a herb-scented stock, Chirent also excels with frogs' legs, boned young pigeon perfumed with tarragon, and an airy millefeuille—all richly deserving of a second toque. The wine list is modest but includes several interesting finds (Arbois, Rully, Saumur); some selections are available by the glass. The first prix-fixe menu (including wine) is excellent.

A la carte: 300 F and up. Menus: 170 F and 250 F (wine incl.).

11/20 Le Comptoir
37, rue Berger
40 26 26 66

Open daily until 1 a.m. Terrace dining.

Sensational prices for tasty tapas (Spanish-style chicken, cold grilled vegetables, spinach-and-ricotta dumplings) served in a lively bistro atmosphere.

A la carte: 150 F.

L'Espadon
Hôtel Ritz
15, pl. Vendôme
42 60 38 30

Closed Aug. Open daily until 11 p.m. Garden dining. Air cond. No pets. Heated pool. Valet parking

From the humble ham sandwich at 90 francs to the rack of lamb sprinkled with chopped parsley at 450 francs (well, it is for two), the grand Ritz style shines through. As one is entitled to expect, the service is among the finest in the world, the clientele prodigiously prosperous. Owner Ali Fayed, ever fond of show, is breaking records for "ritziness" with his grandiose thermal baths, squash courts and rooftop heliport (for *deus ex machina* arrivals to the imperial suite—60,000 francs a night). From the most sumptuous kitchen in France, award-winning chef Guy Legay conjures with increasing grace and inventiveness delightful dishes such as red mullet with tapenade, crispy-skinned sea bass and ris de veau meunière. The 120,000-bottle wine cellar is under the direction of virtuoso Georges Lepré.

A la carte: 700-900 F. Menus: 330 F (lunch only), 550 F (dinner only).

La Fermette du Sud-Ouest
31, rue Coquillière
42 36 73 55

Closed Sun. Open until 10:30 p.m.

Christian Naulet has returned to his native Périgord, leaving a void behind him. But Jacky Mayer, the Fermette's new owner, has remained faithful to the restaurant's Gascon tradition and has kept the same chef. Try the perfect pork grattons, or the excellent duck breast with cèpes and garlicky potatoes. The menu is a bit short, but the welcome is warm.

A la carte: 200-280 F. Menu: 80 F (weekdays lunch only).

Goumard-Prunier
9, rue Duphot
42 60 36 07

Closed Sun. & Mon. Open until 10:30 p.m. Private room: 25. Air cond.

Jean-Claude Goumard has transferred his restaurant to a celebrated Belle Epoque site (note the new address), but he still treks out at 3 a.m. to the Rungis market to net the very best sole and turbot, the fattest lobsters and prawns, for his chef Georges Landriot—fish and crustaceans so perfect that no flambé or croûte is ever allowed to mar them. A pinch of turmeric to enliven the shellfish fricassée; a drop of veal juice with soy sauce to accompany the braised sole; precious little butter all around: in short, nothing that might denature the fresh taste of the sea.

Other dishes include the enormous Brittany prawns baked in their shells, or red mullet dabbed with virgin olive oil and basil. Dessert brings excellent chocolate fondant with coffee sauce. Little remains, alas, of the original décor by Majorelle (the only vestiges are in the toilets); and the less said about the present interior, the better.

A la carte: 500-700 F.

12/20 Le Grand Louvre
At the museum entrance,
under the pyramid
40 20 53 41,
fax 42 86 04 63

Closed Tues. Open until 10 p.m. Private room: 100. Air cond.

Something is cooking under I.M. Pei's glass pyramid. In contrast with the chilly décor, the Louvre's restaurant, directed by the Gascon chef and culinary adviser André Daguin, serves reasonably priced country fare from the south-west: walnut-studded pigeon terrine, hot foie gras with grapes, duck confit with spiced honey, prune nougat glacé. Non-stop service.

A la carte: 210-280 F.

Le Grand Véfour
17, rue de Beaujolais
42 96 56 27,
fax 42 86 80 71

Closed Sat., Sun. & Aug. Open until 10:15 p.m. Private room: 22. Air cond. Valet parking.

Guy Martin got off to a rough start here. Nearly every food critic in town greeted Martin's arrival at Le Grand Véfour with a cutting review. Well, we decided to give the fellow a chance to settle in before sitting in judgment, and for our money, Martin's cuisine is worth a solid double toque. Spiced baked prawns, truffled potato terrine, Bresse pigeon enveloped in cabbage leaves and a delicious, lightly smoked Chateaubriand prepared "à la ficelle" (poached in stock) are just a few of the reasons we're so enthusiastic.

As always, the magic of the Grand Véfour also resides in the fact that were every table empty you would still dine in perfect contentment, free to admire the exquisite surroundings that Jean Taittinger's good taste and family fortune have restored to their former glory: carved boiserie ceilings, graceful painted allegories under glass, plush carpeting, tables covered with white linen and black and gold Directoire chairs. The dining rooms evoke memories of such immortals as Napoléon, Jean Cocteau, Victor Hugo and Colette, who once lounged on these red velvet banquettes in the soft glow of the Palais-Royal gardens.

The service, under the expert and charming guidance of Béatrice Ruggieri, is as elegant as the clientele. The à la carte bill is astronomical, but the fixed-price lunch menu—which offers a wide variety of dishes—is fair value: With a modest Bordeaux, you'll spend about 400 francs and walk away with an unforgettable memory.

A la carte: 700-1,000 F. Menu: 305 F (lunch only).

A la Grille Saint-Honoré
15, pl. du Marché-St-Honoré
42 61 00 93,
fax 47 03 31 64

Closed Sun., Mon., Aug. 7-23 & Dec. 24-31. Open until 10:30 p.m. Private room: 30. Terrace dining. Air cond.

The eyesore (a multi-storey concrete garage) that currently mars the centre of the place du Marché Saint-Honoré will soon be replaced by a glass gallery designed by Riccardo Bofill. Thus transformed, this historic market square should flourish once again.

No surprise then that Jean Speyer, formerly cramped in an eighth-arrondissement basement restaurant, recently took over what had been a shabby corner bistro and gave it a new lease on life. In the sparkling pink-and-grey décor Speyer serves tasty, imaginative "market cuisine": roast veal kidneys with anchovies, pumpkin and mussel soup, crispy mackerel with onion fondue, blanquette of young rabbit. The desserts and affordable wines are Speyer's strongest suit.

A la carte: 320-380 F. Menus: 180 F, 230 F.

11/20 Lescure
7, rue de Mondovi
42 60 18 91

Closed Sat. dinner, Sun., Aug. & Dec. 24-Jan. 1. Open until 10:15 p.m. Terrace dining. Air cond.

Tried-and-trusted French fare served in a feverishly *gai Paris* bistro atmosphere. Sample the hearty veal sauté or duck confit. Game dishes are highlighted in the autumn and winter hunting season.

A la carte: 150 F. Menu: 98 F (wine incl.).

11/20 Le Louchebem
10, rue des Prouvaires
42 33 12 99

Closed Sun. Open until 11:30 p.m. Terrace dining.

Carnivores can count on satisfaction here: huge portions of grilled or roasted beef, lamb and pork, tripe, pigs' trotters and the like are served in a butcher's shop décor (rather cold with all those tiles). Modest, well-chosen wine list.

A la carte: 200 F. Menu: 85 F.

 La Main à la Pâte
35, rue St-Honoré
45 08 85 73

Closed Sun. Open until 12:30 a.m. Private room: 30. Garden dining. Air cond.

The plastic plants and conservatory décor may be ghastly, but the pasta from Annita Bassano's kitchen (10 eggs per kilo of pasta) is *squisita*. So too are the rich polenta alla bolognese, the osso buco and one of the finest Italian wine cellars in Paris.

A la carte: 300-350 F. Menus: 114 F (weekdays lunch only), 176 F.

 Mercure Galant
15, rue des Petits-Champs
42 96 98 89

Closed Sat. lunch & Sun. Open until 10:30 p.m. Private room: 35.

The service in this grand old restaurant is charming, the décor elegant and the cuisine better than ever. Chef Pierre Ferranti cooks with admirable brio, producing such delectable dishes as gratin of just-caught lobster, tournedos de lotte with herby butter, warm oysters with endive fondue, and for dessert, the famous "mille et une feuilles". Interesting cellar with a wide range of Bordeaux; smoothly impeccable service.

A la carte: 380-530 F. Menus: 250 F (lunch only), 280 F and 400 F (dinner only).

 La Passion
41, rue des Petits-Champs
42 97 53 41

Closed w.-e., holidays & July 24-Aug. 24. Open until 10:30 p.m.

Private room: 10. Air cond. No pets.

Gilles Zellenwarger's *trompe-l'œil* and woodwork décor is rather more elegant than passionate. And his rigorously correct cuisine enhanced by subtle sauces shows great respect for tradition. Notable progress is evident in his young pigeon with cabbage and foie gras, truffled blanc de volaille en vessie, and sole with fresh mint. Excellent fixed-price menus, improved wine list, with several selections available by the glass.

A la carte: 220-300 F. Menus: 170 F, 200 F, 360 F.

 Chez Pauline
5, rue Villedo
42 96 20 70

Closed Sat. dinner, Sun. & Aug. 1-17. Open until 10:30 p.m. Private room: 16. Air cond.

André Genin has taken over from his father Paul and slapped a fresh coat of paint on this wonderful old bistro, with its huge mirrors, glowing woodwork, zinc bar and red-velvet banquettes. An almost imperceptible touch of modernity has crept into the menu: old-time specialities like young rabbit in white-wine aspic, or daube of pork cheek now flank steamed fish and fresh pasta with truffles and foie gras. The cellar holds memorable Burgundies, and there is an excellent selection of coffees.

A la carte: 400-450 F. Menu: 190 F (lunch only).

12/20 **Au Pied de Cochon**
6, rue Coquillière
42 36 11 75

Open daily, 24 hours. Private room: 50. Terrace dining. Air cond.

The atmosphere is at once feverish and euphoric in this Les Halles institution, renowned for serving thundering herds of pigs' trotters (85,000 annually) and a ton of shellfish every day of the year.

A la carte: 250-300 F.

 Pierre au Palais-Royal
Au Palais-Royal
10, rue de Richelieu
42 96 09 17

Closed Sat., Sun., holidays & Aug. Open until 10 p.m.

Country delights from the four corners of France fill the lovely handwritten menu of this traditional bistro. The cuisine is in the reliable hands of Roger Leplu, who uses top-quality ingredients to produce such pillars of French cooking as boudin with onions, mackerel in cider and bœuf à la ficelle, as well as stuffed cabbage bourguignonne or sheep's tripe and trotters à la marseillaise. Superb desserts.

A la carte: 300-350 F. Menu: 250 F (wine incl.).

12/20 **La Pomme**
18, pl. Dauphine
43 25 74 93

Closed Wed. off-season & Dec. 20-Jan. Open until 10:30 p.m. Terrace dining.

This restaurant may become the apple of your eye. La Pomme, a modest and charming little establishment on the leafy place Dauphine, serves good, honest food (fish soup, tête de veau, pot-au-feu).

A la carte: 200-250 F.

 Le Poquelin
17, rue Molière
42 96 22 19,
fax 42 96 05 72

Closed Sat. lunch, Sun. & Aug. 1-20. Open until 10:30 p.m. Private room: 8. Air cond.

Regulars rejoice in the unfailing inventiveness of Michel Guillaumin, a chef renowned for his desserts (the honey ice cream and nougat with apricot coulis are exquisite). Guillaumin lightens and updates traditional recipes such as wild-mushroom feuilleté and freshwater perch cooked in Saint-Pourçain wine. There are two worthwhile fixed-price menus and many fine wines this side of 150 francs.

A la carte: 300-350 F. Menus: 154 F, 185 F.

11/20 La Providence
6, rue de la Sourdière
42 60 46 13

Closed Sat., Sun. & holidays. Open until 11 p.m. Air cond.

Hearty Alsatian specialities such as presskopf and baeckeoffe are godsends for avid appetites. Bustling *winstub* atmosphere.

A la carte: 170 F. Menus: 78 F and 109 F (lunch only), 119 F (dinner only).

Saudade
34, rue des Bourdonnais
42 36 30 71

Closed Sun. Open until 10:30 p.m. (w.-e. 11 p.m.). Air cond. No pets.

Skilfully prepared Portuguese dishes have a pinch of nostalgia for Old Lusitania: marinated roast suckling pig alentejana, cod (bacalhau) and robust boiled-beef cozido. Magnificent Portuguese wines and vintage ports.

A la carte: 220-320 F.

La Terrasse Fleurie
Hôtel Inter-Continental
3, rue de Castiglione
44 77 10 44,
fax 44 77 10 94

Closed Dec. 20-30. Open until 10:30 p.m. Private room: 15. Terrace dining. Air cond. No pets. Valet parking.

Dine amid flowers year round in the palatial décor of the Inter-Continental Hotel's candlelit terrace. The service is excellent and the cuisine surprisingly fine. Try chef Jean-Jacques Barbier's lightly smoked lotte in a warm vinaigrette, or the saddle of young rabbit with potato and celery gratin. The prices (unsurprisingly) are pretty stiff.

A la carte: 400-550 F. Menus: 270 F (lunch only), 450 F (dinner only).

Chez la Vieille
37, rue de l'Arbre-Sec
42 60 15 78

Open for lunch only. Closed Sat., Sun. & Aug. No pets.

The obsessive media cult that surrounds chef Adrienne Biasin hasn't corrupted her culinary talents. A regular circle of bankers, press barons and show-business personalities fill this tiny rustic-kitsch restaurant and worship Adrienne's legendary pot-au-feu, hachis Parmentier and sublime stuffed tomatoes.

A la carte: 300-350 F.

12/20 Willi's Wine Bar
13, rue des Petits-Champs
42 61 05 09,
fax 47 03 36 93

Closed Sun. Open until 11 p.m.

Mark Williamson, alias Willi, is an extremely knowledgeable British wine expert. He has wisely reverted to a low-price policy and simple cooking. The food served in the smallish dining room (whiting with olives en croustade, ragoût d'encornets printanier, Stilton served with a glass of cream sherry) now makes a better match for the wonderful Côtes-du-Rhônes and other wines on offer. If you can't get a table, join the customers sitting elbow-to-elbow at the polished wood bar.

A la carte: 220-300 F. Menu: 148 F.

Plan to travel? Look out for the other RAC GaultMillau Best of guides to France and Germany, and for the RAC French Hotel and Holiday Guide and the RAC European Hotel Guide plus maps and atlases of France and Europe.

2nd arrondissement

12/20 Café Runtz
16, rue Favart
42 96 69 86

Closed Sat., Sun., holidays, 1 wk. in May & 3 wk. in Aug. Open until 11:30 p.m. Private room: 45. Air cond.

This is an 1880s Alsatian *winstub* whose classic fare ranges from foie gras to choucroute or potato salad with pork knuckle. Good French Rhine wines.

A la carte: 180-240 F.

14 Le Céladon
Hôtel Westminster
15, rue Daunou
47 03 40 42,
fax 47 60 30 66

Closed Sat., Sun., holidays & Aug. 1-29. Open until 10 p.m. Private room: 40. Air cond. Valet parking.

Tastefully lit, flower-filled and impeccably elegant dining rooms in what is possibly the loveliest *restaurant de palace* in Paris form the perfect setting for a romantic dinner. Le Céladon's remarkable young chef creates delicious and resolutely refined dishes such as scrambled eggs with sea urchins, grilled coquilles Saint-Jacques, smoked breast of duck and cumin-spiced sweetbreads with chicory. Desserts are generally less successful, but we liked the crisp lemon millefeuille.

A la carte: 450-600 F. Menu: 300 F.

La Corbeille
Hôtel Cyrnos
154, rue Montmartre
40 26 30 87

Closed Sat., Sun. & holidays. Open until 10:30 p.m. Private room: 20. Air cond.

When he abandons his penchant for "virtuoso" turns and manneristic touches, chef Jean-Pierre Cario excels at such delightfully simple dishes as cold oysters with cabbage, monkfish bourride, or a perfect filet de bœuf à la ficelle. We heartily approve of the Provençal lilt he has given his latest menu. Comfortable, lavishly lacquered 1930s décor. Superb wine cellar.

A la carte: 300-350 F. Menus: 280 F (dinner only), 150 F and 220 F.

12/20 Coup de Cœur
19, rue St-Augustin
47 03 45 70

Closed Sat. lunch & Sun. Open until 10:30 p.m. Private room: 60. Air cond.

The reception, service and cuisine are thoroughly professional. Appetising entrées (spinach salad with strips of smoked duck breast) lead into tasty "neo-bourgeois" main courses (pigeon gros sel) and the nice little house Bourgueil is a bargain. The monochromatic postmodern décor was designed by Philippe Starck.

A la carte: 180-230 F. Menu: 170 F (wine incl.), 135 F.

Delmonico
39, av. de l'Opéra
42 61 44 26

Closed Sat., Sun. & Aug. Open until 10 p.m. Private room: 14. Terrace dining. Air cond.

The new manager of this old standby has lightened the décor and livened up the atmosphere. In the kitchen, Alain Soltys (also a recent arrival) prepares fresh, modern dishes (artichoke and truffle salad, brill in puff pastry with sea-urchin cream) which we far prefer to the sad (veal chop flamed in Calvados) and distressing (kidneys cooked in whisky) creations formerly on offer. The service is uniformly charming. And note that a fast pre-theatre supper or business lunch can be served in 45 minutes.

A la carte: 250-350 F. Menu: 148 F.

Drouant
18, rue Gaillon
42 65 15 16,
fax 49 24 02 15

Open daily 10:30 pm (12:30 a.m. at Le Café). Private room: 50. Air cond. Valet parking.

Louis Grondard has descended from his eyrie at the Jules Verne (second storey of the Eiffel Tower), bringing with him well-deserved laurels and a repertoire of modern gastronomic classics. After his Robuchon-like success on high, Grondard is bidding fair to keep the 200 seats at Drouant (restaurant, Café, and salons) packed year-round. Appropriately enough, the Goncourt literary prize is awarded here each year, and the monthly literary luncheons of the jury are held in a handsome room with charming Art Deco pastiche décor that features a splendid wrought-iron and marble staircase. The masterly touch of the great sauce-maker is evident in Grondard's baby turbot with a beurre blanc redolent of lemon grass, the long-simmered curried suckling pig, or the pigeon in a potato crust. Few palates would fail to appreciate desserts like spiced vanilla crème brûlée, croquant aux marrons, and honey-gentian ice cream.

The Café Drouant is the haunt of businessmen in search of reasonably priced bourgeois cuisine.

The wine cellar's rare bottles at 5,000 francs are flanked by a selection of fine wines priced between 100 and 200 francs. Efficient, workmanlike service.

A la carte: 600-850 F. Menus: 320 F (weekdays lunch only), 200 F (at Le Café; dinner only).

12/20 Gallopin
40, rue N.-D.-des-Victoires
42 36 45 38

Closed Sat. & Sun. Open until 11:30 p.m. Terrace dining.

The brassy Victorian décor is a feast for the eyes. The food at Gallopin isn't bad either. Try the house speciality: sole à la crème. Jolly service.

A la carte: 220-300 F. Menu: 150 F (dinner only, wine incl.).

11/20 Le Grand Colbert
2, rue Vivienne
42 86 87 88

Closed Aug. Open daily until 1 a.m. Air cond.

Classic brasserie cuisine (oysters and shellfish, andouillette ficelle, bœuf gros sel and poached chicken) served in a freshly restored historic monument with frescoes and ornate plasterwork, brass railings and painted glass panels.

A la carte: 200-250 F.

11/20 La Movida
14, rue M.-Stuart
42 21 98 60

Closed Sat., Sun. & Mon. Open until 2 a.m. Air cond.

Tattooed guitarists incite wild flamenco dancers barely visible through the haze of cigarette smoke. Unspectacular tapas, astonishingly good Spanish sweets.

A la carte: 150-200 F.

12/20 Pierre
A la Fontaine Gaillon
Pl. Gaillon
42 65 87 04

Closed Sat. lunch, Sun. & Aug. Open until 12:30 a.m. Private room: 30. Terrace dining. Air cond.

The menu is long, but short on ideas. You're better off sticking to the plats du jour, which are always ably prepared. The delightful old hôtel particulier décor was recently restored, and the grand terrace's fountain is spectacular when lit at night.

RESTAURANTS – 3rd arrondissement

A la carte: 250-400 F. Menu: 160 F (dinner only).

Pile ou Face
52 bis, rue N.-D.-des-Victoires
42 33 64 33
Closed Sat., Sun., holidays, Dec. 24-Jan. 1 & July 26-Aug. 22. Open until 10 p.m. Private room: 20. Air cond.

A pretty, if ruinously expensive, little establishment run by three associates proud of their success and determined to keep standards high. The stockbroker lunch crowd gives way in the evening to a pleasant mix of bourgeois provincials and foreigners. The first floor's red-and-gold décor, with *fin de siècle* touches, perfectly matches chef Claude Udron's cuisine. Sometimes slightly off the mark, but mostly on target, Udron scores with delicious duck liver coated with gingerbread crumbs, roast pigeon with truffled oil and the many other dishes on the "special" menu, which showcases the restaurant's farm products (rabbit, poultry). A very fine wine cellar.

A la carte: 400-450 F.

Le Saint-Amour
8, rue de Port-Mahon
47 42 63 82
Closed Sat. lunch, Sun. & holidays. Open until 10:15 p.m. Air cond.

Impeccable service and a simple, fresh, generous cuisine distinguish Le Saint-Amour. The new chef has a pronounced penchant for fish and seafood: try, for example the tasty Marennes oysters, or the turbot baked in a salt crust and served with a chervil-scented beurre blanc. Concise but interesting wine list.

A la carte: 300-370 F. Menus: 145 F (dinner only), 165 F (lunch only).

La Taverne du Nil
9, rue du Nil
42 33 51 82
Closed Sat. lunch, Sun. (except dinner in Aug.). Open until 11 p.m. Air cond.

The setting is rather down-at-heel but lightened and brightened by pink upholstery and *naïf* paintings representing the River Nile. Straightforward Lebanese country dishes (hummus with meat and pine nuts, mezes, keftedes with onions and parsley, delicious garlicky grilled chicken) at exceptional prices. Belly dancers sometimes shake things up at the weekends.

A la carte: 180-220 F. Menus: 45 F and 60 F (lunch only, except holidays), 120 F and 165 F (wine incl.), 80 F.

3rd arrondissement

Ambassade d'Auvergne
22, rue du Grenier-St-Lazare
42 72 31 22,
fax 42 78 85 47
Closed 15 days in summer. Open until 10:30 p.m. Private room: 35. Air cond.

Each visit to this embassy brings the same delightful experience. The Petrucci tribe's hospitality knows no bounds. The décor, featuring timbers hung with hams, is worn but authentic; the atmosphere very convivial.
Authenticity is equally present in the house specialities: real country ham, cabbage and Roquefort soup, boudin with chestnuts, cassoulet of lentils from Le Puy, legendary sausages served with slabs of delicious bread, duck daube with fresh pasta and smoky bacon, and so forth. Good desserts (try the aumônière à l'orange, or the mousseline glacée à la verveine du Velay).

The cellar is vast and boasts some little-known Auvergnat wines (Chanturgue, Saint-Pourçain) in a wide range of prices.

A la carte: 220-300 F.

L'Ami Louis
32, rue du Vertbois
48 87 77 48
Closed July 12-Aug. 30. Open until 11 p.m.

Despite its improbably shabby décor (note the peeling, brownish walls), L'Ami Louis jealously claims the title of "the world's costliest bistro". It is certainly dear to the hearts of the tourists, suicidal over-eaters and skinny fashion models who battle to book a table at this famous *lieu de mémoire*. The heirs of old Père Magnin carry on the house tradition of huge portions, but the ingredients are not so choice as they once were. And nowadays the sauces are sometimes thick or sticky, the chips greasy and the meat overcooked. What a joy, though, to sit down to a Gargantuan serving of foie gras fresh from the Landes, giant escargots de Bourgogne, whole roast chickens, the incomparable gigot of baby Pyrénées lamb. The desserts are insignificant, the cellar respectable.

A la carte: 700-750 F.

12/20 ### Le Bar à Huîtres
33, bd Beaumarchais
48 87 98 92
See *14th arrondissement*.

12/20 ### Chez Janou
2, rue R.-Verlomme
42 72 28 41
Closed Sat. & Sun. Open until 11 p.m. Terrace dining.

An honest little old-fashioned bistro with turn-of-the-century décor and a pleasant terrace. The neighbourhood (place des Vosges/Bastille) has gone up-market and so have Janou's prices, but the country cooking (Jerusalem artichokes tossed in hazelnut oil, duck confit) still tastes authentic. Improved wine list.

A la carte: 180-250 F. Menu: 160 F.

Market culture

A stroll round a Parisian *street market* is one of the best ways to see, smell and sample French food. Start out early to admire the carefully constructed stacks of fruits and vegetables—and stick around for bargains when stallholders shut up shop at about 1 p.m. The speed with which they dismantle their stalls and pack up their produce is a spectacle in itself. Most markets are held twice a week, some three times a week, and there are 57 sites to choose from. For contrasting views of Parisian shopping and eating habits, visit the resolutely up-market Saint-Didier market in the 16th arrondissement (go down the rue Mesnil from place Victor-Hugo) held on Tuesday, Thursday and Saturday, and the lively, multicultural market on the place de la Réunion in the 20th arrondissement on Thursday or Sunday.

11/20 Chez Jenny
39, bd du Temple
42 74 75 75

Open daily until 1 a.m. Private room: 120. Terrace dining. Air cond.

This grand, historic monument of a brasserie, with lovely marquetry upstairs, is on the upswing. Many good "world-famous" choucroutes and superb Alsatian charcuteries.

A la carte: 220-270 F. Menu: 160 F (wine incl.).

12/20 Le Souvré
10, rue Fts-du-Temples
42 72 35 71

Closed Sat. lunch, Sun., holidays & Aug. Open until 10 p.m.

A sombre décor is relieved by lovely candlelit, lace-covered tables. The cooking has a regional (south-west) slant and is simple and carefully prepared (foie gras, magret, cassoulet). Try the copious salmon with dill, or the boned saddle of young rabbit with parsley and garlic, followed by a strawberry pastry brimming with Chantilly cream.

A la carte: 250-300 F. Menu: 120 F.

4th arrondissement

L'Ambroisie
9, place des Vosges
42 78 51 45

Closed Sun., Mon., Feb. school holidays & 3 1st wks. of Aug. Open until 10:15 p.m. Air cond. No pets. Valet parking.

Bernard and Danièle Pacaud transformed this former goldsmith's shop under the arcades of the place des Vosges into the most gracious, charming and refined salon in the Marais. The dining room is worthy of a château, with high ceilings and inlaid stone and parquet floors, book-lined shelves, and a sumptuous 17th-century tapestry adorning the beige walls. Others may find the rigorous and restrained atmosphere rather "cold." We don't. It has the lived-in feel of a beautifully maintained private home, of which Danièle is the charming hostess. Don't expect to see much of Bernard, a retiring chef who prefers the sizzling sounds of his kitchen to the applause of an appreciative public. The influence of his mentor, Claude Peyrot, is perceptible everywhere in Bernard's finely chiselled, architectural cuisine. We used to find it a bit cool, but recently it has been warmed with sunny spices and herbs.

For example, an almost imperceptible touch of aniseed gives a new, needed dimension to a highly concentrated jus of mushrooms and cream, made with baby field mushrooms, morels and chanterelles. Red mullet with cumin and carrots, curried prawns with sesame crêpes, calf's liver with sherry vinegar and a hint of honey have won us over and warmed our hearts.

Vive the new Pacaud! And hats off too to the fantastic profiteroles with vanilla ice cream and warm chocolate sauce, as well as the florentines topped with a saffron-scented crème anglaise. Another round of applause for Pierre Le Moullac, the maître d'hôtel-sommelier, who seems to have countless magical bottles up his sleeve.

A la carte: 650-1,000 F.

The A la carte restaurant prices given are for a complete three-course meal for one, including a half-bottle of modest wine and service. Menu prices are for a complete fixed-price meal for one, excluding wine (unless otherwise noted).

RESTAURANTS – 4th arrondissement

11/20 Auberge de Jarente
7, rue de Jarente
42 77 49 35
Closed Sun., Mon., Aug. & 1 wk. beg. April. Open until 10:30 p.m. Air cond.
Here you'll find unpretentious Basque dishes served in a charming old Marais atmosphere (skip the prawns cooked in whisky and the sole au Noilly). The fixed-price menu, which includes pipérade de Saint-Jean, cassoulet, cheese and gâteau basque, is irreproachable.
A la carte: 170 F. Menus: 120 F (wine incl.), 108 F, 160 F.

 Benoit
20, rue St-Martin
42 72 25 76
Closed Sat., Sun., & Aug. Open until 10 p.m. Private room: 18. Air cond.
The more things change, the more Benoit's solid, bourgeois cooking stays the same. This is the archetypal Parisian bistro, with red-velvet banquettes, brass fixtures, lace curtains and a polished zinc bar. Chef Michel Petit (who is anything but!) continues the lusty tradition begun before the Great War by his grandfather. His repertoire consists of simple, modest marvels: bœuf mode, foie gras with lentils, beef tongue in port, salt cod with aïoli, accompanied by luscious desserts (try the chocolate fondue). An excellent cellar is stocked with reasonably priced bottles from Mâcon, Sancerre, Beaujolais, Saumur-Champigny, and Burgundy. Benoit numbers among Paris's best—and most expensive—bistros.
A la carte: 420-570 F.

The prices in this guide reflect what establishments were charging at the time going to press.

10/20 Brasserie de l'Ile Saint-Louis
55, quai de Bourbon
43 54 02 59
Open daily until 1 a.m.
Choucroute, sausages and cassoulet terrine are washed down here with torrents of frothy draught Mützig. This is a favourite haunt of both islanders and famished outlanders.
A la carte: 200 F.

 Coconnas
2 bis, pl. des Vosges
42 78 58 16
Closed Mon., Tues. & Jan. 13-Feb. 11. Open until 10:15 p.m. Terrace dining. Air cond.
Claude Terrail (La Tour d'Argent) saw a good thing coming when nearly 40 years ago he bought and transformed this old tourist bistro on the lovely place des Vosges. The tourists still flock here, and in recent years the cuisine has become reliable and remarkably well-prepared. Sample traditional favourites such as poule au pot with a "garden of vegetables", salt-cured duck or tournedos in a gingerbread croûte. The fixed-price lunches offer excellent value.
A la carte: 280-400 F. Menus: 105 F (weekdays lunch and Sat., wine incl.), 150 F (weekdays lunch and Sat.).

12/20 Le Coin du Caviar
2, rue de la Bastille
48 04 82 93
Closed Sat. lunch & Sun. Open until midnight. Private room: 14. Air cond.
Greece, Russia, Iran and France meet here under the sign of the salmon. Upstairs, in the rather precious dining room, choose from among a variety of salmon dishes (raw and smoked) or an authentic beef Stroganov. In the noisier, more switched-on downstairs bar, you can order bortsch, blinis, smoked fish—or even caviar. For dessert, there's a delicious apple strudel.
A la carte: 300-400 F (without caviar). Menu: 180 F (lunch only).

12/20 Au Franc Pinot
1, quai de Bourbon
43 29 46 98,
fax 42 77 28 16
Closed Sun. & Mon. Open until 11 p.m. Private room: 30. Air cond.
Napoleonic iron gates stand guard before this historic cave on the Ile Saint-Louis. We can't really fault the cuisine, which is serious enough, but we resent the recently inaugurated high-price policy.
A la carte: 500-600 F. Menu: 195 F (weekdays lunch only).

10/20 Jo Goldenberg
7, rue des Rosiers
48 87 20 16
Open daily until midnight. Terrace dining.
This is the archetypal, and most picturesque, of the Goldenberg restaurants in Paris (see 17th arrondissement). The Central European Yiddish cuisine is served in the heart of the Marais's Jewish district. Prepared foods are sold in the take-away shop.
A la carte: 200-250 F.

11/20 Au Gourmet de l'Isle
42, rue St-Louis-en-l'Ile
43 26 79 27
Closed Mon. & Tues. Open until 10 p.m.
The reception is charming, the crowd young and cheerful, the stone-and-beams décor suitably rustic. Au Gourmet de l'Isle has enjoyed over 40 years of deserved success for one of the city's surest-value set menus priced at 120 francs: boudin with apples, beef and lentil salad, andouillette with kidney beans.

A la carte: 170 F. Menu: 120 F.

 Miravile
72, quai de l'Hôtel-de-Ville
42 74 72 22

Closed Sat. lunch & Sun. Open until 10:30 p.m. Terrace dining. Air cond. Valet parking.

Right, left, right: this remarkable establishment has shifted back and forth over the Seine several times, but is now permanently installed in a beautifully restored building on the quay between the Hôtel de Ville and Châtelet. Marble floors, trompe-l'œil paintings and warm colours give the surroundings—the comfortable creation of chef/owner Gilles Epié and his wife Muriel—a charming Mediterranean feel. The kitchen has been revamped and expanded, a good thing as the talented young Gilles needs plenty of elbow room. It comes as no surprise that Gilles's cuisine, which was shaped under the tutelage of Alain Passard, is now better than ever. Gilles is determined to join the ranks of the great toque-laden chefs. And his further ascent will doubtless be hastened by such acutely flavourful, imaginative dishes as céleri rémoulade with duck foie gras, baked tuna with cumin and cèpes, saddle of rabbit with olives or sea bream with baked figs. The desserts are a delight (macaroons with raspberries, chocolate-caramel millefeuille, pistachio-cherry gratin), and the four-course lunch prix-fixe menu is excellent value.

A la carte: 450-600 F. Menus: 150 F (weekdays lunch only), 280 F, 480 F.

Some establishments change their closing times without warning. It is always wise to check in advance.

 Le Monde des Chimères
69, rue St-Louis-en-l'Ile
43 54 45 27

Closed Sun., Mon. & Feb. school holidays. Open until 10:30 p.m.

A delightful old "island bistro" now run by former TV personality Cécile Ibane. The food is reminiscent of Sunday dinner en famille—if, that is, your family included a French granny who was also a marvellous cook! We recommend the oxtail terrine with its garnish of sweet-and-sour quince and cherries, the veal paupiettes with tomatoes, the chicken sautéed with 40 cloves of garlic and a smooth, creamy brandade de morue with milk and olive oil. Delicious homemade desserts and an expertly chosen wine list.

A la carte: 270-350 F. Menu: 150 F (lunch only).

 Wally Saharien
16, rue Le Regrattier
43 25 01 39

Closed Mon. lunch & Sun. Open until 11:30 p.m. Private room: 20. Air cond. No pets.

Wally's desert empire is the place to sample authentic Saharan couscous—served dry and sans vegetables—and classic, festive delights such as harira, pigeon pastilla, stuffed sardines and North African pastries.

Menu: 300 F (wine incl.).

5th arrondissement

 Auberge des Deux Signes
46, rue Galande
43 25 46 56,
fax 46 33 20 49

Closed Sat. lunch, Sun., May 1 & Aug. Open until 10:30 p.m. Private room: 70.

If there is one restaurant in Paris that must be seen to be believed, it is this medieval hostelry lovingly restored and run by Georges Dhulster. Solid oak beams, Gothic vaults and windows that frame Notre-Dame: the setting is nothing short of spectacular (despite the somewhat heavyhanded neo-Louis XIII touches). And now the menu, which was not always so appealing as the surroundings, is packed with delicate, imaginative dishes like boiled-beef ravioli with ginger-scented cabbage, mackerel tart with leek fondue, and warm pear croquant laced with Cointreau. Courteous service.

A la carte: 400-500 F. Menus: 140 F and 230 F (lunch only).

11/20 **Le Balzar**
49, rue des Ecoles
43 54 13 67

Closed Dec. 24-Jan. 1 & Aug. Open until 12:30 a.m.

This Left-Bank/Sorbonne haunt, with its Art Deco woodwork and mirrors, is faithful to traditional brasserie fare (calf's liver, choucroute).

A la carte: 200-250 F.

 La Bûcherie
41, rue de la Bûcherie
43 54 78 06

Open daily until 12:30 a.m. Private room: 45 Terrace dining. Air cond.

Bernard Bosque is built like a Breton buccaneer and has been running his "Hôtel du Bon Dieu" (the Bûcherie's name at the turn of the century) for over 30 years with winning talent and with great success. Handsome woodwork and good contemporary engravings adorn the walls, and there are views of Notre-Dame through the windows of the comfortable covered terrace. The cuisine is rich and rather too predictable (poached eggs meurette, brandade de morue, lamb sauté with aubergines), but satisfying nonetheless. The wine cellar boasts a magnific-

ent selection of Bordeaux.
A la carte: 240-400 F. Menu: 220 F (wine incl.).

 ### Chieng-Mai
12, rue F.-Sauton
43 25 45 45

Closed Sun., Aug. 1-15 & Dec. 16-31. Open until 11:30 p.m. Air cond. No pets.

Its cool, stylised atmosphere, efficient service, and increasingly interesting Thai menu have won Chieng Mai a growing corps of admirers (it is therefore wise to reserve your table). The repertoire features several delicious new dishes: shrimp and spiced roe salad, steamed spicy seafood served in a crab shell, duck breast with basil and young peppercorns and a remarkable coconut-milk flan.

A la carte: 200-300 F. Menus: 91 F (lunch only), 136 F, 159 F, 173 F.

 ### Clavel
65, quai de la Tournelle
46 33 18 65

Closed Sun. dinner, Mon., Feb. school holidays & Aug. 7-30. Open until 10:30 p.m. Air cond.

Chef Frédéric Mignot is the new hand in the kitchen; he plans to update the repertoire of this small, quiet restaurant by the Seine. The décor has been redone in a spare Japanese style; the soft lights and pleasant service create a cosy, intimate atmosphere. The lunch menu is particularly appealing, the à la carte selections rather costly (especially the entrées). Try the generously served Brittany lobster ravioli with chives, the duck and foie gras tourte and finish with the dark, bewitching African chocolate cake.

A la carte: 400-450 F. Menus: 160 F (weekdays lunch and Sat.), 350 F.

 ### Les Colonies
10, rue St-Julien-le-Pauvre
43 54 31 33

Dinner only. Closed Sun. & Aug. Open until 1 a.m. Private room: 38. Air cond.

The decorator of L'Ambroisie took this old building, which faces the church of Saint-Julien-le-Pauvre, and transformed it with subtle refinements such as painted woodwork, luxurious fabrics and fine china. A mild breeze from the colonies stirs many of chef Spyros Vakanas's creations, witness his goat-cheese toasts enhanced with the warm flavour of nutmeg, the rib steak coated with crushed spices, or the chocolate "shell" with sweet saffron cream sauce. Charming service and a high-society clientele. Book ahead for late dining.

A la carte: 280-350 F. Menu: 170 F.

11/20 Délices d'Aphrodite
4, rue Candolle
43 31 40 39

Closed Mon. Open until 11:30 p.m. Air cond.

You'll find a catering service, two take-away shops and a small, summery dining room at this likeable Greek spot. The food is hearty and authentic: fried octopus, stuffed cabbage dolmades, moussaka.

A la carte: 200-220 F.

 ### Diapason
30, rue des Bernardins
43 54 21 13

Closed Sat. lunch, Sun. & Aug. 1-15. Open until 10:30 p.m.

A nicely kept, flower-filled establishment crowded with tiny tables pushed up to comfortable banquettes. The cuisine is rigorously classic (warm oysters with lemon butter, sole and salmon à l'orange, grenadin of young pigeon with truffles and foie gras).

Good desserts, fine Loire wines.

A la carte: 350-400 F. Menus: 165 F, 300 F.

 ### Dodin-Bouffant
25, rue F.-Sauton
43 25 25 14,
fax 43 29 52 61

Closed Sun. Open until 11 p.m. Terrace dining. Air cond.

Prepare yourself for the sound and fury of high and not-so-high-society diners jostling for a table in this cigar-box of a bistro. Dodin-Bouffant is renowned for its charming owners (Danièle and Maurice Cartier) and its delicious, no-nonsense cooking (the work of chef Philippe Valin, disciple of the late Jacques Manière). Two hundred people eat here daily, enjoying the wonderful oysters and seafood (duo of lotte and lobster with mild garlic), the robust bistro fare (daube de joues de bœuf, calf's head) and the many special "market" dishes (sea bream with basil and fennel, roast kid with oyster mushrooms). The very fine wine cellar is in the manner of Manière—full of finds at the right price. Offhand but cheerful service.

A la carte: 350-400 F. Menu: 170 F (lunch only).

 ### Les Fontaines
9, rue Soufflot
43 26 42 80

Closed Sun. & Aug. Open until 10:30 p.m.

Roger Lacipière was right to set aside the back room of his otherwise banal corner café and turn it into a delightful restaurant. Jolly waiters bring on generously robust and reasonably priced dishes like fricasséed young rabbit, Dijon-style kidney, and Bresse pigeon in a sauce thickened with foie gras. Fine selection of Loire and Bordeaux wines, and Beaujolais by the carafe.

A la carte: 200-300 F.

5th arrondissement – RESTAURANTS

Moissonnier
28, rue des Fossés-St-Bernard
43 29 87 65

Closed Sun. dinner, Mon. & Aug.-Sept. 7. Open until 10 p.m.

Reserve your table on the ground floor, where Jeannine trots to and fro serving the regulars from the university nearby, her arms laden with filling Lyonnais specialities (tablier de sapeur, quenelles, andouillette au vin blanc) and *pots* of Morgon, Brouilly and other Beaujolais wines drawn from the barrel. A delightful bistro run by the Moissonnier family for the last 30 years.

A la carte: 220-280 F.

Au Pactole
44, bd St-Germain
46 33 31 31,
fax 46 33 07 60

Closed Sat. lunch & Sun. Open until 10:30 p.m. Private room: 12. Terrace dining.

Roland Magne's policy of serving laudably lightened traditional food at attractive prices has finally paid off. Au Pactole was for years an inexplicably under-appreciated restaurant, but now the lovely dining room is full at lunch and dinner (perhaps the news that François Mitterrand and Helmut Kohl—both known for their love of fine food—had engaged in some dinner diplomacy here early in 1992 gave the restaurant a boost). Try the excellent ox-cheek terrine with onion confit, the perfect crab ravioli, or one of the best rib steaks in Paris (it's roasted in a salt crust), followed by a tasty apple tart with sabayon sauce for dessert. Nice but pricey wine list.

A la carte: 300 F. Menus: 139 F, 279 F.

11/20 Perraudin
157, rue Saint-Jacques
46 33 15 75

Closed Sat. lunch, Sun., Mon. lunch & last 2 wks. of Aug. Open until 10:15 p.m. Terrace dining. No cards.

This establishment is run by one of the city's specialists in homely, country-style cooking, formerly of Le Polidor (see the sixth arrondissement). Heartwarming Vouvray andouillette, bœuf bourguignon, and duck confit. Modest but charming early 1900s décor.

A la carte: 150 F. Menu: 59 F (lunch only).

12/20 Le Petit Navire
14, rue des Fossés-St-Bernard
43 54 22 52

Closed Sun., Mon., 1st wk. of Feb. school holidays & Aug. 1-16. Open until 10 p.m. Terrace dining.

For over 20 years regulars have been flocking here for tapenade, garlicky shellfish soup, grilled sardines and delightful growers' wines that sell for under 80 francs.

A la carte: 400 F. Menu: 120 F.

11/20 Le Petit Prince
12, rue Lanneau
43 54 77 26

Open daily until 12:30 a.m.

A modest Latin-Quarter restaurant serving classic, honest food (confit and magret de canard, lamb curry) and good little wines at low prices.

Menus: 82 F, 146 F.

Restaurant A
5, rue de Poissy
46 33 85 54

Closed Mon. Open until 11 p.m. Air cond.

Huynh-Kien regales clients with his spectacular vegetable and rice-paste sculptures and beguiles their taste buds with his all-but-forgotten Chinese dishes from the 18th-century Imperial court: duck cooked in mustard leaves, sautéed pork with spicy leeks or the Imperial chicken. Order the lychee-nut sorbet for dessert.

A la carte: 200-350 F. Menu: 108 F.

12/20 Rôtisserie du Beaujolais
19, quai de la Tournelle
43 54 17 47

Closed Mon. Open until 11:15 p.m. Terrace dining. Air cond.

Claude Terrail of the Tour d'Argent (across the road) opened this traditional Lyonnais bistro in 1989. It's still a nice little place to spend an animated evening with friends. The roast Challans duck is a delight; the saucisson pistaché and the salad of boiled beef and lentils are equally delicious. Exemplary Beaujolais from Dubœuf, impersonal service.

A la carte: 160-250 F. Menu: 150 F (weekdays lunch and Sat., wine incl.).

La Timonerie
35, quai de la Tournelle
43 25 44 42

Closed Sun., Mon., 1 wk. in Feb. & last wk. of Aug. Open until 10:30 p.m. Air cond.

La Timonerie is a handsome, lively little establishment taken over and redecorated a few years ago by Philippe de Givenchy, a disciple of Senderens and Chibois. Givenchy's technical precision is coupled with a knack for harmonising flavours, as you will discover when you taste his potato and chèvre tart accompanied by chive cream, his freshwater perch with crisp fried cabbage and celery or spiced crab with an orange brunoise. The tarte au chocolat is one of several enchanting desserts. Short, frequently changing menu, good wine cellar, attractive set lunch.

A la carte: 350-450 F. Menu: 185 F (lunch only).

RESTAURANTS – 6th arrondissement

La Tour d'Argent
15-17, quai de la Tournelle
43 54 23 31,
fax 44 07 12 04
Closed Mon. Open until 10 p.m. Private room: 60. Valet parking.

We hope the sight of those sweet little ducks and drakes bobbing on the Seine between the Ile Saint-Louis and your panoramic table doesn't take away your appetite for the best canard aux cerises you'll ever taste—a pressed duck paddling in a deeply flavourful sauce which has been the house speciality for 100 years. Chef Manuel Martinez, now a Tour d'Argent veteran, knows better than anyone how to work wonders with the web-footed fowl.

Don't expect any audacious novelties or revolutionary changes in the Tour d'Argent tradition. Claude Terrail, eternally youthful, charming and diplomatic, has chosen his field of honour once and for all. And what better aide-decamp than Martinez, battle-tested at the Relais Louis XIII? Within the limits of a "noble"—but not boring—repertoire, he imbues his creations with such flavour and harmony that you might be too delightedly dazed to notice the astronomical bill. But then, who notices the bill when it's time to buy the Rolls and the diamonds?

You can easily waste 400 francs on a ghastly meal elsewhere, and though it might seem galling to spend four or five times that here, you will never question the excellence of the food. Your meal might feature luscious, large prawns with tiny cèpes, tantalising truffled brouillade sauce Périgourdine, lobster-stuffed cabbage escorted by lobster ravioli or a voluptuously tender double veal chop. And what of the *nec plus ultra* of ice creams, the Tour d'Argent's vanilla or pistachio? A year from now you won't have forgotten it! Nor will you forget the sight of dusk's golden light on Notre-Dame or the impressive cityscape spread out before you.

The fabled cellar, skilfully managed by David Ridgway, harbours bottles with prices in four and even five digits—but it also holds unsung marvels costing less than 200 francs. And do remember: the lunch menu is only 375 F—put aside a franc and a centime each day for a year and there you are!

A la carte: 1,000 F and up. Menu: 375 F (weekdays lunch and Sat.).

Chez Toutoune
5, rue de Pontoise
43 26 56 81
Closed Mon. lunch, Sun. & Aug. Open until 10:45 p.m. Terrace dining.

Owner Colette Dejean, alias Toutoune, has put her restaurant right. It now has charming service and a delicious prix-fixe menu which offers fragrant soups, tasty terrines, a hearty sauté of duck and artichokes, chocolate soufflé and riz au caramel. To drink, there's a perfectly decent wine from Roussillon at just 65 francs. Lively atmosphere.

A la carte: 220-320 F. Menu: 179 F.

6th arrondissement

Allard
41, rue St-André-des-Arts
43 26 48 23
Closed Sat., Sun., Dec. 23-Jan. 3 & Aug. Open until 9:45 p.m. Private room: 25. Air cond.

Fernande Allard would still feel at home in the enchanting establishment she and her husband founded several decades ago. For practically nothing has changed, from the décor to the handwritten daily menu of escargots, turbot au beurre blanc, pigeon aux petits pois, duck with olives, and gâteau moka for dessert. The charm and chic of Allard are alive, but the wines are overpriced and the bill often overblown.

A la carte: 370-420 F. Menu: 250 F (lunch only).

Le Bélier
L'Hôtel
13, rue des Beaux-Arts
43 25 27 22,
fax 43 25 64 81
Open daily until 12:30 a.m. Private room: 80. Air cond.

The picturesque, theatrical setting features a tree trunk, a fountain, a huge bouquet of flowers and an elegant, cosmopolitan clientele. The chef turns out a rather classic repertoire, occasionally leavened with a spark of imagination (salmon sauté with aubergine pâté, sea bream with a hint of ginger, duck confit and tapenade). The à la carte offerings are considerably more tempting (and costly) than the dishes that make up the prosaic set menus.

A la carte: 300-400 F. Menus: 150 F (lunch only), 170 F (dinner only).

12/20 Bistro de la Grille
14, rue Mabillon
43 54 16 87
Open daily until 12:30 a.m. Terrace dining.

Fine shellfish at reasonable prices (offered at dinner only), appealing prix-fixe menus, and good homely dishes (skate, pot-au-feu) attract a handsome Left-Bank crowd to this bustling bistro hung with photographs of early film stars.

Menu: 140 F (dinner only).

12/20 Brasserie Lutétia
Hôtel Lutétia
23, rue de Sèvres

6th arrondissement – RESTAURANTS

49 54 46 76,
fax 49 54 46 64
Open daily until midnight. Air cond. Valet parking.
The no-nonsense country cooking is prepared with considerable finesse in the same kitchens as Le Paris. Superb seafood is available except for two months in summer. Brunch on Sundays.
A la carte: 200-250 F. Menus: 95 F (weekdays lunch and Sat.), 135 F (weekdays and Sat.), 165 F.

Jacques Cagna
14, rue des Grands-Augustins
43 26 49 39,
fax 43 54 54 48
Closed Sat. (except dinner twice a month), Sun., 3 wks. in Aug. & Christmas. Open until 10:30 p.m. Private room: 10. Air cond.
The roaring success of his bistro annexe has not distracted Jacques Cagna from the business of pleasing the moneyed, cosmopolitan gourmets who prefer to dine at the "old original". The witty, charming Cagna spends most of his time presiding over the prettiest tavern in old Paris, with its oak beams and woodwork, its Flemish still lifes and discreet lighting. But happily, this is not a museum and food, drink, and—measured—merriment are perfectly at home.
Jacques Cagna's guardian angel is his sister Anny, who glides among the tables dispensing smiles and good counsel. She will not, however, try to pull the wool over your eyes: there is nothing Jacques Cagna likes less than foolery (except, perhaps, fusty cooking). He is at once a Left-Bank sophisticate and a peasant, attached to the solid, lusty fare of his native Normandy. We used to think his classic training had bred in him a secret preference for dark, murky sauces—but we see that in fact his "jus" are wonderfully clean, light and tasty. Take for example the deeply flavourful rabbit essence he drizzles over a sea bass meunière with puréed celery and fried celery leaves, or the polished-but-rustic oyster-stuffed brill bathed in a reduction of watercress, or a sensational consommé simmered with a divinely tender shin of veal and perfumed with foie gras.
And what happy harmony Sauternes and honey bring to the Brittany pigeon with carrots and sweet onions! Or the sauce of shallots, bone marrow, and meat juices to an incomparable Angus rib steak, hung for a full three weeks and served with a satisfying side dish of puréed potatoes. Finish with the delightful baba au kirsch topped with whipped cream and cherries, and your palate will have known an hour of unalloyed bliss... To drink? of course there are ruinously expensive bottles of Côte-Rôtie, Hermitage, Burgundy or Bordeaux. On the other hand, you don't have to break the bank to feast on Cagna's astonishingly good fixed-price lunch menu.
A la carte: 600-900 F. Menus: 260 F (weekdays lunch only).

12/20 Le Caméléon
6, rue de Chevreuse
43 20 63 43
Closed Sun., Mon. & Aug. Open until 10:30 p.m.
An archetypal Montparnasse bistro dripping with memories and bustling with lively patrons, Le Caméléon serves uncomplicated, homely dishes (braised veal with fresh pasta, cod Provençal, pear clafoutis). Charming service and an excellent list of growers' wines.
A la carte: 160-230 F.

Aux Charpentiers
10, rue Mabillon
43 26 30 05,
fax 46 33 07 98
Closed Sun. & holidays. Open until 11:30 p.m. Terrace dining.
Pierre Bardèche has opened a new fish restaurant across the street (L'Ecaille de PCB) but continues to serve his renowned honest cooking in this former carpenters' guild hall. The menu revolves around full-flavoured *plats du jour* such as cod aïoli, stuffed cabbage and veal sauté, accompanied by pleasant little wines.
A la carte: 180-260 F.

Le Chat Grippé
87, rue d'Assas
43 54 70 00
Closed Sat. lunch & Mon. Open until 10:30 p.m. Air cond.
Chef Eric Thore, trained at Taillevent, cooks in a classic vein to which he lends many a judicious personal touch. Seafood is his strong suit—witness the delicious fresh cod minestrone, casserole of shellfish, oysters and crustaceans with ginger. But this establishment's roots in the Quercy region are commemorated with warm foie gras with celery and apples, honeyed roast pigeon with spices, cabécous goat cheese and a magnificent gratin aux poires. The robust red wines of Cahors hold a place of honour on the wine list.
A la carte: 320-450 F. Menus: 180 F (weekdays lunch only), 325 F (dinner, except holidays).

12/20 Dominique
19, rue Bréa
43 27 08 80
Closed July 17-Aug. 16. Open until 10:30 p.m. Private room: 40. Air cond.
This famed Montparnasse Russian troika—take-away shop/bar/restaurant—stead-f astly refuses perestroika when

it comes to cuisine and décor: purple-and-gold walls, steaming samovars and goulash Tolstoy. Delicious smoked salmon, bortsch and blinis. And vodka, of course, both Russian and Polish.

A la carte: 240-310 F. Menu: 154 F.

11/20 Drugstore Saint-Germain
149, bd St-Germain
42 22 92 50

Open daily until 1:30 a.m. Air cond.

The reliable, unpretentious cuisine (salads, grilled sausage, hamburgers) is served in a handsome, comfortable setting designed—wouldn't you know it—by Slavik.

A la carte: 200 F. Menu: 78 F.

 ### L'Ecaille de PCB
5, rue Mabillon
43 26 73 70,
fax 46 33 07 98

Closed Sat. lunch & Sun. Open until 11 p.m. Private room: 10. Air cond. Valet parking.

Pierre Bardèche, owner of the renowned Aux Charpentiers across the way, recently bought this old Basque *auberge* and transformed it into one of the city's better fish restaurants. Simple dishes, fresh ingredients and a frequently-changing menu spell success. Try the oysters, the baked fish assortment, or the fine fish soup, as well as Brittany lobsters offered here at very low prices. Short but shrewdly chosen wine list.

A la carte: 300-350 F. Menu: 125 F.

11/20 Guy
6, rue Mabillon
43 54 87 61

Dinner only (and lunch Sat.). Closed Sun. & Aug. 8-31. Open until 12:45 a.m. Air cond.

This is a Brazilian dinner club with festive décor and atmosphere (guitars, killer batidas, bossa-nova...). The cuisine is modest, but portions are generous.

A la carte: 220-320 F. Menus: 97 F (Tues.-Thurs. dinner only), 188 F (Sat.lunch).

12/20 Chez Henri
16, rue Princesse
46 33 51 12

Closed Sun. Open until 11:30 p.m.

Regulars flock here for the good-value bistro cooking by chef Henri Poulat: calf's liver with creamed onions, farm chicken in vinegar, roast lamb, apple clafoutis.

A la carte: 100 F. Menu: 160 F.

11/20 La Hulotte
29, rue Dauphine
46 33 75 92

Closed Sun., Mon. & Aug. Open until 10:15 p.m.

The proof is in the pudding: Bernard Güys is mad about desserts, especially chocolate mousse (he makes it in six delicious variations). Start your meal with tasty grilled meats, coq au vin and other traditional dishes, made with love and generously apportioned.

A la carte: 180 F. Menu: 150 F (wine incl.).

12/20 Joséphine
Chez Dumonet
117, rue du Cherche-Midi
45 48 52 40,
fax 42 84 06 83

Closed Sat., Sun., July 3-31 & Dec. 18-27. Open until 10:30 p.m.

Joséphine is an honourable early 1900s bistro frequented by prominent jurists, journalists and an intellectual theatre crowd. The chummy atmosphere is animated by owner Jean Dumonet and fuelled by the perennially popular cuisine, a heady mix of bourgeois and south-west fare. Humble herrings with warm potatoes at 59 francs flank truffle feuilleté at 530 F; leg of lamb with beans, or leeks in vinaigrette vie for attention with truffled andouillette in flaky pastry. Appropriately, the wine cellar abounds in Bordeaux, both modest and mighty.

A la carte: 300-400 F. Menu: 170 F (lunch only, wine incl.).

Lapérouse
51, quai des Grands-Augustins
43 26 68 04

Closed Sun., Sat. & Mon. lunch, Aug. Open until 10:30 p.m. Private room: 50. Air cond.

For years we felt a pinch at our heartstrings each time we strolled along the Left-Bank quais past Lapérouse. A landmark restaurant, founded in 1766, it was once among the best places to eat in Paris. Here Belle Epoque *cocottes* flirted—and more—in ravishing little private salons (and used the diamonds they earned with their naughtiness to scratch their names in the mirrors). But the once-noted cuisine slipped badly in the 1970s, and gourmets abandoned Lapérouse. What a delight, then, to learn that new owners have restored the décor to its former lustre, and put a brilliant young chef in the kitchen. Gabriel Biscaye, late of the Royal Monceau, has a rare gift for combining tastes and textures in unusual but utterly satisfying ways. A glance at the new *carte* reveals a host of surprising, appetising dishes like tête de veau caramélisée aux huîtres, assiette de poissons à l'encre de seiche, rognon de veau rôti à la moutarde de violette, and a rich array of desserts. Lapérouse is once again an enchanting choice for a romantic dinner by the Seine.

A la carte: 400-600 F. Menus: 250 F (lunch only), 370 F, 480 F.

12/20 Lipp
151, bd St-Germain
45 48 53 91,
fax 45 44 33 20
Open daily until 1 a.m. Air cond.

The interregnum is over: Lipp has lost both the legendary Roger Cazes and his heir-apparent, Michel Cazes. The new *patron* is an interior architect named Perrichon. Despite the often disappointing food (choucroute, bœuf gros sel) and the cruel whims of fashion, this glossy turn-of-the-century brasserie still manages to serve some 400 to 500 customers a day. Of course, the clientele is not what it was, though one still catches sight of a powerful politician or a beauty queen ensconced at a ground-floor table, admiring the gorgeous décor.
A la carte: 270-320 F.

11/20 La Lozère
4, rue Hautefeuille
43 54 26 64
Closed Sun., Mon., Aug. & 1 wk. at Christmas. Open until 10:30 p.m.

You can smell the bracing air of the rural Lozère region in the warm winter soups, herby sausages and pâtés served in this charming old-Paris establishment, a regional tourist office, crafts shop and restaurant combined.
A la carte: 150 F. Menus: 82 F (lunch only, wine incl.), 106 F, 129 F.

La Marlotte
55, rue du Cherche-Midi
45 48 86 79
Closed Sat., Sun. & Aug. Open until 11 p.m. Private room: 9. Terrace dining. Air cond.

This timbered restaurant's pleasant rustic setting is softened by madras upholstery and candlelight in the evening. The food, full of hearty country flavours, is meticulously prepared. Try the homemade terrines, the veal kidney with mustard sauce and the delectable chocolate gâteau. Crowded both at lunch and dinner, often with the smart set.
A la carte: 220-280 F.

Le Muniche
22, rue G.-Apollinaire
46 33 62 09
Open daily until 1:30 a.m. Terrace dining. Air cond.

In its new location (just around the corner from its former site) across from the Church of Saint-Germain-des-Prés, the Muniche remains the liveliest, most feverishly overcrowded of Parisian brasseries. The Layrac brothers and their attentive, smiling staff will regale you with oysters, choucroute garnished with veal knuckle, thick-sliced calf's liver and grilled pigs' ears, washed down with perfect little *pots* of red, white and rosé.
A la carte: 210-260 F. Menu: 140 F.

11/20 Le Parc aux Cerfs
50, rue Vavin
43 54 87 83
Closed Aug. Open daily until 11 p.m. Air cond.

This was one of the first Montparnasse "neo-bistros"—with revisited Lyonnais specialities served in a jovial, youthful atmosphere. Inexpensive lunch menu, and good Rhône wines (by the bottle or carafe).
A la carte: 180-200 F. Menus: 92 F, 120 F.

Le Paris
Hôtel Lutétia
45, bd Raspail
49 54 46 90,
fax 49 54 46 64
Closed Sat., Sun. & Aug. Open until 10 p.m. Air cond. Valet parking.

Philippe Renard, the young chef, still can't decide whether his style should be classic or inventive, but delicious dishes like the glorious crab and green cabbage ravioli attest to his progress and have won back the two toques he earned at the Hôtel Scribe. If only the décor wasn't so dreary and the wine list so depressingly expensive, this restaurant would enjoy the popularity the food and pleasant service deserve.
A la carte: 450-550 F. Menus: 295 F (lunch only), 395 F (dinner only).

10/20 Le Petit Mabillon
6, rue Mabillon
43 54 08 41
Closed Sun., Mon. lunch & 1 wk. at Christmas. Open daily until 11 p.m. Terrace dining.

The good Italian home cooking features two daily pasta choices (fusilli, lasagne). Picturesque bistro décor, garden.
A la carte: 180-200 F. Menu: 72 F.

10/20 Le Petit Saint-Benoît
4, rue St-Benoît
42 60 27 92
Closed Sat. & Sun. Open daily until 10 p.m. Terrace dining.

An unfading coachman's eating-house whose crowded pavement terrace is a refuge for fashionable fast-food haters in search of a cheap meal: hachis Parmentier, bacon with lentils.
A la carte: 100 F.

Le Petit Zinc
11, rue St-Benoît
46 33 51 66
Open daily until 1 a.m. Terrace dining. Air cond.

Le Petit Zinc shares the same kitchen and country cooking as the equally popular Le Muniche next door, but with an emphasis on south-west specialities: oysters, shellfish, poule au pot, thick-sliced calf's liver, leg of duck with apples. In summer the terrace spreads its fluttering tablecloths across the pavement.

A la carte: 210-260 F. Menu: 140 F.

13/ La Petite Cour
8, rue Mabillon
43 26 52 26

Open daily until 11:30 p.m. Garden dining.

Owners and chefs may come and go, but the discreet charm of this old restaurant with its garden and splashing fountain remains. The dining room's Napoleon III décor is equally appealing and the cuisine, though not terribly ambitious, is fresh and generous: skate with cabbage, beef stew with carrots. Tasty, low-priced Saumur and Valençay wines.
A la carte: 270-370 F. Menus: 160 F (lunch only), 180 F (dinner only).

11/20 Polidor
41, rue Monsieur-le-Prince
43 26 95 34

Open daily until 12:30 a.m. (except Sun. 11 p.m.).

Authentic country fare (boudin with mashed potatoes, rabbit in mustard) and attractive little wines are served in a dining room that has not changed much in 100 years.
A la carte: 100 F. Menus: 50 F (weekdays lunch only), 100 F.

15/ Princesse
Castel
15, rue Princesse
43 26 90 22

Dinner only. Closed Sun. & Aug. Open until 5 a.m. Private room: 40. Air cond.

In 1992 owners Jean and Yolande Castel celebrated 30 years of undisputed success for their exclusive club-restaurant. Unfortunately, if you aren't a member you probably won't get in, and will therefore have to settle for imagining the Belle Epoque décor and chef Didier Aupetit's succulent cuisine, which features skate with cabbage and boned saddle of rabbit aux fines herbes.
A la carte: 500-800 F (at Le Foyer: 250-350 F).

11/20 Le Procope
13, rue de l'Ancienne-Comédie
43 26 99 20

Open daily until 1 a.m. Private room: 80. Terrace dining.

The capital's oldest café was recently restored to its original 17th-century splendour and now serves good, simple brasserie food to a clientele in which tourists predominate. Try the oysters (reasonably priced), merlan Colbert, and calf brawn.
A la carte: 200-350 F. Menus: 98 F (lunch only), 289 F (wine incl.).

15/ Relais Louis XIII
8, rue des Grands-Augustins
43 26 75 96,
fax 44 07 07 80

Closed Mon. lunch, Sun. & July 24-Aug. 24. Open until 10:15 p.m. Private room: 22. Air cond.

Louis XIII was proclaimed King of France in this luxurious 17th-century tavern with its beams and polished panelling. The cuisine may not be inspired but it is reliably rich and classic: lobster fricassée, sole and prawns with coriander, and truffled filet de bœuf. In addition to the stupendous and shockingly expensive 1934 Latour (8,750 francs) or 1921 Quarts de Chaume (2,000 francs), the wine cellar boasts a few accessibly priced bottlings.
A la carte: 400-500 F. Menu: 240 F (lunch only).

13/ La Rôtisserie d'en Face
2, rue Christine
43 26 40 98

Closed Sun. Open until 11 p.m. (Mon-Thurs.), 11:30 p.m. (Fri-Sat). Air cond.

Jacques Cagna's smart new annexe with its single-price menu (160 francs) encountered immediate success with Parisians hungry for rousing bistro food at reasonable prices. Start off a satisfying meal with crisp, deep-fried smelts or ravioli stuffed with escargots, then follow with a civet of pork cheek and carrots or Challans chicken with mashed potatoes, and finish with an Alsatian apple tart. Whatever you choose, you'll find a frisky, inexpensive wine to accompany it from among the 20 or so on offer. Rumour has it that another Rôtisserie is in the planning stages for the 17th arrondissement.
Menu: 180 F.

12/20 La Rotonde
105, bd Montparnasse
43 26 68 84

Open daily until 1 a.m. Terrace dining. Air cond.

Along with La Coupole, Le Dôme, and Le Select, La Rotonde belongs to the pantheon of Montparnasse brasseries. No earthshaking food, but the scallop salad with coriander dressing is delicate and fresh, the steak "Prince Albert" (with wine sauce and potato cake) delicious, and the Berthillon sorbets splendid, of course.
A la carte: 250-330 F. Menu: 165 F.

11/20 Chez Claude Sainlouis
Le Golfe Juan
27, rue du Dragon
45 48 29 68

Closed Sat. dinner, Sun., Aug., 2 wks. at Easter & 2 wks. at

Red toques signify modern cuisine; white toques signify traditional cuisine.

Christmas. Open daily until 11 p.m. Air cond.

Reliable salads and steaks are served here amid amusing, theatrical décor.

Menu: 200 F (wine and dessert incl.).

12/20 La Table de Fès
5, rue Sainte-Beuve
45 48 07 22

nner only. Closed Sun. & Aug. 10-26. Open until 12:15 a.m.

The owners have changed, the chef has not: Zohra continues to turn out authentic pastillas, couscous, and tajines as she has for the past 25 years. Fès can get crowded and stuffy in the evening.

A la carte: 200-250 F.

Yugaraj
14, rue Dauphine
43 26 44 91

Closed Mon. lunch. Open until 11 p.m. Private room: 18. Air cond.

Yugaraj's out-of-the-ordinary Indian cooking is served in a pleasant, spotless setting reminiscent of a native temple. The generous and warming specialities such as tandoori lamb are flanked by rather disappointing samosas and pastries. Well-chosen wine list. Interesting game dishes in season.

A la carte: 260-300 F. Menus: 130 F (lunch only), 180 F, 220 F.

7th arrondissement

12/20 Chez les Anges
54, bd de Latour-Maubourg
47 05 89 86,
fax 45 56 03 84

Closed Sun. dinner. Open until 10:30 p.m. Private room: 15. Air cond.

Former owner Armand Monassier, a wine grower, continues to supply this comfortable Burgundian restaurant with barrels of his delicious Rully. To accompany them, ever-reliable chef Bernard Labrosse trots out his classic ham in parsley aspic, coq au vin, and rosy, thick-sliced calf's liver. The atmosphere and setting are refined. Splendid Burgundy wine list, regular clientele studded with senators and deputies.

A la carte: 400-500 F. Menus: 320 F (wine incl.), 230 F.

Antoine et Antoinette
16, av. Rapp
45 51 75 61

Closed Sat. & Sun. Annual closings not available. Open until 10 p.m. Terrace dining.

Chef Jean-Claude Pernot has no quarrel with classic cuisine, and in the best tradition offers a winter menu and a summer menu. The dependable quality of his cooking accounts for the success of his cosy little restaurant, which sparkles with fine silver, crystal and lovely linen. We recommend the squid en escabèche, honeyed roast pigeon, fish tartare and kidneys with mustard. Modest bottles available for around 80 francs.

A la carte: 220-320 F. Menu: 160 F.

Arpège
Alain Passard
84, rue de Varenne
45 51 47 33,
fax 44 18 98 39

Closed Sun. lunch & Sat. Open until 10:30 p.m. Private room: 14. Air cond.

The 260-franc lunch menu is so outstanding that the waiters seem to want to keep it all to themselves. You must ask for it specifically or wind up ordering à la carte—not a bad thing really, as Arpège's stellar young chef Alain Passard has earned his four toques for far more than a fine prix-fixe meal. Allow us to harp on for a moment: Passard began his career in Rheims under Gérard Boyer, then worked as an assistant to Senderens at this same address when it housed L'Archestrate. After proving himself at the Duc d'Enghien, and later at the Carlton in Brussels, he returned here as owner.

At age 38, Passard is a virtuoso. Light though his touch may be, you will never catch him indulging in legerdemain. His inventiveness and imagination are always precisely controlled. Passard's compositions, whether variations on well-known themes (sweetbreads with chestnuts and truffles; saddle of hare with walnuts and cèpes), or new symphonies of taste (crab with mustard butter and cabbage; scallops with leeks and garlic oil), are uniformly harmonious. We single out the John Dory baked with bay leaves inserted under the skin: a masterpiece. How can we sum up the secret of Passard's success in a few words? He is blessed with the touch of the master which pares away superfluities to reveal flavours in all their brilliant clarity. And now, in addition to his fine wine cellar, proven staff, and adoring public (he ministers to many in the local ministries), Passard finally possesses decent kitchens and a sleek, sophisticated setting in tune with his symphonic cuisine.

A la carte: 550-900 F. Menus: 260 F (weekdays lunch and holidays), 350 F (lunch only), 590 F, 690 F.

Bellecour
22, rue Surcouf
45 51 46 93

Closed Sat. (except dinner Oct.-May), Sun. & Aug. 10-30. Open until 10:30 p.m. Terrace dining. Air cond.

A new chef has stepped into the shoes of Stéphane Pruvot, the star pupil of Lorain at

RESTAURANTS – 7th arrondissement

Joigny, now off to seek his fortune in the Marquesas. Denis Croset will henceforth oversee the preparation of the traditional *cuisine lyonnaise* that has made Gérald Goutagny's establishment—a vintage bistro with a vaguely colonial setting—a perennial favourite with the well-heeled locals. The featherlight desserts are the handiwork of Gérald Goutagny himself (a former pastry chef), and are among the best to be found in Paris.

A la carte: 330-480 F. Menus: 180 F (lunch only), 380 F.

11/20 Le Bistrot de Breteuil
3, pl. de Breteuil
45 67 07 27

Open daily until 10:30 p.m. Terrace dining.

An old corner café converted into an up-to-date bistro, the Breteuil serves traditional dishes such as foie gras, smoked salmon and escargots aux noisettes. The fixed-price menu is remarkably good value (it includes an apéritif and coffee as well as wine). Pleasant terrace.

Menu: 165 F (wine and coffe incl.).

La Boule d'Or
13, bd de Latour-Maubourg
47 05 50 18

Closed Sat. lunch & Mon. Open until 10 p.m. Private room: 25. Air cond.

Prim and proper provincial décor, a steady clientele, and a charming proprietor: the Boule rolls on. François Le Quillec, the new chef, complicates some dishes unduly, but we have nothing but praise for his truffled young guinea fowl. Stiffish prices.

A la carte: 300-400 F. Menus: 195 F, 360 F.

Le Bourdonnais
113, av. de La Bourdonnais
47 05 47 96,
fax 45 51 09 29

Open daily until 11:30 p.m. Private room: 25. Air cond.

Owner Micheline Coat earns this year's "Warmest Welcome" award. Never before has her cheerfully redecorated restaurant been so crowded with the chic and powerful. Success has been borne on a south wind, for the keen flavours of Provence pervade chef Philippe Bardau's short but appetising menu. A disciple of Outhier and Maximin, Bardau excels with his tuna gazpacho and grilled artichokes, his sea bass and fennel with a touch of tomato, a pigeon sandwich with celery and Parmesan, rabbit fillet with cabbage and bacon and a luscious fig gratin with almond cream. The fixed-price menus at lunch (220 francs) and dinner (280 francs) are outstanding value.

A la carte: 350-500 F. Menus: 220 F (lunch only, wine incl.), 280 F (dinner only), 380 F.

Clémentine
62, av. Bosquet
45 51 41 16

Closed Sat. lunch, Sun. & Aug. 15-30, Dec. 25 & Dec. 31-Jan. 1. Open until 10:30 p.m. Private room: 25. Terrace dining. Air cond.

Michèle and Bernard Przybyl (you're right, that's Polish) pay homage to the cuisine of their respective/adopted homes: Languedoc (duck cassoulet) and Brittany (skate with capers, lobster à la nage). The rosy décor is attractive, but the tables are still a bit too close for comfort. Pretty people, modest prices and an ever-expanding wine cellar.

A la carte: 230-300 F. Menu: 168 F.

Aux Délices de Szechuen
40, av. Duquesne
43 06 22 55

Closed Mon., Aug. 2-22 & Dec. 24-28. Open until 10:30 p.m. Terrace dining. Air cond.

Fresh and tasty Chinese specialities are served here with flair. The chef has a ten-year track record of reliability. Try the Peking duck (in three courses), the grilled won tons served with a ginger-scented sauce and the beef fillet with orange peel. Elegant décor, excellent service.

A la carte: 180 F. Menu: 96 F (weekdays and Sat.).

Duquesnoy
6, av. Bosquet
47 05 96 78,
fax 44 18 90 57

Closed Sat. lunch, Sun. & Aug. Open until 10:30 p.m. Air cond.

The top drawer of business and TV flocks to Jean-Paul Duquesnoy's comfortable little restaurant, filling both lunch and dinner sittings year round. The light touch extends from the décor and service (directed by the discreet and charming Françoise Duquesnoy) to the cooking. Jean-Paul steers a skilful course between classicism and novelty, pleasing his elegant patrons with turbot and bacon bathed in a rich veal jus, Bresse chicken in a sauce enlivened with sherry vinegar, or sardines accompanied by lasagne layered with black-olive purée. Luscious desserts include honey-nougat ice cream, walnut crème brûlée, and an assortment of milk and bitter chocolates. Exquisite wines from the Loire, Burgundy and Côtes-du-Rhône swell the rather stiff à la carte prices. Excellent prix-fixe lunch menu.

A la carte: 500-650 F. Menu: 250 F (weekdays lunch only).

Une heure et demie passée dans votre établissement est le premier des privilèges. Le second est d'y boire de l'eau d'Evian.

EVIAN. L'EAU MINERALE DES MEILLEURES TABLES DU MONDE.

CHÂTEAU CHEVAL BLANC

PREMIER GRAND CRU CLASSÉ "A"
SAINT-ÉMILION

Ecaille et Plume
25, rue Duvivier
45 55 06 72

Closed Sat. lunch & Sun. Open until 10:30 p.m. (upon reservation). Private room: 10. Air cond.

A master matchmaker, Marie Naël puts heart and soul into her innovative cuisine. Seasonal game specialities and seafood are her strong points: try the briny salade océane, foie gras en terrine with potatoes or, in its short season, Scottish grouse flambéed with single-malt whisky. The décor is cosy, the wines well chosen but oh-so-expensive.

A la carte: 280-400 F.

 La Ferme Saint-Simon
6, rue Saint-Simon
45 48 35 74,
fax 40 49 07 31

Closed Sat. lunch, Sun. & 1st 3 wks. of Aug. Open until 10:15 pm. Private room: 20. Air cond.

Parliamentarians, publishing magnates and food-loving executives savour succulent specialities in the intimate little dining rooms of "the farm" (rustic only in name). Owner Francis Vandenhende dashes from La Ferme to his other, equally renowned restaurant, Le Manoir de Paris in the 17th arrondissement. The cooking here is generous and traditional, but with a modern touch: homemade duck foie gras, brill with veal jus, a hearty pie filled with oxtail and ox cheek, caramelised almond pastry and bitter-chocolate tart. Large and small appetites—and thick and thin wallets—will be equally satisfied.

A la carte: 300-400 F. Menu: 170 F (lunch only).

11/20 **Aux Fins Gourmets**
213, bd St-Germain
42 22 06 57

Closed Sun., Mon. lunch & 1 wk. at Christmas. Open until 10 p.m. Terrace dining.

Hearty Basque/Béarnaise cooking served in a lively family-run bistro frequented by a smart old-Paris set. The charcuteries and confits are good, but skip the desserts. Nice choice of wines from the south-west.

A la carte: 180 F.

12/20 **La Flamberge**
12, av. Rapp
47 05 91 37,
fax 47 23 60 98

Closed Sat. lunch, Sun., Dec. 22-31 & Aug. 10-20. Open until 10:30 p.m. Private room: 24. Air cond. Valet parking.

The prices are so steep in this pretty little establishment swathed in rosy chintz that soon only millionaires and big-spending senators will be able to afford them. Perfect oysters, grilled sea bass with fennel (250 francs, if you please!), baked sea bream. Well-chosen wines in a wide range of prices.

A la carte: 350-500 F. Menu: 230 F.

11/20 **La Fontaine de Mars**
129, rue St-Dominique
47 05 46 44

Closed Sun., Dec. 25 & Jan. 1. Open daily until 11 p.m. Terrace dining.

Check tablecloths, low prices and hearty country food are the perennial attractions of this modest establishment (andouillette, duck fricassée, Cahors at around 50 francs a bottle).

A la carte: 200 F (wine incl.). Menu: 85 F (lunch only).

12/20 **Chez Françoise**
Aérogare des Invalides
47 05 49 03

Closed Sun. & May 1. Open until midnight. Terrace dining. Valet parking.

Chez Françoise is an immense subterranean hall decorated in a pseudo-tropical style that has somehow retained its charm, despite 30 years of wear and tear. This is a favourite haunt of hungry parliamentarians. They blithely ignore the good fixed-price menu and opt instead for the pricier, terribly conservative à la carte fish dishes, grilled lamb and foie gras.

A la carte: 250-300 F. Menu: 160 F.

Les Glénan
54, rue de Bourgogne
45 51 61 09

Closed w.-e. (except Sun. dinner) & Aug. Open until 10:30 p.m. Private room: 20. Air cond.

Fresh seafood is the Glénan's strongest suit: John Dory with garlic cream sauce or red mullet with mascarpone. The new owner has revamped the décor and put capable Thierry Bourdonnais (who earned 15/20 at his last post) in the kitchen.

A la carte: 300-350 F. Menus: 150 F (lunch only, wine incl.), 240 F (dinner only), 350 F.

 Le Divellec
107, rue de l'Université
45 51 91 96,
fax 45 51 31 75

Closed Sun., Mon., Dec. 24-Jan. 4 & Aug. Open until 10 p.m. Air cond. No pets. Valet parking.

France's *Présidents de la République*—past and present—honour Jacques Le Divellec with their presence, as do press moguls, TV idols and other high-class patrons

---

The A la carte restaurant prices given are for a complete three-course meal for one, including a half-bottle of modest wine and service. Menu prices are for a complete fixed-price meal for one, excluding wine (unless otherwise noted).

who fill this "yacht-club" dining room noon and night. But let's be frank: it's not the bigwigs that make this establishment great: it's the fish! We think Jacques Le Divellec is now at the top of his form: he bowled us over on a recent visit with his sublime prawns in walnut oil with slivers of truffle, flavourful smoked whiting covered with herbs and delectable braised sole coated in a fish-fumet-based hollandaise enhanced with Pouilly-Fuissé and fresh cream. The desserts (vacherin à l'orange, strawberry chaud-froid) are better than ever. Pangloss would be proud: the service is efficient, the wine waiter shrewd, and the hostess smiling. In short, all is for the best at Le Divellec.

A la carte: 650-950 F. Menus: 270 F and 370 F (lunch only).

 Chez Marius
5, rue de Bourgogne
45 51 79 42

Closed Sat., Sun. Dec. 24-Jan. 2 & Aug. 5-30. Open until 10:30 p.m. Air cond.

Restaurant pro Michel Perrodo took over this long-lived establishment a few years back, and has no intention of fiddling with a successful formula. Still present on the menu are the famed "bouillabaisse Marius", succulent shellfish dishes and tasty standbys like grilled red mullet or roast saddle of lamb. Mixed clientele, with a sprinkling of parliamentarians. Superb wine cellar.

A la carte: 370-520 F. Menu: 180 F.

12/20 **L'Œillade**
10, rue St-Simon
42 22 01 60

Closed Sat. lunch & Sun. Open until 11 p.m. Air cond.

Things are looking up: the dynamic duo of Huclin and Molto, late of Chez Toutoune, have recently taken over this charming bistro. The prices are as reasonable as ever, the food hearty and unpretentious: mackerel with mustard, calf's liver with gratin dauphinois. Selected wines are available by the glass.

Menu: 145 F (except holidays).

 Le Petit Laurent
38, rue de Varenne
45 48 79 64

Closed Sat. lunch, Sun. & 15 days in Aug. Open until 10:30 p.m. Private room: 16.

Robust cooking is served here in an ultraclassic, comfortable Louis XVI décor. Try the terrine of sweetbreads, the skate in truffled butter, or the roast sea bream with mango: you'll appreciate, as we do, their precise, clearly defined flavours. The cheerful Monsieur Pommier is making an admirable effort to keep prices down. In fact, his appetising 175-franc menu is one of the best deals on the Left Bank. A perfectly decent Entre-Deux-Mers sells for just 98 francs.

A la carte: 250-300 F. Menu: 175 F (except holidays).

11/20 **La Petite Chaise**
36, rue de Grenelle
42 22 13 35

Open daily until 11 p.m.

This charming little restaurant has been serving since the days of Louis XIV (1680). Sit elbow-to-elbow with university students and publishing people and tuck into the fixed-price menu (Baltic herrings, tripe baked with onions and white wine, and so on).

Menu: 170 F (wine incl.).

10/20 **Au Pied de Fouet**
45, rue de Babylone
47 05 12 27

Closed Sat. dinner, Sun., Aug. & Dec. 24-Jan. 3. Open until 9 p.m.

In an authentic coaching inn, enjoy such simple classics as nicely seasoned lentil salad, blanquette de veau, poule au pot and clafoutis.

A la carte: 100 F.

 Le Récamier
4, rue Récamier
45 48 86 58

Closed Sun. Open until 10:30 p.m. Private room: 15. Garden dining. Air cond.

Martin Cantegrit, the courtly owner of this elegant Empire-style establishment, has been working with chef Robert Chassat for more than 15 years, a most felicitous union. Burgundian classics (game pâtés, jambon persillé, beef bourguignon with fresh tagliatelle) flank subtly lightened dishes (tiny scallops with mushrooms, fried tuna with pesto sauce) and great desserts. Cantegrit's farm supplies the fresh produce. Le Récamier's clientele— politicians, publishers and media moguls—also enjoy tapping the 100,000-bottle cellar, surely one of the city's best. In summer the restaurant's lovely terrace spills across a sheltered pedestrian zone for fume-free outdoor dining.

A la carte: 500-600 F.

 Chez Ribe
15, av. de Suffren
45 66 53 79

Closed Sun., Dec. 24-Jan. 2 & Aug. 8-30. Open until 10:30 p.m. Private room: 30. Terrace dining.

You can still eat here for not much more than 200 francs, including a Bordeaux *primeur* or a tasty little white Saumur. Granted, a 178-franc prix-fixe meal is not—yet—hard to find, even in Paris, but chef Pérès's frequently changing menu is always delicious, well prepared and generously served. Our last visit yielded a delicate shellfish sauté, sautéed veal kidneys with fresh pasta and a luscious puff-pastry tart, all

8th arrondissement – RESTAURANTS

graciously served in comfortable turn-of-the-century surroundings.
Menu: 178 F.

 Tan Dinh
60, rue de Verneuil
45 44 04 84

Closed Sun. & Aug. Open until 11 p.m. Air cond. No cards.

Tan Dinh's huge wine list (best Pomerols in Paris) has few equals, even among the city's top restaurants—some say it outclasses the food. One almost suspects that for the Vifian brothers, cuisine is an afterthought, though it was they who 20 years ago introduced Paris to the newest, most refined and creative Vietnamese cooking. Though that early thrill has gone, Robert Vifian acquits himself admirably of such delicious dishes as a fondant of steamed scallops, langoustines with aubergine, and subtle prawns sautéed with scallop coral. If one resists the pricier temptations of the wine list, a dinner here amid the select and stylish Left-Bank crowd need not lead to financial disaster.
A la carte: 300-400 F.

11/20 Thoumieux
79, rue St-Dominique
47 05 49 75

Open daily until 0:30 a.m. Air cond.

A busy, successful bistro where you can tuck into the hearty classics of Auvergne and the south-west: terrines, cassoulets, pigs' trotters, etc. Don't overlook the fine calf brawn, or the cheap-and-cheerful wine list. The dinner crowd is surprisingly glossy.
A la carte: 180-200 F. Menu: 62 F.

Remember to call ahead to reserve your table, and please, if you cannot honour your reservation, be courteous and let the restaurant know.

 Jules Verne
Tour Eiffel, 2nd floor
45 55 61 44,
fax 47 05 94 40

Open daily until 10:30 p.m. Air cond. No pets. Valet parking.

The restaurant with the most beautiful view in Paris has an ambitious new chef in the kitchen. Alain Reix has entirely revamped the Jules Verne's menu, and put his personal stamp on the house repertoire. His is a virile, bold, self-assured style that makes no concessions to prevailing culinary mannerisms, or to the current fashion for old-fashioned fare. Each dish has a distinct personality, a "signature" purely its own. Take, for example, the sauté of langoustines and mackerel given a raffish touch with strips of pig's ear and a sauerkraut salad sparked with cumin; or a fricassée of frogs' legs and escargots with bone-marrow quenelles in a parsley jus; or a fillet of freshwater perch admirably seasoned with a smoky bacon sauce and flanked by irresistible little stuffed crêpes; or turbot cooked on the bone (for juiciness), topped with a brunoise of vegetables tenderly simmered in the most fragrant olive oil, and escorted by a suave aubergine mould. The superb ingredients express all their intrinsic flavours in a harmony that never falters.

Though Reix was trained by master seafood chef Jean Le Divellec (now his neighbour in the seventh arrondissement) he hasn't turned the Jules Verne into a *restaurant de la mer*. Witness a succulent aile de pigeon with a spice and gingerbread sauce, milk-fed veal with a fresh garnish of grapes and grapefruit, and Sisteron lamb in a tasty jus, accompanied by olives and a Provençal vegetable casserole. For a fitting finale to the feast, there is an outstanding apple strudel with caramel suce, or a warm chocolate-cherry cake.
A la carte: 550-800 F. Menus: 290 F, 660 F.

 Vin sur Vin
20, rue de Monttessuy
47 05 14 20

Closed Sat. lunch, Sun. & Mon., Aug. 15-Sep. 1 & Dec. 23-Jan. 2. Open until 10 p.m.

Former sommelier Patrice Vidal has assembled a first-rate cellar made up exclusively of growers' wines, from which he selects a few each week to sell by the glass. The same infectious enthusiasm inspires his brother Marc to concoct inventive dishes that complement the wines: rabbit sausage studded with peanuts, monkfish brochette and scallops with citrus fruit. It's a shame the prices are high and climbing, with no prix-fixe relief in sight.
A la carte: 300-350 F.

8th arrondissement

12/20 Al Ajami
58, rue François-1er
42 25 38 44

Open daily until midnight. Terrace dining. Air cond. Valet parking.

Fortunately the menu's perfunctory French offerings are outnumbered by authentic dishes from the Lebanese highlands—assorted mezes, chawarma, keftedes and deliciously sticky pastries. The wines contribute a dash of local colour to the refined, grey-and-blue dining room.
A la carte: 200-300 F. Menus: 99 F and 109 F (weekdays only), 119 F.

12/20 L'Alsace
39, av. des Champs-Elysées

43 59 44 24,
fax 42 89 06 62
Open daily 24 hours. Terrace dining. Air cond.

Since this lively brasserie never closes, you can go there any time at all to enjoy perfect oysters, delicious sauerkraut and the fresh white wines of Alsace.

A la carte: 250-300 F.

 Les Ambassadeurs
Hôtel de Crillon
10, pl. de la Concorde
44 71 16 16,
fax 44 71 15 02
Open daily until 10:30 p.m. Private room: 120. Air cond. No pets. Valet parking.

The magnificent and intimidating dining room, rich in gold and marble, seems more fitting for an ambassadors' banquet than an intimate dinner or a joyous feast. Customers eat with their voices kept low and their elbows off the table, terrified someone will drop a fork. At least you'll enjoy the cooking of Christian Constant, who after a tentative start is now giving full rein to his talent and personality. His dishes have a reassuringly rural feel that contrasts with the coolly formal setting: wild mushrooms in a bordelaise sauce, duck and spinach sausage, turbot barded with bacon, oxtail and bone marrow, and a braised Bresse chicken with baby onions. Just two small criticisms—we'd like to see rather less formal service and more flattering lighting in the evenings. The excellent wine list can make an already stiff bill harder to swallow, but sommelier Jean-Claude Maître is always willing to recommend some more affordable selections. Menus: 320 F (weekdays lunch only), 570 F.

11/20 **Aux Amis du Beaujolais**
28, rue d'Artois
45 63 92 21
Closed Sat. dinner & Sun. Open until 9 p.m.

The full gamut of French bistro food is represented here—poule au riz, rabbit in mustard sauce, calf brawn, roast beef and chips—washed down with one of the ten tasty *crus* of Beaujolais, which the jolly owner bottles himself. Friendly prices, full plates, forgettable décor.

A la carte: 150-180 F.

12/20 **Baumann Marbeuf**
15, rue Marbeuf
47 20 11 11,
fax 47 23 69 65
Closed 2 wks. in Aug. Open until 1 a.m. Private room: 22. Air cond.

Patrons perch on stools at the bar, or sit at convivial round tables amid the splendid marbles and mirrors of designer Slavik's décor, to feast on shellfish, baroque choucroutes (not all equally successful), and properly hung meats from Scotland and south-west France. We like the chocolate cake, too, and the thirst-quenching Alsatian wines.

A la carte: 260-350 F.

12/20 **Bice**
6, rue Balzac
42 89 86 34
Closed Sat. lunch, Sun., Dec. 23-Jan. 4 & Aug. 3-17. Open until 11:30 p.m. Private room: 48. Air cond. Valet parking.

Amiable Italian (or Italian-style) waiters leap and dash among the young, moneyed clientele (Saint-Tropez, *prêt-à-porter*, the Levant) that gathers in this refined, blond-wood version of Harry's Bar. The food used to be pretty good but that is no longer the case: we were disappointed by the insipid roast peppers, over-

cooked lamb and lamentably unauthentic tiramisù. It's not cheap either and the Italian wines are expensive. The dining room gets terribly crowded after 10 p.m.

A la carte: 340-420 F.

13 **Le Bistrot du Sommelier**
97, bd Haussmann
42 65 24 85
Closed Sat. dinner, Sun. & Aug. 1-29. Open until 10:30 p.m. Private room: 25. Air cond.

Thanks to a new chef, the cooking is now on a par with this bistro's fabled wine cellar: we can recommend the fresh tuna steak with mild garlic, young rabbit with tiny onions and Chablis, and rib steak in red wine sauce (a robust Syrah, in this case). Owner Philippe Faure-Brac, one of the city's most worthy wine buffs, was crowned "World's Best Sommelier" in 1992.

A la carte: 280-400 F. Menu: 350 F (weekdays dinner only, wine incl.).

12/20 **Le Bœuf sur le Toit**
34, rue du Colisée
43 59 83 80,
fax 45 63 45 40
Open daily until 2 a.m. Air cond.

From a seat on the mezzanine watch the dazzling swirl of diners and waiters reflected a hundredfold in this mirrored, flower-filled room. But don't get so distracted that you can't enjoy the faultless seafood, copious brasserie food or the fruity young wines served in *pichets*.

A la carte: 230-280 F.

 Chez Bosc
7, rue Richepanse
42 60 10 27
Closed Sat. lunch, Sun. & Aug. 1-15. Open until 10:30 p.m.

Yves Labrousse transferred his restaurant last year from the Left Bank to this new, elegant, streamlined setting. Happily, he brought along his penchant for moderate prices (the price of the set lunch hasn't changed in three years). Unfortunately, our last visit left us wondering if he hadn't lost some of his formerly flawless technique. Alongside a flavourful, perfectly cooked dish of sweetbreads and morels, we sampled a tasteless sole soufflé and a severely oversalted mussel feuilleté. The staff, kept to a minimum, do what they can—but the service is not so gracious as it once was.

A la carte: 350-400 F. Menu: 190 F.

Le Bristol
Hôtel Bristol
112, rue du Faubourg-St-Honoré
42 66 91 45,
fax 42 66 68 68

Open daily until 10:30 p.m. Private room: 60. Air cond. No pets. Heated pool. Garage parking.

The atmosphere and prices are what you might expect in this heavily guarded hotel near the French President's residence and surrounded by embassies and high-class shops. Seated in the sumptuous dining room lined with Regency wood panelling or outside on the patio with its potted orange trees, you'll find no jarring notes from the dishes prepared by Emile Tabourdiau. Impeccably trained staff will serve you langoustine salad, crab and avocado ragoût, brill with spinach, or saddle of rabbit in a delectable crust of sliced potatoes. The desserts are equally tempting and the cellar boasts a breathtaking array of expensive vintages.

A la carte: 700-800 F. Menus: 440 F and 590 F.

Find the address you are looking for, quickly and easily, in the index.

Le Carpaccio
Hôtel Royal Monceau
35-39, av. Hoche
45 62 76 87,
fax 45 63 04 03

Closed Aug. Open until 10:30 p.m. Air cond. No pets. Heated pool. Valet parking.

A warm Italian atmosphere awaits you beneath the chandeliers, where you can sample the sunny cuisine of Italy at its best. Start off with the eponymous carpaccio, paper-thin raw beef further glorified with aged Parmesan, olive oil and a squirt of lemon juice. Save room for the fresh pasta with pesto sauce and veal escalopes stuffed with aubergine and herbs, and wash down these delightful dishes with a slightly chilled Valpolicella.

A la carte: 450-650 F. Menus: 280 F (lunch only, wine incl.), 340 F (dinner only, wine incl.).

12/20 ### Caviar Kaspia
17, pl. de la Madeleine
42 65 33 32

Closed Sun. Open until 12:30 a.m. Private room: 25. Air cond.

The fine-feathered folk who frequent this dark but charming upper room opposite the Madeleine come to nibble (caviars, salmon roe, smoked sturgeon) rather than feast (smoked fish assortments, bortsch, etc.). But all the offerings, large and small, are quite good and are courteously served.

A la carte: 300-350 F (without caviar).

Chiberta
3, rue A.-Houssaye
45 63 77 90,
fax 45 62 85 08

Closed Sat., Sun., Dec. 24-Jan. 3 & Aug. 1-29. Open until 11 p.m. Air cond.

Along with Fouquet's, Chiberta is the only haunt of *le Tout-Paris* left on the Champs Elysées. Nabobs from the worlds of finance and television gather here for lunch, relayed by the *beau monde* in the evening. The dining room is discreet, the modern décor is ageing gracefully, the floral displays are as sumptuous as ever and—the big news—the food has never been better. Chef Philippe Da Silva was number two here for ten years, but since his recent promotion he has surpassed both himself and his predecessor in the execution of a menu that highlights sublime sauces and a sophisticated use of herbs and seasonings. Examples are cold crayfish consommé with crème au caviar; lobster cannelloni with a truffled shellfish fumet; cod sautéed with a coulis of wild mushrooms and Belgian endive; red mullet in a curried Sauternes sauce; veal kidney cooked whole in its juices with horseradish and capers. All these dishes attest to Da Silva's finesse and good taste. Proprietor Louis-Noël Richard's passion for red Burgundies is infectious but ruinous. Remarkable desserts.

A la carte: 500 F and up.

Clovis
Pullman Windsor
4, av. Bertie-Albrecht
45 61 15 32

Closed Sat., Sun. & holidays. Open until 10:30 p.m. Air cond. Valet parking.

The chef, a former assistant to Michel Rostang, is a master of culinary technique, and we are pleased to announce that he seems to have developed an appealing style all his own. Gone are the heavy hand and the *tours de force*; instead, there are bright-tasting dishes such as terrine de jarret de veau à l'orange, pork tenderloin garnished with a carrot galette and a sprightly salad of squid and baby artichokes. Clever, tasty desserts, and an interesting wine list. Service is flawless in the pretty pink-and-beige dining room.

A la carte: 400-500 F. Menus: 175 F (dinner only), 190 F, 345 F.

 Copenhague
142, av. des Champs-Elysées
43 59 20 41,
fax 42 25 83 10

Closed Sun., holidays, 1st wk. of Jan. & Aug. 2-29. Open until 10:30 p.m. Air cond.

Salmon—smoked, pickled, marinated or grilled—and delicious tender herring prepared in every imaginable way are the stars of this limited menu. The other dishes are dull and terribly expensive. If the weather is fine, ask to be seated on the patio behind the Flora Danica.

A la carte: 350-550 F.

 La Couronne
Hôtel Warwick
5, rue de Berri
45 63 14 11,
fax 45 63 75 81

Closed holidays & Aug. Open until 10:30 p.m. Private room: 120. Air cond.

Winner of international cooking awards, chef Van Gessel is into his stride once more. The delicious prix-fixe lunch (a bargain compared to the costly à la carte offerings) might consist of warm salad of lotte and duck liver, sole matelote with onion confit, excellent cheeses and apple macaroon. The newly redone dining room will not win any awards for interior decoration, and it is unfortunately stuck into a corner of the Hotel Warwick lobby. Van Gessel's fine work deserves a larger audience than just the hotel guests and business people at lunch.

A la carte: 420-500 F. Menu: 220 F (weekdays lunch only), 270 F (weekdays & Sat. dinner), 390 F (weekdays dinner & Sat., wine incl.).

12/20 Diep
55, rue P.-Charron
45 63 52 76
22, rue de Ponthieu
42 56 23 96

Open daily until 11:45 p.m. Air cond.

This is the flagship of the Diep family's three-restaurant fleet. The décor is Bangkok swank and the food Asian eclectic; the grilled chicken with lemon grass and the garlic pork are successful, but the shrimp and rice crêpes and the heavy fish fritters are not. Desserts are worth a try (we like the sticky-rice cake with coconut), but the wines are too expensive. Other address: 28, rue Louis-le-Grand in the second arrondissement.

A la carte: 240-310 F.

11/20 Drugstore des Champs-Elysées
133, av. des Champs-Elysées
47 23 54 34

Open daily until 1:30 a.m. Terrace dining. Air cond.

Believe it or not, the food at this landmark of 1960s chic is not bad at all. The 78-franc two-course meal is more than acceptable, and the main-course salads, grills and crisp pommes frites go very well with the vibrant, bustling atmosphere.

A la carte: 150-200 F. Menu: 78 F.

 Chez Edgard
4, rue Marbeuf
47 20 51 15

Closed Sun. & Aug. 1-23. Open until 12:30 a.m. Private room: 35. Terrace dining.

Just because it has often been said that the *gratin* of French politics eats here, don't expect to see Michel Rocard or Laurent Fabius seated across from you. "Monsieur Paul" serves up to 500 meals here each day, and in any case the Parisian powers-that-be are always whisked off to the quiet private rooms upstairs. Downstairs, amid the typically Gallic brouhaha, the rest of us can choose from a wide range of dishes, from fresh thon à la basquaise to onglet à l'échalote, all prepared with care and skill.

A la carte: 300-400 F.

 Elysée-Lenôtre
10, av. des Champs-Elysées
42 65 85 10,
fax 42 65 76 23

Closed Sat. lunch & Sun. Open until 10:30 p.m. Private

The milk of Sacré-Cœur

An evergreen favourite with amateur artists and the most popular subject of Parisian postcards, the Sacré-Cœur owes its dazzling whiteness to a stone that secretes a milky substance when it rains. Whether you love or loathe its striking Byzantine architecture, it's hard to escape the basilica, which stands atop the highest point of Montmartre. It took more than 40 years to build and since its consecration in 1919 a continuous succession of faithful volunteers have been praying round the clock to atone for the sins of humanity. Climb up to the dome for a sweeping view that takes in Montmartre cemetery and a patchwork of private walled gardens.

8th arrondissement – RESTAURANTS

room: 150. Terrace dining. Air cond. Valet parking.

Business was so bad in this Belle Epoque pavilion, once dear to the hearts of Edward VII and Alphonse XIII, that the proprietors were rumoured to be on the verge of throwing in the towel. But things began to look up, and now tables are much in demand. It's hard to imagine a better spot for a restaurant: in the middle of gardens in the middle of the city, just over the wall from Mitterrand's flower beds. The 340-franc prix-fixe luncheon has been a great success with a select clientele, who choose from among ten first courses (mallard terrine with juniper berries, for example) and ten main dishes (an excellent breast of Loire chicken with endive is popular). There are cheeses to finish, along with desserts in the grand tradition (we applaud the caramelised pears with liquorice flan). If you order à la carte, be prepared to pay more (much more).

A la carte: 500-800 F. Menus: 340 F (lunch only), 580 F (dinner only).

 Les Elysées du Vernet
Hôtel Vernet
25, rue Vernet
47 23 43 10

Closed Sat., Sun & Aug. Open until 10 p.m. Air cond. No pets. Valet parking.

Which way is the Riviera please? We'd suggest this elegant address just off the Champs Elysées. Although you won't have a view of the Mediterranean, Bruno Cirino's cuisine brings the perfumes and flavours of Provence into the glass-roofed dining room. This talented chef often flies home to Nice at weekends to fetch the vegetables, herbs and other specialities he finds it hard to cook without. You might like to whet your appetite with a dish of tiny fish (red mullet, fresh anchovies, squid and langoustines) with garlic mayonnaise before moving on to lobster with smoked bacon or a roast farmhouse duckling scented with mushrooms and olives and so tasty you'd swear it was a wild bird. Bruno Cirino's desserts are still improving too: try the warm bitter chocolate tart or the aromatic coffee ice-cream. Let's hope his honeymoon at Les Elysées du Vernet lasts and that the prices stop their ever-upward spiral.

A la carte: 400-500 F. Menus: 270 F (lunch only), 420 F (dinner only).

11/20 **Elysées Mandarin**
23, rue Washington
42 25 71 20

Closed Sun. & Aug. 6-15. Open until 11:30 p.m. Air cond.

Book a table in the front room (which is fridge-and-microwave-free, unlike the rear dining room), and enjoy the good Thai food: grilled ravioli, prawn salad, Szechuan shrimp and shellfish soup scented with lemon grass.

A la carte: 190-240 F. Menus: 80 F, 85 F, 129 F.

 Fakhr el Dine
3, rue Q.-Bauchart
47 23 74 24

Open daily until 12:30 a.m. Air cond. Valet parking.

Ignore the insipid décor, and focus instead on the delicious Lebanese mezes, which dazzle the eye as they delight the palate: bone-marrow salad, brains in lemon sauce, spinach fritters, fried lamb's sweetbreads, etc. These titbits are offered in batches of 8, 10, 15 or 20, depending on the size of the company and your appetite.

A la carte: 220-300 F. Menus: 210 F, 230 F.

 La Fermette Marbeuf 1900
5, rue Marbeuf
47 20 63 53,
fax 40 70 02 11

Open daily until 11:30 p.m. Terrace dining. Air cond.

Jean Laurent wisely decided not to send prices skyward after genuine Belle Epoque décor—now listed by the Beaux-Arts—was discovered during renovations some years ago. Reasonable prices still prevail at the Fermette for superb andouillette, saddle of lamb, and hearty stewed pork cheek with a hint of ginger, and there is a delicious 160-franc prix-fixe dinner. Moderation, quality and affability are the rule here. As a result, customers quickly become regulars and the staff remains the same—both good signs.

A la carte: 280-300 F. Menu: 160 F.

 Fouquet's
99, av. des Champs-Elysées
47 23 70 60,
fax 47 20 08 69

Open daily until 12:30 a.m. Private room: 200. Terrace dining. Valet parking.

Aesthetically speaking, Fouquet's décor is nothing to write home about, but in the end the only way to save this nerve centre of Parisian high life was to have it listed. At the same time the management has attracted some young bloods from the film and advertising world, so the tone of the place is lively once more. The menu can be a bit of a minefield, but you won't go far wrong if you order the perennially perfect merlan Colbert, the daube of beef with carrots or the charcoal-grilled steak. Paradoxically, the food is considerably better at the two new Fouquet's restaurants (at the Bastille and La Défense) than here at the old original.

A la carte: 300-600 F. Menu: 250 F.

Chez Francis
7, pl. de l'Alma
47 20 86 83,
fax 45 56 98 42

Open daily until 1 a.m. Private room: 70. Terrace dining. Air cond.

The smart patrons are reflected and multiplied by rows of engraved mirrors—so much the better for them, since they obviously take more pleasure in who they're seeing than in what they're eating (though the canard en daube au gratin de macaroni is quite good, as are the shellfish).

A la carte: 300 F. Menu: 180 F (wine incl.).

Les Géorgiques
36, av. George-V
40 70 10 49

Closed Sat. lunch & Sun. Open until 10:30 p.m. Private room: 18. Air cond.

Twenty years' training with the masters of the old school (Rostang, etc.) have left Katsumaro Ishimaru forever stranded in a culinary time warp, surrounded by tournedos Rossini, turbot stuffed with foie gras in Madeira and similar dinosaur dishes. It's a pity his fine technique is chained to so banal a repertoire. The décor is downright funereal; prices are chilling.

A la carte: 350-600 F. Menus: 180 F (lunch only), 360 F.

11/20 Germain
19, rue Jean-Mermoz
43 59 29 24

Closed Sat., Sun., Aug. & holidays. Open until 9:30 p.m.

One of the last bastions of French home cooking anywhere near the Champs Elysées, this restaurant which seats 30 people offers beef bourguignon, coq au vin, and so on at reasonable prices.

A la carte: 150-180 F.

Le Grenadin
44-46, rue de Naples
45 63 28 92

Closed Sat., Sun., wk. of July 14 & wk. of Aug. 15. Open until 10:30 p.m. Private room: 16. Air cond.

A lovely dining room of little nooks and different levels, enlarged with mirrors, is a very pleasant setting for Patrick Cirotte's flavourful, adventurous cooking. Ingredients are the key here—they are uniformly first-rate and handled with respect and simplicity, from the foie gras sautéed without a speck of fat and served with a lentil salad, to the delicious sea bass fillet baked in a salt crust. Desserts are far above average.

A la carte: 350-400 F. Menus: 200 F, 320 F, 370 F.

Au Jardin du Printemps
32, rue de Penthièvre
43 59 32 91

Closed Sun. & Aug. Open until 11:30 p.m. Private room: 30. Air cond.

The three Tan brothers tend to fawn over the political and social celebrities who over the years have come to regard their restaurant as an unofficial clubhouse. Alongside some decent Chinese standards, Tan Le-Huy prepares some very good Vietnamese specialities, many of which are given an appealing personal twist. Try the pho soup, peppery grilled beef fillet and spare ribs in black bean sauce. Elegant lacquered décor.

A la carte: 200-350 F.

Le Jardin du Royal Monceau
Hôtel Royal Monceau
35, av. Hoche
45 62 96 02,
fax 45 63 04 03

Open daily until 10:30 p.m. Garden dining. Air cond. Heated pool. Valet parking.

You step into another world when you enter the bright dining room, its french windows opening onto manicured lawns and immaculate flower beds. Surrounded by buildings, this garden seems to have been brought to central Paris by the wave of a magic wand. The same spell operates in the kitchen, where Bernard Guilhaudin conjures up delectable food with no unnecessary embellishments, each dish the object of infinite care. The ox cheek cooked in celery stock or cabbage stuffed with veal and shellfish are as tasty as they are unpretentious. This talented chef handles desserts with similar passion: try the blancmange or the banana and mango millefeuille. The service is impeccable and the young sommelier provides excellent advice on a well-chosen wine list.

A la carte: 400-550 F. Menus: 280 F (weekdays lunch and holidays), 420 F (dinner except Sun., wine incl.).

Lasserre
17, av. F.-Roosevelt
43 59 53 43,
fax 45 63 72 23

Closed Mon. lunch, Sun. & Aug. Open until 10:30 p.m. Private room: 55. Air cond. Valet parking.

One of the few surviving examples of le grand restaurant à la française, this grandiose establishment merits your attention for the ethnological interest it presents. Nowhere else is the service so minutely choreographed, the atmosphere so festive yet well-bred (piano music, soft lights, glowing silver, silken carpets...). Don't forget to look up as

Lasserre's retractable roof brings you (weather and visibility permitting) the stars. As you look back down you'll notice that the menu is a rich man's dream of French cuisine: duck à l'orange, tournedos béarnaise and crêpes flambées. Look more closely and you'll find some lighter, more interesting options like freshwater perch with crab, precisely cooked scallops with asparagus, Bresse chicken en papillote... But no matter how hard you squint at the wine list, you won't find a bottle of wine for less than 300 francs!

A la carte: 600-800 F.

Laurent

41, av. Gabriel
42 25 00 39,
fax 45 62 45 21

Closed Sat. lunch, Sun. & holidays. Open until 11 p.m. Private room: 84. Terrace dining. Air cond. Valet parking.

Parisians are talking about Laurent's new décor: has Jimmy Goldsmith opened his wallet wide enough to restore a gastronomic pleasure dome on the opulent order of Ledoyen and Elysée-Lenôtre? The debate is still open. A talented young chef from Robuchon's stable, Philippe Braun, has joined a team that includes an intelligent manager, a virtuoso maître d'hôtel and one of the world's best sommeliers. His food is not flashy, but it is based on ingredients that are absolutely prime: pearly turbot with fresh pasta and morels, kid with thyme and mild garlic, sea bream with baby onions and asparagus all evince clean-cut, clearly focused flavours. The desserts, by comparison with the rest of the menu (or the fabulous wine list), seem lacklustre.

A la carte: 800 F and up.
Menus: 380 F (lunch only), 880 F.

Ledoyen

Carré des Champs-Elysées
47 42 23 23,
fax 47 42 55 01

Closed Sun. Open until 10:30 p.m. Private room: 250. Air cond. Valet parking.

Régine has ended her association with this gilt-edged restaurant, and chef Philippe Dorange followed right on her heels. Sous-chef François Lemercier is now in charge of Le Carré (the establishment's elegant grill) and the best news is that Ghislaine Arabian, the toast of Lille, has been lured to head the prestigious *restaurant gastronomique*. A three-toque (18/20) winner at her last establishment, Madame Arabian plans to seduce the Parisian dining public with her signature dishes based on northern ingredients: smoked mussel soup, turbot poached in beer, vanilla cream with gingerbread... As soon as she's settled in, we'll sample her menu and report back.

Menus: 350 F (lunch only), 600 F (dinner only).

Lucas-Carton

9, pl. de la Madeleine
42 65 22 90,
fax 42 65 06 23

Closed Sat. lunch, Sun., 3 wks. in Aug. Open until 10:30 p.m. Private room: 14. Air cond. Valet parking.

Will Alain Senderens be remembered as the inventor of ravioli de pétoncles? It is easy to make fun of this culinary wizard, as his cultural significance (and pretensions?) continue to grow. His meteoric rise from apprentice to legendary chef has not stopped at the kitchen door; just as Bocuse cast off his apron to become a roving "ambassador of French cuisine", Senderens is bidding fair to become the philosopher of Gallic gastronomy.

A literate chef was once as astonishing a rarity as Dr. Johnson's woman preacher, but with more and more young *cuisiniers* entering the kitchen from university, the craft of cookery has acquired a cultural dimension. Having said that, however, anyone with normally tuned tastebuds is sufficiently equipped to savour Senderens's extraordinary inventions. So, as the French say: *à table*.

Eventhia Senderens's skills as a hostess have greatly improved, so that the ambience in this stunning Belle Epoque dining room, panelled in glowing blond wood, has warmed up considerably, making the food seem more wonderful still. And at its best, Senderens's cooking is wonderful beyond words. Yet as some disgruntled readers have not failed to point out, when you pay more than 300 francs for roast lamb, or 480 francs for the famed homard à la vanille, you are not willing to countenance anything but perfection. And when flaws do occur, it is natural to blame Senderens for straying from his kitchen. In all fairness, though, one ought not to confuse his role with that of his head chef. For even in the master's absence the thoroughly drilled staff, led by Bertrand Guéneron and Philippe Peudenier, deliver perfect versions of such Senderens creations as a sublime confit of foie gras with tiny artichokes, or prawns sautéed in tarragon butter served with a heavenly bouillon, or cod cooked in its skin to retain all the juices, accompanied by fragrantly herby "crumbled" potatoes, or lapin Isidoria (the saddle roasted with mustard, the hind legs shredded and tossed with foie gras). Not every dish is above criticism: a perfectly cooked sea bream with a bracing touch of vinegar sported a fussy, purely "decorative" garnish of almonds and cuttlefish ravioli. And pink peppercorns—that plague of nouvelle cuisine—added nothing to a tasty pigeon cressonnière. But our pleasure in his gâteau au chocolat croustillant, or the aumonière au coulis d'abricots, or the sublime vanilla ice cream hasn't diminished. And Lucas-Carton is surely the place where today's most thrilling marriages of food and wine are arranged (Dominique Derozier presides over the unparalleled cellar).

Menus: 420 F (lunch only), 990 F (wine incl.) 750 F.

12/20 Le Manoir Normand

77, bd de Courcelles
42 27 38 97

Closed Sun. & July 10-18, wk. of Aug. 15. Open until 10:30 p.m. Terrace dining. Parking.

In France, a restaurateur named Pommerai (roughly equivalent to "apple orchard"), can hardly do otherwise than give his restaurant a Norman accent. But apart from some fish in cream-based sauces and a fine apple tart, the menu is agreeably free from regional chauvinism. Delicious *plats du jour*, and excellent meats grilled in the big fireplace. Glass-enclosed terrace.

A la carte: 280-350 F. Menus: 100 F (except holidays), 145 F.

La Marée

1, rue Daru
43 80 20 00,
fax 48 88 04 04

Closed Sat., Sun. & Aug. Open until 10:30 p.m. Air cond. Valet parking.

At a restaurant named for the tide—La Marée—you would naturally expect to eat fish. But the best meal we've ever had here was a juicy saddle of rabbit served whole with small onions, chanterelles and courgettes. The old-fashioned pâté en croûte is still among the best in Paris and the once-famous selection of pastries has regained its former glory. The best news, however, is that the fish are no longer drowned in creamy sauces or cooked to the point of no flavour-return. After an exquisite skate terrine with a herby vinaigrette or a luxurious lobster carpaccio, you might move on to the bracingly briny sea bream with its unusual accompaniment of Swiss chard cooked in meat glaze. These and other dishes are served, as always, by a courteous, even benevolent staff. Take your time over the wine list, which features some exceptional bargains (like the '85 white Burgundy Les Perrières from Simon Bize, priced at 140 francs).

A la carte: 550 F and up.

Maxim's

3, rue Royale
42 65 27 94,
fax 40 17 02 91

Open daily (except Sun. in July-Aug.). Open until 11:30 p.m. Private room: 90. Air cond. Valet parking.

Now that Maxim's once-frightful prices are common currency at many another less glamorous establishment, is this glorious Belle Epoque monument doomed to become just another restaurant? Heaven forfend! The trouble is, times have changed. The chic, sleek Parisians who made Maxim's a legend now keep their jewels locked up in the family safe, and leave revelry to the young and the hoi polloi; the day of the dapper *boulevardier* is long over. But Maxim's remains, its marvellous mahogany, bronzes and glass sparkle and glow—it has become a mausoleum for an era whose passing it refuses to acknowledge. The ghost of Maxim's former gaiety occasionally returns at lunch, when an urbane crowd fills the place with sophisticated chatter as they pick at their food. Speaking of the food, chef Michel Menant does an admirable job, considering the hundreds of meals he is obliged to serve each day. We were enchanted, on a recent visit, by the prawns en gelée, delectable fried baby red mullet and delicious bœuf mode. Hats off to him and to the invariably stylish, civilised serving staff.

A la carte: 500-700 F (lunch only), 900 F and up (dinner only).

Daniel Metery

4, rue de l'Arcade
42 65 53 13

Closed Sat. lunch, Sun. & 1st wk. of Aug. Open until 10:15 p.m.

Metery, a dedicated and hard-working disciple of the renowned Michel Guérard, not long ago took over this pretty pink-and-beige restaurant. Though he has yet to realise his full potential, we are delighted with his pigeon salad, his exotically flavoured lamb with vegetable ravioli and a luscious honey-apricot pastry. The cellar is expanding, and some good wines are offered by the glass.

A la carte: 340-400 F. Menus: 230 (dinner only), 175 F.

11/20 Mollard

113, rue St-Lazare
43 87 50 22

Open daily until 1 a.m. Private room: 100.

An extraordinary turn-of-the-century ceramic mural depicts destinations of the trains that depart from the Gare Saint-Lazare across the street. The food is not nearly so enchanting. Safe bets include the platter of shellfish, the

Chateaubriand and the omelette surprise, but skip the sandre à la vanille. Courteous welcome, discreet service.

A la carte: 220-280 F. Menu: 178 F.

 Napoléon
Hôtel Napoléon
38, av. de Friedland
42 27 99 50,
fax 47 66 82 33

Closed Sat., Sun. & Aug. Open until 10:30 p.m. Private room: 20. Air cond.

Better known as the sauerkraut king, Guy-Pierre Baumann is now branching out into seafood. He has opened for business with brand-new décor and a Senderens-trained chef. So far, however, the results aren't entirely convincing. The food is delicate and imaginative, yes, but also fussy and complicated. Nicely garnished with Jerusalem artichokes and mangetout peas, the skate was more than a shade overcooked; a commendable sea bream baked in a salt crust was needlessly encumbered with vegetable chips. Desserts are quite good, and the cellar is stocked with some wonderful white wines.

A la carte: 400-500 F. Menu: 240 F.

12/20 L'Obélisque
Hôtel de Crillon
10, pl. de la Concorde
44 71 15 15,
fax 44 71 15 02

Closed holidays & Aug. Open until 10:30 p.m. Air cond. Valet parking.

To eat at the Hôtel Crillon without breaking the bank, try its other, less formal restaurant. You'll still benefit from top-notch service and a menu supervised by Christian Constant, chef of Les Ambassadeurs (see above). The food is classic and filling: pig's trotter sausage with potato purée, tongue and foie gras wrapped in flaky pastry, fresh rhubarb tart.

A la carte: 250-350 F. Menu: 230 F.

 Au Petit Montmorency
26, rue J.-Mermoz
42 25 11 19

Closed Sat., Sun. & Aug. Open until 10:30 p.m. Private room: 20. Air cond.

Twenty years ago we discovered Daniel Bouché at Le Petit Montmorency, in the Marais district of Paris, and enthralled by the aromas that emanated from his cupboard-sized kitchen, we predicted a great future for this bold, inventive chef. We later tracked him down to the rue Rabelais, where Au Petit Montmorency was surrounded by barricades and soldiers assigned to protect the nearby Israeli embassy. But luck smiled on Bouché, who recently acquired the shop next door to his restaurant, giving him a new address and an unimpeded entrance.

Inside, the restaurant is pleasantly old-fashioned, and eclectically decorated with culinary prints and bric-a-brac. Bouché's tastes are eclectic too, but he has successfully struggled to tame his more outlandish fantasies, and now gives disciplined expression to his culinary imagination. The result is a pure, luminous cuisine that fully deserves three toques.

Bouché dazzled us not long ago with sublime fresh truffles veiled in a diaphanous crust and heightened by a lightly creamy, boldly spiced truffle jus; afterwards came a sumptuous turbot steak (he fetches the fish himself, from Normandy) simply baked with tomatoes and olive oil. Meat-lovers will go for the rosy, peppery veal kidney, or the beef entrecôte en pot-au-feu, the stuffed rabbit with wild rice, or a sweet-and-sour duck with turnips. Finish with cheese, if you like—you'll rarely encounter a better Livarot or a more expertly aged Cantal—but you really should save room for the souffléed lemon crêpes, or a coupe of caramelised honey ice cream with gingerbread croûtons. Nicole Bouché tends the splendid cellar, and greets customers with disarming warmth. Lulled by this deliciousness, your shock may be all the greater when the waiter presents the bill.

A la carte: 450-900 F.

 Le Pichet
68, rue P.-Charron
43 59 50 34

Closed Sat., Sun., Dec. 19-Jan. 3 & Aug. 10-30. Open until midnight. Air cond.

New owners have scrubbed and polished this old Pichet, which is currently enjoying considerable success with its excellent shellfish assortments, plats du jour and some creditable fish dishes (skate in warm vinaigrette; cod à l'unilatérale). These and other simple dishes please a sporty but urbane crowd, which sometimes includes François Mitterrand.

A la carte: 350-400 F.

 Le Prince de Galles
Marriott Prince de Galles
33, av. George-V
47 23 55 11

Open daily until 10:30 p.m. Private room: 180. Garden dining. Air cond. Valet parking.

The Prince of Wales beats King George (see below) hands down in the culinary arena. Ex-Robuchon disciple (and former chef to the Rothschilds), Dominique Cécillon has emerged from a barren patch and is now back in peak form, preparing a cuisine laudably free of hotel-dining-room pomposity, but which maintains a suitably high tone. Warm prawns with chanterelles, turbot à la nage, lobster in Sauternes cream, and pot-au-feu of beef fillet are very nearly as delicious as they are expensive. In contrast, the set menus are incredible bargains, especially considering the luxurious setting and service. But please, chef Cécillon, do get rid of the fussy, precious menu descriptions that make your wonderful dishes sound ridiculous.

A la carte: 400-700 F. Menus: 250 F (Sun. lunch only, wine incl.), 235 F.

 Les Princes
George-V
31, av. George-V
47 23 54 00

Open until 10:30 p.m. Private room: 54. Terrace dining. Air cond. Valet parking.

This dog-eared hotel dining room is undergoing renovations at last. But the facelift alone won't lure back the public—chef Pierre Larapidie should consider revamping his menu, which could also do with some grace and style. In fine weather, book a table on the beautiful flower-covered patio. And when the winter winds blow, give the Prince a cold shoulder and head instead for the Grill George-V, a convivial venue where prices are more affordable and Larapidie's repertoire shows flashes of its former verve.

A la carte: 600-750 F. Menus: 350 F (weekdays lunch only, wine incl.), 450 F (except weekdays lunch and holidays).

 15 Montaigne
La Maison Blanche
15, av. Montaigne
47 23 55 99

Closed Sat. lunch & Sun. Open until midnight. Private room: 40.

Terrace dining. Air cond. Valet parking.

José Martinez now presides over the dazzling, ultra-modern kitchens built for his brother-in-law, the late, lamented José Lampreia. Lampreia's inventive, very personal style still marks the menu: cod with lemon tajine, pigeon with dates, potato galette with salt cod and aïoli are all fresh and appealing, though the portions are skimpy. The young serving staff is far more competent than at the restaurant's debut, and the welcome has warmed up a few degrees as well.

A la carte: 500-600 F.

 Régence-Plaza
Plaza Athénée
25, av. Montaigne
47 23 78 33

Open daily until 10:30 p.m. Private room: 110. Garden dining. Air cond. Valet parking.

The new chef, Gérard Sallé from Deauville, has brought a breath of fresh air to what had been a rather stuffy menu. Lobster soufflé and seafood mixed grill have made way for scallops simmered with coriander, delicate veal sweetbreads perfumed with sage and braised crab brimful of natural flavour. Gérard Sallé will probably find it harder to modify the menu at the hotel's grill restaurant, Le Relais. Opulent flowers, traditional service, musical luncheons et tout le tralala.

A la carte: 500-600 F. Menu: 330 F (lunch except weekdays).

 Le Relais Vermeer
Hôtel Golden Tulip
218, rue du Faubourg-St-Honoré
49 53 03 03

Closed Sat. & Sun. Evenings only a "Brasserie" carte. Open until 10 p.m. Heated pool.

A luxurious restaurant for a luxurious hotel, owned by the Dutch Golden Tulip chain. In a restful grey-blue-and-pink dining room, sample Scandinavian fare full of piquant contrasts between sweet and salty flavours: reindeer fillet with an onion and orange confit, smoked eels in puff pastry and salmon in every possible permutation. Good hot cheese dishes. Chilly service. Steven Spurrier designed the wine list.

A la carte: 300-500 F. Menu: 195 F.

12/20 **Le Saint-Germain**
74, av. des Champs-Elysées
45 63 55 45

Closed w.-e. Open until 9:30 p.m. Air cond.

Buried beneath the Claridge's shopping arcade, this pleasant establishment boasts a new chef, who offers careful, thoughtful cooking: seafood ragoût with fresh pasta, roast lamb au jus with fresh mint. Appealing pastries and good set menus.

Menus: 65 F, 98 F, 165 F, 280 F.

 Saint-Moritz
33, av. de Friedland
45 61 02 74

Closed Sat. & Sun. Open until 10:15 p.m. Terrace dining.

Chef Alain Raichon hails from the Jura, and his cooking too is rooted in that mountain region. Sample his Morteau sausage with warm potato salad, fresh morels and asparagus tips in puff pastry, or sole fillets cooked in Arbois white wine. Fresh seasonal specialities (red-mullet terrine with dill; fig and citrus soup) are featured on the single-price menu, which makes this elegant dining room a very popular choice for business luncheons.

Menu: 185 F.

8th arrondissement – RESTAURANTS

12/20 Savy
23, rue Bayard
47 23 46 98
Closed Aug. Open until 11 p.m.

Cramped, ill-lit, with ancient imitation-leather banquettes and an even more ancient ceiling fan, Savy has a hard-to-fathom charm that keeps customers (including some of the capital's most noted radio personalities) coming back for robust country cooking: stuffed cabbage, Auvergne-style calf's liver, tripe, and so on.
A la carte: 220-300 F.

12/20 Sébillon Elysées
66, rue Pierre-Charron
43 59 28 15
Open daily until midnight. Air cond.

As in the sister establishment in Neuilly (see Suburbs), excellent but expensive shellfish platters are followed here by Sébillon's famous leg of lamb, cooked to rosy tenderness and carved before your eyes. Elegant décor, energetic service.
A la carte: 300-350 F.

 Stresa
7, rue de Chambiges
47 23 51 62
Closed Sat. dinner, Sun., Dec. 20-Jan. 3 & Aug. 3-31. Open until 10:30 p.m. Private room: 12. Terrace dining. Air cond.

This shabby but somehow soothing dining room is always full of press, fashion and theatre people who love the antipasti drizzled with fruity Tuscan olive oil, the toothsome osso buco and the smooth tiramisù prepared by Marco Faiola. Claudio and Toni seat their guests with a sure social sense.
A la carte: 350-450 F.

Red toques signify modern cuisine; white toques signify traditional cuisine.

 Taillevent
15, rue Lamennais
45 63 39 94,
fax 42 25 95 18
Closed Sat., Sun., Feb. 13-21 & July 24-Aug. 22. Open until 10:30 p.m. Private room: 32. Air cond. Valet parking.

Having narrowly escaped expropriation, Taillevent's proprietor, Jean-Claude Vrinat, can concentrate on other pressing matters, like enlarging the restaurant's antediluvian kitchens and, even more critically, reaching a new equilibrium now that chef Claude Deligne has retired after more than 30 years of brilliant service.

His successor, Philippe Legendre, a Robuchon disciple, was formerly number two at Taillevent, and is behind the recent shift towards a more creative, perhaps more subtle menu featuring dishes like a delicious cold cream of rock lobster dotted with minuscule diced vegetables, baked crayfish tails coated with a divine, lightly spiced cream sauce, tiny red mullet with basil in a delicate wine sauce, or suprême de pigeon with its giblets in Médoc wine.

It is safe to say that the future of this noble institution will be guided by Vrinat's policy of grounding the kitchen's innovations in the classics and altering the menu prudently, to suit evolving tastes. It will be interesting to observe how Legendre's talent accommodates itself to the Taillevent tradition. In short, the good life, the hushed business luncheons, the quiet cosmopolitan soirées will certainly continue here in a setting of rich hangings, wood panelling, and old pictures (we wouldn't shed a tear, however, should the drab blue velvet and the knick-knack cabinets suddenly disappear). Didier Bordas guides guests through Taillevent's justly vaunted wine list, and the service functions at the highest level of efficiency and discretion.
A la carte: 700-900 F.

 Chez Tante Louise
41, rue Boissy-d'Anglas
42 65 06 85,
fax 42 65 28 19
Closed w.-e. & Aug. Open until 10:30 p.m. Private room: 14. Air cond.

A regular clientele loves being pampered in this snug little restaurant. The Lhiabastres (from Aveyron) know how to make their guests comfortable, feeding them very good south-west cooking that features (slightly) lightened versions of foie gras, snail fricassée, duck à l'orange and crêpes Suzette.
A la carte: 300-400 F. Menu: 200 F.

 Le Trente
Fauchon
30, pl. de La Madeleine
47 42 56 58,
fax 47 42 28 71
Closed Sun. Open until 10:30 p.m. Garden dining. Air cond. Valet parking.

Whoever dreamed up the name (Le Trente—30—is the building's address) of Fauchon's new restaurant won't win any prizes for creativity, but the decorator might, for his "Roman fantasy" interior complete with atrium, columns and trompe-l'œil paintings. Bruno Deligne, son of Taillevent's Claude Deligne, has yet to affirm a clear personality in the kitchen. The menu is too timid by half, particularly since Fauchon is (with Hédiard) the city's temple of rare and exotic foodstuffs. The cuisine is skilful, however, and based on superior ingredients. Desserts are superb, and the wine list is surprisingly affordable.
A la carte: 400-500 F.

12/20 Le Val d'Or
28, av. F.-Roosevelt
43 59 95 81

Open for lunch only. Closed w.-e.

Madame Rongier holds firmly to the traditions of French home cooking, pleasing her patrons with beef in bone-marrow sauce and lapin à la moutarde, escorted by well-chosen wines at reasonable "bistro" prices. The ground-floor bar stays open at night, serving wine by the glass, charcuterie and sandwiches.

A la carte: 200-300 F.

12/20 Chez Vong
27, rue du Colisée
43 59 77 12,
fax 43 59 59 27

Closed Sun. Open until 9:30 p.m. (midnight on Sat.). Private room: 60. Air cond. Valet parking.

Here's everyone's dream of a Chinese restaurant: embroidered silk, furniture inlaid with mother-of-pearl, lots of little nooks, an air of mystery and dishes named "dancing eels", or "plate of the five happinesses". The cooking is generally well done. Oddly enough, the cellar is rich in fine claret.

A la carte: 290-360 F.

Yvan
1 bis, rue J.-Mermoz
43 59 18 40,
fax 45 63 78 69

Closed Sat. lunch & Sun. Open until midnight. Air cond. Valet parking.

Yvan Zaplatilek spells it out for his customers on the restaurant's sign: "Yvan - Cuisine Française". The food is indeed primarily French, and quite creditably done, with an occasional Belgian touch here and there (scallops accompanied by a mousseline flavoured with Gueuze beer; pheasant garnished with endive). Yvan also has a penchant for exotic seasonings, and turns out an excellent lotte with ginger, and veal kidneys spiced with cumin. Not the least of this establishment's virtues are the affordable prices, unmatched in this top-drawer neighbourhood.

A la carte: 250-350 F. Menus: 168 F, 228 F and 278 F (dinner only), 188 F.

9th arrondissement

11/20 Anarkali
4, pl. G.-Toudouze
48 78 39 84

Open daily until 12:30 a.m. Terrace dining.

One of the first Indian restaurants in Paris, this little spot on a quiet, shady square is still one of the best. The tandooris and chicken tikka are good, authentic and inexpensive.

A la carte: 150 F. Menu: 61 F.

Auberge Landaise
23, rue Clauzel
48 78 74 40,
fax 48 78 20 96

Closed Sun. & Aug. 3-25. Open until 10 p.m. Private room: 35. Parking.

In a rustic atmosphere conducive to a hearty tuck-in, Dominique Morin treats his customers to the best cassoulet in town (served piping hot in an individual earthenware pot), pipérade landaise, braised duck with wild mushrooms, foie gras and an array of sturdy south-west wines. Do not overlook the collection of Armagnacs, a perfect way to end a meal in this friendly, relaxed restaurant.

A la carte: 250-350 F.

Find the address you are looking for, quickly and easily, in the index.

Le Bistrot Blanc
52, rue Blanche
42 85 05 30

Closed Sat., Sun., Aug. 1-Sep. 6. Open until 10 p.m.

Bruno Borni, a Marseille native who held the rank of sauce chef at La Tour d'Argent (indeed, his sauces are excellent, well concentrated, light and fragrant), deserves his first toque. Recommended are his tasty ravioli stuffed with fresh sheep cheese, pigeon baked in a salt crust and, to finish, the citrus fruit "marvel". The atmosphere of this soft-pink dining room manages to be charming, despite the standoffish service. Limited cellar.

A la carte: 250-300 F. Menu: 79 F.

12/20 La Champagne
10 bis, pl. de Clichy
48 74 44 78,
fax 42 80 63 10

Open daily until 3 a.m. Private room: 30. Air cond.

Until the small hours you can join the carefree, festive crowd that pays high prices for homard flambé, onion soup, oysters and sauerkraut at this effervescent restaurant. Clever, cheerful staff.

A la carte: 300-400 F.

Charlot
Roi des Coquillages
81, bd de Clichy (pl. de Clichy)
48 74 49 64,
fax 40 16 11 00

Open daily until 1 a.m. Air cond.

A fine view of the Place de Clichy, a warm welcome, and attentive service will take your mind off the overbearing Art Deco interior. Sparkling fresh oysters, spectacular shellfish assortments, a generous bouillabaisse à la marseillaise and lobsters prepared every possible way are the staples here.

A la carte: 330-430 F. Menu: 250 F (lunch only, wine incl.).

9th arrondissement – RESTAURANTS

10/20 Chartier
7, rue du Faubourg-Montmartre
47 70 86 29
Open daily until 9:30 p.m.
Nothing has changed since 1896 at this rigorously preserved bistro, including the classics (roast chicken, calf brawn) offered at obstinately philanthropic prices.
A la carte: 70-100 F. Menu: 82 F (wine incl.).

11/20 L'Echiquier
48, rue St-Georges
48 78 46 09
Closed Sun. & Mon. Open until 10 p.m. (11 p.m. w.-e.).
This is a good spot for after-theatre suppers, so long as your tastes run to simple dishes like terrines, duck breast, confits and fruit tarts.
A la carte: 180-350 F. Menu: 95 F (until 9:30 p.m.).

12/20 Le Grand Café Capucines
4, bd des Capucines
47 42 19 00
Open daily 24 hours. Terrace dining. Air cond.
The waiter won't pull a face if you order just one course—a shellfish assortment, for example, or a grilled pig's trotter. The extravagant décor is a replica of a Belle Epoque *café boulevardier*.
A la carte: 240-310 F. Menus: 195 F, 256 F, 370 F.

 Les Muses
Hôtel Scribe
1, rue Scribe
44 71 24 26,
fax 42 65 39 97
Closed w.-e., holidays & Aug. Open until 10:30 p.m. Private room: 70. Air cond. Valet parking.
The muse of interior design was off duty the day this basement restaurant was designed. On the other hand, chef Patrice Guibert seems privy to a regular fount of inspiration judging by his technically rigorous, beautifully presented cuisine. He earned a second toque for dishes that bear an appealing personal stamp, like a perfect saumon glacé au vin, a peppery lamb fillet tinged with coffee flavour, osso buco of monkfish with crab, and heavenly pastries (tarte Tatin, bitter-cherry clafoutis, caramelised apple millefeuille). The wine list is notable for balance rather than length.
A la carte: 400-500 F. Menus: 210 F (lunch only), 350 F (dinner only).

 Opéra Restaurant
Café de la Paix
3, pl. de l'Opéra
40 07 32 32,
fax 42 66 12 51
Closed w.-e. Open until 11 p.m. Air cond.
How lucky that the untold sums spent restoring, regilding, re-marbling and reappointing this vast temple of Second Empire opulence did not make it solemn, stuffy and boring. *Au contraire* the atmosphere is exuberant, animated by whirling waiters who juggle the Baccarat crystal, fine china, and gilded silver with aplomb. But chef Jacky Fréon, lured away from the kitchens of the Hôtel Lutétia, has yet to get into his stride here. We can't believe that this award-winning *cuisinier* cannot do better than the overcooked John Dory with scallops that disappointed us the other day, or the gummy mashed potatoes that ruined an otherwise delicious truffled boudin blanc. We're taking back the second toque until Fréon finds his bearings again.
A la carte: 500-600 F.

12/20 Au Petit Riche
25, rue Le Peletier
47 70 68 68
Closed Sun. Open until 12:15 a.m. Private room: 45.
The brass trim, mirrors and woodwork of this nostalgic bistro are sparkling once again. This is everyone's preferred after-theatre spot (an excellent all-in fee procures an orchestra seat in one of eight surrounding theatres, plus dinner) for top-notch chicken liver mousse, braised cod with cabbage, andouillette simmered in Vouvray and delicious wines from the Touraine region.
A la carte: 250-300 F. Menu: 180 F (wine incl.).

12/20 Chez Roger
52, rue de Douai
48 74 77 19
Closed Sun. dinner, Mon., July-Aug. & Christmas wk. Open until 10:30 p.m. Air cond.
The jovial host, Roger Sebban, chats and jokes with his guests, telling improbable stories of colonial life in North Africa. The couscous is decent, the paella fragrant, and the pastries are bought in from Dalloyau.
A la carte: 220-280 F.

12/20 Le Saintongeais
62, rue du Faubourg-Montmartre
42 80 39 92
Closed Sat., Sun., Dec. 25-31 & Aug. 9-29. Open until 9:30 p.m. Private room: 10.
The décor is a study in brown (walls, imitation-leather upholstery...); the menu is rather more cheerful, with good mouclade, fish soup and other specialities from the French Atlantic coast. Attractive selection of wines from the Loire.
A la carte: 230-300 F. Menu: 135 F (weekdays dinner only).

 La Table d'Anvers
2, pl. d'Anvers
48 78 35 21
Closed Sat. lunch, Sun. & Aug. Open until 11:30 p.m. Private room: 35. Air cond.
Cooking, as he does, not far from the city's more fashionable districts, chef Christian

Conticini perhaps feels freer to flout culinary trends. As ever, his knack for creating novel flavour combinations is nothing short of staggering. But we now find that his technique is more finely honed, and his cuisine is a marvel of balance and character.

So put aside your prejudices, and prepare for a real gastronomic adventure: try Conticini's gâteau of oysters and bone marrow heightened with balsamic vinegar; or his tart filled with snails, tomato, chanterelles and spinach, seasoned with a saffron vinaigrette; or a fricassée that brings together morels, tiny peas, asparagus tips, baby broad beans, carrots and turnips in tarragon and chicken juices. Complicated? Trust us: what looks like a litany of disparate ingredients will burst into a harmony of delicate nuances on the palate.

Conticini is equally adept at bringing out the best in a single, perfect ingredient, witness his roast foie gras "steak", well-seared on the outside, very rare within; or the lightly cooked skate, moist and pearly under a crust of mace-scented hazelnuts.

We could go on about all these exciting new ideas, but we must leave room to mention the fabulous cheeses, and the astonishing desserts crafted by Christian's brother, Philippe Conticini. Don't be put off by the latter's imposing waistline: his chocolate-banana-coffee "combo", his macaron au fromage frais, lait d'amande et griotte, or mango-rhubarb puff pastry with a hint of cinnamon are all light as a summer breeze... Now that the dismal service has been overhauled by top professional Serge Calvez, it only remains to revamp the unattractive décor (clumsily camouflaged under an avalanche of plants). Although a meal costs much less than this sort of food would command in a more up-market area, the wine tends to be overpriced.

A la carte: 500-700 F. Menus: 190 F (lunch only), 240 F, 290 F and 320 F (dinner only).

12/20 Taverne Kronenbourg

L'Ambassade d'Alsace
24, bd des Italiens
47 70 16 64

Open daily. Open until 3 a.m. Private room: 100. Terrace dining. Air cond.

The last of the *cafés-concerts* on the Grands Boulevards (live music nightly) serves robust, unpretentious brasserie fare: shellfish, pork knuckle with cabbage, sauerkraut and fine Alsatian wines.

A la carte: 190-260 F.

10th arrondissement

12/20 Brasserie Flo

7, cour des Petites-Ecuries
47 70 13 59

Open daily until 1:30 a.m. Air cond. Valet parking.

The archetypal Alsatian brasserie, Flo is a jewel: nowhere else will you find the atmosphere, the superb décor, the lively patrons, delicious sauerkraut washed down with carafes of frisky Riesling.... Note the "night owl" supper, offered after 11 p.m.: a main dish, dessert and wine cost only 99 francs.

A la carte: 200-300 F. Menu: 99 F (weekdays lunch only, wine incl.).

Au Chateaubriant

23, rue de Chabrol
48 24 58 94

Closed Sun., Mon., 1 wk. in winter & Aug. Open until 10:15 p.m. Air cond.

A very cosy, elegant little restaurant decorated with prints by modern masters (Picasso, Foujita, Chagall...). The menu offers no-nonsense Italian cuisine: scampi fritti with tartare sauce, ravioli stuffed with foie gras and truffles, delicious pasta and fine desserts (zabaglione al Marsala). Lately chef-proprietor Guy Bürkli has been experimenting most successfully in a Mediterranean vein, with dishes that give starring roles to fruit and vegetables, for example skate with fresh figs in raspberry butter, or young rabbit in aspic with fennel and artichokes.

A la carte: 350-500 F. Menu: 150 F (weekdays only).

12/20 Les Deux Canards

8, rue du Faubourg-Poissonnière
47 70 03 23

Closed Sat. lunch & Sun. Open until 10 p.m. Air cond.

The naïve charm of this dining room crammed with bric-a-brac close to the Grands Boulevards is sure to win you over. The voluble owner (a former dentist) does not allow smoking—*nous aimons les fumeurs, pas la fumée*—so diners may enjoy the delicious duck terrine, sardines with pesto, Barbary duck à l'orange, and Provençal mussels in an unpolluted atmosphere. Admirable cellar.

A la carte: 250-400 F.

> **RAC MOTORING ATLAS FRANCE**: Our fully revised and well-established large format RAC Motoring Atlas France, Belgium and Luxembourg at 1:250,000 (approximately 4 miles to 1 inch) now has even more features to improve journey planning and to make driving in France more enjoyable. Clear, accurate and detailed road maps make RAC Motoring Atlas France the ideal atlas for the independent traveller in France. Price: £ 11.99 (spiral bound).

11th arrondissement – RESTAURANTS

12/20 Julien
16, rue du Fg-St-Denis
47 70 12 06

Closed Dec. 24 dinner. Open until 1:30 a.m. Air cond. Valet parking.

For the pleasure of dining in these exuberant surroundings (vintage 1880), we are willing to put up with mediocre food; frankly, the kitchen turns out more than its share of botched dishes. But if you stick to the oysters, the cassoulet or eggs poached in red wine, you'll probably leave with a pleasant memory.
A la carte: 210-310 F. Menus: 99 F (weekdays lunch only, wine incl.), 143 F (w.-e. lunch and holidays).

 Le Louis XIV
8, bd St-Denis
42 08 56 56

Closed June 1-Aug. 31. Open until 1 a.m. Valet parking.

The décor is more Louis XV (Pompadour period!) than Louis XIV, but no one seems to mind. The festive, dressy clientele that dines here is too busy tucking into succulent roast duck, roast lamb, roast pigeon or juicy ribs of beef—preceded, ideally, by a sparkling assortment of fresh shellfish. Other seafood dishes are systematically overcooked. Jolly atmosphere.
A la carte: 300-550 F.

 Chez Michel
10, rue de Belzunce
48 78 44 14

Closed Sat. & Sun. (summer). Open until 10:30 p.m. Private room: 40. Air cond. Parking.

Sauces seem to be the chef's strong point, going by the rich beurre blanc that accompanies chive-steamed turbot, or the sauce diable adorning grilled Bresse chicken. We were also impressed by the suave salad of foie gras and artichoke bottoms and a rich lobster omelette. Prices are outlandish, but the faithful do not appear to notice or care.
A la carte: 400-450 F. Menus: 175 F (weekdays lunch and Sat.), 250 F (weekdays dinner and Sat.).

11/20 Da Mimmo
39, bd de Magenta
42 06 44 47

Closed Sun. & Aug. Open until midnight. Terrace dining.

Neapolitan Domenico (Mimmo) Sommella serves wonderful spaghetti seasoned with hot-pepper oil and topped with tender clams. Delicious Italian cold meats, wonderful pizzas and good tiramisù round out the list of specialities, which the regulars wash down with carafes of tasty Apulian wine.
A la carte: 180-230 F. Menu: 90 F (wine incl.).

 La P'tite Tonkinoise
56, rue du Faubourg-Poissonnière
42 46 85 98

Closed Sun., Mon., Dec. 22-Jan. 4 & July 26-Sep. 7. Open until 10 p.m.

Old Indochina hands come regularly for a whiff of the nostalgia that is virtually palpable in this quiet establishment. The Costas, who ran a restaurant in Haiphong, have put their son Michel in charge of the kitchen, where he prepares an authentic repertoire of spring rolls, ginger-sautéed crab and mi-xao with seven vegetables in a crispy rice galette.
A la carte: 200-250 F.

12/20 Terminus Nord
23, rue de Dunkerque
42 85 05 15

Closed Dec. 24 dinner. Open until 12:30 a.m. Private room: 10.

Now part of the brasserie group of which Flo (see above) is the flagship, the Terminus serves exactly the same food as the rest of the fleet. Enjoy the lively atmosphere, the gay 1925 décor, and look no farther than the sauerkraut, briny oysters and steak with chips for a satisfying meal. Nimble service.
A la carte: 250-350 F. Menu: 108 F (after 11 p.m. only).

11th arrondissement

 L'Aiguière
37 bis, rue de Montreuil
43 72 42 32

Closed Sat. lunch & Sun. Open until 10:30 p.m. Private room: 45. Air cond.

Elegant down to the last meticulous detail, this little restaurant serves romantic dinners with candlelight and piano music. The chef spurns simplicity, but his first-rate ingredients are prepared with care: try the prawn ravioli with sweet peppers, or tournedos with sweetbreads and truffles, then finish with a feuillantine de poires en chaud-froid. Excellent set menus.
A la carte: 350 F. Menus: 115 F (weekdays lunch only), 175 F.

 Astier
44, rue J.-P.-Timbaud
43 57 16 35

Closed Sat., Sun., Dec. 18-Jan. 4 & July 30-Sep. 6. Open until 10:30 p.m. Air cond.

For 130 francs, choose from a dozen first courses, another dozen main dishes (several featuring seafood), a huge array of cheeses and at least six excellent desserts. This is French home cooking at its seasonal, market-fresh best: red mullet cooked in olive oil, magret de canard au cidre, skate with capers, rabbit in mustard sauce, yellow-plum clafoutis, and so on. The atmosphere is good-humoured and noisy. Intelligent, wide-ranging cellar.
Menu: 130 F.

RESTAURANTS – 11th arrondissement

La Belle Epoque
Holiday Inn
10, pl. de la République
43 55 44 34

Closed Sat. lunch, Sun. & Aug 1-29. Open until 10:30 p.m. Air cond.

Chef Patrice Trincali's subtle, sure, personal cuisine comes as something of a surprise in the hotel dining room of a Holiday Inn. The recent renovation of the premises will, we hope, attract the wider, more attentive public that this valiant young *cuisinier* deserves. You'll echo our praise after tasting his delicate prawn salad with potatoes and cream, lobster in an aromatic stock with Thai-spiced ravioli or the delectable salmon baked with honey and spices. Remarkable service; serious cellar.

A la carte: 350-450 F. Menus: 245 F (lunch only), 305 F and 405 F (dinner only).

Cartet
62, rue de Malte
48 05 17 65

Closed Sat., Sun. & Aug. Open until 9 p.m.

The half-dozen tables and faded furnishings are a throwback to the days of the Front Populaire. The cooking is equally nostalgic, with no concessions made to calorie counters: sheep's trotters in sauce poulette, tripe à la lyonnaise flambée, quenelles, croûte aux morilles and delicious sugar-dusted bugnes (fritters) that go down wonderfully with the wines of Bugey.

A la carte: 250-320 F.

Remember to call ahead to reserve your table, and please, if you cannot honour your reservation, be courteous and let the restaurant know.

Chardenoux
1, rue J.-Vallès
43 71 49 52

Closed Sat. lunch, Sun. & Aug. Open until 10:30 p.m. Parking.

In the heart of the old cabinet-makers' district, this graceful (listed) corner bistro displays its charms of marble, mouldings and etched glass. Chef Dominique Mazelin blends country and bourgeois cooking in a most appealing manner: there's a novel salad of boudin and bitter cherries, braised leg of lamb Auvergne-style, perfect aligot (garlicky mashed potatoes with cheese) and a wonderfully flaky apple tart. Connoisseur's cellar.

A la carte: 200-270 F.

Chez Fernand
17, rue de la Fontaine-au-Roi
43 57 46 25

Closed Sun., Mon. & 3 wks. in Aug. Open until 11 p.m. Air cond.

This simple little bistro celebrates the culinary glories of Normandy, with (in particular) an astonishing array of Camemberts, lovingly matured by the owner (who also makes his own bread and butter). An enthusiastic corps of regulars is regaled with tasty terrines, a salad of marinated sardines with crisp vegetables, numerous duck dishes and an apple tart flamed with Calvados. Good wines from the south-west and the Loire, at pleasing prices. (You'll spend even less at the restaurant's annexe, Les Fernandises, two doors away.)

A la carte: 200-270 F. Menu: 130 F (weekdays lunch only).

11/20 Nioullaville
32-34, rue de l'Orillon
43 38 30 44

Open daily until 12:30 a.m. Parking.

Most of the hundreds of dishes served to thousands of customers in this huge Chinese food factory are quite good. Dim sum and roast meat are dispensed from trolleys rolled along by rude, glowering waiters. But never mind. The atmosphere is noisy and effervescent, and there is a dizzying selection of set menus (don't expect much help or advice from the aforementioned waiters).

A la carte: 180-250 F.

Chez Philippe
Auberge Pyrénées-Cévennes
106, rue de la Folie-Méricourt
43 57 33 78

Closed w.-e., holidays & Aug. Open until 10:30 p.m. Air cond. Parking.

The menu written in purple ink is nothing if not eclectic: herrings Bismarck, grilled lobster, a monumental cassoulet, paella (the best in Paris), York ham with macaroni au gratin, beef bourguignon, turbot Dugléré, rock lobster in port and an old-fashioned braised hare. Believe it or not, it's all delicious and satisfying. Best of all, these earthy delights are served in the most convivial atmosphere imaginable, complete with a jovial host. Great Burgundies at giveaway prices only add to the gaiety.

A la carte: 300-400 F.

Le Repaire de Cartouche
99, rue Amelot or 8, bd des Filles-du-Calvaire
47 00 25 86

Closed Sat. lunch, Sun. & Aug. 1-25. Open until 10:30 p.m.

Emmanuel Salabert, a young chef whose career has got off to a brilliant start, presides over this shrine to south-west cooking. The prices and repertoire have so far remained stable, but the execution suffers occasional lapses—as does the slowcoach service. Try the warm foie gras wrapped in cabbage leaves, the lotte stewed in Madiran wine or the Landais pie laced with Armagnac.

A la carte: 230-300 F. Menus: 220 F (Sat. dinner only), 150 F, 350 F.

12th arrondissement

12/20 La Connivence
1, rue de Cotte
46 28 46 17

Open daily until 11 p.m. Private room: 50.

The endearingly low prices make the short, seasonal *carte* that much more appealing: lentil salad with stuffed pig's tail, sautéed mussels with parsley, and a potée of guinea fowl, cabbage and Lyonnais sausage with a hint of cumin are enjoyed by a trendy, slightly bohemian Bastille bunch.

A la carte: 140-200 F. Menu: 120 F.

12/20 Fouquet's Bastille
130, rue de Lyon
43 42 18 18

Closed Sat. lunch & Sun. Open until midnight. Air cond.

Sign of the (economic) times: Fouquet's Bastille has lowered its "gastronomic" profile for a much-simplified, cheaper menu. Instead of bills reaching 400 francs and more, patrons now shell out about half that sum for curried seafood salad, veal kidneys béarnaise, millefeuilles, all served with style and a smile. But the creative current has been cut... We'll let you know what happens next.

A la carte: 200-250F. Menu: 165 F.

> Some establishments change their closing times without warning. It is always wise to check in advance.

La Frégate
30, av. Ledru-Rollin
43 43 90 32

Closed Sat., Sun. & Aug. Open until 10 p.m. Air cond.

The huge menu of this friendly haven for bons vivants is dedicated to seafood. In addition there is an ample list of fresh, bountiful *plats du jour*, marred only by an occasional lapse in execution. We like the prawns served in their shells, the sea bass in Bouzy wine and the tasty marmite du pêcheur.

A la carte: 350-450 F. Menus: 200 F, 300 F.

La Gourmandise
271, av. Daumesnil
43 43 94 41

Closed Sun., Mon., May 1-8 & Aug. 8-28. Open until 10:30 p.m. Parking.

Gourmand or gourmet, you'll be tempted to indulge in Alain Denoual's creative cuisine, served amid new, chic décor of beige and blue. We were bowled over by the sheer inventiveness of his steamed sea bream cleverly heightened by black olives in vinaigrette, the duo of foie gras and magret backed up by a potato gratin, and the timbale de lapin aux choux. Cinnamon ice cream with an apple sablé is a dreamy dessert. The cellar (and the prices) are progressing slowly but surely.

A la carte: 360-510 F. Menus: 190 F, 340 F.

Le Mange Tout
24, bd de la Bastille
43 43 95 15

Closed Sun. & Aug. 15-30. Open until 11:30 p.m. Private room: 18. Terrace dining.

A refugee from the Latin Quarter, the Mange Tout has transferred its kitchens to the new Eldorado of the Bastille. The move didn't harm Michel Simon's tasty south-west repertoire, which he has extended to include some creditable fish dishes (rascasse à l'orange, grilled salmon béarnaise). Note the good regional wines (Gaillac, Cahors) and the irresistible prix-fixe menus. Well worth a toque.

A la carte: 200-250 F. Menus: 98 F, 380 F (for 2, wine incl.).

12/20 Chez Marcel
Restaurant Antoine
7, rue St-Nicolas
43 43 49 40

Closed Sat., Sun., Aug. & holidays. Open daily until 9:30 p.m.

Neither Marcel—nor Antoine, for that matter—mans the kitchen here any more. Jean-Claude Trottet gets the credit for the classic pig's trotters (served in pairs), tripe, charcuterie and good baby lamb with beans. The décor is tumbledown, but the atmosphere wins you over with its friendly warmth. A wonderful spot.

A la carte: 200 F and up. Menu: 150 F.

Au Pressoir
257, av. Daumesnil
43 44 38 21,
fax 43 43 81 77

Closed Sat., Sun., 1st wk. Feb. school holidays & Aug. Open until 10:30 p.m. Private room: 35. Air cond. Valet parking.

Forgotten by most Parisians since the Colonial Exposition closed 60 years ago, the Porte Dorée district is home to a covey of fine restaurants of which Le Pressoir is no doubt the best. Henri Séguin is a chef unmoved by trends who pursues his search for exciting flavours wherever it may lead him. We quiver with pleasure at the memory of a cassolette of Swiss chard, Jerusalem artichokes and truffles; a crusty salmon with vegetable marmalade; lotte with split peas and bacon; veal kidneys à l'orange with mushroom mousse; and roast capon with asparagus. Nor are we likely to forget such unprecedented desserts as hot quince with nougat or chocolate soup with warm brioche. The décor, which was degenerating from dog-eared to dilapidated, recently underwent a facelift.

A la carte: 450-600 F. Menu: 360 F.

 Le Quincy
28, av. Ledru-Rollin
46 28 46 76

Closed w.-e., Mon. & Aug. 8-Sep. 10. Open until 10 p.m. No cards.

Here is a small, friendly, countrified restaurant that features hearty, simple dishes from rural France, washed down with Loire and Rhône Valley wines.

A la carte: 250-400 F.

 Sipario
69, rue de Charenton
43 45 70 26

Closed Sat. lunch & Sun. Open until midnight.

Not your corner pizzeria, Sipario has pretensions both aesthetic (the cool, airy dining room decorated with giant-vegetable frescoes is most attractive) and culinary. Regional Italian dishes, so hard to find in Paris, are proposed by a chef who claims that they are absolutely authentic versions. But though we salivate as we peruse the menu, we are sometimes disappointed by the reality (an insipid bollito misto, for example, and a guinea fowl that tasted distinctly of reheating). Yet the crostino al prosciutto is gooey and good, the involtini di vitello plump and tender, and the tiramisù, for those who like it, probably the best version around. The Italian wine list is wonderful.

A la carte: 230-330 F. Menu: 220 F (weekdays and Sun. dinner).

 La Sologne
164, av. Daumesnil
43 07 68 97

Closed Sat. lunch, Sun. & holidays. Open until 10:30 p.m. Parking. Air cond.

Koji Kaeriyama, the Japanese chef who purchased this restaurant not long ago, shows touching dedication to tradition: he maintains not only the house repertoire of game dishes offered in autumn and winter, but the restaurant's dated hunting-motif décor as well. The original, regularly renewed menu lists a delicious half-cooked, half-smoked duck with horseradish, galette de langoustines, and a filet de pigeon with truffle juice (the sauce is admirably light). Reasonable prices—particularly for the enticing set menus—and deft, professional service.

A la carte: 350-400 F. Menus: 175 F, 250 F.

 Le Temps des Cerises
216, rue du Faubourg-St-Antoine
43 67 52 08

Open daily until 10:30 p.m. Private room: 20. Terrace dining. Air cond.

A toque for Bernard Bergounioux's sagaciously seasonal cooking, which pays fragrant homage to the southwest. Order the generously served and well seasoned terrine of young rabbit and prunes, the duck fillet sprinkled with sesame or a light navarin of lamb with young vegetables, and finish with the delectable crème brûlée flavoured with roast chicory. The set menu is a bargain.

A la carte: 200-280 F. Menus: 95 F, 200 F.

The prices in this guide reflect what establishments were charging at press time.

Le Train Bleu
Gare de Lyon, 1st floor
20, bd Diderot
43 43 09 06,
fax 443 43 97 96

Open daily until 10:30 p.m. Private room: 100.

The extravagant, colossal, delirious, dazzling décor of Le Train Bleu has always been more than adequate compensation for the boring, "standard French" cooking (veal chop Foyot, quenelles, coquelet Val-de-Saône...) served here. But the arrival of Michel Comby, a talented (though conservative) veteran chef, is bound to bring the menu in line with the glorious surroundings. We'll let you know.

A la carte: 330 F. Menu: 195 F.

12/20 **Le Traversière**
40, rue Traversière
43 44 02 10

Closed Sun. dinner, holidays & Aug. Open until 10 p.m.

Here is the little French restaurant of your dreams: a peaceful, provincial oasis where charming hosts are happy to serve you their hearty, delicious cooking. Don't miss the duck terrine, the leek gratin with lardons, or the young boar with pears cooked in wine. The cellar features wonderful Chinons.

A la carte: 230-280 F. Menu: 150 F.

 Au Trou Gascon
40, rue Taine
43 44 34 26,
fax 43 07 80 55

Closed Sat., Sun., Aug. & Christmas wk. Open until 10 p.m. Air cond.

As chef Alain Dutournier tells it, a boyhood spent roaming the Gascon countryside inspired his deep-rooted devotion to the region's fresh produce. Though he now spends most of his time at his three-toque restaurant, Le

Carré des Feuillants (see first arrondissement), Dutournier oversees the menu of the Trou Gascon, and develops new dishes which are prepared on a daily basis by the talented Jacques Faussat, who trained with Michel Guérard. Even Dutournier's oldest and most faithful fans would be hard put to say whether he or Faussat is behind the toothsome medley of asparagus and broad beans with well-cured ham, the warm pâté of cèpes with a parsley sauce, the hot foie gras, the calf's brains with morels, or the rich duck and pork cassoulet.

Game dishes are also close to Dutournier's heart (his spiced saddle of hare is pure magic), and they are best washed down, as is all this robust fare, by the cellar's marvellous Madirans and Jurançons. The lunch-hour set menu (the price hasn't budged for three years) is a delicious bargain.

A la carte: 380-550 F. Menus: 200 F (lunch only), 450 F.

13th arrondissement

12/20 Bœuf Bistrot
4, pl. des Alpes
45 82 08 09

Closed Sat. lunch, Sun., Dec. 25, 2 wks. in March & Aug. Open until 10:30 p.m. Private room: 50. Terrace dining.

Carnivores have a treat in store: a prime selection of fried, boiled, grilled and roast beef awaits you here in this oxblood-coloured bistro. Between salad and dessert, admire the enviable collection of prints and drawings by Szafran, Giacometti, Van Velde and others displayed on the walls. Though the atmosphere is agreeably relaxed and casual, the prices are quite high.

A la carte: 290-360 F.

Menus: 120 F (weekdays lunch only), 155 F (except holidays lunch).

 Les Marronniers
53 bis, bd Arago
47 07 58 57

Closed Sun. & July 27-Sep. 9. Open until 11 p.m. Terrace dining. Air cond. Valet parking.

In fine weather one may choose between a table in the pretty pink interior or one on a pleasant patio under the eponymous chestnut trees. The *plats du jour* are usually the best part of chef Lorenzati's reliably appealing menu. Look for a good cassolette of wild mushrooms and shallots, Auvergne-style turbot, or succulent rabbit à la piémontaise.

A la carte: 280-350 F. Menu: 200 F.

 Le Petit Marguery
9, bd de Port-Royal
43 31 58 59

Closed Sun., Mon., Dec. 23-Jan. 2 & July 27-Sep. 3. Open until 10:15 p.m. Private room: 15. No cards.

Michel and Jacques Cousin cook in a virile vein (game, offal, fresh fish, regional dishes) for an appreciative and very faithful public. Their bright, old-fashioned bistro is a most convivial spot; Alain Cousin directs fleet-footed waiters who deliver generous platefuls of braised wild mushrooms, gratin of cod with oysters and asparagus or partridge purée with juniper berries, as well as robust bourgeois classics like tête de veau ménagère and salt-cured duck à la poitevine. Delicious wines, improved desserts. Prices are still on the rise.

A la carte: 350-450 F. Menus: 160 F (lunch only), 320 F, 450 F.

 Les Vieux Métiers de France
13, bd A.-Blanqui
45 88 90 03

Closed Sun. & Mon. Open until 10:30 p.m. Private room: 16. Air cond.

Onto an austere modern building, chef Michel Moisan (with considerable help from his friends) has grafted the most amazing medieval décor of sculpted wood, stained glass, ancient beams and antique paintings. What saves all this quaintness from tipping over into kitsch is Moisan's flavourful, personalised cuisine: pig's ear with prawns, seafood minestrone, spiced shoulder of lamb with pearl barley and an array of luscious desserts. The cellar is an oenophile's dream.

A la carte: 350-400 F. Menus: 165 F, 290 F.

14th arrondissement

 L'Amuse Bouche
186, rue du Château
43 35 31 61

Closed Sat. lunch, Sun. & wk. of Aug. 15. Open until 10:30 p.m.

A former bouillabaisse restaurant has been transformed into an elegant apricot-coloured dining room, where well-heeled patrons enjoy light dishes with clear, focused flavours. We suggest you sample the delicate warm artichokes with vegetables in vinaigrette, freshwater perch bathed in a fragrant prawn coulis, or meltingly tender young pigeon with a Provençal garnish of baby broad beans and tomatoes, then finish with the superb gâteau mousseux au chocolat amer. Succinct, well-designed wine list.

A la carte: 280-340 F. Menu: 145 F (lunch only).

RESTAURANTS – 14th arrondissement

Les Armes de Bretagne
108, av. du Maine
43 20 29 50
Closed Sun. dinner, Mon. & Aug. Open until 11 p.m. Air cond.
Here is an establishment that proudly upholds the old-fashioned traditions of hospitality, service and French culinary showmanship in a luxurious Second Empire dining room. Top-quality seafood from Brittany stars in William Dhenin's best dishes: fresh oysters, sea bass en croûte with beurre blanc, abalone fricassée and grilled lobster.
A la carte: 300-500 F. Menu: 200 F (weekdays only).

L'Assiette
181, rue du Château
43 22 64 86
Closed Mon., Tues., Aug. & 2 wks. in Dec. Open until 10:30 p.m.
Lucette Rousseau ("Lulu"), the temperamental owner of this pretty, very Parisian spot, is first and foremost an excellent cook. Behind the bantering charm she applies to her many celebrated customers (Françoise Sagan, Karl Lagerfeld...) lies the dedicated soul of an inspired chef. We adore her generous, polished versions of south-west country classics: salad of duck breast and foie gras, braised vegetable medley with fresh truffles, sweetbreads with field mushrooms, or fine Pyrenees lamb. Prices are terrifying, but that is only to be expected when a potato and truffle salad contains nearly equal rations of both ingredients!
A la carte: 400-500 F.

12/20 Le Bar à Huîtres
112, bd du Montparnasse
43 20 71 01
Open daily until 2 a.m. Private room: 15. Terrace dining. Air cond.
Everything's improving, even the service, at this popular oyster bar where, if you wish, you can order and eat just one oyster—but that would be a shame. Six or a dozen belons, fines, or spéciales would surely be more satisfying. Or book a table in the dining room and sample, in addition to the excellent shellfish, some good salt cod with aïoli or salmon with broccoli. Interesting cellar of white wines.
A la carte: 220-350 F.

La Cagouille
In front of
23 rue d'Ouest,
12, pl. C.-Brancusi
43 22 09 01
Closed April 13, April 25-May 3, June 1, Aug. 8-30 & Nov. 2. Open until 10:30 p.m. Terrace dining.
Gérard Allemandou has a rare talent for drawing hordes of seafood lovers to the most improbable locations. Three years ago, even Parisian taxi drivers had never heard of the place Brancusi. Now the address is noted in every restaurant guide in the city, thanks to La Cagouille. The décor is a little cool (and awfully noisy), the welcome is lukewarm and the service often clumsy, but then this is not a grand restaurant—it is a *bistro du port*, where dishes made from the very freshest fish and shellfish (delivered direct from Atlantic ports) are chalked on a blackboard: depending on the day's catch, they might include tiny black scallops from Brest, fresh fried anchovies, red mullet with sea salt, cod and cabbage, plump whiting with mustard sauce or thick, juicy sole. If you are content to drink a modest Aligoté or Quincy, your bill will not rise much above 350 francs. But beware if you succumb to the temptations of the finest Cognac collection in Paris (and maybe the world).
A la carte: 350-500 F.

La Chaumière des Gourmets
22, place Denfert-Rochereau
43 21 22 59
Closed Sat. lunch, Sun., Aug. & 1st wk. of March. Open until 10:30 p.m. Terrace dining.
The new owners, Jean-Paul and Nicole Huc, have not altered the cosy provincial décor, but the menu has been instilled with welcome new vigour: tuna carpaccio with fresh truffles, a very successful salad of sweetbreads and turnips, refreshing jellied bouillabaisse with garlic mayonnaise and a good thin apple tart with bilberry coulis. Attractive list of white wines.
A la carte: 340-440 F. Menus: 165 F, 240 F.

12/20 La Coupole
102, bd du Montparnasse
43 20 14 20,
fax 43 35 46 14
Closed Dec. 24 dinner. Open until 2 a.m. Air cond.
This Montparnasse landmark has survived the takeover by the Flo brasserie group with its mystique intact, indeed improved after a most successful facelift (layers of grime were removed from the famous murals). La Coupole's traditional lamb curry, fried whiting with tartare sauce and cassoulet à l'oie are still on offer (and carefully prepared to boot), as are the exemplary shellfish assortments. Carafes of sprightly house Riesling delivered by swift, efficient waiters add to the charm.
A la carte: 230-280 F. Menu: 109 F (after 11 p.m. only, wine incl.).

11/20 La Créole
122, bd du Montparnasse
43 20 62 12
Open daily until 10:30 p.m. Air cond.
Tropical delights spill out onto the pavement from the

14th arrondissement - RESTAURANTS

plant-filled veranda. A warm, smiling staff serves rum punches and cod fritters as preludes to tasty Creole specialities like stuffed sea urchin, octopus fricassée and more. Prices are on the way up.

A la carte: 220-250 F. Menu: 120 F.

 Le Dôme
108, bd du Montparnasse
43 35 25 81,
fax 42 79 01 19

Closed Mon. Open until 12:45 a.m. Private room: 10. Air cond.

A second toque for Le Dôme, in recognition of chef Franck Graux's wonderful *carte*, which now extends well beyond the traditional house specialities of bouillabaisse and lobster. His prawns wrapped in paper-thin pastry and served with a shellfish bouillon are brilliant; bracing is the word that comes to mind for his tartare of sea bream and salmon with watercress; the cod with vegetables and garlicky aïoli is superb. The desserts are worth saving room for: we loved the warm citrus baba topped with custard sauce. Service, of late, is more precise and cheerful, and the cellar is filled with bottles that invite you to splurge.

A la carte: 400-500 F.

 Le Duc
243, bd Raspail
43 20 96 30

Closed Sat., Sun., Mon., Dec. 21-Jan. 4 & wk. of Aug. 15. Open until 10:30 p.m. Air cond. No cards.

Jean Minchelli is no more, but his brother Paul (*"le génie du poisson"*) has returned from a lengthy sabbatical and is running Le Duc's kitchen in person. It was he who taught Parisians to love raw fish; today, with his faithful disciple—Tonio—he continues to prepare raw sea bass fillets rubbed with shallots, cloves and Cognac, "petals" of coquilles Saint-Jacques, tiny clams sautéed with thyme, red mullet with pesto, and steamed turbot cooked in his own inimitable fashion. A high-class clientele still graces Le Duc's dining room, where the service is skilfully orchestrated by Dominique Turpin. The cellar is a treasure trove of fabulous white wines, from Meursault-Les Charmes to the more modest (but excellent) Muscadet-sur-lie. Did we mention that prices are very high? Or that the chocolate cake is the only decent dessert? In parting, we must warn you that while all our experiences at Le Duc have been memorable, some readers and colleagues have not always been so lucky...

A la carte: 500-850 F.

11/20 Au Feu Follet
5, rue R.-Losserand
43 22 65 72

Closed Sat. lunch, Sun., Aug. 9-25. Open until 10:15 p.m.

The chef-proprietor knows his traditional bistro repertoire inside out. The duck confit and the tarte Tatin will never disappoint, nor will the wines or hospitality offered at this modest but attractive little spot.

A la carte: 180-230 F. Menu: 72 F (weekdays only).

11/20 Giovanna
22, rue E.-Jacques
43 22 32 09

Closed Sat. lunch, Sun. & Aug. 24-Jan. 2. Open until 10:30 p.m.

You, your companion and 16 other diners can tuck into perfectly wrought fresh pasta and other tasty Italian dishes in this minute *trattoria*. Don't miss the osso buco.

A la carte: 120-160 F. Menu: 65 F (lunch only).

 Aux Iles Marquises
15, rue de la Gaîté
43 20 93 58

Closed Sat. lunch, Sun. & Aug. 1-17. Open until midnight. Private room: 15.

Once a favourite haunt of Edith Piaf and her friends, the Iles Marquises is now decked out with fresh nautical décor (shrimp-coloured walls with seascape frescoes) which has effectively erased any raffish air that may have hung about the place. Owner-chef Mathias Théry, a "disciple", so he claims, of the Troisgros brothers, ought to put a bit more of his own personality into such technically flawless dishes as delicious braised prawns and courgettes or the tender young pigeon roasted with garlic. Dessert brings an outstanding sabayon of pears and citrus fruits. The cellar is rich in fine white wines.

A la carte: 350-400 F. Menus: 130 F and 150 F (except holidays).

12/20 Justine
Le Méridien Paris-Montparnasse
19, rue du Commandent-Mouchotte
43 20 15 51

Open daily until 11 p.m. Air cond. Valet parking.

A winter conservatory overlooking a lawn is the backdrop to Raoul Caïga's fine buffet lunch, one of the best bargains in Paris. For 185 francs you can help yourself to any amount of soup, crudités, mixed salads, terrines, fish, oyster and crab dishes, not to mention three hot dishes, cheese, pastries and desserts.

A la carte: 250-300 F. Menu: 185 F (except Sun. lunch).

 Lous Landés
157, av. du Maine
45 43 08 04

Closed Sat. lunch, Sun. & Aug. 1-29. Open until 10:30 p.m. Priv-

ate room: 14. Terrace dining. Air cond.

Hervé Rumen's south-west specialities range from the frankly robust to more refined versions of country cooking: salad of quail and smoked duck breasts in truffle juice, superb sautéed wild mushrooms, a cassoulet which would be exceptional with less mealy beans, and delicious quail's legs grilled with foie gras (oddly garnished with raspberries and asparagus tips). Desserts are all you would expect from a former colleague of Christian Constant. A good cellar with some excellent Cahors and Madirans. Pretty green décor, a charming hostess and attentive service.

A la carte: 330-430 F. Menu: 290 F.

 Le Moniage Guillaume
88, rue de la Tombe-Issoire
43 22 96 15

Closed Sun. & Aug. Open until 10:30 p.m. Private room: 25. Terrace dining. Valet parking. Hôtel: 5 rms, 240-320 F.

A good address for fish. Prices are steep and the rustic inn look is not wildly attractive (though the fireside tables and the terrace are quite pleasant), but Nelly Garanger's welcome is wonderful and the dishes prepared by her husband Michel are always top quality. You're sure to enjoy the fresh shellfish (available all year round), baked turbot, seasonal game and fine apple tart. Wide-ranging cellar.

A la carte: 330-600 F. Menus: 195 F (weekdays lunch only, wine incl.), 260 F, 420 F.

 Montparnasse 25
Le Méridien Paris-Montparnasse
19, rue Cdt-Mouchotte
44 36 44 25,
fax 44 36 49 01

Closed Sat., Sun. & Aug. Open until 10:30 p.m. Private room: 15. Air cond. Valet parking.

The Art Deco interior opens onto a tiny garden, bringing a note of idyllic charm to the surrounding concrete jungle. Chef Jean-Yves Guého, imported from the chain's Hong Kong hotel, entices appetites with turbot and wild mushrooms, succulent duck stew with potato gnocchi and one of the most remarkable cheeseboards in Paris. Delicate desserts round off an elegant and memorable meal. The young sommelier is happy to offer an excellent choice of wines by the glass.

A la carte: 400-500 F. Menus: 230 F (lunch only), 290 F and 380 F (dinner only).

12/20 **L'Olivier-Ouzerie**
9, rue Vandamme
43 21 57 58

Closed Sun. & Aug. Open until 11:30 p.m.

A small patio off a quaint stone-and-tile interior provides the setting for an authentic repertoire of Greek dishes: squid à la grecque, moussaka, spala and so on.

A la carte: 120-180 F. Menus: 59 F (weekdays lunch only, wine incl.), 89 F.

 Pavillon Montsouris
20, rue Gazan
45 88 38 52,
fax 45 88 63 40

Open daily until 10:30 p.m. Private room: 40. Garden dining. Valet parking.

A walk across the Parc Montsouris at sunset will help you work up an appetite for a fine feast in this turn-of-the-century greenhouse overlooking the park, once a favourite rendezvous of the beautiful spy, Mata Hari. Stéphane Ruel's 255-franc menu adds allure to this charming Parisian spot, bringing plenty of custom for his basil-scented bouillon of langoustines, or a deluxe hachis Parmentier made with duck, truffles and foie gras—every bit as good as Michel Guérard's. The honey-spiced duck served in two courses is a truly great dish, and for dessert, try the triple-chocolate concoction; our only cavil is that the vanilla-pod ice cream with candied oranges tastes very little of vanilla.

Yvan Courault, who used to manage the Grand Véfour, excels in the art of greeting his clients.

Menu: 255 F.

 Les Petites Sorcières
12, rue Liancourt
43 21 95 68

Closed Sat. lunch & Sun. Open until 10:30 p.m. Terrace dining.

Christian Teule is a talented chef of the Robuchon school. Helped by his wife Carole, he has worked up a remarkable repertoire of simple and hearty dishes in his modest bistro: moules marinière, duck consommé with ravioli or filet de rascasse au pistou. Good wines are available by the carafe.

A la carte: 180-230 F. Menu: 110 F (lunch only).

11/20 **Aux Petits Chandeliers**
62, rue Daguerre
43 20 25 87

Open daily until 11:30 p.m. Private room: 50.

Creole décor around a flowered patio where you can drink an excellent rum punch and eat sunny dishes such as duck curry, enhanced with the spicy island sauces known as rougails.

A la carte: 150-250 F.

15th arrondissement – RESTAURANTS

11/20 Rendez-Vous des Camionneurs
34, rue des Plantes
45 40 43 36
Closed Sat., Sun., Aug. & 1 wk. Feb. school holidays. Open until 9:30 p.m. Air cond.
We've never actually spotted a lorry driver here, but all sorts of people crowd this friendly bistro where a big-hearted *patron* serves up toothsome pâté de campagne followed by a rack of lamb or flank steak with tasty white beans. Carafes of wine are bargain-priced at 5 francs.
A la carte: 100 F. Menu: 58 F.

11/20 Le Restaurant Bleu
46, rue Didot
45 43 70 56
Closed Sat., Sun., July & Aug. Open until 10 p.m.
Hearty and generous food—pork rillettes, mutton tripe, confits, and omelette with cèpes—are served here in a dining room decked out in blue.
A la carte: 200-220 F. Menu: 80 F.

 Vassanti
3, rue Larochelle
43 21 97 43
Closed Tues. lunch & Mon. Open until 11 p.m. Air cond.
Tucked away in a cul-de-sac, this vintage Indian restaurant has just inaugurated a good-looking Mogul-style décor. Mother presides at the stove, producing admirably light vegetable samosas, a creditably moist chicken tikka and some superb rice dishes. All would be perfect if the spicing were just a pinch more bold...
A la carte: 200-250 F. Menus: 99 F and 130 F (lunch only).

 Les Vendanges
40, rue Friant
45 39 59 98
Closed Sat. lunch, Sun. & Aug. Open until 10 p.m.
Here is a newcomer to the south-west scene. The enchaud en gelée (pork terrine) merits a recommendation, as does the filet de saumon au lard et aux cèpes, the magret with apples and potatoes and the prunes poached in tea. The Madiran wines are good (but not cheap), and the old-fashioned décor is not without charm.
A la carte: 270-370 F. Menu: 155 F.

12/20 Le Vin des Rues
21, rue Boulard
43 22 19 78
Lunch only (and dinner Wed. & Fri. upon reservation). Closed Sun., Mon., Feb.14-21 & Aug. Terrace dining. No cards.
Ex-baker Jean Chanrion's noisy, cramped bistro offers an exemplary Lyonnais repertoire, ranging from pot-au-feu to coq au Beaujolais and salt cod à la lyonnaise. The Beaujolais and Mâconnais wines are sold by the *pichet*, of course.
A la carte: 100-150 F.

 Vishnou
13, rue du Cdt-Mouchotte
45 38 92 93, fax 42 89 90 18
Open until 11:30 p.m. Private room: 60. Terrace dining. Air cond.
Silken saris line the walls of this uncommonly luxurious Indian eating house. Distinguished-looking staff serve forth fragrant dishes that are finely wrought and full of exotic flavours. Savour the subtel hyderabadi beef or one of the good vegetable curries; only the lamb biryani seemed a triffle lacking in authenticity. For dessert, look no farther than the delicious bisan barfi. Amazingly, the wine list is diverse and informative.
Menus: 95 F and 150 F (lunch only, wine incl.), 230 F (dinner only, wine incl.), 220 F.

15th arrondissement

12/20 L'Armoise
67, rue des Entrepreneurs
45 79 03 31
Closed Sat. lunch, Sun., Feb. school holidays and Aug. 5-23. Open until 11 p.m.
Done up in sugar-pink inside and out, this little restaurant has a frilly, feminine air that the cooking belies. Chef Georges Outhier goes in for solid, robust fare, for which he charges commendably low prices. An 89 francs two-course offering stars fresh tagliatelle with smoked salmon, and a lusty confit de canard with crisp sautéed potatoes.
Menus: 89 F, 163 F (wine incl.).

 L'Aubergade
53, av. de La Motte-Picquet
47 83 23 85
Closed Sun. dinner, Mon., Dec. 27-Jan. 5, April 12-22 & Aug. Open until 10:30 p.m. Private room: 15. Terrace dining.
Pierre and Rosanna Moisson have turned in their mournful décor for something fresh. Jean-Claude Poulnais is a gifted chef who aims straight for the taste buds with his salmon and tomato compote, andouillette de Troyes au Chablis and a delicate apple tart. The remarkable all-in business menu includes kir, wine and coffee.
A la carte: 330 F. Menu: 150 F (lunch only).

Le Barrail
17, rue Falguière
43 22 42 61
Closed Sat. & Sun. Open until 10 p.m. Private room: 15. Air cond.
An attractive spot done up in soft pink tones. The cooking is polished but low-key, and the prices won't cause a heart attack. Alain Magna's superb langoustines au foie gras and canard confit aux haricots retain the succulent savours of the south-west. Unbeatable prices for lobster and even for such luxurious dishes as rémoulade de truffes aux girolles au foie gras cru. Average cellar.
A la carte: 240 F. Menus: 100 F (lunch only), 150 F, 198 F.

 Bistro 121
121, rue de la Convention
45 57 52 90,
fax 45 58 07 59
Open daily until midnight. Air cond. Valet parking.
This 30-year-old bistro, founded by Jean Moussié and decorated by Slavik, faithfully serves the sort of classic, heavily sauced dishes that will always be considered by some to be "real" French cooking. Hare à la royale and poached stuffed chicken are two relics of the Bistro's early days, but the current chef, André Jalbert, now concentrates on a repertoire of rich, seasonal, mainly seafood dishes: scallops with three sauces, panaché de sole au homard et langoustines, roast baby lamb with a (pedestrian) gratin dauphinois. While à la carte prices are steep, the two set menus offer excellent value.
A la carte: 300-400 F. Menus: 150 F and 200 F (wine incl.).

Red toques signify modern cuisine; white toques signify traditional cuisine.

 Le Bivio
101, rue de la Croix-Nivert
48 28 31 88
Open daily until 11 p.m. Private room: 60. Terrace dining.
A broad glass front opens onto a coldly modern interior, but conviviality reigns in this lively Italian restaurant run by the jovial Ermanno Chioda. Wonderful hams, pappardelle ai porcini and sage-scented saltimbocca are just a few of the appetising dishes on offer. To help them on their way, choose from an extensive selection of fine Italian wines.
A la carte: 160-250 F. Menu: 120 F.

12/20 Le Bouchut
9, rue Bouchut
45 67 15 65
Closed Sat. (except dinner Oct.-April), Sun. and Aug. Open until 10 p.m. Terrace dining.
Philippe and Martine Métais left their native Tours to try their luch in the capital. And good luck it is, for them and for us. This intimate little spot, set back from the Avenue de Breteuil, quickly attracted a faithful clientele, who return again and again for such classic dishes as grilled yellowtail tuna, steamed lotte, parmentier de gésiers de canard confit (the richly flavourful duck gizzards are topped with a layer of mashed potatoes), and for dessert, a lush charlotte aux marrons glacés laced with Armagnac. The fine cellar highlights wines from the Loire Valley.
Menu: 152 F.

12/20 Casa Alcalde
117, bd de Grenelle
47 83 39 71
Closed Mon. lunch & Dec. 20-Jan. 6. Open until 10:45 p.m. Private room: 40. Terrace dining. Air cond.
A rustic tavern where you eat at blue-tiled tables amid resolutely Spanish décor. Tasty, straightforward food with strong Hispano-Basque overtones: delicious chistorras (grilled sausages with peppers), confit de canard à l'eskualduna (ratatouille), paella, and salt cod à la luzienne. Judiciously selected Spanish wines.
A la carte: 200-300 F.

 Les Célébrités
Hôtel Nikko
61, quai de Grenelle
40 58 20 00,
fax 45 75 42 35
Open daily until 10 p.m. Private room: 22. Air cond. Heated pool. Valet parking.
The Roman emperors who stare down at the perpetual parade of roast lobster and stuffed pigs' trotters passing under their plaster noses don't seem as bored as we now are with them—and with the rest of this pompous, passé décor. Still, there is the view of the Seine beyond the bay window, the comfort of well-spaced tables, soft seating, the attentive, well-trained staff and above all, the artful cuisine of Jacques Sénéchal. This former Tour d'Argent chef has adroitly stepped into the shoes of Joël Robuchon, the Nikko's old star. His repertoire may be a bit static, but we always welcome an opportunity to sample Sénéchal's virtuoso cooking. Prices are steep, but the quality of the food is irreproachable. We cannot speak highly enough of the risotto with prawns, turbot, and a sprightly touch of tomato and basil; or the monumental volaille de Bresse aux morilles et à la crème; or desserts like the sparkling raspberry clafoutis or creamy tiramisù.
The superb cellar is less pricey than you might think. Impeccable service. Note the worthwhile prix-fixe lunch: it's the only bargain in sight.

15th arrondissement – RESTAURANTS

A la carte: 700-800 F. Menus: 250 F (lunch only), 610 F, 710 F.

Le Clos Morillons
50, rue des Morillons
48 28 04 37
Closed Sat. lunch, Sun., Feb. 22-28 & Aug. 8-24. Open until 10:15 p.m. Air cond.
Since he took over this quiet neighborhood bistro from Pierre Vedel some years ago, Philippe Delacourcelle has served consistently good food at reasonable prices. His menus, including the more expensive one which includes fine Loire wines (Pierre and his brother Marc are connoisseurs) offer a selection of dishes that combine innovation and tradition in a most satisfying synthesis: terrine pressée de pommes de terre et foie gras au gros sel, baked salt cod with bacon and a smoky-flavoured purée, young pigeon with sesame seeds. The many delectable desserts (Delacourcelle was once a pâtissier at Fauchon) provide instants of pure bliss in light, charming new décor.
A la carte: 275-375 F. Menus: 150 F (dinner only), 220 F, 285 F.

L'Entre-Siècle
49, av. Lowendal
47 83 51 22
Closed Sat. lunch, Sun. & Aug. Open until 10:30 p.m. Air cond.
Olivier Simon is a young Belgian chef out to conquer Paris with a repertoire that mixes Belgian dishes such as carbonnade à la flamande and waterzoï de volaille à la gantoise with more exotically inspired dishes such as a "beggar's purse" (crêpe) filled with Tunisian-spiced duck, or salmon with leeks and a hint of curry. Desserts are interesting too (try the pear steamed with spices and served with orange sauce). A small, eclectic wine list includes Belgian teas and beers.
A la carte: 280-350 F. Menus: 160 F (lunch only), 210 F and 240 F (dinner only).

11/20 L'Epopée
89, av. E.-Zola
45 77 71 37
Closed Sat. lunch, Sun. dinner & Dec. 24-Jan. 3. Open until 10:30 p.m. Terrace dining.
An earnest little restaurant, recommended for its hospitality, fine cuisine and value for money. Starters (seafood salad, vegetable terrine with tomato purée) are often priced under 50 francs, while main dishes (calf brawn ravigote, pané de bœuf grillé sauce marchand de vin) cost from 80 to 100 francs. Suggestions change daily. To drink, order a tasty Coteaux-du-Tricastin red from the Domaine de Grangeneuve—at 90 francs, you could hardly do better.
A la carte: 230-280 F. Menus: 145 F, 175 F, 225 F.

Erawan
76, rue de la Fédération
47 83 55 67,
fax 47 34 85 98
Closed Sun. & Aug. 2-Sep. 2. Open until 10:30 p.m. Air cond.
A noisy clientele crowds into the little dining rooms of this appealing Thai bistro. The food is exciting and exotic, some of the best of its kind in Paris. Try the bite-sized prawns, the pork and corn, fish steamed in a banana leaf, and beef with basil and green peppercorns.
A la carte: 180-380 F. Menus: from 132 F to 175 F.

12/20 La Farigoule
104, rue Balard
45 54 35 41
Closed Mon. dinner, Sun. & Aug. 14-30. Open until 10 p.m.
At nearly 60, Jean Gras is a colourful character if ever there was one. He has gone back to concocting the fragrant bouillabaisses and bourrides that made his former restaurant, Aux Senteurs de Provence, a fixture in the 15th arrondissement. This is the best place in town for authentic sheep's tripe and trotters à la marseillaise.
A la carte: 250-300 F.

Jacques Hébert
38, rue S.-Mercier
45 57 77 88
Closed Sun., Mon. & Aug. 1-20. Open until 10 p.m. Private room: 18.
Once the bulldozers have finished tearing up this arrondissement a number of excellent bistros will come to light, courageously peeking out of the rubble. Jacques Hébert is already on the scene, patiently waiting for success. After working under Robuchon and being the chef at the Sofitel-Invalides hotel for six years, Hébert decided to strike out on his own, in a small restaurant that is a jewel of simplicity and taste. Try his saddle of rabbit with tarragon, or the calf brawn with baby vegetables. The wines are astutely chosen.
A la carte: 350-450 F. Menu: 260 F (dinner only).

Kim-Anh
15, rue de l'Eglise
45 79 40 96
Dinner only. Open until 11:30 p.m. Air cond.
Charming Kim-Anh runs this tidy, flower-filled little Vietnamese restaurant while his wife Caroline practises her culinary craft in a lilliputian kitchen made for contortionists. She prepares her dishes with fresh herbs, delectable leaves and shoots, subtle spices and light sauces. Try the shredded beef fried with peanuts and vinegar, steamed snails Tonkin, caramelised prawns and the best spring rolls in Paris. Quite a good wine selection and some

surprisingly good desserts.
A la carte: 250-330 F.

Morot-Gaudry
8, rue de la Cavalerie
45 67 06 85,
fax 45 67 55 72

Closed Sat. & Sun. Open until 10:30 p.m. Private room: 20. Terrace dining. Air cond.

It would be hard to find a more ample or appetising lunch for 200 francs, a price unchanged for years and served by Jean-Pierre Morot-Gaudry on the roof of this 1930s building. He offers a choice of five first courses, such as a very good house-smoked salmon or soft-boiled eggs with prawn coulis. Five main dishes include a fabulous tête de veau and a chervil-scented lamb blanquette. Cheese is followed by a lovely selection of desserts: buckwheat crêpes filled with fruit and spices, or an excellent crème brûlée. A charming little wine—Coteaux-du-Lyonnais, Gaillac, or Haut-Poitou—is included. Danièle Morot-Gaudry's welcome is wonderful, and from the verdant terrace you can glimpse a corner of the Eiffel Tower.

But Morot-Gaudry doesn't stop there. His à la carte menu is a subtle marriage of classic, rustic and contemporary dishes such as lasagne de petits-gris (small snails) with morels, a ragoût of salmon and perch with fennel and rosemary, or mouthwatering beef sauce béarnaise.

Some impressive and costly wines are available such as a Montrachet "Marquis de Laguiche" or a Gruaud-Larose '28. But what thrills us at Morot-Gaudry is the selection of Jurançons, Chinon Vieilles Vignes, Savennières and Vouvrays which give enormous pleasure without breaking the bank.

A la carte: 400-550 F.

Menus: 200 F (lunch only, wine incl.), 520 F (wine incl.), 370 F.

L'Oie Cendrée
51, rue Labrouste
45 31 91 91

Closed Sat. lunch, Sun., holidays & July 14-Aug. 15. Open until 10 p.m. Private room: 15.

The two rooms could do with a dash of gaiety and better-spaced tables. The new chef's cuisine is a faithful interpretation of south-west specialities, based on top-quality ingredients: slightly bland goose quenelles with spinach, foie gras, cassoulet and prunes in Armagnac. A tiny cellar of regional wines.

A la carte: 170-250 F. Menus: 95 F, 125 F.

Olympe
8, rue N.-Charlet
47 34 86 08,
fax 44 49 05 04

Closed Mon., Sat. lunch & Sun., Aug. 14-17 & Dec. 23-25. Open until 11 p.m. Air cond.

Now that she is working on other projects, notably at the Virgin Megastore on the Champs-Elysées (a resounding success, we might add), Dominique Nahmias no longer rules over Olympe. But Albert Nahmias is still on hand, and has relaunched the restaurant as a fashionable bistro, serving food that is rather more clever and robust than sophisticated. The now-famous sautéed crayfish are still available, but there is also a 200-franc menu (served at lunch and dinner) which offers calf-brains fritters with capers, roast rabbit with artichoke pesto, duck ravioli au jus, and for dessert, a Paris-Brest or crémet à l'orange. In the same spirit, Albert hunts down good little wines at pleasing prices. The à la carte menu retains the distinctive house style, prepared (successfully, so far) by a well-trained team. The Orient-Express décor could do with a facelift but the largely Parisian and Californian clientele isn't complaining.

A la carte: 300 F. Menus: 200 F (lunch only, wine incl.), 160 F (lunch only), 285 F.

11/20 ### Le Patio Montparnasse
30-32, bd de Vaugirard
43 22 30 25

Closed Sat. lunch, Sun. & 2 wks. in Aug. Open until 10:30 p.m. Terrace dining.

Reasonable décor and a good little set menu: curried fricassée of cockles and mussels, braised kidneys and brains, frozen nougat with caramelised almonds. Interesting cellar, too.

Menus: 110 F (lunch only), 125 F (dinner only).

12/20 ### Le Petit Mâchon
123, rue de la Convention
45 54 08 62

Closed Sun. & July 20-Aug. 20. Open until 11 p.m. Terrace dining.

This is Slavik's re-creation of an old-fashioned bistro and it's devoted to the filling, warming food of Lyon: first-rate charcuterie, caviar lyonnais (hot lentils with shallots), pigs' trotters, and tripe. Ice cream from Berthillon for dessert.

A la carte: 130-190 F.

La Petite Bretonnière
2, rue de Cadix
48 28 34 39

Closed Sat. lunch, Sun. & Aug. Open until 10 p.m. Parking.

In eight years, Alain Lamaison and his wife Georgia have perked up this little restaurant with modest, charming décor worthy of the splendid, essentially south-west cuisine. Lamaison's dishes are lively and daring, particularly in their treatment of vegetables and fruit. Prices are no longer what they were, but the food is worth the money: pigeon roasted in spiced wine, served with a date purée; warm foie gras with a pear-and-celeriac gratin; and a crisp honey-sweet pastry with dried fruits and nuts. Very good cellar, rich in Bordeaux.

A la carte: 400-450 F. Menu: 240 F (lunch only).

12/20 Chez Pierre
117, rue de Vaugirard
47 34 96 12

Closed Sun., Sat. lunch, Mon. & Aug. Open until 10:15 p.m. Air cond. Parking.

Some good country dishes such as bœuf bourguignon aux pâtes fraîches, cassoulet, and confit de canard in an exemplary neighbourhood restaurant.

A la carte: 250 F. Menus: 120 F (lunch only), 175 F.

 ### Raajmahal
192, rue de la Convention
45 33 29 39

Open daily until 10:45 p.m. Air cond.

You can still feast your eyes on the lavish Hindu décor of this temple of North Indian cuisine, and you won't tire of the wonderful selection of breads. The famous lamb curry, the meat samosas, the boti tandoori aren't quite as irresistibly scrumptious as they once were, but the food is more than respectable and portions are generous too. Perfect service. The economical prix-fixe lunch includes one appetiser plus a main dish for just 59 francs.

A la carte: 230-300 F. Menu: 59 F (lunch only).

 ### Le Relais de Sèvres
Hôtel Sofitel Paris
8-12, rue L-Armand
40 60 30 30

Closed Sat., Sun., Aug. & Dec. 23-Jan. 1. Open until 10 p.m. Private room: 15. Air cond. Heated pool. Valet parking.

Roland Durand is off on his own now. He has passed on his apron to his former second-in-command, 33-year-old Martial Enguehard. In order to encourage the latter's efforts, the Sofitel has finally given the dining room a long-overdue facelift. The pale-blue walls and Champagne-coloured tablecloths may not be stunning, but they are fresh and inviting. The cuisine retains Durand's inimitable touch: sample the crab with foie gras and broccoli, ravioles d'escargot en gelée, turbot with mustard, or veal kidneys with a bright garnish of sorrel and caramelised tomatoes, before choosing one of the superb desserts: creamy soupe de semoule aux mangues, or gingery nougat glacé. The question is: will Enguehard develop his own style, or continue to serve Durand's repertoire? An excellent, reasonably priced cellar; exceptionally varied set lunch.

Menus: 290 F and 430 F (dinner only), 320 F (lunch only).

 ### Aux Senteurs de Provence
295, rue Lecourbe
45 57 11 98,
45 58 66 84

Closed Sun., Mon., Aug. 2-24 & 1 wk. in winter. Open until 10 p.m.

The owner is Tuscan and his new chef is a native of Burgundy, but they remain faithful to the Provençal repertoire long prepared here by former owner Jean Gras. Every Wednesday in the long, narrow dining room with cork-covered walls and jaunty nautical prints, the plat du jour is a wonderful aïoli complete with garlicky rouille and fat sea snails. Bouillabaisse and daube d'agneau provençale can be had any day of the week. To drink, order one of the good wines from the Coteaux-d'Aix.

A la carte: 250-350 F. Menus: from 195 F to 225 F.

 ### Uri
5, rue Humblot
45 77 37 11

Closed Sun. & Aug. Open until 10:30 p.m. Air cond.

Paris boasts few good Korean restaurants, so it's not difficult to understand why you can hardly get through the door of this one. It's always packed with homesick exiles in search of kimchee, raw skate salad, and any number of fiercely salted and vinegary native dishes. Cordial welcome from the Cho family.

A la carte: 170-270 F.

 ### Pierre Vedel
19, rue Duranton
45 58 43 17,
fax 45 58 42 65

Closed Sat. & Sun. Annual closings not available. Open until 10:15 p.m.

Be sure to book your table, because Pierre Vedel's warm Parisian bistro is invariably jam-packed. Little wonder the place is popular with dishes like shellfish ravioli, chicken-liver terrine with lobster coulis and sweetbreads en blanquette with wild mushrooms on the menu. True to his southern roots, Vedel also prepares an admirably authentic bourride de lotte à la sétoise (a garlicky monkfish soup), and a satisfying nougat glacé studded with candied fruit. If you order one of the more modest growers' wines from the interesting list, you can rest assured that the bill won't be too bad—Vedel's clients are friends, and he means to keep them!

A la carte: 300-350 F.

Red toques signify modern cuisine; white toques signify traditional cuisine.

RESTAURANTS – 16th arrondissement

12/20 Le Volant
13, rue B.-Dussane
45 75 27 67
Closed Sat. lunch, Sun. & Aug. 1-15. Open until 11 p.m.
Georges Houel is a former racing champion who wears his four-score years very lightly. He's a winner in the kitchen too, where he turns out superb red meats, top-flight ris de veau and succulent veal kidneys. All washed down with Georges Dubœuf's fruity Beaujolais.
A la carte: 180-250 F.

12/20 Le Western
Hilton
18, av. de Suffren
42 73 92 00
Open daily until 11 p.m.
Serving staff in jeans and check shirts welcome you to the Hilton's American-style restaurant, Le Western, which overlooks the garden with its cacti and Indian statuary. Chef Alain Bertrand prepares Tex-Mex favourites and Stateside specialities such as spare ribs, mixed grill and jumbo prawns with peppercorn sauce. Starters include guacamole and crab fritters, and there's cheesecake, brownies, and apple and pecan pie for dessert. On weekdays the "Pony Express" menu—starter, choice of two main courses, dessert and coffee—lets you lunch in 45 minutes flat.
A la carte: 250-300 F. Menu: 150 F.

16th arrondissement

 Amazigh
2, rue La Pérouse
47 20 90 38
Closed Sat. lunch, Sun. & Aug. Open until 11 p.m. Air cond.
Antiques and Oriental knick-knacks against a brick-coloured background make up the décor of this elegant dining room. You can expect attentive and courteous service, and highly refined North African cuisine: try the unusual stuffed sardines, the seafood briouat, tajines of fresh broad beans or lamb and aubergine, or a good couscous royal (the vegetables and stock would benefit from bolder seasoning). A few African wines are on hand, as well as a wider selection of French ones, but the latter fetch fearsome prices.
A la carte: 300-350 F.

10/20 Auberge du Bonheur
Bois de Boulogne
Allée de Longchamp
42 24 10 17
Closed Fri. & Sat. (Nov.-April). Open until 11 p.m. Garden dining. Valet parking.
Happy indeed are the patrons seated in sun-dappled comfort under parasols and plane trees at this delightful Bois de Boulogne restaurant. Charming service (quite a feat, considering the crowds) and simple, unpretentious food: salads, grilled meats, good desserts.
A la carte: 200-270 F.

 La Baie d'Ha Long
164, av. de Versailles
45 24 60 62
Closed Sun. & Aug. Open until 10:15 p.m. Air cond.
Roger, the proprietor of this small Vietnamese spot, is far more interested in his collection of birds and exotic fish than in food. It is his wife Nathalie who works away in the kitchen producing delicious, exotic dishes from her native Vietnam: spicy soups, brochettes made with fresh herbs, duck grilled with ginger. Generous portions. The cellar holds some surprisingly good wines.
A la carte: 200-240 F. Menu: 95 F (lunch only).

12/20 Bellini
28, rue Le Sueur
45 00 54 20
Closed Sat. lunch, Sun. & Aug. 3-29. Open until 11 p.m. Air cond.
Comfy banquettes, smoked mirrors, grey marble and peach-toned walls create a cosy setting for Bellini's somewhat Frenchified Italian fare. Sample the risotto with white truffles (or black truffles, when the short season for tartufi bianchi ends), spaghetti alla bottarga (with mullet eggs), fresh vegetables in olive oil and a smooth tiramisù, all washed down with appealing wines from Friulia, Tuscany and the Veneto. The set lunch is good value.
A la carte: 250-350 F. Menus: 150 F (lunch only), 200 F (dinner only).

 Paul Chène
123, rue Lauriston
47 27 63 17
Closed w.-e., July 31-Sep. 1 & Dec. 23-Jan. 3. Open until 10:30 p.m. Private room: 30. Air cond. Parking.
Paul Chène has turned over his popular restaurant to new owners, but the spirit of his provincial cooking is carried on by his chef, André Ravigneau. Some improvements have been made, and now the food shows a lighter touch and more vigorous flavours. All the more reason to rediscover the fresh mackerel in Muscadet, flawless breast of duckling with foie gras in a light aspic, or daube de bœuf à l'ancienne. For dessert, there are dainty apple fritters with redcurrant jelly. The cellar boasts a varied, judicious selection, but the house Bordeaux is not to be neglected.
A la carte: 350-450 F. Menu: 250 F.

16th arrondissement – RESTAURANTS

Conti
72, rue Lauriston
47 27 74 67
Closed 3 wks. in Aug. Open until 10:30 p.m. Air cond.

Slavik has refurbished Conti's rather Satanic décor of mirrors with black and gold highlights. Chef Michel Ranvier took the cue, and has revamped his repertoire of provincial Italian dishes, giving them a vigorous, modern— French!—zest. His puff-pastry tart of fennel and fresh anchovies is the lightest "pizza" you are likely to encounter; equally appetising are the Gorgonzola flan with Marsala butter, scallops bristling with rosemary leaves, and a poached chicken breast with anchovies and truffles. The best tiramisù in Paris is to be found here, along with a superb Italian cellar, excellent service and a chic, well-bred clientele.

A la carte: 400-500 F. Menu: 265 F (weekdays lunch only, wine incl.).

L'Estournel
Hôtel Baltimore
1, rue L.-Delibes
44 34 54 34,
fax 44 34 54 44
Closed Sat., Sun., Aug. 1-29. Open until 10 p.m. Private room: 80. Air cond. Parking.

The new décor features admirably executed frescoes, but their charm is more or less cancelled out by the bland furnishings. At least the room is spacious and comfortable, and the elegant staff warm up the atmosphere nicely. Chef Daniel Le Quéré works in a classic mode, with considerable success. Despite a flawed dish or two (the prawn and basil salad lacked character, we thought) we recently enjoyed a meal that included a flavourful chartreuse of red mullet and an exceptional tarte Tatin. Encyclopaedic cellar; high prices.

A la carte: 400-500 F. Menu: 250 F (weekdays only).

Fakhr el Dine
30, rue de Longchamp
47 27 90 00
See 8th arrondissement.

Faugeron
52, rue de Longchamp
47 04 24 53,
fax 47 55 62 90
Closed Sat. (except dinner Oct.-April), Sun., Dec. 23-Jan. 3 & Aug. Open until 10 p.m. Private room: 14. Air cond. Valet parking.

Golden oak panelling now enhances Faugeron's large blue-and-saffron dining room, a décor that some find rather chi-chi, but which everyone finds comfortable. Under the smiling supervision of hostess Guerlinde Faugeron, prize-winning sommelier Jean-Claude Jambon and a whole squadron of courteous (but never obsequious) waiters tend to the patrons, while chef-proprietor Henri Faugeron runs the kitchen. Although he is not obsessed by novelty, Faugeron renews his menu often enough to keep our mouths watering and our curiosity alive. We never tire of such classics as soft-boiled eggs with truffle purée, admirable house-smoked salmon, wild mushrooms with foie gras, Challans duckling with turnips, or tender fillet of beef with bone marrow; yet we are delighted to discover new dishes like prawns in a spiced vinaigrette with fried celery, salmon steak with muscat butter and a touch of mint, or a truly memorable combination of young rabbit and potatoes perfumed with fresh dill.

A pear millefeuille with honey cream sauce, or pistachio-caramel ice cream are a final thrill to be savoured along with the last drops of a great Bordeaux, a voluptuous Burgundy, or a more modest Chinon or Sancerre. The calm, unruffled ambience attracts a high-class clientele; the impressive four-course set lunch has many fans.

A la carte: 650-850 F. Menus: 320 F (lunch only), 550 F (dinner only, wine incl.), 780 F (truffles in seas.), 500 F.

Jean-Claude Ferrero
38, rue Vital
45 04 42 42,
fax 45 04 67 71
Closed Sat. (lunch in winter), Sun., holidays, May 1-18 & Aug. 10-Sep. 5. Open until 10:30 p.m. Private room: 35. Valet parking.

If you're looking for a winter treat, book a table here when Jean-Claude Ferrero is serving his famous "all-truffle" menu. Throughout the winter months, this Second Empire *hôtel particulier* welcomes a faithful, very Parisian crowd keen to sample those irresistible, earthy delights in many guises. Less expensive and just as delicious are Ferrero's aïoli with salt cod, blanquette de veau à l'ancienne, and bœuf aux carottes, dishes which are regularly featured in the prix-fixe lunch. But Ferrero earned his third toque last year for more spirited, often ingenious creations that make dining here an adventure. We're thinking of the fragrant prawns "Monsieur le Préfet", or truffled calf's foot and sweetbreads, or the wonderful langoustes aux huiles douces, or a garlic-studded leg of Pauillac lamb served with a creamy gratin dauphinois. Other choices include bouillabaisse raphaëloise and sea bass à la porquerollaise. Our sole quibble is that desserts do not always live up to the standards set by the rest.

A la carte: 450-800 F. Menus: 220 F (lunch only), 350 F.

RESTAURANTS – 16th arrondissement

12/20 Les Filaos
5, rue Guy-de-Maupassant
45 04 94 53
Closed Sun. & 2 wks. in Aug. Open daily until 10:30. Air cond.

The dining room is tidy and neat, the cuisine straight from the island of Mauritius—its spicy Creole fare (deliciously fiery rougails) with a strong Indian influence (Madras-style curry). The pork curry with red beans will put tropical sunshine in your veins and fire in your belly!
A la carte: 200 F. Menu: 82 F (lunch only).

 La Fontaine d'Auteuil
35 bis, rue La Fontaine
42 88 04 47
Closed Sat. lunch, Sun., Feb. 21-28 & Aug. Open until 10:15 p.m. Private room: 12.

Shy, modest Xavier Grégoire, late of the Hilton's Toit de Paris, has spread his wings since he came to this flower-filled establishment next to the Maison de la Radio. Try his marinated sardines—rollmop style—his coquilles Saint-Jacques sprinkled with chopped nuts and garlic, his luscious vanilla ice cream, and an airy millefeuille. A la carte prices are too high, but the set menu served at lunch is very good value. Attractive wines.
A la carte: 380-450 F. Menu: 170 F (lunch only).

 Chez Géraud
31, rue Vital
45 20 33 00
Closed off-season Sat. lunch, Sun. & Aug. Open until 10 p.m. Air cond.

Right across the street from Jean-Claude Ferrero, Gérard Rongier has converted a former bakery into a cosy restaurant complete with banquettes, Sarreguemines tiles, immaculate linen and attentive service. Géraud packs in an appreciative audience with a menu that features sole aux morilles, raie à la moutarde à l'ancienne, roast rabbit with garlic and succulent roast Bresse chicken. And the patrons keep coming back for more.
Fans of Côtes-du-Rhône, Savigny-lès-Beaune or Pineau des Charentes (the latter a golden nectar to sip as an apéritif) will love the wine list. The desserts, though improving, still need work.
A la carte: 250-330 F.

 Le Grand Chinois
6, av. de New-York
47 23 98 21
Closed Mon. & Aug. Open until 11 p.m. Private room: 30.

The Peking duck is still golden and crisp, but the other dishes we've tried here recently seem to indicate that the chef is losing his touch. How else can we explain the unpleasantly sticky, greasy sautéed prawns and vegetables? Or the bland, uninteresting sautéed turbot? Owner Colette Tan's warm smile didn't allay our disappointment—or soften the sting of the bill! Sorry, but we're knocking two points off the rating this year.
A la carte: 220-300 F.

 La Grande Cascade
Bois de Boulogne
Near the race-track
45 27 33 51,
fax 42 88 99 06
Closed Dec. 20-Jan. 20. Open until 10:30 p.m. Private room: 50. Garden dining. Valet parking.

In springtime everyone (it seems) heads to the half-moon terrace of Napoléon III's former pleasure pavilion, shaded by a graceful glass-and-iron marquee. This stylish Belle Epoque establishment offers the reassuring culinary repertoire of Jean Sabine, an enlightened classicist who doesn't mistake tradition for stuffiness. Try his scallop salad sprinkled with walnut oil, salmon with bits of bacon and curly Savoy cabbage, sautéed veal kidneys, or rack of lamb with wild thyme. The cellar houses 80,000 bottles, service is formal, and though à la carte prices are anything but rustic, the set lunch is relatively economical.
A la carte: 600-800 F. Menu: 270 F (weekdays lunch only).

 Marius
82, bd Murat
46 51 67 80
Closed Sat. lunch, Sun. & Aug. Open until 10:30 p.m. Terrace dining.

Come summer, the bright little dining room is enlarged by a terrace, nicely shaded by a row of spindle trees. The new owners have brought a youthful, energetic tone to this old bouillabaisse institution, and have improved the quality considerably (the prices remain reasonable, we are glad to report). Try the bracing crab salad, or the simple, satisfying smoked haddock with butter sauce. Delicious desserts. Smiling (but often slow) service.
A la carte: 250-320 F.

11/20 Mexico Café
1, pl. de Mexico
47 27 96 98
Open daily until 11 p.m. (Sat. & Sun. until midnight). Terrace dining.

Amusing retro décor, attentive service and a professional in the kitchen: fresh pasta salad, andouillette, magret de canard. Cheerful spot, beloved of young trendies.
A la carte: 200-250 F. Menu: 135 F (lunch only).

Red toques signify modern cuisine; white toques signify traditional cuisine.

Verre Harcourt, créé en 1825.

SUR LES AILES DU TEMPS UN BACCARAT S'ENVOLE.

16th arrondissement – RESTAURANTS

Al Mounia
16, rue de Magdebourg
47 27 57 28
Closed Sun. & mid-July-Aug. Open until 11 p.m. Air cond.
The owner, his chef, and the sous-chef all hail from Casablanca. They produce some fine tajines and a delectable lamb couscous served in a seductive Moorish setting. A tiny cellar offers the usual Moroccan wines.
A la carte: 300 F.

Passy-Mandarin
6, rue Bois-le-Vent
42 88 12 18
Closed 2 wks. in Aug. Open until 11:15 p.m. Air cond.
Lots of local colour in the three bright, spacious dining rooms. Dashing waiters in white serve dishes prepared by a chef at the top of his form. Highly original stews (cockscombs, fish...), lotte with soy beans, and excellent stuffed frogs' legs keep the Mandarin's toque firmly in place. Cheerful service.
A la carte: 160-320 F.

Le Pergolèse
40, rue Pergolèse
45 00 21 40,
fax 45 00 81 31
Closed Sat., Sun. & Aug. Open until 10:30 p.m. Private room: 25.
The pastel-pink décor of this stylish establishment is as elegant as the service. A well-bred, well-heeled clientele converses in hushed tones while chef Albert Corre pampers them with scallops and thyme flowers, scrambled eggs with snails and chanterelles, braised sweetbreads with cèpes and other less complicated but clever dishes. Delectable desserts, good regional wines.
A la carte: 440-500 F.
Menus: 230 F, 300 F.

Le Petit Bedon
38, rue Pergolèse
45 00 23 66,
fax 45 01 96 29
Closed Sat. (except Sep. 15-April 15), Sun. & July 31-Aug. 29. Open until 10 p.m. Air cond.
Chef Pierre Marchesseau is known for his television appearances and as a cookbook author. He won over the chic clientele of Le Petit Bedon's little dining room (the décor is straight out of a glossy magazine) with spirited renditions of culinary classics (now more often prepared, as Marchesseau admits, by his associate chef, Bernard Troullier). Try the filets de rouget à la fondue de foie gras et d'oignon, duck with lentils, rack of lamb with gratin dauphinois, or plump poularde au vin jaune. The desserts—profiteroles au chocolat, honey-caramel-pistachio ice cream, cherry fondue—will titillate even the most jaded palates. A fine cellar, professional service, dizzying prices.
A la carte: 500-600 F.
Menus: 185 F (lunch only), 250 F, 350 F.

Le Port Alma
10, av. de New-York
47 23 75 11
Closed Sun. & Aug. Open until 10:30 p.m. Private room: 15. Air cond.
"Scandalous", we wrote a while back, having noticed all the empty seats in one of the finest fish restaurants in town. Luckily, a lot of Parisian seafood aficionados took our protest to heart, for things are definitely looking up in this bright (too bright? maybe even loud?) dining room. Madame Canal's welcome is lovely and warm, and the fresh crustaceans and fish are prepared with a light touch by the Dôme's former chef. Sample the wonderful hot oysters with cockles, a fillet of turbot scented with thyme and escorted by a delicate ragoût of fresh broad beans, or the engaging fricassée of sole with foie gras; for dessert, choose a walnut crème brûlée or a thin apple tart. Wash it all down with a bottle of Roger Neveu's Sancerre or an Hermitage from Guigal, and you'll know the meaning of bliss. Paul Canal is a chef who doesn't skimp on quality ingredients or mask their flavours with superfluous sauces. For committed carnivores the menu lists just one meat dish, but it is a côte de bœuf de Salers: a rib of some of the finest beef in France.
A la carte: 400-600 F. Menu: 200 F (lunch only).

Le Pré Catelan
Bois de Boulogne
Rte de Suresnes
45 24 55 58,
fax 45 24 43 25
Closed Sun. dinner, Mon. & Feb. school holidays. Open until 10 p.m. Private room: 30. Garden dining. Valet parking.
Colette Lenôtre has retired to her vineyard in Bordeaux, leaving this Second Empire landmark in the capable hands of Roland Durand. Working in brand-new kitchens, this talented chef has thoroughly revamped the house repertoire, marking it with his personal stamp and style. Judging by diners' reactions, Durand's menu is a rousing success. They—and we—applaud the rich gratin de macaroni au foie gras, the truffled rabbit terrine, scallops with a dash of cinnamon to underscore their natural sweetness, and the rib of prime Bavarian beef bathed in a parsley and bone marrow jus.
A la carte prices continue to spiral skywards; do we recommend that you take a close look at the appealing new "menu-carte" (a fixed-

price formula which offers a wider choice than the traditional set menu). The cellar is large and reasonably priced.
A la carte: 700-1,000 F. Menus: 550 F, 650 F.

 Quach
47, av. R.-Poincaré
47 27 98 40

Closed Sat. lunch. Open until 11 p.m.

Aquariums decorate this elegant dining room where Monsieur Quach serves some delectable Cantonese and Vietnamese dishes: prawns grilled with lemon grass, squid with red peppers, and grilled lamb with five spices. But it's the Peking duck that keeps the high-class patrons coming back for more. Served, as it should be, in three separate courses, the duck is indeed a delight. Prices are quite reasonable—for the area.
A la carte: 220-280 F. Menus: 92 F (weekdays lunch only), 109 F.

 Le Relais d'Auteuil
Patrick Pignol
31, bd Murat
46 51 09 54

Closed Sat. lunch, Sun. Annual closings not available. Open until 10:15 p.m. Air cond. Valet parking.

Patrick Pignol is a young chef in a hurry, eager to earn recognition for his inventive, resolutely contemporary cuisine. His dishes often combine flavours in provocative, unexpected ways that can perk up the most jaded appetite. How about delicate scallops served in their shells with a thyme-scented stock, or a plump, juicy pigeon cooked en cocotte with Chinese truffles, or, for dessert, a buttery madeleine with the haunting taste of heather honey? All the dishes are most attractively presented, with painstaking attention to detail.

Interesting cellar; charming welcome.
A la carte: 400-500 F. Menus: 200 F (lunch only), 410 F.

12/20 Le Relais du Bois
Bois de Boulogne,
Croix-Catelan
Rte de Suresnes
42 88 08 43

Closed Sun. dinner. Open until 10 p.m. Private room: 250. Terrace dining.

This rustic rendezvous—a Second Empire hunting pavilion where naughty ladies and gentlemen once engaged in rather outrageous behaviour—is now the backdrop for tame family parties and corporate banquets. The comfortable dining room has its charms, but the huge summer garden is truly delightful. Good—if unexciting—food: fish soup, grilled andouillette, confit de canard.
A la carte: 150-250 F.

 Le Relais du Parc
55, av. R.-Poincaré
44 05 66 10

Open daily until 10:30 p.m.

By late 1993 Joël Robuchon will have taken possession of a splendid 1900 townhouse adjoining (and owned by) the Parc Victor-Hugo hotel. While awaiting his removal, Robuchon has undertaken to supervise the hotel's restraurant, Le Relais du Parc. In a British colonial setting (straight *Out of Africa*) Robuchon has placed his prize pupil, Gilles Renault, who skilfully prepares the roster of simple, brasserie-style dishes. Although the marinated herring with warm potato salad hardly rises above the ordinary, the Asian-spiced vegetable salad or the mélange of mushrooms, vegetables, and grapes perfumed with coriander are perky appealing preludes to a perfectly baked lotte à l'ail with saffron-sauced pasta, or to long-simmered oxtail with flavourful carrots. Also featured is spit-roast poultry (the ducks and pigeons are particularly succulent). Dessert brings ably executed standards: floating island, cup custards, and tarte aux pommes. Fascinating, affordable wine list.
A la carte: 250-300 F.

 Robuchon
32, rue de Longchamp
47 27 12 27

Closed Sat., Sun. & July 5-31. Open until 10:15 p.m. Private room: 14. Air cond. Valet parking.

We would love to think it was just a joke, but knowing Joël as we do, we're pretty sure he means it: on his 50th birthday—in 1995—Robuchon will doff his toque and hang up his apron to write *the* cookbook, become a much-sought-after restaurant consultant and manage the soon-to-open restaurant/château he and his associates have built in Tokyo. All the more reason, then, to hurry and put your name on the interminable waiting-list presided over by manager Jean-Jacques Caimant. There's no point in pretending to be a personal friend of François Mitterrand, or Jacques Chirac's long-lost cousin—you just have to wait until the day you too can be one of the 45 privileged people seated in the celadon-coloured dining room or in the charming first-floor private salon that seats 15. We've said everything there is to say about Robuchon's brilliant talent, we've praised his technique, his taste for perfection and the passion for detail which he dins into his disciples like a drill sergeant. But what stuns us still is the ability of this craftsman (he's too modest to call himself an artist) to thrill and surprise us at every visit. The first time you taste his crab perfumed with thyme, saffron

16th arrondissement – RESTAURANTS

and curry, or the sesame sole, or a poulet de Bresse au jus à l'ancienne et aux truffes, you could be forgiven for thinking you had reached the summit—but then next time Robuchon astounds you with his soupe chaude à la gelée de poule, with the intense tastes of truffle and black pepper. Each mouthful of his creamy fennel and sea-urchin soup, spaghetti tossed with prawns and white truffles, his roast milk-fed kid with a persillade of green garlic, or his farm-bred guinea fowl set atop a slice of roast foie gras will make you groan with delight.

Frankly, we would love to catch him out just once—but no luck. Neither the cristalline de chou aux ris de veau with its garnish of grilled morels and asparagus, nor the extraordinary lamb steak with baby broad beans and tiny artichokes, nor the much-touted mashed potatoes (often imitated, never duplicated!) is open to the slightest criticism, any more than desserts like the turban de pommes à la cannelle, the frozen feuillantine made with almond milk and diaphanous apple slices, Robuchon's peerless crème brûlée, or the wines chosen with unmatched flair by sommelier Antoine Hernandez.

Gone, however, is the legendary 160-franc set lunch. Today's soaring prices may well appal you, but this degree of perfection is necessarily costly. And remember, to serve 45 customers, Joël Robuchon employs a staff of 35.

A la carte: 750-1,500 F. Menu: 890 F.

Sous l'Olivier
15, rue Goethe
47 20 84 81

Closed Sat., Sun. & holidays. Open until 10:30 p.m. Terrace dining.

We aren't wild about the eau-de-nil décor or the harsh lighting that does little for patrons' complexions, but summer lunches on the terrace are engagingly lively. The food is uneven (the seasonings in particular lack gusto) but the crab pâté with braised leeks, herring fillets with warm potatoes and bacon and the chocolate feuillantine are creditable enough.

A la carte: 300-350 F.

Le Sully d'Auteuil
78, rue d'Auteuil
46 51 71 18,
fax 46 51 70 60

Closed Sat. lunch & Sun., Aug. 10-30 & Dec. 25-Jan. 1. Open until 10:30 p.m. Private room: 70. Terrace dining. Air cond.

The exaggeratedly precious nomenclature of the overlong menu has been toned down a bit, but Gil Bourgeois remains faithful to the spirit of a sauce-rich—technically accomplished—cuisine. The rich note blends in perfectly with the elegant décor designed by Michel Brunetière in this idyllic pavilion attached to Auteuil railway station. There's an attractive summer terrace, and a large clientele not put off by staggering bills for foie gras with quail eggs and bacon, sole soufflé with shellfish, or calf brawn sauce tortue with essence of sherry. Luscious desserts and a tempting array of old brandies.

A la carte: 450-500 F.

Le Toit de Passy
94, av. Paul-Doumer
45 24 55 37,
fax 45 20 94 57

Closed Sat. lunch, Sun. & Dec. 22-Jan. 4. Open until 10:30 p.m. Private room: 25. Terrace dining. Air cond. Parking.

Check your bank balance before you book a table at Yannick Jacquot's rooftop restaurant. If you're feeling flush, treat yourself to a meal in this pleasant, plant-filled dining room, with its broad terrace overlooking Paris and retractable roof for dining (weather permitting) under the stars. Jacquot is not an innovator, but he has an almost infallible knack of combining flavours in utterly convincing ways. Try his exquisite consommé de langoustines en gelée de petits légumes, the croustillant of frogs' legs with garlic cream sauce, the gently spiced aiguillettes of Challans duck breast, or his perfect chocolate millefeuille layered with praline cream and topped with a chicory-flavoured sauce. The cellar holds 45,000 bottles, so the wine list will take some perusing. Good cigars, too.

A la carte: 500-600 F. Menus: 275 F and 295 F (lunch only), 485 F.

Villa Vinci
23, rue Paul-Valéry
45 01 68 18

Closed Sat., Sun. & Aug. Open until 10:30 p.m. Air cond.

Business people at lunch and an up-market local clientele in the evening frequent this comfortable, luxurious restaurant. Though the pasta is still remarkable, the hors-d'œuvres are ordinary, and the Venetian calf's liver bland and pedestrian. Desserts (like tiramisù) save the day, along with the rich and varied Italian cellar.

A la carte: 350-450 F. Menu: 170 F (lunch only).

Vivarois
192, av. V.-Hugo
45 04 04 31,
fax 45 03 09 84

Closed Sat., Sun. & Aug. Open until 10 p.m. Private room: 10. Air cond. Parking.

If we'd known how happy and serene a fourth toque would make chef Claude Peyrot, we might have been tempted to award it sooner. His life has changed, his restaurant is full, and he's no longer talking of retiring to his native Ardèche or of opening a bistro at the North Pole. This versatile chef sticks faithfully to a concise repertoire enriched daily with a half-dozen dishes created on the spur of the moment. The maître d'hotel might announce the presence of a fondant of vegetables with black-olive purée, dartois de sole that combines light puff pastry and succulent layers of fish, or pigeon sauce au vin, or, in season, hare à la royale garnished with quince. Neither classic nor modern, this cuisine is uniquely Peyrot's. An unrivalled technician, he also possesses a sensitivity and grace all his own. To add to the pleasure, there are wines, magnificent and modest, discovered by sommelier extraordinaire Jean-Claude Vinadier, and served under the benevolent but vigilant eye of Jacqueline Peyrot. We are relieved to report that the rather cold and much-criticised décor is due for a change.

A la carte: 600-800 F. Menu: 385 F (lunch only).

17th arrondissement

Amphyclès
78, av. des Ternes
40 68 01 01,
fax 40 68 91 88

Closed Sat. lunch, Sun. & July 10-31. Open until 10:30 p.m. Air cond. Parking.

Chef Philippe Groult's cuisine resembles the man himself: strong, full of character, absolutely unaffected and often diabolically subtle. His flair with herbs and spices lends extra spark to daring liaisons of textures and tastes. But the combinations are never gratuitous: the well-matched ravioli of pigeon and crayfish are admirable plate-fellows, though we wonder why they're blanketed with a dull veal-based sauce. Other happy marriages include a velouté of langoustines given extra flavour by cumin and marjoram, mitonnée de porcelet aux condiments and an exemplary canard de Challans au coriandre.

Cheeses are something special here, and the fine choice of desserts features caramelised apples with almonds, soufflé chaud au chocolat and simple yet sublime vanilla ice cream. The cellar is still young but interesting, overseen by a shrewd young sommelier who trained with Robuchon, Guérard and Lameloise. A final tip: Groult's set lunch, which features a first course, a hearty main dish (casseroled veal with lentils, joues de bœuf braisées aux carottes confites...), cheeses and dessert, must be one of the best deals around.

A la carte: 500-800 F. Menus: 220 F (lunch only), 580 F, 680 F.

Apicius
122, av. de Villiers
43 80 19 66

Closed Christmas wk. & Aug. Open until 10 p.m. Air cond. Valet parking.

Jean-Pierre Vigato looks more like a film star than a cook, but this shy *cuisinier* prefers to keep hard at work in his kitchen. Vigato is a master of two distinct but complementary culinary styles: an imaginative, modern, highly refined register, and a heartier, more rustic mode steeped in the traditions of the French countryside. They co-exist in harmony, and both bear Vigato's unmistakable stamp, whether it's the robust tête de veau en ravigote or the delicate bouillon of lobster with bone marrow brightened with piquant Thai herbs, the light and engaging steamed skate garnished with fruit and capers, or a succulent filet de bœuf topped with a rich sauce.

We think Vigato's cooking is better than ever—a recent fabulous meal consisted of lamb carpaccio with Parmesan on a salad of fresh herbs; plump prawns flash-fried in a diaphanous batter of spices, Japanese flour and egg white; spiced steamed cod; and crisp morsels of sweetbreads en brochette with a light coating of breadcrumbs, parsley, tarragon and chervil. In the dessert league, Vigato's incredible chocolate-based creations—gâteaux, mousses, shells and sorbets—take top honours. Madeleine Vigato supervises the two warmly decorated dining rooms with smiling courtesy.

A la carte: 500-850 F.

Augusta
98, rue de Tocqueville
47 63 39 97

Closed Sat. lunch, Sun., Aug. 7-23. Open until 10 p.m. Air cond.

Scrupulously seasonal, rigorously precise, based on the freshest seafood: Lionel Maître's cuisine is all this and more. Desserts, somewhat neglected in the past, have greatly improved and the langoustines à la vanille on a salad of lamb's lettuce, the saffron-tinted red mullet and courgettes, the turbot baked with honey and lemon, and scallops on a bed of bean sprouts perfumed with basil have hoisted Augusta high into the ranks of the best fish restaurants in Paris. Lionel Maître is still young, yet his technique is astonishingly mature, and he is quite a hard taskmaster too, judging from the choleric commands that resound in the kitchen (and sometimes carry into the slightly fusty blue dining room). The cellar boasts a superb collection of white

17th arrondissement – RESTAURANTS

wines.
A la carte: 450-500 F.

La Barrière de Clichy
1, rue de Paris
92110 Clichy
47 37 05 18

Closed Sat. lunch, Sun. & 2 wks. in Aug. Open until 10 p.m. Air cond.

Superchefs Guy Savoy and Bernard Loiseau cut their teeth here. Now in charge of the Barrière's kitchen is 34-year-old Gilles Le Gallès, who trained with Loiseau. The establishment suffers from being cut off by the ring road that separates Paris from Clichy. Confronted with that concrete problem, Gilles Le Gallès's preferred weapons are patience—and his talent to surprise. His light, inventive cuisine (he prefers cooking juices to sauces) is marked by interesting marriages: tiny squid stuffed with chicken livers on a bed of courgette fondue, escargots paired with ris de veau, fillets of young rabbit matched with Camembert, or goat cheese with lamb. Most chefs couldn't pull it off, but Le Gallès does—beautifully. The menu lists a few classics too: warm oysters wrapped in spinach leaves and dressed with shallot vinaigrette, salmon steak with sea salt and pigeonneau aux choux. To finish, bold and conservative tastes alike plump for the tarte fine Verger aux pommes. The cellar leans heavily towards fine Bordeaux.
A la carte: 350-450 F. Menus: 220 F (weekdays only), 270 F (weekdays lunch only, wine incl.), 370 F.

Les Béatilles
127, rue Cardinet
42 27 95 64

Closed Sat. & Sun. Open until 10:15 p.m.

A light, easily digestible, nearly irreproachable cuisine that aims for simplicity. Join the well-heeled locals at one of the pretty tables in the intimate white dining rooms for foie gras aux lentilles, red-mullet lasagne, a lamb daube with fresh pasta, or a rich and flaky duck tourte dressed with a meat-juice vinaigrette. When it's time for dessert, the gingery charlotte aux épices will make you glad you came.
A la carte: 300 F. Menus: 130 F (lunch only), 180 F and 290 F (dinner only).

Billy Gourmand
20, rue de Tocqueville
42 27 03 71

Closed Sat. lunch, Sun. & 3 wks. in Aug. Open until 10 p.m. Private room: 14. Air cond.

Philippe Billy, a young pupil of Jacques Chibois and Claude Deligne, has managed to elbow his way into an already restaurant-saturated *quartier*. Against a backdrop of mirrors and large potted plants you can choose from a classic yet personalised menu: a fragrant ragoût of baby scallops and mushrooms with fresh herbs, turbot piccata with mussels, fillet of Angus beef and some pleasing traditional desserts. Good wines by the glass.
A la carte: 280-380 F. Menu: 150 F (dinner, except holidays).

Le Bistrot d'à Côté
10, rue G.-Flaubert
42 67 05 81,
fax 47 63 82 75

Closed Sat. lunch & Aug. 1-15. Open until 11:30 p.m. Terrace dining. Valet parking.

All you want from a bistro: hustle, bustle and cheeky waiters. After a slight falling off, this cheery place has bounced back to become a perfect Lyonnais-style *bouchon* with a few unexpected dishes—lamb curry mauricienne—thrown in for good measure. The warm lentil salad with cervelas saus-

---

New Bridge is old

Despite its name, the *Pont-Neuf* ("new bridge") is the oldest bridge in Paris. Completed in 1604, it was the first in Paris to be built without houses blocking the view of the river. It even had pavements—quite a novelty at the time—and a series of semicircular bays whose stone benches still make an ideal stopping place during a romantic stroll. In its early days, the bridge buzzed with a gaudy population of charlatans, traders and troubadours (who satirised unpopular politicians or the king's latest mistress). The Pont-Neuf's most recent claim to fame came in 1985 when the American sculptor Christo wrapped it lovingly in bridal white to fashion a two-week work of art.

---

age, corn and salmon galette and smooth crème brûlée have won over a faithful corps of customers. The wines, however, are too expensive for this sort of establishment. Another Bistrot d'à Côté is located at 16, avenue de Villiers, 47 63 25 61.
A la carte: 260-320 F.

RESTAURANTS – 17th arrondissement

Le Bistrot de l'Etoile-Niel
75, av. Niel
42 27 88 44

Closed Sun. Open until midnight. Terrace dining. Air cond. Valet parking.

Guy Savoy has gone into partnership with his former pupil, Bruno Gensdarmes, to assure the success of this bistro, now as popular as the one on rue Troyon (see below). Try the museau ravigote au chou craquant or gratin d'épaule d'agneau aux aubergines, followed by one of the irresistible desserts. The house wine, a Merlot, is served "en pot", Lyonnais-fashion; other choices from the limited cellar are rather pricey.

A la carte: 200-260 F.

Le Bistrot de l'Etoile-Troyon
13, rue Troyon
42 67 25 95

Closed Sat. lunch & Sun. Open until midnight. Air cond.

Old-fashioned bistro cooking is here given a youthful touch by William Ledeuil, who spent three years with Guy Savoy. The latter oversees this successful and busy bistro from his own establishment across the street. Specialities include cuisse de canard aux haricots rouges, braised tuna and a pudding aux griottes. Drink the tasty house Merlot served in carafes.

A la carte: 220-300 F.

12/20 Le Cadre Noir
4, rue Gounod
40 54 02 29

Closed Sat. lunch & Sun. Open until 10:30 p.m.

It would be hard to find a more clever or varied menu—95 francs for a starter and a main dish—than the one on offer in this discreetly elegant little restaurant. It's a shame the tiny wine list doesn't follow suit. We enjoyed the crab terrine spiced with saffron and a good noisette de veau with an artichoke galette.

Menus: 95 F, 169 F (dinner only, wine incl.).

Charly de Bab-el-Oued
95, bd Gouvion-St-Cyr
45 74 34 62,
fax 45 74 35 36

Open daily until 11:30 p.m. Air cond.

An inviting place to dream of the *Arabian Nights* amid colourful tiles, cedarwood and palm trees. Feast on excellent couscous, pastillas and tajines, followed by sweet Eastern pastries made on the premises. Perfect service.

A la carte: 200-300 F.

Clos Longchamp
Le Méridien Paris-Etoile
81, bd Gouvion-St-Cyr
40 68 30 40

Closed Sat., Sun. & Aug. 14-22. Open until 10:30 p.m. Private room: 20. Air cond. Valet parking.

Chef Jean-Marie Meulien is at the top of his form this year. Not content with being a master craftsman, he combines the flavours of the Mediterranean with the spices of South-East Asia to produce tempting dishes in which the influence of his mentor, Louis Outhier, still lingers. This year we especially enjoyed the steamed crevettes perfumed with Champagne vinegar, sea bream and young leeks, red mullet on a bed of crisp aubergine, ginger-scented lobster, crawfish with Thai herbs, and spicy duck steak. Not to mention fillet of lamb coated in an astonishing but delicious coffee sauce and tender veal chops sprinkled with pollen and topped by a sauce delicately flavoured with honey. Hot chocolate tart and candied chestnut charlotte are among the delightful deserts and award-winning sommelier Didier Bureau is sure to recommend just the right wine to complement the meal. The exuberant central garden has flourished so well you would think you were in sunnier climes, and almost makes you forget the strange, banana-shaped dining room that surrounds it.

A la carte: 550-800 F.
Menus: 250 F (lunch, except holidays), 450 F (dinner, except holidays).

12/20 Le Congrès
80, av. de la Grande-Armée
45 74 17 24

Open daily, 24 hours. Air cond.

A huge barracks-like brasserie, open all day and all night, vigilant about the consistent quality of its classics: shellfish (fresh all year) and large slabs of charcoal-grilled meat: beef fillet, T-bone steak and huge ribs of beef. A good tarte Tatin ends the meal nicely and the decent selection of house wines will not empty your wallet.

A la carte: 200-250 F.

La Coquille
6, rue du Débarcadère
45 72 10 73

Closed Sun., Mon., Dec. 23-Jan. 3 & July 27-Sep. 2. Open until 10:30 p.m. Air cond.

There aren't many restaurants like this well-bred bistro where today's patrons may order exactly the same dishes (just as overcooked and heavily sauced) as their parents and grandparents before them. Examples are the eponymous coquilles Saint-Jacques au naturel, sea bass Escoffier, jugged hare, boudin grillé aux pommes and the seemingly immortal hazelnut soufflé. Exceptional cellar.

A la carte: 330-430 F.

17th arrondissement – **RESTAURANTS**

 Le Cougar
10, rue des Acacias
47 66 74 14
Closed Sat. lunch & Sun. Open until 10:30 p.m. Air cond.
Taïra Kurihara, a brilliant star in the galaxy of Japanese practitioners of French cuisine, is engaged like many of his colleagues in turning out Gallic dishes influenced by master chefs (in this case, Robuchon, Cagna, Besson). Kurihara's technique has gained authority, and he has developed a knack for creating subtle flavours and vibrant seasonings. In view of all these pluses we feel we can overlook a few errors (a salad of terribly overcooked prawns), and encourage you to sample the perfect John Dory with rice vinegar and sesame oil, or cod with seaweed and olive oil. The menu is deliberately short on meat dishes. Fine cellar, improved décor.
A la carte: 330-430 F. Menu: 320 F (dinner only).

 L'Ecrin d'Or
35, rue Legendre
47 63 83 08
Closed Sat. lunch, Mon. & Aug. 4-25. Open until 11 p.m. Private room: 16. Air cond. Parking.
Huge mirrors, mouldings, Venetian chandeliers and great swathes of velvet make this a supremely comfortable restaurant, and the cuisine of the young chef, Gilles Cendres, is a most pleasant discovery. Sample his precise, personal interpretations of rockfish with red-pepper coulis, salade de jarret de veau, duckling à l'orange and bitter-chocolate fondant. Judicious cellar.
A la carte: 260-330 F. Menus: 95 F, 155 F.

Red toques signify modern cuisine; white toques signify traditional cuisine.

 Epicure 108
108, rue Cardinet
47 63 50 91
Closed Sat. lunch & Sun. Open until 10:30 p.m.
Here's a quiet little restaurant with a pretty, well-lit interior and a decidedly up-market tone. The frequently changing menu attracts a good lunchtime turnout with consistent, palatable dishes (sometimes a bit light on seasonings) by chef Tetsu Goya. The 170-franc set lunch features an exquisite shellfish and courgette galette, delicious sea bream baked with herbs and a dessert (the desserts need work). Good cellar, and the reception has warmed up lately by several degrees.
Menus: 230 F (for 2), 170 F.

 L'Etoile d'Or
Hôtel Concorde-La Fayette
3, pl. du Gal-Kœnig
40 58 50 68
Closed Sat. lunch & Sun. Open until 10:30 p.m. Private room: 40. Air cond. Valet parking.
Jean-Claude Lhonneur, formerly of Le Grand Véfour and La Tour d'Argent, produces precise, tasty cuisine that lacks only a hint of boldness. An attractive seafood assortment and lamb noisettes with juniper berries are among the highlights. Comfortable setting, fine cellar with some affordable bottles, and irreproachable service.
A la carte: 500-600 F. Menu: 250 F.

 Faucher
123, av. de Wagram
42 27 61 50,
fax 46 22 25 72
Closed Sat. lunch, Sun. & wk. of Aug. 15. Open until 10:30 p.m. Terrace dining. Valet parking.
Gérard and Nicole Faucher have embraced the *beaux quartiers*: they are the proud proprietors of a very handsome dining room embellished with paintings, sumptuous bouquets and elegant table settings. Nicole welcomes patrons while a bevy of nimble young waiters serve Gérard's exciting dishes. We tucked into a light, fresh millefeuille of thinly sliced raw beef and spinach leaves, a remarkable galette combining potatoes and cod (the latter in both its fresh and salted forms) bathed in meat juices, a flavourful osso buco with a "minestrone" of vegetables and braised short ribs with a beurre aux truffes. Desserts are equally gorgeous. The cellar is a bit too expensive, but the summer terrace is irresistible.
A la carte: 350-500 F. Menus: 180 F (lunch only), 390 F.

11/20 **Chez Fred**
190 bis, bd Pereire
45 74 20 48
Closed Sun. & 2 wks. in Aug. Open daily until 11 p.m.
An influx of trendies has not spoiled the service, the simplicity of the setting, or the heartwarming sincerity of Fred's cuisine: bacon with lentils, pot-au-feu and blanquette de veau. No-nonsense wines sold by the *pichet*.
A la carte: 200-220 F. Menu: 145 F (lunch only, wine incl.).

 La Gazelle
9, rue Rennequin
42 67 64 18
Closed Sun. Open until 11:30 p.m.
The prettiest, most distinguished and exotic African restaurant in Paris, La Gazelle boasts a surprising range of intensely tasty dishes prepared by the *patronne*, who comes from Cameroon: n'dolé of dried salt cod with chopped bitter spinach, tender and delicious prawns in a spicy sauce, marinated kid en papillote with African corn. Slow-paced service.

A la carte: 200-250 F. Menu: 48 F (weekdays lunch only), 95 F, 130 F.

Chez Georges
273, bd Pereire
45 74 31 00,
fax 45 74 02 56

Closed Aug. Open until 11:30 p.m. Private room: 30. Terrace dining.

The quintessential brasserie-bistro with all its little flaws—some dishes are a bit too expensive, a few of the first courses lack zest, the upstairs dining room has all the warmth and charm of Siberia—and its immense virtues: appealingly worn décor (downstairs, of course), an effervescent clientele (tourists, TV personalities, celebrities) and swift, professional waiters who set before you platefuls of perfect bistro fare: saucisson chaud, juicy roast beef with gratin dauphinois, tête de veau, rare roast lamb with tender beans.
A la carte: 280-350 F.

Graindorge
15, rue de l'Arc-de-Triomphe
47 54 00 28

Closed Sat. lunch & Sun. Open until 10:30 p.m.

Bernard Broux, for six years the chef at Alain Dutournier's Trou Gascon, has struck out on his own. What's more, he has forsaken the south-west and its earthy tastes in favour of the cuisine of his native Flanders. Broux's inaugural menu features unpretentious ingredients handled in clever, original ways: there's a salad of potatoes and sardine "rollmops" (that is, pickled like herring in spiced vinegar), pork braised in a sauce spiked with gin, and caramelised brioche "French toast". The wine list merits your attention, but beer lovers will be knocked out by the superb selection of rare brews.

A la carte: 200-250 F. Menus: 160 F (lunch only), 180 F (dinner only).

12/20 Goldenberg
69, av. de Wagram
42 27 34 79

Open daily until midnight.

Patrick Goldenberg creates a typically Yiddish atmosphere of good humour and nostalgia, Jewish jokes and anecdotes in which to enjoy delicious smoked and corned beef, veal sausage and other Central European classics. There's also a delicatessen and a sunny terrace for fine weather.
A la carte: 200-250 F. Menu: 98 F (wine incl.).

Guyvonne
14, rue de Thann
42 27 25 43

Closed Sat., Sun., Dec. 24-Jan. 3 & Aug. 6-30. Open until 10 p.m. Private room: 11. Terrace dining.

Guy Cros is a charming chap, a great upholder of the French culinary tradition. With renewed vigour, he has lately applied his skill to country dishes, updated classics and "market" cuisine. A large and faithful clientele flocks to Cros' (rather dreary) beige-and-blue dining room and to the terrace a stone's throw from the Parc Monceau, for Guyvonne is justly considered one of the best seafood restaurants in Paris. We won't argue with that: we love the prawns with chanterelles and artichokes, the crayfish with chervil root, and the oysters with Chinese truffles (tasty little violet potatoes). Desserts are guaranteed to make you break your diet, and the cellar is stocked with first-rate Bordeaux.
A la carte: 350-400 F. Menu: 230 F.

Find the address you are looking for, quickly and easily, in the index.

L'Impatient
14, passage Geffroy-Didelot
43 87 28 10

Closed Sat., Sun., 15 days Easter & Aug. 15-Sep. 10. Open until 10 p.m. Air cond.

The new owners are a hard-working pair: they do everything themselves, from picking flowers to adorn their three comely Art Deco dining rooms to gathering fresh fruit and vegetables and then preparing them in novel, amusing ways. Try the warm sardine terrine with apples, rabbit croustade, and potato crêpes studded with corn kernels. Good prix-fixe menus, attentive service.
A la carte: 200-280 F. Menus: 98 F (lunch only), 280 F (dinner only), 145 F.

Chez Laudrin
154, bd Pereire
43 80 87 40

Closed Sat. lunch, Sun. & May 1-9. Open until 10:30 p.m. Air cond.

Age settles gently but graciously over Jacques Billaud's "yacht-club" dining room, his regional repertoire and the moustached smile with which he has greeted customers for 30-odd years. Wines are served by the magnum and charged by "the centimetre" (so you only pay for what you drink). Some of the best tripe dishes in Paris are made in this kitchen, as well as cod with aïoli, grilled stuffed scallops, goujonnettes de sole and a hearty bourride de lotte (fish soup). The obligatory dessert here is the house baba au rhum.
A la carte: 320-420 F. Menu: 250 F.

Chez Lee
13, rue Rennequin
43 80 91 48

Closed Sun. & Aug. 1-26. Open until 11 p.m. Air cond.

For highly original, light and flavourful Chinese cooking,

come to see Mr Lee (and his associate, Mr Lo). Treat yourself to the unusual steamed dumplings, the prawns with savoury salt, Szechuan duck, and pork in a spicy sauce served by slightly furtive waiters in an elegant dining room dotted with silk screens.

A la carte: 150-250 F. Menus: 78 F (weekdays lunch only), 99 F.

12/20 Chez Léon
32, rue Legendre
42 27 06 82

Closed w.-e., Aug. & 1 wk. in Feb. Open until 9:45 p.m.

A traditional bistro with the usual robust food—terrines, tête de veau and cassoulets. But our old friend Léon had better stop serving tough haricot beans with his gigot d'agneau, and pull the ears of the cook responsible for our unevenly baked apple tart! Service is pleasant, and so are the Beaujolais wines.

A la carte: 210-290 F. Menu: 160 F.

Le Madigan
22, rue de la Terrasse
42 27 31 51

Closed Sat. lunch, Sun. & holidays. Open until 9:30 p.m. Terrace dining. Air cond.

The owner is a music lover and his chef a fervent disciple of Escoffier. They have combined their talents to launch a perilous enterprise: the musical supper, a rarity in this city. When it's time for the liqueurs, Le Madigan's sober yet sumptuous dining room is transformed into a concert hall. Hopeful young talents and international prize-winners take their place at the Steinway grand for what are often remarkable recitals. The bearded young chef ably turns out some 19th-century dishes: poached eggs Rossini, lobster Cardinal and sweetbreads à la Demidoff. Top-notch ingredients and subtle prepara-tion ensure a harmonious evening on every scale.

A la carte: 310-475 F. Menus: 150 F and 250 F (lunch only), 180 F and 280 F (dinner only).

Le Manoir de Paris
6, rue P.-Demours
45 72 25 25,
fax 45 74 80 98

Closed Sat. lunch & Sun. Open until 10:30 p.m. Private room: 50. Air cond. Valet parking.

When Philippe Groult left the Manoir to open his own Amphyclès just down the road, Francis Vandenhende and Denise Fabre (the latter a native Niçoise whose heart belongs to the south) encouraged their new chef, Gilles Méry, to give the menu a Mediterranean slant. And now the Manoir's lavish dining room with its mirrored pilasters, intricately carved woodwork and abundant flowers and greenery has a Provençal flavour thanks to a menu studded with southern flavours: langoustines rôties aux blettes et fumet de truffe, herb and mushroom cannelloni served with a mouth-watering roast veal gravy, an ambrosial pumpkin soup with tiny cheese gnocchi and crisp lardons, baked lotte with caramelised tomatoes and braised fennel, and pigeon-neau en cocotte à la polenta with a wild-mushroom sauce. Desserts include a creamy tiramisù and a warm hazelnut-cocoa gâteau accompanied by a glass of Beaumes-de-Venise Domaine de Coyeux from sommelier Remy Aspect's impressive—and costly—cellar.

A la carte: 620-800 F. Menus: 290 F (lunch only), 380 F, 460 F.

> *Remember to call ahead to reserve your table, and please, if you cannot honour your reservation, be courteous and let the restaurant know.*

La Niçoise
4, rue Pierre-Demours
45 74 42 41,
fax 45 74 80 98

Closed Sat. lunch & Sun. Open until 11 p.m. Private room: 50. Air cond. Valet parking.

Honest, simple Niçois specialities. The fresh, flowery décor is reminiscent of Nice at holiday-time, or of a stage set for a turn-of-the-century operetta. An inexplicably tense staff serves robust, full-flavoured ravioli de daube, stuffed sardines, pasta with pistou and for dessert a pinenut tart, all dishes which deserve a round of applause—and a toque. Perfect Provençal cellar.

A la carte: 200-280 F. Menu: 145 F (lunch only).

Le Petit Colombier
42, rue des Acacias
43 80 28 54,
fax 44 40 04 29

Closed Sun. lunch, Sat. & July 21-Aug. 17. Open until 10:30 p.m. Private room: 30. Air cond. Parking.

Bernard Fournier is a wise restaurateur. When you are lucky enough to inherit a delightful "provincial" *auberge* from your father, the sort of place they stopped making in the 19th century, you don't ruin it with trendy lacquered ceilings, salmon-coloured fabrics and halogen lighting. In fact, the patrons of Le Petit Colombier (which has just celebrated 60 years of family management) wouldn't stand for it. They come here to tuck a napkin under their chins, make themselves comfortable in the glow of burnished copper and wrought iron, and discover anew the reassuring flavours of classic French food, a repertoire that will never grow stale in the capable hands of Bernard Fournier. For Le Petit Colombier is not a fusty sanctuary of dyspeptic pre-war cuisine. New dishes often slip onto the menu, and a bit of seaweed mixed with pâtes fraîches or a hint of dill in a seafood pot-au-feu doesn't create a ripple among the clientele. But Bernard Fournier's brigade can also put fresh spirit into a traditional salad of potatoes with fresh truffles, or a gratin de homard à la Newburg, or roast to rosy perfection a young partridge which actually tastes like a partridge and not a chicken reared on fishmeal. And respect for tradition doesn't mean you can't keep up-to-date; air-conditioning, a "smoking" area, bilingual staff, and a computer are all part of the mod cons here—as is a business menu which is one of the best (and least known) bargains in the city. To toast all these delights, there is a fabulous cellar with some 50,000 bottles.

A la carte: 400-550 F. Menu: 200 F (lunch only).

12/20 Le Petit Salé
99, av. des Ternes
45 74 10 57

Open daily until 11 p.m. Terrace dining.

The young chef has changed nothing in the generous house repertoire of petit salé aux lentilles, confits and tarte Tatin which has made the reputation of this solid old bistro. The dining room has been renovated, however: with the bar removed, twice as many diners can contribute to the always-jolly ambience.

A la carte: 180-230 F.

La Petite Auberge
38, rue Laugier
47 63 85 51

Closed Sun. dinner, Mon. & Aug. Open until 10:30 p.m. Private room: 14.

Veteran chef Léo Harbonnier has handed over to Joël Ducloux, a pupil of Paul Bocuse. The dining room and the menu have both been spruced up a bit. Fine, fresh ingredients are the basis for succulent foie gras with shallot purée, snail ravioli with Roquefort butter, a fish assortment with cockle-flavoured butter and a Grand Marnier soufflé. Cheerful welcome, good cellar.

A la carte: 270-400 F. Menu: 160 F.

12/20 Petrus
12, pl. du Maréchal-Juin
43 80 15 95

Open daily until 11 p.m. Private room: 22. Terrace dining. Air cond. Valet parking.

Petrus has ridden the waves of change through new chefs, new owners, new managers; the excellence and variety of the seafood have remained constant in this luxurious restaurant, with its spacious dining room and terrace. But we are obliged to revise our rating, for our most recent meal here certainly did not deserve two toques. A turbot with the texture of cotton, a mediocre shellfish platter and an assortment of fish sauced with an insipid Armoricaine are inexcusable in a restaurant famed for its seafood. So it's no toque at all, we're afraid, until the kitchen comes out of its current careless slump.

A la carte: 450-500 F. Menu: 250 F.

Michel Rostang
20, rue Rennequin
47 63 40 77,
fax 47 63 82 75

Closed Sat. lunch (& dinner May-Sep.), Sun. & Aug. 1-15. Open until 10:15 p.m. Private room: 25. Air cond. Valet parking.

Though his serene demeanour doesn't betray the fact, Michel Rostang is a busy man, with a triumphant New York restaurant, his Bistrots d'à Côte in Paris, a luxury hotel in the Caribbean, La Bonne Auberge in Antibes overseen by his brother, Philippe, and the restaurant that bears his name and occupies most of his time. Nevertheless this youthful 45-year-old manages to keep his composure, even when he is putting his kitchen brigade through its paces like a ringmaster.

To call a chef "industrious" may sound like a back-handed compliment, but we only mean that Michel Rostang works hard at his craft. And he knows how to improvise too, creating a subtly nuanced, colourful, intensely pleasing cuisine. A menu of ten appetisers and a dozen fish and meat dishes always offers a core of tried-and-true classics (roast Sisteron lamb flanked by lamb sweetbreads and a compotée of lamb's trotter with salsify; Bresse duck with a wine sauce enriched by a foie-gras liaison) along with a bouquet of personal creations, like asparagus tips "breaded" with a cèpe duxelles, a superlative terrine de langoustines in a vigorously seasoned shellfish gelée, a delectable Provençal-inspired sea bass with olives and fennel purée, or curried saddle of young rabbit cleverly garnished with a purée of spinach and pears. Though Michel's gratin dauphinois is perhaps a shade less good than his father's—the benchmark of the genre—his poularde à la crème aux morilles is a monument. For dessert, choose a grilled pear with tea sauce, or prune "bonbons" coated in rosemary-flavoured sugar accompanied by an astonishing pepper sorbet, or tarte chaude au chocolat. Alain Ronzatti administers the select, high-priced wine cellar.

A la carte: 650-950 F. Menus: 285 F (lunch only), 495 F, 660 F (except holidays).

17th arrondissement – RESTAURANTS

 Guy Savoy
18, rue Troyon
43 80 40 61,
fax 46 22 43 09
Closed Sat. lunch (& dinner Easter-Sep.) & Sun. Open until 10:30 p.m. Private room: 35. Air cond. Valet parking.

If a client requested it, the ever-so-affable Guy Savoy would probably provide a chauffeur-driven car to drive him home—free of charge. But who would ever want to leave this beautiful, welcoming establishment, a haven of charm and grace? What luxury to be a "*regular*" *chez* Savoy, with a special table reserved in the spacious green-and-rosy-beige dining room dotted with contemporary prints and paintings—an original, elegant setting, surely one of the most attractive in the city.

For bearded, eternally youthful Guy Savoy life is beautiful—his dining room is full and there's a smile on every customer's face. Routine never casts its pall over Savoy's kitchen—every day he fashions new, exquisite, unexpected flavours into fascinating meals. If we had to pin it down with a single adjective, we would call Savoy's cuisine "intelligent". Textures and aromas are brought together with astonishing skill; they are never masked by superfluous sauces, but highlighted by the judicious use of jus, coulis, essences and spice blends that give each dish its singular style and cachet. Beyond Savoy's technical skill lies his acute perceptions of taste, those of a country lad who has never forgotten the taste of fresh garden vegetables, farmyard poultry or the good smells of provincial cooking.

Guy Savoy is not out to dazzle his patrons. He pleases himself first, and if others like the results, so much the better. But frankly who wouldn't like his ragoût of sea urchins and Chinese artichokes, or fat, tender frogs' legs served with a garlicky green-bean jus, or saddle of wild rabbit stuffed with foie gras and casseroled to juicy perfection, or John Dory with basil leaves, presented on a bed of sautéed dandelion greens?

Savoy's imagination works at lightning speed, and we leave you to discover the latest creations on a constantly changing menu. If, when you visit, the risotto with mascarpone, shellfish and a touch of arugula is still on offer—order it! Desserts are voluptuous (grapefruit terrine with a tea-scented sauce, vanilla millefeuille in a ruby pool of berry coulis) and the wines, delicate or full-bodied, as you prefer, are overseen by Eric Mancio, a sommelier with the soul of a poet.

A la carte: 650-1,000 F. Menu: 650 F.

 Sormani
4, rue du Général-Lanzerac
43 80 13 91
Closed Sat., Sun. & holidays. Open until 10:30 p.m. Private room: 18. Terrace dining. Air cond. Valet parking.

Indisputably the best Italian restaurant in Paris, Sormani is the first non-French establishment to win three Gault Millau toques. Pascal Fayet is from Savoie, so he is not, strictly speaking, a "foreign" chef. He owes his passion for Italian cuisine to his Piedmontese grandmother. Fayet's *cucina italiana* is indisputably Frenchified; for him, the Italian repertoire is more a source of inspiration than a model to be followed to the letter.

This sensitive artist works with flavours and ingredients from Florence, Genoa and Tuscany but he is never shy about adding his personal signature to a dish. A trickle of truffled oil on the carpaccio and scallop salad, and suddenly a classic dish is reborn. Lasagne layered with foie gras and truffles, or squid sautéed with hot peppers and salt pork scratchings arranged on a bed of potatoes, or a hot soufflé of brandade de morue (puréed salt cod), or a thin slice of veal wrapped around a fat black truffle make your taste buds snap to delighted attention. Fayet's vegetables are uniformly delicious, for he oven-roasts them *à l'italienne* instead of blanching them in the more usual French style. Thoroughly Italian too is his sensual tiramisù, a poem of mascarpone, chocolate and caramel ice cream. Among the treasures in the cellar are a Venetian Pinot Grigio, a Peppoli Antinori '86, and other superb Italian wines that the French too often neglect. Aspects of his baroque-style décor are in dubious taste, but the overall effect of the frescoes and *faux-marbre* is amusing.

A la carte: 400-650 F. Menus: 300 F, 400 F, 450 F.

 La Soupière
154, av. de Wagram
42 27 00 73
Closed Sat. lunch, Sun. & Aug. 9-22. Open until 10:30 p.m. Terrace dining. Air cond.

The pretty décor is *trompe-l'œil*, but chef Christian Thuillart's cuisine definitely isn't. His straightforward menu shows a distinctive personality at work, as in the lobster salad, salmon à l'unilatéral or roast Pauillac lamb. A passionate connoisseur of rare and expensive mushrooms, he has built special menus around truffles and morels, served when their season is at its height.

A la carte: 250-350 F. Menus: 160 F (weekdays only), 185 F (Sat. only), 240 F.

18th arrondissement

Le Timgad
21, rue Brunel
45 74 23 70

Open daily until 11 p.m. Private room: 15. Air cond. Parking.

With its moulded-plaster arabesques and enamelled tiles, the extravagant palatial décor is one of the most successful of its kind in Paris. On his good days, Ahmed Laasri's couscous is perhaps the best in town, but don't neglect his admirable pastilla, the lamb's-brain tajine with pickled lemons, or the out-of-this-world spit-roasted lamb. A comprehensive cellar of North African wines, curiously all at the same price. Remember to book at this understandably popular restaurant.

A la carte: 300-350 F.

La Toque
16, rue de Tocqueville
42 27 97 75

Closed Sat., Sun., Dec. 24-Jan. 2 & July 23-Aug. 22. Open until 9:30 p.m. Air cond.

Jacky Joubert's cuisine is light, refined, seasonal, and highly inventive—though never "precious" (a failing not infrequent among certain of Michel Guérard's disciples). Laudably low prices add to the pleasure you'll derive from a terrine de joue de bœuf with tiny vegetables, filets de rougets cooked with smoked-salmon butter, and the unusual hot game pie with apricots. Prepare to rub elbows with your neighbours in this tiny dining room swathed in yellow crushed velvet.

A la carte: 280-330 F. Menus: 160 F, 210 F.

Plan to travel? Look out for the other RAC GaultMillau Best of guides to France and Germany, and for the RAC French Hotel and Holiday Guide and the RAC European Hotel Guide plus maps and atlases of France and Europe.

18th arrondissement

A. Beauvilliers
52, rue Lamarck
42 54 54 42,
fax 42 62 70 30

Closed Mon. lunch, Sun. & Aug. 30-Sep. 13. Open until 10:45 p.m. Garden dining. Air cond.

If ever there was a restaurant designed for *fêtes* and celebrations, it is surely Beauvilliers. Owner Edouard Carlier has lovingly fitted out three irresistible dining rooms with Louis-Philippe-era paintings, old prints, damask table linen and fanciful floral displays; and then there's the adorable little "newlywed" salon with its soft lighting and collection of wedding garlands once worn by country brides, pinned like butterflies in glass vitrines; and now, there are even three outdoor terraces with wonderful views of Montmartre.

Michel Deygat, who officiated in the kitchen for the last five years, has been replaced by his former chef-saucier, Gilles Renault. Yet the change is barely perceptible, for the menu was conceived by Carlier (himself a trained chef) and bears his inimitable stamp. Refinement, classicism and rustic touches blend beautifully in dishes like boned rabbit with chopped parsley aspic, or a salad of haricots verts topped with tiny fried squid, or a guinea fowl rubbed with spices then roasted and served with a parmentier of potatoes and mushrooms, a "gigot" of monkfish, a baby pigeon with young peas and lettuce, or a lordly loin of veal presented complete with the kidneys, coated with a fragrant truffle jus. Only a heavy, dizzyingly rich pie filled with sweetbreads, foie gras and lobster strikes a false note.

To accompany these splendid dishes there is a huge selection of rare Champagnes, old port and some glorious wines.

We are always surprised when others criticise the welcome as "cold" not to say "glacial". His plumpness King Edouard is the cream of hosts. But perhaps he has too many chums to greet, and thus ignores some first-time visitors?

A la carte: 600-900 F. Menus: 185 F (weekdays lunch only), 300 F (lunch only, wine incl.).

Charlot Ier
Les Merveilles des Mers
128 bis, bd de Clichy
45 22 47 08,
fax 44 70 07 50

Closed Mon. (July-Aug.). Open until 1 a.m. Air cond. Parking.

An able new chef is handling the traditional house repertoire of no-nonsense seafood classics (bouillabaisse, braised skate, red mullet in aromatic stock). More meat-based and seasonal dishes have appeared on the menu, but the best bets here remain the simplest preparations, starting with the extraordinary assortments of raw shellfish.

A la carte: 350-500 F. Menus: 150 F (dinner, except holidays), 200 F (weekdays lunch and Sat.).

Clodenis
57, rue Caulaincourt
46 06 20 26

Closed Sun. dinner, Mon. & Jan. 10-31. Open until 11 p.m.

Some genuine sun-kissed Provençal specialities distinguish this charming little restaurant set in a highly touristic area of Montmartre. Prices are as steep as the Butte, but the food is first-rate and the brandade de morue, lapin au thym or stuffed courgette blossoms won't disappoint. Wine prices are climbing too.

A la carte: 250-370 F. Menu: 200 F (lunch only).

Le Cottage Marcadet
151 bis, rue Marcadet
42 57 71 22
Closed Sun., April 30-May 16 & Aug. 14-31. Open until 10 p.m. Air cond.
The location is not exactly a Montmartre charm spot but the Cottage itself is appealing. Even more so is the appetising *carte* with its mussel galette with apples, cockle ravioli with a chicken-based cream sauce, and honey-roasted spare ribs. As for the wine list, it is small but perfectly formed for the food at hand (nice prices, too). The set menu, served at lunch and dinner, is good news—and good value.
A la carte: 260-400 F. Menu: 200 F (wine incl.).

12/20 Chez Frézet
181, rue Ordener
46 06 64 20,
fax 46 06 10 79
Closed Sat. lunch, Sun. & Aug. Open until 10:45 p.m. Garden dining. Valet parking.
Christian Marie is the proud owner of this freshly decorated neighbourhood restaurant which overlooks a minuscule back garden. In the evening, people come for the carefully prepared *plat du jour* (turbot hollandaise, leg of lamb in a flaky crust) and the rest of the time for generous portions of decent smoked haddock with cabbage, kidneys with mustard sauce, or grilled duck breast.
A la carte: 200-400 F. Menu: 150 F (weekdays and Sat. dinner).

 Grandgousier
17, av. Rachel
43 87 66 12
Closed Sat. lunch & Sun. Open until 10 p.m. Parking.
Léon Marzynski and his wife, Renée, have got out of the doldrums of their sleepy corner of Montmartre, near the entrance to the famous cemetery. The new décor is a great success with its bright, flower-filled dining room and large, well-spaced tables, and the cooking has kept pace. Léon prepares a scrumptious salad of boned quail with foie gras, an original fillet of sole with Belgian endive and blackcurrants, salmon with capers and cranberry butter and a fine guinea fowl roasted with basil in a Beaujolais-based sauce. The set menu hasn't gone up a single *centime* in five years.
A la carte: 280-320 F. Menu: 145 F.

 Langevin
Au Poulbot Gourmet
39, rue Lamarck
46 06 86 00
Closed Sun. Open until 10:30 p.m. Private room: 34. Air cond.
This small establishment delivers high quality, but few surprises. Run by Normandy native Jean-Paul Langevin, it serves cuisine based on top-notch seasonal ingredients, with a few discreet nods to traditional country cooking. Try the "tournedos" of salmon with boletus mushrooms, roast saddle of hare, and the frozen charlotte aux deux chocolats. Tables are a bit crowded, the background music a little too loud, but the typically Montmartrois décor complete with terrace is sure to delight you.
A la carte: 240-300 F

11/20 Chez Marie-Louise
52, rue Championnet
46 06 86 55
Closed Sun. lunch, July-beg. Sept. & holidays. Open until 10 p.m.
Kidneys with Madeira, coq au vin du patron, clafoutis of seasonal fruits—here's honest bistro cooking, unchanged for 30 years, served amid copper saucepans and prints of carousing monks.
A la carte: 180-200 F. Menu: 120 F.

12/20 Aux Négociants
27, rue Lambert
46 06 15 11
Closed Sat., Sun., Mon. & Wed. dinner & Aug. Open until 10:30 p.m. No cards. Parking.
Jean Navier, a winner of the *Meilleur Pot* ("best glass of wine award"), has recently spruced up his bistro, where he serves a wonderful selection of modest but tasty growers' wines, with an emphasis on the Loire. Wine lovers should sample a Jasnières or a Bourgueil at the bar, but the Rhône wines are velvet on the tongue when married to the hearty dishes produced by *la patronne*. Forget frills like tablecloths and concentrate instead on robust rillettes, farm-reared veal en cocotte, and cassoulet.
A la carte: 150-200 F.

11/20 Palais de Kashmir
77, rue du Poteau
42 59 40 86
Open daily until 11:30 p.m. Air cond.
Exoticism abounds here with fountains, glass, carved wood and other Kashmiri delights but the Indo-Pakistani cuisine lacks similar brilliance: try a modest butter chicken, rice biryani with 25 spices, Indian hot breads and refreshing salted lassi.
A la carte: 180-200 F. Menu: 119 F.

 Le Restaurant
32, rue Véron
42 23 06 22
Closed Mon. lunch & Sun. Open until 11 p.m.
Yves Peladeau worked his way up from junior waiter to owner-chef of his Restaurant at the foot of the Butte Montmartre. It is as modern, bright and appetising as the

imaginative dishes he concocts, for example the braised squid with spicy chorizo sausage, red peppers, leeks and shellfish jus, or a crystalline salad of fresh artichokes, mango, cockles and lobster made punchier with piquant chutney, or a savoury veal steak with meat juices and (yes!) vanilla-scented carrots. Desserts include a seductive warm chocolate tart. The wine list is short but to the point.

A la carte: 240 F. Menu: 148 F (except Sat. dinner and holidays).

12/20 Wepler
14, pl. Clichy
45 22 53 24

Open daily until 1 a.m. Air cond.

A deluxe brasserie with a well-conceived menu and good service. The shellfish is some of the freshest in Paris; other interesting options are the hearty (and truly delicious) brawn, oxtail stew and a copious choucroute garnie. Fine bouillabaisse too.

A la carte: 200-400 F. Menu: 150 F.

19th arrondissement

 Au Cochon d'Or
192, av. Jean-Jaurès
42 45 46 46

Open daily until 10:30 p.m. Private room: 40. Air cond. Valet parking.

Times have changed since the Ayral family set up shop here in 1924. The nearby slaughterhouses are now defunct; butchers and meat-packers have given way to the cultured, worldly crowd disgorged by the Cité des Sciences at La Villette. But the restaurant has evolved along with its clientele. Under René Ayral's management, and with 30 years experience, chef François Médina continues to grill, roast and fry the choicest morsels of beef: filet mignons, prime ribs and sirloin steaks. Earthier choices include pigs' trotters served with sauce Choron, boudin and apples, or calf's-head salad. An excellent sommelier oversees the wines.

A la carte: 300-450 F. Menu: 240 F.

12/20 Dagorno
190, av. J.-Jaurès
40 40 09 39

Open daily until 12:15 a.m. Air cond. Valet parking.

Here's a comfortable deluxe brasserie that serves perfectly honourable, uncomplicated food. You won't be disappointed by the oysters, the calf brawn with lentils, or the enormous côte de bœuf sauce bordelaise. Some original desserts, and an unbeatable set menu.

A la carte: 300-400 F. Menu: 168 F (wine incl.).

11/20 Ly-Ya
5, rue du Hainaut
42 08 34 98

Closed Mon. Open until 10:30 p.m.

A benevolent Buddha, arms upraised, presides over the dining room. In terms of value for money this tasty, fresh, mainly Vietnamese cuisine wins hands down. Try the fritot de crevettes, spicy prawn soup, stuffed crab and chicken with lemon grass and ginger.

A la carte: 100-120 F. Menus: 45 F and 65 F (weekdays lunch only, wine incl.).

 Le Pavillon Puebla
Christian Vergès
Parc des Buttes-Chaumont
42 08 92 62,

Closed Sun., Mon. & 2 wks. in Aug. Open until 10 p.m. Private room: 80. Garden dining. Valet parking.

This stylish Napoléon III hunting lodge, nestled in greenery at the foot of the Buttes Chaumont park is a joy for all seasons. When the weather is clement, you can sit under leafy trees and parasols on the terrace (the interior décor suffers from a heavy hand). Christian Vergès has been in residence here for five years, always touched by the Catalan spirit that inspires his rich, varied and vigorous cuisine. Mediterranean flavours and strong colours bring a singular charm to his red mullet and John Dory perfumed with basil, his terrine of tomatoes and smoked salmon, the poached salt cod with lentils, or the gently spiced galette of potatoes and sweetbreads. One of the city's best crème brûlées is made here and some splendid Banyuls can be found on the extensive wine list.

A la carte: 380-530 F. Menu: 230 F.

12/20 Le Sancerre
13, av. Corentin-Cariou
40 36 80 44

Closed Sat. & Sun. Annual closings not available. Open until 10:30 p.m.

The new management hasn't changed the nostalgic atmosphere of this vestige of the old abattoir district of La Villette. But the chef has been ill-advised to introduce a number of Americanised salads. His talent seems surer in traditional dishes such as lamb stew, braised top rib of beef and juicy double lamb chops. As for wines, look no further than the wonderful Morgon and Sancerre sold by the centimetre (you pay only for what you drink from the bottle placed on the table). It is wise to book ahead for lunch.

A la carte: 250-300 F. Menus: 169 F (wine incl.), 110 F.

THE SUBURBS – RESTAURANTS

20th arrondissement

 Aux Becs Fins
44, bd de Ménilmontant
47 97 51 52
Closed Sun. & Sep. 5-21. Open until 9:30 p.m.

This winsome little bistro is alongside the Père Lachaise cemetery. The colourful owner (Edith Lefebvre) relies on a faithful clientele of regulars who no longer notice the hideous décor (the centrepiece of which is a ghastly old fridge!). The cuisine sometimes backfires, but the pied et tête de veau sauce gribiche and the terrines and cassoulet "mère Edith" keep the toque in place...for now.

A la carte: 220-400 F. Menus: 240 F (except Sun., wine incl.), 180 F.

THE SUBURBS

ARGENTEUIL
95100 Argenteuil – (Val-d'Oise)
Paris 14 · Pontoise 20 · St-Germain-en-L. 15

 La Closerie Périgourdine
85, bd J.-Allemane
39 80 01 28
Closed Sat. lunch & Sun. dinner. Open until 10 p.m. Private room: 30.

Despite the fussy décor—stone walls, velvet-covered beams and corner fireplace, the menu offers a promising list of regionally based specialities: chanterelles en feuilleté, duck confit, escargots aux cèpes, lotte with mustard and thyme, and walnut cake. The wine list includes a good selection of Cahors, Bordeaux and fine Burgundies.

A la carte: 280-400 F. Menus: 159 F and 198 F (wine incl.), 135 F.

ASNIÈRES
92600 Asnières – (Hauts/Seine)
Paris 9 · Argenteuil 6 · Saint-Denis 8

 L'Ecurie
4 bis, Grande-Rue-Ch.-de-Gaulle
47 90 91 30
Closed Sat. lunch, Sun. & Aug. 2-29. Open until 10 p.m. Private room: 15.

An intelligent and generous prix-fixe menu is offered during the week at lunch and dinner (98 francs for a starter plus main course, such as a delicious blue-cheese tart followed by a mildly spiced chicken fricassée). One of the good desserts, like the walnut soufflé, will cost extra but won't ruin you. The charming *patron*, André Fontaine, also makes excellent sole fritters, quick-cooked turbot with citrus fruit and rognons de veau au Margaux. Fresh new pastel décor.

A la carte: 200-300 F.

 Le Van Gogh
2, quai Aulagnier
47 91 05 10,
fax 47 93 00 93
Closed w.-e., Dec. 18-Jan. 6 & Aug. 13-24. Open until 10 p.m. Private room: 12. Terrace dining. Air cond. Valet parking.

Robert and Pierrette Daubian have dropped anchor in this ultramodern establishment on Robinson island. The dining room resembles the interior of a luxury liner, with portholes and bay windows offering views of the Seine. The cuisine looks out to sea, with dishes like lobster and prawn feuilleté, and filet de bar royal cooked with the freshest produce. Desserts are superb (try the delicious berry gratin with Champagne), and there are fine Bordeaux to wash it all down.

A la carte: 400-500 F.

BLANC-MESNIL (LE)
93150 Blanc-Mesnil (Le) – (Seine-St-D.)
Paris 12 · Bobigny 6 · Aulnay 3

12/20 **La Vallière**
8, av. Paul-Vaillant-Couturier
48 69 52 01
Closed Sat. lunch, Sun. & Aug. 7-30. Open until 9:30 p.m. Private room: 30.

This small, provincial restaurant stands in dreary surroundings but the food, honest and simple (and improving, we note) is carefully prepared: crêpes filled with basil-scented escargots, andouillette sausage, salmon with citrus fruit, and banana bavarois with apricot coulis. The chocolate mousse is excellent, and we appreciate the detailed (even didactic) wine list.

A la carte: 230-280 F. Menu: 90 F.

BOULOGNE-BILLANCOURT
92100 Boulogne-Billancourt – (Hauts/Seine)
Versailles 11

 L'Auberge
86, av. J.-B.-Clément
46 05 22 35,
fax 46 05 23 16
Closed Sat., Sun., holidays & July 31-Aug. 29. Open until 10 p.m. Terrace dining. Air cond.

Both the décor and the cooking have undergone a radical change of style in this restaurant once devoted to the regional food of Franche-Comté, but the owners and chefs are still the same. Cancoillotte, a soft, pungent cheese spread, and mountain sausages have disappeared from the menu to be replaced by cabbage stuffed with pigeon and foie gras, mussels with basil butter, and nougat glacé au Grand Marnier (a bit too sweet but nice and creamy). The traditional duck terrine is still available however, and there are Jura wines in the excellent cellar.

A la carte: 350-400 F. Menus: 150 F (dinner only), 190 F.

La Bretonnière
120, av. J.-B.-Clément
46 05 73 56

Closed Sat. & Sun. Open until 9:45 p.m.

A former head waiter, René Rossignol, has switched to cooking and brought this restaurant back up to standard. Taste the marinated sardines, Angus beef with mashed potatoes, and uncomplicated desserts like chocolate mousse with orange sauce. Excellent Loire wines.

A la carte: 300-350 F. Menus: 150 F (dinner only), 200 F (lunch only).

Au Comte de Gascogne
89, av. J.-B.-Clément
46 03 47 27,
fax 46 04 55 70

Closed Sat. lunch & Sun. Open until 10:30 p.m. Private room: 15. Garden dining. Air cond. Valet parking.

Three palm trees, a fountain and lots of flowers make it feel like spring all year in the delightful courtyard garden. Business lunches actually become enjoyable, while dinner in the suburbs turns into an exotic outing. Gérard Vérane, the jovial Gascon who created this tropical greenhouse with its sliding roof, has handed over the kitchen to Henri Charvet, who once served the best meals in Aix-en-Provence. The Gascon flavour lingers on in the seven or eight variations on foie gras, including the wonderful smoked duck foie gras with cucumber and bacon, and in the world-class collection of Armagnacs. But it was the sun-kissed Provençal dishes that really captured our attention: smoked salmon with fennel confit, lobster soup with ravioli filled with green-tomato "jam", red mullet braised in a basil jus flanked by delicious stuffed vegetables, and steamed cod drizzled with Maussane olive oil. The young sommelier, Patrice Marchand, will help you choose from among the 10,000 wines on offer.

A la carte: 500-700 F.

12/20 Le Poivre Vert
1, pl. B.-Palissy
46 03 01 63,
fax 47 12 08 27

Closed dinner Dec. 24, 25 & 31. Open until 11 p.m. Air cond.

Book early for a top-value meal in this modern, plant-filled setting: the 99.50-franc formula (a starter and main course) is understandably much in demand. Try the seafood bouchée, the crisp roast leg of rabbit and the flaky feuillantine of caramelised pears. Well-chosen wines. The waiters are very efficient, but there just aren't enough of them.

A la carte: 170 F.

BUC
78530 Buc – (Yvelines)
Paris 22 - Versailles 5 - Sceaux 8

Relais de Courlande
2, rue Collin-Mamet
39 56 24 29,
fax 39 56 03 92

Closed Sun. dinner, Mon. & Aug. 1-23. Open until 10 p.m. Private room: 35. Garden dining. Hotel: 12 rms 250-360 F. Parking.

The pretty garden and terrace of this former coaching inn are becoming popular for business lunches. Besides its central location, the restaurant's success can be attributed to Ivan Vautier's lively cooking. He makes a fine salad of prawns dressed with mango mayonnaise, a tasty pigeon roasted with cinnamon honey and an interesting lamb dish with walnuts and tomatoes enhanced by caraway seeds and dragon grass. All are served by a professional, smiling staff.

A la carte: 400-460 F. Menus: 130 F, 240 F, 380 F.

CELLE-SAINT-CLOUD (LA)
78170 Celle-Saint-Cloud (La) – (Yvelines)
Paris 16 - Saint-Cloud 5 - Bougival 2

Au Petit Chez Soi
Pl. de l'Eglise
39 69 69 51

Closed Sun. dinner off-season. Open until 10 p.m. Private room: 60. Terrace dining.

Just outside Paris, on an authentic village square complete with fountain, this adorable *auberge* offers modern, flavourful food prepared by Louis Lavandier. Follow our lead and order the lemon-marinated salmon, flawlessly cooked lotte in a creamy sauce, or a succulent filet de bœuf. The wine list is short but offers some well-chosen bottles, and we appreciate the obvious effort made to keep prices down. Charming welcome from the cheerful *patronne*.

A la carte: 220-320 F. Menu: 155 F.

CHÂTEAUFORT
78117 Châteaufort – (Yvelines)
Paris 28 - Versailles 10 - Orsay 11

La Belle Epoque
10, pl. de la Mairie
39 56 21 66

Closed Sun. dinner & Mon. Open until 10 p.m. Private room: 6. Terrace dining.

From the terrace shaded by lime trees just 20 minutes out of Paris, you can enjoy a splendid view of the Mérantaise Valley. Inside, Alain Rayé (fresh from his restaurant near the Champs Elysées) has just taken over from Michel Peignaud. In fact, since our deadline coincided with his opening, we visited La Belle Epoque the day after Rayé moved in! He and his staff were still getting their bearings (hence, we suppose, the excess salt in one dish and the insipid gelée that marred another), but they managed to turn out a refreshing vegetable starter featuring courgette "marmalade", green-bean salad and cauliflower with cumin, an enormous sole brightened with the sunny tastes of lemon and rosemary, a superb chop of veal perfumed with sage, and several luscious old-fashioned desserts (blancmange, waffles with rhubarb compote). Vivacious welcome from Brigitte Rayé.

A la carte: 350-400 F. Menu: 350 F.

CHAVILLE
92370 Chaville — (Hauts/Seine)
Paris 13 - Versailles 9 - Meudon 1 - Boulogne 2

 La Tonnelle
29, rue Lamennais
47 50 42 77

Closed Mon., Feb. school holidays & Aug. 5-25. Open until 10:30 p.m. Private room: 15. Terrace dining. Air cond.

Pretty pink-and-blue curtains and new wallpaper make for an elegant interior, while the garden-terrace with its old wine press is a winner on sunny days. Guy Tardif's cooking is scrupulously classic and ever more skilful: fine hot foie gras set atop an artichoke bottom, perfectly cooked red mullet, pigeon with citrus fruit and a scrumptious vanilla millefeuille. Smiling staff; plenty of attractive half-bottles on the wine list.

Menus: 240 F (except holidays), 180 F (except dinner holidays).

CHENNEVIÈRES-SUR-MARNE
94430 Chennevières-sur-Marne — (Val/Marne)
Paris 17 - Lagny 20 - Coulommiers 51

12/20 L'Ecu de France
31, rue de Champigny
45 76 00 03

Closed Aug. 30-Sep. 6. Open until 9:30 p.m. Private room: 50. Terrace dining. Valet parking.

Lots of people were vying for tables the last time we visited this exceptionally well situated restaurant on the banks of the River Marne. But to tell the truth, we ended up wondering why: after listening to the hostess argue with the head waiter, after learning that our reservation had been lost, after refusing the outrageously expensive wine that the sommelier brought us instead of the bottle we had ordered, after searching in vain for the sweetbreads in our champignons farcis aux ris de veau, and after paying crippling prices for those plus a dried-out curried sole. No toque this year.

A la carte: 400-600 F.

 Au Vieux Clodoche
18, rue de Champigny
45 76 09 39

Open daily until 10 p.m. Garden dining. Parking.

On the riverside terrace in summer or near the fireplace in winter, Brigitte Huerta's cooking will capture your attention—and not only because of the high prices it commands. The delicate duck foie gras au torchon, turbot in a spice crust, tender seven-hour leg of lamb, rich sweetbreads en feuilleté and lively ginger soufflé are all winners, but we repeat: they are too costly by half.

A la carte: 400-500 F.

CHESNAY (LE)
See Versailles

CLICHY
92110 Clichy — (Hauts/Seine)
Paris 7 - Saint-Germain-en-Laye 17

 La Barrière de Clichy
1, rue de Paris
47 37 05 18
See Paris 17th arr. page 69.

The toque, circa 1700

Have you ever wondered about the origin of that towering, billowy (and slightly ridiculous) white hat worn by chefs all over the world? Chefs have played an important role in society since the fifth century B.C., but the hats didn't begin to appear in kitchens until around the eighteenth century A.D. The toque is said to be of Greek origin: many famous Greek cooks, to escape persecution, sought refuge in monasteries and continued to practice their art. The chefs donned the tall hats traditionally worn by Orthodox priests but to distinguish themselves from their fellows, they wore white hats instead of black. The custom eventually was adopted by chefs from Paris to Peking.

RESTAURANTS – THE SUBURBS

La Bonne Table
119, bd J.-Jaurès
47 37 38 79

Closed Sat. lunch, Sun. & Aug. 4-Sep. 2. Open until 10 p.m. Air cond.

Gisèle Berger is a true *cordon bleu*, respected for her talent and adherence to tradition. We find her prices a bit high for the suburbs, but there's the recent redecoration to pay for as well as the top-quality seafood Gisèle demands for her dishes. You'll enjoy her warm oysters with salmon, lobster lasagne, brandade en aïoli, bouillabaisse and the refreshing white wines selected by René, the *patron*.

A la carte: 350-450 F.

COURBEVOIE
92400 Courbevoie – (Hauts/Seine)
Paris 11 · St-Germain-en-Laye 13 · Levallois 4

Les Feuillantines
23, pl. de Seine
La Défense 1
47 73 88 80,
fax 40 90 96 03

Closed dinner & w.-e. (except upon reservation). Terrace dining. Air cond. Parking.

A largely business clientele enjoys a view of the Seine and the Ile de la Jatte from the second-floor terrace. The menu is rather long and expensive, but proposes carefully cooked dishes like a ragoût of snails and artichokes, scallops with chicory, pintade aux choux and luscious lemon-filled crêpes. The "diet" menu keeps your calorie consumption down to just 1,000...

A la carte: 320-450 F. Menu: 220 F.

Le Monarque
pl. des Reflets
La Défense 2 - 48, espl.
du Gal-de-Gaulle
47 78 84 59

Closed w.-e., holidays & Aug. 1-23. Open until 9:45 p.m. Private room: 25. Terrace dining. Air cond. Parking.

The pretentious décor was probably intended for important tête-à-têtes and VIP luncheons. But if you go past the velvet-covered armchairs and Oriental carpets, you'll find a splendid outdoor terrace shaded by young plane trees and looking towards the Arc de Triomphe through the Arche de La Défense. Whichever setting you choose, you can expect the same faultless service from waiters dressed in wing collars and striped jackets. The cooking of Antoine Gayet is delicate, innovative and expensive. But tell yourself that luxury doesn't come cheap and savour the scallops baked in their shells, red mullet paired with foie gras, roast pigeon with a shirred egg and to finish, a kirsch-flavoured peach gratin. Search the wine list and you may find a bottle for under 200 F...

A la carte: 380-530 F. Menus: 220 F and 250 F and 300 F and 320 F (wine incl.).

La Safranée sur Mer
12, pl. des Reflets
La Défense 2
47 78 75 50

Closed Sat., Sun., Dec. 24-Jan. 2. & Aug. Open until 10:30 p.m. Private room: 30. Terrace dining. Air cond. Valet parking.

With its luxurious wood-panelled décor and fine service, this seafood restaurant is a favourite lunch venue for business people with clients to impress. The chef purchases premium ingredients, but a bit more care could be taken in their preparation (our sole fillets were slightly undercooked). Other more successful dishes include warm red-mullet salad, scallops with oyster jus and fricassée de lotte.

A la carte: 400-500 F. Menus: 220 F (dinner only), 300 F, 350 F, 370 F.

Les Trois Marmites
215, bd St-Denis
43 33 25 35

Closed Sat., Sun. & Aug. 1-27. Open until 10 p.m. Private room: 16. Air cond.

This comfortable, elegant restaurant has maintained a traditional bistro décor set off by indirect lighting. Marc Faucheux's honest, seasonal dishes include cockle salad with beurre blanc sauce, filet de turbot au cidre, roast pigeon with pommes boulangère and freshwater perch with leeks. The regional wines are good, but just as costly as the rest.

A la carte: 280-400 F. Menu: 200 F.

CRÉTEIL
94000 Créteil – (Val/Marne)
Paris 12 · Evry 20 · Melun 35 · Bobigny 17

Le Cristolien
29, av. P.-Brossolette
48 98 12 01

Closed Sat. lunch & Sun. Open until 10 p.m. Terrace dining. Air cond. Parking.

It's no surprise that every senior executive and managing director in Créteil comes here to eat; it's the best spot in this huge, modern suburb. Alain Donnard delights his customers with carefully prepared classic dishes like tuna carpaccio rémoulade, salt-cured duck with orange sauce, turbot in an aromatic stock and a chocolate-and-caramel millefeuille. The business lunch is excellent value. Pleasant but frankly amateurish service.

A la carte: 250-320 F. Menu: 180 F.

CROISSY-BEAUBOURG
77183 Croissy-Beaubourg — (Seine/Marne)
Paris 29 - Melun 34 - Meaux 30

L'Aigle d'Or
8, rue de Paris
60 05 31 33,
fax 64 62 09 39

Closed Sun. dinner & Mon. Open until 9 p.m. Private room: 30. Garden dining. Parking.

The Gilliams brothers have created a discreet and elegant décor in pink and white, with a huge fireplace and mezzanine. Hervé Gilliams carefully tends to his long repertoire of regional dishes: sweetbreads with chestnuts and almonds, salmon on a bacon-studded biscuit, truffled boudin blanc with warm duck foie gras, and a scrumptious fruit cake with plum liqueur. Jean-Louis Gilliams oversees the attentive service. Alas, prices are high and rising.

A la carte: 450-550 F. Menus: 250 F (except holidays), 450 F.

ENGHIEN
95880 Enghien — (Val-d'Oise)
Paris 18 - Argenteuil 16 - Chantilly 32

Duc d'Enghien
3, av. de Ceinture
34 12 90 00

Closed Sun. dinner, Mon., Jan. 4-13 & Aug. 2-Sep. 1. Open until 10:30 p.m. Terrace dining.

The nicest spot is outdoors on the lakeside terrace with its geranium beds. In the recently decorated dining room, huge bouquets of flowers do their best to cheer up the ugly airport-style ceiling. Michel Kéréver confirms his triple-toque rating with a menu that, under a fairly classical guise, offers dishes of rare astuteness and acute flavours. Yes, the food is expensive, but paying the bill is sure to be less painful than losing a similar sum in the casino next door! Here the choices are all winners, as you'll agree after tasting the red mullet in a saffron stock, or lobster with tiny légumes à la grecque, or the thin tomato tart perfumed with pesto, or the regal fillet of lamb with its liver, sweetbreads and kidney. Desserts are better than ever; our favourite is a peach roasted in its juices and served with a scoop of delicate verbena ice cream. The wine list now proposes a few modest bottles and half-bottles alongside the *grands crus* of Bordeaux. Graceful service, directed by Michel Santier.

A la carte: 600-700 F. Menus: 325 F (weekdays lunch and Sat., wine incl.), 340 F (weekdays dinner only), 460 F.

EURO DISNEY
See Marne-la-Vallée.

FONTENAY-SOUS-BOIS
94120 Fontenay-sous-Bois — (Val/Marne)
Paris 7 - Saint-Mandé 2 - Nogent-sur-Marne 3

La Musardière
61, av. du Mal-Joffre
48 73 96 13

Closed Sun., Mon. & Tues. dinner, & Aug. Open until 9:45 p.m. Air cond.

This bright, comfortable restaurant lies in the heart of a huge new administrative and shopping centre largely composed of glass and ceramic. The *patron*, formerly of the Savoy Hotel in London, is an attentive host, and his chef, Christian Landier, produces handsome classic dishes with a light touch: saumon au gros sel, smoked haddock and lentils, and kidney with mustard sauce. The excellent fish dishes vary with the market and the set menu is good value. Attractive cellar.

A la carte: 250-350 F. Menu: 140 F.

GARENNE-COLOMBES (LA)
92250 Garenne-Colombes (La)— (Hauts/Seine)
Paris 12 - Courbevoie 2 - Asnières 4

Auberge du 14-Juillet
9, bd de la République
42 42 21 79

Closed w.-e., holidays & 2 wks. in May. Open until 9:30 p.m.

Regular customers are happy to see that this family-run restaurant has new décor. In contrast to the nearby concrete structures of La Défense, it is a charming, intimate place offering several excellent duck specialities and good seafood, prepared with increasing confidence by Jean-Pierre Baillon. His son Laurent helps out with the day's catch to make dishes like freshwater perch with Loire wine and bacon, bass quenelles perfumed with lemon grass, and salmon sprinkled with fragrant olive oil. Charming welcome.

A la carte: 300-450 F. Menu: 220 F.

Aux Gourmets Landais
Hôtel de Paris
5, av. Joffre
42 42 22 86

Closed Sun. dinner & Mon. Open until 10:45 p.m. Private room: 35. Garden dining. Hotel: 12 rms 180-250 F.

Josette Velazco's south-west hospitality routine contributes to the success of this excellent establishment, which now boasts a small garden with sliding roof. Her husband Alain adds the same regional flavour to his much-improved cuisine, which features salade landaise rich with foie gras and fatted duck breast, suprême of sea bass with aromatic vegetables, and light, tender tourtière (apple pie) laced with Armagnac. Tempting selection of affordable regional wines.

RESTAURANTS – THE SUBURBS

A la carte: 300-400 F.
Menus: 120 F, 200 F.

12/20 Rose
10, pl. J.-Baillet
42 42 22 07

Closed Mon., Feb. 15-22 & Aug. 1-22. Open until 9 p.m. Private room: 50. Garden dining.

Cosy and full of flowers, this increasingly charming restaurant has recently added tables outside in the courtyard. The *patron*'s rich, intricate dishes would gain from a little lightening, but they are well prepared and full of flavour: millefeuille of celeriac and salmon, Chateaubriand flavoured with a quartet of spices, confit de canard with baby broad beans, all served in a pretty dining room where everything is pink.

A la carte: 320-480 F. Menu: 180 F (except Sun. dinner).

ISSY-LES-MOULINEAUX
92130 Issy-les-Moulineaux — (Hauts/Seine)
Boulogne-Billancourt 1

 ## La Manufacture
20, espl. de la Manufacture
40 93 08 98

Closed Sat. lunch, Sun. & 2 wks. in Aug. Open until 10:30 p.m. Terrace dining. Air cond.

Jean-Pierre Vigato, who also runs the three-toque Apicius in Paris, hasn't opened a second restaurant just to make more money; he sees it as an outlet for another aspect of his personality. Unlike Apicius, Manufacture is a bright, spacious restaurant converted from an old tobacco factory. Vigato's former number two, David Van Laer, is the chef, putting his all into making this an exciting, original counterpart to Apicius. All the dishes are appetising, but the execution occasionally suffers. After a delicious feuille à feuille d'escargots, we were disappointed by a rather bland casserole of pork and root vegetables; the chocolate cake is rich and scrumptious, but we didn't see the point of the accompanying coffee coulis. Short but pertinent wine list; cheerful yet scatterbrained service.

A la carte: 260-330 F. Menu: 190 F (weekdays lunch only).

JOUY-EN-JOSAS
78350 Jouy-en-Josas — (Yvelines)
Paris 21 - Versailles 4 - Rambouillet 35

 ## Fondation Cartier
Restaurant du Château
3, rue de la Manufacture
39 56 46 46

Closed Mon., Tues. & Wed. dinner, Sat. lunch, Dec. 19-Jan. 3 & July 20-Aug. 16. Open until 10 p.m. Private room: 80. Garden dining. Air cond. Parking.

It's probably because he counts cooking as one of the fine arts that Alain-Dominique Perrin called on master chef Gérard Vié to oversee the kitchens of this restaurant filled with prestigious works of modern art by César, Garouste, Arman and others. All Vié has to do in practice is to let the capable chef, Christian Aubertin, turn out the lamb terrine with figs, steamed sole roulades in a gingery stock, and tulipe au chocolat with orange sauce. The ideas are fine, but the execution occasionally lags. Top Bordeaux and Cahors (of which Perrin is himself a producer) round out the meals taken amid elegant black, white and grey décor.

A la carte: 350-400 F. Menus: 230 F (weekdays lunch only), 280 F (weekdays dinner and Sat., Sun. lunch & holidays), 380 F (except Sun. dinner).

Remember to call ahead to reserve your room, and please, il you cannot honour your reservation, be courteous and let the hotel know.

LEVALLOIS-PERRET
92300 Levallois-Perret — (Hauts/Seine)
Neuilly 4

 ## Gauvain
11, rue L.-Rouquier
47 58 51 09

Closed Sat., Sun. & Aug. Open until 10 p.m. Air cond.

A commendable establishment, driven by the talent of a creative young chef whose personal, regularly renewed repertoire fully merits a toque. The single-price menu might suggest threadfin (a tropical fish) with baby green peppercorns, sea bream with shallots stewed in red wine, followed by floating island in a pool of chestnut coulis. The wine list needs filling out (though the selection of Loire wines is adequate), and the staff needs training in the service of wine: a bottle should never be brought to the table already opened!

A la carte: 250-280 F. Menu: 190 F.

12/20 Le Jardin
9, pl. J-Zay
47 39 54 02

Closed Sat. lunch, Sun. & wk. of Aug. 15. Open until 10 p.m. Terrace dining. Parking.

Just off the ring road, a relaxing country atmosphere has been created here. The *patron*, who is not above leaving the kitchen to chat with his customers, prepares rich, generous dishes such as terrine de confit de canard with fresh foie gras, and sole in trout mousse.

A la carte: 300-350 F. Menu: 155 F.

12/20 Le Petit Poste
39, rue Rivay
47 37 34 46

Closed Sat. lunch & Sun. Open until 10:15 p.m.

Fifteen tables crowded around the bar—this is exactly the type of bistro Brassens used to write about in his songs. Now it is a favourite with Levallois office workers, who come to enjoy the cooking of Pierre Leboucher, formerly of Lucas-Carton and La Marée: rissole d'artichaut au foie gras, navarin of sole à la vanille, lamb sweetbreads sauce diable, and a delicious pineapple terrine. Wash these good dishes down with one of the fine Loire wines.

A la carte: 230-280 F.

 Pointaire
46, rue de Villiers
47 57 44 77

Closed w.-e. & Aug. 1-23. Open until 9:30 p.m.

Père Pointaire remains a legend within the prettily renovated walls of this rustic bistro because of the dishes which were his glory: freshwater perch in butter sauce and beuchelle tourangelle (a regional speciality involving cockscombs and kidneys). But the current chef has some nicely prepared suggestions of his own: sea urchin flan, pheasant in Champagne with chanterelles, and a darkly delicious chocolate marquise. We would love to see a better selection of wines to complement the good food.

Menu: 180 F.

LINAS
91310 Linas — (Essonne)
Paris 25 · Etampes 23 · Orsay 13 · Montlhéry 2

 L'Escargot de Linas
136, rue de la Division-Leclerc
69 01 00 30

Closed Sun., Mon. lunch & Aug. 9-31. Open until 9:30 p.m. Terrace dining. Parking.

Those who love the good old-fashioned style of careful cooking will delight in this elegant, mannered Louis XVI restaurant, offering omelette Curnonsky, fricassée périgourdine, and tournedos à la bordelaise with bone marrow. But Maurice Comte is capable of more adventurous creations, using seasonal produce from nearby Rungis market in a wide selection of dishes such as gratin of shellfish with saffron, asparagus flan flavoured with chervil, and breast of pheasant with juniper berries and buttery cabbage. If the prices hadn't become so steep, we would come here more often in summer to dine on the flowery terrace.

A la carte: 300-400 F. Menu: 200 F (weekdays and Sat.).

LIVRY-GARGAN
93190 Livry-Gargan — (Seine-St-D.)
Paris 17 · Senlis 42 · Aubervilliers 13

 Auberge Saint-Quentinoise
23, bd de la République
43 81 13 08

Closed Sun. dinner & Mon. (except holidays). Open until 10 p.m. Private room: 15.

The courtyard terrace with its ivy-covered walls is clearly the star attraction, although the elegant, newly renovated dining room is now doing its best to compete. The classic dishes skilfully prepared by Michel Nicoleau come as a real surprise in this glum suburb: méli-mélo de sole au citron vert, lobster in an anise-scented stock with mild garlic, tender lamb cooked to perfection (no need for the sauce), and a rich chocolate-truffle cake. Satisfactory service and a good wine list, rich in Bordeaux.

A la carte: 280-450 F. Menu: 180 F.

LOUVECIENNES
78430 Louveciennes — (Yvelines)
Paris 24 · Versailles 7 · St-Germain-en-Laye 6

 Aux Chandelles
12, pl. de l'Eglise
39 69 08 40

Closed Sat. lunch, Wed., & Aug. 15-31. Open until 10 p.m. Private room: 20. Terrace dining.

The upstairs dining room offers a view of the enclosed garden. The young owner-chef, Stéphane Dohollon, who studied with Gérard Besson, produces dishes that are so delicate you could almost accuse him of pretension. The set meals are excellent value, particularly the 260-franc menu which includes wine and features saffron-flavoured perch and a civet de joues de cochon. Perfect service in an ideal setting for romantic dinners.

A la carte: 300-370 F. Menus: 160 F (weekdays lunch only), 260 F (except weekdays lunch, wine incl.).

MAISONS-LAFFITTE
78600 Maisons-Laffitte — (Yvelines)
Paris 21 · Pontoise 18 · St-Germain-en-L. 8

 Le Laffitte
5, av. de Saint-Germain
39 62 01 53

Closed Sun. dinner, Mon., Feb. 7-14 & Aug. Open until 10 p.m.

Offering good seafood, classic cooking and a long list of carefully prepared dishes, André Laurier's restaurant is an address worth noting and just the place for hearty appetites. Sample the escargots in crisp pastry accented with pistou, lotte au curry, skate with cabbage, veal tenderloin

---

Plan to travel? Look out for the other RAC GaultMillau Best of guides to France and Germany, and for the RAC French Hotel and Holiday Guide and the RAC European Hotel Guide plus maps and atlases of France and Europe.

RESTAURANTS – THE SUBURBS

en persillade and dark-chocolate fondant.
A la carte: 280-440 F. Menus: 220 F, 320 F.

Le Tastevin
9, av. Eglé
39 62 11 67
Closed Mon. dinner, Tues. Open until 10 p.m. Terrace dining.

The wine list is still out of this world, but we found our last meal here terribly disappointing, despite the handsome presentation. The gazpacho with prawns was notable only for its lack of flavour, an oyster terrine was coated with a boring curry sauce, and the baked turbot was ruined by an excess of salt. Things started looking up, however, with the pigeon en confit flanked by foie-gras croquettes and a wonderful little fried potato basket. The superb chocolate mousse was counterbalanced by an alarmingly bad crème brûlée. We wonder too why the *plats du jour* listed on the menu had nothing to do with the dishes actually available, and why the *menu dégustation* was described to us with every detail except the price! This year we feel obliged to suspend the rating, in the hope that Le Tastevin will win back its two toques next time.
A la carte: 470 F. Menu: 230 F.

La Vieille Fontaine
8, av. Grétry
39 62 01 78,
fax 39 62 13 43
Closed Sun., Mon. & Aug. Open until 10 p.m. Garden dining.

Manon Letourneur and François Clerc treat all their customers with the same consideration as the many celebrities (like Catherine Deneuve) who dine here. Even with a thriving catering business to take care of, François Clerc is always on duty in the kitchen when the restaurant is open. We just wish he would add some new dishes to his repertoire to vary the pleasures procured by his classic braised lobster with baby vegetables, pigeon stuffed with four kinds of cabbage, calf's kidney accented with a touch of liquorice, and saddle of rabbit with mustard meringue. The menu, available at both lunch and dinner, offers excellent value: you might choose mixed salad with rosy cold roast beef, tarragon-flavoured chicken ham, thyme-scented hot goat cheese, and pain perdu aux fruits. You'll also appreciate the romantic setting and the gracious hospitality of Manon Letourneur.
A la carte: 550-900 F. Menus: 230 (dinner only), 250 F (lunch only, wine incl.).

MARNE-LA-VALLÉE
77206 Marne-la-Vallée – (Seine/Marne)
Paris 28 · Meaux 28 · Melun 40

In nearby Euro Disney
(Access by A4)
77206 Marne-la-Vallée – (Seine/Marne)

Blue Lagoon
In the Park,
Adventureland
64 74 20 74
Open daily until 11 p.m.

Palm trees and a tropical lagoon are the setting for agreeably spicy dishes: grilled swordfish and shrimps, chicken curry, Jamaican nougat and coconut ice cream. Nearby are the boats that ferry passengers into the *Pirates of the Caribbean*, one of the park's most popular attractions.
Menu: 125 F.

Some establishments change their closing times without warning. It is always wise to check in advance.

California Grill
Outside the Park
60 45 65 00,
fax 60 45 65 33
Private room: 80. Air cond. Valet parking.

The "gastronomic" restaurant of the Disneyland Hotel offers inventive dishes based on premium ingredients. In his ultramodern kitchens, the (French) chef and his team prepare warm goat-cheese tart, beef carpaccio strewn with basil and anointed with drops of fruity olive oil, salmon with a maple-syrup glaze, a thick veal chop with black olives and polenta and, for dessert, an ethereal honey-walnut millefeuille. Impeccable service; crippling prices.
A la carte: 450-550 F.

12/20 **Cape Cod**
Disney Festival
60 45 55 93
Open daily until 11 p.m.

To allay pre-dinner hunger pangs, servers dressed in sailor suits bring appetisers of hot garlic bread drizzled with olive oil to every table. But be sure to leave room for the good things that follow, like generous portions of coquilles Saint-Jacques with bacon or swordfish grilled with fresh herbs. You can also dine at the (more expensive: 350 francs) Yacht Club, on crabcakes, shellfish, lobster and the like.
Menus: 180 F (dinner only), 280 F (lunch only).

Key West Seafood
Disney Festival
60 45 70 61
Open daily until 11 p.m.

Overlooking the (artificial) lake is a huge space decked out to resemble an unpretentious Florida fish house. Would real Florida fishermen pay these prices, we wonder, for garlicky blue crab, spicy giant prawns, seafood stew

THE SUBURBS – RESTAURANTS

(195 francs) and Key Lime pie? The wine cellar is Californian.
A la carte: 250-350 F.

12/20 Los Angeles Bar
Disney Festival
60 45 71 14
Open daily until 11 p.m.
Also lakeside is this bright, airy and modern dining room where you can enjoy gazpacho with a well-seasoned crab croûton, a grilled vegetable platter with goat cheese and caramelised garlic, grain-fed chicken with tomatilla sauce and other satisfying, well-prepared dishes. Pizza and light snacks are available upstairs.
Menu: 225 F.

Manhattan Club
Outside the Park,
near the lake
60 45 73 50,
fax 60 45 73 55
Open daily until 11 p.m.
At 7 p.m. sharp, an orchestra in white tie and tails strikes up a cha-cha to kick off the soirée. Waiters in equally formal dress skim over the thick carpet, bearing caviar, smoked salmon, foie gras, lobster Thermidor, tournedos Rossini and other rich and famous dishes concealed under silver serving bells. The scene is perfect—everyone feels like a film star...until the bill arrives.
A la carte: 500-700 F.

12/20 Park Side
Outside the Park
60 45 75 13
Open daily until 11 p.m.
Good, simple American food prepared while you watch: chicken-noodle soup, grilled salmon with bacon, veal loaf with mushroom gravy and celeriac purée.
Menu: 195 F.

10/20 Silver Spur Steakhouse
In the Park, Frontierland
60 45 70 50
Open daily until 11 p.m.
Hearty appetites meet their match here, with huge portions of barbecued chicken wings and prime ribs of beef served in a reconstituted Wild West saloon (but don't ask for a whisky: no alcohol is permitted in the Park!).
A la carte: 250-300 F.

10/20 Walt's An American Restaurant
In the Park, Main Street
64 74 24 08
Open daily until 11 p.m.
A stairway decorated with photographs of Walt Disney leads to a series of charming little dining rooms; one is less taken by the food, however, which is only mildly interesting (good orange and prawn salad, overcooked meat dishes, boring desserts).
Menu: 145 F.

MARNES-LA-COQUETTE
92430 Marnes-la-Coquette – (Hauts-de-Seine)
Paris 15 - Versailles 4 - Vaucresson 1

11/20 Les Hirondelles
18, rue G.-et-X.-Schlumberger
47 41 00 20
Closed Sun. dinner, Wed., Aug. & Dec. 23-Jan. 2. Open until 9:30 p.m.
Traditional cooking prevails at this friendly little bistro, but sometimes the chef decides to surprise his customers with a deftly grilled salmon and cèpes à la provençale.
A la carte: 150-250 F.

La Tête Noire
6, pl. Mairie
47 41 06 28
Closed Sun. dinner & Mon. Open until 9:30 p.m.
A pretty view of a leafy little square and the minuscule church just opposite add to the charm of this establishment, which is popular with the local gentry. Christian Lièvre's cooking is characterised by straightforward flavours and a judicious dose of invention. We can recommend his tourte of frogs' legs and spinach, a rich sculpin fillet souffléed with lobster sauce, and the luscious coffee-and-chocolate entremets. The wine cellar is small but well composed.
A la carte: 240-340 F.

MEUDON
92190 Meudon – (Hauts/Seine)
Paris 12 - Versailles 10 - Boulogne 3

Relais des Gardes
42, av. du Gl-Gallieni
45 34 11 79
Closed Sat. lunch, Sun. dinner & Aug. 6-Sep. 6. Open until 10 p.m. Terrace dining.
Jean-Claude Cahagnet is in command of the kitchens of this handsome brick restaurant where a classical repertoire and style reign supreme. The atmosphere in the formal beige dining room is quite serious and the maître d'hôtel positively solemn, but the cooking is well done with no redundant frills: tricoloured vegetable terrine, oxtail vinaigrette with a robustly flavoured aspic, poularde braisée en paupiette and a superb baba au rhum, rivalled only by the délice aux abricots confits. The wine list is excellent, prices high and hostess Madame Oudina smilingly omnipresent.
A la carte: 300-400 F.
Menus: 290 F (wine incl.), 190 F.

Gault Millau's ratings are based solely on the restaurants' cuisine. We do not take into account the atmosphere, décor, service and so on; these are commented upon within the review.

RESTAURANTS – THE SUBURBS

MONTMORENCY
95160 Montmorency — (Val-d'Oise)
Paris 18 - Pontoise 20 - Enghien 3 - St-Denis 8

12/20 Au Cœur de la Forêt
Av. du Repos-de-Diane
39 64 99 19

Open daily until 9:30 p.m. Terrace dining. Parking.

Next time you go walking in the Montmorency forest, ferret around until you find this establishment hidden among the trees. You'll enjoy the family atmosphere and the nicely crafted, seasonal cuisine, for example a delicate turbot with herby aspic, sole with mussel butter, a bright-tasting duck with apricots, and a good warm banana-rum tart.
A la carte: 260-370 F. Menus: 125 F, 185 F.

NANTERRE
92000 Nanterre — (Hauts/Seine)
Paris 13 - Neuilly 5 - St-Germain 8 - Boulogne 7

12/20 L'Ile de France
83, av. du Mal-Joffre
47 24 10 44

Closed Sun. & Aug. Open until 9:30 p.m. Terrace dining. Parking.

Don't be put off by appearances! This is not a disused warehouse but a serious restaurant that caters for business people. Seated at one of the large, comfortable, well-spaced tables, you can enjoy a generous set menu of seafood salad, beef sauté spiced up with green peppercorns.
A la carte: 280-330 F. Menu: 155 F (except holidays).

NEUILLY-SUR-SEINE
92200 Neuilly-sur-Seine — (Hauts/Seine)
Argenteuil 9 - Versailles 16

Le Bistrot d'à Côté
4, rue Boutard
47 45 34 55
See *Paris 17th arr.*

12/20 Brasserie des Arts
2, rue des Huissiers
46 24 56 17

Closed Sun. Open until 11 p.m.

A simple and unpretentious address often filled with celebrities from this chic suburb. They come for the brioche with bone marrow, chicken-liver terrine, smoky finnan haddie in a beurre blanc sauce, good grilled meats and crème brûlée. The prices are geared to local incomes.
A la carte: 180-250 F.

12/20 Café de la Jatte
60, bd Vital-Bouhot
47 45 04 20,
fax 47 45 19 32

Open daily until midnight. Private room: 250. Terrace dining. Air cond. Valet parking.

The décor revolves around the giant skeleton of a pterodactyl surrounded by a jungle of plants. Wicker furniture, gay colours and lots of space and light provide the rest of the atmosphere. Young waiters zoom around serving plentiful, fresh, and surprisingly well-presented dishes to tables of tanned people "in advertising": raw tuna with sesame seeds, pot-au-feu of beef and veal, noisettes of lamb with fresh vegetables. The cellar could be a little more inventive.
A la carte: 260-350 F.

Carpe Diem
10, rue de l'Eglise
46 24 95 01

Closed Sat. lunch, Sun., Dec. 24-Jan. 4 & Aug. 1-28. Open until 9:30 p.m. Air cond.

This little bistro's faithful customers are obviously drawn to the warm, simple décor, the *patronne's* gentle attentions and the diligent service. Serge Coquoin's soigné menu features a thin asparagus tart with calf's liver and kidneys, baked tuna with celery and scampi, and delicate chocolate and praline beignets. Portions could be larger, and prices lower.
A la carte: 300-400 F. Menu: 180 F (dinner only except holidays).

Jacqueline Fénix
42, av. Charles-de-Gaulle
46 24 42 61,
fax 46 40 19 91

Closed Sat., Sun., Aug. & Dec. 25-Jan. 2. Open until 10 p.m. Air cond.

Jacqueline Fénix is now actively involved in getting a new restaurant off the ground, so she has delegated her authority to Patrick Rozeau, who greets and seats patrons at well-spaced, beautifully set tables. A new chef, Patrick Juhel, makes the most of premium ingredients, creating elegant, harmonious dishes that display a pleasing personal touch: cold oyster soup with winkles, brill baked in a black-olive "crust", and silken crêpes filled with pineapple and swathed in an apricot coulis. A solid toque, then, for the restaurant's promising new departure.
A la carte: 450-550 F. Menu: 330 F.

Les Feuilles Libres
34, rue Perronet
46 24 41 41

Closed Sat. lunch, Sun. & Aug. 1-23. Open until 10 p.m. Terrace dining. Air cond.

Every second Tuesday of the month, a harpsichord concert adds a tinkling accompaniment to dinners served in this charming, peaceful dining room. Patrick Hardy prepares a repertoire that sparkles with lightness and personality, as well as an occasional touch of bold invention. We enjoyed the clever presentation of a "coupelle", or cup of cauliflower and veal, as well as the earthy pork-cheek daube with apples. A good cellar also keeps the local clientele happy.

A la carte: 350-450 F. Menus: 160 F (weekdays lunch only), 255 F (wine incl.).

 Focly
79, av. Charles-de-Gaulle
46 24 43 36

Open daily until 11 p.m. Private room: 22. Air cond.

This elegant dining room is a pleasant change from the bogus exoticism of many Asian restaurants. The talented chef proposes a repertoire of appealing Chinese, Vietnamese, Cambodian and Thai dishes somewhat confusingly presented on an interminable menu. Among the best bets are the smoked prawns with bananas, spare ribs cooked with Champagne and spiny lobster prepared with Chinese wine. Delightful welcome.

A la carte: 200-250 F. Menus: 105 F and 125 F (weekdays lunch only).

 La Guinguette de Neuilly
Ile de la Jatte
12, bd de Levallois
46 24 25 04

Closed at Christmas. Open until 11 p.m. Garden dining.

Trendy artists are drawn to this old barge and its handful of tables for a cuisine that we think merits a toque: leeks with fresh prawns, salmon en papillote with green vegetables and a long-simmered pot-au-feu made with no fewer than five kinds of meat. In fine weather, ask for a table on the terrace by the Seine.

A la carte: 200-260 F.

12/20 **Chez Livio**
6, rue de Longchamp
46 24 81 32

Closed Sat. & Sun. in Aug., May 1, Dec. 24 & Dec. 31. Open until 10:45 p.m. Private room: 18. Garden dining. Air cond.

A real Italian trattoria in the heart of Neuilly, manned by the Innocenti clan. Here you'll find generous and simple cuisine featuring ravioli al magro, gnocchi with basil, pizzas, osso buco and *tutti quanti*. The roof of the dining room rolls back so that you can dine under a canopy of blue sky or stars. Reservations (sometimes hard to come by) are a must.

A la carte: 170-250 F.

 San Valero
209 ter, av. Charles-de-Gaulle
46 24 07 87

Closed Sat. lunch, Sun. & Dec. 24-Jan. 1. Open until 10:30 p.m.

Come for a fiesta and a feast at Valero's Spanish restaurant: the menu offers paella of course, but also more authentic dishes such as squid and sole with a julienne of vegetables, scallops in a garlicky sauce scattered with dried tuna, and baby lamb marinated in herbs, a speciality of the Rioja region. The Spanish offerings on the wine list are worthy of your attention.

A la carte: 250-300 F. Menus: 150 F (weekdays only), 190 F (except holidays).

 Sébillon
Paris-Bar
20, av. Ch.-de-Gaulle
46 24 71 31

Open daily until midnight. Air cond. Valet parking.

The chefs come and go, the menu stays the same. The pride of the house is its famous Sébillon roast lamb and the giant éclair. Add to that the magnificent rib of beef and the tarte Tatin "à l'ancienne," as well as some good fresh seafood and a thick salmon steak grilled with fennel. A selection of nice Loire wines at affordable prices.

A la carte: 300-350 F.

12/20 **La Tonnelle Saintongeaise**
32, bd Vital-Bouhot
46 24 43 15

Closed Sat., Sun., Aug. 2-22, Dec. 24-Jan. 6. Open until 10 p.m.

In summer crowds tend to gather under the trees and parasols of this Ile de la Jatte terrace. The cuisine is pleasant enough, without being challenging. There are poached eggs bordelaise to start, followed by (for example) calf's liver with raisins and salt pork, or mouclade. The cellar leans heavily towards Bordeaux.

A la carte: 220-320 F.

ORLY
94396 Orly – (Val/Marne)
Paris 16 - Corbeil 17 - Villeneuve-St-Georges 12

 Maxim's
Aérogare d'Orly-Ouest
46 87 16 16

Closed Sat., Sun., holidays & Aug. Open until 10 p.m. Air cond.

A complete overhaul has resurrected Maxim's Orly, even giving it some of the cachet of the illustrious mother house. Gil Jouanin, a talented *cuisinier* formerly of the Café de la Paix, is in command of the kitchen. His new job seems to have inspired him to reach for new culinary heights, for he makes the most of excellent ingredients in subtle dishes like a juniper-scented grouse terrine with foie gras, red-mullet fillets set atop tomato fondue with a lively citrus butter, and a remarkably tender veal en casserole. Succulent figs baked in port round out a thoroughly successful meal. The 30,000-bottle cellar holds wines in every price range, from modest to outrageous. Next door, the Grill serves a quality set menu, including

RESTAURANTS – THE SUBURBS

wine and coffee, for 250 francs.

A la carte: 500-600 F. Menu: 250 F (wine & coffee incl., at the Grill).

ORSAY
91400 Orsay — (Essonne)
Paris 27 - Versailles 20 - Evry 24

 Le Boudin Sauvage
6, rue de Versailles
69 28 42 93

Closed Sat. & Sun. Open until 10 p.m. Private room: 20. Garden dining.

Anne-Marie de Gennes is turning away customers these days; we wonder if it has to do with the popularity of her spicy boudin sauvage which gives this establishment its name (but is served only in winter) or the fact that her husband Pierre-Gilles has just won the Nobel Prize for physics! Anne-Marie works with top-quality ingredients to produce her prawns with coriander-scented tomato fondue, noisettes of lamb roasted with sea salt and a delectable crème brûlée. The charming décor looks out over an old garden where you can sit in fine weather.

A la carte: 400-500 F. Menu: 260 F (lunch only).

OZOIR-LA-FERRIÈRE
77330 Ozoir-la-Ferrière — (Seine/Marne)
Paris 34 - Melun 27 - Lagny-sur-Marne 21

12/20 **La Gueulardière**
66, av. du Gal-de-Gaulle
60 02 94 56

Closed Sat. lunch, Sun., winter school holidays & Aug. Open until 9:30 p.m. Garden dining.

Double glazing has made Alain Bureau's intimate and rustic restaurant an even quieter and more charming spot in which to savour his rich, classic cuisine: foie gras, marinated scallops and

salmon, sole meunière and veal tournedos with Parma ham. The cellar is improving, but prices are on the increase. All the more reason to be thankful for the attractive set meals.

A la carte: 350-400 F. Menus: 140 F (except holidays), 210 F.

PERREUX (LE)
94170 Perreux (Le) — (Val/Marne)
Paris 15 - Créteil 11 - Vincennes 6 - Lagny 17

 Les Magnolias
48, av. de Bry
48 72 47 43

Closed Aug. 1-15. Open until 10 p.m. Air cond.

Gérard Royant simply won't let the sorry sight of the surrounding suburbs get to him. Each year he does something to improve his cosy décor of oak panelling, red velvet curtains, deep-pile carpeting and well-spaced tables. But his cuisine seemed less interesting and refined to us this year. The prawn ravioli with shellfish butter were disappointing, while the abalone with garlic and parsley lacked defined flavours. A pear and almond feuillantine saved the day, and then there is always the remarkable cellar, with its treasure trove of vintage Champagnes.

A la carte: 400-500 F. Menu: 280 F (lunch only).

PONTAULT-COMBAULT
77340 Pontault-Combault — (Seine/Marne)
Paris 26 - Melun 29 - Coulommiers 41

 Le Canadel
Aire des Berchères
64 43 45 47

Closed Sat., Sun. & Aug. Open until 10 p.m. Air cond. Parking.

Jean-Pierre Piovan's cooking is rich and admirably traditional: grilled red mullet with a lemony sabayon, sweetbreads with creamed spinach,

chicken pot-au-feu, cold chocolate soufflé. The décor is luscious too: chandeliers, murals, stucco columns, comfortable chairs and well-spaced tables. Stylish service; top-notch cellar.

A la carte: 300-400 F. Menus: 175 F, 245 F.

PONTOISE
95300 Pontoise — (Val-d'Oise)
Paris 34 - Beauvais 55 - Rouen 91 - Mantes 39

In nearby Méry-sur-Oise
(5 km E on N 322)
95540 Pontoise — (Val-d'Oise)

 Le Chiquito
La Bonneville
30 36 40 23

Closed Sat. lunch, Sun., Dec. 23-Jan. 1 & Aug. Open until 9:30 p.m. Air cond. Parking.

Pleasant décor topped with painted beams opens out onto a flowered courtyard. Still only 30, talented chef Alain Mihura has worked with Savoy and Kéréver among others and is currently developing a personal style. You'll enjoy his braised salmon and vegetables, marinière of fish in a delicately flavoured cockle sauce, and the noisettes and paupiettes of lamb with thyme served with a vegetable marmalade. Papa Mihura and his offspring provide the affable welcome and service.

A la carte: 400-450 F. Menu: 240 F.

PORT-MARLY (LE)
78560 Port-Marly (Le) — (Yvelines)
Paris 21 - Versailles 10 - Louveciennes 3

 Auberge du Relais Breton
27, rue de Paris
39 58 64 33

Closed Sun. dinner, Mon., & Aug. Open until 10 p.m. Private room: 35. Garden dining.

Here is an attractive place for a winter meal when a fire is roaring in the immense fireplace, but not to be overlooked in summer when you can sit in the lovely garden and be serenaded by birds while enjoying rather staid, but fresh and carefully executed cuisine. We liked the fricassée of lobster with tiny vegetables, steamed turbot and a fragrant cassolette de lotte. Desserts are so-so, but the cellar is judiciously stocked. Very attractive set menus.

A la carte: 250-300 F. Menus: 209 F (wine incl.), 159 F.

12/20 Les Danaïdes
1, rue Jean-Jaurès
39 16 44 88

Closed Sat. lunch & Sun. dinner. Open until 10:30 p.m. Garden dining.

The old Port-Marly post office has a country look thanks to its delightful terrace and garden. But success has taken its toll on Alain Houdayer's cooking: the ingredients seem to be of lower quality, and the portions have shrunk noticeably! A seafood salad dressed with truffle vinaigrette was served in stingy portions, and the prawns sautéed with chanterelles were microscopic (though nicely cooked). Despite a very good tarte aux pommes, we're obliged to shave a point off the rating.

A la carte: 220-300 F. Menus: 128 F, 155 F.

PRÉ-SAINT-GERVAIS (LE)
93310 Pré-Saint-Gervais (Le) — (Seine-St-D.)
Lagny 27 - Meaux 38

Le Pouilly-Reuilly
68, rue A.-Joineau
48 45 14 59

Closed Sun., holidays & end July-Sep. 6. Open until 10 p.m. Private room: 25.

Jovial Jean Thibaut has been at the helm of this authentic and popular suburban bistro-inn for a quarter of a century. You pass by the kitchen full of nose-tingling aromas to reach the dining room with its yellow tables and zinc-topped bar. Lately, though, the traditional bistro dishes appear to have lost some of their former sparkle. A point less this year for the meagre portion of fried smelts and the bland chicken jambonnette with morels, followed by a decent tarte Tatin. An imprecise wine list doesn't do full justice to the cellar, which is rich in fine Bordeaux.

A la carte: 230-350 F.

PUTEAUX
92800 Puteaux — (Hauts/Seine)
Paris 10 - Versailles 14 - St-Germain-en-Laye 11

Les Communautés
Paris-la-Défense, in the CNIT
2, pl. de la Défense
46 92 10 10,
fax 46 92 10 50

Closed Sat. & Sun. Open until 10 p.m. Air cond. Valet parking.

Pierre Miécaze is well into his stride here at the Sofitel hotel restaurant at La Défense. He works tirelessly with fine ingredients, searching for bold new flavour harmonies; he keeps a close eye on what his colleagues are cooking too, and doesn't hesitate to try out a rare condiment or spice. To sum up, Miécaze works on the principle that cooking is a constantly evolving art. The results of his research are often dazzling, even astonishing: take, for example, his crispy tart of wild mushrooms and hazelnuts; or the red mullet with braised lettuce, shallots and strips of pig's ear; or roast duck breast in a bewitching sweet-and-sour sauce; or a brioche topped with poached green apples and acacia honey—so much talent and brio are fully deserving of two toques. What's more, this interesting cuisine is well served by the elegant surroundings of the Sofitel dining room, the superb cellar and the stylish staff.

A la carte: 350-450 F. Menus: 200 F and 400 F (dinner only, wine incl.).

Les Deux Arcs
34, cours Michelet
La Défense 10
47 76 44 43,
fax 47 73 72 74

Closed Sat. & Sun. lunch. Open until 10:30 p.m. Private room: 100. Terrace dining. Air cond. Valet parking.

This is the elder of the two Sofitel hotels at La Défense. The cooking is serious, executed by a shy young chef who lacks the boldness of his colleague at the CNIT (see above). Yet some delicious meals are served here, composed maybe of crab ravioli, salmon grilled à l'unilatéral or sea bass with artichoke fricassée, and a crisp raspberry croustillant for dessert. The cellar, we are happy to report, is growing and service has improved.

A la carte: 350-400 F. Menu: 180 F (dinner only).

Fouquet's Europe
CNIT, Paris-La Défense
46 92 28 04,
fax 46 92 28 16

Closed Sat. & Sun. Open until 10:30 p.m.. Terrace dining. Air cond. Valet parking.

The stark and austere CNIT tower at La Défense is the last place you would expect to find modern French cooking that pays homage to its regional roots. But that is just the sort of satisfying food that 28-year-old Alexandre Faix is regaling his patrons with at Fouquet's Europe. An exceptionally bright pupil of the great Robuchon, Faix cooks with imagination, enthusiasm

and—this is his secret—a rare sense of split-second timing. His dishes are invariably perfectly cooked. You'll see we aren't exaggerating when you taste the suckling pig stuffed with foie gras, the gurnard fillet spiced with coriander, a succulent grain-fed Loué chicken or buttery shortbread topped with apples and rhubarb. Opulent cellar; top-drawer service.
A la carte: 450-500 F.

11/20 Le Vercanaille
6, bd R.-Wallace
45 06 05 24
Closed Sat. lunch. Open daily until 11 p.m. Private room: 25. Valet parking.
A wine bar where you can drink delicious little wines and enjoy simple but nicely prepared dishes like vegetable terrine, calf's liver with lime, or herring with potato salad. There's a 100-franc lunch formula (starter plus main course) and a take-away shop as well.
A la carte: 230-250 F. Menus: 100 F, 150 F and 200 F (weekdays dinner and Sat.).

ROISSY-EN-FRANCE
95700 Roissy-en-France — (Val/d'Oise)
Paris 26 · Meaux 36 · Senlis 28 · Chantilly 28

Maxim's
Aéroport
Charles-de-Gaulle
48 62 16 16,
fax 48 62 45 96
Open daily. Lunch only. Air cond.
As we go to press, we learn that two-toque *cuisinier* Alain Bariteau of the Jules Verne in Paris is scheduled to pilot the kitchen here... We wish him a happy landing, and will report back to you soon.
A la carte: 350-600 F.

ROMAINVILLE
93230 Romainville — (Seine-St-D.)
Paris 10 · Livry-Gargan 9 · Aulnay-sous-Bois 9

 Chez Henri
72, rte de Noisy
48 45 26 65,
fax 48 91 16 74
Closed Sat. lunch, Mon. dinner, Sun., holidays & Aug. 7-24. Open until 9:30 p.m. Private room: 18. Air cond. Parking.
Car parks and warehouses are not the ideal environment for a fine restaurant. But Henri Bourgin takes it in his stride, as does his clientele of regulars, who know that behind the sombre, unobtrusive facade lies a comfortable dining room where an instinctive, expert chef is at work. You'll soon forget the charmless surroundings when you tuck into a superb salad of skate with asparagus and orange vinaigrette, or lobster with coriander-scented baby vegetables, suprême de pintade en tapenade, or veal en gelée with black and green olives, followed by a walnut, hazelnut and almond craquelin topped with Sauternes sabayon. A keen-flavoured, appetising style of cooking. Fine cellar, diligent service.
A la carte: 300-400 F. Menus: 145 F, 200 F.

RUEIL-MALMAISON
92500 Rueil-Malmaison — (Hauts/Seine)
Paris 15 · Versailles 11 · Argenteuil 12

12/20 El Chiquito
126, av. P.-Doumer
47 51 00 53,
fax 47 49 19 61
Closed Sat., Sun. & 15 days in Aug. Open until 9:45 p.m. Garden dining. Air cond. Valet parking.
Chefs come and go here, and the latest is perhaps not the most gifted. His cooking, while respectable, surely doesn't justify the stiff prices: we sampled a decent salade

gourmande followed by a marinated red mullet sauce aigrelette with oddly undefined flavours, and then a tasty crème à la vanille served with over-baked madeleines. On the plus side, there's a good cellar and at the back is a wonderful garden which blots out the traffic noise.
A la carte: 400-600 F. Menu: 250 F (dinner except holidays).

12/20 Relais de Saint-Cucufa
114, rue du Gal-de-Miribel
47 49 79 05
Closed Sun. dinner, Mon. & Aug. 15-30. Open until 9 p.m. Garden dining.
A terrace and garden enlarge the rustic dining room in fine weather. The Breton *patron* welcomes guests warmly, and sings the praises of his Italian wife's cooking. Indeed, she chooses her ingredients with care, and turns them into generous, delicious dishes. Try her turbot with prawns, the escalope of sweetbreads with morels, and finish with a perky fruit charlotte. Small but choice cellar, reasonably priced.
A la carte: 350-400 F.

RUNGIS
94150 Rungis — (Val/Marne)
Paris 13 · Corbeil 26 · Longjumeau 1

 La Rungisserie
20, av. Ch.-Lindbergh
46 87 36 36,
fax 46 87 08 48
Open daily until 11 p.m. Private room: 60. Garden dining. Air cond. Valet parking.
A huge and happy hotel restaurant with a soothing, modern décor. The good lunch menu, which includes wine, and the large hors-d'œuvre buffet attract a faithful clientele from the Rungis market. The à la carte menu

includes some solid dishes such as scallops in buttery pastry, aiguillettes de canard and delicious desserts. The wide-ranging wine cellar (with bottles from California, Chile and Spain) is over-priced.

A la carte: 300-500 F. Menus: 185 F (weekdays only, wine incl.), 210 F.

SAINT-CLOUD
92210 Saint-Cloud — (Hauts/Seine)
Paris 12 - Boulogne 3 - Versailles 10

12/20 La Désirade
2, bd de la République
47 71 22 33,
fax 46 02 75 64

Open daily until 10 p.m. Garden dining. Air cond. Parking.

Colourful fabrics make for lively décor, but the chef needs rousing, we think. Our last experience here (duo de saumons with crisp-cooked cabbage, fillet of salt cod with julienne vegetables, apricot parfait) left an impression of imprecise cooking and blurred flavours. And the service is still less than spirited.
Menu: 150 F.

11/20 Vanida
6, rue Dailly
47 71 31 05

Closed Sat. lunch, Sun. & Aug. 1-23. Open until 11 p.m. Private room: 50.

A benevolent Buddha beams out over the fresh, white décor of this establishment, which is unfortunately going a bit off course. On our last visit the Thai fish fritters were doughy and the rice sautéed with prawns definitely lacked its usual flavour.

A la carte: 150-200 F. Menus: 85 F (weekdays lunch only), 112 F, 145 F.

> *Red toques signify modern cuisine; white toques signify traditional cuisine.*

SAINT-DENIS
93200 Saint-Denis — (Seine-St-D.)
Paris 10 - Argenteuil 10 - Chantilly 30

La Saumonière
1, rue Lanne
48 20 25 56

Closed Sat. lunch, Sun. & Aug. Open until 10 p.m. Air cond.

You'd be wise to follow the maître d'hôtel's suggestions, for he is well-versed in the talented new chef's repertoire of specialities. They include a very fresh scallop and lobster salad, numerous dishes based on foie gras, an admirably seasoned turbot aux pommes de terre and a fine tarte Tatin. In fact, the food is so good that we would happily dine more frequently here amid the slightly overstuffed décor—were it not for the ever-rising prices!

A la carte: 250-550 F. Menu: 180 F.

SAINT-GERMAIN-EN-LAYE
78100 Saint-Germain-en-Laye — (Yvelines)
Paris 21 - Chartres 81 - Dreux 70 - Beauvais 69

Cazaudehore
1, av. du Président-Kennedy
34 51 93 80

Closed Mon. (except holidays). Open until 10 p.m. Private room: 140. Garden dining. Parking.

On the edge of the forest in a wonderful setting of greenery and flowers sits this charming establishment decorated with old prints and English chintzes; for summer dining, there's a huge terrace that looks out over the trees. It is at this point that the superb and unshakeable "Cazau" sometimes goes off track, its luxurious cuisine suffering under the pressure of numbers. Still, irregularities are not the rule and you are sure to enjoy dishes like an elegant veal terrine. Superb cellar, stylish service.

A la carte: 350-500 F. Menu: 240 F (weekdays lunch only).

12/20 La Feuillantine
10, rue des Louviers
34 51 04 24,
fax 39 21 07 70

Annual closings not available. Open until 10 p.m. Air cond.

Full (and delicious) meals at 130 francs don't grow on trees in affluent Saint-Germain. That is why La Feuillantine's dining room is so crowded these days: taste the baked salmon with tender chicory, chicken blanquette with basmati rice and morels, and a rich fondant au chocolat. The service remains cheerful, even amid the crush—our only complaint is that portions have grown noticeably smaller.
Menu: 130 F.

12/20 Les Nuits des Thés
17bis, rue des Coches
34 51 65 64

Open noon-7 p.m. Closed Mon., Aug. & holidays.

The décor is rich: white lacquer, pink upholstery, mercury mirrors, damask tablecloths, antique furniture and watercolours on the walls. The welcome may be cool if you aren't a regular, but the clientele is noticeably at ease, chatting about such weighty topics as dog pedigrees, boating and the latest literary successes. They nibble on salads and main-dish pies and tarts of all sorts, but in our view only the desserts are really exceptional (caramelised cream cheese tart, for instance, or the raspberry macaroons). You'll spend something over 100 Francs for lunch, half that for tea and a pastry.

A la carte: 100 F.

RESTAURANTS – THE SUBURBS

 Le Pavillon Henri-IV
21, rue Thiers
34 51 62 62,
fax 39 73 93 73
Open daily until 10:30 p.m. Private room: 350. Terrace dining. Air cond. Parking.
Neither the staff nor the patrons appear to be having much fun, but the cuisine fully merits a gourmet's attention. It encompasses dishes so classic as to have nearly disappeared from most modern menus, all deftly prepared. As a result, a meal here resembles nothing so much as a trip to some gastronomic museum; the attractive wine list is a plus.
A la carte: 350-400 F. Menu: 240 F (weekday lunch only).

SAINT-OUEN
93400 Saint-Ouen – (Seine-St-D.)
Paris 7 · Saint-Denis 4 · Chantilly 34

 Le Coq de la Maison Blanche
37, bd J.-Jaurès
40 11 01 23
Closed Sun. & Aug. 1-15. Open until 10 p.m. Private room: 120. Terrace dining.
The long and lovely menu is handwritten daily to entice diners with jambon persillé, coq au vin or grilled kidneys. Seasonal dishes also take pride of place and are prepared in grand bistro tradition with a touch of youthful exuberance. The salad of Breton crab claws, the saddle of lamb with white beans, or the eel sautéed in white wine with spinach and broccoli perfectly suit the convivial atmosphere of this likeable establishment run by a sensational *patron*, Alain François.
A la carte: 300-400 F.

Gault Millau's ratings are based solely on the restaurants' cuisine. We do not take into account the atmosphere, décor, service and so on; these are commented upon within the review.

 Chez Serge
7, bd J.-Jaurès
40 11 06 42
Lunch only (& dinner Thurs.). Open until 9 p.m. Air cond.
Short, simple and sweet—that sums up the menu chez Serge Cancé, and it's a policy that has brought enviable success to this bistro set in a bleak *banlieue* north of Paris. Chef Fabrice Gay's cooking is more noted for its generosity than for its finesse: a copious portion of the house terrine was disappointingly bland on our last visit, and so was the lotte au safran. But the pork knuckle with lentils could not have been better, and it was followed by an exceptional chocolate cake. The cellar, however, is unworthy of a bistro with a reputation for serving well-chosen wines. A point less this year.
A la carte: 220-320 F.

SCEAUX
92330 Sceaux – (Hauts/Seine)
Paris 12 · Versailles 16 · Antony 3 · Bagneux 3

12/20 L'Orangerie
13, rue M.-Charaire
43 50 83 00
Closed Sun. dinner, Mon. & Aug. Open until 9 p.m.
The cooking is generally consistent, the service pleasant and comfort is assured in this peaceful spot situated in a pedestrian zone. But muddled flavours mar some of Jean-Pierre Baudoin's dishes, and the quality of certain ingredients could be improved (such as the gizzards and foie gras in a very mediocre salade périgourdine). Though a copious portion of grilled fish was overcooked, the roast rack of lamb we tried was irreproachable. All in all, it didn't add up to a toque this year.
A la carte: 300-390 F.

SÈVRES
92310 Sèvres – (Hauts/Seine)
Paris 12 · Boulogne 3 · Versailles 8

11/20 Phileas Fogg
5, pl. Pierre-Brossolette
46 26 48 80
Closed Sun. dinner & Mon. Open until 10:30 p.m. Terrace dining.
Travel no farther than Sèvres railway station to go around the world in eighty dishes. The cooking is nicely handled by the wife of a former scriptwriter for the vintage TV series *The Avengers*, repeated ad nauseam on late-night French television. Try the tasty jambalaya, fish pie or lamb with apricots. Simple décor and a smiling welcome. Superb whiskies.
A la carte: 170-200 F.

VARENNE-ST-HILAIRE (LA)
94210 Varenne-St-Hilaire (La) – (Val/Marne)
Paris 16 · t-Maur 3 · Chennevières 2

 La Bretèche
171, quai de Bonneuil
48 83 38 73,
fax 42 83 63 19
Closed Sun. dinner, Mon. & Feb. school holidays. Open until 10 p.m. Private room: 18. Garden dining.
Chef Philippe Regnault has lots of bright ideas, but the flavours of his fine ingredients cry out for more definition. Creamy scrambled eggs with fresh truffles suffered from a bit too much salt; a beautifully cooked sea bream with potatoes and bay leaves was insufficiently seasoned; the prune-studded chocolate ganache, however, was perfectly focused. The cellar is well stocked with bottles in a wide range of prices. The sunny décor is seductive, but when the weather is fine we

opt for the terrace, overlooking the soothingly verdant banks of the Marne.
A la carte: 270-370 F. Menu: 150 F.

 Le Pavillon Bleu
66, prom. des Anglais
48 83 10 56,
fax 43 97 21 21

Open daily until 11 p.m. Private room: 80. Terrace dining.

Once a former suburban dance-café, Le Pavillon Bleu is now a luxurious riverside restaurant. Though prices are high and rising, the cuisine is on a definite downswing. Readers echo our disappointment with reports of botched dishes (like the soft-boiled egg with caviar served with a severely undercooked potato) and lacklustre flavours (if there were any pistachios in our crème brûlée à la pistache, they were imperceptible). Owing to a perfectly prepared cod with garlic purée we'll leave the toque in place, but we're subtracting a point. If the dining room's thick carpet and heavy curtains don't appeal, try the leafy terrace on the water's edge.
A la carte: 350-450 F. Menus: 200 F (weekdays lunch and Sat.), 300 F (weekdays dinner and Sat. lunch).

VARENNES-JARCY
91480 Varennes-Jarcy — (Essonne)
Paris 29 - Corbeil-Essonnes 14 - Melun 30

12/20 **Hostellerie de Varennes**
14, rue de Mandres
69 00 97 03

Closed Tues. dinner, Wed. & Aug. 2-27. Open until 9:30 p.m. Private room: 85. Terrace dining. Parking.

Francis Gautier's charming establishment is graced with a delightful garden full of flowers. The cuisine strikes a pleasing balance between simple (young rabbit terrine, grilled andouillette, and duck confit) and rich dishes (scallops in chervil cream sauce; tantalising desserts).
A la carte: 250-380 F. Menu: 195 F.

VERSAILLES
78000 Versailles — (Yvelines)
Paris 23 - Mantes 44 - Rambouillet 31

11/20 **Brasserie du Théâtre**
15, rue des Réservoirs
39 50 03 21

Open daily until 12:30 a.m.

Classic brasserie food (brawn, pepper steak, sauerkraut, steak tartare), served in a supremely Gallic décor of mirrors, glowing woodwork and leather banquettes.
A la carte: 160-260 F.

12/20 **Au Chapeau Gris**
7, rue Hoche
39 50 10 81,
fax 39 02 77 46

Closed Tues. dinner, Wed. & July. Open until 10 p.m. Private room: 80.

As the ancient exposed beams attest, this is the oldest restaurant in Versailles, and it attracts an extremely well-heeled crowd. The cuisine is honest enough, though not always precise. Traditional dishes are the house speciality: eggs scrambled with fresh truffles, soufflé of turbot with saffron sauce, nougat glacé with blackcurrants. Exceptional wine list. Classic, thoroughly professional service.
A la carte: 300-400 F. Menu: 155 F.

11/20 **La Flotille**
in the Château
de Versailles park
39 51 41 58

Open for lunch only. Parking.

Set on the edge of the château's Grand Canal with a marvellous view of Le Nôtre's gardens, this restaurant serves unpretentious, tasty food like rabbit cooked with mustard, baked salmon with pasta and duck confit. Delightful summer terrace.
A la carte: 160-260 F. Menu: 125 F.

12/20 **Le Lac Hong**
18, rue des Frères-Caudron, D 91
30 44 03 71

Closed Wed. Open until 9:30 p.m.

Fine Chinese-Vietnamese cuisine at low prices (caramelised fresh tuna, quail with five-spice powder, grilled crab). Exceptionally affordable wines, charming welcome.
A la carte: 130-200 F. Menu: 120 F (except holidays).

12/20 **Le Pot-au-Feu**
22, rue de Satory
39 50 57 43

Closed Sat. lunch, Sun. & Aug. 10-17. Open until 10 p.m. Private room: 12.

Pot-au-feu in its classic or seafood versions get star billing, but the chef's repertoire also includes mussels à la sétoise, plaice poached in dry cider and veal confit à l'indienne. Attractive set meals.
A la carte: 220-280 F. Menus: 115 F, 175 F.

 Le Potager du Roy
1, rue du Mal-Joffre
39 50 35 34

Open daily until 10:30 p.m. Air cond.

Gérard Vié's former "Trois Marches" has lost its old magic. Though chef Philippe Letourneur, Vié's one-time associate, started out here creditably enough, our recent experiences have been unfortunate, to say the least. Even if we were to disregard the non-existent welcome, the fearsomely expensive cellar and the flustered service, we could not in all conscience bestow a two-toque rating on cuisine that has lost its creativity and finesse. Did this restaurant's success come too quickly? Is it too late to hope for a turnaround? We'll let you know.

A la carte: 300-400 F. Menus: 120 F (weekdays and Sat.), 165 F (weekdays, Sat. and holidays).

12/20 Le Quai n°1
1, av. de St-Cloud
39 50 42 26

Closed Sun. dinner & Mon. Open until 11 p.m. Terrace dining. Air cond.

A dependable address for fine shellfish and skilfully prepared seafood dishes at reasonable prices. Try the exemplary 115-franc menu: mussels marinière, tuna provençale, Roquefort with figs and walnuts, plus dessert. Amusing nautical décor.

A la carte: 220-370 F. Menus: 115 F, 160 F.

Rescatore
27, av. de St-Cloud
39 50 23 60

Closed Sat. lunch & Sun. Open until 10 p.m. Air cond.

Jacques Bagot is a native of the Norman port of Granville; his speciality is vibrantly fresh fish and seafood prepared in refined, imaginative ways. Try the sea bass in a morel fumet, the unusual combination of oysters and duck breast called rôti d'huîtres au magret, or a keen-flavoured ballotine of prawns with ratatouille. Fine cellar.

A la carte: 380-480 F. Menus: 200 F (weekdays lunch only), 375 F.

Les Trois Marches
1, bd de la Reine
39 50 13 21,
fax 39 51 66 55

Closed Sun., Mon. & Aug. Open until 10 p.m. Private room: 20. Terrace dining. Air cond. Valet parking.

Gérard Vié and his brigade have moved *en masse* to the Trianon Palace, where they now benefit from the most technically sophisticated equipment imaginable. But despite the high-tech surroundings, Vié remains loyal to his country roots.

This chef's cuisine has what it takes to thrill and captivate: warm belon oysters with foie gras, duck liver with strong rancio wine, rabbit gelée with leeks, fillets of sole marinated—almost conserved—in olive oil, baked lobster with thyme, turbot with onions and pommes Anna, braised young pigeon with spices and apricots, and duck with turnips and truffles, simmered for four hours. Even Vié's simple country-style dishes are delicious and full of provincial goodness (beef braised with carrots, cassoulet with Couïza sausages).

The formidable cellar's grand wines push the bill skywards, but the prices are not out of line given the quality. There are many fine bottlings at around 100 francs, and the fixed-price lunch menu is a marvel.

A la carte: 600-800 F. Menus: 260 F (weekdays lunch only), 395 F.

In nearby Le Chesnay

(NE)
78150 Versailles — (Yvelines)

Le Chesnoy
24, rue Pottier
39 54 01 01

Closed Sun. dinner, Mon. & Aug. 4-25. Open until 10 p.m. Garden dining. Air cond.

Bustling and brimming over with *bon vivants*, Le Chesnoy is a welcome oasis in the built-up surroundings. The sunny dining room opens onto a summer terrace. Late of Les Glénan and Marius et Janette, chef Georges Torrès excels with fish dishes such as lightly smoked sea bass with leek sabayon, and a crispy salmon cooked in its skin within a salt crust. There are also several fine meat dishes on the menu (veal sweetbreads cooked with rum and nutmeg). Monsieur Baratin, the owner, will guide you expertly through his wine list.

A la carte: 250-320 F.

Le Connemara
41, rte de Rueil
39 55 63 07

Closed Sun. (except lunch 1st & 2nd Sun. of the month), Mon. & Aug. 1-20. Open until 9:30 p.m. Private room: 15.

Ireland features only modestly on the Connemara's menu: succulent smoked salmon, Aran scallop soup, and a dizzying choice of whiskeys. The rest of chef Pascal Eynard-Machet's repertoire plays variations on classic themes, which are tunefully updated with fruit (sole and salmon served with grapefruit) or vegetables (lamb mignon with fresh white beans, small turbot with a turnip and apple gratin). The handsome décor is in salmon hues, and the restaurant is set in a swathe of greenery.

A la carte: 250-360 F. Menu: 145 F.

L'Etoile de Mer
17, rue des Deux-Frères
39 54 62 70

Closed Sun. dinner, Mon. & Aug. Open until 10 p.m. Air cond. Parking.

L'Etoile de Mer's intimate, modern dining room opens onto the town marketplace. The view features a crowded lobster tank, and beyond it, the fishmonger's shop attached to the restaurant. This is where chef Yann Cadiou takes the freshest, best fish and shellfish, and transforms them into spectacular

THE SUBURBS – RESTAURANTS

assortments and cooked dishes: superb lightly grilled scampi, magnificent sea bass, and fresh summer soup made with large prawns. Charming welcome. Negligible wine cellar.

A la carte: 250-450 F. Menus: 90 F (weekdays lunch only). 155 F.

VILLEBON-SUR-YVETTE
91120 Villebon-sur-Yvette — (Essonne)
Paris 23 · Versailles 21 · Evry 22 · Etampes 31

 La Morvandelle
86, av. du Général-de-Gaulle
60 10 29 61

Open daily until 10 p.m. Private room: 40. Garden dining. Parking.

Yvon Blandin has a knack for preparing seafood, and lots of innovative ideas. Try the tasty ragoût of lobster and escargots, or the firm and flavourful turbot aux épices. To finish, you could order the outstanding tarte Tatin made with figs instead of apples. Decent cellar. Sunny, elegant décor and a pleasant terrace.

A la carte: 300-450 F. Menus: 165 F, 360 F.

VILLENEUVE-LA-GARENNE
92390 Villeneuve-la-Garenne — (Hauts/Seine)
Paris 11 · St-Denis 2 · St-Germain 18

 Les Chanteraines
Av. 8-Mai-1945
47 99 31 31

Closed Sat., Sun. dinner & Aug. 15-31. Open until 10 p.m. Terrace dining. Parking.

This smart new restaurant is lost in the leaden suburbs north of Paris. The décor has a 1930s feel, and the dining room looks out on the municipal park and pond. Though more modern and less Burgundian, the food here is not unlike that of the Coq de la Maison Blanche (see above, Saint-Ouen), which is run by the proprietor's husband. Dishes include a classic asparagus sauce mousseline, scallops set on a bed of lamb's lettuce, finnan haddie with green lentils, and leg of lamb with gratin dauphinois. Great chocolate cake; interesting wine list.

A la carte: 300-360 F. Menu: 170 F.

VILLIERS-LE-BÂCLE
91190 Villiers-le-Bâcle — (Essonne)
Paris 24 · Trappes 15 · Chevreuse 11

 La Petite Forge
1, rte de Gif
60 19 03 88

Closed Sat., Sun., Aug. 2-16, Dec. 24-Feb. Open until 9:30 p.m.

This charming little stopping place at the mouth of the Chevreuse Valley boasts an intimate, roughcast décor with exposed beams. It's a pity the frightfully high prices keep all but the wealthiest away, although owner-chef Kleber Ernimo does his utmost to justify the cost. His cuisine is based on top-quality ingredients and prepared with loving care. The fish are fabulous and fresh, the game delicious, and the farmhouse cheeses remarkable. The cellar is home to many excellent Bordeaux.

A la carte: 330-430 F.

ALLIANCE AUTOS

Rents chauffeur-driven limousines

RELIABILITY – PRESTIGE

Business – Touring – Events

All types of vehicles
Air conditioning – Telephone
Multilingual chauffeurs

(1) 43 28 20 20

24-hour reservation and service

5bis, avenue Foch – 94160 Saint-Mandé
Fax: (1) 43 28 27 27
Licence de Grande Remise n° 10

HOTELS

INTRODUCTION	*100*
SYMBOLS & ABBREVIATIONS	*101*
LUXURY	*102*
FIRST CLASS	*105*
CLASSICAL	*109*
CHARMING	*115*
PRACTICAL	*120*
AIRPORT	*126*
THE SUBURBS	*126*

HOTELS – INTRODUCTION

INTRODUCTION

Paris hotel rooms come in every possible style, size and price range. But whatever the category of the room you seek, remember to book well in advance to get exactly what you want. Our selection ranges from sumptuous suites to far humbler lodgings, but note that certain hoteliers put as high a price on charm or modern facilities as others do on pure luxury, so don't assume that "charming" means "cheap". The prices quoted include taxes and service.
Hotels are classified as follows: Luxury, First Class, Classical, Charming, Practical, Airport and The Suburbs.

RESERVATION SERVICE

Les Hôtesses de Paris can arrange a same-day reservation in any hotel in Paris or the rest of France. The service costs 18 to 55 francs, depending on the hotel. These friendly hostesses also provide tourist information for Paris and France. All you need to do is drop in (don't telephone) at one of the locations listed in *Basics* under Tourist Information.

NO ROOM AT THE INN?

If your every attempt to find a hotel room has failed, you needn't panic. Here are two companies that can track down a room for you or even rent you a high-class studio or apartment. The latter come with every guarantee of home comforts, security and such options as maid, laundry and repair services. Prices range from 450 to 2,500 francs and upwards, depending on the size and type of accommodation. Townhouses and houseboats are available too.
Contact: *Paris-Séjour-Réservation*, 90, avenue des Champs-Elysées, Paris 8th arr., tel. 42 56 30 00, Monday to Friday 9 a.m.-7 p.m., Saturday 10 a.m.- 6 p.m.; or *Paris Bienvenue*, 10, avenue de Villars, Paris 7th arr., tel. 47 53 80 81, Monday to Friday 8:30 a.m.-7:30 p.m., Saturday 10 a.m.-5 p.m.

APARTMENT HOTELS

At the apartment hotels listed below, you'll enjoy the same service you would find in a hotel, for a lower price. Rates start at about 600 francs per night for a studio for two.
• *Carré d'Or*, 46, av. George-V, 8th arr., 40 70 05 05, fax 47 23 30 90. 23 stes 3,950-17,350 F. No pets. Parking.

INTRODUCTION – **HOTELS**

- *Les Citadines-Austerlitz,* 27, rue Esquirol, 13th arr., 44 23 51 51, fax 45 86 59 76. 2 apts 870 F. 49 studios 490-610 F. Bkfst 38 F. Parking.
- *Les Citadines-Bercy,* 14-18, rue de Chaligny, 12th arr., 40 01 15 15, fax 40 01 15 20. 97 apts 540-870 F. Bkfst 38 F. Parking 35 F / day.
- *Les Citadines-Montparnasse,* 67, av. du Maine, 14th arr., 40 47 41 41, fax 43 27 29 94. 72 studios 550-950 F. Garage parking.
- *Les Citadines-Trocadéro,* 29 bis, rue Saint-Didier, 16th arr., 44 34 73 73, fax 47 04 50 07. 6 apts 920-1,150 F. 66 studios 464-660 F. No pets. Garage parking.
- *Flatotel,* 14, rue du Théâtre, 15th arr., 45 75 62 20, fax 45 79 73 30. 247 rms & apts 490-3,900 F. Bkfst 45 F. Parking.
- *Flatotel,* 52, rue d'Oradour-sur-Glane, 15th arr., 45 54 93 45, fax 45 54 93 07. 179 rms & apts 600-1,950 F. Bkfst 45 F. Parking.
- *Flatotel Porte de Versailles,* 52, rue d'Oradour-sur-Glane, 15th arrondissement, 45 54 93 45.
- *Métropole Opéra,* 2, rue de Gramont, 2nd arr., 42 96 91 03, fax 42 96 22 46. 6 apts 950-1,300 F. 27 studios 600-1,200 F. Bkfst 50 F.
- *Orion Les Halles,* 4, rue des Innocents, 1st arr., 45 08 00 33, fax 45 08 40 65. 55 apts 960-1,050 F. 134 studios 620-700 F. 1 appt for disabled.
- *Orion La Défense,* 8, bd de Neuilly, La Défense 1, 92400 Courbevoie, 47 62 55 55. 130 apts 740 F. 104 studios 480 F.
- *Résidence du Roy,* 8, rue François-Ier, 8th arr., 42 89 59 59, fax 40 74 07 92. 31 apts & 51 rms 1,140-2,950 F. Bkfst 65 F. Parking.

SYMBOLS & ABBREVIATIONS

Our opinion of the comfort level and appeal of each hotel is expressed in the following ranking system:

🏰	Very luxurious
🏛	Luxurious
🏠	Very comfortable
🏚	Comfortable
🌲	Very quiet

Symbols in red denote charm.
Rms: rooms.
Stes: suites.
Air cond.: air conditioning.
Half-board: rate per person for room, breakfast and one other meal (lunch or dinner).
No cards: no credit cards accepted.

HOTELS – LUXURY

LUXURY

Beverly Hills
8th arr. - 35, rue de Berri
43 59 55 55,
fax 42 56 52 75

Open year-round. 14 stes 2,500-9,900 F. Parking.

The extravagant décor of marble, mirrors and precious woods reeks of money: this apartment-hotel is designed for millionaires, emirs and merchant princes who want to wallow in luxury. Security is provided for with total electronic surveillance. The huge suites offer every imaginable amenity, from dining rooms to wide-screen TV. Piano bar and restaurant.

Le Bristol
8th arr. - 112, rue du Faubourg-Saint-Honoré
42 66 91 45,
fax 42 66 68 68

Open year-round. 45 stes 6,250 F and up. 152 rms 2,450-4,150 F. Bkfst 140 F. Restaurant. Air cond. No pets. Heated pool. Valet parking.

The elegance of its décor (genuine period furniture, as well as lovely reproductions), the comfort of its rooms, the luxury of its suites and the prestige of its clientele make Le Bristol one of the rare authentic luxury hotels in Paris (as well as one of the most expensive). The Bristol's two distinct wings comprise 35 newer, modern suites housed in a former Carmelite convent, and 150 more traditionally decorated rooms and suites. Among the innumerable amenities are video surveillance, ultramodern conference rooms, a heated swimming pool, a superb laundry service and a hair salon. An extraordinary restaurant (Le Bristol) opens onto the lawn and flowers of a formal French garden, see *Restaurants*. The staff is both cordial and impressively trained.

Hôtel de Crillon
8th arr. - 10, pl. de la Concorde
42 65 24 24,
fax 44 71 15 02

Open year-round. 33 stes 4,600-52,000 F. 130 rms 2,350-3,800 F. Bkfst 130 F. Restaurants. Air cond. Valet parking.

The Crillon, originally an 18th-century palace, is the last of the Parisian luxury hotels to have remained authentically French: inner courtyards; terraces overlooking the place de la Concorde; extravagantly sumptuous public rooms; guest rooms that, though not always immense or well soundproofed, are exquisitely decorated; and the most splendid suites one could hope for. Let's not forget the well-trained staff. Yes, the Hôtel de Crillon has re-established its link with the elegant, magnificent ambience of years past (Louis XVIth-style furniture, silk draperies, pastel walls and woodwork ornamented with gold leaf, cleverly concealed minibars). Relais et Châteaux. Restaurants: Les Ambassadeurs and L'Obélisque, see *Restaurants*.

George-V
8th arr. - 31, avenue George-V
47 23 54 00,
fax 47 20 40 00

Open year-round. 53 stes 6,500-14,500 F. 298 rms 2,300-5,500 F. Bkfst 115 F. Restaurants. Air cond. Valet parking.

The new management has made a Herculean attempt to instil new life and spirit into this "monument in decline." The bar and the restaurant (Les Princes, see *Restaurants*; both open onto a delightful patio) have been redecorated, a Grill has been added, and many of the rooms have been renovated, with as much concern for elegance as for modernity (electronic panels located at the head of the beds allow guests to close the venetian blinds, control both the television and the air conditioning, call room service and so on). The Galerie de la Paix (recently converted into a chic tea room, see *Tea Rooms*), as well as the pictures, rare ornaments and lovely furniture in the public rooms still radiate the legendary George V charm. But such surroundings cry out for absolutely first-rate maintenance and service, neither of which is provided here. How distressing for guests to feel that they are disturbing the personnel when they make a request...

Le Grand Hôtel
9th arr. - 2, rue Scribe
40 07 32 32,
fax 42 66 12 51

Open year-round. 16 stes 4,000-15,000 F. 482 rms 1,750-2,500 F. Bkfst 150 F. Air cond. Valet parking.

The renovation of this grand hotel, built in 1862, is now complete. In the past ten years, this monumental Second Empire building has recovered all the splendour it displayed when Empress Eugénie inaugurated it. The huge central lobby, topped with a glittering glass dome, is a wonder to behold. Guest rooms provide everything the international traveller could require in the way of amenities, as well as the most up-tp-date business equipment available, a health club and much more. Excellent bar, see *Cocktail Bars*.

Remember to call ahead to reserve your room, and please, if you cannot honour your reservation, be courteous and let the hotel know.

LUXURY – HOTELS

Inter-Continental
1st arr. - 3, rue de
Castiglione
44 77 11 11,
fax 44 77 14 60

Open year-round. 70 stes 2,800-12,000 F. 380 rms 1,650-2,450 F. Bkfst 100 F. Restaurants. Air cond.

Garnier, the architect of the Opéra, designed this vast hotel; three out of its seven immense and spectacular salons are listed as historic monuments. With its remarkably equipped conference rooms, it responds perfectly to the business world's needs; and as for charm and comfort, you'll find them both in the lovely patio filled with flowers, in the décor and the incomparable loveliness of many of the rooms (though some are tiny and dark), as well as in the small singles located in the attic, from which there is a fine view of the Tuileries. Bathrooms are often old-fashioned and on the small side. The suites (with Jacuzzi) are luxurious. Three restaurants: La Rôtisserie Rivoli, Le Café Tuileries and La Terrasse Fleurie, see *Restaurants*; and a bar.

Hôtel Lotti
1st arr. - 7, rue de
Castiglione
42 60 37 34,
fax 40 15 93 56

Open year-round. 7 stes 4,500-6,000 F. 133 rms 1,320-3,000 F. Bkfst 120 F. Restaurant. Air cond. Pets 50 F. Valet parking.

This elegant hotel is very popular with members of the European aristocracy. Each of the spacious rooms, whose comfort is worthy of their clientele, is uniquely decorated and offers excellent facilities. The restaurant, the lobby and all the rooms were recently renovated. The staff's standards are not so high as they used to be: the concierges and receptionists are occasionally careless. The charming attic rooms are reserved for non-smokers.

Marriott Prince de Galles
8th arr. - 33, avenue
George-V
47 23 55 11,
fax 47 20 96 92

Open year-round. 30 stes 2,500-8,000 F. 140 rms 1,700-2,400 F. Bkfst 95 F. Restaurant. Air cond. Valet parking.

The open-roofed patio encircled by columns is a delightful place to have lunch on a warm day; the panelled Regency Bar is another pleasant spot, distinguished by excellent service. But upstairs in the guest rooms, the facilities show their age, a fact which, given the price policy practised here, we find more than difficult to swallow. Yet for many travellers, those very flaws are part of this establishment's "Old World" charm. The service can be offhand. Restaurant: Le Prince de Galles, see *Restaurants*.

Meurice
1st arr. - 228, rue de
Rivoli
44 58 10 10,
fax 44 58 10 15

Open year-round. 36 stes 5,000-15,000 F. 143 rms 2,200-3,500 F. Bkfst 130 F. Restaurant. Air cond. in 125 rms. Valet parking.

The Meurice has undergone substantial renovation in the past few years, to restore its glamour and prestige. Most recently, the admirable salons on the main floor were refurbished; the guest rooms and suites (which offer a view of the Tuileries) were equipped with air conditioning and tastefully redecorated; and the pink-marble bathrooms are now ultramodern. The Meurice has regained its place as one of the best and most elegant grand hotels in Paris. The newly designed restaurant, Le Meurice, is now lodged in the salon des Tuileries, which overlooks the gardens. Tea and cocktails are served to the sound of discreet piano music in the salon Pompadour, see *Cocktail Bars*. A free secretarial service is available, and hotel guests are given free use of the hotel's box at the Longchamp race track during the season.

Plaza Athénée
8th arr. - 25, av.
Montaigne
47 23 78 33,
fax 47 20 20 70

Open year-round. 42 stes 6,000-9,390 F. 210 rms 2,630-5,520 F. Bkfst 110 F. Restaurants. Air cond. Valet parking.

At the Plaza, one finds nothing but discretion, efficiency and friendly courtesy. The rooms and suites are bright, generous in size and fitted with every available hotel amenity. The rooms overlooking avenue Montaigne are perfectly soundproofed. At about 11 a.m., guests gather in the bar (Plaza-Bar Anglais, where Mata Hari was arrested), see *Cocktail Bars*; and, from 4 p.m. to 7 p.m. in particular, you'll see them in the gallery (of which Marlene Dietrich was particularly fond). Two restaurants, Le Relais and Le Régence-Plaza, are located just across from the wonderful patio, where tables are set in the summer among cascades of geraniums and ampelopsis vines, see *Restaurants*. Dry-cleaning services are provided, as well as a beauty salon.

Raphaël
16th arr. - 17, av. Kléber
44 28 00 28,
fax 45 01 21 50

Open year-round. 35 stes 2,800-6,500 F. 52 rms 1,700-2,300 F. Bkfst 100 F. Restaurant. Air cond. in 40 rms. Valet parking.

Built between the wars, the Raphaël has maintained an atmosphere of refinement and

HOTELS – LUXURY

elegance. The Oriental rugs strewn upon the marble floors, the fine woodwork, old paintings and period furniture make Le Raphaël a luxurious place to stay, preferred by a wealthy, well-bred clientele. The spacious rooms (all with two beds) are richly furnished in various styles; the wardrobes and bathrooms are immense. Top-drawer reception and service. Bar, see *Cocktail Bars*.

Résidence Maxim's de Paris
8th arr. - 42, av. Gabriel
45 61 96 33,
fax 42 89 06 07

Open year-round. 37 stes 3,000-22,000 F. 4 rms 2,250 F. Bkfst 110 F. Restaurant. Air cond. Valet parking.

Pierre Cardin himself designed the hotel of his dreams, a small but palatial establishment that may well be the world's most luxurious. The landings of each floor are decorated like elegant salons, with beautiful and unusual antique pieces and paintings. Polished stone and sumptuous murals adorn the bathrooms. The suites must be seen to be believed, particularly those on the top floor, which are lacquered in vivid colours and furnished with pieces designed by Cardin. Obviously, accommodation like this is well beyond the bank balances of most ordinary mortals.

Ritz
1st arr. - 15, place Vendôme
42 60 38 30,
fax 42 60 23 71

Open year-round. 45 stes 3,900-49,000 F. 142 rms 2,100-3,500 F. Bkfst 160 F. Restaurant. Air cond. No pets. Heated pool. Valet parking.

The most famous hotel in the world is poised to enter the 21st century with state-of-the-art facilities, but without having in the least betrayed the distinctive character that won the Ritz its reputation. In other words, even if nowadays you can change the video programme or make a phone call without leaving your bed or marble bath (Charles Ritz was the first hotel owner to provide private bathrooms for his clients), nothing has altered the pleasure of stretching out on a wide brass bed surrounded by authentic antique furniture. Add to that a full view of one of the city's most spectacular squares, in an atmosphere of old-fashioned luxury so distinguished that a new word ("ritzy") had to be coined for it. The liveried staff knows the difference between courtesy and obsequiousness. Recent improvements include an 18-metre swimming pool, a squash court, a health club built to resemble a thermal spa of antiquity, and a rooftop heliport. The restaurant, L'Espadon, see *Restaurant*, has its own garden. Additional entertainment possibilities include a nightclub and several bars.

Royal Monceau
8th arr. - 37, av. Hoche
45 61 98 00,
fax 42 56 90 03

Open year-round. 40 stes 4,200-11,000 F. 179 rms 1,950-2,950 F. Bkfst 130 F. Restaurants. Air cond. No pets. Heated pool and beauty centre. Valet parking.

This large, luxurious and discreet hotel attracts politicians, foreign business people and entertainers with spacious rooms, magnificent marble bathrooms and all the usual ingredients of hotel comfort (including excellent room service). Extras include a fashionable piano bar, a spacious health club (with sauna, Jacuzzi, swimming pool and a massage service), outstanding ultramodern conference rooms and a well-equipped "business club." The rooms overlooking the charming flowered patio are the most sought-after by the hotel's habitués. Restaurants: Le Carpaccio see *Restaurants* and Le Jardin.

Saint-James et Albany
1st arr. - 202, rue de Rivoli
42 60 31 60,
fax 40 15 92 21

Open year-round. 56 stes 1,400-2,500 F. 155 rms 850-1,050 F. Bkfst 65 F. Restaurant. Garage parking.

The new management is working hard to make this hotel worthy of its four-star rating and its exceptional location facing the Tuileries Gardens. For reasonable prices, the Saint-James et Albany provides studios, two-room apartments, suites and two-level suites equipped with kitchenettes; the rooms overlook a courtyard or an inner garden and are perfectly quiet. Other amenities include a sauna, a cosy bar with background music (see *Cocktail Bars*) and a restaurant, Le Noailles.

Scribe
9th arr. - 1, rue Scribe
44 71 24 24,
fax 42 65 39 97

Open year-round. 11 stes 2,800-5,400 F. 206 rms 1,450-2,100 F. Bkfst 130 F. Restaurant. Air cond. Valet parking.

Behind the Scribe's Napoléon III façade stands a prime example of the French hotelier's art. All the rooms, suites and two-level suites (the latter are composed of a mezzanine bedroom, a living room that also serves as a dining room/office, a bathroom, dressing room and two entrances) are comfortably furnished in classic style, and boast huge bathrooms. Streetside rooms have double windows and either contemporary or Louis XVIth–style furniture; those overlooking the courtyard are furnished with Louis-Philippe–style pieces and are perfectly quiet. Nineteen TV channels are available, as well as 24-hour room service. Restaurant: Les Muses, see *Restaurants*; and a bar, see *Cocktail Bars*.

 Westminster
2nd arr. - 13, rue de la Paix
42 61 57 46,
fax 42 60 30 66

Open year-round. 17 stes 2,700-4,300 F. 84 rms 1,650-2,450 F. Half-board 2,060 F. Bkfst 95 F. Restaurant. Air cond. in 73 rms. Valet parking, 120 F/day.

Recent and extensive renovation has completely transformed this charming mid-size luxury hotel advantageously situated between the Opéra and the place Vendôme. The pink-and-beige-marble lobby is splendid and luxurious; the bar (with piano) is more than comfortable, see *Cocktail Bars*; the conference rooms are superbly equipped; and the elegant rooms are handsomely decorated with attractive fabrics, chandeliers and Louis XV–style furnishings and are fitted with minibars, safes and satellite TV. Restaurant: Le Céladon, see *Restaurants*.

FIRST CLASS

 Ambassador-Concorde
9th arr. - 16, bd Haussmann
42 46 92 63,
fax 40 22 08 74

Open year-round. 2 stes 3,000-3,500 F. 296 rms 1,300-2,000 F. Bkfst 100 F. Restaurant. Air cond. Valet parking.

A fine traditional hotel, proud of its luxurious fittings. The relatively spacious guest rooms have been modernised in excellent taste with sumptuous fabrics, thick carpeting

and Art Deco furniture. The lobby and public rooms are imposing: pink marble columns are topped with gilded Corinthian capitals; the floors are marble too, and Aubusson tapestries hang on the walls. The penthouse suites look out over Sacré-Cœur. Bar.

 Astor Madeleine L'Horset
8th arr. - 11, rue d'Astorg
42 66 56 56,
fax 42 65 18 37

Open year-round. 128 rms 860-920 F. Bkfst 70 F. Restaurant.

Marble, dark-oak woodwork, inviting leather sofas and huge vases of flowers can be found year-round in the lobby, with its English-style bar. Guest rooms are handsomely decorated in excellent taste. A major renovation is planned for 1993. Restaurant: La Table de l'Astor.

 Baltimore
16th arr. - 88 bis, av. Kléber
44 34 54 54,
fax 44 34 54 44

Open year-round. 1 ste 3,200 F. 104 rms 1,600-2,500 F. Bkfst 95 F. Restaurant. Air cond. Parking.

Six fully equipped meeting rooms are located in the basement; the largest and most luxurious is the former vault room of the Banque Nationale de Paris. The comfortable guest rooms are decorated with understated elegance, in keeping with the neighbourhood and the tastes of the clientele. Restaurant: L'Estournel, see *Restaurants*.

 Hôtel Balzac
8th arr. - 6, rue Balzac
45 61 97 22,
fax 42 25 24 82

Open year-round. 14 stes 3,000-6,000 F. 56 rms 1,380-2,100 F. Bkfst 90 F. Restaurant. Air cond. No pets. Valet parking.

A discreet and luxurious establishment near the place de

l'Etoile, frequented by celebrities and jet-setters. The huge rooms are decorated in delicate tones, with lovely furniture, beautiful chintzes and thick carpeting. Most have king-size beds, all have superb modern bathrooms. Unobtrusive yet attentive staff. Restaurant: Bice, see *Restaurants*.

 California
8th arr. - 16, rue de Berri
43 59 93 00,
fax 45 61 03 62

Open year-round. 16 stes 3,300-8,000 F. 156 rms 1,100-1,900 F. Restaurant. Half-board 1,350-

---

Hidden treasures in the Marais

Since 1960, many of the aristocratic homes in the Marais district (which started life as a swamp) have been restored to their former glory.

Just 30 years ago, the splendid hôtels particuliers—townhouses—were practically invisible, lurking behind blackened and weather-beaten façades. Nowadays, you can spend a marvellous afternoon taking in such architectural treasures as the Hôtel Carnavalet at 23 rue de Sévigné, the Roman-inspired Hôtel d'Hallwyll at 28 rue Michel-le-Comte and the imposing Hôtel de Soubise at 60 rue des Francs-Bourgeois.

HOTELS – FIRST CLASS

2,150 F. Bkfst 100 F. Air cond. Valet parking. Fitness club.

A light-filled lobby and a sunny lounge provide a good first impression, and then there are cheerful, adequately sized rooms decorated with chintzes and neo-18th-century furniture, spacious marble bathrooms and extremely pleasant service. Accomodation overlooking the courtyard is amazingly quiet, despite the proximity of the Champs-Elysées. Restaurant on the premises.

Castille
1st arr. - 37, rue Cambon
42 61 55 20 (will change)

Open year-round. 15 stes 3,000 F. 73 rms 1,300-1,600 F. Restaurant. Air cond. No pets.

After a thorough renovation, this hotel next door to Chanel and just opposite the Ritz was due to reopen in April 1993 with even more luxurious amenities.

Château Frontenac
8th arr. - 54, rue Pierre-Charron
47 23 55 85,
fax 47 23 03 32

Open year-round. 4 stes 1,480 F. 102 rms 850-1,300 F. Bkfst 75 F. Restaurant. Air cond. in 20 rms.

A reasonably priced hotel (given the location), with various sizes of room done in vaguely Louis XV style. Superb marble bathrooms. The soundproofing is effective, but the rooms overlooking the rue Cérisole are still the quietest. Restaurant: Le Pavillon Russe.

Chateaubriand
8th arr. - 6, rue Chateaubriand
40 76 00 50,
fax 40 76 09 22

Open year-round. 28 rms 1,400-1,700 F. Bkfst 65 F. Air cond. No pets.

Built in 1991, this luxury hotel tucked away behind the Champs-Elysées is still fresh and pristine, but has yet to develop a personality, an atmosphere.

Claridge-Bellman
8th arr. - 37, rue François-ler
47 23 54 42,
fax 47 23 08 84

Open year-round. 42 rms 1,100-1,300 F. Bkfst 70 F. Air cond. No pets. Restaurant.

A small, unpretentious hotel with rooms of reasonable size, each of which boasts a special feature, be it a crystal chandelier, antique furniture, a fine print or painting, or a marble fireplace. Friendly, stylish service.

Concorde-La Fayette
17th arr. - 3, pl. du Général-Koenig
40 68 50 68,
fax 40 68 50 43

Open year-round. 28 stes 3,000-8,000 F. 970 rms 1,350-2,100 F. Bkfst 95 F. Restaurants. Air cond. Parking.

The Concorde-La Fayette is immense: a huge oval tower that houses the Palais des Congrès and its 4,500 seats; banquet rooms that can accommodate 2,000; scores of boutiques; four cinemas; nightclubs; and 1,500 parking places. The hotel's 1,000 rooms are neither spacious nor luxurious, but they offer all the modern amenities guests have come to expect: magnetic locks, TV, adjustable air conditioning, soundproofing, minibars and clock radios. Airport shuttles can be relied upon to stop here. The hotel's upper floors lodge the Top Club, whose members benefit from luxurious rooms and personalised service. Panoramic bar, three restaurants, including L'Etoile d'Or, see *Restaurants*.

Concorde Saint-Lazare
8th arr. - 108, rue Saint-Lazare
40 08 44 44,
fax 42 93 01 20

Open year-round. 6 stes 1,950-3,500 F. 300 rms 1,150-1,950 F. Restaurant. Bkfst 90 F. Air cond. in 150 rms. Valet parking.

An enormous hotel, built in 1889 by Gustave Eiffel. The rooms have been thoroughly renovated with pink or beige fabric, attractive lamps and English-style mahogany furniture. Streetside rooms offer the most spacious accommodation. Though large, the bathrooms are a bit old-fashioned. The hotel's most arresting feature is the lobby, a listed architectural landmark, that soars three storeys up to coffered ceilings aglitter with gilt, marble and crystal chandeliers. A magnificent billiard room on the main floor is open to the public, as are the cocktail lounge and brasserie.

Elysées Star
8th arr. - 19, rue Vernet
47 20 41 73,
fax 47 23 32 15

Open year-round. 4 stes 2,400-3,000 F. 38 rms 1,410-2,400 F. Bkfst 80 F. Restaurant. Air cond. Valet parking.

Different decorative styles—from Louis XV to Art Deco—distinguish the various floors of this prestigious hotel near the Champs-Elysées, a paradise for business people. Superb facilities.

Golden Tulip
8th arr. - 218-220, rue du Fg-St-Honoré
49 53 03 03,
fax 40 75 02 00

Open year-round. 20 stes 2,300-3,700 F. 52 rms 1,550-1,750 F. Bkfst 95 F. Restaurant. Half-board 1,840 F. Air cond. Pool. Garage parking.

Owned by a Dutch chain, this comfortable hotel is decorated in modern style using traditional materials (marble, wood, quality fabrics, *trompe-l'œil* paintings). The spacious rooms offer every amenity; all are air conditioned, with splendid marble bathrooms. Restaurant: see *Le Relais Vermeer*.

Hilton
15th arr. - 18, av. de Suffren
42 73 92 00,
fax 47 83 62 66

Open year-round. 35 stes 3,500-12,000 F. 456 rms 1,500-2,300 F. Bkfst 130 F. Restaurants. Air cond. Valet parking.

The city's first postwar luxury hotel is still living up to Hilton's high standards. Rooms are airy and spacious, service is courteous and deft, and children—of any age—can share their parents' room at no extra charge. Closed-circuit TV shows recent films. Ten storeys up are the two "Executive Floors", with their particularly fine rooms (spectacular views of the Seine) and special services. The Hilton houses two restaurants, La Terrasse and Le Western (see *Restaurants*), and three bars, (Lobby Bar, Bar Suffren and Bar du Toit de Paris, see *Cocktail Bars*), as well as a hair salon and prestigious boutiques. 24-hour room-service.

Lancaster
8th arr. - 7, rue de Berri
43 59 90 43,
fax 42 89 22 71

Open year-round. 10 stes 3,500-7,200 F. 50 rms 1,590-2,500 F. Bkfst 110 F. Restaurant. Air cond. in 30 rms. Valet parking.

Once you recover from the immense, breathtaking bouquet of flowers in the lobby, you'll be able to admire the general setting—furniture, wall hangings, paintings, ornaments—of this refined and luxurious hotel. The ravishing indoor garden, with its flowers, fountains and statues (meals are served there on sunny days), lends an unexpected rural touch to this hotel located only a few steps from the Champs-Elysées. The rooms and suites all have period furniture and double windows; their comfort is much appreciated by the aristocrats, statesmen and business tycoons who frequent the Lancaster. Excellent reception; attentive and punctual service. The small conference rooms have fine equipment.

Littré
6th arr. - 9, rue Littré
45 44 38 68,
fax 45 44 88 13

Open year-round. 4 stes 1,280 F. 96 rms 660-875 F. Bkfst 50 F. Air cond. No pets.

The style and décor of this four-star hotel are out of tune with the times, but the Littré's many habitués find the old-fashioned comfort and service entirely satisfactory. In the spacious rooms you'll find high, comfortable beds, ponderous furniture, enormous wardrobes and huge bathrooms. English bar.

Hôtel du Louvre
1st arr. - Pl. André-Malraux
44 58 38 38,
fax 44 58 38 01

Open year-round. 22 stes 3,500-5,000 F. 178 rms 1,300-2,500 F. Restaurant. Bkfst 90 F. Air cond. Valet parking.

From the door of this comfortable, classic hotel, you can see the Gardens of the Palais-Royal, the Louvre and the Tuileries. While most of the guest rooms are spacious and high-ceilinged, offering the décor and all the conveniences we have come to expect from this chain, others are on the small and gloomy side. Brasserie, piano bar.

> *Monday, like Sunday, is a day of rest for many shopkeepers.*

Lutétia
6th arr. - 45, bd Raspail
49 54 46 46,
fax 49 54 46 00

Open year-round. 27 stes 3,000-4,000 F. 276 rms 1,100-2,200 F. Bkfst 115 F. Restaurants. Air cond. in 190 rms. Valet parking.

A Left-Bank landmark, the Lutétia is a noteworthy example of Art Deco furnishing. Marble, gilt and red velvet grace the stately public areas where government bigwigs, elected officials, captains of industry and well-heeled travellers come and go. Leading off the imposing entrance are the lounge, a bar, a brasserie, a restaurant, (Brasserie Lutétia and Le Paris, see *Restaurants*) and conference rooms. The large and expensive suites are done up in pink, with understated furniture and elegant bathrooms—the overall look is very 1930s. As for the service, though occasionally impersonal, it is dependably efficient and precise.

Le Méridien Paris-Etoile
17th arr. - 81, bd Gouvion-Saint-Cyr
40 68 34 34,
fax 40 68 31 31

Open year-round. 17 stes 3,800-7,500 F. 989 rms 1,400-1,950 F. Bkfst 85 F. Restaurants. Air cond. Valet parking. 3 rms for disabled.

The Méridien is the largest hotel in Western Europe, and one of the busiest in Paris. The rooms are small but remarkably well equipped. A variety of boutiques, a nightclub, the Hurlingham Polo Bar (see *Cocktail Bars*) and four restaurants (Le Café Arlequin; La Maison Beaujolaise; the Yamato; and the excellent Clos Longchamp, see *Restaurants*) liven things up, as does the popular cocktail lounge where top jazz musicians play, (Club Lionel Hampton, see *Live Music*). Other services include Le Café

HOTELS – FIRST CLASS

Arlequin, spacious conference rooms, a sauna and travel agencies.

Le Méridien Paris-Montparnasse
14th arr. - 19, rue du Cdt-Mouchotte
44 36 44 36,
fax 44 36 49 00

Open year-round. 15 stes 4,000-6,000 F. 950 rms 1,200-1,800 F. 3 rms for disabled. Bkfst 78 F. Restaurants. Air cond. Valet parking.

Luxurious, soigné and comfortable—that's the Méridien in a nutshell. Try to reserve one of the newer rooms, which are particularly bright and spacious. Or the Presidential Suite, if your means permit. Certain rooms are for non-smokers only; all afford fine views of the city. Three restaurants: Café Atlantique; Justine and Montparnasse 25, see *Restaurants*; bar, Le Platinium; boutiques.

Montalembert
7th arr. - 3, rue de Montalembert
45 48 68 11,
fax 42 22 58 19

Open year-round. 5 stes 2,400-3,000 F. 51 rms 1,450-1,850 F. Bkfst 90 F. Restaurant. Air cond. No pets. Valet parking.

The new management has been unstinting in its efforts to restore this 1926 hotel to its former splendour with luxurious materials (marble, ebony, sycamore, leather), designer fabrics and linens. Guests love the huge bath towels, cosy dressing gowns and premium toiletries they find in the rooms. Restaurant open at lunch only; breakfast buffet. The hotel bar is a favourite rendezvous of writers and publishers.

Pergolèse
16th arr. - 3, rue Pergolèse
40 67 96 77,
fax 45 00 12 11

Open year-round. 40 rms 850-1,500 F. Bkfst 70 F. No pets.

A brand-new deluxe hotel, the Pergolèse provides a top-class address as well as first-rate service and amenities for what are still (relatively) reasonable prices.

Pont-Royal
7th arr. - 7, rue de Montalembert
45 44 38 27,
fax 45 44 92 07

Open year-round. 75 rms 850-1,550 F. No pets.

Business people and cinema actors have taken over the fairly spacious, traditionally furnished rooms where writers—from Faulkner to Sagan—have stayed. On the ninth floor, three rooms have terraces with views all over Paris. Bar: Pont-Royal, see *Cocktail Bars*; restaurant.

Régina
1st arr. - 2, place des Pyramides
42 60 31 10,
fax 40 15 95 16

Open year-round. 10 stes 2,200-3,200 F. 120 rms 900-2,000 F. Restaurant. Half-board 890-1,240 F. Bkfst 80 F. Air cond. in 7 rms. Valet parking.

Opposite the Tuileries is one of the city's most venerable luxury hotels, with immense rooms, valuable furnishings (Louis XVI, Directoire, Empire) and—a practical addition—double-glazed windows. The grandiose lobby is graced with handsome old clocks that give the time of all the major European cities. A quiet bar and a little restaurant that opens onto an indoor garden are pleasant places to idle away an hour.

> A red hotel ranking denotes a place with charm.

Saint James Paris
16th arr. - 5, pl. du Chancelier-Adenauer
47 04 29 29

Open year-round. 31 stes 2,200-3,500 F. 17 rms 1,350-1,900 F. Bkfst 120 F. Restaurant. Air cond. in 48 rms. Valet parking.

Since its purchase by a hotel group, the hotel part of this private club has been open to the public. A staff of 100 looks after the 48 rooms and suites—a luxury level of attention with prices fixed accordingly. The sizeable rooms are decorated in an austere 1930s style, with flowers, plants, and a basket of fruit adding warmth. Marble bathrooms.

San Régis
8th arr. - 12, rue Jean-Goujon
43 59 41 90,
fax 45 61 05 48

Open year-round. 10 stes 2,800-4,000 F. 34 rms 1,325-2,525 F. Bkfst 100 F. Restaurant. Air cond. in 35 rms. Valet parking.

This jewel of a hotel, much appreciated by celebrities from the worlds of show business and *haute couture*, provides a successful mix of traditional comfort and the latest technology. Beautifully kept rooms boast splendid period furniture and paintings, sumptuous bathrooms and lots of space, light and character. The staff are irreproachable.

La Trémoille
8th arr. - 14, rue de La Trémoille
47 23 34 20,
fax 40 70 01 08

Open year-round. 14 stes 2,750-5,100 F. 96 rms 1,600-2,900 F. Bkfst 100 F. Restaurant. Air cond. Valet parking.

Cosy comfort, antique furniture, balconies with window-boxes filled with bright flowers and service worthy of a grand hotel. Several suites are brand new and remarkably comfortable; all the rooms have lovely bathrooms. The delightful dining room/salon is warmed by a crackling fire in winter. Restaurant: Le Louis d'Or.

Hôtel Vernet
8th arr. - 25, rue Vernet
47 23 43 10,
fax 40 70 10 14

Open year-round. 3 stes 3,200 F. 54 rms 1,400-1,950 F. Bkfst 100 F. Restaurant. Air cond. Valet parking.

This is one of the city's finest hotels, combining the best of modern and traditional comforts. The rooms and suites are handsomely decorated with genuine Louis XVI, Directoire or Empire furniture, and walls are hung with sumptuous blue or green fabric. Jacuzzi in all the bathrooms; guests have free access to the luxurious Thermes du Royal Monceau health spa. Restaurant: Les Elysées du Vernet, see *Restaurants.*

La Villa Saint-Germain
6th arr. - 29, rue Jacob
43 26 60 00,
fax 46 34 63 63

Open year-round. 4 stes 1,600-1,950 F. 30 rms 800-1,250 F.

A laser beam projects room numbers onto the doors; the bathroom sinks are crafted of chrome and sanded glass; orange, violet, green and red leather furniture stand out vividly from the subdued grey walls: Marie-Christine Dorner has created a high-tech environment for this new hotel, which attracts a trendy, moneyed clientele. Jazz club on the lower level (La Villa, see *Live Music*), with known performers.

Warwick
8th arr. - 5, rue de Berri
45 63 14 11,
fax 45 63 75 81

Open year-round. 5 stes 3,160-8,100 F. 141 rms 1,620-2,420 F. Bkfst 105 F. Restaurant. Air cond. Valet parking.

Luxurious and modern, just off the Champs-Elysées, this hotel offers bright, spacious rooms done up in pastel colours and chintz—they are designed more for relaxing and living in than for a quick stopover. Efficient soundproofing and air conditioning. There is an attractive bar with piano music in the evening and pleasant rooftop terraces. Room service available 24 hours a day. Restaurant: La Couronne, see *Restaurants.*

CLASSICAL

Agora Saint-Germain
5th arr. - 42, rue des Bernardins
46 34 13 00,
fax 46 34 75 05

Open year-round. 39 rms 530-640 F. Bkfst 40 F. No pets.

A very well-kept establishment which was completely renovated in 1987. Bright rooms with comfortable beds, minibar, radio and television. Bathrooms with such welcome amenities as hairdryers.

Alexander
16th arr. - 102, av. Victor-Hugo
45 53 64 65,
fax 45 53 12 51

Open year-round. 3 stes 1,950 F. 59 rms 830-1,370 F. Bkfst 65 F. Air cond. in 7 rms. No pets.

Stylish comfort and impeccable maintenance distinguish this peaceful establishment. Rooms are decorated with slightly outmoded elegance (leaf-patterned wallpaper, grey carpeting). Nice big bathrooms with all modern fixtures. The reception is most courteous. No restaurant.

Aramis Saint-Germain
6th arr. - 124, rue de Rennes
45 48 03 75,
fax 45 44 99 29

Open year-round. 41 rms 500-750 F. Bkfst 45 F.

These new, well-soundproofed and attractively decorated rooms have soft lighting, modern equipment and perfect bathrooms. The service is especially attentive. Piano bar; no restaurant.

Bastille Speria
4th arr. - 1, rue de la Bastille
42 72 04 01,
fax 42 72 56 38

Open year-round. 42 rms 460-690 F. Bkfst 35 F. No pets.

The interior was renovated in a restrained modern style in 1988. The rooms, though not large, are perfectly quiet thanks to double windows. Very pleasant reception and service.

Bradford
8th arr. - 10, rue Saint-Philippe-du-Roule
43 59 24 20,
fax 45 63 20 07

Open year-round. 2 stes 1,100 F. 46 rms 700-950 F. Bkfst 30 F. No Air cond. No pets.

A traditional hotel, where elegant simplicity combines with exemplary service to give guests true comfort. Decorated in a predominantly Louis XVI style, the rooms are slightly old-fashioned, but spacious and soothing. Good singles; rooms ending with the numbers 6 and 7 are the largest. No restaurant.

Hôtel de la Bretonnerie
4th arr. - 22, rue Ste-Croix-Bretonnerie
48 87 77 63,
fax 42 77 26 78

Closed Aug. 2-29. 1 ste 800-900 F. 30 rms 530-750 F. Bkfst 40 F. No pets.

A 17th-century townhouse, tastefully renovated and redecorated. Spacious rooms with beams and antique furniture; modern bathrooms. The pink-and-white suite is much in demand.

Britannique
1st arr. - 20, av. Victoria
42 33 74 59

Open year-round. 40 rms 490-680 F. Bkfst 40 F. No pets.

A warm welcome and good service characterise this family-run hotel. The rooms are tastefully decorated with pale walls, dark carpeting, minibar and comfortable modern furniture. Satellite television.

Cayré
7th arr. - 4, bd Raspail
45 44 38 88,
fax 45 44 98 13

Open year-round. 126 rms 900-1,300 F. Bkfst 50 F.

A pink-and-grey marble floor, glass pillars and red-leather furniture lend an air of luxury to the lobby. The rooms, modern and thoroughly soundproofed, are completely impersonal. Marble bathrooms.

Claret
12th arr. - 44, bd de Bercy
46 28 41 31,
fax 49 28 09 29

Open year-round. 52 rms 320-490 F. Bkfst 40 F. Restaurant. Half-board 420-590 F.

This neat, modernised hotel with a family atmosphere features a wine bar in the basement.

Colisée
8th arr. - 6, rue du Colisée
43 59 95 25,
fax 45 63 26 54

Open year-round. 44 rms 580-850 F. Air cond. in 19 rms.

Rooms are on the small side (those whose numbers end with an 8 are more spacious), but quite comfortable, with floral décor and tiled bathrooms. The four attic rooms have beamed ceilings and considerable charm. There is a bar and lounge, but no restaurant.

Commodore
9th arr. - 12, bd Haussman
42 46 72 82,
fax 47 70 23 81

Open year-round. 11 stes 2,150-3,500 F. 151 rms 1,000-1,800 F. Bkfst 80 F. Restaurant. Valet parking.

This commendable traditional hotel is located a few steps away from the new Drouot auction rooms and car park. Some of the hotel rooms have just been fully renovated in a bright, elegant style. As for the others, the less said the better. All, however, are spacious; newlyweds should request the honeymoon suite, which must be seen to be believed.

Courcelles
17th arr. - 184, rue de Courcelles
47 63 65 30,
fax 46 22 49 44

Open year-round. 42 rms 530-670 F. Bkfst 40 F.

All the rooms here are equipped with remote-control TV, direct-line telephones, clock-radios and minibars. Walls are covered with pink or green fabric that co-ordinates with the bedspreads and curtains; the furniture is of the modern, lacquered variety. Very pleasant reception and service.

Duminy-Vendôme
1st arr. - 3, rue du Mont-Thabor
42 60 32 80,
fax 42 96 07 83

Open year-round. 79 rms 590-850 F. Bkfst 22 F.

Duminy-Vendôme's rooms have impeccable bathrooms and 1920s–style furnishings. Rooms on the sixth and seventh floors have slightly sloping ceilings, and those with numbers ending in 10 are larger than the rest. A small summer patio is located on the main floor, as is the rather amazing bar, swathed in red velvet.

Edouard VII
2nd arr. - 39, av. de l'Opéra
42 61 56 90,
fax 42 61 47 73

Open year-round. 4 stes 1,800 F. 70 rms 750-1,080 F. Bkfst 50 F. Restaurant. Half-board 948 F. Air cond. in 33 rms.

A certain 1960s-style luxury characterises this hotel near the Opéra. Half the rooms were redecorated last year. Well-equipped bathrooms. Restaurant: Le Delmonico, see *Restaurants*.

Elysa
5th arr. - 6, rue Gay-Lussac
43 25 31 74

Open year-round. 30 rms 450-660 F. Bkfst 35 F. No pets.

In the heart of the Latin Quarter, near the Luxembourg Gardens. The pretty pink or blue rooms with white-lacquered furniture are soundproofed. Buffet breakfast.

Elysées-Maubourg
7th arr. - 35, bd de Latour-Maubourg
45 56 10 78,
fax 47 05 65 08

Open year-round. 2 stes 800-1,200 F. 28 rms 520-690 F. Bkfst 40 F. Air cond.

The 30 rooms of this Best Western hotel are decorated without much originality in green, blue or beige tones, but they are superbly equipped and very comfortable. There is a Finnish sauna in the basement, a bar and a flower-filled patio. No restaurant.

Frantour Suffren
15th arr. - 20, rue Jean-Rey
45 78 50 00,
fax 45 78 91 42

Open year-round. 11 stes 1,900-3,400 F. 396 rms 810-990 F. Bkfst 70 F. Restaurant. Air cond. Garage parking.

The Frantour Suffren is a large, modern hotel located next to the Seine and the

CLASSICAL – HOTELS

Champ-de-Mars. The simple rooms are regularly refurbished and offer excellent equipment. There is an attractive, plant-filled restaurant (Le Champ de Mars), and a garden where meals are served in summer.

 Holiday Inn (République)
11th arr. - 10, pl. de la République
43 55 44 34,
fax 47 00 32 34
Open year-round. 4 stes 2,200-3,200 F. 314 rms 1,190-1,990 F. Bkfst incl. Restaurant. Air cond.

The architect Davioud, who designed the Châtelet, built this former Modern Palace in 1867. Today it belongs to the largest hotel chain in the world, which completely restored and modernised it. The rooms and suites are functional, pleasant and well soundproofed; the most attractive ones overlook the flower-filled covered courtyard. Restaurant: La Belle Epoque, see *Restaurants*.

 Le Jardin de Cluny
5th arr. - 9, rue du Sommerard
43 54 22 66
Open year-round. 40 rms 525-695 F. Bkfst 45 F. No pets.

A perfectly functional hotel, with comfortable rooms and modern bathrooms.

 Kléber
16th arr. - 7, rue de Belloy
47 23 80 22,
fax 49 52 07 20
Open year-round. 1 ste 950-1,250 F. 21 rms 670-780 F. Bkfst 45 F. Parking.

A family-run hotel managed in a thoroughly professional way, this impeccable little establishment has about 20 rooms spread over six floors. All are equipped with double-glazed windows and pretty bathrooms. The décor is modern but warm. Bar, no restaurant.

 Latitudes Saint-Germain
6th arr. - 7-11, rue Saint-Benoît
42 61 53 53,
fax 49 27 09 33
Open year-round. 117 rms 610-890 F. Bkfst 58 F. Air cond.

This large, modern hotel, opened in 1988, is located in the heart of Saint-Germain-des-Prés; it used to be a printing works, and its gracious turn-of-the-century façade has been preserved. The spacious rooms are well equipped, attractively decorated in pastel shades. A cellar jazz club provides hot and cool live music every night except Sunday, from 10:30 p.m.

 Lenox
14th arr. - 15, rue Delambre
43 35 34 50,
fax 43 20 46 64
Open year-round. 6 stes 890 F. 46 rms 490-610 F. Bkfst 45 F.

The lobby is cold rather than inviting, but the penthouse suites are attractive. Rooms vary in size, yet are uniformly comfortable and well maintained. Light meals are served at the bar until 2 a.m. (there is no restaurant).

 Madison
6th arr. - 143, bd St-Germain
43 29 72 50,
fax 40 51 60 01
Open year-round. 55 rms 680-1,220 F. Bkfst 60 F. Air cond.

A comfortable hotel with some antique furniture, and pretty Provençal tiles in the bathrooms. Very well equipped: double-glazing, air conditioning, minibar, satellite television, hairdryer. Smiling service and a generous buffet for breakfast.

 Mercure Paris-Bercy
13th arr. - 6, bd V.-Auriol
45 82 48 00,
fax 45 82 19 16
Open year-round. 89 rms 540-800 F. Restaurant. Air cond.

A modern hotel near the Bercy sports complex and the Gare d'Austerlitz, the Mercure offers easy access from the *périphérique* (the Paris ring road). Well suited to the needs of business people, the rooms are soundproofed and have a large desk area. Some rooms have a terrace.

 Mercure Paris Montparnasse
14th arr. - 20, rue de la Gaîté
43 35 28 28
Open year-round. 7 stes 1,100 F. 178 rms 590-900 F. Bkfst 35 F. Restaurant. Air cond. Garage parking.

The comfortable rooms are just big enough, with double-glazing, minibar, direct-line telephone and ten television channels. Functional bathrooms; generous breakfast buffet.

 Mercure Paris-Vaugirard
15th arr. - 69, bd Victor
45 33 74 63,
fax 48 28 22 11
Open year-round. 91 rms 680-1,500 F. Restaurant. Air cond. Garage parking.

The well-designed, air conditioned (with individual controls) and soundproofed rooms all offer modern amenities; the remarkable bathrooms are equipped with radios, hairdryers and magnifying mirrors. Perfect for business people (the Exhibition Centre is close at hand).

Remember to call ahead to reserve your room, and please, if you cannot honour your reservation, be courteous and let the hotel know.

111

HOTELS – CLASSICAL

Modern Hôtel Lyon
12th arr. - 3, rue Parrot
43 43 41 72

Open year-round. 1 ste 770-875 F. 47 rms 510-660 F. Bkfst 36 F. No pets.

The location is most convenient (near the Gare de Lyon). Rooms are comfortable, unpretentious and equipped with minibars. Thoughtful service.

Montana Tuileries
1st arr. - 12, rue St-Roch
42 60 35 10

Open year-round. 25 rms 580-1,050 F. Bkfst 50 F.

This very chic little hotel doesn't actually overlook the Tuileries Gardens, but they are only a stone's throw away. All double rooms, well equipped. Numbers 50 and 52 have balconies.

Napoléon
8th arr. - 40, av. de Friedland
47 66 02 02,
fax 47 66 82 33

Open year-round. 36 stes 1,550-4,500 F. 66 rms 800-1,950 F. Bkfst 75 F. Restaurant. Air cond. in 6 rms. Valet parking.

Admirably situated, this fine hotel provides top-flight service along with excellent equipment and amenities. The spacious rooms have classic (though not very cheery) décor. The pleasant banquet rooms (L'Etoile, for example) are much in demand for receptions and conferences. Restaurant: Le Napoléon, see *Restaurants*.

Hôtel des Nations
5th arr. - 54, rue Monge
43 26 45 24,
fax 46 34 00 13

Open year-round. 38 rms 550-580 F. Bkfst 50 F.

At this well-kept, functional hotel the curtains and bedcovers match the paper or fabric wallcoverings. Tiled bathrooms, double-glazing. Some rooms look out over a garden that in summer is filled with flowers.

Nikko de Paris
15th arr. - 61, quai de Grenelle
40 58 20 00,
fax 45 75 42 35

Open year-round. 9 stes 3,140-7,680 F. 772 rms 1,260-1,880 F. Restaurants. Half-board 1,555 F. Bkfst 75 F. Air cond. Heated pool. Valet parking.

Thirty-one floors piled up to resemble an immense beehive. You can opt either for vaguely Japanese-style or modern, ultrafunctional rooms; the large porthole windows overlook the Seine and the Pont Mirabeau. The six upper floors are reserved for luxury rooms with personalised service. Boutiques, conference rooms, a heated swimming pool with sauna, fitness club and a massage service are just some of the Nikko's attractive features. You'll also find an excellent bar, restaurants (Les Célébrités, see *Restaurants*) and a brasserie within the complex.

Parc Victor-Hugo
16th arr. - 55-57, av. R.-Poincaré
44 05 66 66,
fax 44 05 66 00

Open year-round. 117 rms 1,900-2,500 F. Bkfst 115 F. Restaurants. Air cond. Valet parking.

The management is putting the finishing touches to a full refurbishment of this sumptuous hotel, opened in 1987. You can expect to find perfectly comfortable, impeccably equipped rooms and a glorious large indoor garden.

Pavillon de la Reine
3rd arr. - 28, pl. des Vosges
42 77 96 40,
fax 42 77 63 06

Open year-round. 22 stes 1,800-3,200 F. 33 rms 1,400-1,600 F. Bkfst 90 F. Air cond. Valet parking.

The rooms and suites, all equipped with marble bathrooms, are tastefully decorated; they artfully blend authentic antiques with lovely reproductions. They overlook either the place des Vosges and its garden or a quiet inner patio filled with flowers. No restaurant.

Pullman Saint-Honoré
8th arr. - 15, rue Boissy d'Anglas
42 66 93 62,
fax 42 66 14 98

Open year-round. 7 stes 1,580 F. 112 rms 750-995 F. Bkfst 85 F. No pets.

Comfortable and functional, favoured by business travellers and visitors to the nearby American Embassy, this well-renovated hotel consists of seven storeys of identically furnished, pleasant, modern rooms with impeccable bathrooms. The bar, open from 10 a.m. to 2 a.m., is decorated with marquetry from the trains of the *Compagnie Internationale des Wagons Lits*. Ten duplexes are located on the seventh floor; there is one suite on the eighth floor. No restaurant, but light meals are available around the clock from room service, and the breakfast buffet is open until 10:30 a.m.

This symbol signifies hotels that offer an exceptional degree of peace and quiet.

HÔTEL
PLAZA ATHÉNÉE

25, Avenue Montaigne, 75008 Paris

Téléphone : (1) 47.23.78.33 ★ Téléfax : (1) 47.20.20.70 ★ Télex 650092 Plaza Paris

31, place de la Madeleine
Les grands crus
ont leur adresse.

Tél. : 42 68 00 16

31, place de la Madeleine the place where the best vintages are.

Château d'Yquem	Château Cheval Blanc
Château Margaux	Montrachet
Château Pétrus	Chambertin
Château Haut-Brion	Pommard
Château Latour	Romanée Conti
Château Mouton Rothschild	

*Ouverture de 9 h à 20 h
du lundi au samedi*

VISA - AMERICAN EXPRESS

CLASSICAL – HOTELS

Pullman Saint-Jacques
14th arr. - 17, bd Saint-Jacques
40 78 79 80,
fax 45 88 43 93

Open year-round. 14 stes 1,825-2,000 F. 797 rms 1,095-1,360 F. Bkfst 90 F. Restaurant. Air cond. Valet parking.

The Pullman Saint-Jacques is conveniently close to Orly airport. It offers good-sized rooms with comfortable bathrooms, air conditioning and blackout blinds that allow long-distance travellers to sleep off their jet lag. For entertainment, there are two bars and four restaurants; or you could ask one of the staff to show you the "Deluxe" suite, which has often served as a setting for films.

Pullman Windsor
8th arr. - 14, rue Beaujon
45 63 04 04,
fax 42 25 36 81

Open year-round. 5 stes 1,900-2,700 F. 130 rms 1,250-1,900 F. Bkfst 90 F. Restaurant. Air cond. Valet parking.

This solid, austere building, dating from 1925, houses a comfortable if charmless hotel, whose facilities (ultra-modern equipment for the business clientele) are constantly being updated. The largish, bright rooms are decorated with understated, functional furniture (minibars, TVs and video programming). Room service. Restaurant: Le Clovis, see *Restaurants*.

Quality Inn Paris-Rive Gauche
6th arr. - 92, rue de Vaugirard
42 22 00 56,
fax 42 22 05 39

Open year-round. 6 stes 960-1,025 F. 128 rms 600-890 F. Bkfst 60 F. Air cond. Garage parking. Rms equipped for disabled.

Part of an American chain with about 1,000 hotels worldwide, this is a quiet, elegant establishment. Well-equipped rooms with minibar and satellite TV, some furnished in cruise-liner style. Piano bar filled with plants. Substantial breakfasts are served until 11 a.m. Impeccable service.

Le Relais de Lyon
12th arr. - 64, rue Crozatier
43 44 22 50

Open year-round. 34 rms 400-498 F. Bkfst 35 F. No pets. Garage parking.

This pleasant hotel provides bright, comfortable, well-equipped rooms which are absolutely quiet (double glazing, blinds). Most overlook a little patch of garden, and those on the fifth floor have a terrace. Friendly reception.

Résidence Bassano
16th arr. - 15, rue de Bassano
47 23 78 23,
fax 47 20 41 22

Open year-round. 3 stes 1,600-1,950 F. 27 rms 750-1,150 F. Bkfst 65 F. Air cond. No pets. Parking.

Housed in a building of Haussmann vintage, the high-class accommodation offers impeccable, thoughtfully designed and equipped guest rooms, enhanced with Art Deco–style furniture. Among the amenities are a sauna, Jacuzzi and 24-hour room service.

Résidence Monceau
8th arr. - 85, rue du Rocher
45 22 75 11,
fax 45 22 30 88

Open year-round. 1 ste 820 F. 50 rms 615 F. Bkfst 42 F.

Though it lacks atmosphere, the Résidence Monceau is functional and well kept, and employs courteous staff. All the rooms have private bathrooms, TVs, minibars and automatic alarm clocks. Good privacy; breakfast is served on a patio. No restaurant.

Résidence Saint-Honoré
8th arr. - 214, rue du Faubourg-St-Honoré
42 25 26 27,
fax 45 63 30 67

Open year-round. 91 rms 630-1,000 F. Bkfst 40 F. Air cond. in 70 rms.

A surprising range of styles has been used in the gradual renovation of the spacious rooms, which are more comfortable than luxurious. Dynamic management, uncommonly courteous staff. The Saint-Honoré auction rooms are situated on the hotel's lower level.

Rond-Point de Longchamp
16th arr. - 86, rue de Longchamp
45 05 13 63,
fax 47 55 12 80

Open year-round. 57 rms 590-1,200 F. Bkfst 45 F. Restaurant. Air cond.

The sizeable, comfortable rooms are nicely fitted and prettily decorated (grey carpeting, burr-walnut furniture), and have marble bathrooms. There is an elegant restaurant with a fireplace, as well as a billiards room.

Saint-Ferdinand
17th arr. - 36, rue St-Ferdinand
45 72 66 66,
fax 45 74 12 92

Open year-round. 42 rms 630-820 F. Bkfst 40 F. Air cond. in 27 rms.

This small, functional hotel opened in 1985. The rooms are tiny (the bathrooms even more so), but they are well equipped, with television, minibar, safe and hairdryer. Soothing décor.

HOTELS – CLASSICAL

Saxe-Résidence
7th arr. - 9, villa de Saxe
47 83 98 28,
fax 47 83 85 47
Open year-round. 4 stes 760 F. 48 rms 545-710 F. Bkfst 55 F. Parking. No pets.
Situated between two convents and a bouquet of secret gardens, this hotel is miraculously quiet. The rooms are constantly updated, and there is a 1950s-style bar. Even the singles are of decent size. Courteous reception.

Hôtel de Sévigné
16th arr. - 6, rue de Belloy
47 20 88 90,
fax 40 70 98 73
Open year-round. 30 rms 630-760 F. Bkfst 42 F. Garage parking.
A classic hotel. The modern, comfortable rooms have white walls, flowered curtains and tiled bathrooms. Friendly service and reception.

Splendid Etoile
17th arr. - 1 bis, av. Carnot
45 72 72 00,
fax 45 72 72 01
Open year-round. 7 stes 1,450 F. 50 rms 880-1,150 F. Bkfst 70 F. Restaurant. Air cond. in 30 rms. No pets.
The Splendid Etoile features 50 well-maintained, comfortably furnished, good-sized rooms, all with double glazing (some afford views of the Arc de Triomphe). Attractive English-style bar. Restaurant: Le Pré Carré.

Sofitel Paris
15th arr. - 8, rue Louis-Armand
40 60 30 30,
fax 45 57 04 22
Open year-round. 2 stes & 11 junior stes 1,900-2,250 F. 622 rms 950 F. Bkfst 80 F. Restaurants. Air cond. Heated pool. Valet parking.
Thirty-seven meeting and conference rooms (with simultaneous translation available in five languages) are connected to a central administration office. The hotel also features recreational facilities (exercise room, sauna and a heated swimming pool with sliding roof on the 23rd floor) and a panoramic bar. The rooms, all equipped with magnetic closing systems, were recently renovated. Restaurant: Le Relais de Sèvres, see *Restaurants*.

Terrass Hôtel
18th arr. - 12, rue Joseph-de-Maistre
46 06 72 85,
fax 42 52 29 11
Open year-round. 13 stes 1,330-1,780 F. 88 rms 800-950 F. Bkfst 60 F. Restaurant. Half-board 735-1,000 F. Air cond in 6 rms. Garage parking.
A just-completed renovation has spruced up this excellent hotel. Located at the foot of the Butte Montmartre, the Terrass offers a majestic view of almost all of Paris. Rooms are comfortable and nicely fitted, with some more attractive furniture and Italian-tile bathrooms. Up on the seventh floor, the panoramic terrace doubles as a bar in summer. Restaurant: Le Guerlande.

Victoria Palace
6th arr. - 6, rue Blaise-Desgoffe
45 44 38 16,
fax 45 49 23 75
Open year-round. 110 rms 780-1,320 F. Bkfst 50 F. No pets. Garage parking.
Still a reliable establishment, despite slightly tired décor (currently undergoing renovation). The rooms are sizeable and comfortable, with really spacious wardrobes and good bathrooms. Bar and restaurant.

Vieux Paris
6th arr. - 9, rue Gît-le-Cœur
43 54 41 66,
fax 43 26 00 15.
Open year-round. 7 stes 1,370-1,470 F. 13 rms 1,070-1,270 F. Bkfst 90 F. No pets.
Here's a hotel that wears its name well, for it was built in the 15th century. An overhaul in 1991 turned the Vieux Paris into a luxurious stopover, whose comfort and first-rate amenities fully justify the high rates. Rooms are handsomely furnished and perfectly quiet, with Jacuzzis in every bathroom. Warm reception.

Vigny
8th arr. - 9, rue Balzac
40 75 04 39,
fax 40 75 05 81
Open year-round. 12 stes 2,600-5,000 F. 25 rms 1,700-2,200 F. Bkfst 90 F. Restaurant. Air cond. Valet parking.
A handsome and brand-new hotel, the Vigny offers English mahogany furniture, comfortable beds and fine marble bathrooms: the virtues of another age simplified and brought up to date. The suites provide all-out luxury. Excellent service. Lunch and light suppers are served at the bar (Le Baretto) designed by Adam Tihany.

Yllen
15th arr. - 196, rue de Vaugirard
45 67 67 67,
fax 45 67 74 37
Open year-round. 1 ste 950-1,070 F. 39 rms 490-710 F. Bkfst 40 F.
Yllen's modern, functional rooms have understated décor and are well soundproofed—but they are very small. Corner rooms (those with numbers ending in 4) on the upper floors are the best. Energetic management, friendly reception.

> *Remember to call ahead to reserve your room, and please, if you cannot honour your reservation, be courteous and let the hotel know.*

CHARMING

Abbaye Saint-Germain
6th arr. - 10, rue Cassette
45 44 38 11,
fax 45 48 07 86

Open year-round. 4 stes 1,660-1,900 F. 44 rms 800-1,400 F. Air cond. in 7 rms. No pets. No cards.

Set back from the street, this serene 18th-century residence located between a courtyard and a garden offers well-kept, elegantly decorated rooms which are not, however, particularly spacious; the most delightful are on the same level as the garden (number 4 even has a terrace). No restaurant.

Agora
1st arr. - 7, rue de la Cossonnerie
42 33 46 02,
fax 42 33 80 99

Open year-round. 29 rms 315-580 F. Bkfst 30 F.

In the heart of the pedestrian district of Les Halles, these rooms are exquisitely decorated and well soundproofed. Lovely pieces of period furniture and engravings are everywhere; the cleanliness is impressive. Cheerful reception. No restaurant.

Angleterre
6th arr. - 44, rue Jacob
42 60 34 72,
fax 42 60 16 93

Open year-round. 3 stes 1,100-1,300 F. 26 rms 700-900 F. Bkfst 40 F.

Hemingway once lived in this former British Embassy, built around a flower-filled patio. The impeccable rooms have been completely renovated; some are quite spacious, with high beamed ceilings. Large, comfortable beds; luxurious bathrooms. Downstairs, there is a bar and lounge with a piano.

Atala
8th arr. - 10, rue Chateaubriand
45 62 01 62,
fax 42 25 66 38

Open year-round. 1 ste 1,400 F. 48 rms 750-1,300 F. Bkfst 50 F. Restaurant. Air cond. in 30 rms.

In a quiet street near the Champs-Elysées, this hotel provides cheerfully decorated rooms that open onto a verdant garden. Balconies and terraces come with rooms on the sixth and eighth floors. L'Atalante, the hotel's bar and restaurant, offers garden dining in fine weather. Excellent service.

Banville
17th arr. - 166, bd Berthier
42 67 70 16,
fax 44 40 42 77

Open year-round. 39 rms 550-650 F. Bkfst 40 F.

A fine small hotel, with flowers at the windows (some of which open to panoramic views of Paris) and bright, cheerful rooms, well soundproofed thanks to thick carpeting. Marble or tile bathrooms. Excellent English breakfasts; no restaurant.

Belle Epoque
12th arr. - 66, rue de Charenton
43 44 06 66,
fax 43 44 10 25

Open year-round. 3 stes 800 F. 30 rms 500-740 F. Bkfst 50 F.

Not far from the Gare de Lyon, this well-kept hotel is furnished and decorated in 1930s style. Comfortable beds, modern bathrooms and double-glazing throughout.

Bersoly's Saint-Germain
7th arr. - 28, rue de Lille
42 60 73 79,
fax 49 27 05 55

Closed Aug. 2-30. 16 rms 550-650 F. Bkfst 50 F.

The hotel's furniture is largely provided by the nearby "golden triangle" of antique dealers; reproduction paintings adorn the walls. Breakfast is served in the attractive vaulted basement. Faultless reception.

Brighton
1st arr. - 218, rue de Rivoli
42 60 30 03,
fax 42 60 41 78

Open year-round. 1 ste 1,000 F. 69 rms 360-780 F. Restaurant. No pets.

A dream setting opposite the Tuileries gardens, near the Louvre, is offered at very reasonable prices. The large rooms on the rue de Rivoli have wonderful views, high moulded ceilings, huge brass beds, 19th-century furniture and good-sized bathrooms. The little attic rooms are especially good value.

Centre Ville Etoile
17th arr. - 6, rue des Acacias
43 80 56 18,
fax 47 54 93 43

Open year-round. 20 rms 650-900 F. Bkfst 50 F. Air cond. Restaurant.

A quiet building, tastefully refurbished. The attractive, contemporary rooms boast minitels (electronic telephone directories), satellite TV and spotless bathrooms. Restaurant: Le Cougar, see *Restaurants*.

RAC PARIS STREETS: *The cartography of this city-wide street plan of Paris is clear and easy to use and is supported by a comprehensive index in book form tipped on to the card cover. The map is packed with essential information including the direction of one-way streets. A must for all visitors to Paris. Price: £ 4.50.*

HOTELS – CHARMING

Crystal Hôtel
6th arr. - 24, rue St-Benoît
45 48 85 14,
fax 45 49 16 45

Open year-round. 1 ste 1,000-1,200 F. 25 rms 480-700 F. Bkfst 38 F.

A charming small hotel with a friendly atmosphere, favoured by artists and writers. The rooms are simply decorated with some antique furniture, and there are thoughtfully equipped bathrooms.

Danemark
6th arr. - 21, rue Vavin
43 26 93 78,
fax 46 34 66 06

Open year-round. 15 rms 540-720 F. Bkfst 40 F. Air cond.

This small hotel was carefully renovated in 1930s style. Rooms are not very large, but elegant, with pleasant lighting, mahogany, ash or oak furniture and grey-marble bathrooms (number 10 has a Jacuzzi). No restaurant.

Les Deux Iles
4th arr. - 59, rue Saint-Louis-en-l'Ile
43 26 13 35,
fax 43 29 60 25

Open year-round. 17 rms 620-750 F. Bkfst 39 F. No cards.

This particularly welcoming hotel, like many buildings on the Ile-Saint-Louis, is a lovely 17th-century house. You'll sleep close to the Seine in small, pretty rooms decorated with bright fabrics and painted furniture. No restaurant.

Duc de Saint-Simon
7th arr. - 14, rue Saint-Simon
45 48 35 66,
fax 45 48 68 25

Open year-round. 5 stes 1,500-1,900 F. 29 rms 1,000-1,500 F. Bkfst 70 F. Air cond. in 8 rms. No cards.

Set back from the street between two gardens, this quiet, elegant 19th-century building houses a most appealing hotel. Fully renovated by its Swedish owners, it provides discreet luxury and comfort, with antiques, fine paintings and objets d'art, good lighting and enchanting décor. The four rooms on the second floor have terraces that overlook the garden. There is a bar, but no restaurant.

Ducs d'Anjou
1st arr. - 1, rue Saint-Opportune
42 36 92 24,
fax 42 36 16 63

Open year-round. 38 rms 390-840 F. Bkfst 42 F.

Located on the delightful small place Sainte-Opportune, this ancient building has been restored from top to bottom. The rooms are small (as are the bathrooms) but quiet; rooms 61 and 62 are larger, and can comfortably accommodate three people. Rooms overlooking the courtyard are a bit gloomy. No restaurant.

Elysée
8th arr. - 12, rue des Saussaies
42 65 29 25,
fax 42 64 64 28

Open year-round. 2 stes 1,250-1,450 F. 30 rms 540-950 F. Bkfst 60 F. Air cond. in 2 rms. No pets.

An intimate, tastefully renovated hotel where you will receive a most pleasant welcome. All the rooms are different; the two suites under the eaves are particularly in demand.

Ermitage Hôtel
18th arr. - 24, rue Lamarck
42 64 79 22,
fax 42 64 10 33

Open year-round. 12 rms 320-420 F. No pets. No cards.

This charming hotel occupies a little white building behind the Sacré-Cœur. Personalised décor in each room; pretty bathrooms. There is a garden and terrace for relaxing after a busy day. Friendly reception.

Etoile Park Hôtel
17th arr. - 10, av. Mac-Mahon
42 67 69 63,
fax 43 80 18 99

Open year-round. 28 rms 455-710 F. Bkfst 49 F.

Modern and decorated in understated good taste, this hotel offers refined but somehow cold guest rooms. Well-designed bathrooms. Extremely good-humoured reception.

Etoile-Pereire
17th arr. - 146, bd Pereire
42 67 60 00,
fax 42 67 02 90

Open year-round. 5 stes 900 F. 21 rooms 500-700 F. Bkfst 50 F. No pets.

Attention to detail is a priority at this welcoming hotel. Located at the back of a quiet courtyard, the spacious rooms are most attractive. More than 20 different varieties of delicious jams are served at breakfast. Both the atmosphere and service are charming and cheerful. No restaurant.

Ferrandi
6th arr. - 92, rue du Cherche-Midi
42 22 97 40,
fax 45 44 89 97

Open year-round. 1 ste 850-1,250 F. 41 rms 440-950 F. Bkfst 60 F. Parking.

In a quiet street near Montparnasse, with a reception area that matches the charm of the rooms. Some of the guest rooms have four-poster beds, others a fireplace. All have good bathrooms (with hairdryers) and double-glazing. Delightful reception.

Garden Elysée
16th arr. - 12, rue Saint-Didier
47 55 01 11,
fax 47 27 79 24

Open year-round. 48 rms 800-1,600 F. Restaurant. Half-board

800-1,560 F. Bkfst 80 F. Air cond. No pets. Parking.

Located in a new building set back from the street are elegant, unusually spacious rooms that overlook a bucolic garden (where breakfast is served on warm days). The 1930s décor is fresh and appealing, and the equipment is particularly fine (satellite television, individual safes, Jacuzzi).

Hameau de Passy
16th arr. - 48, rue de Passy
42 88 47 55,
fax 42 30 83 72

Open year-round. 32 rms 480-560 F. Bkfst 25 F.

Tucked away in a flower-filled cul-de-sac, this exceptionally quiet hotel was modernised in 1990. Plain, comfortable rooms, some connecting, all overlook the garden. Smiling service and reception.

L'Hôtel
6th arr. - 13, rue des Beaux-Arts
43 25 27 22,
fax 43 25 64 81

Open year-round. 3 stes 2,700-3,500 F. 24 rms 900-2,100 F. Bkfst 90 F. Restaurant. Air cond.

The little effort given to the renovation explains the slightly faded character of the rooms in this delightful Directoire-style building—whether it's number 16, the room once occupied by Oscar Wilde, the Imperial room (decorated in a neo-Egyptian style), the Cardinale room (swathed in purple) or number 36, which contains the Art Deco furniture from the home of music-hall star Mistinguett. The seventh floor houses two lovely suites. Despite the dog-eared décor, the atmosphere here reproduces that of a private home and is truly unlike what one usually finds in a hotel. Restaurant: Le Bélier, see Restaurants, and piano bar on the premises.

Hôtel du Jeu de Paume
4th arr. - 54, rue Saint-Louis-en-l'Ile
43 26 14 18,
fax 40 46 02 76

Open year-round. 32 rms 770-1,200 F. Bkfst 70 F. No pets.

This is a 17th-century building with a splendid wood-and-stone interior, featuring a glass lift that ferries guests to their bright, quiet rooms. There is a pleasant little garden too.

Hôtel Left Bank
6th arr. - 9, rue de l'Ancienne-Comédie
43 54 01 70,
fax 43 26 17 14

Open year-round. 1 ste 1,100 F. 30 rms 850-950 F. Bkfst 25 F. Air cond.

An 18th-century building, with loads of charm. The tasteful but rather repetitive décor features custom-made walnut furniture in Louis XIII style, lace bedcovers, brass lamps and marble bathrooms.

Hôtel du Léman
9th arr. - 20, rue de Trévise
42 46 50 66,
fax 48 24 27 59

Open year-round. 24 rms 370-710 F. Bkfst 40 F.

This charming, out-of-the-ordinary small hotel has been tastefully modernised. Tuscany marble inlays enhance the modern décor in the lobby. The rooms are pleasantly decorated with attractive bedside lamps and original drawings and watercolours. Some have king-size beds. Generous buffet breakfast served in the vaulted basement.

Lenox
7th arr. - 9, rue de l'Université
42 96 10 95,
fax 42 61 52 83

Open year-round. 2 stes 840 F. 32 rms 510-710 F. Bkfst 45 F. No pets.

These petite but most attractive rooms were recently renovated with elegant wallpaper and stylish furniture; numbers 22, 32 and 42 are the most enchanting. On the top floor are two split-level suites with exposed beams and flower-filled balconies. No restaurant, but cold meals may be served in the rooms.

Hôtel Lido
8th arr. - 4, pass. de la Madeleine
42 66 27 37,
fax 42 66 61 23

Open year-round. 32 rms 730-830 F.

A laudable establishment, situated between the Madeleine and the place de la Concorde. The lobby is most elegant, with Oriental rugs on the floor and tapestries on the stone walls. The guest rooms, decorated in pink, blue or cream, have comfortable beds with white lace covers, modern bathrooms and double-glazed windows. The staff are thoughtful and courteous.

Lutèce
4th arr. - 65, rue Saint-Louis-en-l'Ile
43 26 23 52,
fax 43 29 60 25

Open year-round. 23 rms 590-740 F. Bkfst 42 F. No pets. No cards.

A tasteful, small hotel for people who love Paris, this handsome old house has some 20 rooms (there are two charming mansards on the upper floor), with whitewashed walls and ceiling beams, decorated with bright, cheerful fabrics. The bathrooms are small but modern and impeccably kept. The lobby features lavish bouquets and a stone fireplace which is often used in winter. No restaurant.

HOTELS – CHARMING

Hôtel Moulin
9th arr. - 39, rue Fontaine
42 81 93 25,
fax 40 16 09 90

Open year-round. 2 stes 940 F. 48 rms 520-690 F. Bkfst 50 F. No pets.

A hotel full of charm and surprises near the place Pigalle, with its appealing Pompeii-style lobby and rooms of varying sizes (some are extended by a small terrace overlooking the inner courtyards). An excellent buffet-style breakfast is served until noon. No restaurant.

Majestic
16th arr. - 29, rue Dumont-d'Urville
45 00 83 70,
fax 45 01 21 50

Open year-round. 3 stes 1,600 F-1,800 F. 27 rms 1,000-1,300 F. Bkfst 55 F. Air cond. in 14 rms.

Some rooms are awaiting redecoration, but all boast comfortable beds, thick carpeting and on the top floor, a lovely penthouse features a small balcony filled with flowers. Old-World atmosphere. No restaurant.

Les Marronniers
6th arr. - 21, rue Jacob
43 25 30 60,
fax 40 46 83 56

Open year-round. 37 rms 440-690 F. Bkfst 45 F. No pets. No cards.

Set back slightly from the rue Jacob, this delightful hotel includes a small garden where breakfast is served. Choose a room just above this garden, or one of the rather bizarre but absolutely adorable (and bright) attic rooms on the seventh floor, which have views of the belfry of Saint-Germain-des-Prés. No television, no radio: your tranquillity is assured!

Notre-Dame Hôtel
5th arr. - 1, quai St-Michel
43 54 20 43,
fax 43 26 61 75

Open year-round. 3 stes 1,030 F. 26 rms 570-770 F. Bkfst 35F.

Situated in a noisy area, but the hotel is protected by effective double-glazing. The sixth floor houses three split-level attic rooms with red carpeting, rustic furniture and a mezzanine that affords superb views over Notre-Dame and the Seine.

Panthéon
5th arr. - 19, pl. du Panthéon
43 54 32 95,
fax 43 26 64 65

Open year-round. 34 rms 500-700 F. Bkfst 35 F. No pets.

Clever use of mirrors makes the entrance and lounge seem bigger. The elegant rooms are quite spacious, decorated in Louis XVI or Louis-Philippe style, with fabric wallcoverings in pastel colours. Room 33 has a four-poster bed; all rooms are equipped with minibars and cable television.

Regent's Garden Hôtel
17th arr. - 6, rue Pierre-Demours
45 74 07 30,
fax 40 55 01 42

Open year-round. 39 rms 620-900 F. Bkfst 36 F. Parking.

This handsome Second Empire building, just a stone's throw from the place de l'Etoile, offers large, nicely proportioned rooms with high, ornate ceilings. Comfortable and well kept, the hotel also offers a gorgeous flower garden. No restaurant.

Relais Christine
6th arr. - 3, rue Christine
43 26 71 80,
fax 43 26 89 38

Open year-round. 17 stes 1,950-2,500 F. 34 rms 1,300-1,450 F. Bkfst 80 F. Air cond. No pets. Valet parking.

This 16th-century cloister was transformed into a luxury hotel in the early 1980s. While it has retained some of the peace of its earlier vocation, the hotel now boasts all the comfort and elegance of the present age, from double-glazing to perfect service. The rooms are all decorated in individual styles, with Provençal prints and pink Portuguese marble baths. The best rooms are the two-level suites and the ground-floor room with private terrace, but all are spacious, comfortable, quiet and air conditioned, with marble bathrooms. Courteous reception. No restaurant.

Relais Saint-Germain
6th arr. - 9, carrefour de l'Odéon
43 29 12 05,
fax 46 33 45 30

Open year-round. 1 ste 1,790 F. 10 rms 1,190-1,380 F. Bkfst incl. Air cond.

About ten large rooms, all different, are decorated in a refined and luxurious manner, with superb furniture, lovely fabrics, exquisite lighting and beautiful, perfectly equipped marble bathrooms. The tall, double-glazed windows open onto the lively Odéon crossroads. You are bound to fall in love with Paris staying at this tiny jewel of an establishment. No restaurant.

Saint-Grégoire
6th arr. - 43, rue de l'Abbé-Grégoire
45 48 23 23,
fax 45 48 33 95

Open year-round. 1 ste 1,000-1,200 F. 19 rms 720-1,200 F. Bkfst 60 F. Air cond. in 2 rms. No pets.

The cosy lounge has a fireplace and there's also a small garden. The rooms are painted in attractive shades of yellow and pink, with matching chintz curtains, white damask bedspreads and some fine antique furniture. Double-glazing and modern bathrooms. Perfect breakfasts.

Saint-Louis
4th arr. - 75, rue Saint-Louis-en-l'Ile
46 34 04 80,
fax 46 34 02 13

Open year-round. 21 rms 620-720 F. Bkfst 42 F. No cards.

Elegant simplicity characterises this appealing hotel, where attention to detail is evident in the gorgeous flower arrangements and polished antiques. Small, perfectly soundproofed rooms offer comfortable beds and thick carpeting underfoot. Modern bathrooms, but no lift. No restaurant.

Saint-Louis Marais
4th arr. - 1, rue Charles-V
48 87 87 04,
fax 48 87 33 26

Open year-round. 16 rms 490-690 F. Bkfst 37 F. No pets.

Reasonable prices and a delightful reception at this former convent annexe in the heart of historic Paris. Each room is different, but all are charming and comfortable.

Saint-Merry
4th arr. - 78, rue de la Verrerie
42 78 14 15,
fax 40 29 06 82

Open year-round. 12 rms 400-1,000 F. Bkfst 40 F. No pets. No cards.

A former presbytery, this 17th-century building is home to an original collection of Gothic furniture, which the owner has been buying at auctions for over 30 years. Unusually large rooms with bathrooms not much bigger than cupboards, and no television. But the charm of the place is such that you have to book well in advance during the summer. Renovation work is under way.

Hôtel des Saints-Pères
6th arr. - 65, rue des Saints-Pères
45 44 50 00,
fax 45 44 90 83

Open year-round. 3 stes 1,600 F. 37 rms 400-1,200 F. Bkfst 50 F. Air cond. No pets.

Situated in two buildings, with all the elegantly furnished rooms overlooking a garden. Suite 205 is particularly attractive. Professional service.

Sainte-Beuve
6th arr. - 9, rue Sainte-Beuve
45 48 20 07,
fax 45 48 67 52

Open year-round. 1 ste 1,600 F. 22 rms 600-1,250 F. Bkfst 80 F. No pets.

The Sainte-Beuve is a tasteful, harmonious example of the neo-Palladian style of decoration, promoted in particular by David Hicks. In the guest rooms soft colours, chintzes and the odd antique create a soothing atmosphere. Most attractive too are the marble-and-tile bathrooms, and the elegant lobby with its comfortable sofas arranged around the fireplace. No restaurant.

Select Hôtel
5th arr. - 1, pl. de la Sorbonne
46 34 14 80,
fax 46 34 51 79

Open year-round. 1 ste 980-1,300 F. 67 rms 490-860 F. Bkfst 30 F. Air cond. in 45 rms.

A glass-roofed atrium with an abundance of plants has been built at the heart of this hotel next door to the Sorbonne. The pleasant, spacious rooms are functionally furnished. Generous buffet breakfast.

Solférino
7th arr. - 91, rue de Lille
47 05 85 54,
fax 45 55 51 16

Closed Dec. 23-Jan. 3. 32 rms 245-598 F. Bkfst 35 F. Air cond. No pets.

Almost opposite the Musée d'Orsay, here are simple rooms done in fresh colours, with bath or shower. There is a charming little lounge, a sky-lit breakfast room and charming ornaments everywhere: The Solférino is both relaxing and pleasantly antiquated. Friendly reception. No restaurant.

For whom the clock tolls

The first public clock in Paris, dating from 1370, is still ticking away on a turret of the *Conciergerie* (a medieval fortress on the Ile de la Cité). The clock's darkest hour was during the Revolution, when its chimes told thousands of unfortunate inmates of this palace-turned-prison that their time was up. Prisoners condemned at the courthouse next door spent their last night at the Conciergerie before heading to the guillotine at dawn. Among the famous victims were Queen Marie-Antoinette and the revolutionary leaders Danton and Robespierre.

HOTELS – PRACTICAL

 Suède
7th arr. - 31, rue Vaneau
47 05 18 65,
fax 47 05 69 27
Open year-round. 1 ste 1,050 F. 40 rms 540-850 F. Bkfst 50 F. No pets.

Decorated in tones of grey in a refined but rather austere Empire style, the guest rooms are quiet and nicely equipped. From the third floor up you'll have a view of the foliage and the parties given in the Matignon gardens. No restaurant. Bar and snack service from 6:30 a.m. to 10 p.m.

 Tamise
1st arr. - 4, rue d'Alger
42 60 51 54,
fax 42 86 89 97
Open year-round. 19 rms 450-650 F. No pets.

Designed by the architect Visconti and situated just 20 yards from the Tuileries Gardens, this tiny establishment offers authentic luxury (note the pretty English furniture—in keeping with the hotel's name which is French for "Thames") at astonishingly low rates.

 Université
7th arr. - 22, rue de l'Université
42 61 09 39,
fax 42 60 40 84
Open year-round. 27 rms 600-1,400 F. Bkfst 50 F. No pets. No cards.

Comfortable beds and modern bathrooms are featured in an intelligently renovated 17th-century residence that is most appealing with its beams, half-timbering and period furniture.

 Varenne
7th arr. - 44, rue de Bourgogne
45 51 45 55,
fax 45 51 86 63
Open year-round. 24 rms 470-630 F. Bkfst 37 F.

A cheerful reception is assured at this small hotel whose provincial air is underlined by a courtyard filled with flowers

and trees (where breakfast is served on sunny days). The rooms overlooking the street have double windows. No restaurant.

 La Villa Maillot
16th arr. - 143, av. de Malakoff
45 01 25 22,
fax 45 00 60 61
Open year-round. 3 stes 2,200-2,400 F. 39 rms 1,680-1,800 F. Bkfst 100 F. Restaurant. Air cond. Valet parking.

Formerly an embassy, this recent conversion is sophisticated and modern: an exemplary establishment. The very comfortable rooms, equipped with kitchenettes, have a grey and beige colour scheme that gives them an Art Deco feel. Pink-marble bathrooms; wonderful breakfast buffet served in an indoor garden.

PRACTICAL

 Alison
8th arr. - 21, rue de Surène
42 65 54 00,
fax 42 65 08 17
Open year-round. 35 rms 420-690 F. Bkfst 45 F. No pets.

The 35 modern, functional rooms are bright and cheerful, with tidy, tiled bathrooms. Bar and lounge on the ground floor. Two mansard rooms on the top floor can be combined to form a suite. No restaurant.

 Ambassade
16th arr. - 79, rue Lauriston
45 53 41 15,
fax 45 53 30 80
Closed Aug. 38 rms 440-550 F. Bkfst 35 F.

The rooms behind a lovely façade are decorated with printed wallpaper and lacquered cane furniture. Small grey-marble bathrooms. Ask for a room overlooking the courtyard and you'll think

you're in the country. No restaurant.

 Aurore Montmartre
9th arr. - 76, rue de Clichy
48 74 85 56,
fax 42 81 09 54
Open year-round. 24 rms 370-420 F. Bkfst 35 F.

A simple hotel offering smallish rooms, soundproofed and perfectly kept. Minibar. Friendly reception.

 Beaugrenelle St-Charles
15th arr. - 82, rue St-Charles
45 78 61 63,
fax 45 49 04 38
Open year-round. 51 rms 350-440 F. Bkfst 32 F.

Near the Beaugrenelle shopping complex, this friendly hotel provides modern, well-equipped rooms decorated in restful colours. Breakfast is served in the rooms upon request. Good value.

 Bergère
9th arr. - 34, rue Bergère
47 70 34 34,
fax 47 70 36 36
Open year-round. 134 rms 490-890 F. Bkfst 45 F.

All the quiet rooms (most of which overlook a courtyard garden) have been freshened up and modernised, including the bathrooms. The setting is modern and simple, with country-style furniture. Fine equipment.

 Le Bois
16th arr. - 11, rue du Dôme
45 00 31 96,
fax 45 00 90 05
Open year-round. 41 rms 395-58 F. Bkfst 40 F.

This simple hotel offers excellent value. In addition to a warm welcome, guests find small, well-kept rooms, which were attractively redecorated in 1990 with Laura Ashley fabrics and wallpaper.

Hôtel des Chevaliers
3rd arr. - 30, rue de Turenne
42 72 73 47,
fax 42 72 54 10

Open year-round. 24 rms 530-580 F. Bkfst 40 F. Parking.

In the heart of the Marais, a small hotel frequented by cinema people. The rooms are bright and pleasantly furnished; some are perfectly quiet. Warm reception.

Hôtel du Collège de France
5th arr. - 7, rue Thénard
43 26 78 36,
fax 46 34 58 29

Open year-round. 29 rms 480-530 F. Bkfst 30 F. Air cond. No pets.

The simple rooms of Hôtel du Collège de France, located on a quiet little street, are tidy and comfortable. Most charming are the garret rooms, with their wooden beams and a view of the towers of Notre-Dame. No restaurant.

Eber Monceau-Courcelles
17th arr. - 18, rue Léon-Jost
46 22 60 70,
fax 47 63 01 01

Open year-round. 5 stes 995-1,260 F. 13 rms 580-630 F. Bkfst 50 F. No pets.

This former bordello has been totally renovated, and "adopted," so to speak, by people in fashion, photography and the cinema. Rooms are on the small side, but they are tastefully decorated and furnished, with good bathrooms. A large, two-level suite on the top floor has a lovely terrace. Breakfast is served on the patio in summer. No restaurant.

Etoile
17th arr. - 3, rue de l'Etoile
43 80 36 94,
fax 44 40 49 19

Open year-round. 25 rms 820-920 F. Bkfst 50 F.

L'Etoile is strategically located between the place de l'Etoile and the place des Ternes. Rooms are clean, modern and functional (renovated in 1991). A little expensive for the level of comfort and service. No restaurant. Courteous reception.

Favart
2nd arr. - 5, rue de Marivaux
42 97 59 83

Open year-round. 37 rms 495-600 F. Bkfst incl.

Goya stayed here when he fled to Paris in 1824. Set on a quiet square opposite the Opéra Comique, this hotel exudes a certain faded charm. Reasonable rates.

Hôtel Flora
10th arr. - 1-3, cour de la Ferme-St-Lazare
48 24 84 84,
fax 48 00 91 03

Open year-round. 45 rms 525-610 F. Bkfst 40 F.

Near the Gare du Nord and the Gare de l'Est, the Flora offers pleasant, well-equipped, modern rooms decorated in pastel shades.

Folkestone
8th arr. - 9, rue Castellane
42 65 73 09,
fax 42 65 64 09

Open year-round. 50 rms 680-950 F. Bkfst 45 F.

The beamed rooms, decorated with fabric wallcovering or Japanese wallpaper, have Art Deco armchairs and comfortable beds. Generous buffet breakfasts, with sweet rolls and pastries baked on the premises. Gracious reception.

Fondary
15th arr. - 30, rue Fondary
45 75 14 75,
fax 45 75 84 42

Open year-round. 20 rms 365-405 F. Bkfst 38 F. Air cond.

A neat and tidy hotel with pretty pastel décor. Service is warm and efficient. No restaurant.

Grands Hommes
5th arr. - 17, pl. du Panthéon
46 34 19 60,
fax 43 26 67 32

Open year-round. 32 rms 500-700 F. Bkfst 35 F. No pets.

Opposite the Panthéon. The fairly spacious rooms are decorated with pink, cream or floral fabric wallcoverings. Room 22 has a four-poster bed, 60 and 61 boast balconies and pleasant views. Cable television, minibar. The staff are friendly and efficient.

Ibis Jemmapes
10th arr. - 12, rue Louis-Blanc
42 01 21 21,
fax 42 08 21 40

Open year-round. 1 ste 1,000-1,200 F. 50 rms 370-445 F. Bkfst 35 F. Garage parking.

Near the Canal Saint-Martin, this well-designed business hotel is perfectly tailored for a busy clientele attending conventions and seminars. The rooms (which we found to be on the chilly side) are spacious, modern and fully equipped. Generous breakfast buffet. No restaurant.

Ibis Paris-Bercy
12th arr. - 77, rue de Bercy
43 42 91 91,
fax 43 42 34 79

Open year-round. 368 rms 455 F. Bkfst 35 F. Restaurant. Half-board 640 F. Parking.

This very professional establishment, surely one of the best in the chain, has a superb marble lobby. Guest rooms have blue-and-white décor and dark carpeting. One room on each floor is reserved for

HOTELS – PRACTICAL

the disabled. Plain, well-kept bathrooms.

Istria
14th arr. - 29, rue Campagne-Première
43 20 91 82,
fax 43 22 48 45

Open year-round. 26 rms 440-540 F. Bkfst 40 F.

Elm furniture and pastel colours grace the rooms and bathrooms of this well-kept hotel, where Mayakovski, Man Ray and Marcel Duchamp have slept. The building was fully modernised in 1988.

Le Jardin des Plantes
5th arr. - 5, rue Linné
47 07 06 20,
fax 47 07 62 74

Open year-round. 33 rms 390-640 F. Bkfst 40 F. Restaurant. Air cond.

This hotel, set in a quiet street behind the Botanical Gardens, has appealing, delightfully decorated rooms—flowers and floral motifs abound. On the sixth floor, there is a terrace with a lovely view; in the basement, a sauna and an ironing room. Restaurant-tea room on the ground floor.

Les Jardins d'Eiffel
7th arr. - 8, rue Amélie
47 05 46 21,
fax 45 55 28 08

Open year-round. 44 rms 530-850 F. Air cond. in 20 rms. Garage parking.

Some rooms are awaiting renovation, but 44 have already been redecorated in attractive colours and re-equipped with double-glazing, minibars, hairdryers and trouser presses. The upper floors overlook the Eiffel Tower. Sauna, many services, charming reception. No restaurant.

A red hotel ranking denotes a place with charm.

Le Laumière
19th arr. - 4, rue Petit
42 06 10 77,
fax 42 06 72 50

Open year-round. 54 rms 230-350 F. Bkfst 30 F. Parking.

This meticulously kept small hotel is located a few steps away from the Buttes-Chaumont park, in a district where modern hotels are not exactly plentiful. Convenient for the La Villette exhibition centre. Rooms are well soundproofed and moderately priced. No restaurant.

Longchamp
16th arr. - 68, rue de Longchamp
47 27 13 48,
fax 47 55 68 26

Open year-round. 23 rms 580-750 F. Bkfst 50 F.

The quiet, comfortable rooms are equipped with minibar, direct line telephone and television with two channels in English. Intimate atmosphere, charming reception.

La Louisiane
6th arr. - 60, rue de Seine
43 29 59 30,
fax 46 34 23 87

Open year-round. 1 ste 600 F. 77 rms 300-600 F. Bkfst 25 F. No pets.

An artistic clientele (writers, dancers, models, musicians) frequents this large Art Deco hotel that stands right in the middle of the Buci street market. Regulars know they will find a warm reception, and rooms that are simple and comfortable, either painted or hung with Japanese wallpaper.

Luxembourg
6th arr. - 4, rue de Vaugirard
43 25 35 90,
fax 43 26 60 84

Open year-round. 34 rms 450-685 F. Bkfst 40 F. Air cond.

Near the Luxembourg Gardens, in the heart of the Latin Quarter. The pleasant rooms have minibar, hairdryer, and individual safe; small bathrooms. Gracious reception by the charming owner.

Magellan
17th arr. - 17, rue Jean-Baptiste-Dumas
45 72 44 51,
fax 40 68 90 36

Open year-round. 75 rms 390-515 F. Bkfst 35 F. No pets. Parking.

Business people will appreciate the quiet and comfort of the rooms (more functional than luxurious) in this creditable hotel, known for the regularity and quality of its service. Attractive garden. No restaurant.

Marais
3rd arr. - 2 bis, rue de Commines
48 87 78 27,
fax 48 87 09 01

Open year-round. 39 rms 320-480 F. Bkfst 30 F.

A simple, neat hotel between Bastille and République offers small, bright, modern rooms. The connecting rooms on the first, second and fifth floors are ideal for families.

Hôtel de Neuville
17th arr. - 3, place Verniquet
43 80 26 30,
fax 43 80 38 55

Open year-round. 28 rms 610-680 F. Bkfst 40 F. Air cond. Restaurant.

This pleasing hotel on a quiet square offers simple rooms, tastefully decorated with floral fabrics and equipped with fine bathrooms. Pleasant salon/winter garden and basement restaurant, Les Tartines.

Nouvel Hôtel
12th arr. - 24, av. du Bel-Air
43 43 01 81,
fax 43 44 64 13

Open year-round. 28 rms 275-490 F. Bkfst 40 F. No pets.

The rooms of the Nouvel Hôtel are peaceful and attractive, though rather eclectically furnished (the prettiest is number 9, on the same level as the garden). Good bathrooms; hospitable reception. No restaurant.

Novanox
6th arr. - 155, bd du Montparnasse
46 33 63 60,
fax 43 26 61 72

Open year-round. 27 rms 540-660 F. Bkfst 45 F. No pets.

The owner of this hotel, opened in 1989, has used a judicious mixture of 1920s, 1930s and 1950s styles for the décor. On the ground floor, a large, cheerful room serves as lounge, bar and breakfast room.

Novotel Bercy
12th arr. - 85, rue de Bercy
43 42 30 00,
fax 43 45 30 60

Open year-round. 1 ste 1,170-1,300 F. 128 rms 690-730 F. Bkfst 55 F. Restaurant. Air cond.

An ultramodern steel-and-glass structure, next door to the Bercy sports complex. The rooms are furnished and equipped to the chain's standards, with minibars, direct line telephones and room service from 6 a.m. to midnight. In addition to meeting rooms and business facilities, there is a large terrace, used for receptions in fine weather.

Novotel Paris Les Halles
1st arr. - 8 pl. Marguerite-de-Navarre
42 21 31 31,
fax 40 26 05 79

Open year-round. 5 stes 1,500 F. 280 rms 790-860 F. Bkfst 55 F. Restaurant. Air cond.

This ultramodern building constructed of stone, glass and zinc is located in the heart of the former market district, near the Pompidou Centre and the Forum des Halles. The huge rooms offer perfect comfort, but their air conditioning prevents you from opening the windows. The restaurant is open from 6 a.m. to midnight, and there is a terrace bar. The conference rooms can be tailored to size by means of movable partitions. Other services include a travel agency and a duty-free shop.

Odéon Hôtel
6th arr. - 3, rue de l'Odéon
43 25 90 67,
fax 43 25 55 98

Open year-round. 34 rms 650-1,000 F. Bkfst 50 F. Air cond. No pets.

The 34 smallish but pleasant and beautifully furnished rooms in this listed building have recently been redecorated. The hotel is located on a strategic street between the Odéon theatre and the square of the same name. No restaurant.

Orléans Palace Hôtel
14th arr. - 185, bd Brune
45 39 68 50,
fax 45 43 65 64

Open year-round. 92 rms 470-520 F. Bkfst 45 F.

A quiet and comfortable traditional hotel that offers good value. The well-equipped and soundproofed rooms are in need of redecoration. Indoor garden.

Ouest Hôtel
17th arr. - 165, rue de Rome
42 27 50 29,
fax 42 27 27 40

Open year-round. 50 rms 300-380 F. Bkfst 30 F.

This cosy establishment has thick carpeting, efficient double-glazing and modest, modern rooms that are well maintained. No restaurant.

Parc Montsouris
14th arr. - 4, rue du Parc-Montsouris
45 89 09 72,
fax 45 80 92 72

Open year-round. 7 stes 470 F. 35 rms 310-480 F. Bkfst 35 F. Air cond.

This small, quiet hotel, recently modernised, features plainly furnished white rooms with bright, new bathrooms. The lovely Parc Montsouris is just a short walk away.

Passy Eiffel
16th arr. - 10, rue de Passy
45 25 55 66,
fax 42 88 89 88

Open year-round. 50 rms 500-620 F. Bkfst 30 F.

Five storeys of spotless, comfortable rooms (though not all equally attractive); four are large enough to suit families. A pleasant breakfast room faces a tiny, glass-enclosed indoor garden. No restaurant.

Perreyve
6th arr. - 63, rue Madame
45 48 35 01,
fax 42 84 03 30

Open year-round. 30 rms 415-500 F. Bkfst 35 F. No pets.

Near the lovely, leafy Luxembourg Gardens, the Perreyve's 30 comfortable rooms have small but faultless bathrooms. There is a little salon on the main floor with mahogany furniture and inviting armchairs. No restaurant.

Hôtel de la Place du Louvre
1st arr. - 21, rue Prêtres-St-Germain-Auxerrois
42 33 78 68,
fax 42 33 09 95

Open year-round. 20 rms 480-800 F. No pets.

This totally renovated hotel is decorated with paintings and sculptures throughout. Fairly large rooms, all comfortably furnished and with good bathrooms. Breakfast is served in a vaulted cellar that dates from the 16th century. The owner gives a warm welcome.

Hôtel du Pré
9th arr. - 10, rue
P.-Sémard
42 81 37 11,
fax 40 23 98 28

Open year-round. 41 rms 395-490 F. Bkfst 35 F.

Actually two hotels, comfortable and close to the Gare du Nord and the Gare de l'Est. Downstairs, guests have the use of a bar, a bright lounge and a pleasant breakfast room. The guest rooms sport painted wood panelling or Japanese wallpaper, paired with cane and bamboo furniture. Good bathrooms.

Queen's Hôtel
16th arr. - 4, rue Bastien-Lepage
42 88 89 85,
fax 40 50 67 52

Open year-round. 23 rms 290-510 F. Bkfst 40 F. No pets.

For an "English" atmosphere and rather petite but delightful modern rooms, try this modest little hotel with a lovely white façade and flower-filled balconies. Excellent reception. No restaurant.

Regyn's Montmartre
18th arr. - 18, pl. des Abbesses
42 54 45 21,
fax 42 54 45 21

Open year-round. 22 rms 360-440 F. Bkfst 38 F.

Each of the rooms in this excellent renovated hotel has a direct line telephone, radio, TV and bathroom; the décor is simple but pleasant. Charming reception. No restaurant.

Le Relais du Louvre
1st arr. - 19, rue Prêtres-St-Germain-Auxerrois
40 41 96 42,
fax 40 41 96 42

Open year-round. 2 stes 1,100-1,400 F. 18 rms 570-880 F. Bkfst 50 F.

The original façade of this historic building opposite the Tuileries Gardens has been preserved, but the interior is fully modernised. The rooms, decorated by Constance de Castelbajac, overflow with charm. Those with numbers ending in 1 are slightly smaller than the rest. Wonderfully hospitable reception.

Résidence des Gobelins
13th arr. - 9, rue des Gobelins
47 07 26 90,
fax 43 31 44 05

Open year-round. 32 rms 350-450 F. Bkfst 35 F. No pets.

A delightful small hotel not far from the Latin Quarter and Montparnasse. The warm welcome of the young owners merits a detour. Rooms are decorated in blue, green or orange, a different colour for each floor.

Résidence Saint-Lambert
15th arr. - 5, rue E.-Gibez
48 28 63 14,
fax 45 33 45 50

Open year-round. 48 rms 380-550 F. Bkfst 38 F.

This pleasant, quiet hotel near the exhibition centre at Porte de Versailles has tidy, smallish but nicely equipped rooms, some overlooking the garden. A laundry and bar are on the premises.

Résidence Trousseau
11th arr. - 13, rue Trousseau
48 05 55 55,
fax 48 05 83 97

Open year-round. 9 stes 780-1,300 F. 57 rms 354-510 F. Garage parking.

Completed in 1989, this self-service hotel is situated in a quiet side street. Pleasant, modern décor and all mod cons: sink, refrigerator, electric hotplates, dishes, coffee machine and microwave oven.

Riboutté-Lafayette
9th arr. - 5, rue Riboutté
47 70 62 36,
fax 48 00 91 50

Open year-round. 24 rms 360-450 F. Bkfst 28 F.

This small and charming hotel faces rue La Fayette and is located within walking distance of the Opéra, the Bourse (Stock Exchange) and the *grands boulevards*. Its quiet rooms are small and attractive. Very hospitable management.

Royal Médoc
9th arr. - 14, rue Geoffroy-Marie
47 70 37 33,
fax 47 70 34 88

Open year-round. 41 rms 550-680 F. Bkfst incl. No pets.

Ten minutes away from the Opéra and close to the main boulevards, this modern, functional hotel (with tidy rooms, direct line telephones and helpful, multilingual staff) near the Bourse is perfect for international business travellers. No restaurant.

Saint-Dominique
7th arr. - 62, rue Saint-Dominique
47 05 51 44,
fax 47 05 81 28

Open year-round. 34 rms 450-690 F. Bkfst 40 F. Air cond.

This most modest of the three "Centre Ville" hotels is also the most charming, and the location is excellent. The delightful little rooms are homely and comfortable. No restaurant.

Hôtel de Saint-Germain
6th arr. - 50, rue du Four
45 48 91 64,
fax 45 48 46 22

Open year-round. 30 rms 500-690 F. Bkfst 50 F. Air cond. in 5 rms. Parking.

This small hotel with its delightful décor and English furniture offers round-the-clock room service, babysitting and various tours of Paris (by helicopter, minibus or on foot).

Saint-Romain
1st arr. - 5-7, rue St-Roch
42 60 31 70,
fax 42 60 10 69

Open year-round. 1 ste 900-1,020 F. 33 rms 470-760 F. Bkfst 40 F. Air cond. No pets.

Recently renovated, this small hotel offers business services that many of its classier cousins do not, such as typing, photocopying,
fax and telex. Simple, comfortable rooms decorated in pretty colours, and marble baths.

Sénateur
6th arr. - 10, rue de Vaugirard
43 26 08 83,
fax 46 34 04 66

Open year-round. 42 rms 550-1,080 F. Bkfst 40 F.

A comfortable, modern hotel with a huge mural and plenty of greenery brightening up the ground floor. The rooms, decorated in grey or beige, are rather impersonal. Fine views from the top floor.

Hôtel du 7e Art
4th arr. - 20, rue St-Paul
42 77 04 03,
fax 42 77 69 10

Open year-round. 22 rms 260-600 F. Bkfst 35 F.

Posters and photographs evoking the cinema—known in France as the seventh art—paper the walls. Small, comfortable rooms with tiny, well-equipped bathrooms. No room service, but there is a restaurant (City Light).

La Tour d'Auvergne
9th arr. - 10, rue de La Tour d'Auvergne
48 78 61 60,
fax 49 95 99 00

Open year-round. 25 rms 550-650 F. Bkfst 45 F. Air cond. No pets.

A competently run, no-nonsense hotel. Each room has décor from a different period; all rooms are furnished with four-poster beds and double-glazed windows. A fine little establishment, ideal for business travellers.

Trocadéro
16th arr. - 21, rue Saint-Didier
45 53 01 82,
fax 45 53 59 56

Open year-round. 23 rms 495-595 F. Bkfst 35 F.

The smallish rooms are done up in soothing pale tones, and the bathrooms are well equipped. The management and staff are unfailingly cheerful. Note the relatively low prices (considering the neighbourhood). No restaurant.

Tim'hôtel Montmartre
18th arr. - 11, rue Ravignan
42 55 74 79,
fax 42 55 71 01

Open year-round. 63 rms 312-430 F. Brkfst 39 F.

On an adorable little square near the Bateau-Lavoir (where Picasso painted the *Demoiselles d'Avignon*, this hotel gives guests a taste of Montmartre's "village" life. Book a room on the upper floors for the best views.

Utrillo
18th arr. - 7, rue A.-Bruant
42 58 13 44,
fax 42 23 93 88

Open year-round. 30 rms 280-410 F. Bkfst 35 F. No pets.

Located behind the rue Lepic in a still-typical part of Montmartre, this former boarding house has been totally renovated. The new rooms feature freshly whitewashed walls, and the upholstery and bedding are in cheerful fabrics. Clean and hospitable. No restaurant.

Vieux Marais
4th arr. - 8, rue du Plâtre
42 78 47 22,
fax 42 78 34 32

Open year-round. 30 rms 350-550 F. Bkfst 30 F. No pets.

Small, friendly hotel in a quiet street. The rooms are simply decorated and well equipped.

Villa des Artistes
6th arr. - 9, rue Grande-Chaumière
43 26 60 86,
fax 43 54 73 70

Open year-round. 59 rms 480-780 F. Air cond. No pets.

An oasis of calm amid the urban noise and bustle. Luxury, quiet and comfort are assured in this hotel, built around a garden patio in the heart of Montparnasse. Excellent value for this district.

Wallace
15th arr. - 89, rue Fondary
45 78 83 30,
fax 40 58 19 43

Open year-round. 35 rms 530-570 F. Bkfst 40 F.

This hotel exudes old-fashioned charm. Most of its small but cheerful rooms overlook a quiet garden.

Welcome Hôtel
6th arr. - 66, rue de Seine
46 34 24 80,
fax 40 46 81 59

Open year-round. 30 rms 300-475 F. No pets. No cards.

You can almost forget the busy intersection of the nearby boulevard Saint-Germain behind the double windows in these small, cosy, tidy rooms. And if you want a taste of the bohemian life, you'll find it on the sixth floor (though you can take the lift!) where you will discover a quaint beamed attic. No restaurant.

This symbol signifies hotels that offer an exceptional degree of peace and quiet.

HOTELS – AIRPORT

AIRPORT

ORLY
94396 Orly – (Val/Marne)
Paris 16 - Corbeil 17 - Villeneuve-St-Georges 12

Altea Paris-Orly
Orly-Ouest
94547 Orly-Aérogare
46 87 23 37,
fax 46 87 71 92
Open daily. 1 ste 900-1,100 F. 193 rms 600-930 F. Restaurant. Air cond. Parking.
The hotel has recently been renovated, and provides soundproof rooms decorated in lively, bright colours. The bathrooms are excellent. Rooms can be rented for the day only (10h-18h) for 220 francs. Minigolf and airport shuttle bus.

Hilton International Orly
Aérogare Orly-Sud
46 87 33 88,
fax 49 78 06 75
Open daily. 359 rms 880-1,180 F. Air cond.
Functional, comfortable rooms near the airport with a free shuttle service. Excellent facilities for conferences or seminars. Round-the-clock room service. Bar and shops.

ROISSY-EN-FRANCE
95700 Roissy-en-France – (Val/d'Oise)
Paris 26 - Meaux 36 - Senlis 28 - Chantilly 28

Holiday Inn
1, allée du Verger
34 29 30 00,
fax 34 29 90 52
Open daily. 245 rms 800-1,030 F. Restaurant. Half-board 980-1,200 F. Air cond. Heated pool. Parking.
Situated in the old village of Roissy. Rooms are large, bright and functional. There's a health club for use by hotel guests (sauna, gym, Jacuzzi, etc.). Free shuttle to the terminals and the exhibition grounds at Villepinte.

Sofitel
Aéroport
Charles-de-Gaulle
48 62 23 23,
fax 48 62 78 49
Open daily. 8 stes 1,500 F. 344 rms 850-950 F. Restaurant. Air cond. Heated pool. Tennis. Valet parking.
A comfortable airport hotel with a discothèque, sauna and coffee shop. Round-the-clock room service and a free shuttle to the airport. There are two restaurants, one with a panoramic view.

THE SUBURBS

AULNAY-SOUS-BOIS
93600 Aulnay-sous-Bois – (Seine-St-D.)
Paris 16 - Senlis 38 - Meaux 30 - St-Denis 13

Novotel
4 km NW on N 370, carrefour de l'Europe
48 66 22 97,
fax 48 66 99 39
Open daily. 138 rms 450-490 F. Restaurant. Half-board 630-850 F. Air cond. Heated pool. Parking.
This handsome modern hotel is located near the Villepinte exhibition centre. Surrounded by gardens, it is especially suitable for families. Good conference facilities.

Les Relais Bleus
Rue L.-de-Vinci
48 66 99 46,
fax 48 66 99 21
Open daily. 117 rms 260-310 F. Restaurant. Parking.
A stone's throw from the exhibition centre and only minutes from Charles de Gaulle airport, this small hotel has pleasant, convenient rooms.

Hôtel de Strasbourg
43, bd de Strasbourg
48 66 60 38,
fax 48 66 15 71
Open daily. 1 ste 300-340 F. 23 rms 225-280 F. Air cond.
This small suburban hotel offers conventional rooms that are charming, comfortable and now soundproofed as well. Bar.

BAGNOLET
93170 Bagnolet – (Seine-St-D.)
Paris 6 - Meaux 41 - Lagny 27

Novotel Paris-Bagnolet
1, av. de la République
49 93 63 00,
fax 43 60 83 95
Open daily. 9 stes 950 F. 602 rms 615-660 F. Restaurant. Air cond. Heated pool. Parking.
Just outside Paris, this is a good address for seminars and conferences. The rooms are modern, functional and well soundproofed. Piano bar.

BLANC-MESNIL (LE)
93150 Blanc-Mesnil (Le) – (Seine-St-D.)
Paris 12 - Bobigny 6 - Aulnay 3

Novotel Paris-Le Bourget
2, rue J.-Perrin
48 67 48 88,
fax 45 91 08 27
Open daily. 143 rms 450-490 F. Restaurant. Half-board 580 F. Air cond. Heated pool. Parking.
Five miles from the permanent science exhibition at La Villette and close to the Aeronautics and Space Museum. The rooms are bright and functional.

RAC MOTORING ATLAS FRANCE: Our fully revised and well-established large format RAC Motoring Atlas France, Belgium and Luxembourg at 1:250,000 (approximately 4 miles to 1 inch) now has even more features to improve journey planning and to make driving in France more enjoyable. Clear, accurate and detailed road maps make RAC Motoring Atlas France the ideal atlas for the independent traveller in France. Price: £ 11.99 (spiral bound).

THE SUBURBS – HOTELS

BOULOGNE-BILLANCOURT
92100 Boulogne-Billancourt – (Hauts/Seine)
Versailles 11

Hôtel Adagio
20-22, rue des Abondances
48 25 80 80,
fax 48 25 33 13
Open daily. 75 rms 695-790 F. Restaurant. Parking.

This modern, glass-and-concrete hotel has bright, spacious rooms fitted with every convenience and pleasantly furnished. The basement houses a vast complex of conference rooms. Brunch served on Sundays until 3 p.m.

CERGY
95000 Cergy – (Val-d'Oise)
Paris 30 - Conflans-Sainte-Honorine 7

Novotel
3, av. du Parc
30 30 39 47,
fax 30 30 90 46
Open daily. 191 rms 450-490 F. Restaurant. Air cond. Heated pool. Parking.

Twenty minutes from Paris and Versailles, this newly renovated hotel has quiet rooms and activities such as table tennis and French billiards. Special weekend rates.

CRÉTEIL
94000 Créteil – (Val/Marne)
Paris 12 - Evry 20 - Melun 35 - Lagny 26

Climat
Rue des Archives
49 80 08 00,
fax 49 80 15 99
Open daily. 51 rms 320 F. Restaurant. Parking.

This well-kept hotel offers simple but cosy rooms three minutes from the métro.

Novotel Créteil-le-Lac
N 186, rue J. Gabin
42 07 91 02,
fax 48 99 03 48
Open daily. 110 rms 470-520 F. Restaurant. Air cond. Heated pool. Parking.

The rooms in this lakeside hotel have recently been modernised. Sports complex with windsurfing nearby.

ENGHIEN
95880 Enghien – (Val-d'Oise)
Paris 18 - Argenteuil 16 - Chantilly 32

Le Grand Hôtel
85, rue du Gal-de-Gaulle
34 12 80 00,
fax 34 12 73 81
Open daily. 3 stes 1,400-2,680 F. 48 rms 690-1,100 F. Restaurant. Half-board 1,260-1,680 F. Air cond. Valet parking.

This bleak building stands in lovely grounds next to the spa. The spacious, comfortable rooms are decorated with period furniture.

EURO DISNEY
See Marne-la-Vallée.

KREMLIN-BICÊTRE (LE)
94270 Kremlin-Bicêtre (Le) – (Val/Marne)
Paris 8 - Boulogne-Billancourt 10 - Versailles 22

Les Relais Bleus
6, rue Voltaire
46 70 15 35,
fax 46 70 58 10
Open daily. 152 rms 340 F. Restaurant. Half-board 450-550 F. Parking.

This hotel is close to the Paris ring road and the Porte d'Italie. The rooms are welcoming and well equipped.

MARNE-LA-VALLÉE
77206 Marne-la-Vallée – (Seine/Marne)
Paris 28 - Meaux 28 - Melun 40

In nearby Euro Disney
(Access by A4)
77206 Marne-la-Vallée – (Seine/Marne)

Disneyland Hotel
Outside the Park
60 45 65 00,
fax 60 45 65 33
Open daily. 21 stes 3,100-8,750 F. 479 rms 1,950-2,500 F. Air cond. Pool. Restaurant.

This enormous candy-pink Victorian pastiche is the *nec plus ultra* of Euro Disney hotels. Sumptuous suites, first-class service; but the pseudo setting and stiff atmosphere are surely not everyone's cup of tea, and the prices are simply staggering. Restaurant: California Grill, see *Restaurants.*

Cheyenne Hotel
Desperado Road
60 45 62 00,
fax 49 30 71 00
Open daily. 1,000 rms 550-750 F. Restaurant.

Perhaps the most amusing of all the Euro Disney hotels: 14 separate structures recall the frontier towns of the Far West. It's not luxurious, but the rooms are tidy and spacious. Tequila and country music in the saloon, restaurant, and a playground for the kids.

New York Hotel
Outside the Park, near the lake
60 45 73 50,
fax 60 45 73 55
Open daily. 26 stes 1,600-2,750 F. 574 rms 1,100-1,600 F. Restaurant. Pool. Tennis.

Manhattan in the 1930s is the theme, complete with skyscrapers, Wall Street and Rockefeller Centre. The Art Deco guest rooms feature mahogany furniture, king-size beds and well-equipped bathrooms. Among the many amenities are a beauty salon, athletic club and conference

---

We're always happy to hear about your discoveries and receive your comments on ours. Please feel free to write to us stating clearly what you liked or disliked.

HOTELS – THE SUBURBS

centre. Restaurant: Manhattan Club, see *Restaurants*.

Newport Bay Club
Disney Festival
60 45 55 00,
fax 49 30 71 00

Open daily. 21 stes 1,150-2,000 F. 1,098 rms 750-1,100 F. Restaurant. Pool.

Were it not so enormous, the Newport Bay Club would be an almost-convincing facsimile of a summer resort in New England. Perhaps it is in an effort to make the place even more lifelike that Disney officials have decided to close the hotel (just months after the official opening) until sometime in the spring of 1993... Restaurant: Cape Cod, see *Restaurants*.

Santa Fe Hotel
In the Park,
near the Pueblos Indian village
60 45 78 00,
fax 49 30 71 00

Open daily. 1,000 rms 550-750 F. Restaurant.

Forty-two "pueblos" make up an ersatz Indian village, dotted with giant cacti; the parking lot is built to look like a drive-in cinema. Games rooms for the children.

Sequoia Lodge
In the Park, near Buena Vista lake
60 45 51 00,
fax 49 30 71 00

Open daily. 1,011 apts 750-1,100 F. Restaurant. Pool.

Bare stone and rough-hewn wood evoke a Rocky Mountain lodge. The sequoias have yet to reach their majestic maturity but guests will find plenty of entertainment at the hotel's restaurants, shops, piano bar, or exercise room.

A red hotel ranking denotes a place with charm.

NEUILLY-SUR-SEINE
92200 Neuilly-sur-Seine — (Hauts/Seine)
Argenteuil 9 - Versailles 16

Hôtel International de Paris
58, bd V.-Hugo
47 58 11 00,
fax 47 58 75 52

Open daily. 3 stes 1,850-3,900 F. 327 rms 850-1,300 F. Restaurant. Air cond. Parking.

A large, contemporary hotel surrounded by lawns and gardens, which has just undergone a luxurious renovation. Elegant, utterly comfortable rooms with every amenity. Sumptuous breakfast buffet.

Neuilly Park Hôtel
23, rue M.-Michelis
46 40 11 15,
fax 46 40 14 78

Open daily. 30 rms 650-770 F. Restaurant.

One of the more recent additions to Neuilly's clique of fine hotels. This is a luxurious and refined establishment with perfectly appointed rooms, understated, soothing décor and some superb bathrooms.

Hôtel du Parc
4, bd du Parc
46 24 32 62

Open daily. 71 rms 295-450 F.

Between the Porte de Champerret and La Défense, on the Ile de la Jatte facing the Seine, is this small 1930s hotel with well-equipped, regularly renovated rooms.

NOGENT-SUR-MARNE
94130 Nogent-sur-Marne — (Val/Marne)
Paris 11 - Créteil 7 - Lagny 17 - Montreuil 5

Nogentel
8, rue du Port
48 72 70 00,
fax 48 72 86 19

Open daily. 60 rms 540-580 F. Restaurant. Parking.

This is a modern hotel in the Nogent marina, well equipped for receptions and seminars

(250-seat auditorium). Panoramic restaurant and grill.

PONTAULT-COMBAULT
77340 Pontault-Combault — (Seine/Marne)
Paris 26 - Melun 29 - Coulommiers 41

Saphir Hôtel
Aire des Berchères
64 43 45 47,
fax 64 40 52 43

Open daily. 21 stes 895 F. 159 rms 495-535 F. Air cond. Heated pool. Tennis. Restaurant.

A brand new hotel next to Euro Disney. Rooms are airy, pleasant and well equipped. Facilities include conference rooms, sauna and a superb indoor swimming pool. Grill. Restaurant: Le Canadel, see *Restaurants*.

PUTEAUX
92800 Puteaux — (Hauts/Seine)
Paris 10 - Versailles 14 - St-Germain-en-Laye 11

Les Communautés
Paris-la-Défense,
in the CNIT
2, pl. de la Défense
46 92 10 10,
fax 46 92 10 50

Open daily. 6 stes 2,500-3,200 F. 141 rms 1,300 F. Air cond. Restaurant.

The hotel is aimed at business clientele with its huge rooms (some boast a view of the Grande Arche), luxurious bathrooms, and 24-hour room service. Restaurant: Les Communautés, see *Restaurants*.

Dauphin
45, rue J.-Jaurès
47 73 71 63,
fax 47 75 25 20

Open daily. 30 rms 450 F. Tennis. Valet parking.

The Dauphin stands opposite the Princesse Isabelle, and is run by the same family. Generous buffet breakfasts are set up in the sitting room; guest rooms are comfortable and pretty, with cable television. Some rooms are reserved for non-smokers. Free shuttle to the RER station.

Sofitel Paris La Défense
34, cours Michelet
La Défense 10
47 76 44 43,
fax 47 73 72 74

Open daily. 1 ste 2,500 F. 149 rms 1,200 F. Air cond. Restaurant.

A new link in the chain, warmly decorated with gilt mirrors and pale marble. Rooms are quiet with superb pink-marble bathrooms. Service is top-notch and breakfasts are delicious. Good facilities for conferences. Restaurant: Les Deux Arcs, see *Restaurants*.

Hôtel de Dion-Bouton
19, quai de Dion-Bouton
42 04 35 54,
fax 45 06 39 51

Open daily. 33 rms 450-520 F.

On the Seine with pleasant, English-style rooms. Pretty bathrooms and an indoor patio.

Princesse Isabelle
72, rue J.-Jaurès
47 78 80 06,
fax 47 75 25 20

Open daily. 1 ste 850 F. 29 rms 620 F. Tennis. Air cond in 4 rms. Valet parking.

The rooms of this hotel near La Défense are prettily decorated, and have Jacuzzi bathtubs or multi-jet showers. Some open onto the flowered patio. There's a free chauffeur service to the RER and the Pont de Neuilly métro station.

> Remember to call ahead to reserve your room, and please, if you cannot honour your reservation, be courteous and let the hotel know.

Syjac Hôtel
20, quai de Dion-Bouton
42 04 03 04

Open daily. 7 stes 850-1,500 F. 29 rms 550-800 F. Parking.

A recently built hotel which has managed to shun the concrete solidity of nearby La Défense. Rooms are very pleasing, large and well appointed. There are some nice two-level suites overlooking the Seine (with fireplace) and a pretty flowered patio. Free sauna. Meals on trays.

Le Victoria
85, bd R.-Wallace
45 06 55 51,
fax 40 99 05 97

Open daily. 32 rms 390-540 F.

Not far from the Arche de La Défense, this recently opened hotel offers comfortable, well-equipped rooms.

RUNGIS
94150 Rungis – (Val/Marne)
Paris 13 - Corbeil 26 - Longjumeau 10

Holiday Inn
4, av. Ch.-Lindbergh
46 87 26 66,
fax 45 60 91 25

Open daily. 168 rms 795-995 F. Half-board 985-1,185 F. Air cond. Parking.

Comfortable and well-kept rooms near Orly airport (free shuttle). A view of the Rungis halles (the Paris wholesale food market). Shops.

Pullman Paris-Orly
20, av. Ch.-Lindbergh
46 87 36 36,
fax 46 87 08 48

Open daily. 2 stes 1,400 F. 196 rms 600-750 F. Air cond. Heated pool. Restaurant.

A reliable, comfortable chain hotel with excellent soundproofing, air conditioning, television and direct telephone lines. Among the amenities on offer are a non-stop shuttle to and from the airports, a panoramic bar, a sauna, shops and a swimming pool. There are deluxe rooms ("Privilège") and several lounges. Restaurant: La Rungisserie, see *Restaurants*.

SACLAY
91400 Saclay – (Essonne)
Paris 21 - Versailles 11 - Palaiseau 8

Novotel Saclay
Rue Ch.-Thomassin
69 35 66 00,
fax 69 41 01 77

Open daily. 136 rms 450-490 F. Restaurant. Half-board 685 F. Air cond. Heated pool. Tennis. Parking.

Part of the Novotel chain with functional, comfortable rooms, recently renovated, and air conditioning. Minigolf, bar. Summer barbecues.

SAINT-CLOUD
92210 Saint-Cloud – (Hauts/Seine)
Paris 12 - Boulogne 3 - Versailles 10

Hôtel Quorum
2, bd de la République
47 71 22 33,
fax 46 02 75 64

Open daily. 58 rms 440-550 F. Restaurant.

A bright new hotel with quietly elegant, modern public rooms, and spacious guest rooms with grey marble baths. The best are on the upper floors with a view over the Parc de Saint-Cloud. The race track and Saint-Cloud golf club are nearby. Restaurant: La Désirade, see *Restaurants*.

Villa Henri IV
43, bd de la République
46 02 59 30,
fax 49 11 11 02

Open daily. 36 rms 420-500 F. Restaurant. Parking.

A pleasant address off the boulevard. Rooms are decorated in Louis XVI, Louis-Philippe or Norman style and are huge, bright and well equipped.

HOTELS – THE SUBURBS

SAINT-GERMAIN-EN-LAYE
78100 Saint-Germain-en-Laye — (Yvelines)
Paris 21 - Chartres 81 - Dreux 70 - Beauvais 69

La Forestière
1, av. du Président-Kennedy
39 73 36 60

Open daily. 6 stes 1,000-1,300 F. 24 rms 680-850 F. Restaurant.

Thirty rooms and suites have been recently renovated and pleasantly furnished in an old-fashioned style with fresh, spring-like fabrics. The hotel sits on extensive, flower-filled grounds at the edge of the forest. Relais et Châteaux. Restaurant: Cazaudehore, see Restaurants.

Le Pavillon Henri-IV
21, rue Thiers
34 51 62 62,
fax 39 73 93 73

Open daily. 3 stes 1,900 F. 39 rms 400-1,300 F. Half-board 660-1,010 F. Restaurant.

This is where Louis XIV was born, Alexandre Dumas wrote The Three Musketeers, and Offenbach composed a number of operettas. Total comfort inhabits the 45 huge rooms and suites. The public rooms are magnificent and there's a splendid view over the immense park. Restaurant: Le Pavillon Henri-IV, see Restaurants.

SURVILLIERS
95470 Survilliers — (Val-d'Oise)
Paris 30 - Chantilly 14 - Senlis 18 - Lagny 32

Novotel Paris-Survilliers
A 1 then D 16
34 68 69 80,
fax 34 68 64 94

Open daily. 79 rms 470-520 F. Restaurant. Air cond. Heated pool. Parking.

This rather nice modern hotel is set in the middle of a park just three miles from the Chantilly forest. Meeting and conference rooms. Bar and grill open from 6 a.m. to midnight.

VÉLIZY
78140 Vélizy — (Yvelines)
Paris 15 - Versailles 7 - Jouy-en-Josas 4

Holiday Inn
22, av. de l'Europe
39 46 96 98,
fax 34 65 95 21

Open daily. 182 rms 725-965 F. Restaurant. Air cond. Heated pool. Parking.

Situated near a shopping centre, the Holiday Inn offers functional rooms and excellent facilities. Free shuttle to the Pont-de-Sèvres métro station.

VERSAILLES
78000 Versailles — (Yvelines)
Paris 23 - Mantes 44 - Rambouillet 31

Bellevue Hôtel
12, av. de Sceaux
39 50 13 41,
fax 39 02 05 67

Open daily. 24 rms 380-520 F.

The Bellevue's Louis XV/XVI-style rooms are soundproofed and well equipped (new beds) but rather worn, despite a recent remodelling. Located near the château and conference centre.

Eden Hôtel
2, rue Ph.-de-Dangeau
39 50 68 06,
fax 39 51 35 23

Open daily. 25 rms 210-340 F.

Eden lies between the railway station and the château, in a quiet street near the police station. The rooms are regularly refurbished and updated.

Home Saint-Louis
28, rue St-Louis
39 50 23 55,
fax 39 21 62 45

Open daily. 27 rms 160-315 F.

This family-style hotel is located in the quiet Saint-Louis neighbourhood.

Pullman
2 bis, av. Paris
39 53 30 31

6 stes 1,300 F. 146 rms 690 F. Restaurant. Air cond. in 75 rms. Valet parking.

Exceptionally well situated near the place d'Armes and the château but set back from the street, this Pullman offers spacious, modern rooms and prestigious amenities. Excellent reception. Piano bar.

Richaud
16, rue Richaud
39 50 10 42,
fax 39 53 43 36

Open daily. 39 rms 250-390 F. Parking.

A small, quiet hotel in the centre of the shopping district. Recently remodelled rooms.

Trianon Palace
1, bd de la Reine
30 84 38 00,
fax 39 51 66 55

Open daily. 32 stes 2,200-7,500 F. 62 rms 1,300-2,000 F. Restaurants. Heated pool. Tennis. Parking.

After sprucing up the place to the tune of £40 million, owner Yusake Miyama has thrown open the gilded gates of his stupendously lavish hotel. From videoconference equipment to a medically supervised spa, it is the last word in luxury. Restaurant: Les Trois Marches, see Restaurants.

Le Versailles
7, rue Ste-Anne
39 50 64 65,
fax 39 02 37 85

Open daily. 48 rms 370-480 F. Parking.

Conveniently situated near the entrance to the château and facing the convention centre, Le Versailles has modern rooms and recently refitted bathrooms. Direct lift access to the car park. Garden and patio.

CAFES

& QUICK BITES

CAFES	*132*
QUICK BITES	*133*
TEA ROOMS	*137*
WINE BARS	*144*

CAFES

Café Beaubourg
4th arr. - 43, rue Saint-Merri - 48 87 63 96
Open 8 a.m.-1 a.m. (Sat. & Sun. 8 a.m.-2 a.m.).

The vast central space is punctuated by eight columns. To your left, as you enter, a section is reserved for reading French and foreign newspapers. Relatively private spots can be found on the upper level, where the efforts of budding artists are displayed. And virtually every seat affords a view of the esplanade of the Centre Pompidou, with its buskers, fire-eaters and mad poets. Though the coffee, salads and croque-monsieurs are fine, the sandwiches are not up to scratch.

Café Costes
1st arr. - 4-6, rue Berger, Place des Innocents - 45 08 54 39
Open 8 a.m.-2 a.m. (Dec. 24 until 8 p.m.).

Designer Philippe Starck may be justly proud of his glass-and-steel temple of postmodern leisure. Paris hadn't seen a café of this calibre open in a good 50 years. Starck's metal café chairs turn out to be more comfortable than they look, perfect for observing the action on the place des Innocents. The smartly turned-out waiters serve good coffee (16 francs) and tasty croque-monsieurs.

Café de Flore
6th arr. - 172, bd Saint-Germain 45 48 55 26
Open daily 7 a.m.-1:30 a.m.

Guillaume Apollinaire and Jean-Paul Sartre are gone, but less illustrious writers still frequent the Flore, as do a few actors, many locals and a plethora of tourists. The café's upper room is no longer an exclusively homosexual haunt; it is now a quiet spot where one may read or write in peace while sipping the house tipple (Pouilly-Fumé from Ladoucette) or tucking into the good Welsh rarebit.

Café Mouffetard
5th arr. - 116, rue Mouffetard 43 31 42 50
Open 7 a.m.-9 p.m. Closed Sun. p.m. & Mon.

Brimming over with the charm of *vieux Paris*—and with patrons, especially on weekend mornings—this café is an obligatory stop for anyone visiting the picturesque open-air market on the rue Mouffetard. The croissants are marvellous.

Café des Musées
3rd arr. - 49, rue de Turenne - 42 72 96 17
Open 7 a.m.-8 p.m. (Sat. & Sun. 7 a.m.-10:30 p.m.).

What looks like a typical French café is in fact a special spot where the boss pampers clients with excellent expresso, sandwiches made with choice charcuteries and cheeses, abundant salads and remarkable hot *plats du jour*. What's more, this tiny but exemplary establishment is within a stone's throw of the Musée Carnavalet, the place des Vosges and the Musée Picasso.

Café de la Paix
9th arr. - 12, bd des Capucines 40 07 30 20
Open daily 10 a.m.-1:30 a.m.

Is it just us, or have the waiters at this Parisian landmark grown terribly blasé? Too much fame, too many tourists seem to have taken their toll of this once-glorious café. Sneak inside for a peek at the Second-Empire toilets (on the first floor), but avoid the crowded, noisy tables. In all fairness we must say that the coffee (six varieties) is pretty good.

La Coupole
14th arr. - 102, bd du Montparnasse - 43 20 14 20
Open daily 7:30 a.m.-2 a.m. Closed Dec. 24 evening.

Back in 1988, the Coupole's new owners promised not to alter this hallowed monument to the creative energy of Montparnasse, its writers, artists and hangers-on; on the whole, they kept their word. The terrace of the restored and refurbished Coupole is a fine place to sit with a beer or a coffee and watch Parisian life go by.

Les Deux Magots
6th arr. - 170, bd Saint-Germain 45 48 55 25
Open 7:30 a.m.-1:30 a.m. Closed Jan. 18-24.

Over there, a group of Japanese tourists sip the famous "old-fashioned chocolate"—made from chocolate bars melted in rich milk, and whipped to creamy lightness. Beneath the eponymous Magots (the twin bronze figures perched at ceiling level), a German couple enjoy the house Muscadet. Out on the newly remodelled terrace, Americans try out their French on the weary waiters, while nattily dressed locals gossip over jugs of coffee. The legendary habitués of the postwar era have long since vanished, but an air of excitement still floats about this archetypal Parisian café.

Aux Deux Saules
2nd arr. - 91, rue Saint-Denis - 42 36 46 57
Open 11 a.m.-midnight. Closed Tues.

For nearly a century this appealing café has served mussels and chips, as well as the usual drinks and snacks, to famished denizens of Les Halles. The clientele changed considerably as the district was transformed from the city's food market to an art/fashion centre, but the gra-

QUICK BITES – CAFES & QUICK BITES

cious wood, tile and enamel décor has not lost its charm.

Le Fouquet's
8th arr. - 99, av. des Champs-Elysées - 47 23 70 60
Open daily 7 a.m.-2 a.m.

Historically, this is *the* café on the Champs-Elysées, with its sprawling terrace on the "good" side of the avenue. True, some TV and film stars can be spotted here, but mainly one sees tourists and other ordinary folk (who are willing, that is, to spend 25 francs on a cup of coffee) soaking up the morning sun or the evening neon.

La Palette
6th arr. - 43, rue de Seine - 43 26 68 15
Open 8 a.m.-2 a.m. Closed Sun., Aug. & 1 wk. Feb. school holidays. No cards.

Painters, gallery owners, antique dealers and art students are the pillars of this venerable café, an unofficial annexe of the nearby Beaux-Arts college. When the weather is clement, it's fun to sit at one of the pavement tables that stretch half-way up the rue Jacques-Callot, order a beer and a *guillotine* (a ham sandwich made with chewy Poilâne bread), and take in all the details of this delightful Left-Bank scene.

Au Roi du Café
15th arr. - 59, rue Lecourbe - 47 34 48 50
Open 7 a.m.-11 p.m. (Sun. 8 a.m.-4 p.m.).

Here is that rare find, a café for coffee lovers. We mean people who know and care about the differences between beans grown in Costa Rica and Brazil, Colombia or New Guinea. Good *plats du jour* are on offer at lunch; service is helpful and jolly.

Le Sancerre
18th arr. - 35, rue des Abbesses 42 58 08 20
Open daily 7 a.m.-1:30 a.m.

As you enter, look up and admire the mermaid painted on the ceiling. This is a café with character, near the pretty and very lively place des Abbesses. The patrons are a colourful mixture of local tradesmen, workers, rockers and Bohemians, artists and the odd tourist. For your refreshment, the menu offers good wines by the glass, sandwiches and salads.

Le Select
6th arr. - 99, bd du Montparnasse - 45 48 38 24
Open daily 8 a.m.-2 a.m. (w.-e. until 4 a.m.).

A more select class of eccentric prefers this café to other, flashier Montparnasse venues. An unusual place to rendezvous before a seafood dinner at Le Dôme or Le Duc.

Le Train Bleu
12th arr. - 20, bd Diderot - 43 43 09 06
Open daily 9 a.m.-10 p.m.

Many people know that Le Train Bleu restaurant in the Gare de Lyon boasts a stunning interior; but not everyone is aware that this Belle Epoque gem is also a bar and café. Why waste time in the lugubrious buffets and bistros on the station level when a beautiful, comfortable (though admittedly more expensive) place of refreshment awaits up one flight of stairs?

QUICK BITES

Al Diwan
8th arr. - 30, av. George-V - 47 20 84 98
Open daily 8 a.m.-11:30 p.m.

The take-away shop of the Al Diwan restaurant has all you need for an impromptu Lebanese picnic: choose chawarma (marinated beef), labneh (fresh cheese), makanek (spicy sausages) or felafel sandwiches on the bread of your choice, top up your basket with some baklava and walnut cakes, pick a bottle of Lebanese wine (don't forget the corkscrew), and off you go!

Bastille Corner
12th arr. - 47, rue de Charenton 43 47 12 17
Open noon-3 p.m. & 7:30 p.m.-12:30 a.m. Closed Sun., Aug., Dec. 25 & Jan. 1.

Hankering after an enchilada? Make for this Mexican-American hangout, where you can also snatch a spicy lunch or late supper of nachos and chili con carne followed by an ice-cream sundae.

La Boutique à Sandwichs
8th arr. - 12, rue du Colisée - 43 59 56 69
Open 11:45 a.m.-1 a.m. Closed Sun. & Aug.

On the first floor of this restaurant you might see a few famous faces seated together around raclette, vegetable soup and other modest but tasty dishes. For our part, we remain loyal to the ground floor, where some of the best sandwiches in Paris are put together, featuring shrimps, chicken and smoked ham. Try the excellent corned beef (pickelfleisch), served hot or cold with horseradish, pickles and Poilâne bread. A great spot for a quick, cheap lunch.

Café de Mars
7th arr. - 11, rue Augereau - 47 05 05 91
Open noon-2:30 p.m. & 8 p.m.-11:30 p.m. (Sat. 8 p.m.-11:30 p.m.; Sun. noon-4 p.m. & 8 p.m.-11:30 p.m.). Closed 10 days in Aug.

An American menu, a jovial atmosphere and a cosmopolitan crowd account for the Café's swift rise to success.

Brunch-style dishes are served any day, any time, but the staff goes all out to produce a traditional brunch on Sunday.

Café des Lettres
7th arr. - 53, rue de Verneuil - 42 22 52 17
Open noon-3 p.m. & 7 p.m.-11 p.m. Closed Sun. & last 2 wks. of Dec.

This annexe to the very serious Maison des Ecrivains (a writers' centre) eschews French food in favour of Italian and Scandinavian dishes. Herring, shrimps and salads dominate the lunch offerings, along with a few hot dishes. After 3 p.m. tea, cakes, Swedish waffles and assorted light refreshments are served.

Coffee-Parisien
7th arr. - 5, rue Perronet - 45 44 92 93
Open daily 11 a.m.-7 p.m. (Fri. until midnight). Closed Aug. No cards.

For a mile-high sandwich (hot smoked or roast beef, tuna or chicken salad, from 30 to 70 francs) perch on a stool at this likeable little café. If you like, the sandwiches can be packed to take away... how about a picnic in the Luxembourg?

Cosi
6th arr. - 54, rue de Seine - 46 33 35 36
Open daily noon-11 p.m. No cards.

Don't let the long queue discourage you—just listen to the music, and study the sandwich fillings listed on the blackboard: fresh goat cheese, cucumber, smoked Italian ham, prosciutto, salmon and more can be stuffed in any combination into oven-fresh pitta bread (35 to 45 francs). Wash your sandwich down with a glass of good Italian wine and finish with an American-style dessert: a brownie, fruit crumble or Häagen-Dazs ice cream. These goodies may be consumed upstairs (one of

the two rooms is reserved for non-smokers), at a communal board or a table for one, as you wish.

Cuisine Gourmande
4th arr. - 63, rue Saint-Louis-en-l'Ile - 46 33 33 33
Open daily 11 a.m.-11 p.m.

A jolly crew of regulars keeps the atmosphere lively at this "island" hangout. Granted, the dishes on the menu are pre-cooked but look who did the cooking: top French chefs Morot-Gaudry, Dutournier, Faugeron, Fournier, who specialise in hearty dishes from the south-west. Petrossian, no less, supplies the salmon and the cheeses come from Androuet. To irrigate all these goodies, there is of course an appropriate range of wines.

Danny Rose
15th arr. - 41, bd Pasteur - 45 66 82 82
Open daily 11 a.m.-9:30 p.m. Closed Dec. 25 & Jan. 1.

Here's fast food with variety—and it's excellent value to boot! In addition to the usual hamburgers, you'll find chili, Texas meatballs and beef kebabs on menus that range from 24 to 37 francs. For dessert, try one of Cynthia's brownies, or a gooey ice-cream sundae.

Eggstra
10th arr. - 66, rue du Faubourg-Poissonnière & 31, rue de Paradis
48 00 01 80
Open 11:30 a.m.-4 p.m. Closed Sun.

Inventive, high-quality fast food does exist in Paris, and it's prepared by an American chef! Her delicious pitta-bread sandwiches (15 to 20 francs), fresh salads, crunchy chips and tongue-tingling chili are winning new converts to the American way of lunch. Even if you finish with a brownie, cheesecake or pecan tart, you

---

A precarious perch

The column that towers over the *Place Vendôme* seems to be equipped with an ejector seat. More than one famous figure has experienced the precariousness of that particular perch since the first version was erected in 1686. The statue of the Sun King, Louis XIV, destroyed during the Revolution, was followed by Napoleon in a number of guises, briefly interrupted by King Henri IV when the monarchy was restored in 1814. Henri, who reigned in the late 16th and early 17th centuries, was the father of the Duke of Vendôme who gave his name to this magnificent square. The present Napoleon—dressed, like the original, in Roman garb—watches over the jewellers, couturiers and furriers of this opulent district.

Cafétéria du Musée Picasso
3rd arr. - 5, rue Thorigny - 42 71 25 21
Open 9:15 a.m.-5:15 p.m. Closed Tues.

Even if you aren't a Picasso fan, you can still slip into his museum, housed in the noble Hôtel Salé, for a bite in the cafeteria—a ticket isn't required. Salads, quiches, savoury tarts and pastries comprise the list of light offerings.

won't spend over 50 francs. American beer, fresh fruit juices and California wines will wash these treats down.

Fauchon
8th arr. - 30, place de la Madeleine - 47 42 60 11
Open 9:40 a.m.-7 p.m. Closed Sun.

The drill for getting through this place would drive anyone but a Frenchman bonkers. First you queue up to choose your main dish, dessert and coffee, then you take your ticket to the cash register (another queue), wait again to retrieve your meal, and finally set off in search of a place to eat it (don't hope for a table). The plus side? Well, the food is very good indeed—and so is the coffee. Plan to spend 100 to 140 francs for a full meal, 12 to 35 francs for a cake and coffee.

Flora Danica
8th arr. - 142, av. des Champs-Elysées - 43 59 20 41
Open daily noon-2:30 p.m. & 7:15 p.m.-11 p.m. Closed Dec. 24 evening.

This Danish outpost at the top of the Champs-Elysées is as popular as ever. After a film, come here for a plate of Baltic herring (smoked or with cream) and potato salad, or gravlax or smoked salmon, along with a chilled Tuborg beer and perhaps a Danish pastry.

Fructidor
9th arr. - 46, rue Saint-Georges 49 95 02 10
Open 11 a.m.-3 p.m. Closed Sat. & Sun.
9th arr. - 67, rue de Provence 48 74 53 46
Open 11 a.m.-3 p.m. Closed Sun.

Anti-stress dishes are accompanied by vitamin-packed fruit and vegetable cocktails. Fortunately, there is as much flavour as nutrition in the onion pie, the salade paysanne and the leek quiche. Both establishments feature identical food, but the rue Saint-Georges address is more pleasant.

Lina's
2nd arr. - 50, rue Etienne-Marcel 42 21 16 14
Open 10 a.m.-6 p.m. (Sat. 10 a.m.-6:30 p.m.). Closed Sun. & holidays.
8th arr. - 8, rue Marbeuf - 47 23 92 33
Open 10:30 a.m.-5 p.m. (Sat. 10 a.m.-6:30 p.m.). Closed Sun.

The friendly, swift staff work as you watch, building delicious, obviously fresh sandwiches. Shrimps, cucumber, bacon and smoked beef are but a few of the many options you can take away, or munch on a stool behind the broad glass shopfront. With a dessert (brownies, pecan pie, ice cream...) and a glass of Bordeaux, you'll spend 50 to 60 francs.

Lord Sandwich
1st arr. - 15, rue Duphot - 42 60 55 94
8th arr. - 134, rue du Faubourg Saint-Honoré - 42 56 41 68
Open 11 a.m.-5 p.m. Closed Sat. & Sun.

By now, no doubt everyone is familiar with the tale of John Montagu, Lord Sandwich, who had a passion for all-night card games and who accidentally invented the sandwich one night towards dawn, when he ordered his butler to bring him a slice of ham between two slices of bread to avoid getting the cards greasy. This Lord Sandwich offers some of the best-tasting creations in Paris along with the widest choice, from simple to sophisticated. Vegetarians and weight-watchers have an array of salads to choose from. The cafeteria format is reminiscent of a fast-food restaurant, but on the first floor there is a garden-style dining room.

Marais Plus
3rd arr. - 20, rue des Francs-Bourgeois - 48 87 01 40
Open daily 10 a.m.-7:30 p.m.

Though the décor does not amount to much and the food is no more than decent, this is a handy address to know if you're in the Marais, dying of hunger, and unwilling to spend too much on your late breakfast, lunch, tea or Sunday brunch.

Le Melrose
3rd arr. - 8, rue du Pas-de-la-Mule 40 29 90 50
Open noon-4 p.m. & 7 p.m.-11 p.m. (Sat. noon-11 p.m. & Sun. noon-7 p.m.).

Revel in the splendid view of the place des Vosges and discover what French "fast food" is all about: *tartines* (open sandwiches) of goat cheese, country ham or smoked duck breast, plates of carpaccio or satisfying quiches and tarts may be followed by gooey chocolate cake, or a simple and refreshing fruit cocktail. This sumptuous snack will cost you approximately 80 francs.

Le Mexico
16th arr. - 1, place de Mexico 47 27 96 98
Open noon-3 p.m. & 7:30 p.m.-11 p.m. (Sat. & Sun. noon-midnight).

In choosing Le Mexico as their *cantina*, the neighbourhood's gilded youth have shown that their good taste extends beyond their signed and logo'd clothes. Follow their lead and try the good fresh pasta, shrimps in sherry, plates of smoked salmon or duck breast and the cool, inventive salads. But for dessert, sneak off to Angélina, across the street.

Some establishments change their closing times without warning. It is always wise to check in advance.

CAFES & QUICK BITES – QUICK BITES

Midi Trente
14th arr. - 56, rue Daguerre - 43 20 49 82
Open 11 a.m.-6 p.m. Closed Sun.

Actresses and cover girls congregate in this refined and very feminine lunch spot. Your hostesses will advise you on whether to choose their rich chicken liver pâté, or the refreshing courgette terrine with a perky tomato and pepper coulis, then guide you on to pick a hot *plat du jour* or a plate of smoked salmon. Even with a lemon tart or fragrant orange fondant for dessert, you're sure to spend under 100 francs.

Pain, Salade et Fantaisie
5th arr.- 22, rue Gay-Lussac - 40 51 05 01
Open 9 a.m.-8 p.m. Closed Sun. & holidays.

The irresistible fragrance of freshy-baked bread wafts out of this appealing sandwich shop, just a stone's throw from the Luxembourg Gardens. Impeccably fresh fillings—goat cheese, salmon, braised or country ham, mortadella and more—are stuffed into wholemeal pitta bread, or piled onto chewy Poilâne bread (9 to 23 francs). Shrimp or chicken salads, brownies and great raspberry muffins round off the bill of fare. The unfailingly cheerful proprietors of this family-owned shop promise that the menu will soon be expanded to include chili, strudel, cheesecake and teas from Mariage Frères.

Pastavino
1st arr. - Forum des Halles, 9, Grande-Galerie - 40 26 54 62
Open 9 a.m.-7:30 p.m. Closed Sun.

If you've descended into the Forum des Halles for a non-stop shopping spree, you needn't resurface for lunch. Perch on a stool at Pastavino's black-marble counter and enjoy a reviving bowl of fresh pasta or a refreshing plate of tomatoes, mozzarella and Parma ham, followed by a serious dessert (tiramisù, Italian pastries) and excellent expresso. Or you can snack while you shop, with a take-away sandwich made with crusty Italian bread (18 to 28 francs).

Au Plaisir des Pains
6th arr. - 62, rue de Vaugirard 45 48 40 45
Open 10 a.m.-8 p.m. Closed Sun.

What this sandwich shop lacks in warmth it makes up for in the freshness of the food on offer: we recommend the hot pitta-bread sandwiches filled with grilled peppers, or herb-flavoured ham, aubergine pâté or tomatoes and mozzarella (20 to 25 francs), as well as the delicious tomato tart, the Roquefort turnover, and the "special" salad, which includes peppers, aubergine, herbs and fromage blanc. A 10-franc surcharge is added if you eat in the shop, but why not save money and take your goodies over to the nearby Luxembourg Gardens?

Au Régal
16th arr. - 4, rue Nicolo - 42 88 49 15
Open 9 a.m.-11 p.m. (Sun. 10 a.m.-3 p.m. & 6 p.m.-11 p.m.). Closed 2 wks. wk. of Aug. 15.

A sudden craving for caviar can be satisfied (at a price) in this traditional Russian grocery-cum-restaurant. More modestly priced and perfectly delicious are the salmon eggs, zakuski, herring any way you like it, borscht and pirozkis, and the wonderful vatrouchka (Russian cheesecake). We hear that Brigitte Bardot occasionally comes in for blinis and smoked salmon.

Seine Rive Gauche
13th arr. - 3, rue Louise-Weiss 44 23 80 02
Open 8 a.m.-7 p.m. Closed Sun. & holidays.

The demanding clientele that the new Finance Ministry and the future Bibliothèque de France are bringing into the neighbourhood have been delighted to discover this elegant, resolutely modern tea room. A well-designed menu features inventive cold dishes (smoked salmon, avocado and grapefruit), generous salads, warming gratins and savoury tarts, all made with top-quality ingredients chosen fresh every morning at the market. Breakfast and teatime treats include homemade jams and chocolate prepared the old-fashioned way, which patrons may enjoy while glancing at the newspapers and magazines put at their disposal by the friendly, efficient staff.

Sydney Health Food
2nd arr. - 46, passage Choiseul 49 26 01 71
Open 9:30 a.m.- 6 p.m. Closed Sat. & Sun.

Low-fat, low-salt and low-cost, Sydney's health food specialities are nevertheless packed with flavour. The fresh-fruit juices, soups, savoury tarts, salads and sandwiches made with wholemeal bread are uniformly delicious and served in generous portions. Eat-in facilities are barely functional (a tiny counter downstairs, a small dining room up a rickety flight of stairs), but the food will be packed in sturdy take-away containers on request.

Virgin Café
8th arr. - 56, av. des Champs-Élysées - 42 89 46 81
Open 10 a.m.-11:30 p.m. (Sat. & Sun. 10 a.m.-12:30 a.m.).

The gallery-restaurant that crowns the Virgin Megastore is a surprisingly pleasant and comfortable spot for lunch,

TEA ROOMS – CAFES & QUICK BITES

tea or light refreshments at any time of day. Celebrity chef Dominique Nahmias ("Olympe" to her friends) has concocted a simple, appetising menu based on fresh ingredients: sautéed shellfish scented with thyme, garlicky brandade of sole, scrambled eggs and polenta... The Virgin Afternoon Tea offers the tea of your choice accompanied by little sandwiches, scones with jam and the pastry *du jour*, all for just 55 francs.

West Side Café
17th arr. - 34, rue Saint-Ferdinand - 40 68 75 05
Open 10 a.m.-6 p.m. Closed Sun. & holidays.

This American-style diner looks like something Edward Hopper might have painted. At noon, customers cluster around the counter for tasty turkey, smoked salmon, shrimp or guacamole sandwiches (25 to 45 francs), or the chicken and West Side salads. It's fun to munch on a brownie or some biscuits and contemplate this very Parisian take-off of an old Yankee tradition.

Xavier Gourmet
8th arr. - 89, bd de Courcelles
43 80 78 22
Open daily noon-3:30 p.m. & 7 p.m.-11:30 p.m.
9th arr. - 19, rue Notre-Dame-de-Lorette - 45 26 38 46
Open daily 9 a.m.-4 p.m. & 6 p.m.-11:30 p.m. (Sat., Sun. & holidays noon-11:30 p.m.).

For a quick bite before or after the play, this pleasing little place in the heart of the theatre district offers sandwiches made with Poilâne's wonderful sourdough bread filled with smoked salmon, tarama or tomatoes and mozzarella drizzled with fruity olive oil, as well as salads and an all-in grill menu (meat, salad and sautéed potatoes for 59 francs). If you want to end with a sweet, steer clear of the mediocre pastries, and go for the Häagen-Dazs ice cream instead.

TEA ROOMS

A Priori-Thé
2nd arr. - 35-37, galerie Vivienne
42 97 48 75
Open noon-7 p.m. (Sun. 12:30 p.m.-6 p.m.). Closed Dec. 25 & Jan. 1.

We would be hard pressed to come up with a prettier or more charming spot in Paris than the passage Vivienne. You slip beneath a glass roof supported by bas-relief carved goddesses and horns of plenty, to reach this honey-coloured room (the scrap of a terrace in front is filled with cane armchairs). From noon until 3 p.m. fashion fiends, journalists and intellectuals lunch on interesting cold dishes, tempting *plats du jour* (try the welsh rarebit) and desserts like fruit crumble and pecan pie. At teatime, you'll find a nice selection of teas served with scones, muffins and jam. Main dishes cost between 70 and 100 francs; Sunday brunch will set you back 145 francs.

Angélina
1st arr. - 226, rue de Rivoli - 42 60 82 00
Open 9:30 a.m.-7 p.m. (Sat. & Sun. 9:30 a.m.-7:30 p.m.). Closed Aug.
16th arr. - 10, place de Mexico - 47 04 89 42
Open daily 8:30 a.m.-8 p.m.
17th arr. - Palais des Congrès, Porte Maillot - 40 68 22 51
Open daily 9 a.m.-8 p.m.

This is it, the high-water mark of posh Paris society—or at least it used to be. Angélina still appears to be *the* elegant tea room in town, a kingdom of elderly grandes dames in green hats. But has it really maintained its once-lofty social position? Not according to the aforementioned grandes dames, who sniff at the increasingly common clientele—rich young bourgeois in leather jackets and young ladies just out of convent schools, smoking and squealing. And perhaps these newcomers *are* out of place in this room, with its bronzed mouldings, coral-coloured pilasters and faded Côte d'Azur frescoes.

But for those with a soft spot for this sort of place, there's still plenty of charm in the heavy curtains, the wealth of gilt moulding and the motherly waitresses bustling about with silver trays. And there are plenty of calories in the notorious Mont-Blanc (sweet chestnut purée in a meringue shell, heaped with whipped cream) and the legendary thick hot chocolate.

L'Arbre à Cannelle
2nd arr. - 57, passage des Panoramas - 45 08 55 87
Open 11 a.m.-6 p.m. Closed Sun. & holidays.

You'll find this charming Second Empire tea room sheltered in the newly refurbished, wonderfully luminous passage des Panoramas. Stockbrokers and people in advertising drop by here for lunch; they are joined, at teatime, by a clutch of elegant elderly ladies. We're particularly fond of the homemade apple crumble and the excellent walnut tart, perfect with one of the many fine teas.

L'Auberge du Bonheur
16th arr. - Bois de Boulogne, av. de Longchamp (behind Grande Cascade restaurant)
42 24 10 17
Open daily May.-Oct. noon-10:30 p.m. Closed evenings & Fri. & Sat. in winter, & 3 wks. in Feb.

This little country inn in the heart of the Bois de Boulogne has the special attraction of a lovely terrace for long summer evenings. But the Auberge is a treat in winter, too, when you squeeze into a comfortable

CAFES & QUICK BITES – TEA ROOMS

banquette after a stroll in the Bois de Boulogne. These former stables have been done up prettily: exposed beams, red-and-white-checked curtains, lots of plants and a smartly turned-out staff. In this utterly cosy little spot, grandmas chat with their little darlings over a cup of tea and a treat, perhaps a tart or ice cream. At noon, people who work near the Bois show up for the 135-franc lunch menu (the children's menu costs 55 francs).

Boissier
16th arr. - 184, av. Victor-Hugo
45 04 87 88
Open 9 a.m.-7:30 p.m. (Sun. 10 a.m.-7 p.m.).

This elegant, traditional tea room overlooks the square Lamartine. Inside, little girls in kilts and white ankle socks devour such house specialities as enormous chocolate cakes and delicately flaky apple tarts. Their mothers, no doubt more concerned about their figures, order mushroom salads or the superb *Marceau* platter of Parma ham, mozzarella, tomatoes and raw mushrooms, along with a glass of Château de Lussac. Among the desserts, our vote goes to the Breda (a rich coffee mousse), and the hazelnut-based Noisettine. And on a chilly afternoon, nothing comforts like Boissier's divine hot chocolate, which comes in five different flavours. Tea or chocolate and a pastry will cost about 50 francs.

Brocco
3rd arr. - 180, rue du Temple
42 72 19 81
Open daily 6:30 a.m.-7:30 p.m.

Piping hot bittersweet chocolate, a creamy rhubarb Chiboust with a touch of lemon and a crunch of caramel, a Royal rich with praline—these are just a few of the superior sweets on offer at Brocco, an unassuming, old-fashioned cake shop near the place de la République.

La Bûcherie
5th arr. - 41, rue de la Bûcherie
43 54 24 52
Open daily 3 p.m.-6 p.m.

There are surely better ways to spend blustery afternoons than before the Bûcherie's crackling fire, with a cup of fine tea, a slice of tart lemon meringue pie, a view of Notre-Dame and a book from Shakespeare & Co. (right next door)—but we can't think of a single one.

Cador
1st arr. - 2, rue de l'Amiral-Coligny - 45 08 19 18
Open 9 a.m.-6:30 p.m. Closed Mon. & Aug. 15-Sept. 15.

Utterly worthy of its prestigious setting just opposite the Louvre, Cador is a regal little cake shop with gilt décor fit for a king. Seated at pink and taupe marble tea tables, tourists and locals alike make short work of the dainty cakes that provide such a mouthwatering display in the window. The Petits Cadors (chocolate and orange peel on a shortcrust base) and the mousseline, a recent creation that is accompanied by a luscious Grand Marnier custard sauce, attract their fair share of customers.

Carette
16th arr. - 4, pl. du Trocadéro
47 27 88 56
Open 8 a.m.-7 p.m. Closed Tues. & Aug.

Carette is famous for its macaroons—chocolate, vanilla, lemon—and its coffee. The wealthy heirs and heiresses of the avenue Mozart have long come here to chat over tea. But now the younger generation is moving in; if their racket is not to your liking, remember that Carette is also a cake shop and caterer: you can stop to pick up some macaroons and go away to eat them in peace.

Casta Diva
8th arr. - 27, rue Cambacérès
42 66 46 53
Open 11:30 a.m.-6:30 p.m. Closed Sun., holidays, Sat. in June & in July & in Aug. No cards.

These two quite chic white rooms under the arcades, with their spacious alcoves and heavy pistachio-coloured curtains, shelter a posh, well-shopped-for clientele. The furniture, all in mahogany, is richly evocative of the Empire. Even the salads and savoury tarts are rich. Desserts uphold the house standards very well (try the apple délice with Calvados or the chocolate mousse cake). The tea list features rare selections from Mariage Frères, and Verlet supplies the coffee. Either beverage and a pastry will set you back about 60 francs.

La Charlotte de l'Isle
4th arr. - 24, rue Saint-Louis-en-l'Isle - 43 54 25 83
Open 2:30 p.m.-4 p.m. (Wed. 2 p.m.-8 p.m.). Closed Mon. & Tues.

Tea tins piled everywhere, posters, paintings, old mirrors, hats, bouquets of dried flowers and, yes, even a piano: such are the elements of its wonderful, artistically disordered décor. Fruit tarts sit nicely with any of the 30 teas (we like the spice tea), served with dignity on small etched trays, in antique teapots and cups, with silver carafes for the hot water. Hot-chocolate lovers will be more than happy with the old-fashioned version offered here, which carefully preserves the aroma of the chocolate.

Find the address you are looking for, quickly and easily, in the index.

TEA ROOMS – CAFES & QUICK BITES

La Chocolatière
6th arr. - 5, rue Stanislas - 45 49 13 06
Open 9 a.m.-7 p.m. Closed Sun.

At lunch and teatime, people from the nearby TV station, teenagers (Lycée Stanislas is next door) and Luxembourg Garden strollers all gather in this cosy spot. At noon, order a quick lunch of a salad, pie and dessert for 59 francs. We recommend you skip the tabouleh, but the gratins are tasty and warming. For afternoon snacks, there is caramel tea, lovely with dark-chocolate cake, or old-fashioned hot chocolate, served in a china chocolate pot, with crème fraîche and a glass of iced water (30 francs). This goes nicely with the hot apple and almond fondant (26 francs) or light fruit cake—homemade, of course.

Concertea
7th arr. - 3, rue Paul-Louis-Courier - 45 49 27 59
Open 11:30 a.m.-7 p.m. (Mon. 11:30 a.m.-4 p.m.). Closed Sun.

If you like Mozart with your chocolate tart, Verdi with your lemon meringue pie, or Bach with your vegetable quiche, this charming spot will suit you to a... tea. Check out the menu (written on a musical stave), then enjoy the concert while sipping smoky Lapsang Souchong from Mariage Frères or nibbling on one of the fresh and delicious homemade gâteaux (30 francs).

Coquelin Aîné
16th arr. - 67, rue de Passy - 45 24 44 00
Open 9 a.m.-7:30 p.m. Closed Sun.

Coquelin Aîné—what a truly Parisian treat. Yes, my dear, we know exactly where we are the moment we enter this tea room and see Hermès scarves in the necks of Burberry raincoats. Sweet, snobby little things from the local private school come in for tea and a tart, éclair, meringue or Coquelin's famed macaroon. In warm weather, we like to lunch on the terrace (135 francs) and enjoy the view of the pretty place de Passy.

A la Cour de Rohan
6th arr. - 59-61, rue Saint-André-des-Arts
43 25 79 67
Open noon-7:30 p.m. Closed Mon., Aug., Dec. 25 & Jan. 1. No cards.

Tucked away in a little passage off the boulevard Saint Germain is this cosy tea room that's as comfortable as a private home: dishes designed by Cocteau, Louis XVI furniture and old Limoges china. Patrons seated at chintz-skirted tables murmur quietly over lunch (good chicken-liver salad) or teatime treats (yummy rhubarb crumble), while the charming hostess attends to their comfort. The delicious homemade jams and scones are sold to take away.

Dalloyau
2nd. - 25, bd des Capucines - 47 03 47 00
Open 8:30 a.m.-7:30 p.m. (Sat. 9 a.m.-7:30 p.m.). Closed Sun.
6th arr. - 2, pl. Edmond-Rostand
43 29 31 10
Open daily 9 a.m.-6:45 p.m.
8th arr. - 99-101, rue du Faubourg-Saint-Honoré
43 59 18 10
Open daily 8:30 a.m.-9 p.m.
15th arr. - 69, rue de la Convention - 45 77 84 27
Open daily 9:30 a.m.-7:30 p.m. (Sun. 9 a.m.-19 p.m.).

Dalloyau will always be Dalloyau. Nothing changes: grandmothers from the sixth arrondissement still chat together or bring their grandchildren in for a treat, schoolgirls still sit telling each other schoolgirl stories, and the young couples still smile timidly at each other after a walk around the Luxembourg Gardens across the street. The conscientious staff serves a substantial choice of teas, fruit juices, good hot chocolate, delicate cakes and sumptuous ice cream concoctions. The lunchtime crowd favours fresh salads and tasty *plats du jour* that don't cost the earth.

Aux Délices de Scott
17th arr. - 39, av. de Villiers - 47 63 71 36
Open 8:30 a.m.-8 p.m. Closed Sun. & holidays.

Aux Délices is nothing short of an institution. The grand chandelier is hung so high up in the vault of the ceiling that it looks small. The huge room, tiled in blue and sienna with ivory woodwork and endless mirrors, was once graced by the likes of Sarah Bernhardt and Sacha Guitry. Tea is served with all due ceremony, and may be accompanied by ethereal macaroons or a

---

Heroic taxpayers

After the architectural free-for-all of the Middle Ages, the development of the *place des Vosges* in the early 17th century heralded an era of elegance and symmetry with its arcades, stone-and-brick façades and steep slate roofs. Despite various renovations, the 36 houses have retained their homogeneous aspect. The place des Vosges was given its present name in 1800 in honour of the first French department to pay its taxes after the Revolution.

nougat parisien, among other excellent cakes.

Les Deux Abeilles
7th arr. - 189, rue de l'Université
45 55 64 04
Open 9 a.m.-7 p.m. Closed Sun. & Aug. No cards.

The classically elegant décor reflects the well-bred, well-heeled clientele that swarms to Les Deux Abeilles for breakfast, lunch and tea. The place buzzes most busily at noon, when inventive salads, smoked salmon feuilleté and an uncommonly good tomato tart appear on the menu (a full lunch costs 80 to 100 francs). Later in the afternoon pastries are featured, including an unusual chestnut cake; and for those who don't fancy tea, may we suggest the lemony ginger drink that is a speciality of the house.

Djarling
15th arr. - 45-47, rue Cronstadt
45 32 47 17
Open noon-6 p.m. (Fri. & Sat. noon-8 p.m.).

Come teatime, the pretty cups on the pink paisley tablecloths sit patiently waiting to be filled with one of 15 premium teas (the classics plus rare blends, including sturdy brews from Kenya) that the house offers. All the appropriate accompaniments are on hand: fruit cake, scones, crêpes and wonderful ice creams. Sunday brunch is served from noon to 6 p.m.

Les Enfants Gâtés
4th arr. - 43, rue des Francs-Bourgeois - 42 77 07 63
Open daily 12:30 p.m.-8 p.m. (Sat. & Sun. noon-7 p.m.). Closed 3 wks. in Aug.

The atmosphere is soft, the lighting subdued, and the round tables and deep armchairs are arranged between tall ivory-painted columns beneath whirling ceiling fans. An ideal place for tea (or even better, hot chocolate) and conversation. If your sweet tooth demands indulgence, order the brownie (the waitress may try to convince you to order the *tarte du jour*, but stand your ground!). Stiffish prices.

La Fourmi Ailée
5th arr. - 8, rue du Fouarre - 43 29 40 99
Open noon-7 p.m. Closed Tues., Dec. 25 & Jan. 1.

From the outside, La Fourmi Ailée looks like a bookshop. Inside, why, it is a bookshop, but one that artfully conceals a tea room—a blissfully intimate, casual tea room. Awaiting you on a rustic sideboard sit a fresh, fragrant spice cake, a Norman tart and scones served with two kinds of jam. Wisps of steam rise from the spouts of a mixed assortment of teapots set on the tables (16 types of tea are offered). One could easily while away the better part of an afternoon in so inviting a spot, with a newly purchased volume of, say, Virginia Woolf (most of the books are by women authors, and the selection is international).

Les Fous de l'Ile
4th arr. - 33, rue des Deux-Ponts 43 25 76 67
Open noon-11:30 p.m. (Sat. 3 p.m.-11:30 p.m., Sun. 11 p.m.-6 p.m.). Closed Mon.

The upper levels above this large, windowed room are lined with books, china is displayed in glass cases, and here and there hang black-and-white photographs. It's a busy place, very relaxed and pleasant, with a student atmosphere. The clientele is young, cosmopolitan and at ease, and the waiters officiate in T-shirts and jeans. A variety of teas are offered, including Sakura (green tea flavoured with cherry) and Caraibes (Indian, Ceylon and Caribbean flowers), all of which go well with the creamy house cheesecake. The popular Sunday brunch (100 to 160 francs) is served from 11 a.m.

Galerie Gourmande
3rd arr. - 38, rue de Sévigné - 42 74 48 40
Open noon-7 p.m. Closed Mon.

The scrumptious orange fondant, clafoutis and fruit cake are baked according to old family recipes and daintily served on immaculate tablecloths along with a steaming cup of tea. What could be more restorative after a visit to the Musée Carnavalet or a tour of the Marais's town houses? The Galerie Gourmande can also set you up with fresh, delicate salads at lunchtime, and the house hot chocolate is a creamy, fragrant masterpiece.

Galerie de la Paix
Hôtel George-V
8th arr. - 31, avenue George-V
47 23 54 00
Open daily 9 a.m.-7 p.m.

The power tea, it seems, has replaced the power breakfast as an occasion for wheeling and dealing. The best place in Paris to perform this new ritual of ambition is the stately *salon de thé* recently inaugurated in the Hôtel George V. Cement an alliance, plan a merger or acquire an adversary's assets over a cup of Japanese Matcha Uji or Russian Czar Alexander tea (prepared according to the "five essential laws of tea brewing") from Mariage Frères, and a plate of miniature French pastries or sandwiches. These delicacies are served beneath the benevolent gaze of Peace and Abundance, allegorical figures who star in an immense tapestry that is the Galerie's most prominent feature. And an abundance of money is what you'll need when the bill comes: 35 to 50 francs for coffee, tea or chocolate, 50 francs for fruit juice and for pastries or sandwiches (note, however, that a club sandwich will set you back 130 francs).

L'Heure Gourmande
6th arr. - 22, passage Dauphine
46 34 00 40
Open 11:30 a.m.-7 p.m. Closed Sun., 3 1st wks. of Aug., 1 wk. at Christmas-New Year's & 1 wk. at May 1.

Sheltered in the picturesque passage Dauphine is a perfect little tea room that offers handsome surroundings, a hospitable welcome, fabulous cheesecake and the peace necessary to enjoy it all—stay an hour, or two hours if you like. For tea and cake, you'll pay about 65 francs; a light lunch costs about 100 francs.

L'Heure des Thés
9th arr. - 1, rue Chaptal - 45 26 85 94
Open 11 a.m.-7:30 p.m. Closed Sat., Sun. Aug. & holidays.

Yellow rattan chairs, pine furniture and cheerful flowered tablecloths make an ideal setting in which to dream of country life. Let a pot of smoky Chinese tea soothe away the urban blues, and indulge in a slice of lemon tart or chocolate fondant. Luncheon dishes (tarte provençale and the like) are priced between 37 and 49 francs; the relaxing atmosphere carries no extra charge.

Ladurée
8th arr. - 16, rue Royale - 42 60 21 79
Open 8:30 a.m.-7 p.m. Closed Sun., Aug. & holidays.

Cherubs on faded frescoes, plush red carpet, oak woodwork and round tables in veined black marble are all part of the charm of this tiny institution, which is always full. Especially on Saturdays, when lovely ladies from the best parts of Paris put down their Hermès shopping bags for a few minutes to enjoy tea with a macaroon or two (they are the best in Paris, you know). Lunchtime is surprisingly lively: choices include omelettes, chicken, hot dishes such as cassoulet, or minuscule crab and salmon sandwiches that will empty your purse long before they fill your stomach.

Le Loir dans la Théière
4th arr. - 3, rue des Rosiers - 42 72 90 61
Open noon-7 p.m. (Sun. 11 a.m.-7 p.m.). Closed 3 1st wks. of Aug., Dec. 25 & Jan. 1. No cards.

Young women as graceful as nymphs ferry bulbous teapots among the low sofas. A faint feeling of nostalgia, a faded carpet, old armoires from Normandy, soft lights and frescoes on the walls give the place a gentle provincial charm. The atmosphere is quaint and slightly intellectual. This tea-room is run on a kind of co-operative basis, and since the waiters and cooks are constantly changing, it is impossible to recommend specific dishes. The clientele, which is more bourgeois and conventional than the place itself, tends to favour the straightforward pastries and the hazelnut cake called Alice's Secret (though we've found it to be rather heavy). The service, although a little too frenetic, is friendly and engaging. Expect to spend 60 francs for tea and a pastry, and about 80 francs for lunch.

Maison du Chocolat
8th arr. - 52, rue François-Ier - 47 23 38 25
Open 9:30 a.m.-7 p.m. Closed Sun. & holidays.

Both haven and heaven—for the truly devout chocoholic, that is—can be found here. Maison du Chocolat is a tea room that lives up to its name by serving neither tea nor coffee, just hot chocolate. And the house drink has but one fault: it's too small. Poured from a hot chocolate pot into Limoges china cups, the divine stuff comes in five incarnations: Guayaquil, a classic and elegant brew; Caracas, bitter, full-bodied, recommended for true lovers of chocolate; Brésilien, lightly flavoured with coffee; Seville, spiced with a hint of cinnamon; and Bacchus, which leaves you dreaming of the Caribbean. All are accompanied by whipped cream. You can also try the worthy chocolate frappé, with either ice cream or sorbet. If you're still not sated, try one of the pastries, perhaps the Gounod with bits of orange peel or the Mokambo with its fresh raspberry flavour, or an assortment of 15 chocolates lovingly dreamed up by Robert Linxe, the guiding spirit of the place.

Mariage Frères
4th arr. - 30, rue du Bourg-Tibourg - 42 72 28 11
Open daily noon-7 p.m.
6th arr. - 30, rue des Grands Augustins - 40 51 82 50
Open daily noon-7 p.m.

A jungle of teas, teapots, teacups, tea balls—Mariage Frères is, in short, a tea-ocracy. For more than a century it has sold tea, 350 kinds of it, from the strongest Imperial Slavic blends to the most delicately perfumed varieties. Non-smokers may station themselves at a table on the ground floor beneath the exotic palms and the ceiling fans. Those dedicated to tobacco as well as tea leaves climb, at their own risk, the steep stairs to a place in which they will be welcomed. Everybody is kept happy here. The teas, prepared with filtered water, are served at the appropriate temperatures in insulated infusion-style teapots, and the waiters respect the ritual of tea. Watching them wheel between the tables, impeccably garbed in something vaguely Indian, one wonders when they have time to read their Kipling. Delicate homemade cakes valiantly accompany these sublime teas. Lots of brunch items are served on Sundays.

La Mosquée de Paris
5th arr. - 39, rue Geoffroy-Saint-Hilaire - 43 31 18 14
Open daily 11 a.m.-9 p.m. Closed July 27-Sept. 10. No cards.

When you emerge—skin softened, hair shining and scented—from the hammam that is part of the Paris Mosque complex, prolong your sense of well-being with a stop at the Mosque's tea room. In a cool, dim atmosphere, with music playing in the background, sample North African and Middle Eastern pastries accompanied by strong, sweet mint tea, Turkish coffee or barley water.

Muscade
1st arr. - 36, rue de Montpensier & 67, galerie de Montpensier, Jardin du Palais Royal
42 97 51 36
Open daily 3 p.m.-6 p.m. Closed 1 wk. at Christmas-New Year's.

A wall of mirror and another of window give the actors (from the nearby Comédie Française) and government officials who frequent this chic little tea room a many-angled view of the Palais-Royal gardens. In fine weather, take a cue from the regulars: lay claim to a table outside, then go inside to inspect the pastries and make your choice.

Les Nuits des Thés
7th arr. - 22, rue de Beaune - 47 03 92 07
Open noon-7 p.m. Closed Sun., Aug. & holidays.

The décor is rich: white lacquer, pink upholstery, mercury mirrors, damask tablecloths, antique furniture and watercolours on the walls. The welcome may be cool if you aren't a regular, but the clientele is noticeably at ease, chatting about such weighty topics as dog pedigrees, boating and the latest literary successes. They nibble on salads and main-dish pies and tarts of all sorts, but to tell the truth, only the desserts are really exceptional (we're thinking of the caramelised cream cheese tart and the raspberry macaroons). You'll spend something over 100 francs for lunch, half that for tea and a pastry.

Pandora
2nd arr. - 24, passage Choiseul 42 97 56 01
Open 11:30 a.m.-7 p.m. Closed Sat., Sun. & Aug.

Take a good look at the cakes as you cross the front room, then proceed to the chocolate-coloured salon in the back, where daylight pours down from the glass ceiling. At lunchtime, crisp toast and fresh butter are already set out on the well-spaced round tables; the menu offers courgette flan, a remarkable chicken salad and other light dishes. Late afternoon is a quieter time, perfect for indulging in Pandora's chocolate-chestnut cake, or the rhubarb or coffee tarts. Reasonable prices. It is advisable to book for lunch.

La Pâtisserie Viennoise
6th arr. - 8, rue de l'Ecole-de-Médecine - 43 26 60 48
Open 9 a.m.-7:15 p.m. Closed Sat., Sun., mid July-end Aug. & holidays.

Medical and literature students are among the enlightened crowd who fill this citadel of the Latin Quarter, its seats worn smooth and shiny by generations of devotion. La Pâtisserie Viennoise opened in 1928, and the youthful atmosphere remains as tasteful as the cakes are tasty—the strudel and the poppy-seed cake (called the *flanni*) are among our favourites. The teas are perfect and the Viennese hot chocolate is a dream; they all marry beautifully with a croissant or a raisin brioche. Everything is made on the premises and everything is good. There's only one drawback: the place is always packed. But so what—just pile in or find a stool at the bar. It's worth it. You'll think you've been transported from Paris to a *Konditorei* in Vienna.

Le Ritz
Hôtel Ritz
1st arr. - 15, place Vendôme - 42 60 38 30
Open daily 4 p.m.-6 p.m.

A harpist adds a magical note to this enchanted garden where classical busts, plane trees and elegant patrons create an otherworldly haven. A discreet, attentive staff serves decent tea; for our money (130 francs, to be precise) only the millefeuille rises above the ordinary. But the atmosphere is worth the price of admission.

Rose Thé
1st arr. - 91, rue Saint-Honoré 42 36 97 18
Open noon-6:30 p.m. Closed Sun. No cards.

Your grandmother would love it here: tasteful paintings, subdued lighting, antiques, plants and a sideboard displaying some luscious-looking cakes. Tea lovers will certainly fall for the rose-thé, an exquisite blend of Bulgarian rose with a touch of jasmine and lotus. Devotees of something more solid will find no fault with the old-fashioned rich chocolate cake made from real chocolate bars. And the hot chocolate is not to be missed. Between noon and 2 pm, the regulars, including local antique dealers, come to nibble on gratins, quiches and the famous meat pie. In summer a sheltered terrace provides a spot of calm in the madding heart of Paris.

TEA ROOMS – CAFES & QUICK BITES

Le Salon du Chocolat
8th arr. - 11, bd de Courcelles
45 22 07 27
Open 2:30 p.m.-6:30 p.m. Closed Sun., Aug. 15, Easter & 4 wks. at Christmas.

Not content with offering wonderfully intense chocolates (try the palets made with cocoas from Java, Ghana and Colombia), the Salon now proposes rich pastries, too. Lunch brings an appealing selection of hot dishes, but the place really comes into its own at teatime, with a wide choice of brews from China and India, and a sublime version of hot chocolate, served in a Limoges chocolate pot. The triple-chocolate cake, we might add, is in a class by itself. Plan to spend 50 francs for a beverage and cake.

Le Stübli
17th arr. - 11, rue Poncelet - 42 27 81 86
Open 10:30 a.m.-6:30 p.m. (Sun. 10:30 a.m.-1 p.m.).

In the ground-floor shop you can choose from among the best German and Viennese pastries in Paris—Linzertorte, Sachertorte, Black Forest cake and, of course, apple strudel (about 25 francs). On the first floor, in the warm atmosphere of an Austrian chalet, all these and more can be tasted along with a hot chocolate or a cup of Viennese coffee. It's *Stüblime*! And in case you're really hungry, there's Bavarian salad, Swabian onion tart (38 francs), an assortment of smoked fish and the Stübli, hot beef sausage and potato salad.

RAC PARIS STREETS: The cartography of this city-wide street plan of Paris is clear and easy to use and is supported by a comprehensive index in book form tipped on to the card cover. The map is packed with essential information including the direction of one-way streets. A must for all visitors to Paris. Price: £ 4.50.

Tarterie
11th arr. - 10, rue Saint-Sébastien - 43 55 27 31
Open 11:30 a.m.-15:30 p.m. Closed Sat. & Sun. No cards.

What sets this former dairy shop apart from the common run of tea rooms is the menu's South American (Colombian, to be specific) accent. Alongside the leek and mushroom quiche, you'll find corn cakes with meat and a rousing chili sauce. Traditional sweets like dark-chocolate cake and fruit crumble appear at teatime. You'll spend about 60 francs at lunch, 40 francs for tea and a pastry.

The Tea Caddy
5th arr. - 14, rue Saint-Julien-le-Pauvre - 43 54 15 56
Open noon-7 p.m. (Sun. 11:30 a.m.-7 p.m.). Closed Tues., Wed. & 3 wks. in Aug. No cards.

This place has a medieval feel about it, with exposed beams and stained-glass windows. It's famous for a warm atmosphere and reasonable prices, and its clientele tends to be young and international (we overheard Swedes discussing with Parisians in English the relative merits of Australian cinema). The cake list has an English and Austrian accent: chocolate Sachertorte, Linzertorte with cinnamon and raspberries, fruit pies with cream, scones and muffins are complemented by six or seven types of tea. Unfortunately, the quality is uneven.

Tea Follies
9th arr. - 6, pl. Gustave-Toudouze - 42 80 08 44
Open 9 a.m.-9 p.m. (Sun. 9 a.m.-7 p.m.). No cards.

The refurbishment did away with the 1930s-style facade. Those who used to hide behind the green carved shutters must now wear sunglasses, for a big window is all that separates Tea Follies from the square outside. Another change, an air-filtering device, allows one to breathe more easily in the smokers' dining room (another area is reserved for non-smokers). The white walls are enlivened with watercolours, and the friendly service remains thoroughly professional. At lunch, the savoury tarts, the famous chicken pie or a refreshing tuna tartare with apples get to the table in record time. Afternoons are more leisurely: young ladies murmur demurely over tea, scones and jam.

Tea and Tattered Pages
6th arr. - 24, rue Mayet - 40 65 94 35
Open 11 a.m.-7 p.m. Closed Sun., Dec. 25 & Jan. 1.

Why do we feel like putting on bell bottoms and a flowered waistcoat when we come here? Must be the atmosphere redolent of hippiedom that floats among these used English-language books, and over the tea tables laden with brownies, muffins, scones and delicious cheesecake. Americans, Canadians and Britons gather here to chat and joke noisily in their native tongue(s). Tea and a cake will cost you about 50 francs.

Thé Cool
16th arr. - 10, rue Jean-Bologne 42 24 69 13
Open noon-7 p.m. (Sun. 11 a.m.-6 p.m.). Closed wk. of Aug. 15.

Thé Cool exudes the charm of an airy English garden—it's a haven of calm in the middle of a busy district. At lunch, enjoy the view of the pretty square opposite while tucking into an attractive dish of, say, mozzarella, salmon, or air-dried beef. Those who live for teatime will rejoice at the selection of 30 rare and wonderful brews, which may be accompanied by a mouthwatering range of sweets (chocolate marquise with crème anglaise, fruit tarts, apple crumble...).

Thé au Fil
2nd arr. - 80, rue Montmartre
42 36 95 49
Open noon-5 p.m. Closed Sat., Sun., Aug. & holidays.

From the apricot walls plastered with posters, the newspapers and magazines neatly arranged on poles and the paisley tablecloths, we knew immediately we were in a tea room. But the liveliness of the place is closer in feel to a bistro. Be that as it may, the tea list is exceptional, the atmosphere convivial, and the appetising luncheon salads are reasonably priced. Teatime treats include poppy-seed strudel and Russian-style cheesecake.

La Théière
14th arr. - 118, bd du Montparnasse - 43 27 22 00
Open 10:30 a.m.-7:45 p.m. Closed Sun. & holidays.

At this mecca for tea lovers, you will also find excellent coffees, jams, chocolates and appealing breads, fudgy brownies, an exceptionally good pear tart, and a tea cake imported from England. Simple but delicious hot dishes appear at lunchtime (salmon en papillote, salads and such).

Toraya
1st arr. - 10, rue Saint-Florentin
42 60 13 00
Open 10 a.m.-7 p.m. Closed Sun.

Westerners may be disconcerted by the taste of green tea, which the courteous staff serves on a tray that is itself a work of art. Or by the pastries with their transcendent, poetic names: in spring you'll be offered the toyamazakura (*the cherry trees on the far mountain*), in summer the semi no ogawa (*the red fish*) and in winter the matso no yuki (*snow-covered pines*). Each of these exotic delights bears a resemblance to its name. Strange, very strange, is the colourless agar-agar (gelatine substitute) topped with an aduki bean paste. The staff will probably tell you that Japanese pastry has something for all five senses: the pleasure of the sound of the name, the treat for the eyes, the pleasant contact of the red-bean paste with the tongue and teeth, and the pleasing sound of the rice crunching. All that remains then is to define the pleasure of the taste. Well, it must be delicious—after all, Toraya has been purveyor to the Emperor of Japan since 1789.

Verlet
1st arr. - 256, rue Saint-Honoré
42 60 67 39
Open noon-6:30 p.m. Closed Sun. & Mon., Easter Sat. & Sun., Oct. 1, Aug., Dec. 25, Jan. 1 & May 1.

At Verlet, it isn't Champagne or the proximity of your beloved that goes to your head, but rather the delicious aromas of tea and coffee. Once inside the door and in the presence of sacks and sacks of both of these earthly delights, we lose all desires except to be served a steaming cup of *something*. This is one of the best places in Paris for either tea or coffee. Seated on the rickety chairs (which, by the way, are few in number and hotly fought over at lunchtime), in its all-wood décor dating from 1880, coffee devotees sip Jamaican, an excellent Mocha or the house blend, Grand Pavois. For tea drinkers, there are more than 30 varieties, including a nicely perfumed Chinese tea called White Flowers and, of course, the famous Darjeeling, which seems particularly soft and subtle here. If you want a snack, there is silky Viennese strudel.

WINE BARS

L'Ange-Vin
11th arr. - 24, rue Richard-Lenoir
43 48 20 20
Open 11 a.m.-8:30 p.m. (Tues. & Thurs. 11 a.m.-2 a.m.). Closed Sat., Sun., July & holidays.

The luscious wines for which Anjou is famous—Montlouis, Coteaux-de-l'Aubance, Vouvray and Coteaux-du-Layon—here get the star billing they deserve. The '89 and '90 harvests yielded some stellar examples, which owner Jean-Pierre Robinot would be only to happy to pour for you (16 to 24 francs a glass).

Les Bacchantes
9th arr. - 21, rue Caumartin - 42 65 25 35
Open 11:30 a.m.-5:30 a.m. (Sun. 11:30 a.m.-10 p.m.).

We're happy to report that the service has greatly improved at this all-night wine bar, where judiciously chosen charcuteries, superb cheeses and tasty hot dishes provide ideal company for the Minervois, Béarn rouge, Pacherenc de Vic Bilh and other unusual bottlings selected by owner Raymond Pocous.

Bar du Caveau
1st arr. - 17, pl. Dauphine - 43 54 45 95
Open 8:30 a.m.-8 p.m. Closed Sat., Sun. & last 2 wks. of Dec.

Lawyers, it seems, will always be lawyers. And lawyers can always be found at the Bar du Caveau, discussing their cases over glasses of Bordeaux. In winter, when the interior of this well-heeled establishment gets a bit cramped, their verbal antics can wax tiresome. You may prefer to sit quietly with a Parisian daily, presented in the old reading-room style on a thin pole, or simply to enjoy a salad, an open sandwich and a glass of one of the excellent

Quality Inn Paris
Rive Gauche

Your right choice in the heart of Paris

LOCATION
In the heart of the left bank, walking distance of
St-Germain des Prés, Jardin du Luxembourg and Montparnasse.

ACCOMODATION
134 rooms including 6 Junior Suites, all fully air conditionned
with bath, shower, hairdryer, digital safe, mini-bar, radio,
local and satellite TV including C.N.N. international
direct dial telephone. No smoking rooms.

FACILITIES
Piano-bar GREGORY'S, meeting room for 15 people.
Buffet breakfast in Café des Fontaines.
Change service, theatre bookings, car rental, excursions,
laundry/dry cleaning, in house parking.

RATES
Single rooms from 600 FF. Double rooms from 670 FF.
Junior Suite from 930 FF.
(Taxes and services included).
All major credit card accepted.

CHOICE HOTELS
INTERNATIONAL

92, rue de Vaugirard - 75006 PARIS
Tél. : (1) 42 22 00 56 - Fax : (1) 42 22 05 39

WINE BARS – CAFES & QUICK BITES

Bordeaux selected by the management, which also runs the restaurant next door. In summer the tiny pavement terrace on the place Dauphine is a treat.

Le Baron Rouge
12th arr. - 1, rue Théophile-Roussel - 43 43 14 32
Open 10 a.m.-2 p.m. & 5 p.m.-9:30 p.m. (Sat. 10 a.m.-8 p.m.; Sun. 10 a.m.-2 p.m.). Closed Mon. & holidays.

New owners have laid in a new selection of wines and spruced up the dining room. The same colourful clientele of trendies, old-time Parisians, craftsmen and artists drops in for a plate of charcuterie and incredibly low-cost wines (Côtes-du-Rhône goes for 22 francs a litre).

Beaujolais Saint-Honoré
1st arr. - 24, rue du Louvre - 42 60 89 79
Open daily 6 a.m.-2 a.m.

Ever since the Pyramide du Louvre became one of the world's top tourist attractions, this venerable bistro (sometime winner of the "Best Jug of Wine" award) has had a new lease on life. Though the décor remains somewhat sad and weary, you can rely on the quality of the Beaujolais, the charcuteries and the perfectly ripened cheeses.

La Bergerie
16th arr. - 21, rue de Galilée - 47 20 48 63
Open 8 a.m.-8 p.m. Closed Sat., Sun., Aug. & holidays.

Another award-winning wine bar, notable not only for its Beaujolais, but also for a deliciously fruity Bourgueil. The hearty *plats du jour* bring in an enthusiastic crowd at lunchtime.

> The prices in this guide reflect what establishments were charging at the time of going to press.

Bistrot des Augustins
6th arr. - 39, quai des Grands-Augustins - 43 54 41 65
Open daily 11 a.m.-2 a.m.

At the bottom of the boulevard Saint-Michel, amid the fast food and cheap cafés, stands this honest bistro, unflagging in its devotion to French culinary tradition. Robust homemade terrine, a satisfying cheeseboard and delicious omelettes are solidly supported by a range of proprietors' wines: Muscadet, Cérons (a honeyed dessert wine), Sinard's Côtes-du-Rhône sell for 12 to 18 francs a glass.

Le Bistrot du Sommelier
8th arr. - 97, bd Haussmann - 42 65 24 85
Open noon-2:30 p.m. & 7:30 p.m.-10:30 p.m. Closed Sat. eve., Sun. & July 24-Aug. 24.

Despite the name, this is hardly a bistro; it's more like a classic restaurant. But there's certainly a sommelier: Philippe Faure-Brac, elected World's Best Sommelier in 1992. His own predilection is for wines from the Rhône valley, of which he is a native, and Bordeaux from the other side of the country (Saint-Emilion, Pomerol). An excellent address for people who wish to learn more about wine and about matching wines with food. No concessions are made to accessibility or easy drinking: here you'll find neither Sancerre nor Beaujolais nor Muscadet. Prices are high.

Aux Bons Crus
1st arr. - 7, rue des Petits-Champs - 42 60 06 45
Open noon-10 p.m (Sat. 10 a.m.-5:30 p.m.). Closed Sun. & Aug. 15.

After a thoroughgoing facelift, this ultra-Parisian institution is now a wine bar that manages to be both rustic and elegant—perfectly in tune with its location near the fashionable place des Victoires. The food still runs to bistro dishes with a Lyonnais accent, accompanied by a wide and clever range of wines from the Loire Valley, Beaujolais and Bordeaux.

Le Bouchon du Marais
4th arr. - 15, rue François-Miron 48 87 44 13
Open noon-3 p.m. & 6 p.m.-2 a.m. Closed Sun. & Dec. 25.

Just opened in 1992, this bar is already a favourite. In a convivial atmosphere, you can down some choice Loire Valley vintages (the proprietor himself owns a vineyard in Chinon), along with the usual selection of sandwiches, grilled andouillette or, for a change, the Savoie potato-and- cheese dish known as raclette.

Ma Bourgogne
8th arr. - 133, bd Haussmann 45 63 50 61
Open 7 a.m.-8:30 p.m. Closed Sat. & Sun.

Nothing ever seems to change at this temple to Beaujolais, a friendly place where a faithful lunchtime crowd returns religiously for coq au Juliénas, boeuf bourguignon and ham terrine with parsley. The owner, Burgundy-born Louis Prin, continues to purchase his wines direct from the producers, as he has for the past 30 years. His Hautes-Côtes-de-Beaune possesses rare finesse.

La Cave Drouot
9th arr. - 8, rue Drouot - 47 70 83 38
Open 7:30 a.m.-9:30 p.m. Closed Sun. & July-Sept.

This long-lived establishment opposite the Drouot auction rooms is at once a wine bar, a brasserie and a restaurant, so the choice of food ranges from open sandwiches to fully fledged cuisine gastronomique. Antique dealers, auctioneers and collectors rely on Jean-Pierre Cachau to select the perfect wine to accompany their meal: perhaps the Ladoix from Burgundy, which he bottles himself, or a slightly sweet Pacherenc de Vic Bilh, from his native Béarn.

Caves Bailly
5th arr. - 174, rue Saint-Jacques
43 26 80 74
Open 6 p.m.-midnight. Closed Sun. & Mon.

What more pleasant place for a selection of cheese or cold meat and a glass of Bordeaux than this ancient wine shop in the heart of the Latin Quarter? We would surely make it a more frequent stop if the prices were a bit more reasonable: 37 francs for a glass of Ermitage de Chasse-Spleen 1988 is a few francs too much.

Les Caves Petrissans
17th arr. - 30 bis, av. Niel - 42 27 83 84
Open noon-10:15 p.m. Closed Sat., Sun., holidays & 3 wks. in Aug.

This wine shop, one of the most prestigious in Paris, will soon be 100 years old. Down the years a cavalcade of literati and bon vivants have drunk the good wines and Champagnes of Martin Petrissans and his descendants. Currently Christine, the great-granddaughter, and her husband, a former lawyer who left the bar (so to speak), run the establishment. Now it includes a restaurant which offers splendid regional menus with wines to match. For 170 francs you might dine on soup, poulet au vinaigre de cidre, cheese and crème brûlée; attractive accompaniments would be Dauvissat's Chablis (210 francs) or a Beaujolais from Jean-Charles Pivot (95 francs).

Les Caves Solignac
14th arr. - 9, rue Decrès - 45 45 58 59
Open noon-2 p.m. & 7:30 p.m.-10 p.m. Closed Sat., Sun., 2 wks. at Christmas & holidays.

With vaguely Italian décor highlighted by lots of old posters and a curious collection of antique siphons, this well-run *bistrot à vin* balances on the cusp of the fashionable. Owner Jean-François Banéat takes great pains to serve only the freshest food (the house foie gras is a marvel) backed up by a tantalising wine list. Nor does he hesitate to transfer any wine that needs it into a (lovely) decanter—a laudable practice we don't often encounter in the city's wine bars.

La Cloche des Halles
1st arr. - 28, rue Coquillière - 42 36 93 89
Open 8 a.m.-10 p.m. (Sat. 10 a.m.-6 p.m.). Closed Sun.

The wooden clock is still there, a small replica of the bronze one that used to ring to signal the closing of the huge central markets. The bistro itself has gracefully survived the great changes in the area. Serge Lesage, who recently took over the reins, is scrupulously maintaining tradition. There are always several special dishes in addition to the excellent open sandwiches, quiches and good wines bottled on the premises. At lunchtime, a bit of patience is in order; people stand three-deep around the bar, a friendly mixture of youngsters elbow-to-elbow with police inspectors, solicitors and shopkeepers. Fully refreshed, you'll have spent a few dozen francs at most.

Clown Bar
11th arr. - 114, rue Amelot - 43 55 87 35
Open noon-3:30 p.m. & 6:30 p.m.-1 a.m. (Sat. 6 p.m.-1 a.m.). Closed Sun. & Aug. No cards.

Countless drawings, figurines and posters of clowns, clowns and more clowns fill this historic establishment. While the 1919 décor alone is worth the trip, why neglect the marvellous wines and good food served here? Tables are few and hotly contested, so remember to book.

La Côte
2nd arr. - 77, rue de Richelieu 42 97 40 68
Open 7:30 a.m.-8:30 p.m. Closed Sat. & Sun.

The fleet-footed Fabre brothers are famed for their victories in waiters' races around the world (the object of these contests is to run carrying a tray with two full glasses and a bottle of wine). Both also run Paris wine bars: this one is a simple bistro that offers good and hearty dishes (rabbit in mustard sauce, boeuf bourguignon), excellent cheeses and a varied choice of wines from the Loire Valley and Beaujolais. A large, eclectic clientele moves in at lunchtime, and the service sometimes suffers from the crush.

Les Coteaux
15th arr. - 26, bd Garibaldi - 47 34 83 48
Open 10 a.m.-10 p.m. (Mon. 10 a.m.-7:30 p.m.). Closed Sat., Sun., Aug. & holidays.

This attractive newcomer looks like a winner to us. In the bright little dining room cheerful staff serve generous charcuteries (the house terrine is left on the table so you can help yourself), warming *plats du jour* (we liked the sage-scented veal stew on a bed of fresh pasta) and nicely matured cheeses. The owners,

---

We're always happy to hear about your discoveries and receive your comments on ours. Please feel free to write to us stating clearly what you liked or disliked.

who formerly ran a wine shop in Montmartre, have put together an intelligent wine list that includes an ample choice by the glass.

Le Coude-Fou
4th arr. - 12, rue du Bourg-Tibourg - 42 77 15 16
Open daily noon-4 p.m. & 7 p.m.-2 a.m. (Sun. 7 p.m.-2 a.m.).

This place doesn't empty until late, mostly because the customers feel so at home. Conversations flow freely among the tables. The cooking is simple and straightforward (boudin, poultry dishes and the like). If you prefer the bar to a table, the wines by the glass and the charcuterie will keep you happy and speed you on your promenade through the Marais. The house usually offers about 30 wines, half of them by the glass. The Côtes-du-Rhône wines and those from the Loire are well chosen, and there are some nice little wines from Savoie. Honesty obliges us to note, however, that we have on occasion encountered a few oxydised examples.

La Courtille
20th arr. - 1, rue des Envierges 46 36 51 59
Open daily noon-11 p.m.

On the picturesque heights of Belleville, a working-class district where Edith Piaf and Maurice Chevalier played as children, two noted wine buffs, François Morel of the neighboring Cave des Envierges (see below) and his associate, Bernard Pontonnier, preside over La Courtille, a sparkling new wine bar-cum-brasserie. From before noon till nearly midnight you can feast here on such earthy delights as oxtail salad, boudin with caramelised apples or blanquette de veau, all perfect foils for the astutely chosen growers' wines (we like Foillard's manly Morgon). Photos by Willy Ronis of Belleville in the 1950s punctuate the airy, ivory and pine-green décor.

L'Ecluse Bastille
11th arr. - 13, rue de la Roquette 48 05 19 12
Open noon-1:30 a.m. (Thurs., Fri. & Sat. until dawn). Closed Dec. 25 & Jan. 1.

The latest link in the Ecluse chain boasts the chic atmosphere, trendy clientele, stylish staff and huge range of Bordeaux that are the company's time-honoured trademarks. For a festive apéritif, sample the bubbly Lassime Crémant de Bordeaux (17 francs), then move on to steak tartare (75 francs) with a glass of Ségur de Cabanac '87, followed by warm apple pie laced with Armagnac (a glass of Sauternes—perhaps a Château Coutet '84—would be ideal at this juncture). To wind up the evening, a smooth Calvados: Lemorton '55 (25 francs), would be just the ticket.

L'Ecluse François-Ier
8th arr. - 64, rue François-Ier - 47 20 77 09
Open daily noon-1:30 a.m.
See *text above*.

L'Ecluse Les Halles
1st arr. - 5, rue Mondétour - 40 41 08 73
Open noon-1:30 a.m. Closed Sun., Dec. 25 & Jan. 1.

A high-class operation like L'Ecluse is rare in these parts, where tourist traps and greasy cafés abound. You'll spot the familiar facade at the end of the rue Rambuteau, tucked behind the Forum des Halles. Inside, a comfortable room and a hospitable welcome await you, along with some good—though expensive—dishes (carpaccio, foie gras, smoked goose breast...) and a wide-ranging selection of red, white and even sparkling Bordeaux. L'Ecluse makes extensive use of the recent inert-gas replacement devices that allow an opened wine to be maintained in perfect condition for up to ten days. This allows for a top château by the glass (for 60 francs and up) to be offered each week.

L'Ecluse Madeleine
8th arr. - 15, pl. de la Madeleine 42 65 34 69
Open daily noon-1:30 a.m.
See *L'Ecluse Bastille*.

L'Ecluse Saint-Michel
6tht arr. - 15, quai des Grands-Augustins - 46 33 58 74
Open daily noon-1:30 a.m. Closed Sun., Dec. 25 & Jan. 1.
See *L'Ecluse Bastille*.

L'Enoteca
4th arr. - 25, rue Charles-V - 42 78 91 44
Open noon-2 a.m. Closed Dec. 24-Jan. 2.

Should you be seized by an irresistible urge for a bottle of Brunello di Montalcino, Sassicaia or a lush Malvasia dei Lipari, head for the Marais and L'Enoteca, the city's first Italian wine bar. Already a hit with journalists and people in politics, this engaging trattoria features succulent pasta dishes, authentic Italian snacks and a mind-boggling, 100 per cent Italian wine list. We can't think of a better place for a Sunday-night supper (neither can a lot of other folk—remember to book your table).

L'Entre-Deux-Verres
2nd arr. - 48, rue Saint-Anne - 42 96 42 26
Open noon-3 p.m. Closed Sat., Sun., Aug. & holidays.

The food, the wines, the owners: every element of this charming establishment, lodged in an ancient coaching inn, hails from Bordeaux. Lampreys from the Gironde are a fixture on the menu, as are wines from the family vineyards in Entre-Deux-Mers and Fronsac.

Les Envierges
20th arr. - 11, rue des Envierges
46 36 47 84
Open noon-2 a.m. (Sat. & Sun. noon-8 p.m.). Closed Mon. & Tues.

Renaissance man (he holds diplomas in philosophy and art history) and wine master François Morel is the proud proprietor of one of the city's most successful *bars à vins*, where customers can enjoy a glass or buy a bottle to take away. Loire Valley bottlings take pride of place but Morel is not averse to promoting his finds from Roussillon or the Jura. Keeping good company with these choice wines is Nadine's generous, warming bistro cooking.

L'Espace Hérault
5th arr. - 8, rue de la Harpe - 46 33 00 56
Open noon-2 p.m. & 7:30 p.m.-10:30 p.m. Closed Sun. & Aug.

Fragrant wines and homely dishes from the Languedoc-Roussillon region top the bill at this jovial bistro, an annexe to Patrick Pagès' popular restaurant of the same name next door.

Au Franc Pinot
4th arr. - 1, quai de Bourbon - 43 29 46 98
Open 11:30 a.m.-3 p.m. & 7 p.m.-midnight. Closed Sun. & Mon. lunch.

Another annexe to a well-known restaurant; the Franc Pinot is one of the oldest taverns on the banks of the Seine, and you couldn't ask for a more picturesque spot. The lower levels (the cellars are said to descend to river-bottom level) are reserved for dining, but the ground-floor entry, with its centuries-old walls, is a comfortable wine bar. Loire and Burgundy wines made from the Pinot grape figure prominently on the list.

Le Griffonnier
8th arr. - 8, rue des Saussaies
42 65 17 17
Open 8 a.m.-9 p.m. Closed Sat., Sun., July & holidays.

Listening to the witty exchanges between the boss and his waiter is a great way to hone your repertoire of snappy retorts in French—if, that is, you can cut through the *patron*'s Auvergnat accent! Robert Savoye's bistro is a favourite with couturiers and gallery owners, who "ooh" and "aah" over the perfectly ripened Fourme d'Ambert (a buttery blue cheese from Auvergne), the collection of Beaujolais and the remarkable Mâcon-Chaintré.

Juvenile's
1st arr. - 47, rue de Richelieu - 42 97 46 49
Open 10 a.m.-midnight. Closed Sun.

Juvenile's is new and improved: and the overhaul, by owner Tim Johnston's account, is not over yet—just wait till the air-conditioning is installed! But with or without added creature comforts, we've always felt perfectly at ease in this hybrid wine-and-tapas bar, where the Queen's English is spoken. The rare sherries that headline the wine list are ideal companions to the Spanish-style bar snacks (chicken wings, marinated fish, country ham and such) that are the house speciality. But the vineyards of southern Burgundy, the Rhône and Bordeaux are not neglected; and the menu even sounds a British note with a roast beef sandwich and nursery puddings.

Jacques Mélac
11th arr. - 42, rue Léon-Frot - 43 70 59 27
Open 9 a.m.-midnight. (Mon. 9 a.m.-6 p.m.). Closed Sat., Sun., Aug. & 1 wk. at Christmas-New Year's.

The proud father of a southern vineyard, Jacques Mélac is brimming with joy. Just thinking about the latest vintage on his three-year-old property in Lirac is enough to set his moustache quivering. Over the years he has kept in training by vinifying the harvest from his Parisian vines, making the Château Charonne which he sells at auction for the price of Lafite. In his bistro, one of the most successful ones around, you can choose between Chinon, Cahors, Chignin or Coteaux-du-Layon. You'll do well to avoid the Chinon white, rare but overrated, and the Saint-Joseph, which the staff has a tendency to push. Yes, it's a little crowded and noisy, but the simple, authentic fare is worth it: try the blue-cheese omelette, the tripe from Aveyron or the plate of charcuterie from remote Rouergue. Reservations are not accepted, so either come early or come prepared to wait.

Le Millésime
6th arr. - 7, rue Lobineau - 46 34 22 15
Open daily 11 a.m.-1 a.m.

No fewer than 32 wines are offered by the glass, priced from 8 to 32 francs. Now, that's a lot of open bottles, and since we must confess that we haven't tasted them all, we can't swear that none of them is oxydised. But we like the bar (the back room is well insulated from street noise), the generous open sandwiches, the charcuterie (49 francs), some of the *plats du jour* and the cheerful, friendly staff.

Plan to travel? Look out for the other RAC GaultMillau Best of guides to France and Germany, and for the RAC French Hotel and Holiday Guide and the RAC European Hotel Guide plus maps and atlases of France and Europe.

WINE BARS – CAFES & QUICK BITES

Le Moulin à Vins
18th arr. - 6, rue Burq
42 52 81 27
Open 11 a.m.-2 a.m. Closed Sun., Mon. & 2 wks. in Aug.

Charming Danièle Denis-Bertin presides over this convivial wine bar perched on the flank of the Butte Montmartre. Let her help you choose from among her attractive bottlings, a selection that has won the hearts and minds of the finicky local connoisseurs. The quality of the *plats du jour* has risen noticeably; so why not order a generous plate of boeuf mode along with a glass (or three) of Guerbois's Gamay de Touraine (13 francs a glass), then finish up with a delicious sweet Jurançon? Don't be surprised if the regulars decide to strike up a song, and someone brings out an accordion—it's a great way to spend an evening in Montmartre.

Aux Négociants
18th arr. - 27, rue Lambert - 46 06 15 11
Open noon-10:30 p.m. (Mon. & Wed. noon-8 p.m.). Closed Sat., Sun., holidays & Aug.

A Montmartre landmark; one of the pillars of this wine bar is a man dressed up like Aristide Bruand, complete with a jaunty red muffler tossed over his shoulder. But this is no self-consciously picturesque tourist attraction—no, Aux Négociants is a place for serious drinking, as you will observe from the mouthwatering multiregional wine list that features (among others) bottles from Jasnières and Gaillac. And serious eating: the food is robust, all homemade and perfectly delicious (try the rillettes de canard and other excellent poultry dishes).

> Don't plan to do much shopping in Paris in August—a great many stores are closed for the entire holiday month.

La Nuit des Rois
11th arr. - 3, rue du Pasteur-Wagner - 48 07 15 22
Open 7 p.m.-5 a.m. Closed Sun.

Since this Champagne bar is now in the hands of a new owner, we'll have to reserve judgment on the quality of the food. But we can vouch for the attractive selection of Champagnes from large firms and small growers.

L'Œnothèque
9th arr. - 20, rue Saint-Lazare - 48 78 08 76
Open noon-10:30 p.m. Closed Sat., Sun., 2 wks. Feb. school holidays, May 1-9 & last 3 wks. of Aug.

Not so much a bar as a *restaurant à vin* (and one of the best in the city, at that), Daniel Hallée's Oenothèque offers simple yet refined cuisine that perfectly complements his fabulous wine collection. If only the welcome were as warm as the attractive décor.

Le Pain et le Vin
16th arr. - 1, rue d'Armaillé - 47 63 88 29
Open 11:30 a.m.-3 p.m. and 7 p.m.-12:30 a.m. Closed Sun., evening of Dec. 24 & 31, Dec. 25 & Jan. 1.

Improved service and fresher, more appealing cuisine have brought us back to this wine bar, created by four enterprising chefs (Dutournier, Morot-Gaudry, Fournier and Faugeron). The food is hearty and simple (steak tartare, tête de veau), but the main attraction is the wine list: 120 different bottlings, chosen by the chefs themselves, of which no fewer than 40 are available by the glass.

Bernard Péret
14th arr. - 6, rue Daguerre - 43 22 57 05
Open 9:30 a.m.-8 p.m. Closed Sun., Mon., Aug. & holidays.

With all the little food shops along this street, we always work up quite a hunger and thirst. But Bernard Péret is here to remedy that, as were his father and grandfather, with mountain sausage and a fine glass of Morgon. The wine cellar is immense—the shop sells wine on the pavement—but the bistro is tiny, six tables and a *zinc* (bar counter), offering about 15 wines by the glass. English connoisseurs in Paris, who consider Péret's Chénas and the Beaujolais nouveau the best available, can often be found here towards the end of the business day, elbow-to-elbow with the butcher and the baker.

Les Pipos
5th arr. - 2, rue de l'Ecole-Polytechnique - 43 54 11 40
Open 8 a.m.-8:30 p.m. (Sat. 8 a.m.-2 a.m.). Closed Sun. & Aug.

Christine and Jean-Michel Delhoume are a couple of pros in the wine business, and their long experience serves their patrons well. This establishment across from the old Ecole Polytechnique (whose graduates are known as *Pipos*) smells of aged wood and polished metal. It makes for a warm and convivial atmosphere in which to partake of Guerbois's excellent Gamay (13 francs) or René Sinard's fine Côtes-du-Rhône. Inspired by the 1910 phonograph, patrons occasionally burst into song, much to the enjoyment of the owners who indeed seem in perfect harmony with themselves, their work and their customers.

Le Relais Chablisien
1st arr. - 4, rue Bertin-Poirée - 45 08 53 73
Open 8 a.m.-11 p.m. Closed Sat., Sun. & last 3 wks. of Aug.

As its name suggests, this inviting bistro promotes the wines of northern Burgundy: Aligoté (10 francs a glass at the bar), Servin's crisp Chablis (14 francs), a delicious Irancy and a Givry from Parize (88 francs a bottle). But Christian Faure is no chauvinist—his wine list features fine bottles from all over France. Copious *plats du jour* at 80 francs can be savoured near the bar, or under the beams of the tiny mezzanine. Booking is recommended.

Le Relais du Vin
1st arr. - 85, rue Saint-Denis - 45 08 41 08
Open 10 a.m.-1:30 a.m. Closed Sun. & 1st wk. of Aug.

The rue Saint-Denis is famed for appealing to appetites somewhere south of the taste buds, but at this Relais, only your palate will be titillated by the likes of Henri Clerc's Burgundy, a green-tinged Saint-Véran or Guiton's Ladoix Premier Cru. Solid bistro food is also served here, in an atmosphere reminiscent of the now-vanished Halles.

Le Repaire de Bacchus
6th arr. - 13, rue du Cherche-Midi - 45 44 01 07
Open 10:30 a.m.-8:30 p.m. Closed Sun., Mon. & holidays.

The best butcher in town and some eminent wine writers frequent this wine shop-cum-bistro, where the "discoveries of the month" are always worth a look and a taste (recent examples have included a suave Montlouis and a floral Crozes-Hermitage blanc). A well-turned-out local crowd drops in around 1 p.m. for a glass of something good and a plate of charcuterie.

Le Réveil du Xe
10th arr. - 35, rue du Château-d'Eau - 42 41 77 59
Open 7 a.m.-8 p.m. (Tues. 7 a.m.-11:30 p.m.). Closed Sat., Sun. & holidays.

Every first Tuesday of the month, Marie-Catherine Vidalenc cooks a huge pot of aligot (garlicky mashed potatoes with cheese) that brings a tear of nostalgia to the eye of every native-born Auvergnat who tastes it. Her potato pâté, stuffed cabbage, tripe and homely charcuteries have a similar effect. Meanwhile, Daniel Vidalenc, son and grandson of bistro proprietors, serves the wines he chooses, purchases and bottles himself (the Chénas and Morgon go for 15 francs a glass), as well as excellent growers' wines like Amirault's stunning Bourgueil and Delubac's Cairanne from the Côtes-du-Rhône.

Le Rouge-Gorge
4th arr. - 8, rue Saint-Paul - 48 04 75 89
Open 9 a.m.-2 a.m. Closed Sun., holidays & Aug. 16-25.

After a stroll among the antique dealers (one of whom boasts an enviable collection of corkscrews), why not drop in here and see what good bottles the "theme of the week" has brought forth? Every two weeks, in fact, a different region of France is highlighted. Recently the Jura was featured; we sampled Rolet's sherry-like vin jaune, and his sturdy red Poulsard. Hot dishes are served at lunchtime (and in the evening, if the midday crowd hasn't gobbled everything up).

Le Rubis
1st arr. - 10, rue du Marché-Saint-Honoré - 42 61 03 34
Open 7 a.m.-10 p.m. (Sat. 9 a.m.-4 p.m.). Closed Sun. & 2 wks. in Aug.

Ages ago, at this very spot, old Léon Gouin first raised the banner for good wine and excellent charcuterie. In his honour, the regulars, from firemen to fashion models, continue to call the place by its former name, Chez Léon. After all, the menu has never veered off course, and the selection of wines is still pretty good, though there are some who say they notice some weaknesses in the Beaujolais. The food includes a daily hot dish in addition to the customary array of open sandwiches, cheese and cold meat. The real problem of the place is its size; it's just too small to handle all its devotees. In the summer, after doing elbow-to-elbow combat to get a glass of wine and some food from the bar, you can carry your conquest out to the pavement, where upended wine casks serve as tables.

Le Sancerre
7th arr. - 22, av. Rapp
45 51 75 91
Open 7:30 a.m.-8:30 p.m. (Sat. 7:30 a.m.-4 p.m.). Closed Sun., holidays & wk. of Aug. 15.

Reserve a table if you want to eat lunch here; in a fancy area where good bistros are rare, this one fills up fast. And it doesn't lack personality, especially that of the owners, the Mellot family. They also own the Domaine de la Moussière vineyard in Sancerre, and they sell their wine here direct from their cellars. Omelettes, andouillette (sausage) and crottin de Chavignol (small, round goat cheeses) are the rule here, but then they always have been, even before that sort of thing was in style. And don't be put off by the slick window dressing—Le Sancerre is very comfortable.

Au Sauvignon
7th arr. - 80, rue des Saints-Pères
45 48 48 02
Open 8:30 a.m.-10 p.m. Closed Sun., Aug., 2 wks. Feb. school holidays & holidays.

The changing of the guard (now the "youngsters" have taken over) and the extension of the terrace have fortunately done nothing to alter the style and tone of this excellent bistro. The formula for success is simple: a few good wines (oh, that Quincy!) and some appetising *tartines* of tangy goat cheese and top-class charcuterie (on neighbour Lionel Poilâne's bread, of course).

WINE BARS – CAFES & QUICK BITES

Au Soleil d'Austerlitz
5th arr. - 18, bd de l'Hôpital - 43 31 22 38
Open 6 a.m-9 p.m. (Sat. 7 a.m.-6 p.m.). Closed Sun. & Aug.

An immutable institution, without which the district wouldn't be the same. Where to go after meeting a friend at the station? Or after a wander through the nearby Jardin des Plantes? Come here, for fruity Régnié (the most recently proclaimed *cru* of Beaujolais) or owner André Calvet's latest discovery. As for solid sustenance, you can count on earthy charcuterie from Aveyron and warming main dishes (try the boeuf bourguignon).

Tabac de l'Institut
6th arr. - 21, rue de Seine - 43 26 98 75
Open 8:30 a.m.-8 p.m. Closed Sun. & Aug.

From the outside, it's just another newsagent/tobacconist with a long row of tables in the back. But on entering, you find yourself in a quiet, dark, wood-panelled bar, where you can taste some excellent wines: Mâcon-Viré, various Beaujolais and Sauvignons and so forth. This is a surprising address—right in the middle of the Beaux-Arts college area—for an intimate conversation.

La Tartine
4th arr. - 24, rue de Rivoli - 42 72 76 85
Open 8:30 a.m.-10 p.m. (Wed. noon-10 p.m.). Closed Tues. & Aug. 1-20.

It's easy to picture Trotsky here, seated at a table in the back or with his elbows up on the big marble bar, in a debate with his cronies over a glass of red wine. His followers, and his opponents, still come to listen for his echoes and to mix with the varied crowd on this end of the rue de Rivoli in the Marais. The complete range of Beaujolais, from generic to Villages all the way through the ten *crus* is available, and there's a different hot dish offered for lunch every day. And of course, open sandwiches (*tartines*) are served at any time.

Taverne Henri-IV
1st arr. - 13, pl. du Pont-Neuf 43 54 27 90
Open noon-10 p.m. (Sat. noon-4 p.m.). Closed Sun. & 3 wks. in Aug.

For more than 30 years the fruits of Beaujolais, Montlouis and the greater and lesser Bordeaux vineyards have been flowing through this old so-called bistro. It continues to fill with advertising types, travel agents, publishers, journalists, lawyers and so forth, not to mention tourists fresh from excursions on the Seine. Behind the counter—or seated with one of the regulars—you'll find the owner, Robert Cointepas, loud and ruddy-faced, and his wife, a vintner's daughter. Cointepas knows how to buy wine even better than he knows how to sell it. He travels to the vineyards to select his wines in October, then offers them in peak condition all year, including the Beaujolais in its traditional pint *pot*. The standard open sandwiches are of good quality, and fine charcuterie and wines are available to take away.

Le Val d'Or
8th arr. - 28, av. Franklin-Roosevelt - 43 59 95 81
Open 8 a.m.-9 p.m. (Sat. 8 a.m.-5 p.m.). Closed Sun., Dec. 25, Jan. 1 & holidays.

Géraud (not Gérard, thank you) Rongier, who hails from deep in the Auvergne, is one of the grand masters of the wine profession. He trains good wine stewards and some excellent colleagues, such as Serge Lesage, who now runs Rongier's former establish-

---

Art on the wall

Paris is officially encouraging the revival of a forgotten art form —the painted wall. The first *mural advertisements* that emerged in the 19th century had some artistic merit, but as the suburbs and the Métro spread they lost their impact in a morass of mediocre slogans. In 1943 a law was passed limiting the size of such dubious decoration to a measly 50 square feet. However the work of some talented fly-by-nighters during the 1960s and 1970s put mural art back on the Paris map, and in 1979 companies were once again allowed to tout their wares on walls. Since 1976 the city authorities have financed the decoration of between five and seven walls a year. Artists are invited to submit designs and a jury selects which ones will give a facelift to some of the city's bleaker buildings. The best way to appreciate a wall painting is probably to come across one by chance, but here are some starters: Philippe Rebuffet's firemen at 45 rue Saint-Fargeau in the 20th arrondissement; "trompe-l'œil" workmen putting up a sign at 52 rue de Belleville, also in the 20th; Cueco's little girl playing in the passage Gatbois, in the 12th; "Shadow of a tree", a reflection of reality at 47 boulevard de Strasbourg in the 10th arrondissement.

ment, La Cloche des Halles. Several years ago Rongier took over this unknown little bistro near Saint-Philippe-du-Roule and, with his personal renown, it has attracted a wide following. At midday, it's filled with advertising executives, civil servants from the Ministry of the Interior, fashion-industry women and television folk from the nearby TV business centres. One of the old Gallic guard of the wine profession, Rongier has harsh words for many of the upstarts who are invading it. And it's hard to argue with him when you taste his selection from the Loire, his Côte-de-Brouilly, his Mâcon-Clessé, his Bordeaux or his Aloxe-Corton. All of these are offered at highly competitive prices. As for more solid sustenance, Rongier himself prepares ham cooked on the bone, rillettes and cheeses that he ages himself.

Au Vin des Rues

14th arr. - 21, rue Boulard - 43 22 19 78
Open 10 a.m.-8 p.m. (Wed. & Fri. dinner at 9 p.m.). Closed Sun., Mon., Aug. & holidays. No cards.

Jean Chanrion sold his Moulin de la Boulange to open this place. Combined with the recent takeover of the nearby Cagouille by another fine specialist, and the established presence of Bernard Péret, the opening practically transforms the area into a wine-lover's crossroads. The atmosphere of this Everyman's bistro is only bolstered by the qualities we expect of Chanrion: the excellent choice of Beaujolais and Mâcons and the hot dishes made from the best ingredients, such as the baked andouillette with a little white wine...

Willi's Wine Bar

1st arr. - 13, rue des Petits-Champs - 42 61 05 09
Open 11 a.m.-11 p.m. Closed Sun.

The Englishmen who founded this establishment are probably the best connoisseurs in Paris (among the English, that is) of wines from the Côtes-du-Rhône, which figure prominently on their wine list both in quality and number. We never grow weary of trying new ones, red and white. At the bar, Williamson and Johnston have a habit of offering discoveries from other regions, such as Australian novelties, a wonderful Vouvray, wines from Madeira or sweet wines from all over. The marble and blond-wood dining room is comfortable and frequented by an unobjectionable crowd: bankers and art experts at noon, high-class regulars at night. You can expect to spend 300 francs for dinner (by the way, we think the food gets better here all the time).

RAC MOTORING ATLAS FRANCE: Our fully revised and well-established large format RAC Motoring Atlas France, Belgium and Lu- xembourg at 1:250,000 (approximately 4 miles to 1 inch) now has even more features to improve journey planning and to make driving in France more enjoyable. Clear, accurate and detailed road maps make RAC Motoring Atlas France the ideal atlas for the independent traveller in France. Price: £ 11.99 (spiral bound).

NIGHTLIFE

CABARETS	*154*
COCKTAIL BARS	*154*
LIVE MUSIC	*157*
NIGHTCLUBS	*158*
PUBS	*161*

NIGHTLIFE – CABARETS

CABARETS

Crazy Horse
8th arr. - 12, av. George-V - 47 23 32 32

For two-score years now, saloon-keeper Alain Bernardin has entertained convoys of tourists with his bevy of buxom beauties. Clad only (and only briefly!) in leather wasp-waisters, these *femmes fatales, the most sophisticated in the universe,* (so says the programme) cavort and form—supposedly—erotic tableaux. But for our money, the most exciting aspect of the show is the astonishingly inventive lighting, which clothes Lova Moor, Betty Buttocks and their cohorts with laser beams. Herculean bouncers stationed at the doors make sure that the atmosphere doesn't turn too steamy. The show is stylish and professional, yes; but is it sexy...?

Folies Bergère
9th arr. - 32, rue Richer - 42 46 77 11

The Folies-Bergères is as famous for its fabulous décor as for its glittering floor shows, but you'll have to wait to get a peek at either. Let's hope the new show scheduled for September 1993 is also more polished than the rather tame productions of late.

Le Lido
8th arr. - 116 bis, av. des Champs-Elysées - 40 76 56 10

Closer in spirit to an athletic event than a cabaret performance, this fast-moving show features grandiose stage sets, magnificently costumed dancers (including the 60 leggy, toothy, busty Bluebell Girls) and a host of occasionally breathtaking novelty acts. Need we mention that most Parisians have never—would never—set foot in the place? "Who cares?" reply the wide-eyed tourists for whom a night at Le Lido is a dream come true.

Le Moulin Rouge
18th arr. - 82, bd de Clichy - 46 06 00 19

You've all seen the film; now you can see the genuine article—in the flesh! Tradition is everything here, and the famous Doriss Girls scrupulously respect it: twice a night, seven nights a week, they prance on stage and cancan the night away.

Le Paradis Latin
5th arr. - 28, rue du Cardinal-Lemoine - 43 25 28 28

What can be said about a cloyingly sweet floor show led by dancers who look as though they have swapped their twinsets and pearls for feathers and rhinestones? *Viva Paradis,* a revue in 24 tableaux, delivers all the obligatory numbers—French cancan, erotic tango and so on. Yet a few stars manage to shine through: Ursuline Kairson, with her warm, thrilling voice; the energetic Lucien who puts the troupe through their paces; and Mister Sergio, the house MC, who could liven up a funeral. Nevertheless, this splendid Belle-Epoque theatre designed by Gustave Eiffel deserves a kinder fate.

Les Trottoirs de Buenos Aires
1st arr. - 37, rue des Lombards 40 26 28 58
Open 10:30 p.m. (Sun. 4 p.m.; Tues. 9 p.m.). Closed Mon.

Nostalgic expatriates meet at this concert-café to drink and listen to the passionate, plaintive strains of *el nuevo tango.* Argentine jazz-fusion bands are featured as well, and they play for a switched-on, appreciative audience. The atmosphere varies nightly: Tuesdays, Wednesdays and Sundays are tango nights, when couples can demonstrate their technique on the dance floor (novices can take lessons on Sunday afternoons).

COCKTAIL BARS

Banana Café
1st arr. - 13, rue de la Ferronnerie 42 33 35 31
Open 4:30 p.m.-5 a.m. (Fri. & Sat. 4:30 p.m.-6 a.m.).

A trendy venue with a tropical twist for a young, clean-cut crowd. Sip cocktails or wines-by-the-glass at the bar, or lend an ear to the improvised jazz and pop concerts staged downstairs.

Le Bélier
L'Hôtel
6th arr. - 13, rue des Beaux-Arts 43 25 27 22
Open daily noon-2 a.m.

A half-dozen tables, a few stools, the gentle sound of a fountain, warm colours, a cheeky bartender... and the cocktails—such as the Bélier (vodka, Curaçao, grenadine, fruit juices)—are good, too. This is an ideal spot to wind up an evening.

Birdland
6th arr. - 8, rue Guisarde - 43 26 97 59
Open 8 p.m.-dawn. (Sun. 10 p.m.-dawn). Closed Dec. 25 & Jan. 1.

The owners recently refurbished this cosy nest for jazz-loving night owls, situated in the heart of Saint-Germain-des-Prés. Sip a cocktail (a few non-alcoholic offerings are available) and wallow in what is surely one of the finest collections of jazz recordings in town.

La Casbah
11th arr. - 18-20, rue de la Forge-Royale - 43 71 71 89
Open daily 9 p.m.-5 a.m.

A neo-Moorish nightspot with fascinating "pre-worn" décor, La Casbah draws a hip, handsome crowd with its exotic cocktails and feverish atmosphere. You can join these trendy revellers if (and only if) the surly doorman/bouncer likes the look of you.

Chapman
2nd arr. - 25, rue Louis-le-Grand
47 42 98 19
Open 5 p.m.-2 a.m. Closed Sun. & holidays.

Just a short putt away from the Opéra, this wood-panelled bar festooned with golfers' paraphernalia plays the "English club" card to the hilt. Bernard, the owner and chief cocktail creator, is a graduate of the famed Harry's Bar. He welcomes a clean-cut crew of habitués (stockbrokers and such) with cleverly concocted cocktails and a soothing atmosphere.

Le China Club
12th arr. - 50, rue de Charenton
43 43 82 02
Open 7 p.m.-1:30 a.m. Closed Dec. 25 & Jan. 1.

The chic denizens of the Bastille nightlife district like to gather at this glamorous, multi-level club: either at the long ground-floor cocktail bar, upstairs in the smoky *fumoir* where choice Cognacs and Armagnacs are poured, or downstairs in the new jazz club dubbed "Le Sing Song," where live music can be heard from Tuesday to Saturday from 11 p.m.

Closerie des Lilas
6th arr. - 171, bd du Montparnasse - 43 26 70 50
Open daily 10:30 a.m.-2 a.m.

This place once served the likes of Hemingway and Gide, though now only Jean-Edern Hallier (who?) holds court at his table by the door. But there is still a superb décor, particularly inviting in warm weather with the laurel-enclosed terrace, the high-class, polished service and the excellent cocktails. Snobbish and expensive? Definitely. But remember, you're not out for a beer at the local.

Le Comptoir
1st arr. - 14, rue Vauvilliers - 40 26 26 66
Open noon-2 a.m. (Fri. & Sat. until 4 a.m.).

Here's a splendid place to mingle with a very Parisian throng, and down a selection of their delicious tapas accompanied by an appealing choice of spirited libations. On Friday and Saturday nights, the presence of a DJ keeps things lively but effectively thwarts any effort at conversation.

Le Dépanneur
9th arr. - 27, rue Fontaine - 40 16 40 20
Open daily 24 hours.

"Tequila, tequila, arriba!" Here comes Miss Tequila, packing icy bottles of Jalisco in her holsters, a cartridge belt loaded with shot glasses slung across her chest, ready to serve a "rapido" to her hard-drinking customers. Strategically located within shooting distance of the big guns on the Pigalle nightlife circuit, this neo-postmodern watering hole is open 24 hours a day.

Le Forum
8th arr. - 4, bd Malesherbes - 42 65 37 86
Open 11:30 a.m.-2 a.m. (Sat. & Sun. 5:30 p.m.-2 a.m.). Closed holidays.

This is the archetypal French cocktail bar, with flawless service, lovely décor (even the cocktail shakers are a work of art) and an iron-clad policy of discretion. At about seven in the evening, couples (legit and less so) drift in for an intimate chat before heading home. The 150 cocktails and the selection (one of the best in Paris) of Scotch whiskies are accompanied by olives and peanuts. The armchairs are comfortable, and the touch of nostalgia in the atmosphere is quite soothing.

George-V
Hôtel George-V
8th arr. - 31, av. George-V - 47 23 54 00
Open daily 11 a.m.-1:30 a.m.

The clientele comes from top-drawer conferences, seminars and other such gatherings. Where are the film stars you'd expect to see? The atmosphere is a little chilly in this otherwise comfortable bar, which opens onto a series of intimate salons where you can engage in quiet conversation while nursing a whisky selected by Monsieur Jacques, who is fluently conversant on the subject.

Le Grand Hôtel
Le Grand Hôtel
9th arr. - 2, rue Scribe
40 07 32 32
Open daily 11 a.m.-2 a.m.

Come cocktail time, dandies, loafers and other elegant fauna gather beneath the Grand Hôtel's immense glass-and-steel dome to see and be seen. It's by no means intimate, but the scene is amusing, and the expertly mixed drinks are served with style.

Harry's Bar
2nd arr. - 5, rue Daunou - 42 61 71 14
Open daily 10:30 a.m.-4 a.m. Closed Dec. 24-25.

Time weighs lightly on this Parisian landmark, which looks much the same today as it did at the Liberation. The main bar is a bustling, convivial place where sporting types (particularly rugby fans) discuss their favourite teams; the downstairs piano bar is more conducive to quiet conversation.

The prices in this guide reflect what establishments were charging at the time of going to press.

NIGHTLIFE – COCKTAIL BARS

Hurlingham Polo Bar
Le Méridien Paris-Etoile
17th arr. - 81, bd Gouvion-Saint-Cyr - 40 68 34 34
Open daily 11:30 a.m.-2 a.m.

A pleasant place to have a "wee dram" in good company. Georges and his staff will initiate you into the lore of rare old whiskies amid improbably British surroundings—leather armchairs, tartan fabrics, a gas-log fire... Champagnes and judiciously chosen wines are also on offer.

Meurice
Hôtel Meurice
1st arr. - 228, rue de Rivoli - 44 58 10 60
Open daily 10 a.m.-2 a.m.

One visits this bar chiefly to sip tea or nibble on a toast au caviar (365 francs) amid sumptuous "Pompadour" décor (Madame herself would have loved it). But if the need for something stronger arises, the waiter can provide a classy selection of whiskies and Armagnacs.

Le Moloko
9th arr. - 26, rue Fontaine - 48 74 70 76
Open daily 8 p.m.-dawn.

White-hot nights are the rule at Serge Krüger's happening nightspot, a *bar de nuit* where the chic and eccentric feed the juke box and commune over cocktails in its wildly eclectic, vaguely Russian décor. Though this is not a private club, first-time patrons should expect to get a cool once-over at the door.

Le Normandy
1st arr. - 7, rue de l'Echelle - 42 60 30 21
Open daily 11 a.m.-1 a.m. (Sat. & Sun. 11 a.m.-1 p.m. & 6 p.m.-1 a.m.).

The Normandy's comfy chesterfield armchairs don't attract the preen-and-be-seen set, but you may hear the confidential murmurings of journalists and others enjoying a pre–Comédie Française drink. This is a bar where women alone can feel at ease, and the cocktails shaken by Serge, Jean and Xavier are as fine as every other feature of this mellow hotel bar. There is a fine choice of brandies, featuring Cognacs from Delamain and a superb Armagnac 1957, Cuvées Normandie.

La Perla
4th arr. - 26, rue François-Miron
42 77 59 40
Open daily noon-2 a.m.

La Perla was a pioneer in the wave of Mexican bars that hit Paris a few years ago. The corner premises on a charming street in the Marais give patrons a wide-angle view of the passing scene, which they may contemplate while enjoying a Dos Equis, a shot of tequila, or an exotic cocktail. A short menu offers decent tortillas, enchiladas and chili con carne.

Plaza Bar Anglais
Plaza Athénée
8th arr. - 25, av. Montaigne - 47 23 78 33
11 a.m.-1:30 a.m.

You can't get any classier than this. Here is a bar where you can talk business or speak of love, safe in the knowledge that you will be neither interrupted nor importuned. Service is impeccable and discreet; in the evening, a piano provides unobtrusive background music.

Pont-Royal
Hôtel Pont-Royal
7th arr. - 7, rue de Montalembert
45 44 38 27
Open noon-midnight (Sat. noon-10 p.m.). Closed Sun. & Aug.

Publishers, writers and agents regularly meet for apéritifs and literary chit-chat at this dark, wood-panelled bar. At off-peak hours, the leather club chairs are just as inviting, and the atmosphere far more calm: perfect for correcting the manuscript of one's memoirs, or for making sentimental conversation.

Raphaël
Hôtel Raphaël
16th arr. - 17, av. Kléber - 44 28 00 28
Open daily 11 a.m.-midnight.

The bar of the Hotel Raphaël is opulent and refined, with bronze sculptures, carved wood, plush carpets and expertly mixed cocktails. Exclusive and very expensive, this bar is a favourite watering hole for stars seeking a respite from their admiring throngs.

Le Rosebud
14th arr. - 11 bis, rue Delambre
43 35 38 54
Open 7 p.m.-2 a.m. Closed Aug.

With each passing decade, a new generation of fans is introduced to this great Montparnasse landmark, where intellectuals and other observers of the urban scene exchange ideas over a drink and a bowl of the bar's famous chili.

Saint-James et Albany
Hôtel Saint-James & Albany
1st arr. - 6, rue du 29-Juillet - 42 60 31 60
Open daily 10 a.m.-1 a.m. (dawn).

In fine weather, the doors open onto a pretty garden—a plus that few hotel bars can boast. On the other hand, the list of cocktails is on the skimpy side, and the service does not always live up to the grandeur of the setting.

Le Scribe
Hôtel Scribe
9th arr. - 1, rue Scribe
44 71 24 24
Open daily 9 a.m.-2 a.m.

Along with the rest of the hotel, Le Scribe's bar got a much-needed facelift which transformed it into a perfect hotel bar, where guests and visitors may enjoy excellent cocktails, soft piano music and private conversation in newly luxurious surroundings.

Choiseul et Montgolfier
Hôtel Sofitel Paris
15th arr. - 8, rue Louis-Armand - 40 60 30 30
Open daily 8:30 a.m.-1 a.m. (Choiseul); open daily 6 p.m.-2 a.m. (Montgolfier).

The Choiseul and Montgolfier bars (the latter famous for nightly jazz) are the only more-or-less quiet (or appropriately lively) spots in this area surrounding the huge exhibition complex known as the Salons of the Porte de Versailles. They are good meeting spots, where you needn't fear being overwhelmed by a tidal wave of show visitors and exhibitors.

Le Suffren et Le Toit de Paris
Hôtel Hilton
15th arr. - 18, av. de Suffren - 42 73 92 00
Le Suffren: open 7 a.m.-11 p.m. (Sun. until 2 a.m.). Le Toit de Paris: 6 p.m.-2 a.m., closed Sun.

Le Suffren manages to maintain a relaxed, friendly atmosphere—no mean feat in this sort of place. Big-business types from nearby offices meet here to settle deals discreetly. Meanwhile, up on the tenth floor, wealthy foreign visitors unwind in the Toit de Paris bar, sipping cocktails made by Christian Viel, mixmaster extraordinaire, and enjoying a splendid view of the Eiffel Tower. On Sundays Le Toit de Paris gives you a glass of Champagne with brunch, a hearty spread featuring roast rib of beef and *plats du jour* like lobster or salmon along with eggs prepared to order and a choice of desserts.

Le Vigny
Hôtel Vigny
8th arr. - 9-11, rue Balzac - 40 75 04 39
Open daily 7 a.m.-2 a.m.

A beautiful bar in an equally beautiful hotel, just off the Champs-Elysées. Polished wood, mellow leather and soft lights create a luxurious setting that is dependably quiet and discreet—unless, of course, a gaggle of groupies awaiting the appearance of their idol has taken over the turf! A glass of premium whisky will set you back about 80 francs.

Le Westminster
Hôtel Westminter
2nd arr. - 13, rue de la Paix - 42 61 57 46
Open daily 9 a.m.-midnight.

Ensconced in a stylish hotel between the Opéra and the place Vendôme, this posh, polished bar is a convenient spot for a pre-prandial drink. In our estimation, though, the atmosphere is not conducive to leisurely conversation.

LIVE MUSIC

Le Baiser Salé
1st arr. - 58, rue des Lombards - 42 33 37 71

For jazz fans eager to discover talented musicians destined for fame (if not fortune, the jazz life being what it is); years from now, you'll be able to say "I saw them play in Paris before anybody had heard of them..."

Caveau de la Huchette
5th arr. - 5, rue de la Huchette - 43 26 65 05

This is a shrine to good old-fashioned swing and Dixieland, situated in a cellar in the Latin Quarter. You'll feel you've been transported back to the 1950s: there's a live band, clouds of smoke, romantic young tourists, eternal students, and some veteran dancers with a real sense of rhythm for the jitterbug and bebop.

Club Lionel Hampton
Le Méridien Paris-Etoile
17th arr. - 81, bd Gouvion-Saint-Cyr - 40 68 34 34

A *Who's Who* of jazz and blues greats have played in this plush, comfortable lounge, located in one of the city's finest hotels. We can recall spending memorable evenings here with Fats Domino, Monty Alexander, John Hendrix, the Count Basie orchestra, Screamin' Jay Hawkins and many more.

Au Duc des Lombards
1st arr. - 42, rue des Lombards - 42 33 22 88

A popular jazz venue somehow reminiscent of an English pub, where prices are comparatively low (the first drink costs 65 francs). The audience doesn't listen in religious silence, but musicians like to play here anyway because the acoustics are just right. Relaxed atmosphere, quality bands. Jam sessions on Tuesdays.

L'Eustache
1st arr. - 37, rue Berger - 40 26 23 20

Lots of people, lots of noise: L'Eustache is one big party, night after night. The more solemn sort of jazz buff spurns it absolutely, but L'Eustache does not pretend to be a concert hall. The acoustics are so-so, yet we've heard some terrific hard-bop horn blowing.

Le New Morning
10th arr. - 7-9, rue des Petites-Ecuries - 45 23 51 41

Unquestionably the city's premier jazz club, the scene of unforgettable evenings with the late Chet Baker and Stan Getz, Gary Burton, Betty Carter, Oscar Peterson, Archie Shepp... The New Morning's 400-seat auditorium boasts surprisingly comfortable seating and superb acoustics. You can purchase tickets at the door an hour before the gig.

NIGHTLIFE – NIGHTCLUBS

Opus Café
10th arr. - 167, quai de Valmy
40 38 09 57

Now for something completely different. The Opus Café is a former British officers' mess from World War I which has been transformed into a classical music venue. Why should the background music for cocktails for two be loud and strident? Here, by the Canal Saint-Martin, you can sip a highball while you listen to a Mozart string quartet or a Schumann sonata—Cheers!

Le Petit Journal Montparnasse
14th arr. - 13, rue du Commandant-Mouchotte - 43 21 56 70

Le Petit Journal Montparnasse features first-rate jazz musicians in a room with good sight lines, good acoustics and a long, comfortable bar. A good time is guaranteed. Its sister establishment at 71, boulevard Saint-Michel, leans to swing and Dixieland bands, but the Claude Bolling trio plays there with some regularity, as does saxophonist Benny Waters and plenty more. Both clubs offer a constantly rotating roster of musicians for a solid selection of contemporary and classical jazz.

Le Petit Opportun
2nd arr. - 15, rue des Lavandières Ste-Opportune - 42 36 01 36

An evening at the Petit Op' is musically rewarding, but physically resembles a descent to hell. A dark, cramped, smoky cellar is the scene of remarkable concerts by the distinguished likes of Steve Lacy and Steve Potts, Barney Wilen and hosts of lesser-known but always exceptional jazz musicians.

Le Sunset
2nd arr. - 60, rue des Lombards
40 26 46 60

Improbably neat and shipshape, this jazz cellar presents an unusual programme of modern, expressive, sometimes over-the-top music. An offbeat spot for a nightcap (cover and first drink, 120 francs), where you can catch a whiff of things to come in the world of jazz.

Utopia
14th arr. - 9, rue Champollion
43 26 84 65

No way you can feel bad when the music is so good and the atmosphere so laid-back and friendly. Nearly every night brings a rock or blues concert (sometimes several!) to this hip Montparnasse nightspot.

La Villa
Hôtel La Villa Saint-Germain
6th arr. - 29, rue Jacob - 43 26 60 00

Top jazz personalities from Europe and the U.S. are charmed by this intimate club, hidden away on the lower level of a Saint-Germain hotel. Here is where the great drummer Billy Hart chose to play when he came through town a few months back (cover and first drink, 120 francs).

NIGHTCLUBS

Les Bains
3rd arr. - 7, rue du Bourg-l'Abbé
48 87 01 80
Open daily 11:30 p.m.-dawn. Restaurant: open daily 9 p.m.-4 a.m.

Stars, dandies and young beauties who live to preen and be seen haunt this exclusive venue, where they rub shoulders (and more!) with poohbahs from the worlds of show biz, advertising and fashion. Mike Tyson has been seen here; so have Madonna, Jean-Paul Gaultier, Roman Polanski, Linda Evangelista and Jack Nicholson. In order to get through the door, jealously guarded by Marilyn, it helps to be insanely chic, madly elegant or wildly notorious. Otherwise, it's advisable to be (or be with) an habitué. At 3 a.m. *El Divino*, the private club-within-a-club, opens its doors to a select group. How do you rate your chances of getting in?

Le Balajo
11th arr. - 9, rue de Lappe - 47 00 07 87
Open 3 p.m.-6:30 p.m. & 11:30 p.m.-5 a.m. (Thurs.

The Ile Saint-Louis opens up

Instead of huddling behind high walls as was usual for many of the capital's finest residences, the townhouses here were built facing the Seine to give their occupants the benefit of a view and fresh air. King Louis XIII acquired the two separate islands that today constitute the Ile Saint-Louis in 1611, had them joined with two stone bridges and started 50 years of building work under the supervision of architect Louis Le Vau. The result is a harmonious architectural whole, best enjoyed during a leisurely stroll. The Church of Saint Louis-en-l'Ile, with its original ironwork clock and wooden sculptures, is the only monument on the island open to the public.

11:30 p.m.-5 a.m. & Sun. 3 p.m.-6:30 p.m.). Closed Tues.

In the 1980s mega-DJs Serge and Albert made Le Balajo a byword among night owls from Manhattan to Tokyo, Copenhagen and Buenos Aires. Alas, the two have parted company, and now Albert makes only occasional appearances. The end of an era? Perhaps, but a new generation is poised to take over, dancing to newly popular mambo and rumba rhythms under the benevolent gaze of the burly bouncers whose bored faces say, "This trend, too, shall pass."

Castel-Princesse
6th arr. - 15, rue Princesse - 43 26 90 22
Open 11:30 p.m.-dawn. Restaurant: 9 p.m. Closed Sun.

But for rare exceptions, this club is strictly members-only. The Castel gang numbers 3,000 and constitutes a private community honoured members: upper-crust Parisians, show biz personalities, literary celebrities, and affiliated members who belong to other exclusive clubs. They sup (very well), drink and dance and gossip together, far from the night's vulgar rabble. To join this late-night coterie, you need two sponsors, a file on your life history, and several thousand francs to cover application and fees. Only 50 new members are admitted per year. Now, if you are still interested, good luck!

La Chapelle des Lombards
11th arr. - 19, rue de Lappe - 43 57 24 24
Open 8 p.m-dawn. Closed Sun.

This is the land of rum punch, Afro-Cuban music, the samba and the tropics. It is here that sunshine breaks through grey Paris skies and the beat is hot. Mingle with the reggae crowd—they're on to a good thing, and they know it.

Keur Samba
8th arr. - 79, rue de La Boétie 43 59 03 10
Open daily midnight-dawn.

Le Keur starts to samba when other clubs are winding down. Even a slow night goes on until 7 or 8 in the morning, but some nights go on until 11... tomorrow. The African jet set, fashion models, diplomats, wealthy business people and carefree youth party here, overseen by N'Diaye Kane: he keeps the dancers happy with an unending wave of West Indian, Brazilian and Afro-Cuban rhythms. If this sounds like your idea of a good time, don your smartest togs, put on a smile and forget "attitude": the man at the door likes easy-going elegance.

La Locomotive
18th arr. - 90, bd de Clichy - 42 57 37 37
Open 11 p.m.-6 a.m. Closed Mon.

Young night hawks adore the Locomotive. It's so big you can get lost in it, and it draws the rockers like moths to a flame. The menu is unchanged since the great days of rock 'n' roll... in the '60s this was the land of the Who, the Rolling Stones and the Kinks. Today the Locomotive claims to be at the cutting edge of rock (well, that's what the bouncer told us, anyway). Dress in your best sneakers, Levis and a clean T-shirt and you'll fit right in with the dancing, flirting, youthful mob.

Le Niel's
17th arr. - 27, av. des Ternes - 47 66 45 00
Open daily 12:30 a.m.-dawn. Restaurant: open daily 9:30 p.m.- 12:30 a.m.

No noise, no glare, no uncouth behaviour disturb the well-mannered revels at this posh, wood-panelled club, a new stopping place on the Paris night circuit. Le Niel's is semi-private, so the chances of your getting in are slim unless you come with a regular, or have an introduction—the concierge of your high-class hotel could perhaps arrange for one.

Olivia Valère
8th arr. - 40, rue du Colisée - 42 25 11 68
Open daily 23:30 pm-dawn. Restaurant: open daily 9:30 p.m.-2 a.m.

Thanks to lots of panache and sleepless nights, Olivia Valère has pushed her club up into the lofty ranks of hot Parisian nightspots. There is a piano bar for intimacy, a discreet and comfy restaurant and a dance floor for the young and energetic. The question now: is Olivia Valère or Régine the reigning queen of the night? It's not an easy choice. Nightclubbers are quite demanding, after all. What is essential is to be seen... and Olivia's club, where the Middle East meets Deauville and Saint-Tropez, is an excellent showcase.

La Poste
9th arr. - 34, rue Duperré - 42 80 66 16
Open 11 p.m.-2 a.m. Closed Sun. & Mon.

Near the seamy, steamy place Pigalle, the town house where Bizet composed *Carmen* and which in later incarnations became a bordello and a post office, is now an exuberantly ornate supper club. A dressy, young crowd comes here to dine, drink and dance before moving on to the area's more down-to-earth nocturnal attractions.

Régine's
8th arr. - 49, rue de Ponthieu 43 59 21 13
Open 11:30 p.m.-dawn. Restaurant: open 9 p.m.-11 p.m. Closed Sun.

The envious (those who get turned away at the door) will tell you it's a dump. Régine's flamboyant friends, ignore the critics and continue to spend large sums of money with total insouciance. But one unmistakable sign of the club's vitality is the fact that a younger crowd comes to dance here now: the children of film stars and the scions of wealthy families all seem to have membership cards in their pockets. They sail in the door, no questions asked. But for the common run of mortals, Régine's door is still irrevocably shut.

Rex Club
2nd arr. - 5, bd Poissonnière - 42 36 10 96
Open 11 p.m.-dawn (Wed. 11:30 p.m.-dawn). Closed Sun. & Aug.

Dance to a different beat every night of the week (but never on Sunday) at the Rex Club's wild theme parties. Midweek is your best bet: Tuesday is *New Jack Swing* time; Wednesday brings *Metallic Jungle Rock*; and on Thursday, DJ Laurent Garnier hosts *Wake Up, Paris*, a soirée of garage, disco and techno-house sounds.

Le Shéhérazade
9th arr. - 3, rue de Liège - 48 74 41 68
Openings vary.

Bewitching, beguiling Shéhérazade! The place to dance and party with a cosmopolitan crowd, in an extravagant setting straight out of the *Arabian Nights*. Raï, jazz-rap and English house music keep the incredibly pumped-up dancers strutting their stuff far into the night. A cosy downstairs bar offers a respite from the frenetic action.

Slow Club
1st arr. - 130, rue de Rivoli - 42 33 84 30
Closed Sun. & Mon.

A jitterbugging couple flashes on the neon sign outside: the retro mood is set. When you hear the swing and big-band sounds inside, you may think you've walked into a 1940s time warp. The middle-aged dancers are sure they've recaptured their youth. But this is no old folks' home: there's great music on tap, performed by first-rate (mostly French) dance and Dixieland bands who have plenty of youthful fans. For a cheap and cheerful night on the town (admission is only 65 francs at weekends) you couldn't do better!

Le Tango
3rd arr. - 13, rue au Maire - 42 72 17 78
Open Tues. 1:30 p.m.-6:30 p.m., Thurs. 10 p.m.-4 a.m., Fri. & Sat. 11 p.m.-5 a.m., Sat. 2 p.m.-6:30 p.m., Sun 2 p.m.-8 p.m. & 10 a.m.-4 p.m. Closed Mon.

Thanks to Serge Krüger, Afro-Latin music is back, alive and well, from Wednesday to Friday in this old dance hall. Black and white members of the Paris African scene flock here to warm their hearts (and shake the rest) to the beat of the beguine, the calypso and the salsa. If you're the type who hates nightclubs, fashion and Top 40 hits, but likes chance encounters and cha-cha, head over here for one last tango in Paris.

Le Timmy's
6th arr. - 76, rue de Rennes - 45 44 22 84
Open 11:30 p.m.-6 a.m. (Sun. 5 p.m.-midnight). Closed Mon.

This up-market address near Saint-Germain swings to an Afro-Creole beat and caters to black jet-setters. To fit in with this dressy crowd, only your smartest clothes will do.

Opera in Paris

There's no opera at the Opéra any more: the richly ornamented Palais Garnier, for over a hundred years the city's temple of lyric art, is now the scene of ballet and other dance performances, as well as the occasional concert. The Opéra Bastille, one of President Mitterrand's most controversial contributions to Parisian architecture, now hosts the official opera season. Lately, however, some of the most acclaimed opera productions in Paris have been staged at the Théâtre de la Ville. Other venues that regularly present operatic performances are the Théâtre des Champs-Elysées and the Opéra Comique. For information about specific productions, check *Le Monde* or *Le Figaro's* magazine supplement on Wednesdays, or *Pariscope* or *L'Officiel des Spectacles*, which also appear on Wednesdays.

Opéra Palais Garnier, **place de l'Opéra, 9th arr. Reservation: 47 42 53 71.**

Opéra de Paris Bastille, **20 rue de Lyon, 12th arr. Reservations: 44 73 13 00.**

Théâtre de la Ville, **2 place du Châtelet, 4th arr. Reservations: 42 74 22 77.**

Théâtre des Champs-Elysées, **15 avenue Montaigne, 8th arr. Reservations: 49 52 50 50.**

Opéra Comique (Salle Favart), **5 rue Favart, 2nd arr. Reservations: 42 86 88 83.**

Find the address you are looking for, quickly and easily, in the index.

Le Bristol
Paris

112, rue du Faubourg Saint Honoré - 75008 Paris
Tél. : 33 (1) 42 66 91 45 - Fax : 33 (1) 42 66 68 68 - Télex : 280961

PUBS

L'Académie de la Bière
5th arr. - 88 bis, bd de Port-Royal
43 54 66 65
Open noon-2 a.m. (Sun. noon-midnight).

As the name suggests, those dedicated to the immortal delights of Gambrinus (the mythical king/inventor of beer) gather here to clink mugs into the night. University types from the surrounding district sit alone resting their eyes on the collections of bottles and labels that adorn the walls. The wooden benches are a bit hard, and at busy times elbows get rubbed together, but these quibbles are small beer compared to the tasty house brew, drawn perfectly under the practised eye of a true artist of the tap, Pierre Marion.

Bar Belge
17th arr. - 75, av. de Saint-Ouen
46 27 41 01
Open daily 11 a.m.-3 a.m.

Two of the many strong beers on tap at this authentically Flemish watering hole are a Lindermans kriek and a Lambic Vieux Bruges; the superb list of bottled beer is topped by Belgium's famous Judas-sur-Lie. Like the other jolly habitués who gather here, we always order a plate of the excellent jambon d'Ardenne to accompany our brew.

Bedford Arms
6th arr. - 17, rue Princesse - 46 33 25 60
Open 10 p.m.-dawn. Closed Sun.

Whether or not you gain admittance to this classy pub will depend on your demeanour (smile!) and your possession of a valid passport. Once inside, you can order a cool lager, a pint of ale or a fine malt whisky, in the company of actors, TV personalities and other urbane night hawks (the ultra-exclusive Castel's is just next door).

Le Café de la Plage
11th arr. - 59, rue de Charonne
47 00 91 60
Bar: open 8 p.m.-2 a.m. Downstairs: open from 11 p.m. Closed Sun. & Mon.

A trendy, eclectic nightspot which features live music (downstairs in the cave: jazz, salsa, blues or fusion), and is the haunt of a cosmopolitan young crowd. Beer—particularly Smithwicks—is the tipple of choice.

Finnegan's Wake
5th arr. - 9, rue des Boulangers
46 34 23 65
Open 10 p.m.-midnight (Sat. & Sun. 4 p.m.-midnight. Closed 1 wk. at Christmas.

Though it is a recent addition to the Latin Quarter scene, Finnegan's Wake is already a popular student haunt (they work up a powerful thirst poring over dusty tomes in the library around the corner!). English is spoken in this friendly Irish pub, where the draught beer is drawn as it should be: slowly and carefully.

Flann O'Brien
1st arr. - 6, rue Bailleul
42 60 13 58
Open daily 4 p.m.-2 a.m. Closed Dec. 25 & Jan. 1.

The most authentically Irish of the city's pubs. James, the owner, makes sure that the Guinness is served just as it would be in Dublin or Cork: rich, smooth, with virtually no head.

Le Général La Fayette
9th arr. - 52, rue La Fayette - 47 70 59 08
Open 10 a.m.-3 a.m. (Sat. 3 p.m.-3 a.m.). Closed Sun.

Join the jolly jostlers around the convivial bar for a cool pint of Guinness or a Belgian brew, or else choose a table inside or on the terrace for a light meal (salads, charcuterie, herrings, cheese…). The service is simpatico, and so is the cosmopolitan clientele.

Gobelet d'Argent
1st arr. - 11, rue du Cygne - 42 33 29 82
Open daily 4 p.m.-1 a.m.

This is the place in town for Guinness and loads of Irish ambience.

La Gueuze
5th arr. - 19, rue Soufflot - 43 54 63 00
Open noon-2 a.m. Closed Sun.

One is surprised by the size of this immense but discreet establishment located halfway between the Pantheon and the Luxembourg Gardens. From the nearby Sorbonne, teachers and students alike flock here at noon and in the evening. The classic array of Belgian beers is sufficiently inclusive to satisfy any lover of fine ale. Of the bountiful food offered here, we prefer the herby white cheese, which you spread on slices of chunky bread and wash down with a solid Duvel beer.

Irish Pub
2nd arr. - 55, rue Montmartre
42 33 91 33
Open daily 4 p.m.-12:30 a.m. Closed 2 days at Christmas.

The convivial Irish atmosphere is accented by ditties and ballads direct from the Emerald Isle, and Guinness stout served at precisely the right temperature, topped with the correct amount of foam.

James Joyce
1st arr. - 5, rue du Jour - 45 08 17 04
Open daily noon-1 a.m.

The great Irish writer, who liked to take a drop himself now and again, is the presiding spirit at this immense beer hall. Film director John Ford might well have dreamed up the

PUBS - NIGHTLIFE

NIGHTLIFE – PUBS

décor, reminiscent of a Hibernian port town.

Kitty O'Shea's
2nd arr. - 10, rue des Capucines 40 15 00 30
Open noon-1:30 a.m. (Fri. & Sat. until 2 a.m.). Closed Dec. 25.

Kitty doesn't have any culinary ambitions; one comes here to put down a few Smithwicks and Guinnesses, served on tap at ideal temperature and pressure—as in Dublin. The smoked salmon, the chicken pie and the Irish coffee never fail to be everything the regulars expect them to be. The décor, which is half-bar, half-dining room, has its charm. But you can't be in too much of a hurry or too fussy about the selection.

La Marine
6th arr. - 59, bd du Montparnasse - 45 48 27 70
Open daily 6:30 a.m.-2:30 a.m. (Fri. & Sat. until 3:30 a.m.).

Thankfully, the sanitising and bleaching of the once-colourful Montparnasse area has not yet reached La Marine; it still retains its folkloric charm—even if little except the varnished tables and copper portholes remains of the nautical motif. A big sign (which we've translated for you) announces *Our job is to serve a good beer, so leave us the choice and have no fear,* thereby setting the tone: beer is queen here. Dark, light or amber, it is accompanied at any hour by Nuremburg sausages or weisswurst (or a combination plus apples and chips), or mussels in beer sauce.

Mayflower
5th arr. 49, rue Descartes - 43 54 56 47
Open daily 10:30 a.m.-4 a.m.

While we wouldn't call it puritanical, this classy British-style pub in the heart of the Latin Quarter stands apart from the more down-to-earth establishments that surround it. By day, weary pilgrims wander in for a quiet drink and a snack, but at nightfall a livelier crew takes over.

La Micro-Brasserie
2nd arr. - 106, rue de Richelieu 42 96 55 31
Open 8 a.m.-2 a.m. Closed Sun.

Yes, the house beers are actually brewed on the premises, in huge copper vats that make up a big part of the interior décor. To accompany the delicious amber brew (far better than the house lager), try some of the surprisingly light fare that incorporates hops and malt: prime rib *marchand de bière*, filets of rockfish cooked in pale ale and so forth. Some excellent cheeses from the north and east of France can be found here as well. It's a pity that the salmon-and-black postmodern décor is so cold and noisy, for overall this is really a very successful experiment.

L'Oiseau de Feu
11th arr. - 12, place de la Bastille 40 19 07 52
Open daily 9 a.m-5 a.m.

An offshoot of the popular Général Lafayette tavern (see above), this splendid establishment offers a fine selection of draught beers and a short menu of homely dishes. The view of the new Opera house is a plus—or a minus, depending on your tastes in architecture.

Sous-Bock Tavern
1st arr. - 49, rue Saint-Honoré 40 26 46 61
Open 11 a.m.-5 a.m. (Sun. 3 p.m.-5 a.m.).

No fewer than 400 beers and 180 whiskies are on offer at this bustling bar, a recent but very welcome addition to the Paris pub scene. The concise but appealing menu features classic brasserie fare (we can recommend the excellent rillettes and civet de sanglier).

La Taverne de Nesle
6th arr. - 32, rue Dauphine - 43 26 38 36
Open daily 8 p.m.-dawn.

Hundreds of beers and 17 krieks (a Belgian brew) are served in this tavern, where you can while away a pleasant evening, if you don't mind the noise of the last-round revellers who drift in after energetic soirées in the area. The video entertainment does its best to thwart all conversation. We prefer to come here around 8 p.m. for an apéritif, such as the good draught beer, and a relaxed chat.

Kiosques

Two popular addresses with folk who decide to go to the *theatre* at the last minute. You're likely to get a good seat because this is where *tickets* that originally went to booking agencies wind up when they're not sold and they're half price. But you'll probably have to queue.

1st arr. - Metro station: Châtelet-les-Halles, open 12:30 p.m.-7:30 p.m., closed Sun. & Mon.
8th arr. - Place de la Madeleine, open 12:30 p.m.-8 p.m. (Sun. noon-4 p.m.), closed Mon.

SHOPS

ANTIQUES	*164*
AT YOUR SERVICE	*179*
BEAUTY	*185*
BOOKS & STATIONERY	*190*
CHEAP CHIC CLOTHES	*195*
CHILDREN	*197*
CLOTHES FOR HIM & HER	*203*
DEPARTMENT STORES	*207*
EYEWEAR	*210*
FLOWERS & PLANTS	*210*
FOOD	*212*
GIFTS	*235*
HOME	*237*
IMAGE & SOUND	*249*
JEWELLERY	*251*
LEATHER & LUGGAGE	*255*
MENSWEAR	*257*
OPEN LATE	*262*
SPORTING GOODS	*263*
TOBACCONISTS	*266*
WOMEN'S WEAR	*268*

ANTIQUES

ANTIQUES CENTRES

La Cour aux Antiquaires
8th arr. - 54, rue du Faubourg-Saint-Honoré - 42 66 96 63
Open 10:30 a.m.-6:30 p.m. Closed Sun., Mon. & July 20-Sept. 5.

Aspects of the art and antiques market are brought together in these small, immaculate boutiques. Eighteen shops offer inlaid furniture of the 17th to 19th centuries, paintings, engravings, ceramics, jewellery and quality *bibelots* for a refined clientele.

Le Louvre des Antiquaires
1st arr. - 2, pl. du Palais-Royal 42 97 27 00
Open 11 a.m.-7 p.m. Closed Mon. (Sun. & Mon. in July & Aug.). No cards.

Le Louvre des Antiquaires, a marketplace for objets d'art, is the greatest success of its kind in France and probably the world. The former Magasins du Louvre department store has been beautifully renovated and now houses some 250 dealers on three levels. These merchants are the most select, professional and scrupulous in the trade, if not the most famous. There isn't a single piece offered for sale whose authenticity and quality is not guaranteed. Of course, the prices reflect this. Thirty specialities are represented—from archaeological artefacts to 18th-century furniture, from 19th-century minor masters to Art Deco ornaments, from old porcelain to rare stamps and from animal bronzes to lead soldiers and ship models, fans, rare books and fabulous jewels. Le Louvre des Antiquaires also provides a delivery service, a club, exhibition halls and bars. Its annual exhibitions are mounted around selected themes on the second floor.

Village Saint-Paul
4th arr. - 23-27 rue St-Paul
Closed Tues. & Wed. No cards.

A new area of antique dealers was developed between the rue Saint-Paul and the rue Charlemagne about 15 years ago. Encompassing some 70 shops, the Village is a good source of jewellery, pictures, glass and crystal, country furniture and decorative objects from the 1900–1930 period.

Le Village Suisse
15th arr. - 78, av. de Suffren and 54, av. de la Motte-Piquet
Open Thurs.-Sun. 10:30 a.m.-7 p.m.

With 150 dealers offering everything from "junque" to rare and precious pieces, this "Village" is a popular attraction for dedicated antique-hunters and Sunday strollers alike. Among the top merchants are Maud and René Garcia, for African art; Michel d'Istria, for 16th and 17th-century wooden furniture from France, Spain, Italy and England; Jeannine Kugel, for animal bronzes; and Antonin Rispal, for Art Nouveau

---

Le Marché aux Puces

Each weekend some 150,000 visitors trek out to Saint-Ouen, a northern suburb just beyond the 18th arrondissement, to the world's largest antiques market. From dawn on Friday until Monday afternoon, dealers sell everything from used kitchen utensils to vintage jeans, from Art Deco clocks and knick-knacks to signed 18th-century writing desks. The Marché Biron boasts the classiest merchandise—crystal chandeliers, rare silver and such; the Marché Serpette draws clients from the fashion and entertainment fields with trendy retro and Art Deco pieces; the open-air Marché Paul-Bert is an eclectic treasure trove where early birds can unearth some terrific finds; the Marché Vernaison, the heart of the flea market, has 400 stands offering vintage linens, crockery, stamps and miscellaneous collectibles; the tiny, tidy shops of the Marché Malassis present cleaned-up, restored merchandise in a modern, high-tech setting; the newest arrival, the Marché Dauphine, is still seeking to carve out its own niche. 93400 Saint-Ouen

Marché Biron: **85, rue des Rosiers;**
Marché Serpette: **110, rue des Rosiers;**
Marché Paul Bert: **104, rue des Rosiers & 18, rue Paul Bert;**
Marché Vernaison: **99, rue des Rosiers & 136, rue Michelet;**
Marché Malassis: **142, rue des Rosiers;**
Marché Dauphine: **138, rue des Rosiers.**

ANTIQUES – SHOPS

glass by Daum, Gallé, Carabin and Majorelle.

FRENCH ANTIQUES

ART NOUVEAU, ART DECO & 1930s

Maria de Beyrie
6th arr. - 23, rue de Seine - 43 25 76 15
Open 11 a.m.-1 p.m. & 2 p.m.-7 p.m. (Mon. 2 p.m.-7 p.m.). Closed Sun., Aug. & holidays. No cards.

Lovely antiques from the turn of the century can be found in this shop, as well as pieces by the great designers from the years 1925–1930: Legrain, Rousseau, Printz, Ruhlmann and others. And that is not to mention the architect-designed furniture, particularly pieces crafted in metal, from 1925 to 1950. You will also find the creations of the Union des artistes modernes, run by René Herbst with Le Corbusier, Chareau, Mallet-Stevens, Charlotte Periand, Eileen Gray and others.

Jean-Jacques Dutko
6th arr. - 13, rue Bonaparte, corner rue des Beaux-Arts - 43 26 96 13
Open 10:30 a.m.-12:30 p.m. & 2:30 p.m.-7 p.m. Closed Sun., Mon. & Aug.

Dutko was one of the early promoters of Art Deco, particularly at the Paris Biennale. Clustered all around him are the top designers of the period (Gray, Ruhlmann, Printz, Dunand). Modern art, Dutko's second love, is represented by paintings and sculptures by Fautrier, Bourdelle and Poliakoff, Léger, as well as by paintings and drawings by André Masson (whose prices he has driven considerably higher).

Félix Marcilhac
6th arr. - 8, rue Bonaparte - 43 26 47 36
Open 10 a.m.-noon & 2:30 p.m.-7 p.m. Closed Sat., Sun., Aug. & holidays. No cards.

Félix Marcilhac, one of the leading lights in Art Deco, is also recognised far and wide for his expertise in other areas. He sells to the grandest museums in the world, and his top-quality objects attract a rich and famous clientele.

Le Roi Fou
8th arr. - 182, rue du Faubourg-Saint-Honoré - 45 63 58 91
Open 10:30 a.m.-7 p.m. Closed Sun., Mon., Aug. & holidays.

Alexandre Mai has accumulated a considerable pile of all sorts of objects from 1880 to 1930: furniture, bronzes, ivories, porcelain, clocks, jardinières (flower stands) and Art Deco chandeliers. If you are willing to rummage a bit, your efforts will often be rewarded.

DIRECTOIRE, EMPIRE, RESTORATION & CHARLES X

Au Directoire
7th arr. - 12, bd Raspail - 42 22 67 09
Open 10:30 a.m.-noon & 2:30 p.m.-7 p.m. (Mon. 2:30 p.m.-7 p.m.). Closed Sun. & Aug. No cards.

In 1982 Thierry Winsall opened this shop on the boulevard Raspail, where the Dubreuil family once sold Empire furniture. He maintained his own speciality from his former shop on the rue de Grenelle: the end of the 18th century to the beginning of the 19th, featuring desks, bookcases, commodes, bronzes, lamps and, his special interest, chairs. There is lots of mahogany, and the prices are sufficiently reasonable to attract other, mostly foreign, dealers.

Raoul Guiraud Brugidou-Malnati
7th arr. - 90, rue de Grenelle - 42 22 61 04
Open 10:30 a.m.-12:30 p.m. & 2:30 p.m.-7 p.m. Closed Sun., Aug. & holidays. No cards.

A shop that celebrates the pleasure of objects that combine beauty and utility, such as scientific instruments, marine objects, curiosities, and seascapes from the 19th and 20th centuries.

Mancel-Coti
7th arr. - 42, rue du Bac - 45 48 04 34
Open 10 a.m.-1 p.m. & 2 p.m.-7 p.m. (Mon. 2:30 p.m.-7 p.m.). Closed Sun., (Sat. in summer), Aug. & holidays. No cards.

This is a venerable establishment reputed for its furniture, clocks and porcelain of the Directoire, Consulate and Empire periods. Its clients are eminent connoisseurs, and have included Prince Murat and the Legion of Honour museum.

Renoncourt
6th arr. - 1-3, rue des Saints-Pères 42 60 75 87
Open 10 a.m.-12:30 & 2 p.m.-7 p.m. Closed Sun. No cards.

A wide-ranging selection of mahogany and fruitwood furniture from the Empire, Restoration and Charles X periods. The objects are of the highest quality, and the Renoncourts are generous in sharing their charm and their extensive knowledge.

LOUIS-PHILIPPE, NAPOLEON III & LATE NINETEENTH CENTURY

Calvet
9th arr. - 10, rue Chauchat - 42 46 12 36
Open 9:30 a.m.-12:30 p.m. & 2:30 p.m.-6:30 p.m. (Sat. by

appt.). Closed Sun., Aug. & holidays. No cards.

Calvet is the third generation of specialists in furniture built during the Second Empire in the manner of the great 18th-century masters; in fact, the best cabinetmakers of the period were those who worked in that classic style, perfected during the Age of Enlightenment.

Madeleine Castaing
6th arr. - 21, rue Bonaparte - 43 54 91 71
Open 10 a.m.-1 p.m. & 3 p.m.-7 p.m. Closed Sun., Mon. & holidays. No cards.

Madeleine Castaing, a renowned decorator, friend to painters, patron of Soutine, was one of the first to rediscover these dainty little furniture pieces and decorative objects of the Second Empire, which she sells at imperial prices. She also carries a substantial selection of carpeting and fabrics which she designs herself.

MEDIEVAL & RENAISSANCE

Jacqueline Boccador
7th arr. - 1, quai Voltaire - 42 60 75 79
Open 10 a.m.-7 p.m. (Mon. 2 p.m.-7 p.m.). Closed Sun., Aug. & holidays. No cards.

Often called to act as expert witness for the French Customs, Jacqueline Boccador (the "High Priestess of Medieval Sculpture") combines her remarkable familiarity with medieval antiques with an equally profound knowledge of Renaissance pieces. She is the author of several superb scholarly works, and is endowed with the ability to communicate her passion for furniture, statues and tapestries to her customers. She recently left her shop on the rue du Bac for new, more impressive premises on the quai Voltaire.

Edouard et Gabriel Bresset
7th arr. - 5, quai Voltaire - 42 60 78 13
Open 10 a.m.-12:30 p.m. & 2:30 p.m.-7 p.m. Closed Sun., Aug. & holidays. No cards.

No-one will dispute the fact that the Bressets are the world's top specialists in medieval statuary, whether in wood or stone, unpainted or polychrome. They also sell Gothic tapestries to major museums, as well as paintings, furniture and carved wood— wonderful cabinets inlaid with tortoiseshell or ebony—and bronze, ivory and enamelled sculpture from the Middle Ages and Renaissance. When you visit, be sure to explore the superb vaulted cellars on the quai Voltaire.

Jean-Claude Edrei
7th arr. - 44, rue de Lille - 42 61 28 08
Open 10 a.m.-7 p.m. (Mon. from 2 p.m.). Closed Sun., Aug. & holidays.

Here is a huge, beautiful shop dedicated in part to the medieval period, and in particular to china and pewterware, for which Edrei is well known as a top-quality dealer. You can also find tapestries here, which enhance some massive furniture pieces from the 17th and 18th centuries.

Antony Embden
7th arr. - 15, quai Voltaire - 42 61 04 06
Open 10:30 a.m.-12:30 p.m. & 2:30 p.m.-7 p.m. Closed Sun., Mon., Aug. & holidays. No cards.

A rich source of Renaissance sculpture in bronze, marble and ivory, as well as some exquisite old faïence and a wide selection of high-quality objects from the 16th and 17th centuries.

Don't plan to shop on Sundays, the vast majority of Paris shops are closed.

Perpitch
7th arr. - 240, bd Saint-Germain 45 48 37 67
Open 9 a.m.-12:30 p.m. & 2 p.m.-6:30 p.m. Closed Sun., Aug. & holidays. No cards.

With 50 years of experience, Antoine Perpitch is a renowned expert on the Flemish and Italian Renaissance, as well as on French Gothic and medieval statuary. Louis XIII chairs, credenzas and tables, including some enormous monastery pieces, and tapestries from the 16th and 17th centuries are on display in his spacious shop, on the corner of the rue du Bac.

SEVENTEENTH & EIGHTEENTH CENTURIES

Didier Aaron
8th arr. - 118, rue du Faubourg-Saint-Honoré - 47 42 47 34
Open 10 a.m.-12:30 p.m. & 2:30 p.m.-6:30 p.m. (Sat. from 11 a.m.). Closed Sun., Aug. & holidays. No cards.

In London, New York and Paris, Didier Aaron enjoys a brilliant reputation for his prestigious collection of 18th-century inlaid furniture and objets d'art. He has extended his interests to the purchase and sale of fine paintings and the art of interior decoration: his firm now includes a design office headed by celebrity decorator, Jacques Grange.

Antiquités de Beaune
7th arr. - 14, rue de Beaune - 42 61 25 42
Open 11 a.m.-12:30 p.m. & 2:30 p.m.-7 p.m. (Mon. 2:30 p.m.-7 p.m.). Closed Sun., Aug. & holidays. No cards.

A noted specialist in French 18th-century country furniture crafted in cherry, maple, sycamore and walnut, Monsieur Horowitz also possesses a large selection of porcelain from the 18th and early 19th centuries.

ANTIQUES – SHOPS

Aveline
8th arr. - 20, rue du Cirque - 42 66 60 29
Open 9:30 a.m.-7 p.m. Closed Sun., Aug. & holidays. No cards.

Here is a respected establishment whose 18th-century "museum quality" furniture and paintings are indeed often purchased by major museums (the Louvre, the Getty, the Musée de Compiègne, to name but a few). Jean-Marie Rossi is also known for his collection of outstanding curiosities that are always both beautiful and strikingly original. Naturally, all of these treasures fetch stratospheric prices.

Bernard Baruch Steinitz
9th arr. - 75, rue du Faubourg-Saint-Honoré - 47 42 31 94
Open 10 a.m.-7 p.m. Closed Sun., 1 wk. in Aug. & holidays. No cards.

An inveterate traveller in search of unusual objects, Steinitz has left his former shop near the Drouot auction rooms for brand new premises on the Faubourg, opposite Le Bristol hotel. The quality of his mainly 18th- and 19th-century furniture and ornaments is beyond question, and the pieces reflect Steinitz's eclectic tastes. In his workshops, 30 top-flight craftsmen maintain the highest tradition of restoration. The prices are also in the highest tradition. But you can visit simply for a look round.

Etienne Lévy La Cour de Varenne
7th arr. - 42, rue de Varenne - 45 44 65 50
Open 10 a.m.-1 p.m. & 2 p.m.-7 p.m. (Sat. until 6 p.m.). Closed Sun., Aug. & holidays. No cards.

This lovely shop opens not only onto the street but also onto a beautiful inner courtyard, around which stand the outbuildings of the former residence of Madame de Staël. Claude Lévy has accumulated some real treasures: 17th- and 18th-century clocks and furniture with secret compartments. Despite astronomical prices, these peerless pieces find buyers in the four corners of the globe. On the ground floor, a gallery displays a wonderful collection of mostly 19th-century paintings.

Fabius Frères
8th arr. - 152, bd Haussmann 45 62 39 18
Open 9:30 a.m.-noon & 2:30 p.m.-6 p.m. Closed Sat. (except appt.), Sun., Aug. & holidays. No cards.

Since 1867 the Fabius family have been antique dealers in Paris—the business handed down from father to son (except when a son named Laurent chose the political scene instead). The firm's clients are museums and the high and mighty who appreciate the choice collection of 17th and 18th-century furniture and objects. Also on view are impressive quantities of Empire pieces, as well as 19th-century paintings and animal bronzes by Barye and Carpeaux.

Galerie Camoin-Demachy
7th arr. - 9, quai Voltaire - 42 61 82 06
Open 10 a.m.-7 p.m. Closed Sun. & Aug. No cards.

This is perhaps the most beautiful antique shop in Paris, with magnificent pieces magnificently presented. Decorator Alain Demachy has done things just right, and his plan is ambitious: to bring together rare and lovely furniture of the 18th and 19th centuries, including Russian, Italian and Austrian creations, with objets d'art and decorative ornaments from diverse periods and styles. The result is strikingly luxurious and more than a little intimidating.

Galerie Perrin
7th arr. - 3, quai Voltaire - 42 60 27 20
8th arr. - 98, rue du Faubourg-Saint-Honoré - 42 65 01 38
Open 10 a.m.-1 p.m. & 2 p.m.-7 p.m. (Mon. 2 p.m.-7 p.m.). Closed Sun. & Aug. No cards.

Perrin can be counted among the major players in the antiques business. In a flamboyant décor of lacquer and black aluminium, Patrick and Philippe Perrin stage a presentation of some spectacular pieces from the 17th and 18th centuries: Boulle commodes, Mazarin desks and other signed masterpieces of the period.

Gismondi
8th arr. - 20, rue Royale - 42 60 73 89
Open 10 a.m.-7 p.m. Closed Sun., Mon., 1 wk. at Christmas-New Year's Day, Aug. & holidays. No cards.

Already well known among collectors for his Antibes shop, Gismondi now also occupies a prestigious address on the rue Royale, which he has placed under the supervision of his daughter, Sabrina. With a pronounced predilection for spectacular baroque pieces, such as sumptuous German and Italian cabinets, gilded bronzes and desks by Boulle overlaid with copper and tortoiseshell, she also presents a magnificent variety of decorative objets d'art and paintings from the 17th and 18th centuries. And the luxurious, theatrical setting with a distinctly Italian feel is itself something to behold.

Kraemer
8th arr. - 43, rue de Monceau 45 63 24 46
Open 9 a.m.-7 p.m. Closed Sun., Aug. & holidays (except appt.). No cards.

It is possible to be one of the world's top experts on the French 17th and 18th centuries, to sell to museums and top-flight collectors a range of furniture, chairs, bronzes and objets d'art and yet to remain charmingly modest. For such are the accomplishments of Philippe Kraemer, who now works in collaboration with his son. Their mind-boggling gallery is as fascinating as a world-class museum.

Jean de Laminne
8th arr. - 148, bd Haussmann 45 62 08 15
Open 10 a.m.-12:30 p.m. & 2 p.m.-6 p.m. Closed Sat., Sun., Aug. & holidays. No cards.

Since 1937, in his 2,000-square-foot shop, Jean de Laminne (now working in tandem with his son) has displayed stunning pieces of furniture from the 18th century. Devotees of Regency furniture crafted in ebony or black wood with copper finework won't go wrong with purchases of Laminne's superb commodes and mirrors, which still bear their original patina.

Michel Meyer
8th arr. - 24, av. Matignon - 42 66 62 95
Open 10 a.m.-1 p.m. & 2 p.m.-7 p.m. (Mon. 2 p.m.-7 p.m.). Closed Sun., Aug. & holidays. No cards.

Meyer grew up in a veritable palace crammed with antiques, and it shows. The ever-replenished stock of furniture and objects from the 18th century reflects a fondness for chased bronzes and mounted objects. With his excellent reputation, Meyer is an influential figure in the Paris biennial shows.

Maurice Segoura
8th arr. - 20, rue du Faubourg-Saint-Honoré - 42 65 11 03
Open 9 a.m.-6:30 p.m. (Sat. 9 a.m.-12:30 p.m. & 2 p.m.-6 p.m.; Mon. 9 a.m.-6 p.m.). Closed Sun. & holidays. No cards.

Segoura is yet another heavyweight among Parisian antique dealers. Three floors of furniture, objets d'art and spectacular decorative arts are destined for an international clientele and for prestigious private collections. He has also developed a reputation for buying and selling works by such French painters as Greuze, Watteau and Fragonard, whose canvases are scattered here and there in the shop, further enhancing the beautiful furniture.

■ FOREIGN ANTIQUES

AFRICAN, OCEANIC & PRE-COLUMBIAN

Arts des Amériques
6th arr. - 42, rue de Seine - 46 33 18 31
Open 10:30 a.m.-7:30 p.m. (Mon. from 3 p.m.). Closed Sun. & holidays.

Within this friendly little shop is an enormous selection of primarily pre-Columbian art, from Mexico, Costa Rica and Colombia. The statues, stones and terracotta objects are all sold with a photograph and a certificate of authenticity.

Galerie Carrefour
6th arr. - 141, bd Raspail - 43 26 58 03
Open 9 a.m.-noon & 2 p.m.-6:30 p.m. Closed Sun., Aug. & holidays. No cards.

Monsieur Vérité has assembled here a huge, diverse but well-selected wealth of mostly African objects: Ibéji, Yoruba and Dan masks, Ibo statues, Ashanti bronzes, Senufo doors, Akan jewellery, Baoulé statuettes and so forth. The range of prices is as wide as the turnover is high. In addition, there's a department of Mediterranean Basin antiques (displaying about 300 objects).

Galerie Mermoz
8th arr. - 9, rue du Cirque - 42 25 84 80
Open 10 a.m.-12:30 p.m. & 2 p.m.-7 p.m. Closed Sun., Aug. & holidays. No cards.

This is a highly specialised shop of the finest sort. It is well known at all the Paris shows on account of its rigorously selected array of pre-Columbian works. Prices to match.

BRITISH

British Import
92200 Neuilly - 23, bd du Parc, Ile-de-la-Jatte - 46 37 27 75
Open 11 a.m.-7 p.m. (Sun. by appt.). Closed Aug.
1st arr. - 4, allée Topino, Louvre des Antiquaires - 42 60 19 13
Open 11 a.m.-7 p.m. Closed Mon. & Aug.
15th arr. 78, av. de Suffren, Swiss Village - Sous-Sol, n° 3 - 45 67 87 61
Open 11 a.m.-12:30 p.m. & 3 p.m.-7 p.m. Closed Tues., Wed. & Aug.

This establishment has just one speciality: English furniture of the 18th and 19th centuries, primarily in mahogany. At the Ile de la Jatte (a popular subject of Seurat) there's a restoration workshop for repairs and French polishing. Approximately 100 pieces arrive every few months.

Andrée Higgins
7th arr. - 54, rue de l'Université 45 48 75 28
Open 9:30 a.m.-1 p.m. & 2 p.m.-5 p.m. Closed Sun., Mon., Aug. & holidays. No cards.

She was one of the first to introduce Paris to the taste for things English, just after the Second World War. She chooses her furniture from the 18th and 19th centuries with the utmost care. The renewed popularity of the colonial style has led her to collect lovely Chinese lacquer-panel tables and writing desks, which were fashionable in England at the turn of the century. On our last visit, we also spotted some superb French furniture from the 17th and 18th centuries. The stock is always changing, and presentations can be given in customers' homes.

Aliette Massenet
16th arr. - 169, av. Victor-Hugo
47 27 24 05
Open 10 a.m.-6:30 p.m. Closed Sun., Aug. & holidays. No cards.

Every month the charming owner, Aliette, takes delivery of British specialities such as furniture and 19th-century objects, tea services, fish knives and forks, porcelain, sporting prints, silver and bronze frames, pipe racks and costume jewellery.

FAR EASTERN

Beurdeley
7th arr. - 200, bd Saint-Germain
45 48 97 86
Open 10 a.m.-12:30 p.m. & 2:30 p.m.-7 p.m. Closed Sun., Mon., Aug. & holidays. No cards.

An expert if ever there was one, Jean-Michel Beurdeley is recognised as one of the great specialists in Far Eastern art. He supplies the big museums, and though you'll rarely see him in Paris—he travels extensively—his gallery continues to bring together some of the best work from China and Japan.

La Boutique du Marais
4th arr. - 16, rue de Sévigné - 42 74 03 65
Open 10:30 a.m.-1 p.m. & 2 p.m.-7 p.m. Closed Sun., Mon., 3 1st wks. of Aug. & holidays.

From opium pipes to Japanese cupboards (tansu), Marie-Anne Baron specialises in works from India, China and Japan. Recently, though, the craft work of India is giving way more and more to the antique furniture of China and Japan. A second shop displays Far Eastern graphic arts: screens, miniatures, paintings and kakemonos.

Bernard Captier
7th arr. - 25, rue de Verneuil - 42 61 00 57
Open 10:30 a.m.-7 p.m. (Mon. from 2:30 p.m.). Closed Sun. & Aug. No cards.

This specialist in Japanese antiques is known to give excellent value for the money his clients invest. Perhaps it's because he is one of the few Paris dealers to travel to Japan several times a year in search of 19th-century objects and furniture (chests, commodes), which he restores in Paris for his wife to sell. (Note: He will also buy them back at the selling price plus inflation.) China and Korea are also represented, and on our last visit, we noticed some very handsome screens.

Compagnie de la Chine et des Indes
8th arr. - 39, av. de Friedland - 42 89 05 45
Open 9:30 a.m.-noon & 2 p.m.-6:30 p.m. Closed Sun., Aug. & holidays. No cards.

Here you will find the entire Far East under one roof. A top-notch selection of Chinese porcelain, pottery, furniture, Indian and Khmer sculpture, paintings and screens is displayed on three floors. Some of the objects are truly museum quality, and the head of the shop, Jean-Pierre Rousset, can be counted on for good advice.

Gérard Lévy
7th arr. - 17, rue de Beaune - 42 61 26 55
Open 10 a.m.-1 p.m. & 2 p.m.-6 p.m. (& 2 Sun. in Dec.). Closed Sun. & Aug.

Lévy is a most reliable guide to the art of China, Cambodia, Japan, Korea and Thailand, and in his pretty shop we've encountered some ardent collectors. He sells important pieces to museums, but there are more accessible items as well—always of a refined and high quality. Lévy is also an antique photograph devotee, and is an official expert on the subject.

March on the Arch

When Napoleon Bonaparte had the *Arc de Triomphe* built to celebrate his battlefield victories, it stood on the outer edge of Paris and the view took in the surrounding countryside. Nowadays you look out over the ultra-chic 8th and 16th arrondissements while to the northwest the Arch's modern cousin, the *Grande Arche de la Défense*, guards the city's newest business district. Twelve broad avenues compose the "star" that radiates from the *place de l'Etoile*, former name of the place Charles-de-Gaulle. The best way to appreciate this urban galaxy is to climb (or take the lift) to the top of the Arc de Triomphe. At the foot of Napoleon's monument an eternal flame burns over the *Tomb of the Unknown Soldier*, chosen among the many unidentified victims of the First World War. The eternal flame symbolises the nation's enduring sorrow and pity.

We're always happy to hear about your discoveries and receive our comments on ours. Please feel free to write to us stating clearly what you liked or disliked.

SHOPS – ANTIQUES

Jan et Hélène Lühl
6th arr. - 19, quai Malaquais - 42 60 76 97
Open 2 p.m.-7 p.m. Closed Sun., Mon., Aug. & holidays. No cards.

These knowledgeable collectors of engravings will sweep you along in their enthusiasm. Their shop is in what was once the gallery of the famous collector Ernest Le Veél (whose prints and engravings were dispersed in three historic auctions at the Hôtel Drouot). They have examples from all fields—we found some fascinating culinary etchings from Japan.

Yvonne Moreau-Gobard
6th arr. - 5, rue des Saints-Pères 42 60 88 25
Open 10 a.m.-12:30 p.m. & 2 p.m.-7 p.m. Closed Sun. & Aug. No cards.

The wife of the noted appraiser Jean-Claude Moreau-Gobard, Yvonne offers a comprehensive range of archaeological objects from China, India and Cambodia. The number of pieces displayed here is as impressive as their quality.

Orient-Occident
6th arr. - 5, rue des Saints-Pères 42 60 77 65
Open 10 a.m.-12:30 p.m. & 2 p.m.-7 p.m. Closed Sun. & Aug. No cards.

The totally unassuming and media-shy Jean-Loup Despras, who reads hieroglyphs as other people read comic strips, is a specialist in Egyptian antiques. He shares the premises with Yvonne Moreau-Gobard (see above), a first-rate expert on Indian and Far Eastern arts. Gobard's bronzes, pottery and ceramics are on display.

Janette Ostier
3rd arr. - 26, pl. des Vosges - 48 87 28 57
Open by appointment only. No cards.

This charming little boutique is primarily devoted to Japanese art; included are drawings, etchings, pictures, painted screens, masks, and lacquered boxes. Janette Ostier gives each client her full attention, since she now receives them by appointment only.

ISLAMIC

Arts de l'Orient
6th arr. - 21, quai Malaquais 42 60 72 91, fax 42 61 01 52
Open 10:30 a.m.-12:30 p.m. & 2:30 p.m.-7 p.m. Closed Sun., Aug. & holidays. No cards.

Annie Kevorkian is one of France's top specialists in Middle Eastern art. She has a magnificent collection of Islamic ceramics, in addition to miniatures, antique glass and terracotta objects and some exquisite bronzes.

Philippe et Claude Magloire
4th arr. - 13, pl. des Vosges - 42 74 40 67
Open 1 p.m.-6 p.m. Closed Mon.

Claude and Philippe Magloire, who are geologists and collectors as well as expert appraisers attached to the French Court of Appeal, spent ten years in Iran. In 1981, they opened a gallery on the place des Vosges to introduce and promote Iranian art, a refined but little-understood tradition in the West. Treasures such as bronzes from Luristan, Islamic ceramics from Nishapur, and antique carpets form a good collection of Asian art and archaeology.

Jean Soustiel
1st arr. - 146, bd Haussmann - 45 62 27 76
Open 9:30 a.m.-1 p.m. & 2 p.m.-7 p.m. Closed Sat., Sun., Aug. & holidays. No cards.

This gallery celebrated its 100th anniversary in 1983; four generations of the family have promoted Islamic art here. Jean Soustiel, a highly regarded expert among his colleagues, runs one of the most famous and reputable galleries in the world. He is also the author of an exhaustive study of Islamic ceramics, which has become the collector's bible. His associate, Marie-Christine David, specialises in Indian ceramics.

MEDITERRANEAN

Nina Borowski
7th arr. - 40, rue du Bac - 45 48 61 60
Open 10:30 a.m.-12:30 p.m. & 2 p.m.-7 p.m. (Mon. 2:30 p.m.-7 p.m.). Closed Sun., Aug. & holidays. No cards.

Daughter of the great Borowski of Basel, the erudite and charming Nina Borowski displays a significant collection of pottery, vases, bronzes and marbles of Greek, Roman and Etruscan origin. Each year, she organises an exhibition of archaeological artefacts. It's possible here to find small Greek terracotta pieces at reasonable prices.

Mythes et Légendes
4th arr. - 18, pl. des Vosges - 42 72 63 26
Open 10 a.m.-12:30 p.m. & 2 p.m.-7 p.m. Closed Sun. & 2 wks. in Aug.

Gilles Cohen has assembled a major collection of antiquities from Egypt, Rome, the Far East and pre-Columbian America. Pieces on display include Egyptian amulets as well as some rare and important Cambodian finds. He offers a certificate of expertise and a mail-order catalogue.

RAC PARIS STREETS: *The cartography of this city-wide street plan of Paris is clear and easy to use and is supported by a comprehensive index in book form tipped on to the card cover. The map is packed with essential information including the direction of one-way streets. A must for all visitors to Paris. Price: £ 4.50.*

ANTIQUES – SHOPS

A la Reine Margot
6th arr. - 7, quai de Conti - 43 26 62 50
Open 10:30 a.m.-1 p.m. & 2 p.m.-7 p.m. Closed Sun. & holidays.

This is the oldest gallery of its kind in Paris. These days more and more space is being devoted to archaeology. Michel Cohen (father of Gilles, see above), the proprietor, mounts excellent exhibitions each year and publishes fascinating catalogues. There are, as always, medieval, Renaissance and 17th-century pieces on display, to admire or buy.

RUSSIAN

Artel
6th arr. - 25, rue Bonaparte - 43 54 93 77
Open 10:30 a.m.-12:30 p.m. & 3 p.m.-7 p.m. Closed Sun., Mon., Aug. & holidays. No cards.

Though the supply of objets d'art from tsarist Russia is increasingly rare, the demand remains high. Martine Cuttat's Russian and Greek icons span the 15th to 19th centuries, and she also sees to the restoration of these fragile pieces.

A la Vieille Cité
1st arr. - 350, rue Saint-Honoré 42 60 67 16
Open 10:30 a.m.-6:30 p.m. Closed Sat., Sun., July 14-Sept. 1. & holidays.

This very Louis Philippe–style décor showcases a treasury of hammered silver, beautiful icons, Fabergé pieces, porcelain, Russian painting and a collection of delicately worked stone Easter eggs, over which presides collector and expert appraiser Alexandre Djanchieff.

> *Don't plan to do much shopping in Paris in August—a great many stores are closed for the entire vacation month.*

■ SPECIALISTS

BANKING, STAMPS & STOCKS

Le Marché aux Timbres
8th arr. - av. des Champs-Elysées, Carré Marigny
Open Thurs., Sat., Sun. & holidays 10 a.m.-6 p.m. No cards.

On the right-hand side of the Champs-Elysées near the corner of the avenues Marigny and Gabriel, 70 licensed sellers set up booths along the pavement. They are there almost all day buying, selling and swapping pieces.

Numistoria
2nd arr. - 49, rue Vivienne - 42 33 93 45
Open 11 a.m.-7 p.m. (Sat. by appt.). Closed Sun. & July 14-Aug. 31. No cards.

This huge and constantly changing presentation of all kinds of banknotes and certificates offers everything from stocks and bonds to coins and old deeds. There's nowhere like it this side of Ali Baba's cave.

BRONZES

Moatti
6th arr. - 77, rue des Saints-Pères 42 22 91 04
Open 10 a.m.-13 p.m. & 2 p.m.-7 p.m. Closed Sun. & Aug. No cards.

In his townhouse on the rue des Saints-Pères, this dealer shows almost exclusively by appointment. The collection of rare pieces represents what connoisseurs consider to be the world's most judiciously selected Renaissance bronzes. Here prices are whispered in a way that suggests that art is beyond any valuation. Every piece must first pass a three-part scrutiny verifying its authenticity, quality and rarity. An artwork purchased from Moatti bears the additional value of the firm's worldwide renown.

COINS & MEDALS

Emile et Sabine Bourgey
9th arr. - 7, rue Drouot - 47 70 35 18
Open 9:15 a.m.-noon & 2 p.m.-6:15 p.m. (Sat. 9 a.m.-noon). Closed Sun. & Aug. No cards.

Located in a Belle Epoque apartment opposite the salesroom of the Drouot auctioneer's, Emile Bourgey's offices have maintained the plush, discreet atmosphere of an earlier age. For over 30 years, everything here has been dedicated to coin collecting: the exquisite display cases, the library of several thousand titles on the subject and the pains that Bourgey and/or his daughter take to initiate clients into the realm of numismatics.

Numismatique et Change de Paris
2nd arr. - 3, rue de la Bourse - 42 97 46 85
Open 9 a.m.-5:30 p.m. Closed Sat. (except in summer 9:30 a.m.-12:30 p.m.), Sun., Aug. & holidays. No cards.

While he reserves the trade in collectors' pieces for his boutique, at this address Jean Vinchon leaves his daughter Annette in charge of buying and selling gold coins, ingots, tokens and old banknotes. Gold pieces are sealed into transparent plastic sachets in the presence of the buyer, a unique procedure that provides a valuable guarantee. If you are interested in selling gold here, you should know that there is a 10 per cent commission.

Jean Vinchon
2nd arr. - 77, rue de Richelieu 42 97 50 00
Open 9 a.m.-6 p.m. Closed Sat., Sun., Aug. & holidays. No cards.

Jean Vinchon is not only one of the world's foremost

171

coin experts, he was also among the first to recognise that coin collecting is more than a hobby or an esoteric speciality. He has worked diligently for its acceptance as an art. In the hushed atmosphere of his shop, great collectors argue the merits of individual coins each worth a fortune, while Vinchon advises those interested in less exalted pieces with the same careful attention.

CRYSTAL & GLASS

L'Arlequin
4th arr. - 19, rue de Turenne - 42 78 77 00
Open 2:30 p.m.-7 p.m. Closed Sun., Mon. & Aug. No cards.

This is the kind of shop whose address gets passed from family to family when one of the children has broken an heirloom wineglass or the stopper to the carafe has mysteriously vanished. L'Arlequin stocks hundreds of styles from every period (the house speciality is 19th century), and at a wide range of prices.

La Brocante de Marie-Jeanne
17th arr. - 14, rue Saussier-Leroy 47 66 59 31
Open 11 a.m.-7 p.m. Closed Sun., Mon. & Aug. No cards.

Among all the glasses and crystal, sold in sets or individually, and the liqueur decanters and toiletry accessories, it would be surprising if Marie-Jeanne Schuhmann couldn't find that tiny, out-of-the-ordinary decanter you've been hunting for. But if she can't, you can console yourself with a beautiful Art Deco vase, or perhaps a lamp or bedside carafe.

Galerie Altero
7th arr. - 21, quai Voltaire - 42 61 19 90
Open 10:30 a.m.-12:30 p.m. & 2:30 p.m.-7 p.m. (Mon. 2:30 p.m.-7 p.m.). Closed Sun., Aug. & holidays. No cards.

This is another one of those places worth seeing even if you are not a devotee; 17th-century furniture and 18th-century glass cases function as the décor for the display of glasses and carafes from all periods from Louis XIV to Napoleon III.

CURIOS & UNUSUAL OBJECTS

Air de Chasse
7th arr. - 8, rue des Saints-Pères 42 60 25 98
Open 11 a.m.-1 p.m. & 2:30 p.m.-7 p.m. Closed Sun., Aug. & holidays. No cards.

Here in Jeanine Gerhard's shop is everything you can imagine that is connected in some way or other with hunting or shooting: 18th, 19th and 20th-century prints, decorative objects, bronze animal statuettes, duck decoys, birds in terracotta.

Aux Fontaines de Niepce et de Daguerre
18th arr. - 20, rue André-del-Sarte - 42 54 27 13
Open 10:30 a.m.-5 p.m. Closed Sun., Mon., Aug. & holidays.

This superb shop, with its Second Empire décor, is home to the best-known antique photographic equipment specialist in Paris. Between the walls of this huge shop/museum, Monsieur Bomet has amassed a fine collection of seemingly every sort of apparatus. Bomet's gems include the 18th-century grandfather of all cameras, the *camera oscura*, the first Eastman from 1885 and a rare Sigrist stereoscope. In all there are close to 500 pieces, displayed with the daguerrotypes and ambrotypes also collected by Bomet.

Brocante Store
6th arr. - 31, rue Jacob - 42 60 24 80
Open 10:30 a.m.-7 p.m. Closed Sun. & Mon. No cards.

Amid the pretty English antiques lurk innumerable charming objects, including little chests, instruments and lamps.

Galerie 13
6th arr. - 13, rue Jacob - 43 26 99 89
Open 2:30 p.m.-7 p.m. Closed Sun. No cards.

Once a specialist in antique games, Martine Jeannin is now more interested in charming decorative objects and curiosities. She carries wood carvings from the 18th century, overmantels and folding screens alongside whimsical and strange items such as bird cages, romantic baubles, embroidery, expensive turned-wood objects from Florence, as well as naive artworks.

Nicole Kraemer
1st arr. - 5, allée Desmalter, Louvre des Antiquaires - 42 61 57 95
Open 11 a.m.-1 p.m. & 2 p.m.-7 p.m. Closed Mon. (Sun. & Mon. in July & Aug.).

This pretty shop belongs to an enthusiastic connoisseur of decorative objects and curios. Small 18th-century French pill boxes and fans are her speciality, but Nicole Kraemer's tastes are quite catholic, extending for example to surgical instruments.

Magnolia
7th arr. - 78, rue du Bac - 42 22 31 79
Open 10 a.m.-7 p.m. Closed Sun.

This congenial assemblage of bric-a-brac is crowned by a display of turn-of-the-century bridal bouquets kept under glass. We've also come across chromo-lithographs, busts in plaster or bronze, pill boxes, powder boxes, engraved flasks, antique jewellery, baptismal medals and several beautiful Art Deco lamps.

Emmanuel Thiriot Bernard Escher
16th arr. - 29, rue de la Tour - 45 04 46 54
Open 10:30 a.m.-7:30 p.m. (Sat. & Mon. 2 p.m.-7:30 p.m.). Closed Sun. No cards.

Original, top-quality decorative pieces collected with unfailing but highly eclectic taste. On our last visit we came upon a beautiful piece of furniture from the 1950s next to a lovely Chinese cabinet, and a ship model from the turn of the century beneath a large decorative lacquered panel signed by Jouve. Don't come here looking for something practical; everything is devoted to the decorative arts, and everything has loads of flair.

FABRICS

Aux Fils du Temps
7th arr. - 33, rue de Grenelle - 45 48 14 68
Open 2 p.m.-7 p.m. Closed Sat., Sun., Mon., Aug. & holidays. No cards.

In an early 19th-century décor, Marie-Noëlle Sudre sits amid her treasures: bolts and bolts of antique fabric from all over the world. These are piled up like the crates of an explorer back from a long voyage through time and space—in Sudre's case, it is from the 18th century to the 1950s. If you're looking for something specific, you should call ahead, and Sudre will have things ready when you arrive.

Les Indiennes
4th arr. - 10, rue St-Paul - 42 72 35 34
Open 2:30 p.m.-7:30 p.m. (morning & Aug. by appointment only). Closed Sun.

The Silk Road passes through the rue Saint-Paul: here is a wonderland of shimmering brocades, damasks and satins, many from the 18th century. Exotic and colourful samples of silken fabrics from the East are on view here, crying out to be fashioned into cushions, curtains or fashion accessories.

FANS

Georges Antiquités
1st arr. 26, rue de Richelieu - 42 61 32 57
Open 12:30 a.m.-6:30 p.m. (Sat. by appt.). Closed Sun., Aug. & holidays. No cards.

A most refined presentation of ivory objects and various collectibles. From every period from Louis XIV to Louis-Philippe comes a display of fans made of tortoiseshell, lace, feathers, mother-of-pearl, tulle with sequins, finely worked bone, painted parchment, ostrich plumes and more. Prices vary drastically.

FIREPLACES

Michel Elbaz (S.C.A.D.)
10th arr. - 29 bis, rue de Rocroy 45 26 40 00
Open 9:30 a.m.-6:30 p.m. (Sat. until 12:30 p.m.). Closed Sun. & Aug. No cards.

Elbaz's selection of fireplaces from the 17th century to 1900 come mainly in marble, and prices start at around 2,000 francs. You can also obtain older examples in stone or wood through this knowledgeable dealer. A wide range of attractive prices.

Fernandez-Blanchard
11th arr. - 36, rue Sedaine - 47 00 67 59
Open 10 a.m.-5 p.m. Closed Sat., Sun. & Aug. No cards.

The selection is enormous, and the fireplaces are all beautiful old specimens in marble, wood and often Burgundian stone. There are also some garden fountains, and a restoration service is available.

Jean Lapierre
3rd arr. - 58, rue Vieille-du-Temple - 42 74 07 70
Open 11 a.m.-7:30 p.m. Closed Sun., Mon. & Aug. No cards.

Oak doors, parquet floors, stairs and other antique architectural elements are sold either "as is" or nicely restored. But the chief attraction is the stonework from (primarily) the Mâcon area: fireplaces in their entirety or in separate pieces, mostly 18th century, as well as some interesting carved well copings. In short, this is the place to go if you're looking for any manner of stone objects and sculpture from the 18th century, even the occasional terracotta tiles.

Pierre Madel
6th arr. - 4, rue Jacob
43 26 90 89
Open 3 p.m.-7 p.m. Closed Sun., Mon. & mid July-beg. Sept. No cards.

The impressive array of wrought-iron articles from the 17th century to 1900 includes fire irons, pokers, ash pans, mechanical roasting spits and so forth.

FOLK ART

Georges Bernard
8th arr. - 1, rue d'Anjou - 46 65 23 83
Open 10:30 a.m.-6:30 p.m. Closed Sun. & holidays. No cards.

Here you'll find original objects and documents in the domains of science, industry and commerce. Monsieur Bernard is an ardent student and collector of implements, especially antique tools, and anything that pertains to the history of cooking. From a Gallo-Roman cooking pot to an old-fashioned cake tin, there's a panoply of antique objects and rare literature on such subjects as winemaking.

Yet another speciality is scale models of machinery.

Galerie d'Art Populaire
7th arr. - 10, rue de Beaune - 42 61 27 87
Open 2:30 p.m.-7 p.m. Closed Sun., Aug. & holidays.

This gallery, located on the site of the barracks of Dumas' Musketeers, is permeated with the pleasant smell of furniture polish. It is filled with beautiful old country furniture, wrought-iron and folk-art objects, such as butter moulds, salt boxes and sheep collars.

L'Herminette
1st arr. - 4, allée Germain, Louvre des Antiquaires - 42 61 57 81
Open 11 a.m.-7 p.m. Closed Mon. (Sun. & Mon. in July & Aug.).

A fine, highly specialised establishment that features the art of ironwork, locks and old tools. Prices range from a few hundred to several thousand francs.

JEWELLERY

Gillet
4th arr. - 19, rue d'Arcole - 43 54 00 83
Open 11 a.m.-6 p.m. Closed Sun., Mon. & Aug.

Hidden away among the souvenir shops that surround Notre Dame, this charming boutique stands out with its 18th-century décor and its covetable selection of romantic jewellery: you'll find authentic antique pieces as well as fashionable ornaments from the 1940s.

Jacqueline Subra
6th arr. - 51, rue de Seine - 43 54 57 65
Open 11:30 a.m.-12:30 p.m. & 2 p.m.-6:30 p.m. Closed Sun., Mon., Aug. & holidays.

Whether from the end of the 19th century, Art Nouveau, Art Deco or the 1950s, the jewellery sold by Jacqueline Subra is always of the best quality, in both materials and design.

Garland
2nd arr. - 13, rue de la Paix - 42 61 17 95
Open 9:30 a.m.-1 p.m. & 2 p.m.-6:30 p.m. (Sat. from 10 a.m.). Closed Sun. & 10 days in Aug.

Minouche Messager never sells one of her rare and antique jewels without a twinge of regret. She is the queen of antique jewellery in Paris; some of the pieces that have passed through her shop are such treasures as the bracelet given to Sarah Bernhardt by the Tsar, and a superb 19th-century necklace that belonged to King Farouk of Egypt. Recently her husband, Bernard Messager, a former craftsman at Cartier, has joined her and makes fine contemporary jewellery that is sold in the shop.

C. Gustave
8th arr. - Carré d'Or, 46, av. George-V - 47 23 03 03
Open 11 a.m.-7 p.m. Closed Sun., Mon., Aug. & holidays.

Founded in 1874, this long-established firm was the first in Europe to import cultured pearls. Here you'll find some lovely antique ornaments, stones of a quality rarely seen nowadays and pieces signed by Van Cleef and Boucheron.

MINERALS, GEMS & SHELLS

Claude Boullé
6th arr. - 28, rue Jacob - 46 33 01 38
Open 10:30 a.m.-12:30 p.m. & 2 p.m.-7 p.m. (Mon. 2 p.m.-7 p.m.). Closed Sun. No cards.

Boullé is a top specialist in the field with a taste for rare and unique minerals. Among the famous collectors of "pretty stones" who have frequented this shop are André Breton, Roger Caillois and Vieira da Silva. Beautiful limestone bowls from Tuscany, marble from Bristol, jasper from Oregon, sandstone from Utah... the list seems endless.

Michel Cachoux
6th arr. - 16, rue Guénégaud - 43 54 52 15
Open 11 a.m.-2:30 p.m. & 2:30 p.m.-7:30 p.m. Closed Sun., Mon. & Aug. (except by appointment).

Several times a year Michel Cachoux travels to Brazil, the United States, Madagascar or simply down to the Alps, to track down dazzling minerals. We still remember the one-ton amethyst geode he exhibited in his shop window several years ago. These days he is also going in for fossils and objects in hard stone, such as boxes and jewellery. And his prices are, if anything, falling. His theme exhibitions are invariably fascinating.

Deyrolle
7th arr. - 46, rue du Bac - 42 22 30 07
Open 9 a.m.-12:30 p.m. & 2 p.m.-6:15 p.m. (Sat. until 5 p.m.). Closed Sun. No cards.

This fabulous shop in a sumptuous mansion houses an astonishing array of minerals of every size and description. In addition, there are displays of shells, fossils, butterflies, botanical specimens and stuffed animals—from partridges to polar bears. Kids love it.

Sciences, Art et Nature
5th arr. - 87, rue Monge - 47 07 53 70
Open 10 a.m.-6:30 p.m. Closed Sun. & Mon. No cards.

Inheritor of the famous house of Boubee, founded in 1846 but now defunct, Françoise Morival still deals in the treasures of the natural world: among her teeming collections are minerals, fossils, shells, rare insects and other delights of taxidermy. Each piece sold is accompanied by a card guaranteeing that it is a unique object.

ANTIQUES – SHOPS

MIRRORS & FRAMES

Georges Bac
6th arr. - 37, rue Bonaparte - 43 26 82 67
Open 10 a.m.-noon & 2 p.m.-6:30 p.m. Closed Sun., Aug. & holidays. No cards.

Museums and major art dealers have long known of the impressive inventory of gilded wood frames, consoles and mirrors from the 17th and 18th centuries housed in this gallery, which enjoys the highest reputation.

Marguerite Fondeur
7th arr. - 24, rue de Beaune - 42 61 25 78
Open 2 p.m.-6:30 p.m. Closed Sun., Aug. & holidays. No cards.

There is no risk of getting stuck with a tarted-up false cherub from the Italian or Spanish trade here in this fine old establishment founded by Madame Fondeur's parents. But the acquisition of a gilded-wood piece or a mirror from the 18th century, with full proof of authenticity, involves a significant investment. There are also lovely, if not gilded, furniture, chairs and objects of the period.

Lebrun
8th arr. 155, rue du Faubourg-Saint-Honoré - 45 61 14 66
Open 2:30 p.m.-7 p.m. Closed Sat., Sun. & Aug. No cards.

Mirrors, consoles, barometers and sculpted wood can all be found here in addition to some magnificent frames from the 15th to the 19th century that constitute one of the largest collections in Paris. Annick Lebrun is the fifth generation of her family to run this establishment, founded in 1847. The restoration work is top-notch.

> *Find the address you are looking for, quickly and easily, in the index.*

Navarro
6th arr. - 15, rue Saint-Sulpice 46 33 61 51
Open 2:30 p.m.-7 p.m. Closed Sun., Mon., Aug. & holidays. No cards.

Colette Navarro is mad about gilt and gold leaf. Her mirrors, barometers and gilded wood from the 17th, 18th and 19th centuries are graciously loaned out for "home trial" before purchasing. Certificates of authenticity, as well as an inventory that covers different price ranges (and attracts an international clientele), are available upon request.

MUSICAL INSTRUMENTS

André Bissonnet
3rd arr. - 6, rue du Pas-de-la-Mule 48 87 20 15
Open 2 p.m.-7 p.m. Closed Sun., Aug. & holidays. No cards.

Brother of the noted Parisian butcher Jean Bissonnet, André—himself a butcher for years—one day exchanged his cleaver and apron for the antique musical instruments he loves—and can play very well. He transformed his butcher's shop (the décor is still virtually intact) into a shrine to the ancient muses of harmony and music; it is surely one of the more amusing and astonishing boutiques in all Paris.

PORCELAIN & CHINA

Dominique Paramythiotis
1st arr. - 170-172, galerie de Valois - 42 96 04 24
Open 1 p.m.-7 p.m. (Sat. from 2 p.m.). Closed Sun. & holidays. No cards.

Displayed here are various styles of china service from the beginning of the 19th century to the 1930s: Limoges, Gien, Sarreguemines, Creil, as well as various Paris manufactures—in every conceivable shape, colour and price range (except, of course, cheap!).

Hélène Fournier-Guérin
6th arr. - 25, rue des Saints-Pères 42 60 21 81
Open 11 a.m.-1 p.m. & 3 p.m.-7 p.m. (Mon. 3 p.m.-7 p.m.). Closed Sun., Aug. & holidays.

Here is a tasteful selection of mostly 18th-century porcelain and faïence primarily from the houses of Moustiers and La Compagnie des Indes. Also: painted faïence from Marseille, Strasbourg, Rouen and Nevers. This show is run by certified experts.

L'Imprévu
6th arr. - 21, rue Guénégaud - 43 54 65 09
Open 2:30 p.m.-7 p.m. Closed Sun., Aug. & holidays. No cards.

Under the sign of the unexpected, you'll discover poured ceramic ware, brightly coloured and fashioned in relief, such as those pieces that flourished in the last 30 years or so of the 19th century: dessert plates, asparagus plates, oyster plates, plates from Salins, Sarreguemines, Clement, Longchamp and plates created by Delphin Massier at Vallauris. Then there's the stock of 19th-century printed plates from such manufacturers as Creil-Monsereau, Choisy-le-Roi and Sarreguemines. And finally, the house speciality, trompe-l'oeil platters adorned with fish or reptiles in the style known as "Bernard Palissy." Recently L'Imprévu has begun to deal in Second Empire objects and furniture.

Lefebvre et Fils
7th arr. - 24, rue du Bac - 42 61 18 40
Open 10 a.m.-12:30 p.m. & 2 p.m.-7 p.m. Closed Sun. & Aug.

Parisian society heads here to purchase their faïence, porcelain and sculpture from the 16th to the 18th century. This respected establishment is run by the city's leading expert in antique ceramic ware and celebrated its centennial in 1980. Lefebvre lists among its former clients Victor Hugo and Marcel Proust.

Nicolier
7th arr. - 7, quai Voltaire - 42 60 78 63
Open 10:30 a.m.-noon & 2:30 p.m.-6:30 p.m. Closed Sun., Mon., Aug. & holidays. No cards.

For three generations this establishment has presented an astounding collection of faïence from the ninth to the 19th centuries: Iranian pieces, 17th-century china, decorated ceramic ware from the Italian Renaissance (Urbino, Gubbio), vases, platters and statuettes in faïence and porcelain from all over Europe, including Delft, Sèvres, Saxony, Rouen, Moustiers, Nevers and Chantilly. Of course, it is all of the best quality and in perfect condition. All sales are accompanied by a certified guarantee.

Trésors du Passé
8th arr. - 131, rue du Faubourg-Saint-Honoré - 42 25 05 39
Open 10 a.m.-1 p.m. & 2:30 p.m.-7 p.m. (Mon. & Sat. 3 p.m.-7 p.m.). Closed Sun., Aug. & holidays. No cards.

Stunning pieces of antique faïence from the 17th and 18th centuries are on sale here, including Sèvres porcelain and high-quality china. The walls are adorned with a number of 18th-century prints in black and white and in colour, as well as drawings, all of which are also for sale.

Vandermeersch
7th arr. - 27, quai Voltaire - 42 61 23 10
Open 10 a.m.-12:30 p.m. & 2 p.m.-6:30 p.m. Closed Sun., Mon., Aug. & holidays.

One of the founders of the Paris biennial shows, Pierre Vandermeersch was a major figure in the world of antiques. His son, Michel, carries on the business in a new shop on the ground floor of the Villette mansion (where Voltaire died). The stock is small but very select: this is a prestigious address for porcelain and faïence.

CARPETS & TAPESTRIES

Berdj Achdjian
8th arr. - 10, rue de Miromesnil 42 65 89 48
Open 10 a.m.-12:30 p.m. & 2 p.m.-6:30 p.m. (Sat. 2 p.m.-6:30 p.m.). Closed Sun., Aug. & holidays.

Berdj Achdjian receives by appointment collectors looking for old and rare carpets. Here, for excellent prices, you can find every manner of old Oriental rug: Caucasian, Armenian, Chinese and Turkish. Achdjian has some rare gems in its collection, dating back to the 16th century, to complement the modern and highly decorative carpets.

Benadava
8th arr. - 28, rue de la Boétie - 43 59 12 21
Open 9:30 a.m.-1 p.m. & 2 p.m.-6:30 p.m. Closed Sun., Aug. & holidays. No cards.

Benadava is a specialist in the restoration, appraisal and cataloguing of rare carpets from the Far East. In addition, the shop carries tapestries from Flanders, Aubusson and the Gobelins, as well as a sizeable collection of European carpets from Spain, France and Portugal.

Jacqueline Boccara
8th arr. - 184, rue du Faubourg-Saint-Honoré - 43 59 84 63
Open 10:30 a.m.-1 p.m. & 2:30 p.m.-6:30 p.m. Closed Sun., Mon. & Aug. No cards.

No need to look any further for that tapestry you have been wanting to hang in your *salon*. From the Middle Ages, the Renaissance, the Baroque era or the Age of Enlightenment, Jacqueline Boccara has them. She supplies tapestries to the big European sales and auctions as well as to museums. If there is something she doesn't have, she will find it for you. She also displays a choice of collector's items and old drawings that she sells for reasonable (considering...) prices.

Chevalier
7th arr. - 15, quai Voltaire - 42 60 72 68
Open 10 a.m.-1 p.m. & 2 p.m.-7 p.m. (Sat. 11 a.m.-6:30 p.m., Mon. 2 p.m.-7 p.m.). Closed Sun., Aug. & holidays.

You'll think you're in a gracious private home, with glowing woodwork and soft lighting. This firm opened in 1917, and today two of the founder's grandsons carry on the work of restoring carpets and tapestries. Certified experts, the Chevalier team sells pieces of the highest quality, be they Oriental or European. The carpets are complemented by a fine selection of very beautiful and decorative cushions (ask to see them).

Lefortier
8th arr. - 54, rue du Faubourg-Saint-Honoré - 42 65 43 74
Open 10 a.m.-12:30 p.m. & 2 p.m.-6:30 p.m. Closed Sat., Sun. & Aug.

When a firm of this quality turns 100, it may safely be regarded as an institution. Heads of state come to Lefortier from all over the world for gifts of state, and for appraisals of old carpets. Madame Potignon-Lefortier, who runs the establishment, is an official expert on carpets for the Customs department and for the Paris Court of Appeal.

Robert Mikaeloff
8th arr. - 23, rue de la Boétie - 42 65 24 55
Open 9 a.m.-noon & 2 p.m.-7 p.m. Closed Sun., Aug. & holidays. No cards.

To get the full effect of Robert Mikaeloff and his

passion for silk carpets from Tabriz, or the rarest Keshans, you must see him in action. It is more accurate to say that he *stages* his carpets rather than exhibits them. For the convenience of his clients, he maintains a restoration service.

SCIENTIFIC & NAUTICAL INSTRUMENTS

Arts et Marine
8th arr. - 8, rue de Miromesnil
42 65 27 85
Open 11 a.m.-7 p.m. (Sat. 2 p.m.-6 p.m.). Closed Sun., Aug. & holidays.

Jean-Noël Marchand-Saurel is the sort of expert who knows about everything from shipbuilders' large-scale models to miniature vessels in ivory. All those afflicted with nostalgia for things marine come here to fish for dioramas, sperm-whale teeth, 18th and 19th-century hourglasses, and antique ships in a bottle (starting at 1,500 francs). Restoration services are provided.

Balmès-Richelieu
3rd arr. - 21, pl. des Vosges - 48 87 20 45
Open 10 a.m.-noon & 2 p.m.-7 p.m. (Mon. 2 p.m.-7 p.m.). Closed Aug. & holidays. No cards.

Here are some of the most beautiful marine articles in Paris. Nevertheless, Monsieur Balmès's great speciality remains clocks and scientific instruments from the 16th to the 19th centuries.

Alain Brieux
6th arr. - 48, rue Jacob - 42 60 21 98
Open 10 a.m.-1 p.m. & 2 p.m.-6:30 p.m. (Sat. 2 p.m.-6 p.m.). Closed Sun., Aug. & holidays.

Here you can find astrolabes (compact instruments used to observe the position of celestial bodies before the invention of the sextant) of course, but collectors from all over the world depend on Alain Brieux as a source of medical and scientific antiques: wooden anatomy models, anatomical tables, surgical or optical instruments. Brieux takes great care in his selections, and is currently one of the most important figures in his field.

Galerie Atlantide des Cinq Sens
1st arr. - 3, rue Sauval
42 33 35 95
Open 11 a.m.-7:30 p.m. (Sat. 1:30 p.m.-7:30 p.m.). Closed Sun., 2 last wks. of Aug. & holidays.

The objects in this shop constitute a veritable nautical history. Among the treasures are handsome ships in bottles and scale-model reproductions, porthole covers, sea chests and seascapes in watercolours or oils. The shop also provides a restoration service for ship models and paintings.

Olivier Roux-Devillas
7th arr. - 12, rue Bonaparte - 43 54 69 32
Open 10 a.m.-noon & 2 p.m.-7 p.m. (Mon. 2 p.m.-7 p.m.). Closed Sun. & holidays. No cards.

A superb shop with the lovely patina of graceful age, it presents a remarkable collection of marine, optical and scientific instruments. Look for antique nautical charts, maps and documents concerning scientific and geographical subjects.

SILVER & GOLD

J.P. de Castro
4th arr. - 17, rue des Francs-Bourgeois - 42 72 04 00
Open 10:30 a.m.-1 p.m. & 2 p.m.-7 p.m. (Sun. 11 a.m.-1 p.m. & 2 p.m.-7 p.m.). Closed Mon. No cards.

This is a magical place for lovers of old silver. It's full of delightful objects to give or to keep, all at reasonable prices. The recent enlargement of the shop now permits display of one of the largest collections of silver in Paris. Every style is represented: Victorian, Napoleon III, bistro and classic. Collectors in search of the hard-to-find piece will find happiness here in the form of samovars, chafing dishes, rare tableware and silver-plated cutlery sold by the kilo.

Eléonore
8th arr. - 18, rue de Miromesnil
42 65 17 81
Open 10 a.m.-noon (noon-2 p.m. by appt.) & 2 p.m.-6 p.m. Closed Sat., Sun., July 15-end Aug. No cards.

Claude-Gérard Cassan and Sophie de Granzial are walking catalogues of French silver—from the Renaissance to the 1880s—and they offer a remarkable range of old silver and curiosities. The two regularly exhibit their best pieces at the Paris shows: stamped silver from the 18th century with full documentation. They also offer restoration work.

A l'Epreuve du Temps
7th arr. - 88, rue du Bac - 42 22 11 42
Open 10 a.m.-6:30 p.m. Closed Sun. & Aug.

If you're in the mood for shopping for charming old pieces, little boxes, knick-knacks and period jewellery, all at reasonable prices, this is the spot. Restoration services, as well as the manufacture of silver-plated flatware, are also available.

Jacques Kugel
8th arr. - 279, rue Saint-Honoré
42 60 86 23
Open 10 a.m.-1 p.m. & 2:30 p.m.-6:30 p.m. (Mon. 2:30 p.m.-6:30 p.m.). Closed Sun., Aug. & holidays.

Devotees the world over speak with pride simply of having had the good fortune to visit this illustrious establishment and witness one of the most magnificent displays of

SHOPS – ANTIQUES

silver and gold objects ever assembled. Since Jacques passed on, Nicolas and Alexis (his two sons) have carried on the family tradition. The shop's three levels brim over with lordly silver pieces, 17th-century paintings, furniture and all sorts of rare and curious objects of great beauty.

Au Vieux Paris
2nd arr. - 4, rue de la Paix - 42 61 00 89
Open 10 a.m.-12:30 p.m. & 2 p.m.-6:30 p.m. (Mon. 2 p.m.-6:30 p.m.). Closed Sun. & Aug. No cards.

Founded in 1849, this is the oldest establishment of its kind in Paris. Michel Turisk has a reliable eye for old gold and presents a selection of fine work, such as gold boxes from the Regency and Empire periods and watches and precious objects of interest from the 17th, 18th and 19th centuries.

TOYS, GAMES & DOLLS

Robert Capia
1st arr. - 24-26, galerie Véro-Dodat - 42 36 25 94
Open 10 a.m.-7 p.m. Closed Sun. & holidays. No cards.

This expert, known far and wide by collectors, is the city's foremost specialist in antique dolls. He has set up shop in one of the most picturesque passages of Paris, the Véro-Dodat gallery, which was opened in 1826 by porkbutchers Véro and Dodat. His dolls are all signed by the top names of yesteryear (Jumeau, Steiner, Bru, Rohmer, Gaultier, Schmitt) and are available for hire. The prices are high, but justified by the quality. Also on display are charming toys: ivory dominoes, construction sets with engraved illustrations and some mechanical toys. The workshop takes care of all after-sales service. We also particularly enjoyed the large selection of phonograph cylinders that played Sarah Bernhardt and Enrico Caruso for us.

Aux Soldats d'Antan
7th arr. - 67, quai de Tournelle 46 33 40 50
Open 2 p.m.-7 p.m. Closed Sun., Aug. & holidays. No cards.

Jacques Stella boasts one of the best collections in the antique-toy soldier business; his sideline is chivalric medals and insignias, of which he is a noted connoisseur.

La Tortue Electrique
5th arr. - 5-7, rue Frédéric-Sauton 43 29 37 08
Open 2 p.m.-7 p.m. Closed Sun., Mon. & holidays. No cards.

The electric turtle referred to in the shop's name is actually an obstacle-course game. Stacked into this shop opposite Notre Dame are games of strategy or skill, chess pieces, puzzles, tops, target games and antique slot machines.

Vieille France
1st arr. - 364, rue Saint-Honoré 42 60 01 57
Open 10:30 a.m.-6 p.m. Closed Sun., Mon. & holidays. No cards.

This place more than lives up to its name (which, of course, translates as "Old France"); it is packed with lovely sets of the kings of France, heroes of the Ancien Régime, military paintings, medals and insignias, antique flags and more. The France of yesteryear lives again, among miniatures of the great moments of its history.

UMBRELLAS & WALKING-STICKS

Antoine
1st arr. - 10, av. de l'Opéra - 42 96 01 80
Open 10 a.m.-7 p.m. Closed Sun., & holidays.

In 1745 Monsieur and Madame Antoine moved up from the Auvergne and set themselves up at either end of the Pont-Neuf, renting out umbrellas to bridge-crossing pedestrians. In 1760 they opened a shop in the galleries of the Palais-Royal, specialising in walking-sticks, umbrellas and parasols. Today the worthy descendant of this dynasty, Madame Lecarpentier-Purorge, offers a collection of antique umbrellas, sticks and riding crops, and has a steady stream of customers.

Lydia Bical
92200 Neuilly - 31, rue de Chartres - 46 24 14 30
Open 3 p.m.-7:30 p.m. Closed Sun., Mon., Aug. & holidays. No cards.

This remarkable spot features hundreds of walking-sticks produced in the years preceding 1930: sticks by Dandy with gold knobs, sticks carved by infantrymen in the trenches, sticks identifying the owner as a Dreyfus supporter, sticks depicting Georges Clemenceau. Then, of course, there are the sword-sticks, rifle sticks, cosh sticks and professional sticks (for undertakers and police, for instance). And we must not forget the absinthe sticks, the blowgun sticks, fire-starting sticks and the rather salacious model with a set of mirrors that permits the voyeur to peek beneath ladies' skirts.

Madeleine Gély
7th arr. - 218, bd Saint-Germain 42 22 63 35
Open 9:30 a.m.-7 p.m. Closed Sun., Mon. Aug. & holidays. No cards.

Madeleine Gély offers hundreds of sticks in astonishing forms—from antique sticks and collector's items to utilitarian and ceremonial sticks. Equally fascinating are the dual-function sticks, such as watch sticks, pipe sticks, cigarette-holder sticks, horse-measurer sticks and a whisky stick with the original flask, stopper and glass intact. Her selection of antique and new umbrellas is the most complete (and attractive) in town.

AT YOUR SERVICE

BABY-SITTERS

Ababa
15th arr. - 8, av. du Maine - 45 49 46 46
Open 7:45 a.m.-8 p.m. Closed Sun. & holidays.

Ababa leaves us agaga: It comprises Ababa "show" (organising children's parties), Ababa "granny" (elderly ladies' companions), Ababa "clean" (housework, particularly day-after-party cleaning), Ababa "grosses têtes" (tutorial support in all subjects), Ababa "commensal" (practising foreign languages) and Ababa "tonus" (getting in shape). Although we haven't yet had the opportunity to personally try every one of their services, the word-of-mouth reports are excellent. There is a fixed price per month or per quarter, plus hourly charges such as babysitting at 28 francs.

BEAUTY & HEALTH

Ismery-James Agency
9th arr. - 55, rue La-Bruyère - 48 74 33 16
Open daily 24 hours.

Put your feet up at home and have them pampered by professionals. Pedicures and manicures are among the services provided by the Ismery-James Agency.

CLOTHING REPAIR

Mermoz Retouches
8th arr. - 21, rue Jean-Mermoz 42 25 73 36
Open 9 a.m.-6 p.m. Closed Sun., Mon. & Aug.

This is an address to hold on to, since good alterations specialists are so rare. Nothing daunts them, whether it's a matter of lengthening, shortening or inserting shoulder pads. Prices are according to estimate.

> **Two reliable au pair services are:**
>
> *L'Accueil Familial des Jeunes Etrangers,* **23 rue du Cherche Midi, 6th arr., 42 22 50 34, open 10 a.m.-4 p.m. (Sat. until noon), closed Sun.;** and
> *L'Amicale Culturelle Internationale,* **27, rue Godot-de-Mauroy, 9th arr., 47 42 94 21, open 10 a.m.-12:30 p.m. & 1:45 p.m.-5:30 p.m., closed Sat. & Sun.**

DRY CLEANERS & LAUNDRY

Delaporte
8th arr. - 62, rue François-Ier - 43 59 82 11
Open 9 a.m.-7 p.m. (Sat. until 5 p.m.). Closed Sun.

The Delaporte dry cleaning shop is owned by Jean-Claude Lesèche, a famous name in Paris dry cleaning specialising in garments that need special attention such as those decorated with lace and sequins. His mother taught him everything, on the job, and he was an excellent student. All the tailors and dressmakers on avenue Montaigne use him.

Gallois
1st arr. - 215, rue Saint-Honoré 42 60 44 00
Open 9 a.m.-12:30 p.m. & 1:30 p.m.-6 p.m. Closed Sat. & Sun. No cards.

These cleaners will give your spots and stains the care they deserve. They'll cope with the trickiest problems, but the best doesn't come cheap...

Huguet
16th arr. - 47, av. Marceau - 47 20 23 02, 47 23 81 39
Open 9 a.m.-7 p.m. Closed Sat. & Sun.

Behind the imposing facade lies an 18th-century shop interior that is home to seemingly perfect dry cleaning services, relied upon by the haute couture neighbours and Paris celebrities, at astonishingly reasonable prices, including free delivery. And there's an extra attraction: hand-washed and ironed men's shirts for 40 francs.

Letourneur-Lesèche
17th arr. - 8, bd de Courcelles 47 63 24 33
Open 8:30 a.m.-6 p.m. Closed Sat., Sun. & holidays. No cards.

Excellent, speedy work and some of the fairest prices. This shop is happy to handle delicate fabrics, suede, leather and lampshades—and delivery is free.

Vendôme
1st arr. - 24, rue du Mont-Thabor 42 60 74 38
Open 8 a.m.-5:30 p.m. (Sat. 8 a.m.-4 p.m.). Closed Sun.

Just as in the previous century, the laundry maids here wash by hand, using soap flakes, and hand-iron delicate finery, Chantilly lace and all. A cambric handkerchief is laundered for 15 francs, but a baptismal robe costs 500 francs. Vendôme also takes care of embroidered tablecloths and men's shirts, and they deliver.

> Plan to travel? Look out for the other RAC GaultMillau Best of guides to France and Germany, and for the RAC French Hotel and Holiday Guide and the RAC European Hotel Guide plus maps and atlases of France and Europe.

SHOPS – AT YOUR SERVICE

■ GENERAL REPAIRS

Réparation-Service de Lazuli
9th arr. - 39, rue Saint-Georges
42 85 24 46
Open 1:30 p.m.-6 p.m. Closed Sat, Sun., Aug. & holidays.
17th arr. - 9, bd Péreire - 42 27 02 70
Open 1:30 p.m.-6 p.m. (Sat. from 2 p.m.). Closed Sun., Aug. & holidays.

Before throwing out anything that is broken or doesn't work, ask these experts if they can mend it. You might be pleasantly surprised.

■ HIRED HANDS

Les Grooms de Paris
16th arr. - 73, av. Paul-Doumer
45 04 45 05
Open 9 a.m.-8 p.m. Closed Sun. (Delivery 24 hours).

A clutch of waiters in livery from this elegant stable will give your parties a certain style and cost you 800 francs for an evening. And while you might find it over the top to hire one of their high-class delivery men just for a bottle of Roederer Champagne, it would be more than appropriate for a piece of Van Cleef jewellery. Les Grooms de Paris will deliver within three hours after you call, every day until midnight. Within the city they charge 180 francs, to which you must obviously add the cost of the gift. Catalogue of services available on request.

Ismery-James Agency
9th arr. - 55, rue La-Bruyère - 48 74 33 16
Open daily 24 hours.

Originally a hairdresser's, this business has expanded into an institution. After moving from the occasional home hairdo to a team of "flying stylists," they incorporated manicures, make-up, leg-waxing and massage before becoming a business willing to tackle anything. Nowadays services include delivering flowers, Champagne or cigarettes (even at 2 am), baby-sitting, taking the dog for a walk, organising children's tea parties, painting, housework or gardening. They'll send a cook to concoct the exotic dish of your choice or a student to wait in for the meter reader. You can subscribe to some services for 200 francs a month or 1,000 francs a year. Estimates and further details available on request.

Ludéric
16th arr. - 20, rue Pétrarque - 45 53 93 93
Open 9 a.m.-1 p.m. & 2 p.m.-7 p.m. (Sat. until 1 p.m.). Closed Sun. & 1 wk. in Aug.

The "Ludériciens" all look like their boss, Olivier Maurey: stylish, chic, glowing with health and bursting with enthusiasm. Founded in 1975, this is the best known of the multiservice agencies, and it remains true to its slogan, "Everything is possible." You can ask just about anything of the rapidly growing company. At first, when it was Ludéric Service, they baby-sat, shopped, chauffeured, served, dog-sat and so forth. Some years later Ludéric Evénement joined the family, organising receptions and promotional events. Then came Ludéric Traiteur (caterer), when hungry Ludéric bought up a catering company. Since then we've seen Haute Tension (for launching new products), Kiosque Théâtre (for last-minute tickets, see p. 162), Boutique Ludéric (for caviar, salmon and Champagne at low prices) and lastly, a bit of whimsy, the historic bistro L'Ami Louis that Ludéric bought to preserve it intact. By the time you read this Ludéric will no doubt have created a new service to meet the needs of some new client. The only question that remains is whether Ludéric can continue to cater to individual needs in the face of its growing corporate clientele and as it expands into the provinces and overseas. We'll let you know in a year or two. The yearly membership (750 francs for individuals, 1,900 francs for corporate accounts) provides access to all services.

■ HOME DELIVERY

BREAKFAST

Mille Break First
12th arr. - 7-9, pl. Abel-Leblanc
43 45 76 53
Open daily 24 hours. Free delivery in Paris. A newspaper is included in the price.

Ordered the night before, breakfast is delivered any time from 7 a.m. to 1 p.m. There are all sorts of fixed formulas (14), including the traditional continental breakfast (220 francs for two), the "brunch" (430 francs for two) and the "morning after," which includes a revitalising cocktail of white wine, grape juice, Alka-Seltzer and a small bottle of Perrier, plus grapefruit juice (60 francs). There are breakfast or brunch menus for company and group functions (special discount). Cigarettes and flowers are provided free with orders priced at 580 francs or more.

FOOD

L'Asie à Votre Table
48 40 50 30
Open 9 a.m.-7 p.m. Closed Sun.

For a Chinese, Vietnamese or Thai dinner, phone your order to Laurence Nguyen in the morning. Cost is around 120 francs per person, plus 120 francs for delivery.

AT YOUR SERVICE – SHOPS

Aux Délices de Scott
47 63 71 36
Open 8:30 a.m.-8 p.m. (Sat. & Mon. 10 a.m.-7 p.m.). Closed Sun.

For people who like to lunch in the office or don't have time to cook, this fine caterer offers a choice of 12 meals-on-a-tray. Prices range from 90 to 145 francs per person and delivery is free in the 8th and 17th arrondissements when you order at least four trays.

Fauchon Service Plus
47 42 60 11 - ext. 317
Open 9:40 a.m.-9:30 p.m. Closed Sun.

Seven choices of quality cold meals-on-a-tray, costing from 150 to 400 francs. Free delivery within Paris if you spend at least 600 francs.

Les Frères Layrac
6th arr. - 29, rue de Buci - before 3 p.m.: 43 25 17 72; after 3 p.m.: 46 34 21 40
Open 9:30 a.m.-midnight. Closed Sun. & Mon.

If you can't go to the shop in the rue de Buci, home delivery is only a phone call away. Festive and varied ideas for dinners organised at the last minute. The seafood platter at 385 francs for two is a real treat. Delivery: 100-150 F.

Jacques Hesse
40 93 05 05. By Minitel, 3615 code Jacques Hesse.
Open 9 a.m.-11 p.m. (Sat. & Sun. 6 p.m.-11 p.m.). Free delivery in Paris.

Hesse delivers to companies and individuals, changes his menu daily, and comes up with novel ideas, like the bachelor tray during August. Service is fast and efficient, but the portions are on the skimpy side.

FRUIT BASKETS & FLOWERS

Interfruits Service
17th arr. - 89, av. de Wagram
47 63 10 55
Open 9 a.m.-7 p.m. Closed Sun.
& Aug. 70 F delivery charge.

Baskets of in-season or exotic fruit are nicely done up and delivered. Interfruit has swiftly become a classic in its field (about 500 to 1,000 francs for a lovely basket).

Téléfleurs France
10th arr. - 15, rue Martel - 05 21 72 17
Open 8:30 a.m.-7 p.m. (Sat. until 6 p.m.) Closed Sun.

This chain of florists delivers anywhere in France, with 3,000 shops at your service.

■ LOCKSMITHS

Clé-Flash
15th arr. - 162, bd de Grenelle
47 83 33 18
Open 8:15 a.m.-12:30 p.m. & 1:15 p.m.-6:30 p.m. (Fri. until 6 p.m.; Sat. 9 a.m.-noon). Closed Sun., 15 days in Aug. & holidays.

Give them a key or lock to work from and they'll quickly make you a copy. The cost is 280 francs per hour. Estimates free.

■ MAID SERVICE

Maison Service
16th arr. - 10, rue Mesnil - 45 53 62 30
Open 9 a.m.-noon & 2 p.m.-6 p.m. Closed Sat. & Sun.

You ought to know from the start that the personnel here are top-notch—and temporary. The woman who deigns to answer the telephone will inform you in no uncertain terms that Maison Service hires only French people from France between 30 and 60 years old, with five years of certified experience and excellent references, and ready to serve "a privileged social class." If that sounds as if it fills the bill, you will pay 150 francs an hour for someone to do your ironing, your cleaning, your cooking, all for a minimum of four hours. Ladies' companions and governesses can be hired on the same basis, for four or five months, but be advised that these grand ladies of household help have never heard of volume discounts. Rates go up by 50 per cent on Sundays and 100 per cent on holidays.

Sélection Suzanne Reinach
92100 Boulogne - 11, rue Thiers
46 08 56 56
Open 9:30 a.m.-7 p.m. Closed Sat., Sun., Aug. & holidays. No cards.

This agency is proud of picking its butlers, servants, cooks, drivers, secretaries and so on out of the top drawer. New household staff are given a trial run before being offered a permanent contract. Registration fees vary from 6,000 to 10,000 francs, depending on the type of staff you want to hire.

■ MESSENGERS

Bunny Courses
92150 Suresnes - 3-5, rue Curie
45 06 45 06
Open 8 a.m.-6.30 p.m. Closed Sat. & Sun.

These are the people to call for urgent transport and deliveries. A messenger in Paris costs 60 francs, with an express service at 240 francs. Delivery with a driver and vehicle is possible, and transport and handling are available in Paris and the suburbs. All the firm's delivery workers keep in touch by radio.

■ RENT-A-...

AIRPLANE

Euralair
93350 Le Bourget - Aéroport du Bourget - 49 34 62 00
Open 24 hours.

This is a wonderful service if you have the means. A Mystère Falcon 20 is yours for 11,450 francs per day, to which you add 21,600 francs

181

per hour of flying time, as well as lodgings for the two pilots and the stewardess if you are gone for more than two days. Should a Mystère be too small, ask for one of the nine Boeing 737s.

BICYCLE

Paris Vélo
5th arr. - 2, rue du Fer-à-Moulin 43 37 59 22, fax 47 07 67 45
Open 10 a.m.-12:30 p.m. & 2 p.m.- 6 p.m. (until 7 p.m. during summer). Closed Sun. & holidays.

A wide range of town and mountain bikes, but nothing for children—unless they're small enough to sit in one of the children's seats for hire. Daily rates range from 90 to 140 francs, a weekend costs from 160 to 220 francs and a week from 420 to 495 francs. Deposits from 1,000 to 2,000 francs.

BOAT

Rive de France
17th arr. - 172, bd Berthier - 46 22 10 86
Open 9 a.m.-7 p.m. (Sat. 10 a.m.-4 p.m. Jan-June). Closed Sat. & Sun.

Little barges, 30 feet by 9 feet, that sleep six are available here, for 9,310 francs a week (in season). Weekend prices equal 60 per cent of the charge for a week. A boat licence is preferred. Departures from all over France.

COMPUTERS

LocaMac
11th arr. - 5, passage Turquetil 43 73 51 51
Open 9:30 a.m.-1 p.m. & 2 p.m.- 7 p.m. Closed Sat. & Sun. No cards.

Various kinds of personal computer but especially Macs, famed for their user-friendliness. You can hire a Mac SE or Mac II for 48 hours, a week, a month or a year, all at very reasonable tapering rates. The machine is delivered to your home, collected at the end of your contract and exchanged immediately if it goes wrong.

THE EIFFEL TOWER

Salle Gustave-Eiffel
7th arr. - Champ-de-Mars - 45 50 34 56
Open daily 9 a.m.-12:30 p.m. & 2 p.m.-6 p.m.

For a really chic reception with a panoramic view, why not hire this room on the first floor of the Eiffel Tower, 185 feet up? You can even rent a private lift. The soundproofed, air-conditioned room will accommodate 450 people for a cocktail party, 300 attending a meeting or show, and 140 sitting down to dinner. Equipment includes projection equipment, sophisticated lighting, stages and podiums.

EQUIPPED OFFICE

Club Sari Affaires
La Défense, CNIT, 2, pl. de La Défense 46 92 24 24, fax 46 92 24 00
Open 8:30 a.m.-7:30 p.m. (Sat. 9 a.m.-1 p.m.). Closed Sun.

Fully equipped offices measuring between 145 and 600 square feet cost from 1,000 to 3,000 francs a day. A private phone line and Minitel are already installed and a computer is provided on request, while a team of full-time secretaries will handle the mail, messages and word processing. Those who need a year-round base in the Paris area might prefer the yearly rate with additional services at 36,500 francs. Meeting rooms come in various sizes and cost from 1,100 to 4,100 francs a day. Restaurant service.

FORMAL OUTFIT

Eugénie Boiserie
9th arr. - 32, rue Vignon - 47 42 43 71
Open 10 a.m.-noon & 1 p.m.- 6 p.m. Closed Sun., Mon. & Aug.

In business for over 30 years, Eugénie Boiserie carries a stunning collection of haute-couture gowns for hire (800 francs, plus a 2,000-franc deposit). The huge selection of dresses is hidden away in the back of the shop (the front is given over to old-fashioned gift items), where they are shown to customers by appointment. No accessories are available, but alterations can be arranged.

Le Cor de Chasse
6th arr. - 40, rue de Buci - 43 26 51 89
Open 9 a.m.-noon & 1:30 p.m.- 6 p.m. Closed Sun., Mon. & Aug.

Famous since 1875 and loved by several generations of Parisians, this stylish shop hires out morning clothes, top hats, dinner jackets and other formal apparel for men (hire fees are between 700 and 800 francs). Shirts and accessories are on sale, and alterations are handled by expert tailors.

Les Costumes de Paris
9th arr. - 21 bis, rue Victor-Massé 48 78 41 02
Open 10 a.m.-7 p.m. Closed Sun. & Mon.

Among the charming, droll and zany costumes fit for the fanciest fancy-dress ball is an enchanting collection of evening gowns by Loris Azzaro, Thierry Mugler, Diamant Noir and others, in sizes 36 to 44 (which roughly translates to British sizes 8 to 16). All these gowns are in excellent condition. Hire prices are from 500 to 2,000 francs.

Since the company started in 1952 it has created more than 20,000 costumes for cinema and television. They take up four floors and range from caveman outfits to fashions from the 1970s, and hiring one will cost you between 400 and 600 francs plus VAT for a weekend. It's best to book a week ahead in case alterations are needed. You can even

AT YOUR SERVICE – SHOPS

have a costume made to measure —ask for an estimate.

Velleda
10th arr. - 206, rue Lafayette - 42 05 81 93
Open 10 a.m.-6:30 p.m. Closed Sun.

If you have nothing to wear to the fancy-dress ball you must see the incredible selection of costumes and disguises at Velleda; people have been known to hire the shop's bridal "costume" to wear to their own wedding! Just as authentic are the medieval get-ups and the beaded twenties frocks. Rates go up to 600 francs for a weekend, plus a deposit of 1,500 to 3,000 francs.

FURNITURE

ABC Ruby
16th arr. - 11, rue Chanez - 46 51 06 42
Open 9 a.m.-noon & 2 p.m.-6 p.m. Closed Sat. & Sun. No cards.

Furnish your apartment in 48 hours with this all-inclusive service that provides furniture, fabrics (except net curtains), tableware and electrical goods. Short or long-term hire. They don't have much on display so it's best to send details of what you require for an estimate.

HELICOPTER

Hélicap
15th arr. - Héliport de Paris, 4, av. de la Porte-de-Sèvres - 45 57 75 51
Open 9 a.m.-7 p.m. Closed Sat. & Sun. No cards.

See Paris and La Défense from the air, or Versailles and its surroundings, or take a trip to the Château d'Esclimont for dinner, touching down on the lawn in front. The possibilities are endless: the cliffs at Etretat on the Norman coast, Mont Saint-Michel, the Loire châteaux. By now you're probably wondering what the price for such trips could be... Versailles and the châteaux de la Loire for 15,200 francs (five people) makes a very nice gift.

HOT AIR BALLOON

Air Ballon Communication
6th arr. - 12, rue Bonaparte - 43 29 14 13
Open 10 a.m.-12:30 p.m. & 2 p.m.-7 p.m. (Mon. from 2 p.m.). Closed Sun.

For your first view of France from a balloon. You take off near the Château de Maintenon, 50 minutes' drive from Paris, but there's no telling where you'll touch down. In any case the flight lasts about an hour and there'll be a car waiting to take you back to Paris. Be sure to book several weeks ahead for an unforgettable flight over the Beauce country and the valley of the Eure. Demand varies according to the time of year. The cost, including insurance, is 1,500 francs for one person or 2,500 francs for two, plus VAT.

Don't plan to shop on Sundays, the vast majority of Paris stores are closed.

> ## The mysterious shrinking tower
>
> What would the Paris skyline be without this most Parisian of silhouettes? Yet the *Eiffel Tower*, a masterpiece of engineering conceived by the genius of Gustave Eiffel, had a close shave with the demolition men in 1909. Luckily, the pioneers of radio and telephone saw the tower's potential value and came to the rescue. The tower's height can vary by as much as six inches depending on the temperature: the hotter, the higher. When completed in time for the World Exhibition in 1889 it was the tallest construction on earth, standing 300 metres (975 feet) high on its four steel feet. For the best view, tackle the 1,652 steps to the top (the short of stamina can take the lifts) an hour before sunset.

LIMOUSINES

Alliance Autos
94160 Saint-Mandé - 5 bis, av. Foch - 43 28 20 20, fax 43 28 27 27
Open daily 24 hours.

The new leader in chauffeur-driven limousines, Alliance Autos has conquered a demanding clientele of company executives, film stars and media moguls. But you needn't be a celebrity to benefit from Alliance's personalised service. Harried business people and travellers touring the capital are all accorded the "star treatment." Instead of fighting for a taxi, why not arrive in Paris in a chauffeured Mercedes Class S (or a Renault Safrane)? A bilingual driver will be your guide. To give you an idea of the prices: transfer from Roissy-Charles de Gaulle to Paris, 1,000 francs; a half-day (four hours), 2,100 francs; a full day (nine hours), 3,000 francs. You can also hire any kind of vehicle at Alliance Autos (buses, lorries, vans, motorcycles).

SHOPS – AT YOUR SERVICE

SAFE

Solon
11th arr. - 126, bd Richard-Lenoir - 48 05 08 34
Open 8:30 a.m.-noon & 1:30 p.m.-6 p.m. Closed Sat., Sun. & Aug.

A safe or strongbox is yours for 500 francs a month. This doesn't include transport, which varies according to distance, the weight of the safe and how many floors there are to walk up. Same-day opening service.

SKI & CLIMBING EQUIPMENT

La Haute Route
4th arr. - 33, bd Henri-IV - 42 72 38 43
Open 9:30 a.m.-1 p.m. & 2 p.m.-7 p.m. Closed Sun.

This is the place to hire ski equipment in winter and climbing gear in summer, for two days, a week, a month or longer. Tapering rates and reasonable deposits.

TELEVISION & STEREO

Locatel
92100 Boulogne - 31, rue de Solférino - 46 09 94 90
92300 Levallois-Perret - 16, rue Barbès - 47 58 12 00
93100 Montreuil - 13, av. Gabriel-Péri - 48 58 91 92
Open 10 a.m.-7 p.m. Closed Sun.

One of the oldest TV hire services, with ten branches in Paris and 15 or so in the surrounding area. They'll deliver within 24 hours and lend you a set while they repair yours. The cheapest TV costs 160 francs a month to rent (for a minimum of six months), a video recorder 190 francs and a hi-fi with CD player 190 francs (minimum period two years). Locatel also hires answering machines, car telephones and satellite dishes.

TRAINS

SNCF
10th arr. - 162, rue du Faubourg-Saint-Martin - 40 18 84 24, fax 40 18 84 40
Open 8:30 a.m.-12:30 p.m. & 1:30 p.m.-5:15 p.m. (Fri. until 3:50 p.m.). Closed Sat. & Sun. No cards.

The French railway company hires out 80-seat second-class carriages, sleeping carriages, a restaurant car, a disco car or even a whole train. You have to phone them two months ahead and they'll give you an estimate based on your requirements.

TYRES (STUDDED SNOW)

Le Relais du pneu
4th arr. - 33, bd Bourdon - 42 72 01 12
Open 8 a.m.-noon & 1:30 p.m.-6 p.m. (Sat. until noon; Mon. 2 p.m.-6 p.m. Closed Sun. & Aug.
12th arr. - 29, bd Diderot - 43 07 46 46
Open 8 a.m.-noon & 1:30 p.m.-6:30 p.m. (Sat. 8 a.m.-noon & 1:30 p.m.-3:30 p.m.; Mon. 1:30 p.m.-6:30 p.m.). Closed Sun. & Aug. 15-30.

Hiring studded snow tyres costs between 300 and 400 francs for ten days, depending on the size of the wheels.

SECRETARIAL SERVICES

Agaphone
17th arr. - 68 bis, bd Péreire - 44 01 50 00
Open 8 a.m.-8 p.m. (Sat. 9 a.m.-noon). Closed Sun. & holidays. No cards.

No need to miss any phone calls when you go away. For 890 francs a month plus VAT, you can have them transferred to Agaphone, who will take messages or orders and record appointments. When you return the details are phoned or faxed to you, or sent by Minitel. The firm also offers typing and word-processing services.

SHOE REPAIR

Central Crépins
3rd arr. - 48, rue de Turbigo - 42 72 68 64
Open 8 a.m.-2:30 p.m. & 3:30 p.m.-7 p.m. (Sat. until 1 p.m.). Closed Sun. & 2 wks. in Aug.

Bags, suitcases, saddles and clothes, Central Crépins repairs everything in leather. Discounts are available to regulars with a membership card. (Check the address before going, since the shop may move).

La Cordonnerie Anglaise
4th arr. - 28, rue des Archives 48 87 11 43
Open 9:30 a.m.-7 p.m. (Sat. from 10:30 a.m.). Closed Sun., Mon., 1 month during summer & holidays.

For a payment of 500 francs in advance, you can have your shoes waterproofed in this attractive shop using a process perfected by Goodyear.

Cordonnerie Vaneau
7th arr. - 44, rue Vaneau - 42 22 06 94
8th arr. - 34, rue Jean-Mermoz
16th arr. - 35, rue de Lonchamp
16th arr. - 8, rue Mignard
17th arr. - 51, bd Gouvion-Saint-Cyr
92200 Neuilly - 37, rue de Chézy
Open 9 a.m.-1 p.m. & 2 p.m.-7 p.m. Closed Sun. Call 42 22 06 94 for information.

The best for the finest. Vaneau is where the finest feet of Paris, shod by Lobb, Weston or Aubercy, go to have repairs done. Their impeccable workmanship can restore footwear that only looks fit for the dustbin. It costs 550 francs to give a pair of men's shoes a new lease of life.

Pulin
8th arr. - 5, rue Chauveau-Lagarde - 42 65 08 57
Open 9 a.m.-7 p.m. Closed Sun. & Mon.

Gérard Pulin's wide range of services includes changing the colour of your shoes, raising and lowering heels and mixing custom-made polish—all within 48 hours. And for 70 francs there's a home pick-up and delivery service.

BEAUTY

■ BEAUTY SALONS

Carita
8th arr. - 11, rue du Faubourg-Saint-Honoré - 44 94 11 00
Open 9 a.m.-7 p.m. Closed Sun. & Mon.

Carita's famous name now belongs to Shiseido, the Japanese cosmetics company. Completely redesigned by Andrée Putman, the salon's luxurious but minimalist décor is in tones of beige and brown. The ground floor is now occupied by a reception area and private rooms. The salon's hair stylists practise their art on the upper floor, where other beauty services are also available (stars are pampered in royally appointed private booths). Carita treatments have fully earned their excellent reputation; expert beauticians can impart a permanent curl to eyelashes or shape eyebrows and lips with a special tattooing technique, perform facials that will make your skin look fresh and firm, or soothe muscles and stimulate circulation with professional massage. Men are welcome too at Carita, and have a realm all their own on the third floor.

Guerlain
6th arr. - 29, rue de Sèvres - 42 22 46 60
Open 9:45 a.m.-6:45 p.m. (Sat. 10 a.m.-7 p.m.). Closed Sun.
8th arr. - 68, av. des Champs-Elysées - 47 89 71 80
Open 9 a.m.-6:45 p.m. Closed Sun. Perfumes & cosmetics only: 1st arr., 15th arr. & 16th arr.

Guerlain is tops in beauty care. Expert technicians dispense the very latest skin-care treatments—they'll even restructure your wrinkles—you can rest assured that your face is in the very best hands. So lie back and enjoy the luxurious surroundings while the excellent Issima line of skin-care products is applied to your face for a relaxing hour and a quarter (495 francs, including makeup). Manicure, pedicure and epilation services are available as well. Be sure to stop at the perfume counter to try some of the enchanting house fragrances.

Lancôme
8th arr. - 29, rue du Faubourg-Saint-Honoré - 42 65 30 74
Open 10 a.m.-7 p.m. (Wed. 1 p.m.-7 p.m.). Closed Sun.

Isabella Rossellini's haunting beauty projects Lancôme's public image, but top beautician Béatrice Braune (director of the Lancôme institute) is the woman behind the scenes here who makes sure the products deliver what they promise. An exclusive "beauty computer" measures the skin's smoothness, elasticity, moisture level and degree of dryness and/or oiliness, then produces a prescription for personalised skin care. Services offered in the institute's handsome, comfortable salons include a Niosome treatment, a bioenergising massage and body exfoliation followed by a lymphatic draining massage.

Monday, like Sunday, is a day of rest for many shopkeepers.

Ingrid Millet
8th arr. - 54, rue du Faubourg-Saint-Honoré - 42 66 66 20
Open 9 a.m.-6 p.m. Closed Sun.

Madame Millet doesn't eat the quantities of caviar she buys; no, she smothers her clients' faces with it (in cream form). Her specialised skin-care services include a facial mask/tonic/rejuvenation treatment, an energising facial (590 francs) and an all-over body treatment with a particularly effective exfoliating action (790 francs). The salon's soothing green-and-white décor makes it an oasis of calm and relaxation on the busy Faubourg-Saint-Honoré.

Sothys
8th arr. - 128, rue du Faubourg-Saint-Honoré - 45 63 98 18
Open 9:30 a.m.-7:30 p.m. (Sat. 10 a.m.-5 p.m.). Closed Sun.

In Sothys' 15 private air-conditioned booths (all equipped with cellular phones), a capable staff dispenses a wide variety of beauty treatments, ranging from deep facial cleansing (260 francs) to slimming techniques (which include baths in highly carbonated water paired with hydromassage). It's quite pleasant, if you don't mind being tickled!

■ EPILATION

Ella Baché
2nd arr. - 8, rue de la Paix - 42 61 67 14
Open 10 a.m.-6:30 p.m. (Mon. 11 a.m.-6:30 p.m. & Sat. 9:30 a.m.-5 p.m.). Closed Sun.

Cold wax is Ella Baché's secret weapon against unwanted hair. The treatment starts with a mentholated disinfecting lotion, then waxing and the application of a soothing moisturising cream. Prices? Legs, 140 francs; bikini line, 85 francs; underarms, 50 francs. Facials are performed here too (235 to 275 francs).

SHOPS – BEAUTY

Institut George-V
8th arr. - 17, av. George-V - 40 70 99 70
Open 10 a.m.-6:30 p.m. Closed Sun. & Mon.

Not one unwanted hair will survive once Antoinette has finished with you: she has 25 years' experience in the art of epilation. The salon is unprepossessing (just two rooms on the fifth floor), but the service and products are first-rate. Antoinette swears by a special pale-pink beeswax, made especially for her, and her famous technique leaves legs smooth and silky for at least three weeks. By appointment only, from 180 francs.

■ HAIR SALONS

Patrick Alès
8th arr. - 37, av. Franklin-Roosevelt - 43 59 33 96
Open 9 a.m.-6 p.m. (Wed. 10 a.m.-6 p.m.). Closed Sun. & Mon.

Patrick Alès is the mind behind the excellent "Phyto" line of hair-care products. Formerly a stylist with Carita, Alès developed them in his spare time (in his garage, no less) with the help of his friend and collaborator, Olga. She tried each formula personally, and numbered them according to how many times each had been tested (shampoo S88: 88 trials). Today, Alès continues to come up with new products, which you can try out for yourself at his Paris salon. Henna treatments, for example, to strengthen fine, lifeless hair, cost from 200 to 400 francs.

Alexandre
8th arr. - 3, av. Matignon - 42 25 57 90
Open 9:30 a.m.-7 p.m. Closed Sun.

Even if it's only once in your life, you really should visit this lovely old Art Deco salon, where socialites and celebrities have been elegantly coiffed for years and years. Alexandre is so passionate about hair that he has devoted a museum to it. Formal styles for weddings and gala evenings are a speciality.

Camille Darmont
16th arr. - 61, rue de la Tour - 45 03 10 99
Open Tues. & Wed. & Fri. 10 a.m.-7 p.m.; Thurs. 1 p.m.-8 p.m.; Sat. 9 a.m.-1 p.m. Closed Sun. & Mon.

Camille Darmont, who holds diplomas in dermatology and pharmacy, was for many years the principal assistant of hair guru René Furterer. Now working on her own, she is one of the most esteemed hair specialists in Paris. A two-hour treatment in her salon includes a thorough massage of head, neck and shoulders to improve circulation, followed by a mud pack and a hot-towel wrap. The client's individual hair problems are then treated with products formulated by Madame Darmont herself.

Jean-Louis David International
8th arr. - 47, rue Pierre-Charron 43 59 82 08
Open 10 a.m.-7 p.m. (Wed. 11 a.m.-7 p.m.). Closed Sun.

Businessman/coiffeur Jean-Louis David has done it again. His most ambitious venture, on the rue Pierre-Charron, is always swarming with heads eager to wear the latest JLD style. We must say, he is a first-rate manager, and he knows how to keep his customers satisfied, notably with innovative ideas like Quick Service for women in a hurry (dry cut, mousse and gel, you're out in 20 minutes), or the Mistershop (same principle, for men). Jean-Louis David International, the top-of-the-line division, charges about 400 francs for a shampoo, cut and style, while the "diffusion" sector, less chic, charges 300 francs for the same services.

Desfossé
8th arr. - 19, av. Matignon - 43 59 95 13
Open 9 a.m.-6:30 p.m. Closed Sun.

For men only. Executives, politicians, socialites and others who pay close attention to their image frequent Desfossé. In addition to hair care (200 francs for a wash, cut and style), skin care, massage, manicure and pedicure services are offered. Pressed for time? You can grab a quick lunch here while having your nails buffed or your pores deep-cleansed.

Jacques Dessange
8th arr. - 37, av. Franklin-Roosevelt - 43 59 31 31 (also: 3rd arr., 4th arr., 6th arr., 7th arr., 11th arr., 15th arr., 17th arr.)
Open 9:30 a.m.-6:30 p.m. Closed Sun.

With commendable concern for his customers' hygiene, Jacques Dessange has decreed that a brand-new brush be used for each client. Efforts have also been made to warm up what was once a pretty uppity reception. But best of all, the stylists no longer systematically impose Master Dessange's latest creation on every head that passes through the salon's front doors. Good hair treatment products for use at home; stylists can give highly effective hair masks or split-end treatments if you wish.

René Furterer
8th arr. - 15, pl. de la Madeleine 42 65 30 60
(also: 17th arr., 15th arr.)
Open 9 a.m.-7 p.m. Closed Sun.

Back when perms meant frizz, and hairstyles were inevitably the product of rollers and pincurls, René Furterer virtually invented the science of hair care. Now retired, he leaves an impressive legacy: an institute that bears his name where scientific hair treatments continue to be formulated. Here specialists offer clear explanations, technical advice and a treatment programme that may include massage or plant-based rinses. You are never urged to buy more than two or three products, which are always reasonably priced.

Léonor Greyl
8th arr. - 15, rue Tronchet - 42 65 32 26
Open 9:30 a.m.-6:30 p.m. (Thurs. 11 a.m.-8 p.m.). Closed Sun.

With the help of her husband, a chemist who formulates her products, Léonor Greyl works wonders on dull, lifeless hair with her various powders, freeze-dried roots, wheat-germ oil and sundry other secret ingredients. But make no mistake: there's nothing hocus-pocus about her hair-care treatments (shampoo, manual and electric massage, scalp packs and the list goes on), and they yield excellent results. Women pay about 300 francs, men around 200 francs for a treatment. A simple cut costs 150 francs.

Harlow
1st arr. - 24, rue Saint-Denis - 42 33 61 36
Open 10 a.m.-7 p.m. (Wed. noon-9 p.m.). Closed Sun. & Mon.
9th arr. - 4, rue de Sèze - 47 42 40 67
Open 10 a.m.-7 p.m. (Thurs. noon-9 p.m.). Closed Sun. & Mon.
16th arr. - 70, rue du Ranelagh 45 24 04 54
Open 9:30 a.m.-6:30 p.m. Closed Sun. & Mon.

Many women want a good haircut that doesn't require elaborate upkeep. For them, Harlow and company have come up with wash-and-wear hair. The salon's atmosphere is relaxed, and service is fast. A shampoo and styling is 150 francs; with a cut, the price is 300 francs.

Lazartigue Traitement du Cheveu
8th arr. - 5, rue du Faubourg-Saint-Honoré - 42 65 29 24 (also: 6th arr., 9th arr., 14th arr., 15th arr.)
Open 9:30 a.m.-6:30 p.m. Closed Sun.

Decorated in tonic tones of green and white, the Lazartigue salon presents the highest standard of creature comforts. Each private booth boasts a telephone and an individual cupboard (including, of course, a lock for your fur). The staff are perfectly charming, too. There's just one hitch: for an examination and assessment of your hair problems, treatments and a "prescription" for Lazartigue products, the bill will come to well over 1,000 francs. Now for that kind of money, wouldn't you think the ingredients would be listed on the label of the products you've been strong-armed into buying? We suppose that Monsieur Lazartigue wants to keep his "miracle" formulas secret.

Jean-Marc Maniatis
8th arr. - 18, rue Marbeuf - 47 23 30 14 (also: 1st arr., 6th arr.)
Open 9:30 a.m.-7 p.m. Closed Sat. & Sun.

His first clients were photo stylists from the fashion press; they raved about the Maniatis technique of precision scissoring one tiny section of hair at a time for chic, superbly shaped cuts. His reputation grew, and now Maniatis is one of the city's best-known coiffeurs. The stylists who work with him are well trained and fast; they do a lot of work for celebrities, models, journalists and so on. The salon is friendly, noisy and always busy. Be prepared to wait. A shampoo, cut and styling cost about 500 francs for a woman, under 300 francs for a man.

Mod's Hair
8th arr. - 64, rue Pierre Charron 42 25 14 29
(also : 1st arr., 6th arr. 7th arr., 11th arr., 14th arr. 16th arr.)
Open Tues. & Thurs. & Fri. 10 a.m.-6:30 p.m.; Wed. noon-7:30 p.m.; Sat. 9 a.m.-5 p.m. Closed Sun. & Mon.

At its salon near the Champs-Elysées, Mod's Hair caters to the younger crowd, with saucy, fashionable styles. The walls of the salon are decorated with the work of talented artists, giving you something to contemplate besides your face in the mirror.

Alexandre Zouari
16th arr. - 1, av. du Président-Wilson - 47 23 79 00
Open 9:30 a.m.-6:30 p.m. Closed Sun.

Celebrities seem to appear wherever you look in this luxurious (but ever-so-slightly gaudy) salon. Figure on spending 350 francs for a shampoo, cut and blow-dry styling, and throw in another 100 francs for a "transformation".

■ MANICURE & PEDICURE

Carita
8th arr. - 11, rue du Faubourg-Saint-Honoré - 42 65 79 00
Open 9 a.m.-7 p.m. Closed Sun. & Mon.

Entrust your feet to Monsieur Ho, and he will work his brand of Oriental magic to make your tired tootsies feel like new again. Carita is also the place to come for an expert "French manicure": white polish is applied to the very end of the nail, resulting in an impeccably groomed finish (but don't even contemplate it unless your hands are in perfect condition).

Don't plan to shop on Sundays, the vast majority of Paris stores are closed.

SHOPS — BEAUTY

Institut Laugier
17th arr. - 39 bis, rue Laugier - 42 27 25 03
Open 10 a.m.-7 p.m. Closed Sun. & Aug. 15-30.

The best manicures and pedicures in Paris are performed at the Institut Laugier. Hands are cared for on the ground floor, where the exclusive Supernail treatment is yours for the asking, as are vitamin baths and artificial nails for both sexes. Downstairs, feet are pampered with massage, vibrating baths, pumice stones and an exfoliation treatment. Before they leave, clients are strongly encouraged to purchase a whole range of (effective, but costly) products to prolong the benefits of the salon's treatments.

Institut Yung
9th arr. - 22, rue Caumartin - 47 42 20 63
Open 9 a.m.-7 p.m. Closed Sat. & Sun. No cards.

No mere cutters or scissors are used here: Monsieur Yung's Chinese pedicure equipment is limited to a simple series of steel blades of varying lengths with more or less sharp points. In just 30 minutes, his fancy footwork will rid you of calluses, bumps, corns and dead skin. Treatment and polish cost just 150 francs.

L'Onglerie de la Madeleine
9th arr. - 26, rue Godot-de-Mauroy - 42 65 49 13
Open 10 a.m.-7 p.m. Closed Sun. & Mon.

The house speciality is American-style artificial nails, made of the same tough resins used in dentistry. These nails are absolutely "unchewable," besides, they taste revolting! Complete manicure and pedicure services are also offered.

Revlon
16th arr. - 19, rue de Bassano
47 20 05 42
Open 9:30 a.m.-6:30 p.m. Closed Sat. & Sun.

Revlon's reputation for nail care is worldwide and well deserved. The institute near the Champs-Elysées employs four medically certified pedicurists, as well as seven manicurists who will take your hands in hand and make them as lovely as they possibly can be. The house products are excellent and most effective. Manicures cost 175 francs (195 francs with a hot-cream treatment), pedicures 280 francs (nail polish included).

■ SCENT & COSMETICS

L'Artisan Parfumeur
9th arr. - 22 rue Vignon - 42 66 32 66 (also: 7th arr.)
Open 10:30 a.m.-2:30 p.m. & 3:30 p.m.-7 p.m. (Mon. 11:30 a.m.-7 p.m.). Closed Sun.

This perfumer's shop looks like a stage set, rich with gilt and velvet drapery. The fragrances are equally voluptuous, based on musk, gardenia, rose, iris... not, we emphasise, the sort of perfumes worn by shrinking violets. His two best-sellers are L'Eau du Grand Siècle and L'Eau du Navigateur. Quite popular as well are the aromatic pomanders that diffuse these heady perfumes (200 to 350 francs and 600 francs) and an exquisite selection of gift items: jewellery, fans, combs and other decorative trifles.

Body Shop
6th arr. - 7, rue de l'Ancienne Comédie - 44 07 14 00
Open 10 a.m.-8 p.m. (Sat. 10 a.m.-11 p.m. & Sun. 2 p.m.-8 p.m.).

Anita Roddick's renowned cruelty-free cosmetics are available here. Try the banana shampoo for dry hair, the menthol lotion to refresh your tired feet, or the unscented bath oil that won't clash with your favourite perfume. The lip balms come in several tasty flavours: rum-raisin, apricot and kiwi for example.

Comptoir Sud-Pacific
2nd arr. - 17, rue de la Paix - 42 61 74 44
Open 9:30 a.m.-7 p.m. Closed Sun.

Josée Fournier has a passion for Polynesia. She was the first to market Monoï oil in Paris some years ago, and followed up that initial success with a line of perfumes that recall her beloved Pacific islands, perfumes with such delicious names as Cherry Vanilla and Barbier des Iles (a kind of Bay Rum). The scents also come in the form of candles, sprays and diffusers. A line of exotic cosmetics, travel toiletries and bath fragrance is the most recent addition to Comptoir's considerable inventory.

Diptyque
5th arr. - 34, bd Saint-Germain
43 26 45 27
Open 10 a.m.-7 p.m. Closed Sun. & Mon.

Diptyque is now over 30 years old, but the shop doesn't show its age. The exclusive fragrances are as appealing as ever; the fresh L'Ombre dans l'Eau is a perennial bestseller; the latest addition to the line is Virgilio, a green perfume with

---

RAC MOTORING ATLAS FRANCE: Our fully revised and well-established large format RAC Motoring Atlas France, Belgium and Luxembourg at 1:250,000 (approximately 4 miles to 1 inch) now has even more features to improve journey planning and to make driving in France more enjoyable. Clear, accurate and detailed road maps make RAC Motoring Atlas France the ideal atlas for the independent traveller in France. Price: £ 11.99 (spiral bound).

notes of basil and cedarwood. You'll find all the house fragrances available in candle form, and there is also a pretty selection of Shetland car rugs.

Annick Goutal
1st arr. - 14, rue de Castiglione 42 61 52 82 (also: 7th arr., 17th arr.)
Open 9:30 a.m.-7:30 p.m. Closed Sun.

Annick Goutal's unique fragrances are sold in their own elegant boutiques decorated in beige and gold tones. Our favourites are the deliciously citrus-scented Eau d'Hadrien, the romantic Heure Exquise and the ultra-feminine Rose Absolue. Goutal's soaps, bath oils and scented pebbles (to scatter in lingerie drawers) make wonderful gifts.

Grain de Beauté
6th arr. - 9, rue du Cherche-Midi 45 48 07 55
Open 10:30 a.m.-7 p.m. Closed Sun., Mon. morning & Aug.

Traditional English furniture and chintzes make an appropriate setting for traditional English fragrances by such renowned perfumers as George F. Trumper, Penhaligon's, Floris and Czech & Speake.

Maître Parfumeur et Gantier
1st arr. - 3, rue des Capucines 42 96 35 13
Open 10:30 a.m.-6:30 p.m. Closed Sun.

Jean-François Laporte's extravagant perfumes are for those who like to leave a trail of lingering fragrance in their wake. Both men and women can find intense, assertive toilet waters here, with evocative names like Rose Muskissime or Fleurs de Comores. Laporte's signature perfumes are also sold as potpourri or room fragrances. Don't miss his elegant perfumed gloves.

Patricia de Nicolaï
7th arr. - 80, rue de Grenelle - 45 44 59 59
Open 10 a.m.-2 p.m. & 3 p.m.-7 p.m. (Sat. 10 a.m.-2 p.m. & 3 p.m.-6:30 p.m.). Closed Sun. & Mon.

Guerlain's granddaughter, Patricia de Nicolaï, perpetuates the family tradition of creating divine perfumes. To date, her collection comprises six for women and three for men. We especially like her Mimosaïque and Jardin Secret. Alongside perfumed candles (200 francs), room sprays and potpourris, you'll find delicate carved crystal flacons, which can be engraved with your name.

Sephora
16th arr. - 50, rue de Passy - 45 20 03 15 (also: 1st arr., 9th arr., 13th arr., 14th arr.)
Open 10 a.m.-7:15 p.m. (Mon. until 7 p.m. & Sat. until 7:30 p.m.). Closed Sun.

If you'd rather avoid dealing with salespeople, and prefer to read labels, look at bottles and decide for yourself what make-up you need, then Sephora, the "beauty supermarket" is for you. Cosmetics and perfumes of every type are on offer: face creams, body-care products, cosmetics and accessories (hairbrushes, mirrors...) from major manufacturers are all neatly displayed.

Shu Uemura
6th arr. - 176, bd Saint-Germain 45 48 02 55
Open 10 a.m.-7 p.m. (Mon. 11 a.m.-7 p.m.). Closed Sun.

As soon as they cross the threshold, even the most freshly-scrubbed women are suddenly possessed by the urge to try the lipsticks, powders (fluffed on with bamboo brushes), pencils and shadows. A Japanese-style décor of wood and glass is the handsome setting for these no-less-handsomely packaged cosmetics, many of which come in reusable containers.

Silver Moon
8th arr. - 12-14, av. des Champs-Elysées - 45 62 94 55 (also: 1st arr., 6th arr., 7th arr., 9th arr., 15th arr., 16th arr.)
Open 10 a.m.-7:30 p.m. Closed Sun. Discounts available.

All the major brands of cosmetics and perfumes are sold (many at discount prices) in Paris' several Silver Moon shops. Sales staff are generally competent and helpful. Two of the branches also provide beauty services (hair removal, facials and so on).

Sur La Place
6th arr. - 12, pl. Saint-Sulpice - 43 26 45 27
Open 10 a.m.-7 p.m. (Mon. 1 p.m.-7 p.m.). Closed Sun.

An appealing range of pretty toiletries and bath accessories, reasonably priced.

■ THALASSO-THERAPY

Biocéane
19th arr. - 22, rue de Flandres 40 36 58 01
Open 10 a.m.-7:30 p.m. Closed Sun. & Mon.

Now you can enjoy the benefits of sun and sea in the 19th arrondissement. Seawater whirlpool baths, seaweed wraps, and a wealth of beauty treatments based on elements taken from the sea will restore your skin tone and boost your morale. Traditional beauty treatments are available as well, from massage to "permanent" makeup for brows, eyelashes and lips. An in-house boutique sells natural cosmetics, vitamins, sea-shell meal and herbal teas.

Villa Thalgo

8th arr. - 218-220, rue du Faubourg Saint-Honoré - 45 62 00 20
Open Mon. noon-8 p.m., Tues. & Thurs. 10 a.m.-8 p.m., Wed. & Fri. & Sat. 9 a.m.-8 p.m. Closed Sun.

Take a sea-cure in the heart of Paris. Below the Golden Tulip Hotel is the city's first thalassotherapy centre, with a (reconstituted) sea-water swimming pool. A multitude of seaweed-based body- and skin-care treatments is offered, as well as more traditional beauty care (manicure, lymphatic draining, sauna, Turkish baths...). After a morning of pampering yourself, you can lounge by the pool and nibble on a nutrionally balanced lunch. Prices vary according to the length and type of treatment; membership available.

BOOKS & STATIONERY

■ ART

Artcurial

8th arr. - 9, av. Matignon - 42 99 16 19
Open 10:30 a.m.-7:15 p.m. Closed Sun. & Mon. (except before Christmas), Aug. & holidays.

One floor up from Artcurial's lively contemporary art gallery, this fabulous bookshop boasts some 8,000 works on fine art, graphic arts, and crafts. Look here for the exquisite and erudite books on art, design and fashion from the Editions du Regard (e.g. Anne Bony's monumental series on 20th-century design), as well as an interesting selection of works (primarily Japanese) on fashion and textiles.

Image et Page

4th arr. - 25, rue du Renard - 42 71 70 77
Open daily 10 a.m.-9 p.m.

Luxuriously produced art books and exhibition catalogues are sold at discount prices at this bookshop just steps away from the Centre Pompidou. Contemporary painting is well represented, but the stock is changed often and has works to interest just about any art lover; books in many languages are available here.

Lecointre et Ozanne

6th arr. - 9, rue de Tournon - 43 26 02 92
Open 10 a.m.-7 p.m. (Sat. until 6 p.m.). Closed Sun. & Mon.

The history of architecture will be an open book to you after a visit to this impressive bookshop, which offers an unequalled selection of rare and important works on the subject. Catalogue available.

Librairie Maeght

4th arr. - 12, rue Saint-Merri - 42 78 27 64
Open 10 a.m.-1 p.m. & 2 p.m.-7 p.m. Closed Sun., Mon. & holidays.

Vying for your attention with lithographs by the Galerie Maeght's stable of artists (more affordable, incidentally, than you might think) are all the most important books on every aspect of contemporary art. In many languages.

Nobele

6th arr. - 35, rue Bonaparte - 43 26 08 62
Open 9 a.m.-noon & 2 p.m.-7 p.m. Closed Sat. & end July-end Aug.

Belgian by birth and over 100 years old, Nobele is the benchmark bookshop when it comes to the fine arts, decorative arts, works on collectible antiques and on the history of books. An extraordinary stock of old or rare art books, at astonishingly reasonable prices. Catalogue on request.

■ ENGLISH-LANGUAGE

Attica 1

5th arr. - 23, rue Jean-de-Beauvais - 46 34 62 03
Open 10 a.m.-7 p.m. Closed Sun. & Mon.

The lack of order that reigns here is either appealing or off-putting: the interpretation depends on your personality. We happen to like it, and often while away a bookish afternoon browsing through the rich and eclectic collections. Helpful, literate staff; good service.

Brentano's

2nd arr. - 37, av. de l'Opéra - 42 61 52 50
Open 10 a.m.-7 p.m. (Sat. 10 a.m.-noon & 2 p.m.-7 p.m.). Closed Sun.

Brentano's deservedly remains a favourite among English-speakers in Paris for its remarkable array of English, American and French books, periodicals, records and art books. Bestsellers of the week are always displayed at the entrance. There is also a large children's section.

Galignani

1st arr. - 224, rue de Rivoli - 42 60 76 07
Open 10 a.m.-7 p.m. Closed Sun.

Galignani, purported to be the oldest English bookshop on the continent, was established in 1805 in the rue Vivienne by Giovanni Antonio Galignani, descendant of a famous 12th-century publisher from Padua, Italy. In the mid-1800s Galignani moved to the rue de Rivoli, near the terminus of the Calais-Paris train, and the shop has passed from father to son ever since. Featured are English, American and French hardbacks and paperbacks, lots of children's literature,

BOOKS & STATIONERY – SHOPS

plus a fabulous international selection of art books.

Le Nouveau Quartier Latin
6th arr. - 78, bd Saint-Michel - 43 26 42 70
Open 10 a.m.-7 p.m. Closed Sun.

The Nouveau Quartier Latin carries a wide selection of English, American, Spanish and German literature, plus dictionaries and paperbacks in English (over 10,000). Also featured are books on painting, design, architecture, photography, graphics and music. An entire section is given over to books on teaching or learning English. The adjacent room is equipped so that you may listen to and watch audiotapes and videotapes before buying. The book-ordering service is fast and efficient, and sales go on throughout the year. Catalogues are available.

Shakespeare and Company
5th arr. - 37, rue de la Bûcherie 43 26 96 50
Open daily 11 a.m.-midnight.

Shakespeare and Co. on the quai by Notre-Dame is the late-night favourite of buyers and browsers in search of second-hand English and American books (see *Open Late*).

W. H. Smith
1st arr. - 248, rue de Rivoli - 42 60 37 97
Open 9:30 a.m.-7 p.m. Closed Sun.

This is the closest thing to the perfect self-service bookstore: it is easy to locate almost any item among the more than 40,000 English and American titles, from cookery books to travel guides to children's books, videos, cassettes... The selection of periodicals is huge and the staff efficient and friendly.

Tea in the Pagoda

The cinema saved *La Pagode* ("the Pagoda") from the threat of demolition. Since 1931 it has been one of the city's most attractive film theatres. The French architects responsible for La Pagode fell under the collective fin-de-siècle enchantment with all things Oriental; the structure's elegant dcor delighted guests at high-society receptions in the 1890s. Later the Chinese Embassy dropped plans to buy La Pagode (the ambassador apparently objected to some wall paintings depicting Chinese warriors being soundly defeated by the Japanese). The oriental flavour lingers on in the tea rooms and garden, additional reasons to visit this pagoda at 57bis rue de Babylone in the seventh arrondissement. Across the street at number 68, Ciné-images sells posters and other souvenirs of the world's greatest films.

Tea and Tattered Pages
6th arr. - 24, rue Mayet - 40 65 94 35
Open 11 a.m.-7 p.m. Closed Sun.

A charming place to browse through a wide selection of English and American used books, and to enjoy a leisurely cup of tea (see *Tea rooms*).

Tonkam
11th arr. - 29, rue Keller - 47 00 78 38
Open 10:30 a.m.-noon & 1 p.m.-7 p.m. (Sat. 2 p.m.-8 p.m.). Closed Sun.

Sylvie Tonkam is the resident expert on *bandes dessinées*—comic strip books and albums. Her vast inventory includes an impressive collection of American comics, some old and collectible. She sells T-shirts too.

The Village Voice
6th arr. - 6, rue Princesse - 46 33 36 47
Open 11 a.m.-8 p.m. (Mon. from 2 p.m.). Closed Sun. No cards.

Nowadays the Village Voice controls the turf once so jealously guarded by Sylvia Beach's original Shakespeare and Co.—a mecca for Americans in Paris, especially writers, journalists and literary types. The Village Voice hosts well-attended poetry readings and book-signing parties, and supplies voracious readers with an intelligently chosen selection of titles. The friendly, literate staff will order books for you.

■ **FILM & PHOTOGRAPHY**

La Chambre Claire
6th arr. - 14, rue Saint-Sulpice 46 34 04 31
Open 10 a.m.-7 p.m. (Mon. 2 p.m.-7 p.m.). Closed Sun. & holidays.

This bookshop is given over entirely to photography—with some 5,000 editions, it is the official supplier to several of the world's greatest museums. A truly remarkable place; some discounted books are available.

Ciné Doc
9th arr. - 43-45, passage Jouffroy 48 24 77 36
Open daily 10 a.m.-7 p.m.

This flea market–style shop in the delightful passage

Jouffroy boasts an admirable jumble of publications pertaining to the cinema, plus posters, postcards and original photographs. The interesting displays in the shop windows change often and add to the already lively atmosphere. Aficionados take note: Ciné Doc possesses a fascinating collection of highly literary erotica.

■ FOOD & COOKING

La Librairie Gourmande
5th arr. - 4, rue Dante - 43 54 37 27
Open 10 a.m.-7 p.m. (Sun. from 3 p.m.).

At La Librairie Gourmande you will find a mouthwatering array of cookery books for amateurs and professionals alike, as well as works on the history of French and foreign cooking (some volumes date from the 16th century). Books on traditional and nouvelle cuisine, recipes by Balzac and Dumas, plus a wide range of works on wine make this one of Paris' most appetising bookshops, despite the high prices. You can bank on a warm welcome and excellent service from owner Geneviève Baudon.

Librairie des Gourmets
5th arr. - 98, rue Monge - 43 31 16 42
Open 10:30 a.m.-7 p.m. Closed Sun. & Mon.

A bright and tidy shop where gourmets and good cooks will feel at home, thanks to the owner's warm welcome. All the latest French cookbooks are on hand, as well as a wide selection of gastronomic classics.

Find the address you are looking for, quickly and easily, in the index.

Le Verre et l'Assiette
5th arr. - 1, rue du Val-de-Grâce 46 33 45 96
Open 10 a.m.-12:30 p.m. & 2:30 p.m.-7 p.m. (Mon. from 2:30 p.m.). Closed Sun. & 2 wks. in Aug.

Too many chefs may well spoil the broth, but they certainly don't spoil Le Verre et l'Assiette. Feast your eyes on the window display: a potpourri of books and accessories about gastronomy and oenology—from unique corkscrews to rare editions on Celtic cooking. This is the bookshop most frequented by famous chefs, and lovers of food and wine. In addition to the thousands of volumes on the subject, there is a fine selection of gift ideas (the wine taster's ideal travelling case, for example). *Bon appétit!*

■ GENERAL INTEREST

Gibert Jeune
5th arr. - 23-27, quai Saint-Michel - 43 54 57 32
5th arr. - 4-6, pl. Saint-Michel - 43 25 91 19
2nd arr. - 15, bd Saint-Denis - 42 36 82 84
Open 9:30 a.m.-7:30 p.m. Closed Sun.

This multi-storey emporium of books is renowned among the city's huge student population for its large inventory, special sales and second-hand hardbacks and paperbacks. A fine selection of English and American books (you might consider selling your own used or unwanted books here).

La Hune
6th arr. - 170, bd Saint-Germain 45 48 35 85
Open 10 a.m.-midnight. Closed Sun.

La Hune is a favourite among Paris intellectuals, bibliophiles and browsers. It stays open late and stocks an impressive array of books on architecture, contemporary art and design, as well as classics and contemporary literature. The mezzanine houses works on the graphic arts, photography, theatre and cinema.

Librairie Delamain
1st arr. - 155, rue Saint-Honoré 42 61 48 78
Open 10 a.m.-7 p.m. Closed Sun.

Delamain is the oldest bookshop in France, founded in 1710 under the arcades of the Comédie-Française. About 100 years ago the original shop burned down, and Delamain was forced to move. Its current location is on the rue Saint-Honoré. Thousands of volumes on French literature, travel, history and art (French only) are available, new or used. The first floor is given over to the graphic arts, photography, film and theatre.

FNAC
1st arr. - Forum des Halles - 40 41 40 00
6th arr. - 136, rue de Rennes - 49 54 30 00
17th arr. - 26, av. des Ternes - 44 09 18 00
Open 10 a.m.-7:30 p.m. Closed Sun.

FNAC is the biggest chain of bookstores in Europe, with a low-price policy that means you can read more for less: French books sell for five per cent less than the standard retail price, while foreign editions are discounted even more. Miles of shelves are packed with a vast and varied stock of volumes ranging from do-it-yourself manuals, cookery books and guides to highbrow fiction, poetry and philosophy. The shops are immense and densely packed with book lovers, particularly at weekends. The sales staff are qualified and knowledgeable, though it often feels as if they are rarer than first editions (which means,

BOOKS & STATIONERY - SHOPS

however, that you can browse for hours undisturbed).

La Librairie des Femmes
6th arr. - 74, rue de Seine - 43 29 50 75
Open 10 a.m.-7 p.m. Closed Sun.

This is not a feminist bookshop. It is a publisher/bookseller's showcase that highlights books written by or about women (including many books by men). The first-floor sales area is one of the most attractive in Paris—light, spacious and user-friendly. The shop also organises photo and print exhibitions.

Librairie Thomas
5th arr. - 28, rue des Fossés-Saint-Bernard - 46 34 11 30
Open 9 a.m.-7 p.m. (Mon. 2 p.m.-6:30 p.m.; Sat. 9:30 a.m.-12:30 p.m. & 2 p.m.-6:30 p.m.). Closed Sun.

This charming little shop features more than 10,000 works on the natural sciences (in several languages). It has recently been remodelled and is now managed by specialists affiliated to the natural history museum. You will find nature guides, works on gardening, ecology, history and much more, plus a large children's section. A wealth of guidebooks is on hand as well.

La Maison du Dictionnaire
14th arr. - 98, bd du Montparnasse - 43 22 12 93
Open 9 a.m.-6:30 p.m. Closed Sat. & Sun.

This ever-expanding shop in the Montparnasse shopping centre features more than 4,000 new and used dictionaries (general, technical and special-interest) in more than 100 languages. Even more astounding is the Pivothèque reading room, open to the public, in which you may sit and browse through any book before buying it.

▶ RARE BOOKS

Pierre Bérès
8th arr. - 14, av. de Friedland - 45 61 00 99
Open 9 a.m.-6 p.m. Closed Sun. No cards.

The grand old man of the city's rare-book trade possesses one of the world's most precious inventories, which includes illuminated manuscripts, incunabula (pre-16th-century printed books) and works illustrated by contemporary artists. Even if like most mortals you lack the wherewithal to purchase one of these treasures, if you are a true bibliophile, you owe it to yourself to visit this remarkable address.

Carnavalette
3rd arr. - 2, rue des Francs-Bourgeois - 42 72 91 92
Open daily 10 a.m.-6:30 p.m. No cards.

Some rare 20th-century volumes are on sale here, but what we find most interesting is the shop's collection of museum posters, highly decorative and ready to frame.

Courant d'Art
6th arr. - 79, rue de Vaugirard 45 49 30 08
Open 9 a.m.-8 p.m. Closed Sun.

Art is the passion of bookseller Marie-Josée Grandjean. Her rue de Vaugirard shop is a showcase for books on art—from studies and monographs of painters, sculptors and artisans, to sales catalogues from Christie's, Sotheby's or the French auctioneers Drouot. On display is a large collection of engravings, reproductions, exhibition catalogues, back issues of art magazines and all sorts of other unfindables. Not to mention the noteworthy collection of books on cinema and photography. In addition to her Left-Bank shop, Grandjean runs a stand at the Saint-Ouen flea market (from 9 a.m.-6 p.m. on Saturday, Sunday and Monday; Marché Jules-Vallès, 40 11 43 88).

Librairie du Cygne
6th arr. - 17, rue Bonaparte - 43 26 32 45
Open 3 p.m.-7 p.m. Closed Sat., Sun. & Aug.

The Librairie du Cygne seems to have tumbled out of a Balzac novel. The old oak bookcases of this austere shop groan with signed first editions and illustrated works by the greats—Stendhal, Molière, Anatole France, Maupassant, Zola and Hugo. A wide-ranging array of books on the decorative arts is another speciality of the house.

Pont-Neuf
6th arr. - 1, rue Dauphine - 43 26 42 40
Open 9:30 a.m.-noon & 2 p.m.-6:30 p.m. (Sat. until 5 p.m.). Closed Sun., Mon. & Aug. No cards.

This charming shop run by Claude Coulet features a 19th-century reading room, with shelves packed with first editions, illustrated works and reprints by Carteret, Vicaire and Pia. The lovely setting, just across from the Pont-Neuf, and one of the best selections of antiquarian books in Paris make the Librairie du Pont-Neuf a must for bibliophiles and curious browsers alike.

▶ TRAVEL BOOKS

Institut Géographique National
8th arr. - 107, rue de La Boétie 43 98 85 00
Open 9:30 a.m.-7 p.m. (Sat. 10 a.m.-12:30 p.m. & 2 p.m.-5:30 p.m.). Closed Sun.

Need a map? Of course you do! Those published by the IGN are meticulously detailed, and will delight travellers, tourists, hikers and bikers who

SHOPS – BOOKS & STATIONERY

like to know exactly where they are.

Le Tour du Monde
16th arr. - 9, rue de la Pompe - 42 88 73 59
Open 10 a.m.-1 p.m. & 2 p.m.-7 p.m. Closed Sun., Mon. & holidays. No cards.

Travel-book lovers take note: Jean-Etienne and Edmonde Huret have earned their reputation as the Sherlock Holmes(es) of the book world. Their shop is chock-a-block with hard-to-find, out-of-print and rare works on the far-flung and the right-next-door. They also stock a fine selection of children's books.

■ STATIONERY

Armorial
8th arr. - 98, rue du Faubourg-Saint-Honoré - 42 65 08 18
Open 9:30 a.m.-1 p.m. & 2 p.m.-6:30 p.m. Closed Sun.

The desk sets and other sophisticated accessories crafted by this prestigious firm can be found in the offices of many cabinet ministers and executives with refined tastes.

Cassegrain
8th arr. - 422, rue Saint-Honoré - 42 60 20 08
Open 9:30 a.m.-6:30 p.m. Closed Sun.

This venerable institution on the rue Saint-Honoré, founded in 1919, is aiming to update its image (while preserving its reputation for fine engraving, of course). A new line of "youthful" leather accessories has been introduced: brightly coloured lizard diaries and address books, boxes covered with marbled paper, more boxes and picture frames in burled elm and amusing gadgets for children. Cassegrain is one of the rare sources in France of the legendary notebooks from Smythson of Bond Street (bible paper, sewn bindings, leather covers—they cost a fortune, but they're worth it). Another Cassegrain store is located at 81, rue des Saints-Pères, in the sixth arrondissement.

Les Crayons de Julie
16th arr. - 17, rue de Longchamp - 44 05 02 01
Open 10:30 a.m.-7 p.m. (Mon. from noon). Closed Sun.

Traditionalists who still write letters and thank-you notes love to browse in Julie's charming shop for old-fashioned fountain pens and pretty stationery.

Dupré Octante
8th arr. - 141, rue du Faubourg-Saint-Honoré - 45 63 10 11
Open 9:15 a.m.-6:30 p.m. (Sat. 10 a.m.-12:30 p.m. & 2 p.m.-6 p.m.). Closed Sun.

Every illustrator and graphic designer in Paris can be found, at one time or another, in this vast stationery shop in the Faubourg-Saint-Honoré. Many different kinds of letter paper are available in lovely, exclusive colours, as well as a full range of office accessories. In the equally large shop nearby in the rue d'Artois is a complete line of drawing materials—from pencils to computer software. You can expect to find even the most arcane art supplies, but don't expect service with a smile from the staff—we found them rather surly.

Elysées Stylos Marbeuf
8th arr. - 40, rue Marbeuf - 42 25 40 49
Open 9:30 a.m.-7 p.m. Closed Sun. & Aug.

If it's a fountain pen you're seeking, this is the place. The selection of famous French and imported brands is quite astonishing; repairs are also performed here (though no cheap pens will be considered). The solid-gold pens and luxurious gold and silver desk accessories make sumptuous, impressive gifts.

Marie-Papier
6th arr. - 26, rue Vavin - 43 26 46 44
Open 10 a.m.-7 p.m. Closed Sun.

Marie-Paule Orluc launched the trend of fashionable stationery when she opened her enchanting little shop, where all the different papers are conveniently displayed on the walls at eye-level. We don't know of anyone who offers a wider choice of coloured letter and note paper, albums, folders and boxes; each season brings a new crop of lovely hues. Unfortunately, there are a few catches here: the merchandise is extremely expensive, the atmosphere very snobbish and the salespeople are hard put to it to hide their annoyance when a customer walks through the door.

Mélodies Graphiques
4th arr. - 10, rue du Pont-Louis-Philippe - 42 74 57 68
Open 11 a.m.-7 p.m. Closed Sun. & Mon.

This pretty boutique, done up in blond wood, features desk accessories covered in marbled paper. The paper, ten styles in all, is made by the well-known Florentine firm, Il Papiro, according to 16th-century methods. A selection of unusual decorative objects—carnival masks and such—is also sold.

Papier Plus
4th arr. - 9, rue du Pont-Louis-Philippe - 42 77 70 49
Open noon-7 p.m. Closed Sun.

Both this shop and Mélodies Graphiques, just opposite (see above), carry quality stationery, but each has its speciality. In Papier Plus, you'll find writing paper sold by the kilo, blank notebooks, photograph albums and files, in a host of pastel shades.

Note that national museums are generally closed on Tuesdays.

CHEAP CHIC CLOTHES – SHOPS

Sennelier
7th arr. - 3, quai Voltaire - 42 60 29 38
Open 9 a.m.-6:30 p.m. (Mon. 9 a.m.-12:15 p.m. & 2 p.m.-6:30 p.m.). Closed Sun.

Appropriately located next to the Ecole des Beaux-Arts, Sennelier has, in its 100 years of existence, sold tons of art supplies to many well-known and aspiring artists. Here they find the best brands of paints and pigments, paper and sketch pads of excellent quality, canvas, easels and framing equipment.

Stern
2nd arr. - 47, passage des Panoramas - 45 08 86 45
Open 9:30 a.m.-12:30 p.m. & 1:30 p.m.-5:30 p.m. Closed Sat., Sun. & Aug. No cards.

Stern started in 1830, when the *grands boulevards* were the epicentre of elegant Parisian life. Now known throughout the world as engraver to royalty, aristocrats and people of taste, Stern carefully conserves its tradition of using only the finest paper, crafted and engraved by hand. The firm has models available for every type of visiting or business card, invitation and announcement, but Stern's draughtsmen can also produce designs to your specifications.

CHEAP CHIC CLOTHES

Alaïa
4th arr. - 7, rue de Moussy - 42 72 19 19
Open 10 a.m.-7 p.m. Closed Sun.

Sexy knits and winsome accessories (shoes, gloves, hats, belts) all bearing the unmistakable stamp of the Tunisian designer. The clothing comes from the previous year's collections, and sells at half the original price.

Bargain City

Manufacturers' outlets offer unbeatable bargains in clothes, shoes and accessories on the rue d'Alésia (14th arrondissement, between the place Victor-et-Hélène-Basch and the rue des Plantes). Head to *Dorotennis* **(n°74) for sportswear by top designer** *Dorothée Bis***, to** *Mac Douglas* **(n°120) for fashionable leather gear, to** *Stock 2* **(n°92) for designs by Daniel Hechter for the entire family, to** *Cacharel* **at n°114 (something for everyone here, too) and to** *SR Store* **(n°64) for greatly reduced fashions by Sonia Rykiel. Across town on the** *Rue de Meslay* **(3rd arr.) fine Italian footwear is sold at cut-rate prices. And discount houses stand cheek-by-jowl with the most prestigious names in tableware on the** *Rue de Paradis* **(10th arr.). Remember, though, that finding a bargain requires considerable time and patience!**

L'Astucerie
15th arr. - 105, rue de Javel - 45 57 94 74
Open 11:30 a.m.-2 p.m. & 3 p.m.-7 p.m. (Sat. 11:30 a.m.-6 p.m.). Closed Sun. & Mon.

Previously owned but hardly worn top-label clothing for women and children is the backbone of this boutique's inventory. Insiders know that they can buy Hermès silk-twill scarves here for 700 francs, as well as Kelly bags in box calf, Vuitton luggage and the occasional Chanel accessory (all in perfect condition).

Catherine Baril
16th arr. - 14 & 25, rue de la Tour 45 20 95 21
Open 10 a.m.-7 p.m. (Mon. from 2 p.m.). Closed Sun. & 3 wks. in Aug.

Catherine Baril, a pioneer of the sale-or-return deposit system in Paris, pampers her elegant clientele with barely used couture and designer clothing and accessories at truly unbeatable prices. The shop at number 25 offers the lowest prices of all.

Chipie Stock
14th arr. - 82, rue d'Alésia - 45 42 07 52
Open 10:15 a.m.-7 p.m. (Mon. 2 p.m.-7 p.m. & Sat. 10 a.m.-7 p.m.). Closed Sun.

"Stock" is the way the French say "designer outlet." Chipie Stock sells seconds and previous-season models of the youthful, cheerful Chipie label: look for lots of stylish sweaters, jeans, jean jackets (285 francs) and colourful sneakers, all of which look best on under-30s.

Le Dépôt des Grandes Marques
2nd arr. - 15, rue de la Banque 42 96 99 04
Open 10 a.m.-7 p.m. Closed Sun.

Rack after rack of designer menswear is set out for your inspection at this first-floor shop near the stock exchange. All the best labels are represented: Renoma, Cerruti, Louis Féraud, Jacques Fath and more, costing an average of 40 per cent less than normal retail prices. Suits, jackets, trousers, shirts and ties make up the stock. Expect to find top-name suits (Renoma, for example) from current collections, Cacharel silk ties, Harris tweed and pure cashmere jackets. Take note that the most complicated alterations will be done by in-house tailors. Lots of stockbrokers invest their clothing budgets here, but so do many executives and politicians who know a bargain when they see one.

Les Deux Oursons
15th arr. - 106, bd de Grenelle
45 75 10 77
Open 10 a.m.-7 p.m. (Mon. 2 p.m.-7 p.m.). Closed Sun.

Pre-worn furs, many with designer labels, all in excellent condition, keep women coming winter after winter to the sign of the "Two Teddy Bears." Blue fox or mink jackets start at 2,000 francs; furs from such prestigious designers as Ricci, Dior and Revillon go for 30 per cent less than elsewhere. Some shearling and leather coats are usually in stock as well. A full range of services includes repairs, expert cleaning and hire purchase.

Diapositive Stock
14th arr. - 72, rue d'Alésia - 45 39 97 27
Open 10:15 a.m.-7 p.m. (Mon. 2 p.m.-7 p.m.). Closed Sun.

At this outlet store prices are slashed on attractive print bodysuits, nicely tailored wool flannel suits, leggings with colourful floral or animal motifs and much more. The clothes all date from the preceding season, but sell for a full 50 per cent below the original price.

Dorothée Bis Stock
14th arr. - 74, rue d'Alésia - 45 42 17 11
Open 10:15 a.m.-7 p.m. (Mon. 2 p.m.-7 p.m.). Closed Sun.

Even if the clothes are two seasons old, their avant-garde design means they still look very fashionable when you buy them—at a quarter of their usual price. Evening clothes in particular are excellent value. Summer collections arrive in mid-December, winter clothes at the end of July. Expect to pay about 700 francs for a pretty dress in top condition.

Fabienne
16th arr. - 77 bis, rue Boileau
45 25 64 26
Open 10 a.m.-1:30 p.m. & 3 p.m.-7 p.m. Closed Sun. & Mon.

A sale-or-return shop for men's clothing is rare indeed, so here is a good one to keep in mind. The inventory changes regularly of course, but you can usually count on finding Façonnable suits, Burberry trench coats and exclusive John Lobb shoes.

Fabrice Karel Stock
14th arr. - 105, rue d'Alésia - 45 42 42 61
Open 10:15 a.m.-7 p.m. (Mon. 2 p.m.-7 p.m.). Closed Sun.

Classic knitwear that never goes out of fashion is sold here for half its original price. From June to August, prices are slashed by an additional 30 per cent.

Réciproque
16th arr. - 89 & 123, rue de la Pompe - 47 04 30 28
Open 10:15 a.m.-6:45 p.m. Closed Sun., Mon.

Thrifty ladies of the jet-set, showbiz and business worlds bring the clothes they no longer want (but can't bear to give away—how do you think they got so rich?) to Réciproque. Manager Nicole Morel displays only the finest designer clothing from recent collections (Chanel, Mugler, Alaïa, Lacroix...), all of it in excellent condition. The spacious, quiet store is a delightful place in which to browse; the atmosphere is nothing like that of a second-hand shop. Men's clothing is sold at 101 rue de la Pompe.

Dépôt Vente de Paris
20th arr. - 81, rue de Lagny - 43 72 13 91
Open 9:30 a.m.-7:30 p.m. Closed Sun. No cards.

Modern and antique furniture, knick-knacks and bric-a-brac, dishes, jewellery, used appliances... everything but clothing can be bought or sold on deposit (the fee is 25 per cent) at this huge old warehouse. Professionals generally cream off the best of the jewels and antiques, but if they've got a sharp eye, even non-professional shoppers

---

Marché Saint-Pierre

18th arr. - Pl. du Marché Saint-Pierre
"None priced lower!" "Sensational bargains!" "Special one-day sale!" Such are the slogans (which we've translated freely for you) that lure crowds of shoppers to the Marché Saint-Pierre, the foremost fabric discount market in Paris. On the ground floor of *Tissus Reine*, (open 9:15 a.m.-6:30 p.m., Mon. 2 p.m.-6:30 p.m. & Sat. until 6:45 p.m.; closed Sun.; 46 06 06 31), carrying the largest choice of fabrics, look for cottons priced as low as 15 francs per metre, silk, velvet, satin (29 francs per metre), and felt (perfect for lining drawers and cupboards). The first floor is devoted to woollens, fake fur, sewing notions and patterns. On the second floor, upholstery and furnishing fabrics are grouped; all the designers are here. On the third floor, you will find curtain materials. Before you leave, look out from the store and admire the fabulous unobstructed view of Sacré-Cœur.

CHILDREN - SHOPS

can come up with some interesting bargains. New stock arrives daily.

Les Deux Portes
16th arr. - 35, rue de l'Annonciation - 45 25 31 97
Open 10 a.m.-6:30 p.m. Closed Sun. & Mon.

Designer fabrics for the home (curtains, upholstery, wallpapers) and top-of-the-line household linens are sold at extremely attractive prices at the four Paris Deux Portes shops. Many items are manufacturers' discontinued lines, others are the firm's own exclusive designs. Also available is a range of sofas, custom-made curtains and a decorating service.

CHILDREN

■ BOOKS

Chantelivre
6th arr. - 13, rue de Sèvres - 45 48 87 90
Open 10 a.m.-6:50 p.m. (Mon. from 1 p.m.). Closed Sun., 1 wk. in Aug. & holidays.

This is the place for the younger generation of bibliophiles. Among the 10,000 titles to choose from are illustrated story books, fairy and folk tales and novels, as well as records and educational games. There is a small selection of books and games in English. In a back corner of the shop is an area open for children—to draw, look at books or listen to a story (in French).

> See also: *Brentano's, W.H. Smith, Attica* in Books, pages 190 and 191.

■ CLOTHING

Baby Dior
8th arr. - 28, av. Montaigne - 40 73 54 44
Open 9:30 a.m.-6:30 p.m. (Sat. & Mon. from 10 a.m.). Closed Sun. & holidays.

If you can afford to buy an entire set of baby clothes, wonderful; if you can't... at least let yourself get one teeny little shirt with a ruffle (400 francs), a pair of sheets for the cradle or a dressing gown. The bootees (200 francs) make a darling baby present, and there are also some other nice items—picture frames (650 francs) and silver cups from about 1,450 francs. Abominably expensive smocked dresses are available in sizes up to eight years (640 to 4,000 francs, for a one-year-old).

Bonpoint
7th arr. - 67 & 86 rue de l'Université
45 55 63 70 & 45 51 17 68
7th arr. - 65 & 82, rue de Grenelle - 47 05 09 09 & 45 48 05 45
7th arr. - 7, rue de Solférino - 45 55 42 79
Open 10 a.m.-7 p.m. Closed Sun.

The styles are most suitable for French yuppie children, but without too much chi-chi. For the last few years, Bonpoint has been trying to lower prices yet maintain its renowned high quality. Trousers are lined so they won't itch, hems are huge, and fabrics are of first-rate quality. A blouse costs about 350 francs; a pair of Bermuda shorts, so well cut that they grow with the child, is also about 350 francs; and a pleated or quilted skirt around 400 francs. The boutique specialises in children's formal dress: white gloves, hats and other such romantic attire.

Cacharel
9th arr. - 34, rue Tronchet - 47 42 12 61
Open 10:15 a.m.-7:30 p.m. (Sat. from 9:30 a.m.). Closed Mon.

Cacharel carries parkas, jackets and blazers, as well as pleated skirts, Bermuda shorts and dresses for children aged four to 18. Girls look fetching in Liberty-print dresses, and boys handsome in the striped shirts. A word of warning: the clothes are cut small, so remember to buy a size larger than usual.

Caddie
8th arr. - 38, rue François-ler - 47 20 79 79
Open 10 a.m.-7 p.m. Closed Sun. & holidays.

From the cradle to sixth-form college, kids can be clothed here in designer clothes with the most fashionable labels: Armani, Dior, Kenzo, Moschino, Rykiel... Luxurious sportswear by Donaldson is embroidered with Disney cartoon characters.

La Châtelaine
16th arr. - 170, av. Victor-Hugo 47 27 44 07
Open 9:30 a.m.-6:30 p.m. Closed Sat. 12:30 pm-2:30 p.m., Sun., Mon., 3 wks. in Aug. & holidays.

This is the most luxurious children's clothing shop imaginable. Dresses, vests and shirts are perfectly finished, and the babywear is the finest, most elegant in Paris. It is designed exclusively for La Châtelaine by Molli, a Swiss lingerie firm. Clothes for any age can be custom-made and will be delivered free of charge; alterations, too, are done gratis. This isn't so surprising when you consider that a size-five Liberty dress is priced at 1,200 francs.

Chevignon Kids
6th arr. - 4, rue des Ciseaux - 43 26 06 37
Open 10:15 a.m.-7 p.m. Closed Sun. & holidays.

This is the place to find hideously expensive children's wear inspired by the clothes American teenagers wore in the 1950s. Practically every item is stamped with the

197

SHOPS – CHILDREN

firm's logo—they should pay their customers for the free advertising.

Gina Diwan
15th arr. - 20, av. du Maine - 42 22 27 09
Open 10:30 a.m.-7 p.m. Closed Sun.

Adorable, dressy rompers for babies are featured (380 francs for a three-month-old), as well as hand-smocked dresses, embroidered shirts and blouses with petal collars. Alongside these are clothes for children aged up to 14.

Jacadi
17th arr. - 60, bd de Courcelles 47 63 55 23
(also in 1st arr., 2nd arr., 4th arr., 5th arr., 6th arr., 7th arr., 8th arr., 9th arr., 13th arr., 14th arr., 15th arr., 16th arr., 18th arr., 19th arr., 20th arr.)
Open 10 a.m.-6:45 p.m. Closed Sun. & holidays.

Given the prices French parents are obliged to pay for children's clothes, Jacadi's merchandise offers pretty good value. The styles are attractive, though rather sedate...formal short trousers for little boys for example. At any rate, there are some beautiful shirts and blouses, sturdy outer garments and lots of lovely accessories (headbands, socks, hats, mittens and scarves). Sizes start at birth and go to age 14.

Naf-Naf
17th arr. - 10, av. des Ternes - 42 67 30 30
Open 10 a.m.-7:30 p.m. Closed Sun.

If you like jogging suits, sweatshirts and dungarees, trot along to Naf-Naf. Everyone knows it as much for its styles as for its recent advertising campaign: piglets in a display of doubtful taste. We think you could do better elsewhere, and price-wise too.

New Man
6th arr. - 12, rue de l'Ancienne-Comédie - 43 54 44 95
Open 10 a.m.-7:30 p.m. Closed Sun.

From the tender age of six months babies, toddlers and older kids can wear the rough-and-ready styles of this fashionable firm's Miniman line. Their range offers a welcome compromise between sloppy sweatshirts and restrictive (and itchy) formal clothes.

Du Pareil au Même
12th arr. - 122, rue du Faubourg Saint-Antoine - 43 44 67 46
Open 10 a.m.-7 p.m. Closed Sun.

This is the biggest of the chain's 12 Parisian stores. The low prices are enough to motivate mothers to dig through piles of pants, shirts, skirts, pyjamas and so on. Surprisingly, the clothes are of more-than-respectable quality, and stylish to boot.

Petit Faune
6th arr. - 33, rue Jacob - 42 60 80 72
Open 10:30 a.m.-7 p.m. Closed Sun. & holidays.

Flowered dresses, hand-knitted baby clothes and separates for children from birth to age 12 in traditional styles to which bold, bright colours give a fashion lift. As for the prices, they really do defy common sense.

Tartine et Chocolat
6th arr. - 90 & 105, rue de Rennes 42 22 67 34 & 45 62 44 04
Open 10 a.m.-7 p.m. Closed Sun. & Mon.
Open 10:30 a.m.-1:30 p.m. & 2:30 p.m.-7 p.m. Closed Sun., Mon. & Aug. 1-15.
16th arr. - 60, av. Paul Doumer 45 04 08 94
Open 10 a.m.-7 p.m. (Mon. from 2 p.m.). Closed Sun. & Aug. 1-15.

The famous little blue and pink stripes that made the brand a success have survived, though these days they represent only three per cent of the collection. Aside from the clothes (up to eight years), Tartine et Chocolat also sells lots of appealing accessories, children's furniture and baby equipment. Little girls love the firm's fresh, innocent eau de cologne (with no alcohol), "P'titsenbon", in its pretty frosted-glass bottle.

Sonia Rykiel Enfants
6th arr. - 4 rue de Grenelle - 49 54 61 10
Open 10 a.m.-7 p.m. Closed Sun.

When Sonia Rykiel became a grandmother, she realised

Tiny togs for less

Dents de Lait ("Milk Teeth") is a brand-new, sparkling white shop that discounts the top brands of clothing for children from birth to aged eight. Here, even chic labels like Petit Faune and Baby Dior can be purchased for less (15, rue Vavin, 6th arr. - 46 33 90 92). For more cut-rate kids' clothes, try *Le Mouton à Cinq Pattes*—it's a madhouse, but the prices are lowest (10, rue Saint-Placide, 6th arr. - 45 48 20 49); *Magic Stock*, same street, same price policy (60, rue Saint-Placide, 6th arr. - 45 44 01 89). For excellent prices on warm outdoor and ski wear by French manufacturers, head for *Mi-Prix* (27, boulevard Victor, 15th arr. - 48 28 42 48).

CHILDREN – SHOPS

that there was nothing in her collections for her darling little Lolita and Tatiana, her two granddaughters. So she got her own daughter, Natalie, to oversee a children's line, and it's a success. Clothes are embroidered with gold-coloured teddies, there's plenty of sharp red, violet, grey and fuchsia jersey, long sweaters over miniskirts and velvet jogging outfits.

SHOES

Bonpoint
7th arr. - 86, rue de l'Université 45 51 17 68
Open 10 a.m.-7 p.m. Closed Sun.

Having outfitted your children at Bonpoint No. 67, what could be easier than to cross the street for footwear to match? There are black Paraboots (extremely difficult to find anywhere else) for macho minimen, pastel-coloured ballet slippers, tennis shoes, boots and classic styles for school.

Find the address you are looking for, quickly and easily, in the index.

Cendrine
6th arr. - 3, rue Vavin - 43 54 81 20
Open 9:30 a.m.-12:30 p.m. & 2 p.m.-7 p.m. (Mon. 2 p.m.-7 p.m.). Closed Sun., last wk. of July & 3 1st wks. of Aug., holidays.

Does your child have delicate or hard-to-fit feet? If so, Cendrine is the place to go. Not that these shoes are orthopaedic. On the contrary, these are classic styles, but Cendrine will fit your baby with a half-sole or advise you on the best model to buy. Anxious mothers emerge confident that their children are correctly shod.

Froment Leroyer
16th arr. - 50, rue Vital - 42 24 82 70
(also 6th arr., 7th arr., 8th arr.)
Open 10 a.m.-7 p.m. Closed Sun., Mon.

Froment Leroyer provides sturdy Start-Rite shoes (but they're much more expensive than in Britain), leather slippers, canvas sandals—all those unchanging models that have become reassuring symbols of continuity. Here you'll find everything from classics

---

Budget busters

Some people, we realise, are not happy unless they've paid a fortune to expand their children's wardrobes. For that segment of the population, we list the following addresses, where the children's clothes are dependably *chic et chers*: **Miki House** makes absolutely adorable trendy togs for toddlers, as well as the cutest sneakers imaginable (1, place des Victoires, 1st arr. - 40 26 23 00); *Claude Vell* dresses kids aged up to 18 in a rainbow of subtle colours (8, rue du Jour, 1st arr. - 40 26 76 70); *Cyrillus* provides outfits for well-bred little ladies and gentlemen—kilts, tiny blazers, flannel bermudas, gorgeous plaid bathrobes (11, av. Duquesne, 7th arr. - 47 05 99 19).

N.B.: like other French retailers, these shops put on worthwhile sales in January and July.

---

to the more avant-garde styles in children's shoes.

Till
6th arr. - 51, rue de Sèvres - 42 22 25 25
Open 9:30 a.m.-7 p.m. (Mon. from noon). Closed Sun.

You can be sure that your little darlings will be properly shod here. Till, the largest chain of its kind in Europe, hires only experienced sales staff and will not sell any shoes that haven't been impeccably finished. Kids' tennis shoes have spongy linings, babies' shoes are reinforced and finished in leather. Till staff will explain to you that children's feet have special requirements, and that successive generations need bigger and bigger shoes. There are 300 designs displayed—from plimsolls to dress shoes to sandals and slippers. This is a serious shoe-shopping stop.

■ JUNIOR & TEENS

Autour du Monde
3rd arr. - 10, rue des Francs-Bourgeois - 42 77 46 48
Open 10:30 a.m.-1 p.m. & 2 p.m.-7 p.m. (Sun. & Mon. from 2 p.m.).

All the brands that French teenagers love—Bensimon, Cimarron, Chipie, Ninos de Lorca—are sure to appeal to their British counterparts. All kinds of jeans, naturally, in all sorts of colours, escorted by the indispensable accessories: bandanas, thick socks, sunglasses and more.

Benetton
16th arr. - 82, av. Victor-Hugo 47 27 73 73
(also 1st arr., 3rd arr., 6th arr., 7th arr., 8th arr., 9th arr., 15th arr., 16tharr., 17th arr.)
Open 10:30 a.m.-7:30 p.m. Closed Sun.

Let's face it, what youngster would leave home without a Benetton sweater slung over his/her shoulders? Having grown far beyond their just-sweater beginnings, United Colors of Benetton is a worldwide success, and is unfortunately neglecting quality in favour of a lot of high-profile advertising. Great colours and co-ordinates unfortunately do not always pass the first test wash. For the price (and the colourful look), you may find it worthwhile.

Chevignon Girl
2nd arr. - 5, pl. des Victoires - 42 36 10 16
Open 10:15 a.m.-7 p.m. Closed Sun. & 2 wks. in Aug.

The spirit of the 1950s lives on, in the form of cotton dresses, jeans, heavy-canvas trousers, motorcycle jackets and all manner of accessories. Chevignon pioneered this casual look, which we would like a lot more without the overdose of insignias and labels vaunting the brand's name. Prices fluctuate between modest and prohibitive.

Chipie
1st arr. - 31, rue de la Ferronnerie 45 08 58 74
6th arr. - 49, rue Bonaparte - 43 29 21 94
Open 10 a.m.-1 p.m. & 2 p.m.-7 p.m. (Mon. from 11 a.m.). Closed Sun.

The brand's motto is: "Quality and fun since 1967." We can only assume that the *fun* comes from the label being pasted all over the front of the clothing, and the *quality* is in the cloth (which has a tough time surviving from one season to the next)... But who cares? This is carefully coded fashion for kids who want to look like all their friends. Prices are high; service is pushy.

Creeks
1st arr. - 98, rue Saint-Denis - 42 33 81 70
Open 10 a.m.-7 p.m. (Mon. 11 a.m.-7 p.m.). Closed Sun.

This Creeks shop in Les Halles was designed by (who else?) Philippe Starck. Marble, granite and chrome predominate, and the huge spaces are filled by blasting FM music. People buy what they recognise: old friends include the Chevignon, Liberto, Levi's, Paraboot and Bowen brands. Creeks aims essentially at the 15-to-25 age group, and prefers its customers slim.

Détails d'Hérald
1st arr. - 15, rue du Jour - 40 26 75 65
Open 10:30 a.m.-7:15 p.m. (Mon. noon-7:30 p.m.). Closed Sun.

Adèle and Patricia are two sisters who present an eclectic panorama of up-to-the-minute clothes ranging from streetwise to sedate. Young fashion fiends will love the colourful collection, and the "graffiti room" at the back of the shop.

Kenzo Enfants
1st arr. - 3, place des Victoires 40 39 72 87
Open 10 a.m.-7 p.m. (Mon. from 11 a.m.). Closed Sun., 2 wks. in Aug. & holidays.

Kenzo captures the younger set with his signature prints, vivid colours and splendid accessories, priced markedly lower than his first-tier line. The clothes are of good quality, and easily identified as "Kenzo".

Naf-Naf
17th arr. - 10, av. des Ternes - 42 67 30 30
Open 10 a.m.-7:30 p.m. Closed Sun.

The little pink pig, Naf-Naf's mascot, has a very bright and tidy new home here, filled to bursting point with relatively inexpensive, youthful clothes that mirror current trends. Amusing and cheerful prints cover leggings, T-shirts, bare little cotton dresses that look great on teenage girls; pretty too are the ribbed-silk T-shirts and lively skirts and sweaters. Boys will love the baggy casual trousers and flashy print shirts. Kids willingly whip out their wallets and spend weeks' worth of pocket money on the huge range of Naf-Naf accessories.

New Man
6th arr. - 12, rue de l'Ancienne-Comédie
43 54 44 95
Open 10 a.m.-7:30 p.m. Closed Sun.

Not just for men. These two stores have recently been redecorated and, by offering extra-large men's sizes, are attracting a new clientele. Casual clothes with considerable cachet are crafted in denim, gabardine and cotton or *cupro*, an attractive new fibre blend.

SHOES

Free Lance
6th arr. - 30, rue du Four - 45 48 14 78
Open 10:15 a.m.-7 p.m. Closed Sun.

Rusted metal seems to be the dominant note in the décor, but never mind. Free Lance has the footwear that teenagers want: lace-ups with rubber or "tyre" soles, post-punk wedgies, 1950s patent leathers, pretty ballet slippers, hobnail boots and leather sandals. They may not be the most comfortable of shoes, but that's not what's important here.

Gelati
6th arr. - 5, rue de Sèvres - 42 22 68 08
Open 10 a.m.-7 p.m. Closed Sun. (Mon., Wed., Thurs. 1 p.m.-2 p.m.).

This is Italian fashion at its most fun and inventive. Prices are reasonable (from 400 francs) for some brash, vividly-coloured shoes with square toes and small heels. Shoes that are destined to be worn with absolute intensity will probably last for just one season.

Marie Lalet

4th arr. - 16, rue du Bourg-Tibourg - 40 27 08 05
Open 11 a.m.-7 p.m. Closed Sun. & Mon. & 2 wks in Aug.

Essentially a boutique for heavy-duty footwear by Doc Martens, this shop also presents some 45 other models (for men, women and children) that offer just about anything you could wish for in the way of colour and style. Many different leathers too (aged, oiled, patent, suede...).

■ TOYS

Ali Baba

7th arr. - 29, av. de Tourville - 45 55 10 85
Open 10 a.m.-1 p.m. & 2 p.m.-7 p.m. Closed Sun. & holidays.

Ali Baba has three floors of quality games and toys for children of all ages. The basement level is a kingdom of scale models and electric trains. The ground floor is devoted to card and board games. Do not miss the superb collection of hand-painted tin soldiers.

Jouets & Cie

1st arr. - 11, bd de Sébastopol - 42 33 67 67
Open 10:30 a.m.-7:30 p.m. Closed Sun.

The gigantic gold baby doll that serves as this company's mascot is rather alarming. He presides over a vast emporium of games, scale models, toys, puzzles, costumes and, yes, dolls that sell for ten to 20 per cent less than in traditional toy shops or department stores. The latest electronic games and cassettes are here, as well as outdoor games, craft sets, robots and baby toys. Shopping baskets are a welcome convenience; sales are held throughout the year.

Don't plan to shop on Sundays, the vast majority of Paris stores are closed.

Multicubes

4th arr. - 5, rue de Rivoli - 42 77 10 77
Open 10 a.m.-7 p.m. (Mon. from 2 p.m.). Closed Sun., 2 1st wks. of Aug. & holidays.
15th arr. - 110, rue Cambronne - 47 34 25 97
Open 10:30 a.m.-2 p.m. & 2:30 p.m.-7 p.m. Closed Sun., Mon. & July 20-Aug. 20 & holidays.

Every year sees a new collection from Erzgebirge, the land of wooden-toy makers. Some of the toys are pure marvels and quite expensive, coveted by the old and young alike. There are mobiles, yoyos, model farms and animals, as well as dolls with real hair made by Käthe Kruse (a Bauhaus disciple); prices start at 1,200 francs. There are also lots of wooden Christmas decorations from Germany and Scandinavia.

Au Nain Bleu

8th arr. - 406-410, rue Saint-Honoré - 42 60 39 01
Open 9:45 a.m.-6:30 p.m. Closed Sun.

Don't be put off by the 32,000-franc price tag on the miniature Bugatti in the window. This illustrious shop does have other wonderful and less expensive toys to tempt you. On the lower level live old friends like Mickey Mouse and Babar, and you can hitch a ride on some fine rocking horses, some of which boast real leather trappings. There's a great variety of enchanting dolls and dolls' clothes (accessory kits start at 500 francs), plastic and china tea services, lots of remote-control cars and motorcycles and a costume and make-up section. Miniature French grocery shops start at 700 francs; stuffed animals in every size and shape cost from 250 to 3,500 francs. Many of the toys sold here are exclusive models which you won't find elsewhere.

L'Oiseau de Paradis

7th arr. - 211, bd Saint-Germain - 45 48 97 90
Open 9:30 a.m.-7 p.m. Closed Sun.

This is the traditional toy shop *par excellence*, chock-a-block from floor to ceiling. Tricycles, rocking toys and scooters hang from the rafters, and we're always greeted with a smile. Apart from the standard variety of toys, there are some fine tin soldiers, handmade wooden puzzles and a collection series of miniature cars. Electronic games are now in stock as well—a sign of the times.

Pain d'Epice

9th arr. - 29, passage Jouffroy - 47 70 82 65
Open 10 a.m.-7 p.m. (Mon. from 12:30 p.m.). Closed Sun.

Tucked away in the lovely passage Jouffroy, just opposite the Musée Grevin (see below) this shop is surely one of the most delightful in town. Reproductions of old-fashioned toys—tops, hoops, gyroscopes, puppets, pretty cut-outs and the like—make charming gifts for good little children.

La Pelucherie

6th arr. - 74, rue de Seine - 46 33 60 21
Open 10:30 a.m.-7:30 p.m. Closed Sun.
8th arr. - 84, av. des Champs-Elysées - 43 59 49 05
Open 10 a.m.-midnight (Sun. & holidays 11:30 a.m.-7:30 p.m.).

A boon for night owls, this stuffed-animal kingdom of soft toys stays open until midnight. You'll find everything here from the tiniest teddy bear to a gargantuan elephant in every colour of the rainbow. Dogs of every breed, raccoons, bees, Bambis and Dumbos (alongside the other Disney characters) coexist in exemplary harmony here. There's also a baby clothes section. La Pelucherie delivers

SHOPS – CHILDREN

within Paris and all over the world.

Si Tu Veux
2nd arr. - 68, Général-Vivienne
42 60 59 97
Open 11 a.m.-7 p.m. Closed Sun. Mail-order sale catalogue.

Nestled cosily in the heart of this lovely gallery is a goldmine for children's parties. Games and toys are attractive and reasonably priced. There are wooden blocks, washable dolls, a great choice of marbles and a panoply of appealing, educational playthings. For children's birthdays and party occasions, there are ready-to-wear as well as ready-to-make costumes (from 150 francs for a kit), easily removable play make-up, hats, magic wands and party kits for 200 francs. Right next door is a space reserved for nostalgic grown-ups. Remember those teddy bears stuffed with straw that you loved as a child (185 francs for the smallest)? Well, you can buy one here as well as painted tin toys, little china services and charming Victorian paper dolls.

■ WHERE TO TAKE THE KIDS

MUSEUMS

The following is a list of museums of special interest to children.

Centre Georges-Pompidou
4th arr. - 120, rue Saint-Martin, entrance pl. Georges-Pompidou ou "Piazza Beaubourg" - 44 78 49 17
Open 2 p.m.-6 p.m. Closed Tues. & holidays.

This Parisian cultural centre hosts a children's workshop with facilities for theatre, dance, video and film shows. Children are usually delighted by the pop-art fountain by Nikki de Saint-Phalle outside the Centre.

Cité des Sciences et de l'Industrie
19th arr. - 30, av. Corentin-Cariou - 40 05 70 00
Open 10 a.m.-6 p.m. Closed Mon.

The Cité des Sciences may make your head spin, but, curiously, we don't notice this happening with children. They delight in the "Géode," a kind of geodesic dome that houses a huge panoramic cinema screen, the Planetarium and the Inventorium. There are also any number of video games for hands-on play. It's a user-friendly spot where a child would find it hard to get bored.

For more details on museums in Paris, consult the *Arts & Leisure* chapter.

Musée de l'Armée
7th arr. - Hôtel des Invalides - 45 55 37 70
Open 10 a.m.-6 p.m. (Oct. 1-March 31 until 5 p.m.). Admission: 30 F, reduced rate: 20 F, children under 7: Free.

This military museum displays arms, uniforms and scale models of famous battle scenes, and screens films of World Wars I and II.

Musée National des Arts d'Afrique et d'Océanie
12th arr. - 293, av. Daumesnil 44 74 84 80
Open 10 a.m.-noon & 1:30 p.m.-5:30 p.m. (Sat. & Sun. until 6 p.m.). Closed Tues.

This museum located on the edge of the Bois de Vincennes (which also has a zoo) features the largest aquarium in Paris. Children adore the crocodile pit.

Musée Grévin
9th arr. - 10, bd Montmartre - 42 46 13 26
Open daily 1 p.m.-7 p.m.

Founded in 1882, this waxworks features historical figures and distorting mirrors to amuse those of all ages.

Musée de la Marine
16th arr. - Palais de Chaillot, pl. du Trocadéro
45 53 31 70
Open 10 a.m.-6 p.m. Closed Tues.

Exhibits and scale models on naval history and marine archaeology are favourites with older children at the Musée de la Marine. The museum also displays maritime art and artefacts of the technical, historical and scientific development of navigation.

Palais de la Découverte
8th arr. - av. Franklin Roosevelt 40 74 80 00
Open 9:30 a.m.-6 p.m. (Sun. 10 a.m.-7 p.m.). Closed Mon., Jan. 1, May 1, July 14, Aug. 15 & Dec. 25. Restaurant.

This museum is an excellent place for children interested in science. Experiments are conducted by staff members every afternoon for the public. A list of daily activities is posted to the left of the museum's entrance.

Muséum National d'Histoire Naturelle
5th arr. - 57, rue Cuvier - 40 79 30 00
Open 10 a.m.-5 p.m. (Sat. & Sun. 11 a.m.-6 p.m.). Closed Tues. & holidays.

Located within the Jardin des Plantes (home to a zoo), this museum houses fascinating exhibits on palaeontology, palaeobotany and mineralogy. Of more interest to older children.

Rock'n'Roll Hall of Fame
1st arr. - Forum des Halles, Porte du Louvre
40 28 08 13
Open daily 10:30 a.m.-6:30 p.m.

When it's raining and the kids can't stand the thought of another museum, try taking them here. The history of rock, from Elvis to Madonna, is illustrated by wax models, animated scenes, all-around sound and lots of special effects. Good fun.

■ PARKS & GARDENS

Here are some city parks with particular appeal for children.

Bois de Boulogne
16th arr.
Entrances are located at the Porte Maillot, Porte Dauphine and Les Sablons. This enormous wooded park, which covers part of the 16th arrondissement and the suburb of Neuilly, features a lake, horse-riding clubs, a lovely children's park and zoo (Jardin d'Acclimatation), a marvellous floral garden (Parc de Bagatelle) and numerous paths that wind through trees and lawns. Bicycles for adults and children are available for hire.

Jardin du Luxembourg
6th arr. - Main entrance: bd Saint- Michel, near place Edmond- Rostand - 40 79 37 00
Open daily dawn-dusk.
Within these attractive gardens, situated between Saint-Michel and Montparnasse, there are pony rides, a puppet theatre, sandpits, jungle gyms and a small children's park for toddlers up to five.

Jardin des Plantes
5th arr. - Main entrance: 57, rue Cuvier - 40 79 30 00
Open daily dawn-dusk.
The Botanical Gardens (Jardin des Plantes) contain more than 10,000 classified plants. There is also a Winter Garden (Jardin d'Hiver), with many tropical plants, and an Alpine Garden (Jardin Alpin), which includes mountain- and polar-region plants. The open-air zoo is a big hit with youngsters.

> For further details about parks and gardens in Paris, as well as information on swimming pools and other sports, see the *Arts & Leisure* chapter.

Parc de la Villette
19th arr. - Main entrance: av. Jean-Jaurès, near Porte de Pantin - 42 40 76 10
Hours vary, call for information.
Lots and lots of space, with seven theme gardens, broad lawns and a fantastic sliding board. Kids can unwind here after an educational tour of the Cité des Sciences.

Parc Floral
12th arr. - Esplanade du Château de Vincennes, Rond-Point de la Pyramide - 43 74 60 49
Open Nov.-Feb. 9:30 a.m.-5 p.m.; March & Oct. until 6 p.m.; April-Sept. until 8 p.m. Entrance: 10 F; 6-10: 5 F; 0-6, 65 & over: Free.
A small fee admits kids to a playground full of delightful things to do. Amusement park rides cost another five francs a go, and the miniature golf course (dotted with reproductions of famous Parisian landmarks) commands an extra fee of 25 francs.

CLOTHES FOR HIM & HER

Agnès B.
1st arr. - 2-3-6-8, rue du Jour - 42 33 04 13
6th arr. - 13, rue Michelet - 40 51 70 69
16th arr. - 17, av. Pierre Ier de Serbie (Women) - 47 23 36 69
16th arr. - 25, av. Pierre Ier de Serbie (Men) - 40 70 06 98
Open 10 a.m.-7 p.m. Closed Sun.
Above all, Agnès B. designs an ageless collection of

Bonjour Mickey!

All the familiar Disney characters have a European headquarters now: *Euro Disneyland* opened its doors in April, 1992. Situated some 20 miles east of Paris, accessible by car or by public transport (the RER), the park is an easy day trip from the capital. It is also a mighty expensive one. A one-day admission to the park costs upwards of 200 francs (140 francs for children aged 11 and under). Even the simplest meals (pizza, hotdogs, hamburgers and the like) add up quickly to 75 or 100 francs per person. Note too that visitors are not permitted to bring in any food from outside (the guards will even confiscate your leftover "baguette"). If you plan to buy a souvenir or two—and what kid will be willing to leave without one?— you should plan on spending a minimum of about a fiver. Please turn to Marne-la-Vallée in the "Suburbs" chapter, p. 86 for restaurants and p. 127 for hotels.

SHOPS – CLOTHES FOR HIM & HER

fashionable clothing that virtually anyone can live with. In fact, if these casual classics didn't wear out so quickly, you could keep them in your wardrobe for decades! Agnès B. presents comfortable, easy styles for the entire family at relatively affordable prices: jogging outfits, sweatshirts and sweaters for a sporty look, lots of stripes and, for more dressy occasions, garments in silk, linen and leather.

Anvers
7th arr. - 7-16, rue du Pré-aux-Clercs - 42 86 84 40
Open 10:30 a.m.-7 p.m. Closed Sun.

In recent years the rue du Pré-aux-Clercs has become one of the most fashionable stretches of street in Paris. The Belgian city of Anvers (Antwerp to us) is the home of this young design firm's guiding spirits, Martine Hillen and Anne Kegels. Their two beautiful boutiques present clothes for women (at number 7) and men (number 16) crafted in fine natural fabrics—wool, cotton, linen, silk. Muted shades like beige, silvery green, sand, rust or chocolate are used for their collection of stretchy dresses (500 francs), fluid dresses (850 to 1,650 francs), trousers (745 to 1,000 francs) and nicely cut men's suits (2,900 francs).

APC
6th arr. - 4, rue de Fleurus - 42 22 12 75 (Women)
6th arr. - 7, rue de Fleurus - 45 49 19 45 (Men)
Open 10:30 a.m.-7 p.m. Closed Sun.

APC stands for *Atelier de Production et Création*, a label dreamed up by the creative Jean Touitou. Understated elegance is the key to his fashion vision: for women, slimline trousers, simple but beautifully crafted blouses, alluringly feminine suits; for men, tasteful sweaters (not so easy to find these days) and casual trousers in oiled canvas—very rugged and masculine.

Armani
8th arr. - 6, pl. Vendôme - 42 61 55 09
Open 10 a.m.-7 p.m. Closed Sun.

Armani's Parisian outpost is a cathedral of mirrors, furnished with cubical seating crafted from glowing wood: a cross between an Egyptian mausoleum and a hall of mirrors—and just as disorienting! Armani has a couple of thousand stores worldwide, and hundreds of thousands of faithful customers: it's a marketing miracle, because the price of a typical off-the-peg Armani suit is about the same as a ticket on Concorde from Paris to New York! But do go in for a look (the sales staff may not seem glad to see you, but never mind them), and bring plenty of money in case you find something irresistible. If you can't bear to leave the shop empty-handed, there's always the Armani cologne; it's far more reasonably priced than the clothes. A few Left Bank boutiques now offer a selection of the Emporio Armani line.

Arnys
7th arr. - 14, rue de Sèvres - 45 48 76 99
Open 10 a.m.-7:30 p.m. (Mon. 10 a.m.-1 p.m. & 4 p.m.-7 p.m.). Closed Sun.

There are always lots of window-shoppers in front of Arny's boutique, admiring the beautifully co-ordinated ready-to-wear on display. Inside, you'll find a huge selection of three-ply cashmere sweaters in some 20 different shades, an equally vast array of men's sports jackets (3,400 to 5,000 francs), silk (1,200 francs) and cotton (800 francs) shirts, as well as a dizzying collection of limited-edition ties. Upstairs in the tailoring department, women can choose from a number of models of chic suits which can be made to measure.

Barbara Bui
1st arr. - 23, rue Etienne Marcel 40 26 43 65
Open 10:30 a.m.-7 p.m. Closed Sun.

For women, designer Barbara Bui blends European style and Oriental silhouettes, using delicate, fragile fabrics (silk, velvet, airy organza). Check out her beautiful skin-coloured blouses. The shop's basement level is reserved for the menswear collection (look for cool wools, heavy cottons and linen), remarkable for its bold designs.

Cerruti 1881
8th arr. - 27, rue Royale - 42 61 11 12
Open 10 a.m.-7 p.m. Closed Sun.

Nino Cerruti runs this family business, which was established in 1881. His self-appointed role is to keep alive the tradition of the Italian suit—as classy as a Ferrari, with its unusual colour combinations and the use of top-quality fabrics: silk, linen or soft wools. A few years back, Cerruti launched a collection for women of rather austere but elegant "executive" clothing. There are also lingerie and sportswear lines for both men and women.

Charvet
1st arr. - 28, pl. Vendôme - 42 60 30 70
Open 9:45 a.m.-6:45 p.m. Closed Sun.

Charvet is an institution. It has been serving the same clientele from generation to generation. Clients' measurements are kept for decades, so the faithful can order their shirts and whatnot by telephone and have them delivered. Whether you're in search of 20 fine Egyptian cotton shirts or a simple pair of cuff links, the welcome and

CLOTHES FOR HIM & HER – SHOPS

deference extended to you will be the same. The women's styles are classic, not to say severe (suits, blouses and blazers). Another classic is the paisley silk dressing gown, a gift for men that women love to wear. Prices are steep.

L'Eclaireur
4th arr. - 3 ter, rue des Rosiers
48 87 10 22
Open 11 a.m.-7 p.m. (Mon. 2 p.m.-7 p.m.). Closed Sun.

For women: Dolce & Gabbana, Moschino Couture, Helmut Lang, Martine Sitbon, Ann Demeulemeester, Martin Margiela, John Galliano—all the hot, hip clothes you want right *now*. For men: Paul Smith, Juliano Fujiwara, Dries van Noten, Momento Due—gear with a definite downtown attitude. To create the proper environment in which to wear these clothes, L'Eclaireur's owners Armand and Martine Hadida present furniture and trendy trinkets by Borek Sipek, Hilton McConnico, André Dubreuil and Fornasetti (whose eerie designs are now furiously fashionable).

Jean-Paul Gaultier
2nd arr. - 6, rue Vivienne - 42 86 05 05
Open 10 a.m.-7 p.m. (Sat. 11 a.m.-7 p.m.). Closed Sun.

The welcome is astonishingly courteous, the clothes are pressed together in glass wardrobes, accessories gleam... there is electricity in the air. The salespeople know what they're talking about. Clothes are beautifully cut and yet extremely provocative: rubber sweaters, tight-knit T-shirts, shoes with astrakhan trimmings; it's an inimitable mix of materials, styles and looks. The Junior Gaultier line is a boon for Jean-Paul's younger fans on smaller budgets. The bronze-green decor with video screens built into the floor is whimsical and fun. (A new Gaultier palace is scheduled to open soon near the Bastille... Watch this space).

Marithée et François Girbaud–Halles Capone
1st arr. - 38, rue Etienne Marcel
42 33 54 69
Open 10 a.m.-7 p.m. (Mon. 11 a.m.-7 p.m.). Closed Sun.

This Mecca for many a fashion pilgrim is a huge, three-level high-tech commercial space, crammed with the famous Girbaud jeans (including the Métamorphojean line), the dressier (and pricier) Sport City collection for men and women, Maillaparty knitwear and leather gear that has all the girls saving up their baby-sitting money.

Hémisphères
17th arr. - 22, av. de la Grande Armée - 42 67 61 86
Open 10:30 a.m.-7 p.m. Closed Sun.

If you want to look like all those chic French people who wander round the Luxembourg Gardens on Sundays in their smart casual clothes, nip over to this sophisticated shop near the Etoile. Then (if you are willing to pay the price) you too can clothe yourself in top-quality cashmere, the softest corduroy shirts, chic duffle coats, parkas and more, all manufactured or selected by Hémisphères.

Kenzo
1st arr. - 3, pl. des Victoires - 40 39 72 03
7th arr. - 16, bd Raspail - 42 22 09 38
Open 10 a.m.-7 p.m. (Mon. 11 a.m.-7 p.m.). Closed Sun.

Kenzo was the first of the Japanese designers in Paris. Now he's everywhere. He designs for the whole family, has a collection of bed and bathroom linens and accessories such as watches and spectacles. He's also jumped into sportswear. Vivid colours, soft shapes, ethnic prints and billowing shirts remain his trademark. N.B.: the twice-a-year sales in January and July lower prices by as much as 50 per cent.

Michel Léger
2nd arr. - 22, pl. du Marché Saint-Honoré - 42 60 47 90
Open 10 a.m.-7 p.m. Closed Sun.

Michel Léger's talents surface equally in his designs for men and women. His supple, simple, refined clothing is made in quality materials: thick cottons lined with alpaca for coats, a wool-silk mix for suits, and viscose for knitwear. His signature style is elegant and urban. You won't find anything sporty here. The service and the welcome, like the well-lit boutique, is warm.

Magic Circle Espace Mode
11th arr. - 9, bd Richard Lenoir
40 21 01 07
Open 10 a.m.-8 p.m. (Sun. 2 p.m.-6 p.m.). Closed Mon.

An immense hangar with cold, grey stone floors, cement pillars, 70s-style orange light fixtures and graffiti on the walls is home to a host of hot designers: Etienne Brunel, Helmut Lang, Dolce & Gabbana and Philippe Model. Men and women will find the latest fashion trends, including clothes by English designer Helen Storey and Gossip (terrific biker-style leather gear).

Mettez
8th arr. - 12, bd Malesherbes
42 65 33 76
Open 10 a.m.-7 p.m. Closed Sun.

This venerable establishment has a faithful clientele, most of whom come from the world of politics or the theatre. Since 1947 Mettez have consistently found buyers for their linen hunting and hacking jacket (3,500 francs), as well as Austrian jackets by

SHOPS – CLOTHES FOR HIM & HER

Confidential Cinema

Want to see a forgotten or rare film from New York, New Delhi or New South Wales? Join the fans who haunt a host of tiny art cinemas in the area bounded by the quai Saint-Michel, boulevard Saint-Michel, rue Saint-Jacques and rue Soufflot. These cinemas often feature avant-garde and foreign films in their original languages. Action Christine in the rue Christine is devoted mainly to Hollywood classics. The projectionist takes special pride in his work, and you can ask when buying your tickets whether the copy is of good quality. Also worth a visit: Cinoche in the rue de Condé, Saint André des Arts, in the street of the same name, and Les 3 Luxembourg, rue Monsieur-le-Prince.

Giesweisen or Staff. Knickerbockers (from 575 francs), capes and corduroy trousers abound, as do Gloverall duffle coats (1,600 francs).

Missoni
7th arr. - 43, rue du Bac - 45 48 38 02
Open 10 a.m.-7 p.m. Closed Sun.

This conservative yet sumptuously crafted collection of fashion is aimed primarily at people who love contrasting colours, changing textures, novel shapes, mossy mohair and (for summer) glazed linen.

Claude Montana
1st arr. - 3, rue des Petits-Champs - 40 20 02 14
Open 10:15 a.m.-1 p.m. & 2 p.m.-7 p.m. Closed Sun.

Claude Montana cultivates an ambiguous look—his style is fierce and uncompromising; he goes in for stark, geometrical silhouettes with loads of accessories (metal belts, zips everywhere). Double knits, quilted cottons, wide belts and bright colours remain the trademark of the Montana style. The leather clothing for men and women is of the highest quality, and superbly designed. Montana boutiques are uncomfortably bare, but attendants are courteous—a detail worth mentioning because it is increasingly rare these days.

Thierry Mugler
8th arr. - 49, av. Montaigne - 47 23 37 62
Open 10 a.m.-7 p.m. Closed Sun.

Thierry Mugler's new premises, done up by Andrée Putman in blinding blue, look a bit like something from outer space. A master of such materials as whipcord, jersey, piqué and gabardine, he goes in for strict lines with no frills. His high-tech designs are for glamorous women and exuberant men; colours are generally muted but can sometimes flare into electric blue, tobacco brown or even pine-green. Prices, too, are fiery—but just consider your purchase as an investment; the Mugler style is already beyond fashion.

Old England
9th arr. - 12, bd des Capucines 47 42 81 99
Open 9:30 a.m.-6:30 p.m. (Mon. 9:30 a.m.-12:30 a.m. & 2 p.m.-6:30 p.m.). Closed Sun.

This 100 per cent French firm, founded in 1867, embodies English elegance with blazers, jackets, suits, raincoats, sweaters and myriad accessories from Britain—at French prices. Should your Chester Barrie suit need alterations, the advice of the in-house tailors is invaluable.

Sonia Rykiel
1st arr. - 70, rue du Faubourg-Saint-Honoré
42 65 20 81
6th arr. - 175, bd Saint Germain
49 54 60 60
Open 10 a.m.-7 p.m. Closed Sun.

Sonia Rykiel's flamboyant red fringe hides a piercing look. This pioneer-cum-diva of fashion recently moved to roomier premises on the boulevard Saint-Germain, bringing with her the soft silhouettes, knits, wide trousers, sombre colours (often shot through with gold) and striped jerseys. The men's shop has been transferred too, and is now just across the street. Inscription Rykiel, the second-tier line, remains on the rue de Grenelle.

Scapa of Scotland
16th arr. - 38, av. Victor Hugo 45 00 31 31
Open 10 a.m.-6:45 p.m. (Mon. 1 p.m.-6:45 p.m.). Closed Sun.

Brian Redding designs these pleasingly classic collections brightening them with a touch of pastel or a colourful ribbon. The chic and attractive sportswear on offer includes long and short duffle coats, gorgeous Irish sweaters, pure wool blazers and coats. Helpful but unobtrusive service.

Ventilo
2nd arr. - 27 bis, rue du Louvre 42 33 18 67
Open 10:30 a.m.-7 p.m. (Mon. 2 p.m.-7 p.m.). Closed Sun.

Earth and wood tones dominate both the shop and the clothing on display. The lower level is reserved for the menfolk, the main and first floors for women. Lots of cotton shirts and jeans are on offer for both sexes. On the top floor, decorative objects for the home share space with a pleasant tea room, bathed in restful light.

Gianni Versace
8th arr. - 62, rue du Faubourg Saint Honoré - 47 42 88 02
Open 10 a.m.-7 p.m. Closed Sun.

Versace's newest shop in Paris was designed by Pizzi (who creates the marvellous stage sets at La Scala opera house in Milan). This wildly extravagant decor is reason enough to wander over for a look, even if you don't want to pay 11,000 francs for a sequin-spangled mini or 1,100 for Versace jeans. If you do, well then walk upstairs for the women's wear, downstairs for the Versace tots collection; men's clothing is displayed on the main level.

Yohji Yamamoto
1st arr. - 25, rue du Louvre - 42 21 42 93 (Women)
1st arr. - 47, rue Etienne Marcel 45 08 82 45 (Men)
Open 10:30 a.m-7 p.m. (Mon. 11:30 a.m.-7 p.m.). Closed Sun.

"Minimalism forever" is Yamamoto's enduring credo. His faith is justified by the pure lines of his gabardine jackets and the flawless form of his classic white shirt. This year, look also for blood-red mohair sweaters, skinny-ribbed extra-long rollnecks, and even a few leopard prints.

■ AND ALSO . . .

Aquascutum
1st arr. - 10, rue de Castiglione 42 60 09 40
Open 10 a.m.-7 p.m. Closed Sun.

Since 1850, quality and comfort: suits, sweaters and the famous Kingsway trench.

Burberrys
6th arr. - 55, rue de Rennes - 45 48 52 71
8th arr. - 8-10, bd Malesherbes 42 66 13 01
16th arr. - 56, rue de Passy - 42 88 88 24
Open 10 a.m.-7 p.m. Closed Sun.

Great trench coats, rain hats, cashmere scarves and sweaters; unbearable sales assistants.

Delaunay
1st arr. - 6, rue de l'Oratoire - 42 60 20 85
Open 10 a.m.-12:30 a.m. & 2 p.m.-6 p.m. Closed Sun. & Mon.

Beautiful handmade casuals and boots will cost up to 10,000 francs and require a two-month wait.

Ralph Lauren
8th arr. - 2, pl. de la Madeleine 44 77 53 00
Open 10 a.m.-7 p.m. Closed Sun.

For a look at what one of America's top designers has on offer, stop for a browse round the authentic, country-style clothes in Ralph Lauren's Paris boutique. But if several items take your fancy, you'll probably save the air fare by hopping on a plane to New York to make your purchases. Excellent window displays.

DEPARTMENT STORES

BHV
4th arr. - 52-64, rue de Rivoli - 42 74 90 00
Open 9 a.m.-7 p.m. (Wed. until 10 p.m.). Closed Sun.

From foreign visitors in search of adapters for their electrical appliances to do-it-yourselfers in need of a handful of nails, everyone in Paris ends up in the BHV basement, a treasure trove of tools, hardware and home-improvement items. Whether it's a brass washer or a gold-plated tap you need, seek it here and you're sure to find. What's more, you can count on competent advice from the sales staff on how to use or instal your purchases. Artists and sculptors also appreciate the BHV's first floor, which is stocked with canvases, easels, brushes and clay at unbeatable prices. Features and services include: in-house specialists to instal goods and materials, from wallpaper to floor tiles to convertible car roofs and more; wedding list service with complimentary "house kit" and a five per cent discount on anything the couple buys in the store during their first year of wedded bliss; an engraving service for adorning china and glass with initials or the family coat of arms; repairs of all sorts, done on the premises (you can have your pearls restrung or your fishing reel adjusted) purchases totalling over 1,000 francs delivered free of charge.

Le Bon Marché
7th arr. - 38, rue de Sèvres - 44 39 80 00
Open 9:30 a.m.-6:30 p.m. (Sat. until 7 p.m.). Grocery store 8:30 a.m.-9 p.m., Fri. until 10 p.m. - 44 39 81 00. Closed Sun.

The good old Bon Marché is cultivating its chic new look with sharper advertising and a greater emphasis on fashion, home décor and gastronomy. This full-service store has vastly improved its clothing departments (take a look at the new first-floor women's shop), and holds frequent sales that are not to be missed. Top features (in addition to unusually courteous staff) include an eye-catching collection of expertly chosen Oriental carpets (store number 1, third floor), and the largest gourmet grocery shop in Paris, which is open every day except Sunday until 9 p.m. La Grande Epicerie stocks 150 types of tea, 240 kinds of cheese and over 200 different products "imported" from Fauchon. Discover the "daily menu" service (they deliver) and tasty health foods from La Vie Claire. A huge and enticing choice of wines is overseen by bistro-owner and winegrower Jacques Mélac. The grocery prices are competitive; in fact, Le Bon Marché promises to pay you the difference if you find a better deal in another Parisian supermarket. The store also provides a convenient in-house travel agency, a ticket agency and a bank. Other services include custom-tailored clothing for men; fur storage and restoration, and Oriental-carpet restoration. And, of course, you can leave your wedding list here, as well as birth and baptism lists.

Les Galeries Lafayette
9th arr. - 40, bd Haussmann - 42 82 34 56
Open 9:30 a.m.-6:45 p.m. Closed Sun.

On an average day, 100,000 women between the ages of 20 and 40 stroll through Les Galeries. What draws them is an enormous selection—three full floors—of clothing and accessories, ranging from such avant-garde designers as Jean-Paul Gaultier, Yohji Yamamoto and Azzedine Alaïa, to the classics, Cacharel, Dior and Guy Laroche. The store labels (hip "Avant-Première," "Briefing" career clothes and feminine casual clothes signed "Jodhpur") offer high fashion at attractive prices. The "Mode Plus" service offers free fashion advice on putting together a look that fits a woman's personality and lifestyle. There's also a comprehensive tableware and kitchen department on the basement level—a paradise for anyone who loves cooking and entertaining. Three restaurants offer a wide selection of refreshments for weary shoppers and there is a Jean-Marc Maniatis beauty salon. A separate building houses the men's store (the Galfa Club), and a smart new food emporium, Lafayette Gourmet. Modelled on Harrod's Food Hall, Lafayette Gourmet bulges with goodies from all over the world. More than just a supermarket (catfood and oven-cleaner share shelf space with high-priced edibles), it is a gastro-playground, with a multitude of stands for snacking and sampling: Petrossian's for caviar and smoked salmon, Lenôtre for pastries and takeaway, there's a Champagne bar, an oyster bar, a salad bar and a "Steak Point" serving Angus beef.

Marks & Spencer
9th arr. - 35, bd Haussmann - 47 42 42 91
Open 9:30 a.m.-7 p.m. (Tues. 10 a.m.-7 p.m.). Closed Sun.

Ever faithful to its mission, this Paris branch brings a touch of British cosiness to the French capital. The store is always busy, particularly at back-to-school time (the children's clothing is sturdy and adorable; older children like the lambswool and cashmere sweaters, the tartan kilts and Oxford shirts) and at Christmas (for the traditional holiday foods, decorations and gifts). Among the features and services are all the requirements for an authentic English tea: tea, of course (loose and in teabags), biscuits, marmalades, scones, crumpets, muffins and so on. Delicious, reasonably priced packaged smoked salmon is available whole, in slices or marinated with dill. The drinks section includes a range of single-malt whiskies, several types of sherry and good English beer. The women's clothing is solid, with skirts available in three lengths and in large sizes. Men's jackets (excellent quality Harris tweed) come in three sleeve-lengths; no alterations are done in the store.

Monoprix
9th arr. - 97, rue du Provence 48 74 37 13
(also: 2nd, 3rd, 4th, 5th, 6th, 8th, 9th, 10th, 11th, 12th, 13th, 15th, 17th, 18th, 19th)
Open 9 a.m.-8 p.m. Closed Sun.

"The basics are what we do best." That's the Monoprix motto. A big factor in the stores' success is their strategic locations in the busiest parts of the capital. Monoprix has its own-label clothing and toiletries of good quality at rock-bottom prices. Lately, successful efforts have been made to give added fashion oomph to the ready-to-wear, with lines designed by young stylists. In another popular move, Monoprix regularly puts so-called luxury goods (caviar at Christmas, for example, or cashmere sweaters in autumn) within reach of the average consumer. The supermarket selection is constantly growing, with heat-and-serve dishes, catering services (at some stores) and the excellent Monoprix Gourmet line, which includes coffee, pasta, vacuum-packed ready-cooked entrées, low-calorie products and a new line of quick-cooking dishes.

Printemps
9th arr. - 64, bd Haussmann - 42 82 50 00
13th arr. - 30, av. d'Italie, centre commercial Galaxie
40 78 17 17
20th arr. - 25, cours de Vincennes - 43 71 12 41
Open 9:35 a.m.-7 p.m. Closed Sun.

Printemps cultivates an image of quintessentially Parisian chic and elegance. The store targets a slightly less youthful clientele than its neighbour, Galeries Lafayette. The ideal Printemps customer is a woman of style and taste who appreciates refinement in both her dress and her surroundings. Top-of-the-line women's fashions are presented on the fourth floor in the Rue de la Mode shop; a wide and appealing array of menswear is found in the Brummel shop, a separate annexe that carries everything from underwear to cashmere overcoats. Features and services: the Boutique Blanche is the top wedding list service in France; Le Printemps de la Maison is an entire store (eight floors) devoted to home décor and household goods, its private "Primavera" collection ranges from attractive handcrafted gift items to furniture designed by the likes of Andrée Putman and Philippe Starck. The ground floor was recently revamped in lavish style (marble and crystal everywhere) to create Le Printemps de la Beauté, a showcase for perfumes, cosmetics and other beauty products by top manufacturers. The free fashion-consultation service shows customers how to put together a stylish, individualised wardrobe. Following a marathon shopping session, it's a pleasure to relax in the Brasserie Flo set up under the gorgeous stained-glass dome (Flo also runs Le Printemps' two cafés, and there is a Flo Prestige take-away shop on the premises as well).

Prisunic
8th arr. - 109, rue de la Boétie
42 25 27 46
Open 9:45 a.m.-midnight. Closed Sun.
(also: 2nd, 11th, 12th, 13th, 15th, 16th, 17th, 18th, 19th, 20th.)
Open 9 a.m.-8 p.m. or 8:30 p.m. depending on stores. Closed Sun.

Never content to rest on its marketing laurels, Prisunic has practised the art of creative retailing ever since it opened for business some 50 years ago. The newly renovated branch on the Champs Elysées is now open until 10 p.m. (midnight in summer). Every week, its inventive merchandising team comes up with a new theme or sales promotion to spark shoppers' enthusiasm. Features include: clever, colourful household goods at affordable prices—dishes, linens, lamps and gadgets; a grocery section that offers fresh, fine-quality produce every day (Forza is the house brand of tinned and packaged goods); a wide range of make-up and toiletries; and sturdy, adorable children's clothing, all at excellent prices.

La Samaritaine
1st arr. - 19, rue de la Monnaie
40 41 20 20
Open 9:30 a.m.-7 p.m. (Wed. until 10 p.m.). Closed Sun.

There's a revolution going on at La Samaritaine. Having cast off its image as a jumble of miscellaneous merchandise, the city's biggest bazaar, the four-store complex known as the "Samar" has entered the era of specialisation. Every department has been overhauled, modernised and streamlined. To top it all, the interior has been spruced up and polished to its original brilliance: the etched glass, steel beams, lacquered ceramic tiles and exuberant floral motifs haven't looked so good since opening day. Among the store's features is one of the finest views of Paris, enjoyed (from April to October) from the Samaritaine's rooftop terrace. The recently renovated restaurant and tea room now serve breakfast, lunch and brunch. Sporting goods and clothing occupy an entire store. What's more, on the second floor you can practise your putting, scale a climbing wall, test a tennis racket or play a little table tennis. The pet shop, on the sixth floor, is a treat for children. On the fifth floor of the main store are the most complete sewing and haberdashery departments in town. Just a few of the services available at La Samaritaine: golf lessons, courses in tailoring and bicycle-repair and maintenance, an in-house astrologer who'll tell you your horoscope and/or read your palm (for 450 francs; call two days ahead), lampshades made to order, resilvering of flatware, and picture framing. Mothers shopping with young children can change their nappies and warm their bottles in the store nursery. And nearly every item on sale at La Samaritaine can be ordered by mail or phone, with payment on delivery.

Aux Trois Quartiers
1st arr. - 23, bd de la Madeleine
Open 10 a.m.-7 p.m. Closed Sun.

If you haven't been near Aux Trois Quartiers for several years, you won't recognise the place. Though the name is the same, the interior was recently gutted, expanded and transformed into a deluxe, three-level shopping centre. Formerly the preserve of tastefully dressed matrons and their prim daughters, Aux Trois Quartiers now draws crowds of customers—including a large percentage of tourists—with its critical mass of 75 chic shops. Madelios, a quality men's store, is here alongside the colourful clothing of Kenzo, Dorothée Bis and Tehen for women, Bang & Olufsen audio, restaurants, take-away shops and much more.

Don't plan to do much shopping in Paris in August—a great many stores are closed for the entire vacation month.

EYEWEAR

Gualdoni
1st arr. - 228, rue de Rivoli - 42 60 77 44
Open 9 a.m.-12:30 p.m. & 1:30 p.m.-6:30 p.m. (Mon. 2:30-6 p.m.). Closed Sun. & 3 wks. in Aug.
16th arr. - 8, av. Mozart - 42 24 77 87
Open 9 a.m.-7 p.m. (Mon. 2:30-6 p.m.). Closed Sun. & 1 wk. in Aug.

Gualdoni specialises in tortoiseshell. The prices vary according to thickness and colour; the darker the frame, the lower the cost (about 3,500 francs). Prices for lighter-coloured frames can zoom up to 25,000 francs. Come down to earth with the eye-catching Silhouette brand, the top-of-the-line in imitation tortoiseshell; coloured plastic frames are cheaper still. There is a children's section as well as a selection of designer frames (Lafont, Cartier, Vuarnet and so forth). Lots of fashionable sunglasses, too, by Ray-Ban, Beausoleil and Persol.

Lunettes Beausoleil
4th arr. - 21, rue du Roi de Sicile - 42 77 28 29
Open 9 a.m.-12:30 p.m. & 2 p.m.-7 p.m. Closed Sat. & Sun.

Miles Davis used to wear them; Stevie Wonder and Jean-Michel Jarre still do: Frédéric Beausoleil's super-sexy specs are made to measure, personalised and utterly unique. Behind those sunglasses fashioned in "tortoiseshell" (it's really cellulose) or metal, you too can look like a star.

Alain Mikli
4th arr. - 1, rue des Rosiers - 42 71 01 56
Open 11 a.m.-7 p.m. (Mon. 2 p.m.-7 p.m.). Closed Sun.

Mikli, with its sleek blond-wood interior and comfortable armchairs, is the hottest place to shop for glasses. Mikli still goes in for extravagant, Hollywood-style frames in large voluptuous shapes, but a glance at the new collection shows that more classic trends are coming to the fore (straightforward round frames). His latest creations incorporate technical innovations such as a combination of metal and plastic in matte or glossy colours. Allow a two- to ten-day wait for a pair of glasses, depending on how much work is involved. You can expect to pay between 800 francs for classic frames and 5,000 francs for a pair of the most sophisticated specs.

Latin Optique
5th arr. - 31, bd Saint Michel 43 29 31 79
Open 9 a.m.-12:30 p.m. & 2 p.m.-7 p.m. Closed Sat., Sun. & holidays.

The owner is a *visagiste*, which means that he specialises in suiting the glasses he makes to the specific contours of your face. Monsieur Raymond measures and studies your features before proposing a frame that he can (if you wish) hand-craft for you in about 48 hours. Latin Optique also has a huge stock (some 20,000) of ready-made frames and a workshop on the premises to assure quick service.

Bastille Optic
11th arr. 38, rue de la Roquette 48 06 87 00
Open 10 a.m.-7:30 p.m. Closed Sun., Mon., 1 wk. in Aug. & holidays.

When Bastille trendies need glasses, this is where they come for funny or fashionable frames by Mikli, Claude Montana, Agnès B. and Alfred Paris. Don't miss the batwing frames by Eye-Wear; another pair mimics the Eiffel Tower—a perfect souvenir (for the near-sighted) of a Parisian holiday.

FLOWERS & PLANTS

■ FLOWER SHOPS

Céline et Jérôme
18th arr. - 83, rue du Mont-Cenis 46 06 30 91
Open 9 a.m.-8 p.m. (Sun. 9:30 a.m.-1 p.m.).

Simple flowers enhanced by exotic foliage and the occasional rare blossom (lotus or papyrus flowers, for instance) are arranged here into splendidly original, inventive bouquets. At weekends, bunches nearing their peak—but with lots of life still left in them—are sold on the pavement at bargain prices.

Patrick Divert
16th arr. - 7, place de Mexico 45 53 69 35
Open 8:30 a.m.-8 p.m. (Sat. from 9 p.m. & Sun. 10 a.m.-1 p.m.).

Subtle interplays of textures—barks, wood, moss and braids of aromatic plants—mark the style of Divert's rustic yet extremely refined bouquets. Wild flowers add their charm to these inventive compositions.

Elyfleurs
17th arr. - 82, av. de Wagram 47 66 87 19
Open daily 24 hours.

It's 2 a.m. and you're seized with the urge to send a sumptuous bouquet to a friend in Berlin. No problem: your thoughtful present will be delivered in France or in any major European city in double-quick time thanks to the efficient service provided round the clock by Elyfleurs.

Some establishments change their closing times without warning. It is always wise to check in advance.

FLOWERS & PLANTS – SHOPS

Guillet
7th arr. - 99, av. La Bourdonnais
45 51 32 98
Open 9:30 a.m.-12:30 p.m. & 2 p.m.-7 p.m. Closed Sun. & Mon.

This long-established florist specialises in floral decorating schemes and, in its own workshop, creates silk flowers, centrepieces and bridal head-dresses to order. Faithful clients include the Opéra and the Comédie-Française, as well as some of Paris's big department stores.

Un Jardin en Plus
7th arr. - 224, bd Saint-Germain
45 48 25 71
Open 10 a.m.-7 p.m. Closed Sun. & Mon. in July & Aug.

It's a floral, floral world. At least in this shop, where there are flowers everywhere: cut flowers, potted flowers, garlands, flowers on fabric, wallpaper, sheets, towels, dishes, furniture and more.

Lachaume
8th arr. - 10, rue Royale - 42 60 57 26
Open 8:30 a.m.-7:30 p.m. (Sat. until 6 p.m.). Closed Sun. & Aug.

This is probably the most famous florist in Paris, and it's been here for over a hundred years. Marcel Proust called in every day to pick out the orchid he wore in his lapel (you can get the same kind today for 140 francs). The quality of the flowers is perfection itself. Short of buying a bouquet, you can admire the 150 varieties of flowers arranged in enormous vases in the shop window. Full bouquets start at about 400 francs.

Mille Feuilles
3rd arr. - 2, rue Rambuteau - 42 78 32 93
Open 9 a.m.-8 p.m. Closed Sun.

Arguably the best florist in the Marais, bursting with blossoms in the most delicate hues. Come here for the freshest flowers, both rare and familiar, artfully disposed in antique or contemporary vases. Like us, you'll want to buy the whole shop!

Au Nom de la Rose
6th arr. - 4, rue de Tournon - 46 34 10 64
Open 10 a.m.-9 p.m. (Sun. 10 a.m.-1 p.m. & 3 p.m.-6 p.m.).

Dani is the name of the rose who runs this shop; she's an ex-pop singer who now spends her time in the fragrant company of roses, nothing but roses! From ultra-sophisticated blooms that look as if they were made of porcelain, to old-fashioned roses that bring back memories of grandmother's garden, all these flowers are sublime. You can purchase an armful for a bouquet, or buy a single, perfectly graceful rose (from 20 francs).

Emilio Robba
1st arr. - 47, rue Etienne Marcel
42 36 66 48
Open 10 a.m.-7 p.m. (Sat. 11 a.m.-7 p.m.). Closed Sun.

Emilio Robba composes some exquisite artificial bouquets, but it's really his vases that will bowl you over, including cloth-draped ones that can double as lamps. He has recently branched out into garden-style furniture (rattan, wrought iron, braided leather); try out his seductive room perfumes.

Christian Tortu
6th arr. - 6, carrefour de l'Odéon
43 26 02 56
Open 9 a.m.-8 p.m. Closed Sun.

Christian Tortu is a gifted flower designer, probably the most talented of his generation. He has an inimitable knack - and many imitators - for blending rare and delicate flowers with simple greenery or tropical plants. Tortu's bouquets are perfect and quite natural-looking, yet they're also sophisticated and somehow wild... His prices have risen just as rapidly as his popularity with the media.

René Veyrat
8th arr. - 168, bd Haussmann
45 62 37 86
Open 8:30 a.m.-7 p.m. Closed Sun.

You'll be captivated by the window displays of this corner shop on the boulevard Haussmann. The flowers and plants are of exemplary quality, the service is charming. Large bouquets start at about 450 francs.

Vilmorin
1st arr. - 2 ter et 4, quai de la Mégisserie
42 33 61 62
Open 9:30 p.m.-7 p.m. Closed Sun. June-Feb. & Mon. July-Aug.

Gardeners should plan to spend at least a few hours browsing among the shrubs, rosebushes, bedding plants, herbs and bulbs on display at the biggest garden store in town. The seed department alone has been known to absorb the green of thumb for entire afternoons. Gardening accessories and house plants are on sale here as well.

> ## Flowers, flowers everywhere
>
> Some 1,800 varieties of flowers are grown in Paris's greenhouses, located in the Auteuil area, and from time to time marvellous flower exhibitions are held. You can pick up timetables at the city hall), or contact the Direction des Parcs et Jardins de la Ville de Paris, 3, av. de la Porte d'Auteuil, 16th arr., 40 71 74 00.

SHOPS – FOOD

FLOWER MARKETS

Marché aux Fleurs de l'Ile de la Cité
4th arr. - Pl. Louis-Lépine (quai de Corse)
Open 8 a.m.-7:30 p.m. Closed Sun. No cards.

Flower supermarkets

These establishments sell remarkably fresh flowers, and they'll deliver anywhere in Paris:
Monceau Fleurs, open 9 a.m.-8 p.m. (Sun. 9 a.m.-1 p.m.) (delivery is 20 francs), 4th arr., 2 quai Célestins, 42 72 24 86; 6th arr., 84 bld Raspail, 45 48 70 10; 8th arr., 92 bd Malesherbes, 45 63 88 23; 16th arr., 60 av. Paul Doumer, 40 72 79 27; 17th arr., 2 place Général Koenig, 45 74 61 39.
A prosperous atmosphere can be found at *La Grange*, 6th arr., 7, rue de Buci, 43 26 19 34, open daily 9:30 a.m.-8:30 p.m. (Sun. until 7 p.m.); delivery is 35 francs, even in an emergency, and credit cards are accepted.
Other addresses: *Lamartine Fleurs*, 16th arr., 188, av. Victor Hugo, 45 04 29 50, open 9 a.m.-7:30 p.m. (Mon. 2:30 p.m.-7:30 p.m.), closed Sun.
And *Nice Fleurs*, 15th arr., 19-21, rue de Lourmel, 45 78 95 14, open 9:30 a.m.-7:30 p.m. (Sun 9:30 a.m.-1:30 p.m.), closed Mon.; 8th arr., 5, rue de Régny, 45 55 85 70, open 9 a.m.-7 p.m. (Sun. 9:30 a.m.-6 p.m.).

Marché de la Madeleine
8th arr. - Pl. de la Madeleine
Open 8 a.m.-7:30 p.m. Closed Sat., Sun. & Mon. (except holidays). No cards.

Marché des Ternes
17th arr. - Pl. des Ternes
Open 8 a.m.-7:30 p.m. Closed Mon. No cards.

FOOD

A yen for the exotic and a return to French culinary roots are the two most prominent—and paradoxical—features of the current Paris food scene. Palates titillated by travels to far-off lands crave those same foreign flavours when they get home: hence the proliferation of shops offering foodstuffs and prepared dishes from all over the world. It's an amazing development; less than a generation ago, the French were particularly insular in their eating habits. But their current flirtation with foreign cuisines doesn't mean they've forsaken their native gastronomy. *Au contraire*, demand is increasing for fine matured cheeses and bread with old-fashioned flavour. And sales of sweets—pastries, ice cream, chocolate—are booming: People are ready to lay out lots and lots of francs to buy the very best.

BAKERIES

Au Panetier
2nd arr. - 10, place des Petits-Pères - 42 60 90 23
Open 8 a.m.-7:15 p.m. Closed Sat., Sun., 1 month during summer & holidays. No cards.

Even if you don't want to buy one of the old-fashioned loaves of hazelnut bread, raisin bread or the house speciality pain de Saint-Fiacre (all baked in a wood-fired oven), this excellent bakery is worth a visit just for a look at the adorable etched-glass and tile décor.

Au Bon Pain d'Autrefois
11th arr. - 45, rue Popincourt
43 55 04 48
Open 6:30 a.m.-8 p.m. Closed Sat., Sun., end Dec. No cards.

The delicious smell of sourdough wafts out of this pretty bakery (a listed building), which features superb pain de campagne (the classic country loaf), rustic rye loaves and delicious brioches. Jean-Pierre Leroy's special rotating oven also produces delectable pastries.

Le Fournil de Pierre
15th arr. - 3, rue du Commerce
45 75 16 48 (also: 2nd arr., 4th arr., 6th arr., 7th arr., 8th arr., 9th arr., 12th arr., 14th arr., 17th arr.)
Open 8:30 a.m.-7:30 p.m. (Mon. 11:30 a.m.-7:30 p.m. & Sun. until 1 p.m.).

The chain's many shops in the greater Paris area sell home-style breads whose sole flaw is that they are not always as oven-fresh as we might wish. But the variety of loaves is astonishing (there are over 20), and we like the plain buns, biscuits and pastries.

Ganachaud
20th arr. - 150-154, rue de Ménilmontant
46 36 13 82
Open 7:30 a.m.-8 p.m. (Tues. 2:30 p.m.-8 p.m. & Sun. 7:30 a.m.-1:30 p.m.). Closed Mon. & Aug.

Bernard Ganachaud has sold his shop, but the new owner still works with the original team of bakers to produce the same fabulous breads from Ganachaud's wood-fired ovens. The nut breads sold here still contain fresh walnuts, the raisin breads are still loaded with fruit, and the traditional country loaf turned out 15 to 20 times daily is still crusty perfection. Meanwhile, Isabelle and Valérie Ganachaud keep the family bread-baking tradition alive a few streets away, selling their father's renowned sourdough flûte, as well as a wonderfully chewy organic bread and a wide variety of homely pastries and brioches (A La Flûte Gana, 226 rue des Pyrénées, 20th arr., 43 58 42 62, closed Sun. and Mon.).

Marcel Haupois

4th arr. - 35, rue des Deux-Ponts
43 54 57 59
Open 6:45 a.m.-1:30 p.m. & 3 p.m.-8:30 p.m. Closed Thurs., Fri. & 1 month during summer.

Out of this small old-fashioned bakery emerge wonderful hand-formed loaves that rank among the finest in Paris. The country-style bread merits particular mention, as do the rye and other whole-grain specialities.

Poilâne

6th arr. - 8, rue du Cherche-Midi
45 48 42 59
Open 7:15 a.m.-8:15 p.m. Closed Sun.
15th arr. - 49, bd de Grenelle
45 79 11 49
Open 7:15 a.m.-8:15 p.m. Closed Mon.

Lionel Poilâne is probably the world's best-known baker; he can be found hawking his famous sourdough bread in magazines and on television screens in all corners of the globe. And even though his products are sold all over Paris in charcuteries and cheese shops, many Poilâne fans think nothing of crossing town and queuing to *personally* buy their favourite bread still warm from his ovens. Poilâne's walnut bread is delicious and we are also particularly fond of the shortbreads (sablés) and the rustic apple turnover (which makes a delicious and inexpensive dessert, accompanied by a bowl of thick crème fraîche).

Max Poilâne

14th arr. - 29, rue de l'Ouest - 43 27 24 91
15th arr. - 87, rue Brancion - 48 28 45 90
Open 7:15 a.m.-8 p.m. Closed Sun. No cards.

An attractive bakery, located across from the old Vaugirard slaughterhouse, which has recently been transformed into a lovely park. His bread follows the family tradition fairly closely, though we find it less sour and perhaps more pleasant than the more famous loaf baked on the rue du Cherche-Midi. Max also turns out a fine walnut bread, and his croissants, brioches and chaussons (turnovers) are huge hits with the locals.

Poujauran

7th arr. - 20, rue Jean-Nicot - 47 05 80 88
Open 8 a.m.-8:30 p.m. Closed Sun. & Mon. No cards.

Jean-Luc Poujauran's bakery may be in an upper-class area, but he hasn't let it go to his head, even though food writers regularly wax lyrical over his talent. And though he bakes a wonderful country loaf with organically grown flour, he's not the type to think he's the best thing since sliced bread. Let's just hope he never changes and that we won't have to give up his delicious little rolls (or his olive or poppy seed or walnut bread), his old-fashioned pound cake (quatre-quarts), his buttery fruitcakes and those delicious frangipane-stuffed galettes that he bakes for Epiphany (Twelfth Night, January 6).

René Saint-Ouen

8th arr. - 111, bd Haussmann
42 65 06 25
Open 8 a.m.-7 p.m. Closed Sun., Aug. & holidays. No cards.

René Saint-Ouen has two passions in life: bread and sculpture. He brings the two together in his bakery on boulevard Haussmann, where he makes and sells golden loaves of bread (sourdough, raisin-nut and bacon, among others) fashioned into classic and fabulous shapes. Special orders are welcome. The bakery also serves light lunches and tea.

▍CATERERS

François Clerc

92210 Saint-Cloud - 3, rue Dantan - 46 02 88 88
Open 9 a.m.-7 p.m. Closed Sun. & holidays.

Backed up by a team of more than 100 professionals, François Clerc moved quickly into the top rank of French caterers. Clerc, a skilled and innovative chef, is passionate about food and cooking. Among his most notable creations, we highly recommend the magnificent pike "Harlequin" served with a subtle shellfish coulis, his unusual casserole of turbot with sea urchins and, among the sweets, the peerless coffee macaroons.

Dalloyau

15th arr. - 69, rue de la Convention - 45 77 84 27
Open 9:30 a.m.-7 p.m.

The oldest catering firm in Paris (founded in 1802), Dalloyau is also one of the best. The dishes on its appetising menu are fit for a king (in case one is coming to your party). Choose from oysters gently stewed in Champagne, Bresse chicken with prawns, stuffed suckling pig and a fine selection of desserts (the famous Dalloyau chocolate macaroons are our favourite).

Potel et Chabot

16th arr. - 3, rue de Chaillot - 47 20 22 00
Open 8 a.m.-7 p.m. Closed Sun.

Potel et Chabot is an old-established Parisian caterer—and perhaps the most successful. It

SHOPS – FOOD

handles cocktail parties, receptions and other soigné soirées for the Opéra, the prime minister's office and the president himself. The food includes well-prepared classic dishes (stuffed saddle of lamb, chicken stuffed with foie gras and truffles), but of late, we've noticed some innovative specialities on the menu: tagliatelle with scallops, shellfish terrine served with a smooth lobster coulis, and a delicate, delicious blanquette of turbot and cucumbers.

■ CHARCUTERIE & TAKE-AWAY

Charcuterie Charles
6th arr. - 10, rue Dauphine - 43 54 25 19
Open 8 a.m.-2 p.m. & 4 p.m.-8 p.m. Closed Sat., Sun. & holidays.

This prize-winning charcuterie, one of the finest in Paris, is the city champion when it comes to boudin blanc (white sausage). During the Christmas season, when boudin blanc is a traditional component of holiday meals, Charles displays some 20 varieties, all with different flavourings (truffles, prunes, pistachios and such). Andouillette (tripe sausage) is another speciality, and we are great fans of Charles's sumptuous terrines (sweetbreads, duck breast and foie gras, herby ham), his tarts and delicious hams.

Au Cochon d'Auvergne
5th arr. - 48, rue Monge - 43 26 36 21
Open 9 a.m.-1 p.m. & 4 p.m.-7:30 p.m. (Sun. & holidays 9 a.m.-1 p.m.). Closed Mon., Jan. 1 & Dec. 25. No cards.

José Léon really knows how to cook a juicy ham—his is certainly one of the most toothsome in town. Equal praise is due to his brawn, and the rich rillettes and confits he fashions from south-west geese. Make a point of sampling his excellent sugar-free compotes, made from prime, organically grown fruits.

Coesnon
6th arr. - 30, rue Dauphine - 43 54 35 80
Open 8:30 a.m.-8 p.m. Closed Mon., Sun. (except 3 wks. in Dec.), 1 wk. at Easter school holidays, Aug. & holidays.

Because true practitioners of the charcutier's art are becoming ever harder to find, and because Gérard Robert is one of its most eminent representatives, we recommend that you make a special point of visiting this wonderful pork emporium. Robert's boudin blanc and boudin noir are legendary (his chestnut-studded black pud-ding has won award after award). What's more, his salt- and smoke-cured pork specialities are top-notch—especially when accompanied by the crisp yet tender sauerkraut he pickles himself. Step up to the counter with confidence, knowing that you will be competently and courteously served.

Flo Prestige
16th arr. - 61, av. de la Grande-Armée
45 00 12 10
16th arr. - 102, av. du Président-Kennedy - 42 88 38 00
1st arr. - 42, pl. du Marché-Saint-Honoré - 42 61 45 46
Open daily 8 a.m.-11 p.m. Delivery.
7th arr. - 36, av. de La Motte-Picquet - 45 55 71 25
Open daily 9:30 a.m.-9:30 p.m. Delivery.
9th arr. - 64, bd Haussmann, Printemps - 42 82 58 82
Open daily 9:30 a.m.-7 p.m. Delivery.
12th arr. - 211, av. Daumesnil 43 44 86 36
Open daily 8 a.m.-9:30 p.m. Delivery.
12th arr. - 22, av. de la Porte de Vincennes
 43 74 54 32
Open daily 9:30 a.m.-11 p.m. Delivery.
15th arr. - 352, rue Lecourbe - 45 54 76 94
Open daily 10:30 a.m.-9:30 p.m. Delivery.

Early or late, every day of the year, you have a sure source of delicious bread, fine wine and delicious desserts at Flo Prestige. The selection of foodstuffs is varied and choice, and covers a wide price range, from the excellent house sauerkraut to prestigious Petrossian caviar. There are now eight Flo Prestige shops in Paris.

Gargantua
1st arr. - 284, rue Saint-Honoré 42 60 52 54
Open 8 a.m.-9 p.m. (Sun. 9 a.m.-8 p.m.). Closed May 1.

The opulent window displays of this well-known charcuterie could satisfy even the gigantically robust appetite of its Rabelaisian namesake. There are cured meats, foie gras and terrines, of course, but Gargantua also carries an abundance of prepared dishes, breads, wines, pastries and ice cream. It's a fine place to go to put together a picnic.

Layrac
6th arr. - 29, rue de Buci - 43 25 17 72
Open daily 9:30 a.m.-2 a.m.

What better place to compose an elegant late-night supper for two than this bright and inviting garden of gourmandise, which overflows with delicacies both savoury and sweet. Prepared dishes can be delivered to your door.

Pou
17th arr. - 16, av. des Ternes - 43 80 19 24
Open 9:30 a.m.-7:15 p.m. Closed Sun. & Mon.

Pou is an excellent charcuterie whose sober décor and rich displays resemble nothing so much as a pal-

FOOD – SHOPS

ace of earthly delights. A look in the window is an enticing, irresistible invitation to buy and taste: black and white boudin sausages, duck pâté en croûte, glittering galantines, cervelas sausage studded with pale-green pistachios and now, sumptuous pastries too. Since everything really is as good as it looks, making a choice is quite a task. And given the prices, paying isn't very easy, either.

Schmid
10th arr. - 76, bd de Strasbourg
46 07 89 74
Open 9 a.m.-7 p.m. (Sat. 8:45 a.m.-6:45 p.m.). Closed Sun. & holidays.
17th arr. - 36, rue de Lévis - 47 63 07 08
Open 9 a.m.-7:30 p.m. (Sun. until 1 p.m.). Closed Mon.
18th arr. - 199, rue Championnet - 46 27 68 24
Open 9 a.m.-7 p.m. Closed Sun. & holidays.

Naturally, with a name like Schmid, you would expect this shop to specialise in sauerkraut. And you wouldn't be wrong. It is excellent—fine, crisp and sharp. But don't overlook the matured Munster cheese, the light and airy Kugelhopf cake and other Alsatian treats.

Vigneau-Desmaret
6th arr. - 105-107, rue de Sèvres
42 22 23 23
Open 9 a.m.-8:30 p.m. Closed Sun.

If ever you should lose your appetite, come over to this old-fashioned charcuterie... we guarantee you'll find it again. Whose mouth wouldn't water at the sight of succulent ham wrapped in a linen cloth and poached in aromatic stock? Who wouldn't long for a bite of perfectly dried saucisson? There are also light vegetable or fish terrines and a whole range of groceries, vegetables, cheeses and fruits.

Vignon
8th arr. - 14, rue Marbeuf - 47 20 24 26
Open 8 a.m.-8:30 p.m. (Sat. 9 a.m.-7:30 p.m.). Closed Sun. & holidays.

A rather grand marble facade sets the luxurious tone for this respected Parisian charcuterie. Monsieur Vignon, president of the professional association, turns out a superb terrine of foie gras, remarkable galantines of chicken and duck studded with truffles or pistachios, game pâtés and delicious, old-fashioned brawn. Parma ham–fanciers should note that Vignon stocks the excellent La Slega brand from Langhirano.

■ CHEESE

Androuët
8th arr. - 41, rue d'Amsterdam
48 74 26 90
Open 10 a.m.-1:30 p.m. & 2:30 p.m.-7:30 p.m. Closed Sun. & holidays.

Since Pierre Androuet, that most renowned *fromager*, retired and sold this medieval-looking cheese shop near the Gare Saint-Lazare, nothing has been quite the same. Quality varies: superbly matured cheeses sit side by side with far less worthy examples...the rule of thumb for purchasing cheese at Androuët is now "Let the buyer beware!".

Marie-Anne Cantin
7th arr. - 12, rue du Champ-de-Mars - 45 50 43 94
Open 8:30 a.m.-1 p.m. & 4 p.m.-7:30 p.m. (Sat. 8:30 a.m.-1 p.m. & 3:30 p.m.-7:30 p.m., Sun. 8:30 a.m.-1 p.m.). Closed Mon.

Like father, like daughter: Marie-Anne Cantin is a worthy successor to the late Christian Cantin. Her customers and her cheeses benefit from large doses of tender loving care. She is an ardent defender of real (which means unpasteurised) cheeses and one of the few merchants in Paris to sell Saint-Marcellins as they are preferred on their home turf—in their creamy prime, not in their chalky youth. And so it is with her other cheeses, all of which retain the authentic flavours of their country origins.

Créplet-Brussol
8th arr. - 17, pl. de la Madeleine
42 65 34 32
Open 9 a.m.-7:30 p.m. (Sat. until 7 p.m., Mon. from 2 p.m.). Closed Sun.

Former supplier of Mimolette (a firm, nutty-flavoured Dutch cheese) to General de Gaulle, Créplet-Brussol still boasts a large number of celebrities among its clientele. But what really counts here is the cheese: nicely matured Camembert, creamy Brillat-Savarin, farmhouse Reblochon and tangy faisselle (fresh cream cheese) made in the shop. The butter, cream and crème fraîche are divine, and there is an appetising selection of foreign cheeses.

Alain Dubois
17th arr. - 80, rue de Tocqueville
42 27 11 38
Open 8 a.m.-1 p.m. & 4 p.m.-7:30 p.m. (Sun. 8 a.m.-1 p.m.). Closed Mon.
17th arr. - 79, rue de Courcelles
43 80 36 42
Open 8:30 a.m.-1 p.m. & 4 p.m.-7:30 p.m. (Mon. from 4 p.m.) Closed Sun. & Aug.

Alain Dubois's Gruyère, matured for at least two years in his cellars, is a royal treat. And there's more: Dubois offers farmhouse goat cheeses, unpasteurised Camembert and authentic Epoisses (which he rinses religiously with marc de Bourgogne). The problem is, now that his shop has expanded, this expert cheese merchant has filled it with so many enticements that we don't know which way to turn. You will not be astonished to learn that Dubois supplies top-class cheeses to such great restaurants as Lucas-Carton, Guy Savoy, Michel Rostang, Laurent and others.

Ferme Poitevine
18th arr. - 64, rue Lamarck - 46 06 54 40
Open 8 a.m.-1 p.m. & 4 p.m.-7:45 p.m. (Sun. 8 a.m.-1 p.m.). Closed Mon., Feb. school holidays & Aug.

Jack Chapu, the cheese man, is a Montmartre personality. He serves all his clients with the same warmth, whether they're famous or not. His many perfectly matured cheeses come from all over the French countryside. We particularly enjoy the flavourful Munsters, the rich Camemberts and the tender little goat cheeses marinated in herby olive oil.

La Ferme Saint-Hubert
8th arr. - 21, rue Vignon - 47 42 79 20
Open 8:30 a.m.-7:15 p.m. Closed Sun.

Cheese seller Henry Voy is so passionate about his vocation that he has no time for anything else. Morning and night you can find him tending to his Beauforts (matured for over two years), his farmhouse goat cheeses or his exclusive Saint-Hubert. He travels all over France, seeking out the best farmhouse cheeses. For true aficionados, Voy unearths such rarities as unpasteurised butter churned with spring water, and delicate goat's-milk butter. You can sample these extraordinary wares in the restaurant next to the shop.

La Fromagerie Boursault
14th arr. - 71, av. du Général-Leclerc - 43 27 93 30
Open 8 a.m.-12:30 p.m. & 4 p.m.-7:15 p.m. (Sun. 8 a.m.-12:30 p.m.). Closed Mon.

It was here that Pierre Boursault created the famous cheese that bears his name. And it is here, naturally enough, that you will find Boursault at its creamy, golden best. Current owner Jacques Vernier has made the shop one of the most pleasant in Paris, a showcase for the rare specimens that he seeks out himself in the French provinces. Like incomparable Beauforts matured under his supervision in their native Alpine air; farmhouse goat cheeses (try the Picodons); hand-crafted Saint-Nectaire from Auvergne, which has nothing in common with the industrially produced variety; and flawless Camemberts. This is one of the few places on earth where you can buy Bleu de Termignon, a blue-veined summer cheese from Savoie.

Ferme Saint-Aubin
4th arr. - 76, rue Saint-Louis-en-l'Ile - 43 54 74 54
Open 8 a.m.-1 p.m. & 3:30 p.m.-8 p.m. (Sun. & holidays 8 a.m.-1 p.m.). Closed Mon.

The best cheeses on the Ile-Saint-Louis are available at this recently renovated shop, now under the management of new owner Odette Jenny. In the vaulted cellars beneath the store she pampers her Pavés d'Auge from Normandy, Epoisses rinsed in marc de Bourgogne, hand-crafted Cantal from Auvergne and robust Reblochon. The fresh cream cheeses, made in the shop, are a delight, as are the goat cheeses from Périgord and the Aveyron region. Madame Jenny is doing a roaring business with her latest innovation: full prepared meals on trays, complete with wine and Poilâne bread.

Barthélémy
7th arr. - 51, rue de Grenelle - 45 48 56 75
Open 8:30 a.m.-1 p.m. & 3:30 p.m.-7:30 p.m. (Sat. 8:30 a.m.-1:30 p.m. & 3 p.m.-7:30 p.m.). Closed Sun. & Mon.

Roland Barthélémy reigns over a treasure trove of cheeses that he selects from farms all over the French countryside, then brings to perfect ripeness in his cellars. He is also the creator of several specialities that have the Who's Who of French officialdom beating a path to his door (he supplies the Elysée Palace, no less). The Boulamour (fresh cream cheese enriched with crème fraîche, currants, raisins and Kirsch) was Barthélémy's invention, as was a delicious Camembert laced with Calvados. We also enjoy the amusing Brie Surprise. But not to worry, tradition is never neglected here, witness the rich-tasting Alpine Beaufort, French Vacherin and the creamy Fontainebleau (the latter is made on the premises). Take one of the attractive cheese trays sold here as your contribution to a dinner party: your hostess will love it.

Tachon
1st arr. - 38, rue de Richelieu - 42 96 08 66
Open 9:30 a.m.-1:30 p.m. & 4 p.m.-8 p.m. Closed Sun., Mon., July, Aug. & holidays.

Jean-Claude Benoit is a native of Sainte-Maure, like the goat cheese of the same name. His personal network of top-quality producers stretches throughout Touraine, and down into Poitou and the Yonne. He also stocks excellent sheep's-milk cheeses from Corsica and the Pyrenees; and to round out the meal, Benoit sells a choice of hand-made sausages.

■ CHOCOLATE & CONFECTIONARY

Bonbonnière de la Trinité
8th arr. - 28, rue de Miromesnil
42 65 02 39
Open 10 a.m.-7 p.m. Closed Sat. & Sun.

FOOD – SHOPS

9th arr. - 4, pl. d'Estienne-d'Orves - 48 74 23 38
Open 9 a.m.-7 p.m. (2 Sun. in Dec.). Closed Sun. & holidays.

This charming little store dates from 1925. A real sweetshop, it stocks some 60 kinds of jam, 25 types of honey, 60 varieties of tea and countless sweets. The chocolate truffles are quite good, but for us, the irresistible attraction here is the range of bitter and extra-bitter chocolates sold in great, thick slabs, perfect for cooking or guilty nibbling.

Les Bonbons
6th arr. - 6, rue Bréa
43 26 21 15
Open 10 a.m.-8 p.m. (Mon. from 2:30 p.m., except July 14-Oct. 1). Closed Sun., Aug. & holidays.

Madame Lesieur's miniscule shop will bring out the child in even the most straitlaced adult. We admit that toffees (hard and soft), candied violets, nougats and barley-sugar sticks are terrible for your teeth, but what a lift they give your spirits! All the traditional sweets of the French provinces are gathered here: cocons de Lyon, ardoises d'Angers, bêtises de Cambrai and more, alongside sticky gingerbread from Basle or Dijon, and satisfyingly substantial slabs of handmade chocolate.

Au Chocolat de Puyricard
7th arr. - 27, av. Rapp
47 05 59 47
Open 9 a.m.-7:30 p.m. (Mon. from 2 p.m.). Closed Sun., Aug. & holidays (except at Christmas).

This shop is the exclusive Parisian source of the sweet (some might say, too sweet) chocolate truffles produced by the Provençal firm, Puyricard. Like the chocolates, the delicious calissons d'Aix (iced marzipan diamonds) are made by hand in small batches. New this year is the *clou de Cézanne*, a chocolate with a light nougatine and pinenut filling shaped like the paving nails used in the streets of Aix-en-Provence in Cézanne's time.

Christian Constant
6th arr. - 37, rue d'Assas - 45 48 45 51
Open daily 8 a.m.-9 p.m.
7th arr. - 26, rue du Bac - 47 03 30 00
Open daily 8 a.m.-8 p.m.

Christian Constant is mad about chocolate; in fact, not long ago he wrote a definitive book on the subject. His innovations include a line of flower-scented chocolates (try the ylang-ylang, vetiver or jasmine varieties), chocolates filled with delicately spiced creams, others spiked with fruit brandies or cordials, still others incorporating nuts and dried fruit (the conquistador is loaded with hazelnuts, honey and cinnamon).

Debauve et Gallais
7th arr. - 30, rue des Saints-Pères
45 48 54 67
Open 10 a.m.-7 p.m. Closed Sun. & holidays.

With its picturesque shopfront designed by renowned 19th-century architects Percier and Fontaine (it's listed by the Beaux-Arts) and its interior decorated with painted pillars, orange-wedge mirrors and antique lamps, Debauve et Gallais has lots of charm. Their filled chocolates, soft caramels, hazelnut pralines and chocolate truffles, all prettily displayed in glass jars, are perfectly delectable and sell for 360 francs a kilo.

Au Duc de Praslin
16th arr. - 125, av. Victor-Hugo
44 05 07 01
Open 10 a.m.-7 p.m. Closed Sun., Aug. & holidays.

Named after a 17th-century aristocrat whose cook invented the confection known as praline, the Duc de Praslin specialises in crunchy caramel-coated almonds (229 francs per kilo). You'll also want to sample some of the delicious variations on that basic theme: amandas (almonds, nougatine and cocoa), mirabos (nougatine and orange, covered with milk chocolate) and passions (chocolate-coated caramelised almonds). An assortment of seven varieties sells for 270 francs.

A l'Etoile d'Or
9th arr. - 30, rue Fontaine - 48 74 59 55
Open 10:30 a.m.-8 p.m. Closed Sun. & holidays (except at Christmas).

Denise Acabo does not make her own chocolate; rather, she is a true connoisseur who selects the best hand-crafted chocolates made in France, and presents them, in a laudable spirit of impartiality, to her delighted customers (while explaining to interested parties the connection between chocolate and eroticism...). The famed Bernachon chocolates from Lyon are sold in this beautiful turn-of-the-century shop, as well as Dufoux's incomparable palets and wonderful soft-centred bouchées from Voiron.

Fontaine au Chocolat
1st arr. - 193, rue Saint-Honoré
49 27 01 30
Open 10 a.m.-6:50 p.m. Closed Sun., Aug. & holidays.

Pervading Michel Cluizel's shop is a smell of chocolate so intense that your nose will flash an alert to your sweet tooth, and, we guarantee, have you salivating within seconds. Whether you try one of the five varieties of palets au chocolat or the croqu-amandes (caramelised almonds coated with extra-dark chocolate), the mendiants studded with nuts and dried fruit or the bold Noir Infini (99 per cent cocoa, perfumed with vanilla and spices), you're in for an unforgettable treat.

SHOPS – FOOD

Godiva
8th arr. - 102, av. des Champs Elysées
45 62 55 17
1st arr. - 237, rue Saint-Honoré
42 60 44 64
Open 9:30 a.m.-7 p.m. Closed Sun.
16th arr. - 157, av. Malakoff - 45 00 39 24
16th arr. - 96, av. Paul Doumer
42 88 59 79
Open 10 a.m.-7 p.m. Closed Sun.

These renowned chocolates are superbly packaged, but we still find them (though we've tried our best not to) far too sugary-sweet. The sales staff in all the Godiva shops are uniformly courteous and helpful.

Jadis et Gourmande
3rd arr. - 39, rue des Archives
48 04 08 03
Open 9:30 a.m.-7 p.m. (Sat. from 10 a.m., Mon. from 1 p.m.). Closed Sun.
5th arr. - 88, bd de Port-Royal
43 26 17 75
Open 9:30 a.m.-7 p.m. (Mon. from 1 p.m.). Closed Sun.
8th arr. - 49 bis, av. Franklin-Roosevelt - 45 25 06 04
Open 9:30 a.m.-7 p.m. (Sat. from 10 a.m., Mon. from 1 p.m.). Closed Sun.
8th arr. - 27, rue Boissy-d'Anglas
42 65 23 23
Open 9:30 a.m.-7 p.m. (Sat. 10:30 a.m.-12:30 p.m. & 1:30 p.m.-7 p.m., Mon. from 1 p.m.). Closed Sun.

It is delightful to browse round this sugarplum palace, where you are tempted in turn by delicious bonbons, boiled sweets, caramels and chocolate in myriad forms. The thick slabs of cooking chocolate make you want to rush to the kitchen and whip up a wickedly rich cake. Our favourite confection here is a thick braid of dark chocolate studded with candied orange peel and hazelnuts. Prices range from 210 to 320 francs per kilo.

Lenôtre
7th arr. - 44, rue du Bac - 42 22 39 39
8th arr. - 15, bd de Courcelles
45 63 87 63
15th arr. - 61, rue Lecourbe - 42 73 20 97
16th arr. - 44, rue d'Auteuil - 45 24 52 52 et 49, av. Victor-Hugo
45 01 71 71
17th arr. - 121, av. de Wagram
47 63 70 30
92200 Neuilly - 3, rue des Huissiers - 46 24 98 68
Open daily 9 a.m.-9 p.m.
16th arr. - 193, av. de Versailles
45 25 55 88
Open daily 9 a.m.-10 p.m.
8th arr. - 5, rue du Havre - 45 22 22 59
Open 10 a.m.-7 p.m. Closed Sun.
9th arr. - Lafayette Gourmet, 40, bd Haussmann - 42 80 45 75
Open daily 9 a.m.-7:45 p.m. Closed Sun.
92100 Boulogne - 79 bis, route de la Reine - 46 05 37 35
Open daily 9 a.m.-9 p.m. (Sun. until 1 p.m.).

Gaston Lenôtre's range of chocolates includes classic, intensely flavoured truffles and remarkable palets d'or filled with rich, subtle butter cream. Brisk turnover ensures the freshness of all these confections. In addition to chocolates, Lenôtre produces creamy toffee, nougatines and, around Christmas, meltingly tender *marrons glacés*. These beautifully packaged delights cost from 355 to 500 francs per kilo (the higher price is for liqueur-laced specialities).

La Maison du Chocolat
8th arr. - 52, rue François-Ier - 47 23 38 25
8th arr. - 225, rue du Faubourg Saint-Honoré - 42 27 39 44
Open 9:30 a.m.-7 p.m. Closed Sun. & holidays.

There's something of the alchemist about Robert Linxe: never satisfied, he is always experimenting, innovating, transforming mere cocoa beans into something very precious. His chocolates are among the finest in Paris, maybe even in the world. His renowned butter cream fillings—lemon, caramel, tea, raspberry and rum—will transport you to gourmet heaven.

Peltier
7th arr. - 66, rue de Sèvres - 47 83 66 12
Open 9:30 a.m.-7:45 p.m. (Sun. 8:30 a.m.-7 p.m.).
7th arr. - 6, rue Saint-Dominique
47 05 50 02
Open 8:15 a.m.-7:45 p.m. (Sun. 8:30 a.m.-7 p.m.).

Peltier's palets d'or (dark chocolates filled with chocolate butter cream and topped with a dab of real gold leaf) are among the capital's finest: light, smooth and balanced. The legion of fancier varieties, made with superb ingredients, are at least equally luscious (try the liquorice or ginger soft centres to see what we mean). Expect to pay between 380 and 400 francs per kilo for these superb sweets.

Richart
7th arr. - 258, bd Saint-Germain
45 55 66 00
Open 10 a.m.-7 p.m. (Mon. & Sat. from 11 a.m.). Closed Sun. & holidays.

A top-notch *chocolatier* from Lyon has established a Parisian outpost near the parliament building. This elegant emporium houses superbly presented chocolates with smooth, scrumptious butter cream fillings (380 francs per kilo) and addictive dark-chocolate bars made from Venezuelan cocoa beans.

Tholoniat
10th arr. - 47, rue du Château-d'Eau - 42 39 93 12
Open 8 a.m.-7 p.m. (Sun. 8:30 a.m.-6 p.m.). Closed Wed. & July 14-Sept. 1.

Within these walls a master pastry chef spins, sculpts, blows and shapes sugar and chocolate into tiny people, landscapes, fruit, flowers and even miniature houses (with furniture). Incredibly enough, his creations taste as good as they look. Special applause goes to Tholoniat's delicious and unusual pear- and orange-flavoured chocolates.

■ COFFEE & TEA

Betjeman and Barton
8th arr. - 23, bd Malesherbes 42 65 35 94
Open 9:30 a.m.-7 p.m. Closed Sun. & holidays.
11th arr. - 24, bd des Filles-du-Calvaire - 40 21 35 52
Open 10 a.m.-7 p.m. Closed Sun. & Mon.

The name on the sign and the shop's décor are British, but the firm itself is 100 per cent French, run nowadays by Didier Jumeau-Lafond. The range of top-class teas on offer is extensive, comprising over 150 natural and flavoured varieties. Indeed, B and B's teas are of such high quality that Harrod's deigns to market them. To help you choose your blend, the staff will offer you a cup —a comforting and highly civilised custom. Vera Winterfeldt's excellent jams and a line of refreshing fruit "waters" intended to be consumed ice-cold in summer, are worth seeking out here.

Brûlerie des Ternes
16th arr. - 28, rue de l'Annonciation - 42 88 99 90
Open 9 a.m.-7:30 p.m. (Sun. & holidays until 1 p.m.). Closed Mon.
17th arr. - 10, rue Poncelet - 46 22 52 79
Open 9 a.m.-1:30 p.m. & 3:30 p.m.-7:30 p.m. (Sun. & holidays until 1 p.m.). Closed Mon.

Coffees from all over the world are roasted and ground to perfection in this commendable shop, which draws a clientele made up, in part, of the chic and famous. Featured is the fabled Blue Mountain coffee from Jamaica, a rare and costly treat (380 francs per kilo). Each customer's individual blend is automatically recorded on a computer, so the recipe need never be lost or forgotten. Flavoured coffees (orange, chocolate, vanilla...) are justly popular, and there are 70 kinds of tea in stock.

L'Espace Café
11th arr. - 89, bd de Charonne 43 70 28 92
Open 10 a.m.-7 p.m. Closed Sun., Mon., Aug. & holidays.

Michel Toutain has a futuristic outlook on coffee. The shop's computer produces a sensory analysis that allegedly matches the customer's personality with a particular bean or blend. But, of course, you may simply go in and ask for your preferred brew: Javanese, Moka, Negus, Mexican or one of a number of house specialities such as the excellent Pantagruel. All beans sold are carefully selected and roasted.

Mariage Frères
4th arr. - 30-32, rue du Bourg-Tibourg - 42 72 28 11
Open daily 10:30 a.m-7:30 p.m.
6th arr. - 13, rue des Grands-Augustins - 40 51 82 50
Open daily 10:30 a.m-7:30 p.m. Closed Mon.

Founded by a family of explorers, one of whose ancestors participated in a delegation sent by Louis XIV to sign a trade agreement with the Shah of Persia, Mariage imports no fewer than 350 varieties of tea from 30 countries. This comprehensive selection, coupled with the firm's unceasing expansion and promotional efforts, makes Mariage Frères the high temple of tea in Paris. Top-class products include the exquisite Bloomfield Darjeeling, a splendid golden-tipped Grand Yunnan and other rarities that may be sampled in the shop's tea room, accompanied by pastries or light snacks (see *Tea Rooms*).

Le Palais des Thés
6th arr. - 25, rue de l'Abbé-Grégoire - 45 48 85 81
14th arr. - 21, rue Raymond-Losserand - 43 21 97 97
Open 10:30 a.m.-7 p.m. Closed Sun. & Mon.
16th arr. - 21, rue de l'Annonciation - 45 25 51 52
Open 10:30 a.m.-7 p.m. (Sun. 10 a.m.-1 p.m.). Closed Mon.

Founded in 1986 by a consortium of 45 tea lovers, this establishment has risen quickly through the ranks of Parisian tea merchants. More than 350 types of tea can be found here, and helpful staff are on hand to guide your choice. Those fond of flavoured teas will appreciate the seven-citrus blend and the monks' tea made with ten aromatic plants. All the paraphernalia required by the tea ritual—from teapots to strainers to cups—is also in stock; true tea fanatics will go overboard for the jellies and sweets perfumed with their favourite brew. Frequent customers should be sure to ask for the shop's *carte de fideli-thé*, which entitles you to a ten per cent discount.

Torréfaction Valade
12th arr. - 21, bd de Reuilly - 43 43 39 27
Open 8:45 a.m.-1 p.m. & 4 p.m.-7:30 p.m. (Sat. 8:45 a.m.-7:30 p.m.). Closed Sun., Mon. & holidays. Annual closings not available.

In his modern, clean-lined shop, Pascal Guiraud celebrates his passion for coffee, a passion that he shares with his equally enthusiastic customers. Beans from Cuba, Brazil, Kenya, Costa Rica, Haiti and elsewhere release an irresistible aroma as they roast (and they are prepared only as needed, so the coffee is absolutely fresh). The house blends are marvellous as well: we like the Italian Roast, which is one of the most popular, the Turkish Special and the spicy Orient

SHOPS – FOOD

Express. Don't overlook the shop's selection of jams, honey and condiments, or the 110 kinds of tea.

Twinings
8th arr. - 76, bd Haussmann - 43 87 39 84
Open 10 a.m.-7 p.m. Closed Sun., Mon. & holidays.

Twinings's utterly English boutique is, so they claim, the only place in Paris to procure genuine Earl Grey tea, the kind still drunk in quantity by the Grey family. Another exceedingly rare variety, Darjeeling Ringtong, is also available, for a rather more hefty sum. Regular customers have their names and favourite blends recorded in a large, bound ledger. Tea fanciers will be glad to learn that Twinings also sells tea in bricks, just as it was purveyed in the 14th century.

Verlet
1st arr. - 256, rue Saint-Honoré 42 60 67 39
Open 9 a.m.-7 p.m. Closed Sun. & Mon. Easter-Oct.; Sat. & Sun. from Oct.-Easter, July 14-Aug. 20 & holidays.

The Verlet family has been roasting and selling coffee beans in their delightful turn-of-the-century shop since 1880. Pierre Verlet imports the finest coffees from Papua, Costa Rica, Colombia, Jamaica, Malabar, Ethiopia and Brazil, and he also produces several subtle and delicious house blends. He will even create one specially for you, for he is a master at balancing different aromas, different degrees of acidity and bitterness to suit personal taste. If you prefer to sample before you buy, take a seat at one of the little tables and try, perhaps, the Petit Cheval blend, a balanced and smooth Moka. Verlet also stocks a selection of teas from all over the world and an appetising selection of dried fruits. At lunchtime, crowds pour into the shop for an excellent croque monsieur or a slice of cake and a cup of fragrant coffee.

■ ETHNIC FOODS

Aux Cinq Continents
11th arr. - 75, rue de la Roquette 43 56 79 69
Open 10 a.m.-1 p.m. & 4 p.m.-8 p.m. (Sun. until 1 p.m.). Closed Sat. & holidays.

The Abramoff family reign over one of the city's most comprehensive ranges of grains, cereals and imported delicacies. No fewer than 15 kinds of rice are stocked here (including wild rice at 90 francs per kilo), along with ten varieties of dried beans (the black beans are wonderful with any kind of smoked meat) and various grades of semolina. Exotica include a delicious dried mullet roe (called "poutargue," 350 francs per kilo), Iranian pistachios, smoked and corned beef, chewy Central European breads and flavoured vodkas. The store also boasts a fascinating supply of arcane kitchen utensils. Aux Cinq Continents is worth a visit for its nose-tickling smells alone.

Davoli
7th arr. - 34, rue Cler 45 51 23 41
Open 8 a.m.-1 p.m. & 3:30 p.m.-7:30 p.m. (Sun., Wed. & holidays until 1 p.m.). Closed Mon. & 1 month during summer.

Fresh stuffed pasta tops the list of specialities here: cappelletti filled with meat, tortellini filled with spinach, and scallop-stuffed ravioli, to name but three. The Parma ham is excellent, and the rosy, smooth mortadella comes straight from Bologna. A selection of fine Italian wines (as well as liqueurs and aperitivi) lets you wash all the good things down in the proper style.

Finkelsztajn
4th arr. - 27, rue des Rosiers - 42 72 78 91
Open 10 a.m.-2 p.m. & 3 p.m.-7:30 p.m. (Sat. 10 a.m.-1:30 p.m. & 3 p.m.-7:30 p.m.; Sun. 10 a.m.-7:30 p.m.). Closed Mon. & Tues. (except holidays).
4th arr. - 24, rue des Ecouffes 48 87 92 85
Open Mon., Thurs. & Fri. 9 a.m.-1:30 p.m. & 2:30 p.m.-7:30 p.m. (Sat. 10 a.m.-1:30 p.m. & 3 p.m.-7:30 p.m.; Sun. 9 a.m.-7:30 p.m.). Closed Tues. & Wed. (except holidays).

In this pretty shop, the hospitable Sacha offers several robust and savoury Yiddish specialities. Among our favourites: the stuffed carp, chopped liver and delicious little piroshki (small turnovers or dumplings filled with a savoury or sweet stuffing). For dessert, try the authentic vatrouchka (Russian cheesecake) or the poppyseed cakes. In the other shop, Sacha's daughter and her husband sell traditional Jewish dishes, all made on the premises, all perfectly delightful.

The General Store
7th arr. - 82, rue de Grenelle - 45 48 63 16
Open 10 a.m.-7:30 p.m. Closed Sun.

Tacos, tortillas and all the other makings of a Tex-Mex feast can be found in this spick-and-span little shop. But the list doesn't stop there: you'll find buttermilk-pancake mix, a selection of California wines, American packaged foods (Karo syrup, cream cheese, tinned pumpkin, chocolate chips, Hellmann's mayonnaise) and even fresh cranberries. If you crave a sweet snack, look for the delectable pecan squares and cookies made freshly every day. As you would expect, English is spoken, and you can count on a warm welcome from the friendly owners (neither of whom, curiously, is American).

FOOD – SHOPS

Jo Goldenberg
4th arr. - 7, rue des Rosiers - 48 87 20 16
Open daily 8:30 a.m.-midnight. (Sat. until 2 a.m.).

For over 60 years, this far-famed little grocery-cum-restaurant has supplied the Ashkenazi community of Paris with stuffed carp, tasty herring with a procession of sauces, smoked salmon, corned beef, smoked tongue and even caviar, which you can wash down with one of the many different vodkas.

Goldenberg
17th arr. - 69, av. de Wagram 42 27 41 85
Open daily 8:30 a.m.-midnight.

Delicatessen fare, made measurably more exotic by the fact that it's served within sight of the Arc de Triomphe. There's herring, there's corned beef, there's gefilte fish (stuffed carp), there's pastrami (smoked beef), and brownies too.

Heratchian Frères
9th arr. - 6, rue Lamartine - 48 78 43 19
Open 8:30 a.m.-7 p.m. (Mon. until 2 p.m.). Closed Sun.

All the mellifluous idioms of the Near East and the Balkans are spoken (and understood) at this fascinating, fragrant bazaar. The sales staff will serve you with fat, purple Kalamata olives, golden thyme-blossom honey, genuine sheep's-milk feta, Salonikan yogurt (made from a mix of cow's and sheep's milk) and savoury kibbeh (bulghur and minced lamb, onions and pinenuts deep-fried or—for the daring—served raw). Nice prices.

Izraël
4th arr. - 30, rue François-Miron 42 72 66 23
Open 9:30 a.m.-1 p.m. & 2:30 p.m.-7 p.m. (Sat. 9:30 a.m.-7 p.m.). Closed Sun., Mon., Aug. & holidays.

Solski and Françoise Izraël are the masters of this colourful, richly scented realm of spices, herbs, exotic foods and condiments. Burlap sacks overflow with basmati rice from Pakistan and perfumed rice from Thailand; crates are filled with fat dates and figs from Turkey; Greek olives soak in barrels of herby, lemony marinades. Curry pastes and powders, chutneys and pink lentils have journeyed from India to this Paris spot; from Mexico, tacos and several types of fiery chillies. Argentinian empanadas, Louisiana pecans, Chinese candied ginger and no fewer than five types of coconut milk are just some of the other international foods found in this unique emporium.

Kioko
2nd arr. - 46, rue des Petits-Champs - 42 61 33 66
Open 10 a.m.-7:30 p.m. Closed Sun. & holidays.

All the hard-to-find ingredients that go into Japanese cuisine can be purchased at this unpretentious little grocery shop. In addition to tofu, taro, Japanese-style rice and wheat noodles, Kioko stocks good Japanese beers, like Kirin and Sapporo. Labels are translated into French.

Marks & Spencer
9th arr. - 35, bd Haussmann - 47 42 42 91
Open 9:30 a.m.-7 p.m. (Tues. from 10 a.m.). Closed Sun.

Marks & Spencer's bacon is wonderful: meaty, smoky, with no nasty bits of bone, no inedible rind. The cheese counter features Stilton, Cheddar, Leicester and so on, and the grocery shelves are crowded with all sorts of piquant condiments and chutneys. Teas, biscuits, jams and marmalades are legion, of course, and a special refrigerated section offers fresh sandwiches for a quick lunch. But be warned: prices in the Paris branch are considerably higher than on Marks & Sparks' home turf.

Mourougane France
10th arr. - 83, passage Brady - 42 46 06 06
Open 9 a.m.-8:30 p.m. Closed Sun.

Over the past decade, Indo-Pakistani cooking has conquered Paris with its sunny, fragrant, spicy dishes. Mourougane, set in the quiet passage Brady, carries marvellous basmati rice, papadums, chutneys and all the spices, chillies and curry pastes and powders needed to produce a full-scale Indian or Pakistani feast.

Au Régal
16th arr. - 4, rue Nicolo - 42 88 49 15
Open 9 a.m.-11 p.m. (Sun. 10 a.m.-3 p.m. & 6 p.m.-11 p.m.). Closed 2 wks. wk. of Aug. 15.

Delicacies from all the Russias are spotlighted here: caviar, vodkas of every description, coulibiac (salmon baked in a pastry crust) and pirozhki (more pastry-wrapped nibbles), marinated herring and blinis, vatrouchka (cheesecake) and walnut tart.

Spécialités Antillaises
20th arr. - 14-16, bd de Belleville 43 58 31 30
Open 10 a.m.-7:15 p.m. (Sat. from 9 a.m.; Sun. 9 a.m.-noon). Closed Mon. & 1st wk. of Jan.

Here's a one-stop shop for Creole ingredients and takeaway foods. Among the latter, we recommend the stuffed crabs, crispy accras (salt-cod fritters), Creole sausage and a spicy avocado dish called féroce d'avocat. The grocery section offers fresh tropical fruits flown in from the West Indies, as well as a selection of exotic frozen fish (shark, gilthead...) and a large choice of rums and punches.

SHOPS – FOOD

Tang Frères
13th arr. - 48, av. d'Ivry - 45 70 80 00
Open 9 a.m.-7:30 p.m. Closed Mon.

Three times a week a cargo plane flies into Paris bearing a shipment earmarked for the Tang brothers. This gastronomic dynasty runs the biggest Asian supermarket in town, stocked with all manner of mysterious (to the uninitiated) roots, powders, dried mushrooms, tinned bamboo shoots, rice and noodles, birds' nests, sharks' fins and so on... and on—there are literally thousands of items to choose from. Don't miss the great ready-to-eat Peking duck.

Than Binh
5th arr. - 18, rue Lagrange - 43 54 66 11
Open 9:30 a.m.-7:30 p.m. Closed Mon. & Aug. 15-22.

From perfumed rice to instant soups, from fresh tropical fruit and vegetables to dried fish, sweet bean cakes and a selection of prepared foods (lovely fresh dim-sum), the Than Binh shops stock a staggering assortment of Chinese, Japanese and Vietnamese food products. Throngs of Asian shoppers come here regularly for their culinary supplies, but the crowds don't seem to worry the calm and amiable staff.

■ FRUIT & VEGETABLES

Palais du Fruit
2nd arr.- 74, rue Montgueil
42 33 22 15
Open 8:30 a.m.-7:30 p.m. (Sun. & holidays until 1 p.m.). Closed Mon., Jan. 1 & Dec. 25.

Superb fruit and vegetables from all over the world, beautifully presented. Even when skies are grey in France, in Chile or the Caribbean gorgeous produce ripens in the sun, then is picked and packed off to this cheerful store. Wide choice, remarkable quality.

Fruits de France
4th arr. - 72, rue Saint-Louis-en-l'Ile - 43 26 83 02
Open 8 a.m.-1 p.m. & 4 p.m.-8:30 p.m. (Tues. from 4 p.m.; Sun. & holidays until 1 p.m.). Closed Mon. & summer.

The freshness of the herbs, fruit and vegetables are above reproach at Jean-Louis Turpin's shop. People in a hurry can have their purchases peeled while they wait (or while they pick up their dry-cleaning down the street).

Le Fruitier d'Auteuil
16th arr. - 5, rue Bastien-Lepage
45 27 51 08
Open 6:30 a.m.-1 p.m. & 3:30 p.m.-7:30 p.m. (holidays until 1 p.m.). Closed Sun. & Aug.

Bernard Rapine, president of the Fruit Retailers' Union, has a personal and professional interest in displaying the best produce he can find. He claims—and we have seen it to be true—that any store displaying the union label (the word *fruitier* printed over a basket of fruit) is honour-bound to provide top-quality merchandise and service. Rapine's shop is a fine example.

■ GOURMET SPECIALITIES

Caves Augé
8th arr. - 116, bd Haussmann
45 22 16 97
Open 9 a.m.-8 p.m. (Mon. from 1 p.m.). Closed Sun. & holidays.

Augé was one of the first shops in town (and maybe the only one) where eccentric gourmets could purchase such rare delicacies as bear steaks, reindeer roasting joints and elephant trunks. Nowadays this rather luxurious little shop specialises in fine wines and brandies. There is still a small grocery section, which includes excellent tinned foods and an enticing assortment of boxed biscuits. But the pride of the house is its wine cellar (the oldest in Paris) which features an exceptional choice of "minor" Bordeaux, great Burgundies, Cognacs and Calvados.

A home for the Nation

The *Triumph of the Nation* is the theme of the bronze group sculpted by Jules Dalou that now stands on the place de la Nation. The work was originally planned for the *place de la République*, but an official jury decided otherwise. For a closer look at the figures, take the underground walkway to the gardens in the centre of the sea of traffic that surrounds the place. Exhaust fumes were less of a problem in 1880, when the first national holiday was celebrated here on 14 July. A short walk away in the *rue de Picpus*, eminent members of the French nobility executed during the Revolution (the guillotine stood for a time on the place de la Nation) are buried in the *Picpus Cemetery*. Today, this green and placid resting place is exclusively reserved for descendants of those same noble families.

FOOD – SHOPS

Detou
2nd arr. - 58, rue de Tiquetonne
42 33 96 43
Open 8 a.m.-6 p.m. (Sat. until noon, except in Dec.: until 5 p.m.). Closed Sun. & holidays.

Home bakers browse happily among the cake-making supplies that comprise Detou's principal stock-in-trade: cooking chocolate, powdered almonds, candied fruit and the like. But there are also rare and delicious jams here, as well as unusual biscuits and tasty tinned goods (the mushrooms are particularly fine), Champagnes and foie gras. Quality merchandise at surprisingly moderate prices.

Faguais
8th arr. - 30, rue La Trémoille
47 20 80 91
Open 9:15 a.m.-7 p.m. Closed Sun. & holidays.

Granny would feel quite at home in this charming gourmet shop. A dizzying variety of temptations is set out neatly on the shelves. Old-fashioned jams, oils, honeys, biscuits, spices, vinegars and condiments fairly cry out to be bought and sampled. As the shop's pervasive fragrance implies, fresh coffee beans are roasted on the premises daily.

Fauchon
8th arr. - 26, pl. de la Madeleine
47 42 60 11
Open 9:40 a.m.-7 p.m. Closed Sun.

In 1886, at the age of 30, Auguste Fauchon opened his *épicerie fine* on the place de la Madeleine, specialising in quality French foodstuffs. The rest is history. After more than a century, Fauchon is the uncontested paragon of what a luxury gourmet emporium should be. The energetic and youthful president of Fauchon, Martine Premat, has brought a new lustre and energy to the firm. All 300 employees are committed to the task of tasting, testing and selling the very finest, the rarest, the most unusual foods in the world. The number of spices alone—4,500—is enough to make your head spin. And you'll find such delicacies as black-fig or watermelon preserves, lavender or buckwheat honey, Mim tea from India or Kee-yu tea from China, lavish displays of prime vegetables and fruits, and a world-renowned collection of vintage wines and brandies. As for the pastries, well...you should know that Pierre Hermé is one of the finest *chef-pâtissiers* in the business.

Fouquet
8th arr. - 22, rue François-ler - 47 23 30 36
Open 9:30 a.m.-7:30 p.m. Closed Sun. & holidays.
9th arr. - 36, rue Laffitte - 47 70 85 00
Open 10 a.m.-6:30 p.m. Closed Sat., Sun. & holidays.

Christophe Fouquet is the most recent representative of the illustrious family of grocers who have been selling choice foodstuffs at this address since 1852. Fine chocolates are a long-standing speciality at this pretty, old-fashioned shop, but don't overlook the rare mustards (flavoured with blackcurrants, oranges or raspberries), appetising bottled sauces, vinegars distilled according to a secret house recipe, liqueur-laced jams, fruity olive oils, imported cakes and biscuits and excellent fruit brandies. All the items are attractively packaged and make much-appreciated gifts.

Hédiard
7th arr. - 126, rue du Bac - 45 44 01 98
8th arr. - 21, pl. de la Madeleine 42 66 44 36
16th arr. - 6, rue Donizetti - 40 50 71 94
Open 9:30 a.m.-9 p.m. Closed Sun.
16th arr. - 70, av. Paul-Doumer 45 04 51 92
17th arr. - 106, bd de Courcelles 47 63 32 14
Open 9:30 a.m.-10 p.m. Closed Sun.
16th arr. - 113, av. Victor-Hugo 44 05 09 88
Open 9:30 a.m.-8 p.m. Closed Sun.
1st arr. - Forum des Halles, 1, rue Pierre-Lescot - 40 39 98 04
Open 10:30 a.m.-7:30 p.m. Closed Sun.
15th arr. - 131, rue Saint-Charles 40 59 86 41
Open 9:30 a.m.-7:30 p.m. Closed Sun.

Only the finest, rarest foodstuffs are deemed worthy of entry into this shrine of epicureanism, founded in 1854. Distinguished smoked salmon from the best "schools," sophisticated sugars and syrups, pedigreed Ports, vintage wines and brandies, and over 4,500 carefully chosen grocery items attract virtually every cultivated palate in town. Even the ordinary is extraordinary here: mustard spiked with Cognac; vinegar flavoured with seaweed; opulent fruits and vegetables, always prime, that hail from the ends of the earth. Many of the items are as costly as they are exotic, but the wines consistently offer excellent value for the money.

CAVIAR & SALMON

Caviar Kaspia
8th arr. - 17, pl. de la Madeleine 42 65 33 52
Open 9 a.m.-12:30 a.m. Closed Sun.

Caviar, it would seem, is best savoured in a setting of serene austerity. Such is the impression made by the stark interior of Caviar Kaspia, where the choicest Russian and Iranian roes are sold, along with an assortment of superb smoked fish. The tender, buttery salmon is flawless, but we come for the fine smoked eel, trout or sturgeon, all of which are models of their kind. Should a hunger pang occur at the sight of these delights (how could it not?), just step upstairs to the first-floor restaurant, where all the house specialities may be ordered à la carte.

Le Coin du Caviar
4th arr. - 2, rue de la Bastille - 48 04 82 93
Open 10 a.m.-2:30 p.m. & 7 p.m.-11:30 p.m. (Sat. 7 p.m.-11:30 p.m.). Closed Sun.

No doubt about it, the area around the Bastille has gone up-market since the new Opéra was built. The Coin du Caviar, right in the thick of things (across the street from the popular Bofinger brasserie), has made faithful customers out of the most finicky caviar and smoked salmon-fanciers. Prime Russian or Iranian caviars are featured (depending on the market); the pale, delicately smoky salmon hails from Denmark.

Comptoir du Saumon
4th arr. - 60, rue François-Miron 42 77 23 08
8th arr. - 61, rue Pierre-Charron 45 61 25 14
15th arr. - 116, rue de la Convention - 45 54 31 16
17th arr. - 3, av. de Villiers - 40 53 89 00
18th arr. - 139, rue Ordener - 42 52 80 73

Open 10 a.m.-10 p.m. Closed Sun. & holidays.

The French are crazy about smoked salmon. And it is this untempered enthusiasm that's behind the success of the Comptoir du Saumon, where Irish, Swedish, Norwegian and Scottish fish are sold at attractive prices. Also stocked are smoked trout and eel, Dutch herring, Danish marinated herring and Iranian caviar. The premium vodkas and aquavits are perfect partners for the fish, and if you really can't wait for a taste, take a table at the shop's snack bar.

Flora Danica
8th arr. - 142, av. des Champs-Elysées - 43 59 20 41
Open 10 a.m.-10 p.m. (Sun. & holidays 11 a.m.-8 p.m.; Dec. 24 until 5 p.m.).

Does the phrase "Danish gastronomy" sound fishy to you? So it should, for salmon in myriad forms is its very foundation. Delicate pink specimens from the Baltic Sea are sold here, both smoked and marinated with dill. We suggest that you sample the delicious Danish herring—in fact, why not the entire array of sweet-and-sour sauces that go with it—then wash it all down with an ice-cold, pale Carlsberg beer.

Dominique
6th arr. - 19, rue Bréa
43 27 08 80
Open daily 9:30 a.m.-2:30 p.m. & 5:15 p.m.-10:30 p.m. Closed 1 wk. Feb. school holidays & mid-July to mid-Aug.

Dominique has been a fixture on the Montparnasse circuit since time immemorial, and will probably remain so, despite occasional lapses in food and service. The takeaway shop remains an excellent source of caviar, Danish smoked salmon and herring, as well as tender blinis, zakuski (traditional Russian hors d'œuvres) and the accompanying heady Russian vodka.

Maxoff
7th arr. - 44, rue de Verneuil - 42 60 60 43
Open 10:30 a.m.-3 p.m. & 6:30 p.m.-10:30 p.m. (Dec. 24 & 31 until 9 p.m.). Closed Sun., Aug. & holidays

Ossetra and sevruga caviars from Iran are featured in the take-away section of this pleasant little restaurant. Smaller spenders may prefer the pressed roe (it's considerably cheaper), or the good Danish smoked salmon, smoked eel, herring (there are ten types) or the assortment of Russian dishes like koulibiac (salmon pie), piroshki and cheesecake. Everything is fresh and of good quality.

Petrossian
7th arr. - 18, bd La Tour-Maubourg - 45 51 70 64
Open 9 a.m.-8 p.m. Closed Sun.

The Petrossian family introduced sturgeon eggs to France in the 1920s, a commercial coup that won them the undying gratitude of the newly born Soviet Union. Today Christian Petrossian still enjoys the rare privilege of choosing the very best roes on site at Caspian fishing ports. In addition to sublime ossetra, sevruga, beluga and pressed caviar, there are remarkably

---

Shopping in the seventh

Ministries, embassies and well-heeled residents of the posh seventh arrondissement are lucky to live amid some of the best food shops in Paris. Quality is the rule and you can fill your basket as fast as you empty your purse in the rue du Bac, the rue Saint-Dominique and the rue Cler. On the way, give your eyes a feast too by peeking into some of the flowered courtyards tucked away behind wrought-iron gates. Try the bread from Jean-Luc Poujauran (20 rue Jean-Nicot), caviar from Petrossian (18 boulevard de Latour-Maubourg), cheese from Marie-Anne Cantin (12 rue du Champ-de-Mars), and chocolates from Debauve et Gallais (30 rue des Saints-Pères).

Depuis des siècles, verriers et tailleurs de Saint Louis soufflent le cristal et le taillent à la main. De la pureté du sable et de l'ardeur du feu naissent des pièces uniques. Au premier plan, deux nouvelles créations de Saint Louis: Tsar, à côtes vénitiennes et jambe torsadée et Crocus, en cristal taillé côtes plates, clair ou doublé rouge.

Le Grand Cristal sort tous les jours.

Les Verreries de Saint-Louis, nées au 16e siècle sont devenues Verreries Royales il y a 225 ans. A l'occasion de cet anniversaire, Saint Louis vous fait un cadeau: du 1er mars 1992 au 31 janvier 1993, à compter de votre date d'achat, Saint Louis s'engage pendant 2 ans, à remplacer à l'identique, 6 verres brisés sur votre service de 36 verres millésimés 225e anniversaire (12 à eau, 12 à vin, 12 flûtes ou coupes à champagne), quel que soit le prix du verre !
Vous pourrez ainsi utiliser sans crainte votre service de verres tous les jours, et même vous en offrir un second !

SAINT·LOUIS
FRANCE

Boutique Saint-Louis. 13, rue Royale, 75008 Paris. Tél. (1) 40 17 01 74.
Liste des points de vente : Saint-Louis. 30, rue de Paradis, 75010 Paris. Tél. (1) 47 70 25 70.

Catherine Baril
Two Boutiques

Deluxe
second-hand
Designer clothing
14, rue de la Tour
Paris 16th
45.20.95.21

Deluxe
second-hand
Designer clothing
25, rue de la Tour
Paris 16th
45.27.11.46

Open Daily 10-7
Monday 2-7

Visa/Carte Bleue Accepted

Saint Laurent   Chanel   Ungaro
Guy Laroche   Givenchy

FOOD - SHOPS

rich Norwegian smoked salmon, smoked eel and sturgeon, Russian salmon roe and a multitude of excellent vodkas. Gift baskets can be composed according to your tastes and budget.

ESCARGOTS

L'Escargot de la Butte
18th arr. - 48, rue Joseph-de-Maistre - 46 27 38 27
Open 8:30 a.m.-7:30 p.m. (Sun. Sept. 1-March 31: until 1 p.m.). Closed Sun. (April 1-Aug. 31), Mon. & July 15-Aug. 15.

"It's really a shame, but there are no more escargots de Bourgogne left in France," laments Monsieur Marchal. He imports them, therefore, from Germany. But his petits-gris come straight from the Provençal countryside, and arrive still frisky at his little shop located at the foot of the Butte Montmartre. He stuffs them with a deliciously fragrant blend of pure butter, garlic and parsley, and they are a remarkable treat.

La Maison de l'Escargot
15th arr. - 79, rue Fondary - 45 75 31 09
Open 8:30 a.m.-8 p.m. (Sun. & holidays 9 a.m.-1 p.m.). Closed Mon. & July 14-Sept. 1.

Snail fanciers from far and wide make the trek to this commendable shop. Live petits-gris and escargots de Bourgogne of all sizes are prepared with a delicious snail butter—which is not too strong, not too bland—it's made according to a secret recipe developed here in 1894. The butter may also be purchased separately. If you want to sample the wares on the spot, cross the street to the little stand opposite the shop.

FOIE GRAS

Comptoir Corrézien du Foie Gras et du Champignon
15th arr. - 8, rue des Volontaires 47 83 52 97
Open 9 a.m.-1:30 p.m. & 3 p.m.-8 p.m. (Mon. from 3:30 p.m.). Closed Sun.

Chantal Larnaudie is an energetic young woman who comes from a long line of foie-gras specialists. The specimens she offers in her shop, whole poached fattened goose liver, preserved in a terrine, are fine indeed, and attractively priced to boot. Don't miss her wide selection of fragrant wild mushrooms, sold fresh in season, or dried.

Le Comptoir du Foie Gras (Bizac)
1st arr. - 6, rue des Prouvaires 42 36 26 27
Open 8 a.m.-7 p.m. Closed Sun.

This shop is the Parisian outpost of Bizac, a renowned foie-gras processing firm from Brive, in south-west France. Foie gras in tins and jars comes fully cooked or, if you prefer, lightly cooked. If you wish to try your hand at preparing your own terrine de foie gras, raw duck and goose livers are available.

Divay (Au Bon Porc)
10th arr. - 52, rue du Faubourg-Saint-Denis - 47 70 06 86
Open 7 a.m.-1:30 p.m. & 4 p.m.-7:30 p.m. (Sun., Wed. & holidays 7:30 a.m.-1 p.m.). Closed Mon. & Aug.
17th arr. - 4, rue Bayen - 43 80 16 97
Open 7:30 a.m.-1:30 p.m. & 3:30 p.m.-7:30 p.m. (Sun. & holidays 7:30 a.m.-1 p.m.). Closed Mon. & Aug.

Priced at 650 francs per kilo, Divay sells the least expensive fattened goose liver to be found in the city. What's more, it's delicious. You'll find great traditional charcuterie here too.

Dubernet
1st arr. - Forum des Halles, 210, porte Lescot, niveau -2 - 42 33 88 46
Open 10:30 a.m.-7:30 p.m. Closed Sun. (except 2 Sun. before Christmas).
7th arr. - 2, rue Augereau - 45 55 50 71
Open 9 a.m.-1:30 p.m. & 3:30 p.m.-7:30 p.m. (holidays 10 a.m.-1 p.m.). Closed Sun., Mon. & Aug. 1-15.
92800 Puteaux - Centre commercial Les Quatre Temps, niveau 1 - 47 73 70 02
Open 10 a.m.-8 p.m. Closed Sun.

These foies gras come from Saint-Sever, in the Landes region of south-west France. Whole fattened goose and duck livers are sold fully cooked in tins or lightly cooked (just pasteurised) in jars. Prices are moderate.

Aux Ducs de Gascogne
1st arr. - 4, rue du Marché-Saint-Honoré - 42 60 45 31
Open 10 a.m.-7 p.m. Closed Sun. & Aug.
4th arr. - 111, rue Saint-Antoine 42 71 17 72
Open 9:30 a.m.-2 p.m. & 5 p.m.-8 p.m. (Mon. from 3 p.m.). Closed Sun.
8th arr. - 112, bd Haussmann 45 22 54 04
Open 10 a.m.-7:15 p.m. (Mon. from noon). Closed Sun. & holidays.
15th arr. - 221, rue de la Convention - 48 28 32 09
Open 9:30 a.m.-1 p.m. & 4 p.m.-8 p.m. (Mon. from 4 p.m.,

RAC PARIS STREETS: The cartography of this city-wide street plan of Paris is clear and easy to use and is supported by a comprehensive index in book form tipped on to the card cover. The map is packed with essential information including the direction of one-way streets. A must for all visitors to Paris. Price: £ 4.50.

SHOPS – FOOD

holidays 9:30 a.m.-1 p.m.). Closed Sun.
20th arr. - 41, rue des Gatines - 43 66 99 99
Open 9 a.m.-12:45 p.m. & 3 p.m.-7:45 p.m. (Mon. from 3 p.m.). Closed Sun. & 3 wks. in Aug.

This multi-store chain specialises in tinned and lightly cooked foie gras, sold at rather steep prices, but the *patron* is a real charmer.

Foie Gras Luxe
1st arr. - 26, rue Montmartre - 42 36 14 73
Open 6 a.m.-noon & 2:30 p.m.-5 p.m. (Mon. from 8 a.m.). Closed Sat. (except morning in Dec.), Sun. & holidays.

This worthy establishment sells raw foie gras all year round, as well as lightly cooked fattened goose and duck livers, and marvellous cured hams from Parma, San Daniele and the Ardennes.

Les Produits Jean-Legrand
8th arr. - 58, rue des Mathurins - 42 65 50 46
Open 10 a.m.-2 p.m. & 3 p.m.-6:30 p.m. (Wed. 10 a.m.-1:30 p.m. & 3:30 p.m.-6:30 p.m.). Closed Sat. (except Nov. & Dec.), Sun., 1 wk. at Easter, Aug. & holidays.
17th arr. - 11, rue Pierre-Demours - 40 55 92 20
Open 8:30 a.m.-2 p.m. & 4:30 p.m.-8 p.m. (Sun. 8 a.m.-1 p.m.). Closed Mon.

This reputable processing concern turns out a fine terrine of fresh fattened goose liver, an equally tasty poached version, duck foie gras in a terrine and some interesting tinned dishes: daube of boar with cranberries, beef goulash and lotte in mustard sauce.

HONEY, JAMS & SYRUP

Daire–Aux Miels de France
8th arr. - 71, rue du Rocher - 45 22 23 13
Open 9:30 a.m.-2 p.m. & 2:30 p.m.-7 p.m. (Mon. from 2:30 p.m.). Closed Sun., Aug. & holidays.

Renée Daire stocks a dozen of the most select French honeys: pine, oak, chestnut, heather, lavender, rosemary, thyme, acacia and more. Pollen and royal jelly are also on sale, as well as a honey-flavoured gingerbread studded with walnuts and hazelnuts. The delicious homemade jams that glitter enticingly on the shelves are prepared by Madame Daire herself.

Le Furet
10th arr. - 63, rue de Chabrol - 47 70 48 34
Open 8:30 a.m.-8 p.m. Closed Sun.

Alain Furet is a *chocolatier* first and foremost, but he also makes fabulous jams from recipes developed by Monsieur Tanrade, for a long time the top name in French preserves. Furet took over the Tanrade plant, and now turns out succulent jams (raspberry, strawberry, apricot, blackcurrant...); he is also putting the finishing touches to a recipe of his own, for *confiture au chocolat*—we can't wait.

Maison du Miel
8th arr. - 24, rue Vignon - 47 42 26 70
Open 9:30 a.m.-7 p.m. (Mon. until 6 p.m.). Closed Sun.

Make a beeline to this "House of Honey" to try varieties from the various regions of France. There's Corsican honey, luscious pine honey from the Vosges mountains (which comes highly recommended for bronchial irritations), Provençal lavender honey, as well as choice varieties from the Alps and Auvergne, all rigorously tested by a busy hive of honey tasters. In addition, you'll find honey "by-products," such as beeswax, candles, pollen and royal jelly, as well as a range of honey-based cosmetics.

A la Mère de Famille
9th arr. - 35, rue du Faubourg-Montmartre - 47 70 83 69
Open 8:30 a.m.-1:30 p.m. & 3 p.m.-7 p.m. Closed Sun., Mon., Aug. & holidays.

Founded in 1761, this adorable emporium is the doyen of Paris sweetshops. Today it is still a showcase for the very best sugarplums that the French provinces produce. You'll find specialities from every region: cakes, glazed chestnuts, exquisite jams and honeys and delicious dried fruits. The current owner, Serge Neveu, is a professional *chocolatier*: his palet guanaja is deep, dark and delicious. Excellent prices.

OILS

A l'Olivier
4th arr. - 23, rue de Rivoli - 48 04 86 59
Open 9:30 a.m.-1 p.m. & 2 p.m.-7 p.m. Closed Sun., Mon. & holidays.

In this freshly refurbished shop connoisseurs will find not only several fine varieties of olive oil but walnut oil, grilled-almond oil, pumpkin-seed oil, hazelnut oil and an incomparable top-secret blend of virgin olive oils as well. We applaud the shop's policy of selling exceptionally expensive and perishable oils in quarter-litre bottles. Fine vinegars and mustards are presented too—everything you need to mix up a world-class vinaigrette.

Jean-Claude Cornu
9th arr. - 82, rue de Clichy - 48 74 60 86
Open 9:30 a.m.-1:30 p.m. & 3 p.m.-8:30 p.m. Closed Sun., Aug. & holidays.

Inside this adorable little shop is a veritable treasure trove of top-quality oils. First pressings of all sorts are featured—from peanut, sunflower and nettle to poppy, walnut and hazelnut. Fragrant, fruity olive oil from Tunisia comes highly recommended, but conspicuous consumers may prefer the horrendously expensive variety from Provence.

PASTA

Biletta
16th arr. - 35, rue d'Auteuil - 42 88 58 88
Open 8 a.m.-1 p.m. & 3:30 p.m.-7:45 p.m. (Sat. from 7 a.m.; Sun. 8:30 a.m.-1 p.m.). Closed Mon. & Aug.

The selection is small—tagliatelle, ravioli, gnocchi, lasagne—but the pasta is golden and finely textured and wonderfully flavoured. Try the fine Italian hams and salamis, too.

Cipolli
13th arr. - 81, rue Bobillot - 45 88 26 06
Open 7 a.m.-1 p.m. & 3 p.m.-7:30 p.m. (Mon. from 3:30 p.m.). Closed Sun. & Aug. No cards.

Monsieur Cipolli kneads and stretches his golden dough into an appetising array of pasta specialities. The tagliatelle and ravioli have an authentic, old-fashioned flavour, while his lasagne is nothing short of sublime. The stuffed pastas (cappelletti filled with minced beef and ham, or mushrooms, or spinach and ricotta; "priests' hats" stuffed with salmon or ricotta and ham) are tender and tasty. Prices range from 43 to 75 francs per kilo.

TRUFFLES

Maison de la Truffe
8th arr. - 19, pl. de la Madeleine 42 65 53 22
Open 9 a.m.-9 p.m. (Mon. until 8 p.m.). Closed Sun.

Alongside extraordinary charcuterie, foie gras, good salmon and prepared foods, this luxurious food emporium offers truffles (both freshly dug and sterilised, and bottled) at prices that are emphatically not of the bargain-basement variety. The season for fresh black truffles runs from October to late March; fresh white truffles are imported from Italy in November and December. Owner Guy Monier recently set aside a corner of his shop for tasting: customers may order from a brief menu featuring dishes made with the sublime fungus (truffes en salade, truffes en feuilleté, truffles with fresh pasta, in risotto...). Look too for the range of oils, vinegars and mustards all perfumed with—truffles, of course.

■ HEALTH FOODS

Herboristerie du Palais-Royal
1st arr. - 11, rue des Petits-Champs - 42 97 54 68
Open 8:30 a.m.-7 p.m. (Sat. 10:30 a.m.-6:30 p.m.). Closed Sun. & holidays.

A venerable herbalist shop that presents a vast and fragrant range of dried medicinal plants and herb teas. The 600 varieties are stocked in a cool, dark cellar to preserve their beneficial properties. Also on hand are plant-based health, beauty products and toiletries.

Grand Appétit
4th arr. - 9, rue de la Cerisaie 40 27 04 95
Open 10 a.m.-8 p.m. (Fri. & Sun. until 4 p.m.). Closed Sat. & 2 wks. in Aug.

Madame David is committed to healthy living and a healthy environment. Her range of macrobiotic and natural foods is supplemented by a selection of "earth-friendly" cleaning products. Her supply of organically grown fruits and vegetables is renewed three times a week for freshness. The shop's annexe restaurant (vegetarian, of course) is very popular—even more so since Elton John was spotted there.

La Vie Claire
6th arr. - 126, bd Raspail - 45 48 82 70
Open 9:30 a.m.-7 p.m. (Sat. 10 a.m.-1 p.m. & 3 p.m.-6 p.m.). Closed Sun. & holidays.

Organically grown fruits and vegetables and wholegrain breads are delivered daily to this pleasant shop, which also carries farm-fresh eggs and milk, and soy-based yogurts. Those of you on salt- or sugar-free diets will find the foods you need here, alongside cosmetics and household products that don't violate the rights of animals or the environment.

Veggie
7th arr. - 38, rue de Verneuil - 42 61 28 61
Open 9:30 a.m.-2:30 p.m. & 4 p.m.-7:30 p.m. Closed Sun., 1 month during summer, & holidays. No cards.

Fresh carrot juice and soy-milk desserts attract a faithful corps of regular customers to Madame Janson's shop. But she also supplies customers with herb teas and plant-based beverages, whole grains, oils and diet supplements, as well as a selection of cosmetics and environmentally sound cleaning products. Busy vegetarians will appreciate her line of meatless take-away dishes (vegetable gratins, couscous, sweet and savoury tarts...).

Le Bol en Bois
13th arr. - 40, rue Pascal - 47 07 07 01
Open 9:30 a.m.-9:30 p.m. Closed Sun. & holidays.

Specialists in macrobiotic fruits and vegetables, the "Wooden Bowl" also imports health foods from Europe and Japan. Whole-grain breads and rice, tofu-based foods, fresh dairy products and vegetables are selected and sold by Monsieur Sakaguchi, who also cooks up tasty vegetarian dishes in his restaurant annexe.

SHOPS – FOOD

Point Nature
17th arr. - 4, rue Lebon - 45 72 11 26
Open 9:30 a.m.-7:30 p.m. (Sun. & holidays 10:30 a.m.-1 p.m.). Closed Mon.

All the best-known names in natural cosmetics and cleaning products are in stock, as well as food supplements and herb teas. But vegetarians (and others) who have a sweet tooth will be especially pleased by the homemade jams and pure honeys, the guaranteed-natural pastries and other guilt-free sweets. If your natural lifestyle does not exclude the pleasures of wine, here you'll find a wealth of organically grown vintages from all over France (don't miss the vin de pays de Pezenas, in red, white or rosé, sold by the litre or in bulk).

■ ICE CREAM & SORBETS

Le Bac à Glaces
7th arr. - 109, rue du Bac - 45 48 87 65
Open 11 a.m.-7:30 p.m. Closed Sun. & holidays.

These guaranteed homemade ice creams and sorbets are crafted from top-quality ingredients, with no artificial additives. Doubting Thomases are encouraged to watch the *glaciers* busily at work in their glassed-in kitchen. Alongside the standards, you'll find some delicious liqueur-flavoured ices and other uncommon concoctions, like Camembert ice cream and carrot and tomato sorbets. We always find it difficult to decide between the scrumptious nougat ice cream and the honey-and-pinenut flavour. All these icy delights may be taken away in cartons or enjoyed on the spot in the tiny ice-cream parlour.

> *Monday, like Sunday, is a day of rest for many shopkeepers.*

Baggi
9th arr. - 33, rue Chaptal - 48 74 01 39
Open 10:30 a.m.-7:15 p.m. Closed Sun., Mon. 2 wks. Feb. school holidays & 2 wks. in Aug.

The Baggis are not newcomers to the ice cream trade. Since 1850 their shop has been a mecca for lovers of frozen desserts. Today, many aficionados consider Guy Baggi, the firm's current creative force, to be the ice prince of Paris. He is forever dreaming up new flavour combinations—and winning prizes for them. Who wouldn't want to pin an award on the Princesse (wild strawberry and chocolate ice creams, pear sorbet and a touch of caramel) or on the Chocolatine (a symphony in chocolate, orange and caramel), or the justly celebrated Biscuit Rothschild. The flavours and dessert creations on hand vary with the seasons and Baggi's mood.

Baskin-Robbins
6th arr. - 1, rue du Four - 43 25 10 63
Open noon-8 p.m. (Fri., Sat. & May 1-Sept. 30 noon-midnight). Closed Sun. & Feb.

The French tend to find Baskin-Robbins ice creams cloyingly sweet and unnecessarily rich; but they are intrigued by the flavours: maple-walnut, banana-chocolate swirl, peanut-butter and chocolate. On summer nights, French ice cream fans join tourists of all nationalities to sip authentic American milkshakes, a Baskin-Robbins speciality.

Berthillon
4th arr. - 31, rue Saint-Louis-en-l'Ile - 43 54 31 61
Open 10 a.m.-8 p.m. Closed Mon., Tues. & school holidays (except at Christmas).

Berthillon is the most famous name in French ice cream. The firm's many faithful fans think nothing of queueing up for *hours* just to treat their taste buds to a cone or dish of chocolate-nougat or glazed-chestnut ice cream. Berthillon's sorbets are our particular weakness: pink grapefruit, fig, wild strawberry... The entire repertoire covers some 70 flavours, including many seasonal specialities.

Glacier Calabrese
14th arr. - 15, rue d'Odessa - 43 20 31 63
Open daily noon-12:30 a.m. Closed Aug. No cards.

The owner's lilting Calabrese accent and welcoming warmth are reason enough to visit this little ice cream parlour. But don't forget to taste his delicious creations. In addition to an assortment of classic ice creams and tropical sorbets, he makes wonderful Italian-style ices: Amaretto, Croccantino (delightfully nutty), mint-flavoured Straciatella and Strega (for a cone with a kick). The prices are not bad either.

Gilles Vilfeu
1st arr. - 3, rue de la Cossonnerie 40 26 36 40
Open daily winter: noon-7 p.m.; from Easter & in summer: noon-1 a.m.

Vilfeu's imaginative productions include surprising and sophisticated novelty flavours—tea, lavender and foie-gras sorbets—an ice based on Beaujolais nouveau, and ice creams flavoured with liquorice, cinnamon and ginger. We strongly encourage you to sample the sumptuous frozen desserts, especially the moulded cream-cheese sorbet served with a raspberry coulis.

Raimo
12th arr. - 59-61, bd de Reuilly 43 43 70 17
Open 9 a.m.-midnight. Closed Mon. & Feb.

Sorbets and ice creams produced according to time-honoured methods, with strictly fresh ingredients.

FOOD – SHOPS

Raimo's strong suit is concocting seductive flavour combinations; some of the most successful are pear-hazelnut, ginger-honey and cinnamon-mandarin orange.

■ MEAT, GAME & FOWL

Au Bell Viandier
6th arr. - 25, rue du Vieux-Colombier - 45 48 57 83
Open 8:30 a.m.-1 p.m. & 4 p.m.-8 p.m. (Sun. until 1 p.m. & holidays until 12:30 p.m.). Closed Mon.

Serge Caillaud is the reigning king of Parisian butchers (and if you want a reference, Joël Robuchon buys his meat here!) Rigorous selection and skilful preparation are the hallmarks of these meats, which hail from the best French producers. There's milk-fed veal and fine beef from the Limousin region, top-quality pork, poultry from Bresse and Challans (including superb capons), and premium game in season. Caillaud's specialities include a truffled roast of beef, veal stuffed with apricots or studded with prunes and pistachios.

Boucherie Lamartine
16th arr. - 172, av. Victor-Hugo 47 27 82 29
Open 6:30 a.m.-7:30 p.m. (Sat. 6 a.m.-3 p.m.). Closed Sun. & holidays.

Christian Prosper sells some of the best meat in France in this pretty, old-fashioned butcher's shop. It's not cheap, but then you can't put a price on perfection, can you? The properly hung beef is sublime. And the milky-pink veal always cooks up to juicy perfection, unlike the more commonly available varieties, which have an annoying tendency to shrink.

Boucherie Marbeuf
8th arr. - 36, rue Marbeuf - 42 25 36 55
Open 7:30 a.m.-2:15 p.m. (Fri. until 3:45 p.m. & Sat. until 12:45 p.m.). Closed Sun. No cards.

This wonderful butcher's shop has a safe place in the annals of Parisian gastronomy. Countless top restaurants rely on the Boucherie Marbeuf's peerless professionals to supply them with superb beef (cuts from several elite breeds, including the rare and costly Simmenthal, said to be one of the world's finest), as well as veal from the Corrèze region, pork from the Auvergne and genuine Sisteron lamb.

Boucheries Bernard
1st arr. - 38, rue du Louvre - 42 21 12 15
Open 8:30 a.m.-7 p.m. Closed Sun.
10th arr. - 221, rue Lafayette - 40 05 07 26
Open 9 a.m.-1 p.m. & 4 p.m.-7:15 p.m. (Fri. 9 a.m.-1 p.m. & 3:30 p.m.-7:15 p.m.; Sat. 9 a.m.-7 p.m. & holidays until 1 p.m.). Closed Sun.
13th arr. - 100, bd Masséna - 45 83 58 20
Open 9:30 a.m.-8 p.m. (Fri. & Sat. from 9 a.m.). Closed Sun.
14th arr. - 55, av. du Maine - 45 38 58 83
Open 9 a.m.-7 p.m. (July & Aug. 9 a.m.-1 p.m. & 3 p.m.-7 p.m.). Closed Sun.
15th arr. - 104 bis, rue Saint-Charles - 45 77 58 46
Open 8:30 a.m.-1 p.m. & 3 p.m.-7:30 p.m. (Fri. 8:30 a.m.-1 p.m. & 2:30 p.m.-7:30 p.m.; Sat. 8:30 a.m.-7 p.m. & Sun. until 1 p.m.). Closed Mon.

Over 20 years ago the Boucheries Bernard came up with a highly successful system for selling good-quality, custom-cut meat at unbeatable prices. The chain now has stores all over Paris and the suburbs, stores that offer excellent pork and lamb. The veal isn't always as appealing, and to spot bargains in the beef section, you need a discerning eye. But the offal counter is admirably stocked, and the poultry selection impressive.

Le Coq Saint-Honoré
1st arr. - 3, rue Gomboust - 42 61 52 04
Open 8 a.m.-1 p.m. & 4:30 p.m.-7 p.m. (Fri. 8 a.m.-1 p.m. & 3:30 p.m.-7 p.m.; Sat. until 1 p.m.). Closed Sun. & holidays.

We might as well make it clear right away: for our money, Le Coq Saint-Honoré is one of Paris's top poulterers. It's no coincidence that the list of its customers boasts such culinary notables as Robuchon, Savoy, Senderens and Terrail of La Tour d'Argent. The refrigerated displays offer choice Bresse chickens and guinea fowl (fast becoming prohibitively expensive), as well as laudable Loué pullets, Challans ducks and plump rabbits from the Gâtinais region south of Paris. In season, there is a fine selection of game, including authentic Scottish grouse.

Maison Queuelevée Rôtisserie Cambronne
15th arr. - 90, rue Cambronne 47 34 36 55
Open 8:30 a.m.-12:30 p.m. & 4 p.m.-7:30 p.m. (Sun. 8:30 a.m.-12:30 p.m.). Closed Mon.

What are the hallmarks of premium fowl? Freshness, first and foremost, because the fresher the chicken, the better

---

RAC MOTORING ATLAS FRANCE: Our fully revised and well-established large format RAC Motoring Atlas France, Belgium and Luxembourg at 1:250,000 (approximately 4 miles to 1 inch) now has even more features to improve journey planning and to make driving in France more enjoyable. Clear, accurate and detailed road maps make RAC Motoring Atlas France the ideal atlas for the independent traveller in France. Price: £ 11.99 (spiral bound).

it tastes. But lineage counts as well, and the birds here are pedigree—from Loué, Périgord and other noted regions—along with ducks from Challans and, in season, one of the city's finest selections of feathered game from Sologne.

Marc Tattevin
Palais de la Viande
7th arr. - 15, rue du Champ-de-Mars - 47 05 07 02
Open 7 a.m.-1 p.m. & 3:30 p.m.-8 p.m. (Sun. 7 a.m.-1 p.m.). Closed Mon. & Aug.

No mere butcher, Tattevin. No, he is a knife- and twine-wielding artist who trusses up an original and delectable roast—our mouths water at the thought of his loin of veal studded with nuggets of Parma ham, and the boned leg of lamb stuffed with kidneys. It goes without saying that Tattevin's raw materials are of the finest quality. House specialities include ready-to-roast truffled chickens, duck with peaches, or leg of lamb boned and stuffed with lamb kidneys.

■ CAKES

Bourdaloue
9th arr. - 7, rue Bourdaloue - 48 78 32 35
Open 7:15 a.m.-7:15 p.m. (Sun. until 6:30 p.m.). Closed Mon.

L'amour, toujours l'amour is what we feel for Bourdaloue's Puits d'Amour, a jam-and-puff-pastry concoction that was created here in the 1800s. We also have an enduring affection for the excellent apple turnovers (among the best we've ever tasted in Paris), the hazelnut delights and Bourdaloue's own ice creams and delectable chocolates. Tea room.

Paul Bugat
4th arr. - 5, bd Beaumarchais - 48 87 89 88
Open 8 a.m.-20 p.m. Closed Mon. & 3 wks. in Aug.

Paul Bugat is a passionate aesthete who orchestrates sweet pastry, chocolate, sugar and cream into exquisite gâteaux. The specialities of the house are delicious, jewel-like petits fours, along with the Clichy (chocolate butter cream and mocha cream on an almond-sponge base), the Pavé de Bourgogne (almond sponge cake and blackcurrant mousse) and the Almaviva (chocolate-mousse cake). Tea room.

Christian Constant
7th arr. - 37, rue d'Assas - 45 48 45 51
Open daily 8 a.m.-8 p.m.
7th arr. - 26, rue du Bac - 47 03 30 00
Open daily 8 a.m.-9 p.m.

After a stroll in the Luxembourg Gardens, why not indulge in a treat from Christian Constant's new shop on the rue d'Assas? You needn't feel too guilty because these cakes are low in sugar, additive-free, all-natural and incredibly light. Try a millefeuille, or Constant's famed chocolate-and-banana tart (we agree with Sonia Rykiel that it is a minor masterpiece), or the intensely chocolatey macaroons. Constant's sorbets (100 francs per litre) and frozen desserts are well worth the money. Tea room.

Coquelin Aîné
16th arr. - 1, pl. de Passy - 42 88 21 74
Open 9 a.m.-7:30 p.m. (Sun. 9 a.m.-1 p.m.). Closed Mon.

Coquelin enjoys a solidly established reputation with its solidly establishment clientele. Joining the traditional treats created for holidays (the Kings' Cake for Twelfth Night is a local favourite) are the shop's occasionally produced, tempting, original desserts, such as the Hérisson d'Automne ("Autumn Hedgehog"), a frozen coffee- and chestnut-flavoured sweet. Excellent ice creams and chocolates may be purchased here too. Tea room.

Couderc
11th arr. - 6, bd Voltaire - 47 00 58 20
Open 8:30 a.m.-8 p.m. Closed Mon., Tues. & Aug.

Michel Couderc takes pride in his sweets, cakes, ice creams and chocolates, all on display in this picturesque shop just off the lively place de la République. We suggest that you at least sample the rustic "peasant" and apricot tarts, and the more sophisticated Turquois (macaroons with chocolate mousse), the Délice (sponge cake, caramelised almonds and whipped cream with vanilla and chocolate) or the Ambre (praline and chocolate mousselines with crushed nougat and walnuts). Good chocolates (350 francs per kilo), authentic Kirsch-soaked cherries and a wonderful bitter-cocoa sorbet are additional reasons to note this fine address.

Dalloyau
2nd. - 25, bd des Capucines - 47 03 47 00
Open 8:30 a.m.-7:30 p.m. (Sat. 9 a.m.-7:30 p.m.). Closed Sun.
6th arr. - 2, pl. Edmond-Rostand 43 29 31 10
Open daily 9 a.m.-6:45 p.m.
8th arr. - 99-101, rue du Faubourg-Saint-Honoré - 43 59 18 10
Open daily 8:30 a.m.-9 p.m.
15th arr. - 69, rue de la Convention - 45 77 84 27
Open daily 9:30 a.m.-7:30 p.m. (Sun. 9 a.m.-19 p.m.)

Deservedly famous, Dalloyau is a temple of gourmandise revered by every discerning sweet tooth in town. Among the most renowned specialities are the memorably good macaroons, the chocolate-and-mocha Opéra cake (created in 1955 and still a bestseller) and the

Mogador (chocolate sponge cake and mousse topped with raspberry sauce). Christmas brings succulent glazed chestnuts and rich Yule logs; Easter offers chocolate hens and bunnies romping among praline eggs and bells in the adorable window displays.

Gallet
16th arr. - 10, rue Mignard - 45 04 21 71
Open 7 a.m.-1 p.m. & 3 p.m.-7:45 p.m. Closed Sun., Mon. & Aug.

A reliable source of English treats for breakfast and tea: buns, muffins, scones and pancakes, always fresh and always delicious. Special orders are gladly accepted for holiday cakes and pies.

Jean-Paul Hévin
7th arr. - 16, av. de La Motte-Picquet - 45 51 77 48
Open 10 a.m.-7:30 p.m. Closed Sun. & Aug.

Jean-Paul Hévin is an artist whose preferred medium is chocolate. His chocolate cakes are inspired symphonies, their deep, dark intensity tempered by fruit, spices, nuts and caramel. Recent compositions include a millefeuille au chocolate, a chocolate-mousse ice cream and (in another register entirely) a fresh gâteau of pears and caramel on an almond-sponge base.

Lenôtre
Information: see Lenôtre page 218.

Normandy native Gaston Lenôtre opened his first shop in Paris in 1957. His pastries and elaborate desserts are now internationally recognised as classics: the Casino, the Plaisir, the Carousel... his latest creation is the Fantasme, a voluptuous fantasy in chocolate (chocolate sponge cake and bitter-chocolate mousse).

A. Lerch
5th arr. - 4, rue du Cardinal Lemoine - 43 26 15 80
Open 7 a.m.-1:30 p.m. & 3:15 p.m.-7 p.m.. Closed Mon., Wed., 2 wks. in Feb. & Aug.

Traditional Alsatian pastries hold the place of honour here, from Kugelhopf (a spongy dome-shaped yeast cake, with or without raisins) to the region's justly famed fruit tarts, featuring bilberries, blue plums or rhubarb topped with meringue. Friendly prices.

Mauduit
10th arr. - 54, rue du Faubourg-Saint-Denis - 42 46 43 64
Open 7:15 a.m.-7:30 p.m. (Sun. 7:15 a.m.-1:30 p.m.). Closed Mon. & Aug.
10th arr. - 12, bd de Denain - 48 78 05 30
Open daily 7:15 a.m.-7:30 p.m. (Sun. 7:15 a.m.-1:30 p.m.).

Mauduit's windows, with their glittering displays of flawless cakes and confections, attract quite an audience. In summer, fruit mousses garnished with fresh fruit or fruit purées sparkle invitingly, while winter brings the delicious Cointreau-flavoured Tambourin, or the Mont-Blanc with caramelised almonds; the refreshing Pacifique dessert (raspberry and lime bavarian creams) is available all year round. Prices are modest for this level of quality.

Millet
7th arr. - 103, rue Saint-Dominique - 45 51 49 80
Open 9 a.m.-7 p.m. (Sun. 8 a.m.-1 p.m.). Closed Mon. & Aug.

Jean Millet, whose shop is almost an institution in this chic neighbourhood, ranks among the foremost practitioners of the art of French pastry. With his executive chef, Denis Ruffel, he turns out superb cakes and desserts that often give starring roles to seasonal fruit. Among Millet's best-sellers are his exceptional pear charlotte, his bitter-chocolate Guanaja and the silken almond-milk Royal with raspberries, pears, oranges and a fresh-tasting raspberry purée.

Gérard Mulot
6th arr. - 76, rue de Seine - 43 26 85 77
Open 7 a.m.-8 p.m. Closed Wed. & 1 month in summer.

Mulot is endlessly inventive, never happier than when he is working out a new idea to complete his line of delectable pastries. The poetically named Nuée d'Or ("Goldlen Cloud") is a divine combination of honey mousseline and candied fruit; Eté Indien ("Indian Summer") combines tea- and orange-flavoured mousselines. In a more down-to-earth vein, Mulot fashions wonderfully flaky, buttery croissants.

Le Moule à Gâteaux
15th arr. - 79, rue Lecourbe - 45 67 78 36 (also: 5th arr., 14th arr., 17th arr., 20th arr.)
Open 8 a.m.-8 p.m. (Sun. until 2 p.m.). Closed Mon.

This prospering chain specialises in traditional, home-style cakes fashioned by young pastry cooks who care about their craft. They use time-honoured recipes that we wish we still had the leisure (and know-how) to prepare in our own kitchens. We love the apricot feuilleté covered with a golden short crust; the Mamita, a poem in chocolate and crème fraîche; and the Carotin: almonds, hazelnuts and carrots, all reasonably priced.

Peltier
7th arr. - 66, rue de Sèvres - 47 34 06 62
Open daily 9:30 a.m.-7:45 p.m.
7th arr. - 1, rue Saint-Dominique 47 05 50 02
Open daily 8:30 a.m.-7:45 p.m.

Lucien Peltier's fame as a master pastry chef is well-earned. His most noteworthy achievements include the Ambre (almond sponge cake,

SHOPS – FOOD

praline-chocolate mousse with caramelised walnuts), the Riviera (almond sponge, lime and raspberry mousses) and a textbook example of Black Forest gâteau, made with real morello cherries. His chocolate tart or the chestnut charlotte spiked with whisky would make wonderful finales for any dinner party. Individual pastries cost between 14 and 25 francs.

Stohrer
2nd arr. - 51, rue Montorgueil
42 33 38 20
Open daily 7:30 a.m.-8:30 p.m.

The shop is decorated with rosy, corpulent allegories of Fame painted by Paul Baudry (he also decorated the Paris Opéra) in 1860; these charming murals are pleasant to contemplate while enjoying a few of Stohrer's pastries: the dark-chocolate Criollo, the refreshing Royal Menthe, the Black Forest gâteau, almond-filled Pithiviers and flaky croissants are all highly recommended.

■ REGIONAL FRENCH SPECIALITIES

Besnier
18th arr. - 28, av. de Saint-Ouen
43 87 65 63
Open 9 a.m.-1 p.m. & 4 p.m.-8 p.m. Closed Sun. & Aug.

Guy Besnier is a hard man to please, and only foods that win his full approval find their way into his shop, a showcase for gourmet specialities from the Auvergne, Brittany and Corsica. Among them are tangy dried sausages from Chassagnard à Egletons, Corsican coppa and figatelli (garlicky liver sausage) and a superb assortment of cheeses, featuring tasty farmhouse goat cheese.

La Cigogne
8th arr. - 61, rue de l'Arcade - 43 87 39 16
Open 8 a.m.-7 p.m. (Sat. 9 a.m.-6:30 p.m.). Closed Sun., Aug. & holidays.

This firm turns out innovative foods rooted in the culinary traditions of Alsace: sweet pretzels, slices of Kugelhopf (a yeast cake) thickly dusted with cinnamon, and a delicious cream-cheese tart. The region's classic dishes are not neglected, however—witness La Cigogne's wonderful strudel, quiche Lorraine, cherry, blueberry and damson-plum tarts and, in the savoury category, cervelas (sausages), weisswurst, bierwurst and bratwurst.

Comtesse du Barry
17th arr. - 23, av. de Wagram
46 22 17 38
Open 10 a.m.-8 p.m. Closed Sun.
4th arr. - 93, rue Saint-Antoine
40 29 07 14
6th arr. - 1, rue de Sèvres - 45 48 32 04
9th arr. - 13, rue Taibout - 47 40 21 01
15th arr. - 317, rue de Vaugirard
42 50 90 13
16th arr. - 88bis, av. Mozart - 45 27 74 49
Open 10 a.m.-7 p.m. Closed Sun.

From the Gers in south-west France comes an extensive line of regional food products: duck and goose confits, foie gras, fattened duck breasts (available fresh, vacuum-packed), as well as galantines, rillettes, excellent little pâtés, good prepared foods (in tins or jars) and frozen dishes.

La Galoche d'Aurillac
11th arr. - 41, rue de Lappe - 47 00 77 15
Open 10 a.m.-midnight. Closed Sun., Mon. & Aug.

Robust fare from the Auvergne may be sampled on the spot or taken home from this colourful shop on the rue de Lappe. We recommend the pounti (a savoury loaf of pork and Swiss chard), the saucisse d'Auvergne, the regional pot-au-feu, the tangy little cabécous goat cheeses and, for dessert, the apple tart flambéed with Calvados. Wash these specialities down with sturdy local wines like Marcillac and Saint-Pourçain. The small selection of rustic brandies includes a Lou Rouergat flavoured with walnuts or peaches (70 francs).

Jean-Claude et Nanou
17th arr. - 46, rue Legendre - 42 27 15 08
Open 9 a.m.-1 p.m. & 4 p.m.-8 p.m. Closed Sun. (except Sept.-April), Mon. & July 14-Aug.

Here's the sort of country food we can never get enough of. Jean-Claude and Nanou sell richly flavoured sausages dried under the ashes of a smouldering fire, aromatic mountain sausage and fresh Tomme (an unmatured cheese with a distinctive "barnyard" taste).

Aux Produits de Bretagne et des Pyrénées
5th arr. - 42, bd Saint-Germain
43 54 72 96
Open 9 a.m.-10 p.m. Closed Mon. & July 1-Sept. 17.

How is it that foods from two such far-flung regions share shelf space in a single shop? Simply because François Miras hails from the Pyrénées, while Madame Miras is a native of Brittany. So alongside the superb mountain-cured bacon, sheep's-milk cheese, Tarbais beans and delicious confits from the south-west, you'll find jars of cèpes preserved in oil, chunky rural breads, sausages and other fine produce from Brittany.

Chez Teil

11th arr. - 6, rue de Lappe - 47 00 41 28
Open 9 a.m.-1 p.m. & 3 p.m.-7 p.m. Closed Sun., Mon. & Aug.

This turn-of-the-century shop is home to a mouthwatering selection of authentic Auvergnat charcuterie, processed by Patrick Teil himself at his family's meat-curing plant in Cayrols. By eliminating the middle man, Teil can market his hams, sausages, spreads, pigs' trotters and pâtés at attractive prices. Try his cheeses too, along with the fine crusty flat bread (fouace) and countrified sweets on display.

Terrier

9th arr. - 58, rue des Martyrs - 48 78 96 45
Open 8:15 a.m.-1 p.m. & 4 p.m.-7:30 p.m. (Sun. 8:15 a.m.-12:45 p.m.). Closed Mon. & Aug.

For generous Lyonnais charcuterie, Terrier is *the* outpost in Paris. Among the typical treats on sale are sausage studded with truffles and pistachios, golden-brown pâtés en croûte, pike and salmon quenelles, Burgundy ham, brawn and genuine rosette sausage, the pride of Lyon.

A la Ville de Rodez

4th arr. - 22, rue Vieille-du-Temple - 48 87 79 36
Open 8 a.m.-1 p.m. & 3 p.m.-7:30 p.m. Closed Sun., Mon. & July 15-Aug.

Alex-Pierre Batût has represented the earthy tradition of Auvergnat charcuterie in Paris for many years. His citron-studded fouace (flat bread) is ambrosial, his terrines are legendary, and his spicy dried sausage is among the most flavourful we've had the pleasure of tasting—anywhere. Ville de Rodez is the place to find all the classic cuts of pork that simmer together with vegetables in a classic potée auvergnate.

■ SEAFOOD

Le Bar à Huîtres

14th arr. - 112, bd Montparnasse - 43 20 71 01
Open noon-midnight.

At the outdoor oyster bar, you can purchase dozens of succulent oysters, opened for you free of charge by the nimble-fingered *écaillers* and neatly arranged on disposable trays (no deposit, no return). A refreshing treat.

Poissonnerie du Dôme

14th arr. - 4, rue Delambre - 43 35 23 95
Open 8 a.m.-1 p.m. & 4 p.m.-7:30 p.m. (Wed. & Sun. until 1 p.m.; Tues. 5 p.m.-7:30 p.m.). Closed Mon. & 1 month in summer.

The lucky residents of Montparnasse can satisfy their urge for seafood at this marvellous fish shop, perhaps the best in Paris. Manager Jean-Pierre Lopez admits only "noble" fish (sole, turbot, lotte, sea bass and the like) to his high-class emporium. The merchandise, from French (particularly Breton) and foreign waters, is snapped up by such eminent restaurants as L'Ambroisie, Duquesnoy and L'Apicius. Need we mention that these rare and succulent denizens of the deep command regally high prices?

■ WINE & SPIRITS

L'Arbre à Vin

12th arr. - 2-4, rue du Rendez-Vous - 43 46 81 10
Open 8:30 a.m.-12:30 p.m. & 4 p.m.-8 p.m. (Sun. 8:30 a.m.-1 p.m.). Closed Mon. & 3 wks. in Aug.

This fascinating wine shop was established in 1893. The superb vaulted cellars house Bordeaux, both great and modest, and a comprehensive range of Burgundies. Rounding out the selection are good *vins de pays*.

Cave de l'Ecole Polytechnique

5th arr. - 48, rue de la Montagne-Sainte-Geneviève - 43 25 35 80
Open 10:30 a.m.-1:30 p.m. & 4:30 p.m.-8:30 p.m. (Sun. 11 a.m.-1:30 p.m.). Closed Mon. & Aug.

In the wine business for more than half a century, Jean-Baptiste Besse must be credited with having converted many a Parisian to the cult of Bacchus. Though the shop may look like a colossal shambles, Besse will unerringly locate the bottle you desire, from a modest red Cheverny to a majestic Château Cheval-Blanc. His choice of dessert wines (Sauternes, Banyuls, Beaumes-de-Venise) always astounds us, as does his judicious selection of Cognacs and ports.

Caves Estève

4th arr. - 10, rue de la Cerisaie 42 72 33 05
Open 9:30 a.m.-12:30 p.m. & 2:30 p.m.-7:30 p.m. Closed Sun. & Mon. (except in Dec.).

5th arr. - 292, rue Saint-Jacques 46 34 69 78
Open 10 a.m.-1 p.m. & 3 p.m.-8 p.m. Closed Sun. & Mon. (except in Dec.).

For Jean-Christophe Estève, wine isn't just a business; it's a sacred vocation. Endowed with a formidable palate, this Gascon native declares that every region of France produces good wines—it's just a question of tracking them down. Given his pedagogic bent (he used to be a Spanish teacher), he'll be happy to help you choose from among 250 Bordeaux, and his expanding collection of Burgundies.

La Cave de Georges Dubœuf

8th arr. - 9, rue Marbeuf - 47 20 71 23
Open 9 a.m.-1 p.m. & 3 p.m.-7 p.m. Closed Sun., Mon. & Aug.

What Lionel Poilâne is to bread, Georges Dubœuf is to

Beaujolais: a guarantee of quality. His Paris shop stocks excellent representatives from all the villages of Beaujolais, but Duboeuf is not parochial by any means. Winemakers from all over France supply him with (for example) fine Burgundies from de Montille, de Vogüé, Rousseau and Trapet, Métaireau's Muscadets, Guigal's Côtes-du-Rhône and Alsatian vintages from Trimbach.

Caves Pétrissans
17th arr. - 30 bis, av. Niel - 42 27 83 84
Open 9:30 a.m.-1:30 p.m. & 3 p.m.-8 p.m. (Sat. 10 a.m.-1:30 p.m.). Closed Sun., 3 wks. in Aug.

For many years this renowned Parisian *cave* has been a magnet for local oenophiles because of its extensive selection of fine wines. A browser might come across an uncommon red wine from Corsica, the appealing Roussette de Seyssel from Savoie, Clos du Marquis ("second" wine of Saint-Julien's Château Léoville-las-Cases), Jaboulet's Saint-Joseph and tasty first-growth Champagne from Chigny-les-Roses. Sharing shelf space with the wines are some highly reputed Cognacs and fruit brandies, Armagnacs (vintages on hand include 1893, 1900, 1912...) and rare whiskies, like the elegant Auchentoshan from the Scottish Lowlands and the peaty, invigorating Bowmore from the Isle of Islay.

Les Caves du Savour Club
14th arr. - 120 or 139, bd Montparnasse - 43 27 12 06
16th arr. - 11-13, rue Gros - 42 30 94 18
Open 10 a.m.-8 p.m. (Sun. until 12:30 p.m.). Closed Mon.

The Savour Club is a wine warehouse that has managed to rise above the greyness of its underground premises with a bright, light décor. Inside, you'll find bottles for every occasion, each with a card bearing an informative description and comments. There are wines for everyday drinking (some cost less than 20 francs), as well as special treats for connoisseurs (Château Haut-Brion '82, Richebourg '84).

Jean Danflou
1st arr. - 36, rue de Mont-Thabor 42 61 51 09
Open 9 a.m.-noon & 2 p.m.-6 p.m. Closed Sat., Sun. & Aug. 1-15.

Pierre Danflou-Glotin, the third generation of Danflous to run this shop, sells absolutely exquisite, fragrant, heady eaux-de-vie (clear fruit brandies) distilled especially for him in Alsace. You must sample his extraordinary aged Kirsch, his Poire Williams, or his perfumed Framboise. A line of elegant Cognacs, Armagnacs and Calvados is also available, along with a small selection of wines from Burgundy and Bordeaux. Prices start at around 200 francs.

Legrand Filles et Fils
2nd arr. - 1, rue de la Banque 42 60 07 12
2nd arr. - 12, galerie Vivienne 42 60 07 12
Open 8:30 a.m.-7:30 p.m. (Sat. 8:30 a.m.-1 p.m. & 3 p.m.-7 p.m.). Closed Sun. & Mon.

Even if the wines were not half so interesting, Legrand's wine shop would be worth a visit for its old-fashioned charm and warm atmosphere. Lucien Legrand's daughter Francine offers a wide selection of carefully chosen, inexpensive wines from up-and-coming growers in the south and the Val de Loire, along with a wide-ranging inventory of prestigious Burgundies and Bordeaux (note the many affordable wines from average years). There are also a few uncommon bottlings: luscious Muscat de Beaumes-de-Venise, Vin de Paille du Jura and some excellent vintage ports.

Nicolas
8th arr. - 21, pl. de Madeleine 42 68 00 16. 250 stores in Paris.
Open 9 a.m.-8 p.m. Closed Sun.

Looking better than ever with smart gold-and-bordeaux décor, the 250 Nicolas stores in the Paris area continue to present a wide and appealing range of wines for every budget. The chain's monthly offers are well worth following: featured are (for example) French wines from unfamiliar or underrated appellations—the Ardèche, Corbières or Bergerac—, imports (Spanish, Italian and even Australian) and the occasional oenological curiosity, all offered at attractive prices. The multi-level flagship store on the place de la Madeleine has more than 1,000 different wines, including rare, old Bordeaux. Nicolas is also an excellent source of fine distilled spirits (there's a good selection of single-malt whiskies). The avenue Wagram shop stays open until 10 p.m., the Ancienne-Comédie store until 9. Home delivery service available.

Le Repaire de Bacchus
17th arr. - 39, rue des Acacias 43 80 09 68
(also: 2nd arr., 6th arr., 7th arr., 9th arr., 15th arr., 16th arr., 18th arr.)
Open 10:30 a.m.-1:30 p.m. & 3:30 p.m.-8 p.m. Closings on Sun. & Mon. vary in the different stores.

Dominique Fenouil continues to inaugurate new branches of his dynamic chain with admirable frequency. Smart marketing isn't everything, of course: the Repaires de Bacchus owe their success to a judicious choice of wines and, perhaps especially, to the excellent advice dispensed by the sales staff (several of whom, in our experience, speak English). From the house-label wines to fine growers' Burgundies, from little-known "village" appellations to Bordeaux's *grands crus*, the wines are selected with an eye to quality and value. Several branches sponsor clubs (membership fee: 200 francs) where you can sometimes enjoy a sip (or two) of a vintage Latour, a Burgundy from the Comte de Lafond, or a rare single-malt whisky.

Au Verger de la Madeleine
8th arr. - 4, bd Malesherbes - 42 65 51 99
Open 10 a.m.-1:30 p.m. & 3 p.m.-8 p.m. Closed Sun.

Jean-Pierre Legras's staggering collection encompasses such unique and extravagant bottles as a Cognac Impérial Tiffon 1810, a Porto Barros dated 1833 (once the property of the French ambassador to Lisbon), a Solera Sercial Madeira from 1835 and a Clos-Peyraguey 1893. Such treasures are not for everyday drinking, but they make impressive, indeed unforgettable, gifts. All the first growths of Bordeaux (Cheval-Blanc, Pétrus...) are on hand as well, along with superb Burgundies from Montrachet and Meursault, and hard-to-find wines like Château-Grillet and Jasnières. Here are also inexpensive offerings from the Côtes-d'Auvergne, Saint-Pourçain and Saumur.

Vins Rares Peter Thustrup
46 33 83 53
The store will open soon. Call for location and information. In the meantime orders can be taken at the above phone number.

Peter Thustrup's unquenchable passion for old, rare vintages leads him to auction rooms all over the world, in search of such finds as antique Yquem, ancient Pétrus and Mouton-Rothschild from another age (which sell, incidentally, for about 18,000 francs—just to give you an idea). Bordeaux, obviously, is well represented, but Thustrup can also show you some exceptional Vendanges Tardives from Alsace, mature Burgundies and collectible Côtes-du-Rhône. He recently added an expanded (and quite attractive) range of younger, lower-priced bottles from other countries.

GIFTS

Un Air de Giverny
7th arr. - 10, rue de Bellechasse 45 55 83 69
Open 11 a.m.-6:30 p.m. Closed Sun. & Mon.

Do you have a passion for the Impressionists? Then this charming boutique is a "must" on your itinerary. Monet's famous blue-and-yellow china is on sale here, of course, but you'll also discover a selection of decorative objects in those colours, and others that date from the Impressionists' heyday, among them household linen from Quimper, handcrafted faïence, watercolours and pretty antique curios.

Axis
11th arr. - 13, rue de Charonne 48 06 79 10
Open 11 a.m.-2 p.m. & 2:30 p.m.-7:30 p.m. Closed Sun.

Witty, imaginative and amusing gift ideas are the Axis trademark. But this policy does not exclude the useful: the Alessi coffeepot and the Dualite toaster are totally trendy, but they also help you get breakfast on the table efficiently. Axis now produces its own collection of vases, picture frames, tableware and rugs, all sporting droll or unusual designs.

La Boîte à Musique
1st arr. - 9, rue de Beaujolais - 42 96 55 13
Open 10 a.m.-7 p.m. Closed Sun.

Music boxes tinkle merrily away in this delightful little shop under the Palais-Royal arcades. The mechanisms are Swiss, dependable and made to last, while the boxes themselves have a pleasingly old-fashioned look. Prices vary according to the complexity of the design and the number of tunes and notes the box plays. The simplest, an ideal gift for a baby (whose name and date of birth can be engraved on the box), costs about 200 francs. The finest music box in the store, made of rare wood with a sophisticated mechanism that plays four tunes and well over a hundred notes, will set you back over 30,000 francs.

Boutique Le Flore
6th arr. - 26, rue Saint Benoît - 45 44 33 40
Open 10 a.m.-1 p.m. & 2 p.m.-7 p.m. Closed Sun.

The Café de Flore now markets a range of merchandise stamped with its famous logo. The heavy, white bistro-style china is a great success: visitors love to buy the cups and saucers to take home as souvenirs. Little silver-plated table decorations, trays, a coffeepot and teapot complete the line. If Saint-Germain-des-Prés has a special place in your heart, you'll love the framed photos of the neighbourhood and the old-fashioned postcards depicting the terrace of Le Flore in different eras (from 85 francs).

Chaumette
7th arr. - 45, av. Duquesne - 42 73 18 54
Open 9:30 a.m.-6:30 p.m. Closed Sat., Sun. & 3 wks. in Aug.

Gérard Chaumette is no ordinary dealer in knick-knacks. He has a genuine passion for faïence (earthenware

SHOPS – GIFTS

decorated with opaque coloured glazes) and glass objects that reproduce and reinterpret nature. On our last visit to his enchanting shop, we found an extraordinary lamp base with mauve-tinged irises; glazed ceramic cachepots displaying bunches of grapes or vegetable still lifes; and stunning reproductions of ancient Roman glass. Prices for these small marvels range from 200 to several thousand francs.

Comptoirs de la Tour d'Argent
5th arr. - 2, rue du Cardinal-Lemoine - 46 33 45 58
Open 10 a.m.-12:30 a.m. (Sun. noon-12:30 a.m.). Closed Mon.

Dinner at the Tour d'Argent may be out of reach, but you can always scrape up a few francs to purchase a small souvenir bearing the restaurant's logo. Classy, classic tableware (crystal, silver, china, embroidered linen) and lots of determinedly tasteful accessories (how about a Tour d'Argent silk tie?). The good tinned foie gras, duck confit, lobster bisque and the Brut Champagne also sport the house colours, and like the rest are high-priced.

L'Entrepôt
16th arr. - 50, rue de Passy - 45 25 64 17
Open 10:30 a.m.-7 p.m. (Sat. until 7:30 p.m.). Closed Sun.

Here's a treasure trove of clever gift items and household gadgets that will charm even the most blasé shopper. We saw a funny little alarm clock disguised as a deep-sea diver, a miniature tool chest hidden inside a model car and an impressively diverse variety of stationery, tableware, clothing—and even jams and jellies. A delightful bazaar, improbably located in the smart Passy district.

Forestier
16th arr. - 35, rue Duret - 45 00 08 61
Open 10:30 a.m.-7:30 p.m. (Mon. from noon). Closed Sun.

In the 1930s, this was a cheese and dairy shop, but an ex-landscape gardener has transformed it into an original boutique that follows the rhythms of the seasons and holidays. Forestier carries all the tableware and decorative touches you need to create a festive atmosphere for Christmas, Valentine's Day, Halloween, April Fools' Day and so on, as well as an attractive selection of hand-crafted pottery and garden accessories for year-round use.

Homme Sweet Homme
4th arr. - 45, rue Vieille-du-Temple - 48 04 94 99
Open 11 a.m.-7:30 p.m. Closed Sun.

Despite the twee name, this shop stocks an interesting variety of (primarily masculine) gifts in a wide range of prices (25 to 2,000 francs). Wallets in all sizes, attractive fountain pens and geometric photo holders from the 1940s are just a few of the clever and useful items on sale. For the man who has everything (including a sense of humour), there's even a little fan in the form of a robot.

Rita Kim
10th arr. - 79, quai de Valmy - 42 39 82 49
Open 1 p.m.-7 p.m. Closed Sun. & Mon. No cards.

We love Rita's collection of plastic items from the 1960s: there's tableware, knick-knacks and irresistibly kitsch costume jewellery—don't miss the "Jesus" watch with the name of an apostle at each hour. Lots of other items are on sale for under 100 francs.

> Monday, like Sunday, is a day of rest for many shopkeepers.

La Maison des Artisans
12th arr.- 14, cours de Vincennes - 43 41 61 63
Open 10:30 a.m.-1:30 p.m. & 2:30 p.m.-7 p.m. Closed Sun., Mon., Aug. & holidays.

For the best in French handicrafts: the Maison des Artisans presents creative, beautifully fashioned objects made according to traditional methods. Come here to admire useful and decorative objects in faïence, pewter and glass (perfume bottles from 160 francs), jewellery crafted in precious wood and silver, or in Altuglas and gilded bronze (brooches from 200 francs).

Pain d'Epices Maison
9th arr. - 35-37, passage Jouffroy 47 70 51 12
Open 10 a.m.-7 p.m. (Mon. from 12:30 p.m.). Closed Sun.

The windows of this delightful shop, situated in the picturesque passage Jouffroy, are a feast for the eyes. Accessories and decorative items that make a home feel inviting and cosy are found here (potpourri, table decorations, lamp shades...), alongside old-fashioned colour prints, picture frames and biscuit tins—everything is beautifully displayed.

Robin des Bois
4th arr. - 15, rue Ferdinand Duval - 48 04 09 36
Open 10:30 a.m.-7:30 p.m. (Sun. from noon).

The headquarters of the Association for the Protection of Humanity and the Environment is also a source of ecologically sound gifts for yourself or your family and friends. Vegetable ivory is carved into pretty ornaments and buttons, jojoba oil replaces whale oil in the body-care products on display, and (naturally) all the stationery is made of recycled paper.

HOME – SHOPS

Shizuka
2nd arr. - 25, bd des Capucines
42 61 54 61
Open 9:30 a.m.-6:30 p.m. Closed Sun.

For years the avenue de l'Opéra has been a mecca for Japanese tourists. But of late they've been joined by Parisians who want to get a look at the best in contemporary Japanese design—and that's at Shizuka, a sleek, upscale emporium. On the ground floor, clean-lined desk accessories and stationery are featured, along with robots and mechanical toys. A downstairs gallery showcases recent creations by Japanese designers, while the top floor is devoted to elegant tableware and cutlery, toilet articles and linens. It's hard to leave empty-handed, especially since prices start at the reasonable sum of 35 francs.

Tant qu'il y aura des Hommes
6th arr. - 23, rue du Cherche-Midi - 45 48 48 17
Open 10:30 a.m.-7 p.m. (Mon. from noon). Closed Sun. & 2 wks. in Aug.

Among the handsome and practical gifts for men on sale here, we particularly liked the silk boxer shorts, the luggage (with lots of detachable pockets) and leather goods that look as if they could withstand hard wear, a classic Irish crewneck sweater and a good-looking leather-trimmed jacket for rough-and-tumble types. The beautiful co-ordinated shirts and ties make highly acceptable gifts.

Territoire
8th arr. - 30, rue Boissy-d'Anglas
42 66 22 13
Open 10:30 a.m.-7 p.m. Closed Sun.

What was once a hardware store is now a bright and spacious shop brimming with ideas for leisure activities. The stock changes with the seasons; in spring, the gardening section offers Wilkinson tools and terracotta pots. In summer, sporting goods take over a greater share of shelf space (we saw an impressive foldable black canvas boat for 5,000 francs), and in winter, fireside games feature more prominently. There are plenty of amusing gifts for children, including reproductions of old-fashioned board games and some spectacular kites. Prices range from about 50 to 5,000 francs.

La Tuile à Loup
5th arr. - 35, rue Daubenton - 47 07 28 90
Open 10:30 a.m.-7:30 p.m. (Sun. until 1 p.m.). Closed Mon.

As peaceful as a village square, this exceptional shop carries traditional handicrafts from all over France. You'll find beautiful glazed pottery from Savoie, Provence, Burgundy and Alsace, and stoneware from Puisaye and Le Maine. There are handmade wooden objects, rustic tableware, wrought-iron weather vanes and decorative tiles for the kitchen, bath or fireplace. Fascinating, too, are the many books documenting popular art forms and regional history.

Michèle Wilson
14th arr. - 116, rue du Château
43 22 28 73
Open 8:30 a.m.-8 p.m. Closed Sun. & Aug.

Puzzle buffs and art lovers alike adore Michèle Wilson's hand-crafted wooden puzzles, which depict paintings or prints from the Louvre, the Musée d'Orsay, the Institut du Monde Arabe and other well-known museums. Some of the puzzles are easy to put together (60 pieces, 110 francs), while others are considerably more mind-bending (5,500 pieces, 6,182 francs). Subjects run the gamut from Persian miniatures to Impressionist paintings or maps. At the workshop next door, you can watch and learn as a puzzle is made.

HOME

BATH & KITCHENWARE

BATH

Le Bain Rose
6th arr. - 11, rue d'Assas - 42 22 55 85
Open 10:30 a.m.-1 p.m. & 2 p.m.-6:30 p.m. Closed Sun., Mon. & Aug.

This is the place for antique washbasins and stands dating from the turn of the century up to the 1950s. Prices are high, but everything works: the taps, the drain, the pipes. Tiles and accessories are available as well—the lighting fixtures are particularly attractive.

A l'Epi d'Or
5th arr. - 17, rue des Bernardins
46 33 08 47
Open 11 a.m.-7 p.m. Closed Sun. & Mon.

After nearly a quarter of a century on the rue Saint-Jacques, this highly reputed bath shop transferred its stock to more spacious quarters, under a vast skylight. Lovely antique and reproduction bathroom sinks are the main attraction, along with period and a few contemporary accessories. A genuine 1930s sink commands a minimum of 7,000 francs, while a reproduction goes for 3,000 francs. An antique soap dish, however, will cost only about 600 francs.

Find the address you are looking for, quickly and easily, in the index.

SHOPS – HOME

CUTLERY

Isler
1st arr. - 44, rue Coquillière - 42 33 20 92
Open 9 a.m.-noon & 2 p.m.-6 p.m. Closed Sat., Sun. & Aug. No cards.

Not a single element of the shop's décor has changed in 50 years, but then neither has the excellent quality of the Swiss knives (including the world-famous Tour Eiffel brand), for which Isler is known. All the great French chefs select their kitchen knives from among the 100 models in stock; and there are 40 types of pocketknife to pick from as well. The firm's latest success is a survival pocketknife with (at least) 29 functions (multi-use pliers, ballpoint pen, mini-screwdriver—you get the idea) which comes in a leather carrying case equipped with a compass, sharpening stone, mirror... The trusty old penknife seems awfully ordinary in comparison.

Kindal
2nd arr. - 33, av. de l'Opéra - 42 61 70 78
Open 10 a.m.-6:30 p.m. (Sat. from 11 a.m.). Closed Sun.

Faithful to its long family tradition, Kindal has carefully preserved its handsome mahogany panelling that dates back to the shop's grand opening in 1905. Knives of every sort are on view: table, hunting and pocket representatives with wooden or precious horn handles. Prices start at about 50 francs and rise to 12,000 francs for certain collectors' items. Knives are also repaired and sharpened on the premises.

KITCHENWARE

La Carpe
8th arr. - 14, rue Tronchet - 47 42 73 25
Open 9:30 a.m.-6:45 p.m. (Mon. from 1:30 p.m.). Closed Sun. & Aug.

For some 70 years the Loiseau family has furnished chefs and knowledgeable home cooks with utensils at the cutting edge of kitchen technology. All the wares are intelligently displayed by type, so that you can find what you want quickly. The sales staff are friendly and generous with good advice. Another nearby store, A la Petite Carpe (13, rue Vignon), carries a selection of gadgets for the table. Catalogue available upon request.

Culinarion
17th arr. - 83 bis, rue de Courcelles - 42 27 63 32
Open 10:15 a.m.-7 p.m. (Mon. from 11:15 a.m.). Closed Sun.

Culinarion is a dependable source of kitchen classics (cast-iron pots and charlotte moulds) at reasonable prices. But adventurous cooks will love the selection of arcana and novelties, like the combination mills that let you salt and pepper with one hand or the shopping bag specially designed for frozen foods. We're also quite fond of the shop's handsome selection of bar accessories and tableware.

Dehillerin
1st arr. - 18-20, rue Coquillière 42 36 53 13
Open 8 a.m.-6 p.m. Closed Mon. 12:30 p.m.-2 p.m. & Sun.

Since 1820, the cream of the French food establishment have purchased their *batterie de cuisine* at Dehillerin. More recently, they have been joined by large numbers of American and Japanese culinary enthusiasts. Dehillerin stocks a truly amazing range of covetable cookware, superb knives and copper pots, and every imaginable baking accessory. We suggest you come early in the day to shop here, and above all, don't be in a hurry. Some of the sales assistants speak English and are quite helpful.

Kitchen Bazaar
15th arr. - 11, av. du Maine - 42 22 91 17
Open 10 a.m.-7 p.m. Closed Sun.

Kitchenware from Kitchen Bazaar is always both high-style and high-performance. The latest small appliances are always available here, with a

---

Thank God, the architect doesn't sing

Good intentions don't always work. The *Bastille opera house* was conceived as a way of bringing opera to the masses, but as a side effect its construction has inexorably turned a traditional working-class part of Paris into a magnet for the trendy and fashionable. Art galleries and night spots are ousting carpenters, craftsmen and cabinetmakers, while many venerable buildings are being demolished to clear the way for up-market apartment blocks. The good news is that this opera house is cheaper and more accessible than its grander counterpart, the Opéra Garnier: you don't even have to dress up. An impressive array of technical devices makes the Opéra Bastille a director's dream—and at least from the inside you can't see the grim grey exterior.

preference for those with the sleekest designs. There's an interesting selection of cookery books too.

Geneviève Lethu
1st arr. - Forum des Halles, level -2 - 40 39 95 94
1st arr. - 91, rue de Rivoli - 42 60 14 90
6th arr. - 95, rue de Rennes - 45 44 40 35
14th arr. - 25, av. du Général-Leclerc - 45 38 71 30
17th arr. - 1, av. Niel 45 72 03 47
Open 10:30 a.m.-7:30 p.m. Closed Sun.

There are Geneviève Lethu shops all over Paris, presenting large selections of bright, practical, cheerful kitchen furniture, utensils, tableware and linen. The ever-growing collections of affordably priced dishes in lots of pretty colours and patterns are co-ordinated with fabric or wipe-clean tablecloths. We also particularly like the attractive, inexpensive glassware in myriad shapes and sizes.

Mora
1st arr. - 13, rue Montmartre - 45 08 19 24
Open 8:30 a.m.-5:45 p.m. (Sat. until noon). Closed Sun.

The shopfront is modern, but Mora is an old established firm dating back to 1814. The most esoteric items of culinary equipment can be found among the astonishing collection of knives and pots and pans in stainless steel, cast iron or copper, and the very best cake and tart tins coated with new-age anti-adhesives (there are 6,000 items in stock). Amateur cooks benefit from the same low prices as restaurant and catering professionals, and they are greeted with the same amiability. The cookery book section boasts over 200 titles; if you think a picture is worth a thousand words, inquire about the cooking-demonstration videos.

A. Simon
2nd arr. - 48, rue Montmartre
42 33 71 65
Open 8:30 a.m.-6:30 p.m. Closed Sun.

This long-established family firm supplies kitchen and tableware to the likes of the Hôtel Méridien, the Café de la Paix and the cooking school in Osaka, Japan. But it also sells its vast range of dishes, glasses and utensils at the same prices to any customer who walks in off the street. For typically French dishes (like the ones you see in traditional brasseries), the prices are unbeatable. You'll also find wine pitchers, carafes and ice cream *coupes* that will add an agreeable Gallic touch to your table. The rue Montmartre store specialises in kitchen supplies, while the shop around the corner on rue Etienne-Marcel (same phone number) deals chiefly in tableware.

Taïr Mercier
5th arr. - 7, bd Saint-Germain
43 54 19 97
Open 11 a.m.-7 p.m. Closed Sat. 1 p.m.-2:30 p.m., Sun. & mid July-mid Aug.

Place mats in appealing shapes (fruits, animals, city skylines) cut out of brightly coloured pieces of plastic are big sellers here. But we also discovered attractive two-tone plastic shopping bags, melamine fish platters, clear plastic knife rests and absolutely stainproof plastic-coated aprons, all of which convinced us that *plastique, c'est chic!*

■ FURNISHINGS

CONTEMPORARY FURNITURE

Academy
6th arr. - 5, pl. de l'Odéon - 43 29 07 18
12th arr. - 68, rue du Faubourg-Saint-Antoine - 43 42 19 19
Open 9:30 a.m.-1 p.m. & 2:30 p.m.-7 p.m. Closed Sun., Mon. & Aug. No cards.

Jean-Michel Wilmotte was the designer selected to decorate the space beneath the Louvre's glass pyramid, and to create the furnishings to be placed throughout the Grand Louvre. The shop that showcases his collection is austere, like the materials Wilmotte prefers: perforated sheet metal, glass slabs, chipboard. Prices for these singular pieces vary widely.

Arredamento
4th arr. - 18, quai des Célestins
42 74 33 14
Open 10 a.m.-12:30 p.m. & 2 p.m.-7 p.m. Closed Sun. & Mon.

In a spacious and handsome two-level shop, Valentine Boitel and Bernard Renaudin present a wide-ranging selection of top Italian furniture and lighting designs. Connoisseurs with a taste for contemporary Italian design (and well-lined wallets) will applaud the modular storage units by Capellini, the sofas by Zanotta (from 22,000 francs), the coffee tables from Fontana Arte and the lamps by Flos. Fine French design is represented as well, though on a smaller scale—there are some marvellous lamps by Gilles Derain.

Avant-Scène
6th arr. - 4, pl. de l'Odéon - 46 33 12 40
Open 10 a.m.-7 p.m. (Mon. from 2 p.m.). Closed Sun.

An eclectic choice of limited-edition furniture and objets d'art by young designers is on display at this beautiful shop on the place de l'Odéon. Elisabeth Delacarte presents unusual sanded-glass candle holders and light fittings by sculptor Marco de Gueltz, as well as furniture by Mark Brazier-Jones, Frank Evennou, François Béliard. Prices start at around 100 francs (for a small gilt dish) and soar up to 45,000 francs and beyond for, say, a table by Dubreuil.

Collectania
1st arr. - 2, pl. du Palais-Royal
42 97 01 30
Open 9:30 a.m.-7 p.m. Closed Sun.

Just opposite the Louvre, Collectania is virtually a museum of 20th-century architect-designed furniture. Beautifully presented in this enormous space are reissues of designs by Le Corbusier, Frank Lloyd Wright, Gerrit Rietveld, Andrea Branzi and Shiro Kuramata. These exclusive pieces obviously command high prices, but the quality of the furniture and the expert advice dispensed by the staff (all professional interior designers) justify the cost.

Ecart International
4th arr. - 111, rue Saint-Antoine
42 78 79 11
Open 10 a.m.-6:30 p.m. Closed Sun. No cards.

The headquarters of Ecart International occupies a townhouse near the Saint-Paul church in the Marais. The bright, spacious, strikingly beautiful showroom presents reissues of pieces by the great designers of the early 20th century, including Mallet-Stevens, Eileen Gray, Pierre Chareau and Le Corbusier. Ecart also displays work by talented young French creators (Sacha Ketoff, Sylvain Dubuisson, Patrick Naggar, Olivier Gagnère), as well as designs by its own star, Andrée Putman. Prices start at about 1,000 francs and shoot up fast to over 30,000 francs.

Edifice
7th arr. - 27 bis, bd Raspail - 45 48 53 60
Open 10 a.m.-7 p.m. Closed Sun.

Each month, Edifice dreams up a splendid setting to highlight a piece or ensemble of pieces by a favourite designer. Owner Sarah Nathan is keen on avant-garde furniture, like Mario Botta's armchair, Guillaume Saalburg's screen, Ingo Maurer's splendid lamp... The store presents almost all of Philippe Starck's creations for the home (his Costes chair and the self-supporting bookcase among them), alongside designs by Ettore Sottsass, Gae Aulenti and Borek Sipek.

En Attendant Les Barbares
2nd arr. - 50, rue Etienne Marcel
42 33 37 87
Open 10:30 a.m.-7 p.m. (Mon. 10:30 a.m.-1 p.m. & 2 p.m.-7 p.m. & Sat. 11 a.m.-6:30 p.m.). Closed Sun.

The vogue for metal furniture bristling with sharp points started here, with designers Garouste and Bonetti. A comprehensive collection of their "Barbarian Baroque" pieces is on view, alongside works by new designers like Marie-Thérèse Migeon (colourful candlesticks and ashtrays), Agnès Pottier and Santiago Santiago.

Etat de Siège
6th arr. - 1, quai de Conti - 43 29 31 60
7th arr. - 94, rue du Bac - 45 49 10 20
8th arr. - 21, av. de Friedland - 45 62 31 02
Open 11 a.m.-7 p.m. (Mon. from 2 p.m.). Closed Sun.

You are certain to find a seat to suit you among the astonishing assortment stocked here. From Louis XIII *fauteuils* to the most avant-garde chair/sculpture, Etat de Siège displays some 150 different designs, many available in a variety of colours and finishes. Prices vary according to the quality of the wood or metal in question, the workmanship (hand- or factory-finished) and the style.

Galerie Neotu
4th arr. - 25, rue du Renard - 42 78 96 97
Open 11 a.m.-7 p.m. Closed Sun. No cards.

Furniture collectors with a taste for the "neo" find this multifaceted gallery a reliable source of aesthetic delight. Some say the furniture and objects displayed here are the rare and precious antiques of the future. Whether or not that will prove to be the case, owners Gérard Dalmon and Pierre Staudenmeyer spotlight works by young artists, painters, sculptors and architects, particularly those pieces that border on the realms of art and design. Most are unique or limited editions, and are thus quite expensive; but the gallery also exhibits some reasonably priced objets d'art.

Modernismes
16th arr. - 16, rue Franklin - 46 47 86 56
Open 10 a.m.-1 p.m. & 2 p.m.-7 p.m. (Sat. 11 a.m.-7 p.m.). Closed Sun. & 2 wks. in Aug.

In this stunning commercial space designed by Gilles Derain, pieces by early-20th-century masters (Eileen Gray, Le Corbusier and others) stand side-by-side with the work of Roberto Mariscal or Boris Sipek, of the current generation. The furniture is austere, but the atmosphere in the shop is warm and cordial, thanks in part to a décor that features art by young painters, Eileen Gray rugs and attractive hand-thrown pottery. Naturally enough, Derain's superb lamps and decorative pieces are given top billing. A lounge chair in leather, wood and fabric, designed by Sipek for Driade, costs around 20,000 francs, but you can walk away with a handsome Derain ashtray for 500 francs.

Monday, like Sunday, is a day of rest for many shopkeepers.

THE LEGEND OF PARIS

The heart of Paris. Scintillating and alive. Legendary. The magic of the Etoile and of the Champs Elysées. The chic of the Faubourg Saint Honoré and the most exclusive shops in the world. □ An encounter between history and modernity... the calm elegance of the Hotel Royal Monceau. A hotel that combines the traditional refinement of Parisian architecture and furnishings with modern facilities and a quality of service which is second to none. □ Savour the superb French haute cuisine of "Le Jardin," and feast on the finest Italian fare served in the sumptuous "Ristorante Carpaccio." □ Jog in the Monceau Park nearby, have a game of squash in the hotel court, then relax in a spa, in the ancient Roman tradition, "Les Thermes." The best equipped water therapy and fitness centre you could ever imagine. □ Whether you are on business or for pleasure, the excitement of Paris is right on your doorstep, when you stay at the Hotel Royal Monceau.

ROYAL MONCEAU HOTEL

SERVICE AND ELEGANCE OF A TRADITIONAL PARISIAN PALACE COMBINED WITH THE "THERMES" SOPHISTICATED HEALTH AND FITNESS FACILITIES IN THE ANCIENT ROMAN TRADITION
See Luxury Hotels — Hotel Royal Monceau and Hotel Vernet.
See Restaurants Eight Arrondissement — Le Jardin, Il Carpaccio, Les Elysées.

| GROUPE | ROYAL | MONCEAU | | THE | ART | OF | TRADITION |

HOTEL ROYAL MONCEAU, 37 AVENUE HOCHE, 75008 PARIS. TEL: (33) 1 45 61 98 00. FAX: (33) 1 42 56 90 03
For Reservations: Contact the Hotel directly, your Travel Agent or our Sales Offices: USA/Canada: 1 800 832 27 91 — Japan: (03) 5434 8060 — United Kingdom: 081 392 99 93
Italy: Cogeta PalaceHotels Associated Hotels: 1678 21057 — Germany: (0) 130 81 79 21 — Belgium: (0) 78 11 95 79 — Switzerland: (0) 155 04 11 or Utell International

francesco smalto

BOUTIQUES : 44 rue François 1er. 75008 Paris / 5 place Victor Hugo. 75016 Paris

HOME – SHOPS

Nestor Perkal
3rd arr. - 8, rue des Quatre-Fils
42 77 46 80
Open 10 a.m.-7 p.m. (Sat. & Mon. from 2 p.m.). Closed Sun. & Aug.

Spaniard Nestor Perkal, interior architect and designer, has a passion for bright, primary colours. So for his marvellous shop, Perkal has selected pieces from Memphis, that crazy bunch of designing Italians, and from the Spanish firm Ediciones. Well before Spain and the *movida* were trendy, Perkal was showing avant-garde designs from Madrid, Seville and, of course, Barcelona.

Protis
8th arr. - 153, rue du Faubourg Saint-Honoré - 45 62 22 40
16th arr. - 22, av. Raymond-Poincarré - 47 04 60 40
Open 3 p.m.-7 p.m. (Sat. 10 a.m.-1 p.m. & 2:30 p.m.-6:30 p.m.). Closed Sun.

White walls and a grey-tile floor set the glass-and-steel furniture off to advantage. Protis presents its own designs (coffee tables in glass and black lacquered metal), Italian pieces by Cattelan, Bieffeplast, Tonon and Technolinea (with a beautiful line of office furniture in walnut or rosewood) and a host of creations by noted architects. A leather-covered high-back chair by Cattelan sells for 3,000 francs or so.

Antoine Schapira
6th arr. - 74, bd Raspail - 45 48 22 80
Open 10:30 a.m.-1 p.m. & 3 p.m.-7 p.m. Closed Sun., Mon. & 2 wks. in Aug.

Antoine Schapira, a designer and cabinetmaker with a diploma from the Ecole Boulle, offers superb contemporary furniture with a strong, singular personality. Schapira crafts and signs each sofa, armchair, bookcase and console himself, using rare and precious woods (palm wood, for example); every piece is custom-made.

VIA
6th arr. - 4-6-8, cour du Commerce Saint-André - 43 29 39 36
Open 10:30 a.m.-7 p.m. Closed Sun. & Aug.

VIA stands for *Valorisation de l'Innovation dans l'Ameublement*; in other words, an association for promoting innovative furniture design. Now housed in spacious new premises on the Left Bank, this gallery/shop/showroom continues to give young designers a boost. VIA alumni include such luminaries as Wilmotte, Starck and Mourgue; among the up-and-coming stars now on view is Kristian Gavoille, elected Designer of the Year in 1992 by a jury of his peers.

OUTDOOR FURNITURE

Le Cèdre Rouge
1st arr. - 22, av. Victoria - 42 33 71 05
Open 10 a.m.-7 p.m. (Mon from 11 a.m.). Closed Sun.
6th arr. - 5, rue de Médicis - 42 33 71 05
Open 10:30 a.m.-7:30 p.m. Closed Sun. & Mon.

Furniture for the patio and garden, in Burmese teak or colonial-style wicker, is the speciality of Le Cèdre Rouge. But you will also find handsome little volcanic stone tables in a score of colours, and copies of 18th-century furniture executed in steel and canvas. We could browse for hours among the many elegant pieces of hand-crafted pottery (over 2,000 in stock) from Biot, Aubagne and Tuscany. A section devoted to decorative objects for indoors includes lamps, Florentine ceramics and lovely rustic baskets.

Jardins Imaginaires
6th arr. - 9 bis, rue d'Assas - 42 22 90 03
Open 10:30 a.m.-1 p.m. & 2 p.m.-6:30 p.m. (Mon. from 2 p.m.). Closed Sun.

A medley of handsome antique furnishings full of grace and wit; a selection of modern furniture and objets d'art for sophisticated gardens and conservatories; an original selection of statuary, pottery, urns and basins... The "imaginary gardens" evoked in this wonderful shop brim over with charm, humour and taste. It's one of our very favourite shops in Paris.

SOFAS & CHAIRS

Duo Sur Canapé
1st arr. - 3, rue de Turbigo - 42 33 37 12
Open 10:30 a.m.-1 p.m. & 2 p.m.-7 p.m. (Mon. 2 p.m.-7 p.m.). Closed Sun.

Contemporary sofas and chairs by top designers. Philippe Starck's recent "Paramount" collection (commissioned by the New York hotel of the same name) is on display.

Un Fauteuil Pour Deux
6th arr. - 9, rue Corneille - 43 29 74 32
Open 10:30 a.m.-7 p.m. Closed Sun. & Mon.

Bernard Maxime updates classic French chairs and sofas by splashing them with brilliant colour or upholstering them with unusual fabrics. A browse around this shop will yield dozens of decorating ideas, even if you don't fancy lugging furniture back home (or paying to have it delivered). Ornamental objects and accessories are also on view, at prices ranging fro 400 to 100,000 francs.

First Time
6th arr. - 27, rue Mazarine - 43 25 55 00
Open 10 a.m.-6:45 p.m. (Mon. from 2 p.m.). Closed Sun. & 3 wks. in Aug.

Noted designer Didier Gomez heads this interior

SHOPS – HOME

decorating firm, which manufactures chairs (7,000 to 10,000 francs) and sofas (17,000 to 20,000 francs) signed by Gomez himself, or by his equally well-known colleagues, Christian Duc and Andrée Putman.

■ HARDWARE

Garnier
12th arr. - 30 bis, bd de la Bastille
43 43 84 85
Open 9 a.m.-12:30 p.m. & 1:30 p.m.-5 p.m. Closed Sat. & Sun. No cards.

Established in 1832, Garnier is a specialist in ornamental hardware and locks. Reproductions of Louis XV, Louis XVI, Directoire, Empire and English locks and plaques are still manufactured and displayed—though not sold—here. Friendly and informative staff can provide a list of dealers who handle any model you might be interested in acquiring.

A la Providence (Leclercq)
11th arr. - 151, rue du Faubourg Saint-Antoine - 43 43 06 41
Open 8:30 a.m.-6 p.m. (Mon. 8:30 a.m.-noon & 2 p.m.-6 p.m.). Closed Sun.

This is undoubtedly the most delightful hardware store on the Faubourg-Saint-Antoine (the cabinetmaker's and woodworker's quarter). Arlette, one of France's few female locksmiths, welcomes you into her domain, where she and her colleagues fashion handmade copies of locks and other hardware, working from antique originals. Some of the hard-to-find items available here are hand-cut crystal knobs for banisters and brass plaques for 1930s armoires.

The prices in this guide reflect what establishments were charging at press time.

■ INTERIOR DECORATION

INTERIOR DECOR

La Chaise Longue
1st - 30, rue Croix des Petits-Champs - 42 96 32 14
Open 11 a.m.-7 p.m. Closed Sun.
3rd - 20, rue des Francs-Bourgeois - 48 04 36 37
Open 11 a.m.-7 p.m. (Sun. from 2 p.m.).
6th - 8, rue Princesse - 43 29 62 39
Open noon-8 p.m. Closed Sun.

A colourful shop chock-full of amusing items to add a touch of whimsy to the house. For the kitchen, there is enamelled metalware (plates, pots, pitchers and so on), multicoloured glasses, special barbecue grills and piles of gadgets; for the office or *salon*, there are hammered metal picture frames, trendy wire baskets by Filo di Ferro, potpourri and papier-mâché vases. Browsing here is lots of fun.

Galerie Acanthe
16th arr. - 18, rue Cortambert
45 03 15 55
Open 11 a.m.-1 p.m. & 2 p.m.-7 p.m. Closed Sun., Mon. & Aug. No cards.

Christian Benais's shop looks like the home of a private collector, where Napoléon III furniture cohabits comfortably with Art Deco ornaments and objets d'art. Benais adores antique linens, and he has amassed a considerable selection of turn-of-the-century embroidered tablecloths, as well as some fine contemporary pieces in embroidered linen and Egyptian cotton. He is also creative director for the Chotard-Brochier textile firm, designing marvellous fabrics (lots of swatches are on view).

Elle
6th arr. - 30, rue Saint-Sulpice
43 26 46 10
Open 10:30 a.m.-7 p.m. Closed Sun.

Chosen by the style-conscious editors of *Elle Décoration*, the dishes, lamps, car rugs and many other decorative and useful objects on display are both lovely to look at and a pleasure to use.

Etamine
7th arr. - 63, rue du Bac - 42 22 03 16
Open 9:30 a.m.-7 p.m. (Mon. from 1 p.m.). Closed Sun. & 2 wks. in Aug.

Etamine's new two-level boutique numbers among the trendiest home-décor shops in Paris, with a superb collection of fabrics from all over the globe: neoclassic prints and cut velvets from Timney and Fowler, a horsehair look-alike made with a vegetable fibre from the Philippines and masses of attractive wallpaper designs. Also on hand is a selection of sofas, lamps, objets d'art and a few choice antique pieces.

Galerie du Bac
7th arr. - 116, rue du Bac - 40 49 03 03
Open 10 a.m.-1 p.m. & 2 p.m.-6:30 p.m. Closed Sun. & Aug.

Galerie du Bac is a handsome, spacious showcase for the latest creations for the home by Missoni—linens and upholstery fabrics, sheets and towels by TJVestor and Mateb. Don't miss the gorgeous Italian wallpapers (crinkled, waxed, "pre-worn"...), or the Woodnotes paper rugs.

Christian Badin
6th arr. - 12, rue de Tournon - 43 26 00 67
Open 10 a.m.-7 p.m. Closed Sat. in July & Aug. & Sun.

A warm, urbane atmosphere reigns in this pretty shop, a showcase for a wonderful collection of fabrics, rugs and decorative objects. The rugs—dhurries, English wool carpeting in 70 different patterns (1,150 francs per linear metre) and tinted coconut matting (160 francs per square metre)—can be made up in the colours of your choice. Christian Badin's beautiful fabrics are inspired by 18th-century designs; the patterns come in bright, slightly acidic colours printed on cotton or silk. Badin's furniture is crafted in natural beech or in sycamore. The splendid decorative objects are not the sort you see everywhere; we were enchanted by some etched Austrian wine glasses, copied from an 18th-century model. Decorating service available.

Juste Mauve
16th arr. - 29, rue Greuze - 47 27 82 31
Open 10 a.m.-7 p.m. (Mon. from 11 p.m.). Closed Sat. (except Nov. 1-end of Feb.), Sun. & Aug.

Anne-Marie de Ganay's shop has all the charm of a cosy home, with its mix of mahogany (coffee tables from 6,000 francs) and flowered chintz, low stools and Chinese cachepots (900 francs), picture frames in burled elm and marquetry (650 francs). Piles of lacy cushions and a selection of ravishing lingerie lend a frothy, feminine note.

Miller et Bertaux
4th arr. - 27, rue du Bourg-Tibourg - 42 77 25 31
Open 11 a.m.-1:30 p.m. & 2 p.m.-7 p.m. Closed Sun. & Mon.

A world that is at once both fragile and rough-hewn, exotic and natural—in any case, brimming with charm and fantasy. The tree-branch lamps, palm-leaf chairs, wrought-iron tables and tulip-printed fabrics perfectly sum up the "ecology-chic" that is the dominant trend in French interior decoration today.

Nicole H.
6th arr. - 28, rue Bonaparte - 43 25 43 60
Open 9:30 a.m.-noon & 1:30 p.m.-6:30 p.m. Closed Sun., Mon. & Aug.

Nicole Hannezo designs delightful furniture with a 1930s feel: writing desks, bars, dining room tables and coffee tables, in wood washed with ceruse (a white pigment), then lacquered or given a sharkskin finish. All the pieces are made to order, and prices are really unbeatable, considering their beauty and exquisite workmanship. An exceptional selection of fabrics from the best manufacturers is available here, as well as a decorating service.

Les Olivades
16th arr. - 25, rue de l'Annonciation - 45 27 07 76
Open 10 a.m.-7 p.m. Closed Sun., Mon. & Aug.

The wonderful warmth and charm of Provence is infused into this tiny shop tucked away behind the rue de Passy. Redolent of olive oil and lavender, bright with the colours of the Midi, Les Olivades displays, among other treasures, traditional Provençal print fabrics. If you're not handy with a needle, there are many small items already made up: bags, spectacle cases, make-up cases, skirts, shawls and even the sunniest umbrellas imaginable.

Souleiado
6th arr. - 78, rue de Seine - 43 54 15 13
16th arr. - 83-85, av. Paul-Doumer - 42 24 99 34
Open 10 a.m.-7 p.m. (Mon. from 2 p.m.). Closed Sun.

Thanks to Charles Demery, Provençal fabrics are known and sought after the world over. Souleiado's original designs, many dating from the 18th century, are available in a riot of cheerful colours. Co-ordinated wallpaper and oilcloth (30 patterns) are on hand too, and the home-décorating department also offers quilted bedspreads with matching sheets, tablecloths, fabric-covered boxes, shopping bags, picture frames and—the firm's best-seller—place mat and napkin sets. The space devoted to fashion continues to grow: wool shawls sell for around 1,000 francs, and

---

A pungent pilgrimage

Paris had a *sewer system* as early as 1370, but the waste emptied straight into the River Seine. Epidemics followed plagues, and public hygiene made little further progress until 1854, when a series of drains and aqueducts channelled the worst of the city's sewage 12 miles downstream. A massive programme to eliminate and purify the last outflows from the capital was launched in 1984. Although we now take the benefits of modern waste-treatment plants for granted, it is interesting to see how a city sewer plant works—and how nasty it smells! Guided tours of the sewer system of Paris leave the quai d'Orsay side of the Pont de l'Alma on Monday and Wednesday afternoons (weather permitting); the tour lasts an hour and a quarter.

there are very trendy men's shirts as well.

Vivement Jeudi
5th arr. - 52, rue Mouffetard - 43 31 44 52
Open Thurs. 10 a.m.-8 p.m.

Open only on Thursdays, this absolutely charming house-within-a-house presents antiques and humbler second-hand (but first-quality) furniture, linens and decorative objects for the home. All the merchandise has been lovingly collected by the shop's two owners, assiduous frequenters of flea markets all over France.

MISCELLANY

Au Chêne-Liège
14th arr. - 74, bd du Montparnasse - 43 22 02 15
Open 9:30 a.m.-6:30 p.m. Closed Sun. & Mon.

A *chêne-liège* is a cork-oak, and cork is the speciality of this well-known Montparnasse emporium. We've seen the most astonishing range of articles, all in cork—accessories for the wine cellar, for the desk and office, luggage and handbags and even women's clothing (believe us, nothing could be less kinky!).

Passementeries de l'Ile de France
11th arr. - 11, rue Trousseau - 48 05 44 33
Open 9 a.m.-5:30 p.m. (Fri. 9 a.m.-5 p.m.). Closed Sat., Sun. & Aug. No cards.

One of the last surviving specialists in silk braid and fringing (to trim curtains, chairs and lampshades, for example), who will design to the customer's specifications. The firm also manufactures reproductions of period trims, as well as a line of contemporary designs.

La Passementerie Nouvelle
1st arr. - 15, rue Etienne-Marcel 42 36 30 01
Open 9 a.m.-6 p.m. Closed Sat., Sun. & Aug. No cards.

When France needs new trimmings for the draperies at Versailles or Fontainebleau, it calls on La Passementerie Nouvelle. In addition to reproductions of historic pieces, the company works with period-style braids, trims and fringing specially adapted for contemporary fabrics.

SMH
11th arr. - 76, bd Richard Lenoir 43 57 47 25
Open 9 a.m.-12:30 p.m. & 1:45 p.m.-6 p.m. Closed Sun.

Single- and double-curved mouldings, cornices, carved door frames, baseboards and rosettes (in pine, oak, tropical wood, polyurethane or even Styrofoam) will dress up even the plainest prefab bungalow. SMH will cut all these elements to measure, then you take them home, paint them, put them up... and hey presto! Goodbye suburbia, hello Versailles! SMH also sells all sorts of supplies for do-it-yourself picture-framers.

CARPETS & NEEDLEPOINT

Brocard
4th arr. - 1, rue Jacques-Cœur 42 72 16 38
Open 9 a.m.-noon & 2 p.m.-5 p.m. Closed Sat., Sun. & Aug. No cards.

If needlework is your favourite pastime, do make time to stop by here. Brocard manufactures all manner of canvases in many sizes. Vintage embroideries and needlepoint receive careful restoration here.

> *The prices in this guide reflect what establishments were charging at press time.*

Casa Lopez
6th arr. - 27, bd Raspail - 45 48 30 97
Open 10 a.m.-1 p.m. & 2:30 p.m.-6:30 p.m. Closed Sun., Mon. & 3 wks. in Aug.

Casa Lopez proposes covetable jacquard rugs in geometric patterns, many of which are reversible. Most designs are available in ten different sizes, in a range of 90 colours, for reasonable prices (8,500 francs for a two by three metre rug). Coconut-fibre mats in plain or houndstooth checks and herringbone patterns have loads of casual charm, and we love the wool carpets with raised lozenge, diagonal or ribbon motifs. Certain designs are also available on canvas, to make co-ordinating petit-point chair backs and seats.

Toulemonde-Bochart
2nd arr. -10, rue du Mail - 40 26 68 83
Open 10 a.m.-7 p.m. Closed Sun. & 3 wks. in Aug.

This award-winning firm's claim to fame is its collection of contemporary carpets designed by the top names: Andrée Putman, Hilton McConnico, Christian Duc, Jean-Michel Wilmotte. Decorative dhurries, sisal and coconut matting are pretty too, and considerably less expensive.

WALLPAPER & FABRICS

Besson
6th arr. - 32, rue Bonaparte - 40 51 89 64
Open 9:30 a.m.-6:30 p.m. Closed Sun., Mon. & 2 wks. in Aug.

The choicest English and French decorator fabrics and wallpapers have been featured at Besson for 30 years. The range of nostalgic, romantic, exotic and rustic patterns is considerable, and the sales staff, bursting with good advice, is also gratifyingly generous with samples.

Manuel Canovas
6th arr. - 5, rue de Furstenberg
43 26 89 31
Open 10 a.m.-7 p.m. (Mon. from 11 a.m.). Closed Sun. & 2 wks. in Aug.

Textile designer and manufacturer Manuel Canovas came up with a style that revolutionised interior decorating in the 1960s. This master colourist drew his inspiration from extensive travels in India, Japan and California, as well as from imagined botanical gardens. Canovas's extraordinary chintzes are done in slightly acid tones, while muted shades are preferred on such sophisticated fabrics as moiré. Co-ordinated wall coverings are available as well, and in the shop next door, fashion and home accessories are made up in Canovas fabrics.

Casal
7th arr. - 40, rue des Saints-Pères
45 44 78 70
Open 9:30 a.m.-6:30 p.m. Sat. (Sept. 1-May 1) & Mon. 10 a.m.-6 p.m. Closed Sun. No cards.

Casal's signature jacquard prints, inspired by traditional paisley patterns and kilim rug designs, look great on sofas. But in this spacious, skylit showroom (formerly an artist's studio) you will also find fabrics by Brunschwig, Jean-Michel Wilmotte and Decortex.

Pierre Frey
6th arr. - 2, rue de Furstenberg
46 33 73 00
Open 10 a.m.-6:30 p.m. Closed Sun. & 3 wks. in Aug.

This firm is a family affair with an international reputation. Although the designers draw a good deal of their inspiration from traditional 18th and 19th-century French patterns, Pierre Frey is also known for its huge—and ever-growing—line of contemporary fabrics and wall coverings. In the *Patrick* Frey home-décorating shops, you'll find a selection of handsome bed linens, cushions, shawls, fabric-covered boxes and laminated trays, all in the Frey signature prints.

Nobilis Fontan
6th arr. - 40, rue Bonaparte - 43 29 21 50
Open 9:30 a.m.-6:30 p.m. Closed Sun.

Since it opened in 1928, this decorating firm has enjoyed a reputation for the high quality and refined taste of its design. Refined, but not conservative, Nobilis Fontan has always managed to evolve intelligently, keeping pace with contemporary designers (recent additions to the Nobilis stable: Robert Le Héros, Ravage and Miller et Bertaux). The wallpapers on display here are relatively expensive, but they are beautifully made. The fabric patterns are inspired by classic English, Japanese and Chinese models, and co-ordinate perfectly with the wall coverings. Nobilis has extended its line of merchandise to include designer furniture and, in a recent development, shoes and *chapeaux*.

Tissus Reine
18th arr. - Place du Marché Saint-Pierre - 46 06 02 31
Open 9:15 a.m.-6:30 p.m., Mon. 2 p.m.-6:30 p.m. & Sat. until 6:45 p.m. Closed Sun.

You will get special attention here with a decorator to guide your choice among all the fabric designers represented. Large upholstery department.

Zuber
6th arr. - 55, quai des Grands-Augustins - 43 29 77 84
Open 10 a.m.-6 p.m. Closed Sun. & 2 wks. in Aug. No cards.

A dynamic new owner has revitalised the venerable firm of Zuber, boosting its level of creativity to new heights. Using time-honoured printing methods and working from a library of more than 100,000 antique patterns, Zuber's is an eye-popping collection of wallpapers: trompe l'œil, panoramas, marbled and damask papers, as well as sublime friezes, cornices and borders of roses and other flowers in the subtlest of tints. Orders (excluding special orders) can be fulfilled in 48 hours.

■ LIGHTING

Antica
7th arr. - 38, rue de Verneuil - 42 61 28 86
Open 10 a.m.-6:30 p.m. Closed Sun., Mon. & Aug. No cards.

Madame Clérin can whip up a lampshade from one of the rich and refined fabrics she has in stock in about ten days, or she'll sell you one ready-made (for about 30 per cent less than the price of a custom-made shade).

Artémide
11th arr. - 6-8, rue Basfroi - 43 67 17 17
Open 9 a.m.-12:30 p.m. & 1:30 p.m.-6 p.m. Closed Sat. & Sun. No cards.

If you are curious to see what sort of lamps and light fittings the best designers have come up with lately, come to Artémide. Mario Botta, Vico Magistretti, Ettore Sottsass and Richard Sapper are just some of the famous names represented in this huge loft showroom.

Capeline
16th arr. - 144, av. de Versailles
45 20 22 65
Open 10 a.m.-7 p.m. Closed Sun., Mon. & Aug. No cards.

In this vast workshop, known to all the best Parisian decorators, craftspeople still turn out pleated, gathered and skirted lampshades as they did in the good old days.

SHOPS – HOME

Ready Made
6th arr. - 38-40, rue Jacob - 42 60 28 01
Open 10 a.m.-7 p.m. Closed Sun. & Mon.

Italian halogens are the speciality of this sleek and trendy shop near Saint-Germain. Flos, Artémide and Arteluce are a few of the manufacturers on sale; we particularly admire the floor lamps designed by Jean-François Crochet in metal and Murano glass. The sister shop next door exhibits furniture that is equally select, with the emphasis on reissues of 1930s classics by Eileen Gray, Breuer, Macintosh and Chareau.

■ LINENS

La Chatelaine
16th arr. - 170, av. Victor Hugo 47 27 44 07
Open 9:30 a.m.-6:30 p.m. (Sat. 9:30 a.m.-12:30 p.m. & 2:30 p.m.-6:30 p.m.). Closed Sun. & Mon.

For superb linens for your bed, bath and table, in satiny cotton, cotton muslin, organdy or linen, this shop is highly recommended. All linens can be embroidered at your request, or you can have pieces specially tailored to your needs (extra-large bath towels, odd-size tablecloths...).

Agnès Comar
8th arr. - 7, av. Georges-V - 47 23 33 85
Open 10:30 a.m.-1 p.m. & 2 p.m.-7 p.m. Closed Sun. & 3 wks in Aug.

Always bubbling with fresh, elegant ideas for the home, international decorator Agnès Comar now has a solution for your dingy living room sofa and chairs: loose, flowing slipcovers in a linen-and-cotton blend that adapt to any shape, virtually any size, and are machine washable (for 3,500 francs). She also makes table skirts to measure, with luxurious quilted borders, and felt bedspreads with adorable appliqués that co-ordinate with curtains and cushions. Sheets come in white or ecru, embroidered or edged with pleats or lace (matched with travel and make-up kits). Expect to pay top prices for these luxurious linens.

Fanette
15th arr. - 1, rue d'Alençon - 42 22 21 73
Open 1 p.m.-7 p.m. Closed Sun. & July 10-Sept. 6.

Fanette's speciality is vintage household linen: embroidered pillowcases, damask tablecloths and Provençal quilted bedspreads. All the pieces are in excellent condition, sold in a charming country-style shop decorated with pretty antiques, curios and baskets (all of which are for sale).

Peau d'Ange
16th arr. - 1, rue Mesnil - 45 53 78 11
Open 10:30 a.m.-noon & 2 p.m.-6:30 p.m. Closed Sun. & Aug. No cards.

A delightfully refined little boutique, Peau d'Ange is awash with frothy vintage linens (embroidered sheets embellished with openwork cost 250 francs; a sheet plus two pillowcases goes for 600 francs). Hand-embroidered tablecloths range between 300 and 6,000 francs, depending on size and quality. Another speciality: old-fashioned bridal gowns, which are altered to the bride's size, then laundered, starched and ironed just before the big day.

Porthault
8th arr. - 18, av. Montaigne - 47 20 75 25
Open 9:30 a.m.-6:30 p.m. (Sat. & Mon. 9:30 a.m.-1 p.m. & 2 p.m.-6 p.m.). Closed Sun.

Everyone who loves luxurious linens knows Porthault. Even if you can't afford these signature prints and exquisite embroideries (they are, of course, very expensive—a tablecloth can cost up to 50,000 francs), you can browse, finger (discreetly!) and admire them in this high-class shop on the avenue Montaigne. A lower-priced line, Porthault Studio, was recently introduced—but even lower-than-usual prices here aren't cheap. A pair of sheets and two pillowcases in embroidered cotton start at 2,500 francs and quickly climb to 35,000.

■ TABLEWARE

CANDLES

Cir-Roussel
6th arr. - 22, rue Saint-Sulpice 43 26 46 50
Open 10 a.m.-7 p.m. (Mon. from 11 a.m.). Closed Sun.

In the wax-processing business since 1643, Cir-Roussel offers a considerable choice of candles in a variety of classic and imaginative shapes. Current bestsellers are "cake," "caviar" and "sandwich" candles. These, like any candle in the shop, may be personalised with your name or initials for a modest fee.

Point à la Ligne
7th arr. - 25, rue de Varenne 42 84 14 45
11th arr. - 28, rue Neuves des Boulets - 43 48 45 84
16th arr. - 67, av. Victor Hugo 45 00 96 80
Open 10 a.m.-7 p.m. Closed Sun.

You are certain to find candles to match your centrepiece or tablecloth (or your eyes, for that matter) in this pretty boutique. There are dozens of shades available, each one co-ordinated with paper napkins, plates and tablecloths. Candle holders are available as well, in clear or coloured glass, along with hurricane lamps and a line of candles in imaginative shapes that echo the seasons or holidays.

CRYSTAL & CHINA

Baccarat
8th arr. - 11, pl. de la Madeleine
42 65 36 26
Open 9:30 a.m.-6:30 p.m. (Sat. & Mon. from 10 a.m.). Closed Sun.

Baccarat now boasts a glittering flagship store on the place de la Madeleine. Guarding the collection of incomparably pure, superbly wrought crystal stemware, decorative items and objets d'art is a fierce 65-pound bear; he, too, is entirely crafted in crystal.

Au Bain Marie
8th arr. - 10, rue Boissy-d'Anglas
42 66 59 74
Open 10 a.m.-7 p.m. Closed Sun.

In a setting that recalls the lobby of a palatial hotel, Aude Clément presents a wide choice of eminently desirable tableware, kitchenware and accessories. Even the items that aren't expensive antiques look as if they ought to be: embroidered table linens, genuine crystal or just-glass glasses (initialled or not, as you wish), real and fake pearl-handled cutlery... Pieces by contemporary designers (watch for Frank Evennou's Champagne bucket) and by talented craftsmen (the hand-decorated faïences are superb) are exhibited alongside witty, inexpensive treasures for the table. Don't miss the huge collection of cookery books and magazines on food and wine.

Bernardaud
8th arr. - 11, rue Royale - 47 42 82 66
Open 9:30 a.m.-6:30 p.m. Closed Sun.

Since 1863, the Limoges-based Bernardaud has been a standard-bearer for French china manufacturers. Following the lead of other prestigious tableware manufacturers, Bernardaud has opened a showcase on the rue Royale to display the full range of its collections. A recent addition is the much-admired *Les Métropoles* service, whose stylised motifs represent the cities of Paris, Berlin, Moscow, London and New York (423 francs for a dinner plate).

Cristalleries Saint-Louis
8th arr. - 13, rue Royale - 40 17 01 74
Open 10 a.m.-7 p.m. Closed Sun.

This venerable firm (founded in 1586) which long crafted crystal for the kings of France, continues to maintain the highest standards of quality. A visit to Saint-Louis' dazzling showplace on the rue Royale will have you longing to adorn your table with blown, hand-cut crystal stemware, decanters encrusted with gold and filigreed or opaline vases.

Daum
2nd arr. - 4, rue de la Paix - 42 61 25 25
Open 10 a.m.-7 p.m. (Mon. from 11 p.m.). Closed Sun.

Daum's elegant dual-level showrooms are situated in premises formerly occupied by the great couturier, Worth. Slate-grey walls and green-glazed bronze furniture form an ideal setting for the firm's latest creations. On the ground floor are the limited-edition (200 or 300 copies) glass pieces in luminous colours: Fassianos's cobalt-blue head, carafes with cactus stoppers by Hilton McConnico, and baroque designs by Garouste and Bonetti. The lower level is devoted to Daum's lovely crystal table services.

Devine Qui Vient Dîner
15th arr. - 83, av. Emile-Zola - 40 59 41 14
Open 10:30 a.m.-7:30 p.m. Closed Sun. & Mon.

This red-and-grey shop is known for its noteworthy assortment of late-19th- and early-20th-century tableware, along with many finely crafted reproductions. Prices are amazingly reasonable for the antique ceramic ware, coloured glasses, silver-plated table accessories and such.

Dîners en Ville
7th arr. - 27, rue de Varenne - 42 22 78 33
Open 11 a.m.-7 p.m. (Mon. from 2 p.m.). Closed Sun.

It's hard not to notice this shop, with its multiple display windows that wrap around the corner of the rue du Bac and the rue de Varenne. It's even harder not to stop and admire the lavish tables draped in old-fashioned paisley tablecloths and set (by owner Blandine de Mandat-Gracey) with turn-of-the-century French or English dishes, colourful Bohemian crystal and antique table decorations. Inside, there are glasses in an enchanting range of tints and, on the upper floor, a section devoted to the ritual of tea, with teapots, tea services, vintage biscuit jars and silver accessories.

La Faïence Anglaise
6th arr. - 11, rue du Dragon - 42 22 42 72
Open 10:30 a.m.-7 p.m. (Sat. from 11 a.m. & Mon. from 2 p.m.). Closed Sun.

Tea fanciers will love the selection of small Victorian antiques, figurines and 1930s lamps available here. But dishes and table and tea accessories are the principal speciality of the house. Teapots, cake plates and tea caddies range in price from about 300 to 500 francs. Fifteen different models of

Wedgwood china are on sale here (plates cost from 56 to 152 francs each).

Gien
1st arr. - 39, rue des Petits-Champs - 47 03 49 92
Open 10:30 a.m.-2:30 p.m. & 3 p.m.-7 p.m. (Sat. & Mon. hours vary). Closed Sun. & Aug. 1-22.

The Gien faïence factory, founded in 1821, has been granted a new lease of life. Noted designers have been commissioned to create new patterns that are now on view in Gien's Paris showroom: Paco Rabanne came up with a service of square plates with delicate ridges, while Jean-Pierre Caillères designed triangular plates edged with black speckles. In a more traditional vein, Dominique Lalande painted his plates with fruit motifs and added a black-and-white border.

Muriel Grateau
1st arr. - 132-133, galerie de Valois - 40 20 90 30
Open 11 a.m.-12:30 a.m. & 1 p.m.-7 p.m. (Mon. from 2 p.m.). Closed Sun. & 3 wks. in Aug.

A talented designer and woman of taste, Muriel Grateau has amassed a highly sophisticated collection of Murano glasses, Limoges china and table linen in a superb palette of muted earth and mineral tones (superb blues, greys, purples and greens). The mix of antique and contemporary pieces on a single table is simply ravishing.

Lalique
8th arr. - 11, rue Royale - 42 66 52 40
Open 9:30 a.m.-6:30 p.m. Closed Sun.

Three generations of creative Laliques have earned an international following with their enchanting crystal designs. Marie-Claude Lalique, who succeeded her father, Marc, at the head of the company in 1977, creates marvellous contemporary pieces in the true Lalique spirit—like her Atossa vase, decorated with a circlet of amber crystal-and-opaline flowers. In the courtyard of the rue Royale shop, Lalique has opened another boutique, devoted to "the art of the table." Accompanying the Lalique crystal glasses and plates are linens, silver and china by prestigious manufacturers.

La Maison du Week-End
6th arr. - 26, rue Vavin - 43 54 15 52
Open 10 a.m.-7 p.m. (Mon. until 6 p.m.). Closed Sun. & Aug.

If your idea of a weekend treat is a shopping spree for linens and dishes to fill up your cupboards, we've got just the address for you. Old-fashioned damask tablecloths, in a range of seven pastel shades, are made to order here (from about 300 francs); damask towels sell for 278 francs with fringe, 178 francs without. You'll also find table services in faïence (earthenware) or china; the most recent addition to the line is a china tea service decorated with tiny old-fashioned blossoms. Do you feel that what is lacking in your life is a gilded garden chair? Look no further.

Manufacture Nationale de Sèvres
1st arr. - 4, pl. André-Malraux 42 61 40 54
Open 11 a.m.-6:30 p.m. Closed Sun. & Mon. No cards.

In an ultra-contemporary setting, with glass-and-brushed-steel shelves, La Manufacture Nationale de Sèvres presents its superb hand-painted, gold-trimmed china. Every piece is a work of art; some pieces are designed by noted artists—Lalanne, Mathieu, Van Lith and Coloretti, among others. Also on display are reproductions of such extraordinary objets d'art as the dancers sculpted by Léonard and Carpeaux. Prices for plates range from 1,000 to 10,000 francs, and the most expensive vase commands 200,000 francs. Special orders are completed in one to three months.

Odiot
8th arr. - 7, pl. de la Madeleine 42 65 00 95
Open 9:30 a.m.-6:30 p.m. (Sat. 10 a.m.-1 p.m. & 2:15 p.m.-6:30 p.m.). Closed Sun.

Silversmiths in Paris since 1690, this illustrious firm maintains its traditions by continuing to reissue pieces cast in 18th- and 19th-century moulds. Odiot will also execute silver or vermeil pieces as requested by a customer (a Napoleon-era desk lamp in gilded silver, priced well over 250,000 francs, is the most expensive object in the shop). For shoppers of more modest means, there are some fine items in silver-plate, china and crystal. Appealing little brooches in the form of a bee cost around 350 francs.

Pavillon Christofle
2nd arr. - 24, rue de la Paix - 42 65 62 43
6th arr. - 17, rue de Sèvres - 45 48 17 83
8th arr. - 9, rue Royale - 49 33 43 00
16th arr. - 95, rue de Passy - 46 47 51 27
Open 9:30 a.m.-6:30 p.m. Closed Sun.

Christofle was born in 1830, and his plated silverware was to make the firm its fortune. Since then, Christofle has become the world's premier exporter of table silver. The current bestseller is the clean-lined, contemporary Aria setting. A recent creation, the Talisman line of Chinese-lacquered settings, owes its beauty and durability to a jealously guarded secret process. Christofle has also enjoyed notable success with reproductions of its designs from the 1920s (like the coveted tea service in silver plate with briarwood handles), and a handsome line of classic china (a dinner plate from the newest service, Orientalys, costs 300 francs).

Peter
8th arr. - 191, rue du Faubourg Saint-Honoré - 45 61 19 37
Open 10 a.m.-6:30 p.m. (Mon. from 1:30 p.m.). Closed Sun. & 3 wks. in Aug.

For a couple of centuries, Peter's exclusive silverware patterns have adorned the dinner tables of the rich and refined (the Aga Khan and Giovanni Agnelli appear on the client list, just to give you an idea). The most sumptuous setting in the shop, fashioned of lapis lazuli and vermeil, is priced just shy of 15,000 francs. But Peter accommodates less opulent tastes as well, with beautifully designed contemporary silver, china services, crystal and small gifts (elegant nail clippers go for around 100 francs).

Puiforcat
8th arr. - 2, av. Matignon - 45 63 10 10
Open 9:30 a.m.-6:30 p.m. (Sat. & Mon. 9:30 a.m.-1 p.m. & 2:15 p.m.-6:30 p.m.). Closed Sun.

A few years ago, Eliane Scali, director of this world-renowned silversmithing firm, had the bright idea of reissuing Jean Puiforcat's stunning 1930s designs (like the table settings for the ocean liner the *Normandie*). More recently Puiforcat added a gift and jewellery department that stocks merchandise for nearly every budget. A silver-plated centrepiece sells for 1,400 francs; but a pretty silver chain bracelet costs only 200 francs. Puiforcat continues to commission pieces from well-known designers such as Andrée Putman and Manuel Canovas.

Quartz Diffusion
6th arr. - 12, rue des Quatre-Vents - 43 54 03 00
Open 10:30 a.m.-7 p.m. (Mon. from 2:30 p.m.). Closed Sun.

There's lots of space in this shop, all of it devoted to the delicate art of the glassmaker. The objects on display are signed by such talented artists as Baldwin, Guggisberg, Bouchard, Hinz, Gilbert and others who research the possibilities of glass for the Musée des Arts Décoratifs. Not everything is terrifyingly fragile or expensive, witness the "laboratory" glass carafe and salad bowl (150 francs and 180 francs, respectively). Glass dinner plates and wine glasses are available as well as glass tabletops, screens and shelves. Quartz is the exclusive source of a layered coloured glass called Décor A IV.

Quatre Saisons
14th arr. - 88, av. du Maine - 43 21 28 99
Open 10:30 a.m.-7 p.m. (Mon. from noon). Closed Sun.

Here's a wonderful collection of high-quality wooden table and kitchenware: carving boards, salad bowls, cheese boards (from 100 francs) and more. Pretty, inexpensive glassware (8 to 80 francs) is also on hand, along with rustic baskets and an assortment of fabric and plastic tablecloths in appealing colours.

IMAGE & SOUND

■ PHOTOGRAPHY

Cipière
11th arr. - 26, bd Beaumarchais 47 00 37 25
Open 9:30 a.m.-12:30 a.m. & 2 p.m.-7 p.m. Closed Sun. Mon. & Aug.

Michel Cipière, a certified appraiser of photographic equipment from every era, sells new and second-hand cameras (the latter in prime condition, of course). Every imaginable brand is in stock; some of the older cameras are rarities that will fascinate collectors. Expect a warm welcome and professional advice.

FNAC
1st arr. - Forum des Halles, level -2 - 40 41 40 00
6th arr. - 136, rue de Rennes - 45 44 39 12
8th arr. - 26, av. de Wagram - 47 66 52 50
Open 10 a.m.-7:30 p.m. (Mon. 1 p.m.-7:30 p.m.). Closed Sun.

You'll find a large selection of top brands at interesting prices at FNAC stores, plus all kind of equipment for developing and printing film. The customer service is excellent. There are over 28 FNAC outlets dotted around Paris, where you can buy rolls of film, spools of super-8 film and blank video cassettes, as well as have your holidays snaps developed.

Immo-Photo-Video-Son
9th arr. - 73, bd de Clichy - 42 82 02 80
Open 11 a.m.-8 p.m. Closed Sun.

You can buy or sell (good) used cameras here, or leave your photography equipment to be sold on consignment. Professionals and amateurs will find a large selection to suit specific needs. The helpful staff are often willing to bargain over prices.

La Maison du Leica
11th arr. - 52, bd Beaumarchais 48 05 77 67
Open 9:30 a.m.-1 p.m. & 2 p.m.-7 p.m. Closed Sun., Mon. & Aug.

For all the lovers of this manufacturer, the Maison du Leica sells new and used equipment and repairs all Leicas. The prices are competitive with those of the big discount store, FNAC, and the service is beyond reproach.

SHOPS – IMAGE & SOUND

RECORDED MUSIC & STEREO EQUIPMENT

Crocodisc
5th arr. - 42, rue des Ecoles - 43 54 47 95
Open 11 a.m.-7 p.m. Closed Sun. & Mon.

In this discount record paradise, you can find reasonably priced imports, used records and compact discs and cassettes. Every genre is represented: rock, reggae, funk, blues, country, film scores, etc. In addition, you can listen to the records, and you can also have them set aside and pay several days later.

Crocojazz
5th arr. - 64, rue de la Montagne-Sainte-Geneviève - 46 34 78 38
Open 11 a.m.-1 p.m. & 2 p.m.-7 p.m. Closed Sun., Mon. & holidays.

This is a branch of the aforementioned Crocodisc, specialising in jazz. Crocojazz is run on the same principles. Lots of interesting imports.

La Dame Blanche
5th arr. - 47, rue de la Montagne-Sainte-Geneviève - 43 54 54 45
Open 10:30 a.m.-1:30 p.m. & 2:30 p.m.-8:30 (Mon. 2:30 p.m.-8:30 p.m.). Closed Sun.

New and used recordings of classical music (mostly on vintage LPs) are this shop's *raison d'être*. Be alert: collectible treasures occasionally come to light here.

Disco Revue
1st arr. - 55, rue des Petits-Champs - 42 61 21 30
Open 11 a.m.-7 p.m. (Sat. 11 a.m.-noon & 2 p.m.-7 p.m.). Closed Sun. & Aug.

You may have to hunt a bit to locate this shop, tucked away in the back of a courtyard, but rock 'n' roll record collectors will find the effort well worth it. Vintage LPs and singles are bought and sold here, and although the management's preferences are for records from the 1950s and 1960s, there are examples from all eras in stock, including many rare and collectible recordings. CDs and laser videodiscs imported from Japan are also available.

FNAC Musique
9th arr. - 24, bd des Italiens - 48 01 02 03
Open 10 a.m.-midnight. Closed Sun.

Opened just a couple of years back, this FNAC is devoted exclusively to music. All types of music are represented on the cassettes, CDs, video and laserdiscs, but rock, jazz and French pop predominate. Plus you'll find a music bookshop, sheet music and a ticket agency for concerts and musical events.

Oldies but Goodies
4th arr. - 16, rue du Bourg-Tibourg - 48 87 14 37
Open 12:30 p.m.-7:30 p.m. Closed Sun.

This shop specialises in used records, including jazz, blues, and rock and roll in French, English and American versions (listen to the hysterical French "covers" of pop songs from the 1960s—the lyrics are even worse!). There are all sorts of goodies, old or rare or cheap. The store boasts a clientele that includes collectors and celebrities (Eddy Mitchell, Bernadette Lafont). Recently they added compact discs, and imports are making more frequent appearances.

Virgin Mégastore
8th arr. - 56-60, av. des Champs-Elysées - 40 74 06 48
Open 10 a.m.-midnight (Fri. & Sat. 10 a.m.-1 a.m.). Closed Sun.

The FNAC's British rival scored a major success when it secured its prime location on the Champs-Elysées. "Mega" only begins to describe Virgin's huge inventory of books, records, stereo gear, video paraphernalia and computer equipment. The staff is young and often only minimally competent (that's why we go elsewhere for expensive electronic merchandise), but the record department is excellent. The newest, the oldest, the best and the weirdest recordings can be found here; new releases are regularly hooked up to earphones, so that you can listen before you buy. You can gloat over your new acquisitions over refreshments at the Virgin Café, at the top of the store's marble staircase.

VIDEO

Playtime
7th arr. - 44, av. Bosquet - 45 55 43 36
16th arr. - 36, av. d'Eylau - 47 27 56 22
Open noon-8 p.m. Closed Sun.

This is the place for cinema fans - they can rent video cassettes from a collection of more than 3,000 titles, including a good selection in English. A nice plus for after shopping: customers can stop for a cup of tea in the adjoining tea room and bar. The assistants are very friendly, and cassette tapes are also available. Non-members pay 45 francs per cassette per day.

Reels on Wheels
15th arr. -35, rue de la Croix Nivert - 45 67 64 99
Open noon-10:30 p.m. (Mon. & Thurs. 10 a.m.-11 p.m.; Fri. noon-11 p.m. & Sun. 6:30 p.m.-10:30 p.m.)

English-language films on cassette are delivered by the friendly crew at Reels on Wheels. Just make sure that your VCR accepts the PAL system, and you're in business. Over 3,500 titles are available; cassettes are also offered for sale.

JEWELLERY

ANTIQUE JEWELLERY

See Antiques section, page 174.

PRESTIGE JEWELLERY

Boucheron
1st arr. - 26, pl. Vendôme - 42 61 58 16
Open 10 a.m.-6:30 p.m. Closed Sun.

Alain Boucheron, the current—dynamic!—bearer of the Boucheron family torch and president of the Comité Vendôme, has led his firm into new areas. In fact, with his Pluriels line of jewellery, he is expanding and developing the notion of what fine jewellery is: changeable gold settings to which you can add rings or links of acacia wood, diamonds, coral or other gems (a Pluriel piece therefore costs 12,500 francs or so). Beautiful jewels are brought out for inspection on plush trays, in an opulent environment of wood-panelling and friezes... such is the luxury for which Boucheron has stood for generations.

Bulgari
8th arr. - 27, av. Montaigne - 47 23 89 89
Open 10 a.m.-1 p.m. & 2:30 p.m.-7 p.m. Closed Sun.

The house of Bulgari started in Rome in 1881 when Sotirio Bulgari began selling jewellery (which he made at night) from a pushcart in the streets. Today Bulgari jewels pay the price of success: they are among the most copied pieces in the world. The Bulgari style is marked by piles of precious stones built up on gold mountings, or hyper-realistic objects with an implicit mocking message.

Cartier
1st arr. - 7, pl. Vendôme - 42 61 55 55
Open 10 a.m.-7 p.m. (until 6:30 p.m. in winter; Mon. & Sat. 10:30 a.m.-7 p.m.). Closed Sun.

"It is better to have authentic junk than fake Cartier," exclaims Dominique Perrin, chief executive of Cartier, the most copied name in the world. The watches can be found all over the globe, as can the wine-red leather goods (from keyholders to spectacle cases). Besides all the *must* Cartier goods, there remains the fine jewellery that made this establishment the most famous house in the world. Traditional jeweller services combined with inventiveness and know-how have conquered the world. In its Paris shops, Cartier will make up from simple sketches engagement rings or wedding bands, or they will rejuvenate—as if by magic—old or poorly cut stones.

Chaumet
1st arr. - 12, pl. Vendôme - 44 77 24 00
Open 9:30 a.m.-1 p.m. & 2:30 p.m.-6:30 p.m. Closed Sun.

Jeweller in Paris since 1780, Chaumet belongs to the highly select association of *Haute Joaillerie de France*, a group that fosters the traditions of French design and craftsmanship in fine jewellery. Though Chaumet's creations have beguiled such connoisseurs as Napoleon, Queen Victoria and countless maharajahs, the firm also produces elegant timepieces, gold jewellery, leather goods and writing instruments that are perfectly appropriate for fast-paced modern life. Prices for the "Boutique" line start at 4,200 francs, watches at 7,800 francs and leather accessories at 600 francs.

Mauboussin
1st arr. - 20, pl. Vendôme - 42 60 32 54
Open 10 a.m.-1 p.m. & 2 p.m.-6:30 p.m. Closed Sun.

Established in 1827, the house of Mauboussin gives off

The hole in Les Halles

Many Parisians still regret that the city's famous food market, installed here since the 12th century, was not preserved when the merchants moved out to Rungis in 1969. The *trou* ("hole") *des Halles* dug after the market was destroyed became a tourist attraction in its own right during the 1970s, while developers argued with the municipality over what should be done with it. One idea was simply to fill it in again; another was to flood it to make a lake linked up to the Seine. A dozen or so architects had their projects rejected before the present Forum shopping centre was approved and built. While indistinguishable from similar emporia worldwide, the Forum at least has the merit of carrying on the centuries-old tradition of trade. Above ground, the site has been attractively landscaped and the surrounding streets are full of echoes of the past for those who care to listen.

SHOP – JEWELLERY

that impression of security and comfort associated with old families, for whom the purchase of fine jewellery is the natural way to celebrate life's big moments. You are warmly welcomed into the discreet little offices where business is conducted. Mauboussin specialises in engagement rings, especially in coloured gemstones (emeralds, rubies, sapphires) set off by diamonds. They are also the creators of the famous Nadia rings in carved mother-of-pearl and gold, set with a diamond or a coloured gem.

Mellerio dits Meller
1st arr.- 9, rue de la Paix - 42 61 57 53
Open 10 a.m.-1 p.m. & 2 p.m.-6:30 p.m. Closed Sun., Sat. in July, Aug. & Sept.

Marie de Medicis had no idea, of course, that she was founding a dynasty of jewellers when she granted her loyal Lombard chimney sweeps (who, from the other side of the flue, had overheard and reported a plot against the Crown) licences first as peddlers, then street vendors and finally jewellers. Now, 14 generations later, the great house of Mellerio is by no means resting on its ancient laurels. The oldest of all the fine jewellers of France, the Mellerio family comb the worldwide gem trade for those outstanding stones, regardless of size, that measure up to their noble tradition. Constituting one of the centres of the *haut monde* of fine jewellery, Mellerio exports half its production to the far corners of the globe.

Poiray
8th arr. - 1, rue de la Paix - 42 61 70 58
8th arr. - 46 av. Georges-V - 47 23 07 41
Open 10:30 a.m.-6:30 p.m. Closed Sat. & Sun.

The house of Poiray is the youngest of the great jewellers. If a fine jewel can be said to have a soul, Poiray endows it with a spirit of youth. The multitinted style of its famous three-gold Tresse ring (13,500 francs), already seen on some very famous fingers, is also available in the form of necklaces and bracelets. There are lots of new items, such as the Three-Gold Heart and the Octogo line of gold-plated pieces, as well as the renowned Poiray watches, which come in round, rectangular or square shapes in gold, steel, gold and steel, or dressed up in precious stones. As for fine jewels, Poiray has the Cascade collection, including a bracelet of gold bangles trimmed in diamonds, rubies and sapphires for 300,000 francs and up. But there are some lovely rings at much more affordable prices.

Alexandre Reza
1st arr.- 23, pl. Vendôme - 42 96 64 00
Open 10 a.m.-1 p.m. & 2 p.m.-6:30 p.m. Closed Sun.

Alexandre Reza, of Russian descent, is a major dealer in precious stones and always seems to have the most beautiful gems around his shop. An expert collector, he has transformed his basement level into a gallery exhibiting reproductions fashioned according to traditional techniques. Take a look, for example, at the necklace of pear diamonds, all in gems by Flowliss, a stunning and priceless piece.

Van Cleef et Arpels
1st arr. - 22, pl. Vendôme - 42 61 58 58
Open 10 a.m.-6:30 p.m. Closed Sun.

The most innovative of the jewellers of the place Vendôme, and originators of the jewelled evening bag of gold and precious gems, this house boasts a unique technique for mounting stones that makes the gem stand out emphatically. The prices reflect the highest level of workmanship and creativity, but even more modest budgets have access to the Van Cleef Boutique where rings, earrings and butterfly pendants, starting at about 4,000 francs, can be found.

Harry Winston
8th arr. - 29, av. Montaigne - 47 20 03 09
Open 9:30 a.m.-1 p.m. & 2:30 p.m.-6:30 p.m. Closed Sat. & Sun.

American jeweller Harry Winston is one of the most prestigious diamond dealers in the world. He sells uncut diamonds from his own mines to other dealers and to retailers, as well as in his own showrooms. Many of the world's best-known diamonds have come from Winston, including five that belong to Queen Elizabeth and one that graced the hand of Elizabeth Taylor, dubbed the Taylor-Burton diamond. Even Marilyn Monroe, for whom diamonds proved to be a girl's best friend, liked to talk about Harry Winston. The entrance to the establishment is discreet and quite intimidating; you must have an appointment and be ready to be virtually frisked. In the two second-floor rooms, decorated in period style, the built-in showcases display diamond jewels, ornaments, earrings and other marvellous creations in a traditional but not ornate style. How much, you ask? Millions of francs... these jewels are intended for an international clientele seeking a recession-proof investment.

■ FINE JEWELLERY

A & A Turner
8th arr. - 16, av. Georges-V - 47 23 88 28
Open 10:30 a.m.-6:30 p.m. Closed Sun. & Aug.

Françoise Turner is one of the more recent arrivals on the fine jewellery scene. Decorated with carved wood and antique red floor tiles, her gallery is nothing if not luxurious. Her striking productions include big rings, some hand-carved (from 5,000 francs), or necklaces of rock crystal tipped in gold (from 40,000 francs). On our last visit there, we also admired large beads in malachite, marble and slate or horn, gold and cut stones that can be worn with a pearl necklace, a large chain or simply strung on a leather thong (from 25,000 francs). More affordable is Turner's new line of solid-gold jewellery, with prices around the 5,000-franc mark.

Arthus Bertrand
6th arr. - 6, pl. Saint-Germain-des-Prés - 42 22 19 20
Open 10 a.m.-6:15 p.m. (Sat. 10:15 a.m.-12:30 p.m. & 2 p.m.-6:30 p.m.). Closed Sun. & Mon.

Opposite the church of Saint-Germain-des-Prés, next door to the Deux Magots, stands Arthus Bertrand, a venerable maker of religious medals and academic swords. Families with a sense of tradition come here for engagement rings wrought in an utterly classic style. No-one, however, comes to Arthus Bertrand for the warm welcome, which is about as friendly as a court martial. The firm also specialises in reproductions of antique jewellery displayed at the Louvre. You'll find 22-carat-gold jewellery, as well as silver and two-headed rings (lion, ram and so forth), and small refined pieces starting at 600 francs.

Chanel Horlogerie
1st arr. - 7, pl. Vendôme - 42 86 29 87
Open 10 a.m.-1 p.m. & 2 p.m.-6:30 p.m. (Mon. & Sat. from 10:30 a.m.). Closed Sun
8th arr. - 40, av. Montaigne - 40 70 12 33
Open 9:30 a.m.-1 p.m. & 2 p.m.-6:30 p.m. (Mon. & Sat. from 10 a.m.). Closed Sun.

The décor of Chanel's newest watch boutique on the place Vendôme is reminiscent of Mademoiselle's private apartment. Japanese screens, suede sofas and lacquered furniture are reason enough to go and take a look. Within the boutique you will find the complete line of Chanel fine timepieces designed by the talented Jacques Helleu, the Chanel Art Director. The Chanel staff will let you discover this beautiful collection ranging from the signature leather and chain model to the ultimate luxury: the all-diamond pavé link bracelet watch.

Cotailys
3rd arr. - 6, rue Réaumur - 42 72 23 79
Open 9 a.m.-6 p.m. Closed Sat. (except in Dec.) & Sun.

Aided by the expert advice of the friendly owner, you can select from a variety of necklaces, bracelets, rings and earrings that combine contemporary taste with timeless classicism. Diamonds, emeralds, sapphires and rubies in myriad sizes are set principally in yellow gold. The shop also takes care of repairs, will make new pieces from your old jewellery, and gladly executes special orders and designs. Wholesale prices.

Ebel
1st arr. - 2, pl. Vendôme - 42 60 82 08
Open 10 a.m.-12:45 a.m. & 2 p.m.-6:15 p.m. Closed Sun. & Mon.

Since 1911 these "architects of time" have been seeking to make the perfect watch. They have succeeded, and you can find it at their gallery on the place Vendôme (with its décor by Andrée Putman): splendid, accurate watches set with cut diamonds and sapphires. The house also offers a designer line of jewellery by Italian Alexandra Gradi, featuring her necklaces and rings fashioned from rounded, tightly linked gold chain, delightful rings composed of coloured gems encircled by large gold bands (ring prices range from 2,300 to 12,000 francs; bracelets, 9,000 francs; necklaces, 77,000 francs). The prices of the watches (from 8,000 francs) are justified by the precious materials and the custom manufacture. An impeccably courteous reception is the house rule.

Fred Joaillier
8th arr. - 6, rue Royale - 42 60 30 65
Open 9 a.m.-6:30 p.m. (Mon & Sat. 9 a.m.-12:30 p.m. & 2 p.m.-6:30 p.m.). Closed Sun.

This is jewellery with a resolutely sportive spin, featuring the Force 10 and Tennis lines. Gold and steel are set with diamonds, flexible bracelets of gold are accessories for the active life. There are some watches in a combination of steel and leather (4,000 francs), and fine jewellery featuring evening bags in mother-of-pearl and precious gems in exotic shapes, butterflies or scarabs. You'll have to fork out a million francs for the latter. Fred Joaillier also has a boutique in the Galerie du Claridge (a shopping arcade off the Champs-Elysées).

Ilias Lalaounis
1st arr. - 364, rue Saint-Honoré 42 61 55 65
Open 10 a.m.-6:30 p.m. Closed Sun.

Here you will find braided gold, gold lions' heads, jewellery inspired by that of ancient Greece, and other creations that are much more con-

SHOP – JEWELLERY

temporary but scarcely more affordable.

Jare
1st arr. - Cour Vendôme - 42 96 33 66
Open by appt. only.

Overrun with business, this jeweller prefers to maintain a peerless standard of quality by limiting orders. Specialising in resetting the jewels that you already own, the magic worked by Jare turns old, tired baubles into contemporary gems.

Jean Dinh Van
2nd arr. - 7, rue de la Paix - 42 61 74 49
Open 9:30 a.m.-6:30 p.m. (Mon. & Sat. 10:30 a.m.-6:30 p.m.). Closed Sun.

Jean Dinh Van was discovered 20 years ago when the fashion world made his square-link chain a must (2,000 francs in silver, 21,000 francs in gold). Since then he has become the recognised leader in modern jewellery for everyday wear. His is a sober style, often featuring square shapes with rounded corners. In the same vein are his heavy square bracelets, his link chains and his famous "handcuff" clasps (from 2,000 francs) for rejuvenating pearl necklaces. His earrings of two large bands in gold or silver (from 2,300 francs) are graceful. And he offers some very pretty necklaces in black pearls, or in steel, gold or semiprecious stones (from 10,500 francs).

O.J. Perrin
16th arr. - 33, av. Victor Hugo 45 01 88 88
Open 10 a.m.-1 p.m. & 2 p.m.-6 p.m. Closed Sun. & Mon.

Elegant, easy-to-wear jewellery: we love the gold Liberty clip, the satin or leather Venetian bracelet with its wonderfully tactile braided-gold clasp, and the Méridienne ring.

La Perle
16th arr. - 85, av. Raymond-Poincaré - 45 53 07 62
Open 10 a.m.-12:45 a.m. & 1:45 p.m.-6:30 p.m. Closed Sat. (except in Nov. & Dec.), Sun. & Aug.

If you care to present your daughter with her first string of pearls or have your old string reset with precious stones, La Perle offers a variety of cultured pearls custom-strung to your liking as bracelets (5,500 francs and up), earrings, ropes or single strands. As well as transforming your old jewellery, the firm designs its own.

Phedra
8th arr. - 1, rue Royale 42 66 97 41
Open 10 a.m.-7 p.m. Closed Sun.

Some magnificent Italian jewels: gold rings covered in cut stones, necklaces of pearls set in rough-finish gold and rectangular watches bordered with gems. The collection here includes some rare and one-of-a-kind pieces.

Pomellato
8th arr. - 66, rue du Faubourg-Saint-Honoré - 42 65 62 07
Open 10 a.m.-7 p.m. Closed Sun.

The headquarters of Pomellato, a famed Milanese jeweller, is elegantly decked out in grey marble with large display windows. The clever, original collection features gold jewellery accented with silver or precious stones. Necklaces and bracelets come in various versions of fine links or in richer braided gold, always involving an invisible clasp as part of the piece. The Pomellato offerings include flat, flexible chains ornamented with cut stones (20,000 to 80,000 francs) and solid-gold rings (6,000 to 40,000 francs).

■ COSTUME JEWELLERY

Artcurial
8th arr. - 9, av. de Matignon - 42 99 16 16
Open 10:30 a.m.-7:15 p.m. Closed Sun. & Mon.

For limited-editions of jewels designed by modern artists, crafted in bronze, vermeil, silver and gold, visit the fascinating shop of this famous art gallery. You'll find "violin" pendants by Arman, Paul Bury's spherical jewels, Piero Dorazio's enamelled-gold ornaments and Claude Lalanne's juicy-looking clusters of glass currants and grapes.

L'Avant Musée
4th arr. - 2, rue Brisemiche - 48 87 45 81
Open 1 p.m.-7 p.m. Closed Sun.

There are 24 craft workers represented here, including Di Rosa (whose badges are creating a sensation), Grosso Modo, Virginia Campion and Happy Fingers. Elbow-to-elbow in the alleyways surrounding the Pompidou Centre, rings, clips, bands, necklaces and bracelets in resin, metal and other materials are sold at moderate prices. These ornaments are far from classic, but collectors are already snapping up the phonecard facsimiles designed by Toffe. Prices start at 75 francs.

Césarée
6th arr. - 43, rue Madame - 45 48 86 86
Open 9 a.m.-1 p.m. & 2 p.m.-7 p.m. Closed Sun.

Laurence Coupelon takes coral, horn, jade, malachite, terracotta, bronze and glass and transforms these disparate elements into highly covetable *bijoux*. Exotic and indefinably ethnic, they don't look like run-of-the-mill costume pieces; what's more, they are not exorbitantly priced.

LEATHER & LUGGAGE – SHOPS

Alexis Lahellec
1st arr. - 14-16, rue Jean-Jacques Rousseau - 42 33 40 33
Open 11 a.m.-7 p.m. (Mon. & Sat. noon-7 p.m.). Closed Sun.

Fabulous fake stones, glass beads, bogus gold and even papier-mâché go into the glorious "gadget" jewellery dreamed up by Alexis Lahellec. A very 1970s look, and prices that range from reasonable to deranged.

Lei
1st arr. - 15, rue des Petits-Champs - 42 86 00 16
Open 11 a.m.-7 p.m. (Sat. 2:30 p.m.-7 p.m.). Closed Sun.

Antonella Grammatico has a knack for choosing custom jewellery from yesteryear to suit contemporary tastes. Her collection includes huge "cocktail" rings from the 1940s, Second-Empire pendants and other baubles and bangles in silver or gold. Interesting prices, from about 500 francs.

Othello
6th arr. - 21, rue des Saints-Pères 42 60 26 24
Open 11 a.m.-7:30 p.m. Closed Sun.

Sheherazade would have loved the jewellery on display at Othello. Terracotta, pink ivorywood, coral, jade beads and even yew-tree roots are used in the creation of these exotic ornaments straight out of a fairy tale. Prices begin at 300 francs.

Yamada
2nd arr. - 30, rue Danielle-Casanova - 42 86 94 81
Open 10:30 a.m.-7 p.m. Closed Sun.

From classic pieces in ivory to hard-lined "design" ornaments in ebony or malachite, this Japanese firm comes up with jewellery for every taste. Prices start at 400 francs.

LEATHER & LUGGAGE

Aïcha
1st arr - 19, rue Pavée - 42 77 62 65
Open 11 a.m.-7 p.m. (Mon. from 2 p.m.). Closed Sun.

Vivid colours—lipstick red, ultraviolet, cobalt blue—amusing shapes and strong, wear-resistant leathers make the hand and shoulder bags sold here an excellent fashion investment.

La Bagagerie
6th arr - 41, rue du Four - 45 48 85 88 (also: 8th arr., 15th arr., 16th arr.)
Open 10:15 a.m.-7 p.m. (Sat. 10 a.m.-7 p.m.).

The prices are rising, but La Bagagerie's colourful bags, belts, luggage and leather accessories are reliably in tune with the season's fashions. Designs run from classic to pure fantasy; we especially like the combinations of timeless shapes (envelopes, bucket bags...) and vivid shades that are the shop's speciality.

Bottega Veneta
6th arr. - 6, rue du Cherche-Midi 42 22 17 09
Open 10 a.m.-7 p.m. Closed Sun.

Expect a grand reception befitting this high-quality Venetian leather-goods establishment. The braided lambskin bags lined in leather are unparalleled. And there are at least 40 models of classic, all-purpose handbags in 11 colours, including bright red and green. The lizard purses are expensive but always in fashion. To the right of the shop there's a handsome line of leather and vinyl luggage, including soft and hard suitcases. Urbane staff proffer advice on how to clean or repair old leather.

William Aimard Camus
6th arr. - 25, rue du Dragon - 45 48 32 16
Open 10:30 a.m.-1:30 p.m. & 2:30 p.m.-7 p.m. (Mon. 2:30 p.m.-7 p.m.). Closed Sun.

Handsome leather backpacks that grow softer and more supple with age are sold here at eminently reasonable prices (800 to 1,500 francs), alongside sturdy suitcases especially designed for air travel.

Gucci
1st arr. - 350, rue Saint-Honoré 42 96 83 27
8th arr. - 2, rue du Faubourg-Saint-Honoré - 42 96 83 27
Open 9:30 a.m.-1 p.m. & 2 p.m.-6:30 p.m. (Wed. 10:30 a.m.-1 p.m. & 2 p.m.-6:30 p.m.). Closed Sun.

Acres of showrooms sumptuously decorated in light marble and lemon wood display leather goods manufactured in Florence by the third generation of the Gucci family. The classic Gucci handbag for day or evening comes in box calf, crocodile, ostrich and wild boar. The leather and vinyl luggage is marked discreetly with the Gucci logo, or in canvas with the distinctive red and green stripes. There's also a fine selection of small leather goods (numerous gift possibilities), as well as silver and gold accessories, costume jewellery and shoes. The store at 27, rue du Faubourg-Saint-Honoré is reserved exclusively for ready-to-wear fashions, such as a classic blazer, straight skirts, silk blouses and lots of covetable leather jackets and trousers.

Henell's
10th arr. - 14, av. Claude-Vellefaux - 42 06 85 94
Open 9 a.m.-noon & 1:30 p.m.-7 p.m. Closed Sun. & Aug.

For high-class leather goods, from shoulder bags to shoes, in ostrich, lizard, buffalo and other rare skins, have a look in here. No, the address is not the

SHOP – LEATHER & LUGGAGE

most fashionable in town, but the service is unbeatable: any item can be custom-ordered in your choice of colour and size (most articles are ready in a month).

Hermès
8th arr. - 24, rue du Faubourg-Saint-Honoré - 40 17 47 17
8th arr. - 42, av. George-V - 47 20 48 51
Open 10 a.m.-6:30 p.m. (Sat. & Mon. 10 a.m.-1 p.m. & 2:15 p.m.-6:30 p.m.). Closed Sun.

Hermès has been selling fine leather goods long enough to reign supreme as the undisputed leader of the pack when it comes to saddles, handbags, luggage and all the accompanying accoutrements of fine living and travelling. But what about the prices? Are they reasonable or completely beyond reality? The answer is both. Check the finish on the leather goods; think of the meticulous hand-work that went into the cutting, sewing and adjusting of these bags and luggage. You still shrug your shoulders? Then go and visit the workshop in the Hermès museum on the fourth floor (by appointment only). That settled, let's move on to the handbags. Will you be tempted by the Kelly design (1949) or the Constance (1969), the red Hermès, the grained leather, the linen-and-leather or the crocodile and ostrich, which are the pride of the house? You really can't go wrong with any of these classically chic styles. The average price for the box calfs is 12,000 francs. There is a prestigious line of handmade luggage in box calf with reinforced corners. If you want something special, such as a leather covering for your bicycle seat or the cockpit of your private jet, the house will gladly oblige.

Monday, like Sunday, is a day of rest for many shopkeepers.

Lancel
9th arr. - 8, pl. de l'Opéra - 47 42 37 29
(also: 6th arr., 8th arr., 17th arr.)
Open 10 a.m.-7 p.m. Closed Sun.

Chic and typically Parisian leather accessories (belts, bags, wallets, key tags...) and fashionable—though never flashy— luggage. Complete lines of the latter are available in canvas as well as leather. On the whole, the craftsmanship is remarkable, and prices are in line with the quality.

Loewe
8th arr. 57, ave Montaigne - 45 63 73 38
Open 10 a.m.-7 p.m. Closed Sun.

Absolutely the last word in leather and suede (clothing, bags, luggage and accessories) from a patrician Spanish firm, recently established at this posh Parisian address.

Longchamp
1st arr. 390, rue Saint Honoré 42 60 00 00
Open 10 a.m.-7 p.m. Closed Sun.

A huge selection of handbags, luggage and accessories in leather, nylon or canvas with leather trim. Attractive detailing sets these bags apart; in addition to being fashionable, they are sturdily crafted to take a lot of heavy wear.

Didier Ludot
1st arr. - 23-24 galerie Montpensier - 42 96 06 56
Open 10:30 a.m.-7 p.m. Closed Sun.

Didier Ludot's shop is located under the arcades of the Palais-Royal, which is a good enough reason to come and see how he lovingly reconditions previously owned bags from Morabito and Hermès. He also carries a line of "surgical" bags used by doctors at the turn of the century and some superb 1920s-to-1930s suitcases lined with suede in box calf or crocodile.

Mac Douglas
8th arr. - 155, rue du Faubourg-Saint-Honoré - 45 61 19 71
Open 10 a.m.-7 p.m. Closed Sun.

Are you a leather lover? If the answer is yes, then you'll want to head straight for Mac and its infinite variety: glossy or dyed lambskin, goatskin, calf-skin, suede and shearling. There are well-cut jackets in crinkled sheepskin and calf-skin coats and dyed lambskin skirts. Prices are on the high side, but the designs are consistent in quality, well made and available in lots of colours. Good sales in January and July.

La Maroquinerie Parisienne
9th arr. - 30, rue Tronchet - 47 42 83 40
Open 9:30 a.m.-7 p.m. (Mon. 1 p.m.-7 p.m.). Closed Sun.

A huge two-level shop filled with an enormous selection of cut-price leather goods, ranging from purses and suitcases (Delsey, Samsonite, Longchamp) to canvas bags and crocodile handbags. Belts, gloves and umbrellas are also featured, and there is a 15 per cent reduction on the list price. Sale time is mid-January to mid-February.

Morabito
1st arr. - 1, pl. Vendôme - 42 60 30 76
Open 9:45 a.m.-6:45 p.m. Closed Sun..

Choose between custom-made luggage and handbags in the skin you fancy (box calf, ostrich or crocodile) and the colour you prefer, or a sportier line of ready-made bags in textured calf (1,000 to 6,0000 francs). The made-to-measure bags are generally ready in two to three days, and prices start at about 6,000 francs. Perfect service, of course, from this long-established firm reputed for quality.

MENSWEAR – SHOPS

Muriel
8th arr. - 4, rue des Saussaies
42 65 95 34
Open 10 a.m.-6:30 p.m. Closed Sun.

A wall lined with neatly organised drawers, a well-polished wooden counter: it's a pleasure to buy gloves at this traditional *gantier*'s shop. For dress or sport, you'll find a wonderful selection of gloves for men and women, crafted in kidskin or pigskin, trimmed with mink or lined with silk.

Renaud Pellegrino
1st arr. - 348, rue Saint-Honoré
42 60 69 36
6th arr. - 15, rue du Cherche-Midi - 45 44 56 37
Open 10:30 a.m.- 7 p.m. Closed Sun.

For the most chic and desirable bags in town, adorned with leather embroidery, grosgrain ribbon, fur and geometrical motifs, visit Renaud Pellegrino's exciting boutique. Top-quality leather in a rainbow of colours are used for these expensive but unique bags which make a definite fashion statement.

Paloma Picasso
2nd arr. - 5, rue de la Paix - 42 86 02 21
Open 10 a.m.-7 p.m. (Mon. 11 a.m.-7 p.m.). Closed Sun.

A jewel of a shop decorated by Jacques Grange is the showcase for Paloma Picasso's pricey and prestigious line of accessories. Red—Paloma's favourite colour—is much in evidence in the belts, bags and small leather goods for active, elegant women.

Prada
6th arr. - 5, rue de Grenelle - 45 48 53 14
Open 10:30 a.m.-7 p.m. (Sat. 10:30 a.m.-1 p.m. & 2 p.m.-7 p.m.). Closed Sun.

Versatile bags whose simple, classic shapes move effortlessly from office to opera house are the strong suit of this renowned Italian firm.

Terre de Bruyère
17th arr - 112, bd de Courcelles
42 27 86 87
Open 10:30 a.m.-7:30 p.m. (Mon. 2:30 p.m.-7 p.m.). Closed Sun.

Canvas, leather, or both together are the materials of choice for a handsome range of hand-crafted bags, backpacks and briefcases. They come in subdued, countrified shades of green, beige and grey-black and (considering the workmanship) are quite reasonably priced.

Louis Vuitton
8th arr. - 54, av. Montaigne - 44 20 84 00
8th arr. - 78 bis, av. Marceau - 47 20 47 00
Open 9:30 a.m.-6:30 p.m. Closed Sun.

Vuitton lovers, here's a test. Put your bag down at the airline counter at an airport. Watch it disappear into a crowd of other Vuittons... now try and identify it! If you haven't marked it somehow, you might be unlucky. The Vuitton madness has taken over the world. For many, the Vuitton bag has become a cult object. It consists of printed linen coated with vinyl, reinforced with lozine (which looks like leather; Vuitton jealously guards the formula) ribs, untreated leather for handles and straps, copper for rivets and hard corners. If the purchase of a Vuitton suitcase doesn't fit into your budget, console yourself with a card holder or racquet cover or even a key ring.

MENSWEAR

Berteil
8th arr. - 3, place Saint Augustin
42 65 28 52
Open 10 a.m.-7 p.m. (Mon. 2 p.m.-7 p.m.). Closed Sun.

Berteil clothes the hunting shooting and fishing set for their sport. But the handsome tweed jackets, well-cut trousers, oiled-canvas coats and nubbly sweaters are more often worn in restaurants, to the cinema, at cocktail parties or for a stroll in the Luxembourg Gardens.

Hugo Boss
1st arr. - 2, place des Victoires
40 28 91 64
Open 10 a.m.-7 p.m. (Mon. 11 a.m.-7 p.m.). Closed Sun.

Philippe Starck designed this three-level boutique, with an atmosphere reminiscent of an English tailor's shop (writ—very—large). Customers come here for the immense choice offered of every item of masculine clothing, from suits to socks. Clothes and accessories are stylish and colourful.

Marcel Bur
8th arr. - 138, rue du Faubourg-Saint-Honoré - 42 56 03 89
Open 9 a.m.-12:30 p.m. & 2 p.m.-7 p.m. Closed Sun. & Aug. 15-30.

Marcel Bur's suits are the stuff dreams are made of. Bur's Saxbury "miracle fabric," made of combed, carded, blended, 100 per cent pure wool, is guaranteed uncrushable. We are pleased to note that Bur's formerly conservative colours have brightened

---

RAC MOTORING ATLAS FRANCE: *Our fully revised and well-established large format RAC Motoring Atlas France, Belgium and Luxembourg at 1:250,000 (approximately 4 miles to 1 inch) now has even more features to improve journey planning and to make driving in France more enjoyable. Clear, accurate and detailed road maps make RAC Motoring Atlas France the ideal atlas for the independent traveller in France. Price: £ 11.99 (spiral bound).*

up a bit. A custom-made two-piece suit costs 10,000 francs upwards, but semi-custom models go for much less. The ground floor boasts several beautiful cashmere items, as well as the house cologne, Marcel Bur pour Homme.

Jean-Charles de Castelbajac Hommes
1st arr. - 31, place du Marché Saint Honoré - 42 60 78 40
Open 10:30 a.m.-7 p.m. Closed Sun.

The world of Castelbajac has finally thrown open its doors to men with a collection of basics, including Ko and Co Intégral plaid coats. The so-called arty ethnic style, with primary colours—so dear to the designer—splashed across jackets, shirts and sweaters, predominates. Knitwear, crafted along rustic lines, is a speciality of the house. The striking window displays lure customers in to buy Castelbajac's line of furniture, rugs, decorative items and luggage.

Cifonelli
8th arr. - 33, rue Marbeuf - 43 59 39 13
Open 9:45 a.m.-7 p.m. (Mon. 9:45 a.m.-1 p.m. & 2 p.m.-7 p.m.). Closed Sun. & 3 wks. in Aug.

When Cifonelli opened for business in the 1930s, he introduced a light, timeless style that immediately won over worldly travellers. The elder Cifonelli's son, Adriano, has perfected his father's designs. The shoulder, back and sleeve fittings are all impeccably precise. So providing the 15,000-franc price tag suits your wallet, you too can have people ask for the address of your tailor. These are noble threads indeed. The ready-to-wear is no less sophisticated, and not much less expensive.

Costardo
2nd arr. - 69, rue de Richelieu 49 27 03 79
17th arr. - 9, av. Niel - 40 55 03 55
Open 10 a.m.-8 p.m. Closed Sun.

A man could easily assemble a complete, reasonably priced and utterly fashionable wardrobe at Costardo. Suits are offered in three different cuts and a wide array of fabrics. Alterations are done in-house, quickly and at no extra charge. Shirts come in three lengths with a choice of two collar styles. For the quality, the prices here would be hard to beat.

Henry Cotton's
2nd arr. - 52, rue Etienne Marcel 42 36 01 22
Open 10 a.m.-7 p.m. Closed Sun.

An Italian take-off of American-style sportswear, sold in a typically trendy Parisian boutique. The clothes are high-class, but rather expensive. The rainwear does have some Italian panache.

Christian Dior Boutique Monsieur
8th arr. - 11, rue François-ler - 40 73 54 44
Open 9:30 a.m.-6:30 p.m. (Mon. & Sat. 10 a.m.-6:30 p.m.). Closed Sun.

Everything you need for an elegant, perfectly balanced wardrobe awaits you here; nowadays, you no longer get the impression that donning a Dior suit is like putting on a suit of armour. The moment you step into the Boutique Monsieur, you are surrounded by traditional Dior good taste: double-breasted suits in striped fabrics, glen plaid wool, cashmere and linen; shirts in cotton poplin with stripes in every colour of the (fashionable) rainbow. And, of course, the Dior accessories are always good value, both chic and functional.

Façonnable
6th arr. - 174, bd Saint Germain 40 49 02 47
Open 10 a.m.-7 p.m. (Mon. 2 p.m.-7 p.m.). Closed Sun.

For work or for play (polo, cricket, golf...), these clothes create an elegant yet easy-going image. Typically French style distinguishes the casual wear: cable-knit sweaters, rugby shirts, twill and canvas trousers. The accessories (socks, ties, underwear) are attractive and well made.

Gianfranco Ferré
8th arr. - 44, av. Georges-V - 49 52 02 74
Open 10 a.m.-7 p.m. Closed Sun.

Though his major focus is the haute-couture line he designs for Dior, Gianfranco Ferré signs a line of men's clothing as well, characterised by perfect shapes, irreproachable collars, light and supple fabrics. Every detail is attentively

---

A village vanishes

The *rue Saint-Blaise* was the main street of the parish of Charonne before it was swallowed up to form part of the 20th arrondissement in 1860. This neighbourhood still has a village atmosphere, and the Church of Saint-Germain-de-Charonne watching over its flock from a broad flight of steps is one of only two left in the capital with its own cemetery.

crafted, as his elegant customers doubtless demand.

Gauno et Chardin
2nd arr. - 8, rue du Mail - 42 96 22 48
Open 10 a.m.-7 p.m. Closed Sun.

In an inviting décor of warm wood, tall mirrors and leather armchairs, this Belgian manufacturer displays a remarkable collection of highly desirable leather coats and jackets. All the finishing touches on the bikers' jackets, parkas and warmly lined car coats are sewn by hand. Most models are in suede, buttery-soft lamb or textured goatskin, in beautiful colours.

Givenchy Gentleman
8th arr. - 56, rue François-ler
40 76 00 21
Open 10 a.m.-7 p.m. Closed Sun.

Blond wood and lots of light are conducive to browsing through Givenchy's refined, beautifully finished ready-to-wear for men. If your taste runs to classic, elegant clothes for the office or casual occasions, you will appreciate the superb poplin shirts, slimline suits and distinguished accessories (pigskin gloves, braces, wristwatches, eau de cologne), all in Givenchy's timeless, never trendy signature style.

Island
2nd arr. - 4, rue Vide-Gousset
42 61 77 77
Open 10 a.m.-7 p.m. Closed Sun.

If you've been invited to a house party in Provence and need a few things to fill out your weekend wardrobe, head over to Island. You'll find the same sort of casual gear—from polo shirts, sweaters, soft trousers and sporty parkas—that all the French guests will be wearing. Dockstep and Bass are the footwear brands on offer.

Lanvin Homme
8th arr. - 15, rue du Faubourg-Saint-Honoré - 44 71 33 33
Open 10 a.m.-7 p.m. Closed Sun.

The venerable Lanvin label has tailor-made itself a place at the forefront of the French menswear world. This shop, which is listed as an historical monument, is a charming product of the Roaring Twenties. It's worth going in just to take the elegant lift. Behind the array of suits, shirts and accessories stands a small army of craftsmen who draw on 50 years of Lanvin experience. Dozens of hours of work are dedicated to each suit. Flawless quality is the key. The Lanvin ready-to-wear line is designed by Dominique Morlotti; his flannel suits with embroidered quilted-silk waistcoats are things of beauty, and far less flashy than they sound.

Lapidus
8th arr. - 35, rue François-ler
47 20 69 33
Open 10 a.m.-6:45 p.m. Closed Sun. & 3 wks. in Aug.

Classic men's clothing with a dash of French chic that makes them interesting—but never eccentric. The accessories are of fine quality, and sufficiently timeless to wear season after season.

Marcel Lassance
6th arr. - 17, rue du Vieux-Colombier - 45 48 29 28
Open 10 a.m.-7 p.m. Closed Sun.

For over a decade now, the Left Bank's upper crust has been donning Monsieur Lassance's fashionable but discreet men's clothes. He will perhaps go down in social history as the man who helped transform President Mitterrand's sartorial habits. The attractive trousers, jackets, suits, shirts and sweaters are designed for intellectuals who like comfortable but elegant clothes.

Pape
7th arr. - 4 av. Rapp
45 55 09 68
Open 10:30 a.m.-7:30 p.m. Closed Sun., Mon., Aug.

Pape is a traditional English haberdasher, ensconced in a two-level wood-panelled shop in the heart of the fashionable seventh arrondissement. In addition to the made-to-measure clothing, Pape sells nicely cut overcoats and classic sweaters in lambswool or cashmere.

Saint Laurent Rive Gauche
16th arr. - 19-21, av. Victor Hugo
45 00 64 64
Open 10 a.m.-7 p.m. Closed Sun.

This former sanctum of the saint of French fashion seems to have slipped into provincial torpor. But lift your gaze beyond the indifferent sales staff to the dizzy décor of mirrors and the maze of dressing rooms...there are suits, jackets, sportswear, swimsuits—all graced by the master's touch. Sumptuous materials come in a regal rainbow of colours: turquoise, saffron, pink, Naples yellow on a black background. Some prices: 1,850 francs for a cotton sweater, 5,000 francs for a classic jacket.

Francesco Smalto
8th arr. - 44, rue François-ler - 47 20 70 63
16th arr. - 5, pl. Victor-Hugo - 45 00 48 64
Open 10 a.m.-7 p.m. Closed Sun.

Francesco Smalto, king of the extravagant fabric, was trained at the renowned Ecole Camps. He continues to uphold his well-earned title of master tailor and serve a clientele that includes celebrities and millionaires. Smalto has even perfected a type of cashmere in which the tennis stripes spell out the name of the customer. His styles appear effortless. No wonder

SHOP – MENSWEAR

his custom suits (with the signature Smalto pinched waist) command 25,000 francs. But take heart: beautiful, less cripplingly expensive ready-to-wear is also available.

Torregiani
8th arr. - 38, rue François-ler
47 23 76 17
Open 10 a.m.-7 p.m. Closed Sun.

Torregiani is an authorised dealer for Brioni suits, but you will also find a wide array of other beautiful, hand-sewn suits in the finest wool (priced from 9,500 to 12,000 francs). Brioni ties are somewhat less expensive, though no less exclusive; also in stock are men's shirts in luxurious printed silk.

Ermenegildo Zegna
2nd arr. - 10, rue de la Paix - 42 61 67 61
Open 10 a.m.-7 p.m. (Mon. 11 a.m.-7 p.m.). Closed Sun.

Renowned the world over, Ermenegildo Zegna is one of the giants of Italian fashion. He invented the pure-wool, no-wrinkle "high-performance" fabric that he uses so skilfully in his custom-made or ready-to-wear suits, costing from 5,600 to 8,750 francs. Zegna's progressive approach to classic clothes includes lively colours and an extensive range of accessories. A sophisticated and charming welcome awaits you in this must for browsers, a favourite with Parisian fashion fiends.

■ ACCESSORIES

BELTS

Losco
4th arr. - 20, rue de Sévigné - 48 04 39 93
Open 11 a.m.-7:30 p.m. (Mon. 2 p.m.-7 p.m. & Sun. 3 p.m.-7 p.m.). Closed 2 wks. in Aug.

The specialist in belts. Leather, lizard, coloured, braided—you name it, all the styles are here. Pick your belt and your buckle, or choose one of the ready-made models. Excellent prices: from 75 to 390 francs; crocodile costs much more.

The Regent Belt Company
4th arr. - 20, rue du Roi de Sicile
48 04 57 52
Open noon-7 p.m. (Sat. from 11 a.m.). Closed Sun., Mon. & 3 wks. in Aug.

A charming, old-fashioned shop in the Marais is the French headquarters of a British belt manufacturer who offers a vast array of leathers, colours, buckles and trims in an appealing range of styles.

HATS

Gélot
8th arr. - 15, rue du Faubourg-Saint-Honoré - 44 71 31 61
Open 10 a.m.-7 p.m. Closed Sun.

Hats off to Gélot, the master headwear maker patronised by Edward VII. Gélot has been working here, at the Lanvin Tailleur shop, since 1968. His made-to-measure fedoras start at 1,400 francs; tweed caps cost from 600 francs.

Motsch
8th arr. - 42, av. George-V - 47 23 79 22
Open 10 a.m.-7 p.m. Closed Sun.

Mad about hats? Motsch has been making and repairing top-notch headgear for over a century. Panamas, Borsalinos, fedoras and even derbies are all hand-crafted according to traditional methods.

SHIRTS

Equipment
2nd arr. - 46, rue Etienne-Marcel
40 26 17 84
Open 10:30 a.m.-7 p.m. (Mon. from 11 a.m.). Closed Sun.

Basic white poplin shirts with *trompe l'œil* buttons, China-blue embroidered shirts, embroidered denim, ruffle-fronted models and so forth—Equipment wreaks havoc on the classics. Things change rather drastically from season to season in this tiny boutique, but Equipment shirts are always exotic and comfortable. Prices for poplin: under 700 francs; silk shirts sell for under 1,000 francs. Sunny decor, and accommodating service.

Alain Figaret
1st arr. - 21, rue de la Paix - 42 65 04 99
7th arr. - 16, rue de Sèvres - 42 22 03 40
8th arr. - 14 bis, rue Marbeuf - 47 23 35 49
16th arr. - 99, rue de Longchamp
47 27 66 81
Open 10 a.m.-7 p.m. (Mon. from 3 p.m.). Closed Sun.

Six collar styles, three sleeve sizes, short-sleeved models, several cuff styles, hundreds of colours for thousands of shirts in 600 types of fabric... you will find—not lose—your shirt at Alain Figaret's shop (prices start at 330 francs). There's always a crowd, so don't bother to wait around for things to slow down. A word of warning: Buy your shirts a size longer in the sleeve (they shrink after the first wash). The button-down collars are often too narrow to cover a tie properly, and anyone with big biceps will probably find their sleeves tight. While Figaret may not be the king of Paris shirtmakers, he's certainly a prince.

Hilditch & Key
1st arr. - 252, rue de Rivoli - 42 60 36 09
Open 9:30 a.m.-6:30 p.m. (Sat. 9 a.m.-6 p.m.). Closed Sun.

Hilditch & Key shirtmakers, established nearly a century ago, is the last bastion of menswear shops in which refinement borders on the sublime. British poplins, fine cottons from France and heavy Japanese silk are among the 500 select fabrics to choose from. Cuffs and collars are made to measure, with extraordinary accuracy. Ready-to-wear shirts are also available. And it's impossible not to mention the celebrated Hilditch & Key sweaters and dressing gowns. Gorgeous two-ply V-neck cashmere sweaters come in 35 colours and cost 3,200 francs. There is also a marvellous selection of camel-hair jumpers, cardigans and sleeveless pullovers.

Sulka & Company
1st arr. - 2, rue de Castiglione
42 60 38 08
Open 9:30 a.m.-6:30 p.m. (Mon. & Sat. from 10 a.m.). Closed Sun.

Sulka is the paragon of refinement, a name with a slightly pre-war ring to it. The discriminating clientele arrives from far-flung nations and provinces to order made-to-measure shirts in sailcloth, poplin, silk, flannel or wool. Timeless classics, these impeccable-quality items are handled by courteous, deferential staff. First-time orders of custom-made shirts must be for six or more (at 2,200 francs each): a pilot shirt is made which you take home, wear, wash and then bring back for Sulka to check for faults. Also available are two-ply cashmere V-necks and cardigans, five-ply cashmere jackets, polo shirts, scarves, ties, umbrellas, socks and a small selection of casual wear.

SHOES

Aubercy
2nd arr. - 34, rue Vivienne - 42 33 93 61
Open 10 a.m.-6:30 p.m. (Mon. from 11 a.m.). Closed Sun. & Mon in Aug.

Aubercy shoes has ridden the waves of fashion since 1935, producing excellent-quality, traditional footwear for discerning customers. Sports and casual shoes, such as the Richelieu buckle casual, are making headway among other offerings, which cater primarily to businessmen and traditionalists. Prices are not excessive.

Carvil
8th arr. - 67, rue Pierre Charron
42 25 54 38
Open 10 a.m.-7 p.m. (Mon. from 2 p.m.). Closed Mon. in Aug. & Sun.
8th arr. - 4, rue Tronchet - 42 66 21 58
Open 10 a.m.-7 p.m. Closed Sun.

At Carvil, the only place the shoe hurts is the wallet. It's known as the playboys' favourite, and it's a good thing that most playboys have large bank balances. But you do get what you pay for: excellent quality and styles ranging from the conservative to the outrageous.

Church's
8th arr. - 23, rue des Mathurins
42 65 25 85
Open 10 a.m.-8:15 p.m. Closed Sun.

These famous and indestructible shoes come in a broad range of widths, in black, bordeaux, cognac, gold and other colours.

Michel Delauney
1st arr. - 6, rue de l'Oratoire - 42 60 20 85
Open 10 a.m.-12:30 a.m. & 2 p.m.-6:30 p.m. Closed Sun., Mon. & Aug.

Welcome to the world of comfortable, solidly built shoes. Models range from moccassins to riding boots. Michel Delauney's walking shoes are elegant and enduring. He will find the right shoe for you according to width, arch and instep—not just try to sell you the most expensive model. Sale shoes are often an excellent deal. Custom-made models cost up to 10,000 francs and require two months of work.

Fratelli Rossetti
16th arr. - 17, av. Victor-Hugo
45 01 63 33
Open 10 a.m.-7 p.m. (Mon. from 11 a.m.). Closed Sun.

In the beginning there were sports shoes... The Rossetti family then launched into the casual and dress shoes market. Success was close on their heels. Nowadays the Fratelli Rossetti line boasts several audacious designs, including white or two-tone Derbys in textured pigskin, rough-cut deck shoe–style casuals or riding boots in kangaroo, zebu or calfskin. They are light on the foot, the summum of casual elegance (for about 1,500 francs).

Stéphane Kélian
7th arr. - 13 bis, rue de Grenelle
42 22 93 03
Open 10 a.m.-7 p.m. Closed Sun.

This sumptuous marble-lined boutique is the lair of Stéphane Kélian, master of the braided-leather shoe and sculptured heel. He also creates strikingly fashionable footwear for the Claude Montana label. A smaller boutique at 6, place des Victoires also features enticing Italian shoes by Cesare Paciotti (42 61 60 74).

John Lobb
8th arr. - 51, rue François-Ier
45 62 06 34
Open 10 a.m.-7 p.m. Closed Sun.

Sublimely comfortable, perfectly proportioned shoes finished to fit the most demanding feet: such are the masterpieces John Lobb makes for his privileged customers. There are hand-decorated, custom-made slippers as well as classic lace-up oxfords, crafted according to traditional methods and commonly requiring a wait of over six months. Prices for custom shoes start at 14,000 francs per pair and require a six-month wait.

SHOP – OPEN LATE

Ready-to-wear shoes include casuals and short boots.

Weston
1st arr. - 3, bd de la Madeleine 42 61 11 87
6th arr. - 49, rue de Rennes - 45 49 38 50
16th arr. - 97, av. Victor-Hugo 47 04 23 75
17th arr. - 98, rue de Courcelles 47 63 18 13
Open 10 a.m.-7 p.m. (Mon. from 2 p.m.). Closed Sun.
8th arr. - 114, av. des Champs-Elysées - 45 62 26 47
Open 9:30 a.m.-7 p.m. (Mon. from 10 a.m.). Closed Sun.

Once upon a time, young men dreamed of handsome, solid, superbly finished Weston shoes (which used to be the finest in ready-to-wear shoes). But Weston's reputation has tarnished of late. The average life of the celebrated "180" moccasin has dropped from eight to two years. Repairs are sometimes shoddy and reports have it that the soles sometimes leak! Faithful customers have turned to the Norwegian Hunter's shoe. A curious note: If you arrive wearing anything but Weston shoes you might receive a stiff welcome. And sale shoes are made especially for the cut-price selling season. At least the prices haven't gone up (but they do start at over 1,200 francs).

UNDERWEAR

Chantal Thomass
1st arr. - 1 rue Vivienne - 40 15 02 36
Open 10 a.m.-7 p.m. (Mon. from 11 a.m.). Closed Sun.

Chantal Thomass, renowned for her lady's lingerie, came up with the idea of launching a men's collection inspired by Hercules. Now that the brawny look is a thing of the past, you will find several attractive lines for men in white cotton, grey chiné, houndstooth, pure black and other colours and fabrics (styles and finishing change according to the type of material). Chantal Thomass's men's undergarments are well made, comfortable and versatile. The only drawback is the price: 250 francs for under-pants, 950 francs for a vest and 1,200 francs for bathing trunks.

Tous les Caleçons
7th arr. - 11, rue du Pré-aux-Clercs - 45 44 32 07
Open 10:30 a.m.-7 p.m. (Mon. from 11:30 a.m.). Closed Sun. & 3 wks. in Aug.

Trying on the merchandise here can be, well...trying. Every figure fault shows in the skimpy tops, hip-hugging shorts and T-shirts sold in this tiny boutique. Lots of nifty underwear, too. For men and women.

OPEN LATE

■ BOOKSHOPS

Shakespeare and Company
5th arr. - 37, rue de la Bûcherie 43 26 96 50
Open daily 11 a.m.-midnight. No cards.

Don't confuse it with the legendary Shakespeare and Company of Sylvia Beach, though owner George Whitman claims that he is carrying on the tradition, albeit in different premises. Shelves are filled to bursting point in this modern Prospero's cell, with books old and new covering every subject imaginable.

La Hune
6th arr. - 170, bd Saint Germain 45 48 35 85
Open 10 a.m.-midnight. Closed Sun.

If you get an urge to reread some Breton or Baudelaire late at night, head over here. Beautiful art books too.

News-stand

If you want to keep up to date with the latest news, kiosks are open 24 hours a day at the following addresses: 33 & 52, av. des Champs-Elysées, 8th arr. - 45 61 48 01; 16, bd de la Madeleine, 8th arr. - 42 65 29 19; 2, bd Montmartre, 9th; Place Charles-de-Gaulle, av. de Wagram, 17th; 16, bd de Clichy, 18th arr.; as well as in railway stations and Drugstores until 2 a.m.

■ DRUGSTORES

Be it premium bubbly or Alka-Seltzer, a little night music or earplugs for a noiseless morning after... they've got it all here.

Drugstore Publicis
6th arr. - Drugstore Saint-Germain - 146, bd Saint-Germain - 42 22 92 50
Open daily 10 a.m.-2 p.m.
8th arr. - Drugstore Champs-Elysées - 133, av. des Champs-Elysées - 47 23 54 34
8th arr. - Drugstore Matignon 1, av. Matignon - 43 59 38 70
Open daily 9 a.m.-2 a.m.

Multistore Opéra
9th arr. - 6, bd des Capucines 42 65 89 43
Open daily 11:15 a.m.-midnight.

■ FLOWERS

Elyfleurs
17th arr. - 82, av. de Wagram 47 66 87 19
Open daily 24 hours.
See in *Flowers* section, page 210.

SPORTING GOODS - SHOPS

FOOD & DRINK

Alsace
8th arr. - 39, av. des Champs-Elysées - 43 59 44 24
Open daily 24 hours.

Beyond the main restaurant is a catering service–cum-boutique where you can purchase essentially Alsatian specialities—sauerkraut, charcuteries, foie gras, etc. There is a take-away service should you be tempted by the idea of a midnight snack.

L'An 2000
17th arr. - 82, bd des Batignolles
43 87 24 67
Open 5 p.m.-1 a.m. (Sun. 11 a.m.-1 a.m.). Closed 2 wks. in Aug.

After an evening at the Théâtre des Arts-Hébertot, you can put together a nice after-theatre supper with provisions from L'An 2000. All sorts of appetising dishes are on display at this spacious emporium. From caviar to charcuterie, from bread and fresh-vegetable terrines to wine, cheese and fresh fruit, you'll find all the makings of a charming midnight feast.

Flo Prestige
1st arr. - 42, pl. du Marché Saint-Honoré - 42 61 45 46
Open daily 8 a.m.-11 p.m. Delivery. See the other branches in Food section page 214.

Flo boutiques are cropping up all over town. They are perfect places for late-night food shopping. Temptations include foie gras from Strasbourg, Norwegian smoked salmon, beautiful cheeses and irresistible pastries, plus Champagne or a robust country wine to wash it all down.

Les Frères Layrac
6th arr. - 29, rue de Buci - 43 25 17 72
Open daily 9 a.m.-2 a.m.

There is a wide selection of prepared dishes, but the pride of Les Frères Layrac is its seafood platter (385 francs for two). Free delivery.

Nocto
8th arr. - 23, bd des Batignolles
43 87 64 79
Open 11 a.m.-midnight (Sun. 4 p.m.-11 p.m.).

A pleasant little supermarket for late-night shopping. The merchandise is of distinctly higher quality than most such establishments offer. Good choice of prepared salads; a take-away meal-on-a-tray costs 60 francs.

CHEMISTS

Pharmacie Azoulay
9th arr. - 5, pl. Pigalle
48 78 38 12
Open 9 a.m.-1 a.m. (Sun. 3 p.m.-1 a.m.).

Pharmacie Les Champs
8th arr. - 84, av. des Champs-Elysées - 45 62 02 41
Open daily 24 hours.

Note the convenient, *all-day-all-night* hours of this drugstore.

Pharmacie Lagarce
11th arr. - 13, pl. de la Nation
43 73 24 03
Open 8 a.m.-midnight (Mon. noon-midnight; Sun. & holidays 8 p.m.-midnight).

24-HOUR POST OFFICE

Poste du Louvre
1st arr. - 52, rue du Louvre - 40 28 20 00
Open daily 24 hours.

The central post office is open 24 hours a day. Long-distance telephone calls can be made from the first floor, ordinary postal transactions on the ground floor. Don't be surprised to find homeless people enjoying some late-night Muzak in the post office's warm recesses.

RECORD STORES

Champs-Disques
8th arr. - 84, av. des Champs-Elysées - 45 62 65 46
Open 9:30 a.m.-1:30 a.m. (Sun. noon-8 p.m.).

Here in this shop on the world's most beautiful avenue is a broad selection of popular and classical music.

Virgin Mégastore
8th arr. - 56-60, av. des Champs-Elysées - 40 74 06 48
Open 10 a.m.-midnight (Fri. & Sat. 10 a.m.-1 a.m.; Sun. noon-midnight).

Jazz, classical, pop and rock, on records, CDs and cassettes—but that's not all: there are books (on the lower level) too, video and audio gear, computer equipment and a terrific restaurant/bar upstairs where a piano player provides evening entertainment (a great place to people-watch).

SPORTING GOODS

CLOTHING & EQUIPMENT (GENERAL)

Chattanooga
7th arr. - 53, av. Bosquet - 45 51 76 65
Open 10:30 a.m.-1:30 p.m. & 2:30 p.m.-7:30 p.m. (Sat. 10:30 a.m.-7:30 p.m.). Closed Sun.

Skateboards, roller skates, surfboards, bodyboards, frisbees, kites and boomerangs: every bit of equipment that today's speed-crazy kids covet can be found here, alongside all the trendy gear that go with it (trainers shoes—wait till you see the prices—tank tops, cycling shorts and the rest). Some

SHOPS – SPORTING GOODS

good-quality second-hand equipment is available as well.

Ekisport
9th arr. - 38, rue Rochechouart
42 80 32 85
Open 10 a.m.-7 p.m. Closed Sun.

It's well worth seeking out this sporting goods store, hidden at the back of a courtyard. Prices are about ten per cent under what you would pay in a department store for tennis equipment (racquets can be restrung while you wait) and for cycling, camping, sailing and skiing gear. Skis can be hired for 200 francs per week.

Go Sport
1st arr. - Pte. Pierre-Lescot, Forum des Halles, level -3 - 45 08 92 96
12th arr. - 110, bd Diderot - 43 47 21 40
13th arr. - 30, av. d'Italie - 45 80 30 05
14th arr. - 68, av. du Maine - 43 27 50 50
15th arr. - 16, rue Linois - Centre Beaugrenelle - 43 47 21 40
16th arr. - 12, av. Porte de Saint-Cloud - 40 71 95 19
17th arr. - 2, pl. de la Porte-Maillot - 40 68 22 46
Open 10 a.m.-7:30 p.m. Closed Sun.

The stores in this fast-growing international chain vary dramatically in size and style from one to another, but all conduct business according to the same successful formula: friendly help, professional advice and quality equipment. Some of the stores specialise in equestrian equipage (the Les Halles and Montparnasse branches). Tennis and fitness equipment are featured at every branch.

K Way
1st arr. - 3, av. de l'Opéra - 42 60 88 20
Open 10 a.m.-7 p.m. (Mon. noon-7 p.m.). Closed Sun.

K Way waterproof parkas and anoraks are lightweight, colourful and attractively fashioned, but best of all, they fold up into tiny packages that can be stowed away with ease. The entire family can be fitted out here from head to toe with rainwear or ski suits.

Lacoste
1st arr. - 372, rue Saint-Honoré
42 61 55 56 (also: 2nd arr., 6th arr., 8th arr., 15th arr., 16th arr., 17th arr.)
Open 10 a.m.-7 p.m. Closed Sun.

There's lots more here besides the famous polo shirts (which come in a dizzying range of colours). The Lacoste flagship store also carries well-made clothing for all sorts of sports, as well as a full line of excellent tennis equipment.

Au Petit Matelot
16th arr. - 27, av. de la Grande-Armée - 45 00 15 51
Open 10 a.m.-7 p.m. (Mon. 2 p.m.-7 p.m.). Closed Sun.

Having celebrated its 200th birthday, Au Petit Matelot is ageing quite gracefully. Striped sailor shirts are less in evidence than they once were, but the rainwear is as good as ever, as are the woollen jackets and oilskins. Ladies and gentlemen come here to dress for the butts, the saddle or the tiller. Be advised that only sporting *clothes* are found here—you'll need to go elsewhere for your equipment.

Au Refuge
6th arr. - 44-46, rue Saint-Placide
42 22 27 33
Open 10 a.m.-7 p.m. (Mon. 2:30 a.m.-7 p.m.). Closed Sun.

Newly renovated and reorganised, Au Refuge specialises in top-quality tennis racquets (the famed Snauwaert sells here for 4,500 francs), but athletes can also find the perfect shoe (140 models to choose from), fitness freaks will be fitted with all the stretchy exercise clothing they might require and downhill racers are sure to locate just the ski equipment they need. Clothes for swimmers and dancers too.

DANCE

Repetto
2nd arr. - 22, rue de la Paix - 44 71 83 00
Open 10 a.m.-7 p.m. Closed Sun.

Repetto has served the dance community since 1947, providing baby ballerinas and professional primas with dainty practice slippers, ballet shoes and tutus. Jazz dancers will find the soft footwear they need, and the leotards and tights (available in a rainbow of colours) are just as suitable for exercise classes as for a session at the *barre*. High prices.

Flashdance
8th arr. - 17, rue de la Pépinière
42 93 05 71
Open 10 a.m.-7 p.m. Closed Sun.

Flashy, stretchy gear for dancing and exercising (brands include Vicard leotards and Freddy tights and slippers), as well as beautiful swimwear by Livia. Friendly, professional staff help clients choose the most flattering fit.

FISHING

Au Martin-Pêcheur
1st arr. - 28, quai du Louvre - 42 36 25 63
Open 9:30 a.m.-7 p.m. Closed Sun. & Mon.

This respected establishment has changed little over the years—it is still one of the most picturesque shops in Paris. In addition to a full range of deep-sea and fly fishing equipment, there's a section for diving accessories, including an underwater-photography department.

SPORTING GOODS – SHOPS

Motillon
15th arr. - 83 bis, rue de l'Abbé-Groult - 48 28 58 94
Open 9 a.m.-7 p.m. Closed Sun. & Mon.

Professional advice is lavished on customers at this venerable institution, which sells the necessities, the accessories and the luxuries for every sort of fishing. What's more, any item can be mail-ordered from its wonderful catalogue. If you would like to try your hand at sport fishing before you invest in the equipment, Motillon rents out tackle for 10 to 15 per cent of its value (plus deposit).

■ GOLF

Comptoir du Golf
17th arr. - 22, av. de la Grande-Armée - 43 80 15 00
Open 9:30 a.m.-7 p.m. (Mon. 2 p.m.-7 p.m.). Closed Sun.

Shoes, clubs, polo shirts and caddy-cars abound, as well as own-brand golf clothes in addition to those of well-known makers'. Reserved reception.

Golf-Plus
17th arr. - 212, bd Pereire - 45 74 08 17
Open 10 a.m.-7 p.m. (Mon. 2 p.m.-7 p.m., Thurs. until 8 p.m.). Closed Sun.

Owner Laurence Schmidlin, several times the French golf champion, offers friendly assistance to his customers. Good-quality clothes and equipment are sold at friendly prices, and if you find what you bought here elsewhere for less, you can come back and receive a credit, plus 10 per cent. Dependable service and advice; equipment rental.

■ HUNTING & SHOOTING

Alex
8th arr. - 63, bd de Courcelles 42 27 66 39
Open 9 a.m.-7 p.m. Closed Sun. & Mon. (except during hunting season: 4 p.m.-6 p.m.).

Traditionally a firearms dealer, Alex has taken over the shop next door and devoted it to clothing, and he has his eye on the bakery next to that. He features the finest brands of rifles, as well as good selections of optical equipment, knives and cartridges. As for shooting clothing, you won't find a collection like this anywhere else: wool socks, elegant and practical storm coats and, of course, Paraboots. There is also an interesting gift department which includes clever little knives in the form of ducks and cuckoos. An excellent store.

Fauré-Lepage-Saillard
1st arr. - 8, rue de Richelieu - 42 96 07 78
Open 9:30 a.m.-7 p.m. Closed Sun.

A specialist in rifles since 1716, this establishment still sells its own make of double-barrelled rifles. Also found here are hand-crafted knives, carbines for target shooting and competition, sights and other such accessories. For collectors, there are sword-canes and rifle-canes, and, for quieter hunting, there's always the Barnett Commando crossbow for around 3,000 francs. On the upper floor, superbly elegant shooting and riding clothes are displayed.

Gastinne et Renette
8th arr. - 39, av. Franklin-Roosevelt - 43 59 77 74
Open 10 a.m.-7 p.m. Closed Sun. & Mon.

This famous emporium markets its own make of rifles. And it doesn't give them away: prices start at 20,000 francs. But there are also used guns at attractive prices. An added feature is the shooting range in the basement, which permits customers to test the merchandise. Extremely diversified, the shop also stocks books, archery equipment and security systems, along with a selection of classic clothing, though not at competitive prices. The gift department is, of course, consistent with the shooting theme.

Tir 1000
13th arr. - 90, rue Jeanne-d'Arc 45 83 34 41
Open 10 a.m.-7 p.m. (Thurs. until 10 p.m., Sat. until 6:30 p.m.). Closed Sun. & Mon.

Tir 1000 stocks a good selection of arms, knives, sights, and offers repair services too. Meanwhile, on the basement level, there's a shooting range for handguns, which is open to members (2,000 francs for an annual membership); beginners can sign up for lessons in target shooting.

■ RIDING

Duprey
17th arr. - 5, rue Troyon - 43 80 29 37
Open 9:45 a.m.-12:30 p.m. & 1:30 p.m.-6 p.m. Closed Sat., Sun. & Aug.

Hidden away on a little street near the Arc de Triomphe since 1902, this reputable shop is a family affair upheld by three generations. Duprey riding equipment is

---

Plan to travel? Look out for the other RAC GaultMillau Best of guides to France and Germany, and for the RAC French Hotel and Holiday Guide and the RAC European Hotel Guide plus maps and atlases of France and Europe.

preferred in the classiest horsey circles. The excellent and comfortable saddles, virtually custom-made, are beautifully crafted (from 9,000 francs). Stirrups, bridles, girths are sold as well; there is no apparel for the rider, but everything in leather for your mount.

Hermès
8th arr. - 24, rue du Faubourg-Saint-Honoré - 40 17 47 17
8th arr. - 42, av. George-V - 47 20 48 51
Open 10 a.m.-6:30 p.m. (Mon. & Sat. 10 a.m.-1 p.m. & 2:15 p.m.-6:30 p.m.). Closed Sun.

Housed in the tasteful luxury of this celebrated store is a complete range of equipment for horse and rider. Hermès turns out roughly 60 saddles a month, all handmade in the firm's workshops. The store will also custom-make and sew saddles made to measure in whatever leather you wish (one well-heeled customer even had a saddle made in crocodile). Should you decide to organise your own racing team, you can have Hermès fit out your jockeys in its famous silks.

Padd
15th arr. - 14, rue de la Cavalerie 43 06 56 50
Open 10 a.m.-7 p.m. (Mon. until 6 p.m.). Closed Sun.

An excellent address for equestrians: in a functional, no-nonsense environment, you'll find every kind of saddle at every sort of price. They come from all over: Spain, England, the United States. The clothing department is well stocked with hacking jackets, helmets, boots, crops and jodhpurs. The store may not be chic (go to Duprey or Equitable for that), but the inventory is complete.

> *Monday, like Sunday, is a day of rest for many shopkeepers.*

■ SKIING

La Haute Route
4th arr. - 33, bd Henri-IV - 42 72 38 43
Open 9:30 a.m.-1 p.m. & 2 p.m.-7 p.m. (Mon. 2 p.m.-7 p.m.). Closed Sun.

You can hire everything here but the mountain: complete ski equipment in the winter, rock-climbing gear in the summer. Camping equipment is also available for hire at utterly reasonable prices.

Passe Montagne
14th arr. - 102, av. Denfert-Rochereau - 43 22 24 24
11th arr. - 39, rue du Chemin-Vert - 43 57 08 47
Open 11 a.m.-7 p.m. (Wed. until 9 p.m., Sat. 10 a.m.-7 p.m.). Closed Sun. & Mon.

Passe-Montagne can outfit you with all the gear you need for virtually any mountain sport, be it climbing, hiking, alpine or cross-country skiing. Both stores are open Wednesday until 9 p.m. Equipment hire is available at the Chemin-Vert store only.

Le Vieux Campeur
5th arr. - 48, rue des Ecoles - 43 29 12 32
Open 10 a.m.-8 p.m. (Mon. 2 p.m.-7 p.m.). Closed Sun.

Actually housed in 14 shops all clustered around the main address. The Vieux Campeur is the place to go for all manner of sporting equipment. The latest innovations and variations on a theme arrive here first. Climbing and mountaineering remain the speciality of the house, but the reputation for quality includes everything from running shoes to tennis racquets, sold with professional advice. We suggest that you avoid a Saturday visit, as the crowds are horrendous. A climbing wall is set up to be used for trying out shoes (and your technique!) before you confront the real thing.

■ WINDSURFING

Mistral Shop
16th arr. - 24, rue Mirabeau - 45 24 38 55
Open 10 a.m.-1 p.m. & 2:15 p.m.-7 p.m. Closed Sun. & Mon.

This windsurfing shop reflects the polish of the surrounding district: the boards are the finest made, the swimsuits are *très chic*, and the staff consists primarily of handsome beach boys. A number of designs are available but only one choice of quality—the best. These are serious boards for the committed windsurfer.

Nautistore
17th arr. - 40, av. de la Grande-Armée - 43 80 28 28
Open 10 a.m.-6:30 p.m. Closed Sun. & Mon.

Nautistore enjoys a solid reputation with windsurfers for its discount prices on new and old windsurfing boards. But the shop can also provide you with fine footwear for boating and sailing, not to mention furred parkas for Arctic expeditions.

TOBACCONISTS

■ ACCESSORIES

Au Caïd
6th arr. - 24, bd Saint-Michel - 43 26 04 01
Open 10 a.m.-7 p.m. Closed Sun.

The charming *mesdames* Schmitt still reign over this pipe-smokers' paradise. Featured is an excellent selection of pipes in clay, porcelain, cherry and briar. Accessories include tobacco pouches and cigar cases, cigar holders and pipe racks, which the Duke of Windsor and Jean-Paul Sartre appreciated in their day. The service is renowned.

TOBACCONISTS – SHOPS

■ CIGARS & TOBACCO

Alfred Dunhill
2nd arr. - 15, rue de la Paix - 42 61 57 58
Open 9:30 a.m.-6:30 p.m. (Mon. & Sat. 10 a.m.-6:30 p.m.). Closed Sun.

The Alfred Dunhill shop remains the domain of men—and women—who have about them the expensive aroma of Havana cigars and fine leather. Foremost among the luxurious items featured around the mahogany-panelled, turn-of-the-century shop are, of course, the famed Dunhill pipes, some of the world's best...and costliest. Collectors will not want to miss the mini-museum of clay, briar and meerschaum pipes. Dunhill is also a gift shop, with a large selection of sunglasses, tie clips, wristwatches and pens (after all, Dunhill owns Mont-Blanc), fine leather goods and hundreds of other gift ideas at reasonable prices. But the lion's share of the shop is given over to smokers' accessories: expensive lighters, cigarette holders, cigar boxes and humidors in rare woods. Dunhill also sells classic menswear and a line of men's toiletries.

Gilbert Guyot
17th arr. - 7, av. de Clichy - 43 87 70 88
Open 10 a.m.-7 p.m. Closed Sun., Mon. & Aug.

Gilbert Guyot is one of the three remaining master pipemakers in France. When we visit his shop, we generally find Guyot (and his son) crafting, repairing, restoring or smoking a pipe and sizing up their customers. Before selling a customer his wares, Guyot personally interviews him, because, as Guyot puts it, "The pipe is the man." All kinds of pipes in every imaginable material and in a wide range of prices are sold in an atmosphere of quality and time-honoured tradition.

NO BARGAINS HERE

As you will have noticed if you're a cigar smoker, they cost an arm and a leg here. Why? The state considers them a "drug" and taxes heavily. But take heart: at the shops we have listed in this section you are sure to find a fresh, high-quality cigar and not, as too often happens, a once-cherished cheroot that has turned into a roll of stale, bitter-tasting compost.

Boutique 22
16th arr. - 22, av. Victor-Hugo 45 01 81 41
Open 10 a.m.-7 p.m. (Mon. 2 p.m.-7 p.m.). Closed Sun.

Cigar lovers consider Boutique 22 the mecca of Davidoffs (even though it is no longer owned by Zino Davidoff). You will find not only Davidoff's "1000" but every other brand of Havana cigar imported in France, including slim Joyitas and thick Hoyo des Dieux and Carousoas. Boutique 22 stocks lesser-known cigars as well and has the exclusive distributorship for the Compagnie des Caraïbes. You will discover such Caribbean delights as sweet and aromatic Cerdeaus, robust Juan Clementes and claro claro/50 Don Miguels, from Cabo Verde. Also featured are 100 models of off-the-shelf humidors and vaults, plus refurbished antique models. For the made-to-measure crowd, you may order haute-couture custom vaults, monogrammed by request (they come equipped with a patented climate-control system that guarantees your cigars' freshness for one month). The accessories department groans with deluxe lighters and fountain pens (Dupont, Cartier, Dunhill, Mont-Blanc), plus crystal wares by Lalique, Daum and Baccarat.

La Cave à Cigares
10th arr. - 4, bd de Denain - 42 81 05 51
Open 8 a.m.-7 p.m. Closed Sat. & Sun.

Owner Gérard Courtial is the inventor of the much-imitated vertical humidifier/display case. Although he is by profession a member of the *confrérie des maîtres pipiers* (brotherhood of master pipemakers), he is nevertheless a cigar connoisseur and an excellent source of information and advice. Do not miss his collection of pipes, including such brands as Chacom, Dunhill and Butz-Choquin. Also, a wide range of smoking accessories, for experts and novices.

A la Civette
1st arr. - 157, rue Saint-Honoré 42 96 04 99
Open 8:30 a.m.-7 p.m. Closed Sun.

Habitués lovingly refer to this venerable establishment as the Civette du Palais-Royal. Founded in 1763, it was the first tobacconist in Paris, for many years *the* place of pilgrimage for cigar and tobacco lovers. Although it is no longer the city's foremost, it remains among its highest ranks. Tobacco goods featured run the gamut from everyday chewing weed to the very best Havanas, including the Hoyo de Monterrey, imported directly from Cuba. La Civette was the first shop in Paris to install climate-controlled vaults for its cigars, and the first to import Monte-Cristos. Also available is a wide range of accessories: deluxe lighters and pipes (Chacom, Butz-Choquin, Dunhill), humidors in all shapes and sizes, pens, leather goods.

SHOPS – WOMEN'S WEAR

Drugstore Publicis
6th arr. - 149, bd Saint-Germain
42 22 92 50
8th arr. - 133, av. des Champs-Elysées - 47 23 54 34
8th arr. - 1, av. Matignon - 43 59 38 70
Open daily 9 a.m.-2 a.m. (Sun. 10 a.m.-2 a.m.).

A large selection of good-quality humidified cigars is available at each of the three Drugstore Publicis year-round and late into the night.

Lemaire
16th arr. - 59, av. Victor-Hugo
45 00 75 63
Open 8:30 a.m.-7:30 p.m. Closed Sun.

Bernard Lecrocq presides over this century-old institution, one of France's most prestigious tobacconists. Of course you will find the cigar of your dreams perfectly preserved and presented with rare flair. Havanas and San Domingos—Zinos, Don Miguels and Juan Clementes—top the list. Lecrocq's astonishing vaults accommodate thousands of cases of cigars in ideal temperature and humidity conditions. Cigar boxes and humidors, humble or extravagant, are guaranteed for workmanship and reliability (the gamut runs from a solid cedarwood three-cigar pocket humidor to a vault the size of a writing desk). Pipe smokers will discover the entire range of tobaccos available in France, plus a large selection of pipes (all major brands, with a particularly good collection of meerschaums). Lemaire's vast array of luxurious accessories includes all the main brands of lighters, cases, pouches, plus 1,100 fountain, ballpoint and felt-tip pens.

WOMEN'S WEAR

■ DESIGNERS

Azzedine Alaïa
4th arr. - 7, rue de Moussy - 42 72 19 19
Open 10 a.m.-7 p.m. Closed Sun.

More women dream of pouring themselves into an Azzedine Alaïa creation than can actually—decently—do so. The Tunisian designer's artful cutting, stretch fabrics and suggestive seaming do wonders for svelte silhouettes. What they do to less-than-heavenly bodies we will leave to your imagination. Still, if Tina Turner dares to wear Alaïa, why shouldn't you? Alaïa's huge new boutique is a must on the fashion circuit. While you're there, try on his newest innovation: a fabric for stress-free dressing said to ward off the evil effects of magnetic fields.

Balenciaga
8th arr. - 10, av. George-V - 47 20 21 11
Open 10 a.m.-7 p.m. (Sat. 10 a.m.-12:30 p.m. & 2 p.m.-7 p.m.). Closed Sun.

With the real Balenciaga long gone, the name is more a label than a creative design philosophy. The strong points of the clothes on display here are their strong colours, structured lines and sophistication. Most successful are the shapely, beautifully cut "power suits" and the rather intimidating evening gowns.

Pierre Balmain
8th arr. - 44, rue François-Ier - 47 20 35 34
Open 10 a.m.-7 p.m. Closed Sat. 1 p.m.- 2 p.m. &Sun.

The fashion world is in a tizzy since word got out that Oscar de la Renta had been named couturier for the venerable House of Balmain. At the age of 60, de la Renta is fearlessly starting a new career; a double career, in fact, since he plans to continue designing for his own label. And why not?

Etienne Brunel
7th arr. - 70, rue des Saints-Pères
45 44 41 14
Open 11 a.m.-8:30 p.m. Closed Sun.

Lyon-native Mireille Etienne designs strikingly original clothes which are also perfectly wearable. Her most recent collections have featured shimmering fabrics (satin, raw silk, wool or velvet mixed with a little Lycra), most effective for strapless tops (1,000 francs) and attractive dresses (1,000 to 4,000 francs). Suits have the polish and meticulous detailing that well-dressed women require. For those with a sense of daring (and humour) there are some daffy little dresses made of straw, plastic, foam, terry towelling (better than they sound!), feathers and lace patchwork.

Cardin
8th arr. - 59, rue du Faubourg-Saint-Honoré - 42 66 92 25
Open 10 a.m.-6:30 p.m. Closed Sun.

Energetic middle-aged ladies (who remember Pierre's heyday back in the 1960s) go for Cardin's city suits, cocktail dresses and nicely structured seven-eighths–length coats. Cardin's ready-to-wear collections and "licensed" accessories lack the whimsical spirit and forward-looking attitude that continue to in-

---

RAC MOTORING ATLAS FRANCE: *Our fully revised and well-established large format RAC Motoring Atlas France, Belgium and Luxembourg at 1:250,000 (approximately 4 miles to 1 inch) now has even more features to improve journey planning and to make driving in France more enjoyable. Clear, accurate and detailed road maps make RAC Motoring Atlas France the ideal atlas for the independent traveller in France. Price: £ 11.99 (spiral bound).*

WOMEN'S WEAR – SHOPS

spire his haute-couture designs.

Chanel
1st arr. - 31, rue Cambon - 42 86 28 00
8th arr. - 42, av. Montaigne - 47 23 74 12
Open 9:30 a.m.-6:30 p.m. (Sat. from 10 a.m.). Closed Sun.

The most famous fashion house on the face of the earth, Chanel is also the most copied. To be sure that your money is going on the *real* house logo (and not just any old intertwined *Cs*), spend it here, at the mother of all Chanel stores. Yes, you'll find the authentic tweed *tailleurs*, the pearls, the bracelets, the chain-link belts, the quilted bags that the world adores. Designer Karl Lagerfeld has done much to redefine the house image.

Chloé
7th arr. - 3, rue de Gribeauval 45 44 02 04
8th arr. - 60, rue du Faubourg-Saint-Honoré - 42 66 01 39
Open 10 a.m.-7 p.m. Closed Sun.

Martine Sitbon's designs have brought a new clientele to Chloé. Sitbon's style has matured—she's more sure of herself—with the result that the clothes are youthful but rigorously styled, perfectly cut and presented in a beautiful palette of colours.

Comme des Garçons
2nd arr. - 42, rue Etienne-Marcel 42 33 05 21
Open 11 a.m.-7 p.m. Closed Sun., Aug. 1-15.

The *vendeurs* size you up as you walk in, and if they don't like your "look," you can expect a pretty frosty reception. Indeed, the store itself exudes precious little warmth. As for the clothes (which, incidentally, the sales assistants just hate to see the customers touch), well... the knitwear is droopy and unattractive; the colours are depressing, the seams are ripped (on purpose, of course) and the fabrics frayed (ditto). Designer Rei Kawakubo's subversive, androgynous styles are not for everyone—at a recent fashion show, even Linda Evangelista looked dowdy in a Kawakubo dress! And they are most definitely not for every budget.

Dior
8th arr. - 30, av. Montaigne - 40 73 54 44
Open 9:30 a.m.-6:30 p.m. (Sat. & Mon. 10 a.m.-1 p.m. & 2:30 p.m.-6:30 p.m.). Closed Sun.

Once you enter Dior's grey-and-white flagship store, you can spend the entire day choosing everything you need to be impeccably attired at all times. From ravishing lingerie to suits, sportswear to ball gowns designed by Gianfranco Ferré (the current Monsieur Dior), chic *chapeaux* to mink-cuffed kid gloves in a rainbow of colours, no detail is neglected. You can also dress your home and your children here.

Dorothée Bis
2nd arr. - 46, rue Etienne-Marcel 42 21 04 40
Open 10 a.m.-7 p.m. Closed Sun.

After a stint in fashion purgatory, the Jacobsons are back with an attractive collection of vampy stretch, Lycra and viscose knits (lots of openwork), fluttery 1940s-style dresses and suits with a masculine, distinctly Dietrich silhouette.

Louis Féraud
8th arr. - 88, rue du Faubourg-Saint-Honoré
42 65 32 84
Open 10 a.m.-7 p.m. (Sat. from 10:30 a.m.). Closed Sun.

Arab princesses and Texan heiresses rub shoulders in these salons during the season. Louis Féraud started his career in Cannes, in the south of France, in the 1950s and dressed such stars as Brigitte Bardot, Kim Novak and Liz Taylor. Today he is dressmaker to France's first lady, Danielle Mitterrand. His creations are feminine and expressive, denoting a man who loves women... His evening bags are divine.

Paco Funada
4th arr. - 17, pl. des Vosges - 40 27 94 29
Open 11 a.m.-7 p.m. (Sat. from 2 p.m.). Closed Sun.

Paco Funada has abandoned menswear (he used to design for Cacharel and Marcel Lassance) for a new career in women's fashion. His is a dramatic, minimalist style which employs a limited palette of muted colours, comfortable fabrics, superb craftsmanship and detailing. The collection is on view in an attractive shop under the arcades of the place des Vosges.

Hélène Gainville
8th arr. - Arcades du Lido, 78, av. des Champs-Elysées 43 59 32 18
Open 10:30 a.m.-7:30 p.m. Closed Sun.

Hélène Gainville designs smart city suits (for your power lunches), frothy cocktail dresses (for your romantic dinners) and gowns for your most extravagant evenings at prices close to what you'd pay for deluxe ready-to-wear. What's more, in her lovely three-level boutique done out in soothing pastel tones and warm wood, she will provide just the right accessories to complete your look, from hats to bags to shoes. And when Prince Charming finally shows up and sweeps you off your feet, Hélène will create a magical gown for the occasion (see *Wedding Gowns*, page 279).

SHOPS – WOMEN'S WEAR

Givenchy
8th arr. - 8, av. George-V - 47 20 81 31
Open 9:30 a.m.-6:30 p.m. (Sat. from 10 a.m.). Closed Sun.

The Givenchy haute-couture look is inaccessible, regal and ethereal. Beautiful cocktail dresses (in fluid jersey), lovely accessories (silk or wool-challis shawls, costume jewellery). Givenchy, who started his career alongside Balenciaga, also produces Good Life, an urbane collection at fairly reasonable prices for mere mortals.

Irié
7th arr. - 8, rue du Pré-aux-Clercs 42 61 18 28
Open 10 a.m.-7 p.m. Closed Sun.

Irié has created a sober yet surrealistic black-and-white setting to show off his collection of hip, sophisticated clothes. Silk, angora, wool gabardine and mousseline are the major components of this designer's ultrafeminine, close-to-the-body creations. Irié is currently one of the darlings of the Left Bank set, who adore his boutique's courteous staff ("Madame, may I say that I think you've made an excellent choice...") and the relatively reasonable prices. Recent collections have featured gay, colourful prints (fish, planets, alphabets, penguins...), oversized transparent shirts in fabulous colours, leggings (of course) and soft panne-velvet tops.

Paule Ka
7th arr. - 192, bd Saint-Germain 45 44 92 60
Open 10:30 a.m.-7 p.m. Closed Sun.

Serge Coifinger's ideal of feminine beauty is to the Grace Kelly or Jackie Kennedy type. One of his most successful creations is a short trench coat in pastel silk organza, guaranteed to turn heads at any cocktail party or theatre evening. Worth a look too are the long velvet skirts and the wide choice of accessories.

Michel Klein
7th arr. - 6, rue du Pré-aux-Clercs 42 60 37 11
Open 10 a.m.-7 p.m. Closed Sun. & 2 wks. in Aug.

Klein's designs have simple yet strong lines and an appealing, timeless style. Easy to wear, versatile and comfortable, his clothes are excellent investments. Lately we've admired his satin Chinese jackets in bright blue, ecru or black, and his remarkably well cut trousers and leatherwear.

Hiroko Koshino
8th arr. - 43, rue du Faubourg-Saint-Honoré - 42 65 83 15
Open 10 a.m.-7 p.m. (Sat. from 11 a.m.). Closed Sun.

This Japanese fixture on the Paris fashion scene creates appealing designs that make his customers feel oh-so-pretty.

Christian Lacroix
8th arr. - 73, rue du Faubourg-Saint-Honoré - 42 65 79 08
8th arr. - 26, av. Montaigne - 47 20 68 95
Open 9 a.m.-7 p.m. (Sat. 10 a.m.-1 p.m. & 2:30 p.m.-7 p.m.). Closed Sun.

Christian Lacroix's vivid, scintillating creations cause women's heads to spin—fast and hard. He marries Provençal folklore with fantasy prints in a style bathed in theatricality. His ready-to-wear is dreadfully expensive, but the accessories—especially the bold, fake-gem-studded jewellery—are accessible (if not exactly affordable), and give lots of fashion "feel" for the money.

Karl Lagerfeld Boutique
8th arr. - 19, rue du Faubourg-Saint-Honoré - 42 66 64 64
Open 10 a.m.-7 p.m. Closed Sun.

Versatile, prolific Karl Lagerfeld, who has infused brilliant new life into the house of Chanel, continues to design clothes and accessories for his personal label. Modern forms and strong colours characterise these witty, irreverent (and extremely expensive) fashions, displayed in rather monumental premises.

Guy Laroche
1st arr. - Forum des Halles, 106, porte Rambuteau, Niveau -1 - 42 21 49 57
Open 10:30 a.m.-7:30 p.m. Closed Sun.
6th arr. - 47, rue de Rennes - 45 48 18 50
8th arr. - 29, av. Montaigne - 40 69 69 51
8th arr. - 30, rue du Faubourg-Saint-Honoré - 42 65 62 74
16th arr. - 9, av. Victor-Hugo - 45 01 82 75
Open 9:30 a.m.-6:30 p.m. Closed Sun.

True to the principles of the late Guy Laroche, the boutique proposes a huge choice of accessories to vary the look of the signature Laroche suits. In daytime and dinner styles, in winter- and summer-weight fabrics, they form the backbone of the house collections.

Lecoanet Hemant
4th arr. - 24, rue Vieille-du-Temple - 42 65 43 37
Open 9 a.m.-6 p.m. (& by appt.). Closed Sat., Sun. & 3 wks. in Aug.

Didier Lecoanet and Hemant Sagar's creations received the haute-couture classification in 1984. The two give shows in unusual venues, and their lucky number is 13, the day they open their salons.

Lolita Lempicka
16th arr. - 7, av. Victor-Hugo - 40 67 15 87
Open 10 a.m.-6:30 p.m. Closed Sun.

Let's be frank, shall we? For our money, designer Lolita Lempicka is more than just a little overrated. Her fussy, pretentious clothes (stiff menswear suits, drop-dead cocktail dresses) are presented in a décor that (we suppose) is inspired by some Vincente Minnelli musical. Lolita Bis is the designer's second-tier line, more youthful, less costly and easier to wear.

Issey Miyake
4th arr. - 3, pl. des Vosges - 48 87 01 86
Open 10 a.m.-7 p.m. Closed Sun.

In a deliberately theatrical setting, Issey Miyake's extravagant, extraordinary designs seem even more dramatic. While they look rather disconcertingly like rags on their hangers, when worn these soft, draped, wrinkled, sculpted and cleverly knotted clothes prove to be impressive, even stately: Miyake's long duster coat, for example, makes the most unassuming individual look like a high priest. The prices these pieces command is terrifying—a plain T-shirt costs about 1,000 francs. His second-tier line, Plantation, is slightly more affordable.

Claude Montana
1st arr. - 3, rue des Petits-Champs - 40 20 02 14
Open 10:15 a.m.-7 p.m. Closed Sun.

Short or long, Montana's clothes show a lot of leg. Zippered sheath dresses, undulating asymmetrical hems, black tulle and silvery mesh compose a wardrobe for a high-tech vamp who isn't afraid to attract a little attention. The clothes are beautifully crafted (Montana's leather trousers and jackets are the definitive statement on the subject).

Popy Moreni
4th arr. - 13, pl. des Vosges - 42 77 09 96
Open 10 a.m.-7 p.m. (Mon. from 11 a.m.) Closed Sun.

Popy Moreni is one of the "grandes dames" of fashion design; her multi-faceted talent extends to clothes, accessories, furniture and houseware. This versatile Italian often looks to the Commedia dell'Arte for inspiration: note the oversized Pierrot collars on tulle dresses and shantung blouses. Her spacious, white boutique is not well organised, but if you persevere, you're sure to find something to covet (we adored a floaty bright-green silk mousseline skirt with a handkerchief hem, paired with a powder-puff angora top). Those who wish actually to buy something, however, should come with plenty of cash.

Hanae Mori
8th arr. - 9, rue du Faubourg-Saint-Honoré - 47 42 78 78
Open 10 a.m.-7 p.m. Closed Sun.

Hanae Mori takes her inspiration from Japanese Kabuki theatre, then translates her designs into a refined and international expression of haute couture.

Thierry Mugler
2nd arr. - 10, pl. des Victoires 42 60 06 37
Open 10 a.m.-1 p.m. & 2 p.m.-7 p.m. (Mon. from 11 a.m.). Closed Sun.

The boutique, designed by Andrée Putman, puts you in mind of a futuristic comic strip. As for the clothes, they are designed for heroines: strong women, sex bombs and glamorous sirens who want structured suits that underline feminine curves. Slit skirts, geometric cutouts and brilliantly coloured leather are the highlights of Mugler's latest collections.

Myrène de Prémonville
8th arr. - 32, av. George-V - 47 20 02 35
Open 10 a.m.-7 p.m. (Sat. 10 a.m.-1 p.m. & 2 p.m.- 7 p.m.; Mon. from 2 p.m.). Closed Sun.

Young, modern women love these sophisticated clothes: dressy suits, crepe trousers, chic jackets with nipped-in waists in gorgeous colours (lilac, raspberry...). This designer has a great sense of graphic style, evident in her strong accessories (we saw a wonderful red-and-black checked silk scarf).

Paco Rabanne
6th arr. - 7, rue du Cherche-Midi 40 49 08 53
Open 10 a.m.-noon & 2 p.m.-7 p.m. Closed Sun., Mon.

Paco Rabanne likes to defy convention. Remember his metal dresses, his use of plastic, the paper clothes? Well, these days he favours structured suits and feminine frocks for women, displayed in his "new age" boutique, designed by Eric Raffy.

Georges Rech
16th arr. - 23, av. Victor-Hugo 45 00 83 19
Open 10 a.m.-7 p.m. (Mon. from 1 p.m.). Closed Sun., 3 wks. in Aug.

Rech makes clothes for active women with lots of personality, as vivacious as they are beautiful. Admire the strapless satin or velvet cocktail dresses striped with multicoloured ribbons (1,650 francs), the angora knit dresses bordered with ostrich plumes, and the city shorts-suits in various beautiful shades of fluid crepe (4,750 francs). The detailing on every item is impeccable, and the Rech sales staff are very nearly perfect too.

Rochas
8th arr. - 33, rue François-Ier - 47 23 54 56
Open 9:30 a.m.-6:30 p.m. (Sat. 9:30 a.m.-1 p.m. & 2 p.m.-6:30 p.m.). Closed Sun.

Rochas's recently launched line of luxurious women's wear is designed with plenty of panache by Peter O'Brien. These are classic clothes given an extra spark of chic by an original approach to fabric:

SHOPS – WOMEN'S WEAR

tweed and silk are juxtaposed, wool shows up for evening alongside mousseline and lace, organza comes out in the daylight escorted by jersey and bouclé knits. Elegant accessories—bags, jewellery, sunglasses, scarves—complete a modern, quintessentially feminine look.

Yves Saint Laurent
6th arr. - 6, pl. Saint-Sulpice - 43 29 43 00
8th arr. - 38, rue du Faubourg-Saint-Honoré - 42 65 74 59
Open 10 a.m.-7 p.m. Closed Sun.
16th arr. - 5, av. Marceau - 47 23 72 71
Open 9:30 a.m.-6 p.m. Closed Sun.

Saint Laurent is a byword for French fashion. For 30 years, Dior's successor has been the standard-bearer of Parisian elegance, with his rigorously conceived, luxuriously detailed collections. His newly redesigned showcase is now twice its former size, the better to display the full range of the Saint Laurent genius: superb furs, opulent evening clothes, incomparably elegant city attire and sportswear, jewellery and accessories. Also on hand are YSL's acclaimed fragrances, cosmetics and the new skincare line represented by Catherine Deneuve.

Jean-Louis Scherrer
8th arr. - 51, av. Montaigne - 42 99 05 79
Open 9:30 a.m.-6:30 p.m. Closed Sun.

Heavily influenced by Yves Saint Laurent, Jean-Louis Scherrer goes in for a classically elegant style. His customers include French television personalities and the Kennedy women. His cocktail dresses and ladylike suits are the highlights of his very attractive ready-to-wear line. Delightful handbags and jewellery.

Elisabeth de Senneville
1st arr. - 3, rue de Turbigo - 42 33 90 83
Open 10:30 a.m.-7 p.m. Closed Sun.

Elisabeth de Senneville designs easy-to-wear fashions in wonderful fabrics. Her "city sportswear" is particularly inventive and flattering, with close-fitting jackets, blazers and blousons paired with wide, flowing trousers. Ecru denim is a big Senneville favourite, shown plain, printed, lined and quilted. The stores also carry an amusing selection of witty and colourful children's clothes.

Angelo Tarlazzi
6th arr. - 74, rue des Saints-Pères 45 44 12 32
8th arr. - 67, rue du Faubourg-Saint-Honoré - 42 66 67 73
Open 10 a.m.-7 p.m. Closed Sun.

Tarlazzi creates sexy, provocative designs for women, with splashes of bright colours in prodigiously worked materials. Prices are high, but, thankfully, there is the Bataclan line to temper the whole. This is fiery fashion that frightens off some—still, try slipping into one of his draped skirts or laced-up cocktail dresses. You'll look so good you may have to buy it...

Téhen
4th arr. - 5 bis, rue des Rosiers 40 27 97 37
Open 11 a.m.-7 p.m. (Mon. from 2 p.m.). Closed Sun.

Designer Irena Gregori gets top billing in the Téhen shops with her fresh, vivid and uncomplicated styles, wearable from morning till night. Her preferences are for fluid fabrics, comfortable knits and stretchy synthetics. Prices are attractive, winter and summer, but at sale time they are downright irresistible.

Chantal Thomass
1st arr. - 1 rue Vivienne - 40 15 02 36
Open 10 a.m.-7 p.m. (Mon. from 11 a.m.). Closed Sun.

The queen of wasp-waists, figure-hugging dresses, ultra-feminine suits and sexy stockings has just inaugurated this huge new emporium. Here, only a stone's throw away from the trendy place des Victoires, spread out over three levels, all of Chantal's multifarious creations are on view. If you don't feel like shopping, head for the *fumoir*, the salon, the library, or the boudoir (no less).

Yuki Torii
2nd arr. - 38-40, galerie Vivienne 42 66 64 66
Open 10 a.m.-7 p.m. Closed Sun.

Don't be misled by the austerity of the boutique; unlike other Japanese stylists, this one does not go in for dramatic, ascetic "draperies." Yuki Torii likes bright colours, exuberant floral prints and amusing details. The clothes are supple, wearable and highly original. And expensive, of course.

Emmanuel Ungaro
8th arr. - 2, av. Montaigne - 47 23 61 94
Open 10 a.m.-7 p.m. Closed Sun.

Emmanuel Ungaro doesn't go in for fashion trends so much as he aims to create torrid "climates." Rousing colours and mad mixes of prints are his signatures: flowers, leopards and geometrical motifs run rampant along his curvy skirts and jackets. His Ungaro Solo Donna and Ungaro Parallèles lines are slightly more affordable than the top-tier ready-to-wear. Marvellous accessories, if you can only afford a "taste" of Ungaro.

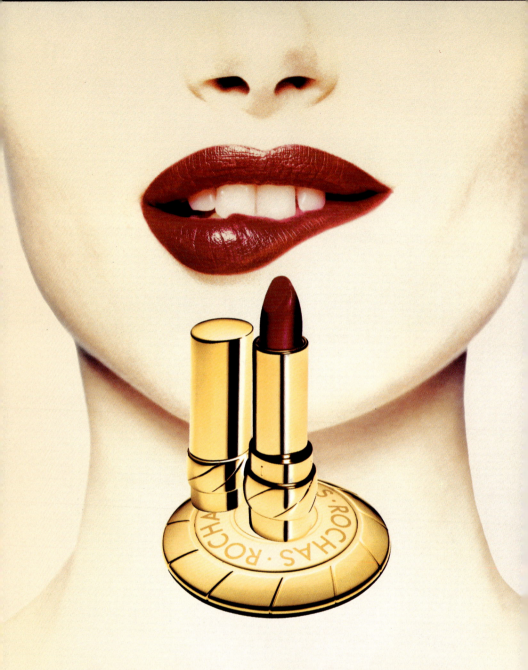

WOMEN'S WEAR – SHOPS

Valentino
8th arr. - 17-19, av. Montaigne
47 23 64 61
Open 10 a.m.-7 p.m. Closed Sun.

Like Caesar, another famous Roman before him, Valentino came, saw and conquered the world of French fashion. Celebrities and common folk alike flock to his boutique in search of classic styles in everything from socks to spectacles. The superbly cut flannel suits, tweed jackets, sweaters and shawls are chic, comfortable and easy to wear. Valentino goes all out for the evening, with frothy silk mousseline frocks, gowns sprinkled with sequins or jet embroidery—we understand why Liz Taylor wanted him to make her umpteenth wedding dress! Everything here is expensive, so be careful not to lose control.

■ EVENINGWEAR

Loris Azzaro
8th arr. - 65, rue du Faubourg-Saint-Honoré - 42 66 92 06
Open 10 a.m.-7 p.m. Closed Sun.

The ground floor of the shop does nothing to prepare customers for the luxury that awaits them in the grey-marble showroom upstairs. There the imperturbable Loris supervises, while his sumptuous gowns are fitted on the fair figures of jet-set celebrities. Though he may be scoffed at by more classic *couturiers*, his customers adore the way Azzaro plunges a neckline, moulds a silhouette. Predictably, his prices are far from negligible, though the ready-to-wear (dresses: 5,000 to 7,000) is obviously more affordable than the couture (10,000 and up).

Hélène Gainville
8th arr. - Arcades du Lido, 78, av. des Champs-Elysées - 43 59 32 18
Open 10:30 a.m.-7:30 p.m. Closed Sun.

See *Designers* page 269.

Narakas
16th arr. - 5, rue Lalo - 40 67 75 96
Open 9 a.m.-6 p.m. Closed Sat. (except appt.), Sun., Aug.

Whether you need a "little" cocktail dress or a gown for a gala dinner, Alexandre Narakas will provide you with a design that won't go unnoticed. In his gilded atelier, aided by Yolande de Gourcuff, he fashions yards of silk, taffeta and satin for spectacular, one-of-a-kind creations priced from 3,000 francs.

Yvan et Marzia
1st arr. - 4, pl. Sainte-Opportune
42 33 00 56
Open 11 a.m.-7 p.m. (Mon. from 2 p.m.). Closed Sun.

If your figure is flawless, you're likely to love Yvan and Marzia's luscious gowns. The lumpy and bumpy among us, however, would do well to look elsewhere. Prices start at about 3,000 francs.

■ FURS

Behar
10th arr. - 45, bd de Strasbourg
47 70 12 33
Open 9:30 a.m.-12:30 p.m. & 2 p.m.-6:30 p.m. Closed Sun., Mon. & 3 wks. in Aug.

Luxuriously full seven-eighths–length coats in dark, lustrous mink are the stars of Behar's collection, but there are beautiful silver-fox coats as well, and blue-fox jackets for 4,000 francs.

Sprung Frères
16th arr. - 5, av. Victor-Hugo - 45 01 70 61
Open 10 a.m.-7 p.m. Closed Sun., 1 wk. in Aug.

Definitely not for dowagers, these superbly cut furs (some designed by Chloé Bruneton) have loads of youthful style and chic.

Révillon
6th arr. - 44, rue du Dragon - 42 22 38 91
Open 11 a.m.-6:45 p.m. Closed Sun.
8th arr. - 17-19, rue du Faubourg-Saint-Honoré - 40 17 98 98
Open 10 a.m.-7 p.m. Closed Sun.

Révillon has been the symbol of furs since 1723. And they are still the most beautiful in the world. Here style goes hand in hand with quality. Of the fur-lined coats, muskrat suits, reversible jackets in blue mink or astrakhan displayed upstairs, none costs under 50,000 francs—in fact, they're generally four times that if you're into sable or chinchilla. Prices on the ground floor are somewhat less fearsome. A men's department with coats and jackets is housed on the lower level.

Riccardo Rozzi
17th arr. - 13, rue de l'Etoile
47 66 37 37
Open 10 a.m.-7 p.m. Closed Sun., Mon. (except Sept. 30-Feb. 28) & Aug.

Furs (including reversible models) in offbeat styles with wonderful, unique sleeves and enamelled with coloured copper make Riccardo Rozzi a designer for the young.

■ KNITS

Chandail
1st arr. - 68, rue Saint-Honoré
40 41 02 72
Open 11 a.m.-2:30 p.m. & 3:30 p.m.-7:30 p.m. (Mon. & Sat. 11 a.m.-1 p.m. & 2 p.m.-7:30 p.m.). Closed Sun.

The sweaters, exotic and eccentric, come from Peru, Norway and Austria and are decorated with dolls from the Andes or strange beasties. Comfort and folksiness is the order of the day. A more run-of-the-mill Italian knitwear collection caps the cosy ambience of this store, where prices range from 500 to 2,500 francs.

273

SHOPS – WOMEN'S WEAR

Crimson
8th arr. - 8, rue Marbeuf - 47 20 44 24
Open 10 a.m.-7 p.m. (Mon. from noon). Closed Sun.

Men and women will find a rainbow selection of colours in lambswool, with twin-sets selling for 700 to 1,400 francs, and long cardigans for 1,370 francs. There are also sweaters as soft as cashmere made from wool from the first shearing of a lamb's underside (700 francs). Rollnecks, V-necks and Irish knitwear in unusual colours are also stocked here at prices from 1,400 to 1,650 francs.

Fac-Bazaar
6th arr. - 38, rue des Saints-Pères 45 48 46 15
Open 11 a.m.-7 p.m. (Mon. from 3 p.m.). Closed Sun. & 3 wks. in Aug.

Fac-Bazaar offers creative designs and attractive pullovers in low-key colours.

Christa Fiedler
16th arr. - 87, av. Paul-Doumer 40 50 84 08
Open 10:30 a.m.-7 p.m. (Mon. from 2:30 p.m.). Closed Sun.

Model-turned-knitwear designer, Christa Fiedler marries comfort and elegance in her upbeat, elegant collections. She uses strong reds, blues and blacks in her lambswool sweaters for the winter months; soft pastel colours and cotton lisle for summer. And she stocks plenty of accessories: turbans, scarves and gloves. Every item is lovingly detailed and finished.

Richard Grand
1st arr. - 229, rue Saint-Honoré 42 60 18 75
Open 10 a.m.-7 p.m. Closed Sun.

This cashmere specialist has been in business for over a quarter of a century. Nobody matches its spectacular range of 70 colours in 100 styles for ladies and men. Richard Grand also manufactures cashmere-and-silk sweaters as light as feathers in a magnificent array of colours. Because the shop controls its own manufacturing, it can offer top-of-the-line chic at prices that start around 850 francs. A must for sweater fanciers in Paris.

Joseph
2nd arr. - 44, rue Etienne-Marcel 42 36 87 83
Open 10:30 a.m.-7 p.m. Closed Sun.

A megastar in London, in Paris Joseph is just, well... Joseph. But glitter and glamour aside, we like his imaginative and colourful knit separates, especially the roomy pullovers.

Aux Laines Ecossaises
7th arr. - 181, bd Saint-Germain 45 48 53 41
Open 10 a.m.-7 p.m. (Mon. from 2 p.m.). Closed Sun.

Top-quality lambswool pullovers, Shetland sweaters (500 francs) and some two-ply cashmere (2,200 francs). Colours are conservative; classic brands include Ballantyne and Gladstone, and there are also Austrian jackets made by Astrifa (1,500 francs) and tartan dressing gowns (1,300 francs).

■ LARGE SIZES

Marina Rinaldi
6th arr. - 56, rue du Four - 45 48 61 57
Open 10:30 a.m.-5 p.m. Closed Sun.

Generous curves are well served by these attractive fashions by an Italian designer. Rather than mask the fuller figure, they underscore its roundness in a most feminine way. Pretty prints, fluid fabrics and three different lines: Marina Rinaldi, the most expensive (and elegant); Marina Sport; and Persona, the least costly collection.

Rondissimo
9th arr. - 42, rue Vignon - 42 66 54 77
Open 10 a.m.-7 p.m. Closed Sun.

In French, women with fuller figures are called *rondes*, hence the name of this chain (with several stores in and around Paris). The fashionable clothes are made chiefly of knits and silky fabrics that flow over the body and flatter the silhouette.

■ LINGERIE

Berlé
1st arr. - 332, rue Saint-Honoré 42 60 42 87
Open 9 a.m.-noon & 1 p.m.-5 p.m. Closed Sat., Sun. & Aug.

For 70 years now, this noble house has manufactured and sold a single style of brassiere, which varies in the material used and how it is adorned. It gives contours to a generous bosom and emphasises a small one. The Queen Mother and Princess Margaret are just two of Berlé's loyal customers.

La Boîte à Bas
16th arr. - 77, rue de Longchamp 47 55 11 55
16th arr. - 16, av. Mozart - 42 24 89 98
Open 10:30 a.m.-7 p.m. (Mon. from 2 p.m.). Closed Sun., July 25-Sept.

It's all stockings and tights here, and all the major brands are represented: Gerbe, Dior, La Perla, Osé (the up-and-comer), Wolford and so forth. There are at least 8,000 pairs in stock and range from the coolest to the warmest (prices from 40 to 500 francs).

Alice Cadolle
1st arr. - 14, rue Cambon - 42 60 94 94
Open 9:30 a.m.-1 p.m. & 2 p.m.-6:30 p.m. (& by appt., except Sat. & Sun.). Closed Sun. & Aug.

Alice Cadolle invented the brassiere in 1889. Sales have been holding up well ever

WOMEN'S WEAR – SHOPS

since; here you can find custom-made, partly custom-made and ready-to-wear bras, lingerie and swimsuits (the latter are housed on the shop's third floor).

Les Folies d'Elodie
16th arr. - 56, av. Paul-Doumer
45 04 93 57
Open 10 a.m.-7 p.m. (Mon. from 11 p.m.). Closed Sun.

Two sisters, Catherine and Nanou, reign over the two Folies boutiques. Their collections are aimed at millionairesses who will settle for nothing less than silk and lace dressing gowns and underwear. Bed linen, wedding dresses and their celebrated blouse with a ribbed yoke are also available. If you need a tulle skirt, a satin strapless top or a transparent organza coat, this is the place.

Natori
1st arr. - 7, pl. Vendôme - 42 96 22 94
Open 10 a.m.-1 p.m. & 2 p.m.-7 p.m. Closed Sat. & Sun.

Seductive lingerie is the speciality here: your eyes will pop (so just think what *his* will do!) when you see Natori's silk negligees, beaded body suits, slinky nightgowns, bathrobes and undies.

Les Nuits d'Elodie
17th arr. - 1bis, av. Mac-Mahon
42 67 68 95

See *Les Folies d'Elodie* above.

Capucine Puerari
6th arr. - 63, rue des Saint-Pères
42 22 14 09
Open 10 a.m.-7 p.m. Closed Sun.

A spacious new boutique gives Capucine Puerari lots of room to display all her designing talents: there's youthful, sexy underwear and lingerie; smoothing, flattering bodysuits; and satiny, beautifully detailed swimsuits. The choice is wide, the staff are helpful,

the prices (for Paris, mind!) are reasonable.

Sabbia Rosa
6th arr. - 73, rue des Saints-Pères
45 48 88 37
Open 10 a.m.-7 p.m. Closed Sun.

This boutique is happy to receive couples in search of a few grammes of satin or an ounce of crêpe de chine with which to spice up an evening...

Chantal Thomass
6th arr. - 11, rue Madame - 45 44 07 52
Open 10 a.m.-7 p.m. (Mon. from 11 a.m.). Closed Sun.

This lingerie is in a class of its own: suspender belts, brassieres, panties and negligees are musts for collectors.

■ READY-TO-WEAR & SPECIALITY SHOPS

Absinthe
1st arr. - 74-76, rue Jean-Jacques-Rousseau
42 33 54 44
Open 11 a.m.-7:30 p.m. (Mon. from 2 p.m.). Closed Sun.

Marthe Desmoulins tracks down designers of the new generation—Dries Van Noten, Christophe Lemaire, Yoneda Kasuko, Costume Nazionale, Charlotte Nilson, among others—and brings their creations together in her trendy boutique. If you want to know what's new in fashion, this is a good place to start.

Inès de La Fressange
8th arr. - 14, av. Montaigne - 47 23 08 94
Open 10 a.m.-6:30 p.m. Closed Sun.

Inès, once the "face" of Chanel (until she fell out of favour with Kaiser Karl) recently launched her own boutique amid much media brouhaha. Set on the ultra-chic avenue Montaigne, the shop has become a roaring success. You'll find impeccably cut wardrobe basics (suits, trousers, jackets) and accessories (a rainbow of suede casuals, jewellery and hats), all produced, designed or selected by Inès herself. A line of household linens and decorative objects is available too.

Kashiyama
1st arr. - 80, rue Jean-Jacques-Rousseau - 40 26 46 46
Open 10 a.m.-1 p.m. & 2 p.m.-7 p.m. (Sat. 11 a.m.-7 p.m.). Closed Sun.
6th arr. - 147, bd Saint-Germain
46 34 11 50
Open 10 a.m.-7 p.m. (Mon. from 11 a.m.). Closed Sun.

The windows that wrap around an entire corner of the boulevard Saint-Germain offer a tantalising sample of what's inside: gorgeous garments by the trendiest designers—Dolce & Gabbana, Jean Colonna, Romeo Gigli, Sybilla and others, all the cream of the current fashion crop. Downstairs, a lavish array of lascivious, lacy lingerie awaits. We cringe at the prices (the twice-yearly sales merit close attention), but we have only praise for the helpful staff.

Maria Luisa
1st arr. - 2, rue Cambon - 47 03 96 15
Open 10:30 a.m.-7 p.m. Closed Sun.

In this chic district, you're unlikely to find a more avant-garde fashion boutique than this one. Maria Luisa is Venezuelan, and she is blessed with an infallible sense of style. Her stable of designing stars includes Martine Sitbon, Helmut Lang, John Galliano and Sybilla. Accessories too are at the cutting edge of fashion, with bags by 31 Février, hats by Le Corre and glorious jewellery by Berao and Valluet.

SHOPS – WOMEN'S WEAR

Songeur Daiya
1st arr. - 245, rue Saint-Honoré
42 60 97 35
Open 10 a.m.-7 p.m. Closed Sun.

The Daiya group (a Japanese concern), opened this spectacular shop to showcase talented designers like Nikita Godart, Brigitte Masson, Laura Caponi and Brazilian stylist, Cristal. An international clientele comes here to look for chic, unusual (and expensive) ensembles for day and evening.

Victoire
2nd arr. - 12 & 10, pl. des Victoires - 42 61 09 02
Open 9:30 a.m.-7 p.m. Closed Sun.

For a comprehensive view of what's new in fashion, Victoire is a good place to start. Young and veteran designers alike make up the eclectic mix of clothing and accessories that reflects owner Françoise Chassagnac's unerring taste: Romeo Gigli, Donna Karan, Callaghan and a handful of newcomers who change each season.

Zenta
8th arr. - 6, rue de Marignan - 42 25 72 47
Open 10 a.m.-7 p.m. (Mon. from 11 a.m.). Closed Sun.

Some 15 designers are represented in this spacious boutique. In addition to confirmed talents like Popy Moreni, Chantal Thomass, Martine Sitbon, Karl Lagerfeld and Lolita Lempicka, you'll discover the creations of the up-and-coming generation.

RAC PARIS STREETS: The cartography of this city-wide street plan of Paris is clear and easy to use and is supported by a comprehensive index in book form tipped on to the card cover. The map is packed with essential information including the direction of one-way streets. A must for all visitors to Paris. Price: £ 4.50.

■ SHOES & ACCESSORIES

Jean Barthet
8th arr. - 13, rue Tronchet - 42 65 35 87
Open 10 a.m.-1 p.m. & 2 p.m.-6:30 p.m. Closed Sat., Sun., 2 wks. in Aug.

Most of the world's celebrities have stuck their heads through the door of this institution—and with good reason. Jean Barthet makes hats that are refined and spectacular. This is high fashion at over-the-top-hat prices!

Isabel Canovas
8th arr. - 16, av. Montaigne - 47 20 10 80
Open 10 a.m.-7 p.m. Closed Sun.

Accessories that lift an outfit out of the banal and into the extraordinary: ants crawl up a pair of silk gloves, cats chase each other round and round a belt, lizards slither up lapels... Nature and Africa are the twin inspirations for Isabel Canovas's fascinating creations. You'll also find lovely handbags, trim little leather envelopes that go beautifully with a tailored suit, glass-bead earrings, shawls, sarongs and much more.

Chéri-Bibi
11th arr. - 82, rue de Charonne 43 70 51 72
Open 11 a.m.-1 p.m. & 2 p.m.-7 p.m. Closed Sun., Mon. & 2 last wks. of Aug.

All manner of adorable little hats (*bibis*) hang on the walls of this trendy shop, where celebrities and anonymous followers of fashion choose their bérets, caps (we love the one with a "target" design), veiled cocktail hats and turbans.

Robert Clergerie
6th arr. - 5, rue du Cherche-Midi 45 48 75 47
Open 9:30 a.m.-7 p.m. Closed Sun.

Clergerie's much-copied wedgies, metallic faux-croco casuals and tall-girl pumps are adored by fashionable *Parisiennes*. Basic shapes vary little from season to season: the designer just changes a detail or two. But the colour schemes are always inventive and up-to-the-minute, with warm, muted shades in winter, pastels and flashy brights in summer.

Un Dimanche à Venise
6th arr. - 50, rue du Four - 42 22 52 38
Open 10 a.m.-7:30 p.m. Closed Sun.

A newcomer to the footwear scene. What makes this shop worthwhile is the selection of more-or-less obvious copies of shoes by more up-scale manufacturers. The quality is perfectly respectable, the styles are always right in fashion and the prices are fine too.

Maud Frizon
6th arr. - 83, rue des Saints-Pères 42 22 06 93
Open 10 a.m.-7 p.m. Closed Sun.

Audacious, feminine styles, with a subtle use of canvas and lizard, suede and leather. There are heels for all seasons and heights, as well as a host of ballet slippers, beach and evening sandals, pumps and dreamy boots. Prices, 1,750 to 2,700 francs.

Harel
8th arr. - 64, rue François-Ier - 47 23 96 57 & 8, av. Montaigne 47 20 75 00
Open 10 a.m.-6:45 p.m. Closed Sun.

If you pride yourself on your elegance, you can't afford to

WOMEN'S WEAR – SHOPS

> ### Confidential Cinema
>
> Want to see a forgotten or rare film from New York, New Delhi or New South Wales? Join the fans who haunt a host of tiny art cinemas in the area bounded by the quai Saint-Michel, boulevard Saint-Michel, rue Saint-Jacques and rue Soufflot. These cinemas often feature avant-garde and foreign films in their original languages. Action Christine in the rue Christine is devoted mainly to Hollywood classics. The projectionist takes special pride in his work, and you can ask when buying your tickets whether the copy is of good quality. Also worth a visit: Cinoche in the rue de Condé, Saint André des Arts, in the street of the same name, and Les 3 Luxembourg, rue Monsieur-le-Prince.

ignore Harel. In fact, you owe it to yourself to own at least one pair of his marvels—sheer, simple luxury: three different arches, three widths and five heel heights. Pumps, sandals and walking shoes, in a choice of satin, lizard, crocodile, ostrich, snakeskin and kid, come in 20 colours and cost from about 1,550 to 3,000 francs. A pair of Harel's shoes lasts a lifetime; if they don't, they'll send them to the factory for repairs.

Charles Jourdan
1st arr. - 5, bd de la Madeleine 42 61 15 89
Open 9:45 a.m.-7 p.m. Closed Sun.
8th arr. - 86, av. des Champs-Elysées - 45 62 29 33
Open 9:45 a.m.-8 p.m. Closed Sun.

There's something here for every taste, including the best. Affordable fine-quality shoes are available in over 20 colours. Plan to spend about 1,050 francs for a pair of pumps.

K-Jacques
4th arr. - 16, rue Pavée - 40 27 03 57
Open 10:30 a.m.-7 p.m. (Mon. & Sun. from 2:30 p.m.). Closed wk. of Aug. 15.

French author Colette launched the K-Jacques sandal in Saint Tropez, some 60 years ago. Reminiscent of the footwear you see Spartans wearing in old films, the sandal comes in every shade from natural brown to metallic turquoise. Lots of other Provençal accessories are on display: great boots like the ones sported by Camargue cowboys, straw bags, ceramics and Biot glassware (the kind with the tiny bubbles locked inside).

Charles Kammer
7th arr. - 14, rue de Grenelle - 42 22 91 19
Open 10 a.m.-7 p.m. Closed Sun.

Shoes as comfortable as bedroom slippers, for trotting about the city in style. In summer, look for lovely sandals and strappy numbers; in winter, you'll find high-rise vamps and thigh boots in softest leather. Kammer gives you lots of fashion for what is, in fact, a reasonable amount of money.

Stéphane Kélian
1st arr. - 6, pl. des Victoires - 42 61 60 74
1st arr. - Les Trois Quartiers, 23, bd de la Madeleine - 42 96 01 99
3rd arr. - 36, rue de Sévigné - 42 77 87 91
7th arr. - 13 bis, rue de Grenelle 42 22 93 03
Open 10 a.m.-7 p.m. Closed Sun.
8th arr. - Galerie Point-Show, 66, av. des Champs-Elysées - 42 56 11 44
8th arr. - 26, av. des Champs-Elysées - 42 56 42 26
Open 10:30 a.m.-7:30 p.m. Closed Sun.

King of the braided-leather shoe, Stéphane Kélian has based his reputation on this technique. He also adds sparkle to classic styles for Claude Montana. Sculptured heels, fine details, fashionable forms—and sniffy service—are found in all the city's Kélian stores. Take note that it is now Kélian, not Maud Frizon, who designs the ultrafeminine Miss Maud shoe collection (rue de Grenelle).

Sidonie Larizzi
8th arr. - 8, rue de Marignan - 43 59 38 87
Open 10 a.m.-7 p.m. Closed Sun.

Sidonie Larizzi designs for couturiers, and also produces a collection with her own label. Her boutique creations blend classicism with originality. Alongside the dressy pumps you'll discover delicious boudoir slippers with swan's down pompons, and handbags to drool over. Studio Larizzi is a lower-priced (but still very stylish) second-tier line.

John Lobb
8th arr. - 51, rue François-Ier - 45 62 06 34
Open 10 a.m.-7 p.m. Closed Sun.

Outrageously expensive shoes for fussy feet whose owners have money to spend. You must place your order six months in advance for a pair of sumptuous, custom-made walking shoes, golf shoes or riding boots. Remarkable foot-

SHOPS – WOMEN'S WEAR

wear from all points of view. Prices are staggering.

Christian Louboutin
1st arr. - 19, rue Jean-Jacques-Rousseau - 42 36 05 31
Open 11 a.m.-7:30 p.m. Closed Sun.

You don't have to have a shoe fetish to find Louboutin's footwear irresistibly sensual and alluring. A student of the great Roger Vivier, he creates jewels for the feet—just look at the gold leaf that adorns the high heels on one of his models. Prices, predictably, are high: around 1,800 francs a pair.

René Mancini
16th arr. - 72, av. Victor-Hugo 45 00 48 81
Open 10 a.m.-7 p.m. (Sat. 10 a.m.-1 p.m. & 2:30 p.m.-6 p.m.). Closed Sun., Mon., Aug.

René Mancini first made the black-tipped shoe for Chanel. In 1964 he introduced square toes. His daughter Claire has carried on the family tradition. A portion of the collection is handmade, and it is possible to match your shoes to your dress for a mere 3,000 francs and a ten-day wait. Mancini's ready-to-wear shoes are made in Italy and are more affordable. Prices at the boutique on avenue Victor-Hugo range from 700 to 1,500 francs.

Laurent Mercadal
1st arr. - 3, pl. des Victoires - 45 08 84 44
6th arr. - 56, rue de Rennes - 45 48 43 87
8th arr. - 26, av. des Champs-Elysées - 42 25 22 70
8th arr. - 31, rue Tronchet - 42 66 01 28
Open 10:30 a.m.-7 p.m. Closed Sun.

Laurent Mercadal makes classic but stylish women's shoes that are always in tune with current fashion trends. A limited number of basic models is offered in a vast assortment of skins and combinations, in beautiful colours. Reasonable prices (from 650 francs).

Marie Mercié
2nd arr. - 56, rue Tiquetonne - 40 26 60 68
6th arr. - 23, rue Saint-Sulpice 43 26 45 83
Open 11 a.m.-7 p.m. Closed Sun.

The Queen of Hats. This tiny boutique is stuffed with chic and shocking *chapeaux* that are guaranteed to grab lots of attention. Marie Mercié designs fantastical headgear that is featured in the fashion shows of many top couturiers.

Philippe Model
1st arr. - 33, pl. du Marché-Saint-Honoré - 42 96 89 02
Open 10 a.m.-7 p.m. (Sat.: March 1-Sept. 30 from 11 p.m.; Oct. 1-Feb 28 from 1 p.m.). Closed Sun.
6th arr. - 79, rue des Saint-Pères 45 44 76 79
Open 10 a.m.-7 p.m. (Mon. & Sat. 11 a.m.-7 p.m.). Closed Sun.

Rare is the woman who would not look fetching in a hat by Philippe Model. His shop overflows with colourful styles: picture hats, fedoras, feathered and beribboned models, airy straw hats and jaunty panamas. Model is currently one of the brightest stars in the fashion-accessory firmament. His beautiful collection of footwear for men and women is displayed in the shop next door.

Oxymuse
7th arr. - 11, rue du Pré-aux-Clercs - 45 44 43 35
Open 11 a.m.-7 p.m. Closed Sun., Aug.

Muriel Jurman, late of Charles Kammer, has launched her own line of shoes under the Oxymuse label. Traditional methods are used to craft her small collection of classic models in stylish colours and leathers. A single price: 650 francs.

Michel Perry
1st arr. - 13, rue de Turbigo - 42 36 44 34
Open 11 a.m.-7 p.m. Closed Sun. & 1 wk. in Aug.

Fashionable to a degree (he was written up by Vogue a few months ago), Perry designs fresh, unusual, always glamorous looks that flatter the feet. His heels are particularly inventive.

Andréa Pfister
1st arr. - 4, rue Cambon - 42 96 55 28
Open 10 a.m.-7 p.m. (Mon. from 2 p.m.). Closed Sun.

Pfister makes fine, delicate shoes to suit the comely foot and well-turned ankle. This is Parisian elegance *par excellence*. Embroidered or sequined evening shoes sell for around 2,000 20francs. The price of a pair of elegant snakeskin shoes can slither up considerably higher. Pfister will also make shoes to measure in the style and leather of your choice. Allow seven weeks with fittings.

Fausto Santini
6th arr. - 4 ter, rue du Cherche-Midi - 45 44 39 40
Open 10 a.m.-7 p.m. (Mon. from 11 p.m.). Closed Sun.

The rue du Cherche-Midi was already chock-a-block with shoe shops, but Santini moved in anyway; in fact, he has made quite a reputation for himself. His handbags and shoes are outstanding for their glowing leathers in myriad hues, delicate curved lines and fashionable finishing touches.

Walter Steiger
6th arr. - 5, rue de Tournon - 46 33 01 45
Open 10 a.m.-7 p.m. (Mon. from 2 p.m.). Closed Sun., Aug.
8th arr. - 83, rue du Faubourg-Saint-Honoré - 42 66 65 08
Open 10 a.m.-7 p.m. Closed Sun.

More foreigners than Parisians pass through the portals of Walter Steiger, women who find his evening sandals, workaday court shoes and weekend boots indispensable. Steiger's fake-lizard (printed on leather) is utterly convincing and much less expensive than the genuine article. Expect to pay from 1,200 to 1,400 for a pair of pumps.

François Villon
6th arr. - 58, rue Bonaparte - 43 25 98 36
Open 10 a.m.-7 p.m. (Mon. 10 a.m.-1 p.m. & 2 p.m.-7 p.m.). Closed Sun.

François Villon's high-quality footwear is beyond fashion. His boots are incomparable (around 2,500 francs). Villon carries pretty dress shoes and casual flatties as well as the celebrated Brides Villon sandals with black tips. Of course, these shoes don't come cheap: between 1,500 and 2,800 francs per pair.

■ SILK

Les Trois Marches
6th arr. - 1, rue Guisarde - 43 54 74 18
Open 12:30 p.m.-7:30 p.m. Closed Sun. & Mon.

Cathy Lullier's pocket-size boutique overflows with vintage gowns and dresses in silk, crêpe de chine and silk mousseline. She personally tracks each treasure down, then proceeds to restore and update it by hand. There is also a delicious selection of frilly cotton and eyelet underthings. Isabelle Adjani and Catherine Deneuve have been spotted shopping here.

Pour Surah
4th arr. - 7, rue du Trésor - 42 77 11 21
Open 11 a.m.-7 p.m. Closed Sun., Mon., 2 wks. in Aug.

Maud Perl wraps women in gorgeous scarves, shawls and sarongs of purest silk, in the most divinely shimmering shades.

■ SWIMSUITS

A la Plage
7th arr. - 6, rue de Solférino - 47 05 18 94
Open 10 a.m.-7 p.m. (Sat. 10 a.m.-1 p.m. & 2 p.m.-7 p.m.). Closed Sun., 1 wk. in Aug.
16th arr. - 17, rue de la Pompe 45 03 08 51
Open 10 a.m.-1 p.m. & 2 p.m.-7 p.m. Closed Sun., 1 wk. in Aug.

The most beautiful swimsuits and cover-ups are available here year-round. There's a children's collection, too.

Erès
6th arr. - 4 bis, rue du Cherche-Midi - 45 44 95 54
8th arr. - 2, rue Tronchet - 47 42 24 55
Open 9:30 a.m.-7 p.m. Closed Sun.
16th arr. - 6, rue Guichard - 46 47 45 21
Open 10 a.m.-7 p.m. Closed Sun.

Erès, the swimsuit specialists, sells two-pieces separately—a brilliant idea. There is an incredible choice of adjustable tops and bottoms to suit just about any figure. What's more, they're beautifully made and as chic as can be. The Beachwear collection includes co-ordinates for before and after *la plage*. Upstairs: a lingerie section.

■ WEDDING GOWNS

Hélène Gainville
8th arr. - Arcades du Lido, 78, av. des Champs-Elysées - 43 59 32 18
Open 10:30 a.m.-7:30 p.m. Closed Sun.

Hélène Gainville and her fairy-fingered seamstresses will create the wedding gown you've dreamed about since you were small. Made to your measurements, hand-beaded and embroidered, in silk, satin, organza or lace, these classic timeless dresses are truly fit for a princess. Naturally, Hélène will be happy to make your veil, headpiece and other accessories too. Chic travelling clothes and ensembles for the mother of the bride can be custom-made here as well.

Monique Germain
6th arr. - 59, bd Raspail - 45 48 22 63
Open 12:30 p.m.-7 p.m. (Sat. 1 p.m.-6 p.m.). Closed Sun. & Mon.

The display window is classic and conventional—anything but exciting. But inside—surprise!—you'll see sculpted tops for bare-shouldered brides, sheath dresses with tulle overskirts, gowns that can be transformed into cocktail dresses after the big day. Alongside is a wealth of stylish accessories.

RAC MOTORING ATLAS FRANCE

Our fully revised and well-established large format RAC Motoring Atlas France, Belgium and Luxembourg at 1:250,000 (approximately 4 miles to 1 inch) now has even more features to improve journey planning and to make driving in France more enjoyable.

An enlarged Paris section now features the capital's rapid transport network, together with a clear map of Paris suburbs, and a simplified access plan to the new Euro Disney resort, while journey planning has been improved by the valuable addition of plans of all the Channel ports, as well as a map of the major French railways.

All this alongside clear, accurate and detailed road maps make RAC Motoring Atlas France the ideal atlas for the independent traveller in France.

RAC Motoring Atlas France £11.99 (spiral bound)

ARTS & LEISURE

ART GALLERIES	282
HOBBIES & SPORTS	287
MUSEUMS	292
PARKS & GARDENS	304

ARTS & LEISURE – ART GALLERIES

ART GALLERIES

GEOGRAPHY

A gallery's address is a fairly reliable indicator of its artistic allegiance. The Right Bank, from avenue Matignon to avenue de Messine, is the place to view established contemporary artists; the Left Bank, from rue Guénégaud to rue des Beaux-Arts, is home to slightly more "advanced" art. The turf of the real avant-garde extends from Beaubourg and Les Halles to the Bastille.

FINE ART

Artcurial
8th arr. - 9, av. Matignon - 42 99 16 16
Open 10:30 a.m.-7:10 p.m. Closed Sun., Mon. (except in Dec.), last 3 wks. of Aug. & holidays.

This artistic offshoot of the L'Oréal cosmetics group is the largest gallery in Paris. Artcurial is a multifaceted gallery that boasts one of the finest art bookshops in all of Europe, in addition to collections of contemporary furniture, carpets and ceramics designed by noted artists, signed lithographs and stunning limited-edition jewellery. Works by de Chirico, Sonia Delauney, Etienne-Martin, Laurens, Masson, Miró and Zadkine may be admired—and purchased—here.

Galeries Beaubourg I et II
4th arr. - 23, rue du Renard - 42 71 20 50
4th arr. - 3, rue Pierre-au-Lard 48 04 34 40
Open 10:30 a.m.-1 p.m. & 2:30 p.m.-7 p.m. Closed Sun., Mon., Aug. & holidays.

Here, at one of the most important galleries in the Beaubourg area, Pierre and Marianne Mahon favour artists of the 1950s, new realists and other contemporaries. Works by celebrated artists (Arman and César, Baselitz, Basquiat, Beuys, Boisrond, Cane, Combas, Dado, Garouste, Klossowski, Monory, Paladino, Raysse, Villeglé, Warhol and Wols, to name only a few) are sold worldwide, including to museums. Some art-lovers whisper that lately the gallery is resting on its laurels, and has lost its sense of adventure. But such talk could just be the price of the Mahons' spectacular success.

Galerie Barbier-Beltz
4th arr. - 7, rue Pecquay - 40 27 84 14
Open noon-7 p.m. (Sat. 10 a.m.-7 p.m.). Closed Sun., Mon., Aug. & holidays.

A discreet, elegant little gallery run by a man who has never hesitated to pursue such "difficult" artists as Barré, Dufour, Kallos, Messagier and Pincemin. They have lately been joined by such estimable newcomers as Barbara Thaden and Christian Sorg.

Galerie Berggruen
7th arr. - 70, rue de l'Université 42 22 02 12
Open 10 a.m.-1 p.m. & 2:30 p.m.-7 p.m. Closed Sun., Mon. & holidays.

H. Berggruen retired and handed over the reins of this traditional gallery to Antoine Mendihara. The solid stock of prints and drawings by Arroyo, Dali, Klee, Masson, Matisse, Miró, Picasso and Zao Wouki are complemented by the works of contemporary artists like Beringer, Janssen and Paguignon. The little catalogues are works of art in their own right.

Galerie Claude Bernard
6th arr. - 7, rue des Beaux-Arts 43 26 97 07
Open 9:30 a.m.-12:30 p.m. & 2:30 p.m.-6:30 p.m. Closed Sun., Mon., Aug. & holidays.

In a district where fine galleries abound, this is surely one of the very best. Bacon and Bonnard have graced these walls, alongside unforgettable works by Balthus, Botero, Giacometti, Hockney and Nevelson. Perhaps understandably, the gallery's atmosphere is weighty and solemn—genius is never stale, but a fresh point of view would be welcome.

Galerie Isy Brachot
6th arr. - 33, rue Guénégaud - 43 29 11 71
6th arr. - 35, rue Guénégaud - 43 54 22 40
Open 2 p.m.-7 p.m. (Sat. 11 a.m.-1 p.m. & 2 p.m.-7 p.m.). Closed Sun., Mon. & July 15-Sept. 1.

Surrealism and fantastic realism are the hallmarks of this originally Belgian gallery. Some of the big names are here: Delvaux, Ensor, Labisse, Magritte. Also present are De Andrea, Dado, Beuys and Roland Cat.

Galerie Jeanne Bucher
6th arr. - 53, rue de Seine - 43 26 22 32
Open 9 a.m.-12:30 p.m. & 2:30 p.m.-6:30 p.m. Closed Sun., Mon., Aug. & holidays.

Faithful to the Ecole de Paris of the 1960s, and to a particularly sensitive vision of painting, typified by Dubuffet, Bissière, De Stael, Viera da Silva and Jean-Pierre Raynaud.

Claire Burrus
11th arr. - 16, rue de Lappe - 43 55 36 90
Open 10:30 a.m.-1 p.m. & 2 p.m.-7 p.m. Closed Sun., Mon., Aug. & holidays.

Claire Burrus, a pioneer in this now-fashionable gallery district, champions post-conceptual artists like Finlay, Thomas, Nils-Udo and Felice Varini. A few of the old guard from her former gallery, Le Dessin, are also present: look for works by Agid, Baruchello, Degottex and Voss.

ART GALLERIES – ARTS & LEISURE

Galerie Farideh Cadot
3rd arr. - 77, rue des Archives
42 78 08 36
Open 10 a.m.-7 p.m. (Sat. 11 a.m.-7 p.m.). Closed Sun., Mon., Aug. & holidays.

Farideh Cadot owns one of the most important galleries in Paris, thanks to his provocative, perspicacious choice of artists. No sectarianism here: painting, sculpture and photography are all (well) represented, with such artists as Boisrond, Favier, Laget, Oppenheim, Raetz, Rousse and Tremblay. And Cadot is always on the prowl for new, exciting work.

Galerie Louis Carré et Cie
8th arr. - 10, av. de Messine - 45 62 57 07
Open 10 a.m.-12:30 p.m. & 1:30 p.m.-6:30 p.m. (Sat. depending on exhibitions). Closed Sun., holidays, Aug. & Dec. 25-Jan. 1.

Patrick Bongers, Louis Carré's grandson, carries on the family tradition by keeping alive the great names of this gallery's past, names like Delaunay, Dufy, Hartung, Léger, Poliakoff and Soulages. He also exhibits more contemporary work by the likes of Estève and Bitran, and even had Di Rosa paint his car!

Galerie Lucien Durand
6th arr. - 19, rue Mazarine - 43 26 25 35
Open 10:30 a.m.-1 p.m. & 2:30 p.m.-7 p.m. Closed Sun., Mon., July & Aug. & holidays.

For 30 years, Lucien Durand has been discovering young artists and organising first exhibitions. This sensitive, eagle-eyed picture dealer introduced César and Dmitrienko to the world at large. Durand's current group of artists includes Braconnier, Canteloup, Frize, Lechner, Nadaud and Vanarsky.

Durand-Dessert
11th arr. - 28, rue de Lappe - 48 06 92 23
Open 11 a.m.-1 p.m. & 2 p.m.-7 p.m. (Sat. 11 a.m.-7 p.m.). Closed Sun., Mon., Aug. & holidays.

In a new gallery that was once a factory, Durand-Dessert display European avant-garde at its loftiest level. You'll find such international high-flyers as Richter, Beuys, Merz, Kounelis, Morellet, Garouste, Lavier and Tosani. The gallery's bookshop is a wonderful place to linger and browse through the latest art publications.

Espace Photographique de Paris
1st arr. - Nouveau Forum des Halles, Place Carrée, Grande-Galerie - 40 26 87 12
Open 1 p.m.-6 p.m. (Sat. & Sun. 1 p.m.-7 p.m.). Closed Mon. & July 15-end of Aug.

After the Palais de Tokyo (see Museums), this is the most comprehensive photographic collection in town. Jacques Lowe, Ralph Gibson, Bill Brandt, Emmet, Gowin and other major figures have shown here; retrospectives and *hommages* bring works of the masters to this fascinating gallery.

Galerie Jean Fournier
4th arr. - 44, rue Quincampoix
42 77 32 31
Open 10 a.m.-1 p.m. & 2 p.m.-7 p.m. (Mon. by appointment). Closed Sun., Aug. & holidays.

Jean Fournier has worked in his vast book-lined premises for 30 years. Though he remains a champion of the post-war abstraction movement, represented by such artists as Buraglio, Sam Francis, Hantai, Joan Mitchell and Viallat, Fournier is also a tireless seeker of new talent. If you are in search of a rare book on contemporary art, this is the place to look.

Galerie de France
4th arr. - 52, rue de la Verrerie
42 74 38 00
Open 10 a.m.-7 p.m. (Mon. 10 a.m.-6 p.m.). Closed Sun., Aug. & holidays.

Huge, museum-like premises that span three floors makes the Galerie de France an ideal venue for sculpture exhibitions and art festivals. Artists represented here include Aillaud, Antoniucci, Brancusi, Degottex, Gonzales, Kantor, Manessier, Matta, Pincemin, Raynaud, Soulages and Zao Wou-Ki. Recent photography exhibitions have displayed works by Alice Springs, Domela and Gisèle Freund. The gallery also actively promotes contemporary Russian artists.

Galerie Maurice Garnier
8th arr. - 6, av. Matignon - 42 25 61 65
Open 10 a.m.-1 p.m. & 2:30 p.m.-7 p.m. Closed Sun., Mon., Aug. & holidays.

Since 1978 Maurice Garnier has represented a single painter: Bernard Buffet, who Picasso believed was the most talented painter of his generation (even geniuses can have an occasional lapse). Each year, in February and March, Garnier mounts a thematic exhibition of Buffet's work.

Galerie Daniel Gervis
7th arr. - 14, rue de Grenelle - 45 44 41 90, fax 45 49 18 98
By appointment only. Closed Sun. & July 15-Sept. 1.

Daniel Gervis, co-producer of the FIAC, Paris's annual International Fair of Contemporary Art, also produces limited editions of engravings and lithographs. His taste runs towards the abstract, exemplified by such artists as Benrath, Olivier Debré,

Dubuffet, Hartung and Malaval.

Didier Imbert Fine Art
8th arr. - 19, av. Matignon - 45 62 10 40
Open 10 a.m.-1 p.m. & 2:30 p.m.-7 p.m. Closed Sun., Aug. & holidays.

Didier Imbert has transformed his gallery into a veritable museum. Exhibits of works by Brauner, Brancusi and the acclaimed *Henry Moore Intime* show, which were as intellectually stimulating as they were thrilling to view, have placed Imbert in the forefront of the Parisian art scene.

Galerie Laage-Salomon
4th arr. - 57, rue du Temple - 42 78 11 71
Open 10:30 a.m.-12:30 p.m. & 2:30 p.m.-7 p.m. (Sat. 11 a.m.-7 p.m.). Closed Sun., Mon., Aug. & holidays.

Gabrielle Salomon's outlook is broadly international. She exhibits the work of German neo-Expressionists (Baselitz, Lüpertz, A. R. Penck and Immendorf) as well as sculpture by Chamberlain (an American), England's Ackling and the French artists Cogné, Mercier, Messager and Di Rosa.

Galerie Yvon Lambert
3rd arr. - 108, rue Vieille-du-Temple - 42 71 09 33
Open 10 a.m.-1 p.m. & 2:30 p.m.-7 p.m. (Sat. 10 a.m.-7 p.m.). Closed Sun., Mon., Aug. & holidays.

Aloof and reserved, Yvon Lambert is an energetic promoter of the avant-garde. A one-time aficionado of minimalist and conceptual art, Lambert now aims in another direction. His enormous gallery is home to works by Lewitt, Oppenheim, Tuttle and Twombly, as well as Christo, Blais, Barcelo and Combas.

Lavignes-Bastille
11th arr. - 27, rue de Charonne 47 00 88 18
Open 11 a.m.-7 p.m. Closed Sun., Mon., Aug., Dec. 25 & Jan. 1.

Since 1985 Jean-Pierre Lavignes has filled his multi-level gallery with fascinating, sometimes violent work by contemporary artists working in the Realist and Expressionist veins: Calum Fraser, Grataloup, Hahn, Lukaschewsky, Rotella, Sandorfi and, occasionally, Andy Warhol (his last Parisian show was held here).

Galerie Baudoin Lebon
4th arr. - 38, rue Sainte-Croix-de-la-Bretonnerie - 42 72 09 10
Open 2 p.m.-7 p.m. (Sat. 11 a.m.-7 p.m.). Closed Sun., Mon., Aug. & holidays.

Allow us to forewarn you: this gallery is a little offbeat. Expect, for example, to see an exhibition of aboriginal art and works by Ben, Bissier, Dado, Dine, Michaux, Pagès, Rauschenberg, Titus-Carmel and Viallat. Photography is another major focus at this eccentric gallery, now established in fabulous new premises.

Galerie Lelong
8th arr. - 13, rue de Téhéran - 45 63 13 19
Open 10:30 a.m.-6 p.m. (Sat. 2 p.m.-6:30 p.m.). Closed Sun., Mon., Aug. & holidays.

Known as the "spiritual son" of Aimé Maeght, Daniel Lelong runs a prestigious gallery that is one of the most important in Paris. In addition to his branches in Zurich and New York, he also has a sideline publishing venture (you'll find the books, catalogues and lithos on the gallery's lower level). Lelong's exhibits encompass works by great 20th-century artists: Bacon, Calder, Chagall, Lindner, Moore, Bram Van Velde, as well as Adami, James Brown, Garcia Sevilla, Kienholz, Tàpies and Titus-Carmel.

Galerie Louise Leiris
8th arr. - 47, rue de Monceau 45 63 20 56
Open 10 a.m.-noon & 2:30 p.m.-6 p.m. Closed Sun., Mon. & holidays. Annual closings not available.

Founded by D. H. Kahnweiler, this "picture dealer of the century" (Picasso, Léger, Gris, Braque and others) is indeed a venerable and historically important gallery that should not be missed. The collections are tops in terms of quality and prestige, with works by Masson, Laurens, Beaudin and, more recently, Elie Lascaux.

Galerie Adrien Maeght
7th arr. - 42-46, rue du Bac - 45 48 45 15
Open 9:30 a.m.-1 p.m. & 2 p.m.-7 p.m. Closed Sun., Mon., Aug. & holidays.

A gallery that bears the name of Maeght is obviously going to have a prestigious catalogue of the highest quality. And indeed, Adrien Maeght, son of Aimé, oversees a tremendous stock of major 20th-century paintings housed in galleries throughout Europe, with works by Matisse, Chagall, Calder and Bram Van Velde. His daughter Yoyo, also a talented picture dealer, has brought a new generation of artists such as Kuroda and Hélène Delprat to the Maeght "stable."

Galerie Daniel Malingue
8th arr. - 26, av. Matignon - 42 66 60 33
Open 10:30 a.m.-12:30 p.m. & 2:30 p.m.-6:30 p.m. (Mon. 2:30 p.m.-6:30 p.m.). Closed Sun., Aug. & holidays.

Twice a year, Daniel Malingue mounts well-publicised exhibitions of important 20th-century artists; recent shows

ART GALLERIES – ARTS & LEISURE

have focused on Dufy, Léger, Matisse and Vlaminck, as well as César, Lobo, Matta and Moore.

Galerie Nikki Diana Marquardt
4th arr. - 9, pl. des Vosges - 42 78 21 00
Open 1 p.m.-7 p.m. Closed Sun. & Mon.

American gallery owner Nikki Marquardt displays a bold approach to contemporary art: she's willing to take a risk, and usually comes up with a winner. She claims that one "doesn't need direction, just vision, to know about art." David Mach has done his special brand of sculpture installation here; sculpture by Vlugt, Flavin and works by Dunoyer, Bader and Kumrov have also been shown, to considerable critical acclaim.

Galerie Marwan Hoss
1st arr. - 12, rue d'Alger - 42 96 37 96
Open 10 a.m.-12:30 p.m. & 2 p.m.-6:30 p.m. (Sat. 10 a.m.-12:30 p.m. & 2 p.m.-6 p.m.). Closed Sun., holidays & mid July-end Aug.

Apart from a few great classics, such as Matisse, Bonnard and Calder, this gallery pipes a contemporary tune from Giacometti to Garcia with some stopovers for Gonzalez, Hayden and Zao Wou-Ki.

Galerie 1900-2000
6th arr. - 8, rue Bonaparte - 43 25 84 20
Open 10 a.m.-12:30 p.m. & 2 p.m.-7 p.m. Closed Sun., Aug. & holidays.

This gallery is best known for its eye-popping exhibitions on such themes as hyper-realism, pop art and fringe artists. Represented are Max Ernst, Hérold, Marcel Jean, Matta, Picabia, Man Ray, Gaston Louis Roux, Takis and Warhol.

Galerie Montaigne
8th arr. - 36, av. Montaigne - 47 23 32 35
Open 11 a.m.-1 p.m. & 2 p.m.-7 p.m. Closed Sun., Mon., Aug. & holidays.

Somewhat isolated here in the sanctuary of *haute couture*, this gallery combines forays into the wild world of contemporary American art with shows of such modern masters as Man Ray and Marcel Duchamp.

Galerie Montenay
6th arr. - 31, rue Mazarine - 43 54 85 30
Open 11 a.m.-1 p.m. & 2:30 p.m.-7 p.m. Closed Sun., Mon., Aug. & holidays.

Marie-Hélène Montenay is the proud possessor of one of the most beautiful galleries in her part of town. From conceptual work to figurative painting, her choices are wide-ranging and always challenging. Friedmann and Bruce Marden have their niche here, and so does Malcolm Morley.

Galerie Odermatt-Cazeau
8th arr. - 85, rue du Faubourg-Saint-Honoré - 42 66 92 58
Open 10 a.m.-6:30 p.m. Closed Sun., Aug. & holidays.

This gallery specialises in works by 19th- and 20th-century masters, Impressionists and post-Impressionists, and has fine sculpture displays (Germaine Richier, Gonzales, Zadkine).

Galerie Proscenium
6th arr. - 35, rue de Seine - 43 54 92 01
Open 10:30 a.m.-12:30 p.m. & 2:30 p.m.-7 p.m. Closed Sun., Mon., holidays & July 20-Sept. 5.

This very pretty gallery often hosts exhibitions of theatre décor and costumes, with an accent on the early 20th century: Bakst, Bérard, Cocteau, Dupont, J. Hugo and Wakevitch are the primary artists, though Erté, Pizzi and even Saint-Laurent are also represented.

Galerie Denise René
7th arr. - 196, bd Saint-Germain 42 22 77 57
Open 10 a.m.-1 p.m. & 2 p.m.-7:30 p.m. Closed Sun. & Aug.

In 1945 Denise René's pioneering gallery became the rallying point for geometrical abstraction. Since then she has sung its praises the world over and adopted the offshoots of constructivism, promoting the works of Agam, Albers, Claisse, Dewasne, Herbin, Naraha, Soto and Vasarely.

Galerie Stadler
6th arr. - 51, rue de Seine - 43 26 91 10
Open 10:30 a.m.-12:30 p.m. & 2:30 p.m.-7 p.m. Closed Sun., Mon., holidays & July 10-Sept. 10.

Since its opening in 1955, Rodolphe Stadler's gallery has been a Left Bank chapel for violent, abstractionist art. Naturally, then, the painters favoured here include Arnulf Rainer, Saura and Antonio Tàpies—artists whose canvases display plenty of texture and relief.

Leif Stahle
11th arr. - 37, rue de Charonne 48 07 24 78
Open 11 a.m.-7:30 p.m. Closings not available.

Leif Stahle, organiser of the Stockholm Festival, came to live in Paris in 1986. His beautiful, well-lit gallery is devoted to contemporary abstract art and, according to Stahle, "not just to lyrical abstraction." Such artists as Choi, Debré, Englund, Gandin, Kallos, Kinahara, Limérat, Rosenthal and Weil have found a home here.

> *Don't plan to do much shopping in Paris in August—a great many stores are closed for the entire holiday month.*

ARTS & LEISURE – ART GALLERIES

King Louis sees the light

It's hardly surprising that Louis XIV, the Sun King, preferred light to shadow—it was he who first had the bright idea of illuminating Paris at night (chiefly to discourage thieves, murderers and other criminals who operate under cover of darkness). Squads of torch-bearers were therefore hired to light up the night. Centuries later, in the 1960s, it occurred to the powers-that-be that they could show off the city's monuments (and discourage unwanted visitors) by floodlighting them after dark. New forms of street lighting are illuminating the nocturnal cityscape; colour has recently added another dimension, brightening the renovated La Villette district with splashes of red and blue.

Galerie Templon
8th arr. - 4, av. Marceau - 47 20 15 02
Open 10 a.m.-7 p.m. Closed Sun., holidays & July 25-beg. Sept.

Daniel Templon has moved out of the Beaubourg area to the sleeker surroundings of the eighth arrondissement. His new upstairs gallery exudes a distinctly New York style, and his choice of painters reflects a contemporary American sensibility. Alongside conceptual and minimalist works by Judd and Serra, there are paintings by Frank Stella and pieces by younger members of the avant-garde, such as Clemente, Chia and Cucchi. French art is represented by the likes of Debré, Appel, Alberola, Giorda and Rouan.

Galerie Patrice Trigano
6th arr. - 4 bis, rue des Beaux-Arts - 46 34 15 01
Open 10 a.m.-1 p.m. & 2:30 p.m.-6:30 p.m. Closed Sun., Mon., Aug. & holidays.

After a spell in rue Beaubourg, Patrice Trigano ferried his pictures across the Seine to the Left Bank where he specialises in art of the 1950s. He exhibits César and Harman (he started out with them) but also Atlan, Hélion, Lanskoy, Lapicque, Schneider, Bram Van Velde and Jenkins.

Galerie Zabriskie
4th arr. - 37, rue Quincampoix 42 72 35 47
Open 11 a.m.-7 p.m. Closed Sun., Mon., Aug. & holidays.

A photographic gallery where photos are presented as if they were sculpture. Weegee, Klein, Friedlander, Peter Briggs and Poivret: the gang are all here, with pictures full of vibrancy and character.

POSTERS & PRINTS

Ciné-Images
7th arr. - 68, rue de Babylone 45 51 27 50
Open noon-7 p.m. (Sat. 2 p.m.-7 p.m.). Closed Sun., Mon., Aug. & holidays. 13-Sept. 6.

Ciné-Images is dedicated to the cinema. According to the professionals, this is an absolute "must" for serious film-poster collectors. All the greats are represented.

Documents
6th arr. - 53, rue de Seine - 43 54 50 68
Open 10:30 a.m.-12:30 p.m. & 2:30 p.m.-7 p.m. Closed Sun., Mon. & 3 1st wks. of Aug.

In 1953 Michel Romand put together a collection of posters amassed by Sagot, his great-grandfather. His stock of superb original posters dating from 1875 to 1930, for sale to the public, has been responsible for his meteoric rise to success. He still has works by Toulouse-Lautrec, Mucha, Chéret, Capiello and Steinlen, among others.

Galerie Princesse, Comptoir de l'Affiche
6th arr. - 18, rue Princesse - 43 25 25 18
Open 10:30 a.m.-7:30 p.m. (Fri. & Sat. 10:30 a.m.-1 a.m.). Closed Sun. & Mon. morning. Annual closings not available.

Hand over a colour slide and 150 francs, and a week later you, too, can be a pin-up (about 15 by 20 inches). Framing is also done here, and there are reproductions—primarily of cinema posters—for sale.

A l'Imagerie
5th arr. - 9, rue Dante 43 25 18 66
Open 10:30 a.m.-1 p.m. & 2 p.m.-7 p.m. Closed Sun., Mon. morning (Mon. in July & Aug.) & holidays.

The selection of old French and foreign advertising posters (selling for 600 to 1,000 francs and up) here is delightful. There are also Belle Epoque lithographs, some 1925 stencils and Japanese prints.

Nouvelles Images
5th arr. - 6, rue Dante 43 25 62 43
Open 11 a.m.-7 p.m. Closed Sun. & holidays.

Among this wide-ranging choice of posters, there are pieces to suit everyone. In addition, you will find postcards, and books on painting, architecture and contemporary photography. Posters from the national museums as well as those issued by major galleries are for sale.

HOBBIES & SPORTS

ART SUPPLIES

Adam Montparnasse
14th arr. - 11, bd Edgar-Quinet - 43 20 68 53
Open 9:30 a.m.-7 p.m. Closed Sun., holidays (except Nov. 11), & 2 wks. in Aug.

For three generations, the Adam family has supplied artists and graphics designers with all the canvas, paper, paint and ink they need, in every possible colour and size. If you want references, how about Braque, Soutine and Modigliani? They have all shopped here, and appreciated the sage advice dispensed by the competent staff.

Sennelier
7th arr. - 3, quai Voltaire - 42 60 72 15
Open 9 a.m.-6:30 p.m. (Mon. & summer 9 a.m.-noon & 2 p.m.-6:30 p.m.). Closed Sun. & holidays.

Appropriately situated next to the Beaux-Arts school, Sennelier has, in its century of existence, sold tons of art supplies to innumerable established and aspiring artists. Here they find the best brands of paints and pigments, paper and sketch pads of excellent quality, canvas, easels and framing equipment. Sculptors too can purchase all their special supplies here.

ASTRONOMY

La Maison de l'Astronomie
4th arr. - 33, rue de Rivoli - 42 77 99 55, fax 48 87 40 87
Open 9:45 a.m.-6:45 p.m. Closed Sun., Mon. & holidays.

This shop specialises in books, posters and sky maps pertaining to astronomy, as well as equipment for searching the heavens: telescopes, photo equipment, binoculars. There are introductory courses in astronomy as well as a course in astronomic photography.

CYCLING

Paris By Cycle
14th arr. - 78, rue de l'Ouest - 40 47 08 04
Open daily 9 a.m.-1 p.m. & 2 p.m.-7:30 p.m.

Rent a city bicycle or a mountain bike by the hour (28 francs) or by the week (300 francs) from this competent, friendly team of specialists. A wide selection of bicycles is available for purchase, and there is a repair shop on the premises.

Paris Vélo (Rent a bike)
5th arr. - 2, rue du Fer-à-Moulin - 43 37 59 22
Open April 1-Sept. 30: 10 a.m.-12:30 p.m. & 2 p.m.-7 p.m.; Oct. 1-March 31: until 6 p.m. Closed Sun.

Bicycle rental by the hour, day or weekend. No racing bikes here, but you'll find plenty of city models and mountain bikes—the most practical varieties for the local terrain.

BOWLING

Bowling Mouffetard
5th arr. - 13, rue Gracieuse - 43 31 09 35
Open daily 11 a.m.-2 a.m.

One of this bowling alley's eight lanes can be yours for 20 francs plus 6 francs for shoe-hire (afternoon rate); or 24 francs plus shoes (evening rate). During weekends and holidays, the cost rises to 30 francs. While you wait your turn, you can play pool or pinball, or have a sandwich at the snack bar.

COOKING

Le Cordon Bleu
15th arr. - 8, rue Léon-Delhomme - 48 56 06 06
Open 9 a.m.-6:30 p.m. Closed Sat., Sun. & holidays.

Cooking enthusiasts can attend daily demonstrations given by master chefs (English-language translation available). If you are more interested in hands-on experience, week-long courses are given in 20 types of regional cuisine, cakemaking, bistro cooking and so on. Professional training leading to a Cordon Bleu diploma is also available (about 30,000 francs a term).

Ecole de Gastronomie Française Ritz-Escoffier
1st arr. - 38, rue Cambon - 42 60 38 30
Open 9 a.m.-6 p.m. Closed Sat. & Sun. Prices: Ritz-Escoffier course 68,400 F / 12 wks.; César-Ritz course 1 to 6 wks 5,550 F / wk. for 28 h.

The school's facilities are set up opposite the kitchens where 19th-century chef Auguste Escoffier exercised his incomparable art. Aspiring cooks can learn every aspect of the trade here, with professional-level courses; amateurs may register for the César-Ritz cycle, which lasts from one to six weeks. Each week, students attend four practical cooking and pâtisserie courses, watch four demonstrations and take one theoretical course (cheese, wine, etc.). For 220 francs, anyone can attend a demonstration performed by a master chef. English-language courses are offered.

Princesse Ere 2001
7th arr. - 18, av. de La Motte-Picquet - 45 51 36 34
Open 10:30 a.m.-2 p.m. Closed Sat. & Sun. Prices: 580 F / course

ARTS & LEISURE – HOBBIES & SPORTS

or 3,000 F for 6 courses, lunch incl.; 650 F / course or 3,400 F for 6 courses directed by G. Sallé, lunch incl.

Regional cooking, market-based cooking, cuisine nouvelle and, as of this year, low-calorie cooking and the art of hospitality make up the curriculum here. Courses are taught by Marie Blanche de Broglie and Gérard Sallé (chef of the Régence restaurant in the Hôtel Plaza-Athénée). In addition to French, the lessons are given in English and Spanish. In August and September, the school takes up its summer quarters in Normandy (11,000 francs per week, full board included).

DANCE

Marais
4th arr. - 41, rue du Temple - 42 72 15 42
Open daily 9 a.m.-9 p.m. Prices: 78 F / course (1h30); 280 F for 4 courses; 480 F for 8 courses.

Everything is taught here—from the Argentine tango and contemporary Japanese *buto* dancing to African dance, flamenco or Brazilian and Asian dances. There are 32 disciplines in all, taught in somewhat tumbledown surroundings but in a friendly, non-threatening atmosphere.

GAMES

Game's
1st arr. - Forum des Halles, level -2 - 40 26 46 06
Open 10 a.m.-7:30 p.m. Closed Sun.

This is a grown-ups' game shop featuring chess sets carved in precious woods or onyx, electronic games, brain-teaser puzzles, billiards, roulette wheels, slot machines and more. Also, role-playing games complete with instruction books (in French and English) and figurines.

Jeux Descartes
5th arr. - 52, rue des Ecoles - 43 26 79 83
Open 10 a.m.-7 p.m. (Mon. 11 a.m.-7 p.m.). Closed Sun.

American games of strategy and intelligence (in English) may be purchased here, as well as collectible historical figurines and old-fashioned board games.

Stratéjeux
14th arr. - 13, rue Poirier-de-Narçay - 45 45 45 87
Open 10:30 a.m.-7 p.m. Closed Sun.

Every Wednesday and Saturday afternoon, Stratéjeux hosts demonstrations of strategy games. All the equipment needed for strategy games and role-playing games are sold in this unobtrusive little shop.

Le Train Bleu
6th arr. - 55, rue Saint-Placide - 45 48 33 78
16th arr. - 2-6, av. Mozart - 42 88 34 70
Open 10 a.m.-7 p.m. Closed Sun.

This is a luxury supermarket for toys and games. The basement level is reserved for adult games, but all ages are amused by the fun buys for kids sold on the other three floors.

GARDENINING & FLOWER ARRANGING

Centre d'Art Floral Ikebana
17th arr. - 26, rue d'Armaillé - 45 74 21 28
Call for information. Entrance fee: 100 F / year; courses: 380 F / day (3 courses incl.).

The tradition of Japanese flower arranging was originally a religious practice developed by Buddhist monks. There are several different schools of Ikebana in Japan. At this address you will be taught the pure and simple style of Ohara. Greenery is included in the price of the lessons, but bring your own shears.

Ecole d'Horticulture du Jardin du Luxembourg
6th arr. - 64, bd Saint-Michel - 45 48 55 55
Open Oct.-Dec.: Thurs. & Sat. 8 a.m.-noon.

Register in May for courses on decorative gardens, or on the proper cultivation of fruit trees. The courses are free, but the number of places is limited.

Société Nationale d'Horticulture de France
7th arr. - 84, rue de Grenelle - 45 48 81 00
Open Tues. & Thurs. 6 p.m.-7 p.m. Entrance fee: 145 F / year.

Only association members are admitted to SNHF courses (the membership fee is 145 francs). Eight different courses are given, including an introduction to gardening, the cultivation of roses, house plants, flower arranging and so on. This is where you can learn to graft trees or create a garden on your balcony.

GOLF

Club de Golf de l'Etoile
17th arr. - 10, av. de la Grande-Armée - 43 80 30 79
Open 8 a.m.-8:30 p.m. (Sat. 9 a.m.-5 p.m. & Sun. 10 a.m.-5 p.m.). Membership: 1,650 F / 6 months; 2,450 F / year; 60 F / 30 mn. Closed Sun. July-Sept.

Polish your putting at this lovely practice range situated in a rooftop greenhouse; you can also loosen up your drive at one of the seven practice tees, or use a video simulation to help improve your swing. Eight highly qualified professionals are on hand to teach beginners the basics, as well as to give veteran players advice on how to achieve a better game. You needn't even bring

HOBBIES & SPORTS – ARTS & LEISURE

your clubs: all equipment is provided free of extra charge.

HEALTH CLUBS

Club Jean de Beauvais
5th arr. - 5, rue Jean-de-Beauvais
46 33 16 80
Open 7 a.m.-10:30 p.m. (Wed. & Fri. 7 a.m.-10 p.m.; Sat. 8:30 a.m.-7 p.m.; Sun. 9:30 a.m.-5 p.m.).

A doctor supervises your progress, a chiropractor advises you, a gym instructor personally takes charge of your training and a nutritionist supervises your diet. For those who have decided, finally, to take themselves in hand, it's a complete overhaul. For sporting types just looking for a tune-up, there's ski readiness in autumn and windsurfing preparation in spring. Annual membership rates range from 3,200 francs (for off-peak hours) to 6,150 francs.

Espace Vit'Halles
3rd arr. - Place Beaubourg, 48, rue Rambuteau - 42 77 21 71
Open 9 a.m.-10 p.m. (Sat. 11 a.m.-7 p.m.; Sun. 11 a.m.-3 p.m.). Closed Dec. 25 & Jan. 1.

Nearly 120 classes per week are given by the centre's 20 instructors in cardiovascular fitness, body-building and strengthening. Body sculpting, stretching and workouts for specific figure problems are just some of the options available. For relaxing after a workout, there are saunas, a Turkish bath, Jacuzzi and massage services. Personal trainers are on hand to design individualised fitness programmes (200 francs an hour); other fees vary. The facilities are well-kept and clean, pleasant to use but unpretentious. Information on short-term rates is available on request.

Gymnase Club
1st arr. - 147 bis, rue Saint-Honoré - 40 20 03 03 (also: 11th, 12th, 13th, 14th, 15th, 17th, La Défense & Neuilly)
Open 7:30 a.m.-10 p.m. (Sat. 9 a.m.-7 p.m.; Sun. 9 a.m.-5 p.m.). Closed May 1, Dec. 25 & Jan. 1. Subcription 3,200-3,650 F / year.

This chain of fitness clubs has centres all over Paris. Several have swimming pools and offer classes in aqua-gym, though this particular centre does not. But the menu of activities does comprise cardio-training, strengthening, body-building and modern jazz dance. Among the post-workout attractions are a whirlpool bath, a sauna and a Turkish bath. Competent staff can design a fitness programme that meets individual needs, and for short-term visitors, books of tickets for a limited number of entries may be obtained at the clubs.

Thermes du Royal Monceau
8th arr. - 39, av. Hoche - 42 25 06 66
Open daily 7 a.m.-11 p.m. Membership: 15,000 F / year.

Sporting-type nymphs lounge by the pool, millionaires pedal away in a superbly equipped, rarely crowded workout room. The personnel are discreetly attentive—from the gym instructor to the masseuse, the make-up artist to the beautician. A classical air is provided by a décor that features Doric columns, an oval pool under a Roman-style glass roof, mosaics, frescoes, lots of plants, comfortable sofas and luxurious Turkish baths. The emphasis here is more on relaxation than on hard-core waistline maintenance. Membership for one year costs 15,000 francs.

Vitatop Club Plein Ciel
15th arr. - 8, rue Louis-Armand
45 54 79 00
Open 7 a.m.-9 p.m. (Sat. 9 a.m.-7 p.m.; Sun. 9 a.m.-5 p.m.). Closed Dec. 25 & Jan. 1.

The membership fees are high (800 francs entrance fee, plus 5,150 francs a year) but the variety of services is undoubtedly the widest in town. Vitatop members have unlimited access to all Gymnase Club centres (see above), and get preferential rates at the chain's tennis courts and golf practice ranges. Vitatop's state-of-the-art fitness equipment includes Stairmasters, electronic stationary bikes, rowing machines and a Gravitron; and each club offers a pool (also used for popular aqua-gym classes), Jacuzzi, comfortable dressing rooms and showers, a sauna and so forth. Courses are offered all

---

Paradise behind the walls

You'll have a better grasp of the original meaning of paradise—"walled garden"—when you visit the flower- and fountain-filled courtyards nestled within the white walls of the *Paris Mosque*. Built in 1922 in a predominantly Moroccan style, it also houses a library, Turkish baths, restaurant and tea rooms. The interior is sumptuous, with stucco, carved wood, mosaics and carpets reminiscent of a more leisurely age. Another view of Islam is afforded by the *Institute of the Arab World* on the nearby quai Saint-Bernard, a futuristic nine-storey structure of glass, concrete and aluminium that includes a museum, art gallery and documentation centre.

ARTS & LEISURE – HOBBIES & SPORTS

day long in fitness and related disciplines (jogging, personal health/nutrition supervision) for no extra charge.

ICE SKATING

Patinoire des Buttes-Chaumont
19th arr. - 30, rue Edouard Pailleron - 42 39 86 10
Open Mon., Tues. & Fri. 4:30 p.m.-6:15 p.m.; Wed. 10 a.m.-5 p.m.; Thurs. 4:30 p.m.-9 p.m.; Sat. 10 a.m.-5 p.m. & 8:30 p.m.-midnight; Sun. 10 a.m.-6 p.m. Closed mid May-beg. Sept. Prices: adults: 25 F; under 16: 20 F; groups: 25 F (skates incl.); skates rental: 15 F.

The one and only ice-skating rink in Paris. Ice dancers and speed-skaters are given run of the rink for 15 minutes each hour.

MUSIC

Andres Serrita
9th arr. - 25, rue de Bruxelles 42 80 40 25
Telephone information available mornings.

This is a friendly place where you can learn how to play the guitar.

François Guidon
9th arr. - 16, rue Victor-Massé 48 78 91 05
Open 2 p.m.-7 p.m. Closed Sat., Sun. & holidays.

François Guidon buys, restores and sells jazz guitars. Moulded instruments command between 8,000 and 12,000 francs, while hand-made guitars (constructed like cellos) go for about twice that price.

Hamm
6th arr. - 135-139, rue de Rennes 44 39 35 35
Open 10 a.m.-7 p.m. (Mon. 2 p.m.-7 p.m.), 2 Sun. in Dec. Closed Sun. & Mon. in July & Aug., holidays.

Hamm's is assuredly one of the city's best sources of all types of musical instruments. Six floors display pianos and synthesisers, percussion and wind instruments, guitars and even a selection of antiques. Small studios can also be hired here, for rehearsals or lessons.

Le Projet Musical
10th arr. - 23, rue du Faubourg-Saint-Denis - 42 46 27 26
Open 11 a.m.-10 p.m. Closed Sun., holidays & school holidays. Price: 62-120 F / h.

Instruments are taught individually, and musical theory in small groups. Top-notch instruction in all instruments, classical or jazz, as well as voice training is offered at this school, which is subsidised by the City of Paris.

NEEDLEWORK

L'Atelier de la Dentellière
13th arr. - 9, rue de Patay - 45 86 14 78
Call for information.

Under the tutelage of Lysianne Brulet, professor of lace-making, you'll learn how to use linen, cotton or silk thread with finesse to make lace trim for curtains, blouses and napkins. This painstaking work teaches the lovely rewards of patience.

La Droguerie
1st arr. - 9, rue du Jour - 45 08 93 27
Open 10:30 a.m.-6:45 p.m. (Mon. 2 p.m.-6:45 p.m.). Closed Sun.

Here is a gold mine for knitting fanatics. Not only will you find the needles and wool you seek, you can also count on the sales staff to help you get the hang of an unusually difficult stitch. And that's not all: the shop stocks a dazzling selection of trims—multi-coloured beads, feathers, sequins and such are stored in antique sweet jars and sold by the ladleful.

R. Malbranche
9th arr. - 17, rue Drouot - 47 70 03 77
Open 9 a.m.-noon & 2 p.m.-6 p.m. Closed Sat., Sun., Aug. & holidays.

For sale here are linen sheets, muslin napkins, linen handkerchiefs and cambric placemats all delicately embroidered by hand—in short, it's the household linen of your dreams. You can learn how to make these masterpieces of patience yourself. Courses are taught by an award-winning needlewoman on Thursday afternoons (eight two-hour classes cost 650 francs). You'll be taught all the basic stitches plus some of the more complicated ones that require real concentration.

RACETRACKS

Hippodrome d'Auteuil
Bois de Boulogne, 16th arr. - 45 27 12 25
Openings vary.

The *Prix du Président de la République*, a race for French steeplechasers, is run here each year.

Hippodrome de Longchamp
Bois de Boulogne, 16th arr. - 42 24 13 29
Openings vary.

Home to the prestigious *Prix de l'Arc de Triomphe*, a highlight of the year's racing calendar.

Hippodrome de Vincennes
12th arr. - Bois de Vincennes, 2, route de la Ferme - 43 68 35 39
Openings vary.

The big event at this track is the yearly *Prix d'Amérique*.

RIDING

Centre Equestre de la Cartoucherie de Vincennes
12th arr. - Rue du Champ-des-Manœuvres - 43 74 61 25
Open 9 a.m.-noon & 2 p.m.-9:30 p.m. (Sun. 9 a.m.-noon). Closed July & Aug. Entrance fee: 150 F (life time). Membership: 400 F / year. Courses: 980 F / term (1 course / wk.).

Indoor and outdoor riding lessons are given here, in the middle of the Bois de Vincennes. Riders who have proved their steadiness in the saddle are permitted to join groups for all-day outings in the forest. Small children may be introduced to equestrian pleasures at the Centre's pony club.

Club Hippique de la Villette
19th arr. - 9, bd Mac-Donald - 40 34 33 33
Open 9 a.m.-noon & 1:30 p.m.-9 p.m. (Sat. 9 a.m.-9 p.m., Sun. 9 a.m.-1 p.m.). Closed July, Aug. & Sept.

On the plus side, this club offers modern facilities, well-cared-for horses reputed for their gentleness, and a spacious indoor ring. Unfortunately, with no woods in the vicinity, students have no opportunities for excursions.

ROCK CLIMBING

La Samaritaine (Magasin 3)
1st arr. - Rue de Rivoli - 40 41 20 20
Open 9:30 a.m.-7 p.m. (Thurs. 9:30 a.m.-10 p.m.). Closed Sun., Dec. 25 & Jan. 1. Free.

Before tackling the Alps or the Pyrenees (or the fascinating rock formations in the Fontainebleau Forest), perfect your rock-climbing technique on this practice wall. Beginners and seasoned climbers alike will be challenged by the wall's hollows, toe-holds, bumps and projections. Equipment for a mountain holiday is sold in the basement of La Samaritaine's shop number three.

SWIMMING

Aquaboulevard
15th arr. - 4, rue Louis-Armand 40 60 10 00
Open 7:30 a.m.-11 p.m. (Sat. & Sun. 8 a.m.-midnight).

Aquaboulevard made quite a splash when it opened its doors in 1989. The centrepiece of this gigantic sports, fitness and leisure complex is an "aquatic park": the biggest pool in Paris, complete with water slides, rapids, toboggans and other fun equipment that drives kids wild with joy. But water sports are only part of the action. Other possibilities include tennis, squash, bowling, billiards, bridge, table tennis and video games. You can work out at the gym, spruce up at the beauty salons or enjoy a meal at one of several restaurants. Examples of the cost: 75 francs for an adult admission at weekends (children: 55 francs), plus 200 francs per hour for tennis, 60 francs per half-hour for squash... The annual fee is 300 francs per person.

Piscine les Amiraux
18th arr. - 6, rue Hermann-la-Chapelle - 46 06 46 47
Hours vary. Entrance: 9.50 F.

This beautiful pool, vintage 1930, is an architectural landmark. Open until 7:30 p.m. on Mondays, for people who like a quick dip after work.

Piscine de la Butte-aux-Cailles
13th arr. - 5, pl. Paul-Verlaine 45 89 60 05
Hours vary. Entrance: 9.50 F.

Set in a picturesque district, this lovely Art Deco establishment offers three pools. The largest is indoors, but the two others are outdoor pools, fed by an artesian well.

> Clean, attractive municipal swimming pools can be found all over Paris; locating one that is open at a given hour is less easy, since timetables vary greatly. A *free booklet*, available from the attendants at any of the city's 28 public pools, will give you specific addresses, opening hours and pool sizes, along with a colour picture of each facility. The entrance fee for city pools is currently 10 francs. Regular swimmers can purchase a three-month pass for 146 francs. Listed below is a selection of some of the prettier pools.

Piscine Champerret-Yser
17th arr. - 32-36, bd de Reims 47 66 49 98
Hours vary. Entrance: Adults: 20 F (under 16: 16 F).

Bright, new and modern, with a spiral sliding board that youngsters adore, this pool is enclosed by tall glass walls. There are tennis courts on the premises.

Piscine Deligny
7th arr. - 25, quai Anatole-France 45 51 72 15
Open 8:30 a.m.-7:30 p.m. Closed Oct. 16-April 30. Entrance: 50 F (students: 40 F, under 16: 35 F, mattress: 70 F).

This privately owned pool, moored along the banks of the Seine, has earned a reputation as a hot spot to flirt. It could hardly be otherwise, given the crowds, the limited space and

ARTS & LEISURE – MUSEUMS

the bathers' skimpy attire. Although (or maybe because) the sunbathing areas are overpopulated, swimmers usually have plenty of room in the pool.

Piscine Henry-de-Montherlant
16th arr. - 32, bd Lannes - 45 03 03 28
Hours vary. Entrance: 9.50 F.

Set in a chic part of Paris close to the Bois de Boulogne, this municipal pool is part of a sports complex that includes tennis courts and a gymnasium.

Piscine Jean-Taris
5th arr. - 16, rue Thouin - 43 25 54 03
Hours vary. Entrance: 10 F (under 16: 5 F).

Students favour this splendid pool, which boasts a view of the Panthéon and the gardens of the Lycée Henri-IV. A special system makes it accessible to disabled people.

Piscine Suzanne-Berlioux
1st arr. - 10, place de la Rotonde 42 36 98 44
Hours vary. Entrance: 20 F (under 16: 15 F).

This new, 50 by 20 metre pool in the Forum des Halles is open several evenings a week.

If you're visiting Paris and wish to play tennis without spending huge sums on private clubs, contact *Allô-Sports* (42 76 54 54), a municipal sports hotline, for information on public and municipal courts. If your French is not up to that try one of the following addresses.

TENNIS & SQUASH

Stade Henry de Montherlant
16th arr. - 48, bd Lannes - 45 03 03 64
Call for information.

When available, these public courts can be reserved 24 hours in advance, for a small fee.

Squash Montmartre
18th arr. - 14, rue Achille-Martinet - 42 55 38 30
Open 10 a.m.-10:30 p.m. (Sat. & Sun. 10 a.m.-7:30 p.m.).

If you schedule your game in off-peak hours (10 a.m. to 5:30 p.m.) you can play at reduced rates on these fine, well-lit courts, then relax in the sauna, on the terrace or in the billiard room. Several different rate structures are offered, and trial memberships are available too.

Tennis du Luxembourg
6th arr. - Jardins du Luxembourg 43 25 79 18
Open 8 a.m.-4:30 p.m. Price: 12.50 F / 30 mn.

The six open courts are usually reserved well in advance by clubs and associations, but there is no reason not to try your luck...

MUSEUMS

MAJOR MUSEUMS

Cité des Sciences et de l'Industrie
19th arr. - 30, av. Corentin-Cariou - 40 05 80 00
Open 10 a.m.-6 p.m. Closed Mon. Cafeterias. Access for the disabled.

A *cité* indeed—or maybe a citadel of knowledge. This gigantic steel, glass and concrete structure—formerly a meat-packing plant—casts a formidable shadow across the Parc de la Villette, with its geodome and moats set along the Ourcq Canal in northeast Paris. It is the world's largest science and industry museum, designed for the 21st century. In the outsized 120-foot-high entrance hall hangs a scale model of a space station with astronauts at work. Yet once you get over that initial dizzy spell, you'll find that the Cité is, paradoxically, on a human scale. Floors are divided into modular cells, which are shuffled around to create scenic effects. Visitors are challenged to penetrate the mysteries of science. And we've found that it is best to be curious—and daring. Get the most out of the Cité by examining and playing with the exhibits. Then sit back and contemplate. Scores of computer terminals beckon, ready to measure your knowledge, to lead you through experiences in weightlessness or travelling at the speed of sound, to activate robots, take you on a trip through outer space, heighten your senses, or put you in touch with experts in myriad fields of knowledge. Of particular interest to children are the Inventorium (Level 3) with its fascinating exhibits that make science "friendly" and fun; and the Géode cinema. Just visiting that imposing stainless-steel sphere is a treat, but actually viewing a film projected by the Omnimax system (enhanced with holograms and lasers) is an experience no child will forget in a hurry.

Galerie Nationale du Jeu de Paume
1st arr. - Jardin des Tuileries, corner place de la Concorde/ rue de Rivoli - 47 03 12 50
Open noon-7 p.m. (Tues. until 9:30 p.m., Sat. & Sun. from 10 a.m.). Closed Mon.

When its treasure trove of Impressionist masterpieces was ferried across the river to the new Musée d'Orsay, the Jeu de Paume lost its *raison d'être*. Then, a few years ago, it was decided that the space could be most advantageously used as a showcase for contemporary art. Magnificently restructured by architect Antoine Stinco, the museum was relaunched in 1991 by a dynamic team of art professionals. The inaugural exhibit, dedicated to Jean Dubuffet, was a resounding success. Subsequent shows featuring Ellsworth Kelly, the Belgian poet/painter Broedthaers and photographers Tunga and Jana Sterbak, among others, also won great acclaim. The new Jeu de Paume combines the prestige of a national art institution with the excitement of an avant-garde gallery, plugged in to the way artists work today.

Musée d'Art Moderne de la Ville de Paris

16th arr. - 11, av. du Président-Wilson - 47 23 61 27
Open 10 a.m.-5:30 p.m. (Wed. until 8:30 p.m.). Closed Mon. & holidays. Temporary exhibitions. Access for the disabled.

The MAM—as this museum is called—has always been a whirlwind of change. But while collections may waltz in and out, the various "isms" of modern art are always represented: from Fauvism (Vlaminck and Derain) to cubism (Picasso and Braque) to cinetism (Vasarely, Agam). It is your opportunity to view a remarkable series of paintings by Rouault and Gromaire, compositions by Robert and Sonia Delaunay, works by Léger, Soutine, Chagall, Pascin and others. And, of course, still on view is the celebrated *Electricity Fairy* by Raoul Dufy and Matisse's terrific triptych, *Dance*. The fourth-level ARC (*Animation, Recherche, Confrontation*) is the liveliest section of the museum, used primarily to showcase contemporary art forms (plastic arts, photography, poetry, contemporary music and jazz). Often, several shows and events run simultaneously, with an accent on new talent. The children's museum is designed to acquaint youngsters (and their parents) with modern art (the entrance is at 14, avenue de New-York).

Musée des Arts Décoratifs

1st arr. - Palais du Louvre, 107, rue de Rivoli - 42 60 32 14
Open 12:30 p.m.-6 p.m. (Sun. noon-6 p.m.). Closed Mon. & Tues. Temporary exhibitions. Access for the disabled.

The Gallic taste for living in beauty and comfort comes vividly alive in the 100-odd rooms and galleries of the Musée des Arts Décoratifs, which traces the history of French homes from the Middle Ages to the present. One-of-a-kind and mass-produced tapestries, ceramics, tableware and furniture demonstrate how taste, form and style have evolved. The exquisite suite of 1920s Art Deco rooms was crafted for fashion designer Jeanne Lanvin. Avant-garde designs by Breuer, Perriand and others flank creations by Eames, Tallon and Paulin in a sweeping panorama of the last 50 years of French and international design. Recent additions: the delightful 18th- and 20th-century toy collection, plus a handsome gift—paintings and sculptures (1942–1966) by Jean Dubuffet. Extensive reference sections cover wallpapers, textiles and patterns (by appointment only). The museum library (109, rue de Rivoli) holds a treasure trove of documentation on arts and crafts, and the museum boutique proposes an alluring collection of books and gifts.

Musée de l'Homme

16th arr. - Palais de Chaillot, pl. du Trocadéro - 45 53 70 60
Open 9:45 a.m.-5:15 p.m. Closed Tues. & holidays.

No longer a daunting jumble amassed over the years, the museum's renovated entrance hall—with its design showcases—as well as the anthropology and Africa sections, are a great success. Descriptions and displays are now easy for the layman to understand. But that's just the tip of the iceberg: the Arctic room is enjoying a warm renaissance, with superb collections unfrozen from the warehouse. The heavenly planetarium whisks visitors across five continents to follow humans and their evolution, their arts and crafts, rites and religions. Don't miss the Chinese theatre costumes, African masks, Indian jewellery, Eskimo sculptures and other oddities from distant lands. But when will the amazing Aztec skull in polished quartz escape from its safe-deposit box?

Musée du Louvre

1st arr. - Cour Napoléon - 40 20 53 17 or 40 20 51 51 (anwsering machine in English)
Open 9 a.m.-6 p.m. (Mon. & Wed. 9 a.m.-10 p.m.). Closed Tues.

The Musée du Louvre, traditionally France's greatest museum, has become the Grand Louvre, reborn with a sparkling glass pyramid designed by Chinese-American architect I. M. Pei. The 200-plus halls and Grande Galerie, the miles of wall space, are still being remodelled and reorganised. Even the once-confusing signs indicating directions to the *Mona Lisa*, the *Venus de Milo* or, for that matter, the toilets, have been rethought. Why? The Louvre's three million or so annual visitors (60 to 80 per cent of whom are foreigners) were exhausted after losing their way among the museum's more than 400,000 catalogued works of art. The prestige of the museum had been in steady decline—hardly surprising since this former palace of kings had remained static for nearly 200 years (it opened on August 10, 1793, as the Muséum Central des Arts). How could the situation be remedied while maintaining the architectural integrity of the buildings (repeatedly stormed, burned, enlarged and redesigned over the last five centuries)? Pei's answer was a huge underground complex with reception and ticket areas, restoration laboratories, gift shops and parking facilities. In addition, the Ministry of Finance offices were transferred from the Rivoli Wing of the palace to a new site at Bercy, on the Seine. (Restoration of the Rivoli Wing and its courtyards will continue for several more years.)

Now that all the hubbub has died down, people are noticing that Pei's controversial glass pyramid rises a mere 67 feet above the Cour Napoléon. Flanked by three smaller pyramids and several reflecting pools, it is in essence a high-tech skylight and entrance. In the vast void beneath, a futuristic helicoidal staircase-cum-lift, plus a bank of double escalators, should help control traffic flow. From inside the pyramid, the view of Lefuel's 1853 facades is marvellous. An unexpected bonus: archaeological excavations uncovered the foundations of the ancient Louvre palace (along with some 25,000 objects from the Middle Ages). The admirably restored crypt, now open to the public, features an imposing section of wall from 1660, the Saint-Louis hall from the 13th century and the Philippe-Auguste tower. Three giant temporary exhibit halls and an auditorium round out the Cour Napoléon complex. If you've been put off by the Louvre in the past, we urge you to give it another go. You're sure to be impressed with the improvements that now make it possible to view 3,000 years worth of world art in a coherent, convenient way (though not, of course, in a single day!).

Crowds in the Louvre

Watch out, the crowds in the Musée du Louvre are heavy in the early morning, especially during summer. To have a quiet look at the Venus of Milo, the Victory of Samothrace, the Mona Lisa or other masterpieces of the collections, come in the afternoon after 3 p.m. And if you dream of being alone—or almost alone—in the galleries, plan your visit on a Monday or a Wednesday at the end of the day: the musuem is then open until 10 p.m.

Musée de la Marine
16th arr. - Palais de Chaillot, pl. du Trocadéro - 45 53 31 70
Open 10 a.m.-6 p.m. Closed Tues. Guided tours, conferences, temporary exhibitions. Access for the disabled.

The world's largest maritime collection is solidly moored at Trocadéro, where waves of enthusiastic youngsters regularly inundate the Musée de la Marine. They may sail right by the magnificent Joseph Vernet paintings, but they always go overboard for the antique and modern navigational instruments, the sidearms and cannons, the old charts and the countless scale-model ships, which cover five centuries of maritime history: caravels (small 15th- and 16th-century sailing ships), galleys, royal vessels, yachts, frigates, trawlers, warships and atomic submarines. Favourites are Napoleon's golden-winged longboat and the stomach-churning wreckage of the *Juste*, which went down in 1725 with over 500 men on board and was discovered in 1968. Deep-sea divers in a grotto, diving suits and the first sailboard to cross the North Atlantic (1985) are among the museum's fascinating flotsam. The library and photo archives are awash with documents. Before setting sail, we like to stop for a view of the Trocadéro gardens or drop anchor on the terrace of Le Totem bar/restaurant.

Musée Marmottan
16th arr. - 2, rue Louis-Boilly - 42 24 07 02
Open 10 a.m.-5:30 p.m. Closed Mon., May 1 & Dec. 25.

This Sleeping Beauty's Castle of a museum (First Empire furniture, knick-knacks and paintings, admirable tapestries from the reign of Louis XII) awoke one day in 1970 in an explosion of colour and light when the works of Claude Monet and fellow Impressionists burst onto the scene. More than 165 oils, sketches and watercolours by Monet were donated, a stunning complement to the Donop de Monchy gift. This is the home of Monet's *Water Lilies*, plus major works by Pierre-Auguste Renoir, Camille Pissarro, Alfred Sisley... a premier Impressionism showcase. In 1987 a new Impressionist collection, the Duhem, was installed on the first floor in newly refurbished rooms. We were as thunderstruck by Paul Gauguin's *Bouquet de Fleurs* as we were thrilled to see Monet's *Impression, Soleil Levant* back in place (stolen in

MUSEUMS – ARTS & LEISURE

1985, it was returned not long ago). Don't miss the Wildenstein collection of illuminated medieval manuscripts—they are extraordinary.

Musée National d'Art Moderne Centre Georges Pompidou
4th arr. - 120, rue Saint-Martin
44 78 12 33
Open noon-10 p.m. (Sat., Sun. & holidays 10 a.m.-10 p.m.). Closed Tues. & May 1. Restaurant, bar, cafeteria. Access for the disabled.

When it opened on 31 January 1977, the Centre Georges Pompidou was called a hideous oil refinery, destined to rust away before the very eyes of a disgusted public. Fifteen years later, it is recognised as an architectural landmark, the embodiment of a certain "romantic" vision of hi-tech. Nearly 100 million visitors have passed through its modern art galleries, museum, cinemas, concert hall, vast library (with many books in English), exhibition areas, industrial creation centre, periodicals room and record archives (with extensive listening facilities). Since space is limited, the Centre is constantly being remodelled and enlarged. The latest metamorphosis of note: the permanent collection rooms on the third and fourth floors, which have been "rebuilt" by Italian architect Gae Aulenti (also responsible for the interior of the Musée d'Orsay). The result was a sorely needed reshuffle of the museum's 17,000 works (exhibits change several times a year). The permanent collection traces the history of modern art from 1914 onwards. Only the Museum of Modern Art in New York rivals it in scope. One of the two screening rooms of the Cinémathèque (National Film Archives) is located in the building. And the sloping plaza in front teems with jugglers, mime artists, palm readers, portrait painters, musicians, fire-eaters and other exotic specimens of humanity. And there's always the astonishing view of Paris rooftops from the top-floor restaurant—from the twin towers of Notre-Dame to the pearly domes of Sacré Coeur. Take note that the Centre's *Librairie* is one of Paris's best-stocked art bookshops, carrying deluxe editions published by the Centre (architecture, film, music and so forth), plus temporary-exhibit catalogues, many of which have become collector's items.

Musée d'Orsay
7th arr. - 1, rue de Bellechasse
45 49 48 14
Open 10 a.m.-6 p.m. (Thurs. 10 a.m.-9:45 p.m. & Sun. 9 a.m.-6 p.m.). Closed Mon., Dec. 25 & Jan. 1.

Storm in a teacup department: just like the Eiffel Tower, the Pompidou Centre and the Louvre Pyramid, the Musée d'Orsay was lashed by waves of criticism when it first opened. And now, just a few years after President Mitterrand snipped the ribbon, there is little or no sign of the appalling verbal squall that surrounded the opening of the museum. The Musée d'Orsay is a resounding success. To think that this former railway station was due for demolition, judged a prime example of horrid *fin de siècle* taste (it was designed in 1900 by architect Victor Laloux). The derelict station's exterior and frame were restored and strengthened—a careful work of preservation and enhancement. Italian architect Gae Aulenti worked her peculiar magic on the vast interior. The result is impressive. Now the Grand Central Terminal of 19th-century art, the Musée d'Orsay's collections trace the jagged path of painting, sculpture, photography, decorative and industrial art from 1848 to 1914. Thanks largely to generous donations from intrepid patrons of the arts, the work of greats formerly outside the mainstream, from Gustave Courbet to Edouard Manet and the Impressionists, now have a stunning home in the Orsay. Among the Orsay's finest: Honoré Daumier's classic 36-bust series *Les Parlementaires* (1832); Claude Monet's *Rue Montorgueil* (1878), bursting with noisy life; Georges Seurat's pointillistic *Poseuse de Dos*, seemingly composed of little more than air and light; and Giovanni Boldini's Proustian *Portrait de Madame Max* (1896). The museum bookshop is large and well stocked; the gift shop displays many lovely and culturally correct trinkets sure to please someone.

Musée du Petit Palais
8th arr. - 1, av. Dutuit - 42 65 12 73
Open 10 a.m.-5:40 p.m. Closed Mon. & holidays.

Built in 1900 For the *Exposition Universelle*, the Petit Palais is distinguished by its stone-and-iron frame, and its rococo galleries decorated with allegories and ornate cupolas are excellent examples of the architecture of the time. Its eccentric permanent collection is largely neglected, which means you'll be able to enjoy an unobscured view of the exquisite Dutuit donation (works from antiquity to the 17th century), featuring rare examples of Egyptian and Greek art, and the sumptuous Rembrandt self-portrait in Oriental garb. The Tuck Collection, comprising furniture, tapestries and other 18th-century items, is also housed here. The municipal collections boast several 19th-century gems: magnificent paintings by Gustave Courbet, Eugène Delacroix, Pierre Bonnard,

ARTS & LEISURE – MUSEUMS

Edouard Vuillard and Paul Cézanne, plus Impressionist works that have escaped the Musée d'Orsay dragnet. An entire hall is given over to a sublime series by Odilon Redon. Elsewhere you'll find sculptures by Auguste Rodin. The inner garden is a delightfully cool refuge during the dog days of summer.

Museum pass

The *Carte Musée et Monuments*, **Museum Pass, available at museums, monuments and main Métro stations, allows you to wander at will through every one of the 62 museums and monuments in Paris and the greater metropolitan area without any need to queue. The single-day pass sells for 55 F, the three-day pass for 110 F, and the five-day pass for 160 F.**

Musée National Picasso
3rd arr. - Hôtel Salé, 5, rue de Thorigny - 42 71 25 21
Open 9:30 a.m.-6 p.m. (Wed. until 10 p.m.). Closed Tues.

This is indeed art in an artful architectural frame. The magnificent 17th-century Hôtel Salé, one of Paris's most spectacular Marais townhouses, was painstakingly restored to house the paintings and artworks of Pablo Picasso (donated to the state by his heirs in lieu of death duties). Here we've rediscovered one of this century's greatest artists through a complete panorama of his favourite works—"Picasso's Picassos" (he selected five of his own paintings each year plus a copy of each lithograph; the sculptures never left his studio). The treasure trove totals 203 paintings, 158 sculptures, 16 collages, 29 montages, 86 ceramics, over 3,000 drawings and engravings, illustrated books and manuscripts, sketchbooks and other original pieces. There's even proof of Picasso's precocity: several astonishingly polished paintings done when the artist was 14 years old— *The Barefoot Girl* and *Man with a Cap* among them. Picasso's private collection of works by his contemporaries—Cézanne, Braque, Matisse, Derain and others—is also on view. Tea room, *see Tea Rooms.*

Muséum National d'Histoire Naturelle
5th arr. - Jardin des Plantes
57, rue Cuvier - 40 79 30 00
Open 10 a.m.-5 p.m. (Sat. & Sun. 11 a.m.-6 p.m.). Closed Tues. & holidays.

Taken bit by bit, this magical, many-faceted museum-cum-garden is a marvel. The lovely Jardin des Plantes (Botanical Garden) that surrounds the natural history museum is a leafy oasis in summer, a riot of colour and fragrance in spring. Its sycamore-lined gravel paths link carefully planted and labeled flower beds and herb gardens, a small zoo and an exotic tropical greenhouse. The museum's galleries tell the tale of the earth—of life and its history. The anatomy and palaeontology hall is a huge, surreal world filled with skeletons and prehistoric monsters. The palaeobotany hall is even odder, with plant specimens from two billion to 250 million years ago. In the cavernous mineralogy hall there are thousands of meteorites, extraordinary crystals, cut gems, precious stones (the Salle du Trésor, or Treasure Hall, reveals an astounding wealth of emeralds, sapphires, rubies, turquoise, platinum and gold nuggets from the Bank of France's safes). A flight of fancy awaits lepidopterists (and all butterfly fanciers) in the entomology hall's collections (45, rue Buffon). In case you're wondering: the museum was originally the modest medicinal plant garden of Louis XIII, later the royal garden. It flowered from 1739 to 1788 under the scientific guidance of Buffon, then was made a natural history museum by decree in 1789. Now the beasts are back in business, with the recent remodelling of the zoology hall and zoo. There are learning laboratoriess on birds, animal languages, minerals and other topics, as well as a museum bookshop.

Palais de la Découverte
8th arr. - av. Franklin-Roosevelt
40 74 80 00
Open 9:30 a.m.-6 p.m. (Sun. 10 a.m.-7 p.m.). Closed Mon., Jan. 1, May 1, July 14, Aug. 15 & Dec. 25. Cafeteria. Access for the disabled.

The futuristic Cité at La Villette has nearly knocked the wind out of this exploratorium. Indeed, the palatial aspect of the Palais de la Découverte has lost lots of lustre. The floor is shedding mosaics while the carpets curl and the *Sciences* and *Techniques* statues collect dust. Still, enthusiastic toddlers, eager adolescents and bemused tourists discover science in the electricity, solar system, nuclear physics and practical chemistry and biology galleries. It's a shame when the computers refuse to play games as programmed or when the knobs and buttons of the touch-me experiential devices come off in your hand... But the planetarium still features star-studded astrological projections. And outer space fans can admire the teeny French flag planted

MUSEUMS – ARTS & LEISURE

on the moon by the Apollo XVII crew.

Palais de Tokyo
16th arr. - 13, av. du Président-Wilson - 47 23 36 53
Open 9:45 a.m.-5 p.m. Closed Tues.

The Palais de Tokyo has finally found its true mission in life: as France's official temple of photography. Visitors may discover the nation's photographic heritage in the permanent collections, or view fascinating thematic shows (aerial photography, for example) and exhibits featuring the work of individual artists (a recent show presented celebrity portraits by Annie Liebowitz).

OFF THE BEATEN TRACK

Cabinet des Médailles et Monnaies Antiques de la Bibliotèque Nationale
2nd arr. - 58, rue de Richelieu 47 03 83 30
Open daily 1 p.m.-5 p.m.

Even hardened numismatists are impressed by this awesome collection of 400,000 coins and medals (the world's largest collection of cameos and intaglios), precious works from antiquity (including a remarkable Hellenistic torso of Aphrodite), the Middle Ages and the Renaissance, plus Persian silverwork and paintings by Boucher and Van Loo. Housed in the Bibliothèque Nationale building, it is one of the most venerable Paris museums, dating from the 1500s.

Plan to travel? Look out for the other RAC GaultMillau Best of guides to France and Germany, and for the RAC French Hotel and Holiday Guide and the RAC European Hotel Guide plus maps and atlases of France and Europe.

Catacombes de Paris
14th arr. - 1, pl. Denfert-Rochereau - 43 22 47 63
Open 2 p.m.-4 p.m. (Sat. & Sun. 9 a.m.-11 a.m. & 2 p.m.-4 p.m.). Closed Mon. Guided tour: Wed. 2:45 p.m. Admission: 16 F (reduced rate: 10 F). Groups w.-e. only by appointment.

The museum of Paris's catacombs is located in the former Montrouge quarry, once outside the city walls and now on the place Denfert-Rochereau. To improve hygiene in the capital, about six million skeletons were brought here in 1786 from the cemeteries and charnel houses of central Paris. About a mile of well-lit section of this immense catacomb is open to visitors. The entrance is in the centre of the place Denfert-Rochereau.

Le Cellier des Bernardins
5th arr. - Caserne de Poissy, 24, rue de Poissy - 47 54 68 18
Open daily by appointment only.

The Poissy fire station was once the refectory of the Collège des Bernardins, whose 14th-century vaulted cellar is one of the largest and finest in the Paris area. To visit, simply ask the firemen on duty for permission.

Espace Grévin
1st arr. - Forum des Halles, level -1, 1, rue Pierre-Lescot - 40 26 28 50
Open 10:30 a.m.-6:45 p.m. (Sun. & holidays 1 p.m.-6:30 p.m.).

The Forum des Halles branch of the Musée Grévin features Paris in the Belle Epoque, a series of animated tableaux and Reynaud's Optical Theatre—the praxinoscope, the predecessor of the Lumière brothers' cinematograph—which he operated in Montmartre from 1892 to 1900.

Historial de Montmartre
18th arr. - 11, rue Poulbot - 42 64 40 10
Open daily 10 a.m.-7 p.m.

We could write a book about the beauty of this museum's location, with its panoramic view across Paris. The amusing historical waxworks evoke vivid images of Montmartre's past and of famous people and places. If Madame Tussaud's is your cup of tea, you'll love this place.

Maison de Balzac
16th arr. - 47, rue Raynouard 42 24 56 38
Open 10 a.m.-5:40 p.m. Closed Mon. & holidays. Temporary exhibitions.

The rustic charm of Honoré de Balzac's modest house and verdant garden—*la cabane de Passy*, where he lived from 1840 to 1847—was only one reason the penurious novelist hid out here. The other is a discreet back entrance and escape route down the rue Berton—because when Balzac wasn't penning immortal prose like *The Human Comedy*, he was keeping his eye out for debt collectors. The flavour of his chequered life comes through in his austere study, which, entirely intact, is stuffed with letters, documents and everyday objects—an inkwell shaped like a padlock and primed for 16 hours of work—and decorated with portraits of the women he loved and admired. Armchairs and tables entice visitors to sit down and have a good read.

Maison de Victor Hugo
4th arr. - Hôtel de Rohan-Guéménée, 6, pl. des Vosges - 42 72 10 16
Open 10 a.m.-5:40 p.m. Closed Mon. & holidays.

Victor Hugo lived from 1832 to 1848 in this 17th-century house on the place des Vosges. He wrote several chapters of *Les Misérables* and scores of other plays and poems here in these seven rooms, which effectively recreate the atmosphere of the *salon rouge*, the Guernesey dining room and the death chamber of the avenue d'Eylau. Family portraits, yellowed souvenirs and piously preserved memorabilia rather blandly trace Hugo's tormented life. But the rooms do provide an excellent idea of how Hugo amused himself when he was not writing: a series of sombre pen-and-ink drawings executed in a state of "almost unconscious reverie" or the eccentric wooden cabinets he cobbled together. The haunting initials V. H. seem to appear everywhere.

Musée de l'Armée
7th arr. - Hôtel des Invalides, 129 rue de Grenelle - 45 51 92 84
Open 10 a.m.-5 p.m. (April 1-Sept. 30 until 6 p.m.). Closed Jan. 1, May 1, Nov. 1 & Dec. 25. Concerts in Saint-Louis des Invalides church; cafeteria.

Arm yourself for the onslaught of countless weapons and machines of war designed to slash, club, explode, flatten, puncture and otherwise exterminate the enemy. Every imaginable type of weaponry is on display in this extremely popular museum (it's in the same league as the Eiffel Tower and the Château de Versailles in terms of tourist visits). Louis XIV had the Invalides built by architects Libéral Bruant and Jules Hardouin as a veterans' hospital. Mansart erected the towering Dôme church, which is visible from all over Paris. The Invalides is still considered one of the city's most handsome architectural ensembles. True to character, Napoleon appropriated the church as a monument to his own glory, and he is entombed in the elaborate carved-porphyry Emperor's Tomb under the cupola. However, we found the astounding engraved sword by Benvenuto Cellini, the gigantic François I on horseback, the 1914-1918 section, with its moving displays, and the 1939-1945 galleries, with their superb model of the Normandy landings, far more interesting. For Napoleon-trivia fans, there's the bizarre stuffed white charger he rode on Saint-Hélène and the dog that kept him company during his exile on the island of Elba. Be forewarned: you will never be able to see the whole museum in one go.

Musée d'Art et d'Histoire de Saint-Denis
93200 Saint-Denis - 22 bis, rue Gabriel-Péri - 42 43 05 10
Open 10 a.m.-5:30 p.m. (Sun. 2 p.m.-6:30 p.m.). Closed Tues. & holidays.

Winner of the coveted Prix Européen du Musée, this former Carmelite convent (17th and 18th centuries), superbly restored in 1981, makes the trip to dingy Saint-Denis worthwhile. On display is a fine collection of religious art and archaeological finds pertaining to the city and the Carmelite order. Easy to reach (the RER suburban express train takes you there from central Paris in just a few minutes), it is located next door to the phenomenal Cathedral of Saint-Denis, resting place of the French kings.

Musée d'Art Juif
18th arr. - 42, rue des Saules - 42 57 84 15
Open 3 p.m.-6 p.m. Closed Fri., Sat. & Jewish holidays.

Objects used at temple services, popular art, scale models of synagogues from the 13th to the 19th century, rare books, contemporary paintings and drawings (Marc Chagall, among them) are on display at this fascinating museum housed in the Montmartre Jewish Centre.

Musée d'Art Naïf Max Fourny-Musée en Herbe
18th arr. - Halle Saint-Pierre, 2, rue Ronsard - 42 58 72 89
Open 10 a.m.-6 p.m. Closed Mon., Jan. 1, May 1 & Dec. 25. Tea room. Admission: 22 F (reduced rate: 16; F).

This two-in-one museum, housed in the bright 19th-century Halle Saint-Pierre, is a charming place to spend an afternoon. A huge second-floor loggia houses Max Fourny's renowned collection of naïf and folk art. The ground floor features theme exhibitions for children that cover an enormous range of subjects. The museum also hosts a number of workshops for kids, spin-offs of the temporary shows.

Musée des Arts Asiatiques-Guimet
16th arr. - 6, pl. d'Iéna
47 23 61 65
Open 9:45 a.m.-5:15 p.m. Closed Tues. Audiovisual & conference rooms.

Ten years of remodelling and enlarging transformed this venerable temple of Asian art from a jumbled bazaar into a shining showcase. Unique treasures have finally been retrieved from the warehouse and put on display. You will be whisked across the vast territory of Oriental art: Khmer statues from 9th to 11th-century Cambodia; smiling gods and eyeless kings that well up in a halo of light. There is also a huge collection of Buddha paintings (from Nepal and Tibet), a cubist-like head of Kasyapa sculpted in grey chalkstone (6thcentury China) and, from the monasteries of Hadda in Afghanistan, delicate, fragile stucco and dried-earth figurines. Chinese ceramics and porcelain fill several halls.

MUSEUMS – ARTS & LEISURE

Musée des Arts de la Mode
1st arr. - 107, rue de Rivoli - 42 60 32 14
Open 12:30 p.m.-6 p.m. (Sun. noon-6 p.m.). Closed Mon. & Tues.

This lovingly restored museum of fashion arts in the Pavillon de Marsan comprises five floors of elegant clothing, accessories, shoes, bags and hats (18th to 20th-century collections from the Arts Décoratifs and the Union Française des Arts du Costume)—in all, about 32,000 pieces of finery. Exhibits change regularly. Don't miss the haute-couture collections by Doucet, Poiret, Chanel and Dior.

Musée Bouchard
16th arr. - 25, rue de l'Yvette - 46 47 63 46
Open Wed. & Sat. 2 p.m.-7 p.m. Closed last 2 wks. of: March, June, Sept. & Dec. Access for the disabled.

Chisels and chips of stone, sketches and photos pinned to the wall in delightful disarray—the liveliest sculptor's studio in town is the Musée Henri Bouchard (1875-1960). The masterful academic's work leaves some people cold, but the guided tours (Wednesday at 7 p.m., limited to 20 participants) and lectures on the sculptor's trade would be sure to convert them.

Musée Bourdelle
15th arr. - 16, rue Antoine-Bourdelle - 45 48 67 27
Open 10 a.m.-5:40 p.m. Closed Mon. & holidays. Access for the disabled.

Riotous green gardens strewn with Antoine Bourdelle's bronzes are hidden in the heart of old Montparnasse. We like to visit in the spring when the trees are bursting with blossoms. This house/museum seems to have been suspended in time since the sculptor's death in 1929. Bourdelle's brawny art represents a powerful reaction to the sculpture of his time (he was, when young, Rodin's assistant). Giant original plasters are featured in the exhibit hall: *The Dying Centaur, The Polish Saga* and the equestrian statue of Alvéar. The Beethoven series of bronze heads overflows with pathos. Don't miss Bourdelle's bas-reliefs (1912-1913, restored in 1987) on the facade of the Champs-Elysées theatre.

Musée Bricard (de la Serrurerie)
3rd arr. - 1, rue de la Perle - 42 77 79 62
Call for information.

This unusual museum holds the key to the locksmith's ancient art. On display are locks from early Christian times, door handles and knobs, ornamental lock casings, bolts, keys, door knockers and all such devices designed to lock, enclose, seal, protect and hide. So what's so special about locks? You may be surprised to find how interesting these odd objects are: the first rudimentary key from Gallo-Roman times, a massive medieval lock, glittering with goldsmithery, 17th-century 12-tooth keys, Napoléon's imperial door bolt, the Marquis de Sade's safe... The museum is in an exquisite 17th-century Marais townhouse (designed by Libéral Bruant, architect of the Invalides) just down the street from the Picasso museum. It was restored by Bricard, the 150-year-old French lock manufacturer, to house its immense collections.

Musée Carnavalet
3rd arr. - 23-29, rue de Sévigné 42 72 21 13
Open 10 a.m.-5:40 p.m. Closed Mon. & holidays.

A vivid panorama of Parisian history is presented here—from the city's ancient origins to the present day. The sound and fury of years gone by, the restitching of the urban fabric, the beautification and destruction of the metropolis are captured in topographical models of different parts of Paris, scale models of monuments, paintings, prints and, for the modern era, photographs. The mansion that houses the museum is itself a prime exhibit: begun in the 1500s by Pierre Lescot, floors were added by François Mansart in the 17th century, and further additions were made in the 19th century. Yet it is one of the most harmonious architectural ensembles in the Marais, with a lovely courtyard garden graced by sculpted shrubs, flower beds and fountains. From 1777 to 1796 the mansion was inhabited by Madame de Sévigné, famed for her letter-writing. French Revolution devotees will not want to miss the blood-stained letter Robespierre was writing when the Terror turned upon him. The temporary exhibitions mounted by the museum are always worthwhile.

Musée de la Chasse et de la Nature
3rd arr. - 60, rue des Archives 42 72 86 43
Open 10 a.m.-12:30 p.m. & 1:30 p.m.-5:30 p.m. Closed Tues. & holidays. Access for the disabled.

Don't be put off by the gory theme—the history of the hunt—for this is a charming museum housed in a magnificent 1654 Marais mansion built by François Mansart. Always a hit with youngsters of all ages are the fine collections of weapons—from flint arrowheads to precision firearms, carved powder horns, gold-inlaid carbines, ancient elephant guns and so on. Impressive trophies from three continents and a superb collection of paintings by Rembrandt, Cranach, Breug-hel and Monet, among others, make this a museum you should be sure to visit.

Musée de la Contrefaçon
16th arr. - 14 ter, rue de la Faisanderie - 45 01 51 11
Open Mon. & Wed. 2 p.m.-4:30 p.m., Fri. 9:30 a.m.-noon. Admission: free.

A curious, sombre little museum, the Musée de la Contrefaçon features famous counterfeits and fakes, from chocolate (*Meinier* instead of Menier) to perfume (*Chinarl* instead of Chanel). Wines, spirits, jewellery, clothing, luggage and so forth—every imaginable item and its dubious double.

Musée du Crystal
10th arr. - 30bis, rue de Paradis
47 70 64 30
Open 9 a.m.-6 p.m. (Sat. 10 a.m.-noon & 2 p.m.-5 p.m.). Closed Sun. & holidays.

After stocking up on china, silver and crystal on the rue de Paradis, where the foremost manufacturers of French tableware cluster in a cosy confraternity, do make time to visit the Musée du Cristal. You'll gasp in amazement at Baccarat's most impressive creations, from stemware and perfume bottles to opaline objets d'art and sumptuous chandeliers.

Musée Ernest Hébert
6th arr. - 85, rue du Cherche-Midi - 42 22 23 82
Open 12:30 p.m.-6 p.m. (Sat., Sun. & holidays 2 p.m.-6 p.m.) Closed Tues., Dec. 25 & Jan. 1.

This is the unjustly unknown museum of forgotten painter Ernest Hébert (1817–1908), all the rage in his day. Here we rediscover the painter of the princesses of the imperial court, winner of the Prix de Rome and countless accolades and the worldly portraitist of the Comtesse Greffulhe, immortalised by Marcel Proust. If you don't care much for Hébert's old-fashioned art, at least come and see the admirable 18th-century mansion furnished with Princess Mathilde's Louis XVI furniture.

Musée Eugène Delacroix
6th arr. - 6, rue de Furstenberg
43 54 04 87
Open 9:45 a.m.-12:30 p.m. & 2 p.m.-5:15 p.m. Closed Tues.

Anyone with a 100-franc note already owns a valuable Delacroix (1798–1863). In a secret garden off the place Furstenberg, romantic as can be, the Eugène Delacroix home/museum (the painter's apartment and sunny studio are linked by a curious footbridge) is one of Paris's great little-known museums. There are no masterpieces here but rather a fine series of drawings, watercolours and pastels (plus studies for such famous paintings as *The Death of Sardanapalus*), an astonishing self-portrait, the palette and easel this Romantic artist used to paint his early works, pages from his journal and various other oddities. We like to follow with a visit to the nearby church of Saint-Sulpice, where Delacroix, advanced in years, decorated the Saints-Anges chapel.

Musée de la Franc-Maçonnerie
9th arr. - 16, rue Cadet - 45 23 20 92
Open 2 p.m.-6 p.m. Closed Sun. & holidays. Admission: free.

This is no ill-lit hideaway for regicides and fearful freethinkers, but a modern, rather stark museum of French Freemasonry. Displayed in glass cases in a sombre hall are paintings, sculptures, engravings and medals, pertaining primarily to political figures, intellectuals and military leaders. You will discover scores of illustrious names: Philippe-Egalité (a royal supporter of the French Revolution who was guillotined during the Reign of Terror), Voltaire, Montesquieu, Marshal Joffre, the Comte de Bourbon-Condé and, surprise, even a Roosevelt.

Musée Grévin
9th arr. - 10, bd Montmartre - 42 46 13 26
Open daily 1 p.m.-7 p.m.

You and the other 650,000 annual visitors to the Musée Grévin will either chuckle at or pale among the petrified personages assembled here. The delirious décor of this monumental waxworks (the fourth most frequently visited museum in Paris) ranges from the Cabinet Fantastique, a charming little theatre done up by Bourdelle and Chéret, to a madcap mob that includes Leonid Brezhnev and Presidents Reagan and Mitterrand all dressed as astronauts with Woody Allen as space cadet floating above. The ground floor features current celebrities. The basement galleries groan with scenes from French history.

Musée Gustave Moreau
9th arr. - 14, rue La Rochefoucauld - 48 74 38 50
Open 10 a.m.-12:45 p.m. & 2 p.m.-5:15 p.m. (Wed. 11 a.m.-5:15 p.m.). Closed Tues.

"If you want a job done properly, do it yourself," thought Symbolist painter Gustave Moreau (1826–1898). So he erected this Renaissance Revival building on the lovely place Saint-Georges, a temple to posterity. It is worth a visit just to see the spectacularly baroque spiral staircase that links the third and fourth floors, where an enormous workshop and grand gallery house Moreau's works. Surrealist writer André Breton was for decades the sole defender of Moreau's prodigious talents, but the admiration of Matisse (whose teacher he was) brought Moreau wider appreciation. We've spent hours rummaging through the nearly 5,000 drawings, studies and watercolours that testify to Moreau's fertile creativity.

Musée de l'Histoire de France
3rd arr. - 60, rue des Francs-Bourgeois - 40 27 61 78
Open 1:45 p.m.-5:45 p.m. Closed Tues. & holidays. Annual closings not available.

What could be more precious than the history of a nation? Which explains the choice for the National Archives: the magnificent Hôtel de Soubise, considered by many to be the finest 18th-century townhouse in Paris. In these exquisite apartments, decorated by some of the most illustrious artists of the time—Boucher, Natoire, Van Loo and Adam—are cases containing medieval manuscripts covering the period from the Merovingians (the dynasty of Frankish kings that flourished from the 5th century to 751) to the Hundred Years War, as well as an impressive collection of documents pertaining to the French Revolution (the *Declaration of the Rights of Man*). Long-running exhibits generally feature some sort of written document, so a working knowledge of French is helpful. Regardless of language, a stroll through the townhouse and inner gardens are worth the visit.

Musée Jean-Jacques Rousseau
95160 Montmorency - 5, rue Jean-Jacques Rousseau - 39 64 80 13
Open 2 p.m.-6 p.m. Closed Mon.

The wandering philosopher and scribe Jean-Jacques Rousseau settled down from 1757 to 1772 in this modest abode and penned *La Nouvelle Héloïse*, *L'Emile* and the *Lettre à d'Alembert*. Rousseau's furniture, various letters and manuscripts are among the memorabilia. The charming garden's path shaded by ancient lime trees—tradition has it that Rousseau planted two of them—leads to a tiny pavilion that houses the philosopher's workroom.

Musée du Jouet
78300 Poissy - 2, enclosure of l'Abbaye - 39 65 06 06
Open 9:30 a.m.-noon & 2 p.m.-5:30 p.m. Closed Mon., Tues. & holidays.

This museum is nothing to toy with—you can look but not touch! It overflows with thousands of exquisite but fragile toys—from porcelain dolls to lead soldiers and mechanical merry-go-rounds from the 19th century. It is housed in an attractive former priory in suburban Poissy.

Musée Lambinet
78000 Versailles - 54, bd de la Reine - 39 50 30 32
Open 2 p.m.-6 p.m. Closed Mon. & holidays. Admission: free.

No pomp and circumstance, as in the neighbouring Château de Versailles. Here you will find a delightful 18th-century townhouse lost in a restful green garden, collections of Sèvres and Saint-Cloud porcelain, sculptures by Houdon, 18th-century paintings, period furniture plus 19th-century statuettes and works by painters Dunoyer de Segonzac and André Suréda, all charmingly displayed.

Musée Mémorial Ivan Tourgueniev
78380 Bougival - 16, rue Ivan-Tourgueniev - 45 77 87 12
Open March 22-Dec. 22: Sun. 2 p.m.-6 p.m. & weekdays by appointment.

This delightful *dacha* was the great Russian writer's slice of home (so what if it looks more like a Swiss chalet!). Turgenev lived here happily, near friends Louis and Pauline Viardot (his pavilion is actually located in their garden; Pauline was his secret lover). And he died here in 1883. A pleasant pilgrimage for Turgenev devotees.

Musée de la Mode et du Costume
16th arr. - Palais Galliera, 10, av. Pierre-Ier-de-Serbie
47 20 85 23
Temporary exhibitions only. Open during exhibitions 10 a.m.-5:40 p.m. Closed Mon. Annual closings depending on exhibitions. Access for the disabled.

Housed here is one of the world's richest wardrobes: 5,000 costumes in a 50,000-piece collection of fashions for men, women and children of all social classes—from the 18th century to the present. You'll admire the remarkable wardrobes that once

---

Museum tours

La Réunion des Musées Nationaux, which organises most of the exhibitions at the national museums in Paris, offers guided tours of the Louvre and other museums and art galleries. For details phone 40 20 51 77 for the Louvre and 40 13 48 00 for the other national museums.

ARTS & LEISURE – MUSEUMS

belonged to the Countess of Greffulhe (Marcel Proust's muse) and the Countess of Castellane. Popular recent exhibits have focused on the designs of Dior, Givenchy and jewellers Van Cleef and Arpels.

Musée de la Monnaie
6th arr. - 11, quai de Conti - 40 46 56 66
Open 1 p m.-6 p.m. (Wed. until 9 p.m.). Closed Mon.

The end of the rainbow for numismatists: a staggering array of precious coins and medals housed in the gorgeous Hôtel des Monnaies. A mere 200 years or so after its creation (1768 by Louis XV), the mint has been reborn as a museum. On display are coins from ancient times to the present, paintings of coin presses, plus scales, tools and books pertaining to minting techniques. The mansion's court of honour and the many superb salons are alone worth the visit.

Musée de Montmartre
18th arr. - 12, rue Cortot - 46 06 61 11
Open 11 a.m.-5:30 p.m. Closed Mon., Jan. 1, May 1 & Dec. 25. Temporary exhibitions.

Relive the notorious Montmartre Bohemia of politicians and artists (which include the likes of Picasso, Utrillo and Renoir) in this bright, charming museum that overlooks the hillside Clos Montmartre, one of the city's last remaining vineyards. Watch for the excellent temporary exhibits (a recent show on Modigliani was a great hit).

Musée National des Arts d'Afrique et d'Océanie
12th arr. - 293, av. Daumesnil 44 74 84 80
Open 10 a.m.-noon & 1:30 p.m.-5:30 p.m. (Sat. & Sun. 10 p.m.-6 p.m.). Closed Tues. Access for the disabled.

Children love this place, with its crocodile pits and an immense aquarium swimming with piranhas. On the edge of the Bois de Vincennes at the Porte Dorée, the massive 1931 former Musée des Colonies is a remarkable example of the architecture of its age. Outside is a gigantic bas-relief of some riotously rich colonial kingdom of flora and fauna. Inside are the marvellous collections of African masks, statues in wood and bronze, jewellery and finery from Africa and Melanesia.

Musée National des Arts et Traditions Populaires
16th arr. - 6, av. du Mahatma-Gandhi, Bois de Boulogne - 44 17 60 00
Open 9:45 a.m.-5:15 p.m. Closed Tues. Access for the disabled.

Another favourite among the young, this is the sort of museum that captivates some and totally fails to interest others. Collections of objects from popular traditions trace the development of rural civilisation in France. Arranged with startling precision and displayed in huge plexiglas cases are a blacksmith's forge, a cooper's shop, the interior of a Breton peasant's house, a wheelwright's and carpenter's workshop, a trawler with sail spread and numerous other life-size models, plus various regional costumes, implements and decorative items. Impressive temporary exhibits, archives, library and other facilities are available to researchers.

Musée National de la Coopération Franco-Américaine
02300 Blérancourt, Château - (16) 23 39 60 16
Open 10 a.m.-noon & 2 p.m.-5 p.m. (in winter 2 p.m.-7 p.m.). Closed Tues. Parking available. Restaurant. Admission: 12 F, 7 F on Sun., free for children under 18, ages 18-21 & over 60: 7 F.

This museum of Franco-American friendship, located in the lovely Château de Blérancourt, belongs to the French National Museums group. The 17th-century château was designed by Salomon de Brosse, architect of the Luxembourg Palace in Paris. Although it has undergone many changes over the centuries, Brosse's ornamented portals, pavilions and portions of the *corps de logis* (the main part of the building) have survived. In 1915 Ann Morgan, daughter of American financier J. P. Morgan, set up a Red Cross infirmary in the château. After World War I she began the painstaking restorations that have only recently been completed. Blérancourt's permanent collection comprises some 50 paintings from the United States and France, formerly displayed at the Musée d'Orsay and the Pompidou Centre, plus a sculpture garden and landscaped grounds. Situated minutes from the forest of Compiègne, where the Armistice was signed, and Viollet le Duc's spectacular Pierrefonds Château, Blérancourt is also a charming

---

RAC MOTORING ATLAS FRANCE: *Our fully revised and well-established large format RAC Motoring Atlas France, Belgium and Luxembourg at 1:250,000 (approximately 4 miles to 1 inch) now has even more features to improve journey planning and to make driving in France more enjoyable. Clear, accurate and detailed road maps make RAC Motoring Atlas France the ideal atlas for the independent traveller in France. Price: £ 11.99 (spiral bound).*

MUSEUMS – ARTS & LEISURE

Picardy village. Trains from the Gare du Nord stop at Noyon; a taxi will take you the rest of the way.

Musée National des Monuments Français
16th arr. - Palais de Chaillot, 1, pl. du Trocadéro - 44 05 39 10
Call for information: temporary exhibitions. Access for the disabled.

This cathedral-size museum is chock-a-block with monumental yet scrupulously accurate phonies—reproductions of France's sculptural monuments from pre-Roman times to the 19th century.

Musée National du Moyen-Age
5th arr. - 6, pl. Paul-Painlevé - 43 25 62 00
Open 9:30 a.m.-5:15 p.m. Closed Tues.

All you need to know about the Middle Ages, from religious relics to everyday objects, is on display in the superb 15th-century Hôtel des Abbés de Cluny. Collections include ivory works, wood sculptures, paintings, stained-glass windows, furniture, jewellery, ironwork, tapestries and such. In the Gallo-Roman baths next door are the barrel-vaulted frigidarium ("cold bath") and other impressive halls (filled with statuary and masterpieces of goldsmithry) restored with rare flair. Do not miss the famed series of 15th-century unicorn tapestries, *The Lady and the Unicorn*.

Musée National de l'Orangerie des Tuileries
1st arr. - Jardin des Tuileries, corner quai des Tuileries/place de la Concorde - 42 97 48 16
Open 9:45 a.m.-5:15 p.m. Closed Tues.

Claude Monet's dazzling *Water Lilies*, painted in Giverny between 1890 and his death in 1926, hang here in the two oval basement rooms, custom-designed according to the wishes of the artist. Upstairs, the Walter-Guillaume collection contains just one Monet but several undisputed masterpieces from the end of the 19th and the beginning of the 20th century (by Modigliani, Renoir, Cézanne, Matisse, Picasso, Soutine).

Musée Nissim de Camondo
8th arr. - 63, rue de Monceau
45 63 26 32
Open 10 a.m.-noon & 2 p.m.-5 p.m. Closed Mon., Tues., Jan. 1, May 1 & Dec. 25.

This grand 1914 townhouse is a nearly exact replica of the Petit Trianon at Versailles. Count Moïse de Camondo built it on the edge of the Parc Monceau and filled it with his priceless collection of 18th-century furniture (designed by such master craftsmen as the Jacob brothers, Riesener and Leleu), paintings (by Vigée-Lebrun and Hubert Robert) and sculptures (by Houdon and Pigalle). Sèvres porcelains, Beauvais tapestries and rare Savonnerie carpets round out the harmonious ensemble, perfectly restored and presented as the count knew it. It's a real labour of love. The only drawback is that you're almost forced to purchase a catalogue in order to follow the exhibits, which are not adequately described.

Musée du Pain
94220 Charenton-le-Pont - 25 bis, rue Victor-Hugo - 43 68 43 60
Open Tues. & Thurs. 2 p.m.-4 p.m. Annual closings not available.

This delightful little museum recounts the history of bread as art. Installed in the granary of a flour mill, the only thing missing is the smell of baking bread. It's up to you to add that pinch of imagination.

Musée Pasteur
15th arr. - 25, rue du Docteur-Roux - 45 68 82 82
Open 2 p.m.-5:30 p.m. Closed Sat., Sun., Aug. & holidays.

The apartment where the great scientist and inventor Louis Pasteur lived is movingly simple, quite a contrast to the Byzantine chapel in which he is buried. The room that displays the souvenirs of science is wonderfully nostalgic.

Musée de la Poste
15th arr. - 34, bd de Vaugirard
42 79 23 45
Open 10 a.m.-6 p.m. Closed Sun. & holidays.

A first-class museum, recently rejuvenated, for philatelists and anyone interested in the history of the postal service. Displays range from Roman wax tablets to featherweight airmail paper, from letterboxes to high-tech video encoders. On our last visit, our favourite piece was a rural postman's bicycle from the 19th century. A word in your ear: bring a magnifying glass for a proper view of the stamp collections.

Musée de la Publicité
1st arr. - 107, rue de Rivoli - 42 60 32 14
Temporary exhibitions only. Open during exhibitions 12:30 p.m.-6 p.m. (Sun. noon-6 p.m.). Closed Mon. & Tues. Documentary centre Mon.-Fri. noon-6 p.m.

The incredibly imaginative, colourful turns of phrase inspired by the profit motive. Thousands of slogans, thousands of posters dating from 1750 to the present are displayed in temporary public exhibits (researchers are not permitted to handle the fragile paper posters but are allowed to view slides). A recent addition: TV and cinema commercials, plus a collection of press, radio, TV and film documents and items used as advertisements.

ARTS & LEISURE – PARKS & GARDENS

Musée Auguste Rodin
7th arr. - Hôtel Biron, 77, rue de Varenne - 47 05 01 34
Open 10 a.m.-5:45 p.m. (Oct. 1-April 30 until 5 p.m.). Closed Mon., Jan. 1, May 1 & Dec. 25. Cafeteria in the park.

As we go to press, Auguste Rodin's *The Thinker*, normally on display in the courtyard entrance, was on loan to an exhibition in China, but there are plenty of other masterpieces by the sculptor on view in the pretty 18th-century garden. Along the lanes stand Rodin's monumental bronzes *The Burghers of Calais*, *The Hell Gate* and the imposing *Balzac*, to name only a few. The 1728 rococo townhouse belonged to the Duchesse du Maine and the Maréchal de Biron before it was divided into apartments where the likes of Matisse, Cocteau and Rilke spent time. Rodin moved in at the peak of his career, and his presence saved the house from demolition. Also on display is an impressive array of sketches and studies. Don't miss the excellent jade carving *Les Bavardes*, by Rodin's lover, Camille Claudel, herself a sculptor of talent. (See the following entry for the Rodin museum annexe.)

Maison d'Auguste Rodin
92190 Meudon - Villa des Brillants, 19, av. Auguste-Rodin - 45 34 13 09
Open June-Sept. 1:30 p.m.-7 p.m.

The Rodin annexe is housed in the red-brick Louis XIII Villa des Brillants and really must be seen. The pastoral setting on a hill is one of the most enchanting locations in the Paris area. Studies for Rodin's masterworks are displayed here.

> *Find the address you are looking for, quickly and easily, in the index.*

Musée de la Sculpture en Plein Air
5th arr. - Jardin et quai Saint-Bernard
Open year-round. Admission: free.

This monumental sculpture garden covers a half-mile stretch of the Seine between the Pont d'Austerlitz and Pont de Sully, featuring works donated or loaned by artists Gilioli, César, Ipoustéguy, Arman and Etienne-Martin. A breath of fresh air in a lovely green setting.

Musée de la Vie Romantique Maison Renan-Scheffer
9th arr. - 16, rue Chaptal - 48 74 95 38
Open 10 a.m.-5:45 p.m. Closed Mon. & holidays. Temporary exhibitions.

Ary Scheffer (1795–1858) was Louis-Philippe's court painter. Ernest Renan (1823–1892), the renowned writer, was Scheffer's nephew. But, surprise, this museum is given over to yet a third celebrity: George Sand (the pen-name of Amandine Dupin). There are a few Scheffer paintings, nothing at all by Renan and an interesting collection of Sand memorabilia that includes furniture and portraits, plus a plaster cast of Sand's and Chopin's hands (the composer was one of her lovers). The real attraction is the house—a handsome Restoration-period mansion with a charming garden at the end of an ivy-draped lane—where time seems to stand still.

Musée Zadkine
6th arr. - 100 bis, rue d'Assas - 43 26 91 90
Open 10 a.m.-5:40 p.m. Closed Mon. & holidays.

The Russian sculptor Zadkine (1911–1967), creator of the celebrated *La Femme à l'Eventail*, lived and worked here for most of his life. Today, a forest of sculptures stands in the tiny garden, an idyllic enclave on the edge of Montparnasse. We like it best in the spring when the daffodils are in bloom.

PARKS & GARDENS

Bois de Boulogne
16th arr. - 40 71 03 43

This immense park, which spreads over more than 2,000 acres on the western edge of the city, is a vestige of the primeval forests that once surrounded Paris. Long a royal domain, the Bois was presented to the capital with imperial munificence by Napoléon III, who stipulated that it be landscaped and maintained with municipal funds. Today the Bois is a paradise for runners, cyclists, riders and strollers. Dogs and

> **Nature walks**
>
> Paris isn't made only of asphalt and stone; nature thrives in parks, squares and odd corners of each arrondissement. For guides to the city's flora and fauna, and some *suggested itineraries* that will allow you to discover them, pick up a Sentiers Nature guide at the local mairie (town hall).

children love to come to the Bois for a romp along the many miles of hiking trails and lawns. Among the myriad attractions are a children's park with a little zoo (Le Jardin d'Acclimatation), a sumptuous rose garden (Le Jardin de Bagatelle), and a lake (le Lac

THE PASS THAT MAKES PARIS YOUR PLAYGROUND.

La carte qui vous ouvre les portes du tout Paris.

ris Visite is an all-in travel pass - valid for 3 or days - giving you access to every part of the city and surrounding areas. By metro, bus or RER, as well as ICF Ile-de-France lines, to Eurodisneyland®-Resort, rsailles, Roissy-Charles-de-Gaulle and Orly airrts. Available at main metro and RER stations.

Paris Visite, c'est un forfait transport de 3 ou 5 jours pour découvrir librement Paris et sa région en métro, bus, RER et trains SNCF Ile-de-France, jusqu'au parc Eurodisneyland®, Versailles et aux aéroports Roissy-Charles-de-Gaulle et Orly. En vente dans les principales stations de métro et gares RER.

'esprit libre

A BETTER WAY FOR VISITING PARIS

PARIS the light city, the capital of France, with all its monuments, its architecture and its Parisian life, were we will be pleased to welcome you.

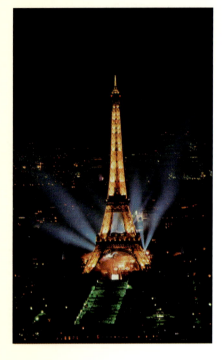

Here are some excursions we can offer you

PICK UP	EXCURSIONS: TOUR
9h et 14h00	Paris 1/2 day
14h00	Versailles 1/2 day
13h30	Giverny 1/2 day
07h00	Loire Valley full day
07h00	Normandy full day
21h30	Illuminations +cruise
20h00	Cruise+ "Milliardaire"
21h30	Illuminations+ Moulin Rouge or Lido.
19h30	Dinner cruise +Moulin rouge or Lido.
20h00	Dinner at the Eiffel Tower + Moulin Rouge or Lido.
19h30	Dinner at the "Paradis Latin"
21h30	Cruise + Moulin Rouge or Lido.
20h00	Dinner at the Eiffel Tower+ Grazy Horse Saloon
21h30	Cruise +Crazy Horse Saloon

TAS travel agency organizes excursions in mini-buses starting and return from your hotel by day and by night in order to help you discover the best places in Paris.

TAS voyages

For any further information,
please contact our North American reservation service:
5720 Buford Highway, Norcross, Georgia 30071 U.S.A.
Telephone: (404) 448-4079
Toll-free: (800) 423-2752
Fax: (404) 447-8475

Inférieur) for boating. Also situated within the park's ample precincts are two racetracks (Longchamp and Auteuil), the Roland-Garros tennis stadium where the French Open is held, equestrian clubs and a couple of first-rate restaurants: Le Pré Catelan and La Grande Cascade (see *Restaurants*).

Bois de Vincennes
12th arr. - 44 06 51 00

Even larger than the Bois de Boulogne, the Bois de Vincennes is similarly endowed with cycling and bridle paths, nature trails and sporting facilities. But it is also home to the city's sole Buddhist temple (complete with a 30-foot statue of Buddha), a world-class zoo where 1,100 animals live in naturalistic surroundings, an arboretum and a fascinating museum of African and Oceanic arts. Our favourite features, though, are the Ferme Georges-Ville, a working farm open to the public during weekends and holidays, where city kids can get close to farm animals; and the Parc Floral, with its bouquet of thematic gardens (herbs, perennials, azaleas, aquatic plants...), its incredible "Valley of Flowers" rich with 100,000 plants, and its superb sculpture garden.

Jardin Albert-Kahn
92100 Boulogne - 1, rue des Abondances and 14, rue du Port 46 04 52 80
Open 11 a.m.-6 p.m. (from May 1-Sept. 30: 11 a.m.-7 p.m.). Closed Mon.

One of Paris's prettiest parks, this landscaped garden on the banks of the Seine was created in the early 20th century by wealthy banker and philanthropist Albert Kahn, who dreamed of bringing together all his favourite scenes of nature in a single park. You may wander through a freshly renovated Japanese garden, a Vosges forest, a formal French garden, a placid lake bordered by trees, a romantic English garden as well as a coniferous and a deciduous wood. We particularly like to visit here from March to June, when the daffodils, hyacinths, azaleas, rhododendrons and roses are in bloom.

Jardin du Luxembourg
6th arr. - Main entrance: bd Saint-Michel, near place Edmond-Rostand - 40 79 37 00
Open daily dawn-dusk.

Head for the Luxembourg Gardens when you need to entertain a couple of energetic kids; or you yearn to sit or stroll in leafy solitude; or you decide to take the pulse of Parisian life on a sunny Sunday afternoon. The Luxembourg offers activities galore for youngsters, from swings and sandpits to pony rides and racing cars, not to mention a pond for launching little sailboats (the sort you push with a stick) and puppet shows manage to amuse even children who don't speak French. Elsewhere, quiet paths wind through lawns and flower beds ornamented with statues that honour the artists and statesmen of France (many of these allegorical tributes are unintentionally hilarious). Inveterate people-watchers should note that the area of the garden closest to the boulevard Saint-Michel is a veritable vivarium of vaguely arty, intellectual Left-Bank types—it's an ideal place to observe Parisians in their natural habitat.

Jardin du Palais-Royal
1st arr. - Main entrances: beg. rue Montpensier & after 1, rue de Valois - 42 60 16 87
Open April 1-May 31 7 a.m.-10:15 p.m., June 1-Aug. 31 7 a.m.-11 p.m., Sept. 1-30 7 a.m.-9:30 p.m., Oct. 1-March 31 7:30 a.m.-8:30 p.m.

For all its serene beauty, this garden maintains an almost secret air; never crowded, it is protected from urban noise by the noble houses that enfold it with their sculpted facades. In summer, it's an enchanting place to sit and watch pigeons bathe in the fountains with little black swifts that have just flown back from Africa; or listen to tiny French toddlers twitter in the sandpits. The architecture embraces the 17th, 18th, 19th and 20th centuries: Richelieu lived in what was known as the Palais-Cardinal, later promoted to royal rank when Anne of Austria and the future Louis XIV moved there from the Louvre. The elegant arcades that run around three sides of the garden date from just before the Revolution, but the buildings behind them, now occupied by the Ministry of Culture and the Constitutional Council, were not completed until the Restoration. The current era is represented by the controversial black-and-white columns designed by Daniel Buren, and the polished steel fountains by Pol Bury.

Jardin des Plantes
5th arr. - Main entrance: 57, rue Cuvier - 40 79 30 00
Open daily dawn-dusk.

Once upon a time, herbs and medicinal plants were cultivated here to treat royal ailments. In 1641 Louis XIV graciously opened his botanical gardens to the public. Ever since, Parisians have promenaded en masse among the charming shaded walks of the maze which encircles the Belvedere, the park's sole surviving edifice from before the French Revolution (note, however, that the garden's centrepiece, a stupendous cedar of Lebanon, also predates that war: it was planted in 1734). You will discover rare species of trees, flowering shrubs and countless other plants from cold climes (in the Jardin d'Hiver, or Winter

Garden) or warm ones (in the huge greenhouse, a jungle of tropical flora and cacti). Reptiles, deer, bears, apes and birds of prey are housed in quaint Second Empire buildings, which have been recently renovated. (See *Museums*, Muséum d'Histoire Naturelle.)

Jardin des Tuileries
1st arr. - Main entrances: place de la Concorde & place du Carrousel - 42 60 27 67
Open 7 a.m. (Sat., Sun. & holidays 7:30 a.m.) -10 p.m. (winter 8 p.m.).

When work is completed in 1995, the Jardin des Tuileries and adjoining Jardin du Carrousel will link the Louvre and the place de la Concorde with an uninterrupted avenue of lawns, walks, flowers, fountains and statuary. For now, this historic area is in a state of disarray. Excavations around the Louvre yielded an unexpected bonanza in the form of a large section of Philippe-Auguste's defensive wall, along with innumerable medieval artefacts. Preserving that archaeological bounty has meant considerable delay in the reconstruction of the Tuileries Gardens. But soon, the authorities assure us, the Tuileries will be a revitalised, coherently landscaped garden worthy of its central place in the capital's geography and the nation's history.

Parc André-Citroën
15th arr. - Main entrances: rue Montagne-de-la-Fage & rue Balard - 45 33 51 97
Open 7:30 a.m. (Sat. & Sun. 8:30 a.m.) to 30 mn before dusk.

With the Parc de la Villette (see below), the 35-acre Parc André-Citroën is the most ambitious project of its kind since the Second Empire, the "Golden Age of Parisian Parks." From the spectacular view of the Seine to the multitude of fountains, the canal and ornamental ponds, water is a dominant theme in this imaginative landscape. Don't look for your garden-variety herbaceous borders here: the visionary architects who designed the park have composed thousands of trees, shrubs and flowers into fantastic themed gardens of extraordinary botanical richness. The dark foliage of the Black Garden sets off the fragrant perennials of the White Garden; the *Jardin des Métamorphoses* changes with the seasons to reflect the alchemical transmutation of lead into gold; then there are the Moss and the Rock Gardens, as well as a series of six gardens, each on the theme of a different colour, metal and sense (the Blue Garden, associated with mercury, is redolent of mint; fruit trees bloom in the Red Garden; a spring bubbles up in the Japanese-inspired Green Garden...). The rarest plants are housed in two tall glass-and-wood conservatories which close the perspective from the Seine. Officially opened late in 1992, the park is still a work in progress. Future plans include the landscaping of the river banks that adjoin the park, and the construction of a footbridge linking the gardens to the 16th arrondissement.

Parc de Belleville
20th arr. - Main entrance: rue Piat, in front of rue des Envierges 43 43 97 27
Open year-round. Hours vary, call for information.

This brand-new park boasts an impressive pergola, an orangery, an open-air theatre and hills landscaped with waterfalls. Topping it all is a panoramic vantage point—the highest in Paris—offering a truly impressive view of the city.

Parc des Buttes-Chaumont
19th arr. - Main entrance: place Armand-Carrel - 40 36 41 32
Open daily 7 a.m.-9 p.m. (summer 11 p.m.).

This romantic park is crossed by creeks and roaring waterfalls fed by the nearby

---

Computerised trees

Despite the ravages of pollution, dogs and Dutch elm disease, Paris still has more trees than any other European capital. Nearly 200,000 trees line its streets and grace its parks and gardens, not to mention another 300,000 in the Bois de Vincennes and Bois de Boulogne. Plane trees are the most common, making up 43 per cent of the total, and one of their number is the city's tallest tree, standing 136 feet high in the avenue Foch. Chestnuts, sophoras and lime trees are also well represented. But if we look on the shady side, the figures also show that 25 per cent of Parisian trees will have disappeared by the year 2000. In an attempt to stop the rot, the city government is keeping a close watch on its woody heritage: every single tree now has a computer file detailing its surroundings, vital statistics and state of health. An experimental greenhouse has been set up to study the effects of traffic pollution on different species, and 4,200 new trees are being planted every year.

Ourcq Canal. A tiny Greek Revival temple perches on a peak in the middle of a swan-filled lake. The temple and panoramic vantage point is reached from below, via a suspension bridge, or from above, by crossing a narrow walkway 100 feet above the lake. The park's main cascade tumbles into a stylised grotto, newly renovated and open to the public for the first time since 1945. This former quarry and dump was, in the late 19th century, transformed into one of Paris' most fashionable public gardens. The mark of the park's designer, Baron Haussmann, is evident in the cast-concrete railings and benches sculpted to resemble tree branches. More than £700,000s been spent on restoring the Buttes-Chaumont to its original splendour, and it's a job well done.

Parc Georges-Brassens

15th arr. - Main entrance: at carrefour rue des Morillons & rue de Cronstadt - 45 33 51 97
Open 7:30 a.m. (Sat. & Sun. 8:30 a.m.) to 30 mn before dusk.

The twin bulls who guard the entrance to this spacious park are survivors, so to speak, of the slaughterhouse that stood on the site until 1975. Other elements from the abattoir were also integrated into the landscape, such as the bell tower that dominates the centre of the park, and the Grande Halle, once a horse's last stop before the glue factory, now the scene of a weekly used-book market. Other opportunities for peaceful pursuits are provided by the park's fragrance garden, a collection of 80 aromatic and medicinal herbs, a vineyard planted with Pinot Noir (a memento of the now-vanished Clos Morillon, a famed Parisian *cru*) and a honey-producing beehives. Children are not forgotten: there are several playgrounds, a puppet theatre and a special wall on which kids and adults too can sharpen their rock-climbing skills.

Parc Monceau

8th arr. - Main entrance: bd de Courcelles, in front of place de la République-Dominicaine - 40 53 00 15
Open daily: Nov. 1-March 31 7 a.m.-8:30 p.m.; April 1-Oct. 31 7 a.m.-10 p.m.

The verdant *allées* of this picturesque park attract large crowds at weekends. But since most of the Sunday strollers are well-mannered inhabitants of the surrounding *beaux quartiers*, no untoward jostling ever seems to occur. Late in the 18th century, the artist and stage designer Carmontelle was hired by a princely patron to create "an extraordinary garden" on this site. Taking his mission to heart, he erected bogus Greek and Egyptian ruins, a Gothic castle, a Dutch windmill and a minaret. Today only a pyramid and an ornamental lake with a colonnade remain of those imaginative edifices. The city of Paris acquired the Parc Monceau in 1860, and is now responsible for its maintenance. We hope that the current replanting and relevelling of the park's grounds will not disturb the stately maple or the Oriental plane tree (note its 22-foot girth), which have spread their branches here for 130 and 170 years respectively.

Parc Montsouris

14th arr. - Main entrance: at the corner of av. Reille & rue Gazan 45 33 51 97
Open 7:30 a.m. (Sat. & Sun. 8:30 a.m.) to 30 mn before dusk.

That energetic architect and engineer, Adolphe Alphand, whose legacy includes the Bois de Boulogne, the Bois de Vincennes, the Buttes-Chaumont, the Parc Monceau and the Square des Batignolles, also supervised the construction of the Parc Montsouris. The lovely English-style gardens were created at the behest of Napoléon III, but were completed only after the fall of the Second Empire, in 1878. On opening day, the artificial lake which was the park's principal attraction suddenly and inexplicably drained dry. The engineer responsible did the only proper thing under the circumstances: he committed suicide. But why let that tragic occurrence spoil your enjoyment? Concentrate instead on the charmingly serpentine paths shaded by Virginia tulip trees, an immense cedar of Lebanon, an American redwood and Siberian elms.

Parc de la Villette

19th arr. - Main entrance: av. Jean-Jaurès, near Porte de Pantin - 42 40 76 10
Hours vary, call for information.

Water, light and greenery guided Bernard Tschumi's design for the Parc de la Villette. The result is an enchanting, indeed poetic "urban park for the 21st century." A long, winding avenue leads visitors through a succession of themed gardens: a bamboo grove signals the Energy Garden, ornamented with sculpture and Bernhard Leitner's *Sound Cylinder*; the Trellis Garden, with its grapevines, hops and perennials, is dotted with seven sculptures by Jean-Max Albert; and the Water Garden is enhanced by F. Nakaya's *Cloud Sculptures*. Along the way are scattered some 30 blood-red "follies" (the colour recalls that La Villette was once the city's abattoir), which house, variously, a snack bar, a restaurant, a gazebo and so on. Philippe Starck is responsible for the benches, lights and other fixtures that strikingly combine function with elegant form. Though the park is difficult to reach from central

ARTS & LEISURE – PARKS & GARDENS

Paris, your kids will thank you for taking them here, where lawns may be walked and picnicked upon and where imaginative playground activities abound (do not under any circumstances miss the *Jardin du Dragon* with its scary sliding board).

Square des Batignolles
17th arr. - Place Charles-Fillion
40 53 00 15
Open 7:30 a.m. (Sat. & Sun. 9 a.m.) to 30 mn before dusk.

Another example of the ubiquitous Alphand's art (see above), the Square des Batignolles delights visitors with its winding paths, running stream and its waterfall edged by weeping willows and ash trees. Hundreds of comically obese ducks paddle on a little lake, which is also home to equally gluttonous carp and goldfish. The only jarring note in this otherwise harmonious ensemble is the incongruous statuary group called *Vultures* that rises up, black and forbidding, from the middle of the water. On weekends a merry-go-round often opens for business, creating a "village fair" atmosphere. Before you go, do walk around to the place Charles-Fillion for a look at Sainte-Marie-des-Batignolles. With its triangular pediment and Tuscan columns, the church resembles a small Greek temple mysteriously set down in a Parisian square.

Montmartre by train

A delightful way to discover the village atmosphere of old Montmartre is from the little train that winds through this attractive part of Paris. Trains leave every day from 10 a.m. to 7 p.m. (midnight at weekends and in summer) from place Blanche (in front the Moulin Rouge) every 30 minutes and the trip takes 40 minutes. You'll pass and hear about all the places that have mattered in Montmartre's history: the Moulin Rouge—home of the Can-Can, Saint Peter's Church—one of the oldest in Paris, the Jewish Art Museum, the Sacré Cœur Basilica with its exceptional views, the Montmartre Museum, Place Pigalle and the charming Place du Tertre. Adults 25 francs; children 15 francs.

OUT OF PARIS

INTRODUCTION	*310*
CHANTILLY	*311*
CHARTRES	*313*
ECOUEN	*315*
FONTAINEBLEAU	*316*
GIVERNY	*319*
RAMBOUILLET	*321*
SAINT-GERMAIN-EN-LAYE	*322*
SENLIS	*323*
VAUX-LE-VICOMTE	*325*
VERSAILLES	*327*

INTRODUCTION

Those lucky Parisians! Not only do they have the rare good fortune to live in a glorious city; that city is ringed with equally glorious forests and accessible countryside. Here are our suggestions for ten easy excursions in the Ile-de-France region, all calculated to combine fresh air and greenery with visits to places of notable historic and/or cultural interest. And naturally Gault Millau wouldn't dream of taking you anywhere without first scouting out the best places to dine and spend the night!

The French monarchy's abiding passion for the hunt dates back to the days when the French were still the Franks. Owing to this regal obsession and to the intense personal interest that kings took in their *chasses royales* (private hunting grounds), the forests of the Ile-de-France, with their ancient stands of oak, beech and hornbeam, have been uncommonly well preserved and responsibly managed over the centuries.

Hugues Capet, founder of the Capetian line and ancestor of the Valois and Bourbon dynasties, was elected king in 987 at Senlis, a thickly forested royal estate north of Paris famed for its excellent hunting. And hunting, in fact, was what made Capet's election necessary in the first place: his predecessor, Louis V (the last of the Carolingians), while in hot pursuit of a stag, had taken a fatal tumble from his horse.

The neighbouring domain of Chantilly, for centuries home to some of France's most powerful lords—the Bouteillers, the Montmorencys, the Condés—was also celebrated for its densely wooded forests, alive with game. The châteaux at Fontainebleau, Rambouillet (where Renaissance monarch François I departed this world with his hunting boots on) and Saint-Germain-en-Laye were all particularly beloved by their royal proprietors for the sport they enjoyed there. Even Versailles, that epitome of regal grandeur, was, before the Sun King transformed it, the preferred (and rather swampy) hunting ground of his father, Louis XIII.

So, like generations of royalty who could pop off to their country castles whenever they got that atavistic urge to bag a boar (or when things got too hot for them in Paris—and we don't just mean the weather), present-day Parisians can hop on a train and, an hour or so later, alight near one of a half dozen splendid forests, all complete with magnificent châteaux.

But even if they don't fancy the primeval forest, nature lovers will find lots to like in the environs of Paris. Admirable parks like those at Ecouen and Rambouillet, and elegant gardens like Le Nôtre's 17th-century *jardins à la française* at Saint-Germain-en-Laye, Vaux-le-Vicomte, Chantilly and Versailles will please those who prefer more manicured landscapes.

Travellers in search of a rural antidote to city stress can head for the farmlands of the Beauce region, south-west of the capital. The soothing sameness of these wheat-bearing plains is broken only by grain-gorged silos (this is the bread basket of France) and by the dramatic spires of the Chartres cathedral. North-west of Paris, along the meanders of the Seine, where the Ile-de-France meets Normandy, lies the Vexin, a region of farmlands and river valleys overflowing with bucolic charm. Here Claude Monet spent the last years of his life, painting in his garden at Giverny.

CHANTILLY – OUT OF PARIS

Thus by venturing just 20, 30 or 50 miles beyond the Paris city limits and the bleaker *banlieues* (suburbs), one can discover a bounty of gently beautiful scenery, bathed in the unique light that inspired not only Monet and the Impressionists, but also Corot, the Barbizon painters, Derain and the Fauvists. Punctuating these luminous landscapes are fascinating historic monuments and landmarks, as well as masterpieces of religious, civil and domestic architecture—any of which would make an ideal destination for a fair-weather *promenade*.

CHANTILLY

Reflected in the shimmering blue waters of its surrounding moat, the Château de Chantilly looks like a fairytale castle, almost too perfect to be true. And in a way, it is: The Renaissance-style Grand Château isn't much more than 100 years old (though the adjoining Petit Château dates from the 16th century). The castle that previously stood on this site was razed during the Revolution by angry citizens for whom Chantilly (about 50 kilometres north of Paris by Autoroute du Nord A1, exit at Survilliers), fief of two ancient warrior families, the Montmorencys and the Condés, symbolised aristocratic privilege and military might.

The Grand Château houses the Musée Condé and its gem of a collection which ranges from the curious—a wax head of King Henri IV, the pink Condé diamond—to the sublime—Piero di Cosimo's *Portrait of Simonetta Vespucci*, Raphael's *Virgin of Loreto*, works by Botticelli, several pictures by Poussin, two masterpieces by Watteau, a splendid series of Renaissance portraits by the Clouet brothers (including the famous *Catherine de Medici* and *Henri III*) and an admirable collection of illuminated manuscripts. Arranged just as the Duc d'Aumale, the last owner of Chantilly, left it (with orders that it never be changed), the museum has the personal and agreeably eccentric style of a private collection.

Connoisseurs of fine horseflesh also know Chantilly as the site of a famous racetrack and Thoroughbred training centre. A fascinating "living museum" devoted to horses occupies the colossal 18th-century stables. From an architectural viewpoint, these Grandes Ecuries are more imposing than the château itself (not so surprising, perhaps, if one considers that the Prince of Condé, who built the stables, was convinced that he would be reincarnated as a horse).

The château's majestic park, complete with a canal, gardens and pools planned by 17th-century landscape artist André Le Nôtre, is crisscrossed by shady walks and velvety lawns. But the immense (nearly 16,000-acre) Chantilly forest, with its hiking paths and ponds (the étangs de Commelles), is by far the best choice for a long woodland ramble. Take care, however, between 9 a.m. and noon—that's when 3,000 Thoroughbreds thunder into the forest for their morning workout!

The **Château de Chantilly** *is open daily, except Tuesday, from March 1 to October 31, 10 a.m. to 6 p.m.; from November 1 to February 28, 10:30 a.m. to 5 p.m. Reservations: (16) 44 57 08 00, Monday to Friday from 9 a.m. to noon, fax (16) 44 51 70 31. Admission: Château and park 35 F, children under 12 9 F; park 15 F, children under 12 9 F.*

The **Musée Vivant du Cheval** *is open daily, except Tuesday, from 10:30 a.m. to*

OUT OF PARIS – CHANTILLY

6:30 p.m.; from November 1 to March 31 2 p.m. to 7:30 p.m. weekdays, and from 10:30 a.m.to 6:30 p.m. at week-ends. Telephone (16) 44 57 40 40 for information, fax (16) 44 57 29 92. Admission: 42 F, children under 16 32 F.

RESTAURANTS & HOTELS

Campanile
60270 Gouvieux, 3 km N on N 16, rte. de Creil (16) 44 57 39 24, fax (16) 44 52 10 05
Open year-round. 47 rms 258F. Restaurant. Parking.

At the edge of the Chantilly forest, the Campanile is quiet, modern but not always well maintained. Restaurant.

Château de Montvillargenne
60270 Gouvieux, 3 km W on D 909, av. F.-Mathet - (16) 44 57 05 14, fax (16) 44 57 28 97
Open year-round. 10 stes 780-980 F. 140 rms 450-490 F. Restaurant. Half-board 440 F. Pool. Tennis. Parking.

Set in extensive grounds, this magnificent 19th-century castle boasts warm wood panelling and a series of elegant linked lounges. Renovated, well-equipped rooms and various leisure facilities.

12/20 Les Etangs
8 km SE, 60580 Coye-la-Forêt, 1, rue Clos-des-Vignes - (16) 44 58 60 15, fax (16) 44 58 75 95
Closed Mon. dinner, Tues., Jan. 15-Feb. 15 & Sept. 6-14. Open until 9:30 p.m. Terrace dining.

Summer visitors should slip under the bower leading to the garden to sample the slightly conventional but well executed cuisine. Top-quality ingredients go into the home-made foie gras, brill sautéed in goose fat, and duck with orange. The wines are good but costly.

A la carte; 270-350 F. Menus: 140 F (except holidays), 200 F (holidays only).

Hostellerie du Lys
60260 Lamorlaye, 7 km S on N 16, 63, 7e-av., Lys-Chantilly, Rond-Point de la Reine (16) 44 21 26 19, fax (16) 44 21 28 19
Closed Dec. 18-Jan. 4. 35 rms 185-510 F. Half-board 350-703 F. Parking.

A beautiful, cosy weekend inn with comfortable rooms and a quiet, pleasant ambience. Tennis, golf and swimming are nearby.

Le Relais Condé
42, av. du Maréchal-Joffre - (16) 44 57 05 75
Closed Mon. dinner off-season & Tues. Annual closings not available. Open until 9:30 p.m. Terrace dining.

The nicest and classiest restaurant in Chantilly is located near the racetrack, under the frame of a 19th-century Anglican chapel. Jacques Legrand, formerly of La Saucière at Tourcoing (14/20), has just taken over in the kitchen. We look forward to his elegant and carefully prepared dishes like lobster and crunchy vegetable terrine, duck breast with spices and honey, and mint-scented peach soup.

A la carte: 300-430 F. Menus: 180 F, 280 F.

COMPIEGNE

Auberge de la Forêt
60350 Trosly-Breuil, 11 km E on N 31, 19, place

des Fêtes - (16) 44 85 62 30, fax (16) 44 85 60 27
Closed Tues. dinner & Wed. Open until 9:30 p.m. Terrace dining.

Gérard Magnan's traditional cuisine has the personal touch and enough originality to provide agreeable surprises. A former colleague of Michel Guérard and a friend of Alain Senderens, he uses only the finest ingredients in the morel mushroom ragoût topped with a poached egg, succulent, bacon-flavoured pike steaks, and veal fillet with pears and tarragon. A smiling Monique Magnan will help you choose a bottle from the carefully constructed wine list.

A la carte: 330-440 F. Menus: 140 F, 180 F and 280 F (except holidays), 250 F (holidays only).

Château de Bellinglise
14 km N on D 142, Route de Lassigny, 60157 Elincourt-Ste-Marguerite (16) 44 76 04 76, fax (16) 44 76 54 75
Open year-round. 3 stes 1,500-1,620 F. 47 rms 680-1,370 F. Restaurant. Half-board 563-753 F. Tennis. Parking.

This immense Louis XIII–era castle on a 600-acre estate has been remarkably preserved and restored; guests can stay in one of the attractive rooms in the hunting lodge. Pond, tennis, riding, archery and conference facilities. Fine wood-panelled restaurant.

See also "Senlis", page 324.

Red toques signify modern cuisine; white toques signify traditional cuisine.

CHARTRES

Long before Christianity had penetrated the Ile-de-France, before Caesar marched into Gaul—even then, Chartres was a holy place. Legend has it that every year Celtic druids assembled in Chartres (90 kilometres southwest of Paris by Autoroute A10) to celebrate their mysteries around a sacred wellspring now immured in the cathedral crypt.

What is certain is that from the fourth century on, a sanctuary consecrated to the Virgin Mary brought the faithful to Chartres. When, in 876, Charles the Bald endowed the church with a precious relic (said to be the Virgin's tunic or veil), it gained even greater importance as a shrine, drawing pilgrims from all over Christendom in a steady stream that neither invasions, fires nor revolutions have stanched. Even today, Catholic students organise a pilgrimage to Chartres each May in honour of the Virgin.

The ancestor of the current cathedral, a Romanesque structure built in the 11th and 12th centuries, was ravaged by fire in 1194. The flames spared only the crypt, two towers and the lower portion of the western façade, with its majestic Portail Royal (royal entrance). But the people of Chartres very quickly set about rebuilding their cathedral, with so mighty a collective will—and generous contributions from rich lords and wealthy townspeople—that it was completed in the impressively short span of just 30 years. It is to the builders' speed that the cathedral owes its exceptional stylistic unity. And it is to their skill in applying new architectural advances—notably the flying buttress—that Chartres owes its soaring height and rare luminosity. Since the buttresses shouldered weight that would otherwise have fallen on the walls, the builders could make the walls higher, with taller windows.

It would be impossible for us to do justice here to the aesthetic and spiritual riches of Chartres. A visitor with plenty of time, patience, curiosity and an observant eye will find innumerable sources of pleasure and interest. Here, however, are a couple of features worth noting, one outside and one inside the cathedral.

The Portail Royal, unscathed by the fire of 1194, represents one of the oldest examples of Gothic sculpture in existence. While the emphasis of the ensemble is on the figure of Christ, depicted in infancy and in majesty above each of the three doors, viewers often feel irresistibly drawn to the 19 elongated figures, a combination of statue and column, that stand aligned on either side of the doors. Interestingly, these Old Testament figures belong to two different eras, the Romanesque and the Gothic; they are the survivors of the old cathedral and, at the same time, heralds of the new sculptural style that first emerged at Chartres. In their extraordinarily sensitive faces, in the contrast between their expressive features and their rigid, stylised bodies, a visitor can trace the mysterious passage from one age—one way of viewing and representing human reality—to another.

Inside the cathedral, among the ravishing, jewel-like shadows and colours of stained glass, there are three windows and a portion of another that, like the Portail Royal, escaped the fire of 1194. They are the windows inserted in the western facade, which depict the genealogy, life and resurrection of Christ, and, to the left, the fragment known as Notre Dame de la Belle Verrière (*The Madonna of the Window*), one of Chartres's most venerated images. They merit your special

OUT OF PARIS - CHARTRES

attention because they are the sole remaining examples of the miraculous *bleu de Chartres*, a blue tint rich (as we now know) in cobalt and copper, but which for centuries no one successfully reproduced.

In medieval times, Chartres was a flourishing town, its wealth based on cloth and farming. It was also an intellectual centre, with a renowned philosophy school. Investigating the many ancient houses and churches in the Old Quarter (the 15th-century Maison Saumon and the Hôtel de la Caige; the medieval church of Saint-Pierre, with its striking stained glass) can be an extremely rewarding way to spend an afternoon.

Agriculture still thrives hereabouts, and the prosperous Beaucerons are fond of the table. Between a tour of the cathedral and a stroll through the town, hungry visitors will find any number of excellent eating places where they may relax and restore themselves.

The **cathedral** is daily open from 7:30 a.m. to 7:30 p.m. from April 1 to September 30; and until 7 p.m. from October 1 to March 31. For additional information, contact the Office du Tourisme, place de la Cathédrale, (16) 37 21 50 00.

RESTAURANTS & HOTELS

 Le Grand Monarque
22, pl. des Epars
(16) 37 21 00 72,
fax (16) 37 36 34 18
Open daily until 9:45 p.m. Terrace dining.

The huge dining room with its handsome wood panelling and beautiful bouquets is just the same and so, unfortunately, is the ultra-classic cuisine of Michel Menier. No doubt it's what the local gentry enjoys, but we're beginning to tire of the same old dishes, especially as they were not all up to scratch during our last visit: we found grit in the mussel salad and the lamb noisettes with tarragon were on the dry side. The pineapple savarin was excellent though, and the wine cellar is just as full of fine Loire vintages. We're awarding a point less this year because for such high prices, we think the cooking ought to be less ordinary.

A la carte: 400-450 F. Menus: 198 F, 288 F.

 Le Grand Monarque
(See restaurant above)
Open year-round. 5 stes 860-1,220 F. 49 rms 460-700 F. Air cond 1 rm.

The best hotel in Chartres has charming new rooms in two turn-of-the-century buildings surrounding a garden. Nice modern suites. Excellent breakfasts.

 Le Manoir du Palomino
28300 Saint-Prest, 10 km NE on N 154 & D 6
(16) 37 22 27 27,
fax (16) 37 22 24 92
Closed Dec. 23-Feb. 15. 20 rms 250-550F. Restaurant. Half-board 305-550F. Tennis. Golf. Parking.

A fine weekend escape from Paris, for relaxing or for conferences. The 40-acre estate provides golf and tennis facilities, and the spacious, quiet, luxuriously decorated rooms have charm, flowers, beams and fine views of the landscape.

12/20 **Relais de la Tour**
28630 Nogent-le-Phaye, 8 km on D 4, N 10, Le Bois-Paris
(16) 37 31 69 79
Closed Tues. dinner, Wed. & July 27-Aug. 15. Open until 10 p.m. Air cond. Parking.

The pleasant service helps customers forget the noisy highway and boring décor, and concentrate on the generous portions of salmon tartare, duck breast with cranberries (slightly overcooked) and delicious crème brûlée. Reasonably priced and well-chosen wines.

A la carte: 160-250 F. Menus: 75 F (weekdays and Sat.), 105 F, 162 F, 175 F.

 La Sellerie
28630 Thivars, 7 km S on N 10, 48, rue Nationale
(16) 37 26 41 59
Closed Sun. dinner (off-seas.), Mon. dinner, Tues., Jan. 4-12 & Aug. 3-24. Open until 9 p.m. Terrace dining. Parking.

Imagination is not Martial Heitz's strong point, but his traditional cuisine is elegant and well prepared. The smiling welcome and excellent Bordeaux add to the enjoyment of a rabbit pâté with tender carrots, stuffed mutton tripe and fresh pasta, and bitter chocolate soufflé. The décor mixes refinement with rustic charm, and there's a pleasant garden for summer lunches.

A la carte: 250-380 F. Menus: 130 F, 270 F.

ST-SYMPHORIEN-LE-CHATEAU

 Château d'Esclimont
(16) 37 31 15 15, fax (16) 37 31 57 91
Open daily until 9:30 p.m. No pets. Parking.

This attractive restaurant could still do better, but our most recent visits have helped to dispel some earlier disappointments. Chef Patrick Guerry is paying more attention to the freshness of his vegetables: we really enjoyed the tender, tasty baby lamb served with asparagus tips and broad beans, although such excellence did make the heavy crème brûlée even harder to bear! The wine list is as magnificent as the Renaissance castle and surrounding countryside. And as for the prices, they seem to scale new heights every year.

A la carte: 400-450 F. Menus: 320 F, 495 F.

 Château d'Esclimont
(See restaurant above)
Open year-round. 6 stes 1,800-2,700F. 48 rms 580-1,500F. Half-board 1,015-1,285 F. Air cond 1 rm. Heated pool. Tennis.

The 48 rooms and six suites of this château are classic, comfortable and well situated in the middle of a 150-acre expanse of completely walled-in grounds at the bottom of a valley, which is traversed by a river and situated near the road that connects Rambouillet and Chartres. Some rooms have been refurbished this year. Guests can play tennis, swim in the heated pool and attend wintertime musical evenings. There's even a helipad. Relais et Châteaux.

> *This symbol signifies hotels that offer an exceptional degree of peace and quiet.*

ECOUEN

You needn't travel all the way to the Loire Valley to view a superb French Renaissance château. Just 20 or so kilometres north of Paris, (Autoroute du Nord A1, exit n°3), stands Ecouen, an admirably preserved castle built between 1538 and 1555 for François I's closest comrade-in-arms, Constable Anne de Montmorency (who also commissioned the first château at Chantilly).

As befitted a great feudal lord and powerful military chief, the constable made Ecouen a formidable fortress. Situated on a hill overlooking the broad plain below, surrounded by moats and fortified by steeply sloping walls, Ecouen was designed to withstand even artillery fire—a wise precaution on the eve of the Wars of Religion, which ravaged the region in the later 16th century.

Yet the constable and his wife, Madeleine de Savoie, were also humanists and patrons of the arts, who engaged the best architects and sculptors of the day to embellish their home. Framed in the portico that leads to the grand courtyard, an equestrian statue of Anne de Montmorency in Roman warrior garb proclaims the constable's taste for antiquity. That taste is also reflected in the château's architecture. Niches in the monumental colonnade of the southern (left-hand) wing once housed Michelangelo's *Slaves* (now in the Louvre), presented to the constable by King Henri II.

In 1632, the constable's grandson, Henri II de Montmorency, was accused of conspiracy against Cardinal de Richelieu, and beheaded. Ecouen then reverted to the Condé family, but they spent little time there, preferring their estate at

Chantilly. During the Revolution, the contents of the castle were confiscated by the state, and eventually dispersed.

Since 1962, Ecouen has housed the Musée de la Renaissance, a unique collection of period French, Italian and Flemish furniture and decorative arts. The most dazzling exhibit is surely the 246-foot-long tapestry displayed in the Galerie de Psyché. Woven in Brussels in the early 16th century, this masterpiece of silk, wool and silver thread relates the story of David and Bathsheba.

What makes all the objects on view particularly interesting is their setting in the château's authentic, beautifully restored Renaissance interior. Do take the time to examine and admire the immense fireplaces, decorated with biblical scenes, for which Ecouen was famous in its heyday. And nothing gives a better idea of the grandeur of a Renaissance lord's castle than the Grande Salle, where the Montmorencys received their vassals. A visitor cannot help but be impressed by the monumental fireplace of porphyry and polychrome marble; or by the magnificent gold-and-cerulean tile floor displaying the entwined initials of Anne de Montmorency and Madeleine de Savoie.

We like to wind up a tour of Ecouen with a stroll in the garden; the park affords an impressive, sweeping view of the plain below. Hardier souls may go and explore the forest that borders the château.

The **Château d'Ecouen** is open daily from 9:45 a.m. to 12:30 p.m. and 2 p.m. to 5:15 p.m., except Tuesday and holidays; telephone 39 90 04 04 for information.

FONTAINEBLEAU

Just as Versailles was created at the whim of young Louis XIV, Fontainebleau owes its splendour to the sudden caprice of Renaissance monarch François I, who in 1528 decided to transform a neglected royal manor near the forest of Bière into a personal residence fit for a king. After his humiliating two-year captivity in Madrid, the Roi Chevalier wanted to prove to Emperor Charles V and King Henry VIII of England (who were then erecting spectacular palaces at Grenada and Hampton Court, respectively) that he could equal, indeed surpass, them in magnificence.

Every aspect of the new château in Fontainebleau (65 kilometres south of Paris by Autoroute du Sud A6) was calculated to glorify France's first absolute ruler (he was the first, for example, to be addressed as "Majesty," a title previously reserved for the emperor). Today, François I's spirit is still tangibly present at Fontainebleau.

Over the centuries the actual architecture of the palace has undergone considerable alteration. The Galerie François I, the most celebrated decorative ensemble of the French Renaissance, was constructed between 1528 and 1530 and embellished with marvellous stuccowork and frescoes by Florentine artist Il Rosso, a pupil of Michelangelo. The recently restored frescoes illustrate a complicated and fairly obscure symbolic scheme. One remarkable figure is an elephant emblazoned with fleur-de-lis and sporting a salamander (François I's emblem) on its forehead, which signifies the royal virtue of wisdom. Other scenes commemorate the king's Italian campaigns or his role as a patron of art and literature.

The Salle de Bal (ballroom) is another impressive Renaissance creation. Commissioned by François I, it was completed under the supervision of his son, Henri II, by architect Philibert Delorme (who also worked on the Louvre). Here the frescoes—superbly restored—were designed by Il Primatice and executed by Niccolo dell'Abbate, two of the foremost Italian artists of what came to be known as the first Fontainebleau school. The ballroom created such a sensation in its day that painters and engravers came from all over to record its sumptuous decoration. Even now, the room provides a fairly accurate idea of the opulence of the Valois court.

Though Fontainebleau was relatively neglected during the second half of the 16th century, it flourished once again under Henri IV. Dated from this era are the Cabinet de Théagène (marvellously preserved, it's the birthplace of Louis XIII) and the Chapelle de la Trinité, decorated with biblical frescoes by Mathieu Fréminet, a French master of the baroque.

The Bourbons made a habit of spending the autumn at Fontainebleau, and continued to embellish and enlarge the palace even after the court officially took up residence at Versailles. Marie-Antoinette, who loved Fontainebleau, completely redecorated several rooms, including the Salon du Jeu (Gaming Room) and the charming Boudoir de la Reine, which was designed by Mique, her favourite architect.

Napoléon too was fond of Fontainebleau, and refurnished the palace entirely. Today it boasts Europe's finest collection of Empire furniture, as well as extensive holdings of Napoleonic relics and memorabilia culled from various national museums.

The palace is surrounded by what is surely one of the most beautiful forests in France. In autumn and winter, hunters still gallop through the russet groves of oak, riding to hounds just as French kings did centuries before them. Less bloodthirsty nature enthusiasts prefer to explore the innumerable bridle and hiking paths, or scramble around the spectacular rock formations, cliffs and gorges that make the Forêt de Fontainebleau an excellent and highly popular training ground for aspiring alpinists.

The **Château de Fontainebleau** is open daily (except Tuesday) from 9:30 a.m. to 12:30 p.m. and 2 p.m. to 5 p.m.; the park and gardens are open from dawn to dusk. Telephone 64 22 27 40 for further information.

The **Musée Napoléonien** is open from 2 p.m. to 5 p.m. (closed Sunday, Monday, September and holidays). Telephone 64 22 49 80 for further information.

RESTAURANTS & HOTELS

12/20 Chez Arrighi
53, rue de France
64 22 29 43
Closed Mon. & Jan. 8-25. Open until 10 p.m.

Some Corsican specialities are still available but traditional French food now tends to be the mainstay of the menu. Prune-stuffed young rabbit, fillet of veal with mushrooms, and crunchy caramel croustine are freshly prepared and generously served.

A la carte: 230-300 F. Menus: 110 F, 139 F, 180 F.

 Le Beauharnais
27, pl. Napoléon-Bonaparte,
64 22 32 65
Closed July 14-aug. 13 & Dec. 23-30. Open until 9:30 p.m. Garden dining. Parking.

Chefs come and go here but the cuisine is so classic it's hard to see the join. Here's a typical 220F menu from this year's new face in the kitchen, Remy Bidron: attractively presented salad of pike roulade, cod in breadcrumbs with mushrooms, a fine cheeseboard, and tasty apple tart. The cellar is superb but too expensive, like the à la carte prices, and the splendid setting would seem more luxurious if the staff could bear to smile.

A la carte: 320-420 F. Menus: 220 F, 300 F.

OUT OF PARIS – FONTAINEBLEAU

 L'Aigle Noir
(See restaurant above)
Open year-round. 7 stes 1,200-2,000 F. 49 rms 950F. Air cond. Heated pool.

Facing the garden or the château, the luxurious rooms are individually decorated in Louis XVI, Empire or Restoration style. Modern comforts include satellite TV, books in English, a gym and sauna. Courteous service.

 Hôtel Legris et Parc
36, rue du Parc - 64 22 24 24, fax 64 22 22 05
Closed Sun. off season, Mon. & Dec. 20-Jan. 28. 5 stes 525-575 F. 26 rms 265-525F. Restaurant. Half-board 385-510 F.

This pleasantly renovated old building is well situated in front of the entrance to the château's grounds. The best of the extremely comfortable rooms look out on the flowers of an interior garden.

BARBIZON

 Le Bas-Bréau
22, rue Grande - 60 66 40 05, fax 60 69 22 89
Closed Jan. 4-30. Open until 9:30 p.m. Garden dining. Parking.

A weekend in the most beautiful inn in the Fontainebleau forest will obviously cost you an arm and a leg, but you'll be rewarded with a veritable feast for the eyes. The food prepared by Alain Tavernier is pricey but delicious: fillets of red mullet and green lentils, lobster salad dressed with olive oil and balsamic vinegar, coriander-scented turbot cooked on the bone and served with artichokes, baby veal chop and button onions, and fine desserts. In winter the log fire crackles away cheerfully and in summer meals can be enjoyed in the shady garden. This place is practically an enchanted forest in itself.
A la carte: 450-700 F. Menus: 300 F and 360 F (weekdays and Sat. lunch only, wine incl.), 360 F (dinner only).

 Le Bas-Bréau
(See restaurant above)
Closed Jan. 4-30. 8 stes 1,700-2,800 F. 12 rms 950-1,500 F. Pool. Tennis.

This Fontainebleau inn, one of the most refined in the Paris region, is where Robert Louis Stevenson wrote *Treasure Island*. Located on the edge of the forest and surrounded by roses and century-old trees, it has a simple, pleasant atmosphere. There's one deluxe, astonishingly comfortable bungalow beyond the vegetable garden and owner Jean-Pierre Fava has recently added a superb heated pool. Relais et Châteaux.

12/20 Les Pléiades
21, rue Grande
60 66 40 25, fax 60 66 41 68
Closed 3 wks in Feb. Open daily until 10 p.m. (10:30 p.m. in summer). Garden dining. Parking.

On a flower-laden terrace on the street or in a quiet garden at the back, you'll enjoy a pleasant meal prepared by the latest chef: roulade of pike served cold, turbot with cockles, and a crisp apple dessert with caramel sauce. The service is slow though, and the bill a bit steep.
A la carte: 270-350 F. Menus: 200 F (weekdays only), 190 F, 295 F.

 Les Pléiades
(See restaurant above)
Closed 3 wks in Feb. 1 ste 680 F. 23 rms 290-490 F. Half-board 460-500F.

The former house of painter Daubigny has attractive, comfortable rooms, and the hotel boasts a beautiful, large flower garden on the edge of the Fontainebleau forest.

See also Melun in "Vaux-le-Vicomte", page 326.

Le Corbusier's design for living

Architect and urban planner *Le Corbusier* is probably best remembered for his rather joyless efforts to rationalise living space into modular units. However, at an earlier stage in his career he made a living by designing houses for the rich. One, the Villa Laroche, (10 impasse du Docteur-Blanche in the 16th arrondissement), is open to the public and affords a glimpse of an architect more concerned with space and light than with political correctness. The house was designed in 1923 for a collector of modern art, its pure lines intended as a backdrop to the works of Braque, Picasso and Ozenfant. You can still see examples of Le Corbusier's furniture there, along with a few Cubist paintings and some striking sculptures.

GIVERNY

It isn't a palace or royal legend that brings travellers to this tiny village 75 kilometres north-west of Paris (55 km on Autoroute A 13, 10 km on N 13BIS and 5 km on D 5), on the border of the Ile-de-France and Normandy regions; what draws crowds to Giverny is the artistic legacy of Claude Monet. From 1883 until his death in 1926, Monet lived and worked in these sublime surroundings, a setting he created largely by and for himself. Giverny provided the light, the multifaceted landscape and the meandering Seine that the painter so loved. But Monet himself supplied the grand design, as well as 40 years of unrelenting efforts to make his ravishing garden a reality. It soon became the central motif of his pictures, and in the end, his garden was the only subject that Monet chose to paint.

Shortly before his death, assailed with doubts about the value of his pictures despite public acclaim for them, Monet came to regard the garden at Giverny as his ultimate creation. He kept six gardeners hard at work in it, full-time. The painter's garden had slowly gone to seed for half a century when in 1977 the American Versailles-Giverny Foundation undertook to restore it, along with Monet's house and studio. Well before Europe recognised his genius, America had embraced Monet at his first New York show in 1889. Now, owing in large part to American generosity, Monet's admirers may visit the house where he worked and entertained fellow artists Mary Cassatt, the poet Mallarmé and many more.

Nothing less resembles a formal French garden than Giverny's glorious, painterly composition of flowers, water and greenery. Ordinary fruit trees were banished from the orchard where the flower garden now blooms; Monet replaced them with exotic Japanese strains of ornamental cherry and apple. With the arrival of spring, perennial beds lose their disciplined, linear look under an exuberance of bright blossoms. Interestingly, except for the roses and peonies, all the flowers at Giverny are humble varieties: iris, foxglove, poppies and lupins. Yet they are planted so artfully and their colours, textures and shapes are arrayed to such advantage that an observer's eye roams over the banks and borders of the garden with as much pleasure as it does over Monet's *Water Lilies*, which hangs in the Orangerie in Paris.

At the far end of the winding central path—take care not to trample the nasturtiums, which grow pretty much wherever they please—is the famous pond that Monet always insisted on showing off to his guests after lunch (he had paid a not-so-small fortune to have it installed). In spring, a curtain of languid wisteria nearly hides the "Japanese bridge," which looks out over a hypnotising profusion of water lilies. Massed on the surface of the pond, they seem to form a huge artist's palette of delicate tints: white, yellow, pink, blue and mauve.

The house and three studios at Giverny—including one Monet had built specially to paint *Les Nymphéas*—give the haunting impression of being actually inhabited; it's as if the people who lived and worked there have only just stepped out for a moment. Everything is exactly as it was on an ordinary day at the turn of the century, from the pots and pans set out in the kitchen (Monet loved rich, complicated cooking), to the master's fascinating collection of Japanese prints. To borrow a phrase from Marcel Proust, Monet's contemporary and admirer, the evocative atmosphere of Giverny rewards the pilgrims who journey there with a sense of time recaptured.

The **Musée Claude Monet** is open every day except Monday—the gardens are open from 10 a.m. to 6 p.m.; the museum is open from April 1 to October 31, 10 a.m. to 6 p.m. Admission: 30 F the house and the gardens; 20 F for the gardens. Telephone (16) 32 51 28 21 for further information, fax (16) 32 51 54 18.

Visit also the **Musée Américain**, 99 rue Claude-Monet. The museum, funded by Chicago art patrons Daniel and Judith Terra, is open every day except Monday from April 1 to October 31, 10 a.m. to 6 p.m. Telephone (16) 32 51 94 65 for further information, fax (16) 32 51 94 67.

RESTAURANTS & HOTELS

PACY-SUR-EURE

Château de Brécourt
27120 Douains, by D 181 - (16) 32 52 40 50
Open daily until 9:30 p.m. Parking.

Admire the exterior of this lovely 17th-century château at the gateway to Normandy rather than reading the menu outside: the one you'll be given in the comfortable dining room is completely different. The 225-franc fixed-price menu is the most interesting: smoked salmon and crab pancakes, carefully cooked cod steak, a good cheeseboard, and a refreshing mango and wild strawberry dessert.

A la carte: 350-450 F. Menus: 350 F (Fri. dinner only), 225 F, 340 F.

Château de Brécourt
(See restaurant above)
Open year-round. 4 stes 1,200-1,400 F. 21 rms 480-990 F. Half-board 730-945 F. Heated pool. Tennis.

Amenities include spacious, comfortable, stylishly furnished rooms (though the bathrooms are a bit small). Most have good views of the marvellous grounds. Conference facilities. Relais et Châteaux.

VERNON

12/20 **Les Fleurs**
71, rue Carnot
34 51 16 80,
fax 32 21 30 51
Closed Sun. dinner, Mon., Feb. school holidays & July 20-Aug. 20. Open until 9 p.m.

Flowers brighten up the walls and chair covers as well as filling vases in the pretty and cheerful dining room. The owner-chef offers an interesting 160-franc menu that includes six oysters (a bit too salty), correctly cooked but under-seasoned pepper steak, and an excellent Grand Marnier soufflé omelet. Enjoyable Coteaux d'Aix served by the carafe.

Menus: 125-240 F (wine incl.).

La Gueulardière
78270 Port-Villez, Lieu dit Le Village
34 76 22 12
Closed Sun. dinner & Mon. (except holidays). Open until 9:30 p.m. Terrace dining. Air cond.

This picturesque site on the Seine, just across from Monet's house and gardens at Giverny, provides a perfect setting for Claude Marguerite's attractive dishes: small snails in sorrel, langoustines and braised peppers, John Dory with asparagus tips, and veal kidney cooked in truffle juice. Excellent wines.

A la carte: 350-400 F. Menu: 160F (weekdays and Sat. only).

Les Jardins de Giverny
27620 Giverny, 6 km E on D 5, chemin du Roy
32 21 60 80,
fax 32 51 93 77
Closed Jan. 4-Fev. 2. Open until 9 p.m. Terrace dining. Parking.

A stone's throw from Claude Monet's house, this fine Norman residence is surrounded by roses and rare trees. The owner-chef, Serge Pirault, bases his cuisine on the seasons: foie gras with apple brandy, hot oysters and seaweed butter, tajine of young turbot, fresh fruit gratin with fluffy sabayon sauce. Michèle Pirault will give you a warm welcome.

A la carte: 300-350 F. 120 F (weekdays and Sat. only), 180 F, 240 F.

Normandy
1, av. Pierre-Mendès-France - 32 51 97 97
Open year-round. 47 rms 380-400 F. Restaurant. Half-board 485 F. Garage parking.

This modern, convenient hotel has just opened in the town centre. The rooms at the back are the quietest; all are comfortable if somewhat lacking in originality. Breakfasts are plentiful and the welcome courteous.

RAMBOUILLET

Although it is now the peaceful summer retreat of the president of France, the château at Rambouillet has witnessed some of the more dramatic moments in the nation's history. In 1547 François I, who enjoyed hunting in the nearby forest, died in a tower of the castle (which then belonged to the captain of his guards). Forty years later, Henri III, driven out of Paris by the League, took refuge at Rambouillet (located about 50 kilometres from Paris by Autoroute Chartres–Orléans A10). In 1815, before his departure for exile, Napoleon spent a last night of melancholy reflection at Rambouillet. It was there, too, that Charles X learned of the Revolution of 1830 and announced his abdication. And it was from Rambouillet, in August 1944, that General Charles de Gaulle gave the order for Leclerc's armoured division to liberate Paris.

Yet Rambouillet has seen more tranquil times as well. Today, little remains of the 16th-century château, save the cool red-and-grey Salle des Marbres (marble room). The 18th century and Empire are the periods now best represented at Rambouillet. The Count of Toulouse, a legitimised son of Louis XIV, purchased the château in 1705. He enlarged the existing structures and had the new west wing decorated with enchanting rococo woodwork. For the garden, he commissioned a system of canals and artificial islands on which magnificent *fêtes* were held throughout the century. The count's son, the Duke of Penthièvre, completed the canals and, in the English garden, had an incredibly kitsch cottage constructed of seashells and slivers of mother-of-pearl.

In 1783, Louis XVI purchased Rambouillet for the exceptional hunting the nearby forest afforded. Marie-Antoinette was less than enthusiastic: she called the place "the toad hole" and longed for her Trianon at Versailles. To appease her, in 1785 Louis had the neoclassic *laiterie* (dairy) constructed, where ladies of the aristocracy came to sip fresh milk and sample cheese. Today the dairy is no longer in operation, but the *bergerie* (sheepfold), built the following year, is still home to some 800 sheep, including 120 merinos descended from a flock presented to Louis XVI by the king of Spain (and those *moutons* of course will have nothing to do with the other 680).

Rambouillet was virtually abandoned during the Revolution, and its furniture removed and sold, but Napoleon took a fancy to the château and decided to restore it. Today, visitors may admire the emperor's study, his private apartments ornamented with "Pompeiian" frescoes and the grand dining room—still used for state dinners—with its enormous, 550-pound bronze chandelier.

The dense forest of Rambouillet, a great favourite with hunters and mushroom gatherers, covers close on half a million acres and begins virtually at the door of the château.

The **Château de Rambouillet** *is open daily, except on Tuesday and when the president is in residence, from 10 a.m. to 11:30 a.m. and 2 p.m. to 5:30 p.m. (until 4:30 p.m. from Oct. 1 to March 31).*

La **Laiterie de la Reine Marie-Antoinette** *is open daily, except Tuesday, March 15 to October 31, from 10 a.m. to noon (last tour: 11 a.m.) and 2 p.m. to 6 p.m. (last tour: 5 p.m.), November 1 to March 14, from 10 a.m. to noon (last tour: 11 a.m.) and 2 p.m. to 4:30 p.m. (last tour: 3:30 p.m.). Telephone 34 83 00 25 for further information.*

RESTAURANTS & HOTELS

12/20 Le Cheval Rouge
78, rue du Général-de-Gaulle
30 88 80 61
Closed Sun. dinner & July 15-Aug. 4. Open until 9:30 p.m. Garden dining. Air cond.
The flower-filled garden of this pleasant inn is just the place to enjoy traditional dishes prepared from the freshest ingredients: crab ravioli, turbot in butter sauce, kid sautéed with garlic purée.
A la carte: 250-350 F. Menus: 120 F (weekdays and Sat. only), 200 F.

 Resthôtel Primevère
ZA du Bel-Air, rue J.-Jacquard - 34 85 51 02
Open year-round. 42 rms 245-260 F. Restaurant. Pets allowed. Parking.
Set back from the main road, this brand-new hotel offers bright, pleasant rooms and buffet breakfasts. The forest is nearby.

MONTFORT-L'AMAURY

 La Toque Blanche
78490 Mesnuls,
12, Grande-Rue
34 86 05 55
Closed Sun. dinner, Mon. & Aug. Open until 10 p.m. Garden dining. Pets allowed. Parking.
Jean-Pierre Philippe, a burly chef with a booming voice, is what you might call a "character" and his clients enjoy distinctive and original cuisine. A native of the coast town of Paimpol, he is at his best when cooking seafood dishes like the basil-scented langoustine ragoût, sea bass and leeks, mussel soup, and John Dory served with fried parsley. None of which come cheap, but the delightful setting helps to take the edge off the bill.
A la carte: 400-450 F. Menu: 360 F.

See also Saint-Symphorien-le-Château in "Chartres", page 315.

> Remember to call ahead to reserve your table, and please, if you cannot honour your reservation, be courteous and let the restaurant know.

SAINT-GERMAIN-EN-LAYE

In 1862 Emperor Napoléon III, an ardent archaeology buff (his great boast was that he had discovered the site of the Battle of Alésia, where Caesar defeated Vercingetorix, leader of the Gauls, in 52 B.C.), established the Musée des Antiquités Nationales at Saint-Germain-en-Laye (about 20 kilometres west of Paris by Autoroute de Normandie A13). The oldest artefacts unearthed on French soil are housed in this fascinating museum, which follows the course of French history up to the time of the Merovingians, the first Frankish dynasty. Today, nothing could be simpler than to take this journey back in time, for the RER links Saint-Germain to the centre of Paris in a matter of minutes.

On the museum's vast mezzanine, exhibits document the millennia that preceded Rome's occupation of Gaul. It is strangely moving to contemplate these age-old vestiges of human artistry. Most of the pieces are quite small, like the *Dame de Brassempouy*, the oldest-known representation of a human face, which is thought to predate Christ's birth by about 20,000 years; or the famous bone carving of a *Bison Licking Its Fur*, from Dordogne (16,000 B.C.); or the many images that remind us that in France too the buffalo roamed and the deer (and antelope) played—at least until the end of the Ice Age.

Even visitors with only a mild interest in archaeology will be riveted by artefacts discovered in the tombs of Celtic princes of the first Iron Age (Hallstatt period), particularly the funeral chariots, which indicate that the entombed were of noble rank, the iron swords, carved daggers and personal ornaments. Other finds verify that Gaulish tribes traded with Greece and Etruria, thus invalidating the theory that Gaul lived in isolation before the Romans burst on the scene. The very existence of coins minted by the principal Gallic tribes, of amphoras and other luxury goods, bears witness to the wealth of Gaul's aristocracy, and to their links with the Mediterranean world.

Exhibits on the upper floor illustrate the period of Roman colonisation and include a model of the Battle of Alésia, which marked the end of Gaul's independence. The number of statues representing Gaulish divinities underscores Rome's generally tolerant attitude toward foreign religions, while an abundance of manufactured goods—ceramics, glass objects—give us a picture of France's earliest industries. The barbarian invasions that followed this period of prosperity are evoked by jewels and impressively worked weapons excavated at Frankish tomb sites.

Though Saint-Germain-en-Laye is now synonymous with prehistory, it holds a significant place in the history of France. A prestigious royal château, it was the birthplace of Kings Henri II, Charles IX and Louis XIV (who preferred it to all his other palaces until he built Versailles). From the 12th to 19th, extensive building and remodelling altered the château's appearance many times over. What the visitor sees today is the Vieux Château, rebuilt under François I. This first important example of brick-and-stone architecture in the Ile-de-France was heavily restored in the 19th century).

The former splendour of Saint-Germain is perhaps best translated by Le Nôtre's magnificent gardens, and the Grande Terrasse bordered with linden trees. Moreover, with its 8,500 acres of flat, sandy paths, picturesque hunting pavilions and majestic stands of oak, the Forest of Saint-Germain offers ideal walking country within easy reach of Paris.

The **Musée des Antiquités Nationales** *is open daily, except Tuesday, from 9 a.m. to 5:15 p.m. Telephone 34 51 53 65 for further information.*
See also "The Suburbs" in the Restaurants (page 93) and Hotels (page 130) chapters.

SENLIS

When you walk through the narrow medieval streets of Senlis (50 kilometres north of Paris by Autoroute du Nord A1), don't be surprised if you suddenly recognise the set from a French costume drama. This compact, well-preserved town on the border of the Ile-de-France and Picardy regions offers a fascinating glimpse into the history of pre-Revolutionary France. Understandably, it is a popular location with film-production companies.

North of the town, the Jardin du Roy (king's garden) lies in what was once the moat surrounding a Gallo-Roman defensive wall. The garden affords a marvellous overall view of Senlis, and of one of the best-preserved Roman fortifications in France. About 13 feet thick and 23 feet high, the wall dates back to the barbarian invasions of the third century. It once linked together 28 watch towers, 16 of which have survived.

The nearby Château Royal, despite its grandiose name, is now nothing more than a park scattered with romantic ruins that date from antiquity to the Renaissance. Built on the site of a first-century Roman fortress, the château was a royal residence from the time of Clovis, in the fifth century, until the reign of Henri IV, early in the

17th century. It was there, in 987, that the Capetian line of monarchs was established, with the election of Hugues Capet, Duke of the Franks, to the throne of France.

If you cross the pretty square in front of the Cathedral of Notre-Dame, you can best admire the monumental portal with its celebrated Gothic sculpture. Begun in 1153, ten years before Notre-Dame de Paris, the cathedral at Senlis served as a model for those at Chartres, Amiens and Reims. Yet by the 16th century, recurrent fires had made it necessary to rebuild the northern and southern façades practically from scratch. The work was directed by Pierre Chambiges, who created one of the finest (and last) examples of flamboyant Gothic architecture. Crowning the northern portal are the initial and emblematic salamander of François I.

After visiting the cathedral, we always take the time to wander through the winding, ancient streets of Senlis: rue de la Tonnellerie, rue du Châtel, rue de la Treille and rue de Beauvais all boast 16th-century houses and mansions with splendid carved entrances (many of which are open to visitors in odd-numbered years, during the month of September for the Rendez-vous de Senlis). You'll end up at the 13th-century church of Saint Frambourg, restored through the efforts of pianist and composer George Cziffra, and now used as a concert hall.

If you have time and a car, drive a few kilometres north to the Italianate Château de Raray, built in the 17th century, where Jean Cocteau filmed his magical *Beauty and the Beast*. Who knows? Perhaps, as you stand admiring the fantastic hunting scenes sculpted on Diana's Gate, your own Beauty—or Prince Charming—will suddenly appear!

*The **Château Royal** and **Musée de la Vénerie** are open daily, except Tuesday and Wednesday morning, from 10 a.m. to noon and 2 p.m. to 5 p.m.*
*The access to the **Jardin du Roy** is permanent.*
*The **cathedral** is open from 7 a.m. to 7 p.m. Telephone (16) 44 53 00 80 for further information.*

RESTAURANTS & HOTELS

 Les Gourmandins
3, pl. de la Halle
(16) 44 60 94 01
Closed Mon. dinner & Tues. (except holidays) & Aug. 5-25. Open until 9:30 p.m.

Other restaurant guides seem slow in "discovering" Sylvain Knecht's excellent cuisine. Never mind, we'll continue to pay tribute to his perfect sense of timing, the subtlety of his sauces and contemporary creations like a Champagne-flavoured lobster and scallop mould, lotte sautéed with chanterelle mushrooms or an olive-studded lamb charlotte. Marie-Christine Knecht makes you feel at home in the cosy dining room.
Menus: 120 F (weekdays only), 210 F, 310 F.

FONTAINE-CHAALIS

11/20 **Auberge de Fontaine**
22, Grande-Rue
(16) 44 54 20 22
Closed Tues. dinner, Wed. & Feb. Open until 9 p.m. Garden dinning.

This charming inn, tucked away in a delightful village, stresses simplicity and sincerity both in the dining room and in the kitchen. Salad of baby rabbit, seafood ragoût and veal kidneys with shallots are among the highlights of the menu.
A la carte: 210-320 F. Menus: 120 F, 190 F.

 Auberge de Fontaine
(See restaurant above)
Closed Tues. & Wed. 8 rms 240-330 F.

Rooms as restful as you could wish for, with flowered wallpaper, wood beams and superbly comfortable beds.

See also Chantilly and Compiègne in "Chantilly", page 312.

> *Red toques* signify modern cuisine; white toques signify traditional cuisine.

VAUX-LE-VICOMTE

As we stand in the unfinished Grand Salon of Vaux-le-Vicomte, looking out over the intricate gardens designed by Le Nôtre, we can almost picture the scene: The dog days of August 1661... Nicolas Fouquet, France's brilliant finance minister, is entertaining his young sovereign, Louis XIV, at an indescribably lavish reception. A thousand fountains play in the magnificent Jardins à la Française, while Molière's troupe performs the comic ballet *Les Fâcheux*. Courtiers applaud the water jousts, the concerts, the fireworks... At dinner—prepared by Vatel, the foremost chef of his day—the king and his retinue are served on solid-gold plates. According to legend, the dinner did not sit well with Louis, whose suspicions—and envy—were aroused by such luxury. Historians claim that Colbert, Fouquet's rival for control of the royal treasury, had slandered Fouquet, insinuating that he was raiding the king's coffers. Or it may have been that the king set Fouquet up himself: wangling an invitation to Vaux, then watching the vainglorious minister flaunt his riches, and thus be hoist by his own petard!

Whoever laid it, the trap was sprung that August day at Vaux-le-Vicomte (about 60 kilometres south of Paris by Autoroute du Sud A6). A few weeks later, Louis sent d'Artagnan, the captain of his musketeers, to arrest Fouquet at Nantes. He then sent workmen to pack up the finest tapestries, furnishings and paintings from Vaux and carry them straight into the royal collection. Louis summoned Fouquet's architect, Le Vau, his decorator, Le Brun and his landscape designer, Le Nôtre, and ordered them all to begin work on the royal showplace at Versailles.

After a trial that dragged out over three years, the courts handed down a sentence of banishment for Fouquet. Louis, implacable, overruled them, and condemned his former minister to life imprisonment. Fouquet was, in all probability, a rascal, yet the story of his fall and miserable end (after 19 years in prison) still colours our view of Vaux's splendours with a tinge of melancholy.

It is largely thanks to Alfred Sommier, a sugar-refining magnate who purchased a dilapidated Vaux-le-Vicomte in 1875, that we can now see the château and gardens much as they were on that fateful day in 1661. He spent prodigious amounts of money and energy to rebuild sagging roofs and walls, to furnish the nearly empty house with 17th-century antiques, and to restore the gardens to their former beauty. That last task alone took a good half century. Using Le Nôtre's plans and contemporary engravings, Sommier was able to reconstruct the terraces, pools and the complex system of pipes that feed the fountains. He planted acres of trees and bushes, and acquired antique statuary for the garden, as well as commissioned pieces from modern sculptors to replace the statues confiscated by Louis XIV.

In addition to the gardens, three levels of the château are now open to the public. On the upper floor are the Fouquets' private living quarters—studies, boudoirs and bedrooms—handsomely fitted out with period furniture and hung with tapestries and reproductions of paintings from the minister's (confiscated) collection. Above the fireplace in Madame Fouquet's study is Le Brun's famous portrait of a smiling Nicolas Fouquet.

OUT OF PARIS – VAUX-LE-VICOMTE

For us, the most appealing aspect of the reception rooms downstairs (the Grands Appartements) is Le Brun's decoration. Actually, the term *decoration* is not adequate to describe this virtuoso performance with paint, stucco, carving and gilt. The scores of rosy nymphs, cherubs, squirrels (Fouquet's emblem) and other allegorical figures that populate the ceilings and woodwork of the Salon des Muses and Cabinet des Jeux (Gaming Room) fill these formal rooms with a rapturous charm. Le Brun's stucco-and-fresco décor in the Chambre du Roi (Royal Chamber) is the model for what later became known throughout Europe as the "French style," which reached its apotheosis at Versailles.

Bereft of its intended decoration, the Grand Salon demonstrates the measure of architect Le Vau's genius; the eye, unsolicited by bright allegories and visions, is naturally drawn outside, to the harmonious perspectives of the gardens, Le Nôtre's masterpiece. In their more modest way, the workrooms and staff quarters on the lower level are also quite interesting. The kitchens (in use until 1956) display a dazzling collection of copper pots and pans buffed to a high polish.

Those in search of rare sensations and exquisite atmospheres will surely want to visit Vaux-le-Vicomte by candlelight on a Saturday evening in summer. The scene is unforgettable—indeed, it is enough to rouse the envy of a king!

The **Château de Vaux-le-Vicomte** is open daily (except Christmas Day) April 1 to October 31, from 10 a.m. to 6 p.m.; November 1 to March 31, from 11 a.m.-5 p.m., except from November 16 to December 18 and January 4 to February 12 when the château is closed. **Candlelight tours** are held on Saturday evenings from May to September (Sunday evenings in July and August), 8:30 p.m. to 11 p.m. **Fountain displays** are scheduled on the second and final Saturday of each month from April to October. Telephone 60 66 97 09 for further information.

RESTAURANTS & HOTELS

MELUN

L'Ecurie
77176 Nandy, 9 km NW by N 446, Ferme de Nandy, 1, rue Arqueil
60 63 63 63
43 rms 300-330 F. Restaurant. Half-board 453 F. Parking.
This solid stone hotel between Melun and Corbeil houses comfortable, well-soundproofed rooms with full bathrooms. Fitness center.

Gault Millau's ratings are based solely on the restaurants' cuisine. We do not take into account the atmosphere, décor, service and so on; these are commented on within the review.

Grand Monarque
Melun-la-Rochette, av. de Fontainebleau
64 39 04 40
Open daily until 9:30 p.m. Garden dining. Parking.
In the middle of the forest stands this restaurant, with well-dressed tables, cheery and comfortable modern décor and a terrace by the pool. Service is attentive and the cooking brings out the best in fine ingredients: duck foie gras cooked with green cabbage, shark steak and basmati rice, and a bitter chocolate dessert coated in orange sauce.
A la carte: 280-400 F. Menu: 145 F (weekends only, wine incl.), 190 F.

Concorde Grand Monarque
(See restaurant above)
Open year-round. 5 stes 700-750 F. 45 rms 450-550 F. Half-board 462-512 F. Heated pool. Tennis.
The small but perfectly equipped rooms open onto the park. Conference facilities. Excellent service.

12/20 **La Mare au Diable**
77550 Moissy-Cramayel, 5 km N on N 6, parc Plessis-Picard
60 63 17 17
Closed Sun. dinner & Mon. Open until 10 p.m. Garden dining. Pool. Tennis. Parking.
Overlooking romantic grounds, this charming inn has warm, rustic décor. The cooking is simple and honest, with succulent grilled meats as the main attraction. The 150-franc menu offers salmon salad, entrecôte steak with shallots, andouillette sausage, and île flottante. The service is pleasant, the bill less so.
A la carte: 270-470 F. Menus: 200 F (lunch only), 150 F, 230 F, 300 F.

VERSAILLES

Versailles, undoubtedly the world's most famous palace, has been a favourite destination for day-tripping Parisians since 1833, when King Louis-Philippe turned the château, which had been abandoned since the Revolution, into a "museum of the glories of France." Today, Versailles (about 25 kilometres west of Paris by Autoroute de Normandie A13) offers pleasures at every season, in every kind of weather. Visitors can amble through parks dotted with romantic statuary, admire a wealth of art, furniture and architecture—comparing Louis this with Louis that—or simply spread out a rug and picnic beside the Grand Canal.

It took Louis XIV just 40 years to build the palace and its park around a hunting lodge erected by his father, Louis XIII. And though his successors made many changes, Versailles still bears the unmistakable stamp of the Sun King, who, from 1682 on, made it the official residence of the court, the sole seat of royal power and the political capital of France. The court's permanent presence explains the colossal proportions of the palace, which housed the royal family, the princes of the blood, the courtiers, the king's counsellors, everyone's servants... it's little wonder that the western facade of the palace stretches out nearly 2,000 feet.

Lodging his considerable household and entourage was not all that Louis had in mind when he built Versailles. He also saw the palace as a powerful propaganda tool, a monument to the glory of the French monarchy and a showcase for masterworks by French artists and craftsmen. Versailles was open to all. The humblest subjects of the realm could wander freely through the Grands Appartements to gape at the cream of the royal collections. Classical statues and busts stood in marble-lined halls; paintings from the French and Venetian schools hung on walls covered in velvet, damask and brocade. Today's tourists are the descendants of those visitors who, at the end of the 17th century, marvelled at the dazzling Galerie des Glaces (Gallery of Mirrors) or the Salon d'Apollon before attending the king's supper or submitting a petition to Louis XIV as he made his way to mass at the royal chapel.

But we have the advantage over those tourists of long ago, for we can visit parts of Versailles that were then out of bounds to the public, even to courtiers. Among the most beautiful of the private quarters is the Petit Appartement, fitted out for Louis XV just above his official suite, a place where he could relax alone—or with friends (like Madame du Barry, who had her own room there).

A similarly intimate mood and scale are evident in the two Trianons, situated about half a mile from the main palace. The Grand Trianon was built in 1687 for Louis XIV, who spent many a quiet summer evening there surrounded by his family. Today it houses heads of state on official visits. The Petit Trianon is an exquisite neoclassic structure designed by Gabriel in 1764 for Louis XV, who wished to live closer to his beloved botanical garden. It was also the preferred residence of Marie-Antoinette, whose spirit still pervades the place. There, on October 5, 1789, she learned of the Parisians' march on Versailles.

In fine weather, the gardens of Versailles are an irresistible invitation to wander. They cover over 200 acres with an enchanting variety of landscapes. The classical French *parterres* (flower beds), with their broad perspectives, ponds and lawns, were designed by Le Nôtre at the height of his powers; his is also the genius behind the marvellous *bosquets* (coppices) that combine thickly massed greenery and spectacular waterworks. Scattered throughout are hundreds of marble and bronze statues, many inspired by the myths of Apollo, with whom the Sun King strongly identified. If you happen to be in Versailles between May and September, make a point of touring the gardens when the Grandes Eaux are scheduled: all over the gardens, in every bed and *bosquet*, the fountains put on a magical display.

And in summer, it is well worth the effort to obtain tickets for a performance at the Opéra Royal, an architectural masterpiece by Gabriel, inaugurated in 1770 for the marriage of the future Louis XVI and the Archduchess Marie-Antoinette. The elegance of its proportions, its superb acoustics and the splendour of its decoration make it perhaps the most beautiful theatre in the world.

The **Château de Versailles** is open daily, except Monday and holidays, from 9 a.m. to 6 p.m. (until 5 p.m. from October 1 to April 31). The **park and gardens** are open daily from dawn to dusk. Fountain displays are scheduled on two or three Sundays a month from May to September at 4 p.m. to 5 p.m. Telephone 30 84 74 00 for further information.

■ RESTAURANTS & HOTELS

See "The Suburbs" in the Restaurants (page 95) and Hotels (page 130) chapters.

■ SIGHTS

Following is a highly condensed list of Versailles's most noteworthy sights.
The **Château de Versailles** (a must!), with more than four million visitors per year (from May to September its parks host the Grandes Eaux and the Fêtes de Nuit); the **Trianon Palaces**; the **Salle du Jeu de Paume**; **Notre-Dame** church (designed by Hardouin-Mansart); the **king's vegetable garden** (school of horticulture); the **Carrés Saint-Louis** (modest lodgings during the time of the Old Régime); the **antiques** and **second-hand market** (passage de la Geôle, next to the colourful market at Notre-Dame); the **Hôtel des Ventes** (former home of the Light Cavalry); the delightful **Musée Lambinet** (with beautiful 18th-century paintings, see *Museums* section page 301); the **Couvent des Récollets**.

BASICS

GETTING AROUND	*330*
TOURS	*331*
AT YOUR SERVICE	*333*
GOINGS-ON	*335*

GETTING AROUND

Paris is a rationally designed city divided into 20 *arrondissements*, or districts. Essential to getting around Paris is knowledge of the excellent transport system and the RAC map *Paris Streets*. Available from bookshops or from RAC Publishing telephone free in UK on 0800 212 713, it includes comprehensive maps of Paris, the underground system (Métro and RER) and an index.

■ BUSES

Taking the bus is an enjoyable—and cheap—way to tour the city. The n° 24 bus, for example, passes by many historic monuments. Buses take you almost everywhere within the metropolitan area for just two tickets (one ticket is valid for two zones). You can purchase tickets (6 francs) on the bus or a book (*carnet*) of ten tickets (36.50 francs—an economical investment) at Métro stations or in some tobacconists. Special three- or five-day tourist passes (*Paris Visite*) allow unlimited travel on buses, the Métro, the RER express line and the SNCF Ile-de-France lines and are sold at major Métro and RER stations. Major bus routes operate from 7 a.m. to 12:30 a.m. every day. Bus numbers are indicated by a coloured number inside a white disc at the bus stops. The less important routes, marked by a white number inside a coloured disc, do not run on Sundays or holidays, nor does the service go on much after 8 or 9 p.m. There is an excellent late-night service (*Noctambus*): Buses leave Châtelet from special stops marked with the night owl–logo every hour on the half hour. Every bus stop in Paris indicates fares, times, routes and bus numbers. When you enter the bus, punch your ticket(s) in the machine next to the driver. Do not punch passes or orange card coupons: simply hold them up for the bus driver to see. When you wish to get off, signal the driver by pressing the red button near your seat. Getting around by bus is a good deal easier than it may sound; and listening to an irate Parisian bus driver caught in rush-hour traffic is also an excellent way to learn some interesting French words that you won't find in the dictionary!

A convenient way to get to the different Paris airports is to take the *Air France Bus*. It leaves every 12, 15 or 20 minutes depending on the destination, from three different points in the capital: the Aérogare des Invalides, Esplanade des Invalides, 7th arr. 43 23 84 49; Le Palais des Congrès, place de la Porte Maillot, near the Air France agency, 16th arr. 42 99 25 00; and near the Arc de Triomphe, at the beginning of avenue Carnot, 17th arr. The bus makes the same stops on the return journey from the airports.

■ LIMOUSINES

See *Alliance Autos*, page 183.

■ MÉTRO

See map, pp. 340-341.

Getting the knack of the Métro system is easy. You'll find a Métro map at each station, outside in the street and inside as well. Let's imagine you want to go from the Gare du Nord to Saint-Germain-des-Prés. Locate the two stations on your map and check whether they are on the the same line (each line is indicated by a different colour). In this case, they are, so follow the line from your station of departure to your station of arrival, then note the name of the station at the end of the line (in this instance it's the Porte d'Orléans). That means that Porte d'Orléans is the name of the direction you will be taking. Inside the station, look for signs indicating "direction Porte d'Orléans," and when you reach the platform, check again on the sign located in the middle of the platform. If you have to change lines to reach your destination, consult a Métro map to ascertain which stop offers the relevant *correspondance*, or change.

A single ticket will take you anywhere on the Métro system and within zones 1 and 2 of the RER system (see RER, below). Don't forget to keep your ticket until you leave the bus or Métro, for you may be asked to produce it by an R.A.T.P. official. Tourist or not, if you don't have it, you will have to pay an on-the-spot fine if you're caught.

> The *R.A.T.P.* runs the Métro, the buses and the RER. Information line: 43 46 14 14 from 6 a.m. to 9 p.m.

■ RER

The *Réseau Express Régional* is a network of fast commuter services linking the centre of Paris to destinations all over the Greater Paris Region. Quite a number of interesting places to visit are accessible by RER, and you can pick up brochures listing these from any Métro information kiosk. There is also a very good bicycle-hire service (*Roue Libre*) run by the RER that allows you to explore some beautiful woodlands around Paris (like the Chevreuse Valley, the Forest of Saint-Germain-en-Laye and so forth). The flat-rate system on the ordinary Métro does not apply to the RER (unless you are travelling within the city), so you must consult the diagrams on the automatic ticket machines to determine the cost of your ticket. It is possible to get return tickets, and the machine will give change for any coins you use (though it doesn't take notes).

■ TAXIS

There are some 14,700 taxis available in Paris (until you really need one!). There are three ways of getting a taxi: The first is simply to flag one down (it is available if its roof light is fully lit); the second is to go to a taxi stand (*Tête de Station*); the third is to call a radio taxi that will arrive five to ten minutes later at your address (the meter will already be running, but don't get in if it's more than 30 francs). Normally, you pay 11 francs to get in the cab and 2.79 francs per kilometre during the day (7 a.m.-7 p.m.) and 4.35 francs at night (7 p.m.-7 a.m.). You'll be charged a supplement if the taxi leaves from a railway station (5 francs), if a fourth person is aboard (5 francs), and for each item of luggage (5 francs). The fare scale is higher on motorways (bear this in mind if you take a taxi to or from an airport). Tip the driver 10 to 15 per cent. If you wish to report a problem or lodge a complaint, you can call 45 31 14 80, or write to Service des Taxis, 36, rue des Morillons, 75732 Paris cedex 15, indicating the taxi's licence number as well as the date and time you were picked up.

Alpha-Taxis
45 85 85 85

Artaxi
42 41 50 50

G7 Radio
47 39 47 39

Taxis-Radio "Etoile"
42 70 41 41

TOURS

■ BY BUS

Cityrama
1st arr. - 4, pl. des Pyramides - 42 60 30 14
Open daily April 1-Oct. 31: 6:30 a.m.-10 p.m.; Nov. 1-March 31: until 8:30 p.m.

Cityrama's double-decker, ultracomfortable tour buses whisk visitors all around Paris morning, noon and night (phone for timetables and fares). A recorded commentary describes monuments, landmarks and points of interest in the language of your choice. For early risers, there is a superb crack-of-dawn tour in spring and summer.

Panam' 2002
8th arr. - 5, rue Lincoln - 45 04 36 78
Open daily 9 a.m.-7 p.m. Guided tours: 1 p.m. & 9 p.m. Fee: 240 F.

A hostess will provide a running commentary while you tour Paris in the comfort of a luxuriously appointed coach. From the place de la Concorde to the Opéra, the Eiffel Tower, the Champs-Elysées and onward, you can even nibble a meal-on-a-tray as you admire the cityscape and watch the locals hustle and bustle about their business.

Paris et son Histoire
9th arr. - 82, rue Taitbout - 45 26 26 77
Open 10 a.m.-noon & 2 p.m.-6:30 p.m. Closed Sun. & holidays. Fee: 330 F, 480 F per couple.

As the name indicates, this association specialises in the history of Paris (and the surrounding Ile-de-France region). Members attend lecture tours throughout the year; and from March to October, bus trips are organised to points of interest in the Paris area. Annual membership fees are 330 francs (480 francs for couples) and include a monthly bulletin of events. Meeting times and other information are provided by phone, or at tourist offices.

Walking tours

Discover the city on foot during a three-hour stroll with a theme. You can choose from luxury fashion, avant-garde fashion, Left Bank fashion, designer fashion, antiques and art galleries, or gift ideas. Cost is 180 francs per person, which includes the services of a bilingual guide and a tea or coffee break. Call *Shopping Plus* at 47 53 91 17 for further details, fax 44 18 96 68.

Paris Passion
17th arr. - 34, rue Chazelles - 42 67 20 73, fax 40 53 85 54
Open 9 a.m.-1 p.m. & 2 p.m.-6 p.m. Closed Sun. Prices vary.

If you like the idea of an informed guided tour but don't like buses, give Emanuelle Darras a call. This young woman has created a series of small, first-class, personalised tours. In a luxurious minivan (stocked with Champagne, no less), a maximum of five people at a time are taken to such places as artists' studios, foie-gras makers, the Cartier workshops and much more.

Paris-Vision
1st arr. - 214, rue de Rivoli - 42 60 31 25
Open daily 8 a.m.-10 p.m.

Paris-Vision conducts guided tours of the city in just about any language you can think of.

R.A.T.P.
8th arr. - Pl. de la Madeleine (behind the flower market) - 40 06 71 45
Open 9 a.m.-7 p.m. (Sat. & Sun. in summer 6:30 a.m.-7 p.m.); winter: until 5 p.m. Closed Sun.

Guided bus tours conducted in every imaginable language.

T.A.S.
43 80 56 56, fax 43 80 04 34
Open daily 7:30 a.m.-midnight.

T.A.S.: a new way to travel. Specialising in tours of Paris and the surrounding area, T.A.S. will pick you up at your hotel in a minibus holding eight to 15 passengers and escort you on a guided tour conducted in your own language, for a day or half-day, morning, noon or night.

■ BY BOAT

Les Bateaux-Mouches
8th arr. - Port de la Conférence, Pont de l'Alma, rive droite - 42 25 96 10
Call for information.

These whales of river cruisers glide down the Seine packed with thousands of tourists, often eliciting a sarcastic smirk from Parisians. But the laugh is on the cynics. These fast, smooth boats provide one of the few ways to see Paris from a new angle. Take an early-morning or dusk cruise, when the light is at its loveliest. On night cruises, the Bateaux-Mouches' floodlights unveil a phantasmagoric cityscape that fascinates tourists and seen-it-all Parisians alike. Lunch and formal dinners are available on board at reasonable prices, considering the incomparable view that accompanies your meal.

Canauxrama
19th arr. - 13, quai de la Loire
42 39 15 00
One day cruise March 15-Nov. 15: 8:30 a.m.-6 p.m.; 3 hours cruise: 9:45 a.m. & 2:45 p.m. Closed Dec. 25 & Jan. 1. Admission: 70-195 F, reduced rate for children.

Did you know that the Saint-Martin and the Ourcq Canals run from the Seine in central Paris as far (upstream) as Meaux? Well, now you do. So why go by bus or underground when you can take a boat back from La Villette's Cité des Sciences? Canauxrama's cruises are one of the city's most pleasant, unhurried, uncrowded excursions. The view of Paris and the Ile-de-France from a comfortable canal boat (sunroof, on-board bar, guided tours) has a special softness. Canauxrama offers a day-long trip on the Canal de l'Ourcq through the charming countryside between Paris and Meaux, with a stopover at Claye-Souilly for a picnic or bistro lunch. Also featured is a tour of the exciting La Villette district, which includes passage through the deepest lock in the Paris region. Departures are from the pier opposite 5 bis, quai de la Loire (19th arrondissement) and from the Paris-Arsenal canal port opposite 50 boulevard de la Bastille (12th arrondissement), just down from the new Opera house.

Paris-Canal et Quiztour Continental
9th arr. - 19, rue d'Athènes
48 74 75 30
Open 9 a.m.-6:30 p.m. (Sat. 10:30 a.m.-4 p.m.). Closed Sun. Admission: 90-200 F, reduced rate for children.

Quiztour offers Canal Saint-Martin and Seine cruises from April 1 to November 13 on board the *Patache* and the *Canotier*, two comfortable riverboats that carry between 50 and 100 passengers. The atmosphere is particularly good in the off-season. Boats are also available for receptions or private cruises, and there are houseboats and canal boat/hotels as well.

Les Vedettes de Paris-Ile-de-France
15th arr. - Port de Suffren
47 05 71 29
Open daily April 1-Sept. 30: 10 a.m.-11 p.m.; Oct. 1-March 31: 10 a.m.-6 p.m. (Sat. & Sun. until 10 p.m.).

A summery dance-hall atmosphere reigns on these tea-dance cruises with such themes as historic Paris or the Val-de-Marne.

Les Vedettes du Pont-Neuf
1st arr. - Square du Vert-Galant
46 33 98 38
Open daily 10 a.m.-11 p.m.

For anyone who knows Paris well, the tour commentary (in several languages) is somewhat bewildering. Les Vedettes du Pont-Neuf runs medium-size boats and is centrally located. Its one-hour pleasure cruises run up and down the Seine. There are departures every 30 minutes from 10 a.m. to noon and from 1:30 p.m. to 6:30 p.m. From May to October there are illuminated tours from 9 p.m. to 10:30 p.m. (departures every half hour). From November to March, call for the times. Tours for groups (minimum 50 persons) and parties can be arranged on request.

AT YOUR SERVICE

■ TOURIST INFORMATION

For all the brochures and other "literature" that the clever sightseer might need:

Eiffel Tower Office
7th arr. - 45 51 22 15
Open May 1-Sept. 30 11 a.m.-6 p.m.

Bureau Gare d'Austerlitz
13th arr. - bd de l'Hôpital - 45 84 91 70
Open 8 a.m.-3 p.m. Closed Sun.
  Located in the international arrivals area.

Bureau Gare de l'Est
10th arr. - bd de Strasbourg - 46 07 17 73
Open 8 a.m.-9 p.m. (off-seas. until 8 p.m.). Closed Sun.
  Located in the arrivals lobby.

Bureau Gare de Lyon
12th arr. - 20 bd Diderot - 43 43 33 24
Open 8 a.m.-9 p.m. (off-seas. until 8 p.m.). Closed Sun.
  Located at the international lines exit.

Bureau Gare Montparnasse
14th arr. - 15, bd de Vaugirard - 43 22 19 19
Open 8 a.m.-9 p.m. (off-seas. until 8 p.m.). Closed Sun.
  Located opposite platform 18.

Bureau Gare du Nord
10th arr. - 18, rue de Dunkerque - 45 26 94 82
Open 8 a.m.-9 p.m., Sun. 1 p.m.-8 p.m. (off-seas. until 8 p.m.). Closed Sun. off-seas.
  Located in the international arrivals area.

Office de Tourisme de Paris
8th arr. - 127, av. des Champs-Elysées - 47 23 61 72, fax 47 23 56 91 (after April 1 '93: 49 52 53 54, fax 49 52 53 00)
Open 9 a.m.-8 p.m. Closed May 1, Dec. 25, Jan. 1.

24-Hour Information Line
47 20 88 98 (after April 1 '93 49 52 53 56)
  In English, of course.

■ ORIENTATION

Here are a few facts of French life for foreign visitors:
When dining out, the service charge (15 per cent) is always included in the bill. An additional tip can be left if you are satisfied with the service. Hairdressers are generally given a 10 to 15 per cent tip. Porters, doormen and room service are tipped a few francs. A hotel concierge makes all sorts of reservations for you (theatre, restaurant, plane, train and so on) and can offer advice about getting around in Paris; don't forget to tip your concierge afterwards for his or her considerable services. Ushers at some cinemas, sporting events, ballets and concerts expect a tip, and can be vengeful if you fail to shell out a couple of francs.

You will doubtless need an adapter to use your shaver or hairdryer in French plugs. They can be obtained in the basement of the Samaritaine or BHV department stores. (See *Department Stores* in the Shops chapter.)

Hallway lighting systems are often manually operated. Just to one side of the entrance, in a conspicuous place on each landing or near the lift, you'll find a luminous switch that is automatically timed to give you one to three minutes of light. To enter many buildings, you must press a buzzer or a numerical code usually located at the side of the front door.

The French telecommunications services (FRANCE TELECOM) have created plastic telephone cards to be used instead of coins in public phone booths. They sell for 96 francs or 40 francs and may be purchased at the post office, cafés and some bookshops. Their microchip technology gives you a certain number of units, which are gradually used up as you make your calls. Don't count too heavily on using telephones in cafés and restaurants unless you have a drink or meal there.

Most modern pay phones have instructions in English printed on them. A local call costs 1 franc. You can phone abroad from most pay phones using either your plastic card or a large supply of 5-franc coins. Reverse-charges calls can be made from pay phones by dialling 19, then 33 after the tone, and then the code for the country you want (Britain, 44; Australia, 61; Canada and the United States, 11).

The Louvre post office (52, rue du Louvre, 1st arr., 40 28 20 00) has a 24-hour international telephone/telegraph/fax service. Also note that Paris telephone numbers have eight figures. If you should come upon an old-style Parisian number with only seven digits, you must dial 4 before the number.

We're always happy to hear about your discoveries and receive your comments on ours. Please feel free to write to us stating clearly what you liked or disliked.

BASICS - AT YOUR SERVICE

■ USEFUL ADDRESSES

Here are some addresses and phone numbers of particular interest to English-speaking travellers:

CHURCHES

American Cathedral in Paris
8th arr. - 23, av. George-V - 47 20 17 92

American Church
7th arr. - 65, quai d'Orsay - 47 05 07 99

Christian Science
14th arr. - 36, bd Saint-Jacques
47 07 26 60

Church of Scotland
8th arr. - 17, rue Bayard - 47 20 90 49

Great Synagogue
9th arr. - 44, rue de la Victoire
45 26 95 36

Liberal Synagogue
16th arr. - 24, rue Copernic - 47 04 37 27, fax 42 27 81 02

St. George's (Anglican)
16th arr. - 7, rue Auguste-Vacquerie
47 20 22 51

St. Joseph's (Catholic)
8th arr. - 50, av. Hoche - 42 27 28 56, fax 42 27 86 49

St. Michael's English Church
8th arr. - 5, rue d'Aguesseau - 47 42 70 88

EMBASSIES

American Embassy
8th arr. - 2, av. Gabriel - 42 96 12 02, fax 42 66 97 83

Australian Embassy
15th arr. - 4, rue Jean-Rey - 40 59 33 00, fax 40 59 33 10

British Embassy
8th arr. - 35, rue du Faubourg-Saint-Honoré - 42 66 91 42, fax 42 66 98 96

Canadian Embassy
8th arr. - 35, av. Montaigne - 44 43 32 00, fax 44 43 34 99

New Zealand Embassy
16th arr. - 7 ter, rue Léonard-de-Vinci
45 00 24 11, fax 45 01 26 39

City lights

Admire Paris in all its splendour during a night-time visit. Hundreds of the city's buildings and monuments are cloaked in illuminations when the sun goes down to show them at their best. Sparkling fountains, shining façades, glowing towers—you'll see the city in a new light.
Monuments: Sun.-Fri. from dusk to midnight; Sat. & eves of holidays until 1 a.m.
Fountains: Daytime April 1-Dec. 31 from 10 a.m. to dusk; Night-time April 1-Dec. 31 Sun.-Fri. from dusk to midnight; Sat. & eves of holidays until 1 a.m.

ENGLISH-SPEAKING ORGANISATIONS

American Centre
12th arr. - 51, rue de Bercy - 44 73 77 77, fax 43 07 11 11
Open 9 a.m.-7 p.m. (Sat. until 2 p.m.). Closed Sun.
Until the Centre's new home, designed by architect Frank Gehry, is completed in September 1993, English courses only are taught (at a temporary address). The other classes for which the Centre is known —yoga, dance, theatre and exercise—will be offered again once the building is complete; at that time dance and theatre performances will be scheduled as well.

American Chamber of Commerce
8th arr. - 21, av. Georges-V - 47 23 80 26
Open 9 a.m.-5 p.m. Closed Sat. & Sun.

American Express
9tht arr. - 11, rue Scribe - 47 77 70 00
Open daily 24 hours.
Here you'll find traveller's cheques and American Express card and travel services. You can also arrange to pick up mail and send or receive money orders.

American Library
7th arr. - 10, rue Général-Camou
45 51 46 82
Open 10 a.m.-7 p.m. Closed Sun., Mon., French hols., July 4 & Thanksgiving.

This privately run establishment houses the largest English-language library on the continent. There is also a selection of records and cassettes. You must, however, be an official resident of France (with a *carte de séjour*) to take books out of the library. A membership fee is required.

British Council
7th arr. - 9, rue Constantine - 49 55 73 23
Open 11 a.m.-6 p.m. (Wed. 7 a.m.). Closed Sat. & Sun.

The council sponsors a wide-ranging library of English books and records.

Canadian Cultural Centre
8th arr. - 5, rue Constantine - 45 51 35 73, fax 47 05 43 55
Open 9 a.m.-5 p.m. Closed Sat. (except exhibitions) & Sun.

The Canadian cultural centre offers dance, theatre and musical performances, as well as a library, art gallery and a student-exchange-programme office.

HOSPITALS (ENGLISH-SPEAKING)

Hôpital Américain
American Hospital of Paris
92200 Neuilly sur Seine - 63, bd Victor-Hugo
46 41 25 25, fax 46 24 49 38

A consultation here is more expensive than at most hospitals in Paris. You can pay in dollars. Dental services are also provided, and there is a 24-hour English-speaking emergency service.

Hôpital Franco-Britannique (British Hospital)
92300 Levallois-Perret - 3 rue Barbès
47 58 13 12

This hospital provides complete services.

PHARMACY

Swann Pharmacy
1st arr. - 6, rue Castiglione - 42 60 72 96, fax 42 60 44 12
Open 9 a.m.-7:30 p.m. Closed Sun.

This is the only pharmacy in Paris where your English-language prescription will be translated and an equivalent medicine made up by a pharmacist.

■ PHONE DIRECTORY

Police/Help
17

Fire Department
18

SAMU (Ambulance)
45 67 50 50

S.O.S. Médecins
43 37 77 77 or 47 07 77 77, fax 45 87 13 47

These doctors make house calls at any hour of the day or night, for about 250-300 francs.

S.O.S. Crisis Line (in English)
47 23 80 80
Open 3 p.m.-11 p.m.

S.O.S. Psychiatrie
47 07 24 24

Emergency psychiatric care.

S.O.S. Dentaire
43 37 51 00

An operator will direct you to a dentist offering emergency care in your district.

Centre Anti-Poisons
40 37 04 04

Poison Control Centre.

GOINGS-ON

As an international city, Paris is the site of many artistic festivals, trade fairs and sporting events. Exact dates vary from year to year, so we've simply listed the month in which they occur.

French national holidays are January 1, May 1, May 8, July 14 and November 11; religious holidays fall on Easter, Easter Monday, Ascension Thursday, Whit Sunday and the following Monday, Assumption Day (August 15), All Saints' Day (November 1) and Christmas. A word of warning: Banks and some shops will close early the day before a public holiday, and the French often take a four-day weekend when holidays fall on a Tuesday or a Thursday.

BASICS - GOINGS-ON

■ JANUARY

Prix d'Amérique
12th arr. - Hippodrome de Vincennes
49 77 17 17
End Jan.
   One of the most prestigious trotting horse races.

■ FEBRUARY

Antiquités-Brocante à Champerret
17th arr. - Porte de Champerret, espace Champerret
Mid-Feb.
   Antiques and bric-à-brac.

Foire à la Ferraille de Paris
12th arr. - Parc Floral de Paris, Bois de Vincennes
End Feb.
   An amusing collection of taste treats and "junque".

■ MARCH

Foire du Trône
12th arr. - Pelouse de Reuilly, Bois de Vincennes
End March-beg. June. Open 2 p.m.-midnight (Fri. & Sat. until 1 a.m.)
   All the fun of a fair.

Jumping International de Paris
12th arr. - Palais Omnisports de Bercy,
8, bd de Bercy - 43 46 12 21
Mid-March.
   International show-jumping trials.

Salon International de l'Agriculture
15th arr. - Parc des Expositions, Porte de Versailles
Beg. March. Open 10 a.m.-7 p.m.
   Bring the kids to this international agricultural show.

Salon du Livre
15th arr. - Parc d'Expositions, Porte de Versailles
Mid-March. Open 9:30 a.m.-7:30 p.m.
   A mammoth book fair.

Salon de Mars
7th arr.- Place Joffre (in front of Ecole Militaire)
Mid-March. Open noon-8 p.m. (Thurs. 11 p.m.), Sat. & Sun. 10 a.m.-8 p.m.
   High-class antiques.

Salon Mondial du Tourisme et des Voyages
15th arr. - Parc des Expositions, Porte de Versailles
Mid-March.
   World tourism and travel.

■ APRIL

Expolangues
15th arr. - Parc des Expositions, Porte de Versailles
End Jan. Open 9:30 a.m.-7 p.m.
   Everything connected with foreign languages.

Foire de Paris
15th arr. - Parc des Expositions, Porte de Versailles
End April-beg. May. Open 10 a.m.-7 p.m.
   Food, wine, household equipment and gadgetry.

Marathon International de Paris
Departure avenue des Champs-Elysées, 8th arr; arrival avenue Foch, 16th arr.
End April.
   26 miles or 42 kilometres, it's all the same to the runners.

■ MAY

Championnats Internationaux de France de Tennis (French Open)
16th arr. - Stade Roland Garros,
2, av. Gordon-Bennett - 47 43 48 00
End May-beg. June
   Top international tennis championship.

Foire du Trône
12th arr. - Pelouse de Reuilly, Bois de Vincennes
   See *March*.

Cinq Jours de l'Objet Extraordinaire (Carré des Antiquaires Rive Gauche)
7th arr. - rue du Bac, de Beaune, de Lille, des Saints-Pères, de l'Université, de Verneuil & quai Voltaire
Mid-May - 10 a.m.-10 p.m.
   Paris's top antiques shops hold open house: rare and unusual objects.

■ JUNE

Course des Garçons de Café
1st arr. - Departure & arrival at L'Hôtel-de-Ville - 40 07 30 12
Beg. June
   Waiters race in the Paris streets balancing a tray with a full bottle and a full glass of beer.

GOINGS-ON · BASICS

Fête de la Musique
Streets of Paris - 42 20 12 34
June 21. All day, all night.
    Anyone who wants to can blow his horn on Music Day.

Foire du Trône
12th arr. - Pelouse de Reuilly, Bois de Vincennes
    See *March.*

Paris Villages
Various Paris districts - 42 74 20 04
From mid-June through summer.
    Local festivities with a working-class flavour: parades, majorettes, folk dancing, fun and games for all.

Prix de Diane Hermès
60500 Chantilly - Hippodrome de Chantilly - (16) 44 62 41 00
Mid-June.
    Wear your classiest *chapeau* to this elegant day at the races, attended by the cream of Parisian society.

Salon International de l'Aéronautique et de l'Espace
93350 Le Bourget - Parc des Expositions du Bourget - 48 35 91 61
Only in odd years. Open 9:30 a.m.-6 p.m.
    Air shows by daredevil pilots; aircraft displays.

■ JULY

Arrivée du Tour de France Cycliste
8th arr. - av. des Champs-Elysées
End July.
    The Tour de France cyclists triumphantly cross the finishing line.

Bastille Day Eve
July 13. In the evening.
    A jolly evening: dance to rock, tango and accordion bands in public squares and at local fire stations. The largest *bal* is the one on the place de la Bastille, 12th arr.

Bastille Day
8th arr. - Avenue des Champs-Elysées
July 14.
    In the morning, a military parade on the Champs-Elysées celebrates the French national holiday. Fireworks display in the evening in the Jardins du Trocadéro, 16th arr.

■ AUGUST

Almost everything is closed in August, but true Paris-lovers regard this as the best month of the year to be in their favourite city.

■ SEPTEMBER

La Biennale des Antiquaires
8th arr. - Grand Palais, av. Winston Churchill.
End Sept.-beg. Oct.
This major antiques show is held every two years, in even years—so look for it in 1994 and 1996.

■ OCTOBER

Fête des Vendanges
18th arr. - Butte Montmartre, corner of rue des Saules & rue Saint-Vincent
First Sat. in Oct.
    A grape harvest at the city's only working vineyard.

Foire Internationale d'Art Contemporain (FIAC)
8th arr. - Grand Palais, av. Winston Churchill
Mid Oct. Open noon-7:30 p.m. (Thurs. 11 p.m.), Sat. & Sun. 10 a.m.-7:30 p.m.
    An international contemporary-art show.

Journée du Patrimoine
44 61 21 50/51
One w.-e. mid Sept.
    A celebration of France's architectural heritage: 300 monuments, ministries, town houses and public buildings open to visitors.

Mondial de l'Automobile
15th arr. - Parc des Expositions, Porte de Versailles
Only in even years. Beg. Oct. Open 10 a.m.-10 p.m.
    The world's second-largest international motor show.

Open de la Ville de Paris
12th arr. - Palais Omnisports de Bercy, 8, bd de Bercy - 43 46 12 21
Beg. Nov.
    The City of Paris Open Tennis Championships.

SICOB
93420 Villepinte - Parc des Expositions, Paris-Nord 48 63 30 30, fax 48 63 31 36
Beg. Oct. Open 9 a.m.-6:30 p.m.
    International office machinery, computers and supplies.

BASICS - GOINGS-ON

Prix de l'Arc de Triomphe
16th arr. - Hippodrome de Longchamp
Beg. Oct. - 49 10 20 30
   A day at the races and a chance to win a lot of money.

Salon International de l'Alimentation (S.I.A.L.)
93420 Villepinte - Parc des Expositions, Paris-Nord
48 63 30 30, fax 48 63 31 36
Only in even years. Mid Oct.
   An international food-products exhibit.

Salon Meubles et Décors
15th arr. - Parc des Expositions, Porte de Versailles
Mid Oct.
   A trade show highlighting the latest innovations in home furnishings and décor.

■ NOVEMBER

Salon d'Automne
8th arr. - Grand Palais, av. Winston Churchill
End Oct. Open 11 a.m.-7:30 a.m. (Thurs. 10 p.m.).
   New art by budding talents.

■ DECEMBER

La Crèche
4th arr.- Place de l'Hôtel de Ville
Dec. 4-Jan. 4. Open 10 a.m.-8 p.m.
   A giant nativity scene, with moving figures and music, set up on the esplanade outside the Town Hall of Paris.

Salon du Chevalet du Poney
15th arr. - Parc des Expositions, Porte de Versailles
Beg. Dec. Open 10 a.m.-7 p.m.
   Horses and ponies galore, and all the trappings.

Salon Nautique International
15th arr. - Parc des Expositions, Porte de Versailles
Beg. Dec. Open 10 a.m.-7 p.m. (Thurs. until 11 p.m.)
   International boat show.

2,000 years of history

The past comes to life in *Paristoric*, a spectacular show in which Paris displays its history and monuments on a giant screen.
Open 365 days a year at 78 bis, boulevard de Batignolles, 17th arr., tel. 42 93 93 46, fax 42 93 93 48. Shows start every hour, on the hour, from 9 a.m. to 6 p.m. (9 p.m. in summer). Adults, 70 francs, children and students, 40 francs.

RAC Motor Insurance

The quickest route to better insurance value

CALL NOW FOR YOUR FREE QUOTATION

0800 678000

or contact your local RAC Insurance branch below during normal working hours

Belfast: (0232) 232640
Birmingham: 021-475 8811
Bournemouth: (0202) 752950
Bristol: (0272) 238499
Cardiff: (0222) 495333
Croydon: 081-681 1546
Darlington: (0325) 369 269
Edinburgh: 031-657 3444
Exeter: (0392) 58335
Glasgow: 041-221 5665
Gloucester: (0452) 300715
Leeds: (0532) 460404

Liverpool: 051-258 1441
Manchester: 061-832 2536
Newcastle: 091-230 0066
Norwich: (0603) 632056
Nottingham: (0602) 691933
Oxford: (0865) 514077
Plymouth: (0752) 228591
Sheffield: (0742) 788044
Southampton: (0703) 335361
Stockport: 061-429 0100
Watford: (0923) 817839

All the cover you'll ever need

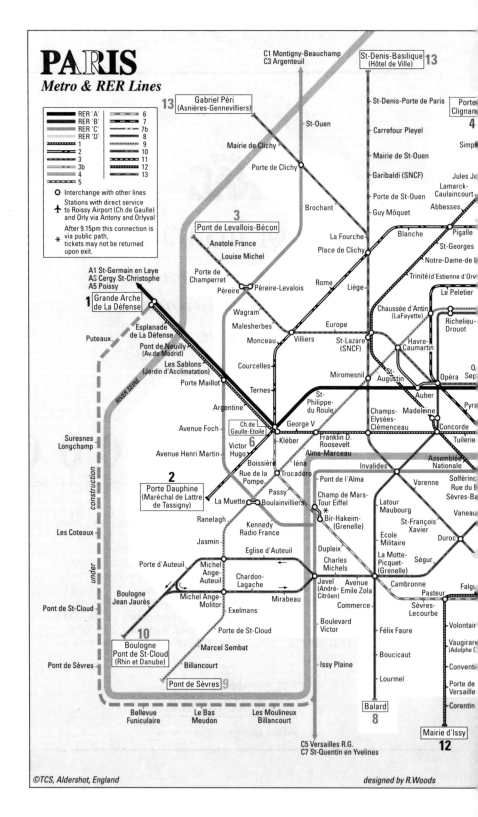

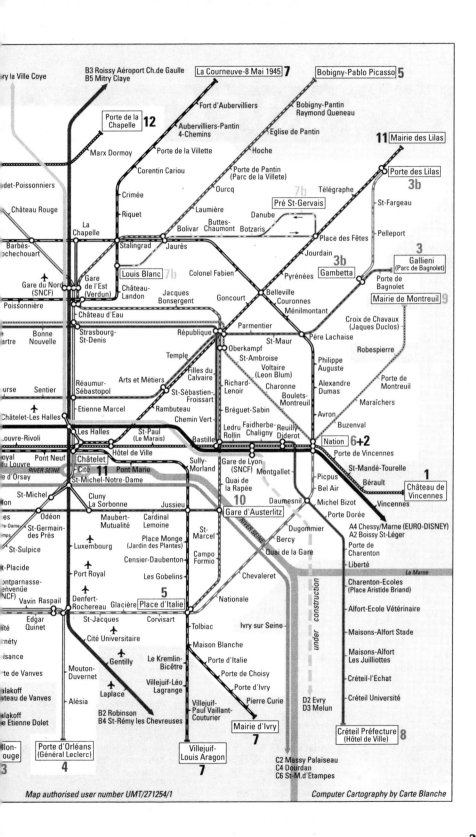

INDEX

Main subject headings and places appear in **bold** print.

A

A & A Turner, 252
A la Plage, 279
A Priori-Thé, 137
A. Lerch, 231
A. Simon, 239
Aaron (Didier), 166
Ababa, 179
Abbaye Saint-Germain, 115
ABC Ruby, 183
Absinthe, 275
Académie de la Bière (L'), 161
Academy, 239
Accessories
- menswear, 260
- tobacconists, 266
- women's wear, 276
Accueil Familial des Jeunes Etrangers (L'), 179
Achdjian (Berdj), 176
Adam Montparnasse, 287
Adrien Maeght, (Galerie), 284
Agaphone, 184
Agnès B., 203
Agnès Comar, 246
Agora, 115
Agora Saint-Germain, 109
Aïcha, 255
Aigle Noir (L'), 318
Aigle d'Or (L'), 83
Aiguière (L'), 49
Air ballon communication, 183
Air de Chasse, 172
Air France (buses), 330
Air de Giverny (Un), 235
Airplane, (rentals), 182
Airports
- hotels, 126
- transportation, 330
Al Ajami, 35
Al Diwan, 133
Al Mounia, 65
Alaïa, 195, 268
Alain Brieux, 177
Alain Dubois, 215
Alain Dutournier, 14
Alain Figaret, 260
Alain Mikli, 210
Alain Passard, 31
Alain Senderens, 41
Alès (Patrick), 186
Alex, 265

Alexander, 109
Alexandre, 186
Alexandre Reza, 252
Alexandre Zouari, 187
Alexis Lahellec, 255
Alfred Dunhill, 267
Ali Baba, 201
Alice Cadolle, 274
Aliette Massenet, 169
Alison, 120
Allard, 26
Allen (Joe), 14
Alliance Autos, 183
Alpha-Taxis, 331
Alsace, 263
Alsace (L'), 35
Altea Paris-Orly, 126
Amazigh, 62
Ambassade, 120
Ambassade d'Auvergne, 20
Ambassadeurs (Les), 36
Ambassador-Concorde, 105
Ambroisie (L'), 21
Ambulance, 335
American
- Center, 334
- Church, 334
- Embassy, 334
- Express, 334
- Hospital, 335
- Library, 335
- Cathedral in Paris, 334
- Chamber of Commerce, 334
Ami Louis (L'), 20
Amicale Culturelle Internationale (L'), 179
Amis du Beaujolais (Aux), 36
Amphyclès, 68
Amuse Bouche (L'), 53
An 2000 (L'), 263
Anarkali, 46
André Bissonnet, 175
Andréa Pfister, 278
Andrée Higgins, 168
Andres Serrita, 290
Androuët, 215
Ange-Vin (L'), 144
Angélina, 137
Angelo Tarlazzi, 272
Anges (Chez les), 31
Angleterre, 115
Annick Goutal, 189
Antica, 245
Antiques, 164

Antiquités de Beaune, 166
Antiquités-Brocante à Champerret, 336
Antoine, 178
Antoine et Antoinette, 31
Antoine Schapira, 241
Antony Embden, 166
Anvers, 204
APC, 204
Apicius, 68
Aquaboulevard, 291
Aquascutum, 207
Aramis Saint-Germain, 109
Arbre à Cannelle (L'), 137
Arbre à Vin (L'), 233
Arc de Triomphe, 169
Argenteuil, 79
Arlequin (L'), 172
Armand au Palais-Royal, 14
Armani, 204
Armes de Bretagne (Les), 54
Armoise (L'), 57
Armorial, 194
Arnys, 204
Arpège, 31
Arredamento, 239
Arrighi (Chez), 317
Arrondissements, 330
Art
- books, 190
- Déco, 165
- Galleries, 282
- Nouveau, 165
- supplies, 287
Artcurial, 190, 254, 282
Artel, 171
Artémide, 245
Arthus Bertrand, 253
Artisan Parfumeur (L'), 188
Arts & Leisure, 281
Arts des Amériques, 168
Arts et Marine, 177
Arts de l'Orient, 170
Asie à Votre Table (L'), 180
Asnières, 79
Assiette (L'), 54
Astier, 49
Astor Madeleine L'Horset, 105
Astronomy, 287
Astucerie (L'), 195
Atala, 115
Atelier de la Dentellière (L'), 290
Attica 1, 190
Aubercy, 261

342

INDEX

Aubergade (L'), 57
Auberge
- du Bonheur, 62, 137
- des Deux Signes, 23
- de Fontaine, 324
- de la Forêt, 312
- de Jarente, 22
- Landaise, 46
- du 14-Juillet, 843
- du Relais Breton, 910
- Saint-Quentinoise, 85
Auberge (L'), 79
Augusta, 68
Aulnay-sous-Bois, 126
Aurore Montmartre, 120
Australian Embassy, 334
Autour du Monde, 199
Avant Musée (L'), 254
Avant-Scène, 239
Aveline, 167
Axis, 235
Azzaro (Loris), 273
Azzedine Alaïa, 268

B

Baby Dior, 197
Baby-sitters, 179
Bac (Georges), 175
Bac à Glaces (Le), 228
Baccarat, 247
Bacchantes (Les), 144
Baché (Ella), 186
Badin (Christian), 242
Bagagerie (La), 255
Baggi, 228
Bagnolet, 126
Baie d'Ha Long (La), 62
Bain Marie (Au), 247
Bain Rose (Le), 237
Bains (Les), 158
Baiser Salé (Le), 157
Bakeries, 212
Balajo (Le), 158
Balenciaga, 268
Balmain (Pierre), 268
Balmès-Richelieu, 177
Baltimore, 105
- restaurant, 63
Balzac, (Maison de), 297
Balzar (Le), 23
Banana Café, 154
Banville, 115
Bar Anglais (Plaza), 158
Bar Belge, 161
Bar du Caveau, 144
Bar à Huîtres (Le), 20, 54, 233
Barbara Bui, 204
Barbier-Beltz, (Galerie), 282
Barbizon, 318
Baril (Catherine), 202
Baron Rouge (Le), 145
Barrail (Le), 58
Barrière de Clichy (La), 69
Barthélémy, 216

Barthet (Jean), 276
Bas-Bréau (Le), 318
Basics, 329
Baskin-Robbins, 228
Bastille
- Corner, 133
- Day, 337
- Day Eve, 337
- Opera, 238
- Optic, 210
- Speria, 109
Bateaux-Mouches (Les), 332
Bath, 237
Baudoin Lebon, (Galerie), 284
Baumann Marbeuf, 36
Béatilles (Les), 69
Beauce (La), 310
Beaugrenelle St-Charles, 120
Beauharnais (Le), 317
Beaujolais Saint-Honoré, 145
Beausoleil (Lunettes), 210
Beauty, 179
Beauty Salons, 185
Beauvilliers (A.), 76
Becs Fins (Aux), 79
Bedford Arms, 161
Beer Bars, 154
Behar, 273
Bélier (Le), 26, 154
Bell Viandier (Au), 229
Belle Epoque, 115
Belle Epoque (La), 50, 80
Bellecour, 31
Bellevue Hôtel, 130
Bellini, 62
Belts, 260
Benadava, 176
Benetton, 199
Benoit, 22
Berdj Achdjian, 176
Bérès (Pierre), 193
Bergère, 120
Bergerie (La), 145
Berggruen, (Galerie), 282
Berlé, 274
Bernard (Claude), (Galerie), 282
Bernard Baruch Steinitz, 167
Bernard Captier, 169
Bernard Chirent, 15
Bernard (Georges), 173
Bernard Péret, 149
Bernardaud, 247
Bersoly's Saint-Germain, 115
Berteil, 257
Berthillon, 228
Bertrand (Arthus), 253
Besnier, 232
Besson, 244
Besson (Gérard), 14
Betjeman and Barton, 219
Beurdeley, 169
Beverly Hills, 102
Beyrie (Maria de), 165
BHV, 207
Bical (Lydia), 178
Bice, 36
Bicycling, 287

- rentals, 287
Biennale des Antiquaires (La), 337
Biletta, 227
Billy Gourmand, 69
Biocéane, 189
Birdland, 154
Bissonnet (André), 175
Bistro 121, 58
Bistro de la Grille, 26
Bistrot
- des Augustins, 145
- Blanc (Le), 47
- de Breteuil (Le), 32
- d'à Côté (Le), 69, 88
- de l'Etoile-Niel (Le), 70
- de l'Etoile-Troyon (Le), 70
- du Sommelier (Le), 36, 145
Bivio (Le), 58
Blanc-Mesnil (Le), 79, 126
Blue Lagoon, 86
Boat
- rentals, 182
- tours, 332
Boccador (Jacqueline), 166
Boccara (Jacqueline), 176
Body Shop, 188
Bœuf sur le Toit (Le), 36
Bois (Le), 120
Bois de Boulogne, 203, 304
Bois de Vincennes, 305
Boiserie (Eugénie), 182
Boissier, 138
Boîte à Bas (La), 274
Boîte à Musique (La), 235
Bol en Bois (Le), 227
Bon Marché (Le), 207
Bon Pain d'Autrefois (Au), 212
Bonbonnière de la Trinité, 216
Bonbons (Les), 217
Bonne Table (La), 82
Bonpoint, 197, 199
Bons Crus (Aux), 145
Books, 190
- art, 190
- children, 197
- cooking, 192
- english-language, 190
- film, 191
- food, 192
- general interest, 192
- open late, 262
- photography, 191
- rare, 193
- travel, 193
Borowski (Nina), 170
Bosc (Chez), 36
Bottega Veneta, 255
Boucherie Lamartine, 229
Boucherie Marbeuf, 229
Boucheries Bernard, 229
Boucheron, 251
Bouchon du Marais (Le), 145
Bouchut (Le), 58
Boudin Sauvage (Le), 90
Boule d'Or (La), 32
Boullé (Claude), 174

343

INDEX

Boulogne-Billancourt, 79, 127
Bourdaloue, 230
Bourdonnais (Le), 32
Bourgey (Emile et Sabine), 171
Bourgogne (Ma), 145
Boutique Le Flore, 235
Boutique du Marais (La), 169
Boutique à Sandwichs (La), 133
Boutique 22, 267
Bowling, 287
Bowling Mouffetard, 287
Bœuf Bistrot, 53
Bœuf sur le Toit (Le), 37
Bradford, 109
Brasserie
- des Arts, 88
- Flo, 48
- de l'Ile Saint-Louis, 22
- Lutétia, 26
- Munichoise, 14
- du Théâtre, 95
Breakfast, 180
Brentano's, 190
Bresset (Edouard et Gabriel), 166
Bretèche (La), 94
Bretonnière (La), 80
Brieux (Alain), 177
Brighton, 115
Bristol (Le), 37, 102
Britannique, 110
British
- Council, 335
- Embassy, 334
- Hospital, 335
- Import, 168
Brocante de Marie-Jeanne (La), 172
Brocante Store, 172
Brocard, 244
Brocco, 138
Brûlerie des Ternes, 219
Brunel (Etienne), 268
Buc, 80
Bucher (Jeanne), (Galerie), 282
Bûcherie (La), 23, 138
Bugat (Paul), 230
Bui (Barbara), 204
Bulgari, 251
Bunny Courses, 181
Bur (Marcel), 257
Burberrys, 207
Burrus (Claire), 282
Buses, 330
- Air France, 330
- rentals, see *Limousines*, 183
- tickets, 330
- tours, 331

C

C. Gustave, 174
Cabarets, 155

Cabinet des Médailles et Monnaies Antiques de la Bibliothèque Nationale, 297
Cacharel, 195, 197
Cachoux (Michel), 174
Caddie, 197
Cadolle (Alice), 274
Cador, 138
Cadre Noir (Le), 70
Café
- Beaubourg, 132
- Costes, 132
- de Flore, 132
- de la Jatte, 88
- des Lettres, 134
- de Mars, 133
- Mouffetard, 132
- des Musées, 132
- de la Paix, 132
- de la Plage (Le), 161
- Runtz, 18
Cafes, 132
Cafétéria du Musée Picasso, 134
Cagna (Jacques), 27
Cagouille (La), 54
Caïd (Au), 266
Cakes, 230
California, 105
California Grill, 86
Calvet, 165
Caméléon (Le), 27
Camille Darmont, 186
Campanile, 312
Camus (William Aimard), 255
Canadel (Le), 90
Canadian
- Cultural Center, 335
- Embassy, 334
Canauxrama, 332
Candles, 246
Canovas (Isabel), 276
Canovas (Manuel), 245
Cantin (Marie-Anne), 215, 240
Cap Cod, 86
Capeline, 245
Capet (Hugues), 310
Capia (Robert), 178
Captier (Bernard), 169
Capucine Puerari, 275
Cars (rentals), see *Limousines*, 183
Cardin, 268
Cardinal de Richelieu, 315
Carette, 138
Carita, 185, 187
Carnavalette, 193
Carpaccio (Le), 37
Carpe (La), 238
Carpe Diem, 88
Carpets, 244
Carré des Feuillants, 14
Carré (Louis) et Cie (Galerie), 283
Cartes Postales (Les), 15
Cartet, 50
Cartier, 251

Cartier (Fondation), 84
Carvil, 261
Casa Alcalde, 58
Casa Lopez, 244
Casal, 245
Casbah (La), 154
Cassegrain, 194
Casta Diva, 138
Castaing (Madeleine), 166
Castel-Princesse, 159
- restaurants, 30
Castelbajac Hommes (Jean-Charles de), 258
Castille, 106
Castro (J.P. de), 177
Catacombes de Paris, 297
Caterers, 213
Catherine Baril, 195
Cave
- à Cigares (La), 267
- Drouot (La), 145
- de l'Ecole Polytechnique, 233
- de Georges Dubœuf (La), 233
Caveau de la Huchette, 157
Caveau du Palais (Le), 15
Caves
- Augé, 222
- Bailly, 146
- Estève, 233
- Pétrissans, 146, 234
- du Savour Club (Les), 234
- Solignac (Les), 146
Caviar, 223
Caviar Kaspia, 37, 223
Cayré, 110
Cazaudehore, 93
Cèdre Rouge (Le), 241
Céladon (Le), 18
Célébrités (Les), 58
Céline et Jérôme, 210
Celle-Saint-Cloud (La), 80
Cellier des Bernardins (Le), 297
Cendrine, 199
Central Crépins, 184
Centre Anti-Poisons, 335
Centre d'Art Floral Ikebana, 288
Centre Equestre de la Cartoucherie de Vincennes, 291
Centre Georges Pompidou, 202, 295
Centre Ville Etoile, 115
Cergy, 127
Cerruti 1881, 204
Césarée, 254
Chairs, 241
Chaise Longue (La), 242
Chambre Claire (La), 191
Champagne (La), 46
Championnats Internationaux de France de Tennis, 336
Champs-Disques, 263
Chandail, 273
Chandelles (Aux), 85
Chanel, 269
- Horlogerie, 253
Chantal Thomass, 262, 272, 275
Chantelivre, 197

INDEX

Chanteraines (Les), 97
Chantllly, 310
Chapeau Gris (Au), 95
Chapelle des
  Lombards (La), 159
Chapman, 155
Charcuterie, 214
Charcuterie Charles, 214
Chardenoux, 50
Charles the Bald, 313
Charles Jourdan, 277
Charles Kammer, 277
Charlot, 46
Charlot Ier, 76
Charlotte de l'Isle (La), 138
Charly de Bab-el-Oued, 70
Charonne, 258
Charpentiers (Aux), 27
Chartier, 47
Chartres, 313
Charvet, 204
Chat Grippé (Le), 27
Château
- de Bellinglise, 312
- de Blérancourt, 302
- de Brécourt, 320
- de Chantilly, 311
- d'Esclimont, 315
- de Fontainebleau, 310, 317
- Frontenac, 106
- de Montvillargenne, 312
- de Rambouillet, 310, 321
- de Saint-Germain-en-Laye, 310
- de Vaux-le-Vicomte, 325
- de Versailles, 327
Chateaubriand, 106
Chateaubriant (Au), 48
Châteaufort, 80
Châtelaine (La), 197, 246
Chattanooga, 263
Chaumet, 251
Chaumette, 235
Chaumière des
  Gourmets (La), 54
Chaville, 81
Cheese, 215
Chêne-Liège (Au), 244
Chène (Paul), 62
Chennevières-sur-Marne, 81
Chéri-Bibi, 276
Chesnay (Le), 96
Chesnoy (Le), 96
Cheval Rouge (Le), 322
Chevalier, 176
Chevignon Girl, 200
Chevignon Kids, 197
Cheyenne Hotel, 127
Chez
- Anges (les), 31
- Arrighi, 317
- Bosc, 37
- Claude Sainlouis, 31
- Dumonet, 28
- Edgard, 38
- Fernand, 50
- Francis, 40
- Françoise, 34

- Fred, 71
- Frézet, 77
- Georges, 72
- Géraud, 64
- Henri, 28, 93
- Janou, 20
- Jenny, 21
- Laudrin, 72
- Lee, 73
- Léon, 73
- Livio, 89
- Marcel, 52
- Marie-Louise, 77
- Marius, 34
- Michel, 49
- Pauline, 17
- Philippe, 51
- Pierre, 61
- Ribe, 35
- Roger, 48
- Serge, 95
- Tante Louise, 46
- Teil, 233
- Toutoune, 26
- Vieille (la), 18
- Vong, 46
Chiberta, 37
Chieng-Mai, 24
Children, 197
- books, 197
- clothing, 197
- discount, 198, 199
- gardens, 203
- juniors, 199
- museums, 202
- parks, 203
- shoes, 199
- teens, 199
China, 247
- antiques, 175
China Club (Le), 155
Chipie, 200
Chipie Stock, 195
Chiquito (Le), 90, 92
Chirent (Bernard), 15
Chloé, 269
Chocolat de Puyricard (Au), 217
Chocolate, 216
Chocolatière (La), 139
Choiseul, 157
Christa Fiedler, 274
Christian Badin, 242
Christian Constant, 217, 230
Christian Dior, 269
- Boutique Monsieur, 258
Christian Lacroix, 270
Christian Louboutin, 278
Christian Science, 334
Christian Tortu, 211
Church of Scotland, 334
Church's, 261
Churches, 334
Cifonelli, 258
Cigars, 267
Cigogne (La), 232
Ciné Doc, 191
Ciné-Images, 286

Cinema, 206
Cinq Continents (Aux), 220
Cinq Jours de l'Objet
  Extraordinaire (Les), 336
Cipière, 249
Cipolli, 227
Cir-Roussel, 246
Cité des Sciences et
  de l'Industrie, 202, 292
City lights, 334
Cityrama, 331
Civette (A la), 267
Claire Burrus, 282
Claret, 110
Claridge-Bellman, 106
Claude Bernard, (Galerie), 282
Claude Boullé, 174
Claude Monet, 310, 319
Claude Montana, 206, 271
Claude Sainlouis (Chez), 30
Claude Vell, 199
Clavel, 24
Clé-Flash, 181
Clémentine, 32
Clerc (François), 213
Clergerie (Robert), 276
Clichy, 81
Climat, 127
Climbing, 291
- equipment, 184
Cloche des Halles (La), 146
Clodenis, 76
Clos Longchamp, 70
Clos Morillons (Le), 59
Closerie des Lilas, 155
Closerie Périgourdine (La), 79
Clothing repair, 179
Clovis, 37, 323
Clown Bar, 146
Club
- de Golf de l'Etoile, 288
- Hippique de la Villette, 291
- Jean de Beauvais, 289
- Lionel Hampton, 157
- Sari Affaires, 182
Cochon d'Auvergne (Au), 214
Cochon d'Or (Au), 78
Cocktails Bars, 156
Coconnas, 22
Coesnon, 214
Cœur de la Forêt (Au), 88
Coffee, 219
Coffee-Parisien, 134
Coin du Caviar (Le), 22, 224
Colisée, 110
Collectania, 240
Colonies (Les), 24
Comar (Agnès), 246
Comme des Garçons, 269
Commodore, 110
Communautés (Les), 91, 128
Compagnie de la Chine et des
  Indes, 169
Compiègne, 312
Comptoir
- Corrézien du Foie Gras
  et du Champignon, 225

INDEX

- du Foie Gras (Bizac) (Le), 225
- du Golf, 265
- du Saumon, 224
- Sud-Pacific, 188
Comptoir (Le), 15, 155
Comptoirs de la Tour
 d'Argent, 236
Computers, 182
Comte de Gascogne (Au), 80
Comtesse du Barry, 232
Concertea, 139
Conciergerie, 119
Concodisc, 250
Concorde Grand
 Monarque, 326
Concorde-La Fayette, 106
- restaurant, 71
Concorde Saint-Lazare, 106
Confectionary, 216
Congrès (Le), 70
Connemara (Le), 96
Connivence (La), 51
Constable Anne de
 Montmorency, 315
Constant (Christian), 217, 230
Conti, 63
Cooking, 287
- books, 192
Coordonnerie Vaneau, 185
Copenhague, 38
Coq de la Maison
 Blanche (Le), 94
Coq Saint-Honoré (Le), 229
Coquelin Aîné, 139, 230
Coquille (La), 70
Cor de Chasse (Le), 182
Corbeille (La), 18
Corbusier (Le), 318
Cordon Bleu (Le), 287
Cordonnerie Anglaise (La), 184
Cordonnerie Vaneau, 184
Cornu (Jean-Claude), 226
Cosi, 134
Cosmetics, 188
Costardo, 258
Costume jewelry, 254
Les Costumes de Paris, 182
Cotailys, 253
Côte (La), 146
Coteaux (Les), 146
Cottage Marcadet (Le), 77
Coude-Fou (Le), 147
Couderc, 230
Cougar (Le), 71
Coup de Cœur, 19
Coupole (La), 54, 132
Cour aux Antiquaires (La), 164
Cour de Rohan (A la), 139
Cour de Varenne (La), 167
Courant d'Art, 193
Courbevoie, 82
Courcelles, 110
Couronne (La), 38
Course des Garçons
 de Café, 336
Courtille (La), 147
Coye-la-Forêt, 312
Crayons de Julie (Les), 194

Crazy Horse, 154
Crèche (La), 338
Creeks, 200
Créole (La), 54
Créplet-Brussol, 215
Créteil, 82, 127
Crillon Hotel, 102
- restaurants, 36, 43
Crimson, 274
Cristalleries Saint-Louis, 247
Cristolien (Le), 82
Crocodisc, 250
Crocojazz, 250
Croissy-Beaubourg, 83
Crystal, 247
- antiques, 172
Crystal Hôtel, 116
Cuisine Gourmande, 134
Culinarion, 238
Cutlery, 238
Cyrillus, 199

D

Da Mimmo, 49
Dagorno, 78
Daire–Miels
 de France (Aux), 226
Dalloyau, 139, 213, 230
Dalou (Jules), 222
Dame Blanche (La), 250
Danaïdes (Les), 91
Dance
- clothing, 264
- sports, 288
Danemark, 116
Danflou (Jean), 234
Daniel Gervis, (Galerie), 283
Daniel Malingue, (Galerie), 284
Daniel Metery, 42
Danny Rose, 134
Darmont (Camille), 186
Daum, 247
Dauphin, 128
Davoli, 220
Debauve et Gallais, 217, 224
Dehillerin, 238
Delaporte, 179
Delaunay, 207
Delauney (Michel), 261
Délices d'Aphrodite, 24
Délices de Scott (Aux), 139, 181
Délices de Szechuen (Aux), 32
Delivery
- breakfast, 180
- flowers, 181
- food, 181
- fruits, 181
Delmonico, 19
Denise René, (Galerie), 285
Dents de Lait, 198
Dépanneur (Le), 155
Department Stores, 207
Dépôt des Grandes
 Marques (Le), 195

Dépôt-Vente de Paris, 196
Desfossé, 186
Designers (Women's wear), 268
Désirade (La), 93
Dessange (Jacques), 186
Détails d'Hérald, 200
Detou, 223
Deux Abeilles (Les), 140
Deux Arcs (Les), 91
Deux Canards (Les), 48
Deux Iles (Les), 116
Deux Magots (Les), 132
Deux Oursons (Les), 196
Deux Portes (Les), 197
Devine Qui Vient Dîner, 247
Deyrolle, 174
Diapason, 24
Diapositive Stock, 196
Didier Aaron, 166
Didier Imbert Fine Art, 284
Didier Ludot, 256
Diep, 38
Dimanche à Venise (Un), 276
Dîners en Ville, 247
Dinh Van (Jean), 254
Dior, 269
- Boutique Monsieur, 258
Diptyque, 188
Directoire (Au), 165
Disco Revue, 250
Discount
- children, 198, 199
- clothes, 195
Disneyland Hotel, 127
Divay (Au Bon Porc), 225
Divellec (Le), 33
Divert (Patrick), 210
Diwan (Gina), 198
Djarling, 140
Documents, 286
Dodin-Bouffant, 24
Dôme (Le), 55
Dominique, 27, 224
Dominique Paramythiotis, 175
Dorotennis, 195
Dorothée Bis, 195, 269
Dorothée Bis Stock, 196
Douains, 320
Drink (open late), 263
Droguerie (La), 290
Drouant, 19
Drugstore
- des Champs-Elysées, 38, 262
- Matignon, 262
- Publicis, 262, 268
- open late, 262
- Saint-Germain, 28, 262
Dry Cleaners, 179
Du Pareil au Même, 197
Dubernet, 225
Dubois (Alain), 215
Duc (Le), 55
Duc d'Aumale, 311
Duc des Lombards (Au), 157
Duc d'Enghien, 83
Duc de Praslin (Au), 217

INDEX

Duc de Saint-Simon, 116
Ducs d'Anjou, 116
Ducs de Gascogne (Aux), 225
Duminy-Vendôme, 110
Dumonet (Chez), 28
Dunhill (Alfred), 267
Duo sur Canapé, 241
Dupré Octante, 194
Duprey, 265
Duquesnoy, 32
Durand-Dessert, 283
Durand (Lucien), (Galerie), 283
Dutko (Jean-Jacques), 165
Dutournier (Alain), 14

E

Ebel, 253
Eber Monceau-Courcelles, 121
Ecaille de PCB (L'), 28
Ecaille et Plume, 33
Ecart International, 240
Echiquier (L'), 47
Eclaireur (L'), 205
Ecluse
- Bastille, 147
- François-Ier, 147
- Les Halles, 147
- Madeleine, 147
- Saint-Michel, 147
Ecole
- de Gastronomie Française Ritz Escoffier, 287
- d'Horticulture du Jardin du Luxembourg, 288
Ecouen, 315
Ecrin d'Or (L'), 71
Ecu de France (L'), 81
Ecurie (L'), 79, 326
Eden Hôtel, 130
Edgard (Chez), 38
Edifice, 240
Edouard et Gabriel Bresset, 166
Edouard VII, 110
Edrei (Jean-Claude), 166
Eggstra, 134
Eiffel Tower, 183
- rentals, 182
- restaurant, 35
- tourist office, 333
Ekisport, 264
El Chiquito, 93
Electrical plugs, 35
Eléonore, 177
Elincourt-Ste-Marguerite, 312
Elisabeth de Senneville, 272
Ella Baché, 185
Elle, 242
Elyfleurs, 210, 262
Elysa, 110
Elysée, 116
Elysée-Lenôtre, 38
Elysées Mandarin, 39
Elysées-Maubourg, 110
Elysées Star, 106

Elysées Stylos Marbeuf, 194
Elysées du Vernet (Les), 39
Embassies, 334
Embden (Antony), 166
Emile et Sabine Bourgey, 171
Emilio Robba, 211
Emmanuel Thiriot–Bernard Escher, 173
Emmanuel Ungaro, 272
En Attendant Les Barbares, 240
Enfants Gâtés (Les), 140
Enghien, 83, 127
English-speaking
- bookstores, 190
- organizations, 334
Enoteca (L'), 147
Entre-Deux-Verres (L'), 147
Entre-Siècle (L'), 59
Entrepôt (L'), 236
Envierges (Les), 148
Epi d'Or (A l'), 237
Epicure 108, 71
Epilation, 186
Epopée (L'), 59
Epreuve du Temps (A l'), 177
Equipment, 260
Equipment, 263
- fishing, 264
- golf, 265
- hunting, 265
- riding, 265
- shooting, 265
- skiing, 266
- sport, 263
- windsurfing, 266
Erawan, 59
Erès, 279
Ermenegildo Zegna, 260
Ermitage Hôtel, 116
Escargot de la Butte (L'), 225
Escargot de Linas (L'), 85
Escargots, 225
Espace
- Café (L'), 219
- Grévin, 297
- Hérault (L'), 148
- Photographique de Paris, 283
- Vit'Halles, 289
Espadon (L'), 15
Estournel (L'), 63
Etamine, 242
Etangs (Les), 312
Etangs de Commelles (Les), 311
Etat de Siège, 240
Ethnic foods, 220
Etienne Brunel, 268
Etienne Levy, 167
Etoile, 121
Etoile de Mer (L'), 96
Etoile d'Or (L'), 71, 217
Etoile Park Hôtel, 116
Etoile-Pereire, 116
Eugénie Boiserie, 182
Euralair, 181
Euro Disney, 203
- hotels, 127
- restaurants, 86

Eustache (L'), 157
Eveningwear (Women's Wear), 273
Expolangues, 336
Eyewear, 210

F

Fabienne, 196
Fabius Frères, 167
Fabrice Karel Stock, 196
Fabrics
- antiques, 173
- clothing, 196
- home, 244
Fac-Bazaar, 274
Façonnable, 258
Faguais, 223
Faïence Anglaise (La), 247
Fakhr el Dine, 39, 63
Fanette, 246
Farideh Cadot, (Galerie), 283
Farigoule (La), 59
Faucher, 71
Fauchon, 223
- home delivery, 181
- quick bites, 135
- restaurant, 46
Faugeron, 63
Fauré-Lepage-Saillard, 265
Fausto Santini, 278
Fauteuil pour Deux (Un), 241
Favart, 121
Félix Marcilhac, 165
Fénix (Jacqueline), 88
Féraud (Louis), 269
Ferme Poitevine, 216
Ferme Saint-Aubin, 216
Ferme Saint-Hubert (La), 216
Ferme Saint-Simon (La), 33
Fermette Marbeuf 1900 (La), 39
Fermette du Sud-Ouest (La), 15
Fernand (Chez), 50
Fernandez-Blanchard, 173
Ferrandi, 116
Ferré (Gianfranco), 258
Ferrero (Jean-Claude), 63
Festivals, 336
Fête de la Musique, 337
Fête des Vendanges, 337
Feu Follet (Au), 55
Feuillantine (La), 93
Feuillantines (Les), 82
Feuilles Libres (Les), 88
FIAC, 337
Fiedler (Christa), 274
Figaret (Alain), 260
Filaos (Les), 64
Film (books), 191
Fils du Temps (Aux), 173
Fine Art, 282
Finkelsztajn, 220
Finnegan's Wake, 161
Fins Gourmets (Aux), 33
Fire Department, 335

INDEX

First Time, 241
Fishing (equipment), 264
Flamberge (La), 33
Flann O'Brien, 161
Flashdance, 264
Fleurs (Les), 320
Flo Prestige, 214, 263
Flora Danica, 38, 135, 224
Flotille (La), 95
Flowers, 181, 108
- arranging, 288
- markets, 212
- open late, 262
- shops, 210
Fnac, 192, 249, 250
Focly, 89
Foie gras, 225
Foie Gras Luxe, 226
Foire
- à la Ferraille de Paris, 336
- Internationale d'Art Contemporain, 337
- de Paris, 336
- du Trône, 336, 337
Folies Bergère, 154
Folies d'Elodie (Les), 275
Folkestone, 121
Fondary, 121
Fondation Cartier, 84
Fondeur (Marguerite), 175
Fontaine d'Auteuil (La), 64
Fontaine-Chaalis, 324
Fontaine au Chocolat, 217
Fontaine de Mars (La), 33
Fontainebleau, 316
Fontaines (Les), 24
Fontaines de Niepce et de Daguerre (Aux), 172
Fontenay-sous-Bois, 83
Food, 212
Forest of Saint-Germain, 323
Forest of Fontainebleau, 317
Forestier, 236
Forestière (La), 130
Formal outfit, 182
Forum (Le), 155
Fouquet, 223
Fouquet (Nicolas), 325
Fouquet's, 39, 133
Fouquet's Bastille, 51
Fouquet's Europe, 91
Fourmi Ailée (La), 140
Fournier-Guérin (Hélène), 175
Fournier (Jean), (Galerie), 283
Fournil de Pierre (Le), 212
Fous de l'Ile (Les), 140
Fowl, 229
Franc Pinot (Au), 22, 148
Francesco Smalto, 259
Francis (Chez), 40
François Clerc, 213
François Guidon, 290
François Ier, 310, 316, 321
François Villon, 279
Françoise (Chez), 33
Frantour Suffren, 110
Fratelli Rossetti, 261

Fred (Chez), 71
Fred Joaillier, 253
Free Lance, 200
Frégate (La), 51
French Open (tennis), 336
Frères Layrac (Les), 181, 263
Fressange (Inès de La), 275
Frey (Pierre), 245
Frézet (Chez), 77
Frizon (Maud), 276
Fromagerie Boursault (La), 216
Froment Leroyer, 199
Fructidor, 135
Fruitier d'Auteuil (Le), 222
Fruit, 181, 222
Fruits de France, 222
Furet (Le), 226
Furniture, 239
- chairs, 241
- contemporary, 239
- outdoor, 241
- rentals, 183
- sofas, 241
Furs, 273
Furterer (René), 186

G

G7 Radio, 331
Gainville (Hélène), 269, 273, 279
Galerie
- Acanthe, 242
- Altero, 172
- d'Art Populaire, 174
- Atlantide des Cinq Sens, 177
- du Bac, 242
- Barbier-Beltz, 282
- Baudoin Lebon, 284
- Beaubourg I et II, 282
- Berggruen, 282
- Claude Bernard, 282
- Jeanne Bucher, 282
- Carrefour, 168
- Farideh Cadot, 283
- Camoin-Demachy, 167
- Louis Carré et Cie, 283
- Lucien Durand, 283
- Jean Fournier, 283
- de France, 283
- Maurice Garnier, 283
- Daniel Gervis, 283
- Gourmande, 140
- Isy Brachot, 282
- Laage-Salomon, 284
- Yvon Lambert, 284
- Louise Leiris, 284
- Lelong, 284
- Adrien Maeght, 284
- Daniel Malingue, 284
- Marwan Hoss, 285
- Mermoz, 168
- Montaigne, 285
- Montenay, 285

- Nationale du Jeu de Paume, 292
- Neotu, 240
- 1900-2000, 285
- Nikki Diana Marquardt, 285
- Odermatt-Cazeau, 285
- de la Paix, 140
- Perrin, 167
- Princesse, Comptoir de l'Affiche, 286
- Proscenium, 285
- Denise René, 285
- Templon, 286
- 13, 172
- Stadler, 285
- Patrice Trigano, 286
- Zabriskie, 286
Galeries Lafayette (Les), 208
Galignani, 190
Gallet, 231
Gallois, 179
Gallopin, 19
Galoche d'Aurillac (La), 232
Game, 229
Game's, 288
Games, 288
- antiques, 178
Ganachaud, 212
Garden Elysée, 116
Gardening, 288
Gardens, 304
- children, 203
Gare
- d'Austerlitz (tourist office), 333
- de l'Est (tourist office), 333
- de Lyon (tourist office), 333
- Montparnasse (tourist office), 333
- du Nord, (tourist office), 333
Garenne-Colombes (La), 83
Gargantua, 214
Garland, 174
Garnier, 242
Garnier (Maurice), Galerie, 283
Gastinne et Renette, 265
Gaultier (Jean-Paul), 205
Gauno et Chardin, 259
Gauvain, 84
Gazelle (La), 71
Gelati, 200
Gélot, 260
Gély (Madeleine), 178
Général La Fayette (Le), 161
General Store (The), 220
Geneviève Lethu, 239
Geography, 282
George-V, 102
- cocktail bar, 155
- restaurant, 44
- tea room, 157
Georges (Chez), 72
Georges Antiquités, 173
Georges Bac, 175
Georges Bernard, 173
Georges Pompidou Center, 295
Georges Rech, 271
Géorgiques (Les), 40

INDEX

Gérard Besson, 14
Gérard Lévy, 169
Gérard Mulot, 231
Géraud (Chez), 64
Germain, 40
Germain (Monique), 279
Gianfranco Ferré, 258
Gianni Versace, 207
Gibert Jeune, 192
Gien, 248
Gifts, 235
Gilbert Guyot, 267
Gilles Vilfeu, 228
Gillet, 174
Gina Diwan, 198
Giovanna, 55
Gismondi, 167
Givenchy, 270
- Gentleman, 259
Giverny, 310, 319
Glacier Calabrese, 228
Glass (antiques), 172
Glénan (Les), 33
Go Sport, 264
Gobelet d'Argent, 161
Godiva, 218
Golden Tulip, 106
Goldenberg, 72, 221
Goldenberg (Jo), 22, 221
Golf, 288
- clothing, 265
- equipment, 265
Golf-Plus, 265
Goumard-Prunier, 15
Gourmandins (Les), 324
Gourmandise (La), 51
Gourmet de l'Isle (Au), 22
Gourmet specialties, 222
Gourmets Landais (Aux), 83
Goutal (Annick), 189
Gouvieux, 312
Grain de Beauté, 189
Graindorge, 72
Grand
- Appétit, 227
- Café Capucines (Le), 47
- Chinois (Le), 64
- Colbert (Le), 19
- Hôtel (Le), 102, 127
- Hôtel (Le) (cocktail bar), 155
- Louvre (Le), 16
- Monarque (Le), 314, 326
- (Richard), 274
- Véfour (Le), 16
Grande Arche de la Défense, 169
Grande Cascade (La), 64
Grandgousier, 77
Grands Hommes, 121
Grange (La), 212
Grateau (Muriel), 248
Great Synagogue, 334
Grenadin (Le), 40
Greyl (Léonor), 187
Griffonnier (Le), 148
Grille Saint-Honoré (A la), 16
Grooms de Paris (Les), 180

Gualdoni, 210
Gucci, 255
- Guerlain, 185
Gueulardière (La), 90, 320
Gueuze (La), 161
Guidon (François), 290
Guillet, 211
Guimet museum, 298
Guinguette de Neuilly (La), 89
Gustave (C.), 174
Guy, 28
Guy Laroche, 270
Guy Savoy, 75
Guyot (Gilbert), 267
Guyvonne, 72
Gymnase Club, 289

H

Hair salons, 186
- service, 333
Halles (Les), 251
Halles Capone, 205
Hameau de Passy, 117
Hamm, 290
Hanae Mori, 271
Hardware, 242
Harel, 276
Harlow, 187
Harry Winston, 252
Harry's Bar, 155
Hats, 260
Haupois (Marcel), 213
Haute Route (La), 184, 266
Health, 179
- clubs, 289
- foods, 227
Hébert (Jacques), 59
Hédiard, 223
Hélène Fournier-Guérin, 175
Hélène Gainville, 269, 273, 279
Hélicap, 183
Hémisphères, 205
Henell's, 255
Henri (Chez), 28, 92
Henri III, 321
Henry Cotton's, 258
Heratchian Frères, 221
Herboristerie du Palais-Royal, 227
Hermès, 256, 266
Herminette (L'), 174
Hesse (Jacques), 181
Heure Gourmande (L'), 141
Heure des Thés (L'), 141
Hévin (Jean-Paul), 231
Higgins (Andrée), 168
Hilditch & Key, 260
Hilton, 107
- cocktail bars, 159
- International Orly, 126
- restaurants, 62
Hippodrome
- d'Auteuil, 290
- de Longchamp, 290

- de Vincennes, 290
Hired Hands, 180
Hiroko Koshino, 270
Hirondelles (Les), 87
Historial de Montmartre, 297
History, (movie), 338
Hobbies, 287
Holiday Inn, 111, 126, 129, 130
Holidays, 336
Home, 237
- delivery, 180
Home Saint-Louis, 130
Homme Sweet Homme, 236
Honey, 226
Hôpital Américain, 335
Hôpital Franco-Britannique, 335
Hospitals, 335
Hostellerie du Lys, 312
Hostellerie de Varennes, 95
Hot air balloon, 183
Hôtel
- Adagio, 127
- Balzac, 105
- de la Bretonnerie, 109
- du Collège de France, 121
- de Crillon, 102
- de Crillon (restaurants), 36
- des Chevaliers, 121
- de Dion-Bouton, 129
- Flora, 121
- International de Paris, 128
- du Jeu de Paume, 117
- Left Bank, 117
- Legris et Parc, 318
- du Léman, 117
- Lido, 117
- Lotti, 103
- du Louvre, 107
- Moulin, 118
- des Nations, 112
- de Neuville, 122
- du Parc, 128
- de la Place du Louvre, 123
- du Pré, 124
- Quorum, 129
- de Saint-Germain, 124
- des Saints-Pères, 119
- du 7e Art, 125
- de Sévigné, 114
- de Strasbourg, 126
- Vernet, 109
Hôtel (L'), 117
Hotels, 99
Hugo Boss, 257
Hugues Capet, 310
Huguet, 179
Hulotte (La), 28
Hune (La), 192, 262
Hunting, 265
Hurlingham Polo Bar, 156

I

Ibis Jemmapes, 121
Ibis Paris-Bercy, 121

349

INDEX

Ice cream, 228
Ice skating, 290
Ile de France (L'), 88
Ile Saint-Louis, 158
Iles Marquises (Aux), 55
Ilias Lalaounis, 253
Illuminations, 286, 334
IMA, 289
Image, 249
Image et Page, 190
Imagerie (A l'), 286
Immo-Photo-Video-Son, 249
Impatient (L'), 72
Imprévu (L'), 175
Indiennes (Les), 173
Inès de La Fressange, 275
Information Line, 333
Ingrid Millet, 185
Institut
- George-V, 186
- Géographique National, 193
- Laugier, 188
- Yung, 188
Institute of the Arab World, 289
Inter-Continental, 103
- restaurant, 18
Interfruits Service, 181
Interior decoration, 242
- decor, 242
- miscellany, 244
Irié, 270
Irish Pub, 161
Isabel Canovas, 276
Island, 259
Isler, 238
Ismery-James Agency, 179, 180
Issey Miyake, 271
Issy-les-Moulineaux, 84
Istria, 122
Isy Brachot, (Galerie), 282
Izraël, 221

J

J.P. de Castro, 177
Jacadi, 198
Jacqueline Boccador, 166
Jacqueline Boccara, 176
Jacqueline Fénix, 88
Jacqueline Subra, 174
Jacques Cagna, 27
Jacques Dessange, 186
Jacques Hébert, 59
Jacques Hesse, 181
Jacques Kugel, 177
Jacques Mélac, 148
Jadis et Gourmande, 218
James Joyce, 161
Jams, 226
Jan et Hélène Lühl, 170
Janette Ostier, 170
Janou (Chez), 20
Jardin
- Albert-Kahn, 305
- de Cluny (Le), 111

- du Luxembourg, 203, 305
- du Palais-Royal, 305
- des Plantes, 203, 305
- des Plantes (Le), (hotel), 122
- en Plus (Un), 211
- du Printemps (Au), 40
- du Royal Monceau (Le), 40
- des Tuileries, 306
Jardin (Le), 84
Jardins
- d'Eiffel (Les), 122
- de Giverny (Les), 320
- Imaginaires, 241
Jare, 254
Jean Barthet, 276
Jean-Charles de Castelbajac
   Hommes, 258
Jean-Claude Cornu, 226
Jean-Claude Edrei, 166
Jean-Claude Ferrero, 63
Jean-Claude et Nanou, 232
Jean Danflou, 234
Jean Dinh Van, 254
Jean Fournier, (Galerie), 283
Jean-Jacques Dutko, 165
Jean de Laminne, 168
Jean Lapierre, 173
Jean-Legrand (Les Produits), 226
Jean-Louis David
   International, 186
Jean-Louis Scherrer, 272
Jean-Marc Maniatis, 187
Jean-Paul Gaultier, 205
Jean-Paul Hévin, 231
Jean Soustiel, 170
Jean Vinchon, 171
Jean-Luc Poujauran, 224
Jean-Pierre Vigato, 68
Jeanne Bucher, (Galerie), 282
Jenny (Chez), 21
Jeu de Paume, 292
Jeux Descartes, 288
Jewellery, 251
Jo Goldenberg, 22, 221
Joe Allen, 14
John Lobb, 261, 277
Joseph, 274
Joséphine, 28
Jouets & Cie, 201
Jourdan (Charles), 277
Journée du Patrimoine, 337
Jouy-en-Josas, 84
Jules Dalou, 222
Jules Verne, 35
Julien, 49
July 13, 337
July 14, 337
Jumping International
   de Paris, 336
Juste Mauve, 243
Justine, 55
Juvenile's, 148

K

K-Jacques, 277
K Way, 264
Ka (Paule), 270
Kammer (Charles), 277
Karel Stock (Fabrice), 196
Karl Lagerfeld Boutique, 270
Kashiyama, 275
Kélian (Stéphane), 261, 277
Kenzo, 205
Kenzo Enfants, 200
Keur Samba, 159
Key West Seafood, 86
Kim-Anh, 59
Kim (Rita), 236
Kindal, 238
Kioko, 221
Kiosques, 162
Kitchen Bazaar, 238
Kitchenware, 238
- cutlery, 238
Kitty O'Shea's, 162
Kléber, 111
Klein (Michel), 270
Knits, 273
Koshino (Hiroko), 270
Kraemer, 167
Kraemer (Nicole), 172
Kremlin-Bicêtre (Le), 127
Kugel (Jacques), 177

L

Laage-Salomon, (Galerie), 284
Lac Hong (Le), 95
Lachaume, 211
Lacoste, 264
Lacroix (Christian), 270
Ladurée, 141
Laffitte (Le), 85
Lagerfeld Boutique (Karl), 270
Lahellec (Alexis), 255
Laines Ecossaises (Aux), 274
Lalaounis (Ilias), 253
Lalet (Marie), 201
Lalique, 248
Lamartine Fleurs, 212
Lambert (Yvon), (Galerie), 284
Laminne (Jean de), 168
Lamorlaye, 312
Lancaster, 107
Lancel, 256
Lancôme, 185
Langevin, 77
Lanvin Homme, 259
Lapérouse, 28
Lapidus, 259
Lapierre (Jean), 173
**Large Sizes (Women's
   Wear), 274**
Larizzi (Sidonie), 277
Laroche (Guy), 270
Lassance (Marcel), 259
Lasserre, 40

INDEX

Late openings, 262
Latin Optique, 210
Latitudes Saint-Germain, 111
Laudrin (Chez), 72
Laumière (Le), 122
Laundry, 179
Laurent, 41
Laurent Mercadal, 278
Lavignes-Bastille, 284
Layrac, 214
Lazartigue Traitement
  du Cheveu, 187
Le Brun, 325
Le Corbusier, 318
Le Divellec, 33
Le Nôtre (André), 310, 311, 323,
  325, 328
Leather, 255
- repair, 184
Lebrun, 175
Lecoanet Hemant, 270
Lecointre et Ozanne, 190
Ledoyen, 41
Lee (Chez), 72
Lefebvre et Fils, 175
Lefortier, 176
Léger (Michel), 205
Legrand Filles et Fils, 234
Lei, 255
Leif Stahle, 285
Leiris (Louise), (Galerie), 284
Lelong, (Galerie), 284
Lemaire, 268
Lempicka (Lolita), 270
Lenôtre, 218, 231
Lenox, 111, 117
Léon (Chez), 73
Léonor Greyl, 187
Lerch (A.), 231
Leroyer (Froment), 199
Les Halles, 251
Lescure, 16
Lethu (Geneviève), 239
Letourneur-Lesèche, 179
Levallois-Perret, 84
Lévy (Gérard), 169
Liberal Synagogue, 334
Librairie
- du Cygne, 193
- Delamain, 192
- des Femmes (La), 193
- Gourmande (La), 192
- des Gourmets, 192
- Maeght, 190
- Thomas, 193
Lido (Le), 154
Lighting, 245
- systems, 333
Limousines, 183, 330
Lina's, 135
Linas, 85
Linens, 246
Lingerie, 274
Lionel Hampton (Club), 159
Lipp, 29
Littré, 107
Live Music, 159

Livio (Chez), 89
Livry-Gargan, 85
Lobb (John), 261, 277
Locamac, 182
Locatel, 184
Locksmiths, 181
Locomotive (La), 159
Loewe, 256
Loir dans la Théière (Le), 141
Lolita Lempicka, 270
Longchamp, 122, 256
Lord Sandwich, 135
Loris Azzaro, 273
Los Angeles Bar, 87
Losco, 260
Lotti Hotel, 103
Louboutin (Christian), 278
Louchebem (Le), 16
Louis Carré et Cie (Galerie), 283
Louis Féraud, 269
Louis XIV, 323, 327
Louis XIV (Le), 49
Louis XVI, 321
Louis Vuitton, 257
Louise Leiris, (Galerie), 284
Louisiane (La), 122
Lous Landés, 55
Louveciennes, 85
Louvre
- des Antiquaires (Le), 164
- museum, 293
Lozère (La), 29
Lucas-Carton, 41
Lucien Durand, (Galerie), 283
Ludéric, 180
Ludot (Didier), 256
Luggage, 255
Lühl (Jan et Hélène), 170
Luisa (Maria), 275
Lunettes Beausoleil, 210
Lutèce, 117
Lutétia, 107
- restaurants, 27, 29
Luxembourg, 122
Ly-Ya, 78
Lydia Bical, 178

M

Mac Douglas, 195, 256
Madel (Pierre), 173
Madeleine Castaing, 166
Madeleine Gély, 178
Madeleine de Savoie, 315
Madigan (Le), 73
Madison, 111
Maeght (Adrien), (Galerie), 284
Magellan, 122
Magic Circle-Espace
  Mode, 205
Magic Stock, 198
Magloire (Philippe et
  Claude), 170
Magnolia, 172
Magnolias (Les), 90

Maid Services, 181
Main à la Pâte (La), 17
Maison
- Auguste Rodin, 304
- des Artisans (La), 236
- de l'Astronomie (La), 287
- de Balzac, 297
- Blanche (La), 44
- du Chocolat (La), 141, 218
- du Dictionnaire (La), 193
- de l'Escargot (La), 225
- du Leica (La), 249
- du Miel, 226
- Queulevée-Rôtisserie
  Cambronne, 229
- Renan-Scheffer, 304
- Service, 181
- de la Truffe, 227
- de Victor Hugo, 297
- du Week-End (La), 248
Maisons-Laffitte, 85
Maître Parfumeur
  et Gantier, 189
Majestic, 118
Malbranche (R.), 290
Malingue (Daniel),
  (Galerie), 284
Mancel-Coti, 165
Mancini (René), 278
Mange Tout (Le), 51
Manhattan Club, 87
Maniatis (Jean-Marc), 187
Manicure, 188
Manoir Normand (Le), 42
Manoir du Palomino (Le), 314
Manoir de Paris (Le), 73
Manuel Canovas, 245
Manufacture (La), 84
Manufacture Nationale
  de Sèvres, 248
Marais, 105, 122, 288
Marais Plus, 135
Marathon International
  de Paris, 336
Marc Tattevin-Palais
  de la Viande, 230
Marcel (Chez), 51
Marcel Bur, 257
Marcel Haupois, 213
Marcel Lassance, 259
Marché
- aux Fleurs de l'Île
  de la Cité, 212
- de la Madeleine, 212
- aux Puces (Le), 164
- Saint-Pierre, 196
- des Ternes, 212
- aux Timbres (Le), 171
Marcilhac (Félix), 165
Mare au Diable (La), 326
Marée (La), 42
Marguerite Fondeur, 175
Maria de Beyrie, 165
Maria Luisa, 275
Mariage Frères, 141, 219
Marie-Anne Cantin, 215, 224
Marie Lalet, 201

351

INDEX

Marie-Louise (Chez), 77
Marie Mercié, 278
Marie-Papier, 194
Marina Rinaldi, 274
Marine (La), 162
Marithée et François
   Girbaud–Halles Capone, 205
Marius, 64
Marius (Chez), 34
Markets
- flowers, 212
- food, 21
Marks & Spencer, 208, 221
Marlotte (La), 29
Marne-la-Vallée, 86, 127
Marnes-la-Coquette, 87
Maroquinerie
   Parisienne (La), 256
Marriott Prince de Galles, 103
- restaurant, 44
Marronniers (Les), 53, 118
Martin-Pêcheur (Au), 264
Marwan Hoss, (Galerie), 285
Massenet (Aliette), 169
Mauboussin, 251
Maud Frizon, 276
Mauduit, 231
Maurice Garnier, (Galerie), 283
Maurice Segoura, 168
Max Poilâne, 213
Maxim's, 42, 89, 92
Maxim's (Résidence
   de Paris), 104
Maxoff, 224
Mayflower, 162
Meat, 229
Mélac (Jacques), 148
Mellerio dits Meller, 252
Mélodies Graphiques, 194
Melrose (Le), 135
Melun, 326
Menswear, 257
Mercadal (Laurent), 278
Mercié (Marie), 278
Mercier (Taïr), 239
Mercure Galant, 17
Mercure Paris-Bercy, 111
Mercure Paris-
   Montparnasse, 111
Mercure Paris-Vaugirard, 111
Mère de Famille (A la), 226
Méridien Paris-Etoile (Le), 107
- restaurant, 70
- live music, 157, 159
Méridien Paris-
   Montparnasse (Le), 108
- restaurants, 56
Mermoz Retouches, 179
Méry-sur-Oise, 90
Messengers, 182
Metery (Daniel), 43
Métro, 330
- map, 340-341
Mettez, 205
Meudon, 87
Meurice, 103
- cocktail bar, 156

Mexico (Le), 135
Mexico Café, 64
Meyer (Michel), 168
Mi-Prix, 198
Michel (Chez), 49
Michel Cachoux, 174
Michel Delauney, 261
Michel Elbaz (S.C.A.D.), 173
Michel Klein, 270
Michel Léger, 205
Michel Meyer, 168
Michel Perry, 278
Michel Rostang, 74
Michèle Wilson, 237
Micro-Brasserie (La), 162
Midi Trente, 136
Mikaeloff (Robert), 176
Miki House, 199
Mikli (Alain), 210
Mille Break First, 180
Mille Feuilles, 211
Miller et Bertaux, 243
Millésime (Le), 148
Millet, 231
Millet (Ingrid), 185
Miravile, 23
Missoni, 206
Mistral Shop, 266
Miyake (Issey), 271
Moatti, 171
Mod's Hair, 187
Model (Philippe), 278
Modern Hôtel Lyon, 112
Modernismes, 240
Moissonnier, 25
Moissy-Cramayel, 326
Mollard, 42
Moloko (Le), 156
Monarque (Le), 82
Monceau Fleurs, 212
Monde des Chimères (Le), 23
Mondial de l'Automobile, 337
Monet (Claude), 310, 319
Monfort-l'Amaury, 322
Moniage Guillaume (Le), 56
Monique Germain, 279
Monoprix, 208
Montalembert, 108
Montana (Claude), 206, 271
Montana-Tuileries, 112
Montgolfier, 157
Montmartre, 302
- by train, 308
Montmorency, 88
Montparnasse 25, 56
Monuments (movie), 338
Mora, 239
Morabito, 256
Moreau-Gobard (Yvonne), 170
Moreni (Popy), 271
Mori (Hanae), 271
Morot-Gaudry, 60
Morvandelle (La), 97
Mosquée de Paris, 142, 289
Motillon, 265
Motorcycles (rentals),
   see Limousines, 183

Motsch, 260
Moule à Gâteaux (Le), 231
Moulin Rouge (Le), 154
Moulin à Vins (Le), 149
Mounia (Al), 65
Mourougane France, 221
Mouton à Cinq Pattes (Le), 198
Movida (La), 19
Movie, (about Paris), 338
Mugler (Thierry), 206, 271
Mulot (Gérard), 231
Multicubes, 201
Multistore Opéra, 262
Muniche (Le), 29
Muriel, 257
Muriel Grateau, 248
Musardière (La), 83
Muscade, 142
Musée
- Grévin, 202
- Américain, 320
- des Antiquités
   Nationales, 322, 323
- de l'Armée, 202, 298
- d'Art et d'Histoire
   de Saint-Denis, 298
- d'Art Juif, 298
- d'Art Moderne de la
   Ville de Paris, 293
- d'Art Naïf Max Fourny-Musée
   en Herbe, 298
- des Arts Asiatiques-
   Guimet, 298
- des Arts Décoratifs, 293
- des Arts de la Mode, 299
- Auguste Rodin, 304
- Bouchard, 299
- Bourdelle, 299
- Bricard (de la Serrurerie), 299
- Carnavalet, 299
- de la Chasse et de
   la Nature, 299
- Claude Monet, 320
- Condé, 311
- de la Contrefaçon, 300
- du Crystal, 300
- Ernest Hébert, 300
- Eugène Delacroix, 300
- de la Franc-Maçonnerie, 300
- Grévin, 300
- Guimet, 298
- Gustave Moreau, 300
- de l'Histoire de France, 301
- de l'Homme, 293
- Jean-Jacques Rousseau, 301
- du Jouet, 301
- Lambinet, 301
- du Louvre, 293
- de la Marine, 202, 294
- Marmottan, 294
- Mémorial Ivan
   Tourgueniev, 301
- de la Mode et du
   Costume, 301
- Monet (Claude), 320
- de la Monnaie, 302
- de Montmartre, 302

INDEX

- National d'Art Moderne, (Centre Georges Pompidou), 295
- National des Arts d'Afrique et d'Océanie, 202, 302
- National des Arts et Traditions Populaires, 302
- National de la Coopération Franco-Américaine–Château de Blérancourt, 302
- National des Monuments Français, 303
- National du Moyen-Age, 303
- National de l'Orangerie des Tuileries, 303
- National Picasso, 296
- Nissim de Camondo, 303
- d'Orsay, 295
- du Pain, 303
- Pasteur, 303
- du Petit Palais, 295
- Picasso, 296
- Picasso (cafétéria), 134
- de la Poste, 303
- de la Publicité, 303
- de la Renaissance, 316
- Rodin (Auguste), 304
- de la Sculpture en Plein Air, 304
- de la Vie Romantique, 304
- Vivant du Cheval, 311
- Zadkine, 304
Muses (Les), 47
Muséum National d'Histoire Naturelle, 202, 296
Museums, 292
- children, 200
- tours, 301
Music, 159, 290
Myrène de Prémonville, 271
Mythes et Légendes, 170

N

Naf-Naf, 198, 200
Nain Bleu (Au), 201
Nandy, 326
Nanterre, 88
Napoléon, 43, 112, 321
Narakas, 273
National holidays, 336
Natori, 275
Nautistore, 266
Navarro, 175
Navig France, 182
Needlepoint, 244
Needlework, 290
Négociants (Aux), 77, 149
Nestor Perkal, 241
Neuilly Park Hôtel, 128
Neuilly-sur-Seine, 88, 128
New Man, 198, 200
New Morning (Le), 157
New York Hotel, 127
New Zealand Embassy, 334
Newport Bay Club, 128

Nice Fleurs, 212
Niçoise (La), 73
Nicolaï (Patricia de), 189
Nicolas, 234
Nicolas Fouquet, 325
Nicole H., 243
Nicole Kraemer, 172
Nicolier, 176
Niel's (Le), 159
Nightclubs, 160
Nightlife, 153
Nikki Diana Marquardt, (Galerie), 285
Nikko de Paris, 112
- restaurant, 58
Nina Borowski, 170
N'ioullaville, 50
Nobele, 190
Nobilis Fontan, 245
Noctambus, 330
Nocto, 263
Nogent-le-Phaye, 314
Nogent-sur-Marne, 128
Nogentel, 128
Nom de la Rose (Au), 211
Normandy, 320
Normandy (Le), 156
Notre-Dame Hôtel, 118
Nouveau Quartier Latin (Le), 191
Nouvel Hôtel, 122
Nouvelles Images, 286
Novanox, 123
Novotel, 126, 127
- Bercy, 123
- Créteil-le-Lac, 127
- Paris-Bagnolet, 126
- Paris-Le Bourget, 126
- Paris-Les Halles, 123
- Paris-Survilliers, 130
- Saclay, 129
Nuit des Rois (La), 149
Nuits d'Elodie (Les), 275
Nuits des Thés (Les), 93, 142
Numismatique et Change de Paris, 171
Numistoria, 171

O

Obélisque (L'), 43
Odéon Hôtel, 123
Odermatt-Cazeau, (Galerie), 285
Odiot, 248
Œillade (L'), 34
Œnothèque (L'), 149
Office (equipped), 182
Office de Tourisme de Paris, 333
Oie Cendrée (L'), 60
Oils, 226
Oiseau de Feu (L'), 162
Oiseau de Paradis (L'), 201
O.J. Perrin, 254

Old England, 206
Oldies but Goodies, 250
Olivades (Les), 243
Olivia Valère, 159
Olivier (A l'), 226
Olivier Roux-Devillas, 177
Olivier-Ouzerie (L'), 56
Olympe, 60
Onglerie de la Madeleine (L'), 188
Open late, 262
- bookshops, 262
- drink, 263
- drugstores, 262
- flowers, 262
- food, 263
- pharmacies, 263
- record stores, 263
Open de la Ville de Paris, (tennis), 337
Opera, 160
- Bastille, 160, 238
- Comique, 160
- Garnier, 160, 238
Opéra Restaurant, 47
Opus Café, 158
Orangerie (L'), 94
Orangerie museum, 303
Orient-Occident, 170
Orientation, 333
Orléans Palace Hôtel, 123
Orly, 89, 126
Orsay, 90
- museum, 295
Ostier (Janette), 170
Othello, 255
Ouest Hôtel, 123
Out of Paris, 309
Oxymuse, 278
Ozoir-la-Ferrière, 90

P

Paco Funada, 269
Paco Rabanne, 271
Pactole (Au), 25
Pacy-sur-Eure, 320
Padd, 266
Pagode (La), 192
Pain d'Epice, 201
Pain d'Epices Maison, 236
Pain, Salade et Fantaisie, 136
Pain et le Vin (Le), 149
Palais
- de la Découverte, 202, 296
- du Fruit, 222
- de Kashmir, 77
- des Thés (Le), 219
- de Tokyo, 297
Palette (La), 133
Paloma Picasso, 257
Panam' 2002, 331
Pandora, 142
Panetier (Au), 212
Panthéon, 118

353

INDEX

Pape, 259
Papier Plus, 194
Paradis Latin (Le), 154
Paramythiotis (Dominique), 175
Parc
- André-Citroën, 306
- de Belleville, 306
- des Buttes-Chaumont, 306
- aux Cerfs (Le), 29
- Floral, 203
- Georges-Brassens, 307
- Monceau, 307
- Montsouris, 123, 307
- Victor-Hugo, 112
- de la Villette, 203, 307
Pareil au Même (Du), 198
Paris (Le), 29
Paris By Cycle, 287
Paris-Canal, 332
Paris et son Histoire, 331
Paris Passion, 331
Paris Tourist Offices, 333
Paris Vélo, 182
Paris Vélo (Rent a bike), 287
Paris Villages, 337
Paris-Vision, 332
Paris Visite, 330
Paristoric, 338
Park Side, 87
Parks, 304
- children, 203
Passard (Alain), 31
Passe Montagne, 266
Passementerie
  Nouvelle (La), 244
Passementeries de l'Ile
  de France, 244
Passion (La), 17
Passy Eiffel, 123
Passy-Mandarin, 65
Pasta, 227
Pastavino, 136
Patinoire des Buttes-
  Chaumont, 290
Patio Montparnasse (Le), 60
Pâtisserie Viennoise (La), 142
Patrice Trigano, (Galerie), 286
Patricia de Nicolaï, 189
Patrick Alès, 186
Patrick Divert, 211
Paul Bugat, 230
Paul Chène, 62
Paule Ka, 270
Pauline (Chez), 17
Pavillon
- Bleu (Le), 95
- Christofle, 248
- Henri-IV (Le), 94, 130
- Montsouris, 56
- Puebla (Le), 78
- de la Reine, 112
Peau d'Ange, 246
Pedicure, 188
Pellegrino (Renaud), 257
Peltier, 218, 231
Pelucherie (La), 201
Péret (Bernard), 149

Pergolèse, 108
Pergolèse (Le), 65
Perkal (Nestor), 241
Perla (La), 156
Perle (La), 254
Perpitch, 166
Perraudin, 25
Perreux (Le), 90
Perreyve, 123
Perrin (O.J.), 254
Perry (Michel), 278
Peter, 249
Petit
- Bedon (Le), 65
- Colombier (Le), 73
- Faune, 198
- Journal Montparnasse
  (Le), 158
- Laurent (Le), 34
- Mabillon (Le), 30
- Mâchon (Le), 60
- Marguery (Le), 53
- Matelot (Au), 264
- Montmorency (Au), 43
- Navire (Le), 25
- Opportun (Le), 158
- Palais museum, 295
- Poste (Le), 84
- Prince (Le), 25
- Riche (Au), 47
- Saint-Benoît (Le), 30
- Salé (Le), 74
- chez Soi (Au), 80
- Zinc (Le), 30
Petite
- Auberge (La), 74
- Bretonnière (La), 60
- Chaise (La), 34
- Cour (La), 30
- Forge (La), 97
P'tite Tonkinoise (La), 49
Petites Sorcières (Les), 57
Petits Chandeliers (Aux), 57
Petrossian, 224
Petrus, 74
Pfister (Andréa), 278
Pharmacies, 335
- Azoulay, 263
- Les Champs, 263
- Lagarce, 263
- open late, 263
- Swann, 335
Phedra, 254
Phileas Fogg, 94
Philippe (Chez), 50
Philippe et Claude
  Magloire, 170
Philippe Model, 278
Photography, 249
- books, 191
Picasso museum, 296
Pichet (Le), 43
Picpus Cemetery, 222
Pied de Cochon (Au), 17
Pied de Fouet (Au), 34
Pierre, 19
Pierre (Chez), 61

Pierre Balmain, 268
Pierre Bérès, 193
Pierre Frey, 245
Pierre Madel, 173
Pierre au Palais-Royal, 17
Pierre Vedel, 61
Pile ou Face, 20
Pipos (Les), 149
Piscine
- les Amiraux, 291
- de la Butte-aux-Cailles, 291
- Champerret-Yser, 291
- Deligny, 291
- Henry de Montherlant, 292
- Jean-Taris, 292
- Suzanne-Berlioux, 292
Place
- de l'Etoile, 169
- de la République, 222
- Vendôme, 134
- des Vosges, 139
Plage (A la), 279
Plaisir des Pains (Au), 136
Plants, 211
Playtime, 250
Plaza Athénée, 103
- cocktail bar, 156
- restaurant, 44
Plaza Bar Anglais, 158
Pléiades (Les), 318
Plugs, 333
Poilâne, 213
Poilâne (Max), 213
Point à la Ligne, 246
Point Nature, 228
Pointaire, 85
Poiray, 252
Poison Control Center, 335
Poissonnerie du Dôme, 233
Poivre Vert (Le), 80
Police, 335
Polidor, 30
Pomellato, 254
Pomme (La), 17
Pont-Neuf, 69, 193
Pont-Royal, 108
- cocktail bar, 156
Pontault-Combault, 90, 128
Pontoise, 90
Pools, 291
Popy Moreni, 271
Poquelin (Le), 17
Porcelain (antiques), 175
Port Alma (Le), 65
Port-Marly (Le), 90
Porthault, 246
Post office, 263, 333
Poste (La), 159
Poste du Louvre, 263
Posters, 286
Pot-au-Feu (Le), 95
Potager du Roy (Le), 95
Potel et Chabot, 213
Pou, 214
Pouilly-Reuilly (Le), 91
Poujauran, 213
Poujauran (Jean-Luc), 224

INDEX

Pour Surah, 279
Prada, 257
Pré Catelan (Le), 65
Prémonville (Myrène de), 271
Pré-Saint-Gervais (Le), 91
Pressoir (Au), 51
Prince de Galles (Le), 43
Princes (Les), 44
Princesse, 30
Princesse Ere 2001, 287
Princesse Isabelle, 129
Printemps, 208
Prints, 286
Priori-Thé (A), 137
Prisunic, 209
Prix
- d'Amérique, 336
- de l'Arc de Triomphe, 338
- de Diane Hermès, 337
Procope (Le), 30
Produits de Bretagne et des Pyrénées (Aux), 232
Produits Jean-Legrand (Les), 226
Projet Musical (Le), 290
Protis, 241
Providence (A la) (Leclercq), 242
Providence (La), 18
Puerari (Capucine), 275
Puiforcat, 249
Pulin, 185
Pullman, 130
Pullman Paris-Orly, 129
Pullman Saint-Honoré, 112
Pullman Saint-Jacques, 113
Pullman Windsor, 113
Puteaux, 91, 128

Q

Quach, 66
Quai n°1 (Le), 96
Quality Inn Paris-Rive Gauche, 113
Quartz Diffusion, 249
Quatre Saisons, 249
Queen's Hôtel, 124
Quick Bites, 133
Quincy (Le), 52
15 Montaigne, 44
Quiztour Continental, 332

R

R. Malbranche, 290
Raajmahal, 61
Rabanne (Paco), 271
Racetracks, 290
Raimo, 228
Ralph Lauren, 207
Rambouillet, 321
Rankings (restaurants), 11
Raoul Guiraud-Brugidou-Malnati, 165

Raphaël, 103
- cocktail bar, 156
R.A.T.P., 330, 332
Ready Made, 246
Ready-to-wear (Women's Wear), 275
Récamier (Le), 34
Rech (Georges), 271
Réciproque, 196
Records, 250
- open late, 263
Reels on Wheels, 250
Refuge (Au), 264
Régal (Au), 136, 221
Régence-Plaza, 44
Regent Belt Company (The), 260
Regent's Garden Hôtel, 118
Régina, 108
Régine's, 159
Regional French Specialities, 232
Regyn's Montmartre, 124
Reine Margot (A la), 171
Relais
- d'Auteuil (Le), 66
- Bleus (Les), 126, 127
- du Bois (Le), 66
- Chablisien (Le), 149
- Christine, 118
- Condé (Le), 312
- de Courlande, 80
- des Gardes, 87
- Louis XIII, 30
- du Louvre (Le), 124
- de Lyon (Le), 113
- du Parc, 66
- du Pneu (Le), 184
- de Saint-Cucufa, 92
- Saint-Germain, 118
- de Sèvres (Le), 61
- de la Tour, 314
- Vermeer (Le), 44
- du Vin (Le), 150
Renaud Pellegrino, 257
Rendez-Vous des Camionneurs, 57
René (Denise), (Galerie), 285
René Furterer, 186
René Mancini, 278
René Saint-Ouen, 213
René Veyrat, 211
Renoncourt, 165
Rentals, 182
- airplane, 182
- bicycle, 182
- bike, 287
- boat, 182
- buses, see Limousines, 183
- cars, see Limousines, 183
- climbing equipment, 184
- computers, 182
- Eiffel Tower, 182
- furniture, 183
- hot air balloon, 183
- motorcycles, see Limousines, 183

- outfit, 182
- RV, see Limousines, 183
- safe, 184
- ski equipment, 183
- stereo, 184
- television, 184
- tires, 184
- train, 184
- trucks, see Limousines, 183
- vans, see Limousines, 183
- office (equipped), 182
Repaire de Cartouche (Le), 50
Repaire de Bacchus (Le), 150, 234
Repairs, 180
Réparation-Service de Lazuli, 180
Repetto, 264
RER, 330
Rescatore, 96
Résidence
- Bassano, 113
- des Gobelins, 124
- Maxim's de Paris, 104
- Monceau, 113
- Saint-Honoré, 113
- Saint-Lambert, 124
- Trousseau, 124
Restaurant (Le), 77
Restaurant A, 25
Restaurant Bleu, 57
Restaurants, 9
- prices, 12
- rankings, 11
- reservation, 10
- service, 11, 333
- what to wear, 10
- when to go, 11
Resthôtel Primevère, 322
Réunion des Musées Nationaux, 301
Réveil du Xe (Le), 150
Révillon, 273
Revlon, 188
Rex Club, 160
Reza (Alexandre), 252
Ribe (Chez), 34
Riboutté-Lafayette, 124
Riccardo Rozzi, 273
Richard Grand, 274
Richart, 218
Richaud, 130
Riding, 291
- equipment, 265
Rinaldi (Marina), 274
Rita Kim, 236
Ritz, 104
- cooking school, 287
- restaurant, 15
- tea room, 142
Robba (Emilio), 211
Robert Capia, 178
Robert Clergerie, 276
Robert Mikaeloff, 176
Robin des Bois, 236
Robuchon, 66
Rochas, 271

INDEX

Rock climbing, 291
Rock'n'Roll Hall of Fame, 202
Rodin, (Auguste)
- maison, 304
- museum, 303
Roger (Chez), 47
Roi du Café (Au), 133
Roi Fou (Le), 165
Roissy-en-France, 92, 126
Romainville, 92
Rond-Point de Longchamp, 113
Rondissimo, 274
Rosa (Sabbia), 275
Rose, 84
Rose Thé, 142
Rosebud (Le), 156
Rostang (Michel), 74
Rôtisserie du Beaujolais, 25
Rôtisserie Cambronne, 229
Rôtisserie d'en Face (La), 30
Rotonde (La), 30
Roue Libre, 330
Rouge-Gorge (Le), 150
Roux-Devillas (Olivier), 177
Royal Médoc, 124
Royal Monceau, 104
- health club, 289
- restaurants, 37, 40
Rozzi Riccardo, 273
Rubis (Le), 150
Rue
- de Picpus, 222
- de Meslay, 195
- de Paradis, 195
- Saint-Blaise, 258
Rueil-Malmaison, 92
- antiques, 176
Rungis, 92, 129
Rungisserie (La), 92
RV (rentals),
  see Limousines, 183
Rykiel (Sonia) Enfants, 198
Rykiel (Sonia), 206

S

Sabbia Rosa, 275
Saclay, 129
Sacré-Cœur, 38
Safe, 184
Safranée sur Mer (La), 82
Saint-Amour (Le), 20
Saint-Cloud, 93, 129
Saint-Denis, 93
Saint-Dominique, 124
Saint-Ferdinand, 113
St. George's, 334
Saint-Germain (Le), 44
**Saint-Germain-en-
  Laye, 93, 130, 322**
Saint-Grégoire, 118
Saint-James et Albany, 104
- cocktail bar, 156
Saint James Paris, 108
St. Joseph's, 334

Saint Laurent Rive Gauche, 259
Saint Laurent (Yves), 272
Saint-Louis, 119
Saint-Louis Marais, 119
Saint-Merry, 119
St. Michael's English
  Church, 334
Saint-Moritz, 44
Saint-Ouen, 94
Saint-Ouen (René), 213
Saint-Prest, 314
Saint-Romain, 125
**Saint-Symphorien-le-
  Château, 315**
Sainte-Beuve, 119
Saintongeais (Le), 47
Salle Favart, 160
Salle Gustave-Eiffel, 182
Salmon, 223
Salon
- d'Automne, 338
- du Cheval et du Poney, 338
- du Chocolat (Le), 143
- International de
  l'Aéronautique
  et de l'Espace, 337
- International de
  l'Agriculture, 336
- International de
  l'Alimentation, 338
- du Livre, 336
- de Mars, 336
- Meubles et Décors, 338
- Mondial du Tourisme et des
  Voyages, 336
- Nautique International, 338
Samaritaine (La), 209, 291
SAMU, 335
San Régis, 108
San Valero, 89
Sancerre (Le), 78, 133, 150
Santa Fe Hotel, 128
Santini (Fausto), 278
Saphir Hôtel, 128
Saudade, 18
Saumonière (La), 93
Sauvignon (Au), 150
Savoy (Guy), 75
Savy, 45
Saxe-Résidence, 114
Scapa of Scotland, 206
Sceaux, 94
Scents, 188
Schapira (Antoine), 241
Scherrer (Jean-Louis), 272
Schmid, 214
Sciences, Art et Nature, 174
Scribe, 104
- cocktail bar, 156
Seafood, 233
Sébillon, 89
Sébillon Elysées, 45
Secretarial services, 184
Segoura (Maurice), 168
Seine Rive Gauche, 136
Select (Le), 133
Select Hôtel, 119

Sélection Suzanne Reinach, 181
Sellerie (La), 314
Sénateur, 125
Senderens (Alain), 41
Senlis, 310, 323
Sennelier, 195, 287
Senneville (Elisabeth de), 272
Senteurs de Provence (Aux), 61
Sephora, 189
Sequoia Lodge, 128
Serge (Chez), 94
Service
- hair salons, 333
- restaurants, 11, 333
- secretarial, 184
- ushers, 333
Service des Taxis, 331
Seventh arrondissement, 224
Sèvres, 94
Sewer, 243
Shakespeare and
  Company, 191, 262
Shéhérazade (Le), 160
Shirts, 260
Shizuka, 237
Shoes
- children, 199
- juniors & teens, 200
- menswear, 261
- repair, 184
- women's wear, 276
Shooting, 265
Shopping Plus, 331
Shops, 163
Shu-Uemura, 189
Si Tu Veux, 202
S.I.A.L, 338
SICOB, 337
Sidney Health Food, 136
Sidonie Larizzi, 277
Silk (Women's Wear), 279
Silver Moon, 189
Silver Spur Steakhouse, 87
Simon (A.), 239
Sipario, 52
Skiing (equipement), 184, 266
Slow Club, 160
Smalto (Francesco), 259
SMH, 244
Smith (W. H.), 191
SNCF, 184
Société Nationale
  d'Horticulture de France, 288
Sofas, 241
Sofitel, 126
Sofitel Paris, 114
- cocktail bars, 159
- restaurant, 61
Sofitel Paris-La-Défense, 129
Soldats d'Antan (Aux), 178
Soleil d'Austerlitz (Au), 151
Solférino, 119
Sologne (La), 52
Solon, 184
Songeur Daiya, 276
Sonia Rykiel, 195, 206
Sonia Rykiel Enfants, 198

356

INDEX

Sorbets, **228**
Sormani, 75
S.O.S. Crisis Line, 335
S.O.S. Dentaire, 335
S.O.S. Médecins, 335
S.O.S. Psychiatrie, 335
Sothys, 185
Souleiado, 243
Soupière (La), 75
Sous l'Olivier, 67
Sous-Bock Tavern, 162
Soustiel (Jean), 170
Souvré (Le), 21
Spécialités Antillaises, 221
Spirits, 233
Splendid Etoile, 114
Sports, 287
- equipment, 263
- events, 336
- goods, 263
Sprung Frères, 273
Square des Batignolles, 308
Squash, 292
Squash Montmartre, 292
SR Store, 195
Stade Henry de Montherlant, 292
Stadler, (Galerie), 285
Stationery, 190, 194
Steiger (Walter), 278
Stéphane Kélian, 261, 277
Stereo, 250
- rentals, 184
Stern, 195
Stock 2, 195
Stohrer, 232
Stratéjeux, 288
Stresa, 45
Stübli (Le), 143
Subra (Jacqueline), 174
Suburbs (The)
- hotels, 126
- restaurants, 79
Suède, 120
Suffren (Le), 157
Sulka & Company, 261
Sully d'Auteuil (Le), 67
Sunset (Le), 158
Sur La Place, 189
Survilliers, 130
Swann Pharmacy, 335
Swimming, 291
Swimsuits (Women's Wear), 279
Syjac Hôtel, 129
Syrup, 226

T

Tabac de l'Institut, 151
Table d'Anvers (La), 47
Table de Fès (La), 31
Tableware, 246
Tachon, 216
Taillevent, 45
Taïr Mercier, 239
Take-away, 214
Tamise, 120
Tan Dinh, 35
Tang Frères, 222
Tango (Le), 160
Tant qu'il y aura des Hommes, 237
Tante Louise (Chez), 45
Tarlazzi (Angelo), 272
Tarterie, 143
Tartine (La), 151
Tartine et Chocolat, 198
T.A.S., 332
Tastevin (Le), 86
Tattevin (Marc)–Palais de la Viande, 230
Taverne Henri-IV, 151
Taverne Kronenbourg, 48
Taverne de Nesle (La), 162
Taverne du Nil (La), 20
Taxis, 331
Taxis-Radio "Etoile", 331
Tea, 219
Tea Caddy (The), 143
Tea Follies, 143
Tea rooms, 137
Tea and Tattered Pages, 143, 191
Téhen, 272
Teil (Chez), 233
Téléfleurs France, 181
Telephone
- card, 333
- international, 333
Television (rentals), 184
Temps des Cerises (Le), 52
Tennis, 292
- French Open, 336
- du Luxembourg, 292
- Open de la Ville de Paris, 338
Terminus Nord, 49
Terrass Hôtel, 114
Terrasse Fleurie (La), 18
Terre de Bruyère, 257
Terrier, 233
Territoire, 237
Tête Noire (La), 87
Thalassotherapy, 189
Than Binh, 222
Thé Cool, 143
Thé au Fil, 144
Theater, 162
Théâtre des Champs-Elysées, 160
Théâtre de la Ville, 160
Théière (La), 144
Thermes du Royal Monceau, 289
Thierry Mugler, 206, 271
Thivars, 314
Tholoniat, 218
Thomass (Chantal), 262, 272, 275
Thoumieux, 35
Tickets
- buses, 330
- métro, 330
- theater, 162
Till, 199
Tim'hôtel Montmartre, 125
Timgad (Le), 76
Timmy's (Le), 160
Timonerie (La), 25
Tir 1000, 265
Tires, 184
Tissus Reine, 196, 245
Tobacconists, 266
- accessories, 266
Toit de Paris (Le), 159
Toit de Passy (Le), 67
Tomb of the Unknown Soldier, 169
Tonkam, 191
Tonnelle (La), 81
Tonnelle Saintongeaise (La), 89
Toque (La), 76
Toque Blanche (La), 322
Toques, 11
Toraya, 144
Torii (Yuki), 272
Torréfaction Valade, 219
Torregiani, 260
Tortu (Christian), 211
Tortue Electrique (La), 178
Toulemonde-Bochart, 244
Tour d'Argent (La), 26
- Comptoirs (de), 236
Tour d'Auvergne (La), 125
Tour de France, 337
Tour du Monde (Le), 194
Tourist information, 333
Tours, 331
- boat, 332
- buses, 331
- limousines, 330
- museums, 301
- walking, 331
Tous les Caleçons, 262
Toutoune (Chez), 26
Toys, 200
- antiques, 178
Trade fairs, 336
Train (rentals), 184
Train Bleu (Le), 52, 133, 288
Travel books, 193
Traversière (Le), 52
Trémoille (La), 108
Trente (Le), 45
Trésors du Passé, 176
Trianon Palace, 130
Trigano (Patrice), (Galerie), 286
Trocadéro, 125
Trois Marches (Les) (restaurant), 96
Trois Marches (Les), 279
Trois Marmites (Les), 82
Trois Quartiers (Aux), 209
Trosly-Breuil, 312
Trottoirs de Buenos Aires (Les), 154
Trou Gascon (Au), 52
Trucks (rentals), see *Limousines*, 183

357

INDEX

Truffles, 227
Tuile à Loup (La), 237
Twinings, 220

U

Underwear (Menswear), 262
Ungaro (Emmanuel), 272
Université, 120
Uri, 61
Utopia, 158
Utrillo, 125

V

Val d'Or (Le), 46, 151
Valentino, 273
Valère (Olivia), 161
Vallière (La), 79
Value Added Tax, 335
Van Cleef et Arpels, 252
Van Gogh (Le), 79
Vandermeersch, 176
Vanida, 93
Vans (rentals), see
 Limousines, 183
Varenne, 120
Varenne-St-Hilaire (La), 94
Varennes-Jarcy, 95
Vassanti, 57
Vaux-Le-Vicomte, 325
Vedel (Pierre), 61
Vedettes de Paris-Ile-de-
 France (Les), 332
Vedettes du
 Pont-Neuf (Les), 332
Vegetables, 222
Veggie, 227
Vélizy, 130
Vell (Claude), 199
Velleda, 183
Vendanges (Les), 57
Vendôme, 179
Vendôme (Place), 134
Ventilo, 206
Vercanaille (Le), 92
Verger de la
 Madeleine (Au), 235
Verlet, 144, 220
Vernon, 320
Verre et l'Assiette (Le), 192
Versace (Gianni), 207
Versailles, 327
- hotels, 130
- restaurants, 95
Versailles (Le), 130
Vexin, 310
Veyrat (René), 211
VIA, 241
Victoire, 276
Victor Hugo, (Maison de), 297

Victoria (Le), 129
Victoria Palace, 114
Video, 250
Vie Claire (La), 227
Vieille (Chez la), 18
Vieille Cité (A la), 171
Vieille Fontaine (La), 86
Vieille France, 178
Vieux
- Campeur (Le), 266
- Clodoche (Au), 81
- Marais, 125
- Métiers de France (Les), 53
- Paris, 114
- Paris (Au), 178
Vigato (Jean-Pierre), 68
Vigneau-Desmaret, 215
Vignon, 215
Vigny, 114
Vigny (Le), 157
Vilfeu (Gilles), 228
Villa
- des Artistes, 125
- Henri IV, 129
- Laroche, 318
- Maillot (La), 120
- Saint-Germain (La), 109
- Thalgo, 190
- Vinci, 67
Villa (La), 158
Village
- Saint-Paul, 164
- Suisse (Le), 164
- Voice (The), 191
Ville de Rodez (A la), 233
Villebon-sur-Yvette, 97
Villeneuve-la-Garenne, 97
Villiers-le-Bâcle, 97
Villon (François), 279
Vilmorin, 211
Vin des Rues (Le), 57, 152
Vin sur Vin, 35
Vinchon (Jean), 171
Vins Rare–Peter Thustrup, 235
Virgin Café, 136
Virgin Mégastore, 250, 263
Vishnou, 57
Vitatop-Club Plein Ciel, 289
Vivarois, 67
Vivement Jeudi, 244
Volant (Le), 62
Vong (Chez), 46
Vuitton (Louis), 257

W

W. H. Smith, 191
Walking tours, 331
Wallace, 125
Wallpaper, 244
Wally Saharien, 23
Walt's An American
 Restaurant, 87

Walter Steiger, 278
Warwick, 109
Wedding Gowns, 279
Welcome Hôtel, 125
Wepler, 78
West Side Café, 137
Western (Le), 62
Westminster, 105
- cocktail bar, 157
- restaurant, 18
Weston, 262
Willi's Wine Bar, 18, 152
William Aimard Camus, 255
Wilson (Michèle), 237
Windsurfing (equipment), 266
Wine Bars, 144
Wine, 233
Winston (Harry), 252
Women's Wear, 268
- accessories, 276
- designers, 268
- eveningwear, 273
- furs, 273
- knits, 273
- large sizes, 274
- lingerie, 274
- shoes, 276
- silk, 279
- specialty shops, 275
- swimsuits, 279
- ready-to-wear, 275
- wedding-gowns, 279

X

Xavier Gourmet, 137

Y

Yamada, 255
Yamamoto (Yohji), 207
Yllen, 114
Yohji Yamamoto, 207
Yugaraj, 31
Yuki Torii, 272
Yvan, 46
Yvan et Marzia, 273
Yves Saint Laurent, 272
Yvon Lambert, (Galerie), 284
Yvonne Moreau-Gobard, 170

Z

Zegna (Ermenegildo), 260
Zenta, 276
Zouari (Alexandre), 187
Zuber, 245

RAC MOTORING ATLAS EUROPE

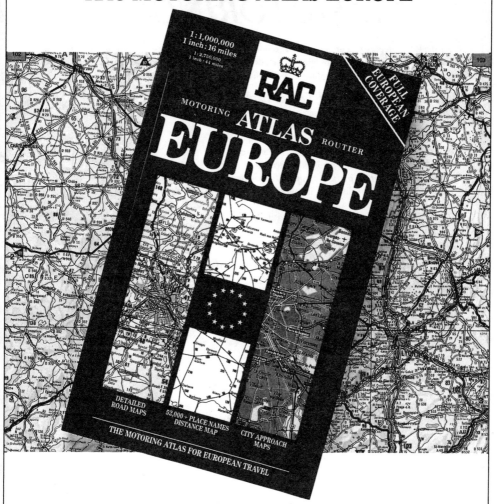

A new, revised edition of our small format RAC Motoring Atlas Europe, ideal for reference at home, at work, and in the car, where it will fit neatly into the glove compartment.

Mapping is clear and detailed, with western Europe at a scale of 1:1,000,000 (16 miles to 1 inch), and eastern Europe at 1:2,750,000 (43 miles to 1 inch), while approach maps to 45 popular European cities will prove invaluable. The atlas is backed up by a comprehensive index featuring over 52,000 place names.

RAC Motoring Atlas Europe
Price: £10.99

YOUR ROUTE TO SUCCESSFUL MOTORING

RAC Travel Services

Let the RAC prepare you an individually tailored route to your holiday destination. We'll take the strain out of your journey by supplying a route designed to your requirements, avoiding major road works and so ensuring a smooth start to your holiday.

1. European Route and Travel Pack
- Choose from: the fastest, most scenic, most suitable for towing or to avoid motorways or toll roads.
- Junction by junction route directions from your port of arrival to your destination *(coverage includes France, Benelux, Germany, Spain, Portugal, Austria and Switzerland. Elsewhere marked mapping is provided).*
- Total and intermediate distances in miles/km.
- Through-route town plans for major centres.
- Route planning maps for every country visited.
- Information booklets for each country.

Member £16.20 Non Member £18.50

2. European Route and Town Plans only Member £11.00 Non Member £13.00

3. UK and European Route and Travel Pack
European Route and Travel Pack plus the best route from your home town to your port of departure, UK town and port plans and UK road map.

Member £18.50 Non Member £20.50

4. UK and Irish Route
Tell us the type of route you want - motorway, picturesque, towing, etc - and receive the best junction by junction driving instructions, information on motorway facilities, road numbers, town plans, UK roadworks report and route planning map of the UK and Ireland.

UK Route: Member £5.00 Non Member £10.00
Irish Route: Member £5.00 Non Member £10.00

> *Express Route Service - Next day delivery guaranteed for a £3.00 supplement.*

To obtain your route:
☎ 0345 333222 - charged at local rate. Please have your credit card details available. Allow 14 days for route preparation and return by post.

RAC Telephone Traffic and Travel Information Lines
Before you set out be prepared:
- ☎ 0891 500242 The latest traffic conditions for London and the UK motorways.
- ☎ 0891 500241 Traffic and roadworks in Europe.
- ☎ 0891 500243 European Touring Information - documentation and motoring regulations - make sure you comply.

RAC Weatherline For UK weather information:
- ☎ 0891 500249 The national 1-5 day weather forecast *(updated daily)* or 30 day weather outlook.

Calls cost 36p per minute cheap rate and 48p per minute all other times.

Contents

Preface		vii
Acknowledgements		ix
Abbreviations		xi
Introduction KEVIN CLEMENTS		1
1	Cambodia SHIRLEY LITHGOW	27
2	The Gulf Crisis: Failure of Preventive Diplomacy CLAUDE RAKISITS	58
3	Somalia: International Intervention in a Failed State BRUCE LENDON	104
4	The Balkans MICHAEL WILSON	140
5	The International Response to Humanitarian Emergencies JAMES INGRAM	163
6	The International Court of Justice STEVEN MCINTOSH	207
7	Arms Control and Disarmament: Prevention and Enforcement JILL COURTNEY	211
8	Managing Potential Conflict in the South China Sea IAN KEMISH	222
9	The Falklands: Failure of a Mission HUGH WYNDHAM	229

10	Mediation - The United Nations Role in Indonesia, 1947-1950 TOM CRITCHLEY	243
11	Peacemaking Diplomacy: United Nations Good Offices in Afghanistan WILLIAM MALEY	250
12	Namibia: A Lesson for Success JANE MADDEN	255
13	United Nations Involvement in the Peace Process in El Salvador DAVID STUART	261
14	Keeping but not Making Peace: The UN Peacekeeping Force in Cyprus DAVID MORRIS	273
15	Traditional Peacekeeping: United Nations Truce Supervision Organisation and the Multinational Force and Observers RICHARD LENNANE AND ROBERT NEWTON	280
16	Kashmir: The Problem of United Nations Peacekeeping Contributing to Political 'Stasis' FELICITY VOLK	288
17	United Nations Angola Verification Mission II DOROTHY HOLT	302
18	Sanctions STEVEN MCINTOSH	311
19	Iraq and the United Nations Special Commission PETER FURLONGER	319

Conclusion   325
   KEVIN CLEMENTS

Index   329

Preface

Most of the case studies in this volume were prepared by serving or former officers of the Australian Department of Foreign Affairs and Trade as an input to the preparation of Senator Evans's book, *Cooperating for Peace: the Global Agenda for the 1990s and Beyond*, which was published by Allen & Unwin in 1993. The project tapped into many areas of the Department and its overseas missions.

In a few cases, such as 'The International Response to Humanitarian Emergencies' by Jim Ingram, formerly Executive Director of the World Food Program, the studies were the work of consultants engaged because they offered a perspective based on a level of experience or expertise which was not then available in the Department.

The topics for the studies were chosen with a mind to covering thoroughly both the range of international security problems and the types of response to them mounted by the international community. A deliberate effort was made to address situations in diverse geographic regions and to look at both contemporary and historic situations. The common focus of almost all the studies was to assess the United Nations' role in responding to major security threats, although many of the case studies also considered the part played by regional organisations or individual countries in trying to maintain or restore peace.

Two types of studies were commissioned. Five general studies examined in detail several key aspects of contemporary security problems: the Gulf Crisis as a failure of preventive diplomacy; Somalia as an example of international intervention in a 'failed state'; the Balkans, combining a situation of ethnonationalist conflict with one which illuminates how regional bodies and the UN work together (or fail to do so); the international response to humanitarian crises; and Cambodia as an example of both concerted international efforts at peacemaking and a new generation of UN peacekeeping. The remaining studies were briefer pieces which drew a broad-brush picture of a wider variety of international security problems and the responses to them and provided a succinct analysis of the reasons for the success or ineffectiveness of these responses.

The case studies were prepared to a tight deadline during the second quarter of 1993. Some required no updating, such as the studies on Namibia and the UN's role in Indonesia from 1947 to 1950, but in the majority of cases authors were asked to revise the studies so that they were current to the end of 1993.

The authors of the case studies were asked to produce an independent analysis of each topic. They were able to draw from material available to the Department, as well as from public sources, but were not expected to confine their views to current Government positions. Hence the views expressed are those of the authors and do not necessarily reflect the policies of the Australian Government.

Acknowledgements

All books are a product of cooperative activity. This one is no exception. In the first place I would like to thank my co-editor Robin Ward for her editorial skills and careful attention to facts and details. She was also responsible for the preparation of the index. Christine Wilson of the Peace Research Centre liaised with the Department of Foreign Affairs and Trade, coordinated the art work and had oversight of the final stages of publication. David Stuart, Bryce Hutchesson and Amanda Hawkins of the Department of Foreign Affairs and Trade, which commissioned the original case studies, were a source of factual and editorial advice. Jan Preston-Stanley of the Peace Research Centre did most of the original word-processing and organised the studies for publication. Carol Staples, also of the Peace Research Centre, worked her magic with the computer and turned all the text into copy ready for publication. Finally, Patrick Gallagher, Managing Director of Allen & Unwin, has from the outset had confidence in the worthwhileness of this project.

To all of these people, my thanks for their professionalism and dedication to the task.

Kevin P. Clements
August 1994

Abbreviations

ACC	Administrative Committee on Coordination; Arab Cooperation Council
AEPU	Advance Electoral Planning Unit
AMM	ASEAN Ministerial Meeting
ARENA	Alianza Republicana Nacional
ASEAN	Association of Southeast Asian Nations
AWEPPAA	Association of West European Parliamentarians for Action Against Apartheid
BJP	Bharatiya Janata Party
BWC	Biological Weapons Convention
CBMs	Confidence-building measures
CCPM	Joint Political-Military Commission (Angola)
CGDK	Coalition Government of Democratic Kampuchea
CIA	Central Intelligence Agency
CIVPOL	civilian police
CMVF	Joint Verification and Monitoring Commission (Angola)
COPAZ	National Commission for the Consolidation of Peace
CPAF	Cambodian Peoples Armed Forces
CPP	Cambodian Peoples Party
CSCE	Conference on Security and Cooperation in Europe
CW	chemical weapons
CWC	Chemical Weapons Convention
DPRK	Democratic People's Republic of Korea
EC	European Community
ECOSOC	Economic and Social Council (UN)
EPC	European political cooperation
FMLN	Frente Faribundo Marti Para La Liberacion Nacional
FRY	Federal Republic of Yugoslavia (Serbia and Montenegro)

FUNCINPEC	United Front for an Independent, Neutral, Peaceful and Cooperative Cambodia
GCC	Gulf Cooperation Countries
GOC	Good Offices Committee
GRUNC	Royal Government of the National Union of Cambodia
IAEA	International Atomic Energy Agency
ICJ	International Court of Justice
ICORC	International Committee on the Reconstruction of Cambodia
ICRC	International Committee of the Red Cross
IGADD	Intergovernmental Authority on Drought and Development
IMF	International Monetary Fund
JNA	Yugoslav National Army
KPNLF	Khmer People's National Liberation Front
LOSC	Law of the Sea Convention
MACs	Mixed Armistice Commissions
MFO	Multinational Force and Observers in the Sinai
MIF	Multinational Interception Force
MOG	Military Observer Group
MPLA	Popular Movement for the Liberation of Angola
MSF	Médecins sans Frontières
MTCR	Missile Technology Control Regime
NATO	North Atlantic Treaty Organisation
NGOs	Non-Government Organisations
NPT	Nuclear Non-Proliferation Treaty
NSS	National Security Service
OAU	Organisation of African Unity
ODA	Official Development Assistance
OIC	Organisation of the Islamic Conference
ONUC	United Nations Operation in the Congo
ONUMOZ	United Nations Operation in Mozambique
ONUSAL	United Nations Observer Mission in El Salvador
OPCW	Organisation for the Prohibition of Chemical Weapons
OPEC	Organisation of Petroleum Exporting Countries
ORCI	Office of Research and the Collection of Information
OSGAP	Office of the Secretary-General in Afghanistan and Pakistan
PGFK	Provisional Government of Free Kuwait
PICC	Paris International Conference on Cambodia
PLO	Palestine Liberation Organisation
PRK	People's Republic of Kampuchea
RTC	Round Table Conference

SCF-UK	Save the Children Fund
SCR	Security Council Resolution
SLOCs	sea lines of communication
SNA	Somali National Army
SNC	Supreme National Council
SNF	Somali National Front
SNM	Somali National Movement
SOC	State of Cambodia
SPM	Somali Patriotic Movement
SRC	Supreme Revolutionary Council
SSDF	Somali Salvation Democratic Front
SWAPO	South West African Peoples' Organisation
SWATF	South West Africa Territory Forces
TNC	Transitional National Council
TRNC	'Turkish Republic of Northern Cyprus'
UAE	United Arab Emirates
UN	United Nations
UNAMIC	United Nations Advance Mission to Cambodia
UNAVEM	United Nations Angola Verification Mission
UNCHR	United Nations Commission on Human Rights
UNCI	United Nations Commission for Indonesia
UNCIP	United Nations Commission for India and Pakistan
UNCURK	United Nations Commission for the Unification and Rehabilitation of Korea
UNDOF	United Nations Disengagement Observer Force
UNDP	United Nations Development Program
UNEF	United Nations Emergency Force
UNFICYP	United Nations Peace Keeping Force in Cyprus
UNFPA	United Nations Fund for Population Activities
UNGOMAP	United Nations Good Offices Mission in Afghanistan and Pakistan
UNHCR	United Nations High Commission for Refugees
UNICEF	United Nations Children's Fund
UNIFIL	United Nations Interim Force in Lebanon
UNIPOM	United Nations India Pakistan Observation Mission
UNITA	National Union for the Total Independence of Angola
UNITAF	United Nations Interim Task Force (Somalia)
UNMOGIP	United Nations Military Observers Group in India and Pakistan
UNO	Union Nacional Opositora
UNOCA	United Nations Coordinator for Humanitarian and Economic Assistance Programmes Relating to Afghanistan

UNOCHA	United Nations Office for the Coordination of Humanitarian Assistance to Afghanistan
UNOSOM	United Nations Operation in Somalia
UNPA	United Nations Protected Area
UNPROFOR	United Nations Protection Force
UNSCOM	United Nations Special Commission
UNTAC	United Nations Transitional Authority in Cambodia
UNTAG	United Nations Transition Assistance Group
UNTSO	United Nations Truce Supervision Organisation
USAID	United States Aid for International Development
USC	United Somali Congress
USI	United States of Indonesia
USSR	Union of Soviet Socialist Republics
WEU	Western European Union
WFP	World Food Program
WHO	World Health Organisation
WMD	weapons of mass destruction
WSLF	Western Somali Liberation Front

Introduction

KEVIN P. CLEMENTS

The papers in this volume were written originally as background case studies for Senator Gareth Evans's book *Cooperating for Peace: The Global Agenda for the 1990s*.[1] They were intended to illustrate how the United Nations had contributed to the maintenance of international peace and security in the past, and what positive and negative lessons might be derived from this experience to guide behaviour in the future. Each one underlines important aspects of the work of the United Nations in relation to peace building, maintaining peace through preventive diplomacy, restoring the peace through peacemaking and peacekeeping processes, and through the enforcement mechanisms available to the United Nations when all other methods fail.

The overwhelming concern of *Cooperating for Peace* and these case studies is to bring some conceptual clarity and positive prescription to the debate about the most effective means for generating stable peaceful relations within and between nations. The current inability of the United Nations to respond adequately to the diverse crises before the international community underlines the failure of the old conceptual frameworks to guide timely analysis and effective multilateral intervention. It is in response to these sorts of problems that these case studies and Evans's book are directed. In *Cooperating for Peace* Evans addresses the problems initially by identifying and analysing the sources of global insecurity and

---

[1] Gareth Evans, *Cooperating for Peace: The Global Agenda for the 1990s* (St Leonards, NSW: Allen & Unwin, 1993). This book was launched at the 48th General Assembly in 1993 as a response to Boutros Boutros-Ghali, *An Agenda for Peace - Preventive Diplomacy, Peacemaking and Peacekeeping* (New York: United Nations, 1992).

then by asking questions about how the United Nations, which was established primarily to counter threats of aggression between states, might now shift its focus to ensure its responses to such problems advances both the security of states and the peoples within them. Taking 'cooperative security' as his central conceptual theme, Evans insists that this is as much about the protection of individuals as it is about the territorial integrity and independence of states.[2]

There are many questions that flow from this assertion. How can an international organisation established primarily to deal with relations between states (despite the preambular 'We the Peoples . . .' in the Charter) ensure that the populations of failed and failing states are protected, since this is where most of the current violent conflicts are occurring?[3] Much of this violence is in fact perpetrated by governments against their own citizens, who cannot avail themselves of the protection of the UN Charter. One major problem with United Nations intervention is that often the UN deals with political and military leaders representing only an élite group, and leaves middle-range and grassroots leadership ignored or marginalised. Effective and durable long-term problem-solving is unlikely without the incorporation of a wider range of actors in the decision-making processes.

Similarly, when the world community is alerted to violent conflicts which threaten large numbers of people, how does it ensure that killing on a large scale, or even genocide, does not occur and that gross and persistent violations of human rights are dealt with quickly? How does the United Nations deal with the forced movements of people, the degradation of the biosphere and other major challenges to peace and security? What are the rights and responsibilities of the United Nations and other multilateral organisations in relation to these questions? What sorts of problems should the international community (through the United Nations) assume responsibility for, and what should it leave to national actors, regional organisations or non-governmental agencies?

These are complex problems demanding some urgent answers. Since the United Nations lacks both resources and the organisational capability to deal with all the problems being directed to it, there is clearly a need to prioritise problems, determine rational responses to them, and to develop a flexible division of labour between the UN, regional organisations, nation

---

[2] Evans, *Cooperating for Peace*, p.16.
[3] For a good description of some of these current conflicts, see Coral Bell, 'The Nature of Contemporary Crises', in Coral Bell (ed.), *The United Nations and Crisis Management: Six Case Studies* (Canberra: Strategic and Defence Studies Centre, Research School of Pacific Studies, Australian National University, 1994) pp.1-8. For an excellent analysis of the relationship between economic dislocation and internal ethnic conflicts, see A. Smith Albion and John Lampe, *Ethnic Conflict in the Post Cold War Era: Strains of Economic Transition and Ethnic Conflict* (Washington DC: Woodrow Wilson Centre, 1994).

states and the expanding network of national and international non-governmental organisations concerned with such problems.[4]

Evans's contribution to this debate begins with a conceptualisation of some of the problems challenging international peace and security. He defines these as 'emerging threats', 'disputes', 'armed conflicts' and 'other major security crises'.[5] These problems are then matched with a range of graduated responses - building peace, maintaining peace, restoring peace, and enforcing peace - which are aimed at exhausting 'softer' options before 'harder' ones are contemplated or applied.[6] The aim of this simple but useful matrix is to alert decision makers to all the measures that may be applied early in the evolution of a dispute. Such measures are intended to avoid coercive military solutions to problems by early and creative non-violent intervention when arguments and disputes are still relatively tractable.[7] Unfortunately, too many of the world's current crises (for example, those in Rwanda, the former Yugoslavia and Somalia) have gone well past the preventive phase of action, and challenge the ability of the United Nations either to solve the underlying political and military problems or to provide protection for human life and the delivery of basic humanitarian assistance. They remain a standing indictment of the international community's ability to respond adequately to the new dilemmas confronting it, and raise some important questions about when a judicious and early application of force may prevent later catastrophe.

As a recent NATO report stated in relation to Yugoslavia:

> [It] has presented the international community with all possible types of armed conflict and commitment. Civil wars, wars of secession, interstate wars and wars of territorial conquest have combined on the ground to justify the successive or simultaneous recourse to traditional peacekeeping operations (in Croatia) and humanitarian intervention (Bosnia), mixed with a dash of peace enforcement (Serbia), an attempt at prevention (Macedonia) and a systematic pretence of impartiality.[8]

The report then goes on to note that while the conflicts have been enormously complex, the response of Western democracies and the United Nations to them have been characterised by 'failure and massive shortcoming'.[9] These case studies and Evans's original book are attempts to discover what sorts of national, regional and global initiatives will prevent these failures in the future, and what is necessary to equip the

---

[4] For an overview of some the dilemmas and a review of Evans's book, see Brian Urquhart, 'Who Can Police the World', *New York Review of Books*, 12 May 1994, p.29.
[5] Evans, *Cooperating for Peace*, pp.6-7.
[6] ibid., p.13.
[7] ibid., p.14.
[8] NATO, *Peacekeeping and the Former Yugoslavia*, NATO Document DSC/DC(94) 2, p.1.
[9] ibid.

United Nations to help the development of a pluralistic security community in order to promote stable peace.[10]

Most recent analyses of effective problem-solving and conflict resolution[11] stress the need to reorient activity away from the application of crisis management techniques after violence has occurred towards the reactivation of familiar but under-used processes of peace building and preventive diplomacy, and the development of institutions and processes aimed at creating a situation where 'habits of willing' rather than 'coerced compliance' prevail.[12]

What these case studies suggest, and what *Cooperating for Peace* underlines, is that building and maintaining international peace and security require much more emphasis on the processes of economic and social development, international regime-building, support for democratisation and the application of non-violent means of managing or resolving conflicts, as well as much less emphasis on coercive conflict management. While this argument seems totally unexceptional, it is not one that has been heard by all nations and peoples in the world.[13] Not all understand that directing attention to these basic elements of peace building tilts the bias towards early and late preventive strategies, alters the ways crises are conceptualised and suggests alternative ways of dealing with them.

There is a synergistic connection between economic development, democratic governance, the promotion of human rights, the protection of individual and collective identities, and the achievement of stable peaceful relations between peoples. Movement towards any one of these objectives tends to generate a positive dynamic in relation to all of the others, although very rapid but uneven development can undermine security, and democracy without order can generate anarchy. Despite these caveats, lack of movement towards these objectives, however, is likely to generate negative stress and disequilibrium. If this stress is sustained, it will result in a diminished acceptance of negotiated solutions to problems and a

---

[10] For an interesting new book that explores the role of the United Nations as a 'central guidance mechanism' in the evolution of a stable security community relying on 'habits of compliance' and 'fair and reasonable' societal norms rather than on threats of punishment, see J. Martin Rochester, *Waiting for the Millennium: The United Nations and the Future of World Order* (Columbia: University of South Carolina Press, 1994).

[11] See Dennis J. Sandole and H. Van der Merwe, *Conflict Resolution Theory and Practice: Integration and Application* (Manchester: Manchester University Press, 1993) for a good recent summary of the literature.

[12] See John Burton, *Global Conflict: The Domestic Sources of International Crisis* (Brighton, Sussex: Wheatsheaf Books, 1984), especially Chapter 16, 'Problem Solving Processes', pp.143-152.

[13] *An Agenda for Development*, UN Document A/48/935, 6 May 1994, which is intended as a companion to *An Agenda for Peace*, acknowledges this by linking political and military security to economic and social security.

willingness to contemplate violence.[14] This becomes most likely when economic underdevelopment is coupled with authoritarian rule and embedded within a generalised 'culture of violence' that eulogises weapons and violent means of settling disputes.[15] It is this combination which is most likely to result in gross violations of human rights, or worse, genocide. Such malevolent conflict cycles are extremely difficult to resolve, and severely tax the ability of the international community to deal with them. Conflicts which emerge in situations where there is little political legitimacy, where sectarian or communal politics have become salient and where factional groups have adopted armed strategies and elicited repressive responses from the incumbent regimes, are likely to result in a breakdown of civil society, the rule of law and open warfare among armed groups.[16]

Conflict resolution experts faced with an entrenched and apparently intractable conflict have to move cautiously in order to 'map' it by identifying the key protagonists, their positions, interests, needs and fears. This involves expert awareness, careful listening, and taking time to break the conflict into its constituent attitudinal, behavioural and situational components. This strategy of 'going slow to go fast'[17] is one that sits uneasily with harassed national and international officials under pressure to develop instant solutions to complex problems. While such analysis might be considered a luxury in terms of crisis management, it is clear from the case studies presented in this volume that good analysis is critical to delivering effective long-term answers to problems. UN intervention based on faulty or wrong analysis is likely to exacerbate rather than alleviate both the presenting and underlying problems. Sophisticated conflict analysis, therefore, far from being an optional extra, is fundamental to effective problem-solving.

While conflict analysis is a necessary condition for the prevention or management of violent conflict, it is still not sufficient, however, to ensure that problems will be solved or conflicts resolved in any final sense. There is quite a lot of evidence to suggest that there is no such thing as a solved problem, only new or reorganised sets of social,

---

[14] See C. R. Mitchell, *The Structure of International Conflict*, (London: MacMillan Press, 1981) pp.54-55 for an excellent introduction to these topics.

[15] See Carolyn Nordstrom, 'Warzones: Cultures of Violence, Militarisation and Peace', Working Paper 145, Peace Research Centre, Research School of Pacific and Asian Studies, Australian National University, 1994.

[16] See Albert Jongman, 'The PIOOM Program on Monitoring and Early Warning of Humanitarian Crises' in Ted Robert Gurr and Barbara Harff (eds), *Early Warning of Communal Conflicts and Humanitarian Crises*, Special issue of *The Journal of Ethno-Development*, 4, 1 (July 1994), pp.65-71.

[17] See *Conflict Resolution Training in the North Caucasus and Georgia*, Report of the Nalchik Seminar (London: International Alert, 1993) p.7.

economic and political relationships which, while solving one type of dilemma, may be generating entirely different ones. In other words, conflict management, conflict resolution and problem-solving are never-ending processes which have to be continually rediscovered and reapplied to new problems and new sets of relationships.[18] Most violent conflicts, for example, derive from highly unequal power relationships. Such conflicts, therefore, are concerned with the dynamics of power, empowerment of the disempowered, mobilisation of resources, confrontation (which may be violent or non-violent) and then the management or resolution of any subsequent conflict.

It is important that those interested in different types of intervention understand the probable trajectories of the conflicts and what sorts of integrative strategies might be employed to deal with them. There are a variety of conflict resolution methods that can be employed to advance win-win solutions. For example, depending on the source of the conflict, intervenors can apply 'differentiated', 'compensatory' or 'expansionist' solutions to problems, or some variation of all three.

> Differentiation refers to integrative solutions in which parties fulfil their needs by getting different parts or aspects of the contested object or issue. . . . compensation is possible when one party can be convinced that its needs can fulfilled through a compensatory gesture. . . . expansion can be a form of integrative solution, if parties find a way to increase the amount, type or use of the contested 'good'.[19]

Different types of conflict, therefore, will require different responses. It is important, therefore, that negotiators, diplomats and conflict resolution experts have a wide repertoire of responses to diverse problems. It is also possible that in some situations none of the current techniques will be appropriate at all, for cultural reasons, or because the conflict in question is not susceptible to integrative 'win-win' solutions. In these instances those involved in conflict avoidance, management or resolution need to be able to know what sort of technique is applicable to the problem in question. What is reasonably clear, however, is that there are normally three general techniques which may be applied to the prevention of violence. Mitchell identifies them as follows:

- avoiding conflicts through ensuring adequate supplies of valued goods, minimising demands, or developing superordinate goals;[20]

- preventing disruptive conflict from crossing the violence threshold, through techniques of suppression, regulation, institutionalisation;[21]

---

[18] See Burton, *Global Conflict*, for the development of this idea.
[19] *Conflict Resolution Training in the North Caucasus and Georgia*, p.9.
[20] Mitchell, *The Structure of International Conflict*, pp.258-263.
[21] ibid., pp.263-271.

- controlling or, more optimally, resolving the conflict. The tactics for this include processes of intervention, imposition, conciliation, mediation or more non-directive techniques, such as controlled communication workshops.[22]

These diverse techniques for resolving conflicts, like the responses outlined in *Cooperating for Peace*, also tilt the balance towards the pre-emptive and preventive side of the conflict management spectrum. The empirical evidence suggests that once antagonists choose violence, the stakes are increased and their 'maximum concession levels' increase until resources are depleted and/or their pain outweighs any prospect of possible gain.[23] Violent disputes are much less likely to be settled as easily as those which are anticipated and prevented, avoided or responded to when the parties in conflict are still flexible and the dispute tractable.

One of the major problems with preventive diplomacy and other early initiatives to deal with potentially violent problems, however, is to work out which agents and institutions can best initiate these processes and what sorts of interventions are likely to result in cooperative rather than coercive outcomes.[24] Nation states remain the primary agents in helping forge some notion of international community. This means that whenever a nation state wishes to act internationally it has to demonstrate the value of this action for its own citizens.

International altruism, in other words, has to be harnessed to national interest if it is to receive domestic political support. Domestic constituencies need to know that being a good 'international citizen' makes both national as well as international sense. The dilemma is that the best way of selling altruistic policies to domestic constituencies is by highlighting the national interests which will be advanced by the international policy (thus, despite the fact that it sometimes antagonises the aid community within a nation, support for international aid and development is sold in terms of domestic business and economic interests). However, this means that whenever nation states become aware of problems in neighbouring states or further afield, the 'states with problems' have difficulty accepting that other states are able either to view their problems impartially or to respond in an unselfish and impartial manner.

This especially applies to relations between neighbouring states where national interests are likely to be finely honed. The 'proximity factor' helps explain why states that are well removed from conflicts are often in a better position to contribute good offices towards their resolution than

---

[22] ibid., p.278.
[23] Mitchell has an interesting discussion of 'maximum concession levels' and 'fuzzy concession zones', ibid., pp. 284-285.
[24] See Kumar Rupesinghe, 'Early Warning and Preventive Diplomacy', in Gurr and Harff (eds), *Early Warning of Communal Conflicts*, pp.88-97.

those with very intimate geographical and other connections.[25] In most cases of relations between nation states there will always be the suspicion that State X is concerning itself with State Y's problems for essentially selfish reasons, even if the rhetoric and stated intention is completely altruistic.

While there will always be a role for unilateral and bilateral diplomacy as long as there are nation states (indeed, there are many problems which cannot be resolved any other way), the most urgent problems on the world agenda (such as international development, global pandemics like AIDS, environmental degradation and violent internal conflicts) cannot be dealt with on this basis, and require regional and global multilateral solutions.

Despite some anxieties about whether organisations reflecting regional and global interests simply provide multilateral cover for the assertion of national interests, there is little doubt that it is easier for multilateral institutions such as the United Nations and regional organisations to allay security concerns and establish altruistic intent than it is for states acting alone or in concert with others.[26] This is why the United Nations has assumed a more central profile since the end of the Cold War. East-West cooperation has resulted in a decline in the use of the veto and a disposition to move from obstructive to constructive policies. In this process the United Nations has become for many the only organisation capable of providing new organising principles for the world as a whole. The External Affairs Committee of the Canadian House of Commons, for example, argued that the United Nations is absolutely critical to the development of 'international community', which is a pre-requisite for the solution of global problems.

> The world needs a centre, and some confidence that the centre is holding: the United Nations is the only credible candidate.[27]

---

[25] This helps explain why Australia, for example, was able to make a more positive contribution to the Cambodian settlement than adjoining states or ASEAN. This same principle probably may explain why a country such as Australia, for example, is not in the best position to provide good offices to help solve problems in Papua New Guinea, whereas countries such as New Zealand may be more acceptable because less directly involved.

[26] This is a concern that has been raised in connection with whether the interests of the Permanent Five members of the Security Council, for example, are synonymous with those of the United Nations as a whole, or whether the decisions made by the Permanent Five really reflect their own national interests. A number of states feel uncomfortable at the ability of the Permanent Five to determine which cases will be responded to and on what terms.

[27] *Minutes of Proceedings*, Issue No. 55, House of Commons, Ottawa, 23 February 1993, quoted in Erskine Childers with Brian Urquhart, *Renewing the United Nations System* (Uppsala: Dag Hammarskjöld Foundation, 1994) p.11. This book is an extremely important contribution to the

It is the shape of this 'centre' and how it can perform its tasks better which is engaging all those concerned with the promotion of stable peaceful relations. The dilemmas facing both nation states (especially those with some global reach) and international organisations concerned with these issues is how to establish impartial credentials alongside a capability for early analytically-based responses to economic, political and security problems.

As mentioned already, it is always hard for states to convey clear, altruistic and unambiguous intentions when it comes to issues of economic, political, military or humanitarian intervention. Therefore, it is important that individual states and multilateral organisations (both regional and global) provide legitimacy to groups and individuals in the non-governmental sector whose objective political interests are less ambiguous and whose professional interest lies in creative problem-solving, effective third-party intervention and conflict management or conflict resolution. These groups and individuals can sometimes act when states are constrained from acting.

Most states have difficulty appealing to neighbours or to regional organisations to help them solve problems, because it looks like an admission of weakness and vulnerability. As a result, many simmering problems have to assume crisis proportions before they are acted upon by governments. In such circumstances, non-governmental organisations or influential individuals (for example, former President Jimmy Carter in relation to North Korea) can sometimes fulfil a very positive role in helping those in dispute understand the likely consequences of different sorts of actions.

James Ingram, in his chapter on humanitarian emergencies, suggests a larger role for non-governmental organisations such as the International Committee of the Red Cross in negotiations with parties engaged in international disputes. This suggestion is made precisely to overcome the suspicions of bias, partiality and self-interest which often seem to accompany unilateral state-sponsored or even UN-sponsored multilateral humanitarian initiatives.

Mitchell gives an historical example of the importance of such bodies, citing the many different inter-governmental, non-governmental groups and individuals who kept communications open between the Nigerian government and the Biafran secessionists between 1967-70. Collectively

---

> evolving debate on the reform of the United Nations and follows earlier work by the same authors on UN leadership and on the UN's humanitarian emergency machinery. The major objective of this book is to examine the UN system as it is now and to suggest changes which will gradually transform it into the effective 'mechanism of a future world community'. While the primary focus of the work is on the machinery dealing with economic and social cooperation, both authors acknowledge that this is critical to 'peacebuilding' and to laying the foundations for dealing with peace and security problems in a more cooperative fashion.

these groups and individuals, including the Catholic Church, the Society of Friends (Quakers), the Commonwealth Secretariat and some prominent personalities, were very influential in helping frame possible solutions to the crisis when 'official' governmental channels were paralysed.[28]

The Quakers, in particular have acquired very extensive experience in this area, in conflicts such as those between Egypt and Israel, India and Pakistan, the United States and Vietnam, and in a variety of civil wars. They were very successful in clarifying different positions and lowering tensions between warring parties in the Nigerian civil war, and in some non-governmental shuttle diplomacy between President Nasser of Egypt and Prime Minister Ben Gurion of Israel in the Middle East.[29]

Non-governmental organisations are important political resources that can and should be drawn on by governments and international organisations when delicate messages need to be transmitted, perceptions clarified, proposals floated, or when there is a desire to do some serious 'costing' of conflicts with those embroiled in them.

An important task facing advocates of preventive diplomacy is to spend time elaborating how and why these strategies are likely to prove more effective than late coercive strategies. In this regard it is important to identify who has standing to alert international organisations to worrying trends and potential threats. Who has both standing and resources to start making contacts with the parties to the conflicts, and who is in a position to help work out the implications of these for antagonists? What sorts of collaborative arrangements are possible between governmental and non-governmental groups? What can NGOs do that governments cannot, and vice versa? In all of these questions it is important to identify networks of conflict resolution professionals, diplomats and organisations that have had experience in national and international problem-solving and mediation. These groups and their experience constitute an important, because relatively un-self-interested, base for developing different modes of problem-solving, new ways of creatively managing and resolving violent conflicts and dealing with catastrophe.

The wisdom of emphasising peace building and of tilting the bias in favour of preventive diplomatic strategies and early intervention in intractable conflicts is borne out by the studies in this volume.

In Cambodia the international community proved powerless to prevent a cycle of war, civil war, genocide, invasion and civil war through the late 1970s and 1980s. It is highly probable that these crises would not have occurred in the first place had Cambodia not been sucked into the Vietnam war. But the fact remains that the international community did not act against the genocide that took place under the Khmer Rouge and did not

---

[28] Mitchell, *The Structure of International Conflict*, pp.302-304.
[29] For a very detailed account of these activities, see C. H. (Mike) Yarrow, *Quaker Experiences in International Conciliation* (New Haven: Yale University Press, 1978).

move very quickly to try and facilitate internal reconciliation after this period. This paralysis undoubtedly reflected superpower conflicts playing themselves out in the periphery, as well as a general uncertainty about how to respond to the unfolding crisis. Irrespective of the particulars, however, it is an indictment of both the United Nations and ASEAN that neither was able to initiate meaningful discussions between the major protagonists within Cambodia until the late 1980s.

In most conflicts there are moments of 'ripeness' for effective third party intervention. In armed conflicts this normally follows some sort of 'hurting stalemate'. It is possible that this point was only reached in Cambodia by the late 1980s. When the Cold War ended, Vietnam started to play a conciliatory role, and states such as Indonesia and Australia decided to adopt a more pro-active approach. Meaningful discussions were problematic until China expressed a willingness to modify and then withdraw its support for the Khmer Rouge. Shirley Lithgow suggests in the case study on Cambodia that even with the impediments to effective negotiation, it would have been desirable for the United Nations or ASEAN to have intervened much sooner than they did to protect the peoples of Cambodia and to facilitate discussions between the different Cambodian factions about ways of ending the civil war. Now that the Cold War has ended, it is easy to suggest such things, but during the 1970s and 1980s the United Nations was much more constrained and was not actively engaged in trying to ameliorate or manage internal conflicts challenging regional peace and security.

In retrospect it is unfortunate that there was no obvious warning of the impending genocide in Cambodia, or that, once aware of it, both the United Nations and ASEAN felt powerless to take action to end it. As it was, when the Paris International Conference on Cambodia finally got under way in 1989, it was clear that Cambodian factional positions had hardened considerably, and neither ASEAN nor the United Nations were in a position to break the impasse. Without astute diplomatic efforts by Australia and Indonesia, it is quite possible that there would still be no political settlement in Cambodia. Indeed, at the time of writing in July 1994, it is by no means clear that the Paris settlement and the UNTAC operation have established the essential preconditions for stable peaceful relations within the country, namely, a viable economic and political infrastructure, respect for the rule of law, and effective internal security arrangements. Lithgow's detailed analysis of the Cambodian experience, therefore, is both sobering and salutary. In addition to highlighting some of the dilemmas of extended peacekeeping, it also underlines many of the problems associated with late intervention in violent internal conflicts.

Claude Rakisits' analysis of the Gulf crisis also suggests that international policy makers should concentrate more attention on developing effective early-warning systems and a range of graduated responses to escalating crises. Iraq's invasion of Kuwait and the subsequent Gulf War were the result of events and attitudes that had been gestating for some time; although the invasion was perceived by many as having come 'out of the blue', a variety of important historical reasons behind Iraq's actions can be identified.

There had been longstanding disputes between Iraq and Kuwait over oil pricing and access to the Gulf, and conflict over the shared Rumaila oil field as well as over control of the Warba and Bubiyan islands. There were a number of specific irritants, such as the failure of Kuwait to cancel Iraq's war debt, but had there been a willingness to move towards negotiated solutions and expert facilitators available, these disputes could have been costed by the parties concerned and the full implications of different actions mapped out.[30] If the Gulf Cooperation Council, the Arab League and the United Nations, for example, had coordinated their good offices at the early prevention phase (before July 1990) the international community might have engaged Iraq and Kuwait in negotiations on each of the issues under contention.

The fact that this did not happen indicates, among other things, how difficult it is for international organisations to intervene in disputes before they have reached a crisis point. The Texas aphorism, 'If it ain't broke, don't fix it', certainly seems to apply to most international disputes. International organisations (unlike individual nation states) have some difficulty intervening early in disputes without being asked to do so. This is especially so in relation to the United Nations Security Council which many states perceive as a punitive and coercive instrument rather than as one which in the first instance advances preventive measures. Because of this there may be merit in nation states, regional organisations and the United Nations utilising 'prominent international personalities' or impartial non-governmental organisations to meet with parties in the early stages of conflicts, before it is appropriate for states to intervene, in order

---

[30] The issue of costing conflicts normally only occurs after they have crossed the violence threshold and antagonists are forced to contemplate the costs and benefits of continuing armed conflict as opposed to seeking a truce or some peaceful solution. These sorts of exercises are very difficult, and as long as there is a chance that there may be military and political advantage from continuing armed struggle, it is difficult for the parties to contemplate its termination. Both sides need to be 'hurting' therefore, or one side staring defeat in the face, for these cost-benefit calculations to be translated into meaningful end game negotiations. If preventive diplomacy and early intervention are to be successful, however, more attention should be given to socio-political, economic and military costing of conflicts prior to their escalation. There is now sufficient evidence to demonstrate the costs of war as opposed to the costs of peaceful solutions. In the Gulf War, for example, it is highly probable that conceding or negotiating some of Iraq's demands and responding to them positively would have involved much less expenditure than the $70 billion cost of the war and its traumatic aftermath in Iraq and Kuwait.

to determine levels of negotiating flexibility and what sorts of procedures might pre-empt violent conflict occurring.[31]

In relation to the Gulf War, it is also true, as Rakisits notes, that neither Iraq nor Kuwait could see any point in moving into negotiations early, since the issues at stake seemed completely non-negotiable. There were a number of other missed opportunities at the late prevention phase (July 1990) as well. The international community, for example, misread Iraqi intentions, and there were unclear and ambiguous signals emanating from the United States. In addition the United Nations was not given full intelligence about troop deployments, all of which meant little acknowledgement or awareness that the dispute was escalating to the point where invasion and annexation were an imminent possibility.

In retrospect, it is unfortunate that existing UN mechanisms (such as Article 35 provisions, under which any member of the United Nations may bring any dispute to the attention of the Security Council or the General Assembly, or Article 99 provisions, which allow the Secretary-General to do the same) were not employed sooner. Similarly, it is unfortunate that regional organisations such as the Gulf Cooperation Council and the League of Arab States had not developed a more effective collaborative relationship with the United Nations in order to work out some appropriate bilateral, regional and global division of labour as well as a strategic response to the unfolding crisis.

It also needs to be kept in mind that if the Iraqi regime had always intended to invade and occupy the whole of Kuwait, no amount of early warning or early intervention would have made any difference.

If more attention had been given to early and late preventive diplomacy coupled to some preventive deployment and deterrent signals prior to Iraq's confrontation with Kuwait, it is possible that the invasion and the Gulf War itself might have been avoided. If nations are determined to achieve their objectives by force, however, it is equally possible that such preventive diplomatic initiatives might simply provide extra time to mobilise military resources. During the Gulf crisis there were a number of indications that the escalation of the crisis might have been pre-empted with appropriate early diplomatic circuit breakers. The fact that these were not tried and exhausted, coupled with persistent Iraqi intransigence, meant a very rapid escalation to coercive diplomacy and the use of armed force.

Somalia, like Cambodia, represents a test of the United Nations' ability to intervene constructively in a deep-seated internal conflict. The Somali civil war left the international community in a quandary. Because Somalia lacked oil reserves and had no particular geopolitical value at the end of the Cold War, it did not rank as highly as Kuwait in the

---

[31] The quality of 'pre-negotiation' will determine whether or not parties to conflict feel comfortable addressing their grievances. See Mitchell, *The Structure of International Conflict*, pp.199-217, for an elaboration of these issues.

consciousness of the West or the United Nations. As Somalia's state system fractured and the warring factions generated more and more civil disorder, there was little international concern about the emergent chaos, nor any particular interest in trying to develop a negotiated solution to the problems. The few efforts initiated by Egypt and Italy in 1990 were viewed with profound suspicion by the antagonists, and that proposed by Kenya met with an equally indifferent response. There was certainly no superpower interest in promoting a negotiated settlement, nor, it must be said, was there any particular inclination on the part of the conflicting parties to proceed in this direction. By the end of 1991, therefore, when Ali Mahdi's regime fell apart and the scope of the humanitarian crisis became apparent, it was too late for either early or late prevention of the ensuing crisis.

As in the Gulf crisis, where Arab regional organisations were powerless to prevent the drift towards war, so too in Somalia the regional organisation with most interest in the conflict, the Organisation of African Unity, both because of its policy of non-interference in the domestic affairs of member states and because it lacked political or financial resources to do so effectively, felt unable to intervene, either to restore some semblance of functional government or to coordinate disaster relief. The United Nations itself was only prodded into action by the efforts of a pro-active Secretary-General, the international media and sustained Third World pressure.[32] The response to both the Somali political and humanitarian crises, therefore, has been characterised as 'too little too late'. As Bruce Lendon outlines in his chapter on Somalia, however, this negative experience has also taught the United Nations some important lessons.

In the first place the Somalia crisis underlined the essential fragility of states formed from former colonial territories, especially where these include a variety of internal societies and peoples. (Rwanda is the most

---

[32] The role of the media in focusing international attention on humanitarian crises has both positive and negative consequences. The positive consequence is that countries which do not rank politically or strategically can be given a heightened profile by the media. (In Australia recently, for example, the Prime Minister announced an increase in Australian aid to Rwanda partly because he and his family were shocked by television pictures of the unfolding horror.) The negative feature of political responses being led by the media, however, is that the world's preventive diplomacy agenda and its response to international humanitarian crises will be shaped by the media rather than by any objective criteria of need or urgency. These criteria may coincide with media interests but such is not necessarily always true. The second problem is that the media demand instant diagnoses and solutions and, as mentioned above, effective conflict analysis and problem-solving have to proceed a lot more cautiously. It is possible that well-intentioned media may in fact generate premature judgements about the sources of problems and possible cures.

tragic recent example of a fractured and failed state where ancient ethnic and territorial identities sit uneasily with colonial and post-colonial boundaries.) There can be no long-term solution to the internal conflicts caused by fracturing and failed states until the underlying contradictions are addressed and the cycles of revenge ended. For this to occur it is important that minorities within these states have political communities with which they can identify and which confer protection in return.

Second, in the absence of a durable political settlement, deployment of troops by the United Nations resulted in what was intended to be a limited operation in support of humanitarian objectives drifting into a Chapter VII enforcement operation (under UNITAF and UNOSOM II), to the great discredit of the United Nations (as has also been the case in different parts of the former Yugoslavia). Movement from peacekeeping operations or limited military operations in support of humanitarian objectives to enforcement procedures raises important questions about whether the use of force by the UN is likely to yield more positive outcomes than the use of force under the aegis of military superpowers. Somalia, like the other two cases mentioned above, highlights the need for greater attention to be paid to clear thinking about the circumstances and conditions for deployment of UN troops and the dilemmas surrounding the use of force in support of humanitarian objectives.[33]

The case study on Somalia analyses these issues, particularly the poorly-defined objectives of the UN mandates, the definite limits on the power and authority of the Secretary-General, the bureaucratic inefficiencies of the United Nations, and the difficulties associated with maintaining costly operations when big powers like the United States withdraw their support.

Fractured and failed states like Somalia and Rwanda are likely to appear elsewhere in Africa before the end of the decade. In fact, Political Risk Services Ltd (who supply national risk assessments to European business) have identified nineteen African countries that are civil war risks.[34] The time for peace building and preventive diplomacy in these countries is now. Much more attention needs to be given to ways and means of dealing with the vestigial remnants of colonialism, to matters such as state boundaries that have been artificially imposed on different tribal and communal groups, and to the negative social and political consequences of economic underdevelopment or maldevelopment. But it is also important that a lot more pre-emptive attention be given to the development of political systems which will ensure the safety and integrity of minority groups within them.

---

[33] For an excellent overview of the Somalia crisis, see Samuel Makinda, *Seeking Peace from Chaos: Humanitarian Intervention in Somalia*, International Peace Academy Occasional Paper Series (Boulder CO: Lynne Rienner Publishers, 1993).

[34] See Jongman, 'The PIOOM Program', p.71.

In relation to those countries that are at high risk of ethnic and communal tension, or which may be subject to political terrorism or civil war, international governmental and non-governmental organisations should direct more attention now to identifying the necessary preconditions, intervening factors and final precipitants of violence, so that responsible agencies know where they should be directing scarce political resources in order to prevent these potential conflicts from crossing the violence threshold.[35]

The experience of the United Nations in the Balkans completes the quartet of cases which have fundamentally challenged the old conceptual and procedural framework of the United Nations in relation to the maintenance of peace and security. As mentioned above, the former Yugoslavia presents the UN and the international community with a whole spectrum of civil war, wars of secession, inter-state wars and wars of territorial conquest. Parties to conflict in the former Yugoslavia, like their counterparts in Rwanda and Somalia, have engaged in war crimes and gross violations of human rights, but the UN and the European Community (EC) have been relatively powerless to stop them.

These instances of violent conflict raise not only important questions about whether or not the United Nations could have anticipated and prevented them from occurring in the first place, but also once they had occurred, what sorts of measures might have been effective in getting a viable political settlement and in providing basic protection to innocent civilians? Would it have been possible, for example, for the United Nations to have preventively deployed more 'Blue Berets' along the borders, pending negotiations about where these borders might be finally fixed? What might the UN have done, that it did not do, in relation to internal inter-ethnic or communal conflicts in the former Yugoslavia? Are there any particular conflict management or resolution techniques that the UN and regional organisations might apply to such conflicts? For example, could states have suspended recognition of the states evolving from the former Yugoslavia until such time as boundary and minority questions were settled? Does the UN have a specific role to play in relation to strengthening civil society in the development of new states from old? How can the UN strengthen civilian capability in relation to the maintenance of law and order? Would it have been useful for the international community to have applied earlier arms control initiatives in order to prevent the massive flow of arms into the different Balkan states? All of these questions flow out of the multiple crises that have afflicted the Balkans over the past four years.

---

35 A very good start in this direction is given in the chapter written by Ted Robert Gurr, 'Testing and Using a Model of Communal Conflict for Early Warning', pp.20-24, and that by Barbara Harff, 'A Theoretical Model of Genocides and Politicides', pp.25-30, both in Gurr and Harff (eds), *Early Warning of Communal Conflicts*.

The United Nations, the EC and NATO have not provided particularly adequate or useful responses to these questions, and they remain upon the international table. Although there are profound historical reasons for some of the deep animosities in the former Yugoslavia (outlined in the chapter by Michael Wilson), the contemporary challenges thrown up by recent experience in the Balkans has much more universal significance. It raises issues about the nature of sovereignty in the last decade of the twentieth century, and important questions about the distinctions between internal and external conflicts and whether or not there is any chance of early intervention when the sources of some of these conflicts go back hundreds of years. As Coral Bell suggested recently, 'the opportunity for early intervention in Yugoslavia passed by three hundred years ago!'[36] While this may be something of an exaggeration, the point is well taken. The experience in Yugoslavia, therefore, suggests the need to develop late prevention methods capable of dealing with the presenting problems, while simultaneously searching for ways of addressing the more deep-seated historical grievances at another stage, when current conflicts have assumed a more manageable form.

Even so, there are a number of salutary lessons that can be drawn from the experience in Bosnia-Hercegovina which relate to the late and indecisive nature of the intervention, the unclear nature of the mandates for UNPROFOR, and the problem, yet again, of slipping from peacekeeping operations in support of humanitarian objectives into partial enforcement operations and then back into more protective peacekeeping roles. While there are no immediate or obvious solutions to the current problems, the task facing the United Nations and regional organisations concerned about preventing similar crises from erupting elsewhere in the world relates to ways of developing political systems which will ensure that ethnic and communal groups can coexist within common boundaries, or, if this proves impossible, of developing modalities for effective territorial separation.

Experiences in Cambodia, Somalia, the Gulf and the Balkans illustrate the difficulties of late intervention in conflicts after they have crossed the violence threshold. The case study by Ian Kemish on managing potential conflict in the South China Sea, on the other hand, describes a good counter-example of early preventive diplomacy in action. In this instance there are a number of competing national claimants to the Spratly and Paracel islands, with their supposed surrounding undersea resources, and also at stake is general control over sea lines of communication in the South China Sea. There have been recent military disputes between China and Vietnam over the islands, and intense political competition between

---

[36] In a conference on Cooperating for Peace, sponsored by the Peace Research Centre and the Department of International Relations with the United Nations Association of Australia, held at the Australian National University in Canberra, Australia, 4-5 July 1994.

China, Vietnam, Taiwan, Malaysia, the Philippines and Brunei over sovereignty and economic development. A number of the claimants have been expanding their military presence on the islands, with the result that the South China Sea has been identified by a number of strategic analysts as a potential military flashpoint.

In response to this anxiety the Indonesian government, with financial assistance from Canada, instituted a series of 'unofficial' workshops, to enable the claimants to focus on ways of cooperating in the areas of resource assessment, management and development while temporarily suspending their territorial claims. As the case study highlights, the workshops aimed to build confidence between the parties, at the same time developing procedures for solving disputes by peaceful means and identifying the possibilities for joint development.

These 'two-track' workshops (which brought together experts and officials in their 'unofficial' capacities) began in January 1990 and continue to the present. They have been extremely important in helping to defuse tensions in the region and build confidence between most of the claimants, and were instrumental in the development of an 'official' ASEAN Declaration on the South China Sea. This declaration calls for the peaceful resolution of sovereign claims, a voluntary exercise of restraint and a willingness to cooperate in the development of underwater and island resources. It is the explicit renunciation of the use of force and a request for all claimants to abide by the provisions of the Treaty of Amity and Cooperation in Southeast Asia, however, which is probably the most important feature of this declaration. Although there is no guarantee that this promise will remain intact forever, it does signal a willingness on the part of the signatories to eschew coercive diplomacy and negotiate solutions to problems.

The crucial challenge facing the different signatories to the Declaration is how to circumscribe potentially provocative unilateral actions on the part of some claimants while strengthening the cooperative processes. (A number of countries, China, Malaysia and Vietnam, for example, have already made unilateral moves to strengthen their national claims, but it is important that these not create a precedent, since they undermine the wider effort to solve the disputes cooperatively.) The other question is whether or not there is any role for the United Nations in relation to the South China Sea dialogue process.

The case study on the South China Sea identifies three possible ways in which the UN might become engaged with this process. The first is by taking a case to the International Court of Justice, seeking a ruling on the claims in terms of existing international law and the Law of the Sea. The second is through working out a legal regime to govern the development of the region (perhaps something equivalent to the Antarctic Treaty). The third is the development of a separate UN-sponsored 'Spratly authority' to manage the resources on behalf of all the claimants. While there is merit in all of these proposals, there is also considerable regional reluctance to bringing in an extra-regional authority when the 'indigenous' regional processes seem to be working satisfactorily. In this instance, therefore, the United Nations should continue to legitimate the processes that are working, by keeping itself informed about the discussions and by making its good offices available should the South China Sea initiative and the current dialogue process with its unofficial expert working groups not prove sufficient to maintain the peace.

This particular case study is a very useful example of the ways in which an impartial state with standing in the region can facilitate positive 'win-win' negotiating processes, address a series of presenting problems in a positive fashion, identify the underlying concerns and develop important dialogues and discussions aimed at cooperative solutions. It is an excellent illustration of the wisdom of preventive strategies, and contrasts dramatically with the late and more difficult engagement of problems after they have crossed the threshold of armed hostilities. This initiative also highlights how one state's 'altruistic' actions can stimulate positive regional processes and generate virtuous and positive global responses as well.

The other national case studies in this volume, covering Indonesia in the period prior to independence, Kashmir, Cyprus, El Salvador, Angola and the Falklands, all draw attention to the diverse difficulties confronting the United Nations or, as in the case of the Falklands, individual mediators, in seeking to respond to the threatened or actual use of force in ways that will generate enduring political and military settlements and the reconstitution of unconstituted societies.

Once force and coercion have been applied to a situation, it is much more difficult to generate non-coercive responses to problems. These particular case studies reinforce the view that settlements which require coercive conflict management are likely to be less stable than those based on non-coercive conflict management processes, because coercive intervention, mediation with muscle, and other forceful techniques of conflict management rarely resolve problems on any permanent basis. This means that the 'peace' which is reached is likely to be precarious rather than stable, and there is always a possibility that the underlying causes and contradictions which generated the problems in the first place will reassert themselves with equally devastating consequences sometime in the future.[37]

Cyprus and Kashmir, for example, are good illustrations of UN interventions which have failed to resolve the underlying sources of conflict, and have either simply frozen them for others to address at a later stage (which is the case with Cyprus) or generated the illusion of engagement without any substantive outcomes (as is the case in Kashmir).

---

[37] See Paul Wehr, *Conflict Regulation* (Boulder CO: Westview Press, 1979) pp.33-34 for an analysis of the likely consequences of coercive or non-coercive conflict regulation.

In Kashmir, the UN Military Observers Group in India and Pakistan (UNMOGIP) has provided a restraining 'trip wire' for military adventurism, but it has not resulted in any increased willingness on the part of either side to enter serious negotiations. United Nations negotiators have never been able to bridge the gulf between the Pakistan and Indian negotiating positions, with the result that both countries are no nearer a solution to the Kashmir problem now than they were in 1947. Similarly, as William Maley notes in the case study on Afghanistan, even when the United Nations is able to broker a deal between external parties to conflict (as was the case with the Geneva Accords on Afghanistan), it is likely to become unravelled unless it is supported by all the key domestic constituencies, and if crucial domestic needs, issues and positions remain unacknowledged or are left unresolved by the negotiators and mediators.

In Namibia, by contrast, although the independence plan mapped out in UN Security Council Resolution 435 of 1978 took nearly ten years to come to fruition, it is a successful instance of diplomatic intervention, and highlights factors critical to the successful solution of an internal conflict. The case study by Jane Madden on Namibia demonstrates the positive benefits of high levels of cooperation between the superpowers, regional players and national and international non-governmental organisations concerned with the issues. It also shows how a patient process of peacemaking can create the conditions in which peacekeeping becomes an effective tool in maintaining political and military stability.

Although there were many aspects of the Namibian operation that could have been improved (such as relationships between the Special Task Force in New York and operations in the field, or the relationships between the civilian and military sides of the operation), overall it must be judged to have been a success. This success in spite of operational problems was due mainly to favourable external conditions and, secondarily, to the fact that the UN took a very inclusive view of its role within Namibia in order to ensure the development of fair and appropriate political processes. To this end it spent much time and energy educating the people, so as to change the internal political atmosphere from one of suspicion to one of trust. It operated on sound assessments of the situation within Namibia, and was guided by very clear Security Council mandates which helped keep the operation tightly focused. Most of all, however, this operation succeeded because the major actors were included in decision making processes. This engagement built considerable commitment to the agreement, and was accompanied by a strong desire to stimulate 'official' processes of cooperation and reconciliation. From 1989, these factors ensured rapid progress towards the realisation of UNSC Resolution 435 and a smooth transition to independence.

Conversely, the United Nations has discovered that where the commitment to cooperative problem-solving is weak, where there is no widespread reconciliation process and little disposition to entertain power-sharing *en route* to elected democracy, the probability of a peaceful settlement is extremely remote.

Angola is a case in point. The case study highlights the factors leading to the failure of peacemaking - no political agreement between conflicting parties, no commitment to national unity and a deteriorating military situation, with internal chaos and violence as the inevitable result. In such circumstances it is extremely difficult for the United Nations to play a constructive role, and that has been the experience of the UN Angolan Verification Mission II (UNAVEM II).

A lesson to be drawn from negative examples such as Angola and from positive examples such as Namibia is that the development of cooperative problem-solving processes by the United Nations and parties in the field is crucial not only to successful peacemaking and peacekeeping but also to the development of institutions and regimes capable of preventing violent conflicts in the future.

Over the course of the last fifty years, the United Nations has developed different processes, organisations, institutions and regimes to help it fulfil its mandate. While many of these have been ad hoc responses to particular crises, others represent more systematic attempts to institutionalise procedures for dealing with disputes and to help ensure negotiated solutions to problems.

Organisationally, the United Nations' principal organs and specialised agencies cover peace and security affairs, economic and social activities, humanitarian affairs and the administration and management of the Secretariat. The demands placed upon it are immense, but its resources remain extremely meagre. The total number of professional and general staff in the UN numbers 51,484. As Childers and Urquhart note:

> ... the entire UN system world-wide, serving the interests of some 5,500,000,000 people in 184 countries, employs no more workers than the civil service in the American state of Wyoming, population 545,000. Its staff is actually smaller than the number of public-service employees of the city of Stockholm in Sweden, with a population of 672,000.[38]

The success of the UN in relation to maintaining international peace and security, delivering effective humanitarian assistance and promoting economic and social development, therefore, depends on member states making available sufficient resources to implement UN decisions, and on a commitment to the development of international norms and obligations to ensure that this will happen. Since the United Nations has no army, no economic resources that are not given to it, and few and limited means of coercing member states to be good international citizens, its importance and its ability to provide international leadership comes primarily from its 'moral value, its credibility'.[39] The major problem with the organisation

---

[38] Childers and Urquhart, *Renewing the United Nations System*, p.28.
[39] Boutros-Ghali, *An Agenda for Peace*, p.36.

in the 1990s, as Urquhart points out, is that 'it is being suffocated by criticism and doubt'.[40]

In the case study on the International Court of Justice, Steven McIntosh notes that the Court, which was established to adjudicate on 'any question of international law', has not worked out as planned by the founders. The body envisaged as the instrument to establish 'World Peace through World Law' has effectively been prevented from doing so, because most nation states have been reluctant to submit disputes affecting national interests to the decision of the Court and because only a tiny fraction of the UN's members have accepted its compulsory jurisdiction. The proceedings of the Court occur at a glacially slow pace, which is an additional impediment to states seeking a quick judgement on matters of international concern.

Despite these criticisms, there are a record number of cases currently before the Court, and there are signs that it is once again being seen as an appropriate vehicle for both airing and adjudicating international disputes. The Court provides an important judicial alternative to the use of force. If all states were willing to accept its compulsory jurisdiction, as proposed by Boutros-Ghali in *An Agenda for Peace*, and if new life could be breathed back into its judicial processes, it would continue to contribute to the 'moral value and credibility' of the United Nations.

The credibility of the United Nations is enhanced by the development of a legal framework of internationally binding agreements, treaties and regimes. The 1982 Convention on the Law of the Sea, for example, helps promote peace, security and international community by regulating conflicting claims over maritime resources, continental shelves and maritime shipping. Although this convention will not come into force until 17 November 1994, it has exerted very strong moral authority over all those states that have acceded to its provisions already. This means that maritime conflicts of the sort which abound in nineteenth and early twentieth century history can now be placed in a quasi-legal framework and negotiated, instead of ending in naval battles. Such rules are an important element in the construction of international community, and there is no indication that this rule-making function of the United Nations is about to cease. On the contrary, more and more problems are demanding something like the functional equivalent of the Law of the Sea Convention. Treatment of nuclear waste, for example, or working to ensure access to major water supplies, or developing regimes to regulate ozone depletion, all require the negotiation of rules and their acceptance.

In relation to disarmament and arms control, the United Nations, like its predecessor the League of Nations, plays an extremely crucial role in relation to rules and regulations controlling the flow of weapons, in promoting disarmament and in articulating ways of generating security at the lowest possible level of armaments, although it is clear that it has not

---

[40] Urquhart, 'Who Can Police the World?'.

been notably successful in inhibiting the overall flows of conventional arms.[41] In her chapter on arms control and disarmament, Jill Courtney argues that there are three different aspects to United Nations arms control and disarmament processes. The first includes the setting up of essentially preventive measures aimed at developing arms control and disarmament agreements and arrangements. The second aspect involves the processes aimed at managing treaty compliance, while the third covers measures aimed at post-conflict or post-treaty violation actions, or enforcement measures aimed at maintaining the integrity of agreements. While many of these agreements are negotiated outside the UN system itself (for example, the Treaty of Rarotonga which established a South Pacific Nuclear Weapon Free Zone), the United Nations remains their inspiration and the Secretary-General is the depository for most recent disarmament conventions.

Considerable progress has been made in relation to developing multilateral treaties and conventions against nuclear, chemical, biological and inhumane weapons, but much remains to be done in this area. The United Nations, through bodies such as the Conference on Disarmament, through General Assembly and Security Council debates on disarmament, and through the work of the United Nations Disarmament Commission, plays a vital role in maintaining pressure on member states to lower their military holdings to levels likely to generate security for all rather than security for some and insecurity for others.

There is a synergistic connection between progress on economic and social development, the creation of more effective mechanisms for the settlement of dispute, and the willingness to contemplate arms reductions and disarmament. The United Nations is the one body capable of making connections between and helping promote these different types of activity. It can do this by facilitating direct arms control and disarmament negotiations in Geneva. But it can also do it by stimulating trust and confidence-building processes between nations. Bilateral, regional and global confidence-building measures enhance moves towards transparency, and generate a momentum in favour of seeking security at lower levels of weaponry.

Generating macro conditions conducive to stable peace and high levels of trust between nations is both a cause and consequence of successful arms control and disarmament measures. Thus this area of the United Nations activity is not an 'optional extra'; it is critical for generating positive conditions for the use of preventive diplomacy, for encouraging

---

[41] The Permanent Five members of the United Nations Security Council, who are responsible for setting much of the 'moral' tone of the organisation, account for 86 per cent of the world's arms trade. If Germany is included, these six countries together account for 93 per cent of the world's arms trade. This fact makes it very difficult for these countries to take the moral high ground in relation to achieving national defence with as few weapons as possible.

cooperative relations between states and peoples, and thus for the resolution or management of potentially violent conflicts.

One positive aspect of arms control and disarmament agreements is that each has processes both for verifying compliance and for dealing with states who break the rules. The fact that there are sanctions for non-compliance built into the agreements is an important element in maintaining the credibility of the United Nations as an effective arbiter of world peace and security. The case study on Iraq and the United Nations Special Commission on Iraq (UNSCOM) describes how UNSCOM, which was authorised to coordinate and supervise the abolition of Iraq's weapons of mass destruction and their delivery systems, has proved to be highly effective. The development of UNSCOM is a particularly graphic example of how the United Nations can act to enforce international disarmament agreements when there is a political will to do so.

Similarly, North Korea's refusal to comply with its international obligations under the Nuclear Non-Proliferation Treaty has provoked a strong response from states parties to the NPT, especially those with interests in the North Pacific. In these instances the United Nations is revealing that it does have the capability to enforce international agreements, and in this way enhances its own moral authority by strengthening internationally agreed norms.

The question of how to enforce compliance with international norms is not, of course, confined to arms control and disarmament agreements. If states are found to be in non-compliance with their Charter obligations, for example, this poses an important challenge to the integrity of the United Nations and demands some appropriate and effective responses. Evans's book and these case studies have attempted to respond to this challenge by mapping out the graduated responses that the United Nations can make to different sets of problems. Evans makes very clear, as do the case studies, that prevention of conflicts is the most cost-effective and politically effective way of dealing with international problems. But movement towards using preventive diplomacy requires that states rethink their orientations towards international problems by developing a willingness to intervene earlier in disputes than is currently the case and to invoke the Article 33 provisions of the Charter in order to ensure that disputes are resolved by peaceful means. To engage in effective preventive diplomacy will require the employment of more skilled conflict resolution professionals, diplomats and analysts and fewer military personnel. These professionals should be given the task of determining when disputes are escalating and what might constitute appropriate and effective interventions.

States or dissident groups determined to break the peace, engage in the gross violation of human rights or foment violent internal conflicts pose direct threats to the integrity of the United Nations. If the protagonists do not respond to peaceful processes, then the United Nations may have to contemplate more coercive responses to fulfil its goals.

The case study on sanctions highlights one set of procedures available to the United Nations to demonstrate opprobrium with the delinquent actions of member states. The threat or application of sanctions is an indication that preventive diplomacy and 'mediation with muscle' have both failed to deliver desirable outcomes. The application of sanctions (which has only occurred eight times in the history of the United Nations) both signifies displeasure with the behaviour of a member state and signals that if the behaviour does not change there is the possibility of an escalation to full Chapter VII enforcement procedures including military action. These procedures also help maintain the integrity of the United Nations by establishing respect for its processes and goals. While there are a number of important problems in relation to their scope and effectiveness, sanctions are an important means of representing the collective determination of the international community to develop effective means of ensuring respect for human rights and for making the world a little less anarchic.

If the threat of sanctions or actual sanctions does not have the desired objective, then the United Nations may be forced to contemplate more extreme Chapter VII coercive measures. There is normally no problem about applying these to international conflicts where there is a clear threat to the peace. The application of force becomes much more problematic, however, in relation to internal conflicts, which are responsible for most of the current violent conflicts on the global agenda and are producing most deaths. The dilemma in regard to the application of force to internal crises is how to establish criteria for military intervention, and whether such intervention is likely to generate better outcomes than non-military intervention or no intervention at all.

It is clear that when there is a major humanitarian crisis, of the sort that is currently afflicting Rwanda, the international community cannot stand on one side and ignore what is happening. Internal conflicts which precipitate widespread loss of life or threatened loss of life, which are accompanied by a breakdown of civil society and multiple claims to political sovereignty, should alert the international community to the possibility of catastrophe and trigger a wide range of responses. These should, wherever possible, be non-violent and non-coercive, but if they fail to achieve the basic objective of protecting innocent lives, then the United Nations has to contemplate applying force itself. Clearly, international community is advanced best by nations and peoples willingly accepting and abiding by their international commitments and obligations. For states that are unwilling to do this the ultimate sanction of force must remain a possibility to be applied when the United Nations has exhausted all other measures. All such actions should take place under properly constituted multilateral authority, the decision making processes that underly enforcement operations should be as transparent as possible, the responses should be proportional to the problem being tackled, and there has to be a reasonable likelihood that the enforcement action will yield more positive than negative outcomes and make a useful rather than an unhelpful contribution to the problem. If the world community cannot be satisfied that these conditions have been fulfilled, then it is probably wise not to proceed towards enforcement activities.

In addition to the question of whether the United Nations can apply force more effectively than nation states acting alone or in alliance with others, the major problem for the UN engaging in coercive diplomacy is what physical resources or means it has for conducting effective operations. It has no standing army, despite appeals from the Secretary-General and Sir Brian Urquhart to establish one, and remains dependent on contributions of troops from member states in response to requests from the Security Council. This would not be a difficulty were it not for the fact that most of the major suppliers of UN troops now feel overstretched, and many are deeply sceptical about the ability of the United Nations to mount effective enforcement operations.

Recent humanitarian crises such as those in Rwanda and Angola have required, but not received, the urgent dispatch of troops in order to prevent immediate bloodshed. Troops from member states were not immediately forthcoming, and the UN has had to stand by and watch the disaster unfolding. Perhaps it is time to contemplate the establishment of some permanent UN enforcement capacity which would be at the disposal of the Secretary-General and the Security Council, for response to those manifest humanitarian crises which require some kind of military intervention in order to generate space for more non-coercive processes to work.

There are many other issues that bear on the development of international community and the role of the United Nations in its evolution. Enough has been said, however, to indicate that the challenge facing the world in the 1990s is to make the world safe for all peoples. There is an urgent need to ensure that nation states, national and international non-governmental organisations, and regional organisations should join the United Nations in ensuring the development of effective institutions and processes for the maintenance of international peace and security within and between nations. These case studies and Senator Evans's book are contributions to the debate. Much remains to be done but there can be no more intellectually satisfying task than working out how to move the world from systems based on coercion and threat to ones based on trust and cooperation. This is the task of the twenty-first century.

1 Cambodia

SHIRLEY LITHGOW

Introduction

The process of finding a negotiated settlement to the Cambodian civil war proved to be very long and complex. At the outset of the final stage - from Vietnam's withdrawal late in 1989 - the chances for a comprehensive settlement were not considered high: no one knew whether a mutually acceptable agreement was impossible to achieve, or merely difficult.[1] There were four internal parties to the conflict: the State of Cambodia (SOC - the pro-Vietnamese communists); the Party of Democratic Kampuchea (the Khmer Rouge - the Maoist Communists); and the two non-communist factions, the Khmer People's National Liberation Front (KPNLF) and Prince Sihanouk's United Front for an Independent, Neutral, Peaceful and Cooperative Cambodia (FUNCINPEC). The Khmer Rouge, KPNLF and FUNCINPEC had been in an uneasy coalition since 1982. All parties were immensely distrustful of each other and reluctant to reach any form of accommodation.

Cambodia was also a focus for great-power conflicts, with China supporting the Khmer Rouge and Prince Sihanouk, the Soviet Union supporting the SOC, and the United States and its allies supporting the two non-communist resistance groups. The regional countries were also involved in the civil war, with Vietnam aligned with the SOC and the Association of Southeast Asian Nations (ASEAN) with the others.

Failure to resolve the Cambodian conflict, therefore, held the potential for increasing regional instability, particularly in the context of

---

[1] Stephen Solarz, 'Cambodia and the International Community' *Foreign Affairs* 69, 2 (Spring1990) p.100.

superpower confrontation, regional polarisation and even a regional arms race.[2] As well, the flow of refugees continued to confront countries in and beyond the region with major moral, economic and social problems.

The best outcome for Cambodia was for a comprehensive political settlement that would demilitarise the internal struggle, neutralise Cambodia as an arena for superpower and regional rivalry, and give the Cambodian people an opportunity for free and fair elections.[3]

Background to the Cambodian conflict

The modern tragedy of Cambodia began in March 1970 when Prince Norodom Sihanouk, the Head of State and head of the government, was overthrown in a military coup led by Marshal Lon Nol. Sihanouk took up residence in Beijing where he set up a government-in-exile, the Royal Government of the National Union of Cambodia (GRUNC). Over the next five years Lon Nol's hold on power declined in the face of the continuing Vietnamese war (which increasingly infringed on Cambodia), internal corruption, and external threat from Sihanouk's supporters allied with the Khmer Rouge guerrillas. On 17 April 1975, the Khmer Rouge captured Phnom Penh and overthrew the Lon Nol regime. Sihanouk returned as Head of State, but when the brutality of Pol Pot's Democratic Kampuchea and the very limited power of his own role became obvious, Sihanouk resigned (in April 1976), and was placed under house arrest.

Under the Khmer Rouge regime foreigners were expelled and the country isolated from the rest of the world. Cities and towns were evacuated and people sent to work in the fields. A severe refugee problem developed as people tried to escape the social dislocation and economic breakdown. A commonly accepted figure is that at least one million died as a result of policies of the Pol Pot regime. Many died from starvation, but many others, including most of Cambodia's intelligentsia, perished from execution, torture or mistreatment.

The virulent anti-Vietnamese attitude of the Khmer Rouge led to serious border clashes with Vietnam and incursions into Vietnamese territory by Khmer Rouge forces. On 25 December 1978, Vietnam launched an invasion of Cambodia. On 7 January 1979, Vietnam captured Phnom Penh and a few days later the People's Republic of Kampuchea (PRK) was proclaimed. The new government comprised pro-Vietnamese Communists who had previously defected from the Khmer Rouge. The Khmer Rouge fled westwards to the mountains and jungles along the Thai border where they were sustained by Chinese arms shipments via Thailand,

---

2   Gareth Evans and Bruce Grant, *Australia's Foreign Relations* (Carlton: Melbourne University Press, 1991) p.208.
3   Solarz, 'Cambodia and the International Community' p.99.

as part of China's and Thailand's strategy to either remove Vietnam from Cambodia, or at least render it incapable of aggression elsewhere.[4]

The PRK (renamed the State of Cambodia in April 1989) held power in Phnom Penh throughout the 1980s. The Vietnamese army reinforced PRK control over most of the countryside, but Vietnam and the PRK could not fully overcome the resistance of the Khmer Rouge, secure in its western bastions.

At a meeting in Kuala Lumpur in June 1982, the Coalition Government of Democratic Kampuchea (CGDK) was established, bringing the two non-Communist parties, FUNCINPEC and the KPNLF together with the Communist Khmer Rouge. The three factions were united only in their opposition to the PRK. They were supported by the Chinese, the Americans and the countries of ASEAN. One reason behind the formation of the coalition was the perceived need to prevent the United Nations from substituting the PRK for the internationally unpopular Khmer Rouge as the occupant of Cambodia's seat in the United Nations or from declaring the seat vacant.[5]

Vietnam and the PRK launched regular offensives against the resistance forces. A major offensive in 1984/85 resulted in heavy fighting and many refugees crossed the border into Thailand. In time Cambodia became a burden on Vietnam, as it was an obstacle to Vietnam's economic development, a drain on Soviet supplied resources and above all a liability in Vietnam's efforts to achieve better international standing and support. Vietnam continued to be subjected to Australian, UN and international pressure to withdraw from Cambodia as a precondition for better relations and restored aid. However, Vietnam's announcement in January 1989 that it would withdraw its forces from Cambodia by September of that year caused some concern in the international community of a possible return to power of the Khmer Rouge.

Efforts to find a solution

Vietnam's announced intention to withdraw its forces from Cambodia met one of the long-standing steps which Australia and others had been working for and thus improved the chances for negotiating a settlement to the Cambodian conflict. By the mid-1980s something of a consensus had emerged on a set of principles first developed in discussions between Australia and Vietnam: there needed to be withdrawal of all Vietnamese forces from Cambodia, matched by an effective arrangement to prevent the Khmer Rouge from returning to power in Cambodia; free and fair elections for Cambodia; the creation of conditions for the peaceful return of

---

[4] Ibid. p.102.
[5] Ibid. p.103.

displaced Cambodians; and guarantees that a post-settlement Cambodia would be neutral, independent and non-aligned.[6]

The crucial factor in bringing about a settlement to the Cambodian conflict was that the Khmer Rouge could not be effectively isolated and marginalised, and its military influence nullified, while it continued to be supplied, especially by China, with arms, money and diplomatic support. Unless China was prepared to modify that support, then irrespective of what efforts were made to negotiate a settlement, the continuation of bloody civil war was inevitable.[7]

China's primary stated objective in Cambodia was to oppose Vietnamese hegemony in Indochina; centuries of Sino-Vietnamese friction underlay China's approach. China saw Soviet influence in Vietnam and Vietnamese influence in Indochina as part of a policy of encirclement by the Soviet Union. As the Soviet Union's interest in regional conflicts waned under Mikhail Gorbachev's leadership and relations between China and the Soviet Union improved, China no longer felt threatened by the Soviet Union, and while it still opposed Vietnamese hegemony in Cambodia, it saw it more in regional rather than global terms. Moreover, China (and for that matter Vietnam) knew that without Soviet support it would not be feasible in the long-run for Vietnam to maintain its position in Cambodia.

China consistently maintained that it would give a commitment to cease military support to the Khmer Rouge, and support a ceasefire, only in the context of a comprehensive settlement agreed to by all Cambodian parties and which guaranteed the future independence and neutrality of the country - that is, a Cambodia which gave no weight or succour to China's enemies around its borders. Only a UN peace settlement seemed capable of delivering that .[8]

Of the four Cambodian factions, the Khmer Rouge was the least inclined to go along with a UN settlement. While any UN settlement would gain the dissolution of the SOC regime, the Khmer Rouge's prospects of seizing power would clearly diminish. However, if China supported a UN settlement, the Khmer Rouge was likely to be compelled to go along, given its dependence on China.[9]

A UN agreement on Cambodia would also enable China (and the ASEAN countries) to verify the Vietnamese withdrawal. Further, a comprehensive UN settlement would reduce the prospect of Vietnam seeing a need for a renewed military involvement in Cambodia to prevent the threat to its security that would result from a Khmer Rouge victory. Such a settlement, for this and other reasons, gave Vietnam an opportunity to end its international isolation.

---

6   Evans & Grant, *Australia's Foreign Relations* p.209.
7   Ibid. p.212.
8   Ibid.
9   Solarz, 'Cambodia and the International Community' p.109.

Paris International Conference on Cambodia July-August 1989

Two ministerial meetings were convened in Paris on 29-31 July and 27-31 August 1989, by France, the former colonial power, and Indonesia. The Paris International Conference on Cambodia (PICC), sought to bring the four Cambodian factions and the principal parties concerned with the Cambodian issue (including the UN Secretary-General) together in an effort to achieve a comprehensive political settlement in association with the withdrawal of Vietnamese troops from Cambodia by the end of September. The hope was that the influence of the Five Permanent Members of the UN Security Council and the participation of a group of interested countries would demonstrate the strength of international concern to resolve the conflict, and help induce the factions to reach some accommodation on power sharing.

Unfortunately, the settlement strategy foundered for a number of reasons, the crucial one being the issue of power sharing. The CGDK, together with its international backers, demanded a place for each of the four Cambodian parties, including the Khmer Rouge, in the transitional administration; a demand which the SOC government of Hun Sen, and its international backers, were not prepared to concede.[10] The stark fact to emerge from the Conference was that the Cambodian factions remained unprepared to reach an accommodation, for all of the reasons that had prevented real progress throughout the 1980s.

The withdrawal of Vietnam's occupation forces from Cambodia in September 1989, was not accompanied by a renewed momentum for peace, despite the efforts of the Paris Co-Chairmen, the Thai Prime Minister and the United States Secretary-of-State. Instead, there was a resurgence of fighting, continued external supplies of materiel, and a general hardening of diplomatic positions. Although international opinion remained overwhelming in favour of a comprehensive settlement, the composition of the proposed transitional authority in Cambodia, in particular the role proposed for the Khmer Rouge, remained a major stumbling block.[11] ASEAN and the US were suspicious of any arrangements that would legitimise the PRK/SOC government.

The Australian proposal

In response to the diplomatic deadlock and deteriorating military situation, on 24 November 1989, the Australian Minister for Foreign Affairs and Trade, Senator Gareth Evans, launched an initiative designed to end the fighting and give the Cambodian people an opportunity to determine their own destiny. Instead of considering the question of how power should be

---

[10] Senator Gareth D. Evans, Ministerial Statement by the Australian Minister for Foreign Affairs and Trade, the Senate (Canberra: 6 December 1990) p.3.
[11] Ibid.

divided between the four Cambodian parties in the interim administration of Cambodia, the Australian proposal addressed the question of how to ensure that the administration of Cambodia in the interim period was carried out so that it gave no political advantage or disadvantage to any political party during the election process. The proposal drew on ideas of a neutral UN interim administration put forward earlier by Prince Sihanouk and US Congressman Stephen Solarz.[12]

The core of the Australian proposal for a comprehensive settlement was that the United Nations would assume responsibility for the administration of Cambodia during the interim period between the establishment of a ceasefire and the emergence of a new government following an election conducted and supervised by the United Nations. A UN involvement in the transitional administration, together with a UN military force to monitor the ceasefire and cessation of external military assistance and a UN role in organising and conducting the elections, was to ensure a neutral political environment conducive to free and fair elections.[13]

An enhanced role for the United Nations that would supervise an interim Cambodian administration circumvented the SOC's objection to the inclusion of the Khmer Rouge in a coalition government and the CGDK's objection to recognising the SOC as a basis for a settlement.[14]

The idea of the UN involvement in a transitional authority was not new. In West New Guinea in 1962, authority was transferred to the United Nations Temporary Executive Authority for the seven month transitional period. A similar arrangement was made in Namibia. However, the degree of UN involvement in a transitional authority as subsequently developed in Cambodia was certainly new.

The Australian proposal also envisaged the formation of a Supreme National Council comprising individuals from the four Cambodian parties serving in their personal capacity as 'prominent Cambodians'. It was proposed that the Supreme National Council would be the repository of Cambodian national sovereignty and national unity during the transitional period. It would be consulted by, and give advice to, those carrying out the functions of civil administration, electoral organisation, and security supervision, monitoring and verification. But the Supreme National Council would devolve government authority in the transitional period to the UN Secretary-General, to ensure that these functions could be carried out in a way that would create the environment of confidence which was necessary if a lasting Cambodian peace was to be achieved.[15]

---

12   Evans & Grant, *Australia's Foreign Relations* p.211.
13   Ibid.
14   Solarz, 'Cambodia and the International Community' p.108.
15   Senator Gareth D. Evans, Introductory Statement by Australian Foreign Minister to the Informal Meeting on Cambodia (Jakarta: 26 July 1990).

While what was being proposed was inherently difficult and complex, a number of factors seemed to indicate that a settlement of the Cambodian conflict might be achievable. The United Nations had been able to demonstrate new vitality and credibility through its success in facilitating an end to the Iran-Iraq war and the Soviet withdrawal from Afghanistan and its role in implementing the Namibian settlement. As well, the transformation of East-West relations brought close collaboration between the US and the Soviet Union in a number of international disputes, including Cambodia, and this had strengthened markedly the collective authority and influence of the Permanent Five Members of the UN Security Council. Further, as the effects of the historic changes in the Soviet Union and Europe worked their way through to the Asia Pacific region, it was becoming clear that the Soviet Union, Vietnam and probably China (which was seeking to restore its international image following the Beijing massacre) were more interested than before in achieving a Cambodian settlement.[16]

While the proposal received unprecedented support from the major powers, there was still a long way to go before a settlement, as a number of factors had to be considered when determining the degree of UN involvement. First, there was the need to continue to respect the sovereignty of the Cambodian nation; second, there was the need for strict impartiality, for without that the creation of an environment of confidence would be impossible; third, there was the need to ensure that any UN role in civil administration would provide for the continued delivery of the normal services of government to the Cambodian people; and finally, there was the need to consider the principle of efficiency and cost-effectiveness.

Informal Meeting on Cambodia, Jakarta, 26-28 February 1990

The Indonesian Foreign Minister, Ali Alatas, a Co-Chairman of the Paris Conference, had been exploring the possibility of an informal regional meeting on Cambodia, and felt sufficiently encouraged to convene a meeting in Jakarta on 26-28 February 1990. In response to a request by Alatas, Australia prepared Working Papers, setting out in detail the Australian plan, for presentation to that meeting. The Working Papers were based on information obtained by the Australian Technical Mission which had visited Cambodia that month.

The Working Papers were prepared on the basis that there were two essential objectives to which all the work of a comprehensive settlement must be directed. These objectives were:

- to achieve conditions in which the Cambodian people could freely, secure from intimidation or coercion, choose their own leaders and determine their own future, by means of free and fair elections; and

---

[16] Evans, Ministerial Statement p.3.

- to achieve a reconstructed Cambodia with internationally guaranteed sovereignty, independence and neutrality.

The central thesis of the Working Papers was that any agreement on a comprehensive settlement of the Cambodian problem could not of itself decide between the competing claims of various parties as to which constituted the legitimate government of Cambodia, or determine what would be Cambodia's constitutional order and social and political system. Only the Cambodian people could make those decisions. The most a comprehensive settlement could do was to provide for conditions in which the Cambodians themselves could decide on these matters through fair elections in a secure environment.[17]

The Working Papers outlined various options on the role of the United Nations in civil administration, organising and conducting elections, and maintaining a secure environment in which Cambodians might exercise their electoral choice free from fear, intimidation and violence. As well, the papers explored a range of costings. Conventional wisdom had it that such an exercise would be beyond the resources of the United Nations. Australian calculations 'showed that such a proposal (estimated ... to cost US$1.3 billion for 18 months) was both practicable and affordable'.[18]

While the Jakarta meeting failed to reach an agreement on a statement of principles providing for an enhanced role for the United Nations in a comprehensive settlement (it became deadlocked over the question of a reference to genocide), nevertheless, there was a large measure of agreement on the central concepts of the Working Papers: the enhanced role for the United Nations in the transitional period; the establishment of a Supreme National Council; and that the United Nations organise and conduct free and fair elections.

It was generally accepted that, if only the political will could be found, the Australian plan offered a practical way forward. In fact, the proposal was considered to be the last substantial hope for a peaceful solution of the Cambodian conflict.[19]

Permanent Five framework

The negotiating process continued throughout 1990. Representatives of the Five Permanent Members of the UN Security Council had met in Paris on 15-16 January and agreed on a set of principles which would form the basis of their future discussions. This meeting of the Permanent Five was significant in that it marked the start of a two-track international approach to the Cambodia problem - the Permanent Five process and the

---

[17] Department of Foreign Affairs and Trade, *Cambodia: an Australian Peace Proposal* (Canberra: Australian Government Printing Service, 1990) p.1.
[18] Evans & Grant, *Australia's Foreign Relations* p.215.
[19] Ibid. p.214.

Paris Conference process - between which a productive interaction was subsequently maintained.[20]

Consultations continued between the Permanent Five and the Paris Conference Co-Chairmen and the UN Secretariat, and by late August 1990 agreement had been reached on a framework document setting out the key elements of a comprehensive political settlement based on an enhanced UN role.

At a meeting hosted by the Paris Conference Co-Chairmen in Jakarta on 9-10 September, the Cambodians accepted the Permanent Five framework in its entirety as a basis for settling the Cambodian conflict, and agreed to establish the Supreme National Council (SNC) as called for in the Permanent Five framework.

The United Nations (in Security Council Resolution 668 of 20 September 1990, and General Assembly Resolution 45/3 of 15 October 1990), endorsed the basic elements of the peace plan, and urged the parties to elaborate the Permanent Five framework into a concluded comprehensive political settlement. These Resolutions also welcomed the agreement of the Cambodian parties to form the SNC 'as the unique legitimate body and source of authority' in which, throughout the transitional period, the independence, national unity and sovereignty of Cambodia was embodied, noting that the SNC would 'designate its representatives to occupy the seat of Cambodia at the United Nations'.[21]

At a meeting in Jakarta on 9-10 November hosted by the Paris Conference Co-Chairmen, agreement was reached on the form and structure of a comprehensive settlement negotiating text. Then on 23-26 November 1990, representatives of the Co-Chairmen and the UN Secretary-General met with Permanent Five officials and reached consensus on a full draft comprehensive settlement.[22]

While the indications were that a settlement of the Cambodian conflict was well on the way, in late 1990 the SOC, supported by Vietnam, expressed a series of reservations about the Permanent Five negotiating text. The SOC was keen to obtain assurances on practical measures which ensured that the Khmer Rouge could not seize power militarily either during or after the transitional period. The SOC's chief concern related to the provisions in the draft agreements on demobilisation. While the SOC accepted regrouping and cantonment of the armed forces of all four parties, it argued against demobilisation on the basis that it did not want to leave itself exposed to attacks from undeclared Khmer Rouge guerrilla forces. Other issues of concern to the SOC were human rights (the non-recurrence of genocide) and sovereignty.

The SOC's stand - based on a view that the settlement process had begun to swing too far against its interests and in favour of the other

---

[20] Ibid.
[21] Evans, Ministerial Statement p.5.
[22] Evans & Grant, *Australia's Foreign Relations* p.216.

Cambodian parties and their international supporters - was a major setback to what had been a mammoth effort on the part of the Permanent Five Members of the Security Council, the Paris Co-Chairmen and the other international players in achieving a full draft comprehensive settlement. As other major issues, such as the Gulf crisis continued to clamour for the attention of most of the Permanent Five countries, the risk was that if the Cambodian parties themselves remained intransigent, the key international players might walk away from the Cambodian problem.

After further diplomatic efforts and consultation between the Cambodian parties, Prince Sihanouk convened a SNC meeting at Pattaya on 26-28 August 1991, and brokered a series of agreements between the four Cambodian parties. The SOC agreed to demobilisation of 70 per cent of each armed force and of 70 per cent of their weapons, with regrouping and cantonment of the remaining 30 per cent and the remaining 30 per cent of arms stored on site under UN supervision. The genocide issue was diffused on the basis of a SOC proposal to include the words 'catastrophe of the past' in reference to the Pol Pot era. As well, there was agreement on SNC decision making processes, and specifically on the relationship between the SNC and the UN Secretary-General's Special Representative. Most importantly, however, the Cambodian parties reiterated their support for the Permanent Five framework, and for a comprehensive settlement in which the United Nations would have a central role.

The Agreements on a Comprehensive Political Settlement of the Cambodia Conflict were signed on 23 October 1991 by the four Cambodian parties and the international participants at the Paris Conference on Cambodia. The settlement committed the Cambodian parties and those supporting them to a permanent ceasefire, the holding of free and fair elections, and the adoption of a new democratic constitution - all under the supervision of the United Nations through the United Nations Transitional Authority in Cambodia (UNTAC).

The Comprehensive Political Settlement

The UN mandate in Cambodia went far beyond that of traditional peacekeeping, and included comprehensive efforts to achieve genuine national reconciliation and a transition to democratic government. In addition to traditional peacekeeping tasks, such as the verification of the withdrawal of foreign forces and the supervision of the ceasefire, UNTAC was responsible for creating a neutral political environment conducive to free and fair elections; a task which involved a 'direct control' function in respect of key areas of the civil administration of Cambodia in the transitional period. As well, UNTAC was responsible for the cantonment and demobilisation of factional forces, the organisation and conduct of the elections (not just to monitor them), the repatriation and resettlement of more than 365,000 Cambodian refugees and displaced persons in camps along the Thai-Cambodia border, advancing efforts to ensure the observation of human rights, and for the rehabilitation of essential Cambodian infrastructure during the transitional period and the post-transitional reconstruction of Cambodia.

Over the period of UNTAC administration, Cambodian sovereignty was vested in the SNC, which was chaired by Prince Sihanouk and comprised representatives of the four Cambodian parties - the SOC, which was the administration in place in Phnom Penh, and the three former resistance parties: the PDK (the Khmer Rouge), FUNCINPEC and KPNLF.

Under Article 6 of the Comprehensive Agreement, the SNC delegated to UNTAC 'all powers necessary' in the transitional period to ensure the implementation of the Agreements. The transitional period began with the signing of the Agreements on 23 October 1991 and concluded on 24 September 1993 when the 120-member Constituent Assembly, elected in the UN-supervised elections, adopted a constitution and transformed itself into a legislative assembly.

An innovative aspect of the comprehensive settlement was that it did not end with the completion of UNTAC's mandate, but was rather a continuing international process to which the signatories were committed in a variety of ways, including the rehabilitation and reconstruction of Cambodia through involvement in the International Committee on the Reconstruction of Cambodia (ICORC); obligations to uphold the sovereignty, independence, territorial integrity and inviolability, neutrality and national unity of Cambodia, with a continuing role for the PICC Co-Chairmen; continuing involvement, through the UN Secretary-General's Special Representative of the Commission on Human Rights, in human rights questions, quite apart from whatever signatories to the Paris Accords choose to do bilaterally.

Given the difficult physical and health environment, the lack of infrastructure, transport difficulties, language difficulties, the potentially fragile character of any ceasefire, the difficulty of monitoring guerrilla forces, and the sheer daunting size of the UN operation in Cambodia, implementing the Cambodian peace settlement was likely to be more difficult than had been experienced in most other UN peacekeeping operations.[23]

Problems posed by diversification of United Nations role

The ambitious nature of the Cambodian peace settlement was to expose a wide range of problems, starting with the inability of the UN machinery to stage a vast and complex operation within the deadlines envisaged in the settlement.

---

[23] Ibid. p.211.

Planning and deployment

The Namibia operation had shown that in planning a peacekeeping operation, there should be an earnest effort to reduce the time taken between the end of the negotiation phase and implementation of the agreement. The UN Secretary-General has embraced also the need for speedy reaction by the UN in conflict resolution, suggesting that such a capability could be derived from a 'force-in-being'.[24]

While in late 1991 there was a real political imperative for the quick deployment of UNTAC, there was also the realisation within the United Nations that early and full deployment was logistically impossible. The United Nations' Field Operations Division, which had responsibility for the day-to-day planning of the UNTAC operation, was stretched to capacity in coordinating and supporting existing peacekeeping operations. The risk of undue delay in the deployment of UNTAC was the possibility of an erosion of commitment to the settlement both on the part of the Cambodian parties and some members of the international community.[25] There was also the risk that the UN operation itself could become too drawn out with a consequent ballooning of costs.

The United Nations Advance Mission to Cambodia (UNAMIC), comprising 268 civilian and military personnel from about 22 countries, was deployed in November 1991, to provide a bridge between the signing of the Peace Accords and the arrival of UNTAC. However, UNAMIC's mandate was too restricted and focused more on maintaining liaison between the Cambodian parties and the monitoring of ceasefire violations, than on preparing the way for UNTAC. The weakness of the UNAMIC mandate meant that the various elements of UNTAC were slower than needed be in establishing a strong and visible presence throughout Cambodia.[26]

On 28 February 1992, the UN Security Council approved the overall plan for UNTAC. The estimated total budget was US$1.58 billion and the plan called for 15,900 military personnel, 3,600 civilian police and 1,020 administrative personnel from more than 30 countries. The Secretary-General's Special Representative, the Head of UNTAC, was Mr Yasushi Akashi of Japan and the UNTAC Military Commander was Lieutenant-General John Sanderson of Australia.

The UNTAC force, however, was not deployed in the effective manner anticipated in the operational plan. The UN Secretary-General's Special Representative was not appointed until January 1992, the Force

---

[24] Boutros Boutros-Ghali, *An Agenda for Peace - Preventative Diplomacy, Peacemaking and Peace-Keeping* (New York: United Nations, 1992) para.43.

[25] Nick Warner, 'Cambodia: Lessons of UNTAC for Future Peacekeeping Operations' paper presented to the International Seminar, UN Peacekeeping at the Crossroads (Canberra: 21-24 March 1993) p.3.

[26] Ibid. p.6.

Commander, until December 1991, the Police Commissioner and the Civil Administration and Human Rights Directors, until March 1992. While the period between the signing of the Paris Agreements and their implementation was five months, it was another five to six months before UNTAC was fully operational. The force's twelve battalions were not fully deployed until mid-1992 and the 3,600 civilian police not until July. The centrally important civil administration component was not in place in the provinces until the end of September, several months behind schedule. Other components were also affected to varying extents.

In part the delays in UNTAC's deployment were due to, or were aggravated by, inadequate planning and preparation. Several UN planning missions visited Cambodia between 1989 and late 1991, reporting on many aspects of the country, its administration and its problems. Because Cambodia at that time was a very remote and inaccessible place, with travel out of Phnom Penh being very difficult, the planning missions could not get to the heart of any issue.[27]

The main exceptions to this paucity of in-field planning was the visit to Cambodia as part of the planning team in December 1991, of Lieutenant-General Sanderson, who would be the Military Commander of the UNTAC force, and the deployment to Cambodia in October-November 1991 of the Advance Electoral Planning Unit to conduct a survey throughout Cambodia for the electoral component.

Administration

The administration division of UNTAC was responsible for a billion dollar budget, massive international procurement, the establishment of offices in more than 300 locations throughout the country, the recruitment of 50,000 local staff for the electoral process, the management and servicing of a fleet of 10,000 vehicles, communications, housing, finance and the management of thousands of personnel - and in a country whose infrastructure was practically non-existent.[28]

The task of the administration division would have been difficult enough with adequate planning in New York. But with the rush to get UNTAC into the field, and with competing priorities like Yugoslavia, it seemed that the administrative blueprint of previous and less complex operations, were simply applied to the Cambodia mission. As a result UNTAC had an inappropriate administrative structure for the scope and magnitude of its responsibilities. At times, the problems of administration in areas such as personnel, finance, procurement, and transportation threatened to bring UNTAC to a standstill, jeopardising the success of the operation.[29]

---

[27] Ibid.
[28] Ibid. p.10.
[29] Ibid.

Defining and redefining the mandate

International and UN response to PDK non-compliance

Failure by the UN Secretariat to ensure that UNTAC was provided with adequate staff and facilities to make a timely beginning to its crucial task of supervising and controlling key areas of the existing Cambodian administration, left an opening for Khmer Rouge allegations of UNTAC bias towards the SOC and an excuse not to fulfil their obligations under the terms of the settlement.

On 9 May 1992, Sanderson, after consultation with the parties, called for the commencement of Phase II of the peace process (the cantonment, disarming and eventual demobilisation of 70 per cent of the four Cambodian armies) from 13 June 1992. It was estimated that about 150,000 soldiers from the four Cambodian armies had to be cantoned and more than 300,000 weapons secured.

The PDK refused to comply with a number of requirements for commencement of Phase II - including refusing full access by UNTAC to all areas under PDK control. The PDK based their refusal to cooperate on two complaints: first, that UNTAC had not taken adequate steps to verify the withdrawal of all Vietnamese forces from Cambodia and, second, the SNC needed to become, in fact, the 'unique' authority in Cambodia.

Vietnam had provided Akashi with information on the withdrawal of Vietnamese forces from Cambodia and had assured him that no Vietnamese forces remained in Cambodia. However, as far as the PDK was concerned 'Vietnamese forces' meant not just military units but also the ethnic Vietnamese settlers who the PDK alleged included large numbers of disguised Vietnamese soldiers and spies. A population of around half a million ethnic Vietnamese had lived in Cambodia before the Khmer Rouge era. Since the signing of the Paris Agreements large numbers of Vietnamese artisans and labourers attracted by the economic opportunities offered by UNTAC, flowed into Cambodia.

Akashi made it clear that he was not prepared to countenance any racially-based discrimination against the Vietnamese in Cambodia and that he regarded the Vietnamese settlers' question as being entirely separate from the question of verification of foreign troop withdrawal. The issue of Vietnamese settlers was one that could only be resolved by a democratically elected government of Cambodia.

As to the issue of SNC authority, the PDK became more insistent that 'the SNC and UNTAC in consultation and cooperation retain State power in Cambodia during the transitional period'. Stated in these terms the PDK's position on the status and powers of the SNC was a clear misinterpretation of the settlement text and a return to their old demand for a share in the interim Cambodian government and the complete dismantling of the SOC administration. Akashi responded that such a demand was quite unacceptable as it undermined the whole basis of the comprehensive settlement.

The Ministerial Conference on the Reconstruction and Rehabilitation of Cambodia in Tokyo on 22 June 1992, provided an opportunity for the international signatories to the settlement to encourage the PDK to comply fully with the terms of the settlement. A 'non-paper' setting out ways in which legitimate PDK concerns might be addressed was passed to the PDK and the other Cambodian parties. The Conference participants adopted a conciliatory approach to genuine PDK concerns that UNTAC should create a neutral political environment, without favouring one party or the other, in which free and fair elections could be held in the first half of 1993. Similarly, PDK concerns that international aid would be used to support any one party over another were addressed. Ways were also suggested of enhancing consultation between UNTAC and the SNC. However, the PDK made no direct response to the proposals in the non-paper.

In response to the deadlock, the UN Security Council adopted Resolution 766 on 21 July 1992, which referred to the refusal of the PDK to proceed with the implementation of Phase II of the settlement, deplored the continuing violations of the ceasefire and urged all parties to cease all hostilities forthwith. The Resolution also called on the UN Secretary-General to ensure that international assistance to Cambodia only went to those parties who were fulfilling their obligations under the Paris Agreements.

Throughout August the international community (China, Thailand and Japan in particular), held a series of meetings with PDK representatives in a further attempt to draw the PDK back into the peace process. By the end of August, however, when there was still no positive response from the PDK, a number of concerned countries expressed the view that the international community should begin to examine alternative options for implementing the settlement.

On 13 October 1992, the UN Security Council adopted Resolution 783 which confirmed the timetable for the implementation of the peace settlement including that elections be held no later than April-May 1993. As well, the military component was to create a secure environment conducive to the preparations for, and subsequent conduct of the electoral process. The Resolution deplored the PDK's non-compliance and demanded that the PDK fulfil its obligations under the Paris Agreements. Thailand and Japan were invited to continue their efforts to find solutions to the problem of the PDK's intransigence. Further, the PICC Co-Chairmen were asked to undertake consultations and these took place in Beijing on 7-8 November 1992. At Beijing the consensus among the major international players was that it should be made clear to the PDK that their non-cooperation could not be expected to be entirely painless.

The key question facing the UN Security Council was what to do about the refusal of the PDK to participate in the settlement process unless their conditions were met, conditions which the international community believed were unacceptable.

In an attempt to overcome the problems of the PDK non-compliance, the UN Security Council adopted Resolution 792 on 30 November 1992. The Resolution reiterated that general elections were to go ahead as scheduled in April-May 1993, in all areas of Cambodia to which UNTAC had full and free access as at 31 January 1993. Also proposed were a number of measures that bore upon the capacity of the PDK to continue to resist the full implementation of the settlement, specifically, that UNTAC establish border checkpoints, and the supply of petroleum products to the PDK areas be prevented in accordance with the military provisions of the Paris Agreements. The Resolution also supported the decision of the SNC to ban the export of logs from Cambodia from 31 December 1992, and called on UNTAC to ensure its implementation. It further requested the SNC to consider similar action on the export of minerals and gems. The PDK was very dependent on the revenue from the export of logs and gems from its areas of control.

China, a key to the successful implementation of the settlement, abstained from voting on Resolution 792. China considered the imposition of sanctions and the possible holding of elections without the Khmer Rouge to be at variance with the Paris Agreements. The international community had been successful up to that time in maintaining a consensus approach on the implementation of the settlement, and China's decision not to support Resolution 792 was a break from that consensus. China, however, later reiterated its commitment to the implementation of the Paris Accords.

With the Khmer Rouge unlikely now to enter Phase II, UNTAC had all but abandoned cantonment. From 31 December, the role for UNTAC's military component changed from the cantonment process to more active patrolling, movement control and more security oriented tasks designed to create a secure environment for the electoral process. However, the continuing existence of large and sometimes undisciplined Cambodian armies, and attempts by some of them to improve their positions on the ground, had an adverse effect on the security situation in the country. In December there was a marked increase in ceasefire violations and attacks against UNTAC personnel and helicopters. The PDK embarked upon a policy of detaining UNTAC military personnel who encroached into PDK claimed areas. As well, there was an increase in politically motivated acts of intimidation and attacks against party offices and officials by the SOC, in addition to the deliberate killing of ethnic Vietnamese civilians.

Although Akashi announced on 25 December measures for protecting officials of political parties, UNTAC was increasingly being accused of weakness in the face of political violence and for not taking sterner action against the SOC. As well, criticism of the military component increased sharply in early January, beginning with Hun Sen's major address to diplomatic representatives and the media on 5 January 1993. Hun Sen warned that the PDK would seek to sabotage the elections and called for UNTAC to be given a stronger mandate to take direct military action against the PDK. Sanderson addressed a number of the criticisms on 14 January. Sanderson's constant position in not wanting to commit troops to internal security operations was that this was outside UNTAC's mandate.

'Internal security operations' in reality meant moving to a Chapter VII mandate, i.e., using force against Cambodians. This would have required the UN Security Council's approval and it was certain some of the key international players, in particular Japan and China, would not have agreed to an offensive role for UNTAC military. Also, UNTAC would have required additional forces to undertake such a role. With UN resources already overstretched it would have taken time to deploy the additional forces. This would have lengthened considerably the UN's presence in Cambodia for there was no guarantee that a conventional force would ultimately defeat the Khmer Rouge guerrilla force, or even force its compliance. The UN's operation in the Congo in the 1960s showed how easily a peacekeeping force could become embroiled in a chaotic internal situation of extreme complexity.

With the continued refusal of the PDK to comply with the terms of the Cambodia peace settlement by 31 January 1993, representatives of the Core Group countries (the Permanent Five Members of the Security Council plus Australia, Japan, Indonesia, Thailand, Germany, Canada and India) met in New York on 16 February to discuss the next steps in the peace process. A general consensus emerged on Security Council action and on 8 March the Security Council unanimously passed Resolution 810, which sought to move the Cambodian peace process along to elections on 23-27 May, without the participation of the PDK.

In his report to the UN Security Council on 3 May, the Secretary-General concluded that while the elections would clearly not be taking place in an environment as disarmed and politically neutral as was envisaged in the Paris Agreements, the UN had an obligation - not least to the 95 per cent of eligible Cambodians who had registered to vote - to proceed with the election 'with all caution and prudence, and with the greatest possible concern for the safety of its own staff and the well-being of Cambodians'.[30]

The Secretary-General also added that if the holding of free and fair elections in Cambodia was a test for the United Nations, it was also a test for the Cambodians themselves. Neither peace nor elections nor national reconciliation could be imposed by force, nor indeed was UNTAC mandated or equipped to use force. The Cambodian parties could not expect the international community to succeed where they themselves had

---

[30] United Nations Secretary-General, *Fourth Progress Report of the United Nations Transitional Authority in Cambodia* (New York: United Nations, 3 May 1993) para.140.

failed.³¹ On 15 May, the Secretary-General acknowledged that the elections were likely to be affected by violence and reiterated that UNTAC would continue to do its utmost in providing security measures. UNTAC, therefore, would be conducting the most impartial elections that was possible in conditions that were not susceptible to its full control.³²

Institutional building and social reconstruction

UNTAC's mandate included comprehensive efforts towards institutional building and social reconstruction as integral parts of a peace building package designed to secure a lasting end to armed conflict and a genuine transition to democracy. In additional to a traditional peacekeeping role, UNTAC had significant civil administration, electoral, police, human rights, repatriation, and rehabilitation and reconstruction functions.

Civil administration

UNTAC was mandated to exercise 'direct control' of the existing administrations of the parties to ensure strict neutrality in the areas of foreign affairs, security, information, finance and national defence in the period leading up to and immediately after the elections. This would be a daunting task in any polity, but was more so in Cambodia where there were ostensibly four separate administrations and police forces to control, little workable infrastructure, and huge language problems.³³

Without the political will of the Cambodian factions to apply the Paris Accords, administrative control by UNTAC could not be effective. The non-compliance of the PDK with the Peace Agreements seemed to signal to the other factions that they could bypass UN rules with impunity.

As well, control over the administrations was to be applied equally to all four factions. As FUNCINPEC and the KPNLF did not have administrative structures to speak of, and UNTAC did not have access to PDK administration, UNTAC's attention was focused on the SOC administration. As a consequence, any guise of impartiality was lost.³⁴

Unfortunately UNTAC did not move quickly to control and supervise the politically sensitive areas of the SOC administration. A major problem was the lack of in-depth planning and consideration of the concept

---

31 Ibid. para.138.
32 United Nations Secretary-General, Report in Pursuance of Paragraph 6 of Security Council Resolution 810 (New York: United Nations, 15 May 1993) para.22.
33 Warner, 'Cambodia' p.12.
34 Lyndall McLean, 'Civil Administration in Transition: Public Information and the Neutral Political/Electoral Environment' paper presented to International Peacekeeping - A Regional Perspective, Seminar (Canberra: 2-4 May 1994).

and requirement of 'direct control' before the deployment of UNTAC. Months after the deployment of UNTAC, debates were still going on in the civil administration component as to what was meant by 'control' and how UNTAC should implement its mandate. Because of the fragility of the peace process, many areas of the civil administration component were reluctant to push the SOC too hard for fear it might refuse to cooperate altogether. As a consequence, the SOC usually was able to bypass UNTAC control.

Another problem was that UNTAC had insufficient staff to take full and effective control over the key sectors of the SOC bureaucracy. The civilian component of UNTAC when fully deployed numbered 1,020, of whom 157 were senior administrators. UNTAC would have needed several thousand officials to have taken effective control of the civil administration throughout the 21 provinces in the country as envisaged in its mandate. As well, the UN Secretariat was slow and inefficient in recruiting and deploying the 157 senior administrators. Five months after the deployment of UNTAC, only 120 of the senior administrators, and about half of the administrative support staff, had been deployed. The slowness in deploying civil administration staff was partly due to the UN's policy of giving preference to UN personnel, many of whom were neither suitable nor qualified for the positions they were assigned.

UNTAC's mandate also included the supervision and control of the Cambodian civilian police. While in Namibia the role of CIVPOL had been central to the success of that mission, in Cambodia, where UNTAC employed 3,600 civilian police, CIVPOL, with a few exceptions, was far from successful. For the most part, the role of CIVPOL centred on monitoring, rather than on control and supervision of the Cambodian police.

The problems of CIVPOL were due largely to the lack of planning and preparation before deployment. The UNTAC Police Commissioner was deployed two weeks after his appointment which meant there was insufficient time for serious planning and for the drawing up of Standard Operating Procedures. As well, there were no proper detention centres to hold accused persons and no courts before which CIVPOL could conduct their cases.[35]

Another problem was the unsuitability of some of the police. The criteria issued by UN Headquarters for CIVPOL called for six years of community policing, with driving skills and competency in English or French. In Cambodia, in far too many cases these criteria were not met by contributing countries, detracting, sometimes seriously, from the performance of the police force. Many in CIVPOL were not community police, but were security guards, border guards or military police. There

---

[35] Mark Plunkett, 'The Establishment of the Rule of Law in the Post Conflict Peacekeeping' paper presented to International Peacekeeping - A Regional Perspective, Seminar (Canberra: 2-4 May 1994) p.7.

were also instances where diplomats and doctors had been sent to UNTAC as police. As well, many in CIVPOL were not proficient in either English or French and many were unable to drive a motor vehicle. The different attitudes to policing and differences in customs of some national contingencies often led to conflict between contingents over their roles and responsibilities. In retrospect, UNTAC CIVPOL probably would have operated more effectively with a smaller, better qualified force, perhaps 1,200 instead of 3,600.[36]

Nevertheless, UNTAC's civil administration component did have some success. In the area of public information, albeit late in the day, UNTAC ensured that registered political parties did have access to the media. In the area of finance, UNTAC succeeded in controlling the issuance of currency and customs activity even though the real budgetary mechanism was diverted beyond its scrutiny. In the area of foreign affairs, UNTAC took control of passport visas.

The mandate for UNTAC's civil administration component was overly ambitious and in some aspects clearly non-achievable given the United Nations' stretched resources and the situation in Cambodia where years of armed struggle had caused enormous damage to both the population and the basic infrastructure of the country. Better analysis was needed of the problems likely to be encountered where there were no human rights protective mechanisms and no effective legal system.

UNTAC's failure to take adequate control of the key areas of the SOC administration and to take corrective action when necessary, meant that UNTAC was unable to deal effectively with corruption and with the continuing SOC intimidation of political figures from other parties during the election period. This and the decision of the PDK not to comply with key provisions of the Paris Agreements, including the cantonment, disarmament and demobilisation process, meant the elections would not be held in a strictly neutral political environment.

Elections

The Constituent Assembly elections were held 23-28 May, in all areas in which UNTAC had access as at 31 January 1993. Three of the four Cambodian signatories to the Paris Agreements took part in the electoral process. Altogether there were twenty political parties standing candidates, and 4.7 million Cambodians had registered to vote (95 per cent of those eligible).

Whereas UNTAC had failed to fulfil its full mandate in regard to controlling the civil administration, its efforts in organising and conducting the elections were an outstanding achievement. This was largely due to three factors. The first was good preparation. Preparation for the electoral process began with the visit to Cambodia in October-

---

[36] Warner, 'Cambodia' p.10.

November 1991, of the Advance Electoral Planning Unit (AEPU), which undertook in-depth planning throughout Cambodia. Development work, as distinct from planning, began in New York in January 1992, with the formation of a team to draft the Electoral Law for Cambodia reflecting the requirements of the Paris Agreements and the recommendations of the AEPU. The team included the future head of the electoral component, Professor Reg Austin from Zimbabwe, and his deputy, Michael Maley of Australia. This continuity proved valuable since it prevented some of the nuances in thinking which underlay the various stages of work from being lost.[37]

The second factor was the professional staff (including UN Volunteers) in the electoral component, their education program and their ability to educate the Cambodians in democratic principles and to convince them to take part in the election. The third factor was the flexibility of UNTAC's mandate to allow the role of the military component to be changed on 31 December 1992, from cantonment, disarmament and demobilisation of the faction's forces to the protection of the electoral process.

The 43 day election campaign saw a high level of SOC intimidation, which ranged from fairly minor incidents, such as the ripping down of posters, threats against members and officials of 'opposition' parties, to the more serious shootings and killings. Unfortunately, the atmosphere of fear that pervaded the early weeks of the campaign, eroded the willingness of many party officials to get out and campaign. As a result, the Cambodian Peoples Party (CPP) dominated the campaign period, holding more than 1,050 of the 1,500 rallies and meetings. The delay by almost twelve months in the establishment of an UNTAC radio broadcast facility covering the whole of Cambodia, hindered UNTAC's ability to counter rumours and spread the word about the secrecy of the vote. Nevertheless, the campaign, on balance, was successful, and gave Cambodians an opportunity to listen to the views of the contending parties.

There was concern that the PDK would continue its attacks against UNTAC personnel and the Cambodian Peoples Armed Forces (CPAF) to destabilise the election and reduce the areas for the free operation of polling stations in order to discredit the election outcome. The UNTAC military component adopted tight security measures for the electoral process. Despite PDK threats, the elections proceeded with only some scattered violence. There was a tremendous response by the Cambodian people in their first country-wide general election in over twenty years, with more than 4.24 million of registered voters (nearly 90 per cent) turning out to vote. The very high level of participation in the elections was indicative of the Cambodians' desire to assume responsibility for the conduct of their national affairs.

---

[37] Michael Maley, 'Reflections on the Electoral Process in Cambodia' in Hugh Smith (ed.), *Peacekeeping: Challenges for the Future* (Canberra: Australian Defence Force Academy, 1993) p.88.

While the electoral process was an achievement for UNTAC, there were a number of areas where UNTAC's arrangements could have been more effective. Experience in Cambodia has shown that there needs to be a better designed ballot box than the one used, and probably stronger seals and locks. The 'tapered' Canadian boxes had a design fault which meant that when stacked for transportation to 'safe havens', the top boxes exerted such pressure on the boxes below that the seals and locks sometimes broke. The SOC seized upon these irregularities following their failure at the polls and demanded an independent inquiry.

There were other problems including the presence of armed SOC police and CPAF within the 200 metre perimeter of some polling stations, and the SOC's use of government transport in some areas to bring voters to the polls. As well, the 1,000 or so International Polling Station Officers, who were to supervise and control the Cambodian Presiding Officers, had a patchy record of performance, with some having no knowledge of the electoral law. On the other hand, the Cambodian electoral staff were well trained and performed extremely well, voter education was shown to have largely worked, and the polling ran smoothly in most areas.

However, the registration process and the elections could not have taken place without the 480 UN Volunteers in the electoral component. Despite problems in the lead up to the elections as the security situation became increasingly fraught, the great majority of volunteers proved to be very capable and professional and worked well with Khmer staff and, in general, performed better than UN personnel. Moreover, the administrative component of the UN Volunteer program displayed a capacity for expeditious recruitment which was lacking in the broader UN administration.[38]

UNTAC achieved its primary objective, namely, organising and conducting the elections so that the Cambodian people could express their collective will in a genuine act of self-determination. At the SNC meeting on 29 May, Akashi declared, on behalf of the UN Secretary-General, that in view of the very high turnout throughout the country, the absence of violence or disruption during the polling, the success of the technical conduct of the poll and the calm and peaceful atmosphere that reigned throughout the polling period, the conduct of the poll had been free and fair. The elections were pronounced as such by the Secretary-General on 10 June. It was a heartening outcome given that the electoral process, as noted by the Secretary-General, had been a 'complex mission [held] under extraordinarily difficult and often dangerous conditions'.[39]

The two major Cambodian parties to gain the most seats in the elections were FUNCINPEC and the CPP. Although FUNCINPEC won

---

[38] Ibid. p.91.
[39] United Nations Secretary-General, Report on the Conduct and Results of the Elections in Cambodia (New York: United Nations, 1993) p.4.

the most seats it did not win a simple majority. These parties, with the third largest party, the Buddhist Liberal Democratic Party (the political wing of the KPNLF), formed a coalition interim administration. On 24 September, the Kingdom of Cambodia was established, the new constitution was promulgated, the Constituent Assembly became the National Assembly and Norodom Sihanouk was installed as king.

Human rights

UNTAC's human rights mandate reflected the growing realisation that ensuring respect for human rights was critical for any comprehensive settlement to a conflict. But unlike other UNTAC components which were given responsibility to supervise and control the existing administration structures, the police and the military, the human rights component undertook a broad monitoring function, particularly of those institutions and structures linked directly to the protection of human rights, such as the police, the prisons, the courts and the legal system generally.

While the human rights component succeeded in increasing awareness of human rights, it failed to deeply inculcate its message. In part this was due to gross understaffing. Initially the component was to consist of just ten personnel (from a force of 22,000) but was eventually expanded to fifteen in Phnom Penh and twenty-one in the provinces, although provincial personnel were from the civil administration, which led to other problems. Another fundamental problem was the component's lack of enforcement capacity, brought about mainly by an unwillingness within UNTAC to take the necessary tough measures.

In response to the urgent problem of political violence, UNTAC authorised UNTAC police and military officers to arrest and detain those suspected of involvement in political violence and appointed a Special Prosecutor to investigate and prosecute serious human rights offenders. Unfortunately this effort foundered once the SOC ordered its courts not to hear such cases.

Nevertheless, UNTAC's human rights component closely monitored the release of hundreds of political prisoners, trained judges, police and administrators in basic human right principles, conducted an education campaign throughout the country, encouraged Cambodia's accession to seven international human rights instruments, and enacted an interim criminal code that introduced procedural safeguards. As well, UNTAC nurtured five human right organisations with offices in nearly all the provinces and a combined membership reportedly approaching 50,000.

Repatriation

The repatriation operation was of paramount importance to the success of the overall peace settlement, for it had to be completed before the elections. With refugee repatriation, it was the first time in the history of the United Nations High Commission for Refugees (UNHCR) that a field operation had been totally managed from the field, with the delegation of authority and financial arrangements to Phnom Penh. UNHCR, therefore, was flexible in planning and better able to respond to changing situations. After a less than auspicious start caused by unrealistic and overly-ambitious planning (including an offer to give every returnee two hectares of land, and the failure of a US$650,000 satellite photo-mapping program of Cambodia), the UNHCR repatriation program was an outstanding success.[40]

In a remarkably smooth operation, more than 365,000 Cambodian refugees were safely repatriated from camps along the Thai-Cambodia border and elsewhere in the region. In addition to rations for 400 days and a domestic kit, the returnees had the choice of several forms of assistance, including agricultural land, a housing plot and a cash grant in lieu of building materials. Most returnees choose the cash grant. In order to assist the reintegration of the returnees, UNHCR, together with the United Nations Development Program (UNDP) and various non-governmental organisations, implemented more than 60 quick-impact projects to help communities absorb the returnees. These projects included road and bridge repair work, mine-clearance, agricultural development, and improvement and construction of health and education facilities.

Rehabilitation and reconstruction

UNTAC made only a small dent in the task of improving the infrastructure of Cambodia, particularly in the areas of communications, road and rail. Some of the work completed by UNTAC (e.g., roads) was of a temporary nature aimed at facilitating the work of UNTAC, rather than the long term development of Cambodia.

In response to the UN Secretary-General's Appeal for US$595 million for the rehabilitation and reconstruction of Cambodia, the international community pledged US$880 million at the Ministerial Conference on the Rehabilitation and Reconstruction of Cambodia in Tokyo on 20-22 June 1992. The conference adopted the Tokyo Declaration which, *inter alia*, set out the international community's agreement to establish the International Committee on the Reconstruction of Cambodia as the international mechanism for coordinating, in consultation with the elected Government of Cambodia, the medium and long term assistance for the reconstruction of Cambodia.

In an environment characterised by armed conflict, and a degree of economic and political disorder, some donors, consciously or unconsciously, slowed the pace of their activity in order to assess the evolution of the political situation in Cambodia. However, at the time of the first meeting of ICORC in Paris on 8-9 September 1993, US$714

---

[40] Warner, 'Cambodia' p.12.

million of the US$880 million pledged in Tokyo had been spent. At the Paris meeting donors responded to an effective Cambodian presentation of needs by pledging an additional US$119 million.

Coordination between the United Nations and national governments

In his *Agenda for Peace*, the UN Secretary-General considered one of the basic conditions for successful peacekeeping to be 'the readiness of Member States to contribute the military, police and civilian personnel, including specialists' as required.[41] In Cambodia, the member states - especially the Core Group countries (the Permanent Five Members of the Security Council plus Australia, Japan, Indonesia, Thailand, Germany, Canada and India) - did far more than just provide personnel for UNTAC. In New York, the Core Group played a vital role in focusing the attention of decision makers, the Security Council and the Secretariat, on the Cambodia problem throughout the implementation process. In Phnom Penh, representatives of the Core Group monitored the process in the field and gave advise to the Secretary-General's Special Representative and to the UNTAC Military Commander. The Permanent Five also participated in SNC meetings, with other Core Group countries attending as observers.

Relations between UNTAC and the Core Group in Phnom Penh were generally cooperative with Akashi and Sanderson and directors of the UNTAC components meeting with the Core Group frequently. Sometimes UNTAC officials were reluctant to acknowledge that the international community had a role to play and a right to suggest proposals. These officials overlooked the fact that had it not been largely to the efforts of the international community, there would not have been a UN operation in Cambodia.

Stationing UN Military Liaison Officers in Thailand, Laos and Vietnam was another way in which UNTAC coordinated its activities in Cambodia with the border countries whose cooperation was vital.

In general, the UN agencies and the international community cooperated well. Meetings between representatives of the international community and UN agencies were held regularly and the mechanism of ICORC ensured there was coordination between donor countries and the various UN agencies.

The economic and social effects of UNTAC

UNTAC had three key economic tasks. First, to oversee the coordination of international aid. Second, in the rehabilitation stage, to ensure the restoration of Cambodia's existing basic infrastructure and public utilities. Third, to control and supervise the SOC Ministry of Finance, including

---

[41] Boutros-Ghali, *Agenda for Peace* para.50.

the right to issue binding directives. UNTAC, however, failed to fully implement these tasks. While the international community had pledged US$800 million for the reconstruction of Cambodia, armed conflict and the uncertain political environment caused some donors to be hesitant in disbursing funds. As well, UNTAC made only a small impression in improving Cambodia's basic infrastructure. In the area of finance, UNTAC succeeded only in controlling the issuance of currency and of legal border trade.

While UNTAC's economic achievements fell far short of Cambodian expectations and what was indicated in its mandate, nevertheless, in the economic sphere, UNTAC set a precedent for a need for probity and for checks and balances. As well, UNTAC clearly identified the key economic problems even though it was unable to adequately deal with them.[42]

At its peak UNTAC employed 22,000 highly paid foreigners, 4,000 locals on a permanent basis and about 50,000 locals during the elections. In less than fifteen months UNTAC poured a total of US$511 million into Cambodia of which at least US$403 million was spent locally. This sheer financial clout fuelled an unsustainable boom. Cambodians were beset on all sides by a 'get-rich-quick' mentality. Corruption for those in positions of responsibility became endemic while smuggling and profiteering became rampant.[43]

It is difficult to underestimate the transformation that UNTAC brought to Cambodian society, particularly in urban areas. Tens of thousands of foreigners and expatriate Khmers exposed Cambodians to the outside world for the first time since 1975. As a consequence, Cambodians became more cosmopolitan, more aware of the world around them, and more eager to further their lot.

However, the behaviour of some UN personnel caused resentment and alienated many Cambodians.[44] There were instances of UN troops being rude and insensitive towards the local population and unacceptable behaviour such as rape, harassment and abuse of women, and not paying for goods was frequently reported.

Conclusion

UNTAC's operation in Cambodia was the United Nations most complex, though no longer its largest, to date. In Cambodia the United Nations expanded its traditional peacekeeping role to bring about an end to hostilities, repatriate and resettle refugees, carry out a rehabilitation and

---

[42] Robin Davies, 'Blue berets, green backs: What was the impact?' *Phnom Penh Post* (22 October-4 November 1993) p.19.
[43] Davies, Robin, The Roots of Violence' *Phnom Penh Post* (5-18 November 1993) p.7.
[44] Sarah Horner, 'Security Breakdown' *Phnom Penh Post* (5-18 November 1993) p.4.

reconstruction program, and ensure the observance of human rights, but it was principally its role in civil administration and in conducting the elections that makes the UN mission in Cambodia such an innovative and ground-breaking aspect of international peacekeeping and conflict resolution. The United Nations was well experienced in peacekeeping operations but had never attempted before anything as intrusive as the direct control of the civil administration of one of its member states. Nor had the United Nations ever taken the primary responsibility for organising and conducting elections as distinct from monitoring them.

The success of achieving the comprehensive settlement to the Cambodian conflict was due to the ASEAN dialogues led by Indonesia, the driving force of the Permanent Five Members of the Security Council, the efforts of other international players such as Australia and Vietnam, and of course the Cambodian parties themselves. The principal countries concerned, and the United Nations itself, unanimously supported the full implementation of the Paris Accords.

While UNTAC was a huge drain on UN resources, any course other than a comprehensive settlement would have been very much a second-best option. Any form of international support for the Phnom Penh government would have meant the continuing civil war and the appalling prospect of a second military takeover by the PDK. As well, the Cambodian conflict would have almost certainly continued as a source of international tension in the region. UNTAC's mandate, however, was overly ambitious in some areas given the stretched resources of the United Nations and the situation in Cambodia where years of civil war had caused enormous damage to both the population and the basic infrastructure of Cambodia.

Despite some setbacks, principally the result of the refusal by the PDK to comply with all the provisions of the Paris Agreements, the UN-supervised settlement achieved its principal aims. The Paris Agreements succeeded in removing the Cambodia conflict as a source of regional tension. Vietnam has entered into more productive relations regionally and internationally. External patrons have withdrawn material support for the various factions, thereby removing the capacity of Cambodians to engage in an endless destructive civil war. The Thai government has cooperated with UNTAC in enforcing measures against the PDK called for by the Security Council, although elements of the Thai military and business community still maintain links with the PDK. As well, more than 365,000 displaced Cambodians on the Thai border have been successfully repatriated.

Most importantly, the United Nations has demonstrably succeeded in giving the Cambodian people the opportunity to exercise their democratic will in a genuine act of self-determination, by means of UN-organised free and fair elections. These achievements far outweigh in significance the failure of the disarmament and demobilisation process and UNTAC's failure to take effective control of the key areas of the civil administration.

Much of UNTAC's success was due to the high degree of flexibility in the mandate and risk taking in problem solving. This was evident in the decision by the Security Council to proceed with the elections even though the PDK continued to refuse to comply with the terms of the Paris Accords. It also meant changing the role of the UNTAC military component from the cantonment, disarmament and demobilisation process to protecting the electoral process, without having to change the mandate. However, the military component was to have stabilised the security situation before the electoral component began the voter registration process. With the PDK refusing to participate in the cantonment phase, the electoral component had to carry out its operations in an insecure environment. Even though the ceasefire held in general, there were numerous incidents of fighting between the armies of the PDK and the SOC and attacks against UNTAC personnel. Fourteen UNTAC personnel were killed as a result of hostile action, including a UN volunteer with the electoral component.

To have postponed the elections risked extending UNTAC's mandate indefinitely at a huge cost to the United Nations. To have withdrawn, which was at least an outside option for UNTAC in mid-1992 when the PDK refused to canton its troops, would have been to abandon the advances that were being made in returning Cambodia to the community of nations. To stay on and try to implement the Agreements as comprehensively as possible meant that UNTAC had to compromise in a number of important areas and risked the operation failing altogether as happened in Angola. The UN Secretary-General rightly decided to continue on to the elections even though one party refused to cooperate.

The flexibility in implementing the peace settlement was in part derived from another innovation - the role of the Core Group countries (a similar, but smaller, group played an equally important role in Namibia). The Core Group, in both New York and in Phnom Penh, maintained a sense of unity of purpose and commitment within the international community, and was useful in focusing pressure and persuasion on the Cambodian factions to comply with the terms of the Agreements. In New York, the Core Group's role in assisting and advising the Secretary-General, the UN Secretariat and the Security Council on the Cambodian peace settlement was vital. While a successful outcome in Cambodia was important to the standing of the United Nations, the Secretary-General could not focus his attention on just Cambodia as happened in the 1960s with the UN operation in the Congo. In the post-Cold War period, with the United Nations involved in thirteen peacekeeping operations, it was no longer conceivable that the Secretary-General could give as much attention to one operation.

The UN operation in Cambodia also demonstrated that the United Nations and the international community are capable of sustaining a very complex operation which included not only peacekeeping, but also conflict resolution, national reconciliation and nation building, and even under extremely difficult and dangerous conditions. The UN operation in Cambodia also demonstrated that it was possible for such a complex operation to be completed within a tight time framework.

Lessons for future operations

Cooperation of the parties to the conflict

The operation in Cambodia has shown that to successfully implement its mandate in all respects, any UN peacekeeping mission requires the full cooperation of all the parties to the conflict. The non-compliance of the PDK with key provisions of the Paris Agreements, and the less than full compliance of the other parties, affected every aspect of the UNTAC operation.

Precipitate deployment

The UN operation in Cambodia has also underlined another well-known lesson - the need for precipitate deployment - not just early deployment, but deployment in force throughout the country. The delays in the deployment of UNTAC were critical in that they cut into the tight timetable outlined in the Peace Agreements, and affected UNTAC's credibility in the eyes of the Cambodian people.[45] Deployment must take place soon after the parties to the conflict have reached agreement so as to build and maintain the confidence of the parties to the conflict and the local population.

Planning in New York

The UNTAC experience has shown the need for structural changes in the UN Secretariat to meet increasing demands and to improve the administration of peacekeeping operations. Multidimensional peacekeeping requires a new or revamped planning structure in the Secretariat, with new or enlarged planning units dedicated to military and political affairs, human rights, elections, police and administration. The Advance Electoral Planning Unit, for example, was a concept that should be built on in future operations with, perhaps, each component of the mission establishing its own advance unit to provide detailed information on local conditions.[46] The Secretariat must also achieve greater integration between planning and operations.

---

[45] Warner, 'Cambodia' p.4.
[46] Ibid. pp.7-8.

Staffing

Appointment of senior staff. UNTAC suffered especially in its early days from a lack of continuity and a lack of institutional memory due largely to the late appointment of many of its senior officers. There is a need for the early appointment of the senior leadership of any peacekeeping force to assist with planning, establishing mission objectives, working out and coordinating policy guidelines and standard operating procedures amongst the different component heads, and of course, building team spirit.[47]

Quality. UNTAC's 21,000 personnel ranged from highly qualified professionals to those who were incompetent. There should be an obligation on the part of the contributing countries to meet the criteria set by the United Nations for personnel, and a right by the United Nations to reject unsuitable or unqualified personnel. Unfortunately, there were far too many instances of unsuitable and unqualified people being sent to UNTAC and who were not rejected, possibly for fear of offending contributing countries. For example, of the 150 qualified military police sent to Cambodia, about a third could not speak either English or French, the designated languages. When UNTAC requested that the number be increased to help clear the backlog of work caused by the provision of the ill-equipped officers, of the first twenty new military police sent, sixteen could not speak either of the designated languages.[48]

Only troops who are professional and well-disciplined should be selected and in a process that includes the Force Commander.[49] There needs to be a code of conduct for UN troops, outlining penalties for misconduct. This code could be incorporated into the Standing Operating Procedures. Pre-deployment training in peacekeeping to a common UN standard, when this is lacking, is essential. As well, all UN troops and police should receive training in basic human rights.

United Nations volunteers. UNTAC's experience of UN volunteers has shown that they work well in areas such as conflict resolution and election supervision. There were just over 700 UN volunteers attached to UNTAC (about 480 in the electoral component, and others in the medical, administration and engineering elements of the force). With few exceptions, UN volunteers performed with dedication and professionalism, and in general, performed better than regular UN personnel. Moreover, employing UN volunteers was very cost effective. The total cost of one volunteer, including salary and travel, was less than the mission subsistence allowance of a staff member from within the UN

---

[47] Ibid.
[48] Ibid. p.9.
[49] Lt-General J.M. Sanderson, AC, Closing Address to International Peacekeeping - A Regional Perspective, Seminar (Canberra: 2-4 May 1994) p.15.

system. UN volunteers should be drawn on in even greater numbers in future operations and used in a wider range of roles.[50]

Administration

As peacekeeping has grown increasingly complex so has the job of administration. Serious consideration needs to be given to strengthening the administration of Cambodia type operations through more thorough planning before deployment, more realistic staffing levels, the timely recruitment and deployment of well qualified staff and to the greater delegation of authority to the mission.

With the Namibia operation the Senior Task Force for Namibia in the Secretariat took a keen interest in the day-to-day operation of the United Nations Transition Assistance Group in Namibia (UNTAG). With the Cambodia operation, however, there was relatively little contact or exchange of views and information between the Secretariat and UNTAC.[51] Visits by senior officials were few and there were instances when UNTAC misunderstood sensitivities felt in New York and vice versa.[52] Communication between the force and the UN Secretariat must be strengthened and with budgetary resources to enable the Secretariat to respond quickly to force recommendations and requests and to permit frequent travel to missions.

The UN Secretariat needs to consider the 'privatisation' of some functions, such as the contracting out to private firms. A number of key elements of the UNTAC operation were affected by slow procurement, as the outdated UN procedures tried to cope with new circumstances and a much larger mission. For instance, UNTAC's plans for the establishment of a UN radio broadcast facility, covering the whole of Cambodia, and for an UNTAC television studio, were delayed by almost twelve months by the need to go through cumbersome New York tender systems, detracting from UNTAC's ability to spread its message about the secrecy of the vote. On the other hand, the UNTAC electoral component was able to let three major supply items - the computer system to support voter registration, the equipment used by registration teams to issue photographic registration cards, and the equipment needed at the polling booths. All were successfully supplied on a turnkey basis, thereby minimising the number of occasions on which purchasing procedures had to be undertaken.[53]

---

[50] Warner, 'Cambodia' p.10.
[51] Ibid. p.4.
[52] Lt-General John M. Sanderson, AO, 'Preparation and Deployment and Conduct of Peacekeeping Operations: A Cambodia Snapshot' paper presented to the International Seminar, UN Peacekeeping at the Crossroads (Canberra: 21-24 March 1993) p.4.
[53] Warner, 'Cambodia' p.11.

2 The Gulf Crisis: Failure of Preventive Diplomacy

CLAUDE RAKISITS

The Gulf War was an extreme case of failure of *preventive diplomacy*. The War might have been avoided if, *before* the invasion, Iraq-Kuwait differences had been either discussed by the United Nations Security Council or the UN Secretary-General had examined the issue. The UN's failure to take an active role in the issue when it was not yet at crisis level meant that all subsequent efforts at diplomacy concentrated on containing the problem.

Peacemaking after the invasion aimed at reaching a peaceful resolution to the problem. This basically involved finding a formula which allowed Saddam Hussein to withdraw his Iraqi forces from Kuwait without appearing to 'reward' him for violating Kuwait's sovereignty. It was the failure to find such a formula - Saddam's price was simply too high - that made the military clash virtually inevitable.

However, preventive diplomacy and peacemaking might not have worked in any case given the Iraqi leadership's perception of itself and the international community. Saddam did not expect the international community's reaction to the invasion, underestimated the Coalition's diplomatic and military resolve not to let Iraq's actions go unpunished and overestimated his armed forces' capabilities. These perceptions were reinforced by the mixed and confused signals which the international community, particularly the Arab States and the United States, was sending Saddam *before* the invasion. Moreover, the international community misread and incorrectly assessed Saddam's intentions, actions and signals. Consequently, all these factors made it extremely difficult, if not outright impossible, for preventive diplomacy and peacemaking to succeed.

Background to the Gulf War

Historical factors

Saddam Hussein attempted to justify Iraq's 2 August 1990 invasion and subsequent annexation of Kuwait on spurious historical claims that had no basis in international law. Moreover, and probably because the Iraqi Government realised its historical claims to Kuwait were at best legally dubious, the Iraqi leadership scarcely troubled to advance a legal justification for its action.[1]

Interestingly, Iraq did not initially justify the invasion on the basis of historical claims. Instead, Saddam claimed that Iraq had invaded Kuwait at the request of the Provisional Government of Free Kuwait (PGFK). The PGFK, which was supposedly made up of Kuwaiti elements opposed to the rule of the Emir, had virtually no following in the Emirate. The PGFK consisted mainly of men who were either unknown in Kuwait or were Iraqi military officers. It was rejected by the Kuwaiti Opposition and had no popular support. By 8 August, realising that the PGFK fig leaf was fooling no one, the Iraqi Government dropped all pretence of collaboration with the PGFK in favour of outright annexation of Kuwait. The PGFK accelerated its own demise by making a formal request to 'return the part and the branch, Kuwait, to the whole and origin, Iraq, in a comprehensive and eternal merger unity'.[2] Given that the PGFK never had any credibility with the international community, this request was regarded as worthless by that community.

Iraq argued that Kuwait had once been a district of the *wilayet* of Basra, one of three provinces which later made up modern Iraq, and that its existence was an artificial creation of the British Colonial Office. Iraq claims that Kuwait was separated from Basra with the 1899 secret agreement between the British Government and the Sheikh of Kuwait, that made Kuwait a virtual British protectorate, and the 1914 British recognition of Kuwait as an independent state in return for Kuwait's support in the war against the Ottoman Empire.[3]

Even on historical grounds, however, this argument is weak. Certainly, Kuwait did come under the suzerainty of the Ottoman Empire during the nineteenth century, although the nature of the relationship with Constantinople remains unclear. Furthermore, the Ottoman ruler never really tried to assert his authority over Kuwait, and the territory was not

---

[1] C. Greenwood, 'Iraq's Invasion of Kuwait: Some Legal Issues' *World Today* 47, 2 (February 1991) p.39.

[2] C. Greenwood, 'New World Order or Old? The Invasion of Kuwait and the Rule of Law' *The Modern Law Review* 55, 2 (March 1992) p.155.

[3] E. Lauterpacht, C. Greenwood, M. Weller and D. Bethlehem (eds), *The Kuwait Crisis: Basic Documents* (Cambridge: Grotius Publications, 1991) pp.9, 37.

treated as simply another part of the *wilayet* of Basra. In any case, Turkey formally relinquished all claims to Kuwait in the 1923 Treaty of Lausanne, by which time Britain had already recognised Kuwait as an independent state under British protection. Kuwait's separate existence was acknowledged by the Prime Minister of Iraq on the eve of the termination of Britain's League of Nation Mandate in Iraq in 1932. In an exchange of letters that year, Iraq recognised the existing border between Iraq and Kuwait.[4]

Irrespective of Iraq's historical claims to Kuwait, developments since 1961 had further destroyed Iraq's legal position on the matter. In that year, Kuwait's status as a protectorate ended and it was recognised as an independent entity by the international community. Iraq raised the claim that Kuwait was part of its territory, moved troops to the border and tried to block Kuwait's admission into the United Nations and the Arab League. At the request of the Kuwaiti Government, a British force was sent to Kuwait to prevent military action by Iraq. The majority of Arab states rejected Iraq's claim and an Arab League peacekeeping force eventually replaced the British troops. This was not the first time that Iraq claimed Kuwait as part of its territory. King Ghazi of Iraq advocated the absorption of Kuwait by Iraq in 1937. In March 1973, Iraqi troops occupied a border outpost close to the Island of Bubiyan. The Iraqis withdrew under pressure from the Shah of Iran. With Kuwait's admission to the UN and the Arab League, Kuwait's claim to exist as a state independent of Iraq was established beyond doubt.

Iraq eventually accepted Kuwait's independence in 1963 in an agreement between the governments of Iraq and Kuwait. It stated, *inter alia*,

> The Republic of Iraq recognized the independence and complete sovereignty of the State of Kuwait with its boundaries as specified in the letter of the Prime Minister of Iraq dated 21.7.1932 and which was accepted by the ruler of Kuwait in his letter dated 10.8.1932.[5]

Iraq has argued that this agreement was invalid because it was not ratified as required by the constitution then in force in Iraq. However, even if this were true, the failure to comply with the Iraqi constitution in 1963 would not be sufficient to invalidate the agreement today. According to international law [Vienna Convention on the Law of Treaties (Art. 46)], 'a State may only invoke a violation of its domestic law as invalidating its consent to be bound by a treaty if the violation was manifest to any State conducting itself in good faith and concerned a rule of domestic law of fundamental importance'. Moreover, even if it did, Iraq would not be entitled to rely upon such a violation 'if, after becoming aware of the facts, it must by reason of its conduct be considered as having acquiesced in the validity of the treaty' [Vienna Convention on the Law of Treaties (Art.

---

4   Ibid. p.49; C. Greenwood, 'Iraq's Invasion of Kuwait' p.40.
5   E. Lauterpacht *et al.* (eds), *The Kuwait Crisis*, p.57.

45)]. Moreover, given that Iraq continued to deal with Kuwait as an independent state up to the invasion, it forfeited any right it might have had to rely upon constitutional defects in the 1963 agreement. It is interesting to note that Iraq's claim to the whole of Kuwait was inconsistent with its demand for border changes prior to the invasion. It is, therefore, not surprising that Iraq's legal claims to Kuwait were overwhelmingly rejected by the international community.

In an attempt to strengthen its legal claim, the Iraqi leadership argued that all boundaries between Arab states should be seen as mere temporary partitions between parts of the Arab nation. According to an August 1990 resolution passed by Iraq's supreme ruling body, the Revolutionary Command Council,

> In the past, the Arab nation was one and indivisible. After independence was gained by the Arab States the many countries of the region were the result of foreign colonizers carving up the territory of the region. The colonizers re-drew the geopolitical map of the region in order to weaken the Arab States. The colonizers did not hesitate to do in Iraq what they did in other countries of the region. That is why the Iraqi Revolutionary Command Council decided to restore to our country the portion taken away from it, thus re-establishing the eternal, indestructible unity of our country.[6]

Certainly, the notion of an 'Arab nation' has a certain degree of appeal with Arab public opinion, as it reminisces to the early years of the Muslim era. However, while there are many transnational issues which unite Arab states, the notion that boundaries between Arab states are less important than in other parts of the world is a fallacy and has no legal basis. The Pact of the League Arab States has as one of its objectives the safeguarding of the members states' independence and sovereignty. Additionally, according to Article 5 of the Pact, 'any resort to force in order to resolve disputes arising between two or more members states of the League is prohibited'.

Strategic Factors

One of the underlying causes behind the war was Iraq's drive to improve its geo-strategic position. Iraq had gone to war against Iran in 1980 determined to have better access to the Persian Gulf, as Iraq is effectively a land-locked country, with only 26 miles of Gulf shoreline and without a port on the Gulf. Having failed to achieve this objective after eight years of war with Iran, Iraq next turned to Kuwait.

Although Iraq and Kuwait had agreed in 1963 on the border demarcation, by 1968, when President Ahmad Hasan al-Bakr and his deputy, Saddam Hussein, came to power, Iraq began to question the border agreement. During the 1970s the Iraqi leaders approached the Kuwaitis on

---

[6]   Ibid. p.109.

several occasions, pressuring them to relinquish or lease the islands of Warba and Bubiyan to Iraq. Iraq wanted control of these islands as that would allow it to control the Khor Abd Allah estuary, a waterway to the Gulf which leads to the Iraqi ports of Umm Qasr and Khor Zubair. Baghdad made it clear that it would recognise the *'de facto* borders only if the islands of Warba and Bubiyan [were] included within Iraq or leased to it'.[7] Kuwait refused to accommodate the Iraqis as Bubiyan Island dominates Kuwait city and Iraqi ownership of the island would constitute a threat to the Emirate. Saddam and the Kuwaiti Crown Prince had an inconclusive meeting in Baghdad on this matter in early 1989. This issue was still unresolved when Iraq invaded Kuwait.

Iraq raised another 'border' issue, that of the Rumaila oil field, part of which extends across the border into Kuwait. Iraq claimed that Kuwait had been pumping oil from the Iraqi side of the field and selling it abroad while Iraq was at war with Iran. The Iraqis had raised this issue with the Kuwaitis on several previous occasions but it had never really become a contentious issue. Certainly the Rumaila oil field issue was not one of the main reasons for the war, although the Iraqi leadership did subsequently attempt to use the issue as an argument for the invasion of Kuwait.[8]

Economic Factors

The Rumaila oil field issue, while important in itself, was part of a bigger and more immediate problem confronting Saddam's government: the dire economic condition of the country. The war with Iran had cost Iraq dearly in financial and human terms. And while it had won - or at least not lost - the war, it lacked the funds for reconstruction, defence and the import of consumer goods. The war had cost Iraq over US$500 billion and throughout most of the conflict, Iraq had spent about 40 per cent of its gross domestic product on military procurement. After the war Iraq had a US$80 billion debt, with nearly half owed to Gulf Cooperation countries (GCC),[9] including US$4 billion to Kuwait.[10] Iraq owed between US$30 billion and US$35 billion in short-term loans to Europe, Japan and the United States, which had to be repaid in hard currency.[11] To make matters worse, between January and June 1990 the average price of oil dropped from US$20.50 to US$13.00 a barrel. Every one dollar drop in the price of oil cost Iraq US$1 billion annually in lost revenue. This loss of

---

[7] L. Freedman and E. Karsh, *The Gulf Conflict, 1990-1991: Diplomacy and War in the New World Order* (London: Faber and Faber, 1993) p.44.
[8] M. Heikal, *Illusions of Triumph* (London: Harper Collins, 1992) p.144.
[9] The GCC is composed of Bahrain, Kuwait, Oman, Qatar, Saudi Arabia and the United Arab Emirates.
[10] J.G. Stein, 'Deterrence and Compellence in the Gulf, 1990-91' *International Security* 17, 2 (Fall 1992) pp. 157.
[11] P. Marr, 'Iraq's Uncertain Future' *Current History* 90, 552 (January 1991) p.2.

revenue created further strains for an economy which was already having difficulties importing essential foodstuffs.[12] Although Saddam managed the economy badly by investing too much in the country's high-technology defence industry, spending on show-case projects and importing consumer goods for the hard-hit middle class, this did not hide the fact that the economy was in dire straits.[13]

Iraq had expected the debt owed to the Arab countries to be forgiven. From Saddam's perspective Iraq had fought Iran for eight years and had lost hundreds of thousands of men, to protect the wealthy Gulf states from Iranian-inspired fundamentalism. This perception was strengthened by the fact that the GCC countries had poured billion of dollars into Iraq to help it fight the Iranians. However, following the end of the war, the Gulf countries' attitudes towards Iraq changed. After the Iran-Iraq War, Iraq was by far the strongest country in the region and, if it so wished, it had the capability to intimidate credibly its neighbours. Kuwait felt particularly uncomfortable with that situation.

On 9 August 1988, a day after the Iran-Iraq ceasefire, Kuwait decided to increase its oil production, in violation of Organisation of Petroleum Exporting Countries (OPEC) accords. Not only did Kuwait pump oil from the Rumaila oil field but the over-production caused the price of oil to drop dramatically, making it more difficult for Iraq to repay its debts. And to add insult to injury, Kuwait refused to convert its war-time loans into gifts, as Saudi Arabia had done, insisting instead that Iraq pay back all its debts.[14] These actions by Kuwait had the opposite effect from what was intended, however. Instead of modifying Iraq's behaviour toward Kuwait, the Iraqi leadership became even more determined to take action against what it perceived to be unjust measures by the Emirate.

Pre-invasion Period

Iraqi Signals

With hindsight five 'signals' that the Iraqi leadership sent to the outside world can be identified, indicating without any doubt that it was unhappy with the status quo regarding the price of oil, Kuwait's insistence that Iraq pay up its debts and Kuwait's exploitation of the Rumaila oil field.

On 24 February 1990, Saddam Hussein made a speech at an Arab Cooperation Council (ACC) meeting.[15] It was an angry speech in which he attacked the United States naval presence in the Gulf. He argued that

---

[12] Stein, 'Deterrence and Compellence in the Gulf' p.158.
[13] Marr, 'Iraq's Uncertain Future' pp.2-3.
[14] R. Springborg, 'Origins of the Gulf Crisis' *Australian Journal of International Affairs* 44, 3 (December 1990) p.230.
[15] The ACC is composed of Egypt, Jordan, Iraq and Yemen.

the US should remove its fleet from the area as this would help to break what he called total US control of the oil market. Saddam included insults to 'cowardly and timid Arab leaders who recognised the US as a superpower'.[16] This was a clear reference to Egypt's President Hosni Mubarak and Saudi Arabia's King Fahd. In a private meeting with Jordan's King Hussein and President Mubarak (conflicting reports make it unclear whether King Fahd was also present at the meeting), Saddam asked those present to inform the Gulf states that Iraq was not only adamant on its demand for a complete moratorium on its wartime loans, but urgently needed an immediate infusion of additional funds of some $30 billion. He stressed that if the Gulf states did not give the funds he asked for, he knew 'how to get it'. This threat was accompanied by Iraqi military manoeuvres in the neutral zone on the Kuwaiti border.[17]

The second signal, and that which was the first evidence of the possibility of war, was at the Arab League Summit in Baghdad on 30 May 1990. In response to Kuwait's and the United Arab Emirate's oil production over their allowed OPEC quota, Saddam warned

> War is fought with soldiers and much harm is done by explosions, killing, and coup attempts - but it is also done by economic means. Therefore, we would ask our brothers who do not mean to wage war on Iraq: this is in fact a kind of war against Iraq.[18]

The third signal came in a speech Saddam delivered on 17 July on the twenty-second anniversary of the coup that brought the ruling Ba'ath Party to power. Alluding to Kuwait's and the United Arab Emirates' (UAE) over-production of oil, Saddam threatened that

> ... if words fail to protect Iraqis, something effective must be done to return things to their natural course and return usurped rights to their owners.[19]

On 18 July, the Iraqi Government delivered its fourth signal with its decision to make public a memorandum Iraqi Foreign Minister, Tariq Aziz, had sent to the Arab League's Secretary-General, Chedli Klibi, on 15 July. In the memorandum Iraq demanded $2.4 billion in compensation for oil that Iraq claimed Kuwait had pumped from the disputed Rumaila oil field; $12 billion in compensation for the depressed oil prices brought about by Kuwait's over-production; forgiveness of Iraq's war debt of $10 billion; and a lease on the strategic island of Bubiyan that controlled access to Iraq's only port, Umm Qasr.[20] Besides these demands, Iraq accused Kuwait of installing military posts inside Iraqi territory; and the UAE and

---

[16] J.K. Cooley, 'Pre-War Gulf Diplomacy' *Survival* 33, 2 (March/April 1991) p.126.
[17] Freedman & Karsh, *The Gulf Conflict* p.45
[18] Ibid. p.46.
[19] Springborg, 'Origins of the Gulf Crisis' p.222.
[20] Stein, 'Deterrence and Compellence in the Gulf' p.150.

Kuwait of being part of a 'Zionist plot aided by imperialists against the Arab nation', with Kuwaiti Foreign Minister Sheikh Sabah al-Ahmad being 'an American agent'.[21]

The fifth signal came progressively but should have, nevertheless, been obvious to most observers. On 27 July - ten days after Saddam's warning that Iraq may need to take 'effective action' - Western intelligence reports confirmed that eight divisions of approximately 100,000 men from the best Iraqi units were positioned on the Iraq-Kuwait border. Senior US officials still believed that these troop movements were more consistent with intimidation than with preparations for an invasion of the Emirate, which would have required a far heavier communications traffic and more substantial artillery stocks, munitions and logistics 'tail'.[22]

Prevention

In this section we will examine the main players who were involved in preventive diplomacy prior to the invasion. And while preventive diplomacy ultimately failed, it is important to examine the process the main actors went through in their attempt to prevent the invasion. Why preventive diplomacy eventually failed will be discussed in a later section.

Arab diplomacy. Relations between Iraq and Kuwait had been tense since the former obtained its independence in 1932. Iraq regularly questioned Kuwait's sovereign independence and consistently pressured Kuwait to lease the islands of Bubiyan and Warba. Broadly and historically speaking, the Iraqis have had contempt for the Kuwaitis whom they see as lazy and living the good life thanks to the luck of having a vast amount of oil reserves. And while the two countries had been on the same side during the Iran-Iraq War, relations became tense after the war in 1988. Not only did Kuwait begin to over-produce oil a day after the end of the Iran-Iraq War, thus forcing the price of oil down, but Kuwait quickly moved to improve relations with Iran, with whom it had not broken diplomatic relations during the War. Moreover, Kuwait lobbied strongly in the GCC against granting Iraq membership in the organisation.[23]

It was clear from the beginning of the crisis that Kuwait had no intention of accommodating Iraq's demands regarding Kuwait's over-production of oil and the leasing of the two islands. On the contrary, the more pressure Iraq put on Kuwait the more the latter resisted. The Iraqi leadership saw this as arrogance and provocation.

In response to Iraq's demand that Kuwait only produce according to its OPEC quota, Kuwait continued to produce well over its quota, arguing that it was only doing what other OPEC countries had the option of doing as well. And while the Emir did replace his oil minister in response to Saddam's threat that Kuwait's actions were tantamount to economic

---

21 Cooley, 'Pre-War Gulf Diplomacy' p.127.
22 Freedman & Karsh, *The Gulf Conflict* p.55.
23 Springborg, 'Origins of the Gulf Crisis' p.230.

warfare and Iraq had 'reached a point where we can no longer withstand pressure', the Kuwaiti Government was determined to maintain a hard line.[24] As far as the Kuwaiti Cabinet was concerned any other course of action was unacceptable, as it would be giving in to threats, blackmail and extortion.[25] Accordingly, not only did Kuwait not reduce its oil production, but it refused both to forgive its war-time loans to Iraq (as opposed to Saudi Arabia which had) and to extend Baghdad US$10 billion worth of additional grants. Instead, the Emir was willing to offer a US$500 million grant, spread over three years, as 'an act of charity to Iraq'.[26] Kuwait was only willing to discuss a production quota on the resolution of the border issue. And although the Kuwaitis did agree at an OPEC meeting on 10 July to a temporary cut in oil production following strong pressure from the Saudis, Iranians and Iraqis, the Kuwaiti Government issued a statement stating that it would reconsider its willingness to observe the OPEC quotas in autumn.[27] This strengthened Saddam's belief that the Kuwaitis would not adhere to their quota.[28]

Throughout the crisis leading to the invasion, the Kuwaiti Government believed that Iraq's threats were only to intimidate Kuwait into submission. The Emir is even reported to have dismissed the crisis as a 'summer cloud' that would soon blow away.[29] Still, on 19 July the Kuwaiti Government suggested in a letter to the United Nations Secretary-General that an Arab Committee be established to examine the Iraq-Kuwait border issue. It appears, however, that this suggestion was either never followed through by the United Nations or was overtaken by events.

The Kuwaitis came under increasing pressure from other Arab states to compromise with Iraq. Saudi Arabia, supported by the Egyptian and Jordanian governments, suggested that Kuwait consider making concessions on Iraq's debts and the Rumaila oil fields and perhaps lease on a long term basis the islands of Bubiyan and Warba to Iraq. The Kuwaitis rejected this proposal, arguing that their constitution did not allow the government to 'give up one inch of Kuwaiti territory'.[30] Moreover, from Kuwait's perspective, while Saudi Arabia was eager to defuse the crisis, Riyadh's perception of the situation was not identical to Kuwait's.

Nevertheless, under Saudi pressure to reach a compromise with Iraq and eager to find an 'Arab solution' to the crisis, the Kuwaitis agreed to meet the Iraqis in Jeddah, Saudi Arabia, on 31 July 1990. The meeting was attended by Iraq's Vice-Chairman of the Revolutionary Command Council, Izzat Ibrahim, Deputy-Prime Minister Sa'adoun Hammadi and Saddam's cousin and confidant, Ali Hasan al-Majid. The Kuwaiti delegation was

---

24 Freedman & Karsh, *The Gulf Conflict* p.46.
25 P. Salinger and E. Laurent, *Secret Dossier* (London: Penguin, 1991) p.43.
26 Freedman & Karsh, *The Gulf Conflict* p.46.
27   Stein, 'Deterrence and Compellence in the Gulf' p.157.
28 Freedman & Karsh, *The Gulf Conflict* p.46.
29 Cooley, 'Pre-War Gulf Diplomacy' p.127.
30 Heikal, *Illusions of Triumph* p.180.

composed of the Crown Prince and Prime Minister and the Ministers for Foreign Affairs and Justice. At the meeting the Iraqi delegation read out a list of charges against Kuwait, which the Kuwaiti delegation refuted point by point. The Iraqis then repeated their earlier demand of a US$10 billion grant; a loan would be acceptable if a gift was not possible. The Kuwaitis offered a US$9 billion loan. King Fahd offered to make up the difference by promising a US$1 billion grant to Iraq. However, the Kuwaiti delegation later told the Iraqis that before the loan could be finalised, the Kuwait-Iraq boundary question would have to be resolved. The Iraqis rejected this suggestion and the meeting ended inconclusively. The Kuwaitis believed the discussion would continue in Baghdad on 4 August, as they had agreed - albeit reluctantly - to meet again at that time.[31]

From the Kuwait Government's perspective, if Kuwait had given in to Saddam's demands after the 17 July threat, a total about-face on the part of the Emir, a peaceful solution to the crisis probably would have been reached. However, what guarantees did Kuwait have that Saddam would not later try to extract more out of Kuwait? And would not submitting to Iraq render Kuwait's sovereignty only nominal?

The GCC's contribution to preventive diplomacy was limited. After the invasion some of its member countries and GCC officials were actively involved in trying to find an 'Arab solution' to the crisis. But by then it was clearly too late. The GCC made two pre-invasion contributions. It called an emergency meeting of the organisation at the request of the Kuwait Government, following Saddam's 17 July threat that Iraq may have to resort to 'effective action', in order to get the Arab League fully involved in the matter.

The second contribution was made by the Kuwaiti Chairman of the GCC, Abdullah Bishara, at the Iraq-Kuwait meeting in Jeddah on 31 July. Bishara suggested to the Kuwaiti Crown Prince that

> ... he put forward a proposal that would allow the two sides to agree on four points: first, the ending of all hostile propaganda - the media, especially in Iraq, should put a stop to all their attacks; second, the demobilization of all the forces stationed on the border between the two countries; third - and this was the most important, from a diplomatic point of view - [implement] measures designed to nurture mutual confidence, through dialogue, visits, etc.; and, finally, agreement about the next meeting.[32]

Except for the agreement to meet again on 4 August - a meeting which never took place - Bishara's suggestion made no headway.

While there had been some diplomatic activity between Iraq and the Arab states since April 1990 regarding Iraq's dispute with Kuwait, the Arab states only seriously embarked on preventive diplomacy after Saddam's 17 July threat. The fundamental principles that the Arab states -

---

[31] Salinger & Laurent, *Secret Dossier* pp.70-5.
[32] Ibid. pp.73-4.

including Iraq, but for different reasons - wished to follow were containment of the crisis to the region and a peaceful 'Arab solution'.

Saudi Arabia's King Fahd, Jordan's King Hussein and Egypt's President Mubarak were actively involved in trying to reach a peaceful solution to the Iraq-Kuwait dispute. These three leaders shuttled on a regular basis between Baghdad and other Arab capitals in a desperate attempt to prevent an armed confrontation. Unfortunately, their eagerness to achieve a peaceful resolution probably led them to misread Iraq's ultimate intentions. Furthermore, the fact that no Arab state had ever previously invaded and annexed another Arab country may have led the Arab leaders to dismiss or at least down play Iraq's aggressive intentions.[33] Perceptions were becoming more important than developments on the ground.

On 24 July, Mubarak and Saddam had a private meeting in Baghdad. The outcome of the meeting remains unclear, as there were no notes taken. According to Mubarak, Saddam told him that Iraq was only trying to scare Kuwait and would not use force. Mubarak reported this back to Kuwait and Saudi Arabia.[34] But according to Saddam's version, and which he passed on to the US Ambassador to Iraq at a meeting on 25 July, he told Mubarak to

> ... assure the Kuwaitis and give them our word that we are not going to do anything until we meet with them. If, when we meet, we see that there is hope, nothing will happen. But if we are unable to find a solution, then it will be natural that Iraq will not accept death, even though wisdom is above everything else.[35]

According to Saddam's version, Mubarak's reporting of the meeting was correct - but only to a point. The crucial point was the 31 July meeting in Jeddah. According to Saddam's version, he made it quite clear that, were Iraq not to get what it demanded, it would not discount the military option as a means of last resort.[36]

President Mubarak, however, cannot solely be blamed for having misread Saddam's signals, as the Iraqi leader was almost certainly deliberately sending confused signals to the outside world about his true intentions. Moreover, according to Iraqi Foreign Minister Aziz, while Saddam decided to invade Kuwait only at the last minute, following the breakdown of the Jeddah meeting, it is also clear that Iraq wished to keep all its options open for as long as possible.[37] For example, on 21 July Saddam reassured the Saudi Foreign Minister, Prince Saud al-Faisal, that while there were troop movements along the Iraq-Kuwait border, they were not there for aggressive purposes.[38]

---

[33] Springborg, 'Origins of the Gulf Crisis' p.222.
[34] Heikal, *Illusions of Triumph* p.179.
[35] Freedman & Karsh, *The Gulf Conflict* p.54.
[36] Ibid. p.53.
[37] Stein, 'Deterrence and Compellence in the Gulf' p.159.
[38] Heikal, *Illusions of Triumph* p.178.

Up to a few days before the invasion, and even in light of the intelligence reports, President Mubarak reassured President Bush that there was no need to worry about the Iraqi troop deployment along the Kuwaiti border. Similarly, to President Bush's question whether Iraq intended to invade Kuwait, Jordan's King Hussein replied that 'there is no possibility for this, and it will not reach this point'.[39]

However, even with their own belief - at least publicly - that Saddam only meant to intimidate Kuwait into accepting Iraq's demands, the Arab leaders urged Kuwait to show restraint in its dealings with Iraq. The Jordanian King warned the Emir to take the Iraqi threats seriously. King Fahd wrote to the Emir making clear that he expected Kuwait to compromise at the forthcoming meeting in Jeddah on 31 July.[40] It was becoming increasingly clear to all that the Jeddah meeting was going to be a turning point in the crisis, one way or another. Still, while all Arab states wished to find a peaceful solution to the crisis, Kuwait's perspective on the situation and what was an acceptable peaceful solution, was understandably quite different from its neighbours.

One individual who had a less optimistic view of the crisis and where it was heading was Arab League Secretary-General Chedli Klibi. He felt that Iraqi Foreign Minister Aziz's 15 July memorandum addressed to him in which he makes the accusations against Kuwait and Saddam's 17 July threat that Iraq may need to take 'effective action', were tantamount to declarations of war against Kuwait.[41] These feelings must have been reinforced when Aziz told him that he believed the Kuwaiti royal family should go.[42] It appears, however, that Klibi was a voice in the wilderness.

Western diplomacy. In the lead up to Iraq's invasion of Kuwait, the United States sent mixed, and at times confusing, signals to Iraq about its attitude towards the Iraq-Kuwait dispute. While one should not exaggerate the importance of these signals in Saddam's decision to invade and annex Kuwait, clearer signals from Washington might have led Saddam to reconsider his position on the issue. The fact of the matter is, however, that the confused American signals were not due to American unwillingness to oppose the Iraqi regime (although there were some in the administration who believed that Saddam's behaviour could be modified through quiet diplomacy) but rather as a result of differences within the US administration and the intelligence agencies as to Saddam's true intentions. Virtually up to the invasion the Americans were of the opinion that the Iraqi troop movements were only for intimidation purposes, and those who thought Iraq was going to invade believed it would only be a limited

---

[39] Freedman & Karsh, *The Gulf Conflict* pp.55, 57.
[40] Ibid. p.56.
[41] Cooley, 'Pre-War Gulf Diplomacy' p.127.
[42] Freedman & Karsh, *The Gulf Conflict* p.56.

invasion. The entire crisis might have been averted if it had not been for this intelligence misjudgement.

Following Saddam's 17 July threat, the United States issued a strong statement declaring that it would defend its interests and friends in the region. Iraq's Ambassador in Washington was told in no uncertain terms that the United States would continue to support the 'sovereignty and integrity of the Gulf states'.[43] The US Secretary of Defence iterated this position two days later when he stated that an American commitment made during the Iran-Iraq War to come to Kuwait's defence was still valid. This was, however, later qualified by a Pentagon spokesperson who said that Secretary Dick Cheney had been quoted by the press 'with some degree of liberty'.[44] Still, on 24 July the US State Department asked its Ambassador in Baghdad, April Glaspie, to stress the friendship of the United States toward Iraq but also to warn that the United States was

> ... committed to ensure the free flow of oil from the Gulf and to support the sovereignty and integrity of the Gulf states. We will continue to defend our vital interests in the Gulf. We are strongly committed to supporting the individual and collective self-defense of our friends in the Gulf.[45]

On the same day, the US announced that it had dispatched refuelling planes at the request of the UAE to take part in an 'emergency training exercise' with UAE fighter jets and that there would also be a joint naval exercise. It is interesting to note that the UAE, clearly worried about the repercussions of such a close US connection, denied that there were going to be such manoeuvres.[46] Nevertheless, these were clear and strong warnings to Baghdad. The warnings, however, were somewhat negated and confused when on the same day State Department spokesperson, Margaret Tutwiler, stated that 'we do not have any defence treaties with Kuwait, and there are no special defense or security commitments to Kuwait'.[47] The following US signals were more ambiguous.

The next crucial step in the United States' approach to the matter was Ambassador Glaspie's private and unexpected meeting with Saddam Hussein on 25 July. Much has been written about the importance of this meeting and how crucial it was in Saddam's ultimate decision to proceed with the invasion. One will never know how prominent this meeting was in Saddam's policy equation, but certainly the Ambassador's weak warnings strengthened Saddam's invasion option.

According to the Ambassador's testimony to the Senate Foreign Relations Committee, she warned Saddam that

---

[43] Ibid. p.51.
[44] Stein, 'Deterrence and Compellence in the Gulf' p.151.
[45] Ibid.
[46] Springborg, 'Origins of the Gulf Crisis' p.222.
[47] Stein, 'Deterrence and Compellence in the Gulf' p.152.

> ... we would defend our vital interests, we would support our friends in the Gulf, we would defend their sovereignty and integrity.[48]

Although she acknowledged that she had told Saddam that the US had no opinion on Iraq's conflict with Kuwait, she insisted that she had warned him that the US

> ... would insist on settlements being made in a non-violent manner, not by threats, not by intimidation, and certainly not by aggression.[49]

However, according to the Iraqi transcript of the meeting or the summary Ambassador Glaspie cabled to the State Department of the meeting, no such strong warning against Iraqi military action appears to have been given to Iraq. Moreover, Saddam reportedly told Ambassador Glaspie that while he preferred a peaceful resolution of the crisis, he did not discount the military option as a means of last resort.[50]

On 27 July, following reassurances from President Mubarak that Saddam had no intention of invading Kuwait, President Bush wrote to President Saddam. While he did warn Iraq not to pursue 'threats involving military force or conflict against Kuwait', he promised him US friendship and expressed a keen interest in improving relations with Baghdad. The letter made no reference to the 100,000 Iraqi troops deployed along the Iraq-Kuwait border. On the same day the Bush administration opposed a Senate vote (80 to 16) imposing economic sanctions against Iraq, including the end of the US$1.2 billion in loan guarantees. By not taking a confrontational approach to the crisis, the Americans were showing their willingness to accommodate the Arab leaders' eagerness to find a peaceful 'Arab solution' to the crisis.

In a testimony to a US House Sub-Committee on 31 July, US Assistant Secretary of State John Kelly stated that the US supported the Gulf states' 'independence and security' and called 'for a peaceful solution to all disputes', and that the 'sovereignty of every state in the Gulf must be respected'. When asked about a possible Iraqi invasion of Kuwait, Kelly replied that the US would be under no treaty obligation to use American forces to defend Kuwait.[51] These words were immediately broadcast by the BBC, and heard in Baghdad.

From Saddam's perspective, the mixed and confused signals emanating from Washington could only mean one thing: the Americans appeared to be putting more value on nurturing their relationship with Iraq than on protecting Kuwait against a possible Iraqi attack. Accordingly, the Iraqi leadership was under virtually no pressure from the US or anyone else to change its approach.

---

[48] Ibid. p.153.
[49] Ibid.
[50] Freedman & Karsh, *The Gulf Conflict* p.53.
[51] Cooley, 'Pre-War Gulf Diplomacy' p.128.

Apart from the Arab world and the United States, virtually no other country involved itself in the crisis or even paid much attention to the worsening Iraqi-Kuwaiti relations. Europe, the only other main player with vital interests in the developing Gulf crisis, was deeply involved in the aftermath of Germany's reunification and in the construction of a European Community monetary structure. As for the Soviet Union, it was too deeply involved in its domestic woes in the dying months of the Communist system to worry about developments in the Gulf.

The British took the same policy line as the Americans in arguing that the dispute should be settled by negotiation and peaceful means. Like the Arab states, the British urged moderation on the part of the Kuwaitis when dealing with Iraq. Although the Foreign Office did not wish to jeopardise the Arab efforts, it did instruct its delegation at the UN to suggest that the border issue be raised among the five permanent members of the Security Council. Reportedly, there was no interest from other members, and no common EC approach was being formulated.[52] That was the only recorded attempt at bringing in the UN before the invasion.

Period between the Invasion and the Gulf War

In the wake of the invasion the international community attempted to apply peacemaking arrangements coupled with enforcement measures, as allowed under Chapter VII of the United Nations Charter, i.e., sanctions. Diplomacy was exhaustively pursued by organisations, countries and individuals up to the time the Western-led Coalition began its military operations to oust Iraq from Kuwait. All diplomatic channels were given ample chance. Saddam was given many opportunities to enter into negotiations between August 1990 and mid-January 1991. But he refused the diplomatic option, choosing instead to lock his country into the military option. In this section we will analyse only the most important initiatives undertaken by the various players in their attempt to resolve peacefully the crisis, as space does not allow an exhaustive examination of all diplomatic efforts. This analysis will not include the numerous and successful diplomatic initiatives that were essentially concerned with the release of the thousands of hostages held by the Iraqi authorities. In the next section, we will examine *enforcement* which, prior to the activation of *Desert Storm* took the form of UN-authorised sanctions and other measures against the Iraqi regime. Both tracks were pursued simultaneously.

Peacemaking

While the actual invasion of Kuwait may not have surprised everyone, the extent of it certainly did. It was generally believed within the intelligence

---

[52] Freedman & Karsh, *The Gulf Conflict* p.55.

communities and foreign ministries that if Iraq were to invade it would limit itself to taking over the two strategic islands and the Rumaila oil field. A comprehensive invasion of Kuwait was generally not envisaged as an option Saddam would consider pursuing.

Arab diplomacy. Although Iraq's invasion shocked the Arab world and its leaders, who felt that Saddam had misled them all along, Arab governments were still keen to find an 'Arab solution' to the crisis. There was a very strong desire to avoid outside involvement in the matter. The Iraqi leadership was aware of these sentiments and exploited these feelings to its advantage. In the first few days after the invasion, Saddam persistently and successfully played the 'Arab solution' card, with promises of leaving Kuwait in the near future. And while Western intelligence indicated that Saddam had no intention of leaving Kuwait, the Arab world, eager to reach a peaceful resolution to the crisis, was generally willing to believe him. However, while Iraq's delaying tactics did work for a while, most Arab leaders had to come eventually to the conclusion that Iraq's 'Arab solution' - which generally included unacceptable conditions - would not work and outside intervention would be necessary to oust the Iraqi forces from Kuwait.

On 3 August, the day after the invasion, Jordan's King Hussein met Saddam in Baghdad. He secured Saddam's pledge to attend an Arab mini-summit in Saudi Arabia, planned for 5 August, and to withdraw from Kuwait if 'differences' with the Emirate were resolved. There are different versions as to what preconditions Saddam was meant to have agreed to before attending the mini-summit.[53] Saddam, however, also threatened that, if the Arab League condemned him, he would announce Kuwait's annexation. On the same day, Saddam also announced that he would begin withdrawing from Kuwait on 5 August but that the Kuwaiti royal family would not be permitted to return. It was an obvious but clever ploy at attempting to divide the Arab community by enticing it to accept a peaceful solution at the expense of the Kuwaiti royal family. Western intelligence saw no evidence of Iraqi troop movements preparing to depart Kuwait. On the contrary, Iraqi troops were massing on the Saudi border.[54]

The Arab League Council, which was meeting in Cairo in an extraordinary session, condemned Iraq, with Jordan, the Sudan, Yemen and the Palestine Liberation Organisation (PLO) voting against it and Libya refusing to vote. In an attempt to seek an 'Arab solution', the Resolution rejected 'strenuously any foreign intervention or attempt at intervention in Arab affairs'.[55] In any case, the League's condemnation probably had little impact on later developments, as Iraq probably had no intention of leaving Kuwait. For example, on 3 August Iraqi Vice-President Izzat Ibrahim told his Saudi hosts in Riyadh that 'there was no way to reverse the clock and

---

[53] Ibid. p.70.
[54] Cooley, 'Pre-War Gulf Diplomacy' p.130.
[55] E. Lauterpacht et al. (eds), *The Kuwait Crisis*, p.293.

that Kuwait was past history'.[56] A similar uncompromising message was delivered by Iraqi Prime Minister Hammadi at the extraordinary session of the Arab League. Saddam's decision to annex Kuwait on 8 August was the next logical step. Iraq did not even bother with the earlier pretence of having been invited into Kuwait by the PGFK. Saddam also withdrew his promise to attend the Arab summit in Saudi Arabia.

At the Arab League Council meeting the Kuwaiti delegation requested immediate application of the Arab League defence pact meant to protect an attacked member. Only the UAE responded positively.[57] Iraq had clearly breached Article 2 of the League's Charter ('safeguard the independence and sovereignty of each state') and Article 8 ('each Member State shall respect the system of government established in the other Member States ... and will pledge to abstain from any action calculated to change established systems of government'). The League's failure to respond firmly to Iraq's actions confirmed its weakness and its inadequacy in resolving the crisis.

The next major turning point in the Arabs' search for a peaceful solution was the Extraordinary Arab League Summit in Cairo on 10 August called at Syria's request. Several resolutions were passed supporting Kuwait's sovereignty and independence, rejecting Iraq's annexation of Kuwait, upholding the UN Security Council resolutions dealing with the Kuwait crisis, and supporting Saudi Arabia's legitimate self-defence in its call for foreign forces. The resolutions also called for the dispatch of a pan-Arab force to Saudi Arabia to protect it against a possible Iraqi invasion. The League split again over the issue. Resolutions were adopted by a slim majority, with Iraq, Libya and the PLO voting against. Algeria and Yemen abstained, while Jordan, Sudan and Mauritania expressed 'reservations', and Tunisia was absent.

The next important development in the search for an 'Arab solution' was Saddam's attempt to link the Kuwait crisis with the Arab-Israeli conflict and other Middle Eastern 'occupations'. In a communiqué the Iraqi Government stated that 'for the occupation of Kuwait' to be solved, Syria had to withdraw from Lebanon; remaining Iraqi prisoners of war returned from Iran; Israel must withdraw from Palestine; and 'arrangements' should be made between Iraq and Kuwait. However, first, UN sanctions against Iraq had to be lifted and Coalition forces had to be withdrawn from Saudi Arabia and replaced by a pan-Arab force which did not include Egyptians.[58] This was a cynical attempt to muddy the water and broaden Saddam's appeal among the people across the Arab world. And while he did achieve some success among the general Arab population in that respect - there were several pro-Saddam demonstrations in various Arab countries - the Arab leaders were not fooled by this transparent ploy. The United States and other members of the anti-Iraq Coalition rejected the linkage.

---

[56] Freedman & Karsh, *The Gulf Conflict* p.71.
[57] Cooley, 'Pre-War Gulf Diplomacy' p.129.
[58] Ibid. pp.132-3.

Nevertheless, Saddam would repeatedly return to this linkage as the months wore on, and he did manage to get some support among some Western leaders, but ultimately this Iraqi diplomatic strategy failed.

If there was any doubt left regarding Saddam's determination to hold on to Kuwait, two developments dispelled it. On 17 August the Iraqi Government decided to make peace with Iran and accept most of Teheran's conditions for a peace agreement, including the medial line as the Iran-Iraq boundary in the Shatt al 'Arab waterway. Iraq also agreed to evacuate Iranian territory which it still occupied, and to an exchange of prisoners. This surprise move allowed Iraq to free up over half a million Iraqi troops protecting the country's eastern flank. Eleven days later Iraq declared the Emirate Iraq's nineteenth province and renamed it Khadima, its name during the Ottoman Empire.

The Council of the League of Arab States met again in Cairo on 31 August 1990. Several resolutions were passed which included condemnation of the invasion of Kuwait, urging the protection of civilians in Kuwait, and calling on the Iraqi authorities not to tamper with the demographic composition of Kuwait. As with the 10 August League Summit resolutions, the Arab world split over these resolutions. Libya opposed them. Algeria, Iraq, Jordan, Mauritania, Palestine, Sudan, Tunisia and Yemen did not participate in the work of the session.[59] In light of the League's failure to move the crisis closer to a resolution and the decision by his own country, Tunisia, to boycott the proceedings, the League's Secretary-General decided to resign on 4 September 1990.

King Hussein, and Yasser Arafat to a lesser extent, engaged in extensive shuttle diplomacy between Baghdad and various Arab and Western capitals in an attempt to find a peaceful and diplomatic solution to the crisis. In late August, King Hussein floated a plan which absorbed the major elements of a PLO proposal suggested earlier. The PLO plan involved freezing the military build-up in the Gulf, withdrawal of Iraqi troops from Kuwait and US forces from Saudi Arabia, and the replacement of both by UN or Arab peacekeeping forces, with a committee set up by the Arab League to discuss the territorial dispute. King Hussein's contribution to the plan was a proposal to model Kuwait on Monaco's relations with France, with a constitutional monarchy conceding certain functions to Iraq. Saddam showed no interest in this plan.[60]

In September, King Hussein, King Hassan of Morocco and President Bendjedid of Algeria proposed a compromise: Iraq would withdraw from Kuwait but the two countries would have a special relationship similar to that of Syria with Lebanon; Kuwait would cede the islands of Bubiyan and Warba and the Rumaila oil field, and a free vote would be held in Kuwait for a successor government; and the Iraqi withdrawal would be tightly coupled to a fixed date for the withdrawal of foreign forces from Saudi

---

[59] E. Lauterpacht et al. (eds), *The Kuwait Crisis* pp.296-9.
[60] Freedman & Karsh, *The Gulf Conflict* p.162.

Arabia and to a discussion of the Palestinian problem.[61] Again, this proposal fell on deaf ears.

In December, King Hussein was urging the convening of an international peace conference on the Middle East on the basis of Saddam's 12 August 'linkage' initiative, simultaneously with the beginning of an Iraqi withdrawal from Kuwait, with some concessions from the Emirate to satisfy Iraq's security and economic concerns.[62] However, even if the international community had been willing to accommodate such a linkage, Iraq's Revolutionary Command Council put to rest any illusions about Saddam's willingness to find a compromise when it stated

> When we stand for linkage as stated in the 12 August initiative, the belief that Kuwait is part of Iraq is unshakeable, and that it is the nineteenth province is a fact treated by our people and their Armed Forces as a great gain ...[63]

One final Arab attempt at preventive diplomacy came from Algerian President Chadli Bendjedid in December 1990. The Algerian leader suggested that a 'concrete signal on the Palestinian question would be decisive step' in solving the crisis. He also told Saddam that Iraq would have to pay 'a certain price to settle'.[64] In the end his proposal was unacceptable to all parties involved and his efforts were unsuccessful.

Western, Soviet and UN Diplomacy. The United States' response to the invasion was quick and effective. The Bush administration was determined to send a clear and unambiguous signal to the Iraqi leadership: the invasion of Kuwait was unacceptable and would not be allowed to remain and the United States was ready to defend Saudi Arabia and the other Gulf states against Iraqi attacks. President Bush warned Iraq against invading Saudi Arabia.[65] The US followed a dual track approach in implementing its Gulf policy. With the *diplomatic* track, the US was willing to consider an 'Arab solution' or any other peaceful resolution of the crisis, but only as long as there was no appeasement nor linkage with other issues, particularly other outstanding Middle East disputes. Iraq could not be allowed - or be perceived - to be rewarded for invading and annexing another Arab state. The second track, *preventive deployment,* required that a substantial military force be stationed quickly in Saudi Arabia. It was only months later, when it became clear that Iraq had no intention of departing Kuwait, that the defensive nature of the multi-national troop deployment in Saudi Arabia (*Desert Shield*) was changed for a possible offensive role (*Desert Storm*).

Saudi Arabia's contribution to the establishment of the multi-national force was vital for both *Desert Shield* and *Desert Storm. Desert Shield*

---

61   Stein, 'Deterrence and Compellence in the Gulf' p.171.
62   Freedman & Karsh, *The Gulf Conflict* p.246.
63   Ibid. p.247.
64   Cooley, 'Pre-War Gulf Diplomacy' pp.134-5.
65   Ibid. p.130.

was not only about the protection of Saudi Arabia and other Gulf states. It also had an essential role to play in supporting diplomatic efforts, as it was the supportive military arm behind the many subsequent diplomatic initiatives. *Desert Shield* allowed the 'Arab solution' approach to be exhausted fully. The multi-national force deployment - which included many Arab armed forces - sent Saddam a clear and unambiguous signal about the international community's determination to correct an unacceptable development.

A few days after the invasion the Americans showed the Saudi monarch intelligence reports that the Iraqis were massing on the Saudi border and argued that it was essential to have a large number of troops to protect the Saudi Kingdom and to back up the economic sanctions against Iraq. The Saudis did not need much convincing given the nature of the Iraqi military threat. US Secretary Cheney signed a secret agreement with Saudi Defence Minister Prince Sultan: American troops would have Saudi aid and logistical support inside the Kingdom, but would be subject to Saudi veto on offensive actions beyond Saudi territory.[66] The US also stressed that it would not be seeking a permanent base in Saudi Arabia. By 8 August the deployment of *Desert Shield* had begun.

Washington's ability to forge an anti-Iraqi Coalition would not have been possible without the Soviet Union's cooperation. This was the first real test for the post-Cold War world, and the international community managed it successfully. Saddam had not expected such close US-Soviet cooperation and resolve to end Iraq's annexation of Kuwait. However, this policy coordination should not have come as a surprise to the Iraqi leadership, as it was US-Soviet cooperation at the United Nations in 1988 which resulted in achieving a ceasefire to the Iran-Iraq War.

Ironically, US Secretary of State James Baker and Soviet Foreign Minister Eduard Shevardnadze were meeting in Irkutsk, Siberia, when Iraq invaded Kuwait. Shevardnadze's reaction to the news was one of 'embarrassment and surprise'.[67] Like the US, the Soviet Union believed the Iraqis were only trying to intimidate the Kuwaitis. Nevertheless, the Soviet Government declared that 'the Soviet Union believes that no contentious issues, no matter how complicated, justify the use of force'.[68] This view confirmed an earlier statement Moscow had issued in July, when it stated that 'the USSR is convinced that there are no conflicts, no matter how difficult, that cannot be settled across the negotiating table'.[69]

This spirit of cooperation was publicly reaffirmed at the Bush-Gorbachev Summit in Helsinki on 9 September 1990. It was agreed, however, that while the United States was building up its forces in Saudi Arabia the Soviet Union would continue to make contacts with Saddam in

---

66 Ibid.
67 Freedman & Karsh, *The Gulf Conflict* p.77.
68 Ibid. p.78.
69 Ibid. p.77.

an effort to find a peaceful solution to the crisis.[70] This was a quid pro quo for the USSR's cooperation with the US. Iraq was one of the Soviet Union's few remaining allies in the Middle East, and decades of close military and political cooperation had forged close ties between the two countries. There was a vigorous debate within the Soviet administration over the extent to which Moscow should cooperate with the US over this issue. The conservatives were against cooperating with the Americans. They felt that by taking an anti-Iraq line the Soviet Union would lose its only remaining ally and this would affect Moscow's influence in the region. The pro-Coalition group, led by Shevardnadze, urged cooperation with the US and joint action against Iraq.[71] In any case, the Soviet Union publicly supported *Desert Shield* and cooperated with the US in the adoption of the twelve UN Security Council resolutions against Iraq. Moreover, Shevardnadze told the United Nations that he believed that the international community had the 'right' to use force against Iraq if it continued with its occupation.[72]

The first Soviet initiative came on 4 September, when Shevardnadze suggested a linkage between the Gulf crisis and the Arab-Israeli conflict, arguing that Israel's agreement to participate in an international conference on the Middle East could exert a 'positive influence' on the events in the Gulf.[73] Nothing came of this diplomatic feeler, however. Instead, President Mikhail Gorbachev placed more hope on the diplomatic initiatives of Evgeny Primakov, a noted Arabist, a member of the Presidential Council and known for his pro-Iraqi leanings. Primakov's major effort was in October when he went to Baghdad. Reportedly, Primakov mooted a proposal which suggested a possible convocation of an international conference following Iraq's withdrawal from Kuwait.[74] In any case, Primakov warned Saddam that he had to withdraw his troops from Kuwait otherwise the Coalition forces would have to use force to oust the Iraqi troops. Although Primakov failed to convince Saddam of the Coalition's resolve, he did manage to have Saddam agree to the release of the 7,830 Soviet hostages, at the rate of 1,500 per month.[75] Even though Saddam was vague and uncompromising, Primakov remained optimistic throughout his shuttle diplomacy between Baghdad, Moscow and the Western capitals. But by the end of October, Primakov's diplomacy had been unsuccessful. The Soviet Union put the blame squarely on Saddam's intransigence.[76]

---

[70] Cooley, 'Pre-War Gulf Diplomacy' p.133.
[71] O. Alexandrova, 'Soviet Policy in the Gulf Conflict' *Aussenpolitik* 42, 3 (1991) p.232.
[72] Freedman & Karsh, *The Gulf Conflict* p.126.
[73] Ibid. p.175.
[74] Ibid.
[75] Heikal, *Illusions of Triumph* p.263.
[76] Freedman & Karsh, *The Gulf Conflict* p.200.

While the Soviet Union was not being successful in its attempt to find a peaceful resolution to the crisis, President Bush was not deterred from trying. Accordingly, on 30 November, the day after the UN adopted Security Council Resolution 678, authorising 'all necessary means' to evict the Iraqi forces from Kuwait, President Bush offered direct talks between the US and Iraq. Bush made this 'extra mile for peace' initiative because as Secretary Baker admitted later,

> ... if force ends up being used we owe it to the American people and to others to show that we left no stone unturned in the search for peace.[77]

Determined to reassure some of his Coalition partners who were worried that the US' resolve to oust Iraq may have diminished, President Bush stated that he had suggested direct talks with Iraq not only to ensure that all attempts to reach a peaceful solution had been exhausted but also to ensure that it was made clear to Saddam that unless Iraq left Kuwait and all UN resolutions were implemented the US-led Coalition forces would use force to expel the Iraqis from Kuwait. Bush also emphasised that no concessions would be made and no negotiations entered into at this meeting.

After Iraq and the United States failed to agree on a date for the talks, Bush suggested that Baker meet Iraqi Foreign Minister Aziz in Geneva instead. Baker and Aziz agreed to meet on 9 January 1991. The meeting held no surprises and no one expected any break through. It is interesting, however, that Aziz did not respond to Baker's suggestion that the US 'supported the idea of settling differences between Iraq and Kuwait peacefully as provided for by Resolution 660'.[78] The US Secretary was referring to Paragraph 3 of UNSCR 660 which 'calls upon Iraq and Kuwait to begin immediately intensive negotiations for the resolution of their differences ...' Finally, while Aziz repeatedly referred to the 12 August 'linkage' during the talks, when asked by the press after the meeting whether Iraq would be willing to leave Kuwait if promised an international conference on the Palestinian problem, he replied with a categorical refusal.[79] The meeting had lasted over six hours, and peacemaking diplomacy had failed once again.

The French were keen to contribute to the diplomatic track. Moreover, France had a long history of relations with the Arab world and felt that it was well placed to seek a peaceful resolution. Nevertheless, while France had been Iraq's foremost Western ally, French President Mitterand condemned Iraq's invasion. He stated

> France has for long had friendly relations with Iraq. You know that we continued to help it during the war with Iran. That allows us to say all

---

[77] Ibid. p.235.
[78] Ibid. p.258.
[79] Ibid. p.259.

the more clearly that we accept neither the aggression against Kuwait nor the annexation which followed.[80]

On 24 September 1990, Mitterand proposed a four-stage process of settlement. Iraq would declare its intention to withdraw from Kuwait and the Kuwaiti people would exercise their 'democratic will'. An international conference would then address the Arab-Israeli conflict and the future of Lebanon. Finally, the states in the Middle East would consider arms control agreements and arrangements.[81] President Mitterand then made the first trip by a Western head of state to the Gulf since the crisis began, meeting with leaders from Saudi Arabia and the UAE. Over the next several months France would send a total of twelve envoys to 24 countries, including to Iraq, in an attempt to find a peaceful solution. However, those who visited Iraq were received with Saddam's usual hardline response.

At an EC meeting on 4 January, France proposed, and Germany supported, a seven-point plan for peace talks. It was suggested that Iraqi Foreign Minister Aziz meet Luxembourg's Foreign Minister on 10 January, the day after the planned Baker-Aziz meeting. However, nothing came of that proposal, as Aziz declined the invitation because the EC had rejected his earlier suggestion for a meeting.

Still, the French believed that there were signs of an Iraqi willingness to withdraw in the event of a major concession on the Palestinian issue. There had never been, however, any firm evidence that Saddam would be satisfied with a promise to convene an international conference on the Palestinian issue.[82] Nevertheless, France made a last attempt at diplomacy. French Foreign Minister Roland Dumas suggested a final UN Security Council resolution. The draft resolution appealed to the Iraqi authorities to 'announce without further delay their intention to withdraw from Kuwait along the lines of a pre-planned schedule, and to begin a rapid and massive withdrawal which is to commence immediately'. This withdrawal would be observed and verified by international observers and an Arab peacekeeping force organised through the UN. In return, Iraq would get a guarantee of non-aggression and, 'in association with Arab countries, necessary measures to promote all useful negotiations to consolidate the process of a peaceful settlement'. Finally, from the moment of this settlement being agreed upon, the Security Council members would provide active participation to the settlement of other regional problems, in particular the Arab-Israeli conflict and the Palestinian problem.[83]

This French draft resolution was unacceptable to the British and American governments as it made too much of a direct link between the

---

80 Ibid. p.115.
81 Stein, 'Deterrence and Compellence in the Gulf' p.171.
82 Freedman & Karsh, *The Gulf Conflict* p.263.
83 Ibid. p.272.

Gulf crisis and the other Middle East problems, and it failed to set a tight deadline for Iraqi troop withdrawal. And, although this draft, as well as a counter British draft, were discussed in the Security Council on 15 January, the Iraqi leadership continued to show no sign of flexibility. Consequently, and as a result of disagreement as to what should be in the draft resolution, the Security Council decided not to proceed any further with the adoption of a resolution.

United Nations Secretary-General Javier Perez de Cuellar made two genuine attempts at peacemaking diplomacy following the invasion. However, de Cuellar was in the awkward position of having to confine his negotiations within the framework of the UN Security Council Resolutions that had been adopted since the crisis had begun. Nevertheless, even with this restriction he felt that it was worth trying in the hope that his attempts would bring the crisis closer to a peaceful resolution.

The UN Secretary-General agreed to meet Iraqi Foreign Minister Aziz in Amman, Jordan, in late August. However, on his way to the meeting, Saddam confirmed the annexation of Kuwait as Iraq's nineteenth province. It did not augur well for the meeting. The Secretary-General did not have any concrete proposal, simply a number of ideas. These revolved around the possibility of a UN peacekeeping force to monitor and police withdrawals, setting up a mechanism for serious negotiations between Iraq and Kuwait, and, if it seemed worthwhile, a personal visit to Baghdad. He could only negotiate for the status quo ante.[84] Talks led to nowhere, however, as Aziz maintained a hardline and proceeded along familiar lines.

De Cuellar's second major attempt was in January 1991. He announced that he would be going to Baghdad on 11 January. And although he had 'no proposals to make', he felt it was his 'moral duty to do everything to avoid the worst'. President Saddam made him wait almost two days in Baghdad before receiving him. When he did see him he was confrontational and showed no sign of flexibility. This was in marked contrast to de Cuellar who showed moderation, going as far as to suggest that Saddam's 12 August 'initiative' had 'not been given due consideration and that it could still form a basis for the resolution of the crisis'.[85] After six hours of talks the meeting closed. This had been the last unsuccessful attempt at direct talks with Saddam.

While not directly relevant to the issue of Kuwait and the demand that Iraq withdraw from the Emirate, a significant number of diplomatic initiatives involved trying to have Saddam release the hundreds of Western hostages - or 'foreign guests' as the Iraqi Government called them - he had been holding since the invasion. The hostage issue was a particularly sensitive matter for President Bush as the presidencies of Carter and Reagan had been badly affected by their own hostage situations. It was

---

[84] Ibid. p.161.
[85] Ibid. p.269.

also a very emotive issue with the American public. Nevertheless, Western countries were determined not to allow the hostage issue influence the bigger question of Kuwait. They proved that with the adoption of UNSCRs 661 (6 August) and 662 (9 August).

However, the Iraqi leadership attempted to exploit this matter to its advantage, and was successful to a certain point. Saddam attempted to achieve several aims with his hostage policy. One of his foremost aims was to get Western domestic opinion to pressure Western governments not to use military force against Iraq. Later, he used approximately 600 hostages as human shields to protect non-conventional arms installations and to attempt to prevent Coalition retaliation against Iraq. Iraq stressed that the 'guests' would remain as long as the threat against Iraq remained.[86] Another objective was to try to undermine the West's resolve in applying the sanctions. Saddam stated that the 'guests' would have to share the same economic and nutritional deprivation as the Iraqi people. Finally, the Iraqi Government 'rewarded' Western governments which were willing, or appeared to be willing, to be more accommodating with Iraq. It was a blatant attempt at divide and rule. Saddam's hostage policy backfired, however, particularly on his decision to use them as human shields. Arab states criticised him and Western public opinion turned against him.

Nevertheless, Saddam managed to have a significant number of prominent individuals go to Baghdad and negotiate the release of hostages. In an attempt to weaken the Coalition, the Iraqis tried to arrange a special hostage deal with the French Government if it would agree to send a senior French political figure to Baghdad. And while the French initially appeared to be willing to be more accommodating with Saddam, in the end the French refused to oblige. Saddam also promised that, if Japan or Germany and one permanent member of the Security Council stated that they opposed military action against Iraq, all hostages would be released. This proposal was rejected by the international community.

After the adoption of UNSCR 678, authorising the use of force against Iraq, the hostages had outlived their usefulness and, accordingly, the Iraqis began to release them. A week after President Bush's 'extra mile' initiative, Saddam released all remaining hostages, believing that, were he to end the hostage issue, a settlement might be possible.

Enforcement

At the same time as diplomacy was being exhaustively pursued, the international community was working on a parallel track in the United Nations. Thanks to a dramatically changed international environment in which traditional superpower rivalry had disappeared, the UN Security Council was able to move the Gulf crisis issue swiftly to Chapter VII of the UN Charter. Chapter VII, which refers to 'Action with respect to

---

[86] Ibid. p.137.

threats to the peace, breaches of the peace, and acts of aggression', allowed the Security Council, and through it the international community, to proceed with mandatory measures against Iraq. The Security Council adopted twelve resolutions between the invasion of Kuwait on 2 August 1990 and 29 November 1990, when it adopted Resolution 678 authorising the use of force to oust Iraq from Kuwait. The non-permanent members of the Council when these resolutions were passed were: Canada, Colombia, Côte d'Ivoire, Cuba, Ethiopia, Finland, Malaysia, Romania, Yemen and Zaïre.

The Twelve UN Security Council Resolutions. The main elements of the twelve Security Council resolutions were:

- Resolution 660, adopted on 2 August 1990. Relating, *inter alia*, to the Council's condemnation of the Iraqi invasion of Kuwait. It was adopted by a vote of fourteen in favour and none against. Yemen did not participate in the vote.

- Resolution 661, adopted on 6 August 1990. Relating, *inter alia*, to the imposition of mandatory sanctions and to the establishment of a committee to undertake certain tasks regarding the implementation of the resolution. It was adopted by a vote of thirteen in favour, none against and two abstentions (Cuba and Yemen).

- Resolution 662, adopted on 9 August 1990. Relating, *inter alia*, to the non-validity of the Iraqi annexation of Kuwait. It was adopted by unanimous vote.

- Resolution 664, adopted on 18 August 1990. Relating, *inter alia*, to the nationals of third countries in Iraq and Kuwait and to diplomatic and consular missions in Kuwait. It was adopted by unanimous vote.

- Resolution 665, adopted on 25 August 1990. Relating, *inter alia*, to measures to ensure implementation of Resolution 661. It sanctioned the formation of the US-led Multinational Interception Force (MIF). It was adopted by a vote of 13 in favour, none against and 2 abstentions (Cuba and Yemen).

- Resolution 666, adopted on 13 September 1990. Relating, *inter alia*, to the determination of humanitarian circumstances. It was adopted by a vote of thirteen in favour and two abstentions (Cuba and Yemen).

- Resolution 667, adopted on 16 September 1990. Relating, *inter alia*, to diplomatic and consular personnel and premises. It was adopted by unanimous vote.

- Resolution 669, adopted on 24 September 1990. Relating, *inter alia*, to requests for assistance under the provisions of Article 50 of the Charter. It was adopted by unanimous vote.

- Resolution 670, adopted on 25 September 1990. Relating, *inter alia*, to the applicability of sanctions to all means of transport, including aircraft. It was adopted by a vote of fourteen in favour and one against (Cuba).

- Resolution 674, adopted on 29 October 1990. Relating, *inter alia*, to the situation of Kuwaiti and third-State nationals in Kuwait and Iraq, to further measures in the event of non-compliance by Iraq with Security Council resolutions and to the good offices of the Secretary-General. It was adopted by a vote of thirteen in favour and two abstentions (Cuba and Yemen).

- Resolution 677, adopted on 28 November 1990. Relating, *inter alia*, to attempts by Iraq to alter the demographic composition of the population of Kuwait. It was adopted by unanimous vote.

- Resolution 678, adopted on 29 November 1990. Relating, *inter alia*, to the use by Member States of 'all necessary means to uphold and implement Resolution 660 and all subsequent relevant resolutions and to restore international peace and security in the area'. It was adopted by a vote of twelve in favour, two against (Cuba and Yemen) and one abstention (China).

Evaluation

The Gulf Crisis: What Kind of Security Problem and Threat to the World?

The invasion of Kuwait presented the international community with a *conflict*-type security problem. The Kuwait crisis was the clearest post-World War II example of a 1930s-type invasion. While there had been cases of countries invading and annexing another territory (Goa by India, the West Bank and the Gaza Strip by Israel and East Timor by Indonesia), not only were these previous cases not as clear cut as the present case but this was the only post-World War II case of the annexation of a sovereign, independent and internationally recognised state. Accordingly, the response was correct and accusations of double standards were not applicable.[87] According to some, this made the war against Iraq a 'just war'.[88] While undoubtedly the oil factor played a significant role in the US' ability to muster the international support for the formation of *Desert Shield* and *Desert Storm* and in the international community's decision to use force to oust Iraq from Kuwait, it was the violation of the fundamental principle of state sovereignty which could not be allowed to go unpunished.

The invasion of Kuwait was a clear violation of Article 2(4) of the UN Charter which effectively outlaws wars and clearly falls within the subject (Breaches of the peace, and acts of aggression) covered by Chapter VII of the Charter. Accordingly, this allowed Kuwait (which had been annexed) and Saudi Arabia (which felt threatened) to resort to Chapter VII's Article 51 of the UN Charter which provides members with the inherent right to self-defence. Article 51 gave the international community the legal sanction for the establishment of *Desert Shield*. Chapter VII is the umbrella under which all subsequent Security Council resolutions were adopted.

The Kuwait crisis also presented the world with a *threatening trends*-type security problem. The invasion and the subsequent military developments revealed the extent to which Iraq had developed - or was in the process of developing - weapons of mass destruction (WMD). The threat and the extent of Iraq's capacity in WMD was real, as has been subsequently revealed through the United Nations Special Commission's systematic destruction of very extensive quantities of biological and chemical products earmarked for Iraq's WMD program.[89] The Iraqi leadership also publicly acknowledged the possession of, and the willingness to use, Iraq's WMD against the country's enemies. On 2 April 1990, in an address to the General Command of the Iraqi armed forces, Saddam threatened that 'we will make fire and eat half of Israel if it tries to do anything against Iraq'.[90]

Both these security problems, conflict and threatening trends, presented the world with a *regional military threat*, with possibly global implications. There was the danger, at least in the early stages, that Iraq might decide to invade Saudi Arabia. The implications if this had occurred would have been widely felt. Not only would have Iraq been in control of 45 per cent of the world's oil reserves (60 per cent of OPEC's oil reserves), and therefore been able to have a greater control over oil pricing, but with

---

[87] G. Evans, 'The Case for Australian Participation' in M. Goot and R. Tiffen (eds) *Australia's Gulf War* (Melbourne: Melbourne University Press, 1992) pp.10-21.

[88] L. Freedman, 'The Gulf War and the New World Order' *Survival* 33, 3 (May/June 1991) pp.202-4.

[89] UNSCOM is the UN body established under UNSCR 687 whose task is to destroy Iraq's WMD program and implement the long term monitoring of Iraq's missile program.

[90] Freedman & Karsh, *The Gulf Conflict* p.32.

Iraq occupying Kuwait *and* Saudi Arabia it would have been significantly harder to liberate Kuwait and Saudi Arabia. Moreover, Iraq's occupation of Saudi Arabia would have made it an even greater regional military power than it already was before the invasion of Kuwait. Such a development would have enabled Iraq to have an unacceptably high degree of influence on Middle East affairs.

But even if Iraq had not intended to invade Saudi Arabia, the annexation of Kuwait already had sufficient regional and international implications to make international intervention not only possible but logical.[91] And it was because of these consequences and the violation of international law that the international community was determined to expel Iraq from Kuwait, either peacefully or by force. Every UN Member State had a vital interest in reversing this massive breach in international law, for allowing it to go unpunished would have set an unacceptable precedent. The international community's commitment to the upholding of international law was demonstrated by the great number of participants in *Desert Shield* and *Desert Storm*. Thirty-eight countries participated directly in the action and another four (including Germany and Japan) contributed major financial and logistical support. And it was the anti-Iraq Coalition's determination to oust Iraq from Kuwait, one way or another, which made it so important that many diplomatic initiatives be undertaken.

The end of the Cold War and the willingness of erstwhile enemies to cooperate in the international arena provided the world with a unique opportunity to use the United Nations as it was originally planned to operate. Failure to take effective action to reverse Iraq's action would have dealt a severe blow to the credibility of the UN in the post-Cold War period. In many ways, the Gulf crisis was as much about stopping an international aggressor as it was about managing the end of the Cold War.

The United Nations' Role

The UN Security Council Resolutions: were they sufficiently clear? The Security Council resolutions confirmed the world's condemnation and rejection of the invasion and annexation of Kuwait. They also made very clear the international community's determination to take measures ensuring Iraq's actions were reversed. Put differently, these resolutions, which slowly tightened the noose around the Iraqi leadership, confirmed the urgency and importance of the diplomatic initiatives which were put forward by various international players. They made it abundantly clear that if the Iraqi leadership did not take up any of the diplomatic opportunities offered to it, armed confrontation would ultimately occur.

Most of these resolutions were triggered by developments on the ground in Kuwait. UNSCR 660, which was adopted on the same day as

---

[91] C. Bell, 'The Gulf and the Great Powers' *Quadrant* 35, 10 (October 1991) p.35.

the invasion, not only demanded that Iraq withdraw, immediately and unconditionally, its forces from Kuwait, but it also called 'upon Iraq and Kuwait to begin immediately intensive negotiations for the resolution of their differences'. The fact that fourteen members of the Security Council voted in favour, including Cuba, and only Yemen abstained, demonstrated that there was widespread consensus on this matter. Over the next five months Iraq never showed any serious interest in entering into negotiations with Kuwait, or with anyone else for that matter.

Iraq having failed to comply with UNSCR 660 after four days, the Security Council decided to impose comprehensive sanctions against Iraq, with the adoption of UNSCR 661 (6 August) and UNSCR 670 (25 September). Although a number of countries, including Australia, had already imposed economic sanctions against Iraq under Article 51 (collective self-defence), it was felt that a Security Council resolution would give the sanctions more legitimacy. The voting pattern on these resolutions were interesting, in that for UNSCR 661 no one opposed it, with Cuba and Yemen abstaining. But for UNSCR 670, which basically dealt with transport sanctions, only Cuba voted against it, with Yemen voting for it along with the other thirteen members. Broadly speaking, this demonstrated that already early in the crisis, Iraq could not muster much international support even among its allies and friends.

UNSCR 670 was also significant, in that it reaffirmed 'the inherent right of individual or collective self-defence, in response to the armed attack by Iraq against Kuwait, in accordance with Article 51 of the Charter'. In other words, it provided further justification and legitimisation for the establishment of *Desert Shield*, which began deployment two days later.

In reaction to Iraq's decision to annex Kuwait, the Security Council adopted UNSCR 662, which decided that the 'annexation of Kuwait by Iraq by any form and whatever pretext has no legal validity, and is considered null and void'. It demanded that 'Iraq rescind its actions purporting to annex Kuwait'. It is interesting that Yemen, which voted for the resolution, abstained the next day on an Arab League Resolution condemning the annexation.

On 6 August Iraq made a formal link between the UN-imposed sanctions and the safety of foreign nationals in Kuwait and Iraq. Lt-Colonel Walid Saud Muammad Abdallah, the Foreign Minister of the puppet government installed in Kuwait, stated

> Countries that resort to punitive measures against the provisional free Kuwaiti Government and fraternal Iraq ... should remember that they have interests and nationals in Kuwait. If these countries insist on aggression against Kuwait and Iraq ... the Kuwaiti Government will then reconsider the methods for dealing with these countries. [92]

---

[92] Freedman & Karsh, *The Gulf Conflict* p.136.

Iraq's decision to adopt this policy of taking hostages and holding them for ransom led to the adoption of UNSCR 664, which demanded that Iraq permit and facilitate the immediate release of the hostages and that 'Iraq take no action to jeopardize the safety, security or health of such nationals'. Saddam again ignored this resolution and only released the hostages in trickles and generally only after negotiating with various emissaries. The demand for the release of all hostages was reiterated in UNSCRs 667 (16 September) and 674 (29 October). UNSCRs 664 and 667 were adopted by unanimous vote. However, Cuba and Yemen abstained on UNSCR 674, which not only covered essentially the same issue, but requested the UN Secretary-General 'to undertake diplomatic efforts in order to reach a peaceful solution to the crisis' and called 'upon all states, both those in the region and others, to pursue on this basis their efforts to this end ...' It is not clear why those two Iraqi allies abstained on UNSCR 674 when it was urging a peaceful resolution of the crisis.

One month later, UNSCR 678 was adopted. China abstained and, predictably, Cuba and Yemen opposed it. This resolution is in marked contrast to UNSCR 674, as it authorised 'all necessary means' to expel Iraqi forces from Kuwait. Although the vote was not unanimous, it had sufficient support to give it credibility. Critics of UNSCR 678 argued that the resolution was invalid because China had abstained. While it is true that Article 27(3) of the Charter provides that decisions on substantive matters require the 'concurring votes of the Permanent members', the practice of the Security Council has been to ignore the abstention of a permanent member when applying this provision.[93] Although it was effectively open-ended as to how much force could be used, it did give the Iraqi leadership 'a pause of goodwill' of about one month and a half before it would implement the resolution. Again Saddam failed to take up this diplomatic opportunity.

The adoption of UNSCR 678 was not necessary in legal terms, as Article 42 of the UN Charter states that 'the Security Council ... may take such action by air, sea, or land forces as may be necessary to maintain or restore international peace and security', but it was essential in political terms. Certainly the US-led forces could have proceeded with *Desert Storm* without UNSCR 678, by simply invoking Article 51 of the UN Charter. However, there already was growing domestic opposition in the West to the US' role in the crisis and the growing possibility that force would be used to expel the Iraqi forces. Accordingly, the international community welcomed UNSCR 678, as it gave the US-led coalition the explicit authorisation to use force against Iraq. Australia supported UNSCR 678 as it had a strong preference that were it necessary to use military force it should be conducted with the explicit authority of the United Nations.[94]

---

[93] Greenwood, 'New World Order or Old?' p.166.
[94] Evans, 'The Case for Australian Participation' p.16.

Article 42 does not require that those military forces be controlled by the UN, i.e., that a Military Staff Committee be established (Article 47). Put differently, there is nothing preventing the UN from authorising a group of states from doing the job and commanding the force, i.e., UNSCR 678. The adoption of UNSCR 678 was necessary not only because Article 43 cannot oblige Member States to contribute to an international force, but because the establishment of a Military Staff Committee was effectively impossible. Not only had the Committee been moribund, but also for purely practical reasons the UN does not have the machinery for controlling operations such as *Desert Storm*. So the activation of the Committee was never seriously considered.[95] Moreover, this Committee is not likely to have much more success in the future, as it is unlikely - as was the case with *Desert Shield* and *Desert Storm* - that the US would want to commit its troops to the UN if an operation of a similar magnitude is considered.[96] The result was that, unlike the Korean operation, no UN flags or symbols were used in *Desert Shield* and *Desert Storm*. Moreover, the US was not responsible to the UN on a daily basis, but, according to UNSCR 678 (Para 4) only required 'to keep the Security Council regularly informed on the progress of actions undertaken'.

UNSCR 678 had two clear purposes. First, it sent an unambiguous message to Saddam that, if Iraq did not abide by all UN Security Council resolutions and Iraqi forces did not leave Kuwait by 15 January, force would be used to expel Iraq from the Emirate. Second, it gave the US-led forces a mandate to implement all twelve UN resolutions relating to Iraq. It was about restoring the legitimate and recognised government of Kuwait. It was not about punishing the Iraqi people who were as much a victim of Saddam's excesses as the Kuwaitis. UNSCR 678 was not about toppling Saddam, as to have tried to include that in the mandate would have run the risk of jeopardising the cohesion of the Coalition. Broadly speaking, the Coalition was a necessary marriage of convenience between democratic Western countries and autocratic Middle Eastern states to ensure that a precedent, the violation of a country's sovereignty, not be allowed to go unpunished. It was therefore essential that *Desert Storm* stay within the UN mandate.

The adoption of UNSCR 678 was not the first departure from the strict interpretation of Article 42. UNSCR 665 (Para 1) called upon

---

[95] Greenwood, 'Iraq's Invasion of Kuwait' p.42; B. Urquhart, 'The Role of the United Nations in the Iraq-Kuwait Conflict in 1990', in the Stockholm International Peace Research Institute *SIPRI Yearbook 1991. World Armaments and Disarmament* (Oxford: Oxford University Press, 1991) p.619; A. Parsons, 'The United Nations after the Gulf War' *The Round Table* 319 (1991) p.270.

[96] G. Evans, *Australia's Foreign Relations* (Melbourne: Melbourne University Press, 1991) p.94.

Member States co-operating with the government of Kuwait which are deploying maritime forces to the area to use such measures commensurate to the specific circumstances as may be necessary ... to halt all inward and outward shipping in order to inspect and verify their cargoes and destinations ...

This resolution delegated UN power to the US-led force and gave further legitimacy and endorsement to the multi-national force (MNF) which was established a few days after the Iraqi invasion of Kuwait. A number of countries had challenged the right of the United States-led naval force to prevent sanctions violations in the absence of a Security Council authorisation.[97] In any case, the US and the other participating countries could claim to be resorting to Article 51 ('Nothing in the present Charter shall impair the inherent right of individual or collective self-defence if an armed attack occurs against a Member of the UN'), as they had been officially requested assistance by Kuwait. The MNF not only contributed to deterring further Iraqi aggression, but provided the clearest signal to Iraq,

... reinforcing both the appearance and the reality of international solidarity against Saddam and giving new weight and credibility to sanctions enforcement as the preferred method of resolving the crisis.[98]

The Roles of the Security Council, the Secretary-General, the General Assembly and the International Court of Justice. The Security Council's role during the crisis was effectively limited to adopting resolutions which provided greater legal authority to measures which had already been taken by Member States under Article 51. UNSCR 665 sanctioned the US-led MNF and UNSCR 678 did likewise for *Desert Storm* (whose predecessor *Desert Shield* had been established using the same legal argument). However, while that may be the case, the Security Council was in no position to assure the protection of other Member States against possible Iraqi attacks and, therefore, had no other choice but to adopt resolutions which sanctioned the Coalition's actions.[99]

In July, using Article 34 ('The Security Council may investigate any dispute ... which might lead to international friction or give rise to a dispute'), the British Government suggested to its delegation at the United Nations that it look into the possibility of bringing the Iraq-Kuwait border issue up for discussion in the Security Council. Reportedly, there was no interest from other Security Council members.[100] The Security Council's failure to discuss this issue even after intelligence reports had confirmed that Iraq had amassed a very significant number of troops on its border with Kuwait was a major deficiency in the UN preventive diplomacy.

---

97   Greenwood, 'New World Order or Old?' p.161.
98   Evans, 'The Case for Australian Participation' p.15.
99   Urquhart, 'The Role of the United Nations' p.619.
100 Freedman & Karsh, *The Gulf Conflict* p.55.

Surprisingly, virtually no mention is made of this major failure in academic studies examining the Gulf crisis.

Similarly, according to public records, the UN Secretary-General did not engage in preventive diplomacy on this matter. This is even though, according to Article 99, he 'may bring to the attention of the Security Council any matter which in his opinion may threaten the maintenance of international peace and security'. And while the Secretary-General's diplomatic initiatives *after* the invasion were welcomed - albeit he had been directed to undertake diplomatic efforts under UNSCR 674 - it is surprising that the Secretary-General had not been more proactive *prior* to the invasion.

The General Assembly also played a very minor role. During the 49th Session of the General Assembly (18 September-21 December 1990), the General Assembly passed only *one* resolution specifically relating to Kuwait. It was adopted 144 for and one against. Having only one resolution on such an important matter not only reflects poorly on the General Assembly but the resolution (The situation of human rights in occupied Kuwait - 18 December), while rightfully concerned with the violation of human rights in Kuwait, hardly mentioned the invasion and annexation of Kuwait and did not even urge that Iraq comply with the Security Council resolution relating to the crisis. Only one other resolution (Respect for the principles of national sovereignty and non-interference in the internal affairs of States in their electoral processes - 18 December) is remotely applicable to the Kuwait crisis, as there is no direct reference to Kuwait in the resolution. It stated, *inter alia*, that the General Assembly should consider making use of the provisions of the Charter in order to discuss disputes or situations when appropriate. The General Assembly failed miserably in preventive diplomacy. However, one needs to recognise that Article 12 of the UN Charter was seen by the delegations as a definite constraint on General Assembly action ('While the Security Council is exercising in respect of any dispute or situation the functions assigned to it ... the General Assembly shall not make any recommendation with regard to that dispute or situation unless the Security Council so requests.') Indeed, even in negotiating the terms of the human rights resolution, there were concerns that Iraq would call the Legal Council to argue that the draft resolution was out of order.

The International Court of Justice (ICJ) played an even more minor role in the crisis. In this case, however, the court is not to be blamed as the jurisdiction of the Court is limited to cases which the parties have voluntarily submitted to it or which the Security Council has decided to refer to the Court (Articles 36 and 37). Neither Kuwait nor Iraq referred their dispute to the Court before or after the invasion. While it is understandable why Iraq did not submit the case to the ICJ, given its spurious legal claims, it is more difficult to understand Kuwait's failure to refer it to the ICJ. As for the Security Council, it still could have referred the case to the ICJ either for a judgement or an Advisory Opinion at the same time as *Desert Shield* was being established.

Had sanctions been given enough time to take effect? UNSCR 678, which authorised the use of force against Iraq, has been attacked on the ground that the Security Council should not have proceeded to a decision on the use of force without first establishing that sanctions were inadequate. Certainly, it is arguable whether by the time UNSCR 678 was adopted sanctions had been given enough time to take effect. Moreover, the Central Intelligence Agency (CIA) director reported to Congress in December 1990 that sanctions had dealt a 'serious blow' to Iraq's economy, shutting off more than 90 per cent of imports and 97 per cent of exports. In January 1991, however, he admitted that 'the ability of Iraqi ground forces to defend Kuwait is unlikely to be substantially eroded over the next six to twelve months'.[101]

While sanctions appeared to have started to take effect by the time UNSCR 678 had been adopted, it was generally assessed that it would have taken at least one year for sanctions to bite so deeply that Iraq would change its behaviour. And even then, given Saddam's attitude toward the needs of the Iraqi people, it is not certain that he would necessarily have changed his Kuwait policy because the Iraqi people were suffering economic hardship. The principal intention of the sanctions was to send a clear message to the Iraqi leadership that the international community was determined not to let the invasion and annexation of Kuwait go unpunished. Sanctions proceeded on a parallel track to peacemaking efforts and were vital in the pursuit of a peaceful resolution of the crisis.

But after nearly four months of sanctions, and certainly by the time UNSCR 678 went into effect, Saddam had shown no willingness to leave Kuwait or to take up any of the many diplomatic initiatives presented to him. Accordingly, the international community decided after 'a pause of goodwill', to proceed with force. It decided to do so because:

- Iraq would have continued the cruel occupation of Kuwait.

- The multinational military force needed a high level of preparedness, and keeping it at that level required heavy expenses. Moreover, a military operation in the summer presented greater difficulty.

- Potential international erosion of outrage with Iraq's invasion.

- The Iraqi people would have suffered even more with continued sanctions.

- The detrimental effect sanctions were having on Third World states.[102]

---

[101] Greenwood, 'New World Order or Old?' pp.166-7.
[102] Evans, 'The Case for Australian Participation' p.22.

A determination that sanctions would not be sufficient was implicit in UNSCR 678. That determination was one which the Security Council could make. Article 42 allows the Security Council to take military action if 'measures provided for in Article 41 (sanctions) would be inadequate'.

Were negotiations sufficiently exhausted before activating UNSCR 678? As discussed earlier, Saddam had ample opportunities to take up any of one of many diplomatic initiatives presented to him. He continued to reject all offers, however, including the ones that came very close to accommodating his 12 August 'linkage' initiative. So, not only was diplomacy being actively pursued by the international community right up to the eve of hostilities, but, according to UNSCR 674 (29 October), all Member States were called upon to pursue their efforts with the specific aim of reaching a peaceful solution. It was only at the end of November that the UN decided that force should be used as a means of last resort. It was hoped that after UNSCR 678 was adopted the Iraqi leadership would change its policy and withdraw from Kuwait.

Critics would argue that, on the contrary, the adoption of UNSCR 678 left Saddam with little room to manoeuvre, as the international community now threatened Iraq with military action if it did not depart Kuwait, and agreeing to leave Kuwait, even under generous conditions, would have been difficult for Saddam without appearing to be avoiding a military confrontation. It appears, however, that all along nothing would have swayed Saddam from changing his policy, short of the international community meeting his demands, and most of them were unacceptable. So while diplomatic efforts were limited by the need to find an 'honourable' way out for Saddam without 'rewarding' him for the invasion, within that framework negotiations were nevertheless exhausted fully.

Why did Diplomacy fail?

The Iraqi leadership's perception of itself and the world. At the time of the invasion of Kuwait, Saddam was at the height of his political career. He had been at the helm since 1979 and had foiled many coup attempts. He had led his country through a gruelling eight-year war with Iran. And even after the war Iraq still had a massive army; he could put together an army of approximately one million men.[103] Iraq had weapons of mass destruction, and had even threatened to hit Israel. Iraq had vast oil reserves, and at the 28 July OPEC meeting Saddam had the other members agree to a production quota. In May 1990, Saddam had chaired the Arab Summit in Baghdad, confirming that he had become a central player in Arab politics. All in all, Iraq was the largest regional power and it had the capability to intimidate its neighbours.

---

[103] Freedman & Karsh, *The Gulf Conflict* p.179.

Iraq's actual military and regional political power, and the objectives it could potentially fulfil with it, were distorted, however, by Saddam's view of the world. Saddam's perception of the world has been influenced greatly by the conspiratorial, underground and ruthless nature of the Ba'ath regime. Saddam has never travelled outside the Arab world. This explains much of his blinkered and narrow view of international affairs. The Iraqi leadership did not understand the dramatic shift in international relations in the post-Cold War period and the change of mood at the UN. Nevertheless, they should have been aware of these changes, given that it was US-USSR cooperation at the UN which led in 1988 to the imposition of a ceasefire in the Iran-Iraq War.

The Iraqi leadership did not take into account either of the radical changes that were taking place in the Soviet Union. At the international level, Moscow had effectively admitted that it could no longer compete ideologically and economically with the US.[104] This would influence strongly Moscow's approach towards the Gulf Crisis. Also important was the Soviet Union's expanded relations with the countries of the region, particularly Iran and Kuwait, over the last few years. Moscow did not wish to jeopardise those budding relations by supporting Iraq on Kuwait. Accordingly, in July the Soviets stressed to Saddam that 'there are no conflicts, no matter how difficult, that cannot be settled across the negotiating table'.[105]

According to Primakov, Gorbachev's personal envoy, Saddam was surprised by the Soviet Union's reaction to the invasion. Saddam believed that Moscow would not endorse American coercion nor agree to UN resolutions which authorised the use of force. His expectations are difficult to reconcile with his own acknowledgment in February 1990 of the decline of the Soviet Union and the emergence of the US as the only remaining superpower. It is not clear how he could later expect that the USSR would not cooperate with the US. However, even when it was evident that Moscow and Washington were cooperating, Saddam continued to reject Gorbachev's diplomatic initiatives.[106]

Saddam also had a poor understanding of the US and of American domestic politics. His fundamental misreading of the US - which ended up costing him dearly - was his belief that the Americans would not have the resolve to go through with a war against Iraq. He believed strongly that the 'Vietnam syndrome' still determined heavily US foreign policy and, therefore, the US President would not wish to get entangled in a far away war. He clearly had failed to realise that eight years of President Reagan had to all intents and purposes expunged that reluctance to intervene militarily abroad. This was confirmed by the fact that although the television was widely reporting the possibility of Iraq using chemical

---

[104] Bell, 'The Gulf and the Great Powers' p.34.
[105] Freedman & Karsh, *The Gulf Conflict* p.77.
[106] Stein, 'Deterrence and Compellence in the Gulf' pp.173-4.

weapons, American public opinion still supported President Bush's position.

Another contributing factor in President's Bush determination to punish Iraq, but which does not necessarily mean that Bush did not believe in the correctness of the US position, was President Bush's low standing in the polls. And while Saddam could afford to disregard popularity polls in Iraq, if he had been more aware of their importance in the US it might have altered his view about President Bush's resolve to engage military force. President Bush was also keen to demolish the 'wimp' image which he had to deal with throughout his presidency. The media had done nothing to diminish that image either. President Bush would later successfully use the electronic media, especially during the war, to break the image. When Saddam finally realised that Bush would indeed go to war, he apparently did not expect the five weeks of intensive aerial bombing which preceded the land war. He based that judgement on the fact that there already was intense domestic debate in the US about the appropriateness of the use of force to drive Iraq out of Kuwait.[107]

From Saddam's perspective President Bush's lack of resolve was confirmed when he made the 'extra mile for peace' initiative. Saddam saw this diplomatic move as an American climb-down, as it was offered at a time when Iraq was at its lowest negotiating point. The government-controlled press in Iraq declared that

> The enemy of God, the arrogant President of the United States, George Bush, had consistently opposed dialogue ... His initiative is [therefore] a submission to Iraq's demand ... [108]

In any case, Saddam strongly believed that there was a US conspiracy against him and that Washington was determined to topple him. In his meeting with Ambassador Glaspie, Saddam said that

> I don't say the President himself - but certain parties who had links with the intelligence community and with the State Department ... some circles are gathering information on who might be Saddam Hussein's successor.[109]

Saddam's belief that there was a US conspiracy against him was confirmed by Iraqi Foreign Minister Aziz, who stated after the war:

> The decision [to occupy all of Kuwait] was predicated on Saddam's belief that it would make no difference whether Iraq chose to take part or all of Kuwait. The Americans had decided long before August 2nd to crush Iraq, and there was nothing [our] government could do to stop them ... We expected an American military retaliation from the very beginning.

---

[107] Ibid. p.174.
[108] Freedman & Karsh, *The Gulf Conflict* p.236.
[109] Stein, 'Deterrence and Compellence in the Gulf' p.164.

Within the leadership we had no dispute - we agreed that we had to go all the way.[110]

Saddam believed the US was behind Kuwait's decision not to abide by its OPEC quota and its refusal to grant Iraq debt forgiveness. Saddam saw Washington's failure to encourage Kuwait to be more forthcoming on the outstanding bilateral issues as proof that it was determined to topple him. While the US had indeed secretly sold equipment to Iran in 1986, the Bush administration had opposed the Senate's drive to impose economic measures against Iraq and had hardly reacted to Saddam's appalling treatment of the Kurds. So it is not clear how Saddam could conclude that there was an American conspiracy against him.[111] But the fact of the matter is that believing that there was a conspiracy against him meant that any US diplomatic initiative would have had little chance to succeed.

Another fundamental misjudgement on the part of Saddam was that he overestimated his ability to appeal to the 'Arab street', with the manipulation of Arab symbols such as showing concern for the Palestinians, promoting Arab nationalism and threatening to 'burn half of Israel'. And while there was a degree of popular support for him across the Arab world, it was not enough to stop Arab leaders, such as Syria's Assad, Egypt's Mubarak and, of course, Saudi Arabia's King Fahd, from participating in the Western-led anti-Iraq military force. In that regard, Saddam made a major strategic miscalculation in assuming that after Iraq had invaded and annexed Kuwait no Arab country would dare ask for US support, let alone allow hundreds of thousands of Western troops to be based in Saudi Arabia.[112]

Saddam also believed that he would be able to get the Arab participants in the anti-Iraq Coalition to break away on the issue of Israel. But their own self-interest in seeing that a border violation precedent not be established, and US financial inducement, convinced the Arab participants that they had more to gain in the long term by siding with the US. Whether the Coalition would have survived if Israel had decided to retaliate for the Iraqi Scud attacks is a moot point.

The Iraqi leadership's misreading of the world's reaction to the invasion was compounded by its overestimation of Iraq's military capability. These two factors led Saddam to overplay his hand. Saddam believed that eight years of war against Iran had prepared his army to withstand any Western onslaught. The Iran-Iraq War, however, was a conflict in which the two countries used World War I-type techniques of warfare. The Western forces used highly sophisticated weaponry against demoralised Iraqi forces, many of whom were poorly trained and poorly equipped conscripts. He also underestimated the Western forces' resolve, capability and massive air

---

[110] Ibid. p.166.
[111] Springborg, 'Origins of the Gulf Crisis' pp.228-9; Stein, 'Deterrence and Compellence in the Gulf' p.162.
[112] Heikal, *Illusions of Triumph* p.192.

power. Airpower had played only a minor role in the conduct of the Iran-Iraq War.[113]

Saddam's many misjudgements were reinforced by the advice which his sycophants and members of the Revolutionary Command Council provided him. Given that it was in no one's self-interest to contradict Saddam, it is understandable that they all gave him self-serving advice. Nevertheless, Saddam always felt that, while he would of course prefer to keep Kuwait without having to go to war, his position at home would be, at best, extremely precarious were he to depart Kuwait *before* hostilities had started. Saddam said so to Soviet envoy Primakov, when he stated that 'the Iraqi people will not forgive me for unconditional withdrawal from Kuwait'.[114]

So Saddam's misjudgements and skewed perception of other countries' behaviour, his personal dislike of Kuwaitis, the low-key US threats and his political insecurity were he to withdraw unconditionally, meant that war was a virtual certainty. Finally, Saddam's firm belief that, while the US was keen to topple him, it would not have the resolve to follow that through by fighting a long war with Iraq, meant that from Saddam's perspective he had nothing to lose and everything to win by taking over Kuwait. Put differently, the potential economic rewards (more vital resources, greater ability to control the pricing of oil and a longer coast line with access to the Gulf) from annexing Kuwait far outweighed any possible international backlash to the invasion. Accordingly, preventive diplomacy and diplomatic efforts at peacemaking following the invasion had little chance to succeed.

The International Community's perception of the Iraqi leadership. Diplomacy also failed because of the international community's mixed and confused signals (particularly from the US), its distorted perception of Saddam and the incorrect assessment of his intentions. These signals in turn reinforced the Iraqi leadership's skewed perceptions and incorrect assessments of how the world would react to an invasion of Kuwait, which in turn was factored into Iraq's cost and benefit analysis of annexing Kuwait.

The US sent mixed and confusing signals *before* and *after* the invasion. Between 1988 and 1990 Washington generally gave the Iraqi leadership either the benefit of the doubt or turned a blind eye to some of its domestic excesses. For example, the US administration's reaction to Saddam's human rights abuses, particularly following the widely-known use of chemical weapons against its own Kurdish population, was relatively muted. President Reagan opposed and defeated a bill in the US House of Representatives which would have imposed economic sanctions against Iraq for having used poisonous gas to subdue the Kurds. The US administration also opposed Congress' attempt to punish Iraq for violating

---

[113] Stein, 'Deterrence and Compellence in the Gulf' pp.174-5.
[114] Freedman & Karsh, *The Gulf Conflict* p.431.

bilateral economic agreements and attempting to smuggle weapons technology out of the US. Instead, the US granted large loans which enabled Baghdad to purchase $5.5 billion in US crops and livestock and extended $270 million in government guaranteed credit from the Export-Import Bank to buy American goods.[115]

As was discussed earlier, right up to the invasion of Kuwait the US continued to send signals to Iraq which must have made it appear to Saddam as if the US were willing to maintain good relations with Iraq at all cost. For example, on 25 July, at a meeting with Saddam, US Ambassador Glaspie gave the impression that the US did not care too much about the Iraqi-Kuwait dispute. On 27 July President Bush wrote a letter to Saddam in which he mildly warned Iraq not to use force to resolve its dispute with Kuwait, promised US friendship and expressed a keen interest in improving bilateral relations. On the same day Bush opposed a Senate vote imposing economic sanctions against Iraq. On 31 July, US Assistant Secretary of State Kelly also adopted a conciliatory tone and told Congress that, while the US supported the Gulf states' 'independence and security' and called 'for a peaceful solution to all disputes', the US had no treaty obligation to use American forces to defend Kuwait. In light of these signals, it appears that US policy makers believed that the best way to have Saddam modify his domestic policies would be by cajoling him rather than by threatening him.

Not all signals emanating from Washington were positive from Baghdad's perspective, however, and this certainly must have led to some confusion in Iraq. For example, between January 1989 and August 1990 the US began placing increasingly severe restrictions on the export to Iraq of technology with potential military applications. In 1989 the US Government stopped the export of an advanced computer, and in April 1990 the US Commerce Department cancelled an aerospace trade mission to Iraq. The Congress was also getting increasingly impatient with Saddam's domestic policies and there was growing pressure on President Bush to change his policy toward Iraq.[116] On 24 July the US dispatched refuelling planes to the UAE and announced that there would be a joint naval exercise with the UAE. These 'negative' signals would have confirmed Saddam's perception that there was a US conspiracy against him and that President Bush was determined to get him. And while there were still many 'positive' signals coming from Washington, Saddam may have decided to pre-empt what he must have thought was a certain change in US policy toward Iraq in the near future. Invading Kuwait at that point, when the US was still ambivalent about Baghdad, would have been perceived by the Iraqi leadership as an opportune moment to act.

Poor and incorrect Western intelligence assessment of Saddam's true intentions and the significance of the troop movements was a major

---

[115] Springborg, 'Origins of the Gulf Crisis' p.227.
[116] Ibid. p.229.

contributory factor to the failure of preventive diplomacy. For if the international community had known how determined Saddam was to act on Iraq's grievances, it could have engaged in more proactive preventive diplomacy.

The general belief was that Iraq had neither the resources nor the desire to take Kuwait, and that it would continue to conduct a moderate foreign policy.[117] Moreover, the international community believed that it would not be in Saddam's interest to invade Kuwait and, therefore, it would be irrational for him to do so. While Western intelligence assessment that Iraq's troop movements in late July were only for intimidation purposes has been subsequently confirmed by Iraqi Foreign Minister Aziz, they failed to assess that from Saddam's perspective Iraq was left with no choice but to invade Kuwait following the breakdown of negotiations at the 31 July Jeddah meeting.[118] Furthermore, the international community's incorrect assessment of the Iraqi leadership's perception of the world and the international community's reaction to an invasion of Kuwait, led it to send either wrong or weak signals to Saddam. This in turn reinforced the Iraqi leadership's incorrect assessment of what would be the world's reaction to Iraq's invasion.

The Arab states also failed to send Saddam unambiguous signals. Most Arab states were willing to accommodate some of Saddam's demands, for example Saudi Arabia's decision to forgive Iraq's debts. Generally speaking, the Arab leaders were willing to accommodate Saddam because they did not believe that Iraq would consider invading Kuwait, as no post-World War II Arab country had ever invaded another. But the Arabs' willingness to accommodate Iraq would have sent Saddam the wrong signal about what would be their attitude to Iraq's invasion of Kuwait. Furthermore, the Arabs' eagerness to find an 'Arab solution' to the crisis would have strengthened the Iraqi leadership's belief that the Arabs would neither seek Western assistance nor allow Western forces to be stationed in an Arab country. Kuwait's and other Arab countries' failure to evoke Article 35 of the UN Charter, which allows Member States to bring a dispute which is likely to endanger the maintenance of international peace to the attention of the Security Council or the General Assembly, *prior* to the invasion would have reinforced Saddam's belief that the countries in the region wanted to find an 'Arab solution' at all cost and would not consider outside intervention.

Throughout the crisis, and notwithstanding pressure from the other Arab states, Kuwait maintained a hard line. While from Kuwait's perspective it would have been giving in to blackmail to accept some of Saddam's demands, particularly with regard to the Rumaila oil field and the possible leasing of the two islands, from Iraq's perspective the Emir's attitude was arrogant and provocative. The Kuwaiti approach to the

---

[117] Ibid. p.223.
[118] Stein, 'Deterrence and Compellence in the Gulf' p.158.

matter, particularly at the 31 July meeting, would have reaffirmed Saddam's disdain for them. Iraqi Foreign Minister Aziz observed about the Kuwaiti attitude at the meeting: '... they were very strange, very pompous, very obstinate'.[119] The Iraqis' negative perception of Kuwait, coupled with the Kuwaiti refusal to enter into negotiations with Iraq on the outstanding bilateral grievances, would have increased further the already high level of tension. The signal this sent Iraq was that nothing would bring the Kuwaitis to negotiate seriously, and given the Iraqi perception that it would probably be able to get away with it, from Baghdad's perspective Iraq had nothing to lose and everything to win by invading Kuwait.

Could more have been done to prevent the crisis from developing into an armed conflict?

The United Nations. The UN failed in preventive diplomacy prior to the invasion. Little was either initiated by the UN and Members States did not refer the matter to the UN. After the invasion, the UN's peacemaking diplomacy was limited to containing the conflict and trying to find a peaceful resolution within the framework of the Security Council resolutions relating to the crisis. The UN's failure in preventive diplomacy is that much more deplorable given that Iraq-Kuwait differences did not suddenly emerge; they had been festering on and off for the last 30 years. Early UN involvement could have led the international community to send different signals to Iraq and possibly increase the chances of avoiding the invasion and the subsequent military confrontation.

The Member States failed to use the UN organs to engage in preventive diplomacy. For example, Kuwait or any other country or organisation could and should have resorted to Article 35 of the UN Charter to bring the matter to the attention of the Security Council or the General Assembly. Except for Britain - which considered bringing it to the Security Council but eventually decided against it due to a lack of interest on the part of the Council members - no one brought the subject up for discussion at the Security Council.

Kuwait probably did not bring it to the attention of the Security Council for fear of sending Iraq a wrong signal. The Kuwaiti Government might have thought that bringing the matter up to the Security Council would have given the perception that perhaps Iraq's claims, legal or otherwise, might have some validity and that the matter was not as clear cut as it might appear. Certainly, the Kuwaitis did not wish to give any credibility to Iraq's claims. Another important reason would have been Kuwait's reluctance to lose control over the matter, as it probably would have, if it had allowed the Security Council to examine the matter.

---

[119] Ibid. pp.156-7.

Saudi Arabia, other Arab states, the GCC and the Arab League could have referred the matter to the Security Council prior to the invasion. However, throughout the crisis, and certainly prior to the invasion, there was a keen desire among Arab states to find an 'Arab solution' to the matter. Accordingly, there would have been a great reluctance on the part of Arab states and organisations to have the UN get involved in the issue, as this would have been tantamount to an admission that an 'Arab solution' was not possible. The Arab states, particularly Saudi Arabia and the other GCC members, would also have been reluctant to bring the matter up to the UN, lest they appeared to be interfering in Kuwait's internal affairs or making an oblique criticism of Kuwait's handling of the affair.

The United States also could have brought the matter up at the Security Council. And with the intelligence it had available, it could have argued for early UN involvement in the matter. Moreover, by sharing the intelligence it would have given the opportunity for others on the Security Council to assess the situation on the ground and possibly avoid misinterpreting the military significance of the troop movement.

The Secretary-General and the UN Secretariat also did poorly in their execution of preventive diplomacy. For example, on 19 July the Kuwait Government suggested to the Secretary-General that an Arab Committee be set up at the UN to examine the Iraq-Kuwait dispute. Oddly, the Secretary-General did not follow this up. Kuwait's request should have been a clear signal to Secretary-General de Cuellar that the Kuwait Government was worried and that the dispute was quickly approaching crisis level. Kuwait's approach had come two days after Saddam publicly stated that Iraq may 'need to resort to effective action' and one day after Iraq's demands had been made public.

As far as is known, the Secretary-General did not engage in informal discussion and consultation with Iraq and Kuwait prior to the invasion. This is a major failure given that the Secretary-General has 'a broad discretion to conduct inquiries and to engage in informal diplomatic activity in regard to matters which may threaten peace and security'.[120] However, even if he believed the problem did not warrant behind-the-scene discussions, he should have resorted to Article 99 of the UN Charter and brought the matter up at the Security Council. Why he failed on both counts is difficult to understand given Kuwait's suggestion and the rapid deterioration in Iraq-Kuwait relations. Perhaps the Secretary-General failed to act early because the then Office of Research and the Collection of Information (ORCI), which was 'set up to collect and analyse information, to provide "early warning" and to suggest options to the Secretary-General'

---

[120] G. Forrester, 'Some Aspects of Preventive Diplomacy' paper presented at a seminar on International Peacekeeping (Canberra: 22 March 1993) p.5.

failed to perform its function.[121] As far is known, the ORCI did not refer the matter to the Secretary-General.

The General Assembly and the International Court of Justice did not perform well either; however, both these UN organs are not well suited for preventive diplomacy. As discussed above, the General Assembly was constrained by Article 12 of the UN Charter which limited its ability to make recommendations on issues which were then being debated in the Security Council. The General Assembly passed two resolutions, including one on human rights in Kuwait, but these had no impact on diplomatic activity or developments on the ground.

As discussed above, the International Court of Justice played no role in the whole matter. Given that Iraq-Kuwait differences had been present since Kuwait's independence in 1961, it is surprising that the matter had not been brought to the ICJ either by one of the two parties or the Security Council for a judgement or at least an Advisory Opinion. And while the ICJ's decisions are not binding, at least it could have assisted preventive diplomacy. Certainly, the case should have been brought to the ICJ following the invasion.

Regional Organisations. Prior to the invasion, the GCC and the Arab League engaged in very limited preventive diplomacy. Although the GCC believes in the principle of collective self-defence, the it gave no signal prior to the invasion that an attack against Kuwait would be considered tantamount to an attack against all other GCC members. To be fair to the GCC, this is probably because no one expected Iraq to follow that course of action. Nevertheless, this failure to send a clear signal to Iraq may have reinforced Saddam's belief that the invasion would only cause a muted response from the GCC countries, particularly from Saudi Arabia. Following the invasion the GCC played virtually no role in diplomatic efforts to find a peaceful solution.

Similarly, the Arab League played hardly any role in preventive diplomacy, although it has the mechanism to do so. According to the charter, the League's Council *'shall* mediate in all differences which threaten to lead to war between two Member States ...' The League did not pursue this duty, however, even after Saddam's 15 July threat, the Iraqi Foreign Minister Aziz's Memorandum to League Secretary-General Kibli and Kibli's belief that the Iraqi statements were tantamount to war.

But it would have been difficult to envisage the League play any effective role in preventive diplomacy given the divisions within the Arab 'nation'. These divisions were confirmed after the invasion when the League split down the middle when voting on resolutions condemning Iraq's actions and when only the UAE responded positively to Kuwait's request for the immediate application of the Arab League's Defence Pact.

---

[121] C. Peck, 'Preventive Diplomacy: A Perspective for the 1990s' paper prepared for the Australian Foreign Minister (Canberra: 1993) p.11.

Conclusion

The human and financial cost of the Gulf War demonstrated dramatically how essential it is that there be effective and credible mechanisms for the implementation of preventive diplomacy. While preventive diplomacy might not have worked in this case (given the Iraqi leadership's perception of itself and the international community), if a mechanism had existed it would have increased the chances of war being avoided. Accordingly, if preventive diplomacy is to be effective, it is essential that the international community take a more active role in disputes *before* they reach crisis level. This can be done in several ways.

First, Member States of the UN, including the parties to a dispute, should resort to Article 35 of the UN Charter and bring the issue to the attention of the Security Council as soon as possible. While this means that the parties to the dispute would probably lose control over the issue, there would be a higher probability that military confrontation could be avoided, given that the international community would then be in a position to send clear UN-sanctioned signals to the parties involved in the dispute.

Second, the UN Secretary-General must engage in informal discussions with the parties to a dispute *before* it reaches crisis level. The Secretary-General has the authority and the credibility to do so when he believes this is necessary. If this approach does not bear results, the Secretary-General should then resort to Article 99 of the UN Charter which allows him formally to bring the matter up at the Security Council.

Third, the International Court of Justice should be used more often. In cases where a dispute has been present for many years, and has the potential to lead to a major crisis, as in this case study, it is essential that either the parties to the dispute or the Security Council bring the matter to the ICJ for a judgement or an Advisory Opinion.

Last, while regional organisations should play a greater role in preventive diplomacy, given that often they are divided and lack credibility and authority, the UN will often be the most suitable forum to deal effectively with a dispute *before* it becomes a crisis.

3 Somalia: International Intervention in a Failed State

BRUCE LENDON

At the end of 1991 Somalia was described as the 'world's greatest humanitarian emergency'. The Somali state had collapsed completely, Somali society was consumed by a many-sided civil war and the country was faced with mass starvation. Over the next year the international community struggled to develop a response to the challenges presented by this situation. The international community has found that it cannot ignore the disaster in Somalia, but its assumption of responsibility for dealing with that disaster has been reluctant and halting. This case study examines the reasons for the failure of the Somali state, the resulting humanitarian crisis and the successive stages in the international community's response to it. In particular, the study examines the reaction of the United Nations to the crisis and some of the problems in its performance in Somalia. The study concludes that there are several pressures for and limitations on UN intervention in crises generated by a failed state. The management of these pressures and limitations will be critical in determining the success or failure of an intervention.

Background

The clan system

A brief outline of the Somali clan system is necessary for an understanding of the current conflicts in Somalia. Unlike the populations of most African states, Somalis are usually said to possess all the major traits of a common nationality. They share a single language and ethnic identity and a largely homogeneous culture. They also possess a highly developed sense of collective unity which is rooted in their belief in descent from a common ancestor. Because they have formed the basis of group formation and loyalty, the genealogical ties that are derived from this belief have played a central role in Somali history.

The Somalis are divided into six major clan families: the Darod, Hawiye, Isaaq, Dir, Rahanweyn and Digil. These clan families are further divided into clans (such as the Marehan, Siad Barre's clan, and the Ogaden), sub-clans and numerous smaller lineage groups. The first four clan families traditionally were nomadic or semi-nomadic pastoralists, but an increasing minority have become settled farmers over the past thirty years.[1] The latter two groups are settled in the intra-riverine region of southern Somalia and rely on a mixture of cattle husbandry and cultivation. Bantu agricultural communities, outside the clan structure but attached to it by client relationships, are also settled in this region. It is these settled communities which have suffered most from the civil wars and famine of the past three years.

Because they were too large, and usually too dispersed, the clan families had no political or economic functions. The most effective unit of cooperation was the *diya* paying group, consisting of kinsmen bound together by contractual obligation for the payment and receipt of blood compensation. Conflict amongst Somalis usually took place at the sub-clan level or below, often involved intra-clan battles and could feature alliances with groups from other clans or clan families. There are apparently no historic examples of warfare between the major clan families.[2]

Lineage segmentation is both the foundation and major weakness of Somali nationalism. This segmentation has been described as '... both centripetal and centrifugal, at once drawing the Somalis into a powerful social fabric of kinship affinity and cultural solidarity while setting them against one another in a complicated maze of antagonistic clan interests'.[3] The strong sense of common identity and the exceptionally fissile nature of Somali society are the outcome of these bonds.

The values associated with this social system have had a profound impact on the political culture. Structural instability is regarded as the norm and social relations institutionalise instability. A leading Somali scholar has written that

> The law of lineage segmentation requires that political interest groups should be in a state of constant motion, expanding or contracting according to the stakes at hand. The stakes may involve competition

---

[1] H.D. Nelson, *Somalia: A Country Study* (Washington, DC: American University, 1982) p.82.
[2] H.M. Adam, 'Somalia: Militarism, Warlordism or Democracy?' *Review of African Political Economy* 54 (1992) p.12.
[3] D. Laitin and S. Samatar, *Somalia: Nation in Search of a State* (Boulder, Col.: Westview Press, 1987) pp.30-1.

over grazing grounds ... or, alternatively, struggle for the resources of the central state.[4]

This 'pastoral ethos' of anarchic individualism in the context of group competition has dominated Somali political life.

Independence and the 1969 Coup

The modern state of Somalia was formed in 1960 by the union of British Somaliland and the Italian Trust Territory. Three Somali inhabited areas, French Somaliland (now the Republic of Djibouti), the Ogaden area of Ethiopia and Kenya's Northern Frontier District, lay outside the boundaries of the new state. The quest to unify all Somalis in a single state was a constant theme in the first two decades after independence, dominating all other political issues. This irredentism has been a continuing source of tension between Somalia and its neighbours.

The constitution of the new state was substantially drafted by Italian and American experts and reflected the usual liberal models. A President elected by the National Assembly served as head of state for a six year term, could dissolve the assembly and had the right to appoint and dismiss the prime minister. The government, composed of the prime minister and subordinate ministers, had the responsibility for implementing the laws of the National Assembly. A judicial system, drawing on Italian, British and Shariah legal traditions, was established independent of the executive and legislature.

The government system established by the constitution was a careful attempt to balance the interests of the different groups in the new state, but because it was associated with the south was nevertheless viewed with suspicion by northerners. A national referendum in 1961 ratified the constitution, but a majority of northerners voted against it.

Although the nationalism on which Somalia was founded aspired to eliminate traditional divisions, the clans rapidly assumed a new importance as mediating institutions between the individual and the state. Governments were constructed on the basis of balanced clan membership (and fell if this was not achieved), political parties were clan based and resources distributed according to clan power. The larger clan families assumed a political significance as politicians exploited ethnic loyalties to build parliamentary and electoral alliances.[5] The resulting instability, corruption, nepotism and governmental paralysis rapidly discredited the parliamentary system.

In October 1969 the President, Abdirashid Ali Shermarke, was assassinated as the result of a private grudge. To the relief of most

---

[4] S. Samatar, *Somalia: A Nation in Turmoil* (London: Minority Rights Group Report, 1991) p.25.

[5] Sixty-four parties, representing the sixty-four important lineage and sub-lineage groups, contested the last free elections in 1969. Ibid., p.17.

Somalis, the army took advantage of the squabbling which followed to stage a coup. The constitution was suspended, a Supreme Revolutionary Council (SRC) established and the army commander, Mohamed Siad Barre, named President. Siad Barre was to rule in an increasingly personal and autocratic manner for the next twenty-one years.

Siad's regime initially enjoyed considerable popularity. The SRC undertook a campaign against government corruption, adopted 'scientific socialism' as its ideology and introduced a number of long delayed social reforms, including a script for the Somali language, mass literacy campaigns, the extension of primary and secondary education and the implementation of legal equality for women. Siad's government also sought to eliminate clan divisions by forbidding references to clan names and membership in 1971.

At the same time, the regime installed an elaborate repressive mechanism modelled on those of the Soviet Union and East Germany. The National Security Service (NSS), created in 1970, established an extensive network of informers and was given wide powers, including the right to detain people without trial. Moreover, despite his attempt to eradicate clan based politics, Siad himself relied heavily on a coalition involving his own Marehan clan, the Ogaden and the Dolbahante.

Somalia's role in the Cold War

Shuttling back and forth between the superpower blocs, Somalia was an unusually promiscuous client state during the Cold War. Its foreign policy, however, was almost entirely driven by the nationalist desire to unite all Somalis in one state. In pursuit of this aim Somalia successively alienated its two colonial neighbours, Britain and France in the early 1960s, fought a border war with Ethiopia in 1964, and supported an ethnic Somali insurgency against independent Kenya in the mid-1960s. When the United States and other Western powers rebuffed its requests for military assistance, Somalia began to develop a security relationship with the Soviet Union. This relationship was substantially strengthened after the 1969 coup and in 1974 Somalia signed a Treaty of Friendship and Cooperation with the USSR. In return for military supplies and advice, the Soviet Union was allowed to build a naval base at Berbera on Somalia's northern coast.

Although the Somalis claimed territory belonging to each of their neighbours, the area that held greatest significance for them was the Ogaden region of Ethiopia. As that country collapsed into turmoil after the 1974 revolution, the Somali Government and military thought they saw their chance to unify the Ogaden with the republic. Following a successful guerrilla campaign by the Western Somali Liberation Front (WSLF), the Somali armed forces invaded the Ogaden in July 1977. The Somalis rapidly drove the demoralised Ethiopians out of much of the region, but in August the Soviet Union cut off all military aid and switched their support to the Ethiopians. Since the 1974 revolution the Ethiopian regime had progressively moved closer to the Eastern bloc and, faced with a choice between Somalia and the Ethiopians, the Soviet Union assessed that the latter were the more useful clients in the region. Assisted by Soviet advice and materiel, and by Cuban troops, the Ethiopians forced the Somalis out of the Ogaden by March 1978.

During 1977 Siad desperately tried to obtain US support to counter the loss of Soviet patronage. The US agreed to supply defensive equipment and economic aid on the condition that the Somalis withdrew from the Ogaden, but only small amounts of military aid were actually delivered in the first few years after the Ogaden War. The Carter administration remained wary of Siad Barre's irredentism and doubted his reliability as an ally.[6] As the US developed its Rapid Deployment Force for use in the Middle East, however, it became interested in obtaining access to the former Soviet naval and air facilities at Berbera. As the US already controlled Diego Garcia and was negotiating for rights in Kenya and Oman, these facilities were regarded as useful rather than essential. Siad Barre sought $2 billion in material aid in exchange for the rights to use the facilities, but was compelled to accept the US offer of $40 million.

As part of its more confrontationist stance, the Reagan administration pursued a policy of countering Soviet influence in the Horn of Africa. After Somali rebels and Ethiopian troops briefly invaded Somalia in 1982, the Reagan administration increased its military support for Somalia. Over the next few years, military assistance became a significant part of the US aid program in Somalia. The Berbera facilities, however, never became a vital part of the US strategic planning in the Indian Ocean and US military personnel were not permanently stationed there. Somalia's chief strategic value to the US lay in its denial to the Soviet Union.

The decline of the regime: 1978-88

The defeat in the Ogaden War severely damaged the prestige of the regime and resulted in a resurgence of tribalism as different groups blamed each other for the disaster.[7] Clans excluded from the system of alliances underpinning the government became increasingly disaffected and the Ethiopians were quick to encourage opposition movements such as the Somali Salvation Democratic Front (SSDF) and the Somali National Movement (SNM). Siad responded by exploiting the divisions and competition inherent in Somali society. Clans identified with the opposition movements were 'punished', either by the military or by inciting traditional rivals against them. The Isaaq, concentrated in the north, suffered particularly severely in this period. The leading British authority on Somalia, I.M. Lewis has noted that the north '... began to

---

[6] Laitin and Samatar, *Somalia* pp.143-4.
[7] I.M. Lewis, 'The Ogaden and the Fragility of Segmentary Somali Nationalism' *Horn of Africa* 13, 1-2 (January/June 1990) p.57.

look and feel like a colony under a foreign military tyranny'.[8] Other clans were bought off by the constant reshuffling of political and bureaucratic appointments or by commercial incentives. Siad also relied increasingly on his own family and clan.

The economic policies pursued by the regime intensified inter-clan competition. Those groups with access to political power enriched themselves by plundering the extensive government controlled sector of the economy and foreign aid. Economic reward became a major incentive to participate in the regime. In contrast, groups identified with the opposition, such as the Isaaq clan family and the Majerteyn clan, were largely excluded from access to government resources. Even amongst these groups, however, Siad played a careful game of divide and rule. Less prominent members of these groups were promoted or rewarded in a constant effort to pit clan against clan, lineage against lineage. Government monopolies on traditional trading activities encouraged smuggling, the organisation of which was conducted on clan lines. Alex de Waal, a former director of Africa Watch, has argued that by the late 1980s, '... the state and the commercial elites associated with it were obtaining their wealth, not through production, but by expropriation ...' Commentators quipped that Somalia was no longer a state - it was a process of commercial predation.[9]

These strategies helped maintain Siad's power, but seriously exacerbated clan rivalry and increased clan identification. In a warning that proved grimly accurate, Laitin and Samatar wrote in 1985 that

> ... interclan enmity is worse and potentially more violent than in any period of Somalia's history ... Because interclan rivalries focus societal attention on the distribution of jobs and contracts and not on the creation of new wealth or development of the society as a whole, this enmity is a disease that has seriously weakened the body politic.[10]

Rebellion against Siad Barre: 1988-1991

The Somali National Movement rebellion

By April 1988 the regime's growing insecurity compelled Siad to strike a deal with the equally precarious President Mengistu of Ethiopia ending support for opposition movements in each other's country. The agreement, however, backfired on Siad. Fearing internment by their former sponsors, the Isaaq dominated SNM crossed into northern Somalia

---

[8] Ibid. p.58.
[9] A. de Waal, 'The Shadow Economy' *Africa Report* 38, 2 (March/April 1993) p.28.
[10] Laitin and Samatar, *Somalia* p.94.

and launched an offensive in which they captured the two major towns of the region. The Somali armed forces replied by bombing Hargeisa, the northern capital, back into submission. Over the next few months thousands of civilians were massacred in reprisals by government troops and at least two hundred thousand people, almost all Isaaqs, fled into Ethiopia.

The SNM's successes accelerated the disintegration of the regime. Clans prominent in the army resented being used to fight what was perceived as a Marehan-Isaaq feud. Unable to contain the insurrection with its own forces, the government armed and encouraged the militias of neighbouring clans to attack the Isaaqs. The Ogaden, a mainstay of the regime, regarded the agreement with Mengistu as a betrayal and in early 1989 Ogaden army units mutinied and formed the Somali Patriotic Movement (SPM). Other units either defected or distributed weapons to their clansmen. In the face of multiple small rebellions and growing tribal war, the government's control of the countryside progressively collapsed. By the middle of 1989, Siad Barre was derisively nicknamed 'the Mayor of Mogadishu'.

At the same time, foreign support for Siad's government was drying up. Three factors were responsible for this. First, donors had become increasingly disgusted by the flagrant corruption and theft of huge amounts of foreign aid that had poured into Somalia in the 1980s. Secondly, human rights groups were focusing on Somalia and lobbying Western governments against continued support for the regime. Amnesty International and Africa Watch published comprehensive reports in 1988 and 1990 documenting the Somali Government's gross human rights violations. The US Congress responded by delaying military and economic aid to Somalia in 1988 and 1989. Thirdly, Western, and particularly US, interest in Africa rapidly declined with the ending of the Cold War. One analyst of US foreign policy, noting the rapid decline in resources committed to Africa after the end of the Cold War wrote that the collapse of the Soviet Union '... set America free to pursue its own interests in Africa - and it found it did not have any'.[11] As Somalia became increasingly chaotic, the US believed there was little to be gained from continued support for Siad Barre.

The fall of Siad Barre

With foreign aid declining and much of the countryside beyond his reach, Siad once again tried to use divide and rule tactics on both his opponents and Western donors. In August 1989, Siad announced that he would hold multi-party elections the following year. The patent insincerity of this proposal, however, was demonstrated by the conditions attached to it. Only two or three opposition parties would be legalised and those in armed

---

[11] M. Michaels, 'Retreat from Africa' *Foreign Affairs* 72, 1 (1992/93) p.94.

rebellion against the government would not be allowed to participate. The SNM rejected the offer and refused to negotiate with Siad Barre. Throughout 1990 Siad manoeuvred desperately to stay in power, trying to mollify both foreign donors and at least some of his domestic opponents. He abolished his security service, the NSS, set a date for unconditional multi-party elections and adopted a new constitution. His opponents, however, rejected all his overtures and by the end of the year he controlled little more than Mogadishu.

Siad's last months in power were marked by widespread factional fighting, murder and looting. Before they retreated, Siad's troops pillaged and destroyed many regional centres. This pattern was repeated in the capital, with nightly murders and looting by government soldiers commonplace. In December 1990, the behaviour of the army provoked an uprising by the Hawiye residents of Mogadishu. Over the next six weeks the rebels, reinforced by Hawiye clansmen belonging to the United Somali Congress (USC) from outside of the city, slowly broke Siad's hold on the capital. He finally fled to his home region in south-west Somalia in late January 1991.

The international community's response to the civil war

For most of 1990 the Siad Barre government had been regarded as a lost cause. For the US, Somalia had lost its strategic value with the end of the Cold War and American policy makers were largely indifferent to the outcome of the war. The ending of superpower competition on the African continent also left the US free to respond more directly to domestic lobbies supporting democratisation and human rights there. As these issues assumed a higher profile, the US was happy to see some distance develop between it and Siad's government, one of the worst human rights abusers on the continent.

In concert with the US, the European Community progressively reduced its aid commitments. This decline in support meant that Western donors rapidly lost their leverage with Siad. The EC issued a series of statements during 1989 and 1990 calling for negotiations between the government and the rebels, but it did not attempt to mediate between the parties. The Somali government was urged to adopt political and economic reforms, but with little thought for what would follow.

Like Somalia's other major aid donors, the UN adopted a passive non-interventionist role during the civil war. The United Nations High Commission for Refugees (UNHCR), the major UN agency present in Somalia, had been attempting to scale down its operations since the peace agreement between Siad and Mengistu in April 1988. Despite strenuous opposition from the Somali government, UNHCR argued that the agreement meant refugees could safely return to Ethiopia and developed a plan to encourage them to go. A number of refugee camps, however, were overrun in clan fighting between 1988 and 1989 and UNHCR, and other

UN aid agencies, withdrew many personnel during 1990. All remaining UN staff were evacuated from Somalia in January 1991. For most of the next year, the UN's Somali offices operated out of Nairobi and Djibouti.

As civil disorder spread the small number of non-government organisations (NGOs) working in Somalia also withdrew their staff in the course of 1990. Only the International Committee of the Red Cross (ICRC) and the Austrian children's charity, SOS Kinderdorf, remained in Mogadishu throughout the civil war.

By the time of the fighting in Mogadishu there was little international interest in the fate of Siad Barre. Much of the world, certainly the US, the UN and the Gulf states (formerly major aid donors), had been preoccupied with the Gulf crisis for the previous six months. As the USC and Siad Barre's Marehan soldiers fought over Mogadishu, the chief concern of the US and EC countries was to withdraw their remaining nationals from the country. While appealing for peace, the US and Italy mounted evacuation operations in early January 1991. Amongst the foreign nationals rescued by the US was the Soviet Ambassador and his remaining staff.

Mediation attempts

There were, nevertheless, a series of attempts to find a peaceful resolution to the civil war. Italy, the only European country with a significant economic interest in Somalia and the largest single aid donor, offered several times during 1990 to mediate between the combatants. In a joint effort with Egypt, Italy attempted to organise a round table conference between the government and opposition groups in Cairo in December. The SNM, however, regarded Italy as one of Siad Barre's chief backers and rejected its mediation offers. The conference proposal collapsed when it was rejected by the SNM, USC and SPM. Italy unsuccessfully tried again early in January 1991. By that time, none of the parties were interested in negotiations.

In late 1990, Kenya proposed an emergency meeting of the Intergovernmental Authority on Drought and Development (IGADD) to deal with the Somali problem. Established to deal with drought issues, IGADD is the only regional organisation in the Horn of Africa.[12] There was little enthusiasm for the idea amongst other members, however and the proposal, designed to secure Siad Barre a graceful exit, lapsed when he was overthrown.

In addition to these efforts, the growing number of rebel organisations held a round table conference in mid-November 1990 in Rome in an effort to coordinate their activities. Participants included the SNM, SSDF, USC, SPM, the Somali Democratic Association (Gadabursi clan) and the Somali Democratic Movement (Rahanweyn clan). Although the SNM and the Aideed faction of the USC agreed to an alliance, little concrete was

---

[12] The organisation consists of Kenya, Ethiopia, Somalia, Djibouti, the Sudan and Uganda.

achieved at this meeting and the clans continued their more or less separate wars against Siad Barre and the Marehans.

Why did mediation fail?

By 1989 Somalia was already deeply fractured along clan lines and the various opposition movements seemed primarily concerned with securing or preserving for their clan a bigger share of diminishing national resources. Beyond the removal of Siad Barre, none had any coherent political or economic program. Most of the movements, moreover, consistently rejected negotiations while Siad Barre remained in office. No faction was prepared to deal with a government headed by him. For Siad and his clan, however, his continuation in power was the only way they could protect the huge gains they had made over the past twenty years. Economic success was identified with political survival. Neither he nor his circle could contemplate a peaceful departure.

The feeble international attempts, particularly those of its former Western patrons, to help resolve Somalia's civil war demonstrates the marginality of the country, both strategically and economically. Neither the US nor any of Somalia's other former supporters had any real interest (other than a humanitarian one) in seeking a resolution of the conflict. Somalia was seen as another African war, the causes of which were remote and irrelevant to the outside world. A US official was quoted as saying 'It is illusory to think we can do anything about the situation'.[13]

The end of the Somali state: 1991

Anarchy

The USC's victory in Mogadishu marked the end of the rebellion against a single government. As the country disintegrated throughout 1989 and 1990 clan militias were established to protect clan interests. The result was the division of the country along clan lines. The USC itself controlled only central Somalia, the traditional lands of the Hawiye clan family, and had been divided by feuds since its formation in 1989. At the beginning of 1991 the major Somali organisations were: the SNM (Isaaq, the north-west); the SSDF (Majerteyn, centre-north); the USC (Hawiye, centre and Mogadishu); and the SPM (Ogaden, south, Kismayu). These organisations exercised only the loosest control over their troops, most of whom owed primary allegiance to their immediate lineage group. In addition to the clan militias, numerous unaffiliated armed bands roamed much of the countryside, looting more or less at will.

---

[13] *New York Times* (4 January 1991).

The clans quickly demonstrated they were unwilling to work together. Several days after Siad's flight, a faction of the USC, without consulting any other group, declared Ali Mahdi Mohamed, a Mogadishu businessman, interim President.[14] This faction represented Ali Mahdi's own clan, the Abgal, concentrated in Mogadishu. Ali Mahdi promised to call a national conference in late February to establish a broad based government. The SNM, SSDF and SPM, however, denounced Ali Mahdi's appointment as President and refused to attend. Unable to gain their participation, or guarantee security in Mogadishu, Ali Mahdi indefinitely postponed his conference.

Fighting quickly broke out between the factions as they jostled for control of territory, particularly the key agricultural areas around the Juba and Shebelle rivers in southern Somalia. In early February clashes occurred at Afgoye, south-west of Mogadishu, between the Ogadeni SPM and USC forces belonging to Mohamed Farah Aideed. Aideed was pursuing Siad Barre's retreating troops in an attempt to establish his control over southern Somalia. Aideed's men were also involved in battles against the Majerteyn based SSDF in central Somalia.

In April 1991, the SNM, in shaky control of northern Somalia, declared its independence as the Republic of Somaliland. Many northerners had resented southern dominance of the country since independence and Siad Barre had frequently accused the Isaaq of harbouring separatist sentiments. These allegations had been denied, but the SNM apparently decided that it would not be subjected to a southern government again. Somaliland has not been recognised by any other state and its independence declaration was criticised by the Organisation of African Unity (OAU).

Mogadishu was partitioned between the major Hawiye clans and little attempt was made to re-establish government services, including water, electricity and the police.[15] Conflict between the militias was common, but relatively contained. In May, Aideed demanded Ali Mahdi's resignation, provoking a number of battles between their forces. Aideed, however, was preoccupied with consolidating his position in southern Somalia and the conflict subsided. Although Ali Mahdi and Aideed both belonged to the USC, the two wings of the organisation they controlled were based on different Hawiye clans and had operated independently of each other. Aideed's hostility to Ali Mahdi owes at least as much to

---

[14] There are reports that the Italian Ambassador, Mario Sica, encouraged Ali Mahdi to declare himself President to pre-empt the claims of Mohamed Farah Aideed, candidate of the USC's other main faction. See Adam, 'Somalia' p.20

[15] Samatar, *Somalia* p.22.

resentment of the latter's seizure of the presidency as to any deep-seated clan rivalry.[16]

The outbreak of fighting, and the SNM's declaration of independence, led to renewed efforts to hold a peace conference. Another joint effort between Italy and Egypt to bring the parties together foundered, but in June the two countries backed a reconciliation bid by Djibouti's President, Hassan Gouled Aptidon, an ethnic Somali. A meeting of the Somali factions was held in Djibouti in early June, and agreed to meet again the following month. The SNM refused to go to either conference, but organisations representing other northern clans did attend. The conference was ultimately attended by the representatives of six Somali factions and observers from sixteen countries (including Egypt, Ethiopia, France, Germany, the USSR, Sudan, the US and the Yemen) and six international organisations (most notably the OAU, UN and the EC).

Although the Somali delegations were deeply divided, the conference agreed to recognise Ali Mahdi as the head of a two year interim administration.[17] Somalia was to be run under the 1960 constitution and free elections were to be held at the end of the two year period. The conference also agreed on a ceasefire. Ali Mahdi was sworn in as Somalia's interim president in August and appointed an eighty member ministry. The size was an effort to appease the clans. Notably excluded from this government were supporters of General Aideed. This was the only practical result of the Djibouti agreement. Ali Mahdi's authority was still recognised only in northern Mogadishu. No ministries began to function and, even in Mogadishu, basic government services were not restored.

The conference, in fact, was deeply flawed. Most of the faction leaders, including Aideed, did not attend the meeting and few of the faction delegates had the authority to bind their movements. Indeed, many lived outside of Somalia and had no influence over the internal leadership of the organisations they purported to represent. Nor did the conference agree on any practical procedures for implementing or enforcing the ceasefire. Although it appealed for foreign observers to monitor the ceasefire, no government or international organisation was willing to undertake the mandate.

The ceasefire agreed upon by the second Djibouti meeting was ignored throughout the country. After a bout of fighting in September 1991, sparked by another demand by Aideed for Ali Mahdi's resignation, the conflict between the two warlords broke out in earnest in November. This round, in which at least 20,000 people were killed or wounded, dragged on

---

[16] Adam notes that both the Abgal and the Habr Gedir have practised reciprocal recognition of each other's claims in the past and that there is no history of fighting between them. Adam, 'Somalia' p.25.

[17] 'Somalia Still Fighting' *Africa Confidential* 32, 16 (9 August 1991) pp.6-7.

into 1992 and brought Somalia to the attention of the international community once again.

By the end of 1991 hundreds of thousands of Somalis had become refugees in neighbouring countries or in Europe and North America. No effective government had functioned since at least the end of 1990. The structures normally associated with the modern state, the civil service, army, schools and utilities, had all collapsed. Ali Mahdi's government was unrecognised by any other country. For all practical purposes, the Somali state had ceased to exist.

The beginnings of a humanitarian emergency

Throughout 1991 much of the worst fighting occurred in the agricultural regions of southern Somalia. These areas were contested by Aideed's USC, the SPM and Siad Barre's newly constituted Somali National Front (SNF). Each time a region was captured it was systematically looted of food and goods. Alex de Waal has noted that the looting was '... not an offshoot of fighting, but how the militias and their leaders sustain themselves'.[18] At the same time Somalia, like much of east and southern Africa, was experiencing its worst drought in memory.

The impact of the drought and the civil wars was quickly felt in Somalia. The ICRC reported in May 1991 that severe food shortages in Somalia were becoming more critical and noted that food input from other organisations, governments and private merchants was insufficient to meet the growing need. By late 1991, it was estimated that at least half of Mogadishu's population of one million people required emergency food assistance.[19]

International responses in 1991

During 1991 there was only limited contact with, and limited information available about, Somalia. There was some awareness of the dimensions of the growing disaster, but very few foreigners were based in Somalia. Only two countries, Italy and Egypt, re-established their embassies after the mass evacuation of January 1991 and both were forced out by the fighting in Mogadishu later in the year. The US investigated conditions in Mogadishu but considered the situation too insecure to reopen its embassy. The unwillingness of Somalia's former allies and patrons to re-establish a presence is indicative of the lack of interest and helplessness with which the country was regarded throughout this time. Foreign attitudes were largely summed up by the comment of a US government

---

[18] de Waal, 'The Shadow Economy' p.28.
[19] P. Biles, 'Filling the Vacuum' *Africa Report* 36, 6 (November/December 1991) pp.35-7.

official who said 'Somalia has ceased to exist and right now, nobody cares'.[20]

The unwillingness of most countries to offer practical assistance after the second Djibouti conference confirms this lack of interest. Most observer countries at the conference appear to have assessed that the agreement had little chance of being implemented and decided to await further developments.

After the failure of the Djibouti peace agreement, there was a pause in attempts to find a diplomatic solution to the civil war. Only after the war in Mogadishu resumed - it was the only part of the country readily accessible to foreign journalists - was Somalia again forced onto the international agenda. The high civilian casualty rate in Mogadishu and its coverage by the international press finally prompted international reaction. Although an observer to the second Djibouti conference, the Organisation of African Unity had played little part in the attempts to establish a workable peace in Somalia. In December 1991, however, OAU Secretary-General Salim Salim offered its services as a mediator. He was unable to secure a ceasefire or even permission for a representative to land at Mogadishu airport. At Egypt's urging, the Arab League also called for a ceasefire and established a committee of foreign ministers to mediate between Ali Mahdi and Aideed. Eritrea, fresh from victory in its own protracted war of independence, also sent two officials to mediate between Ali Mahdi and Aideed. Like all attempts before them, these efforts foundered on the intransigence of the warring parties.

The role of the United Nations

In a number of other humanitarian emergencies in Africa, notably the Ethiopian famine of 1984-85, the UN had assumed a role as coordinator of international, bilateral government and non-government assistance. In Somalia, however, the UN did not assume a major role in organising relief during 1991. Moreover, it played little part in alerting the international community to the scale and potential of the disaster. The reason for this failure can be traced to the UN's absence from Somalia through much of 1991.

Following the evacuation of its staff from Mogadishu, the UN established its Somali offices in Nairobi and Djibouti. During the first half of 1991, several exploratory visits were made to assess both security and food needs, but in July the UN decided the security situation was too unstable to re-establish a resident mission. Some staff were deployed to run emergency operations, but were evacuated from Mogadishu in September. UNHCR staff made short visits to northern Somalia from their base in Djibouti. Concern with the security situation appears to

---

[20] *Washington Post* (6 January 1992).

have been a key factor in determining the scale of UN involvement in Somalia for the remainder of the year.

The UN also declined to assume a political role in finding a solution for the Somali crisis. The second Djibouti conference appealed for international assistance in monitoring a ceasefire, but senior UN officials, concerned with the number of peace keeping operations in which the organisation was already involved and the strains on its budget, refused to provide any forces.[21] This concern was not confined to the UN bureaucracy. The US and other key members of the Security Council were preoccupied with a series of international crises during 1991, including the Gulf War, the Kurdish refugee problem and the collapse of Yugoslavia. Because it was seen as a purely internal situation, Somalia was not regarded as an appropriate arena for UN action. A lack of strategic and economic interest by the major powers, and concern over the UN's ability to sustain another major operation appear to lie behind this reasoning.

The UN was offered another opportunity to address the Somali question in October 1991 when Ali Mahdi appealed for a General Assembly special session on Somalia. The UN again refused to become involved. A senior UN official, James Jonah, advised the UN's office in Nairobi that

> The consensus of views here is that it is most unlikely that the General Assembly could accept the convening of a special session ... We would suggest that you endeavour to discourage at the local level any idea for holding a special session on Somalia. We are following closely the evolution of political and military developments in Mogadishu, and at this time we cannot contemplate any meaningful action by the secretary general.[22]

The UN's unwillingness to become involved in Somalia throughout 1991 fostered an impression of weakness amongst the warlords (particularly in Aideed's faction). The UN already suffered from a lack of credibility because of the evacuation of its personnel during the civil war.

Assessment of the international community's role

The reasons for the non-involvement of the US and other major powers have already been touched upon. These included a lack of any vital interest in Somalia, either strategic or economic, the relative paucity of information about developments in the country and a resulting lack of public attention, and concern about the ability of the UN to undertake another major operation. Behind this last concern, of course, was an awareness that the major powers would be required to fund and support any

---

[21] 'Somalia: Ways to End the Slaughter' *Africa Confidential* 33, 3 (7 February 1992) pp.5-6.
[22] R. Bonner, 'Why We Went' *Mother Jones* (March/April 1993) p.55.

UN operation. Also relevant was the attitude, widespread amongst many Westerners, that Africa should take responsibility for its own problems.[23]

For most of 1991, however, Africa's leading multilateral institution, the OAU, was only peripherally involved in the search for peace. The institution was handicapped by its guiding principle of non-interference in the affairs of member states. A further impediment is the lack of an institutional tradition of coordinating a response to disasters in member states. The organisation instead tends to be driven by the diplomatic agendas of its chairmen.

The failure of the UN to offer mediation or to coordinate a relief effort has been repeatedly criticised.[24] Although Somalia was effectively isolated throughout 1991, the UN had some awareness of the dimensions of the crisis developing there. It ignored these signals, however, preferring to limit its involvement in the affairs of member states along traditional lines. A more activist bureaucracy could have established a role as a mediator by exploiting the opportunities presented by the second Djibouti conference and, later, Ali Mahdi's appeal to the General Assembly. The UN's attitude to relief operations in Somalia also compares poorly with the activities of NGOs such as ICRC. For much of 1991 the ICRC warned of the developing famine in Somalia, but the lack of a host government, coupled with the UN's own withdrawal from the country early in the year, seems to have removed most institutional pressure for action. Because Somalia had neither a government nor friends, it did not appear on the UN's agenda.

Humanitarian intervention: 1992

The United Nations decision to intervene

The conflict in Mogadishu proved to be the catalyst for intervention by the UN. Three factors shaped the UN's renewed interest in Somalia and its decision to intervene.

International media attention. The extended war between Ali Mahdi and Aideed - and the high level of civilian casualties - aroused significant international media attention for Somalia for the first time since the fall of Siad Barre.

Criticism of the UN relief effort. Mogadishu was the principal entry point for aid and the war disrupted the limited relief effort that had been under way in the latter part of 1991. The UN's inaction in seeking a ceasefire in Mogadishu, and the restrictions it placed on its relief operations, prompted trenchant criticism from NGOs. In mid-December,

---

[23] *New York Times* (6 January 1992).
[24] See, for example, Bonner, 'Why We Went' and *New York Times* (26 February 1992).

USAID's Director of Foreign Assistance, Andrew Natsios, expressed his concern at the UN's failure to send medical workers or relief supplies to Somalia.[25] These criticisms prompted the then Secretary General, Javier Perez de Cuellar, to announce that the UN was sending a team into Mogadishu and that relief operations would be expanded '... as soon as the security situation permits ...'

Third World pressure. The dominance of the Security Council's agenda by the interests of the Permanent Five members had been criticised by many Third World countries for some time. Coupled with this was a widespread feeling amongst many Africans that the end of the Cold War had prompted a realignment of the West's interests - and aid - away from Africa towards the former Soviet bloc. These trends seemed confirmed by the preoccupation of the Security Council with the break up of Yugoslavia and other East European problems in 1991 and its comparable neglect of African issues. One analyst has noted the UN's '... institutional resignation to Africa's hopelessness ...'[26] These concerns were echoed by the new Secretary-General, Boutros Boutros-Ghali, and he came to office committed to broadening the Council's agenda and a more activist role for the UN. By the end of 1991, the Security Council's three African members, Cape Verde, Morocco and Zimbabwe, were pressing for greater Security Council consideration of African issues and, in particular, the Somali crisis.

Familiar with the Somali problem from his time as Egyptian Deputy Prime Minister, Boutros-Ghali drew these three strands together in an effort to counter the Security Council's focus on Yugoslavia.

United Nations Security Council Resolution 733

In early January 1992, Boutros-Ghali sent James Jonah, then an Assistant Secretary-General, to Mogadishu to begin negotiations for a ceasefire. Jonah's visit, and his talks with the major factions in Mogadishu, formed the basis of Boutros-Ghali's report in late January to the Security Council on the UN's relief efforts and the attempts to broker a ceasefire in Mogadishu. Using this report as a basis, the African members of the Council prepared a resolution calling for a ceasefire and an increase in humanitarian assistance to Somalia. The language of this draft was not acceptable to the US and a weakened version was passed as UN Security Council Resolution 733 on 23 January 1992. UNSCR 733 requested the Secretary-General

- to increase the UN's humanitarian assistance to Somalia and to appoint a coordinator to oversee the relief effort;

---

[25] *New York Times* (15 December 1991)
[26] J. Stevenson, 'Hope Restored in Somalia?'*Foreign Policy* 91 (Summer 1993) p.144.

- to contact the parties in the conflict and seek their commitment to the cessation of hostilities to permit humanitarian assistance to be distributed, to promote a ceasefire and to assist in the process of a political settlement.

Acting under Chapter VII of the Charter, the Council also imposed an embargo on deliveries of weapons and military equipment to all the factions in Somalia.

There was little discussion at the time of the implications of intervention in the affairs of a member state. The examples of its involvement in protecting the Kurdish population of northern Iraq and its activities in former Yugoslavia were recent and prominent examples of the extension of the UN's competence. UNSCR 733 was justified by reference to the Security Council's '... primary responsibility under the Charter ... for the maintenance of the international peace and security ...', but it clearly raises questions about the extent of state sovereignty and the right of the international community to intervene to protect the citizens of failed or delinquent states. These issues were addressed by implication rather than by any explicit discussion. In the case of Somalia, the complete absence of legitimate state authorities eased the way to international intervention and rendered these questions largely theoretical.

This potentially radical step in theory was balanced by a very cautious approach to intervention in practice. The Security Council authorised the Secretary-General to begin a traditional conciliation process in the dispute between the various Somali factions. The Secretary-General was to

> ... contact all the parties involved in the conflict, to seek their commitment to the cessation of hostilities to permit the humanitarian assistance to be distributed, to promote a cease-fire and compliance therewith, and to assist in the process of a political settlement of the conflict in Somalia ...[27]

The other parts of the resolution dealt with expanding the UN's role in providing relief to Somalia. The resolution, however, did not impose any clear limits on the UN's role in the peace process or in the relief exercise.

The likely success of this traditional approach to conflict resolution in a non-traditional situation, however, was uncertain from the beginning. Although he argued in a report to the Security Council in March that '... new avenues and innovative methods commensurate with the humanitarian and political situation at hand need to be explored to facilitate a political settlement ...',[28] the Secretary-General initially envisaged only a limited commitment of UN personnel to monitor a ceasefire agreement.

---

[27] United Nations Security Council Resolution (UNSCR) 733 (1992).
[28] United Nations Secretary-General, *Reports on the Situation in Somalia*. (New York: United Nations, Report of the Secretary-General, 11 March 1992, UN Document Number S/23693) p.16.

Such an approach certainly satisfied the concerns of the US and other Permanent Five members of the Security Council. The US and other Council members were anxious to avoid the commitment of a peacekeeping force, both because of the cost and the precedent that it would create for UN intervention in other areas.[29] It was also widely doubted whether the UN had the necessary flexibility and resources to mount another peacekeeping operation. Nor was there any support amongst Council members for a peacekeeping operation as long as the fighting in Mogadishu continued.[30]

The connection between political reconciliation and a successful relief effort was recognised by the Security Council in UNSCR 733, but the UN's role was nevertheless conceived of as being primarily humanitarian in nature. The resolution, for instance, did not address the nature or extent of UN involvement in any peace process. The suggestion that a peacekeeping force would be necessary to monitor a ceasefire was canvassed (including by Ali Mahdi, who argued that a monitoring force would be necessary to enforce a ceasefire), but there was no support for this option as long as the fighting continued.

Even at that stage, however, many observers regarded a peacekeeping force as an essential step towards building a ceasefire in Mogadishu, if not the rest of Somalia. Following its attempted mediation, for instance, Eritrea proposed that a regional peacekeeping force, including Eritrean, Ethiopian and Kenyan troops, operating under UN authority be placed in Mogadishu if a ceasefire was agreed upon. Because Eritrea was neither a member of the UN nor an independent state, this plan appears to have been ignored by Jonah or other senior UN officials and was not pursued.[31]

The UN and the warlords

The UN began the search for a ceasefire in early January 1992, when Boutros-Ghali sent James Jonah to Mogadishu as his envoy. An agreement between Ali Mahdi and Aideed was finally signed in early March. Throughout this period - and beyond - the various warlords treated the UN not as a disinterested third party, but as a player to be conciliated and, wherever possible, exploited in pursuit of advantage over their rivals. The manoeuvres of the warlords echo those of post-independence Somali governments which consistently sought to use foreign patronage to further their nationalist or clannist agendas.

The early reactions of the warlords to the UN's peace and humanitarian efforts depended largely on the perceived impact of these operations on the local military situation. Ali Mahdi, the weaker of the two main antagonists in Mogadishu, welcomed UN intervention and called for a peacekeeping force. In contrast, Aideed recognised that UN involvement

---

[29] Jeffrey Clark, 'Debacle in Somalia' *Foreign Affairs* 72, 1 (1992/93) p.119.
[30] *New York Times* (12 January 1992).
[31] Bonner, 'Why We Went' p.56.

would probably work against his attempts to consolidate his power in southern and central Somalia and initially opposed UN action. Aideed realised during Jonah's visit, however, that he was unable to stop some form of UN intervention and thereafter sought to limit its scope. This made the ceasefire negotiations during January and February particularly difficult as Aideed exploited every opportunity to delay the signing of an agreement.

An agreement between the two factions of the USC was finally signed on 3 March. Ali Mahdi and Aideed agreed to disengage their troops, allow the unimpeded flow of relief aid and to encourage a withdrawal of those clan militias occupying the airport and port. It was agreed that a UN technical mission would work out with the two parties the details for the monitoring of the ceasefire. This mission was authorised by the Security Council in SCR 746 of 17 March, but it did not visit Somalia until the end of that month.

Although there were sporadic outbreaks of fighting between the factions in Mogadishu throughout the year, and extensive looting of relief supplies, the ceasefire generally held without effective UN supervision. The ceasefire in Mogadishu, however, left Aideed free to continue the war in other parts of the country. Between April and July he was able to extend his control over large parts of central and southern Somalia. In April, Siad Barre's SNF attacked Aideed's forces around Baidoa, but Aideed turned back the offensive and forced Siad Barre to seek refuge in Kenya by the end of that month. At the same time, Aideed took control of the southern port city of Kismayu in alliance with a faction of the SPM. The ceasefire also enabled Aideed to encroach on territory held by the SSDF in central Somalia. Much of the worst fighting in this period took place in the key agricultural regions of southern Somalia. The systematic looting carried out by Siad Barre's and Aideed's armed bands pushed these areas further towards starvation.[32] By July, the famine was reaching its peak.

At the same time as negotiating a ceasefire agreement, the UN was also proposing to sponsor a conference of national reconciliation. Ali Mahdi initially opposed a conference, claiming that the second Djibouti conference had recognised him as interim President and that negotiations to establish a government of Somalia should be conducted on this basis. Aideed welcomed UN intervention in this area, as he disputed the legitimacy of the Djibouti conference. He believed that his dominant position in southern and central Somalia would give him a key role in another conference. Aideed's efforts to extend his territory in southern Somalia were designed to strengthen his position at a reconciliation conference.

UN efforts to establish a ceasefire initially aggravated the tension in Mogadishu. It has been suggested that the UN's failure to deal with other clans in Mogadishu - and the rest of Somalia - elevated the standing of Ali

---

[32] de Waal, 'The Shadow Economy' p.28.

Mahdi and Aideed and encouraged them to attack their lesser rivals.[33] The UN has also been criticised by a number of journalists and aid workers familiar with Somalia for failing to exploit the opportunity created by the first ceasefire agreement between Ali Mahdi and Aideed.[34] One analyst has argued that

> After the cessation of hostilities U.N. senior diplomats foundered in the field, the Security Council dithered and U.N. relief agencies squandered valuable time. The Security Council's meekness was inconsistent with more forceful actions taken regarding concurrent crises in both Iraq and the Balkans. Great power reluctance to focus on Somalia was unmistakable ...[35]

While the ceasefire was extremely fragile and the space for the UN to move was narrow, its response was certainly too slow. The Security Council did not authorise the formation of the technical mission until two weeks after the ceasefire was signed and the mission itself did not begin its visit to Mogadishu until 23 March.

Doubts about the direction of UN involvement on the part of the US and other Permanent Five members of the Council also contributed to the delays. In the negotiations leading to UNSCR 746, the US initially opposed the dispatch of a technical team and wanted to focus the resolution on the humanitarian aspects of the situation. It argued that the UN could not implement a ceasefire which was not being respected. The African members of the Council (Zimbabwe and Nigeria), however, again raised their concerns about the treatment of Africa relative to other areas, such as Yugoslavia, and the US dropped its opposition to the team. The negotiations over this resolution highlight the confusion evident in the international community's approach to Somalia. A political resolution was an essential precondition for a successful relief operation, but the international community was reluctant to undertake the necessary steps to achieve such a resolution. Instead, it focused on the relief operation as an exercise in logistics.

United Nations operation in Somalia: Mandate and deployment

Because of the continuing insecurity, and the attraction of relief shipments for looters, the UN technical team recommended that a 500 person unit be placed in Mogadishu to guard the airport and port. A fifty person Military Observer Group would monitor the ceasefire. These recommendations were accepted by the Security Council and embodied in UNSCR 751 of 24 April, which created the United Nations Operation in Somalia (UNOSOM). At the same time Boutros-Ghali appointed a Special Representative for Somalia to provide overall direction for the UN's relief

---

[33] Clark, 'Debacle in Somalia' p.115.
[34] Stevenson, 'Hope Restored in Somalia?'
[35] Clark, 'Debacle in Somalia' pp.115-116

efforts and to assist with the consultations for the convening of a national reconciliation conference.

The appointment of a Special Representative by the Secretary-General to coordinate relief and peace efforts had been a relatively common device in previous crises, Ethiopia being a recent example. That this occurred only four months after the UN's first steps towards active intervention in Somalia is indicative of the failure of the UN bureaucracy and of the international community to recognise the dimensions of the crisis with which they were faced. This was despite frequent warnings of the scale of the emergency in Somalia and an acknowledgement by Boutros-Ghali that the country presented '... a special challenge to the international community'.[36]

The UNOSOM security force was limited by its mandate to firing in self-defence. Its task was conceived as providing '... the United Nations convoys of relief supplies with a sufficiently strong military escort to deter attack and to fire effectively in self-defence if deterrence should not prove effective'.[37] This mandate was to prove seriously inadequate.

The passage of UNSCR 751 was followed by a dispute between the US and the UK and other Security Council members over funding for the security element of UNOSOM. This hampered the planning and establishment of the operation and contributed to a delay in the deployment of the security contingent. Further delays arose from negotiations with Aideed and Ali Mahdi to obtain the approval for the deployment of the 50 person Military Observer Group (MOG) and the security contingent. Aideed, in particular, repeatedly blocked the deployment of both groups, and the MOG's advance party consequently did not arrive in Mogadishu until early July. Aideed remained opposed to the deployment of the security unit and the Secretary-General's Special Representative, Mohammed Sahnoun, did not obtain agreement for the deployment of a Pakistani battalion until 12 August. The unit did not arrive in Mogadishu until mid-September.

The failure of UNOSOM

Restricted by their mandate and by the UN's policy of obtaining the cooperation of the warlords, the Pakistanis quickly found they were unable to fulfil their mission. They were unable to secure Mogadishu's main airport or the port and were too weak to mount effective patrols. By November, the Pakistani battalion was largely confined to its camp and it was unable to provide effective security for the food convoys in Mogadishu. The battalion also suffered from inadequate logistics support and, despite the delay between the approval of a UNOSOM security force

---

[36] Report of the Secretary-General, 11 March 1992, UN Document Number S/23693 p.17.
[37] Report of the Secretary-General, 21 April 1992, UN Document Number S/23829 p.7.

(late April) and its deployment (mid-September), the whole operation bore the signs of hasty and makeshift planning by the UN.

The March ceasefire agreement preserved an uneasy peace between Aideed and Ali Mahdi throughout 1992, but the overall situation quickly began to deteriorate. Because it was seen as a weak player with ineffective military forces, the UN was increasingly regarded as a commercial opportunity by the warlords and the other armed bands. As a result looting increased again and Pakistani patrols were subjected to attacks by gunmen. In a report to the Security Council in August, Boutros-Ghali noted that

> ... the problem in Somalia today is not the delivery of humanitarian relief supplies ... but the protection of the convoys that transport supplies from port or airport to warehouses and distribution centres, together with the protection of those stores and centres themselves.[38]

Fighting between the Ali Mahdi and Aideed factions periodically broke out in Mogadishu and food convoys were attacked outside the city. In late October, Aideed declared that the Pakistani battalion was no longer welcome on the streets of Mogadishu and in November a relief convoy was attacked and looted in the city. On 24 November, a World Food Program (WFP) ship was shelled by Ali Mahdi's militia as it entered Mogadishu harbour.

UNOSOM was also beset by other difficulties. Sahnoun proved to be a highly capable representative, but he repeatedly clashed with senior UN officials in New York. He also publicly criticised 'bureaucratic haggling' within the UN and agencies such as the United Nations Children's Fund (UNICEF) and WFP. Sahnoun further irritated the UN bureaucracy by refusing to accept direction from New York and formulating his own policy. Sahnoun was angered by UN actions which tended to undermine his authority in the eyes of the warlords. He was not consulted, for instance, when the Secretary-General proposed to expand the size of the security contingent of UNOSOM to cover the whole country. After receiving a letter in late October from Boutros-Ghali ordering him to refrain from public criticism of the UN, Sahnoun resigned. He apparently hoped to be reappointed with greater authority, but instead Boutros-Ghali accepted the resignation and appointed a new Special Representative, Ismat Kittani. The departure of Sahnoun further weakened the UN's authority in Somalia.

The continuing difficulties facing the UN convinced Boutros-Ghali that a larger security presence was necessary to establish sufficient security for the relief effort and to enable national reconciliation to proceed. In late August, he recommended to the Security Council that the UNOSOM security force be expanded to 4,000 personnel and that it cover the whole

---

[38] Report of the Secretary-General, 24 August 1992, UN Document Number S/24480 p.5.

country in four zones. This was endorsed by the Council in UNSCR 775 of 28 August 1992. Despite their initial approval, some of the factions in whose territory the forces were to be based opposed this decision. The UN also had difficulty in identifying contributors to the force and the estimated date for deployment was repeatedly postponed.

From the beginning of 1992, the UN attempted to obtain the consent of the key parties for its operations in Somalia. Although it was a non-traditional situation, this was essentially a traditional approach to the problem of establishing peace. The warlords, however, were less interested in peace and relief than in self-aggrandisement and the opportunity to profit from UN and NGO operations.[39] The UN's desire for their agreement was seen as a weakness capable of exploitation and manipulation in pursuit of their aims.

Humanitarian intervention without consent: 1992-1993

The development of United States policy

By the middle of 1992 the full extent of the Somali famine was becoming apparent. The UN estimated that up to 4.5 million people in a population of between 6 and 6.5 million required assistance.[40] Of these, it was estimated that 1.5 million people were at risk of starvation. Proportionately, this was the worst famine in Africa for twenty years. The major powers on the Security Council, however, continued to be preoccupied with the war in former Yugoslavia. This preoccupation prompted Boutros-Ghali to condemn the US and other members of the Council as being more concerned with a 'rich man's war'. The size of the disaster also began to attract substantial numbers from the international media. These developments significantly heightened Somalia's profile.

Recognising the need for increased assistance, the Security Council passed a further resolution, 767, on 27 July requesting the Secretary-General to '... make full use of all available means and arrangements, including the mounting of an urgent airlift operation ...'[41] US policy also began to change in this period. Although the US had provided large amounts of emergency aid through NGOs such as ICRC and Médecins sans Frontières (MSF) it had repeatedly attempted to limit UN involvement. Realisation of the extent of the famine, and the growing media attention, focused the minds of US policy makers on the situation

---

[39] In September, for instance, Aideed blocked a UN plan to move relief supplies by land through 'corridors of tranquillity'. *Washington Post* (11 September 1992).
[40] Report of the Secretary-General, 24 August 1992, UN Document Number S/24480 p.3.
[41] UNSCR 767 (1992).

and the UN's difficulties in dealing with it.[42] In mid-August, several days before the Republican National Convention, President George Bush ordered an airlift of relief supplies into Somalia. As they became more closely involved in the relief effort, US officials became increasingly aware of the difficulties in operating in a country with no government and numerous armed groups. In September, for instance, the US airlift into Baidoa was suspended because of factional fighting around the airport.

The origins of United Nations Interim Task Force (Somalia)

The continuing insecurity surrounding UN and other relief operations was intensified by fighting between the factions in south Somalia over Bardera and Kismayu. At the same time, WFP allowed the dissemination of a claim that up to 80 per cent of relief supplies were looted. Although this claim has since been disputed, it contributed to the growing sense of crisis and failure which pervaded UN operations at the time.[43] These events, and the reports he received from his new Special Representative in Mogadishu, Kittani, convinced Boutros-Ghali that a new approach was necessary. This view was widely shared and the UN began to consider the use of force to deliver food supplies.[44] This option had been publicly advocated for several months by some aid groups familiar with Somalia.

On 24 November, Boutros-Ghali wrote to the President of the Security Council advocating a review of the basic principles of the UN relief effort in Somalia. A meeting of the Security Council the following day informally agreed with Boutros-Ghali that the use of force under Chapter VII of the Charter was necessary to ensure the delivery of relief supplies. On the same day, the US informed Boutros-Ghali that, if the Security Council sanctioned the use of force to deliver relief supplies, it was willing to organise an enforcement operation to achieve this. Boutros-Ghali preferred an operation under direct UN command and control, with the US limited to logistic support, but the US insisted that it retain command. On 3 December, the Security Council passed UNSCR 794, authorising the Secretary-General and member states to use 'all necessary means' under Chapter VII of the Charter to establish a secure environment for relief operations.

The US offer seems to have been driven by several factors. Senior US officials, including President Bush, were apparently shocked by the level of suffering in Somalia and the evident inability of existing relief operations to cope with the conditions. There appears to have been a belief that the US could deal with the situation, at least in the sense of establishing a secure environment for relief operations, relatively quickly.

---

[42] *Washington Post* (24 August 1992).
[43] Mark Huband, 'When Yankee Goes Home' *Africa Report* 38, 2 (March/April 1993) pp.20-3.
[44] *Washington Post* (28 October 1992).

As President Bush said in a television broadcast on 5 December, justifying the use of American troops,

... American action is often necessary as a catalyst for broader involvement of the community of nations. Only the United States has the global reach to place such a large security force on the ground in such a distant place quickly and efficiently ...

Somalia also offered President Bush and his administration an opportunity to enhance its internationalist reputation at relatively little cost, either in military terms or to domestic public opinion. US action in Somalia could also help to offset calls for action in former Yugoslavia. The US could argue that it had performed its humanitarian duty where it was possible and that Yugoslavia was a quite different, and much more complex, case.

In passing UNSCR 794, the Security Council recognised that the situation in Somalia had deteriorated 'beyond the point at which it is susceptible to the peace-keeping treatment' and that the Council had no alternative but to '... adopt more forceful measures to secure the humanitarian operations in Somalia'.[45] UNSCR 794 takes a further step towards establishing a right of humanitarian intervention on the part of the international community, and specifically the UN, where a state has collapsed. The resolution begins by affirming the unique character of the situation in Somalia and determines that the magnitude of the tragedy caused by the conflict in Somalia, as well as the obstacles to the distribution of humanitarian assistance, constitute a threat to international peace and security. There is little pretence in the resolution that the intervention is based on the consent of a government of Somalia. The resolution was based on the need to provide assistance to the Somali people. One analyst has argued that, together with other recent interventions by the UN (such as that in the Kurdish parts of Iraq), UNSCR 794 means '[i]t is no longer tenable to assert that whenever a government massacres its own people or a state collapses into anarchy international law forbids military intervention altogether'.[46]

UNITAF: Mandate and operation

The Unified Task Force (UNITAF) was conceived essentially as a police action by member states of the UN with specific goals, the chief of which was to create a secure environment for the distribution of relief. The operation was also intended to be limited in time. After security was established, the UN would again assume direct responsibility for rehabilitation and political reconciliation. The mandate given to UNITAF by the Security Council - to establish a ceasefire, distribute humanitarian

---

[45] Letter from the Secretary-General to the President of the Security Council, 1993.
[46] Christopher Greenwood, 'Is There a Right of Humanitarian Intervention?' *The World Today* 49, 2 (February 1992) p.40.

relief and promote national reconciliation - was essentially similar to that of UNOSOM. As a Chapter VII operation, however, UNITAF was given enforcement powers to achieve this mandate. Member states cooperating in UNITAF were authorised to use 'all necessary means' to establish a secure environment for humanitarian relief operations, language clearly encompassing the use of force against uncooperative Somali groups.

UNITAF gave a new impetus to a relief effort in danger of being overwhelmed by the difficulties it faced. Over the five months of its existence, UNITAF deployed 37,000 troops over 40 per cent of Somalia's area and occupied all of the major population centres in the south. It ensured delivery of relief assistance to the neediest areas and opened many of the more remote regions to relief operations for the first time. It also eliminated extortion at Mogadishu port.

The key to UNITAF's success in these areas was the overwhelming force it deployed. Most of the factions in the country acquiesced in the operation and avoided confrontations with UNITAF troops. The general environment, however, remained insecure. UNITAF did not deploy in some key areas, such as the Somali-Kenyan border region, and was unable to stop completely interclan fighting, notably in the Kismayu area. Many armed bands also turned from attacking heavily guarded food convoys and distribution centres to softer targets such as NGOs and foreign relief workers. Many of the guards hired by these organisations were stripped of their weapons by UNITAF in the first stages of its operation.

Moreover, the US did not regard disarmament of the Somali factions as a primary part of UNITAF's task. In the negotiations leading to the formation of UNITAF, Boutros-Ghali emphasised repeatedly the need to disarm the factions of at least their heavy weapons if long term security was to be established. The US regarded this as potentially costly and only authorised local commanders to disarm the factions when it was considered necessary for operational security. Despite constant pressure from Boutros-Ghali, no general program of disarmament was undertaken by UNITAF.

Faced with overwhelming force, Aideed and Ali Mahdi publicly welcomed the UNITAF intervention and, within days of its arrival, again reached a ceasefire agreement in Mogadishu. Both, however, attempted to turn the intervention to their advantage and courted the US for support against their rivals.[47] Aideed quickly became more critical of the intervention, however, when the arrival of foreign troops effectively removed several towns, including Baidoa, from his control. This hostility was compounded when General Siyad Hersi Morgan's SNF partly overran Kismayu, held by Aideed's ally Colonel Ahmed Omar Jess, in early January 1993.

In an attempt to fulfil the political reconciliation part of the UN's mandate, Boutros-Ghali convened an informal meeting of fourteen factions

---

[47] Stevenson, 'Hope Restored in Somalia?' p.150.

in Addis Ababa on 4 January 1993. Although only scheduled to last two days, it was twice extended until 15 January. The meeting agreed to hold a National Reconciliation Conference in March and established an ad hoc committee to set the agenda and determine participation. The meeting also agreed on a general ceasefire.

Aideed disrupted the ad hoc committee by organising a boycott, but the UN nevertheless obtained agreement on participation and the agenda of the conference by consulting individually with the factions. The Conference met between 15 and 27 March in Addis Ababa. The Conference agreed that general disarmament was essential and requested UNITAF and UNOSOM to help achieve this within ninety days. It also agreed that a two year transitional period was necessary to rebuild political and administrative structures. In the meantime, the country would be governed by a Transitional National Council (TNC) and a network of Regional and District Councils. These Councils were intended to reflect the reality of a splintered country and would encourage rehabilitation from the grass roots. They were to assume responsibility for the implementation of humanitarian, social and economic programs and for the administration of law and order.

Despite the facade of unity at this conference, little progress was made in the following months with the implementation of the Addis Ababa accords. The factions proved to be unenthusiastic about disarmament, particularly after the beginning of conflict between Aideed's SNA and UNOSOM II (see below). The behaviour of most of the factions since March 1993 has shown that they are less interested in cooperation to rehabilitate their country than in consolidating control of their fiefdoms and manoeuvring for advantage against their rivals.

UNOSOM II: Mandate and operation (May-November 1993)

Because UNITAF was envisaged as a temporary operation designed to allow the UN to fulfil its mandate in Somalia, UNSCR 794 requested the Secretary-General to submit a plan to the Security Council for a new UNOSOM within fifteen days. Anxious to establish a clear time limit for the UNITAF operation, the US pressed the Secretary-General to begin planning in early December 1992, but Boutros-Ghali preferred to wait until the success of UNITAF was established and the terms of an authorising resolution were clear. Despite the obvious time pressure, this approach seems to have characterised the preparations for UNOSOM II. In January 1993, for instance, the Secretariat argued that it could not undertake detailed planning of the military and financial aspects of UNOSOM II until an authorising resolution was passed by the Security Council.

The Security Council approved UNSCR 814 authorising a new UNOSOM on 26 March 1993. In the negotiations leading to the adoption of the new resolution, it was widely accepted that UNOSOM II would require a wider mandate and powers under Chapter VII of the Charter. Boutros-Ghali argued that the mandate should

> ... empower UNOSOM II to provide assistance to the Somali people in rebuilding their shattered economy and social and political life, re-establishing the country's institutional structure, achieving national political reconciliation, recreating a Somali State based on democratic governance and rehabilitating the country's economy and infrastructure.[48]

The resolution gave UNOSOM II a broad mandate to assist in the rehabilitation and political reconciliation of Somalia and to help create conditions under which civil society would have a role in the political and physical reconstruction of the country. It was also given enforcement powers under Chapter VII to continue the work of UNITAF in establishing a secure environment in Somalia and, in particular, to pursue the disarmament of the factions.

This mandate was considerably more extensive than those entrusted to the first UNOSOM and to UNITAF. UNOSOM II, for instance, was required to pursue disarmament of the factions, but with fewer troops than those available to UNITAF and over a wider area. Boutros-Ghali also promised that UNOSOM II would be deployed throughout Somalia, including in the north-west, whereas UNITAF concentrated on securing the major population centres. Because of budgetary reasons, the mandate expired in October 1993. Although it was envisaged that the mandate would be renewed, this placed some pressure on UNOSOM II to achieve at least some of its goals by that time.

UNOSOM II was also to be intimately involved in the process of recreating the Somali state. Although the mandate built on the activities of the UN in northern Iraq and Cambodia in recent years, it nevertheless gave the UN an essentially new role which went significantly beyond traditional notions of peacekeeping and humanitarian operations towards peace enforcement and nation building. Apart from relief activities, the UN's task in Somalia was envisaged as assisting with the political and physical reconstruction of the country. UNOSOM II was to assist with the implementation of the Addis Ababa peace accords, as well as develop a comprehensive strategy for the reconstruction of Somalia. Senior UN officials, including the Secretary-General's new Special Representative in Somalia, retired US Admiral Jonathan Howe, regarded UNOSOM's role as that of a catalyst in the formation of a new civil administration.

One of the key elements of the Addis Ababa accords was to be the reconstruction of the Somali state from the local level upwards. The first step in this process was to be the formation of district councils (DCs), representative of all groups in a given locality. The DCs were to elect Regional Councils (RCs), which in turn would choose a Transitional

---

[48] Further Report of the Secretary-General Submitted in Pursuance of Paragraphs 18 and 19 of Resolution 794 (1992) p.19.

National Council to govern the country until elections. Although no specific time frame was fixed for the formation of the DCs and RCs, Admiral Howe planned that elections in January 1995 would be followed by the formation of a new government in March 1995.

Along with its Justice Program, designed to recreate a functioning Somali police and judicial system, UNOSOM regarded the formation of the DCs as one of its principal tasks.

While all major Somali factions had accepted the Addis Ababa accords and, implicitly, continued UN involvement in Somalia, most factional leaders regarded these programs with a certain amount of unease. The idea underpinning the formation of the DCs, widespread local participation in the selection of members, if not formal election, threatened the authority of both factional leaders and traditional authorities. As a result, the formation of the DCs proceeded extremely slowly over the next few months.

UNOSOM II's mandate to actively pursue disarmament also struck directly at the position of the warlords, whose heavily armed faction members underpinned their power and survival. The control of arms was also essential to attract followers. Unsurprisingly, UNOSOM's efforts to contain the number of arms triggered its conflict with General Aideed and his militia.

On 5 June, a Pakistani UNOSOM unit inspecting an SNA weapons storage site was subjected to sniper fire. Other Pakistani units, including one assisting at a feeding station, were ambushed by SNA militia. Twenty-four Pakistani soldiers were killed in the fighting.

Although Aideed's decision to attack UNOSOM highlights the sensitivity of the arms issue to him, it was also consistent with his concerns about the role of the UN in Somalia and its adverse impact on his position. Of all the warlords, Aideed had been most seriously affected by the UN intervention in Somalia beginning in January 1992. Although far from being able to dominate the whole country, Aideed had been gradually consolidating his position in the south, by alliance and conquest, throughout the latter part of 1991 and early 1992. The first UNOSOM had disrupted his activities in Mogadishu, while UNITAF had weakened him in Mogadishu and broken his control over key towns in southern Somalia. An active disarmament policy, coupled with the development of the district and regional councils, would have rapidly eroded Aideed's remaining power base.

UNOSOM responded to the deaths of the peacekeepers by seeking to break Aideed's control of south Mogadishu. The Security Council approved Resolution 837 on 6 June 1993, condemning the attack and authorising the Secretary-General to take all necessary measures against the (unnamed) organisers of the attack to establish UNOSOM's authority and to bring them to trial. UNOSOM proceeded to destroy the SNA's radio station in Mogadishu and, on 10 June, issued a warrant for Aideed's arrest. At the same time, it attacked Aideed's own compound.

Over the next four months UNOSOM increasingly appeared to focus on removing Aideed and crippling his military capacity as a prerequisite for establishing peace in Somalia. Its troops launched a series of operations to find or destroy Aideed, while the SNA conducted its own guerrilla campaign against the UN.

Although entirely confined to south Mogadishu, the fighting prompted growing disquiet in the West about the nature and magnitude of the UN's task in Somalia. Regular television pictures from Mogadishu, and the numerous deaths of women and children (some of them because of 'human shields' tactics by the SNA militia) increased this concern. UNOSOM's critics argued that its approach to Somalia was dominated by the US and that it had become obsessed with the elimination of Aideed. These criticisms escalated as the potential costs of peace enforcement, as opposed to traditional peacekeeping, became clearer. UNOSOM sought to highlight its progress, emphasising the peaceful nature of the country outside of Mogadishu, the end of the famine and the establishment of DCs, but the slow progress towards a political settlement in Somalia contradicted these claims.

These criticisms were not confined to the media and NGOs. Several troop contributors, most notably Italy, became increasingly uneasy about the conduct of UNOSOM. The Italian commander in Somalia was accused of conducting his own policy independent of UNOSOM, including contacts with the SNA. In turn, the Italian Government publicly criticised UNOSOM's approach and indicated it wanted to withdraw from Mogadishu. The UN responded by demanding the recall of the Italian commander in Somalia.

Apart from the policy differences, the friction between Italy and the UN also highlighted another of UNOSOM's problems, the lack of coordination between national contingents in Somalia. This difficulty, and the tendency of some national contingents to refer UNOSOM orders to their capitals for confirmation, appears to have seriously hampered UN operations in Mogadishu during this period.

As the war in Mogadishu developed, concern about the direction of UNOSOM's policy increased in the US Congress and media, particularly after the deaths of four US servicemen in early August. Critics argued that the UN and the US were effectively trapped in Somalia without a coherent policy beyond the elimination of Aideed. Although the US administration argued that the UN effort had been largely successful, Senate Majority Leader Bob Dole called for a reassessment of the US' role in Somalia. On 9 September, the US Senate approved a resolution calling for a report from the administration on its policy and long term goals in Somalia. Several days later, President Bill Clinton acknowledged that 'some renewed political initiative' was necessary.

Against this background of disquiet, the UN Security Council passed Resolution 865 on 22 September. While the resolution affirmed the UN's commitment to the restoration of law and order in Somalia, it also requested the Secretary-General to prepare a detailed plan setting out 'concrete steps' in UNOSOM's future strategy. The Secretary-General was also urged to encourage broad participation in the process of national reconciliation.

The casualties amongst peacekeepers in Mogadishu slowly mounted until, on 3 October, eighteen US servicemen were killed when the SNA succeeded in downing two US helicopters. One US serviceman was captured by the SNA. Televised pictures of the abuse of some of the bodies of the US dead, and of the captured airman, deeply shocked and angered American public opinion. Demands for a complete US withdrawal, already common, became insistent.

The Clinton administration reinforced its troops in Somalia, but also sent a special envoy to explore a political search. On 9 October, Aideed announced a unilateral ceasefire against UNOSOM.

On 13 October, the Clinton administration delivered the report to Congress on its policy in Somalia demanded in the Senate Resolution of 9 September. The report again defined the mission of US troops in Somalia as assisting in the provision of a secure environment to enable the free flow of humanitarian relief. It argued that this mission had been effectively completed and the remaining problems were primarily humanitarian and political. As a result, all US troops would be withdrawn by 31 March 1994.

Although after May 1993 the US component of UNOSOM numbered only about 4,000, they included some of its best trained troops, as well as essential logistic units. From the beginning of the UNITAF operation, the US had also played a decisive role in formulating the UN's strategy in Somalia, and against Aideed. Its decision to withdraw made UNOSOM unviable in its existing form and prompted other troop contributors to reconsider their commitment. The UN was, perforce, compelled to find a new strategy and new approach to Somalia.

UNOSOM II's mandate formally expired on 31 October 1993. The Security Council renewed it for an interim period until 18 November in Resolution 878 on 30 October and asked the Secretary-General to report on the situation. In that report, delivered on 12 November, Boutros-Ghali reaffirmed his view that 'without effective disarmament ... it would not be possible for the country to enjoy lasting peace and stability'.[49] Boutros-Ghali outlined three options for UNOSOM's future mandate.

- Retain the existing mandate, with the exception that UNOSOM would not take the initiative or use coercive methods of disarmament. UNOSOM, however, would have retained the right to use coercive methods of disarmament if necessary. This would have required the maintenance of UNOSOM's then troop strength (about 26,000);

---

[49] Further Report of the Secretary-General, UN Document Number S/26738, 12 November 1993, p.20.

- Confine UNOSOM's mandate to providing security for distribution of humanitarian aid and assisting reconstruction activities, while foregoing efforts to forcibly disarm the factions. Force would be used only in self-defence, in accordance with traditional peacekeeping practices. The troop requirement would have been about 16,000 personnel;

- Confine UNOSOM's mandate to securing the port and airport in Mogadishu and important ports and airfields in other parts of the country. UNOSOM would assist in the delivery of aid and in development projects, as well as continue with the formation of a Somali police force. About 5,000 personnel would have been required under this option.

In an important step away from the policy of the past few months, the Security Council approved Resolution 885 on 16 November, authorising the establishment of a Commission of Enquiry to investigate armed attacks on UNOSOM personnel and suspending arrest actions against those individuals who might be implicated in the 5 June attack on UNOSOM forces. This was followed by Resolution 886 of 18 November 1993, in which the Security Council decided to renew UNOSOM's mandate until 31 May 1994. It also requested a further report from the Secretary-General outlining a more detailed plan for UNOSOM's future strategy and decided to undertake a fundamental review of UNOSOM's mandate by 1 February 1994.

In his report to the Security Council, the Secretary-General briefly raised and quickly dismissed a fourth option, that of complete UN withdrawal from Somalia. He commented that 'total withdrawal would not be a responsible act'.[50] The UN's inadequacies and failures in Somalia have raised large questions about its role in international humanitarian crises, but there is little sign that it will be able quickly to extricate itself from its involvement in Somalia.

Conclusions

The failure of regional organisations

From the very beginning of its commitment to Somalia, the UN sought to involve major regional organisations such as the OAU, the Organisation of the Islamic Conference (OIC) and the Arab League. Their practical contribution, however, was very limited.

The failure of these organisations to become involved in any substantial way in Somalia raises serious doubts about whether they are

---

[50] Ibid. p.23.

able to play a role as effective mediators or peacemakers in national disputes. Their failure to respond to the Somali situation exposes significant institutional and political weaknesses. The executive bodies of these organisations lack the authority and the independence to embark on initiatives of their own. The OAU, at least, is seriously under resourced. Many of its members are in arrears and most of its limited budget is devoted to maintaining its bureaucracy in Addis Ababa.

The failure of these large regional organisations in this situation suggests the need for alternative strategies. The UN and donor countries, for instance, could encourage the development of smaller regional groupings such as the Intergovernmental Authority on Drought and Development. In late 1990 President Moi of Kenya proposed to use IGADD as a forum to discuss the Somali problem. As was noted earlier, there was little enthusiasm at the time for this suggestion, partly because IGADD was seen as a technical rather than a political organisation. Cooperation on a relatively small scale through fora such as IGADD, however, would help build institutional links between countries in particular regions and give them some tangible interests in preserving the stability of their neighbours.

The intensification of cooperation in sub-regional organisations may be a step towards strengthening some weak states, but the underlying problems would remain. The Horn of Africa is one of the poorest areas in the world. There is little intra-regional trade and most economic activity in the border areas of Ethiopia, Somalia and Kenya is dominated by nomadic pastoralists.

Somalia and the United Nations

Pressures for UN action. *International concern over famine and civil war* The international community demonstrated that it was unwilling to tolerate both mass starvation and the large scale theft of humanitarian supplies. In his November 1992 letter to the Security Council Boutros-Ghali raised and rejected the option the withdrawal of military support for humanitarian operations.

Public opinion in the West had a critical role in defining the course of international intervention in Somalia. It was only after the civilian casualty figures from the fighting in November and December 1991 in Mogadishu were widely publicised that pressure developed for the UN to take an active role in reconciling the factions. The first phase in the UN's involvement, UNOSOM, developed out of this pressure. UNOSOM, however, was an entirely inadequate response to the situation and was unable to arrest the slide into mass starvation. The problems surrounding UNOSOM rapidly became apparent, but it took another burst of international publicity, including the arrival of television, to spur the international community and the UN into action again. The support for large scale intervention, and the creation of UNITAF, grew out of media coverage between July and November 1992.

Limitations on UN action. *Poorly defined objectives* The UN was drawn into Somalia as much by the pressure of events as by any coherent set of objectives. As a result, UN activities have been marked by conflict over, and uncertainty about, aims. This uncertainty about the UN's role has reappeared in the debates about the function of UNOSOM II.

Public opinion. Just as the shift in public opinion towards international intervention in the latter part of 1992, so the shift against involvement after fighting began in Mogadishu in June 1993, particularly in the US, but also in other Western countries, influenced policy makers. In many ways, television pictures, of starving children and of wounded civilians and US soldiers, led the shift in opinion. These shifts emphasise the need for careful thought about objectives, both prior to an intervention and during its course. The dramatic potential of television pictures may severely hamper the range of options open to policy makers.

Limits on the authority of the Secretary-General. The development of the UN's response to the Somali crisis illustrates the limitations on the power of the Secretary-General to implement an agenda without the active support of some, at least, of the Permanent Five members of the Security Council. The Permanent Five bear at least part of the responsibility for the UN's lack of interest in the developing Somali problem during 1991. For much of 1992 the Permanent Five acceded only reluctantly to Boutros-Ghali's efforts to expand UN efforts in Somalia.

UN able to act effectively only when great powers engaged. The Secretary-General may have been freed from some of the limits imposed by the Cold War, but he remains dependent on the broader agendas of the Permanent Five. Only when the interest of some, at least, of these powers is engaged, as was that of the US at the end of 1992, will the UN be able to act effectively and with authority.

UN system. Throughout its involvement in Somalia, the UN's activities have been consistently marred by poor planning and slow reaction to the developing situation. There was little contingency planning for recommendations adopted by the Security Council and instructions in resolutions were implemented slowly. Negotiations with countries for financial and military contributions were also protracted. It appears that the UN's bureaucratic culture is ill equipped to deal with emergency situations.

Criteria for UN action when a state breaks down: Lessons of Somalia. *Humanitarian emergency* The Somalia crisis seems to indicate that a major criterion for UN intervention in the crises caused by failed states is the existence of an extreme humanitarian emergency. In the case of Somalia, it was fairly clear to outside observers throughout 1991 that the continuing civil war was generating a major humanitarian crisis. It was only when this situation deteriorated dramatically in the course of 1992 that the UN felt compelled to intervene.

Complete collapse of the state. The UN's intervention in Somalia was made possible by the completeness of the state's collapse. The absence of any state authorities, or of any moral claim by any of the warlords to represent the state, made intervention a comparatively easy choice for the UN and the international community. The issue of consent of any legitimate authorities could be ignored in the interests of the overwhelming majority of the population. It is doubtful whether the UN could have intervened militarily without the consent of legitimate state authorities.

Wide degree of consensus on the need for intervention and on the conduct of operations. Somalia demonstrated that the UN requires the active support of the Permanent Five members of the Security Council to intervene in a crisis resulting from a failed state. This support is likely to be forthcoming only when the interests of those powers are somehow engaged, either because they are strategic interests or because of domestic pressure. The loss of interest in Somalia by the US seriously impairs the ability of UNOSOM II to meet its mandate.

Support from other members of the international community, including major non-governmental organisations, is also highly desirable. The UN's intervention in Somalia has been marked by conflict between the major contributors, and with smaller contributors and NGOs, over aims and means of conducting the operation.

Financial support from the international community. Throughout its operations in Somalia, the UN has been troubled by a shortage of funds and a difficulty in identifying troop contributors. These problems have severely hampered its ability to meet the goals that have been set for it. It is clear that without extensive international financial support, UN intervention in failed states will not be successful.

These considerations appear to have played a critical role in determining whether the UN would intervene in the Somalia. Since that intervention there have been a number of calls for similar UN action in other parts of the African continent, such as the south Sudan. It is unlikely, however, that such intervention will occur. Although the Sudanese state has lost control of much of the south, it nevertheless remains a functioning entity and, to some extent, can block international efforts to provide relief to the south. Moreover, there is no developing international consensus, either among governments or major NGOs, on the need for intervention.

The international intervention in Somalia in many ways broke new ground. The course of the intervention, however, demonstrates that the UN remains dependent on the assistance and goodwill of the great powers which dominate its affairs. Without that assistance, it will be unable to muster sufficient support within the international community to undertake large scale operations in the future.

4 The Balkans

MICHAEL WILSON

Introduction

The end of the Cold War, the collapse of communist rule and the dissolution of the Soviet empire lifted the straitjacket of enforced discipline in Eastern Europe which is now undergoing a fundamental restructuring of state, society and economy. In southern Europe there have been three wars as the Socialist Federal Republic of Yugoslavia broke into five independent states. Two have been fought to protect and advance the minority interests of the Serbs in Croatia and the Serbs and Croats in Bosnia, backed by Serbian and Croatian national ambitions.

Europe has had little post-war experience dealing with minority claims which have hitherto been suppressed or ignored, but since 1990 there have been six such conflicts: three in Yugoslavia and three in the European areas of the former USSR. These events have been described as a process of renationalisation, i.e., the reassertion of independent nations, including the reawakening of nations or nationalities within those countries.[1]

Background

The causes of the Yugoslav wars are embedded in the complexity of history, language, religion and culture of the Balkans. Yugoslavia was divided for centuries between the empires of the Austro-Hungarian Catholic 'civilised' north and the Ottoman East Orthodox Muslim 'Balkan' south.

---

[1] Curt Gasteyger, 'European Security and the New Arc of Crisis', in *New Dimensions in International Security*, Adelphi Papers 265, (Winter 1991/92) pp.69-81.

Strong nationalisms developed: Serbian, Croat, Albanian and Slovenian. After World War II, the Macedonians and the Serbo-Croat speaking Muslims were also recognised as separate national groups, further diversifying the mosaic of peoples spread through the country. The most populous nationality, the Serbs, had led and inspired the way towards independence from the Turks in the 19th century; fought with the French in World War I against the Hapsburg Empire which then included present-day Croatia and Slovenia; and, laying claim to leadership in the new Yugoslavia, sought ascendancy over the other nationalities between 1918 and 1941. Ambivalent towards the occupying enemy in World War II, they were primarily engaged in civil war with Croats and Muslims and gave only qualified support to Tito's communist partisans. Post-war, in the second Yugoslavia, Tito kept Serbian ambitions well in check, even permitting, by the 1974 Constitution, an expansion of Albanian aspirations in Kosovo, the cradle of Serbism: in the Serbian perception an unforgivable act of humiliation and discrimination.

The communist slogan 'unity and brotherhood' was the key to Tito's policies to control nationalism and minorities. Nationalities were encouraged to find in the post-war federal Yugoslavia a higher and broader aspiration towards a new Yugoslav personality; assertive nationalism was discouraged; hostile religious and national differences were suppressed; the Party and the army (JNA) executed Tito's will.

Intense nationalist aspirations re-emerged in official politics in the 1960s and strengthened further after Tito's death in 1980, particularly in Croatia and Serbia. The Serbian leader, Slobodan Milosevic, successfully aroused Serbian grievances into a national movement for the assertion of Serbian hegemony over the federation. Minorities within Serbia suffered. The Albanians of Kosovo and the Hungarians of Vojvodina were by constitutional mugging stripped in 1989 of the autonomy granted under Tito and reduced - in the case of Kosovo - to intense forms of persecution and privation.

An equally intransigent and ambitious nationalism in Croatia resisted Serbian claims to domination within the federation. Croatia and Slovenia overthrew the internal monopoly of the Communist Party, held open elections and referenda and supported national 'sovereignty' within a confederation which, following Serbian intransigence, became support for secession from the federation, and independence. Macedonia followed suit a few months later. Bosnia, because of its three nationalities - Muslims, Serbs and Croats - was ambivalent but finally, because a majority was in favour, and the departure of Croatia and Slovenia made remaining in a Serb-dominated rump Yugoslavia unacceptable, was forced to choose independence, which provoked savage internal conflict - in many ways a rerun of 1941-44.

Civil war: Serbia/Croatia

Croatia and Serbia are each driven by an extreme and combative nationalism. Memories of the mutual (Chetnik/Ustashe) savagery perpetrated during World War II, largely suppressed under Tito, re-emerged in aggressive hostility in the early 1960s and again in the late 1980s when the federation began to break down. Serbia saw its future in a continued Federal state under Serbian domination which it was prepared to fight to maintain. Should the federation collapse the objective would become the achievement of Greater Serbia: the excision from Croatia of those parts where Serbs are the majority or a significant minority. Croatia resisted and in the 1991-92 war lost about one third of its territory where local Serb militias, aided by Belgrade, seized control.

Serbian fears had been intensified by the discriminatory national programs and policies of the Croatian Government. Croatia (and other republics) adopted a system defined as constitutional nationalism:[2] a constitutional and legal structure that privileges the members of one ethnically defined nation over other residents in a particular state. It envisages a state in which sovereignty resides with a particular nation, the members of which alone decide fundamental questions of state form and identity. Thus the Croatian Constitution is based primarily on the sovereignty of the dominant ethnic group rather than on equal citizens of the state. In the 1990 Constitution the Republic of Croatia is 'established as the national state of the Croatian nation and the state of the members of other nations and minorities that live within it'. The Serbian dialect and the Cyrillic alphabet used by Serbs were discarded in the Constitution and numerous practical acts (e.g., the requirement to sign loyalty oaths to Croatia and discrimination in employment) confirmed to Serbs that Croatian policy constituted a narrow ethnic and punitive nationalism which had to be resisted. (Croatia tried to meet these criticisms by adopting a minorities law in May 1992 which, although widely criticised, offered some autonomy in cultural and local administrative matters.) Much the same philosophy and policies were adopted by Serbia to reinforce and institutionalise discrimination in respect of its own Albanian, Hungarian and other minorities.

Tensions seem endemic; the minority believes it has no future in a state created on the basis of discrimination. It thus seeks self-determination, which is resisted on the grounds of the inviolability of frontiers. The choices seem to be the subjugation of the minority; secession of that part of the state, or expulsion of the disloyal minority (ethnic cleansing).

---

[2] R. M. Hayden, 'Constitutional Nationalism in the Formerly Yugoslav Republics', *Slavic Review* 51, 4 (Winter 1992), pp.654-73.

The European Community: Crisis management and Yugoslavia

At the outset of the Yugoslav crisis in 1990-91 Europe was preoccupied with the crisis of Soviet power, the reunification of Germany, proposals to amend the Treaty of Rome and the Single European Act for closer European integration leading up to the EC Summit at Maastricht, and the recent war with Iraq, in which the Europeans had essentially only followed Washington's lead.

The European Community (EC), therefore, approached Yugoslav concerns with reluctance and no very clear purposes, but with some sense of responsibility. It was seen, in geographical and historical terms, as a European problem and the US and the USSR were in the early stages only intermittently active. The EC had apparent leverage in Yugoslavia; more than 50 per cent of its trade was with the EC and there were extensive financial, aid and other arrangements.

Sound reasons of principle and policy caused the Europeans to hesitate to intervene:

- intervention would be regarded as interference in internal affairs, and thus a bad precedent - a view strongly put by the former USSR anxious to avoid any such action in its own territories (e.g., the Baltic States);

- respect for state sovereignty went hand-in-hand with the principle of the inviolability of national boundaries;

- the risk of a growing, expensive and lasting involvement;

- the risk of being shown to be impotent and losing credibility.

The first preference of the majority of EC members was for a political transition within existing constitutional structures (a view shared by Washington) rather than support for secession, most importantly because of the possible precedent of Yugoslavia for the Soviet Union, which the West was trying to keep together. However, a minority wanted to do something to support independence aspirations. The result was caution and extreme reluctance to take any initiative.[3]

There were practical problems in Yugoslavia for the major EC actors, inhibiting the prospects of coherent policy:

- France had close traditional ties with Serbia;

---

[3] Maarten Lak, 'The Involvement of the European Community in the Yugoslav Crisis During 1991' *Yearbook of European Studies* 5 (1992) pp.177-8; Gregory Treverton, 'The New Europe' *Foreign Affairs* 71, 1 (1991/92) pp.94-112; Josef Joffe, 'The New Europe: Yesterday's Ghosts' *Foreign Affairs* 72, 1 (1992/93) pp.29-43.

- Germany had historical (and wartime) connections with Croatia and Slovenia;

- Britain recoiled from a quarrel as prospectively endless as its military action in Northern Ireland.

There were structural difficulties for the EC. Earlier moves towards political integration led in 1969 to what became European political cooperation (EPC), a system involving an organisational order outside the formal treaty framework and based on intergovernmental cooperation. There were political commitments to establish and implement jointly a European foreign policy. But the record of EPC has at best been mixed and, while a pattern of solidarity could be detected, there was no common European policy. Thus the EC's machinery for conflict management and resolution was not highly developed or coherent.

A further and fundamental consideration was that Yugoslavia's significance as an important strategic actor during the Cold War warranting substantial Western political and economic support had disappeared, and some weight was given to the school of thought that would have left it to its own future.

The EC's responses to the very brief conflict in Slovenia (June-July 1991) and the longer war in Croatia (July 1991-January 1992) were slow to get started and operated initially on the erroneous assumption that Yugoslavia's crises could be successfully dealt with seriatim.[4] From the beginning force was excluded. A retrospective report (May 1992) to the European Parliament stated:

> If the EC had a defence policy and a rapid deployment force a threat of military intervention might have served some purpose. Yet intervention by land forces is not easy ... the federal army is strong ... intervention would not result in swift military successes.

It was President of the European Commission Jacques Delors' opinion in September 1991 that the EC had three weapons at its disposal: public opinion, the threat of recognition of Croatia and Slovenia, and economic sanctions. The EC's preventive diplomatic and peacemaking measures can be summarised as a mixture of mediation, conciliation, good offices and pressure (sanctions and recognition). With the exception of the agreement on Slovenia, all other peacemaking efforts were unsuccessful and were, at the end of 1991, undercut by the recognition of Croatia and Slovenia. Sanctions hurt Serbia but were not decisive. The same report to the European Parliament in an assessment up to January 1992 concluded:

> The Yugoslavian crisis has been a harsh reminder to the EC that it is not a superpower in the political and military sense, although it does enjoy such status in economic terms ... The discrepancy between

---

[4] Trevor Salmon, 'Cracks in European Unity?' *International Affairs* 68, 2 (April 1992) pp.233-53.

economic and political power makes the EC a disappointment when it seeks to resolve and control conflicts.

European Community peacemaking efforts

- Ministerial Missions, usually Troika Missions (the past, present and future EC Foreign Ministers). They had one success and subsequent failures. They negotiated a ceasefire in Slovenia (the Brioni Agreement). This came about less because of any intrinsic quality or leverage in the EC activity and more because the Yugoslav Army had decided to abandon Slovenia (where there was almost no Serbian minority) and concentrate its efforts in support of the Serbian minority already fighting in Croatia.

- Monitoring/Observer Missions. Unarmed observers were sent to Slovenia and Croatia, and later to Bosnia, as a preventive factor. Serbia and the Yugoslav Army objected to any moves to increase their number or to give them any rights of peaceful intervention.

- A Peace Conference, chaired by former British Foreign Secretary Lord Carrington (with staff and support from EC members), of all the parties at Head of Government level attempted to draw up a new constitution on the basis of a confederation, without any success. The above quoted report to the European Parliament stated: 'The EC has been faced with negotiating partners who regard the Conference - or its failure - merely as a means of safeguarding their own limited self-interests'. Carrington used his good offices to assist United Nations special envoy Cyrus Vance to negotiate ceasefires in moves towards the introduction of a UN force.

Sanctions. The EC employed its economic and financial leverage against Serbia: the cancellation of credit, suspension of the trade agreement, an arms embargo and an oil embargo. None of the sanctions had much impact. The arms embargo, for instance, had a selective effect to the advantage of the Serbs, who had access, in Bosnia as well as in Serbia, to the large federal arsenal. The lack of success of sanctions was partly because they were not observed by all EC members and principally because they were not being universally applied - a task which had to be taken up by the Security Council.

Recognition. The act of recognition by the EC in mid-January 1992[5] (preceded by a German announcement in mid-December) was a crucial decision. It was the principal lever in the EC's armoury. The threat to grant recognition to Croatia and Slovenia offered leverage with

---

5   John Newhouse, 'The Diplomatic Round: Dodging the Issue' *New Yorker* 68, 27 (24 August 1992).

Milosevic, the threat to withhold it provided leverage with the President of Croatia, Franjo Tudjman. Recognition was a one-time asset - once used, leverage would be lost. Bosnia wanted it withheld, fearing that if the independence of Croatia and Slovenia were recognised, Bosnia would be obliged to declare its independence, thus provoking the Bosnian Serbs, who, fearful for their own future outside the federal structure, would seek forcible redress. The United States, Carrington, Vance, and the UN Secretary-General Perez de Cueller all had warned against *premature* recognition.

Britain and France also opposed premature recognition in the hope that the EC would have some leverage in trying to extract concessions from Serbia and Croatia, but were swept along by their desire to make a success of the proposals for closer European integration at the Maastricht Summit (December 1991), at which Germany's role would be crucial. (The United States held to its view until April 1992.)

Germany and Austria led the way for recognition. The arguments were that :

- recognition would strengthen the position of Croatia and Slovenia;

- the process of separation by Serb-inhabited regions in Croatia was well advanced;

- the principle of self-determination should be upheld;

- the threat of recognition might force the Serbs to be more amenable to peace talks and the maintenance of ceasefires; and,

- recognition would have a beneficial effect, by example, on any territorial claims of successor states of the former USSR.

The decision destroyed Carrington's forlorn efforts to produce a constitution for a confederation of independent republics. Vance complained that it undercut his efforts to negotiate a durable ceasefire in Croatia and get agreement on the introduction of a UN peacekeeping force. It weakened EC influence in Serbia and gave it little over Tudjman. The decision fulfilled Bosnia's worst fears and probably advanced the date of the Serbian onslaught in Bosnia, but it is doubtful whether recognition did much more than to hasten the onset of a conflict which by then was virtually inevitable.

The Badinter Commission, set up by the EC to offer advice on the legal issues in Yugoslavia, did not certify that Croatia had met one of the EC's criteria for recognition - concerning minority rights - but this opinion was ignored.

Role of other European regional organisations

The Conference on Security and Cooperation in Europe (CSCE), the Western European Union (WEU) and the North Atlantic Treaty Organisation (NATO), the other regional organisations concerned with security issues, have had marginal roles in Yugoslavia, inhibited by their charters, their memberships and structures and uncertain or unable to offer more positive contributions. All, moreover, are constrained by the lack of unity of purpose and political will which have characterised the Western response from the outset.

CSCE. The CSCE[6] is the only institution encompassing both Eastern and Western Europe as well as the US, Canada and the former USSR. It has evolved from the Helsinki Act of 1975 into an association of 53 countries (including the former Yugoslavia), operating by consensus. It was created to make Europe more secure and stable by concentrating on its territorial status quo and by attenuating its political divisions.

It is now slowly evolving towards a structural system of political consultation with its own institutions and mechanisms. It ascribed to itself in the Paris Charter (1990) a number of functions in conflict prevention and crisis management that it was not particularly equipped to carry out in respect of Yugoslavia, being handicapped by its unanimity principle (now adapted to consensus minus one in the event of a conflict concerning a Member State). Its role, therefore, in the Yugoslav crisis where protagonists seek to advance the interests of selected minorities and to alter boundaries, if need be by force, to achieve self-determination, could not be anything but marginal. It has been used principally as a sounding board to broaden and endorse the legitimacy of EC claims and actions.

It is now, in the light of the Yugoslav crisis, considering what means of coercion could be taken about defecting states, including more effective decision making procedures, sanctions, peacekeeping and peacemaking.

It is also beginning to grapple with the principles concerning legitimate intervention in cases of aggression directed by a state against its own society - especially aggression directed against the minorities of that society. Consistent with this approach is the French initiative for the negotiated settlement of Eastern European minority population questions, assisted by European mediators/monitors and endorsed in a 'European Pact'. The intense nationalisms in Eastern Europe would make this a task of very considerable complexity.

WEU. Described variously as the European pillar of NATO and the security and defence pillar of European integration, the WEU has only eleven members, all EC, and cannot yet justifiably claim an effective European role. It has no direct security obligations.

---

6 Gasteyger, 'European Security and the New Arc of Crisis'; Ian Cuthbertson (ed.), *Redefining the CSCE: Challenges and Opportunities in the New Europe* (New York: Institute for East-West Studies, 1992).

Its role in Yugoslavia has been at best marginal. France has attempted to enhance the WEU by having it act as the potential military arm of the EC and has attempted to bring it into military planning on Yugoslavia. These endeavours have encountered American concerns that an improved WEU could weaken US influence in Europe and perhaps diminish European interest in NATO. Its practical role has been confined to supporting NATO with military planning for the force required to implement a Bosnian settlement, naval patrols in the Adriatic and measures to strengthen the implementation of the embargo on the Danube.

NATO. NATO seems to be a resource going to waste. It has had difficulty in adapting to the post-Cold War era where the emphasis now is to protect security in Central and Eastern Europe. Efforts persist to 'Europeanise' it which risks alienating the United States. There are conflicting views whether NATO should now be disbanded in favour of the CSCE or whether it is capable of providing the CSCE with support for peacekeeping.

NATO would wish to have a substantial role in Yugoslavia but it seems frustrated by lack of clear objectives from policy makers.

In Bosnia it has done military planning in support of CSCE and UN decisions. It is responsible for enforcing sanctions in the Adriatic and the no-fly zone in Bosnia; it is planning NATO participation in providing protective air power for the United Nations Protection Force (UNPROFOR) as part of the establishment of the safe areas and in the provision of more troops for the Force. It would have a major role in planning for any Force to safeguard a Bosnian peace settlement.

The United Nations in Croatia

The EC peacemaking efforts in Yugoslavia in the second half of 1991 (ministerial 'Troika' missions, observer missions, conference of all parties, sanctions) were achieving little. Ceasefire agreements were repeatedly broken, fighting intensified and the option of the use of a peacekeeping force entered the debate. The mood in the EC, possibly exasperated at its own impotence, was that this was a task for the UN Security Council which had acquired greater authority and stature following the end of the Cold War and the recent success in Iraq. The Security Council became engaged in September 1991 and Vance was appointed as the Secretary-General's envoy to augment the EC's failing efforts.[7] He negotiated ceasefires in November 1991 and January 1992, and pursued discussion with the parties for the possible introduction of a UN peacekeeping force which they indicated they wanted.

---

7 United Nations Document S/RES 713 25 September 1991.

Concept for UN peacekeeping operation

The basic principle of the UN force 'would be an interim arrangement to create the conditions of peace and security required for the negotiation of an overall settlement of the Yugoslav crisis'.[8] The operation would follow standard UN practice and be established by the Security Council on the recommendation of the Secretary-General. It was assumed that the parties ('all concerned') would abide by the arrangements 'in a serious and sustained way' including an unconditional ceasefire and that they would cooperate to enable the peacekeeping operation force to carry out its functions.

- The military and police personnel required would be contributed voluntarily by member states and approved by the Security Council after consultation with the parties; and

- the operation would be established initially for twelve months and financed collectively by member states.

The force would be deployed in regions of Croatia where Serbs constituted the majority, or a substantial minority, of the population and where fighting had taken place. These areas would be designated UN Protected Areas; they would be demilitarised and all armed forces in them would be withdrawn or disbanded. The Yugoslav National Army would withdraw from Croatia. The existing local authorities would continue to function, under UN supervision, pending an overall settlement. Weapons of local units would be placed in secure storage under a two lock system. The UN force would have civilian police monitors to supervise local police and a civilian complement to perform a range of political, legal and administrative functions.

Signalling obstructions to come,[9] the establishment of the force was delayed by the objections of the 'Government' of the self-proclaimed 'Republic of Serbian Krajina'. The reference to the UN Protected Areas as being 'in Croatia' was unacceptable because it prejudged the political solution; demilitarisation of the UN Protected Areas was rejected, and the people of Krajina would not disarm because the UN Force could not protect them from the Croatian Government's public commitment to restore its authority over all the territory of Croatia, including the United Nations Protected Areas (UNPAs). Croatia entered reservations because the plan did not immediately provide for the restoration of that authority. The UN was obliged to clarify its intentions,[10] namely that:

---

[8] United Nations Document S/23280 11 December 1991. Report of the Secretary General Annex III.
[9] United Nations Document S/23513 4 February 1992. Report of the Secretary General.
[10] Ibid.

- the force would not be withdrawn before an overall political solution was found;

- the deployment of the force would not prejudge the outcome of the political process;

- in respect of arrangements for local government and the maintenance of law and order in the UNPAs, the deployment of the force would not change the status quo;

- the UNPAs would continue *not* to be subject to the laws and institutions of Croatia pending a political settlement;

- the force would protect the local population.

Tudjman backed down and reaffirmed his commitment to the force and the Serbian authorities put successful pressure on Krajina:

> ... the decision [of the Krajina Assembly] means the definitive and unconditional acceptance of the UN plan and full readiness to cooperate in its execution.[11]

The Secretary-General, now Boutros Boutros-Ghali, was not wholly convinced of the good faith of the Krajina Serbs who 'constitute a potential danger to implementation of the plan' but concluded that the danger that the plan might fail because of lack of cooperation was less than the danger that delay would lead to a breakdown of the ceasefire and a renewal of fighting.[12] UNPROFOR was established, for a period of twelve months, on the above basis on 21 February 1992. It took four months to get the force of more than 13,000 in place. A statement is attached at Annex A listing the national contributions to UNPROFOR up to 31 May 1993 and the costs of the operation up to 30 June 1993.

Peacekeeping and peacemaking: European Community and United Nations

The Secretary-General saw the UN and the EC Conference on Yugoslavia as mutually supporting roles: 'The Conference ... remains the only forum where all the Yugoslav republics have agreed to participate in an effort to arrive at an agreed negotiated settlement ...' and the UN operation has been 'conceived as being to create the basic conditions for the necessary negotiations between the parties ...'[13]

---

[11] United Nations Document S/23592 15 February 1992. Report of the Secretary General.
[12] Ibid.
[13] United Nations Document S/23363 5 January 1992. Report of the Secretary General.

He also maintained well into 1992, that it might be more appropriate that in Bosnia the EC, rather than the UN, undertake the peacekeeping as well as the peacemaking;[14] that the UN's mandate was uncertain, and that Europe had the primary interest and responsibility. These concerns not only reflected his own appreciation of the risks in Yugoslavia but also his view that the UN was too Eurocentric and should be helping the Third World more with its problems, e.g., Somalia.

Changes in UNPROFOR's mandate. The mandate has been amended seven times, principally:
- to undertake monitoring functions in the Serb controlled areas of Croatia lying outside the UNPAs, the 'Pink Zones'; and
- to carry out immigration and customs functions where the boundaries of the UNPAs coincide with Croatian frontiers.

These later measures indicate the evolution on the ground which has drawn UNPROFOR into quasi-government functions which go beyond normal peacekeeping practice.

Renewal of the mandate. Reviewing the first year of the Force, the Secretary-General advised in April 1993 that:

> UNPROFOR is severely handicapped in performing its functions and its personnel are in peril. In the circumstances it is currently not possible for UNPROFOR to fulfil its mandate in Croatia.[15]

He reported that the Serbs took the presence of UNPROFOR 'as a licence to freeze the status quo in place, under UNPROFOR "protection", while establishing a "state" of the "Republic of Serb Krajina" in UNPROFOR's area of responsibility'. The Croatians insist that since Croatia has been recognised as an independent state and admitted to the UN there is no longer 'an overall political settlement' to negotiate. The issue is the return of the UNPAs to Croatian authority with Serbian minority rights guaranteed in the constitution and legislation.

The International Conference on the Former Yugoslavia (co-chaired by Cyrus Vance and David Owen), which replaced the EC Conference on Yugoslavia, then took the same view: a settlement was to be sought without change to Croatia's borders. The Security Council endorsed this view and supported

> ... the Co-Chairmen ... in their efforts to help to define the future status of those territories comprising the UNPAs which are integral parts of the territory of Croatia.

---

[14] United Nations Document S/23900 12 May 1992. Report of the Secretary General.
[15] United Nations Document S/25777 15 May 1993. Report of the Secretary General.

The three options for the future of UNPROFOR put forward by the Secretary-General in May 1993 indicated the difficulties of any course of action:

- Withdrawal: This would almost certainly precipitate a resumption of hostilities, but where the mandate could not be implemented would not prolongation 'become an expensive and open-ended commitment'?

- Enforcement: this would bring UNPROFOR into direct conflict with the Serbs; would require additional forces (not easily found); and, with the added risks, some contributors might withdraw; others might not be willing to provide the substantial additional forces required.

- Renewal (but with added strength): this would require hope that negotiations and sanctions would moderate Serbian positions and that Croatia would be prepared to 'wait indefinitely for the restoration of its authority'.[16]

The mandate has been renewed on the same basis for three months until the end of September and thus UNPROFOR remains in an invidious position. It has been suggested that the current cooperation between the Croats and Serbs in their planned disposition of Bosnia has led to a temporary coincidence of interest.

Comment

European role. The European engagement in Croatia has been inglorious. It has been characterised by vacillation, a reluctance to intervene in an internal conflict with unknown and indefinite consequences and, above all, by a conflict of policies among the three major EC players.

The shortcomings of the preventive and peacemaking structures of the EC and CSCE have been amply demonstrated: the EC lacked a common will and the CSCE was hamstrung by its unanimity rule and lack of common purpose. Their diplomatic techniques were inadequate: the threat of force was excluded from the beginning and the timing of recognition of Croatia was mishandled. The EC and CSCE will have to improve their planning and systems in preventive diplomacy and deployment. The initiative in Macedonia (see below) is a minor step forward. Intervention on humanitarian grounds may become a norm.

The development of strategies for models for early warning of political crises, particularly in relation to minorities questions, could be a useful ingredient in the development of CSCE principles and mechanisms for preventive diplomacy/deployment, and the French proposal for a European Pact takes account of such shortcomings. NATO's resources could be

---

[16] Ibid.

applied more productively as the CSCE's military planning and executing agent.

UNPROFOR in Croatia. UNPROFOR has had mixed results in the discharge of its mandate. It has managed to maintain a precarious ceasefire but there have been numerous, flagrant transgressions by all sides which have got progressively worse during 1993. The worst was a Croatian attack on the Serb-held positions in January 1993 which led the Serbs to recover their heavy weapons and mobilise their forces (see below).

UNPROFOR succeeded in ensuring the complete withdrawal of the JNA from Croatia (possibly due to the JNA's intention to prepare for deployment in Bosnia); in putting the JNA's heavy weapons into storage (for twelve months), and in partially disarming the militia in the UNPAs.

It has had very limited success in impeding or reversing ethnic cleansing and other human rights abuses and is itself subject to daily manifestations of hostility and restrictions on its freedom of movement. It has been unable to demilitarise the UNPAs, to complete the disarming of local forces or to prevent their re-arming. It has therefore been unable to establish conditions to permit the return of displaced people.

The original concept for the force envisaged that it would remain until the conditions required for the negotiation of an overall settlement had been achieved. In retrospect, this seems an improbable objective, implying an open-ended commitment. Both Vance and the UN Secretary-General were sceptical of the good faith of the parties, however, and hesitated to recommend the Force to the Security Council. There does seem to have been an over optimistic perception and expectation of the capacity for compromise between Serbs and Croats and their willingness to abide by agreements, and too much faith may have been placed in the Peace Conference under Carrington. The misperceptions now seem widespread. But the international community was in a weak position: force had been excluded; its hand had been weakened by recognition and there was a high public expectation and momentum for action to prevent or impede a resumption of the war. Few foresaw the speed and depth of the Bosnian conflict, rendering compromise in Croatia up to the present even less likely.

Faced with a prospectively indefinite engagement in an expensive and apparently insoluble operation the UN may have to consider condoning a settlement between Serbs and Croats involving a tacit, if not legally recognised, redrawing of boundaries within both Croatia and Bosnia, despite the repeated declarations of the international community.

These complexities and difficulties for UNPROFOR raise more general observations:

- the desirability of and adherence to a firm termination point in major UN operations would seem essential to avoid indefinite engagement;

- the record shows that the Secretary-General has consistently advised against over-extending the UN's role (in part because he had his Third World constituency in mind), that he recognised before others the pitfalls for the UN in Croatia (and Bosnia) and that he had an accurate perception of the rightful and primary role of the European regional organisations. This would suggest that the sources of information and intelligence available to the Secretary-General are sufficient and that the weaknesses in the Secretariat's role in peacekeeping lie less in perception than in the lack of resources for the management of major operations.

- on the experience of Yugoslavia, the UN should consider reverting to a more restrictive and limited interpretation of its peacekeeping role and concentrate on actions under Chapter VI, including preventive diplomacy and preventive deployment - as in Macedonia - leaving Chapter VII type actions to individual states and regional organisations except in those very few scenarios where at least four of the permanent members of the Security Council should become willingly and wholeheartedly engaged. (The actions in Yugoslavia have been weakened by the decisions of the US and Russia to confine their roles very largely to diplomacy.)

Bosnia

Bosnia's internal stability had historically been guaranteed by an external force (the Ottoman Empire, the Hapsburg Empire, the royal dictatorship of the 1930s, Tito) which mediated between the communities. When this guarantee broke down between 1941 and 1944, a savage civil war raged. Caught between Croatian and Slovenian moves towards independence in 1990 and demands for unity under Serbian leadership, Bosnia vainly sought protective constitutional expedients.

Croatian and Slovenian independence left Bosnia a terrible choice: staying with Serbia (opposed by Croats and Muslims) or declaring independence (opposed by Serbs), sovereign and recognised, but unable to defend itself. Its hand was forced: the Badinter Report concluded that there should be a referendum to determine whether the demand for independence had public support. The referendum result was for independence but it was boycotted by most Serbs. The Bosnian Serbs assisted by the JNA and the Serbian Government prepared for war. The Serbs claim that they are defending Christendom against the Muslims and point to the imprisonment of Alija Izetbegovic (now President of Bosnia-Hercegovina) by Tito for advocating fundamentalism, the presence of Arab irregulars, and the supply of arms to the Muslims despite the embargo.

UNPROFOR in Bosnia

Foreseeing the ruinous choices, Bosnia in late 1991 appealed for a UN presence as the minimum form of protection. In January 1992 Izetbegovic renewed his request for the 'preventive' deployment immediately of 2,000-3,000 UN peacekeepers. (It had been envisaged as part of the Vance plan for Croatia put forward in December that a small detachment of observers be sent to Bosnia.) The UN Secretary-General preferred to hold over the Bosnian request.

Bosnia repeated its call for the deployment of a UN force after fighting began in April 1992. The UN Secretary-General said UNPROFOR's mandate was confined to Croatia and the Bosnians should address themselves to the EC. But after a report by Vance the deployment of a small contingent of observers was approved at the end of June 1992. A peacekeeping force was ruled out because of the widespread violence. The UN headquarters in Sarajevo, put there before the war to offer Bosnia some diplomatic protection, used its good offices when the city was besieged to provide humanitarian support and to evacuate people. The pattern of the conflict intensified, dispossessed people were moved on a big scale, and the parties broke repeated ceasefire agreements negotiated by the European Community and the United Nations.

In May 1992 the Secretary-General canvassed, but did not press, the possibility of an 'intervention force' to be sent in without the consent of all the parties, to enforce an end to the fighting - as requested by the Bosnian Government. He also canvassed the concept of armed UN forces to protect convoys of relief supplies, but set it aside because of the risks to the UNPROFOR in Croatia.

Driven by events, the mandate of UNPROFOR was extended in June 1992 to permit the deployment of UNPROFOR to protect Sarajevo airport in order that the unimpeded delivery of humanitarian supplies could take place. UNPROFOR's mandate and strength were enlarged in September 1992 to protect convoys of former prisoners. In October 1992 military flights in Bosnia were banned, a symbolic rather than a practical gesture. The concept of safe areas was put to study in November 1992. The Vance/Owen peace talks for a Bosnian settlement intensified and were put forward and rejected in early 1993. By February 1993 the Security Council had adopted the safe areas concept and authorised the use of UN force to protect UNPROFOR troops in them and the use of airpower in support. This was reaffirmed in June, when it also authorised the deployment of reinforcements to UNPROFOR.

Human rights

The scale of human rights' abuses has led the Security Council to establish two new mechanisms to deal with breaches of humanitarian law. One is a Commission of Experts to collect evidence of breaches of Geneva Conventions, etc., and the other, advocated by the Co-Chairmen, is an international tribunal for the prosecutions of violations of international humanitarian law.

The Vance/Owen proposals for the new Constitutional arrangements in Bosnia introduced innovations for the protection of human rights such as a human rights court, a human rights commissioner and an international commission on human rights. These concepts may well be revived in the event of a settlement in Bosnia.

Comment

Bosnia is a sorry tale: both peacekeeping and peacemaking have failed. The UN was faced with an impossible task: UNPROFOR has no clear mandate in Bosnia. Overtaken and almost overwhelmed by the speed and intensity of the war, and driven along by public opinion, the Force and the mandate have been expanded haphazardly to meet humanitarian needs. It lacks authority to coordinate the numerous UN agencies engaged in Bosnia. It has moved from expedient to experiment - secure corridors, no fly zones, safe areas - in its attempts at preventive actions. Since enforcement was ruled out it has had to commit the cardinal error of a peacekeeping presence among warring parties without any worthwhile assurance of their support, let alone cooperation. The public policy disagreements among the permanent members of the Security Council have neither strengthened the authority of the Council nor the prestige of the force on the ground.

UNPROFOR has intervened repeatedly in the past fifteen months to try to negotiate local and temporary ceasefires; to try to protect people against wholesale human rights abuses; to expose and help bring to an end the more systematic patterns of abuse (starvation in prison camps; rape of women); to introduce safe areas. But it has been able to achieve little more than to safeguard relief convoys and secure some people from the fighting. Undoubtedly, however, without the UN presence, more people would have been killed, or died from the conditions under which they have been forced to live.

At the peacemaking level, Co-Chairmen Vance and Owen, put forward the outline of a new constitution for Bosnia - a very loose central government - which was to be the basis for a negotiated settlement. It rested on the unity of Bosnia, the sanctity of national borders and respect for national rights. Bosnian Muslims and Croats agreed to it but Bosnian Serbs rejected it since, *inter alia*, it would have required them to surrender territory acquired forcibly. The Vance/Owen plan is now regarded as dead, even by its authors.

The policy divisions among the major powers, evident in the Croatian conflict, persisted in Bosnia. Britain and France, each of whom has sizeable forces on the ground, have been unwilling to give too much weight to US views while it remains unwilling to commit ground troops (except to help implement a durable peace settlement). There was division over the Vance/Owen plan: the American perception was that it rewarded Serbian gains and was in any event unworkable. The Europeans took the view that it was the only realistic option available.

There is currently division over the best military methods to protect the safe areas. Even more contentious is the argument to lift selectively the Security Council's arms embargo and allow the supply of arms to the Muslims. The US, Third World countries, and now Germany, back the Bosnian argument that a sovereign state, internationally recognised, has the right to obtain arms to defend itself in accordance with Article 51 of the Charter and thus redress the internal military (and political) balance more in its favour. Britain and France say that this course would only intensify and prolong the conflict, bring humanitarian relief efforts to an end and put their troops even more at risk.

- Bosnia is a conflict where the international community is unwilling to intervene with sufficient force for an indefinite time to stop the war and enforce a settlement;

- it illustrates the risks of UN intervention without a clear mandate, without a time limit and without the assured cooperation and support of the parties;

- the evidence of the reluctant, confused and divided EC/UN interventions in Croatia in 1990 and 1991, and similar hesitations in Bosnia, demonstrated to Bosnian Serbs and Croats that they could safely disregard the international community in pursuit of their territorial ambitions in Bosnia;

- the prospect is a Bosnia divided principally among the Serbs and Croats with the Muslims, the most populous of the three groups, coming a poor third territorially should there be a ceasefire. This would point to an indefinite UN involvement, not least in regard to humanitarian issues (it is estimated that some 2.5 millions have been dispossessed), but also towards wider political issues: guarantees for Muslim territory; constitutional arrangements; protection of human rights;

- the pressure of public and government opinion for protective humanitarian measures in Bosnia has carried the UN Secretary-General and the Security Council well beyond the conventional functions of a peacekeeping operation. New concepts and definitions may seem to be emerging regarding the right of international intervention on humanitarian grounds and for the legal protection of human rights.

Macedonia and Kosovo: CSCE/EC/UN

Macedonia

Macedonia is significant in the context of peacekeeping efforts in Yugoslavia because it is a minor innovative exercise in UN/EC/CSCE preventive diplomacy and deployment. A force of 1,000 plus military observers and civil police is deployed along Macedonia's borders with Albania and Serbia.

Macedonia used to be part of Serbia and was awarded republican status by Tito for its part in World War II - 'a weak Serbia is a strong Yugoslavia'. Neighbouring Bulgaria and Greece - and many Serbs, unofficially - dismiss the Macedonian nationality and language as Titoist fabrications.[17] Following Croatia and Serbia, Macedonia declared its independence in 1991, but its existence is precarious. It is a weak, poor state and its very name is challenged by Greece, frustrating the exercise of sovereignty, jeopardising the existing moderate government and denying it international recognition. After a year of Greek obstruction and EC failure to pull Greece into line, Macedonia has been admitted to the UN under the provisional title of 'The Former Yugoslav Republic of Macedonia', but its final name remains unresolved.

Macedonia adjoins Albania and Kosovo (90 per cent or more Albanian) and its future stability and security are interwoven with Kosovo. More than one quarter of Macedonia's population is Albanian, who form a majority in the western communes bordering Kosovo and Albania, but as in the case of minorities in Croatia and Serbia they are not seen as a constituent part of Macedonia and relations are strained between them and the other communities.

A CSCE mission was sent to Macedonia in 1992 but late in the year Macedonia requested a UN presence fearful that if conflict erupted in Kosovo it would be dragged in. Albania had indicated that in the event of conflict it would support Kosovo. What was sought was a force to monitor the borders and report developments which could signify a threat to the territory of Macedonia. A UN presence would also serve as a deterrent to external aggression against Macedonia. The Security Council authorised the deployment of the small force in December 1992[18] and the United States has recently added weight to the UN presence by deploying 300 troops to Macedonia, in 'support of multilateral efforts to prevent spill over and contribute to stability'.[19]

---

[17] Mark Thompson, *A Paper House: the End of Yugoslavia* (London: Hutchinson Radius, 1992).
[18] United Nations Document S/24923 9 December 1992. Report of the Secretary General.
[19] United Nations Document S/25934 11 June 1993. Report of the Secretary General.

The Co-Chairmen of the Conference on the Former Yugoslavia (Vance/Owen) tried in April/May 1993 to put in place additional confidence-building measures in Macedonia. Apart from negotiating with Greece and Macedonia on an acceptable name for Macedonia, they proposed a draft treaty between the two countries, which would confirm the existing frontier and establish measures for confidence-building, friendship and neighbourly cooperation.[20] Nothing firm has yet come of this.

Given the extreme economic and political weakness of Macedonia, (e.g., its inability or unwillingness to prevent Greek sanction breakers traversing its territory), its potentially predatory neighbours and the high risk of a conflagration in Kosovo, the preventive deployment and confidence-building measures are prudent and timely and, with the added presence of US forces, may be some form of deterrent to any moves against, or through, Macedonia.

As an exercise in preventive diplomacy and deployment - the first of its kind - Macedonia deserves the close and continuing attention of the UN and regional organisations, especially in regard to the treatment of its Albanian minority. It is a practical instance where the continued application of preventive measures is necessary and justified. Pressure should continue to be placed on Greece (especially by the EC and the CSCE), in order to get rid of the incubus of the contested name, and a continual effort to get durable bilateral confidence-building mechanisms in place should be maintained.

Kosovo

When the Yugoslav federation began to disintegrate it was widely assumed that the Albanians in Kosovo would seek to break away from Serbia and declare their independence or seek a close association with Albania. Serbs insist that Kosovo must remain an integral part of any Serbian state, and governed by Serbs, since for them it is the 'cradle of Serbdom' (the site of the origins of the Serbian Orthodox Church and of a major medieval defeat at Turkish hands). Mainly to weaken the Serbs, Tito permitted Kosovo the status of an autonomous region: Albanian nationalism flourished and the movement for a republic within the federation grew. Milosevic reversed this: by constitutional chicanery and bullying the constitution was revoked in 1989 and Kosovo reverted to a condition of extreme subordination within Serbia. Most rights have been denied to Albanians and they are treated as 'a captive tribe'.

The mechanisms of early warning and preventive diplomacy could be applied more vigorously in Kosovo, against the widespread predictions of conflict which it is assessed would bring in outside forces. Whereas Croatia and Bosnia are essentially internal conflicts and have not drawn in outside powers (except in the UN context), Macedonia and Kosovo already

---

[20] United Nations Document S/25855 28 May 1993 Report of the Secretary General.

excite the direct attention of Bulgaria, Greece and Turkey. A further conflict involving (Albanian) Muslims could strengthen wider concerns, and perhaps participation among Arab countries, already sensitive to the perceived indifference of the West to the condition of the Bosnian Muslims.

But the UN shows no disposition to push the Serbs to reconsider their refusal to have UN observers in Kosovo nor to press for measures to ease the burden of the Albanians. The CSCE has not done much better. It has a small observer mission Kosovo. The Serbs are applying pressure by asking it to leave in view of the continued exclusion of the former Yugoslavia from CSCE deliberations. Nevertheless, with its spread of European membership involving all the potential participants in any conflict, the CSCE seems best placed to apply more active preventive diplomacy.

ANNEX A

Contributions to UNPROFOR

Country	Civil Police	Troops	Military Observers
Argentina	30	882	4
Australia			1
Bangladesh	44		24
Belgium		802	6
Brazil			13
Canada	45	2,171	15
Colombia	46		4
Czech Rep.		492	19
Denmark	39	1,240 (M)	27
Egypt	17	414	13
Finland		510 (M)	8
France	42	4,954	12
Ghana			17
Ireland	20		6
Jordan	46	931	31
Kenya	44	890	36
Luxembourg		35	
Nepal	45	894	6
Netherlands		1042	38
New Zealand			9
Nigeria	30	871	6
Norway	30	335 (M)	24
Poland	30	903	17
Portugal	35	9	12
Russian Fed'n	36	874	12
Slovak Rep.		409	
Spain		985	10
Sweden	30	360 (M)	5
Switzerland			6
Tunisia	12		
Ukraine		362	
United Kingdom		2453	9
United States		665 (M)	
Venezuela			3
TOTALS	621	23,483	393

(Total UNPROFOR - 24,497)

Notes:

1. Data as of 31 May 1993 except for the recent deployment of 300 US troops to Macedonia Command (included in US total of 665).

2. Figures followed by an (M) include troops deployed to Macedonia Command as a preventive deployment.

Financing of UNPROFOR

Total UN assessments to 30 June 1993: $716,754,979
Amount received: $469,435,688
Additional assessment requested to 30 June 1993: $334,482,200

This provides for the UN to assume all costs of UNPROFOR for the period 1 April -30 June 1993 (see below) plus the expansion into the Former Yugoslav Republic of Macedonia and the 50 observers in Bosnian safe havens.

The estimated monthly cost of UNPROFOR from 30 June 1993 onwards as it is presently established is $77,065,450.

From 1 April 1993, all UNPROFOR activities are to be met from the UNPROFOR account. Prior to that troops deployed in Bosnia were provided at no cost to the UN.

5 The International Response to Humanitarian Emergencies

JAMES INGRAM

Introduction

In this barbarous century the impact of war has greatly changed. According to one estimate[1] only 5 per cent of the casualties in World War I were civilians. The proportion rose to 50 per cent during World War II and is now about 80 per cent, a high proportion being women and children. Most of this suffering arises from armed conflicts, involving massive displacements of peoples. The end of the Cold War and the impact of the electronic media on public opinion has led governments to turn to the United Nations as an instrument for ending conflict and providing more effective succour for its victims. The dimensions of the problem are considerable. The United Nations has estimated current refugees at seventeen million and displaced persons within and beyond national borders at twenty million.[2]

Recent decisions of the United Nations Security Council have authorised the use of armed force in support of relief assistance to suffering civilians and to protect them from violence. Military forces are quite frequently used for relief purposes in natural disasters outside their own country. Historically, justification of the use of force for humanitarian purposes is not new. What is new is that states acting collectively under

---

[1] James P. Grant, *The State of the World's Children* (New York: UNICEF, 1992) p.26.
[2] Boutros Boutros-Ghali, *An Agenda for Peace - Preventive Diplomacy, Peacemaking and Peace-Keeping* (New York: United Nations, 1992) p.7.

the security provisions of the United Nations Charter have used force to intervene in ways which, arguably, are contrary to international law on the sovereignty of states. International humanitarian law, contained in the Geneva Convention of 1949 and Additional Protocols of 1977, is well defined in relation to non-international and national conflicts. However, enforcement is lacking. Through a range of measures, from diplomatic pressure to economic sanctions and military coercion, the Security Council has now established a *de facto* right of intervention on humanitarian grounds that in practice overrides any claim of domestic jurisdiction. However, the Council's decisions are not based on any set of agreed criteria and many grave humanitarian situations go unconsidered. Council action is essentially opportunistic, being reached on political grounds.

The purpose of this study is to explore the relationship between the security and humanitarian functions of the United Nations *from the humanitarian perspective*. The focus is neither on law nor on peacemaking and peacekeeping as such. Instead, the humanitarian impact of selected concrete United Nations interventions is examined to assess two things: first, the degree of success achieved in saving civilian lives and relieving life-threatening suffering; and secondly, the potential incompatibility between the peacemaking/keeping role of the United Nations and the humanitarian requirements of impartiality and neutrality. In this context alternatives to forceful intervention are considered. The cost of international relief operations and peacekeeping for humanitarian purposes, especially when measured against flows of development assistance, is already very high. Having regard to the likelihood that current levels of non-international conflict will continue, and may increase, possibilities for improving the effectiveness and efficiency of the United Nations overall response are considered and recommendations made. In view of the likelihood that the media's focus on suffering will from time to time force the Security Council to consider further coercive interventions on humanitarian grounds a serious attempt to rationalise the current incoherent approach is essential. Possibilities for achieving this are considered.

The developing role of the United Nations

Through the 1980s there had been an explosion in numbers of refugees and displaced persons in Africa, Asia and Central America. This was particularly so in Africa where problems were multiplying and worsening. The combination of recurring drought, falling food production and civil conflict had given rise to intractable relief problems in Mozambique, Angola, Ethiopia and Sudan, to name the more noteworthy examples. The humanitarian interventions of United Nations agencies in these situations were constrained by the requirement that they confine their dealings to governments. In civil war situations this meant that only the needy under government control were reached. Refugees entering neighbouring states could usually be assisted by United Nations agencies operating within the states of refuge. Non-governmental agencies operated across borders to gain access to the suffering, including displaced persons, in areas outside government control. In some instances their work received substantial funding from donor governments. While chaotic in organisation and wasteful of resources - government areas were often relatively oversupplied with food aid, for example - and something of a blunt instrument in terms of reaching the neediest, the system worked reasonably well although it undoubtedly helped to keep tyrannical regimes in power (Ethiopia) and sustained insurgencies (southern Sudan, Namibia, Cambodia). However, donor governments were more concerned by what they saw as poorly coordinated, inefficient operations.

Operation Lifeline Sudan

A catastrophic loss of life in southern Sudan in 1988, due to the on-going civil war in that country and the failure of piecemeal assistance from the International Committee of the Red Cross (ICRC), United Nations agencies and non-government organisations, led in 1989 to the establishment of Operation Lifeline Sudan under the auspices of the United Nations. This was an important development because the Sudanese Government agreed to the United Nations conducting structured discussions with it and the dissidents with a view to reaching agreement about the amounts of food and medical supplies to go to both sides and the conditions of safe passage for their delivery.

The United Nations role would not have been feasible at that time except at the invitation of the Sudanese Government, in view of the weight attached by the organisation to national sovereignty. The idea of a peacekeeping operation was not actively considered. Rather, emphasis was placed on persuading the government that it was entirely consistent with Sudanese sovereignty that the government, given its concern for the welfare of its people, should invite the United Nations to seek to establish conditions that would enable the humanitarian needs of all Sudanese to be met.

It has been argued that Lifeline's principal success lay in reducing hostilities for a time and that, impressive as its delivery of indispensable supplies was, this was not its most important contribution: 'The cessation of violence benefits all. It allows civilian populations that ultimately must provide for themselves to begin to do so, whether or not they are reached with outside aid'.[3] However, there is disagreement that the prospect of provision of relief aid was an important factor in bringing about either the invitation to the United Nations to intervene or the

---

[3] Larry Minear *et al.*, *Humanitarianism Under Siege: A Critical Review of Operation Lifeline Sudan* (Trenton, N.J: Red Sea Press, 1991) p.146.

imperfect and short-lived agreements on 'Corridors of Tranquillity' for the safe passage of relief.[4] Nevertheless, Operation Lifeline Sudan raises a critical issue: namely the extent to which the provision of humanitarian assistance can (or should) be used to get the combatants to cease fire and begin negotiations on the issues dividing them, that is to say whether the provision of relief and the pursuit of peace should be linked in some way and if so how this should be done. Consideration of this issue, which is seen as important by United Nations officials and some non-government organisations concerned that the basic thrust of international interventions should be directed at resolving the root causes of humanitarian disasters, will recur through this study.

Operation Lifeline Sudan raised another issue which should be of concern but is never addressed by the international community, namely the issue of proportionality. In 1989 the cost of Operation Lifeline Sudan was of the order of US$200-300 million. In this, as for virtually all major relief operations, the cost has never been definitively established, even approximately. Equally, under southern Sudanese conditions, there is no reliable data on lives saved or even any means of calculating them since the necessary accurate base-line statistics do not exist. Estimates of deaths are imprecise and numbers tend to be exaggerated, but the aid workers who have made such strong personal sacrifices to the relief of suffering would be less than human not to take pride in their achievements. However, at $1,000-$3,000 per life saved the cost was certainly high measured against per capita expenditure in sub-Saharan Africa on, say, child nutrition, health and education. Moreover, the relief effort has gone on every year since because the war continued. The situation of its victims has never again attracted anything like the same level of international attention given the lack of interest of the electronic media. Though there have been hints of a possible United Nations military intervention the Security Council has not seriously addressed the matter.

The precedent established by Lifeline was followed by the United Nations in other non-international conflict situations, for example, the agreement negotiated by the World Food Program (WFP) for the reopening of the port of Massawa, the apportionment of food aid between Ethiopian and Eritrean forces and delivery of food aid to the besieged city of Asmara. But for the end of the Cold War the international community would have continued on the, by then, established path. The efforts of the United Nations in relation to internal conflict caused by humanitarian emergencies would have remained circumspect and require the assent of the affected state.

---

4   James Ingram, 'The Future Architecture for Humanitarian Assistance' in Thomas G. Weiss and Larry Minear, *Humanitarianism Across Borders: Sustaining Civilians in Times of War* (Boulder, Col: Lynne Rienner, 1993).

The Gulf conflict

Security Council Resolution 688 of 5 April 1991 seemingly changed the situation. The Council condemned the Iraqi repression of the Kurds, the consequence of which, it was said, 'threatened international peace and security in the region'. The Council 'demanded that Iraq end this repression' and 'insisted' that it 'allow immediate access by international humanitarian organisations to all those in need of assistance in all parts of Iraq and to make available all necessary facilities for their operations'.

In retrospect, Resolution 688 should have been made an integral part of Resolution 687, which set out a comprehensive set of conditions to be complied with by Iraq backed up by an elaborate sanctions regime. The reality is that Iraq placed great obstacles in the way of United Nations agencies operating in Iraq. The United Nations was obliged to negotiate a memorandum of understanding dealing with issues such as the numbers of international personnel to be admitted, procedures for the issue of visas and restrictions on the kinds of relief goods to be provided. Negotiations on an extension of the memorandum were equally difficult. At the time of writing a new agreement has not yet been successfully negotiated and the United Nations operates under temporary arrangements. The major powers have shown a diminishing interest over time in relief operations within Iraq, including their funding.

A major issue in initial negotiations with Iraq, was the proposal of the Secretary-General's representative, Prince Sadruddin Aga Khan, that Iraq accept a contingent of 500 United Nations guards to provide symbolic protection in northern Iraq, following the withdrawal of allied military personnel. This experiment is considered a success, not least due to the fact that the guards were backed up by allied fire power based in Turkey. Iraq would not accept formal peacekeepers and the guards were a compromise. While the arrangement was an ad hoc one, its cost was low compared with a peacekeeping operation. There could be advantages in its institutionalisation for use in future humanitarian emergencies arising from intra-state conflict.

A concern of the United Nations humanitarian agencies and non-government organisations throughout has been the unwillingness of the United States and its allies to give sufficient weight to the serious negative impact of the war itself and of economic sanctions on the well-being of Iraqi civilians generally. A United Nations needs assessment mission shortly after the end of the conflict was severely criticised because of its strong language about the extent of the war damage and its impact on civilian welfare. Relative to needs and to the volume of aid provided to the Kurds, only token amounts have been forthcoming for Iraqis generally. As a result United Nations agencies continue to be hindered in their work, being seen not as impartial but as instruments of Western policy. However, as time has gone by and the economy has somewhat recovered, the circumstances of civilians generally have improved. Nevertheless, the

Security Council has not encouraged humanitarian agencies to monitor and publicise the privations endured by the Iraqi people.

The issue of proportionality is raised more dramatically by the Gulf crisis than Operation Lifeline Sudan. The United States military contribution in support of the Kurds, under Operation Provide Comfort, cost US$800 million, more than the entire global United Nations High Commission for Refugees (UNHCR) budget in support of refugees in 1991, or only slightly less than the whole of Australia's overseas aid. At the same time the needs of 1.5 million newly displaced persons in Liberia, whose misery was certainly as great as the Kurds, passed virtually unnoticed. United Nations agencies like UNHCR and WFP struggled to meet their needs with insufficient financial and staff resources.

Evolution of international humanitarian law

The right of humanitarian intervention

Passage of Resolution 688 gave new impetus to the contention that a 'right of humanitarian intervention' exists in international law. However, basing itself essentially on the hard to dispute proposition that the massive movement of Kurds towards and across borders could threaten regional peace and security, that resolution is scarcely grounds for claiming that a generally applicable 'right' of humanitarian intervention has thereby been established. A relevant consideration in this regard is that since the adoption of Resolution 688 analogous humanitarian situations have occurred - for example Armenia's incursion into Azerbaijan and civil war in Rwanda, Georgia and Tajikistan, not to mention Turkey's assaults on its Kurds - which have not led to forceful intervention. The special effort made for the Kurds was a function of the outcome of the Gulf war, the central role of the United States in it and the continuance in power of Saddam Hussein.

While the language of Resolution 688 places relatively little weight on humanitarian considerations Security Council Resolution 794 of 3 December 1992, effectively authorising the deployment of United States forces in Somalia, is much more explicit. The emphasis throughout is on the deterioration of the humanitarian situation, including 'grave alarm' at 'widespread violations of international humanitarian law' and 'dismay' at the 'continuation of conditions that impede the delivery of humanitarian supplies to destinations within Somalia'. The operative paragraphs retain this emphasis. In Resolution 794 and those preceding it, the Security Council asserts that the situation in Somalia 'constitutes a threat to security'. The assertion is linked to phrases describing the situation as one of 'heavy loss of life' (733) or the 'magnitude of human suffering' (746, 751, 767, 775). Resolution 794 expands the phrase so that it is 'the magnitude of the human tragedy caused by the conflict in Somalia, further exacerbated by the obstacles being created to the distribution of humanitarian assistance', that constitutes the threat. However, the 'heavy loss of life' had gone on for one year prior to Resolution 733. In the last resort the legal backing for it and successive resolutions would appear to be 'the request by Somalia' for Security Council consideration, referred to in Resolution 733, rather than the humanitarian situation. There was no functioning government in Somalia from January 1991, but none of the resolutions referred to mentions this. However, the preamble of 794 refers to the 'unique', 'complex' and 'extraordinary' situation in Somalia that requires an 'exceptional' response.

Nevertheless, in terms of the extension of the ' right of intervention' doctrine Resolution 794 may break new ground. International lawyers point to the significance of operative paragraph 10, by which the Secretary-General and the cooperating Member States are authorised 'to use all necessary means to establish as soon as possible a secure environment for international humanitarian relief operations in Somalia'.

Resolution 794 was succeeded by Resolution 814, the first Chapter VII military operation unambiguously under the direct command and control of the United Nations Secretary-General. In June 1993 a further resolution concerning retaliation against General Aideed was adopted.

Enforcement of humanitarian law

Another resolution of great importance in relation to the evolution of humanitarian law through Security Council decision making is number 780, concerning the former Yugoslavia. Recalling that persons who commit or order the commission of grave breaches of international humanitarian law, in particular of the Geneva Conventions, 'are individually responsible in respect of such breaches', the Council requested the Secretary-General to establish an 'impartial Commission of Experts' to analyse relevant information on breaches of law. It is to be noted that Somalia Resolution 794 'affirmed' that 'those who commit or order the commission of acts' violating international humanitarian law, 'including in particular the deliberate impeding of the delivery of food and medical supplies', will be 'held individually responsible in respect of such acts'. However, further follow up action as for Bosnia was not provided for.

In recent civil wars, at least those in the Sudan, Angola, Mozambique, not to mention in the former Yugoslavia and Ethiopia, the deliberate displacement of persons has been an essential element in the policies of one or other of the parties. In view of the great importance attached to the 'right of intervention', the extent of application of international humanitarian law to displaced persons needs to be understood. This would not be the place to give a comprehensive analysis but the essential point to note is that the Geneva Conventions of 1949 and the Additional Protocols of 1977 govern both international and non-international armed conflicts. According to Plattner, the rules in Protocol II relating to military conflict are very specific but have not yet been formally codified in respect of internal armed conflicts.[5] As regards care and relief activities in support of the civilian population, the obligations of States are clear, i.e., they may not prevent people whose lives and health are endangered from receiving assistance from an international organisation *insofar as such assistance is provided in a manner in keeping with the aim of humanitarian law.* Article 1, common to the Geneva Conventions, provides that States have the duty to ensure respect for humanitarian law. The International Court of Justice (ICJ) considers that this duty obtains with respect to non-international armed conflicts. However, assistance in accordance with international humanitarian law is to be provided in accordance with the principles of the International Committee of the Red Cross. In particular, distribution must be made impartially and without discrimination, something that in practice United Nations agencies have not done, for example, in Iraq.

The action of the United Nations in Somalia in using force against General Aideed will be seen by many Somalis as of great benefit to President Ali Mahdi and his faction. My discussions with WFP officials reveal that United Nations agencies in Mogadishu, engaged solely in humanitarian work, are in practice unable to differentiate themselves from UNOSOM II (United Nations Operation in Somalia). In the light of the ICJ ruling the question then arises whether, in the event that there is in future interference by the factions in United Nations relief operations, the Security Council can legally hold the perpetrators to be in breach of humanitarian law.

More broadly, the current situation in Somalia raises in acute form the existence of an underlying, fundamental tension in the twin roles of the United Nations as a peacemaking and peacekeeping organisation on the one hand, and on the other as an impartial and neutral humanitarian organisation. This tension is taken up in detail later in this study.

While the law in relation to non-international armed conflict is clear, its enforcement is problematic. According to the ICRC, what the written law confers on it is essentially the power to negotiate with the parties, though in practice the ICRC has usually been able to operate in conflict zones. The International Conference for the Protection of War Victims, to begin in August, could provide an opportunity to strengthen monitoring and enforcement of humanitarian law, particularly in non-international conflicts. Currently, the Draft Declaration prepared for the Conference goes some way in this direction. One possible further step, in line with Security Council Resolution 780, would be to institutionalise on a permanent basis the impartial Commission of Experts, and to extend its mandate to cover all non-international conflicts. In view of the number of

---

[5] Denise Plattner, 'The Protection of Displaced Persons in Non-International Armed Conflicts' *International Review of the Red Cross No 291* (Geneva: 1992).

governments which have still not recognised the competence of the International Fact Finding Commission established under Article 90 of Protocol I, and the failure of some major powers to ratify the Additional Protocols, substantially more positive action from the Conference may be unlikely. In any event, the matter could be pursued further in the United Nations.

Forceful United Nations intervention and the humanitarian balance sheet

In the three recent cases where the 'right of intervention' issue has arisen, namely Iraq, Somalia and the former Yugoslavia, the critical question from the humanitarian perspective is whether the steps taken have overall saved more lives and relieved more suffering than would otherwise have occurred. 'Humanitarian' is one of those widely used words with multiple meanings, used in pejorative as well as praiseworthy senses. There is no universally accepted definition as such. In this study humanitarian action is action directed at relieving life threatening human suffering, i.e., essentially the position of the ICRC. Many non-governmental organisations involved in conflict situations take a much broader view. Their concept of humanitarian encompasses, for example, wider issues of human rights. However, the right to life is the most basic of human rights. Relief organisations may be mindful of other goals but their primary focus should be on saving life and reducing life threatening suffering.

Iraq and Bosnia

In seeking to answer the question posed in the preceding paragraph, international intervention undoubtedly benefited the Kurds but other Iraqis certainly suffered severely, including southern Shiites. The overall balance is probably positive but is never likely to be definitively established. Nevertheless, the failure of the Security Council to take account of the humanitarian impact of its decisions authorising coercive measures, including sanctions, is of great concern to humanitarians. The most commonly accepted solution is that the Under Secretary-General for Humanitarian Affairs should be 'an advocate for the victims of humanitarian emergencies, a conscience of the international community, an authority which can create and protect humanitarian space between the politicians and peacemakers'.[6] The potential incompatibility between this independent 'ombudsman' type role and the Under Secretary-General's position as a subordinate official of the Secretary-General is, however, rarely recognised or addressed.

---

[6] Jacques Cuenord, *Co-ordinating United Nations Humanitarian Assistance* (Washington, DC: Refugee Policy Group, June 1993) p.2.

From discussions with those having first hand experience of Bosnia, it appears that the decision to open Sarajevo airport, to deploy troops there and to escort relief convoys undoubtedly saved lives. But the United Nations intervention has also probably prolonged the conflict and the likely end result, in terms of the fragmentation of Bosnia, may not be very different than if the United Nations had never interposed forces. Prolongation of the conflict may well have added to life-threatening suffering. At the time of writing donor interest in providing sufficient resources for relief operations has rapidly weakened. Short of a thorough *post-facto* evaluation, involving field visits by a professional team, more definitive conclusions may be hard to reach.

Somalia

The circumstances giving rise to United Nations military intervention in Somalia were quite different from those of Bosnia and Iraq. President Siad Barre had fled Mogadishu approximately eighteen months beforehand, in January 1991. The lack of interest of the major powers (who withdrew their embassies), the absence of the media and the evacuation of United Nations staff meant that the deteriorating situation was ignored for most of 1991. This was in no way due to lack of knowledge among governments that an appalling situation existed. The ICRC, which with a few other organisations had retained a presence, was disseminating accurate information. The will did not exist among the major powers or at United Nations headquarters to seriously address the situation. As well, United Nations organisations lacked the means to operate under the prevailing conditions. However, by January 1992 the Security Council was stirred to action. An ill-conceived United Nations mission was followed by an unrealistic Security Council Resolution (number 733) urging the parties to cease conflict, embargoing the supply of arms (available anyway in quantity as a result of USSR/USA policies over many years) and asking the Secretary-General to 'increase humanitarian assistance to the affected parties'.

The slow pace of action continued through the next few months. After the United Nations had negotiated a ceasefire with President Ali Mahdi and General Aideed in March, the Security Council authorised UNOSOM I. This was very much a case of too little too late. By 23 June the parties had only agreed to the deployment of the authorised 50 military observers along the demarcation line in Mogadishu. Security Council Resolution 751 of 24 April 1992 also provided for the deployment of a security force but the first contingent arrived only by mid September. Meanwhile, the Secretary-General had concluded that the United Nation's efforts should be enlarged to bring about an effective ceasefire throughout the country, while promoting 'national reconciliation'. By 24 August the Secretary-General was reporting that lawlessness prevented unloading in the ports and distribution of relief supplies. Subsequent Security Council decisions endorsed an expansion in UNOSOM to 4,219 personnel.

At the time of the approval by the Security Council on 28 August 1992 of a greatly enlarged UNOSOM there was no large-scale war going on between the various clans which had, by then, staked out areas of the country between themselves. According to the then Special Representative of the Secretary-General, 'each movement controlled a well-defined territory whose dimensions roughly matched its aspirations'.[7] In other words, a status quo situation prevailed and there was no need for a conventional peacekeeping force to separate the combatants. Banditry was the real problem, in particular the looting by gangs of food aid. Food was in very short supply in centres like Baidoa and, therefore, highly valuable. It was simply too hazardous for non-government organisations to be involved in distribution on a large scale. One way or another the country had to be flooded with food, either by injecting it at low cost into the normal marketing channels or by providing armed escorts on the scale required with appropriate fire power and rules of engagement.

Otherwise, on the relief side, the United Nations continued to do poorly through 1992. Finally, under the leadership of the Under Secretary-General for Humanitarian Affairs, a 100-Day Action Program was launched at a meeting of governments and non-government organisations on 12-13 October. Much of the delay can be attributed to structural weaknesses in the United Nations humanitarian relief system. For example, the fiction that no coordinated disaster intervention plan may be produced without bringing in major agencies, whose operational role is non-existent at a time when the primary task is to save lives and reduce suffering, is a recipe for delay. Notwithstanding that there was no functioning government and basic relief work was being harassed, the plan gave roles to the Food and Agriculture Organisation (FAO) for agricultural rehabilitation, to the World Health Organisation (WHO) for health infrastructures (although the ICRC was doing the only such work that could be done) and to the United Nations Development Program (UNDP) for 'infrastructure and other rehabilitation programs'. The production of all such United Nations plans is delayed by the time spent in negotiation with agencies powerful in the United Nations system but irrelevant to the relief stage of emergencies. The British Red Cross has officially stated that 'a large part of the tragedy of Somalia was due to ineffectual co-ordination within the United Nations system and even to institutional rivalry'.[8]

A less tempered critique has been given by Jeffrey Clark who, in a chronological review of the diplomatic and relief efforts of the United

---

[7] Bertrand Le Gendre, 'Use of Force can be Avoided in Somalia' *Le Monde* (9/10 August 1992).

[8] Submission by the British Red Cross to the House of Commons Select Committee on Foreign Affairs, *The Performance of the United Nations in the Field of Humanitarian Assistance* (London: 1993).

Nations preceding Operation Restore Hope, concluded that: 'Neither the operational responses of U.N. relief agencies nor the conflict- mediation efforts of U.N. diplomats were undertaken with visible professionalism'.[9]

Deciding on a Chapter VII intervention is a decision of great consequence. Deficiencies in the United Nations overall management of humanitarian relief was probably a critical factor leading to the necessity for that decision. It follows that improvements in the functioning of the United Nations security system would be incomplete unless problems of United Nations humanitarian relief coordination are also addressed.

The Secretary-General reported on 4 November that the deteriorating situation prevented UNOSOM from implementing its mandate. He cited the failure of factions to cooperate, the extortion, blackmail and robbery affecting the international relief effort and the repeated attacks on United Nations and non-government personnel. In a situation, not of civil war but of widespread lawlessness over-laying a military stalemate between the principal political factions, the situation cried out for decisive action to impose law and order. Under pressure from non-governmental organisations and a public opinion aroused by appalling television images, the United States decided to intervene and exerted the necessary pressure that led to the adoption of Security Council Resolution 794 on 3 December, effectively giving it the freedom it deemed essential. From the perspective of the United Nations humanitarian agencies it was a decision that should have been taken months previously.

Nevertheless, the decision authorising Operation Restore Hope was controversial. While United Nations agencies and non-government organisations such as CARE, which receives most of its funding from the United States Government, were enthusiastic supporters, others such as Save the Children Fund (SCF-UK) were opposed. The ICRC, which had been able to work successfully in many of the most affected areas, reluctantly acquiesced.

The current situation in which UNOSOM II finds itself has sharpened long-felt concerns of many humanitarian agencies about the wisdom of using military force to secure humanitarian objectives. An evaluation of the achievements of the United Nations Interim Task Force (UNITAF) is therefore more than usually important.

Such an evaluation has been carried out by an independent organisation called 'African Rights' headed by two respected social scientists with considerable field experience in Africa.[10] It is rare indeed to get such an outside preliminary assessment, even if incomplete, so close to a major disaster event. African Rights accepts that UNITAF undoubtedly brought about an improvement in the delivery of bulk food aid, while dramatically

---

[9] Jeffrey Clarke, 'Debacle in Somalia' *Foreign Affairs* 72, 1 (1992/93) p.109.

[10] Rakiya Omaar and Alex de Waal, *Somalia. Operation Restore Hope: A Preliminary Assessment* (London: African Rights, 1993).

reducing extortion rackets and looting of food convoys. However, African Rights contends that the extent of losses and diversions, claimed by the then Special Representatives of the Secretary-General as justification for forceful intervention, was grossly exaggerated. It is rightly pointed out that in most relief operations in Africa losses are high. Measures used by agencies like the ICRC for dealing successfully with looting and other diversions are given, and for getting food into Mogadishu port, when it was said to be closed, are described. The report also shows that cereal prices in Mogadishu had returned to normal levels by October from levels four to five times higher in July, the month widely agreed to be the peak of the famine. It is also contended that a sharp fall in death rates had occurred already in September-November and that there was little evidence of a further substantial fall in death rates: 'In Baidoa, the epicentre of the famine, the number of deaths fell from a peak of over 1700 per week at the beginning of September to about 300 per week in mid-November'.

The report contends that security problems were not fully overcome - which in the light of recent developments appears correct - and that the very modes of operation of UNITAF forces in themselves created security problems. To give the flavour of its findings the following is an extract from the report:

> The post-January improvement in food deliveries masks other extremely serious problems. At the beginning of December, as the US marines prepared to land in Mogadishu, hundreds of militiamen with their technicals fled the city. Some went north, to the previously-quiet region of Mudug, where there is now fierce fighting. Others went to Baidoa, where their presence combined with a split between two factions of the local Somali Democratic Movement military to create havoc in the town. Aid workers expected the marines to arrive in Baidoa and Kismayo at the same time as Mogadishu. Their arrival was delayed by about ten days. In that time, gunmen went on a shooting spree. $13000 was taken from CARE-Australia in Baidoa at gunpoint. Their compound was also attacked later. A World Vision guard was short dead by a robber and a guard working for Concern died in a hail of bullets after he went to check out noise in the compound. The Red Cross was also robbed at gunpoint. Six Somali workers with CARE died when their convoy was attacked. The US Air Force, diverted from Operation Provide Relief to assist with Operation Restore Hope, could no longer fly in food, and the aid agencies were unable to supply surrounding areas. Aid workers lived in fortified compounds, fearful for their lives and unable to carry out their work. They were further incensed by the US forces' public announcement of their slow operational schedule. On 13 December, a message from the US commander, General Robert Johnson, telling the agencies that they would not reach Baidoa for another six days was broadcast that evening on BBC Somali service. Aid workers in Baidoa believe that the delay and the announcement cost lives.

More than eighty people were killed in the violence, while disruptions to relief deliveries contributed to a rise in death rates from about forty per day to about one hundred. Only when the marines belatedly reached Baidoa - normally four hours' drive from Mogadishu - were relief activities able to resume.

Unfortunately, Baidoa was not to be the only instance of deteriorating security. In the days before the UNITAF forces arrived in Kismayo, there was a wave of assassinations targeted at leading members of the Harte clans in the city. A list of 128 names of people allegedly killed in this campaign has been widely circulated in Somalia and Kenya. A number of aid workers were taken hostage before the arrival of the troops. Rampages by gunmen forced an end to all relief work and precipitated the evacuation of all foreign nationals. After a short period of calm, insecurity returned to the villages around Kismayo and then to the city itself. First, outlying feeding centres were closed. Finally, in March, almost all humanitarian work save emergency surgery in the hospital was stopped due to fighting between the Somali National Army (SNA), headed by General Mohamed Farah Aideed and the Somali National Front (SNF) headed by General Mohamed Hersi Morgan. MSF doctors are obliged to travel between their house and the hospital in Belgian tanks; their feeding centres and out-patient dispensaries have all been closed.

The looting spree in the interim between the announcement of Operation Restore Hope and the arrival of the US troops also severely disrupted relief operations elsewhere. In the Lower Shebell, the ICRC warehouse in Merca was looted and transport to centres in the region was interrupted for a month. In Baardheere, there was also serious disruption to the relief program.

More widely, security for relief agencies has deteriorated. Three expatriates have been killed since the intervention, compared with two during the previous two years. The UN estimates that more Somali relief workers have also lost their lives since the intervention than during all of 1992. On 28 December five Somali aid workers were short dead in Mogadishu. Four of them were local staff hired by the ICRC who were travelling in a bus in south Mogadishu on their way to work. The other, a security guard employed by CARE, was killed when gunmen hijacked a CARE car. On 12 January, a Somali employee of the Irish agency, Goal, died in a crossfire near the green line. It is no longer possible for expatriates to travel from Mogadishu to Baidoa by road - a trip that had been possible at all times in the seven months before the intervention. MSF is no longer able to send its expatriate staff to supervise its out-patient dispensaries in the villages around Baidoa. Travel by road to Merca and Brava, never difficult before December 1992, is now almost impossible without a heavily-armed military escort. As a result, MSF cannot supervise its 17 feeding centres in the area.

The ICRC has continued to lose vehicles to looters; in one week in February, no fewer than five of its cars were held up at gunpoint - a higher number than ever before. On 18 March, the ICRC office in north Mogadishu was robbed of $180,000 by two gunmen, and the organisation was obliged to close down its operations in that sector. On 15 February, the UNICEF office was robbed by gunmen, who disarmed the guards and stole about $50,000 and some equipment. The office of Pharmacists without Borders was also robbed. The deterioration in security has compelled CARE to consider withdrawing from Baardheere. CARE has also evacuated most of its expatriates from Mogadishu, where its compound is guarded by a platoon of US marines.

Overall, the essential argument of African Rights is that the intervention came too late in addressing the food supply problem and that it otherwise failed to address the main issue, namely disarmament of the factions, which is seen as an essential prerequisite for peace and reconciliation. Allegedly, there was little real encouragement of civil society. Key groups such as Somali humanitarian workers, professionals and traders were being 'marginalised in the political process' and in the international civilian administration. Somali expertise has been little used in planning and managing United Nations aid programs. There was little substantial progress towards political reconciliation. The importance of encouraging reconciliation at the regional level, despite pressure from Somalis, was entirely neglected, it is claimed. The authors are also highly critical of the behaviour and level of accountability of UNITAF forces under 'liberal rules of engagement' and the lack of channels for Somalis to air their grievances.

The highly respected Médecins sans Frontières (MSF), which along with ICRC and two small non-government organisations continued operations throughout the crises, recently gave a brief assessment as follows:

> Military intervention has helped reduce malnutrition by restoring supply lines but there remain pockets of insecurity throughout the country. MSF had to pull out its ten staff members from Baidoa and interrupt its hospital activities at the end of April despite alarming mortality rates. The situation became untenable after a Somali nurse working for MSF was murdered and expatriates were taken hostage by their own guards and threatened with execution. All attempts at negotiating better security conditions with the local leaders had failed. MSF deplored the failure of the United Nations to twin military intervention with genuine efforts to establish a new framework for local politics. By contrast, the easing of tensions in Kismayu has allowed MSF to prepare for medium-term reconstruction projects. Another positive development is that MSF can gradually phase out its intensive feeding centres in many parts of the former famine areas.[11]

---

11 Médecins sans Frontières, *International Newsletter* 6 (1993).

Discussion of the issues raised in the African Rights report with Australian non-government organisations involved in Somalia and with WFP officials, gives a consensus of opinion that African Rights' judgements are too harsh. The bulk distribution of food to Baidoa, for example, was impossible on account of the dangers. Because of scarcity, such food was simply too valuable. Overcoming that problem was essential at the time Operation Restore Hope was launched.

African Rights' criticisms of the failure to disarm and to seek to revive civil society with more energy and commitment would, however, receive broad support, including from United Nations organisations like WFP and UNICEF, though they are unable to say so publicly.

The public disagreements between the United Nations Secretary-General and the United States Secretary of State about disarming dissidents at the beginning of UNITAF's operation revealed a fundamental difference of opinion about the purpose of the operation. According to press reports, General Colin Powell had been reluctant to see United States forces involved. As a compromise, the conditions under which United States forces were utilised were heavily circumscribed. It is not surprising that UNITAF's success was limited at best.

A related question is deciding appropriate rules of engagement. Recent events in Somalia suggest that, if framed too much from the point of view of minimising losses to United Nations forces, they may diminish the chances of building peace and could jeopardise attainment of the humanitarian goal of reducing civilian suffering and loss of life.

To a considerable extent differences among humanitarian agencies about the appropriateness of any military intervention reflect differences about the purpose of humanitarian relief. Many non-government organisations see the relief of suffering as secondary to addressing the causes of suffering and to 'empowering' local people to overcome the causes of their suffering. They are concerned that assistance solely to save life creates dependence on outside assistance, so increasing vulnerability to future disasters. In their view, effective humanitarian action should encompass a comprehensive view of overall needs and of the impact of interventions. For some agencies, encouraging respect for human rights is an essential ingredient in addressing the underlying causes of conflicts.

As already noted in relation to Operation Lifeline Sudan, agencies adhering to this latter view tend to attach more weight to the United Nations' role of promoting potential reconciliation in conflict situations rather than its role as an armed escort for relief deliveries. They were more critical of Operation Restore Hope, expressing doubt as to its necessity and about the extent of its achievements. The same agencies were strong supporters of Mahommed Sahnoun, who resigned as the Secretary-General's Special Representative in Somalia late last year. However, agencies more concerned about immediate relief did not find him as sympathetic to their problems.

Reviving civil society is no easy task and the United Nations has no experience of how to do it. Mounting a Namibia or Cambodia peacekeeping style operation is difficult, though less challenging. Before UNITAF was launched there were those arguing that the situation called for the establishment of a 'new kind of trusteeship' with administration in the hands of the United Nations. 'Somalia's dying from a lack not of food or medicines but of order', it was said.[12] To have to establish even a functioning system of law and order means being in Somalia for years, not months - a very expensive operation requiring the sustained financial support of donors.

Criteria for Security Council intervention

The reasons for the reluctance of General Colin Powell, Chairman of the United States Joint Chiefs of Staff, to use United States ground forces in support of peacekeeping and humanitarian operation are worth examination. On the one hand, Iraq and Somalia demonstrate that without United States forces and leadership interventions outside Europe are unlikely to be effective if it becomes necessary to use force seriously. The United States alone appears to have the capability to project sufficient force far from home. On the other hand, United States rules of engagement, designed to minimise risks to their forces, increase the likelihood that in the longer term the humanitarian benefits are diminished and could even become negative.

For Powell the essential requirement is that objectives must be limited, as well as means. The Gulf War was such a war. The alternative, he claims, would have meant the stationing of 'major occupation forces in Iraq for years to come and a very expensive and complex American proconsulship in Baghdad ...'[13]

In considering whether to commit ground forces Powell has defined the questions to be answered as follows:

> Is the political objective we seek to achieve important, clearly defined and understood? Have all other nonviolent policy means failed? Will military forces achieve the objective? At what cost? Have the gains and risks been analyzed? How might the situation that we seek to alter, once it is altered by force, develop further and what might be the consequences?[14]

Clearly, in the light of hindsight, and no doubt obvious to many at the time, these questions were not examined with sufficient care. Powell's final test is that if the political objective is important and the risks are

---

[12] Charles Krauthammer, 'Trusteeship for Somalia' *Washington Post* (9 October 1992).
[13] Colin L. Powell, 'US Forces: Challenges Ahead' *Foreign Affairs* 71, 5 (Winter 1992/93) p.38.
[14] Ibid.

acceptable then 'clear and unambiguous objectives must be given to the armed forces'. While United States forces were given such objectives, since the other tests were not satisfactorily addressed securing operational success was at best of limited value and duration. All in all the Powell criteria could appropriately be applied by the Security Council when deciding whether to use force in pursuit of humanitarian objectives. One more test would be required. *Are large numbers of people likely to die if there is no forceful intervention, and have all alternative measures been exhausted?* How this test might be established is dealt with later in this study.

An important consideration to note in relation to the establishment of criteria is that there is a hierarchy of possibilities for armed activity in support of humanitarian objectives, as set out in Table 1. The development of clear criteria for the various possibilities adds further complexity to a daunting task.

A further important, though difficult to publicly acknowledge, criterion to be taken into account is cost. In this connection reference to proportionality in relation to Operation Lifeline Sudan and Provide Comfort in Iraq has already been made. The cost of United Nations' humanitarian operations in war situations has become very substantial as will be seen from Table 2. It should be noted that most of the appeals listed are not for the whole of 1992. For the full year the total will have been much higher. For 1993 a total cost of about US$3 billion is anticipated. To the humanitarian costs must be added the peacekeeping bill. Table 3 shows estimated expenditure in 1992. Again, the total will be much higher in 1993. By way of putting these figures into perspective, net disbursements of Official Development Assistance (ODA) from all sources in 1990 for low income countries was only US$29.3 billion.[15] Total ODA is increasing slowly and relief expenditure is charged to it. In effect, the more the international community spends on relief the less it spends on addressing underdevelopment, which to some extent is a causal factor in many situations requiring relief.

To date United Nations interventions have not been decided on the basis of objective criteria. Political considerations, the feasibility of intervention in terms of military risk, and pressure on the industrialised countries from non-government organisations and public opinion, stimulated by television pictures of the dead and dying, especially children, have been decisive. Given the controversy likely to continue to surround forceful humanitarian intervention, the possibility of getting agreement on a useful set of criteria will be difficult. Moreover, assessing the weight to be given to individual agreed criteria in relation to the particular circumstances of each situation will continue to involve considerable exercise of judgement.

---

[15] *World Development Report 1992* (Washington, DC: World Bank, 1992) p.256.

Each of the United Nations' humanitarian interventions discussed has taken place under quite different circumstances. The Kurds were in a defined geographical region and were being oppressed by an aggressor state against whom the international community had taken up arms. The military forces were in place not only to coerce Iraq but to provide relief assistance quickly and effectively to 1.5 million Iraqis. In Bosnia we have had a three-sided war between territorially interspersed and intermixed ethnic/cultural groups. The introduction of military forces *per se* has neither stopped the fighting nor promoted a political settlement. On the other hand, the provision of relief has possibly prolonged the conflict. The application of sanctions, threats of force and the various diplomatic initiatives of the United Nations and European Economic Community could have proceeded without the introduction of armed forces. Moreover, in the absence of protecting forces it is unlikely that relief efforts would have ceased. While major relief operations have been coordinated by UNHCR the ICRC continued, albeit under great difficulty, to work independently. Long before the media focused, in July 1992, on detention camps the ICRC had publicly deplored the arrest of civilians and denounced the so-called 'ethnic cleansing' and other crimes against civilians. Almost certainly the media focus and the presence of the ICRC and other humanitarian organisations would have had some meliorating effect on the parties.

Other non-international humanitarian conflicts

Somalia has been identified with the emergence of what is described as a disturbing new phenomenon: 'the failed nation-state, utterly incapable of sustaining itself as a member of the international community'.[16] It has been lumped along with Haiti, remnants of Yugoslavia, Sudan, Liberia and Cambodia. Just as the situation in Somalia shares few features with Iraq and Bosnia so it does with the ones mentioned. The only way out in Somalia may be the Helman/Ratner remedy, i.e., the assumption by the United Nations of 'nation-saving responsibilities', a form of trusteeship which they call 'conservatorship'. However, civil authority has not collapsed in Haiti, Sudan or even Bosnia. Sudan's situation is more akin to the Kurdish problem in Iraq. Haiti's problems are due as much to outside interference as to any other factor.

The Security Council (and the United States) applied a range of coercive measures against Haiti aimed at placing in office the democratically elected Father Jean-Bertrand Aristide, i.e., an avowedly political goal. The sanctions applied have caused great suffering. In this instance little attention appears to have been given to striking an appropriate balance between the principles of intervention to sustain a

---

[16] Gerald B. Helman and Steven R. Ratner, 'Saving Failed States' *Foreign Policy* 89 (Winter 92/93) p.3.

human right to democratic government and the humanitarian goal of saving lives and diminishing suffering.

In Africa current non-international conflicts or recently concluded ones have been more often wars of insurgency between functioning governments and organised opponents, e.g., Mozambique and Angola. Liberia is the closest parallel to Somalia in that the outside troops involved were authorised to use, and did use, force. However, the documentation available to me has been insufficient to draw useful parallels. Suffice it to say that there are contradictory opinions about the success of the West African states' security operation in that country, which was established in order to achieve security, rather than humanitarian, goals. While Monrovia is peaceful the civil war, which began in 1991, resumed in October 1992 and has spread into Sierra Leone. Some 773,000 refugees in neighbouring countries and in Liberia itself (from Sierra Leone) and 1,455,000 internally displaced persons in Liberia are now being supported by the international community. For WFP the cost of this operation since inception in 1990 is estimated at US$316 million. These figures alone are sufficient to throw doubt on the efficacy of intervention as a humanitarian operation.

Other situations in which far more people have been displaced and endured extreme suffering in life-threatening situations, have not led to United Nations peacekeeping or peacemaking operations, although the United Nations has been involved in negotiations for an end to conflict and United Nations forces have a role in implementation of agreements negotiated between the parties.

Mozambique is an interesting example. The conflict in Mozambique led to the displacement of more than a quarter of the estimated population of 16 million, of whom 1.5 million had fled the country. By the end of the 1980s 85 per cent of food requirements were imported. The war with Renamo, backed first by the then Rhodesia and later by South Africa, began shortly after Mozambique's independence in 1975. From the perspective of this study, three things about the process leading to the peace agreement of 4 October 1992 are noteworthy:

- the United Nations did not play a decisive role in the negotiations, which were initiated by the Catholic Church through the Archbishop of Beira and carried forward largely by the Italian Ambassador. Major contributions were made by the ICRC and by representatives of United Nations humanitarian agencies;

- the extraordinarily severe drought of 1992/93 compounded the collapse of South African support for Renamo as a major factor in bringing about agreement;

- the ICRC was the only agency able to provide humanitarian relief in Renamo held territory.

Under the agreement a United Nations force, the United Nations Operation in Mozambique (ONUMOZ), has several major tasks. To avoid the mistake made in Angola, the Secretary-General has stressed the critical importance of not holding elections until the military provisions of the agreement have been fully implemented. He has also sought a much larger force than in Angola. Despite the delays in establishing ONUMOZ, the peace agreement has generally held, testimony to the exhaustion of the participants and the desire to end violence. However, because of the delays, refugees are slow to return.

The war in El Salvador and the associated peace agreement have points of resemblance to Mozambique (and Angola). A military stalemate was an important factor in persuading the parties to negotiate. Others were the 1989 US invasion of Panama and the 1990 victory of Violetta Barrios di Chamorra in Nicaragua, which destroyed the United States administration's rationale about the threat posed by El Salvador to the United States and regional security. By February 1990 the United States had publicly abandoned the idea of the military defeat of the FMLN. The political conditions had thus been established for the successful negotiation of a peace agreement, which were carried through under the auspices of the United Nations. Their success owed much to the personal involvement of the then United Nations Secretary-General, Javier Perez de Cuellar, and the personal respect in which he was held in Central America and by the parties. The United Nations plays a critical role in the implementation of the agreement including the confinement of rival troops to areas under its supervision.

El Salvador was also a humanitarian disaster, with one quarter of the civilian population being displaced. There, and in Angola and Mozambique, United Nations assistance flowed to those under government control though not exclusively, e.g., UNICEF's, 'days of tranquillity' for country-wide child vaccination in El Salvador. Non-governmental agencies operating across borders provided the bulk of relief assistance outside government held areas.

The saving of civilian lives and the relief of life-threatening suffering is the fundamental justification for international humanitarian relief. From the point of view of the victim as victim it is important that assistance reach him, not who supplies it or whether it resulted from the use of, or threat of, force by the United Nations. The previous analysis suggests that the humanitarian benefits of military intervention in Iraq, Bosnia and Somalia are not clear-cut. Military intervention in Mozambique would have been justifiable in terms of the threat to peace arising from the movement of people and the anti-humanitarian policies of Renamo and its indifference to suffering and death in areas under its control. It is hard to believe that intervention would have brought about a significantly better overall humanitarian balance sheet than what was achieved through the relief work of the ICRC and United Nations relief agencies. As in Mozambique, El Salvador and virtually any other non-international conflict, a peaceful settlement is achieved either through the victory of one side (Afghanistan) or the exhaustion of the parties (Mozambique). Even if one side is victorious the fighting will not necessarily end though the opponents may change (Afghanistan). Bosnia and Somalia are showing that exercise by the United Nations of a 'right of humanitarian intervention' through use of armed forces is not a panacea for the unqualified achievement of humanitarian goals.

The success achieved by the United Nations in El Salvador shows what a prestigious and actively engaged Secretary-General backed by competent staff can do. However, that success would not have been feasible but for the end of the Cold War. The opportunity now exists for the office of Secretary-General to be a more active agent in preventive diplomacy and peacemaking. To the extent feasible, peacekeeping forces should find their place much more as a means of ensuring the successful implementation of agreements already reached by the parties.

Assuming the Secretary-General has the required personal and diplomatic qualities, his success will depend on maintaining the confidence of the United States and at the same time being seen to be independent of the United States. The central role to date of the United States in Security Council decision making and the likelihood that the United States administration seems committed to the exercise of global leadership on security/humanitarian issues, will make this a difficult task. The further reality that United States military power seems indispensable for the effective use of force and the creation of convincing signals that under certain circumstances force will be used (e.g., Somalia) adds even further to the problems of the Secretary-General. On the other hand, United States recognition that to the maximum extent possible its leadership should be exercised within a multilateral framework should be helpful to an astute Secretary-General. Looking ahead to Boutros Boutros-Ghali's successor, it could be timely to revive the Urquhart/Childers proposals for a reformed process for the selection of the Secretary-General.

On the basis of this broad overview of the recent record it is hard to avoid the conclusion that the more active pursuit by the United Nations of the peaceful settlement of conflicts through diplomatic and associated means, e.g., embargoes on supply of arms, coupled with traditional humanitarian relief operations through a variety of actors, including United Nations agencies, is not on balance likely to be a better approach than the use by the United Nations of military forces for humanitarian purposes, except in extreme circumstances. Only in such cases, when practically and politically there is no alternative, should force be used to achieve humanitarian goals. In short, irrespective of the validity of arguments among international lawyers about the right of intervention versus the principle of sovereignty of states, from the point of view of what has been called 'humanitarian pragmatism'[17] the test must be: have interventions by force brought an overall beneficial result in lives saved and suffering averted? The most we can say at this stage is that a clear verdict is not yet possible.

Future Security Council decision making would be assisted by an authoritative evaluation of the humanitarian balance sheet, including the overall cost, of the Iraq, Bosnian and Somalian interventions. The United Nations would not be the most appropriate body to do this, for obvious reasons. An independent study under the auspices of a consortium of foundations might be a better alternative.

Sovereignty and humanitarian principles

Developing countries and other new states fear that an appeal to humanitarian goals by the Security Council might be used as an excuse by more powerful countries to meddle in their affairs. Humanitarian intervention could, in their view, lead to a new imperialism or colonialism. The failed intervention in Bosnia and the morass which is opening up in Somalia, reinforce the weight of legitimate concern that otherwise commendable efforts to extend international humanitarian and related human rights law could undermine the basis for the limited international order that now exists.

Concern about the erosion of national sovereignty seems likely to remain strong and could grow. Much bitter controversy preceded the General Assembly's adoption of resolution 46/182 leading to the establishment of the Department of Humanitarian Affairs. The Under Secretary-General for Humanitarian Affairs, Jan Eliasson, contends that in carrying on this work the sovereignty issue has not been the obstacle he expected. He is an enthusiastic advocate of the view that 'sovereignty is no longer a principle we can recognise as absolute'.[18] In his view the 'United Nations has the moral obligation and authority to continue to expand its role in complex emergencies, in civil wars' and that what is needed is a 'firm commitment to an ethically informed politics of international solidarity'. He appears to believe that since 'nation states are increasingly perceived as societies of human beings' the protection of human rights is a sufficient reason for the United Nations to play an active role in internal crisis situations.

The views of the Secretary-General on the sovereignty issue are more ambivalent. In *An Agenda For Peace* Boutros-Ghali writes:

---

[17] Raymond W. Copson, *The Use of Force in Civil Conflicts for Humanitarian Purposes: Prospects for the Post-Cold War Era* (Washington, DC: Library of Congress, Congressional Research Service, 2 December 1992) p.16.

[18] Jan Eliasson, 'The United Nations in a Changing World' address at Columbia University, New York ,18 May 1993.

> The foundation-stone of this work [i.e., security] is and must remain the State. Respect for its fundamental sovereignty and integrity are crucial to any common international progress. The time of absolute and exclusive sovereignty, however, has passed; its theory was never matched by reality.[19]

Elsewhere in the same document he states:

> In these situations of internal crisis the United Nations will need to respect the sovereignty of the State; to do otherwise would not be in accordance with the understanding of Member States in accepting the principles of the Charter. The Organization must remain mindful of the carefully negotiated balance of the guiding principles annexed to General Assembly resolution 46/182 of 19 December 1991.[20]

Overall, the current Secretary-General's attitude is more cautious than his predecessor's.

The Secretary-General's caution reflects, presumably, the views of states like India and the People's Republic of China. Currently, most developing countries are relatively passive on the sovereignty issue, but this could be misleading. Senior United Nations officials from developing countries privately contend that smaller states, particularly in Africa, are now so dependent on Western goodwill for economic survival, that they feel that they are in no position to resist the pressures of the major powers when it comes to humanitarian intervention or intervention on human rights grounds.

Recent events in Somalia suggest that in failed or failing states successful humanitarian interventions will need to be carried on for a considerable period of time, and will require the establishment and sustenance over time of a civil administration to re-create civil society and to rehabilitate infrastructure essential for the economic functioning of civil society. Apart from the expense - the cost of the United Nations Transitional Authority in Cambodia (UNTAC) gives some idea of magnitude - there must be the gravest doubts about the willingness of governments to provide for extended periods the necessary appropriately manned military and police forces. More than 60 countries currently provide peacekeeping forces numbering about 90,000. It is clear that for their effective operation they require a solid nucleus of well-trained and organised contingents available from only a handful of states. The considerations that Australia sees as limiting its capacity to support substantial numbers of peacekeepers apply equally to others.

The likelihood of more rather than less turmoil, together with these practical limitations on capacity, would also suggest caution in getting United Nations forces involved in new situations of non-international conflict. Before doing so, careful consideration should be given to the risks involved and the capacity in terms of manpower, finance and

---

[19] Boutros-Ghali, *Agenda for Peace* p.9.
[20] Ibid. p.17.

organisational skills to carry interventions to the point where the affected state becomes viable and civil government is assured. Long term international peace and security will not be advanced if sovereignty is overridden in the name of humanitarian rights and principles, but United Nations' use of military force is ineffectual or leaves the affected state in no better, or even worse, humanitarian circumstances. I am not, of course, suggesting that the United Nations should never intervene with armed forces for humanitarian reasons. I am saying only that it should do so cautiously, be ready to see the intervention through to a satisfactory outcome and that action by the Security Council should be taken only on the basis of a high degree of consensus between developed and developing countries.

Further, in order to build consensus and to achieve more consistency the trigger for Security Council decision making on the use of force for humanitarian purposes should be a report from an impartial and neutral source that the humanitarian crisis can no longer be satisfactorily managed. A decision by the Security Council would be taken in the light of this advice and other relevant factors. The balance of this study will be concerned with examining whether and how this would be feasible.

Non-international conflict and the United Nations humanitarian role

It has been argued earlier in this study that the use of force against General Aideed means that the United Nations ceases to be seen to be neutral in the eyes of Somalis. It is equally true that if United Nations forces had intervened in Bosnia in a serious way against one of the parties, even to secure the delivery of relief, it would have ceased to have been seen as impartial. Hence the emphasis always placed when bringing in relief under the protection of UN forces on doing so with the consent of the parties. The denial or provision of food in a conflict situation has tactical and even strategic implications for the parties to the conflict. They either consent to its delivery, or if force is to be used to get it through, then the user of force becomes a party to the conflict.

Bosnia, Iraq and Somalia point up a critical issue, namely the potential incompatibility in the security and humanitarian roles of the United Nations. In Somalia at this moment the UN is not distributing relief food in south Mogadishu, i.e., to the area where General Aideed's forces are located, because of the security situation. However, relief work is proceeding normally in the north of the city, i.e., the area under Ali Mahdi's control. Further, immediately after the first attack on Aideed's headquarters some of his supporters took refuge in the ICRC compound, presumably because it has always been careful to maintain its independence of the United Nations while always cooperating with the them. If the United Nations could confine itself to the role of an impartial mediator in disputes arising from international and non-international conflicts then the problem would not arise. However, if the United Nations is to carry out the purposes set out in Article 1 of the Charter it must play a much broader and more active political role.

The Secretary-General of the United Nations overruled in February 1992 the High Commissioner for Refugees when she suspended most relief shipments in Bosnia in the face of the belligerents' failure to allow access to desperate civilians. Sadako Ogata justified her decision on the grounds that the political leaders on all sides had made a mockery of United Nations efforts. Suspension by the ICRC of its efforts is not unknown in the face of rampant violations of law and humanity in which continuance of activities would bring into question its fundamental integrity. In overruling Ogata, Boutros-Ghali reportedly said, 'I'm supposed to direct this operation'. The incident illustrates that in the last resort United Nations humanitarian agencies are subject to political direction.

Further, UNHCR and the ICRC have not always been in agreement on the most appropriate course of action. In the former Yugoslavia the creation of 'safety zones' for vulnerable ethnic groups has been a subject of disagreement between the two agencies. The UNHCR has not favoured evacuation of civilians from zones of conflict on the grounds that such steps could contribute to the consolidation of ethnic cleansing, i.e., a politically grounded decision, justified on the basis that 'efforts should concentrate first on bringing safety to people, rather than people to safety'.[21] The ICRC maintains 'that this consideration must be secondary to the purely humanitarian consideration of how best to relieve suffering'.

The UNHCR is seen by some non-governmental organisations concerned with human rights as inconsistent in the application of humanitarian principles, in effect too 'political' in its decision making. This is particularly so in its dealings with major donors, e.g., its alleged failure to uphold the rights of refugees from El Salvador in the United States and of the several hundred thousand Cambodian 'non-refugees' who took refuge inside the Thai border. This not to criticise UNHCR but to make the point that the only United Nations organisation with a statutorily defined humanitarian mandate does not act consistently in support of the rights of refugees. Given the pressures from governments on all functional United Nations agencies, UNHCR performs well.

Security Council decision making on the prevention and termination of wars and internal conflicts will continue to be selective. Neither the interests of states, e.g., Australia in relation to Papua New Guinea and the Solomon Islands, nor the likely availability of financial and other resources, would allow any other course.

---

[21] UNHCR, 4 December 1992, quoted in Kathleen Newland, 'Ethnic Conflict and Refugees' *Survival* 35, 1 (Spring 1993) p.98.

Despite the media's role in stimulating United Nations involvement in certain conflicts causing great human suffering, from which states might have preferred to stand aside, the media is fickle and highly selective. To give an example, in 1992 conflict in Rwanda between government and opposition led to the displacement of upwards of 350,000 terrified local villagers. In late 1992 the ICRC found alarming levels of malnutrition among children. In February 1993 all-out war began in the north of the country, leading to the further movement of already displaced persons, the numbers of which have now reached 900,000. As yet none have returned home. While Rwanda is a tiny country in area it is the most densely populated country in Africa. Its population of 7,000,000 is about the same as Somalia's. Yet its plight has not attracted media attention.

However, just as the ICRC was operating in a major way in Somalia long before the Security Council took up the issue, so too is it and other humanitarian organisations working in Rwanda. While it is appropriate for the United Nations to be selective about its political and security interventions, *a genuinely humanitarian organisation cannot be selective about which innocent people in life-threatening situations it will help. All must be eligible, the only practical limitation being set by the availability of money, organisational capability and manpower.*

There is no agreed definition of the meaning of 'humanitarian' either in international law, in the Security Council Sanctions Committee or among non-government organisations. However, there is agreement on the ICRC's definition of humanitarian action, namely: 'action to prevent and alleviate human suffering wherever it is found'. 'It makes no discrimination as to nationality, race, class, religious beliefs or political opinions.' In relieving suffering it is guided solely by the 'needs of individuals'. In order to enjoy the confidence of all, the Red Cross movement 'may not take sides in hostilities' or engage in controversies of a political, racial, religious or ideological nature'.[22]

The President of the ICRC summed up the issues in a major address given on 20 November 1992 to the United Nations General Assembly[23] which deserves extensive quotation:

> The principle of impartiality, which requires that assistance be provided in accordance with the degree of suffering and priority given to the most urgent cases of distress, is crucial. It is observance of this principle that enables humanitarian organizations, in accordance with the acknowledged right of victims to receive assistance, to respond to emergency situations while providing all necessary guarantees of non-interference.

---

[22] *The International Committee of the Red Cross: What it Is, What it Does* (Geneva: ICRC Publications, 1990).

[23] Cornelio Sommaruga, 'Strengthening of the Co-ordination of Emergency Humanitarian Assistance of the United Nations Organisation' *International Review of the Red Cross* 292 (January-February 1993).

The principles of humanity and neutrality are equally important in ensuring that humanitarian activities remain apolitical.

It would be *impossible, and perhaps even undesirable, to dissociate humanitarian endeavour completely from political action.*

Humanitarian work concentrates on the acute symptoms produced by crises, but the crises themselves cannot be resolved without political measures to tackle their underlying causes. Moreover, just as humanitarian work needs political support, political negotiations stand to benefit from the relief afforded by maintaining a measure of humanity in the midst of conflict.

We are nevertheless convinced that *humanitarian endeavour and political action must go their separate ways* if the neutrality and impartiality of humanitarian work is not to be jeopardized.

In any situation in which humanitarian concerns become the overriding issue, it is rather dangerous to regard humanitarian action as just another political tool, or conversely, as an excuse for States to shirk their political responsibilities.

Indeed, to tie humanitarian activities too closely to political concerns is to run the risk of seeing humanitarian work rejected on political grounds.

In this regard, I wonder *how wise it is to resort to military means to support humanitarian activities* and, in certain circumstances, to protect the people who conduct them. The effectiveness of our operations is, admittedly, directly affected by the conditions of extreme insecurity in which we have to work. In the former Yugoslavia, and even more so in Somalia, it has unfortunately proved necessary to use armed escorts to protect humanitarian convoys. This, however, must remain a temporary and exceptional measure, and we must take care not to start thinking of it as an acceptable long-term solution. If we resign ourselves to these means, are we not in fact giving up all hope of persuading the belligerents to respect not only humanitarian work but above all defenceless civilians and prisoners?

For all these reasons we believe that it is *dangerous to link humanitarian activities aimed at meeting the needs of victims of a conflict with political measures designed to bring about the settlement* of the dispute between the parties.

The issue has been put less diplomatically and more starkly by the President of the highly respected private organisation, Médecins sans Frontières, as follows:

Amidst the fear and tension of armed conflict, aid workers have only one set of tactics they can use to secure relatively safe conditions in which to conduct relief efforts: it is to attempt to build a relationship of trust with the local strongmen. This relationship is always fragile, but it is indispensable to non-government organisations' freedom of movement and their ability to assess needs and monitor the delivery of aid.

I am convinced that only private organisations are in a position to build up and maintain this relationship. In other words, our strength in wartime lies in the fact that our motives are so obviously disinterested. You can see evidence of this in Somalia, where we worked under fire for eighteen months without protection. Today however, the military intervention has disrupted relations between non-government organisations and the local people so much that operating without protection has become unthinkable.

Western governments know that their humanitarian assistance pays off in electoral currency. But who can reasonably believe that any government would put its wish to play the Good Samaritan before its customary obligations? Governments' agendas are not and never will be ruled by a concern to do good. By nature they have to pursue the interests of their own countries, for better and for worse. This is what *raison d'état* is all about.[24]

When the United Nations first sought to bring about a ceasefire in Mogadishu during the first months of 1992, the basic concern of the official entrusted with negotiations was to use food aid as an inducement to the parties. Because his goal was political and not humanitarian he gave no serious attention to the extraordinarily complex and urgent problem of getting food to civilian victims under the conditions prevailing. The succession of United Nations failures in Somalia began from that first mistaken judgement, i.e., unwillingness to recognise that bringing about ceasefires and achieving access of relief supplies to victims are driven by different imperatives and practical constraints.

This is a very important point to be clear about. Successful humanitarian action may create a climate that facilitates independently negotiated conflict resolution of some kind. In very special circumstances the same person may be able to pursue negotiations simultaneously towards a peaceful settlement of the conflict and the provision of humanitarian relief. But from my experience it is best to keep separate negotiations that establish the conditions for the provision of humanitarian relief to parties in dispute from negotiations which look to the resolution of the dispute itself. In the United Nations the two functions are mixed up. The structure that is emerging in complex emergencies, e.g., Somalia and Mozambique, is for the Secretary-General's Representative to be in overall charge with a representative of the

---

[24] Rory Brauman, Médecins Sans Frontières, *International Newsletter* 6 (1993).

Department of Humanitarian Affairs in charge of relief coordination and a military officer in charge of peacekeeping. The Under Secretary-General for Humanitarian Affairs is, at the same time, answerable to the Secretary-General.

An alternative international humanitarian relief structure

I have argued elsewhere that because of the difficulty of reconciling the security functions of the United Nations with the principles of humanitarian action a 'reformed' ICRC should be responsible for negotiations with the parties involved in non-international disputes for securing access to the victims of conflict.[25] The reforms would be directed towards turning the ICRC from a private Swiss body into an international agency. As a Swiss, i.e., Western, body it appears to lack full credibility as an apolitical institution with developing countries. In the event that such a body decided that a humanitarian crisis could not longer be satisfactorily managed by the family of humanitarian organisations it could so advise the Secretary-General in a formal report. The Secretary-General in turn could inform the Security Council. Taking account of that report and other relevant criteria the Council would decide what action, if any, should be taken, including the most appropriate form of intervention. Under such an arrangement, the developing countries could be reasonably assured that if the Security Council decided to authorise the use of force, then the humanitarian argument would not be an excuse to cover other reasons. In situations akin to that covered by Resolution 688 action could continue to be initiated by the Security Council without a prior report by the Red Cross, i.e., the Security Council would remain master of its decision making on questions of peace and security.

The basis of this view is that the suffering of more people will be alleviated more quickly if, in non-international conflicts, the political functions of conflict resolution and peace enforcement are separated as much as possible from the function of relieving life-threatening suffering. The United Nations is necessarily a highly political body, the work of whose humanitarian agencies is influenced by the political goals of national governments. Of course, if the primacy of politics over humanitarian principles is seen as appropriate, as no doubt many national political leaders would feel, then the conflict in the security and humanitarian roles of the United Nations can be disregarded. Its continuation may indeed be welcomed in private. From the perspective of a narrow *realpolitik,* ambiguity in United Nations roles may be all to the good. However, the momentum being attained in relation to human rights as a legitimate concern of the international community makes such an attitude increasingly unsustainable.

---

[25] Ingram, 'The Future Architecture for Humanitarian Assistance'.

The Swiss Government and the ICRC may resist attempts to confer such a role on the ICRC, seeing in internationalisation a derogation in some way from its unique situation derived from the neutrality of Switzerland.

The ICRC recognises that it can barely cope with its present responsibilities and does not wish to expand them. It wishes to focus less on humanitarian operations and more on its role as custodian of international humanitarian law and to related functions of protecting war victims, etc. Moreover, governments have made a heavy investment in United Nations relief agencies as humanitarian actors. It may well be considered inappropriate for the Security Council to be advised in a formal way by other than an international organisation. As a matter of practical politics, therefore, the most realistic option for bringing about worthwhile change may be to focus on changes in the United Nations structure which would bring about separation of its security and humanitarian roles. Three possibilities exist.

The first would be to expand UNHCR's functions to include responsibility for internally displaced persons. UNHCR is doing this in Yugoslavia as 'lead agency' for the United Nations system, and for a time did so in northern Iraq. UNICEF has in the past also done so on several occasions. However, many years' experience has shown that the lead agency approach is not a sufficient answer. Setting aside UNHCR's considerable limitations as an effective operational agency in sudden, rapidly developing conflict situations, as compared with the ICRC yardstick, UNHCR's protective functions in regard to refugees proper are and should remain its essential *raison d'être*. Those functions are well established in international law. Refugee problems are clearly issues of state relations. Protection and succour of the victims of internal conflict, if pursued vigorously, is bound to create at times serious problems with states which could affect UNHCR's credibility with developing countries in view of the weight they attach to state sovereignty in this area. The result could easily be that UNHCR's capacity to protect refugees would be weakened. In short, the interests of refugees might well be damaged. As already noted, the fact that UNHCR is a United Nations agency under the direct political influence of governments has not always helped refugees.

A better option would be to create a single United Nations disaster response agency under the aegis of the Secretary-General. This would be an operational body to take over the relief and related basic rehabilitation work of UNICEF, UNHCR and WFP as well as being charged with negotiating, on behalf of the international community, access to the victims of conflict in accordance with ICRC-type principles. It would also advise the Secretary-General when the international relief community was unable to reach victims on account of conflict. To the extent that the skills of other agencies were required - and the need would be small - they would be provided under contract on a fee for service basis. Alternatively, the necessary skills could be purchased elsewhere from non-government organisations and national governments. UNICEF and WFP could continue with their development work and UNHCR would be able to concentrate on its protection work, the reason for its establishment in the first place.

To facilitate cooperation with ICRC and non-government organisations the new agency should be set up in Geneva. This would have the further advantage of underlining the intention to separate as much as possible the United Nations humanitarian and political functions. However, the reality would remain that the organisation would be seen as being, in the last resort, under the Secretary-General's guidance.

A much more substantial step, and the best option, would be the constitution of a specialised agency. The agency would carry out the functions just described, be constituted from the relief arms of the three agencies and set up in Geneva. The post of the Under Secretary-General for Humanitarian Affairs could be used to head up the new agency and suitable personnel on his staff could be transferred to it. A specialised agency staff with requisite skills for emergency work could be recruited and appropriate rules for their work in dangerous situations developed. More importantly, it would not be subject to the *direction* of the Secretary-General and would be able to provide independent advice for transmission to the Security Council on whether conflict situations had reached a point where forcible intervention should be considered if lives were to be saved. It would also be able to provide credible advice to the Security Council on the humanitarian consequences of decisions it was contemplating for other reasons. However, as an inter-governmental body it would be more sensitive to political factors and to donor pressure than an internationalised ICRC. It would not, therefore, be fully reassuring to developing countries.

Creation of a specialised agency would bring an additional significant bonus, namely an opportunity for at last ensuring an efficient and effective United Nations relief capability. *As already noted, to the extent that incompetence in this area was a factor leading to Resolution 794 on Somalia, there is a direct link between an improved security regime and reforms in the relief function.*

A reformed United Nations relief capability

The issue of how to create an effective United Nations disaster response mechanism is a vexing one. Since it established what was expected to be a soundly based, comprehensive United Nations disaster response system over twenty years ago, the General Assembly has on many occasions reviewed that decision, culminating in resolution 46/182 of December 1991 intended to deal comprehensively with this subject. Less than eighteen months later there is a widely held perception that the General Assembly could have done better and that many of the previous weaknesses still exist. According to one recent study, the ability of the United Nations to deal with humanitarian emergencies is increasingly questioned and there are signs that donors are looking around for alternative solutions. This was to be expected since the new institutional arrangements, while an advance in some respects on their predecessors, remained deeply flawed. In particular, every important element embodied in twenty year old resolution 2816 (XXVI) found its place in Resolution 46/182, though there were, of course, important differences of detail and of emphasis. Without root and branch changes, which so far governments have shown little willingness to tackle, at best marginal improvements may realistically be expected.

Structural problems

Structural reasons lie at the heart of United Nations inadequacy as an effective international relief instrument. While the international community has been concerned about the organisation of humanitarian relief for well over a century, neither under the League of Nations nor when establishing the United Nations was serious consideration given to establishing a permanent and comprehensive relief capability.

The post World War II United Nations relief system evolved from a structure created for different purposes. With the exception of UNHCR and UNICEF, the other main agencies now involved in emergencies, i.e., WFP, UNDP, FAO and WHO and various units of the United Nations Secretariat, acquired that role as a secondary function. Their main role was seen as promotion of economic and social development. Emergencies were incidental to their work until the 1980s, as they were for UNICEF, which long before had switched to 'development' as its main focus. At that time, notwithstanding the upsurge in their humanitarian relief work, the organisation of the agencies underwent no fundamental change. Staff recruited for intellectually challenging 'development' work were disdainful of relief. Inter-governmental agencies overseeing their work invariably focused on activities in support of development. This reflected the fact that the officials concerned were drawn mainly from development assistance agencies or technical departments of government, like agriculture. As a rule their understanding of, or interest in, humanitarian assistance was low. The development culture of the United Nations agencies, geared essentially to projects undertaken in the public sectors of developing countries, meant that there was little interaction with non-government organisations working at the local level, often on disaster related activities. Meanwhile, the extraordinary growth in the number of voluntary aid agencies working in developing countries added to the pattern of a chaotic and not very professional international response to successive humanitarian crises.

The system of governance of the United Nations system very much compounded the problem. The specialised agencies of the United Nations system are linked in the loosest way with the United Nations proper. In the principal coordinating body of the system, the Administrative Committee on Coordination (ACC) the United Nations Secretary-General is *primus inter pares*. The functional programs like UNICEF, UNDP, UNHCR and WFP, though legally less independent, in practice operate with much the same autonomy as the specialised agencies. All have separate inter-governmental managing councils. This very loose system of governance grew out of the view that international cooperation was best built around the nations working together in areas of mutual *functional* interest: food and agriculture, education, telecommunications, health, civil aviation and so on. Humanitarian relief was not seen as such a function. There was also fear that if the functional agencies were not kept separate from the United Nations political division in the latter would spill over into the former.

Separate agencies are inevitably in competition for scarce funds and want to be seen to be making a major contribution to a problem exercising donor governments, e.g., any headline catching major humanitarian disaster. This competition and the conflicts between, and gaps in, mandates of agencies prevent the kind of swift and purposeful action required to come to grips with complex, rapidly evolving humanitarian emergencies due to armed conflict, or sudden natural disasters such as regularly afflict Bangladesh. The Secretary-General does not have the authority to adjudicate these conflicts which, to the extent they are resolved, emerge from what is essentially a bargaining process. The governing bodies share with the secretariats of the agencies concerned an interest in their continuing autonomy and prosperity. Accordingly, General Assembly resolutions calling for the pursuit of appropriate coordination policies by the various governing bodies are rarely seriously addressed or followed up over time. In the field, i.e., the point of humanitarian intervention, the system of independent agency representation, reflecting the overall diffuse structure of the system, means that much time there is also spent on coordination. The result is that decisive action is invariably too slow.

None of the attempts so far made to deal with the perceived ineffectuality of the United Nations in dealing with emergencies address these structural problems. Instead they focus on coordination and matters, though of importance in their own right, that are essentially peripheral to the real issue. Examples are the preparation of appeals that consolidate the financial requirements of the various agencies involved in each disaster and the creation of 'effective mechanisms to provide early warning of impending crises, based on independent and unbiased information'.

A detailed discussion of the weaknesses of the system and the reasons for the inevitability of all proposals for change so far advanced by the United Nations or by governments leading to further failure would be out of place in this study. However, in view of the importance attached to early warning and improved information collation in relation to the peacemaking work of the United Nations, some brief comments on the importance of this subject for humanitarian crises management are offered.

Early warning and the humanitarian response

In practice, United Nations agencies collectively have a good sense of emerging humanitarian crises in most developing countries. The principal humanitarian agencies are represented in all but the smallest member states with personnel sensitive to the political, economic and social factors leading to conflict and war. Mr Boutros-Ghali was exaggerating, but not much, when he wrote recently: 'Nothing can match the United Nations' global network of information-gathering ... which reaches from modern world centers of power down to the villages and families where people carry out the irreducible responsibilities of their lives'.[26]

What the United Nations does lack is a means for the systematic collation, analysis and dissemination of information, the presence of which would facilitate decision making at United Nations headquarters and in humanitarian agencies in relation to the on-going management of emergencies. Nothing like the organisation of information in the foreign office of even one of the smaller industrialised countries exists or, in relation to global disaster intelligence, USAID. Vital to a more systematic collation of information is the creation of a unified United Nations field representation under a single individual functioning as the representative of the Secretary-General and responsible not simply for developmental matters but for all United Nations functions, including the political. The heads of the various organisations represented, including UNDP, would be deputies to the representative.

However, it is not a lack of knowledge as such that inhibits an 'appropriate' United Nations response to humanitarian crises as the lack of an effective organisational structure capable of well-planned and executed action, and a dearth of resources. The establishment of a new specialised agency built around the existing emergency functions of WFP, UNICEF, UNHCR and the Department of Humanitarian Affairs would overcome the organisational problem. However, the funding problem should also be addressed.

As regards resources, donors keep agencies on an extraordinarily short leash. They want full flexibility to decide themselves what emergencies to support bilaterally, through non-government organisations, or through the United Nations. By the time they make up their minds the situation has gravely worsened because the resources which in many cases could have led to its rapid containment were not available in sufficient extent at the right time. Innumerable concrete examples can be given.

The President of the ICRC has accurately and diplomatically summed up the situation as follows:

---

[26] Boutros Boutros-Ghali, 'Empowering the United Nations' *Foreign Affairs* 71, 5 (Winter 1992/93) p.99.

Resolution 46/182 provides for early-warning mechanisms, in which the ICRC plays a part on a case-by-case basis and in accordance with its principles. However, more important than early warning, which was in fact given in Somalia, for example, especially by the ICRC, what is sadly lacking at the moment is *a rapid response*.

What worries me personally is the fact that these atrocities inflicted on entire populations, these immense deficiencies in the humanitarian standards that protect each and every one of us, this worldwide upsurge of violence that we see on our television screens all elicit such a feeble and slow response.[27]

Governments have gone some way to recognising the need for establishing a pool of uncommitted resources. In 1991 WFP was given authority to set up a fund of US$30 million to facilitate an immediate response to food emergencies. By resolution 46/182 a US$50 million revolving fund was established for use by the Department of Humanitarian Affairs. Measured against the magnitude of the appeals shown in Table 3, let alone the total anticipated for 1993, these are grossly inadequate amounts.

The recent Ford Foundation Report on Financing an Effective United Nations examined *inter alia* the problem of financing peacekeeping. Among other recommendations it proposed that the United Nations should create a revolving reserve fund for peacekeeping set at $400 million, financed by three annual assessments. If the United Nations is to continue to be at the centre of humanitarian relief then a somewhat similar reserve fund arrangement is almost certainly necessary. *At the very least a serious inquiry by an outside independent advisory group along the lines of the peacekeeping one should be carried out.* If it achieves nothing else it will make donor governments more aware of a problem which so far they are unwilling to face seriously. To date, without exceptions, donors put most of their emergencies funding through non-government organisations. They do so for political reasons. Domestically, non-government organisations become potent lobby groups when the television screens fill with images of starving children. Literally hundreds of non-government organisations are attracted to the high profile emergencies, all fiercely competitive and often acting with a self-righteous inflexibility. The idea of using emergency aid to strengthen bilateral relations is also far from over.

Prospects for change

Current developments at the inter-governmental level suggest that action on the lines recommended, namely creation of a single humanitarian functional body for the United Nations system, could become feasible for

---

[27] Sommaruga, 'Strengthening of the Co-ordination of Emergency Humanitarian Assistance of the United Nations Organisation'.

the first time in United Nation's history. The draft resolution in the name of Uruguay (A/47/L.58) for presentation to the coming General Assembly, concerning the governing bodies of UNDP, UNICEF, WFP and the United Nations Fund for Population Activities (UNFPA), is a radical proposal in United Nations terms. If adopted, it may mean little in practice other than a reduction in the membership of governing bodies. Its significance lies in the demonstration it provides of a willingness on the part of governments to take first steps towards overcoming, albeit in a different context, the essential problem of coordination, namely the autonomy of agencies backed up by inter-governmental bodies sharing many of the ambitions of secretariats. The specialised agencies, which are at the heart of getting better coordination in relation to economic and social development, are not affected, nor is the system of United Nations representation in the field addressed. Moreover, if the Economic and Social Council (ECOSOC) is to be in reality a governing body giving policy direction to the four agencies it will be ineffective without the support of a strong secretariat. Presumably that support is to come from the recently created Department for Policy Coordination and Sustainable Development. The greater the intervention from this Department the more certain is the generation of a high level of friction between it and the four agencies. Moreover, by continuing to put operational activities for development at the centre of its concern the resolution overlooks two things, first, the extent to which UNICEF and WFP have become heavily involved in emergencies and secondly, the necessity of bringing UNHCR into the framework if better coordination is to be achieved in this critical area. Indeed the resolution, by excluding UNHCR, strengthens its relative autonomy.

Despite its serious flaws the resolution is a conceptual step forward and could open the way for more fundamental structural reform along the lines proposed here.

Humanitarian intervention and the causes of conflict

An issue of perennial concern for many years to donors and aid agencies has been the escalation in humanitarian emergencies and the possibility of reversing the trend by addressing more basic causes. Greater emphasis on preventive diplomacy is one approach to this issue. Another, which will be dealt with briefly here, is directed at the economic and social causes of conflict and the displacement of peoples.

There is no doubt that the displacement of peoples is often due to ethnic tensions, and economic decline can be a contributing factor. According to one respected scholar:

> A number of the ethnic conflicts that have erupted into violence and generated refugees in the developing world can be characterized as resource wars, in which battle lines reflect ethnic or tribal affiliations.

Some begin as disputes about grazing, water or agricultural rights, as population pressures or droughts impel people to move beyond the areas they traditionally inhabited.[28]

Clearly, the United Nations has a role in dealing with fundamental causes such as these. However, the language in which the issue is addressed within the United Nations is essentially rhetorical and self-serving, for example the following passage from Mr Boutros-Ghali:

> At the same time inseparable links between peace and development need to be acknowledged and understood. The world has seen the deterioration of economic and social conditions give rise to political strife and military conflict. The activities of the United Nations for peace and security should not be carried out at the expense of its responsibilities for development. It is essential that peace and development be pursued in an integrated, mutually supporting way.[29]

The Under Secretary-General for Humanitarian Affairs used similarly rhetorical language in addressing the last session of the UNDP Governing Council:

> Unchecked population growth, massive movements of people, the poverty gap, environmental degradation have to be tackled if we are to move away from an *ad hoc*, or 'band-aid' approach to ever-increasing emergencies. We have to deal more forcefully with root causes and concentrate more on prevention.

As always, the questions remain: How can these things actually be done? What concrete changes as compared with current practice should be introduced? Where is the money to come from to do them? In terms of the production of first-rate studies dealing with these perennial issues the work of the United Nations is not highly respected. Setting aside the World Bank, it is also a minor player as a provider of development assistance. Overcoming poverty has been the rationale for United Nations and bilateral aid programs for many years, to which has been recently added 'sustainable development', but there has been little real impact. Official aid programs remain politically driven, despite changing rhetoric. If, indeed, root causes can be dealt with in a significant way through external interventions, a fundamental change in the foreign aid regime will be necessary. Meanwhile, the United Nations should focus on what can be done: making the institutional reforms required to reduce death and suffering due to emergencies arising out of armed conflict and sharpening its role in peacemaking.

Moreover, it does not follow that because prevention is better than cure that the provision of aid and other actions to overcome the alleged structural causes of conflict needs to, or should be, addressed at the same

---

[28] Newland, 'Ethnic Conflict and Refugees' p.90.
[29] Boutros-Ghali, 'Empowering the United Nations' p.95.

time as the difficult and complex enough task of saving lives and relieving suffering is being attended to.

In complex situations where everything is inter-related, knowledge is incomplete and the tools at hand inadequate, endeavouring to take a holistic approach is a sure recipe for failing to achieve anything. In emergencies priorities have to be set. Saving life and relieving life-threatening suffering must come first and bringing conflict to an end second. The latter is necessarily difficult to achieve and as the history of every civil conflict mentioned in this study shows, draw out over years. Rehabilitation beyond what is required for well managed relief, e.g., the establishment of potable water supplies and basic health infrastructure and de-mining, must come second.

Summary conclusions and recommendations

The *principal findings* of this study, which has focused in most detail on Somalia as the clearest example of an intervention justified in humanitarian terms, are as follows:

- United Nations failings in relation to the provision, management and coordination of humanitarian relief contributed directly to the situation that led to Security Council decisions to intervene with force in Somalia.

- While the use of force brought certain short term benefits, there is controversy about the necessity for and timing of the intervention and its overall long term humanitarian impact.

- There is an inherent contradiction between the pursuit by the United Nations of its responsibilities for peacemaking and peacekeeping and its capacity to act in accordance with the humanitarian principles of impartiality and neutrality.

- Interventions in situations of unresolved internal conflict under narrow short term goals, i.e., the use of armed forces to establish secure conditions for delivery of relief supplies, are unlikely to be capable of early successful termination.

The principal recommendations are as follows:

- Before deciding on coercive measures specifically to prevent loss of life and prevent human suffering, which should be a rare last resort, the Security Council should receive independent outside advice that the humanitarian situation is such that coercive measures are essential.

- Before deciding on coercive measures against states for other than humanitarian reasons, the Security Council should have before it a report on the likely humanitarian impact (if any) of the contemplated action.

- An internationalised ICRC, which would have all humanitarian crises under scrutiny, could be an appropriate body to provide such advice. As an apolitical, impartial and neutral body the ICRC's performance of these rules should be reassuring to states concerned at the possible misuse of the humanitarian justification for interventions in the affairs of sovereign states.

- In the event that this is not feasible, then a United Nations specialised agency should be set up to provide such reports and to be responsible for humanitarian relief operations and all related matters. Existing United Nations agencies carrying out relief functions would cease to do so. The Department of Humanitarian Affairs would be abolished.

- United Nations forces should not be introduced unless it is agreed that they will remain as long as necessary for the establishment of conditions allowing for sustained relief, rehabilitation and reconstruction activities to continue on their withdrawal.

- The rules of engagement of United Nations forces introduced for humanitarian purposes should be carefully considered for each situation from the perspective of minimising the impact of the use of force on the civilian population.

Subsidiary recommendations, not listed in order of importance, are as follows:

- In deciding to intervene in a humanitarian crises the Security Council has available to it a hierarchy of measures. One measure used with relative success in Iraq, i.e., the provision of unarmed guards, might be an appropriate first response in some crisis situations.

- Measures for the stronger enforcement of international humanitarian law should be considered. For example, in the light of experience of its work, the Impartial Commission of Experts established under Security Council Resolution 780 might be institutionalised on a permanent basis and its mandate expanded to encompass all conflicts in respect of which the ICRC certifies that the relevant principles of the Geneva Conventions and Additional Protocols have been breached.

- The United Nations should provide a *post facto* final report and interim reports on the full peacekeeping and relief costs for each intervention involving the use of armed forces acting under United Nations auspices. To the extent feasible, assessments of the overall humanitarian impact of each such intervention should be included.

- An independent study of how best to provide sufficient resources to allow a prompt and effective multilateral response to humanitarian emergencies should be commissioned.

TABLE 1: Possible Uses of Force for Humanitarian Purposes in Civil Strife

Armed Activity	Possible Humanitarian Objectives
Military forces deliver relief supplies but do not carry weapons.	Provide food and relief to suffering civilian populations while minimising potential for entanglement in local conflict.
Armed forces deliver relief aid, using force only in self defence and to protect relief supplies.	Provide relief aid, with somewhat greater security for personnel, while deterring interference by hostile groups.
Armed monitoring or enforcement of sanctions; blockade.	Pressure the offending government to modify its behaviour to better protect civilians; deprive it of arms that might be used against civilians.
Armed suppression of air traffic in the offending country.	Prevent or reduce air attacks on civilians; protect delivery of relief supplies; pressure the government to modify its behaviour.
Air strikes against selected military targets, such as artillery or airfields.	Prevent use of particular weapons against civilians, punish the offending combatant, demonstrate resolve to protect civilians.
Air, ground, and/or naval action against the armed forces of one or more combatants.	Deter or reduce attacks on civilians or relief shipments; pressure the offending government or other combatants to modify behaviour.
Armed forces create safe havens or 'zones of peace' and defend them against local combatants.	Shelter displaced civilians until the conflict subsides.
Peacekeeping - armed forces monitor a ceasefire or peace agreement with the consent of combatants.	Protect civilians and encourage a resumption of normal life through efforts to prevent a resumption of hostilities.
Imposed peace - armed occupation to enforce terms not accepted by the government and/or other parties.	Restore peaceful conditions and allow resumption of normal life; arrange a transition to a new regime more likely to respect civilian lives.

Source: Raymond W. Copson, *The Use of Force in Civil Conflicts for Humanitarian Purposes: Prospects for the Post-Cold War Era* (Washington, DC: Library of Congress, Congressional Research Service, 2 December 1992).

TABLE 2: United Nations Emergency Appeals

Population (million)	Affected	UN Emergency Appeals Total	$ million	Period
Afghanistan	3.7	16.6	180	6-12/92
Angola	1.4	10.0	81	5-12/92
Ethiopia/Eritrea	9.2	49.2	200	7-12/92
Iraq	0.75	18.9	217	7/92-3/93
Liberia	2.1[a]	2.6	150	12/90-9/92
Mozambique	4.7[a]	15.7	250	5-12/92
Somalia	2.4	6.0	83	10-12/92
Sudan	7.8	25.2	141	7-12/92
Yugoslavia[b]	3.1	23.8	434	9/92-4/93

Source: United Nations Department of Public Information DPI/1320: 'Enlarging the UN's Humanitarian Mandate', *United Nations Spotlight on Humanitarian Issues* (December 1992).

Notes: a. Including refugees in neighbouring countries   b. Former

TABLE 3: Peacekeeping Missions - Assessments in 1992 and Estimated Expenditures

Mission	Authorisation: Assessment ($US million)		1992 Cost ($US million)
UNTSO (Middle East)	Authorised Regular Budget		25
UNMOGIP (India/Pakistan)	Authorised Regular Budget		6
UNFICYP (Cyprus)	Voluntary Contributions		31
ONUCA (Nicaragua)	11/91-4/92:	12	7
UNDOF (Golan Heights)	12/91-11/92: 12/92-5/93:	35 17	39
UNFIL (Lebanon)	2/92-1/93:	144	153
UNIKOM (Iraq/Kuwait)	10/91-10/92: 11/92-4/93:	50 19	68
UNAVEM II (Angola)	1/92-10/92: 11/92-2/93:	56 25	67
ONUSAL (El Salvador)	1/92-10/92: 11/92-2/93:	36 8	35
MINURSO (Western Sahara)	Authorised 9/91: not yet fully operational		18
UNPROFOR (Yugoslavia)	1/92-10/92: 12/92-2/93:	250 298	222
UNAMIC (Cambodia advance mission)	11/91-4/92:	33	20
UNTAC (Cambodia)	5/92-10/92: 11/92-4/93:	802 313	637
UNOSOM (Somalia)	5/92-4/93:	108	390
ONUMOZ (Mozambique)	to be authorised in March, '93 at estimated cost of over $200		-
Total			$1,367

Source: *World Development Report 1992* (Washington, DC: World Bank)

6 The International Court of Justice

STEVEN MCINTOSH

The role of the Court - the theory

What role does the Court have in keeping the peace between nations?

Potentially, a very important role. The Court was set up, after all, to adjudicate on 'any question of international law'. No limit was placed on the subject matter with which it could deal. The Court would seem a logical place to settle disputes before the shooting begins. A place where arguments could be put, and compromises reached, in an atmosphere of scholarship and reason rather than violence and intimidation.

This was the hope of the Court's founders and it is something that today's Secretary-General recognises in his report *An Agenda for Peace*. The report concludes that 'greater reliance on the Court would be an important contribution to United Nations peacemaking'.

How it has worked in practice

Unfortunately things have not worked out this way in practice. There are almost no examples of where it could be said that the Court - by adjudicating on an issue - has prevented the use of force.

Yet there is no doubt that the Court *could* play such a role. The case of *Libya v Chad* offers an interesting - and recent - example of where the Court may be in the process of doing so.

This case involved the submission to the Court of a *compromis* setting out the position of the parties in a long-standing dispute relating to the Aouzou Strip, a mineral-rich rectangle of land which runs the entire length of the boundary between the two states. The area was progressively occupied by Libyan troops beginning in the 1970s, and the dispute manifested itself as a low-level war throughout much of the 1980s, from time to time leading to interventions by outside powers, notably France. At one stage Libya installed a sympathetic government in Chad, but it fell in a civil war some years later. Following that reverse, Libya agreed in August 1989 to submit the dispute to the Court. Oral hearings commenced on 7 June 1993. The case of *Burkino Faso v Mali* provides another interesting example of a border dispute in Africa which was, after a period of prolonged low level armed conflict, referred to the Court for determination. The Court's judgement was publicly accepted and praised by the parties.

Why has the Court's role been so limited?

The fundamental reason why the Court's role has been so limited is that states have not *allowed* it to play a more significant role. It is clear that many states are reluctant to allow a third party to decide issues which they consider vital to their national sovereignty. This has meant that only a small number of states have accepted the compulsory jurisdiction of the Court.

In one sense this reluctance is not surprising. After all, in most situations where the use of force is a possibility, the issues are so fundamental that they usually have implications for the territorial integrity of the state itself or the viability of the government. These are not issues which a leader will lightly place in the hands of a third party, especially if there is a chance that the third party will decide against the leader.

This fundamental political problem will always be a potential barrier to the effective operation of the Court in the area of peacemaking. It would be naive to pretend otherwise.

However there are a number of specific problems - to do with the actual running of the Court - which have made the situation worse. These problems have further discouraged states from submitting to the Court's jurisdiction. By fixing these problems we will have at least maximised the chances of the Court operating effectively in the imperfect world in which it has been cast.

A basic problem is the slowness with which the Court hears cases. This is shown by the timetable for the case of *Portugal v Australia*. Written pleadings in this case closed on 1 July 1993, yet a hearing of the matter is not expected before November 1994. On the pattern set by the *Nauru v Australia* case, a written judgement in the Portugal case could not be expected before March 1995. Parties to disputes which threaten international peace and security especially are likely to feel that such delays compromise their national interests (although in some cases delays may give the parties an opportunity to negotiate a settlement of the dispute before the final judgement of the Court - as in *Nauru v Australia*). This may compound the perceptions regarding loss of national sovereignty referred to above and contribute to an unwillingness to submit to ICJ jurisdiction.

Some of the causes of this slowness could be quite easily addressed - for example the inadequate translation facilities available to the Court, the restricted sitting times and the failure of the Court to advise parties prior to oral proceedings of the points on which the Court desires assistance from counsel.

The chief cause of delays, however, is that the Court, which is usually constituted by the entire fifteen judges, will not consider more than one case at a time. After hearing the oral submissions of the parties, the Court retires to consider its judgement. This is a lengthy process involving a series of formal consultations among members of the Court, the preparation and circulation of written notes by all members of the Court, the election of a drafting committee and the circulation of multiple draft opinions. Until that judgement is delivered the Court will not commence hearing another matter. In the case of *Nauru v Australia*, as noted above, oral hearings on the Preliminary Objections were held in November 1991 and judgement was delivered in June 1992 - some seven months later. During this entire period the Court did not hear any other matters - a practice which is not reflected in domestic jurisdictions.

The only exception is in the case of a request for provisional measures. The Court endeavours to hear arguments and deliver judgement on such applications expeditiously, as it did most recently in the case of *Bosnia and Hercegovina v Yugoslavia (Serbia and Montenegro)*. In that case the Court, at the request of the Bosnian Government, ordered the authorities in Belgrade to take all measures within their power to prevent breaches of the Genocide Convention. The order has had no discernible effect on the conflict in Bosnia-Hercegovina, clearly demonstrating the limits of the Court's power.

There are some procedures available to the Court to alleviate the backlog of work it faces. The Chambers procedure (Articles 26 to 29 of the Statute of the Court), for example, is under-utilised. The use of an ad hoc Chamber (Article 26) enables the parties to a dispute to select five judges from among the members of the Court to hear their Case. The first use of ad hoc Chambers in the Gulf of Maine Case (*Canada v United States of America*) attracted opposition from within the Court on the basis that the parties were choosing 'Western' judges to hear the matter. However, the ad hoc Chambers procedure has been used on a number of occasions since then without objection from other members of the Court.

In addition to these ad hoc Chambers, Article 29 of the Statute provides:

> With a view to the speedy dispatch of business, the Court shall form annually a chamber composed of five judges which, at the request of the parties, may hear and determine cases by summary procedure.

No states have requested that this Chamber, which is a separate body from the ad hoc Chambers constituted pursuant to Article 26, be used. This is probably because states fear that such a procedure will not allow for the full ventilation of their arguments in relation to what are very important questions. Australia has suggested that matters such as disputes under the proposed International Convention on State Immunities could conveniently be heard in the Chamber of Summary Procedure. It certainly offers scope for a swifter resolution of (necessarily minor) matters than is possible by way of the ordinary proceedings of the Court.

The future

There are several ways in which Australia is going to encourage the Court to play a more active role in the UN peacemaking function.

The *first* is to encourage States to accept the compulsory jurisdiction of the Court. Until quite recently this may have seemed nothing more than a pious aspiration. However, the end of the Cold War offers new hope that more disputes can be settled by peaceful means. The list of states accepting the compulsory jurisdiction of the Court has grown by four in the past two years (Bulgaria, Estonia, Madagascar and Hungary), and there is presently a record number of cases before the Court. In *An Agenda For Peace* the Secretary General calls for all states to accept the compulsory jurisdiction of the Court and this is something which Australia will continue to fully support.

The *second* is to try to speed up the rate at which the Court handles cases. The chief way this could be done in the immediate future would be through the greater use of the Court's Chambers procedures. Australia could work on this with other states which have accepted the compulsory jurisdiction of the Court without reservations. The already evident increase in the Court's workload suggests that the time has come for a new procedural approach which enables it to meet the broad Article 29 requirement which envisages 'the speedy dispatch of business'.

The *third* is to encourage UN member states to agree to a full evaluation of the Court and the other organs in the international legal community in the year 1999, which will mark the end of the 'Decade of International Law' referred to by the Secretary-General in *An Agenda for Peace*.

7 Arms Control and Disarmament: Prevention and Enforcement

JILL COURTNEY

Disarmament and arms control processes manifest themselves in three different ways:

- prevention (arms control and disarmament agreements and arrangements);
- preventive diplomacy (managing treaty compliance);
- post-conflict/post-treaty violation actions (enforcement).

While the processes of implementation of these disarmament measures and strategies are different, they all seek the same fundamental goal - the enhancement of security and inter-state trust without impediment to legitimate trade and technology transfer.

Prevention: Arms control and disarmament

There is an intrinsic link between disarmament and arms control and security. No state will enter voluntarily into an arms control process unless it is convinced that it will enhance its security - or at minimum that it is security neutral.

Context

Preventive arms control as a method for security enhancement has been resorted to frequently throughout this century, often when other security promotion mechanisms failed - or were not sought. Frequently, in response to technological developments, treaties were devised to eliminate the use, possession or proliferation of a certain category of weapons.

The 1925 Geneva Protocol banning the use of chemical weapons was an early example. It was a response to use of such weapons in World War I and the common belief of states that such abhorrent weapons should not be used. The Protocol was not verifiable and did not ban possession, relying essentially on the goodwill of the signatory states.

When the UN Charter was drafted in 1945, the rather idealistic approach to disarmament taken by the League of Nations was replaced by the concepts of collective security and the inherent right of self defence. The role of the UN in the field of disarmament receives two mentions in Articles 26 and 47 of the Charter. Article 26 states as follows:

> In order to promote the establishment and maintenance of international peace and security with the least diversion for armaments of the world's human and economic resources, the Security Council shall be responsible for formulating, with the assistance of the Military Staff Committee referred to in Article 47, plans to be submitted to the Members of the United Nations for the establishment of a system for the regulation of armaments.

This literal disarmament role of the Security Council has never been realised and, during the Cold War, the Security Council was unable to agree on any disarmament role for the Council whatsoever. From the outset, however, member states recognised that weapons possession and control, particularly weapons of mass destruction (WMD), were key elements in determining the post-World War II security structure and balance. This was evidenced most clearly by the arms race between east and west - perhaps the single most dominant feature of the Cold War world.

Role of the United Nations

While the UN could not act through its own mechanisms in the face of such arms races, member states perceived the security threat of a possible widespread nuclear arms race, of acquisition of other weapons of mass destruction, and the accumulation of large arsenals of increasingly sophisticated conventional weapons. The result, beginning in the sixties, was the cooperative negotiation and agreement to abide by a number of arms control and disarmament treaties and arrangements.

These treaties derived closely from the international norms established by the General Assembly and the Security Council, even if they were autonomous treaties outside the UN system itself. And while technically outside the UN, the UN performed and continues to perform a constant support function in acting as Secretariat for the review of these treaties. The Secretary-General is depositary of more recent treaties, and the states parties to the treaties report to and take advice from the General Assembly and relevant bodies, as does the multilateral disarmament negotiating forum, the Conference on Disarmament. In a number of cases violations of a treaty are to be reported to the Security Council for follow-up action. Thus, there is a vital relationship between the UN in the development of procedures, norms, rules, conventions and treaties, and the functioning and enforcement of the separate treaties themselves.

Prevention and the Treaties

Prevention in the case of arms control and disarmament could be said to have a number of different aspects:

- the restraint in acquisition, or the elimination, of certain weapons systems promotes security and confidence between states;

- such voluntary cooperative actions demonstrate benign interest of states and thus promote peaceful dispute resolution;

- the voluntary subjection of sovereign territory for verification and inspection to ensure compliance is a major confidence-building and transparency measure between states;

- in the event that conflict does occur the consequences may be less devastating or escalation may be more controlled if a disarmament-limited range of weapons are available for use.

The existing panoply of multilateral treaties covers all weapons of mass destruction and a number of other weapons types:

- The Nuclear Non-Proliferation Treaty (NPT)

- Chemical Weapons Convention (CWC)

- Biological Weapons Convention (BWC)

- Inhumane Weapons Convention

- Partial Test Ban Treaty

- Environmental Modification Treaty

- Seabed Treaty.

There are also notable regional treaties which ban from a zone certain categories of weapons and military activities. These include the Rarotonga Treaty, the Treaty of Tlatelolco, the Outer Space Treaty and the Antarctic Treaty.

The United Nations and the Conference on Disarmament are also in the process of establishing transparency on transfers of armaments, and establishing cooperative norms in respect of acquisition of conventional weapons.

To analyse the effectiveness of preventive measures, the NPT and the CWC are useful examples.

The Nuclear Non-Proliferation Treaty. The NPT provides for *ad interim* possession of nuclear weapons by the nuclear weapon states - that is those five countries which had manufactured and exploded a nuclear weapon or other nuclear explosive device before 1 January 1967 - while committing them to work towards complete disarmament. It obliges all other states to reject the option of possession or control of nuclear explosives in return for access to assistance in peaceful uses of nuclear energy. In preventing the proliferation of weapons to those 152 other states, it has contributed extraordinarily to global and regional security. Prevention has not, of course, applied to those states which have not accepted the obligations of the treaty, some of whom are threshold nuclear weapon states. Paradoxically, those states have gained security benefits from the membership of others, particularly their regional neighbours.

The NPT was the first treaty to establish a routine, intrusive verification regime (International Atomic Energy Agency safeguards) and to require specific commitments by nuclear and non-nuclear weapon states not to transfer nuclear material and equipment to non-nuclear weapon states except under IAEA full-scope safeguards. This far sighted approach process was designed to provide confidence that the states are complying with their obligations; this confidence in turn facilitates legitimate nuclear trade and cooperation. The experience of the United Nations Special Commission (UNSCOM)/IAEA inspections in Iraq demonstrated that the IAEA safeguards system needed to be strengthened, particularly in the area of detection of undeclared facilities.

Chemical weapons. The recently concluded Chemical Weapons Convention goes even further than the NPT by banning completely this category of weapons. It goes beyond the Geneva Protocol in not simply outlawing use but also production, development and stockpiling. Its strictures apply equally to all states. The CWC provides not only for routine monitoring (including monitoring of the world's extensive chemical industry), but also for the challenge inspection of any suspect site, including, if required, of sensitive military sites. The acceptance of such intrusion provides enhanced confidence in the observation of the convention and will facilitate trade in chemical agents, materials and technologies for peaceful purposes. If universally adhered to the Convention will effectively eliminate a weapon that is indiscriminate in its effect and particularly lethal to large unprotected population centres.

As these two examples show, arms control and disarmament agreements are classical examples of cooperative security action whereby a group of states or a state eschew certain types or numbers of weapons in order to promote mutual security. Given the experience with the NPT and BWC, treaties of the future will more likely have verification provisions which cover both declared and undeclared facilities, and are unlikely to entail simply a ban on use or, like the BWC, to be unverifiable in their ban on development and production.

The future

While existing treaties and arrangements in the multilateral field have yielded security benefits to date, the lacunae in the arms control field are many and consequently a number of states continue to possess arsenals containing weapons of mass destruction or large, destabilising arsenals of often sophisticated conventional weapons. And many states direct disproportionate amounts of their scant resources to spending on armaments and armed forces.

There are a number of options for cooperative action to enhance security in these fields. Conventional weapons are yet to be subject to any limitations (except self imposed) in terms of acquisition and transfer. Unsurprisingly, it is regions of tension that tend to acquire increasingly larger arsenals, often through secretive or illicit transfers, thus engendering mistrust and undermining confidence. Enhanced openness about transfer and military matters has commenced but requires greater participation and broader data submission. Cooperative international agreement to a code of conduct in arms transfers and possibly possession - with relevant verification measures - would contribute to enhanced confidence between states and assist with the peaceful settlement of disputes.

Many other gaps exist and there is no reason why traditional cooperative methods of treaty negotiation should not be used as a preventive strategy. Areas where security would be enhanced by such treaties include

- Comprehensive Test Ban Treaty;

- Prevention of an arms race in outer space;

- Negative security guarantees to non-nuclear weapon states.

The United Nations, through General Assembly debates and resolutions, the UN Disarmament Commission and the Security Council, will continue to play a role in the development of international norms in these areas. There is also greater scope than before for the Security Council to take a more active role in the disarmament, non-proliferation and arms control fields:

- as an agent of recourse in the event of treaty violation;

- in promoting non-proliferation objectives, in particular for weapons of mass destruction and their delivery vehicles;

- by high level meetings aimed at accelerating negotiations of extant treaties;

- by proposing, consistent with the Charter, limits on quantities and types of conventional weapons for various regions and globally; and

- increasing its use of arms embargoes as a preventive as well as a punitive measure to limit the armaments of warring factions, in intra-state conflicts or possibly those in inter-state conflicts.

As the establishment of the UN Arms Transfer Register demonstrates, the UN Secretariat, with the support of member states, can also move to more active support of security dialogue through the promotion of measures of transparency and openness. The Secretariat is ideally placed to maintain data bases of military holdings, force structures and related activities and to ensure that these are available to all member states.

There is an intrinsic if obvious logic deriving from the UN Charter that since states are obliged to settle their disputes by peaceful means the possession of weapons should be kept to the minimum for collective or self defence purposes. Arms control and disarmament arrangements, particularly when underscored by balanced effective verification methods, provide a cooperative avenue for creating a global configuration of defence-oriented forces.

Such a process will be step-by-step and will occur only in the context of enhanced dispute settlement mechanisms which render less likely the resort to the use of force in situations of tension or crisis. Thus, close cooperation between the promotion of both avenues of preventive mechanisms will be necessary. Progress in one area is likely to be conducive to progress in the other.

Prevention - managing treaty compliance

The effectiveness of international arms control, non-proliferation and disarmament treaties as instruments of preventive diplomacy can be judged by:

- the normative effect of such treaties (so that remaining outside them or breaching their obligations attracts international opprobrium);

- the effectiveness of verification mechanisms as a deterrent to the development or acquisition of weapons of mass destruction and their delivery systems; and

- the effectiveness of verification mechanisms in uncovering undeclared WMD before these programs reach fruition (so enforcement action can be triggered).

Case studies

Iraq

The United Nations Special Commission (UNSCOM), in cooperation with the International Atomic Energy Agency (IAEA), revealed that Iraq had been developing extensive weapons of mass destruction and ballistic missile programs before the Gulf War. What multilateral disarmament/non-proliferation mechanisms were available to prevent Iraq developing these weapons systems and why did they fail?

Iraq's adherence to multilateral disarmament/non-proliferation instruments before the Gulf War. Iraq had signed but not ratified the Biological Weapons Convention, but its efforts to develop a BW capability were in breach of its BWC obligations. The BWC's lack of specific verification provisions (apart from a series of voluntary confidence-building measures) meant that even if Iraq had been a full Party to the Convention there would have been no available international mechanism to detect non-compliance.

Iraq breached its obligations under the 1925 Geneva Protocol, banning use of chemical weapons, when it discharged chemical munitions during the Iran-Iraq War. Use of chemical weapons during this war provided impetus to the Chemical Weapons Convention negotiations (finally concluded in 1992 in part due to the additional stimulus of the threat of CW use during the Gulf War) as well as successive UN General Assembly resolutions giving the UN Secretary-General unhindered authority to investigate allegations of CW use. Investigations under the UN Secretary-General's authority were important in confirming and bringing to the international community's attention CW use during the Iran-Iraq War.

There was and still is no multilateral treaty to prevent the proliferation of missile technology to which all states can adhere. The only international mechanism is the Missile Technology Control Regime (MTCR), a group of like-minded countries which has developed guidelines to control exports and which meets to share information. So in developing a ballistic missile program, Iraq was not in breach of any international treaty obligations.

However, Iraqi activities to develop nuclear weapons were in breach of its obligations as a member of the Treaty on the Non-Proliferation of Nuclear Weapons. Iraq joined the NPT in 1969 and concluded a full-scope safeguards agreement with the International Atomic Energy Agency in 1972 (as required by the Treaty). This agreement obliged Iraq to accept IAEA inspections on all current and future nuclear activities. The facilities covered under the agreement were two nuclear research reactors, a nuclear fuel fabrication plant and a separate storage facility at the Tuwaitha nuclear complex near Baghdad. The IAEA conducted routine inspections of these safeguarded facilities and found no evidence of diversion of nuclear material from them (i.e., for use in a possible nuclear weapons program). But a significant number of additional covert nuclear facilities and materials, notably concerning uranium enrichment technology and nuclear weapons design, were uncovered by UNSCOM after the war.

This experience with Iraq highlighted the need for the IAEA to strengthen its safeguards system, particularly its capacity to detect undeclared materials and facilities and to extend its interest to possible nuclear weapons related activity. It demonstrated that the IAEA needed greater access in states under full-scope or comprehensive safeguards. It demonstrated that the IAEA needed an improved flow of information on nuclear trade and access to information in the hands of member states. It demonstrated that the IAEA should draw on other sources of expertise, such as on nuclear weapons, when this was required to enable it to carry out effectively its functions. It demonstrated the importance of political and financial support for its verification program by members of the NPT, and of political support for the Agency from its Board of Governors and from the UN Security Council.

The IAEA statute also contains a preventive provision, in the form of the threat of Security Council consideration. Article XII, C requires the IAEA Board of Governors to report non-compliance by member states with their safeguards obligations to the IAEA Director-General and for the Board then to report the non-compliance to all IAEA member states and to the Security Council and General Assembly of the United Nations. On the basis of the results of IAEA inspections as part of the UNSCOM process after the war, the IAEA Board found Iraq in non-compliance with its safeguards obligations in July 1991 and decided to report the non-compliance to all IAEA member states and to the United Nations Security Council and General Assembly.

Conclusions and outcomes. The case of Iraq highlighted the need to develop additional non-proliferation regimes (i.e., to cover CW and missiles) and to develop (for the BWC) or strengthen (in the case of the NPT) the verification provisions of existing treaties. UNSCOM's revelations provided added impetus to the conclusion of the long-running CWC negotiations (also greatly assisted by the end of the Cold War) and led to the strengthening of IAEA safeguards.

The February 1991 meeting of the IAEA Board of Governors reaffirmed the Agency's right of access to sites beyond declared facilities through the conduct of special inspections. It also took action to strengthen the flow of information to the IAEA Secretariat, including requiring member states to provide design information on new nuclear facilities at an earlier stage. In February 1993 the Board approved a universal reporting system to enhance the flow of information on nuclear transfers. Work on strengthening Agency safeguards is continuing.

Democratic Peoples Republic of Korea (DPRK)

While conducting safeguards inspections under the DPRK's NPT agreement to verify the declaration by the DPRK of its holdings of nuclear material, IAEA inspectors uncovered discrepancies between information provided by the DPRK and the results of IAEA sampling. This was a case of international verification provisions detecting anomalies and provided the early warning to the international community for which they were designed. Why were the IAEA's verification activities under the NPT effective on this occasion?

The DPRK's compliance with its NPT obligations. The DPRK joined the NPT in 1985 but only concluded its full-scope safeguards agreement with the Agency in 1992 (i.e., well outside the eighteen months time frame required by the Treaty). Members of the international community had long been concerned that the DPRK was developing a large, unsafeguarded nuclear program, including a sizeable reprocessing plant (to reprocess spent nuclear fuel to produce plutonium). These concerns were confirmed when the DPRK provided the IAEA with an initial inventory of nuclear material in May 1992.

While conducting safeguards inspections to verify the DPRK's initial inventory, IAEA inspectors uncovered discrepancies between information provided by the DPRK and the results of IAEA sampling. The discrepancies revealed a shortfall in the amount of plutonium declared by the DPRK and the amount the IAEA judged had been produced. The DPRK also denied Agency inspectors access to two suspect sites at the Yongbyon nuclear complex. The DPRK claimed, and has continued to claim, that the sites were military facilities and should not be inspected - despite an earlier offer to IAEA Director-General Blix for inspections 'anywhere anytime'. Information provided to the Agency by member states added to the Agency's concerns about the sites.

After numerous attempts to seek adequate explanations and access, the IAEA Director-General requested a special inspection of the sites under the terms of the DPRK's full-scope safeguards agreement with the IAEA on 9 February. This action was endorsed by the IAEA Board of Governors in a resolution of 25 February. Rather than comply with the Board's request, the DPRK announced on 12 March that it would withdraw from the NPT, an action for which three months notice under the Treaty was required. Following the DPRK's continued refusal to cooperate with the Agency in the implementation of its safeguards agreement, the IAEA Board of Governors, in a special session on 1 April 1993, found the DPRK in non-compliance with its safeguards agreement and, in keeping with the provisions of the IAEA statute, reported the matter to all IAEA member states and to the UN Security Council and General Assembly.

The Security Council responded initially with a statement noting the report and expressing its concern, in which it also asked the IAEA to continue consultations with the DPRK. Further correspondence between the DPRK and the IAEA led in late April to a further routine safeguards visit, but no progress was made on the main issue of access to the disputed sites which had been the subject of the request for special inspections.

With the DPRK unable to provide adequate explanation of the discrepancies in its nuclear inventory or otherwise to offer reassurance to the international community about the peaceful nature of its nuclear program consistent with its NPT obligations, the Security Council passed a resolution (UNSCR 825 - passed 13-0-2) on 11 May calling on the DPRK to reverse its withdrawal decision and fulfil its safeguards obligations, and noting its intention to consider further action if necessary. 'Further action' was not defined in terms of any particular response, but carried with it the clear implication that the issue was considered a potential threat to international peace and security under the terms of Chapters VI and VII of the UN Charter. This added an effective threat of sanctions to previous political pressure. The DPRK eventually responded by announcing the suspension of its withdrawal on 11 June - the day before it was to have taken effect - in the context of a package of political 'principles' negotiated bilaterally with the United States.

Conclusions. Strengthened IAEA safeguards after the Gulf War and the provision of information by member states to the Agency enabled Agency inspectors to detect evidence of possibly undeclared nuclear activities in North Korea. The ability of the Agency to respond effectively was aided considerably by the widespread political support from members of the Board of Governors. This highlights the importance of the normative effect of multilateral arms control, disarmament and non-proliferation treaties, of stronger verification measures and of political support for verification action, including from the Security Council, in preventing weapons proliferation. This has been demonstrated by increased international support for multilateral non-proliferation regimes in general - and strengthened IAEA safeguards in particular - after UNSCOMS's revelations of Iraq's clandestine WMD activities.

This case demonstrates, too, that multilateral mechanisms often need to be used in tandem with bilateral or regional consultations in dealing with problems involving states' legitimate or perceived security concerns and military/strategic ambitions. In North Korea's case, bilateral dialogue with South Korea, China and the United States has been important in managing and exploring ways to resolve tensions and has also provided useful opportunities to underline the importance of treaty compliance.

This case also represents one in which the *threat* of punitive or enforcement action - rather than any actual enforcement action - has had an effect in encouraging reconsideration by a state of a course of action that was against that established by international norms, and in reinforcing the mandatory nature of international treaty obligations. It has had a secondary (but nonetheless important) deterrent effect also, in demonstrating that the international community was prepared - for the most part cooperatively - to take action in response to a violation of a treaty obligation which was seen to threaten, or potentially threaten, international peace and security. It is a case where the international community's response was in part preventive, in part enforcement.

8 Managing Potential Conflict in the South China Sea

IAN KEMISH

This study examines the preventive diplomacy role of the 'Managing Potential Conflict in the South China Sea' workshop series organised by the Research and Development Agency of the Indonesian Ministry of Foreign Affairs.

Nature of the problem

The situation in the South China Sea, while not currently one of open conflict, involves a range of disputes which pose a serious threat to the peace and security of the Southeast Asian region. Recent developments in regional military capabilities have contributed to international concern over the destabilising potential of localised armed conflicts in the South China Sea. All of the disputants but one maintain a military presence in the South China Sea, China and Vietnam fought a naval battle in the area in March 1988, and there have been other occasional exchanges of fire among troops stationed in the area. The South China Sea disputes involve the following issues.

Territorial claims. The competing maritime claims in the South China Sea have considerable symbolic significance to the various disputants, with internal political dynamics playing a major role in driving some of the claims.

Access to natural resources. The South China Sea has significant fisheries resources, and certain areas are thought to have considerable hydrocarbon (oil and gas) potential. Oil is of fundamental importance to the rapidly expanding economies of each of the claimant countries.

Control over important sea lines of communication (SLOCs). Major shipping lanes transit the South China Sea. Islands in the area could be used as bases for the surveillance and interdiction of aircraft, surface vessels and submarine traffic.

The disputes in the South China Sea may be divided into two groups, as follows:

- The multilateral dispute over the Spratly Islands, a group of over 100 islands, rocks, reefs and shoals spread over an area of 180,000 square kilometres in the South China Sea. China, Vietnam and Taiwan claim the entire archipelago, and Malaysia, the Philippines and Brunei claim significant parts.

- A number of trilateral disputes involving Vietnam, China and Taiwan: notably over the Paracel Islands, an archipelago covering an area of 46,000 square kilometres in the northern part of the South China Sea; and the Gulf of Tonkin, located between the northern coast of Vietnam and the Chinese island of Hainan. The competing claims of China and Taiwan should be seen in the context of the broader Chinese sovereignty dispute.

The 'South China Sea Initiative'

In January 1990 the Government of Indonesia, a littoral non-claimant, launched a preventive diplomacy initiative which, in the words of Indonesian Foreign Minister Ali Alatas, aims to 'accentuate the positives and eliminate the negatives to create a better climate' (in respect to the South China Sea). The central idea of this initiative for a series of 'unofficial' workshops was to shelve territorial claims for the time being, and to explore the prospects for cooperative activity in the South China Sea.

A gradual confidence-building process

The Indonesian organisers envisaged that the confidence-building process would address less controversial issues first, and then move on to tackle more difficult questions. This process has taken form in the following way.

The **first workshop** in Bali (January 1990), essentially an Association of Southeast Asian Nations 'preparatory meeting', simply discussed the likely scope of the process, and identified a number of possible areas for discussion, including resource management and joint development, shipping, navigation and communication, the environment, political and jurisdictional issues. Participants in the **second workshop** in Bandung (July 1991) expressed support for the principle of resolving disputes in the South China Sea through peaceful means, and cooperative work in those areas considered less likely to pose difficulties between the countries concerned (e.g., navigation, meteorology and marine scientific research). The **third workshop** in Yogyakarta (June/July 1992) made progress on the modalities for joint development, by recommending the establishment of two expert working groups to consider the scope for practical cooperation, one in the area of marine scientific research and the other in the field of 'resource assessment'.

The **Marine Scientific Research Working Group** held its first meeting in Manila in May 1993. This working group submitted three areas of cooperation for consideration by participants in the fourth workshop: database, information exchange and networking; sea level and tide monitoring; and biodiversity studies. The Marine Scientific Research Working Group will meet again in December 1993, probably in Singapore.

The **Resource Assessment/Development Working Group**, which met in Jakarta in July 1993, produced a statement enumerating a number of possible research activities in four resource fields: fisheries, non-hydrocarbon non-living resources, hydrocarbon resources, and non-mineral non-living resources.

The **fourth workshop** in Surabaya in September 1993 discussed and adopted the reports of these two technical working groups. It also agreed, in principle, to convene a working group on environmental issues to be hosted by China; and considered ways to increase safety of navigation in the South China Sea. A number of other ideas were raised, including the idea of a legal working group, an environmental working group and a navigation, shipping and communication working group. The idea of a South China Sea Secretariat to coordinate the activities of the various working groups was also raised.

Graduated participation

Another feature of the workshop series has been the carefully graduated approach adopted on the question of participation. This approach has ensured the participation of all the South China Sea claimants, at the same time retaining an important role for ASEAN in the workshops. The inaugural Bali workshop was attended by officials from each of the ASEAN states, including those with no claim to the area (Indonesia, Singapore and Thailand). Officials from China, Vietnam, Taiwan, and Laos accepted invitations to join these countries at the second and third workshops. The fourth workshop in Surabaya reached agreement that 'non-South China Sea states and other regional or global organisations would also be invited, as necessary, to be involved and to participate in the realisation of specific projects of cooperation' in the South China Sea.

A number of the claimants clearly have reservations about the involvement in the process of 'outsiders'. China has made it clear that it will only support multilateral discussions on the future of the Spratly Islands if these discussions are undertaken exclusively by the littoral states of the South China Sea. Other claimants have been reluctant to countenance 'external involvement' because of their concern to prevent extra-regional powers from using the South China Sea dispute as a pretext for greater involvement in regional affairs.

Although the workshop series has been characterised by both the organisers and participants as having 'unofficial standing', it has the advantage of being officially sanctioned and organised at government level. Academics, scientists and officials participate and while there is an understanding that officials are present in their private capacities, their attendance allows claimant states to remain informed on (if not necessarily influenced by) workshop deliberations. Governments are thus able to 'vicariously' participate in an informal exchange of ideas and information on policy issues, without being bound by the views expressed by their representatives or to workshop outcomes.

Formalisation?

In his opening speech to the fourth workshop in Surabaya, Foreign Minister Alatas stressed the desirability of formalising the workshop as an official inter-governmental forum, particularly following the 1992 Declaration on the South China Sea, where ASEAN governments had taken a collective stance on the resolution of possible conflict in the area (see further details below). Other participants (particularly China and Malaysia) have made it clear, however, that the workshops should not be permitted to evolve into anything resembling a multilateral negotiating forum.

Parallel official exchanges

The South China Sea was brought into the official regional agenda for the first time at the 1992 ASEAN Ministerial Meeting (AMM) in Manila, when ASEAN Foreign Ministers issued a Declaration on the South China Sea. The Declaration called for a resolution of sovereignty in the South China Sea through peaceful means, called on all parties to the dispute to exercise restraint and explore the possibility of cooperation without prejudicing the sovereignty and jurisdiction of claimants, and urged all protagonists to abide by the principles of the Treaty of Amity and Cooperation in Southeast Asia (the Bali Treaty). China and Taiwan are not signatories to the Bali Treaty. This was ASEAN's first post-Cold War attempt at applying preventive diplomacy to a security issue using existing regional mechanisms (the AMM) and instruments (the Bali Treaty).

Through the South China Sea Declaration ASEAN Governments announced their support for the main 'unofficial' conclusions of the second South China Sea workshop. The Declaration was successful in prompting non-ASEAN claimants to join with ASEAN in renouncing force as a mechanism for conflict resolution, and to subscribe to a code of conduct (along the lines of the Bali Treaty) governing action in the South China Sea. In this way they hoped to constrain future Chinese action, or at the least exert pressure on China through the existence of a diplomatic declaration subscribed to by other claimants and regional states. Vietnam welcomed the South China Sea Declaration, and China responded with a statement that it supported a peaceful settlement of territorial disputes through negotiations, and that it had always taken a positive attitude toward joint development in the area.

The Spratly Islands have also been the subject of official bilateral exchanges, notably the 1988-89 negotiations between Malaysia and the Philippines over their conflicting claims in the southern Spratlys and the 1992 agreement between Vietnam and Malaysia on joint exploration of a disputed area in the archipelago.

Outcomes

The South China Sea initiative is an ongoing process, but has so far been successful in: providing a forum for the definition and discussion of the issues involved; promoting general agreement, at least unofficially, that claimants should renounce the use of force and that dialogue should be used to resolve tensions and conflict; building confidence by securing agreement to examine joint cooperation (but with some important caveats, i.e., no diminution of sovereignty); and helping ensure that, by and large, this dispute does not prevent the development in the region of closer economic and political linkages.

Notwithstanding the increased dialogue flowing from the workshop series, claimant countries have continued to take unilateral action to strengthen their claims. In February 1992 China passed legislation stating the basis of its maritime jurisdictional claims and embodying in law its claim to the Spratly and Paracel islands; Malaysia announced in August 1991 that it planned to build an airstrip on Swallow Reef, and has more recently established tourist facilities in a disputed area; China concluded an oil exploration agreement with a United States company in May 1992 covering an area contested by Vietnam; and Vietnam, has recently signed an oil exploration agreement with another US company (in an area contested by China).

A role for the global community?

It has been suggested that there may be a role for the broader international community in advancing the process begun by the South China Sea seminars, by bringing the United Nations and/or international conventions into play. A proposal has been put forward that international law and law of the sea (including the 1982 Law of the Sea Convention) could be applied by the International Court of Justice or another international tribunal to help resolve the legal dispute over ownership of the islands, and to address the questions of maritime delimitation arising in the South China Sea.[1] It has also been suggested that there might be a role for the United Nations or another recognised international forum in sponsoring the negotiation of a treaty regime involving a consensus based and distributive resolution of the issues in the South China Sea.[2] Useful models would include the management regime established for the Antarctic, the Timor Gap Treaty and aspects of the Law of the Sea Convention (LOSC) which deal with the use and management of the high seas and the deep sea bed. One observer has proposed that the UN establish a 'Spratlys authority' to manage the resources of the Spratlys area,[3] and another has suggested that, at some stage in the future, there may even be scope for some form of maritime preventive deployment force.[4]

Previous responses to suggestions of external involvement indicate, however, that the claimants would be strongly opposed to the idea of any extra-regional authority assuming a direct role *vis-à-vis* the disputes in the South China Sea. The underlying concern that claimants might lose control of the decision making process reflects the deep-seated historical, economic and internal political processes which underlie their positions, and the strategic and symbolic value of the islands.

---

[1] B.A. Hamzah, *The Spratlies: What Can Be Done to Enhance Confidence* (Kuala Lumpur: Institute of Strategic and International Studies, 1990) pp.13-18.

[2] Mark Valencia, 'The South China Sea: Potential Conflict and Cooperation', East-West Center, Honolulu, June 1992. This unpublished paper is an updated integration of several media articles by the author, including 'Asia Can Settle the Spratly Dispute' *International Herald Tribune* (13 February 1992).

[3] Valencia, 'The South China Sea' p.4

[4] Michael C. Pugh, 'Maritime Peacekeeping: Scope for Deep Blue Berets?' *Working Paper* 119, (Canberra: Peace Research Centre, Australian National University, July 1992) pp.21-2.

Lessons to be learnt

The experience of the South China Sea workshops contains a number of lessons on the potential security role of regional arrangements as envisaged in the UN Charter, the UN Secretary General's *Agenda for Peace* report and the subsequent UNGA 47 resolution.

The workshops represent an innovative attempt by an impartial neighbouring state to institute an informal preventive diplomacy process: by redefining the task as a search for options which are of mutual interest to the parties, the process promotes problem solving and the beginning of cooperative dialogue. This kind of 'second track' diplomacy provides an excellent basis for later officials' talks. Such a process takes time, but both the process and substance of such workshops can systematically build momentum towards a peaceful resolution. Joint projects which come from working group proposals, if carried forward, will assist in the development of mutual goals and working relationships; this has been shown to be one of the best ways of reversing a competitive process.

The workshops provide a positive example of the kinds of thoughtfully designed regional initiatives which could be undertaken more frequently by regional, sub-regional or unilateral actors.

9 The Falklands: Failure of a Mission

HUGH WYNDHAM

The origin of the dispute

The Falkland Islands[1] may have been first seen by Amerigo Vespucci in 1501. They may also have been first seen by an unknown Spanish vessel in 1540, or by one of two English ships which were in the area about that time. However, the first definite sighting, including an accurate fixing of their position, was by a Dutch explorer, Sebald de Weert, in 1600.

The first settlement was established for France by Louis-Antoine de Bougainville in 1764. His action drew a protest from Spain, which believed the islands were too close to Spanish America for it to be acceptable for France to claim them. The French Government agreed to a transfer to Spain (for a consideration) in 1767.

At the same time, British interest in the islands awoke. Lord Egmont said in 1765 that the Falkland Islands were the key to the whole Pacific and dominated the ports of Chile, Peru, Panama and all the Spanish maritime territory. In January 1765, an English expedition, under Commodore John Byron, claimed the islands for Britain. A settlement was founded at Port Egmont in January 1766.

---

[1] The dispute which is the subject of this study includes a dispute over nomenclature. The English language name is used here for convenience. The French were the first to name the islands, as 'Les Malouines', after Malo, the home town of the man who named them. Argentina knows them by the Spanish version of that name, 'Las Malvinas', and the United Nations by the combination 'Falkland/Malvinas'.

In 1770, the Spanish Governor in Buenos Aires, Francisco de Paula Bucarelli, removed the English. Britain protested, threatening war, and Spain eventually agreed to disavow the action of Bucarelli and allow the English to reoccupy Port Egmont. The exchange of notes incorporating the agreement included a reaffirmation by Spain of its claim. The British reply was silent on the subject. Spanish sources refer to an oral assurance by Britain that it would abandon the settlement shortly after its re-establishment. The agreement was not well received in the House of Commons, because it did not, in the view of many members, adequately protect the British claim. As a result, the withdrawal was delayed. However, the English settlers eventually left the islands in 1774. Spain withdrew its settlement in 1811.

Following their independence, the United Provinces of the River Plate (now Argentina) raised their flag on the Falklands, in November 1820. In 1823, the Government named a military Governor for the islands. In 1829, a decree was issued asserting Argentine sovereignty and regulating fishing around the islands. The British and American consuls in Buenos Aires protested. The latter denied that any Spanish sovereignty existed over the Patagonian or Fuegian coasts to which the United Provinces could be heir. When the United Provinces attempted to implement the fishing regulations against United States vessels, a United States warship, the USS *Lexington*, destroyed military installations and other fixtures on the Falklands and arrested the majority of the settlers. Argentine protests were unavailing.

In September 1832, Buenos Aires appointed a new interim military and political commander and sent the ARA *Sarandi* to the islands to repair the damage and restore law and order. The settlers, however, rebelled after the departure of the warship and killed the governor. The *Sarandi* returned and tried to repress the uprising.

In December, two British frigates called at the old settlement of Port Egmont and then at Port Louis on 2 January 1833. The British Captain informed the Captain of the *Sarandi* that the British flag would replace the Argentine flag the following day. The latter objected, but could do nothing, faced with superior force. Two days later, the *Sarandi* left the islands, taking with it the Argentine soldiers, prisoners from the penal settlement of San Carlos and some of the Argentine settlers. The Argentine Government protested, without effect. The islands were formally declared a colony in 1840. In the ensuing years, opportunities were taken by both sides, especially the Argentine, to protect their legal position, but Argentina's relative weakness and the importance for its development of British trade and investment made more effective action impossible.

In 1960, the United Nations General Assembly adopted Resolution 1514(XV), which called for decolonisation and the self-determination of peoples. Britain had long ago included the Falkland Islands in its list of non self-governing territories. Information on the islands was reported to the committee established pursuant to Resolution 1514, (the 'Committee of 24'), without stimulating any comment, until, in 1965, Uruguay proposed that the British report be put on the agenda. This action coincided with a revival of interest in Argentina. Resolution 2065 (XX) of 16 December 1965 invited Britain and Argentina to proceed with negotiations with a view to finding a peaceful solution to the problem, taking into account the interests of the inhabitants of the islands.

Negotiations began in London in July 1966.[2] In March 1967 Britain stated for the first time that it was willing to cede sovereignty under certain conditions, provided the wishes of the islanders were respected. Negotiations were directed to agreeing a Memorandum of Understanding. Agreement was reached at official level in August 1968. However, it received a critical reception in the British Parliament. Nor was the Argentine Government prepared to agree that transfer of sovereignty would be subject to the wishes of the islanders or to a unilateral British statement to that effect, linked to the Memorandum. Accordingly, the British Government decided not to proceed on the basis of the Memorandum, but to continue negotiations under a 'sovereignty umbrella', that is, without prejudice to either side's position on sovereignty. They were concluded in 1971 and produced some practical results, facilitating travel and communications between the islands and the mainland.

Argentine and United Nations pressure to put the sovereignty question on the agenda led to consideration by the British Government in 1974, eventually with the knowledge of the Argentine Government, of the idea of a condominium. Islander opposition, however, led to this idea also being abandoned.

In 1975, the British Government sent a mission under Lord Shackleton to report on possible economic development. This led to a hostile Argentine reaction, aggravated by the fact that Lord Shackleton arrived on the anniversary of the British occupation of the islands in 1833, timing which the Argentine Foreign Minister described as 'unfriendly and unthoughtful'. In February 1976, an Argentine destroyer fired shots at the RRS *Shackleton*, which was assisting the Shackleton mission, and attempted to board it, after Argentina had warned Britain that the ship would be arrested if it entered Argentine waters.

Following a major review of British policy in March 1976, negotiations resumed in July and August. In December, Argentina surreptitiously established a military/scientific base on South Thule in the South Sandwich Islands. The British Government protested, but took no further action. (The base remained until the 1982 war.) Negotiations

---

[2] The following account of the negotiations is drawn largely from *Falkland Islands Review*, Report of a Committee of Privy Counsellors, (the 'Franks Review') (London: HMSO, 1983). The only excuse for basing the account on it is that it is also heavily quoted in Argentine Foreign Minister Costa Mendez's memoirs (see reference below).

resumed in July 1977. An agreement on scientific cooperation was negotiated in December 1978, but was rejected by the islanders.

The election of the Thatcher Government in May 1979 led to a year's delay in the negotiations, while a policy was developed. Talks resumed in April 1980, with the British Government floating the idea of a transfer of sovereignty and lease back. However, a visit to the islands by Foreign Office Minister Nicholas Ridley in December 1980 revealed such opposition to the idea that it was dropped.

Negotiations continued but Britain now had little to offer of interest to Argentina and Argentine patience wore thin. This was known and a matter of concern to the Foreign Office. However, no decisions were taken to forestall military action by Argentina. On the contrary, plans were made to abandon the British Antarctic Survey base on South Georgia and withdraw the Navy's Antarctic support ship, HMS *Endurance*. The overall impression created on the Argentines was of diminishing British interest.

The Argentine military government decided in January 1982 to initiate a study of a military option, to be used if the negotiations failed. At the same time, it decided to redouble diplomatic efforts to oblige Britain to negotiate the question of sovereignty. Negotiations in New York at the end of February 1982 went better than the Argentine delegation expected and an optimistic communiqué was issued at the end of the talks. However, the Argentine delegation had misunderstood the military Junta's mood. In particular, it required agreement from Britain to a timetable for negotiations leading to recognition of Argentine sovereignty. Foreign Minister Nicanor Costa Méndez issued a declaration reiterating the totality of the Argentine position. This was accompanied in the Buenos Aires press by a number of commentaries, including, not for the first time that year, one by a well informed journalist speculating about the likelihood of a resolution of the problem by force.

Davidoff

Constantino Davidoff was an Argentine businessman who won a contract from a Scottish firm to remove scrap metal left over from whaling days at Leith, Stromness and Husvik in South Georgia. Having failed to gain British agreement to use the *Endurance* to take his party of workmen to the site, he turned to the Argentine Ministry of Foreign Relations and the Argentine Navy. The Navy conceived of the idea of doing the same thing on South Georgia as it had years before on South Thule. Project Alpha was developed. Davidoff made an inspection of the site in late December 1981, assisted by the Argentine Navy icebreaker, the *Almirante Irízar*. The British Foreign Office decided not to react too fiercely, lest an overreaction provoke a more serious incident leading to unforeseeable consequences. A protest note was sent and duly rejected. Meanwhile, a new Junta had taken over in Buenos Aires, which decided to postpone execution of Project Alpha until after the next round of negotiations with Britain. Foreign Minister Costa Méndez was to be consulted before any action was taken.

When, in March, Davidoff again asked for Navy assistance, Admiral Otero, responsible for transport and logistics, and a supporter of Alpha, gave his approval without informing or consulting higher or other authority. Davidoff informed the British Embassy in late February that he was going to Leith. The Embassy informed London and Port Stanley and received no objections. Davidoff's lawyer confirmed on 9 March that 41 men would leave for Leith on an Argentine naval vessel and would be there about four months. He was reminded of the need to go first to Grytviken to obtain authorisation. Having maintained radio silence *en route*, the *Bahia Buen Suceso* arrived at Leith (without going first to Grytviken) on 18 March. There followed a series of events leading by a process of rapid escalation to the occupation of the Falkland Islands by Argentina on 2 April 1982, only two weeks later.

The Haig mediation

In the days before the Argentine occupation of the Falkland Islands, plans had been developed in London for their recapture. Thus, even before the fall of Port Stanley, ships of what became known as the Task Force were heading south. The build-up was to take some weeks. The United Kingdom appealed to the United Nations Security Council, which, on 3 July, adopted a British draft as Resolution 502. It called for a cessation of hostilities and the immediate withdrawal of the Argentine armed forces from the Falkland Islands and on the two parties to find a diplomatic solution which fully respected the purposes and principles of the United Nations. The resolution was carried 10-1(Panama)-4(China, Soviet Union, Poland, Spain). It was a great disappointment to Argentina not to have been able to secure either a Soviet or a Chinese veto.

It was imperative for the United States to avoid, if possible, an armed confrontation between two friendly countries. Britain was a NATO ally and, of all the European countries, had the closest relationship with the United States. Argentina's military government was assisting the United States in its campaign against left-wing subversion in Central America, an important priority for the Reagan administration. Wrote Secretary of State Alexander Haig in his memoirs, 'While my sympathy was with the British, I believed that the most practical expression of that sympathy would be impartial United States mediation in the dispute'.[3] Haig proposed to President Ronald Reagan, who agreed, that he make an attempt to broker a negotiated settlement of the dispute, before the British Task Force reached the Southern Atlantic.

---

[3] Haig, Alexander, *Caveat* (New York: Macmillan, 1984) p.266.

Both sides agreed. Haig had meetings in Washington with the British Ambassador and the Argentine Foreign Minister on 6 April. He put to each the initial ideas generated by the State Department, which involved diverting the British Task Force, withdrawal of Argentine forces, the interposition of a force from Canada, the United States and two Latin American countries. Then, negotiations would begin.[4]

The British Ambassador laid much emphasis on Argentine withdrawal, without which, he said Mrs Margaret Thatcher would fall. He also said that he would prefer to see the United States acting alone as guarantor of the peace. Costa Méndez used the opportunity to go through with Haig the full history of the dispute and the last sixteen years' frustrating negotiations. Haig's approach left him optimistic, the more so as he had dined with the United States Ambassador to the United Nations, Jeane Kirkpatrick, on 2 and again on 4 April and had found her firm on the necessity for a peaceful solution to the dispute. Haig did not condemn the Argentine action, but, according to Costa Méndez, spoke of saving Mrs Thatcher's face and allowing time for a transfer of sovereignty.[5]

On 8 April, Haig arrived in London. After he had explained the American ideas to Mrs Thatcher, she firmly reminded him of the consequences of rewarding German aggression against Czechoslovakia in 1938 and asked the United States not to urge Britain to reward aggression now, which, she said, would send a signal around the world with devastating consequences.[6] More specifically, she said that she was committed to the House of Commons to restore the British administration and that the idea of an interim administration and some arrangement for self-determination was too woolly.[7] Haig's conclusion from his visit to London was that Mrs Thatcher did not have universal support for her hard line.[8] If giving Argentina something meant the fall of Mrs Thatcher, then, equally, giving it nothing meant the fall of the Junta and that was not a basis for a negotiation.

Haig arrived in Buenos Aires on 9 April and had a day of meetings with the Argentine Foreign Minister and the Junta. According to Costa Méndez, the Argentine objective was to obtain a serious and accelerated development of the process for the transfer of sovereignty.[9] To this end, Argentina looked for a solution through one of two routes. It would accept retaining the administration of the islands or jointly administering them with Britain or turning them over to third countries, while negotiations proceeded. Alternatively, it would agree to the return of the

---

4   Ibid. p.271.
5   Freedman and Gamba-Stonehouse, *Senales de Guerra* (Buenos Aires: Vergara, 1992) p.192.
6   Haig, *Caveat* p.272.
7   Ibid. p.273.
8   Ibid. p. 298.
9   Costa Méndez, Nicanor, *Malvinas* (Buenos Aires: Editorial Sudamericana, 1993) p.220.

British administration, while modalities for a transition were discussed, if Britain were to recognise Argentine sovereignty.[10]

Clearly, neither of these propositions was likely to appeal to the British government. Haig tried to impress on the Argentines his judgement that the British were the superior force, that they would fight if there were no prior agreement and that they would win.[11] (This was, in particular, a response to General Leopoldo Galtieri's insistence that the government of the islands must be Argentine.) Galtieri's only accepted too late that the British would fight and that the Americans would not stop them. His response on the first point was that 'That woman would not dare'.[12]

The two sides agreed to try to produce a draft modifying the American proposals. The United States draft called for withdrawal of all forces, a four-power observation team to monitor compliance, maintenance of communications and movement between the islands and the mainland and an undertaking by Argentina and the United Kingdom to conclude negotiations, taking into account the rights and interests of the inhabitants of the islands, no later than 31 December 1982. The traditional local administration would continue, with Argentina naming a senior official as its coordinator on the islands to act as liaison with and to assist the four powers.[13]

The draft did not meet Argentina's requirements. Hours of arduous discussion followed, until Haig had a private discussion with Galtieri, in which he believed he saw a concession. A new version of the American ideas was quickly produced, involving rapid removal of economic and financial sanctions against Argentina, the flags of all six nations would be flown on the islands and national flags could be flown on the residences and official automobiles of the countries represented.[14] However, this document was not discussed before Haig's departure.

Meanwhile, unknown to Haig, the Junta had decided it could not accept the American ideas and decided to put on paper its own, modified in the light of the discussion. These were:

- immediate and simultaneous implementation of Resolution 502;

- adoption of an Argentine administration or a promise that sovereignty would be handed over by 31 December 1982 (i.e., the original two alternatives);

---

[10] Ibid. p. 221
[11] Haig, *Caveat* p.279.
[12] Quoted in Freedman and Gamba-Fieldhouse, *Senales de Guerra* p.199.
[13] Haig, *Caveat* p.281.
[14] Ibid. p.282.

- the participation of the islanders' committees in the administration could be acceptable, as well as the presence of an international organisation to guarantee the new arrangements.[15]

What made Haig think that there had been a break through remains a mystery. Certainly, no Argentine participant saw the night's discussions that way. When, as he boarded the plane the next day to return to London, Foreign Minister Costa Méndez gave him a piece of paper containing 'some personal thoughts of his own', Haig considered it a retreat from everything accomplished the previous night.

When the 'personal thoughts' appeared in the *New York Times* the following day, Haig, by then in London, called Costa Méndez to ask for an explanation. Costa Méndez reiterated the two basic points - Argentine administration and an Argentine flag. Haig refers to this in his memoirs as a blatant double cross.[16] He did not say so to Costa Méndez, however.

In further telephone discussion between them, Costa Méndez indicated that Argentina would not insist on an Argentine Governor, if the agreement contained an undertaking by Britain to decolonise the islands in accordance with General Assembly Resolution 1514. Discussions with Mrs Thatcher and Foreign Secretary Francis Pym indicated that the British were cautious but not negative and thought it was worth pursuing the negotiations. This convinced Haig that it would be worth while to return to Buenos Aires. He arrived on April 15.

He carried with him a proposal, approved by Mrs Thatcher, which called for:

- Argentine withdrawal from the islands;

- a halt of the task force at 1,000 miles from the islands;

- interim administration by Britain and Argentina, with an American presence on the islands;

- an immediate end to sanctions;

- completion of negotiations on sovereignty by the end of 1982. [17]

It did not seem to Haig that a rational government would reject these terms. He presented them to the Argentine Government at a meeting with General Galtieri on the morning of 16 April. They were discussed all day. The Argentines had a number of relatively minor problems, but some fundamental objections as well. In the former category, they wanted to know whether withdrawal of forces included the submarines. In the

---

[15] Freedman and Gamba-Stonehouse, *Senales de Guerra* p.205; Haig, *Caveat* p.282-3.
[16] Haig *Caveat* p.283.
[17] Ibid. p.286; Freedman and Gamba-Stonehouse, *Senales de Guerra* p.217.

latter, the Argentine authorities did not believe that a tripartite administration, with the United States as guarantor, was in their interests. Nor did they feel secure as regards sovereignty. The more they looked at them, the more the American proposals looked like a trap.[18]

Costa Méndez came to Haig at his hotel after discussing the proposals with the Junta and said that they had not accepted them, and presented new terms. They were complex, but contained elements that Haig knew he could not sell in London. They called for shared administrative control and equal rights for Falkland Islanders and other Argentines - opening the possibility of changing the demography of the islands. They also contained conditions on the final settlement which, without saying so in terms, guaranteed that their result would be Argentine sovereignty. 'I am sure that the British will shoot when they receive this message' was Haig's reaction, to which he reports Costa Méndez saying that he was surprised that the British would go to war for such a small problem as these few rocky islands.[19]

Haig had an inconclusive meeting with General Galtieri and it was agreed that he should meet the Junta the next morning. They, in the meantime, had been informed by Costa Méndez of Haig's reaction and had begun to think about how to handle a breakdown of Haig's mission.

The meeting was tense. The Navy member of the Junta and known hardliner, Admiral Jorge Anaya, responded to Haig's warnings about the bloody consequences of failing to be more flexible by referring to the fact that his son was on the Falklands and his family would be honoured if his blood were mingled with the soil of the Falklands. Haig told him 'You do not know the meaning of war until you see the corpses of young men being put into body bags.'[20] The Air Force member, Lt General Lami Dozo was clearly the dove in the Junta, but was also the third in influence. Discussions adjourned to working levels and continued throughout the day and well into the night. By 2.40 a.m., on 19 April, a draft was prepared which Haig, in his memoirs, records as having been acceptable to the Argentines.[21]

However, it was not to be. The Junta insisted on adding additional guarantees for the eventual recognition of Argentine sovereignty. Once again, Costa Méndez gave the bad news to Haig in an envelope as he was boarding his plane. It was, according to Haig, 'an exercise of bad faith that is unique in my experience as a negotiator'.[22] Haig passed the results of the work in Buenos Aires to Britain minus the last minute addition and returned to Washington to see if anything could be salvaged.

---

[18] Freedman and Gamba-Stonehouse, *Senales de Guerra* p.219.
[19] Haig , *Caveat*   p.286.
[20] Ibid. p.288.
[21] Ibid. p.289.
[22] Ibid. p.290

The British reaction was that the document was not balanced. The question of sovereignty was too clearly treated, while the wishes of the islanders had not been taken sufficiently into account.

Absent a miracle, Haig's mission was near its end. Following discussions in Washington with British Foreign Secretary Pym, Haig, on 27 April, sent to Britain and Argentina a new proposal based on the earlier drafts, but more elaborate. It consisted of a Memorandum of Understanding, a protocol and a letter of acceptance. It did not include a time limit for the negotiations or an Argentine role in the island legislative bodies. It included a phrase referring to the will and the desires of the islanders and made no reference to territorial integrity, a critical point for Argentina. Britain would remain in charge for an unlimited time and the sense of the document favoured the self-determination of the islanders, an impossible point for Argentina.

The Argentine Government did not reject the proposal, but the message it sent to Haig on 28 April following his discussions with Costa Méndez in Washington made it clear that the proposal had no future. It referred to recognition of Argentine sovereignty over the Falkland Islands as an 'unrenouncable goal'. The document did not satisfy Argentina's minimum aspirations. Haig informed the press on 30 April that his mission had come to an end and that Argentina was responsible. The United States announced sanctions against Argentina and support for Britain. Costa Méndez for his part, notes in his memoirs that, 'in a month of negotiations, we had not advanced a centimetre.'[23]

An initiative taken on 2 May by Peruvian President Belaunde, briefly awoke hope of a negotiated solution. His text was based on a very simplified version of the last Haig proposal. Argentina did not react to it and Haig's way of passing it to British foreign Secretary Pym meant that London did not know about it until it was already a dead letter.

The lessons

In any negotiation, there are many elements, a number of them critical. The following are the main elements which determined the outcome of the Haig mission.

The parties to the dispute

United Kingdom. Anyone who heard the debate in the House of Commons on Saturday afternoon 3 April would understand the limitations on the freedom of action of the British Government. It was 1939-1940 all over again, with Mrs Thatcher in the role of the warrior queen. The noisy, nationalistic scene left Mrs Thatcher no choice, even if she had wanted it, but to make a serious effort to recover the Falklands. It was not just that

---

[23] Costa Méndez, *Malvinas* p.267.

the Parliamentary mood was bellicose. There were repeated echoes of the history of the 1930s. The human rights record of the Galtieri regime made the image of a latter-day Hitler easy to promote. Appeasement was, therefore, out of the question. Moreover, at a time when the Anglo-United States hard line against the 'evil Empire' (as President Reagan once called the Soviet Union) was at its height, Mrs Thatcher was not about to show any sign of Western weakness. The British objectives were stated in relation to the details of the Falkland Islands dispute, but there was always another, higher objective - to defend the principle that the illegal use of force could not be rewarded. As Haig's objective was to give Argentina enough to secure its agreement to withdraw, without doing violence to any overarching principle, the two objectives were never going to be easily achieved together.

Argentina. The situation in Argentina was in some ways similar and in some ways different. Haig found it frustrating to be negotiating often with people who did not have the final say as to whether a particular point was acceptable or not. The Argentine Foreign Ministry was held in as low regard by the military as the British Foreign Office was by Mrs Thatcher. The difference was that Haig could talk to Mrs Thatcher and what she said went. The Junta itself had to consult within the three services and General Galtieri was not even master of army opinion. Another problem for the Junta was that the public supported the Junta's action in occupying the Falklands, but that it was otherwise very unpopular. Civilian politicians consulted by the Junta from time to time took as hard a line as the military.[24]

The mediator

There have been many comments on Haig's suitability as a mediator. On the one hand, he could talk to the Argentine Junta as one military man to another. He was a tireless worker and determined to leave no possibility unexplored to find a solution. On the other hand, he lacked subtlety and did not readily understand the subtlety of others. Yet his team included people about whom that could not be said (General Vernon Walters and Thomas Enders, in particular). One of his problems was in communication. At times, his English style was difficult enough for the British to follow. He spoke little Spanish and Galtieri little English. General Walters was used as interpreter. He did not give himself or the Junta time to digest or react to new ideas as they came out. His tactic of threatening United States support for Britain and defeat for Argentina, in

---

[24] For example, Costa Mendez's predecessor as Foreign Minister and present Defence Minister, Dr Oscar Camilion, told the weekly news magazine, *Somos*, during Haig's second visit that an Argentine withdrawal as a result of the negotiations could be excluded. 'As a rational attitude, it would be a catastrophe', he said.

the event of an armed conflict, did not convince the Junta and caused irritation.

Haig was also bedevilled by comments made openly or leaked by some of his senior colleagues in Washington. On the one hand, Defense Secretary Caspar Weinberger was an unashamed Anglophile and wanted to support Britain from the outset. On the other, the Ambassador to the United Nations, Jeane Kirkpatrick, was the architect of the Reagan development of relations with Latin America on the basis of an abandonment of the strong Carter human rights policy. The Argentines drew periodical comfort from her public and private statements.

Trust

For a negotiation to succeed, there must be someone in whom each party trusts. If it is not the other side, then it must be a third party. The British did not trust the Argentines. The Davidoff mission to South Georgia had been interpreted as a calculated challenge to British sovereignty and the Argentine Government's denials were disbelieved.[25] In the negotiations, there could be no room for ambiguity.

The Argentines did not trust the British, either. In particular, after sixteen years of frustrating negotiations, during which three chances of success had been torpedoed by the Falkland Islands lobby in the House of Commons, they also could not agree to any ambiguity in a negotiated document. It needed to be clear what the end result would be. Nor could they agree to the islanders being given the last word. It was precisely on these two points, however, that Britain could not satisfy Argentina.

Finally, neither side fully trusted Haig. The British were irritated that the United States should adopt an initial position of neutrality. No assurance by Haig that, in the end, Britain would have United States support removed the necessity to have the British position fully protected in any document. The Argentines, for their part, came to see Haig as a spokesman for, if not the agent of, Mrs Thatcher. They assessed his negotiating efforts as intended to give her time to get the Task Force into position. It is ironical that the British had exactly the opposite concern - that his efforts would impede the operations of the Task Force when it was ready and, towards the end, they accordingly pressed Haig for a speedy resolution of his mediation one way or another.

Timing

Any negotiation requires a cost-benefit analysis by the parties. In a situation such as the one we are considering, it also requires an assessment of one's prospects in the possible armed confrontation. At the time of Haig's mission, neither side had realised how difficult the task was going to be. Although Mrs Thatcher would not hear of the possibility of defeat,

---

[25] See *Falkland Islands Review*, pp.48ff.

military experts in Britain, the United States and among Britain's European allies were not all as confident. Indeed, had the Argentine armed forces used their power better and had a higher proportion of their weapons worked properly, British losses would have been substantially higher. Whether that would have affected the outcome, we will never know, but it certainly would have affected the political climate in Britain, which, in any case, sobered up considerably once the scale of the loss of life became known.

As for Argentina, it, too, started from an exaggerated idea of its capacities and a lack of consciousness of the terrible effect of modern weapons. It was only after the sinking of the Argentine cruiser, *General Belgrano*, on 4 May and of the British destroyer, *Sheffield*, three days later that a new attempt at negotiating a solution, this time by United Nations Secretary General, Perez de Cuellar, came closest to success. There was then more soberness than bravado. Even during Perez de Cuellar's attempts to find a negotiated solution, however, the Argentines tended to exaggerate British losses and thought they were doing better than they were.

Judgement

In any negotiation, both sides need to recognise a good deal when they see one. The atmosphere in Buenos Aires and London during Haig's mission was not conducive to the necessary clear sightedness. There were several occasions, moreover, when the negotiators or expert advisers were overruled by their political masters.

There was also an unfortunate interaction between the negotiations and the preparations for war, which were frequently misread in Buenos Aires. The Junta's decision that the Haig mission had effectively come to an end was premature, but it led the Junta to present to Haig, instead of a serious attempt at a balanced proposal, a document protecting the future Argentine negotiating position.

Having written off the mission, the Junta also declined an offer of a further visit to Buenos Aires. Haig believed that the British would not attack if he were in Buenos Aires and the Junta might have been wise to have realised that, also.

Comments on British judgement properly go more to their policy over the years than to details of their conduct of the negotiations. These are exhaustively set out in the Franks Review. It cannot be said that British strategy during the conflict failed, because they recovered the Falklands and illegal use of armed force went unrewarded - but at a terrible price.

Technique

There are many ways of trying to broker a compromise. One can act essentially as a go-between or one can take a more active role. Haig was an activist. He did not seek to pass on to the Argentines the British position, but, rather, to negotiate with them, indicating where he thought particular Argentine requirements could not be met. He never varied from the basic approach he outlined to the two sides when he first spoke to them in Washington. The problem with that was that the Argentines came to see him, wrongly, as a spokesman for Mrs Thatcher. Perez de Cuellar, later, remained in New York, holding several meetings a day with the British and Argentine Ambassadors, working his way slowly forwards, always passing to each side what he received from the other. Haig's mission was accompanied by extensive press coverage, not always accurate, which added to the political pressures on the negotiators of both sides.

10 Mediation - The United Nations Role in Indonesia, 1947-1950

TOM CRITCHLEY

Like many other parts of Asia, the Netherlands East Indies was transformed by World War II. On 17 August 1945 Soekarno and Hatta proclaimed the independence of the Republic of Indonesia. Refusal by the Netherlands to accept this declaration led to months of negotiations, culminating on 25 March 1947 in the signing by the Netherlands and the Republic of the Linggadjati Agreement as the basis for the formation of a United States of Indonesia (USI). But disagreement between the parties on the interpretation of the Agreement resulted in the Netherlands launching, on 20 July 1947, a military assault on Java and Sumatra which it described as a police action' of a 'strictly limited character'.

When other means to end the fighting proved fruitless, Australia referred the conflict to the Security Council as a breach of the peace under Chapter VII, Article 39 of the UN Charter - the first time this chapter had been invoked. Quickly responding, the Security Council on 1 August called on the parties to 'cease hostilities forthwith' and 'to settle their dispute by arbitration or other peaceful means'. This ceasefire resolution, the first ever adopted by the United Nations, was accepted by the Netherlands and the Republic on 4 August and took effect at midnight.

Requests for arbitration by the Republic were backed by Australia and a number of other Council members, but the United States showed a strong preference for limiting United Nations involvement. Consequently, on 25 August the Council established a three-member Committee of Good Offices on the Indonesian Question with Belgium chosen by the Netherlands, Australia by Indonesia and the third member, the United States, chosen jointly by Australia and Belgium.

Whereas the Good Offices Committee (GOC) sought to assume a role of conciliation and mediation, the Dutch insisted with some success on a much more limited legal interpretation of good offices that excluded authority to arbitrate, mediate or even make public its suggestions to the parties. For the GOC's suggestions to have authority, they had to be unanimous and then either the Netherlands or the Republic could still veto them.

Notwithstanding the Security Council resolution of 1 August, the failure of the Security Council to issue a stand fast order or call for a withdrawal of forces enabled the Netherlands to continue to advance and claim responsibility for areas far beyond what they had controlled when the ceasefire order came into effect.

By December 1947, the military talks had broken down and there was an impasse in the negotiations. Faced with a crisis, the GOC appealed to the two parties in a Christmas Message with suggestions that included nine proposals for a truce based temporarily on the advanced position claimed by the Netherlands and with eight proposals for a political settlement. The Dutch accepted the truce but without provision for the eventual withdrawal of their troops and they rejected the GOC's right to make political suggestions. Instead, they submitted their own twelve principles for a settlement which although based to some extent on the GOC's proposals, seriously disadvantaged the Republic. Netherlands obligations had been completely rewritten. In particular, all reference to the Republic was deleted. Nor was there any guarantee of international observation during the transitional period leading to the transfer of sovereignty. The Dutch insisted that their political principles were final and not open to further discussion. The total package was submitted with the ultimatum that, if it was not accepted within 48 hours of the time the Republicans conferred with the GOC, the Netherlands was likely to resume 'freedom of action'.

Nonetheless, six additional principles introduced by the United States representative on the GOC were accepted by the Netherlands within twenty-four hours. This was a remarkable Dutch reversal only explicable by assuming high level United States pressure as was subsequently confirmed. While the additional principles were not entirely to the liking of the Republic, they strengthened its position by clearly designating it as one of the states in the future USI and assuring continued United Nations involvement during the transition period.

Known as the Renville Agreement, the package was signed on 17-19 January 1948. Although to the disadvantage of the Republic, the Agreement at least ensured that the Republic was a party principle to the dispute and recognised as such by the United Nations. Moreover, the Republican leaders realised the importance of having the United States take a more direct and obvious responsibility for a political settlement.

Nevertheless, the concessions made by the Republic at the time of the Renville Agreement, when its military elements wanted to continue the armed struggle, could only be fully justified if there was early progress towards a political settlement. In the months that followed, such progress was entirely absent. The Dutch continued to stall negotiations and to set up states under their own direction in an attempt to implement their concept of a United States of Indonesia. Furthermore, contrary to the Agreement, the economic blockade of the Republic was maintained.

Faced with a fast deteriorating situation, the Australian representative, seeking to break the deadlock and to give the Republic much needed encouragement, presented a working paper to the GOC. In its final version the plan was known by the names of the Australian and American representatives on the GOC as the Critchley-duBois Plan. Although not accepted by the Belgian representative, it was submitted informally to the parties on 10 June 1948. Not unexpectedly, the Netherlands refused to consider it and insisted that it could not form the basis of a report to the Security Council.

The Australian and United States representatives on the GOC hoped that the Security Council could call for the plan. But when a resolution to this effect failed because of a United States abstention, it appeared that the initiative was lost. However, shortly afterwards when the new United States representative on the GOC, Merle Cochran, came to Indonesia with new proposals (the Cochran Plan), they were based essentially on the Critchley-duBois Plan but with significant new concessions to the Dutch. These, along with further concessions by the Republic, failed to satisfy the Dutch who, having issued what could only be regarded as another ultimatum to the Republic, launched early on the morning of 19 December 1948 their second 'police action'. Yogyakarta, the Republic's capital, was occupied and its main leaders interned. But it quickly became apparent that this most ill advised attack marked, as far as the United Nations was concerned, a major turning point in the dispute.

In a series of strong reports to the Security Council the GOC pointed out that the Dutch military action violated the Security Council's ceasefire resolution of 1 August 1947 and the Renville Truce Agreement. It also stressed that its good offices had 'not been exhausted, much less effectively utilised' and that there was 'no legitimate basis on which a party could forsake the forum of negotiations for that of armed force'.

Moreover, influenced by the Republic's successful suppression of the communist revolt at Madiun some months earlier and by the unprovoked actions of the Netherlands, the United States was no longer inclined to limit United Nations involvement. Instead it was now ready to exert considerable financial pressures on the Dutch. Its Economic Cooperation Administration cut off aid to the Netherlands East Indies on 22 December 1948 and there were threats that Marshal Plan aid to the Netherlands could also be suspended.

In a new atmosphere the Security Council called for a cessation of hostilities on 24 December. Gone was the former sympathy for Netherlands insistence that the dispute was a domestic matter and that the role of the United Nations should be limited to one of good offices. Bolstered by the resolutions adopted at a conference on the Indonesian

Question convened by Prime Minister Jawaharlal Nehru in New Delhi from 22 to 23 January 1949, the Council in its resolution of 28 January at last took firm decisions to settle the dispute. Among other things, it ordered the unconditional release of prisoners, the restoration of the Republican Government at Yogyakarta and outlined the basis for a political settlement that would provide for the transfer of sovereignty to Indonesia no later than July 1950.

Perhaps most significantly, the resolution changed the GOC into the United Nations Commission for Indonesia (UNCI) with the same membership but with specific authority to make proposals and recommendations and take decisions by majority vote to achieve a settlement. In the event, UNCI's formidable powers as the agent of the Security Council never had to be used. But the awareness that they existed helped to ensure cooperation and contributed to the resolution of intransigent problems.

In accordance with the Security Council's resolution, UNCI was able after protracted negotiations to promote the triumphant return of the Republican leader to Yogyakarta. It was the first time that the Dutch had been required to give up the territory they had captured and an overt recognition of the failure of their military action. But, as UNCI noted, it was also 'an important precedent' in that for the first time a Government had been 'restored and returned to its constitutional position and to its capital through the assistance of an international organisation which ... made use not of armed force but of its offices'.

In August 1949, on the basis of a Dutch initiative and negotiations facilitated by UNCI, a Round Table Conference (RTC) was organised to accelerate the transfer of sovereignty to an Indonesian Government for the whole of Indonesia.

As a participant in the Round Table Conference, UNCI was the first United Nations conciliatory body to take part in an international conference called by a member state. In doing so, UNCI was careful to retain its powers, including the right to initiate reports, but left it to the parties to reach their own solutions wherever possible. This was all the more appropriate as there was now a balance of power between the Indonesians and the Dutch. Neither could afford to have the conference fail and both were anxious to achieve an early agreement. In these circumstances, the parties showed no reluctance in seeking advice and help from UNCI when difficulties arose. With that help the RTC came to a successful conclusion on 2 November 1949.

Composition of the GOC

Appointment of a three power Good Offices Committee had advantages over a single conciliatory in giving an assurance of continuity. Since it met the wishes of both parties to be represented, it was also a safeguard against charges of partisanship. The viewpoint of both parties could thus be expressed, while there was a balance through the third and consequently more decisive member.

Australia had suggested that the third member might be appointed by the Council but there was good sense in ensuring that the third decisive member was acceptable to the other two members, Australia and Belgium. It was understandable that they should choose the United States which, as the neutral member, had the power and prestige to make the GOC's work effective.

From the outset the Australian representatives appreciated the importance of gaining the support of the United States representatives and of establishing with them a common understanding of the need to come to terms with the new, powerful force of Asian nationalism and that this was represented in Indonesia by the Republic. Australia achieved some success in this. Certainly the policies and attitudes of the United States members of the GOC, helped no doubt by first hand knowledge of the situation, appeared much more favourable to Indonesia than those of the State Department where European interests tended to predominate. In particular, the six additional principles advanced by the United States at Renville and the support given Australian proposals in the Critchley-duBois Plan were important in sustaining the Republic at critical stages of the dispute. But the decisive action which Australia had sought from the beginning was slow in coming. It came only after the second 'police action'.

Participation of members

Members of the GOC participated in three capacities - firstly as individuals, secondly as representatives of governments and thirdly as agents of the Security Council. It would appear, however, that they were seldom aware of any contradictions in this. The Australian representatives on the GOC kept Canberra informed but received very few instructions and were left with what today would be exceptional discretion. Had their actions not reflected the policy of the Australian Government, they would presumably have been quickly told.

Military observers

The number of military observers made available to the GOC and UNCI from the Consular Commission varied in strength according to the needs at the time. They provided a series of functions, such as helping to keep the Security Council through its agency in Indonesia, the GOC (later UNCI) informed of developments in the field, liaising between the military forces of the two parties, providing the teams to guard the demilitarised zones and maintain the Renville truce, preparing the plans for and helping in the restoration of the Republican Government in Yogyakarta in 1949 and providing teams to facilitate the cease hostilities agreement of 1949. In short, the usefulness of the military elements was an early demonstration of the importance of having international military personnel attached to conciliatory bodies that have been given the task of bringing about an end to hostilities and helping to find a political solution.

Great power conflict

At a time when the Cold War was at its most intense, great power rivalry was always in the background. It was most noticeable when United States and USSR abstentions played a part in the Security Council's failure to adopt resolutions calling for troop withdrawals after the second 'police action'. But, despite differences on how it should be achieved, both the Soviet Union and the United States favoured an independent Indonesia and the USSR did not block any majority decision until the dispute was settled.

Economic

Although there were economists in the delegations and attention was given to the economic blockade of the Republic, little consideration was given to the eventual economic and administrative problems of a final settlement. To a large degree this was dictated by the circumstances of the dispute. But, unfortunately, it meant that such long term issues as how much indebtedness to the Dutch the Indonesians should accept received scant consideration before the RTC. The Australian representative on UNCI was in favour of a Debt Commission considering the issue after the transfer of sovereignty when detailed figures could be reconciled. This was strongly opposed by the Netherlands and the debt negotiations were based on Dutch presentations, resulting in decisions that embittered Dutch-Indonesian relations.

Conclusions

United Nations involvement in the Indonesian dispute went through three stages. The first stage, after the first 'police action' of 1947, lasted for approximately eighteen months. During this period the United Nations relied on good offices with limited success and eventual failure. The failure of the GOC was not because of its composition, which was appropriate in the circumstances, but because the vague mandate of good offices was inappropriate in a situation of military conflict and especially when the opposing parties were of unequal strength. Furthermore, the cease hostilities order was given different interpretations by the parties and demonstrated the need for a ceasefire to include orders for a stand fast and withdrawal of forces. Lack of these and of a clear definition of military terms meant that, with the Republic much weaker militarily, its position was seriously eroded. Under the Renville truce which conceded Dutch advances, the introduction of demilitarised zones ten kilometres in width under GOC control helped to stabilise the situation until the second 'police action'.

Despite its weakness the GOC was a restraining influence that avoided the conflict degenerating into long drawn out guerrilla struggle with the resultant suffering and destruction. The GOC also helped ensure continuing international attention and in particular international and United Nations recognition of the Republic as the main Indonesian party in the dispute. It is worth noting, however, that these limited successes were achieved by initiatives that the Netherlands would have considered in contravention of good offices, notably the Christmas Message, the six additional principles and the Critchley-duBois Plan. It is also worth noting that the Good Offices Committee, principally through its military observers, investigated and thereby limited complaints of breaches of human rights.

The second stage followed the second 'police action' with the United Nations abandoning good offices for a positive role which relatively quickly brought success. In contrast to the lack of guidance given the GOC, the United Nations Commission for Indonesia had clear objectives and an unprecedented mandate to pursue them.

In the third stage, UNCI's participation in the Round Table Conference provided the parties with a respected source from which they could seek help when they were unable to reach agreement on their own and it also made compromises more palatable. UNCI thus made a valuable contribution to the final agreement for the transfer of sovereignty to a United States of Indonesia.

11 Peacemaking Diplomacy: United Nations Good Offices in Afghanistan

WILLIAM MALEY

Introduction

Following the Soviet invasion of Afghanistan in December 1979, successive Personal Representatives of the United Nations Secretary-General exercised the good offices of the UN to encourage a negotiated settlement of the Afghanistan conflict. These efforts resulted in the signing of the Geneva Accords on Afghanistan in April 1988, which provided for the staged withdrawal of Soviet forces. However, the Geneva process failed to deliver an orderly internal settlement between the Afghan parties, and subsequent UN efforts to broker such a settlement failed. With the collapse of the communist regime in April 1992, the UN appeared to abandon an active role in fostering internal political order, although some forms of humanitarian assistance to the Afghan population have continued to be supplied by the United Nations High Commission for Refugees (UNHCR), the World Food Program (WFP), and the United Nations Office for the Coordination of Humanitarian Assistance to Afghanistan (UNOCHA).

Historical background

In April 1978, Afghan President Muhammad Daoud was overthrown in a violent coup mounted by supporters in the Afghan military of the communist *Khalq* and *Parcham* groups. While the new regime which they established received diplomatic recognition and material support from the USSR, it suffered from divisions within its ranks, and its radical policies met with widespread opposition from cohesive social groups in rural Afghanistan, which its ill-advised resort to terror failed to mute. On 12

December 1979, the Politburo of the Communist Party of the Soviet Union authorised an invasion to replace hardline *Khalq* faction President Hafizullah Amin with the more compliant Babrak Karmal. This took place on 27 December 1979.

The invasion prompted a massive outflow of refugees from Afghanistan to Pakistan and Iran; by July 1980 the refugee population in Pakistan exceeded one million, and it eventually grew to around 3.3 million, with a further 2.8 million in Iran. It also prompted the escalation of the pre-invasion insurgency to a full-scale war, in which Soviet forces and the forces of the Karmal regime were confronted by a popular resistance movement, known collectively as the Afghan *Mujahideen*. This movement consisted of (a) exile parties *(tanzeemat)* of varying ethnic and ideological complexion, and enjoying varying degrees of moral and material support from sympathetic member states of the UN; and (b) traditional leaderships and charismatic commanders in particular provinces or regions.

The responses of the UN system

The UN system responded to these events in varying ways. UNHCR and WFP rapidly became involved in efforts to provide assistance to the displaced persons in refugee camps in Pakistan; in general these efforts were carried out with considerable proficiency, and require no further comment. Furthermore, from 1985, a series of reports on human rights in Afghanistan, produced by the Special Rapporteur to the Human Rights Commission of the Economic and Social Council, Professor Felix Ermacora, greatly added to an understanding of the human dimensions of what had become a particularly gruesome conflict. However, the response of the central *political* organs of the UN system was constrained by two specific factors.

The first and obvious restraint was the veto power of the Soviet Union as a permanent member of the Security Council. At a Security Council meeting in the first week of 1980, a draft resolution on Afghanistan was vetoed by the Soviet permanent representative. The second and much more serious constraint arose largely through inadvertence on the part of the member states which responded to the Security Council veto by moving to procure an Emergency Special Session of the General Assembly under the 'Uniting for Peace' resolution. In stark contrast to events following the invasion of Hungary in 1956, the credentials of the representatives of the regime installed by the invasion were accepted, and this accorded the regime a status within the UN system which it subsequently - and predictably - exploited to constrain the ambit of the Secretary-General's good offices. This case presents a very clear illustration of a point which should never be overlooked in the context of peacemaking diplomacy: that issues of credentials are political, *not* merely procedural, and should be approached with the greatest of care.

The Geneva Accords

On 11 February 1981, the then Secretary-General, Dr Kurt Waldheim, named Mr Javier Perez de Cuellar as his Personal Representative to promote 'peace talks between the Parties concerned'. Perez de Cuellar paid several visits to Afghanistan and Pakistan before himself assuming the office of Secretary-General, at which point he appointed Mr Diego Cordovez as his replacement. Between June 1982 and April 1988, Cordovez facilitated a series of exchanges between delegations from Pakistan and Afghanistan in Geneva which addressed the issues of withdrawal of foreign troops, non-interference in each others' affairs, voluntary return of refugees, and international guarantees of a settlement package. Representatives of the Afghan *Mujahideen* were at no time allowed to take part in the discussions, and Mr Cordovez did not attempt to meet any *Mujahideen* leader until late 1986, when the enunciation of a policy of 'national reconciliation' by the new Afghan leader, Najibullah, who had replaced Karmal in May 1986, in effect authorised him to do so.

However, on 13 November 1986, faced with battlefield failure, the Soviet Politburo decided to withdraw Soviet forces from Afghanistan within two years. On 8 February 1988, Soviet General Secretary Mikhail S. Gorbachev announced that beginning on 15 May 1988, Soviet troops would be withdrawn over a ten-month period. This led to the signing on 14 April 1988 of the four Geneva Accords, which provided for the withdrawal of 'the foreign troops' from Afghanistan by 15 February 1989. In a statement to coincide with the signing of the Accords, the Secretary-General asserted that the Accords 'lay the basis for the exercise by all Afghans of their right to self-determination, a principle enshrined in the Charter'. This was exactly what the Accords did not do. They simply required the Soviet leadership to follow the course which it had unilaterally chosen in November 1986. For this reason they were denounced by the *Mujahideen*, the shrewder of whom foresaw further arduous conflict before Najibullah's regime, which continued to receive massive financial and material support from the USSR, would fall.

The signing of the Accords led to the establishment of two significant new bodies. The first was the United Nations Good Offices Mission in Afghanistan and Pakistan (UNGOMAP). This body, which came into being in April 1988, was formally constituted by Security Council Resolution 622 of 31 October 1988, and continued until 15 March 1990, when it was succeeded by the Office of the Secretary-General in Afghanistan and Pakistan (OSGAP). It performed monitoring functions pursuant to a Memorandum of Understanding annexed to the Geneva Accords. The second was the Office of the United Nations Coordinator for

Humanitarian and Economic Assistance Program Relating to Afghanistan (UNOCA), subsequently renamed the United Nations Office for the Coordination of Humanitarian Assistance to Afghanistan (UNOCHA). This office was established by the Secretary-General on 11 May 1988. The experience of UNOCA demonstrates quite clearly that it is inadvisable for the UN to launch humanitarian programs based on *faulty political premises* - in this case, the myth that the Geneva Accords laid the basis for the exercise by all Afghans of their right to self-determination. While some of its 'Operation Salam' programs proved extremely valuable, particularly in the area of mine clearance training, the continuation of war in Afghanistan, and the failure of refugees to return as anticipated, significantly undercut the rationale for UNOCA's existence. It can even be argued that by absorbing donor funds when they could not realistically be used for reconstruction - and in the process exhausting the sense of commitment to Afghanistan of significant donors - UNOCA actually *harmed* Afghanistan's prospects of recovering from years of damaging conflict.

The UN's good offices after the Soviet withdrawal

In November 1989, the General Assembly passed a resolution which encouraged the Secretary-General 'to encourage and facilitate the early realisation of a comprehensive political settlement in Afghanistan in accordance with the provisions of the Geneva Accords and of the present resolution'. With the establishment of OSGAP under the Secretary-General's new Personal Representative, Mr Benon Sevan, the UN moved towards identifying certain common principles which a settlement plan acceptable to the internal and external parties might contain. On 21 May 1991, the Secretary-General issued a new proposal which contained as its key elements an 'intra-Afghan dialogue' to shape 'a credible and impartial transition mechanism' that 'would enjoy the confidence of the Afghan people and provide them with the necessary assurances to participate in free and fair elections, taking into account Afghan traditions, for the establishment of a broadbased Government'; and 'cessation of hostilities during the transition period'.

However, Sevan's strenuous exertions to flesh out this framework were ultimately overtaken by events. The failure of the August 1991 coup attempt in the Soviet Union led directly to a joint US-Soviet agreement to discontinue the dispatch of 'lethal material and supplies' to internal parties to the Afghan conflict; and the loss of Soviet support fatally undermined the position of the Kabul regime, which began to unravel. On 18 March 1992, Najibullah announced that he would resign from the moment when a transitional mechanism took over, a statement which triggered a frenzied attempt by the UN to put together such a mechanism and secure its acceptance by all the significant elements of the *Mujahideen*. The attempt failed, and on 16 April 1992, the regime disintegrated and Najibullah sought and obtained sanctuary in UN premises in Kabul. On 28 April, the leader of a new *Mujahideen* government arrived in Kabul.

There were five main reasons why Sevan's efforts failed. First, the exclusion of the Afghan resistance from the Geneva process had led some of its leading figures to view the UN's good offices with deep suspicion. Second, Sevan was perceived, whether rightly or wrongly, as sympathetic to Najibullah, and consequently lacked the personal authority to salvage the Secretary-General's plan as it was overtaken by events on the ground. Third, his office had not established or maintained adequate contact with important commanders in Afghanistan who stood poised to move on Kabul as the communist regime started to crumble. Fourth, Najibullah's public offer to resign came far too late to satisfy the appetites of those commanders. Finally, the transitional mechanism which Sevan hoped to put in place, made up of 'impartial personalities', lacked an independent power base and as a consequence lacked credibility. All this suggests that a good offices mission is unlikely to succeed unless it manages to secure the confidence of those with whom it is dealing, and deals with the key political actors in a way which realistically reflects their relative power.

The change of government in April 1992 triggered the largest and fastest spontaneous repatriation of refugees in the history of UNHCR, a reflection of the relative stability of the Afghan countryside in the post-communist period. Unfortunately, from August 1992, Kabul was blitzed with rockets by extremist *Mujahideen* groups who accused the new, moderate-dominated government of ruling in the name of 'communists'. While the UN bears no responsibility for these atrocities, they make its failure to develop a credible transition process through its good offices in the period between February 1989 and April 1992 all the more unfortunate. The scope for the constructive exercise of a good offices function is now extremely narrow, and is not assisted by the UN's continuing hospitality to Najibullah in its Kabul office. However, the door is not completely closed on UN involvement in Afghanistan, and supervision of elections is one sphere of activity which the Secretary-General's present Personal Representative, Mr Sotirios Mousouris, has publicly canvassed.

The Afghanistan experience provides sharp lessons for future exercises of the good offices function. It illustrates four key points. First, decisions on seemingly minor questions such as the recognition of credentials can significantly constrain the manner in which a good offices function is subsequently exercised. Second, settlements brokered by the UN can fail to solve difficult problems if crucial parties or crucial issues are excluded or overlooked in order to protect the negotiating process. Third, humanitarian programmes should not be distorted in order to reconcile them with broader UN mythology. Fourth, highly expert, level-headed assessment of complex political situations is required if good offices missions are not to collapse spectacularly.

12 Namibia: A Lesson for Success

JANE MADDEN

Historical background

On 21 March 1990 the United Nations' plan for the independence of Namibia successfully ended and Africa's last colony officially became an independent state. This was an historic event for which the people of Namibia and the international community had long struggled.

More than eleven years earlier, in 1978, the comprehensive settlement plan providing for UN supervised transition to independence had been adopted by the UN Security Council under Resolution 435. This followed the termination of South Africa's mandate by the UN General Assembly in 1966, the transferral of responsibility for the territory to the UN Council for Namibia in the same year and the 1971 declaration by the International Court of Justice that South Africa's continued presence in the country was illegal.

Up until late 1988, only a year prior to the eventual implementation of UNSCR 435, the plan had looked doomed and in many respects out-of-date. Attempts at implementation had come up against South African military ambition in Angola, and United States' attempts to link the withdrawal of Cuban forces from Angola with South Africa's withdrawal from Namibia had failed. The Soviet retreat from sub-Saharan Africa in the second half of the decade, however, dramatically altered the region's balance of power and stimulated South Africa to reassess its position. The door to Namibia's independence was finally opened by peace accords between South Africa and Angola in early 1989.

This door, too, was almost shut because of an incursion by thousands of guerrillas from the South West African Peoples' Organisation (SWAPO) in April 1989. The incursion was a clear breach of the peace accords and the South African Government reacted with force. Hundreds of

SWAPO guerrillas were killed during the next two weeks. The guerrillas had sought to bolster SWAPO's electoral profile with a show of force prior to the implementation of the peace plan.

In the event this incursion did not derail or delay UNSCR 435. The fighting between SWAPO and the South West African Police was curtailed following South African military action and an order issued by SWAPO President, Sam Nujoma, on April 8 that all SWAPO troops inside Namibia stop fighting, regroup and return to Angola within 72 hours under the escort of UNTAG (the UN Transition Assistance Group).

Things moved quickly throughout the rest of 1989. The South African Defence Forces were successfully confined to base by 13 May (some weeks later than originally scheduled because of the SWAPO incursion), reducing in numbers more or less in accordance with the UNSCR timetable until being finally withdrawn on 24 November. The local Namibian force, the South West Africa Territory Force (SWATF), was demobilised. Refugee repatriation commenced on 12 June and was effectively completed by 19 September. About 50 discriminatory or restrictive laws which could have effected the freedom and fairness of the elections were repealed in whole or in part. Political prisoners were released on the advice of an expert independent jurist. Voter registration started on 3 July and was completed by 23 September. Elections were held from 7-11 November 1989 to choose the 72 members of the country's Constituent Assembly under the UN's supervision and control. By Christmas a shadow Cabinet was announced and a draft constitution, acclaimed as one of the most liberal in Africa, was agreed. The stage was set for independence.

Lessons for the UN - what should we try to duplicate?

What were the ingredients behind this relatively smooth timetable and why did the UN operation succeed in Namibia?

One critical factor was that the timing for peacemaking was right. The respective positions of the superpowers, regional players, political organisations and the public were so aligned as to maintain the momentum towards settlement once the key obstacle - South African refusal to withdraw troops - was removed. Amongst the driving forces at play were economic imperatives, growing war fatigue and pragmatic calculation of the odds. Without the cooperation of all the parties to the conflict, the independence process would surely have not succeeded.

Another factor was that UNTAG included a sizeable civilian component. This was appropriate given that the Namibia settlement process was an elaborate exercise in self-determination, in other words a political, rather than military, operation. This made UNTAG quite different to the previous generation of UN peacekeeping operations, which had had a predominantly military orientation. UNTAG had about 400-450 civilian officials in Namibia for much of the transition period supported by about 800 locally engaged staff. During the elections, a further 1,400 civilians were flown in for a month.

The extensive historical involvement which the UN had with the Namibian problem was no doubt another contributing factor to the operation's success. The Special Representative of the UNTAG and his closest advisers, the Force Commander, the Police Commissioner, the Directors of Administration and Elections and the Head of the Special Representative's office, had been employed as a team for ten years before the UNTAG force was deployed. Senior staff, therefore, had detailed knowledge, familiarity with the key players and a good understanding of every nuance and aspect of UNSCR 435. They had all experienced close involvement with the negotiation and planning phases leading up to deployment and implementation.

The established senior personnel also ensured that UNTAG personnel were recruited promptly and member states provided quality staff in a timely manner. With a 4,650-strong military force contributed by twenty-one countries, a US$416.2 million budget, 2,000 civilian staff and 500 professional police officers to monitor the local police forces, UNTAG was the largest operation the UN had organised since the Congo operation in the 1960s. With the wisdom of hindsight, even greater deployment at the earliest stage would have been desirable. For example, as the crisis of April 1989 unfolded, only 100 UN staff and 921 troops had arrived in Namibia. It was more through good luck than any good management on the part of the UN that the SWAPO incursion in 1989 did not bring the peacekeeping effort to an end.

The fact that UNTAG had a wide mandate was also essential to its success. In most previous UN peacekeeping operations, UN forces observed independence elections. In Namibia the mission had a much larger role, supervising and controlling the electoral process and all related aspects. Additional resources were provided to meet this objective. The UN officials originally brought in for electoral tasks had little or no background in electoral matters and it was necessary to bring in a number of experts from Australia, Canada and Britain. These experts contributed significantly to the overall success of the electoral process.

The UN was involved at every stage of the electoral timetable - refugee repatriation and settlement, military and police monitoring, election supervision, public relations, prisoner release, human rights, voter education and information dissemination. Namibia was actually the first occasion outside Cyprus where police had been extensively used in a peacekeeping operation under the term of reference of the military organisation. CIVPOL's track record was quite impressive, despite continuing problems thrown up by the South West African Police.

The multi-dimensional nature of UNTAG allowed it to assert its authority over the South African Government-appointed Administrator-General, thereby securing the confidence of the Namibian people and their parties. This in turn stimulated a greater confidence in the peacemaking process and limited the extent of intimidation. The UNTAG experience reinforces the observation that 'the credibility of any UN force will depend in part on its visibility and legitimacy in the eyes of the population. There is an element of theatre or symbolism involved'.[1]

Of central importance to UNTAG's concept of operations was the need to inform Namibians and to assist in the process of reconciliation. With Namibia's population of only 1.3 million and a very low population density, UNTAG divided the country into ten operational districts and established 42 outposts throughout the country, each staffed by two professionals from the UN system. The regional offices allowed UNTAG to develop good networks of operation across the country and gave UN regional directors considerable autonomy in their areas of control. The regional directors were responsible for coordinating all of UNTAG's operations within their territories including those that were not directly related to the administration such as the civilian police and the military force. Most importantly, these offices gave UNTAG a high profile throughout Namibia and contributed to a positive change in the political atmosphere. UNTAG paid particular attention to the dissemination of information in an effort to counter the effects of the generally slanted reporting in the local press. UNTAG also ran daily radio programs in all the local languages, and had a weekly television slot. UNTAG's role on this area was commendable but as a new experience for UN operations, it lacked some professionalism.

The Joint Commission established by Angola, South Africa and Cuba, with the US, USSR and UNTAG as observers and invitees also proved invaluable to the success of the Namibia operation. The Joint Commission provided the forum for discussion between antagonistic and often suspicious countries during the long and difficult transition period. The Commission enabled the settlement process to weather a number of storms, most notably SWAPO's April 1989 incursion.

A feature of the UNTAG operation which may be worth considering duplicating in future UN operations was the stipulation that the Special Representative of the UN Secretary-General, Mr Martti Ahtisaari, had to satisfy himself at each stage as to the fairness and appropriateness of all measures affecting the political process at all levels of administration before such measures took effect. This effectively gave him a right of veto with regard to political processes in Namibia and strengthened the negotiating position of UNTAG in all its dealings with the South African Government and other parties. In relations between the Special Representative and the Administrator-General, this was particularly important.

---

[1] Nick Warner, 'Cambodia: Lessons of UNTAC for Future Peacekeeping Operations' paper presented at the UN Peacekeeping at the Crossroads International Seminar, Canberra 21-24 March 1993.

Lessons for the UN - what should we try to avoid?

The close working relations between UN headquarters in New York and UNTAG in Namibia were also important but produced some mixed results. There was extremely avid interest by the Special Task Force, established in the UN Secretariat, in the day-to-day operation of UNTAG. The fact that there were no other major peacekeeping efforts at the time in other parts of the world no doubt contributed to this high level of attention. On the positive side, this scrutiny allowed information about the peacemaking process to be disseminated to member states rapidly and decisions regarding personnel and resources to be made quite promptly. One of drawbacks was that the Special Task Force in New York contributed to a muddled division of responsibility between the peacekeeping force and the Secretariat. The Task Force's contribution was therefore sometimes counterproductive - confusing rather than assisting the operation of the force. In hindsight, more authority should have been delegated to the field.

There were other institutional weaknesses in the UN system, evident both in New York and in Namibia. In the field, there was a distinct lack of coordination, and even cooperation, between UNTAG's military and civilian wings. On numerous occasions UNTAG did not operate as a single, united entity, but as two separate, and often competing parts. This was due in part to the UN Force Commander in Namibia adopting an independent role, sometimes communicating directly with the UN Secretariat and by-passing the Special Representative on important policy matters. The result was the forwarding of some contradictory reporting and advice to UN Headquarters and a duplication of functions. Several areas of UNTAG's military and civilian sides established separate structures to perform the same role, notably in logistics and communications.

Shortcomings in the logistics of the UN's operations could be detected throughout the deployment period. For example, one of the most important constraints on UNTAG's mobility and effectiveness in the early stages had been the fear of mines. For several months after the deployment of UNTAG, the force could not operate in a large part of northern Namibia until mine-proof vehicles were purchased. However, the generally sound infrastructure of Namibia, developed largely through South Africa's military engagement, prevented logistical problems becoming a major obstacle.

Conclusion

As the above analysis seeks to show, Namibia holds valuable lessons for future peacekeeping exercises.

The first is that the cooperation of parties to the process is essential. The success or failure of the mission will ultimately depend on this factor. This means that the timing of the operation must be finely judged so that the chances of this cooperation are maximised. Sometimes this may mean delaying the start of the operation.

The second lesson is that an essential condition for any successful peacekeeping operation must be a reasonably clear mandate from the Security Council. Related to this, it may often be desirable to invest the senior UN representative with a power to veto each stage of the political process so as to consolidate the authority of the UN.

Third, the budget of the operation should be approved prior to the implementation date in order to deploy the bulk of the UN forces from the very start of the process.

Finally, the division of responsibility between the military and civilian wings of the UN should be spelt out so that the lines of communication and responsibility are clear.

Cooperation, rather than competition and duplication, should be the hallmark of the operation.

13 United Nations Involvement in the Peace Process in El Salvador

DAVID STUART

Background

After 1931, when a coup saw the installation of military rule in El Salvador, the politics of the country were dominated for generations by a regime based on the alliance between wealthy land owners and the army, and a policy of selective social reform and repression aimed at dividing middle and lower social sectors. During the 1970s freedoms afforded to the middle class were continually reduced. Honduras closed its borders to El Salvador following the 1969 war, and landless farmers who would once have emigrated, migrated to the cities, causing a sudden increase in the marginal population and social conflict. These factors led to the development and expansion of revolutionary forces. Reformist parties united to form the Union Nacional Opositora (UNO) to contest the 1972 elections, and won a majority of votes. The military manipulated the election, however, and claimed victory, the fraudulent result of the elections leading to an unsuccessful coup by a section of the officer corps. These abuses were repeated in Presidential elections in 1977, characterised by intimidation and violent suppression.

From 1969, a succession of extreme right-wing terrorist groups emerged which were responsible for assassinations and other attempts to intimidate those in support of reform and political change. In 1979, increased violence by both right and left-wing terrorist groups and rioting escalated into civil war. In 1980, the growing number of extreme left guerilla groups united to form the Frente Faribundo Marti Para La Liberacion Nacional (FMLN).

In 1984, victory for José Duarte, the civilian candidate exiled after the 1972 elections, saw hopes for reform in El Salvador by democratic means.

However, the Duarte administration made no significant progress towards reform and was defeated in 1988 by the Alianza Republicana Nacional (ARENA), with Alfredo Cristiani elected President in 1989. (ARENA was established in 1981 as a right-wing response to left-wing insurgency).

By 1992 more than 80,000 combatants and civilians had been killed, 550,000 displaced and more than 500,000 had fled the country.

Contacts between the Government and the FMLN were made throughout the armed conflict, but peace negotiations broke down over control of the armed forces and political integration of the FMLN. Duarte's lack of control over the military meant that the Government could not meet FMLN demands. However, following a period of assassinations and counter-assassinations, FMLN and Government representatives met in Geneva in April 1990. An Agreement on Human Rights was concluded on 26 July at San Jose in Costa Rica; it proved to be the first major achievement in a long process of negotiation under the auspices of the United Nations Secretary-General which eventually produced a comprehensive agreement on 31 December 1991.

According to a report of the Secretary-General, agreement was only reached through the determination of both the Government and the FMLN to see an end to armed conflict. Both sides had agreed that a durable peace could only be achieved through significant changes and the assistance of the international community. There is no doubt, however, that the international environment played a major role in resolving the dispute. The Cristiani Government was no doubt influenced by the United States position on military aid, with Congress threatening a 50 per cent cut. The collapse of the former Soviet Union removed support for insurgency groups such as the FMLN. The decline of Cuba as a regional power also decreased the FMLN's chances of expanding its influence. The success in resolving conflict in Nicaragua led to increased pressure on the US to encourage the Government of El Salvador, which was heavily dependent on it for military and other assistance, to develop a peaceful agreement. Joint US and Soviet Union action resurrected the Esquipulas Agreement, signed by the Central American Presidents in 1985, which had committed the five countries to specific measures to achieve regional peace, including dialogue with insurgents. Many of El Salvador's neighbours adopted measures aimed at preventing activities taking place within their territorites that would result in violations of the Esquipulas Agreement.

The Peace Accords were signed by Government and FMLN officials on 16 January 1992 in Chapultepec Castle, Mexico City, and concluded agreement on all outstanding points of substance. The Peace Accords provided that the twelve-year civil war in El Salvador would cease, with a ceasefire beginning on 1 February and an armed peace continuing until 31 October 1992. The comprehensive agreement covered questions concerning socio-economic issues (in particular, that of land tenure), electoral and judicial reform, the establishment of a civilian police force and FMLN demobilisation and participation in the political process.

Following the beginning of the ceasefire on 1 February 1992, the separation of forces was completed without major incident by 6 February. However, the second stage of the Accords, scheduled for March 2, was delayed because of several factors. Difficulties arose over the abolition and incorporation into the army of the Treasury Police and the National Guard, and it appeared that the intentions of the Government to comply with the agreements on these points were questionable. The FMLN did not complete its second stage of demobilisation, citing failure by the Government to comply with other conditions. The peace process was also delayed by suspicions that the FMLN was withholding arms and ammunition. With further United Nation's assistance, a new timetable for land distribution, political participation and recruitment into the new National Civil Police was agreed and FMLN combatants began to demobilise in the second half of the year.

The 16 January 1992 Accords, according to the UN Secretary-General, aimed not only to bring about a cessation of conflict, but also to remove original causes of the conflict and promote democratisation and reconciliation among Salvadorans: 'In that respect, it may serve as an inspiration for the settlement of other conflicts'.

United Nations Observer Mission in El Salvador

Through the Secretary-General's Special Representative for the Central American Peace Process, Alvaro de Soto, the UN had engaged in consultations with the Government and the FMLN early in 1990. The meetings in Geneva in April set the framework for UN-mediated talks. Even though the July Accord contemplated a UN mission only after a ceasefire had been established, both sides were interested in having a UN presence ahead of negotiation of a ceasefire.

On 20 May 1991 the Security Council, under Resolution 693(1991), agreed to create a United Nations Observer Mission in El Salvador (ONUSAL) to monitor all agreements between the Government and the FMLN. The United Nations Development Program (UNDP) was given the role of mobilising and channelling resources to meet ONUSAL needs (the ONUSAL budget, however, is met by assessed contributions of UN member states).

ONUSAL was a departure from previous Security Council mandates for peace keeping in some important respects. It expressly included human rights verification as a function of the UN mission. Its establishment in advance of a ceasefire was also unprecedented, especially when it was not possible to guarantee the safety of UN personnel (and indeed extreme right-wing groups openly threatened UN personnel before and during their deployment).

Following establishment of a small preparatory office in January 1991, ONUSAL deployed in El Salvador in July 1991. The Secretary-General concluded that there was strong support across all sectors of political opinion for the UN commencing the verification of the Agreement without awaiting a ceasefire. Its mandate, in its first phase as a peacekeeping operation, was to verify compliance by the parties to the July 1990 Agreement on Human Rights. In this phase, ONUSAL's tasks included: monitoring the human rights situation in El Salvador; investigating alleged human rights violations; promoting human rights; making recommendations on eliminating violations; and reporting to the Security Council, the General Assembly and the Secretary-General. Under the Human Rights Agreement, which had foreseen a UN role, ONUSAL had powers to visit any place freely and without notice, it could receive communications from any Salvadoran individual or group, conduct direct investigations and even use the media to the extent useful for fulfilling its mandate - these powers gave ONUSAL an unprecedented role as a UN mission. The Secretary-General took the view that the verification of human rights by ONUSAL would not only promote a significant improvement in human rights in El Salvador but would also act as a strong impetus to the negotiations between the Government and FMLN.

By November 1991, ONUSAL comprised 135 international staff members from 31 countries: 57 human rights officers, legal advisers and educators; 15 military liaison officers; 27 police advisers; and 36 administrative and support staff. It seems to have carried out its mandate quite vigorously, travelling, and, subsequently deploying its personnel, throughout the country, establishing a very wide range of contacts including with the FMLN, and setting up coordination mechanisms with human rights non-government organisations as well as a human rights education program. Its effective human rights role was carried out in parallel to the continuing work of the long-standing Special Representative on El Salvador of the UN Commission on Human Rights.

The UN continued to be active in brokering talks between the Government and the FMLN, although it was not until mid-September 1991 after the site of negotiations had moved to the UN Headquarters in New York, with the direct involvement of Secretary-General Javier Perez de Cuellar, President Cristiani and top FMLN Commanders, that significant progress was made towards agreement on a ceasefire. On 25 September the two sides signed the New York Accord in which they agreed to establish a National Commission for the Consolidation of Peace (COPAZ) to provide for overall supervision of the peace agreements, including: reduction and reform of the Salvadoran armed forces; establishment of a National Civilian police to replace the National Guard, the Treasury Policy and the National Police; and land reform. Details and timing were left for further negotiation.

In November, the FMLN announced a unilateral truce and the Government responded by suspending air operations and heavy artillery use. COPAZ, in which ONUSAL and the Catholic Church were observers, began functioning as a multi-party consultative mechanism.

UN-mediated negotiations intensified and, at the very end of 1991 (with the clock stopped on 31 December, with the Secretary-General's term about to expire), a ceasefire agreement was struck in New York.

On the verge of agreement on the January 1992 Peace Accords, the Security Council decided to enlarge ONUSAL's mandate to include verification and monitoring of the agreement. ONUSAL was to verify all aspects of the ceasefire and the separation of forces and to monitor the maintenance of public order during the transitional period while the new National Civil Police was created. ONUSAL played an active role in assisting negotiations so that differences over fulfilment of undertakings by the FMLN to demobilise and by the Government to distribute land more equitably, to allow broad political participation and recruit widely into the new National Civil Police force, were resolved during the course of 1992. The UN presence in this period was divided into a Military Division, a Police Division and a Human Rights Division; total force numbers were 425.

Following the demobilisation of the FMLN, the El Salvador Government requested that the UN extend its mandate to monitor the election scheduled for March 1994. In May 1993 the UN Secretary-General recommended to the UN Security Council the sending of 900 observers to monitor the elections. ONUSAL's mandate was extended by the Security Council on 27 May 1993 to 30 November 1993, and is likely to be extended further.

In addition to verifying the implementation of the peace accord, ONUSAL has been carrying out other tasks in El Salvador. The Military Division monitored the reduction of the armed forces (completed by the end of January 1993) and the introduction of a new Armed Forces Reserve System, and has been supervising clearing minefields and monitoring the situation affecting ex-combatants. The Police Division has been assisting the National Police pending the formation of the new National Civil Police.

The plans for transition to a new national police force which would be, and be seen to be, apolitical and independent from the armed forces, were a key part of the Peace Accords. The two bodies most associated with repression and human rights abuses during the Civil War, the National Guard and the Treasury Police, were to be disbanded and, during the transition period while the National Civil Police was established (expected to take 24 months), the UN police monitors were assigned to assist and escort the existing National Police. This role has been hindered, however, by the difficulty in obtaining sufficient numbers of civilian police from UN Member States to deploy in ONUSAL and by the limited role of ONUSAL in creating the new force.

Economic and social issues

Significant as the January 1992 Accords were, the pressures of negotiating to a deadline meant that the chapter on economic and social issues, including the crucial question of land reform - considered by many to be the root cause of the civil war in El Salvador - received much less attention than the chapter dealing with demobilisation and reform of the Government and FMLN forces. Reinsertion into civil society of combatants on both sides depended greatly on the ability to implement the Accords' provisions for land reform, which relied on 'voluntary' transfer of private land at market prices. But the Chapultepec Agreements did not specify how many were to benefit from land transfers, the size of plots to be transferred or practical arrangements for land transfer, so that this quickly emerged as one of the main obstacles to implementing the peace process. In October 1992 the FMLN stopped the third (of five) phases of demobilisation, accusing the Government of failing to start the land program; the UN Secretary-General negotiated a program acceptable to both sides to supplement the January Accords but this was no more than a partial solution.

Commission of Truth

On 13 July 1992, three notables (from Venezuela, Colombia and the USA) selected by the Secretary-General were appointed to form a 'Commission of the Truth'. The aim of the Truth Commission was to investigate acts of violence between 1980 and July 1991. It was given six months to identify the worst human rights abuses by all sides, to ascertain the degree of impunity with which the military acted, to make legal, administrative or political recommendations so as to prevent repeats of abuses, and to stimulate national reconciliation.

The report of the Truth Commission was released on 15 March 1993, naming predominantly members of the armed forces, the security forces and death squads as responsible for episodes of violence during the civil war. Only five per cent of the episodes of grave violence were attributed to the FMLN. Several prominent figures, including the late ruling party leader Roberto D'Aubuisson, former Defence Minister Casanova, Defence Minister Ponce and FMLN leaders, had specific killings attributed to them.

By 20 March 1993 the ARENA-dominated Congress had passed an amnesty bill introduced only two days before. The UN Secretary-General has nevertheless insisted that El Salvador implement the findings of the Truth Commission as part of the peace agreement. Many expect the US to exert pressure on the Salvadoran Government to conform with the findings.

Why was ONUSAL a success?

While there were difficulties in El Salvador in the process of disarming the FMLN and having the Government and armed forces accept some sharing of power, or at least a reduction in the size of the armed forces and creation of a new National Civil Police force, the situation was much more amenable to solution than in other situations in which the UN has sought to play a role in assisting national reconciliation.

- In El Salvador, both the Government, including ARENA as the dominant party, and the FMLN, had a strong stake in international support and retaining some minimum respectability. President Cristiani needed to maintain US backing and aid; the FMLN valued its standing as a legitimate opposition after its demobilisation. Largely through its political wing, the FDR, it had developed links with democratic socialist and social democrat parties in a range of Western countries in the 1980s.

- The human rights component of ONUSAL was established in response to a formal request from both parties and was on the basis that both would cooperate with ONUSAL. Both sides were therefore willing to support a significant UN role in El Salvador. Notwithstanding extremist threats to ONUSAL personnel, ONUSAL had the unanimous backing of the Legislative Assembly, genuine cooperation from the Cristiani Government and broad public support.

- The intense mutual suspicion and lack of trust between the Government and the FMLN enabled the UN to present itself as a respected arbiter and guarantor, not least in the provision of security for FMLN leaders (an incident or killing involving an FMLN leader would have had the potential to derail the peace process). The Secretary-General's Special Representative for the Central American Peace Process, Alvaro de Soto, has said the UN had been involved in negotiating the agreement in a good officer's role, which is a broad, all-encompassing formula which does not oblige the parties to entertain proposals submitted by the good officer. Both parties were willing to eschew military victory as an option, not least because neither could realistically hope to win militarily, and there was widespread and genuine national yearning for peace and reconciliation. The duration and futility of the civil war were also factors.

- A factor which contributed to reaching a political solution was the parties' concern that their traditional backers and suppliers of arms could no longer be relied on. That said, the FMLN were more prepared to rely on the processes of 'democratisation' of El Salvador than, for example, the Khmer Rouge, and (understandably, as they were not an international pariah) much less willing to flaunt international opinion by dissociating themselves from previous agreements and reverting to armed struggle than disputants in some other countries.

External factors, regional and global, also contributed to the achievement of agreement on a political settlement. The real increase in the willingness of central American Governments to cooperate on security issues and to address the need for national reconciliation, demonstrated in the Esquipulas Agreements, had increased the margin for conflict resolution in the region. The end of the Cold War meant a changed approach for the chief political backers of each side: this clearly was a major reason for the shifts in attitude towards negotiation of both the Government and the FMLN leadership. Cooperation between the superpowers in the Security Council also underpinned the Security Council's newfound ability to respond innovatively - at that stage, concerns about rising peacekeeping costs and threats to blue-helmeted personnel had not yet emerged to constrain the Council's effectiveness. At the same time, the support of middle powers for a negotiated settlement was notable, especially Mexico, Colombia and Venezuela, and others like Canada and Spain.

The role played by individuals in mediating the peace agreements also warrants mention. The then Secretary-General devoted much personal attention to brokering agreement, and senior officials like Alvaro de Soto also seem to have shown no small measure of diplomatic skill and perseverance in keeping the sides talking and promoting an environment of mutual confidence. It has also been suggested that, together with the then United States Permanent Representative in New York, Ambassador Thomas Pickering, UN officials also helped to convince the US administration that peace in El Salvador was possible and that a negotiated settlement which made possible the political survival of the FMLN was consistent with US interests. The Ambassadors of Colombia, Spain, Mexico and Venezuela formed a group called the 'Friends of the Secretary-General' which also contributed actively to the peace making process, for example, in 'operation Palomina' in May 1991 which organised protected transport of FMLN leaders out of El Salvador to participate in ceasefire talks.

ONUSAL as a model

As an exercise in peace making, El Salvador showed that the UN Secretary-General could take the initiative to broker a peaceful solution to a long running civil war. Much can be learnt about the techniques of third party mediation from this experience;[1] it also shows that in the right

---

[1] Alvaro de Soto and Graciana del Castillo, 'Obstacles to Peacebuilding', *Foreign Policy* 94, (Spring 1994) pp. 69-83; Stephen Baranyi and Liisa

circumstances the UN can take the lead effectively and to good effect. An important consideration was that some of the principal actors (including Perez de Cuellar, de Soto, Pickering) were closely familiar with the situation in El Salvador and well informed about developments. Nonetheless, in considering whether the UN's involvement in negotiations was a 'model', we should recognise that its success rested on the convergence of a range of factors, within El Salvador and external to it, which were outside the control of the UN Security Council and the Secretary-General.

Some aspects of ONUSAL's role are interesting for their possible application to other situations, such as Cambodia, where the UN's goals include assisting national reconciliation in the face of violent internal strife and a history of systematic human rights violations:

- Monitoring armed force reduction (though the FMLN claimed that the supposed halving of the armed forces was illusory as the forces had never been as large as the Government claimed).

- Assistance for establishing a new, supposedly neutral, National Civil Police, with the role of monitoring residual functions of the old police force in the transition period (although there were limits in ONUSAL's role in training and establishing the new force).

- The activist human rights role, including with investigatory powers, the complementarity of human rights activities mandated by the Security Council, and the continuing arrangements of the United Nations Commission on Human Rights to remain apprised of developments in El Salvador (in 1992, UNCHR downgraded the Special Representative to an Independent Expert, and from 1993 the situation in El Salvador was moved out of Item 12 scrutiny and into the item on Advisory Services). The powers of investigation, the education program and the resources devoted to human rights work could provide useful precedents for arguing for a more effective UN role in other situations where peace keepers have been deployed and human rights abuse is a critical factor in efforts to restore peace.

The relative weakness of the chapter on economic and social issues of the January 1992 Agreement points to a larger problem of the UN's role in El Salvador. If peace is to endure in El Salvador, the underlying reasons for conflict will need to be resolved; economic domination by an élite, and corresponding domination of political institutions, lies at the heart of armed conflicts in a number of central American countries. Without steps being taken which will ensure the provision of land and other productive assets more broadly, and an attendant improvement in living standards and

---

North, Stretching the Limits of the Possible: United Nations Peacemaking in Central America (Ottawa: Canadian Centre for Global Security, 1992).

democratic incorporation of majorities, social conflict will not be far removed. This is not only a question of the long haul task of post-conflict peace building - the weakness of provisions for land reform in the Chapultapec Accord has already been an impediment to the peace process.

It is argued by de Soto and del Castillo that the approach of the international community to El Salvador is characterised by two parallel processes - restoring peace through UN peacemaking and peacekeeping; and economic stabilisation through the Bretton Woods institutions - and that there is a lack of coordination between these, so that constraints imposed by the Salvadoran economy in general and the stabilisation process in particular make the prospects of financing the peace process and therefore its implementation very difficult and uncertain.[2] They describe how the Salvadoran Government's economic program agreed with the International Monetary Fund (IMF) in May 1993 would mean that peace-related programs (establishment of the new National Civil Police and land transfers) would depend on new external financing. They point to the institutional obstacles to avoiding a collision between these two processes: the fact that the statutes, rules and policies of institutions like the World Bank do not lend themselves to adapting lending programs to efforts to restore peace (or may be based on quite distinct criteria to goals such as the reinsertion of combatants into the work force and land reform); the lack of transparency in decision making so that there is relatively little exchange of information between the UN Secretary-General and the heads of the World Bank and the IMF (the Bretton Woods institutes did not inform the UN of their agreements with the Government of El Salvador in the period of negotiations); and the lack of coordination, by UN Member States in taking decisions in the Council and as IMF or World Bank members (remembering that the Security Council Permanent Members constitute over 30 per cent of the voting power of these bodies) and between different parts of the multilateral system (for example, when the UN began to play a role in negotiations in 1990, it did not consult the IMF or the World Bank on the financial implications of a peaceful settlement - and only did so belatedly when putting forward the October 1992 program of land transfer).[3] Their conclusion, that UN-led peace operations require an integrated approach to ensure success and that this should extend to the Bretton Woods institutions, seems entirely reasonable.

Postscript: November 1993

As El Salvador moves towards elections in March 1994, substantial progress has been made on the implementation of the Peace Accords.

---

[2] de Soto and del Castillo, 'Obstacles to Peacebuilding' pp.76.
[3] Ibid. pp.72-73.

There appears to be a general acceptance that atrocities have been committed by both sides during the conflict, and the desire is now more for reconciliation than revenge for war crimes. The ceasefire has held and there has been a large degree of demobilisation and a reduction in arms. The army has been reduced by 30,000 and the FMLN disbanded (8,000 fighters). During mid-1993, ONUSAL was involved in the discovery and destruction of large quantities of clandestine arms caches belonging to the FMLN in Salvadoran territory as well as in Nicaragua and Honduras. By all indications, the FMLN's military structure has now been effectively dismantled and its former combatants have been demobilised and reintegrated, within a framework of full legality, into the civil, institutional and political life of the country, as outlined in the Peace Accords. The process of verification and destruction of FMLN weaponry was finally completed on 18 August 1993. On 30 September, the Secretary-General reported that given the circumstances surrounding the bitter twelve-year conflict in El Salvador, weaponry was likely to remain in the hands of groups or individuals, including criminal ones, for some time. He noted that the evidence had brought into sharp focus the public's condemnation of armed groups and the futility of arms as a viable means to achieve political aims.

Significant difficulties remain in the implementation of the Peace Accords, however. In October 1993, renewed political violence, particularly against FMLN leaders, threatened to undermine the peace process. The violence substantiated concerns referred to in reports of the Human Rights Division of ONUSAL, including the re-emergence of death squads, and confirmed the need for immediate implementation of the recommendations of the Commission of Truth regarding the impartial and independent investigation of illegal armed groups. Delays in the implementation of provisions of the Peace Accords, including the phasing out of the National Police and full deployment of the National Civil Police, will make it impossible for these provisions to be completed before the 1994 elections, as scheduled. In addition, tension has been created by delays in the implementation of social and economic programs, particularly with regard to land reform.

ONUSAL's mandate has been renewed and an Electoral Division created to observe the elections. It appears likely that its mandate will be further renewed to enable it to complete its verification of the 20 March 1994 elections, which will mark the culmination of the peace process, and to remain in El Salvador for a short transition period immediately after.

Although the peace process still has a long way to go, reflecting the complexity of the transition towards democracy, the UN has contributed greatly to its progress by playing a key role in brokering the Peace Accords. The elections will be the first in which all of the country's political sectors, including the FMLN, will participate. The recent spate of political violence has highlighted the need to accelerate implementation of the Accords in order to lay the foundations for genuinely free and fair elections and thus assist in the process of national reconciliation.

14 Keeping but not Making Peace:The UN Peacekeeping Force in Cyprus

DAVID MORRIS

Twenty-nine years after its establishment, the United Nations Peacekeeping Force in Cyprus (UNFICYP) continues to monitor a *de facto* ceasefire between Turkish forces, Turkish Cypriot security forces and the Greek Cypriot National Guard. In terms of its limited peacekeeping mandate, UNFICYP has been a success, but arguably its success in maintaining the status quo on the island, since the Turkish invasion of northern Cyprus in 1974, has developed into a disincentive to a peace settlement.

The Republic of Cyprus was granted independence from the United Kingdom in 1960, after diplomatic efforts to assure in its constitution a government structure for the harmonious coexistence of the island's Greek Cypriot and Turkish Cypriot communities. The territorial integrity and constitutional guarantees for both communities of the new republic were endorsed and guaranteed in the 1959 Zurich-London accords between the UK, Turkey and Greece and also endorsed by representatives of the Greek Cypriot and Turkish Cypriot communities. The Accords and subsequent treaties established the UK, Turkey and Greece as guarantor powers of the basic articles of the constitution.

From early on, the new republic suffered a number of constitutional crises concerning the Greek Cypriot and Turkish Cypriot elements of the government which were guaranteed in the constitution. After only three years, conflict broke out between the Greek Cypriot and Turkish Cypriot communities, prompted in part by the President's decision to amend the constitution which was seen by the Turkish Cypriots as reducing their equal status rights to those of a minority. The guarantor powers, all of which maintained forces on the island, offered to form a joint peacekeeping force under British command to restore peace and order. The Government of Cyprus accepted the offer and the force was established on 26 December 1963. Three days later a ceasefire was arranged and a neutral zone, or 'green line', was established between the areas occupied by the two communities in Nicosia. The guarantor powers also arranged a conference involving all parties to negotiate a settlement, but negotiations failed. The Government of Cyprus then rejected proposals to strengthen the peacekeeping force and insisted that any force be placed under UN control. The peacekeeping force had failed to prevent the inter-communal fighting and the Government of Cyprus feared military intervention by Greece and Turkey.

The UN Secretary-General appointed a personal representative to observe the peacekeeping operation in January 1964 and, in March, with the consent of the Government of Cyprus, the Security Council established (by Security Council Resolution 186) a UN Peacekeeping Force in Cyprus with a mandate to

> use its best efforts to prevent a recurrence of fighting and, as necessary, to contribute to the maintenance and restoration of law and order and a return to normal conditions.

An initial force of about 6,000 was deployed on the island under a three-monthly mandate. UNFICYP established a number of observation posts throughout the island in areas of tension, on the 'green line', in mixed villages and in Turkish Cypriot enclaves. UNFICYP negotiated ceasefires in numerous, isolated outbreaks of violence and provided humanitarian assistance, in cooperation with other UN agencies and non-government organisations such as the United Nations High Commission for Refugees (UNHCR) and the Red Cross, seeking to ensure the provision of services and return to normality for all sections of the population.

After a severe deterioration in 1967, involving Greek and Turkish forces on the island, the Security Council strengthened the UNFICYP mandate to provide for supervision of the disarmament of forces constituted after 1963 (SCR244). Greek national troops were withdrawn from Cyprus by January 1968, with the exception of small contingents provided for under the treaty of alliance, but, since Greece and Turkey could not agree on reciprocal arrangements for disarmament, UNFICYP did not take on the role of supervision of disarmament. Concerted UN attempts at peace negotiations, including the parties as well as Greece, Turkey and the UK, failed to resolve the conflict between the two communities of Cyprus. UNFICYP's mandate was thereafter extended by the Security Council every six months.

After a coup by the Greek Cypriot National Guard, supported by Greek military authorities, and the subsequent invasion and occupation of part of northern Cyprus by Turkish forces in July 1974, the guarantor powers Turkey, Greece and the UK agreed to an expanded role for UNFICYP (noted by the UN Security Council in SCR 355 of 1974) to establish and secure a security zone, or 'buffer zone', between the opposing parties and to protect Turkish Cypriot enclaves. The expanded mandate gave UNFICYP the force strength to maintain peace in the buffer zone. UNFICYP mapped the territory held by the opposing parties and set up observation posts to mark out and to secure the buffer zone. UNFICYP also took on a greater range of humanitarian functions, which included assisting the movement of people across the buffer zone, allowing farming in the buffer zone and provision of emergency medical services, and which were noted in SCR 359 (1974). Further international mediation efforts since 1974, firstly by the UK and subsequently under the auspices of the good offices of the UN Secretary-General and other attempts by the Commonwealth have failed to achieve a settlement.

The Security Council has continued to routinely extend UNFICYP's mandate each six months. UNFICYP operated with the full consent of all parties until 1983. On 15 November 1983 the Turkish Cypriots proclaimed a 'Turkish Republic of Northern Cyprus' ('TRNC'). The 'TRNC' was declared legally invalid by the Security Council and has been recognised only by Turkey. The 'TRNC' has not accepted Security Council resolutions extending UNFICYP's mandate.

From the beginning of efforts to agree on a constitutional structure for the new state, the three powers, Greece, Turkey and the UK, had different interests which impacted on the development of ethnic tension on the island. Given the continued partisan interests of two of the three 'guarantor powers', the trilateral mechanism established under the Zurich-London Accords proved inadequate as a preventive guarantee for the stability of the new state. Subsequent trilateral peacemaking faced the obstacles of a breakdown in community relations in scattered and mixed-population areas and the difficulty of imposing peace when community faith in the institutions of the new state had deteriorated, possibly beyond repair.

UNFICYP was established as a typical 'peacekeeping' force, i.e., impartial, with the consent of the governments concerned, and with provision to carry arms but only to use them in self-defence. It had no time limit (mandate renewals became routine), no timetable of action, and no built-in incentives or penalties for the parties. The force had no mandate to broker a solution to the conflict.

UNFICYP was not successful in attempts to encourage the parties to demobilise, dismantle fortifications or to restore normalised conditions. While ceasefires were negotiated in many locations, UNFICYP came under fire on numerous occasions and suffered many casualties. UNFICYP subsequently sought pragmatically to maintain the military status quo and prevent deterioration of the situation and, by such action, provide some degree of stability to aid the separate negotiation process.

UNFICYP's hold on the status quo began to slip after the failure of Greece and Turkey to agree on disarmament after the deterioration of the situation in 1967. Despite the subsequent addition of disarmament monitoring to UNFICYP's mandate, it was powerless to carry out this function. Arms imports and military build-ups by opposing sides in the following years, and up to the present day, have contributed to a worsening of the situation, making a political settlement much more difficult. Turkish forces of about 30,000 are stationed north of the buffer zone and the Cypriot National Guard has forces comprising 10,000 regulars and about 65,000 reserves. UNFICYP was unable to establish a demilitarised zone adjacent to the buffer zone. While the parties agreed in high-level talks in 1979 that an objective would be for a future federation to be demilitarised, for the time being fully-armed forces are deployed right up to the buffer zone in numerous locations. Despite arms embargoes by the United States and the United Kingdom against both sides, the international community has not prevented massive imports of arms into Cyprus.

The international hostilities on the island after the coup and invasion challenged UNFICYP's traditional 'peacekeeping' mandate. Rather than withdraw the force, the Security Council called on all parties to cooperate with UNFICYP. The conclusion of a ceasefire allowed UNFICYP to continue under the same mandate, with some additional responsibilities, even though the whole basis of the conflict had changed to one of occupation of part of a state by a foreign power. The Turkish forces established a new status quo on the island which UNFICYP, with its limited peacekeeping mandate, was not equipped to challenge. Arguably, UNFICYP's establishment and maintenance of the integrity of the buffer zone helped to legitimise the Turkish held zone in northern Cyprus by dividing the island from the time of the invasion on the basis of territory held by the opposing parties.

On the ground, UNFICYP established credibility by securing control of Nicosia International Airport and by adequately patrolling the buffer zone. The buffer zone was delineated by the UN in 1974 but not accepted by either side, thus contributing to instability. The original map drawn up in 1974 has been lost. Forces on either side periodically attempt to retake territory within the zone patrolled by UNFICYP, which varies from twenty metres to seven kilometres in width and totals about three per cent of the island's land area. UNFICYP operations have remained constrained by a lack of cooperation by the parties in facilitating access by UNFICYP to certain areas of the island, in particular in the northern zone.

The civilian police component of UNFICYP has generally been recognised as invaluable for functions such as oversight of law and order, oversight of searches conducted by the respective authorities at their request and helping to maintain the integrity of the buffer zone. Australia currently provides a civilian police contingent to UNFICYP of twenty Australian Federal Police officers.

From its establishment, the financing of UNFICYP was insecure, relying on voluntary contributions by force contributors. Other UN peacekeeping forces were funded either by assessed contributions or (at an earlier stage) from the UN regular budget. A financing deficit has been a constant feature of the force, in recent years creating difficulties for the UN in encouraging countries to contribute forces to UNFICYP and, recently, has been a factor in the withdrawal or scaling down of some troop contributions. On 27 May 1993, the Security Council decided (by SCR 831) to change the financing of UNFICYP to assessed contributions for costs in excess of those met by voluntary contributions from Cyprus and Greece, which total over half of UNFICYP's annual cost. At the same time a number of countries, including the United States and Russia, signalled their dissatisfaction with the failure of progress towards a settlement in Cyprus. The Resolution called for a comprehensive reassessment of UNFICYP at the time of the December 1993 mandate renewal, which has subsequently been postponed until February 1994.

The Turkish occupation of northern Cyprus and the subsequent proclamation of the 'TRNC' have continued to be unacceptable to the international community and multilateral peacemaking initiatives have been built on the premise that agreement could be reached on a bi-zonal, bi-communal, federal structure for a reunited Cyprus. Although leaders of the two communities pledged themselves in high-level talks in 1977 and 1979 to the establishment of a bi-communal, Federal Republic of Cyprus, negotiation positions of both sides have placed obstacles before such a settlement.

In recent UN-sponsored negotiations, the parties have concentrated on a number of proposed confidence-building measures (CBMs): establishment of a UN-administered bi-communal zone of Varosha, allowing the return of some of the town's original inhabitants, 90 per cent of whom were of Greek Cypriot origin, with guarantees to protect the economic interests of Turkish Cypriots and the reopening of Nicosia International Airport under UN administration.

While agreement by the two sides on even the proposed CBMs is proving difficult, the concept of CBMs raises an important tactical question: are CBMs likely to assist the peace process along the road to a full settlement (as intended); or are they likely to distract the parties from tackling the substantive issues; and, crucially, in the event that the CBMs should fail to be implemented or fail to be perceived as successful in implementation, would they set back the peace process?

In 1964 Cyprus had 123 ethnically mixed towns and villages. There is now one. Following the Turkish invasion of 1974, Greece, Turkey and the UK agreed in Geneva to allow Turkish Cypriots in the south of the island to move to the north and Greek Cypriots in the north to move to the south with the assistance of UNFICYP. UNFICYP took control from Greek and Greek Cypriot forces of all Turkish enclaves outside the northern zone. The Security Council noted these functions carried out by UNFICYP in SCR 355 (1974). UNFICYP also helped Maronite Greek Cypriots who had fled south to subsequently return to the north. UNFICYP monitors the voluntary nature of subsequent ethnic movements, which are rare. About 500 Greek Cypriots remain in the enclave of Karpas Peninsula in the north east of the island.

The facilitation of ethnic movements by UNFICYP was an assistance measure to save lives. In the course of time, UNFICYP's actions, constrained as they were by the peacekeeping mandate and the lack of a peace settlement between the parties, may in retrospect have made a return to pre-conflict ethnic populations non-viable. UNFICYP has, however, promoted a return to normal conditions, in particular encouraging bi-communal contacts, rapprochement between the communities, farming, small businesses and other humanitarian activities in the buffer zone. Among the growing number of humanitarian tasks included are medical treatment, payment of pensions, delivery of mail, provision of pharmaceuticals and family reunions. As a result of the 'TRNC' preventing applications by Turkish Cypriots living in the south for family visits to the north and preventing all Orthodox Greek Cypriots from entering the north, family reunions with enclaved members of both communities take place at the Nicosia checkpoint.

Although UNFICYP has played an important role in conflict management, it had no responsibility for reaching a political solution. The absence of a time limit or timetable of action (e.g., a plebiscite on the island's future) or any other built-in schedule of incentives or penalties for the parties to reach a political solution has meant that UNFICYP's presence has not given much impetus to finding a long term resolution of the Cyprus problem. The Security Council did take punitive measures against the 'TRNC' (principally non-recognition and consequent restrictions on its international contacts, such as air services), but not as part of any gradated scheme designed to induce the parties to work towards a political settlement. The existence of the force for such an extended period has reinforced the *de facto* division of Cyprus, and UNFICYP has been a part of arrangements which have divided the island for 29 years on the basis of territory held by the opposing sides. Each extra year of this arrangement arguably makes returning to one state on the island less politically realistic.

In terms of conflict management in the absence of a likely peace settlement, UNFICYP remains a necessary interim measure. Cypriot President Glafcos Clerides has expressed concern, as did his predecessor, at the possibility of an escalation in the conflict if UNFICYP were to cease or scale down its operations before a settlement had been achieved. Turkish Cypriot leader Denktash has stated that an observer force would be adequate.

It cannot be assumed that the patience of the international community is limitless. With prospects for an early political settlement in Cyprus uncertain and troop contributors owed large sums in arrears because of the former voluntary financing arrangement, a number of countries, Denmark, Finland, Canada, Sweden and the UK, have withdrawn or foreshadowed withdrawal or reduction of their forces from UNFICYP. However, a number of countries have provided replacement forces, in particular Argentina, which has provided a battalion to replace the departed Canadian battalion. The introduction of assessed contributions for UNFICYP may make it easier for the UN to find countries willing to contribute forces. The UN Security Council asked in SCR 889 (1993) that the Secretary-General keep under constant review the further possible restructuring of UNFICYP. The Security Council's thorough review of UNFICYP, scheduled for February 1994, which will include the future role of the UN, could usefully consider linking continuation of UNFICYP with progress on a peace settlement.

Overall, UNFICYP has been valuable as an exercise in conflict *management*. Its value as an element in conflict *resolution* is, however, dubious and raises questions about constructing mandates for peacekeeping operations which are open-ended and do not link the length of deployment of a UN force to steps towards longer-term resolution of underlying problems.

15 Traditional Peacekeeping: United Nations Truce Supervision Organisation and the Multinational Force and Observers

RICHARD LENNANE AND ROBERT NEWTON

Introduction

The following case studies focus on the United Nations Truce Supervision Organisation (UNTSO) and the non-UN Multinational Force and Observers in the Sinai (MFO), two examples of what could be termed 'traditional' peacekeeping operations, which involve the monitoring, supervising and verifying of agreements once reached. Despite obvious disparities between the organisations, there are areas of commonality in experience and performance which form an important basis for an evaluation of the relevance of these two organisations to future demands for peacekeeping operations.

Case study: United Nations Truce Supervision Organisation

Historical overview

Following the withdrawal of the British Mandate over Palestine and the proclamation of the State of Israel on 14 May 1948, Egyptian, Jordanian, Iraqi, Syrian and Lebanese forces moved against the newly established Israeli state. UNTSO - the United Nations' first peacekeeping operation - was created in 1948 as a 'Truce Commission' as part of United Nations' efforts to bring about a peaceful settlement to what was then called 'the question of Palestine'.

Initially a small force of about 90 observers attached to the United Nations Mediator in Palestine, the Truce Commission was originally composed of 'representatives of those members of the Security Council which have career consular offices in Jerusalem' (Belgium, France and the United States), and, with the Mediator, was under the control of the Security Council. Security Council Resolution 50, adopted on 29 May 1948, called for a four-week truce, and instructed that the Mediator, in concert with the Truce Commission, should supervise the truce and should be provided with a sufficient number of military observers for that purpose.

Following the resumption of hostilities between Israeli and Arab forces after the expiry of the four-week truce, the Security Council ordered a new ceasefire (Resolution 54) which was intended to last until a permanent peace settlement could be reached. The Truce Commission was to supervise this new truce, and was boosted in strength for this task. Despite several outbreaks of fighting during the remainder of 1948, and the assassination of the Mediator by Jewish terrorists, by early 1949 the UN had succeeded in concluding General Armistice Agreements between Israel and its four Arab neighbours: Egypt, Jordan, Lebanon and Syria. The Security Council, in Resolution 73, welcomed the Armistice Agreements, terminated the role of Mediator, and established UNTSO as an independent body (subsuming the Truce Commission) responsible to the Chief-of-Staff and through him directly to the Secretary-General of the United Nations. In this form, UNTSO supervised the Armistice Agreements, through the Mixed Armistice Commissions (MACs) that were established between Israel and each of the four Arab states, until the collapse of the Israel-Egypt Agreement and the Suez Crisis and War in 1956.

In the aftermath of the Suez War, the first United Nations Emergency Force (UNEF I) was created, the first UN peacekeeping *force*. UNTSO observers were attached to this force, and were later to be used in several other UN peacekeeping operations such as UNEF II, the UN Operation in the Congo (ONUC), UNIFIL and UNDOF. In this way, UNTSO was established as a pool of UN peacekeeping personnel which could be rapidly deployed to other operations.

The remaining three Armistice Agreements gradually deteriorated and finally collapsed in 1967 with the outbreak of the Six-Day War. UNTSO played an active role in observing and maintaining the ceasefire that halted hostilities in that war, and was redeployed widely on the Golan Heights and in the Suez canal area. Large scale hostilities commenced again in October 1973 with a surprise attack on Israel by Egypt and Syria. After successful Israeli counter-attacks, a ceasefire was concluded, and UNTSO continued its observation duties until it was effectively replaced in the Israel-Syria sector by the United Nations Disengagement Observer Force (UNDOF) and in the Israel-Egypt sector by UNEF II.

From 1973 onwards, UNTSO maintained a presence in the Israel-Syria, Israel-Egypt and Israel-Lebanon sectors, providing support and assistance to UNEF II, UNDOF, and (following the invasion of Lebanon by Israeli forces in 1978) the United Nations Interim Force in Lebanon (UNIFIL). UNTSO observers operated in Beirut through the 1980s, despite the non-cooperation of Israeli forces. Currently, UNTSO observers remain in the Sinai, the Golan Heights and Lebanon, complementing the activities of the MFO, UNDOF and UNIFIL, and acting as a pool of trained peacekeeping personnel for deployment to other UN operations.

Mandate and objectives

UNTSO has a continuing mandate: no renewal by the Security Council is required.

However, the mandate and objectives of UNTSO have changed several times in response to changing circumstances over its 45 year history. Despite changes in mandate and objectives, the following characteristics of UNTSO have remained constant: UNTSO observers are hired as individuals, on secondment from their own national armed forces - no formal agreement exists between the UN and the contributing governments; and UNTSO observers are unarmed and have no power of enforcement.

Financing

UNTSO is treated for budgetary purposes as a 'special mission', and is financed from the regular budget because it was established before the UN introduced special accounts for peacekeeping.

This form of financing was uncontroversial until 1963 when Soviet bloc countries, following an Opinion of the International Court of Justice on the matter of peacekeeping expenses, refused to pay the parts of their regular budget assessments which were for UNTSO or the UN Commission for the Unification and Rehabilitation of Korea (UNCURK).

However, UNTSO, as a small operation (annual budget around US$30 million), does not constitute a major expense for the UN, and its financing is presently not a significant issue.

Evaluation

Given the scale and complexity of the situation into which UNTSO was introduced, the scope of UNTSO was very restricted. This restricted scope gave UNTSO little chance of effecting a long term peace. In terms of its own modest mandate, however, UNTSO has been moderately successful. Once a ceasefire, truce or armistice had been reached, UNTSO observers were able to:

- move relatively free of restriction along ceasefire lines, and observe movements of troops and equipment and general behaviour of the parties;

TRADITIONAL PEACEKEEPING 283

- liaise with local commanders of the opposing forces, and serve as a means of communication between them;

- mediate and sometimes resolve minor disputes, such as movement of non-combatants across lines, and exchange of prisoners;

- provide relatively accurate and independent information on the situation to the Security Council.

The modest mandate, particularly the lack of enforcement powers and the fact that the observers were unarmed, also ensured UNTSO enjoyed a workable level of consent among its host states, who tolerated UNTSO's presence and usually cooperated, or at least did not interfere, with its operations.

Considered in the broader sense as a UN response to an international conflict of extraordinary complexity and vehemence, UNTSO was patently inadequate. There were a number of reasons for this. The situation of the Middle East as a major 'theatre' of the Cold War largely constricted the options of the Security Council, and precluded the establishment of a larger, more potent force with wider powers. The Soviet Union feared that an armed UN peacekeeping force would amount to a US-controlled military presence, and would lead to greater US influence in the region. There was never, at least until the 1970s, sufficient basis to the truces and armistices reached to enable a permanent settlement. Ceasefires were imposed by the Security Council, sometimes with the threat of enforcement action under Chapter VII of the Charter, but a failure to proceed with a satisfactory resolution of the underlying conflict left UNTSO supervising truces doomed to collapse.

In the light of the above, UNTSO's acceptance by its host states would seem to be more a case of tolerance of its ineffectual presence than support and cooperation.

The UN does not appear to have any long term plans for UNTSO: this raises the question of what to do with old peacekeeping operations that have outlived their original mandate. There is no formal mechanism for review of UNTSO, which means that UNTSO escapes the scrutiny of those who might otherwise ask whether its existence remains a necessity.

Case study: Multinational Force and Observers (MFO)

Historical overview

The MFO was established by agreement between Egypt, Israel and the United States following the Camp David Agreements of 1978 and the Egypt-Israel Peace Treaty of 1979. Annex I to the Peace Treaty detailed the terms of Israel's withdrawal from the Sinai, set the post-withdrawal levels of military personnel and equipment to be allowed in the Sinai and in Israel along the international border, and specified that the parties were to request the UN to 'provide forces and observers to supervise the implementation of this annex and employ their best effort to prevent any violation of its terms'.

Due to the weight of opposition to the Camp David Agreements (among Arab states and the Soviet bloc) it became apparent that obtaining Security Council approval for the stationing of a UN peacekeeping force in the Sinai would be difficult. Following the advice of the President of the Security Council in May 1981 that it would not be possible for the UN to provide a peacekeeping force, negotiations began between Israel, Egypt and the United States aimed at the creation of a multinational force and observer group outside the UN framework. On 3 August 1981, the three parties signed a Protocol which created the MFO, transferred the mission and responsibilities assigned to the UN by the Peace Treaty to the MFO, and established the principle that the two parties would agree on the nations from which the MFO contingents would be drawn.

The MFO took up its duties on 25 April 1982 when the Sinai was returned to Egyptian sovereignty. Comprising about 2,750 personnel from twelve countries, the MFO has continued in operation since that time, despite the assassination of its first Director-General, Leamon Hunt, in Rome in February 1984.

Mandate and objectives

As set out in Annex I of the Peace Treaty, the objectives of the MFO are:

- operations of checkpoints, reconnaissance patrols and observations posts along the international boundary and in specified areas of the Sinai;

- periodic verification of the implementation of the provisions of Annex I;

- additional verification within 48 hours after the receipt of a request from either party; and

- ensuring the freedom of navigation through the Strait of Tiran.

Although it includes a large contingent of troops, the MFO has no power of enforcement. The MFO has no fixed term.

Financing

The MFO is paid for in equal shares by Israel, Egypt and the United States, net of any other funding (such as donations from Germany and Japan). The MFO, being a relatively large scale military operation, is considerably more expensive than UNTSO, with an average annual budget of around US$80 million. The fact that only the parties to the Peace Treaty (and the US as broker of the Treaty) pay for its supervision enhances accountability and efficiency.

Evaluation

The immediate impression of the MFO is one of success. While relations between Israel and Egypt have fluctuated since 1979, the peace has held and there have been no serious incidents in the Sinai. Both Egypt and Israel have expressed their approval of the functioning of the MFO, which has carefully maintained its impartiality. The fact that Egypt and Israel continue to pay the considerable costs of the MFO with little complaint is an indication of their regard and commitment. The MFO reports misdemeanours about once a week, but all breaches so far have been of a technical nature (for example Israeli aircraft oversteering designated flight paths) and have been quickly rectified.

The MFO has survived strident opposition from other Arab states, and the assassination of its first Director-General. This would seem to indicate that the success of a peacekeeping force depends more on the commitment of its host countries to peace than to other international factors. The involvement of the UN is clearly not vital to the success of a peacekeeping operation, but does add a degree of political legitimacy.

The MFO appears to be an example of a timely and proportionate response to the need for independent supervision and maintenance of a sensitive peace treaty in a volatile environment. However, there are two external factors that have aided the success of the MFO: the sparse, flat desert terrain of the Sinai which makes observation easy and violations immediately apparent; and the relative simplicity of the situation (in comparison with that of many other peacekeeping operations): a simple bilateral peace treaty between two sovereign states, dealing with a single well-defined border, and without the complication of significant factions or militias backed by external sponsors.

The MFO has an indefinite mandate, and there is no timetable for its withdrawal. This is perhaps a weakness, as there is a danger that the MFO could become a self-perpetuating entity with little real purpose once peace is cemented. Disbanding the MFO is not likely to occur until a broader regional peace settlement is reached in the Middle East. The MFO's budget has diminished significantly every year since its inception, a sign that it is undergoing some reduction in scale, if not actually being phased out.

The MFO carries potential as a model for future peacekeeping and observer roles in other strategically sensitive parts of the region, such as the Golan Heights, or indeed elsewhere in the world. Advantages of its non-UN status include greater cost-effectiveness and a better integrated command and control structure and more effective and capable organisation overall, largely as a result of greater selectivity of participants.

Other UN Forces in the area

UNDOF

In May 1974, the Security Council set up the United Nations Disengagement Observer Force to monitor an agreement on the disengagement of forces between Israel and Syria which was signed at a meeting of the Military Working group of the Geneva Peace Conference on the Middle East. That agreement provided for a redeployment of the Israeli and Syrian forces, with the establishment of limited forces and armaments on both sides of the buffer zone and a UN force to supervise the implementation. The ceasefire became effective on the conclusion of the disengagement agreement and the area has remained generally quiet since then.

UNDOF, like UNTSO, is limited by its mandate to an observer role. Its success is mainly attributable to the interests of both the states directly involved to maintain the agreement and their capacity to maintain control over irregular forces not party to the agreement. Unlike UNTSO, it has to seek renewal of its mandate from the Security Council.

UNIFIL

On 15 March, 1978, following a Palestinian raid on Israel, Israeli forces invaded southern Lebanon. On 19 March, the Security Council adopted Resolution 425, calling on Israel to cease its military action against Lebanese territory. It also decided to establish immediately under its authority the United Nations Interim Force in Lebanon, for the purpose of confirming withdrawal of Israeli forces, ensuring international peace and security, and assisting the government of Lebanon in returning its effective authority to the area.

Arguably UNIFIL has had some effect in containing the area of conflict and preventing an escalation. It has, however, an unenforceable mandate, with no effective agreement between the states involved. The Lebanese government has been unable or unwilling to prevent irregular forces from striking at Israel, and the Israelis are still in Lebanon and intent on responding with increased force to any attack.

Conclusions

The immediately striking conclusion drawn from an examination of the above case studies is that the most crucial factor to the success of a 'traditional' peacekeeping operation is the commitment of the opposing parties to a peaceful end to their conflict. The fact that the MFO has been so successful owes far more to the fortitude of Anwar Sadat in seeking genuine peace with Israel despite unrelenting Arab hostility than to any aspect of its mandate, composition or organisation. Not only has the MFO succeeded without a UN mandate, it has done so in spite of active opposition (including sabotage and assassination) from non-participating Arab states.

In contrast, UNTSO, with a clear UN mandate and UN authority, on several occasions was simply overtaken by reality as essentially baseless truces inevitably collapsed into outright war. Clearly, truce observation is inherently of little use if the parties to the truce have no interest in - or are incapable of - converting it to a permanent peace treaty. This is, of course, true regardless of whether the observation is being done by a UN or non-UN body.

The ending of the Cold War holds promise for less fettered UN involvement in peacekeeping, particularly in the case of the Middle East. While the UN may have been seen as a discredited player in the Middle East in the past, due to its failure to respond impartially to developments such as the conclusion of the Israel-Egypt Peace Treaty, the removal of superpower rivalries holds promise for renewed legitimacy for the UN in the region. Although the MFO has made an undoubted contribution to international security, it detracts from the concept that the responsibility for maintaining global peace belongs to the world community as a whole, and its partisan composition created unease both within the region and further afield. An impartial UN, if such could be attained, remains the ideal vehicle for 'traditional' peacekeeping responses.

16 Kashmir : The Problem of United Nations Peacekeeping Contributing to Political 'Stasis'

FELICITY VOLK

The differences between India and Pakistan over the State of Jammu and Kashmir (referred to here as Kashmir) remain as they were when Sir Owen Dixon abandoned his United Nations-sponsored efforts at mediation in 1951. Neither side is prepared to accept certain elements of the main UN proposals as they now stand. India clearly has no intention of conducting a plebiscite in Kashmir - it is well aware of the likelihood of an unfavourable response - and the other aspects of the UN resolutions (including troop withdrawals) which it cannot accept are secondary to that. Pakistan could well have major difficulty in accepting provisions such as the prior withdrawal of its forces and the exclusion of the 'Azad' (free) Kashmir government in Pakistan-held Kashmir from the process. The one thing which has become clear over the years, as the Kashmir dispute has dragged on, is that a significant and apparently growing section of the Kashmiri population is in favour, not of acceding to Pakistan, but of independence. Such an outcome would be more likely to be acceptable to Pakistan than to India.

The failure, over 46 years, to achieve progress towards a resolution on the Kashmir issue begs a number of questions:

- Why has UN intervention and the UN presence in Kashmir failed to achieve a settlement in Kashmir?

- Could a different UN response have prompted a permanent settlement?

- To what degree have other factors (including the domestic political situations of both India and Pakistan) impinged on the ability of the UN to promote an enduring political solution to the Kashmir conflict?

Origins

Since 1947, conflict in Kashmir has occurred both in the context of cross-border skirmishes between India and Pakistan and, at times of greatest tension, full-scale war (in September 1965 and in December 1971 when India supported East Pakistan - now Bangladesh - in its independence movement), and in the context of civil strife. Through the 1950s and 1960s, political discontent with the central Indian government's attempts to control politics in the state grew. Militant organisations became increasing active, organising attacks, kidnappings, assassinations, sabotage and bombings. Pro-independence and pro-plebiscite activists were jailed. The conflict escalated sharply in January 1990 when government troops launched a major operation against militant groups in Kashmir. The military offensive was marked by widespread human rights violations including a campaign of raids designed to capture suspected militants and terrorise civilian sympathisers.

The origins of the conflict in Kashmir lie in the subcontinent's partition in 1947 which created the independent states of India and Pakistan. As a result of the partition, hundreds of nominally independent 'princely states' were absorbed into two new nations. However, Kashmir's Hindu ruler refused to accede to either nation, apparently in the hope that the state might be permitted to remain independent. In late 1947, an invasion by Pakistani tribesmen and an uprising among Kashmiri Moslems in the western regions of Kashmir compelled Kashmir's ruler to seek the assistance of Prime Minister Jawaharlal Nehru of India, who agreed to send troops only if Kashmir formally acceded to India. On 27 October 1947, the ruler agreed to Kashmir's accession to India, on the condition that the state be permitted to retain its own constitution. Indian troops succeeded in halting the Pakistani forces, driving them back to the western third of the state, which then acceded to Pakistan as Azad Kashmir.

At the time, British authorities stated that the question of Kashmir's accession should be settled by a plebiscite as soon as law and order was reinstated and the invading forces had left. But the plebiscite was never held. The Indian government argued first that the essential precondition to a plebiscite, the withdrawal of Pakistani troops from Azad Kashmir, had not been met, and later that the Kashmiri people had effectively ratified accession by voting in local elections and adopting a state constitution.

The Kashmir question first came before the Security Council in January 1948, when India complained that tribesmen and others were invading Kashmir, resulting in extensive fighting. India alleged that Pakistan had assisted and participated in the invasion. Pakistan denied these allegations and declared that Kashmir's accession to India in 1947 was illegal.

In 1948, when the Kashmir conflict was being discussed in the Security Council, the British representative, Mr Noel Baker, described it as 'the greatest and gravest single issue in international affairs'. The unsettled Kashmir question continues to be recognised by the international community as one of the most volatile and serious disputes in the South Asian region. The United Nations worked out a solution for Kashmir. It was originally agreed to by the parties concerned. Yet the Kashmir conflict is one which more than forty years of UN scrutiny and resolutions have failed effectively to address. Twice the United Nations achieved a cessation of fighting in Kashmir. Both times it established a ceasefire, frequently violated, for the attempted maintenance of which it provides machinery at a considerable cost. However, the experience of Kashmir has shown that a ceasefire is not a substitute for settlement. Inherent in it is the prospect of a renewal of hostilities. A ceasefire not quickly followed by settlement is a half measure. It indicates that there has been an inconclusive war and underlines the fact that there is still a dispute to be settled. While it cannot be argued that the UN has been satisfied with the mere achievement of a precarious ceasefire in Kashmir, UN efforts have failed to progress beyond poorly-enforced ceasefire arrangements.

The UN Resolutions and peacekeeping operations

There has been a considerable number of UN resolutions on Kashmir since 1948. The most recent, Security Council Resolution 307, was in 1971. The question of Kashmir remains on the agenda of the Security Council.

Most of the resolutions have been variations on the theme of appealing to both sides to withdraw their forces to the ceasefire line and to negotiate, and all of them flow from the main resolution passed by the UN on the Kashmir dispute, Security Council Resolution 47 of 21 April 1948. Essentially, Resolution 47 called for :

- cessation of hostilities to enable the conduct of a free and impartial plebiscite, to decide whether Kashmir should accede to either India or Pakistan;

- the Government of Pakistan to use its best endeavours to secure the withdrawal from Kashmir of tribesmen and Pakistani nationals not normally resident therein who had entered the state for the purpose of fighting;

- once Pakistani withdrawal was under way and the ceasefire effective, the Government of India to withdraw their own forces from Kashmir except for the minimum strength required to maintain law and order, with the minimum number retained in forward areas;

- the Government of India to undertake that there would be a plebiscite as soon as possible on the question of the accession of the state to India or Pakistan.

The significant points of this resolution were that Kashmir was to be offered only the limited option of accession to either India or Pakistan; that Pakistan was to withdraw all its armed forces from Kashmir; that Indian forces would move into the areas vacated by the Pakistanis; and that India was to have the only (but limited) armed forces in Kashmir until after the plebiscite.

Following the adoption of Resolution 47, both the Indian and Pakistani Governments notified the UN that they were unable to commit themselves to acceptance of certain specific parts of it.

- Pakistan wanted an impartial administration under UN auspices established immediately.

- India wanted the provisional government of Kashmir converted into a Council of Ministers to conduct both elections for the National Assembly and the plebiscite (under the aegis of the United Nations Commission for India and Pakistan, UNCIP, established by Security Council Resolution 39 of 20 January 1948).

- Pakistan wanted India to withdraw its forces from Kashmir.

- India maintained that all its forces had to remain in the state until the dispute was resolved.

Both India and Pakistan did, however, accept a subsequent UNCIP resolution of 13 August 1948 which was in essence a modified version of Security Council Resolution 47. The UNCIP resolution provided for a ceasefire, prohibited both sides from taking measures which might augment the military potential of their forces in Kashmir, required Pakistan to use its 'best endeavours' to secure the withdrawal of armed Pakistani nationals and tribesmen from Kashmir, and provided for the evacuated territory to be administered by the local authorities under UNCIP surveillance. India again was to begin a staged withdrawal of the bulk of its forces from Kashmir, retaining 'the minimum strength of its forces considered (by UNCIP) necessary to assist local authorities in the observance of law and order'. The resolution reaffirmed the wish of both Pakistan and India that the future status of Kashmir should be determined in accordance with the will of its people and stated both Governments' agreement to enter into consultations with UNCIP to determine 'fair and equitable conditions whereby such free expression will be assured'.

The ceasefire did not come into effect until 31 December 1948. In the meantime, the Indian position had hardened, following Pakistan's admission that it had moved regular troops into Kashmir to localise the conflict and prevent Indian troops from coming into contact with Pakistan's frontier. Both sides reverted to the policy of demanding the withdrawal of the other side's forces before negotiations could begin. In addition, Pakistan sought to have the Government of Azad Kashmir included as a party to any negotiations.

A further UNCIP resolution (5 January 1949) which sought to determine details for the implementation of a plebiscite was accepted by both India and Pakistan, but no progress was made. However, both countries agreed to a UNCIP plan for the organisation and deployment of the military observers in the area. These observers, under the command of the UNCIP Military Adviser, formed the nucleus of the United Nations Military Observers Group in India and Pakistan (UNMOGIP). The observers were divided into two groups, one attached to each army. The number of observers fluctuated in relation to the level of hostility between India and Pakistan. UNMOGIP's task was to accompany the local authorities in their investigations, gather as much information as possible and report impartially on violations of the ceasefire line. UNMOGIP had no authority or function entitling it to enforce or prevent any situation, or to try to ensure that the ceasefire was respected. Its presence acted to some extent as a deterrent, but that was not always the case.

The Karachi Agreement of July 1949 established a ceasefire line and specified that UNCIP would station observers where necessary. The Agreement detailed prohibited activities including the strengthening of defences and introduction of additional military potential into Kashmir. After the signing of the Agreement, the ceasefire line became more stable. Incidents were generally minor until the hostilities of 1965.

From early 1949, India increasingly procrastinated on the efforts of the Security Council to implement a plebiscite in Kashmir. On 12 December 1949, UNCIP stated in a report to the Security Council that the possibilities of mediation open to it had been exhausted. It recommended the appointment of a single person as a mediator in a bid to maximise flexibility in the negotiations. Neither General Andrew McNaughton (Canada) nor his successor, Sir Owen Dixon (Australia) met with any success. The latter recommended that, as all possibilities of mediation had been exhausted, India and Pakistan should be left to negotiate a settlement between themselves. His final proposals, for a limited plebiscite in the Vale of Kashmir and the partitioning of the rest of the state, were rejected by both sides.

1965 Indo-Pakistan war

Strained relations between India and Pakistan led to the eruption of military hostilities on a large scale along the ceasefire line in Kashmir in 1965. After hostilities spread to the international border between India and West Pakistan, the Security Council adopted a resolution which demanded that a ceasefire take effect and that all armed personnel be withdrawn. The United Nations India Pakistan Observation Mission (UNIPOM), an administrative adjunct to UNMOGIP, was established as a temporary measure for the sole purpose of supervising the ceasefire, but UNIPOM had no authority to order a cessation of firing. Ceasefire violations continued to occur until 1966, despite UN resolutions calling on India and Pakistan to cooperate with the UN and cease all military activity.

Tashkent Agreement

The Tashkent Agreement signed by India and Pakistan in 1966 provided for the withdrawal of all armed personnel, and a general ceasefire observed by UNMOGIP and UNIPOM. Completion of withdrawal in 1966 led to the termination of UNIPOM and from that date until 1971 UNMOGIP functioned on the pre-established basis of the Karachi Agreement.

1971 War

When tension mounted in 1971, the UN Secretary-General expressed concern about the situation and offered his good offices to avoid further deterioration. From October onwards, both India and Pakistan greatly reinforced their forces along the ceasefire line and both sides admitted that violations of the Karachi Agreement were being committed, but they continued to use the machinery of UNMOGIP to prevent escalation. However, hostilities broke out in December. In response to a Security Council resolution calling for adherence to a ceasefire, India stated that Kashmir was an integral part of India and in order to avoid bloodshed, India had respected the ceasefire line supervised by UNMOGIP, but there was a need to make some adjustments in that line and India intended to discuss and settle the matter directly with Pakistan. Conversely, Pakistan insisted that Kashmir was disputed territory whose status should be settled by agreement under the aegis of the Security Council.

In 1972, the Secretary-General reported that, while the Pakistan military authorities continued to submit to UNMOGIP complaints of ceasefire violations by the other side, the Indian military authorities had stopped doing so. India claimed that cross-border disputes had been satisfactorily settled at flag meetings and pressed for direct bilateral negotiations with Pakistan to negotiate a solution to the conflict. India's position was that as a result of the 1971 war, the Karachi Agreement ceased to be operative and the mandate of UNMOGIP had lapsed. Pakistan claimed that the military disputes had not been settled and that investigation by UNMOGIP and continued activation of the UNMOGIP machinery was required.

The Simla Agreement

In July 1972, following the Indo-Pakistani conflict of 1971, India and Pakistan agreed at Simla on a Line of Control to separate the parties to the dispute. The Simla Agreement envisaged that India and Pakistan would 'settle their differences by peaceful means through bilateral negotiations or by any other peaceful means mutually agreed between them'. It is upon this part of the preamble to the Simla Agreement that India relies in its efforts to rebut Pakistani attempts to 'internationalise' the dispute.

The Simla Agreement remains central to the Indian Government's policy approach to a settlement on Kashmir with Pakistan. The Agreement, and not the UN resolutions, is the starting point for India. India has been able to use it as the reference point for the evolution of its Kashmir policy towards a position where it effectively discounts the legitimacy of UN involvement in arriving at an eventual solution to the conflict, and by extension, that of any other third party or agency. As far as India is concerned attempts at outside intervention in the dispute will only derogate from the will of the parties to the conflict to come to a settlement on their own terms. India insists upon cessation of external support for terrorism in Kashmir, that is, active Pakistani support for militants in Kashmir, before it will commence dialogue with Pakistan.

Pakistan, for its part, points to another section of the preamble to the Agreement, which reads in part : '... the principles and purposes of the Charter of the United Nations shall govern the relations between the two countries'. Pakistan argues that this places the entire Simla Agreement in the context of the United Nations Charter and asserts that, in any case, no bilateral agreement can preclude the right of any independent nation to have recourse to the UN, under its Charter. In its most recent statements, Pakistan has said that while proposing bilateral discussions under the Simla Agreement, Pakistan's view was the UN Security Council Resolution calling for a plebiscite in Kashmir remains valid. Pakistan does not regard the Simla Agreement and the UN resolutions as being mutually exclusive. It views the Simla Agreement as providing the means to negotiate and resolve the dispute, and the resolutions as providing the framework for the settlement.

The positions of India and Pakistan on the functioning of UNMOGIP remain unchanged. Since January 1972, India has lodged no complaints and has restricted the activities of the United Nations' observers on the Indian side of the Line of Control. India has, however, continued to provide accommodation, transport and other facilities to UNMOGIP.

The conflict between India and Pakistan over Kashmir is now that of a military stalemate on the Line of Control. The focus has shifted to the struggle within Indian controlled Kashmir by Kashmiris for independence. On the international agenda this surfaces as two elements : allegations by Pakistan (and by international human rights organisations) of human rights violations by Indian security forces in Kashmir, and accusations by India of Pakistan Government meddling in India's internal affairs by supporting terrorism or militants in Kashmir.

Cost and size of current UNMOGIP operations

In its current form, UNMOGIP is a modest program. Thirty-nine military observers are now shared between the Indian and Pakisitani sides of the

Line of Control in eleven or twelve stations which, with the exceptions of the two most northerly stations, operate all year round. The group comprises officers drawn from Belgium, Italy, Uruguay, Chile, Sweden, Finland, Denmark and Norway, supported by 45 administrative personnel. UNMOGIP operates with an annual budget in the order of US$7 million which is small relative to other current UN peacekeeping operations. UNMOGIP is financed from the regular budget of the UN and submits regular reports to the UN Secretary-General. Australia maintained contributions to UN peacekeeping operations in Kashmir for just on 40 years.

Assessment of the UN response

Following 46 years of stalemate, any reinvigorated role for the UN would have to begin from:

- an analysis of UN involvement in Kashmir (both in terms of its political intervention through various resolutions, and its peacekeeping role in the provision of observer missions);

- an assessment of the degree to which UN activity (and its inability appropriately to address the Kashmir conflict) has perpetuated, if not contributed to the political stasis currently afflicting Kashmir; and

- an evaluation of the other factors which have operated to prevent the achievement of a permanent settlement, or even progress towards such a settlement.

Timeliness and magnitude of UN response

The record of UN activity in Kashmir is a chronicle of passive multilateral involvement in the conflict of two intransigent parties. If there ever was a time (and this is highly uncertain) for more active UN involvement it was at, or shortly after, partition in 1947 before Indian and Pakistani attitudes had hardened and there may have been more potential to manoeuvre. UN activities with regard to Kashmir were and continue to be minimal. The Simla Agreement of 1972 was negotiated bilaterally without UN involvement and the UN has since maintained little more than a 'watching' brief as far as Kashmir is concerned: UN resolutions encourage both parties towards peaceful negotiation and the long term UN observer presence has sought to promote an environment conducive to such negotiations. Beyond UNMOGIP's modest (and not always successful) role in keeping the peace, it is difficult to envisage a scenario where the UN could play a more active role to bring about a solution in Kashmir. Indian and Pakistani attitudes on the subject are so far apart that after 46 years neither party to the conflict has been able to seriously consider the variety of compromises suggested by UN mediators.

Protecting national sovereignty

Sir Owen Dixon observed in his report to the UN (1950-51) that a plebiscite was not possible because India and Pakistan had failed to agree on matters, including demilitarisation, which were preliminary to even the commencement of necessary arrangements for holding elections. A further difficulty of the plebiscite solution was ensuring that it would be held in conditions which would make it an effective means of ascertaining the real will of the Kashmiris. India's strong notions of sovereignty, its unwillingness to accept any interference with or restriction of the powers of the government in Kashmir, either in reference to the use of Armed Forces or to the civil administration, would have been a stumbling block to guaranteeing free and fair elections. Further, it was Dixon's view that a plebiscite was not appropriate in view of Kashmir's lack of geographic, demographic or economic unity. He said Kashmir 'is an agglomerate of territories brought under the political power of one Maharaja. That is the unity it possesses'. That unifying force has been withdrawn and if, as a result of a plebiscite Kashmir as an entirety passed to India, a large influx of refugee Muslims would be expected to cross to Pakistan. If the result favoured Pakistan, Hindus and Sikhs would move to India. It was Dixon's assessment that 'the interest of the Kashmiri people, the justice as well as the permanence of the settlement, and the imperative necessity of avoiding another refugee problem all point to the wisdom of adopting partition as the principle of settlement and of abandoning that of an overall plebiscite'.

Dixon's ultimate conclusion was that India and Pakistan should be left to themselves to settle the Kashmir dispute. During the times of actual conflict it had been appropriate for the UN to intervene and propose terms to stop the hostilities, but, the UN having exhaustively investigated possible methods of settlement, the initiative was returned to India and Pakistan to determine how to dispose of Kashmir. Similarly, while Dixon conceded that in 1951 UNMOGIP was a necessary component of the ceasefire arrangements, he underlined that the observer forces should not continue in Kashmir indefinitely: eventually the question of their withdrawal would have to be settled in consultation with the two Governments. Forty years later, UNMOGIP is still active along the ceasefire line, although, in keeping with India's view that Kashmir is a conflict in which the UN has no further role to play, UNMOGIP personnel in India are confined to their field stations and much of UNMOGIP's assessment of Indian activities is based on press reports or information provided by the Indian authorities.

UNMOGIP's achievements

- Credit for the relative peace along the Line of Control since 1971 can be attributed in part to UNMOGIP's presence. The region where heavy fighting has occurred in recent years, the Siachen Glacier, is well beyond the presence of UNMOGIP observers.

- UNMOGIP is essentially a trip-wire. It would be difficult for either side to launch an attack and escape the opprobrium of the international community because the presence of UNMOGIP observers would provide an independent assessment of events. Pakistan's more cooperative attitude to UNMOGIP's presence reflects, at least in part, the fact that it is in a relatively weaker position militarily and has more to gain from the restraining influence which UNMOGIP observers provide.

- Nevertheless, the significance of UN activities in Kashmir in keeping the Indian and Pakistani armies apart is open to argument. One crucial factor has been that the balance of military force makes the achievement of any significant gains through military means improbable. At best, UNMOGIP's presence has discouraged border skirmishing which might then have escalated into a major confrontation. However, there are daily exchanges of small arms fire, and sometimes artillery, along the ceasefire line. On a number of occasions, including two incidents in the first six months of 1993, UNMOGIP observers have been fired upon, despite their presence having been notified and their UN flag being displayed prominently. The effectiveness of UNMOGIP has been curtailed by the antipathy with which India regards the UN observers' presence. The UN experience in monitoring the ceasefire in Kashmir demonstrates the need for full cooperation from all parties involved.

Current international attitudes to the UN resolutions - political reticence

International reluctance to take a position on Kashmir and the UN resolutions is unmistakable. International attention has focused on Kashmir as a result of representations by Pakistan and human rights organisations about allegations of Indian atrocities in Kashmir and representations by India about the interference of Pakistan in the internal affairs of a sovereign state by supporting terrorism in Kashmir. The very limited use that has been made of the UN resolutions in response to these concerns derives not only from the outdated nature of the resolutions themselves, but from the realisation that Pakistan's insistence on them is disingenuous. Pakistan's insistence on 'the UN resolutions' is largely related to the call contained therein for a plebiscite.

The central UN resolution, as it stands, can be supported by neither the Indians nor the Pakistanis. India will not agree to a plebiscite and does not want the issue internationalised because this would hinder Indian efforts to manage the issue. In the event that the matter did come before the UN, Pakistan would also have difficulty with some of the aspects of the issue, such as any requirement for the prior withdrawal of all Pakistani forces not indigenous to Kashmir, and even possibly the question of genuine self-determination for the Kashmiris. Should India agree to the issue being raised in the UN, this could considerably dampen Pakistan's traditional enthusiasm for UN involvement.

Overriding domestic political concerns - impediments to conflict resolution

Domestic political considerations prevent either India or Pakistan from negotiating a settlement along lines detailed in the UN resolutions, or the Simla Accord.

- For India, the loss of the disputed territory would have a destabilising effect and would be likely to bring down the Government which let it come about. Successive Indian Governments have had electorates in which powerful groups have opposed any concessions to, let alone real rapprochement with, Pakistan. Chief among these has been the Bharatiya Janata Party (BJP), the main opposition party which has a Hindu fundamentalist platform. The party presently in power in India, Congress, is equally inclined to use Kashmir as an issue from which it can gain domestic political mileage, drawing on general public disaffection with Pakistan.

- Separatist groups in India would adopt concessions on Kashmir as a clear precedent for their own campaigns for independence. Their causes would be refreshed and enhanced by the example of Kashmir.

- Finally, the loss of India's one Moslem-majority state would effectively put paid to the efforts by successive Indian Governments to build India's identity as a secular, rather than a Hindu, state - with all that would imply for the non-Hindu minorities in India. Were Kashmir to be granted independence (or allowed to join Pakistan, though current opinion is that, in the event of a plebiscite being held, the vote would be for independence) because it had a Moslem majority, it would be tantamount to conceding the notion of religious states.

- Likewise for a Pakistani Government to compromise on the highly sensitive issue of Kashmir, particularly Pakistani (Azad) Kashmir and the Vale of Kashmir, would be political suicide. The Kashmir conflict is one of the most sensitive domestic issues dealt with by any Pakistani leader. Compromise might, however, be possible on the status of the Hindu majority areas of Jammu and the Buddhist region of Ladakh.

- In addition to the sentiments of the general populace with respect to India, Islamic fundamentalists in Pakistan staunchly reject the possibility of any compromise with India.

- A compromise on Kashmir would also require the support of the military which still maintains considerable political influence within the Government of Pakistan.

UN peacekeeping as a factor contributing to political stasis in the Kashmir conflict

It is an unfortunate historical fact that in Kashmir both sides have some historical justification for their position and there is no compromise solution which, even if it could somehow be imposed, would be acceptable to both parties. In the light of the intransigence of both India and Pakistan on the Kashmir issue, it would be difficult to sustain the view that UNMOGIP's presence (similarly UNCIP and UNIPOM involvement) and the UN's general responses to the Kashmir conflict (both through the adoption of resolutions encouraging peaceful negotiations and the appointment of mediators to assist those negotiations), have contributed to political stasis. It could, however, be argued that the mere existence of the UN resolutions has perpetuated the inherent political stasis by providing Pakistan with a counter-position to India's insistence on a bilateral solution.

It is open to debate that the UN could have responded to the emerging conflict over Kashmir in a more pre-emptive fashion in 1947, but the sorts of religious, ethnic and political factors that exist today, existed equally at that time. The past 46 years have served merely to hone areas of dissension. The UN's inclination to tread carefully, respect for the sovereignty of India and Pakistan, and the very limited mandate of the UN observer missions have all been factors (and not necessarily intrinsically negative ones) which have detracted from the effectiveness of a UN response to the Kashmir conflict. The Kashmir problem has been exacerbated by factors unrelated to UN operations, and extrinsic to UN mechanisms. Indian and Pakistani domestic concerns, perceptions of territorial integrity, efforts to avoid political instability and communal discord, and irreconcilable analyses of historical disputes have, more than any action taken by the UN, contributed to political stasis over Kashmir.

On the question of political stasis, the UN presence has been largely irrelevant. To say that UN involvement has contributed to a stalemate over Kashmir, it would be necessary to establish that stasis would have been less likely had the UN either avoided involvement in the dispute, or adopted a radically different approach to settling the conflict. In that the UN has acted as a buffer-zone, it could be argued that:

- *de facto* recognition has been given to an artificially created border (the Line of Control) which is disputed by nations on both sides of the line;

- UNMOGIP has prevented an all out confrontation which might have settled the Kashmir situation one way or another, at least in terms of territorial boundaries (though an enduring solution would still have required the negotiation of a settlement acceptable to all components of the Kashmiri population). For example, in 1965 and 1971, the averting of long term large-scale hostilities, and the re-establishment of the Line of Control, were partly the result of UN intervention. However, as has been previously highlighted, the balance of military force, more than any other factor, has deterred India and Pakistan from engaging in more serious hostilities.

Conclusions

It cannot be convincingly argued that UN peacekeeping has contributed to political stasis in the Kashmir conflict. What is clear from the Kashmir case is that for UN peacekeepers to play an effective role in restoring and maintaining a ceasefire, and promoting an atmosphere in which tension is readily contained and political negotiation possible, the peacekeepers must not only have a sufficiently wide mandate but must command the full cooperation of the parties to the dispute.

In the case of Kashmir, neither side fully accepts substantial elements of the UN proposal for negotiating a settlement, and the Kashmiris themselves appear increasingly interested in independence rather than swapping Indian rule for that of Pakistan.

The UN might have been able to intervene decisively in the relatively fluid circumstances applying immediately after the separation of India and Pakistan in 1947. But since then positions have hardened as India and Pakistan have consolidated their national strength. The only breakthrough - the 1972 Simla agreement - was achieved by the two countries without UN assistance.

Without a UN presence, without UN resolutions, the Kashmir problem would not be significantly different from that which exists today. The UN resolutions may have pointed the way toward areas of negotiation and compromise, and UNMOGIP has played a very modest role in keeping the peace on the ground, making it difficult for any party to resume hostilities without attracting international opprobrium. But it is difficult to envisage a scenario in which the UN could play a more active role: we agree with Sir Owen Dixon's view that India and Pakistan have to be left to themselves to settle the dispute, and the dynamics of their relationship - and their own internal politics - will be more important factors than any UN input.

Nevertheless, the international community's response to the conflict requires reassessment in view of an added dimension (albeit an unlikely scenario) that tension between India and Pakistan could be played out in the nuclear arena. In addition to the international security implications of the threat posed by India's and Pakistan's nuclear programs, India and Pakistan devote a large proportion of their budgets to their military establishments: Kashmir is a large part of the reason. Both countries have been recipients of foreign aid for a considerable period - funds which could have been utilised more effectively had the countries' military expenditure been smaller.

The case study of UN involvement in Kashmir is, therefore, important both in terms of the general lessons that it offers - the limits on effective UN action when the main internal and external parties to a dispute are equivocal about a negotiated settlement - and the more specific need to reassess possibilities for multilateral intervention in the Kashmir conflict itself as part of international concern to develop the role of the UN in preventive diplomacy, to avert a nuclear risk and to ensure the equitable use of development assistance.

17 United Nations Angola Verification Mission II

DOROTHY HOLT

The resumption of civil war in Angola following UN-monitored elections in September 1992 raised serious questions about UNAVEM II's mandate and the political context in which it operates, both internal and external.

The course of events

The first UN Angola Verification Mission (UNAVEM I) was established by UN Security Council Resolution 626 (1988), with a mandate to verify the phased and total withdrawal of Cuban troops from Angola in accordance with a timetable agreed between the Governments of Angola and Cuba. The withdrawal was completed by May 1991 and on 6 June 1991 the Secretary-General of the United Nations reported to the Security Council that UNAVEM I had carried out, fully and effectively, its mandate.

Following the conclusion of the Bicesse Peace Accords signed in May 1991 between the Angolan Government and the opposition movement UNITA, which provided for a ceasefire following sixteen years of civil war and Angola's first multi-party elections, the Angolan government requested that the UN verify 'whether the monitoring groups are assuming their responsibilities' stipulated under the Bicesse Accords. Security Council Resolution 696 (1991) authorised a new mandate for the UN operation, thereafter designated UNAVEM II, for a period of seventeen months. The tasks of the mission included verifying that the demobilisation and confinement to assembly areas of troops was being monitored by joint teams of the two Angolan parties, as provided for in the Bicesse Accords, and monitoring the selection of troops to join the new Angolan Armed

Forces. The authorised strength of the force was 350 military observers, 90 police observers, a civilian air unit, a medical unit, 90 international and 120 local civilian staff.

The Angolan Government further requested, in December 1991, that the UN observe the national elections, and the Security Council, in Resolution 747 (1992), enlarged UNAVEM II's mandate to include election observation and verification. The strength of the police contingent was subsequently increased to 126 officers and the electoral division fielded 400 electoral observers during the polling.

The elections were held on 29-30 September 1992 and were monitored by about 400 further observers representing the Organisation of African Unity (OAU), the International Parliamentary Union, European parliamentarians (AWEPPAA) and individual observers representing various non-governmental groups from countries such as Japan and the United States. The elections proceeded remarkably well, with a significant and generally enthusiastic turnout, and were declared to be free and fair by the UN Secretary-General's Special Representative, Ms Margaret Anstee.

The ruling Popular Movement for the Liberation of Angola party (MPLA) was returned with a majority in the National Assembly (129 of the 220 elected seats). Presidential elections held at the same time did not give either candidate the outright 50 per cent win required by the Angolan Constitution, so a run-off election had to be held. The MPLA leader, Jose Eduardo Dos Santos, won 49.57 per cent of the vote and Dr Jonas Savimbi, the leader of the National Union for the Total Independence of Angola (UNITA), gained 40.07 per cent. Despite widespread acceptance that the poll was fair, Savimbi refused to accept the results of the election, claiming extensive irregularities.

Early October 1992 saw UNITA withdraw its forces from the unified army and attack Government positions. Major outbreaks of violence followed, resulting in the deaths of hundreds of people, particularly in the capital Luanda where civilians were heavily involved in the fighting and several senior UNITA leaders were killed or captured.

On 1 November 1992, a UN-brokered ceasefire was agreed to at talks in Lobito but within days UNITA renewed its attacks. On 6 November, UN Under Secretary-General, Mr Marrack Goulding, arrived in Angola to assist with efforts to commence talks between President Dos Santos and Savimbi as a crucial first step to bringing hostilities to an end and creating suitable conditions for the second round of elections for the Presidency. He met separately with Dos Santos and Savimbi but both adamantly refused to meet face to face. South African Foreign Minister Pik Botha and an OAU mediating group led by Zimbabwean President Robert Mugabe attempted unsuccessfully to broker a ceasefire and facilitate talks between the two leaders.

The two sides held a round of UN-sponsored peace talks in Addis Ababa in late January 1993 but failed to agree to a ceasefire. The second round of talks scheduled for February were postponed and then aborted when the bulk of UNITA's delegation failed to appear.

In circumstances of escalating conflict, on 29 January 1993 the Security Council, in Resolution 804, endorsed a three-month mandate for a reduced UNAVEM II and on 30 April, in Resolution 823, the Security Council rolled over the mandate for a further month. Following Resolution 834 of 1 June 1993, the force strength fell to 50 military observers, eighteen civilian police, 43 international civilian staff, eleven paramedics and necessary local staff largely concentrated in Luanda.

Fighting continued on a large scale throughout the country. The second largest city, Huambo, was eventually won by UNITA after a particularly prolonged, brutal and destructive battle costing thousands of mainly non-combatant lives.

On 19 May, after six weeks of discussion in Abidjan, Ivory Coast, UN-mediated talks failed to reach a ceasefire agreement. The talks were monitored by representatives of the Observer states to the peace process - the United States, Russia and Portugal. The Observer states had prepared a set of principles to facilitate a ceasefire, including a recommendation for a significant increase in the UN involvement in Angola. The Government side agreed to sign the set of principles, entailing incorporation of UNITA in most levels of occupied areas. The following day UNITA re-intensified its attacks on various targets including the key oil city of Soyo in the north-west.

The present situation

Reports vary but estimates are that over 100,000 people (mainly non-combatants) have been killed since the country returned to full-scale war in December 1992. UNITA is reported to control over 60 per cent of Angola's territory, a drop from approximately 75 per cent some months ago; and original estimates of UNITA control over 40-50 per cent of the population have diminished to 35 per cent as refugees continue to seek safety in Government held areas. Fighting since the elections has focused on cities and infrastructure and the level of resulting destruction is worse than that following the sixteen years of civil war prior to the Bicesse Accords.

The humanitarian situation in Angola is grave, with an estimated three million people threatened with hunger and disease. The World Food Program (WFP) remains the only relief agency operational on a large scale within the country, although its relief flights have been attacked and cancelled. The cancellations were not only a result of UNITA's attacks against the planes delivering the supplies, but also UNITA's refusal to allow relief flights into areas held by it. These flights resumed to selected cities in mid-September 1993, following signature by both sides to a document permitting humanitarian deliveries. This has not totally eliminated the problem as UNITA still vacillates over whether planes can land in some cities, leaving civilian populations severely malnourished and with increased child/infant mortality.

Security for UN and other international personnel in Angola has been, and continues to be, a major concern. On 29 November 1992, when UNITA troops occupied the provincial town of Uige, the UNAVEM II camp was caught in cross-fire and a UN police observer was killed. In the week of 11 January 1993, prior to Security Council Resolution 804 concentrating UNAVEM II forces in Luanda, fighting was so intense that 45 of UNAVEM II's 67 locations were evacuated. UNITA rebels have shot down WFP aircraft carrying food and other emergency supplies to the civilian population and staff contracted to the UN have been injured in these attacks.

After requesting on a number of occasions to be permitted to stand down, Ms Margaret Anstee, the Secretary-General's Special Representative, was released from her position in June. Mr Alioune Blondin Beye took over the position on 28 June 1993.

In July, the Observer countries consented to the Government of Angola entering into government-to-government agreements to provide much needed military supplies.

Security Council Resolution 864 extended UNAVEM II's mandate from 16 September to 15 December, and 'demanded' UNITA accept the election results and resume peace negotiations. On 25 September 1993, as determined by Resolution 864, an arms embargo was imposed on UNITA because the demanded ceasefire had not occurred. This embargo would be automatically re-imposed if UNITA were to breach any agreed ceasefire in the future. The embargo covers sale and supply of arms, petroleum and military material to UNITA. In addition, other measures (i.e., trade measures and travel restrictions) will be imposed on UNITA after 1 November 1993 unless the Secretary-General has advised that an effective ceasefire has been established. On 27 October, the Security Council recommended the date of effect be adjusted to 1 December following the resumption of talks between the two sides to the conflict.

With effect from 20 September, UNITA unilaterally declared a ceasefire throughout Angola, and the fighting has diminished since that date. As a sign of the renewed Observer nations efforts to bring about a peaceful solution to the situation in Angola, President Clinton appointed Ambassador Paul J. Hare on 22 October as the US Special Representative to the Angolan Peace Process. UN brokered ceasefire discussions renewed between the Government and UNITA on 25 October 1993 in Lusaka; the outcome of these talks are not known but the number of unsuccessful talks in the past do not encourage the prospect of any early result.

Failure of the peace process

To what extent can the disastrous turn of events in Angola be ascribed to the framing and discharge of UNAVEM II's mandate?

The cause of the renewed war was the adamant refusal of Savimbi to accept that fair elections had denied him power. During years of external support and patronage, including during the lead up to the elections, Savimbi had been encouraged in the belief that he was the rightful president of Angola. UNITA is more of a military than a political organisation, highly authoritarian and resistant to outside argument or internal debate and Savimbi has used extreme measures to maintain control over his supporters, particularly those who have dissented in some way. The assassination of his lieutenants, Pedro Chingunji and Wilson dos Santos, is one example. Comparatively little attempt was made by UNITA during the election campaign to court support in new areas.

UNAVEM II did not have the power to influence Savimbi's attitudes to the democratic process, but recognising the character of his organisation, the failure to disarm UNITA fully prior to the elections and to ensure its withdrawal from occupied areas, as agreed in the Bicesse Accords, was crucial to the ensuing course of events, including the relatively weak negotiating position of the Government. Under the Bicesse Accords, UNITA was required to withdraw immediately from the areas it occupied. It never did so, and faced little effective pressure to do so, thus enhancing its capacity to mobilise quickly and strike hard when it recommenced fighting in October 1992. Savimbi was able to mobilise rapidly as many as 40,000 troops, supporting the claim that he had secreted some of his forces to be prepared for such an event. The Government, by contrast, had to rely on police forces in the early stages of the fighting. That is not to say that had the Accords been fully observed, Savimbi would have been bereft of military options. It was always an option to recall his forces (maximum 20,000) from the unified army (of 40,000). But the strength and speed with which he was able to develop his military campaign would have been greatly reduced and its riskiness much increased - perhaps sufficiently to dissuade him from it altogether.

From the outset, the UN was confronted in Angola with a difficult, if not impossible task. Under the terms of the Bicesse Accords, UNAVEM II was in effect subordinate to the body which had overall supervision of the peace process, the Joint Political-Military Commission (CCPM), comprising the Government of Angola and UNITA as members, and the United States, Russia and Portugal as Observers. UNAVEM II did not attend meetings of the CCPM and was thus excluded from the regular exchange between the main players on key issues, and was unable to directly influence CCPM decisions. It was invited to attend the Joint Verification and Monitoring Commission (CMVF), the body created to monitor the ceasefire, which otherwise had the same membership as the CCPM.

In key areas, therefore, UNAVEM II was given a secondary status. In particular, its role was not to monitor or supervise the demobilisation process directly, but to verify that the monitoring groups, composed of equal numbers of government and UNITA personnel, were 'assuming their responsibilities', and to support investigation and resolution of alleged ceasefire violations.

With a few exceptions, including some military leaders, relations between the two Angolan parties remained characterised throughout the process by profound mistrust and constant manoeuvring for political advantage. Neither party was prepared to see a system of vigorous investigation by the two Commissions of alleged breaches, since both had things to hide.

Following the election, the MPLA offered UNITA minor portfolios in the Government. The UNITA claimed this were not commensurate with the percentage of the popular vote it attained in the Assembly elections.

It was the role of the Observers, rather than UNAVEM II, to cajole the parties within the CCPM towards genuine implementation of the Accords, but their success was limited, especially in regard to UNITA. As the elections approached, the Observers and UNAVEM II had to choose whether to risk jeopardising the process by applying greater pressure on UNITA to abide by its undertakings, or to proceed in the hope that a successful election process would create a new dynamic which would make it difficult for either side to resort to military means. They chose the latter, which proved to be a grave misjudgement in Savimbi's case. Had it lost the elections, the Angolan government's response can only be speculated upon, but its greater investment in the notion of legitimacy, compliance with the demobilisation process and less militaristic character would probably have dissuaded it from taking a similar course.

It is important to recognise that UNAVEM II's contribution to the peaceful and successful conduct of the elections, although overshadowed by the subsequent collapse of the process, was a major achievement in the Angolan context, establishing an important marker in Angola's political development.

The then UN Special Representative, Margaret Anstee, started to assume a more active negotiating role in Angola only after UNITA withdrew from the unified army and launched its attacks. As the Observers proved themselves incapable of reining in the conflict, more was expected of the UN, although the UNAVEM II mandate does not explicitly provide for it. The fact that two of the Observers were Permanent Members of the Security Council, with long-standing links with the respective Angolan parties, made it more difficult for the UN Special Representative to take an authoritative position, since any further UN measures she recommended would have to be agreed by the same parties who were in some respects more directly involved and making their own assessments of the situation. Anstee performed well, with limited mandate and resources, in a messy and frustrating situation. She retained the confidence of the Observers, but faced difficulties with the Angolan parties. The government more than once accused her of bias, and access to decision makers was not easy. Savimbi maligned her at every opportunity and called for her replacement.

It is doubtful whether anyone could have done a better job. One African Ambassador suggested that given gender attitudes in Angola a male might have been a better appointment, but although an African male is now the Secretary-General's Special Representative, he has faced the same frustrations as Anstee, with Savimbi failing to deliver his frequent promises.

Other contributing factors

Despite supporting the election process, former sponsors of UNITA, the United States and South Africa, withheld recognition from the newly-elected Angolan government on the basis that the election was incomplete. By declining to recognise the government they denied it crucial post-election support which, coming from them especially, would have sent a clear message to Savimbi. Instead, US policy remained in the hands of those identified with the Reagan administration's support for UNITA, which failed to persuade Savimbi to return to the peace process. Public remarks by the US Secretary of State relating recognition to the issue of control of territory can only have encouraged Savimbi in his military and political ambitions. The United States eventually recognised the government on 19 May 1993, after the failure of the Abidjan talks and since that time it has increased its condemnation of UNITA.

The slowness of the international community in condemning external intervention may have also strengthened Savimbi by providing time for UNITA to consolidate its arms supplies and its territory. Yet the Observer nations' agreement in July to allow the Angolan Government to obtain much needed military supplies, has contributed to the turning of the military tide against UNITA. Savimbi has played international interest in Angola astutely. His receptive manner at times belies the ruthlessness with which he has pursued new territory in Angola with catastrophic results for the population in the area, particularly those he feels did not vote for him in the elections. He has been encouraged in his tactics by being offered concessions for promises which he does not keep: he is the aggressor and spoiler in the process. Once he resorted to war, international attempts to be even-handed and balanced, including in UN resolutions, only encouraged him to believe that he was paying no price for his actions.

Given that UNITA is well armed and has access to income from illegal diamond sales, the recently imposed embargo can only be described as a token measure. Yet this resolution, along with the lifting of the arms embargo against the Angolan Government has helped to convince Savimbi to return to the negotiating table.

African countries, while deeply concerned about the situation in Angola and its impact on other African countries, have not being as proactive in this crisis as in other cases such as Liberia and border dispute between Somalia and Ethiopia. Savimbi's long-standing personal links with Francophone African leaders, amongst others, are one factor. There has also been an impatience expressed in Southern Africa with the blinkered attitude of the MPLA, while the OAU mediation efforts have been patchy. African representatives argue that given Savimbi's intractability and without military or financial clout to offer, the OAU is not well placed to mediate.

All foreign intervention in Angola was required to have ceased with the signing of the peace accords. Evidence exists that elements located in South Africa and Zaire provided support to UNITA. After many denials, South Africa finally agreed in early March that South African companies had been involved in supplying Savimbi. South Africa has vehemently denied official involvement and has said it is taking steps to tighten up control of its airports to ensure they are not used for unauthorised flights into Angola. Internal preoccupations in South Africa may mean that elements in the South African Defence Force (e.g., Military Intelligence) with established links to UNITA, are continuing covert assistance, out of old loyalty or financial gain, with or without the knowledge of the political stratum.

In the case of Zaire, past links with Savimbi and deals involving participation by Zaire in massive illegal diamond mining in north-eastern Angola make continuing support for Savimbi probable.

Outlook for UNAVEM II

With the collapse of the cease-fire UNAVEM II has little, if any, role to play in terms of its original mandate. Security reasons aside, the withdrawal of its personnel, largely to Luanda, is a holding operation designed to support the efforts of the Special Representative to facilitate a renewed ceasefire and to avoid the impression that the UN has given the situation away. Given the current failure in the peace process, it may be that UN credibility would be better served by the withdrawal of UNAVEM II. However, without an obvious international presence, withdrawal could mean the total abandonment of the suffering Angolan people.

UNAVEM II's mandate gave it only an ancillary role in the peace process, with resources barely to support even that. The collapse of the process owes more to the nature of the Angolan parties and the ambiguities of the external response to UNITA's violations than it does to any specific deficiencies on UNAVEM's part. UNAVEM II could have played a more public cajoling role in trying to correct breaches to the peace accords, but with uncertain consequences.

Any expanded UN role following a renewed ceasefire should provide for UNAVEM II to be recognised as a principal player in the process, on an equal footing with the government and UNITA. Such a role, encompassing peacekeeping on a much larger scale, would require a greatly increased UN presence in Angola: 8-15,000 personnel has been suggested. Control and destruction of arms in the demobilisation process would need to be greatly improved. In the light of security concerns affecting UNAVEM II, an expanded force should carry arms and be entitled to use them in clearly-defined circumstances.

Delays in deploying an expanded UN presence will increase exponentially the chances of a further breakdown, so in the light of the ongoing Lusaka peace talks, the call by the Secretary-General for a strengthening of UNAVEM II's numbers, is heartening.

The Angolan experience has clearly established the difficulties for future UN operations in similar situations in proceeding to elections without the full support of all parties to the peace process. Another critical element in future comparable programs of support and assistance will be to secure guarantees from the parties that they will accept the outcome. Ideally, there should be sanctions for failing to do so which are clearly indicated in advance. The commitment and compliance of external sponsors and supporters of the parties in relation to these undertakings is almost as important as those of the parties themselves.

More generally, in countries where there is no history of the peaceful and regular transfer of power through elections, a winner-take-all approach to elections creates an explosive situation. Initial elections may be better directed at determining relative shares in a power-sharing government of national unity, reducing the stakes and the concomitant incentive for the losers to resort to force.

Although in Angola's case it is doubtful whether anything less than the top job would have satisfied Savimbi, a process directed from the outset at a government of national unity may have created a more constructive atmosphere, particularly if a power sharing arrangement had been instituted for the entire ceasefire period thus exposing UNITA to democratic processes and political responsibility.

Power sharing could be where the present process will end, after the loss of thousands of lives, widespread destruction and the entrenchment of internecine bitterness on an epic scale.

18 Sanctions

STEVEN MCINTOSH

The United Nations has imposed sanctions in seven instances since its inception - Rhodesia, South Africa (arms embargo only), Iraq, Libya (restricted sanctions), Somalia (arms embargo only), the former Yugoslavia (arms embargo against all former republics with additional comprehensive sanctions against the Federal Republic of Yugoslavia - Serbia and Montenegro) and Haiti (oil and arms embargo). The effectiveness of international sanctions generally has been a matter for debate ever since the failure of League of Nations economic sanctions to force Italy to reverse its occupation of Abyssinia in the 1930s. The piecemeal or partial application of sanctions, or flouting of them by trading partners of the target state, undoubtedly reduces their effectiveness. However, an efficient sanctions regime is an important tool in reducing the capacity for aggression on the part of, or changing the behaviour of, errant states. Sanctions are a form of action which the United Nations can take, regardless of their real effect, to show opprobrium and to signal potential Chapter VII action. Even the threat of the imposition of sanctions may at times be sufficient to obtain a response from an errant state. The one factor which needs to be kept in mind is that sanctions take time to work. Expectations that they will result in an instant change of course would generally seem to be unrealistic.

Rhodesia

United Nations Security Council Resolution 232 (1966), imposing sanctions against Rhodesia, was the first instance of mandatory sanctions in United Nations history.[1] Previously, the Security Council had

---

[1] John W. Halderman, 'Some Legal Aspects of Sanctions in the Rhodesian Case' *The International and Comparative Law Quarterly* 17 (1968) p.672.

312 BUILDING INTERNATIONAL COMMUNITY

recommended that states impose arms embargoes on Portugal (Resolution 180, in 1963) and South Africa (Resolution 181, in 1963) and rather vague sanctions against Rhodesia (Resolution 217, in 1965), but had declined to make them mandatory. In following years further measures were imposed against Rhodesia in a rather piecemeal fashion, thus diminishing their effectiveness.[2] Neither Portugal (which controlled Rhodesia's major rail link, the line to Beira in Mozambique), nor South Africa, which was anxious that sanctions not be seen to succeed, took any steps to enforce the sanctions - indeed, they actively took steps to ensure that they would fail.[3] Most Western states also took no action to force their nationals to cease trading with Rhodesia - some, such as France (sale of oil) and the United States (purchases of chrome, ferro-chrome and nickel) actively participated in sanctions-breaking activities. It was only after Portugal's withdrawal from Mozambique, President Jimmy Carter's actions in directing the cessation of purchases of strategic minerals and pressure from South Africa that sanctions began to have a belated effect, reinforcing the effect of the guerrilla warfare conducted by Robert Mugabe's forces, and leading to Ian Smith's preparedness to negotiate.

South Africa

As early as 1963, the Security Council called upon states to cease exports of arms to South Africa. However, it was not until after the Soweto massacre and the murder of Steve Biko in 1976 that serious actions were taken against South Africa by the international community. United Nations Security Council Resolution 418 (1977) imposed a mandatory arms embargo. Although, due to British and United States opposition, no other mandatory measures were imposed by the Security Council, unilateral and multilateral (Commonwealth, European Community) initiatives put in place following the events of 1976 and strengthened in the ensuing years, placed a substantial burden on the South African economy. The imposition of a State of Emergency in 1985 quickened the pace of sanctions implementation. The United States Congress overrode vetoes from President Ronald Reagan to impose strong economic sanctions against South Africa in 1986-87. Much of the action taken against South Africa was private rather than governmental - disinvestment, consumer boycotts, sports and cultural boycotts. Politically motivated disinvestment combined with increased economic uncertainty to reduce foreign investment in South Africa. The overall aim of the sanctions was the destruction of the pillars of apartheid and negotiations for an end to

---

[2] M.S. Daoudi and M.S. Dajani, *Economic Sanctions: Ideals and Experience* (: Routledge & Kegan Paul, 1983) p.82.
[3] Martin Meredith, *The Past is Another Country: Rhodesia 1890-1979* (London: , 1979) p.145.

minority rule.[4] South Africa, which was (and is) a commodity trader with an open economy, a low skills base (which means that high value added goods must be imported) and a dependence on a small number of trading partners,[5] was peculiarly vulnerable to such sanctions.

As the local arms industry was unable to manufacture sophisticated weapons, the arms embargo meant that they had to be purchased on the black market with a markup of 20-100 per cent. The cost of the oil embargo was approximately US$2 billion per annum, whilst the cost of trade sanctions has been estimated at 'several billion dollars [US] annually'.[6] Financial sanctions, although beneficial in the short term as South Africans gained assets at discounted prices and the South African Government imposed restrictions on repatriation of profits from sale of capital assets, led to serious long term effects. The drying up of investment was serious for an economy dependent on capital inflow, leading to a currency crisis. The effects of the economic crisis, to which the imposition of sanctions was a major contributor, have been summed up as follows: '[H]ad the South African economy been able to sustain its growth rates of the 1946-75 period through the late 1980s, real GDP would have been more than 45 per cent higher, and real GDP per capita would have increased rather than diminished'.[7] As sanctions, and particularly financial sanctions, bit, the structural distortions of apartheid contributed to the slowing of growth.

The economic crisis prompted the South African business community to pressure the Government in the direction of political reform. The change in the character of Afrikaner society since 1948 meant that its members were now part of the business and academic élite, which contributed to a weakening of the 'laager mentality'. White South Africans see themselves as part of the West and are therefore hurt by being shunned by the West.[8] In the 1989 Budget speech the Minister for Finance acknowledged that sanctions were destroying the economy. There was therefore no choice for F.W. de Klerk but to initiate negotiations. The support for reform on the part of the white electorate at the referendum of March 1992 illustrated an awareness of this position.

It should not be pretended that sanctions were the only factor pushing South Africa towards reform. The collapse of the Soviet Union removed the 'communist bogey' from South African politics, whilst the end of minority rule in Namibia demonstrated that such an outcome need not entail the loss of economic influence for the white minority. Internal black opposition was always a crucial element in the anti-apartheid

---

[4] Bronwen Manby, 'South Africa: The Impact of Sanctions' *Journal of International Affairs* 46, 1 (Summer 1992) p.202.
[5] Ibid. p.204.
[6] Stephen Lewis, *The Economics of Apartheid* (New York: , 1990) p.114.
[7] Ibid. p.115.
[8] Manby, 'South Africa' pp.211-12.

struggle, and it was the attempts by the South African Government to quell that opposition that prompted the imposition of economic sanctions.

Iraq

Sanctions against Iraq were imposed by Resolution 661 and strengthened by Resolution 670 and a number of subsequent resolutions. The sanctions remain in force pending compliance by Iraq with conditions set by the Security Council (See Resolutions 687 of 3 April and 707 of 15 August 1991) regarding weapons disclosure and destruction, identification of missing Kuwaiti and other third party nationals, return of Kuwaiti property and treatment of the civilian population in the north and south of the country. Due to Saddam Hussein's refusal to cooperate in UN-supervised oil sales, the sanctions continue to have a significant impact on the Iraqi economy and on the living standards of the Iraqi people. The Iraqi regime is anxious to have the sanctions lifted in order that its economy and military power can be rebuilt, but is unwilling to accede to the conditions set down by the Security Council referred to above. The sanctions have not succeeded in forcing compliance with the conditions imposed by the Security Council for three reasons:

- the ability of the political and military élite to escape the impact of the sanctions themselves whilst pushing their worst effects on to their internal opponents, the Kurds and the Shia. Indeed, those in power and those close to them are often in a position to profit from sanctions-busting activities;

- leakage via Jordan, Turkey, Iran and other neighbouring states;

- the agricultural richness of the country and the Iraqi ability (necessarily deteriorating) to continue to maintain machinery and other factors of production.

One view as to why the sanctions have not yet succeeded in forcing Iraqi compliance is that the regime does not see how it could capitulate to UN demands and retain its credibility - indeed, its very survival would be in doubt. On the other hand, given the degree of control exercised over Iraqi society by Saddam and his close associates, the chances of popular anger forcing a change of government, at least in the short term, must be assessed as low. On that scenario, Saddam finds the continuation of the sanctions useful, as they enable him to portray himself as the Arab leader who will not bow to United States aggression. However, there can be no question that the sanctions, together with the United Nations Special Commission's (UNSCOM) activities, have restricted Iraq's ability to rearm and once again threaten the stability of the region and must therefore be counted as a success in that way.

Libya

Sanctions against Libya were imposed by the Security Council on 15 April 1992 following Libya's failure to comply with UNSCRs 731 and 748, which called on Libya to cooperate with investigations into the bombing of Pan Am flight 103 and UTA flight 772 and demanded that Libya cease all forms of terrorist action and all assistance to terrorist groups. Those sanctions are limited to an air embargo, an arms embargo and restrictions on diplomatic staff. Whilst causing some discomfort to the regime and the people, they have not threatened the former's stability and are unlikely to do so in the absence of additional measures. There is, therefore, little prospect that the Libyans will agree to comply with the UN's demands. The action which would be of most effect would be a ban on the export of Libyan oil. It is unlikely that European states would agree to the imposition of such an embargo. However, there has recently been consideration given to a strengthening of sanctions which might include bans on the supply of technology and equipment to the oil industry and the freezing of Libyan assets overseas. In the absence of a significant strengthening of the sanctions, it appears that the present stand off will continue for some time, to the undoubted relief of some neighbouring states to whom the arms embargo has given some peace of mind.

Yugoslavia

The situation in the former Yugoslavia is even more complicated. An arms embargo has been imposed against all the constituent republics of the former Yugoslavia (Resolution 713 of 25 September 1991); given that Yugoslavia was still recognised as a single state at that time, the arms embargo is expressed to be directed against the supply of all deliveries of weapons and other military equipment to Yugoslavia. The effect of the arms embargo has been distinctly uneven, advantaging the Federal Republic of Yugoslavia (Serbia and Montenegro) (FRY) and the Bosnian Serbs and disadvantaging the Bosnian Muslims. Economic sanctions have been imposed against the FRY, and more recently against areas occupied by the Bosnian Serbs in Bosnia-Hercegovina and the United Nations Protected Areas in Croatia, in an effort to stop the fighting (Resolutions 757 of 30 May 1992, 787 of 16 November 1992 and 820 of 17 April 1993). These measures do not appear to be bringing effective pressure for an early just settlement in Bosnia; nor are they likely to influence decisions on a further round of fighting in the Krajina, about which there has been widespread speculation. As in the case of Iraq, the sanctions have had a severe effect on the living standards of the people of the FRY. Sanctions, loosely applied at first, still had a drastic effect on the import and export dependent Yugoslav economy. Industrial production was almost halved, a million people lost their jobs, inflation soared to over 200 per cent a month and average wages sank to the equivalent of US$25 a month. UNSCR 820, which bans transhipment of goods across the FRY, and the gradual toughening of controls on the FRY's borders will mean even more hardship for the majority of the people in the FRY. Nevertheless, sanctions have not discomfited the regime enough to cause a change in policy and some members of the ruling élites in the FRY and Bosnia have been involved in lucrative sanctions-busting operations.

Sanctions have not had a clear cut effect on public opinion in the FRY. Serbia's international isolation was one factor in anti-government demonstrations that took place soon after their introduction, and Serbia's growing economic difficulties enabled Milan Panic to mount a strong challenge to the previously impregnable Slobodan Milosevic in last December's elections. However, sanctions appear to have stiffened the resolve of nationalists to resist the will of the international community. Moreover, the fact that sanctions have not been imposed on Croatia, which most Serbs consider to be equally if not more responsible for the fighting in Bosnia, confirms the view, fostered by government-controlled media, that the international community is biased against Serbia. This undermines popular resolve to mobilise against the regime, despite weariness with the present situation and a disposition to be impatient with the Bosnian Serbs should they be seen to be holding the Serbs of Serbia hostage through unreasonable intransigence. Milosevic seemed to tap such impatience when the Bosnian Serbs refused to sign the Vance-Owen plan. But that sentiment dissipated following the announcement on 22 May in Washington of the Joint Action Plan and a sense that the Vance-Owen option was fading.

Sanctions have also made it harder for the FRY to continue giving military aid to the Bosnian Serbs (although the latter were well-equipped from the outset). They were undoubtedly a factor prompting Milosevic to endorse the Vance-Owen plan at the Athens Conference in May and his announcement of an economic blockade of sorts against the Bosnian Serbs (although the genuineness of the blockade is somewhat doubtful, given Milosevic's refusal to allow the UN to monitor border crossings). The debilitating effect of sanctions on the vulnerable Montenegrin economy has also contributed to the determination of the young Montenegrin leadership to pursue a more independent policy. Montenegro is unlikely to secede because of sanctions alone, but could take that step one day if Serbia continues to ignore its interests. Finally it should be noted that, less than two months after UNSCR 820, it is still early to gauge the effect of the strengthened sanctions regime. Smuggling via the Danube now seems to have been severely curtailed. Although it will be harder to close up land routes, particularly from Macedonia, importing and exporting is getting ever harder and more expensive.

Haiti

On 16 June 1993 the Security Council unanimously passed Resolution 841 imposing sanctions against Haiti which include oil and arms embargoes and the freezing of Haitian assets overseas. The sanctions require the restoration of democratic government to Haiti. In July 1993 the military regime agreed to the restoration of democratically elected President Jean-Bertrand Aristide on the condition that military officers enjoy an amnesty. It appeared that sanctions had in this case been peculiarly effective, and they were lifted on 27 August.

The unintended effects of sanctions on third-party states

An important issue is the difficulty caused by the current lack of an accepted and effective mechanism to deal with the problems of third-party states particularly affected by the imposition of sanctions against a state with which they have no direct quarrel. Article 50 of the UN Charter provides for compensation to be paid; however, in practice the amounts paid, if any, have not been regarded as adequate compensation. Instances are Jordan, in respect of the sanctions against Iraq, and a number of neighbouring states, particularly Romania and Bulgaria, in respect of the sanctions against the FRY. The failure to adequately address this aspect of sanctions enforcement will inevitably reduce the effectiveness of the sanctions regimes. However, questions also arise as to who is going to pay the compensation - virtually all governments in the developed world are facing budgetary problems which make them averse to making significant contributions to third countries adversely affected by sanctions. For example, Egypt has called for the Council to consult with states likely to be affected by the imposition of sanctions both prior to and after such imposition, and for the institution of assessed contributions to meet the costs of Article 50 compensation. On the other hand, consultation, both prior to and during the currency of sanctions, may not result in any consensus, and the use of assessed contributions is not regarded as acceptable by a number of UN member states.

Conclusion

Although comprehensive economic sanctions may not, in the short term at least, compel target states to alter their behaviour, they adversely affect the ability of those states to continue that behaviour.[9] The effectiveness of sanctions is dependent upon their scope and upon the vigour with which they are enforced. It is probably impossible for sanctions to be made

---

[9] Daoudi and Dajani, *Economic Sanctions* pp.160-1.

absolutely watertight, but there are necessarily costs, often significant, involved in circumventing the sanctions.

There are some critical points to be kept in mind when assessing the likely impact of sanctions:

- What matters is the impact of the sanctions on those who control the political (and military) power in the target state. In a Western democracy, pressure from the electorate would influence its government's policies. However, in states with autocratic regimes (which are those more likely to be targeted with sanctions), those regimes are likely to be indifferent to hardships suffered by their people as long as they are not affected directly by them. Further, the distortions in the economy of the target state caused by the imposition of sanctions may benefit certain persons best-placed to take advantage of those distortions. These persons are quite likely to be part of, or associated with, the ruling élites of those states.

- In an environment where strong nationalist sentiments are present, the initial effect of sanctions is likely to stiffen the resolve of the population of the target state to resist the dictates of the international community, particularly of powerful members of the Permanent Five. Sanctions may be portrayed by the governing regime in the target state as victimisation. This may result, at least initially, in increased domestic, and possibly even international, support for the errant regime. However, in the long term local support is likely to be dampened by the on-going effect of economic deprivation.

- The development of an accepted and effective mechanism for addressing the problems of third-party states affected by the impact of sanctions would enhance the effectiveness of sanctions implementation.

19 Iraq and the United Nations Special Commission

PETER FURLONGER

Enforcement of arms control and disarmament measures

The strengthening or introduction of routine, special and challenge inspections which can be carried out by a number of international organisations in support of arms control and disarmament is likely to be an increasing avenue for enforcement of collective security responses.

The terms of the ceasefire resolution

Following the cessation of hostilities by the United Nations coalition forces against Iraq in March 1991, Iraq notified its acceptance of the comprehensive ceasefire resolution, UNSCR 687 (1991), adopted by the Security Council on 3 April 1991. Part C of that resolution set out requirements with respect to Iraqi weapons of mass destruction (WMD) capabilities and their delivery systems, and established a new body, the UN Special Commission (UNSCOM) to ensure Iraq complied with the terms of the resolution. It also directed the Director-General of the International Atomic Energy Agency (IAEA) to assist and cooperate in ensuring Iraq complied in the nuclear field, with UNSCOM being charged with responsibility for overall coordination.

Specific requirements of Iraq contained in Part C of UNSCR 687 were:
Para 7. unconditional reaffirmation of its obligations under the 1925 Geneva Protocol (prohibiting the use of chemical weapons), and ratification of the 1972 Biological Weapons Convention

Para 8. unconditional acceptance of the destruction, removal or rendering harmless, under international supervision, of

- 'all chemical and biological weapons and all stocks of agents and all related sub-systems and components and all research, development, support and manufacturing facilities'

- 'all ballistic missiles with a range greater than 150 kilometres and related parts, and major repair and production facilities'

Para 9. to assist in fulfilling the obligations set out in paragraph 8, Iraq was required to submit a declaration 'of the locations, amounts, and types of all items specified in paragraph 8 and agree to urgent, on-site inspections' as specified later in the resolution.

- this paragraph also required Iraq to yield possession to UNSCOM 'for destruction, removal or rendering harmless, taking into account the requirements of public safety, of all items specified in paragraph 8'

- Iraq was also required to destroy, under UNSCOM supervision, all its missile capabilities including launchers

Para 10. an unconditional undertaking 'not to use, develop, construct or acquire any of the items specified in paragraphs 8 and 9

Para 11. unconditional reaffirmation of its Nuclear Non-Proliferation Treaty obligations

Para 12. unconditional agreement 'not to acquire or develop nuclear weapons or nuclear-weapons-usable materials or any sub-systems or components or any (related) research, development, support or manufacturing facilities'

- submit to the United Nations Secretary-General and to the Director-General of the IAEA a declaration 'of the locations, amounts, types of all items specified above'

- place all of its nuclear-weapons-usable materials under the IAEA's exclusive control, for custody and removal

- accept 'urgent, on-site inspection and the destruction, removal or rendering harmless of all items specified above'

- accept the ongoing monitoring plan to verify compliance with undertakings required by UNSCR 687.

UNSCR 687 thus envisaged a three phase operation:

- a declaration by Iraq of relevant stocks and related facilities, which would then be verified by UNSCOM and the IAEA, including by the use of a series of highly intrusive inspections;

- the destruction, removal or rendering harmless under international supervision of these stocks and facilities;

- an ongoing monitoring plan (detailed in a subsequent resolution UNSCR 715 adopted by the Security Council in October 1991) to ensure Iraq did not rebuild its WMD and missile delivery system capabilities.

Until very recently, Iraq resisted acceptance of the ongoing monitoring plan, which is regarded as the critical element in preventing Iraq from rebuilding the sizeable program of WMD and missile development it had been undertaking prior to Operation Desert Storm. It said implementation of the plan would be a gross infringement of its national sovereignty, and also claimed it conflicted with the UN Charter. The Security Council rejected this position. The Council indicated clearly that it saw the plan as falling within the scope of Chapter VII of the UN Charter, meaning that compliance with the plan was both mandatory and enforceable. In late 1993, Iraq indicated a preparedness to accept UNSCR 715 and UNSCOM has since been engaged in detailed negotiations with Iraqi authorities over the implementation of the plan. The three years of experience with Iraq's relative lack of cooperation with UNSCOM and the IAEA has left a legacy of distrust by the international community of Iraqi intentions. An extended period of cooperation by Iraq in the operation of the monitoring regime, which did not produce new evidence of Iraqi non-compliance with UNSCR 687, is likely to be needed before the Security Council accepts that Iraq has completed all the actions required by Part C of UNSCR 687. Paragraph 22 of that Resolution states that the Security Council needs to come to such a judgement before the sanctions against imports from Iraq (including notably oil) and related financial transactions can be lifted.

UNSCOM in practice

The original three consecutive phase model for UNSCOM operations did not prove accurate in practice - efforts to verify Iraqi declarations regarding stocks and facilities became an ongoing process and coincided with activities under UNSCOM and IAEA supervision to 'destroy, remove or render harmless' declared missile, chemical weapons (CW), nuclear and other facilities.

Iraqi authorities adopted an uncooperative approach toward UNSCOM from the beginning. Its initial declaration of its WMD capabilities was very inadequate. Deficiencies included the listing of only a small fraction of its CW munition stocks and the lack of any reference to biological or nuclear weapons development or capacity. For example, Iraq's 18 April 1991 declaration listed only 11,000 chemical munitions and included no reference to any stocks of the Tabun nerve agent. By early 1993 UNSCOM efforts had resulted in identification of more than 140,000 filled and unfilled chemical munitions and 125 tonnes of Tabun. Evidence also came to light of a large-scale nuclear enrichment program exploring, in parallel, both electromagnetic and centrifuge techniques, to produce fissile material for nuclear weapons. Successive Iraqi declarations, each revealing more details on the scope and numbers of munitions or facilities involved in Iraq's WMD program, have occurred in response to revelations by the UNSCOM/IAEA inspection efforts and Security Council pressure.

The period to the first UNSCOM inspection in mid-May 1991 was occupied by a dispute with Iraq over the terms, including immunities, under which international inspectors would operate within Iraq. Iraq also objected to UNSCOM plans to conduct its own flight operations in Iraqi airspace. In many cases the issue had to be referred to the Security Council for its weight to be added before Iraq backed down. Iraq's lack of cooperation with the initial series of UNSCOM inspections resulted in a further Security Council resolution (UNSCR 707) in August 1991, reiterating the demands contained in UNSCR 687, and specifying in greater detail UNSCOM's inspection rights: unconditional and unrestricted access to all areas, facilities, equipment and records, as well as the conduct of flight operations throughout Iraq to assist UNSCOM in its work. Although there has been repeated reference back to the Security Council for swift political support on more grave incidents, lack of cooperation - which has included various forms of harassment of UNSCOM inspectors - has been a constant feature with UNSCOM activity down to the present day. Iraq's approach to UNSCOM is a large factor behind the observation in mid-1993 by its Executive Chairman, Ambassador Rolf Ekeus, that Iraq's lack of openness meant the organisation still did not have a complete understanding of Iraq's WMD programs. Ekeus added this meant UNSCOM could not certify that Iraq would not move quickly to rebuild its programs if UN efforts ceased, a point reinforced by Iraq's then strong resistance to the ongoing monitoring plan.

Despite Iraq's uncooperativeness, UNSCOM and the IAEA have gone a long way towards fulfilling the mandate given them by UNSCR 687. Although questions remain over some aspects of the CW, missile and nuclear weapons programs, the scope of these programs is believed to have been largely identified, as well as most of the key facilities or stocks which are being progressively destroyed. Destruction of known elements of Iraqi WMD programs is expected to be completed during 1994.

Conclusions

UNSCOM is an innovative and largely effective example of a collective international action to maintain security and order. Iraq's efforts to further develop WMD, particularly acquisition of nuclear weapons, would be destabilising both within the Middle East region and globally (through encouragement to states with similar ambitions).

UNSCOM was established and started effective operations quickly, largely by calling on offers of often highly specialised personnel and other assistance from UN members. Relatively few permanent UN staff have been required, and those principally in coordinating or support roles. Despite some initial tensions in developing a cooperative relationship with the IAEA, UNSCOM benefited greatly from that organisation's capacity, long experience and expertise in inspecting and verifying nuclear activities. No such organisation existed at the time in the chemical or biological weapons areas. The future Organisation for the Prohibition of Chemical Weapons (OPCW), which will come into being when the Chemical Weapons Convention (CWC) enters into force (expected during 1995 once the required 65 ratifications are notified formally), means that the capacity of the UN system to mount a similar operation from international organisational resources will be considerably enhanced. This international capacity will be further enhanced if responsibility is given to the OPCW or another organisation to verify also compliance with the Biological Weapons Convention (BWC), whose lack of verification provisions or machinery is a significant deficiency which is currently being addressed by Parties to the Convention. (The evidence of Iraqi interest in biological weapons has been a key factor in prompting interest in strengthening the BWC.)

UNSCOM's activities have also highlighted the desirability of international non-proliferation controls on the proliferation of missiles, the key delivery system for weapons of mass destruction. There is currently no international treaty-based regime governing the proliferation of missiles.

The conduct of the program as a whole has relied on the political will shared widely among UN members to support the operation, and demonstrated by many members' provision of direct substantial assistance to UNSCOM.

It has operated under clear authority from the Security Council, hich has responded quickly and in most cases unanimously when called on to back UNSCOM in countering acts of Iraqi intransigence. This has been essential as Iraq's approach has been characterised by constant testing of the political will of the international community to back UNSCOM's efforts. Even Yemen and Cuba joined with other Security Council members in calls on Iraq to back down.

The key point of leverage with Iraq underpinning UNSCOM efforts has been continuation of the comprehensive sanctions regime, suggesting that any Security Council action to enforce the CWC or other disarmament or arms control treaties would need to include a sanctions element.

A major conclusion emerging from any review of the UNSCOM program concerns the role of the Security Council. The willingness of the Security Council to take action when needed has been a fundamental element in the effectiveness of the disarmament program in Iraq. The Council's expeditious and often forceful response when called on to reply to Iraqi provocations is particularly encouraging in view of the Council's prospective role under the CWC and future arms control or disarmament treaties. Article XII of the CWC provides for reference to the Security Council (and the United Nations General Assembly) in cases of grave breaches of the Convention. The scope for sanctions within the CWC machinery itself is limited largely to the suspension of rights within the OPCW: more general sanctions in response to a breach of the Convention would have to be mandated by the Security Council.

Conclusion

KEVIN P. CLEMENTS

The case studies in this volume have traversed some of the diverse conflicts that have afflicted the world over the last fifty years. Many of these conflicts are still in process, some are confined and managed, but very few have been finally resolved. Each in its own way challenges nation states, regional organisations and the United Nations to devise more innovative ways of analysing and addressing important social, economic and political problems. The studies underline the need for all these bodies to think afresh about the adequacy of existing institutional mechanisms for responding effectively to situations that threaten stable peace and security.

All of the case studies highlight the complexity of restoring, building and maintaining peace, as well as the central importance of more timely and adequate diagnoses of, and responses to, problems. They emphasise the importance and utility of effective preventive diplomacy and the benefits of settling disputes peacefully.[1] Indeed, the case studies demonstrate the wisdom, outlined in *Cooperating for Peace*, of exhausting all non-military means of persuasion before either contemplating or sanctioning multilateral military responses to threatening political or military developments.

For too long the Security Council has been seen as the 'ultimate stick' to punish those states and peoples who contravene the dictates of the Charter. It is increasingly being recognised that military force and coercion are unable to deliver an enduring, peaceful resolution of conflict. The world community is beginning to realise that there is an urgent need to develop mechanisms that are able to alter undesirable political or

---

[1] See United Nations Office of Legal Affairs, Codification Division, *Handbook on the Peaceful Settlement of Disputes between States* (New York: United Nations, 1992) for an elaboration of the many diverse procedures available to member states of the United Nations.

military behaviour by less coercive means, through processes of rewards and positive incentives rather than through punishment and negative sanctions. Movement in this direction, however, requires some certainty that positive rewarding processes are more likely to secure compliance with international norms than negative sanctions. Consideration of this proposal suggests that policy makers need to rethink how the military can play a positive role in world affairs when rewarding processes fail to prevent military adventurism, internal conflicts or, worse, genocide.

These days national defence forces are rarely deployed unilaterally in support of international peace and security. Rather, military responses to conflict have to be negotiated within regional or global frameworks. In this situation the UN Charter demands that the use of force be conducted under clear multilateral mandates with signposted end-points and exits. Military intervention in response to major humanitarian crisis or act of aggression *must* have an international mandate if it is to have any legitimacy. It is this single fact that challenges old conceptions of national defence, leading to the development of new ways of conceptualising 'collective security' under regional and multilateral auspices.

The case studies demonstrate that among the requirements for effective operation by multilateral organisations in a conflict or crisis situation are sustained strength of will, on the part of both the organisation and its individual member states, as well as clarity of mandate. One of the most important developments of the past five years is a reawakening of the United Nations and its member states to the ways in which the current configurations of military and political power can be harnessed for the maintenance of international peace and security under the auspices of the United Nations. This has produced a number of studies about the relationships between big powers and the work of the United Nations (most focusing on the Permanent Five, and particularly on the United States, which remains the world's single most important military power).

There are two particular problems that have to be addressed. The first is how to ensure that the UN does not become a cloak to legitimise the military and political interests of its most powerful members. The second is how to ensure that these powerful members (the US in particular) serve the interests of the United Nations. The answers to these two questions will determine whether or not the United Nations is able to fulfil its promise of becoming the centre for an emergent world community, or whether it will limp along as an agency of last resort, starved of funds and resources and unable to perform its central tasks.

It is important that regional and global efforts to maintain international peace and security be linked to a clear conflict resolution framework which enables proportionate multilateral responses to different types of problems. Each political or security problem, for example, requires a tailor-made solution. The problems confronting the new international order are so complex, and the responses dictated by *realpolitik* have proven so inadequate to their solution, that there is a need for new paradigms to help decision makers develop some adequate solutions.

Gareth Evans identifies cooperative security as the central basis for this new paradigm. He is certainly right in highlighting that when cooperation breaks down problems become more difficult to resolve. But the critical question is how to ensure that states and peoples do more than pay lip service to the concept of cooperation and actually develop ways and means of enhancing cooperative processes and diminishing those that result in violent conflict. This is a central theoretical and practical task for the last few years of the twentieth century.

How, for example, do nation states, regional organisations and the United Nations cooperate to prevent the savagery that has afflicted Rwanda, Burundi and Bosnia in recent years? How do nations cooperate to restrict the flow of weapons that fuel many of these appalling conflicts? How do nations and peoples cooperate to ensure that the existing provisions of the United Nations Charter are respected and adhered to? How does the United Nations work to ensure the elevation of 'win-win' instead of 'win-lose' solutions to problems? Finally, how can governments insist on cooperative solutions to problems when nations and people are so unequal in terms of power and resources? These questions need to be engaged jointly by academics and policy makers if a new paradigm adequate to the needs of the twenty-first century is to be developed and applied to relations between states and between peoples.

Since these case studies were originally written some of the details need updating. In El Salvador, for example, the elections of March 1994 (despite some anomalies) created new political options where only military conflict existed in the past. While the Security Council still wishes to see a full implementation of the 1992 Peace Accords, particularly in relation to public security and the status of the judiciary, the UN Observer Mission (ONUSAL), whose mandate has been extended, must be judged a quiet success.

In Angola, unfortunately, it is not possible to report the same sort of success, and since the case study was completed the military situation has continued to deteriorate, notwithstanding progress in the Lusaka Peace talks. UNAVEM II is over-stretched and of limited effectiveness. At the time of writing there is still no obvious sign of a sustainable or effective ceasefire, nor of any reconciliation between UNITA and government forces. When or if such a settlement is reached it appears likely that there will be a need for a full-scale UN peacekeeping operation in Angola mandated as UNAVEM III. Such an operation would, however, add to the existing peacekeeping burden of the United Nations and would require vastly expanded peacekeeping resources from member states.

The fact is that many of the problems of the 1980s and early 1990s remain active. Iraq still has not renounced territorial ambitions against Kuwait for example, nor has it improved its human rights record.

Sanctions against Haiti, Yugoslavia and Libya remain in force, and there is still no reconciliation between Turk and Greek on Cyprus.

The United Nations remains the only set of global institutions capable of providing a centre for the incipient world community. It is the difference between civilisation and chaos, it provides the one forum capable of promoting global cooperation. As the world stumbles hesitantly, violently into the twenty-first century, it is absolutely imperative that states and peoples acknowledge this fact and dedicate their intellectual, economic and political resources to ensuring that it fulfils its promise.

Index

Abdallah, Lt-Col Walid Saud Muammad, 87
Abgal clan, 114, 115fn16
Abyssinia, 311
Addis Ababa accords, 131, 132, 133
Afghanistan, 184
  civil war, 251, 253
  human rights, 251
  refugees from, 251, 252, 253, 254
  and Soviet Union, 33, 250, 251, 252, 253
  and UN, 20, 250, 251, 253, 254
  and US, 253
  see also United Nations Security Council, Resolutions
Africa, 15, 119, 127, 182
  and Angola, 309
  and end of Cold War, 120
  and refugees, 164
  and sovereignty, 186
  and UN, 120, 124
  and US, 110
African Rights, 174-5, 177, 178
Africa Watch, 109, 110
Aga Khan, Prince Sadruddin, 167
Agenda for Peace, 22, 51, 185, 228
  and ICJ, 207, 210
Ahtisaari, Martti, 258
Aideed, General Mohamed Farah, 114, 116, 123, 131, 133, 176
  and Ali Mahdi, 114, 115, 117, 119, 122, 126
  and mediation efforts, 112, 115
  and UN, 118, 122, 123, 125, 170, 172, 187
  and UNITAF, 130, 131
  and UNOSOM II, 133, 134, 135
  and UNSCR 814, 169
Akashi, Yasushi, 38, 40, 42, 48, 51
al-Ahmad, Sheikh Sabah, 65
al-Faisal, Prince Saud, 68
Alatas, Ali, 33, 223, 225
Albania, 141, 158, 159
Algeria, 74, 75
Ali Mahdi Mohamed, President, 14, 114, 115, 122, 123
  and Aideed, 114, 115, 117, 119, 122, 126
  and UN, 118, 119, 125, 170, 172, 187
  and UNITAF, 130, 131
Alianza Republicana Nacional (ARENA), 262, 266, 267
Almirante Irízar, 232
Amin, President Hafizullah, 251
Amnesty International, 110
Anaya, Admiral Jorge, 237
Angola, 164, 169, 183, 258, 303, 309
  arms embargo, 308
  civil war, 302, 304, 305, 306
  Joint Political Military Commission, 306, 307

elections, 302, 303, 307, 310
Observer countries, 304, 305, 307, 308
and South Africa, 255
and UN, 19, 21, 183, 303, 304, 305, 310, 327
see also United Nations Security Council, Resolutions
Angola, National Union for the Total Independence of (UNITA), 302-10 *passim*, 327
Angolan Armed Forces, 302-3
Anstee, Margaret, 303, 305, 307
Antarctic, 227
Antarctic Treaty, 213
Aouzou Strip, 207
apartheid, 312, 313
Aptidon, President Hassan Gouled, 115
Arab Cooperation Council, 63
Arab League, 12, 13, 117, 136
Arab League Council, 101, 102
and Iraq, 73, 74, 75, 87
Summit meeting 64, 74
Arab States, 101, 284, 285, 286
and Iraq, 99, 102
and Saddam Hussein, 58, 96
Arab-Israeli conflict, 74
Arafat, Yasser, 75
Argentina
and Falkland Islands dispute, 235, 236, 238, 239, 241
claims to Falkland Islands, 230, 231
occupation of Falkland Islands, 233
and Falklands sovereignty, 234, 235
and Alexander Haig, 241-2
and sovereignty of Falkland Islands, 231, 232, 237, 238
and UK, 240
and US, 233, 236
and UNFICYP, 279

Argentine Navy, 232
Aristide, Father Jean-Bertrand, 181, 317
arms
in Bosnia, 157
control, 211, 213, 214, 215, 216, 220, 319, 324
and UN, 22, 23, 24, 215
in Croatia, 149, 153
in Cyprus, 276
in El Salvador, 271
embargoes, 184, 216, 311, 312
race, 28, 212, 215
ASEAN *see* Association of Southeast Asian Nations
ASEAN Declaration on the South China Sea, 18
ASEAN Ministerial Meeting (AMM), 225, 226
Assad, President, 96
Association of Southeast Asian Nations (ASEAN)
and Cambodia, 8fn25, 11, 27, 29, 30, 31, 53
and South China Sea, 223, 224, 225, 226
Association of West European Parliamentarians for Action Against Apartheid (AWEPPAA), 303
Austin, Reg, 47
Australia, 186
and Cambodia, 8fn25, 11, 29, 31-2, 43, 53
Working Papers on Cambodia, 33-4
and Cyprus, 276
and ICJ, 210
and Indonesia, 243, 245, 247
and Iraq, 87, 88
and Kashmir, 295
and Namibia, 257
and Papua New Guinea, 188
and Vietnam, 29
Austria, 146

Azad Kashmir, 288, 289, 292, 298
Aziz, Tariq, 69, 80, 95
  and Kuwait, 68, 99, 100
  meeting with James Baker, 79
  meeting with Perez de Cuellar, 81
  memorandum to Arab League, 64, 102

Badinter Commission/Report, 146, 154
Baidoa, 123, 128, 130, 173, 175, 177, 178
Baker, James, 77, 79
Baker, Noel, 289
Bali Treaty *see* Treaty of Amity and Cooperation in Southeast Asia
Balkans, 16, 17, 141
Bangladesh, 196, 289
Bardera, 128
Barre, President Siad, *see* Siad Barre
Basra, 59, 60
Belaunde, President, 238
Belgium, 243, 245, 247, 295
Bell, Coral, 17
Ben Gurion, 10
Bendjedid, President Chadli, 75, 76
Berbera, 107, 108
Beye, Alioune Blondin, 305
Bharatiya Janata Party (BJP), 298
Biafra, 9
Bicesse Accords, 302, 304, 306
Biko, Steve, 312
Biological Weapons Convention (BWC) 1972, 213-18 *passim*, 319, 323
biological weapons, 23, 85, 320, 322, 323
Bishara, Abdullah, 67
Blix, Director-General, 219
Bosnia, 145, 148, 160, 327
  and Europe, 151
  and human rights, 155-6, 157
  intervention in, 3, 172, 181, 183, 184, 185
  and secession, 141
  recognition, 146
  and sanctions, 315, 316
  Serbs in, 140
  and UN, 153, 155, 156, 157, 172, 187, 188
  and UNSCR 780, 169
  war in, 140, 154-7
Bosnia and Hercegovina v Yugoslavia (Serbia and Montenegro), 209
Bosnia-Hercegovina, 17, 154, 315
Botha, Pik, 303
Bougainville, Louis-Antoine de, 229
Boutros-Ghali, Boutros
  and Africa, 120, 127
  and Bosnia, 188
  and development, 200
  and ICJ, 22
  and Somalia, 120, 122, 124, 128, 130, 132, 135, 137, 138
  and sovereignty, 185-6
  and Yugoslavia, 150
Brioni Agreement, 145
Britain *see* United Kingdom
British Task Force, 233, 240
Brunei, 18, 223
Bubiyan island, 12, 60, 62, 64, 65, 66, 75
Bucarelli, Francisco de Paula, 230
Buddhist Liberal Democratic Party, 49
Bulgaria, 158, 160, 317
Burkino Faso v Mali, 208
Burundi, 327
Bush, President George
  and Gulf conflict, 69, 71, 79, 82, 95, 98
  and Somalia, 128, 129
Bush administration, 76, 96

Byron, John, 229

Cambodia, 10, 11, 27, 42, 53, 165, 181
  Advance Electoral Planning Unit (AEPU), 39, 47, 55
  Agreements on a Comprehensive Political Settlement of the Cambodia Conflict, 36, 37, 53
  background to conflict, 28-9
  Cambodian People's Party (CPP), 47, 48
  civil administration of, 44-6, 53
  Core Group countries and, 43, 51, 54
  efforts to find solution to civil war in, 29-36
  elections in, 42, 43, 46-9, 53, 54, 57
  human rights in, 35, 37, 49, 53
  Informal Meeting on, Jakarta, 1990, 33-4
  infrastructure of, 50, 51-2
  international aid for, 50, 51
  Ministerial Conference on the Reconstruction and Rehabilitation of, 41
  refugees from, 49-50, 52, 188
  sovereignty, 35
  Supreme National Council (SNC), 34, 36, 37, 40
  and UN, 11, 29, 34, 52, 53, 54, 57, 179
    peace settlement, 30-9 *passim*, 51
    volunteers in Cambodia, 47, 48, 54, 56-7
  see also Cambodia, State of; International Committee on the Reconstruction of Cambodia (ICORC); Kampuchea, Coalition Government of Democratic (CGDK); Kampuchea, People's Republic of (PRK); Khmer People's National Liberation Front (KPNLF); Khmer Rouge; Royal Government of the National Union of Cambodia (GRUNC); United Front for an Independent, Neutral, Peaceful and Cooperative Cambodia (FUNCINPEC); United Nations Advance Mission to Cambodia (UNAMIC); United Nations General Assembly, Resolutions of; United Nations Security Council, Resolutions; United Nations Transitional Authority in Cambodia (UNTAC)

Cambodia, State of (SOC), 27, 29, 54
  and Cambodian elections, 47, 48
  civil administration of, 44
  and comprehensive settlement, 35, 36
  human rights in, 49
  and Khmer Rouge, 32
  and the PICC, 31
  and UN settlement in Cambodia, 30
  during UNTAC administration, 37, 46
Cambodian Peoples Armed Forces (CPAF), 47, 48
Camilion, Oscar, 239fn24
Camp David Agreements, 1978, 283, 284
Canada v United States of America, 209
Canada, 18, 43, 234, 257, 278
Cape Verde, 120
CARE, 174, 175, 177

INDEX 333

Carrington, Lord, 144, 145, 146, 153
Carter, President Jimmy, 9, 312
Carter administration, 108, 135
Catholic Church, 10, 182, 264
Central America, 233
Central Intelligence Agency (CIA), 92
CGDK *see* Kampuchea, Coalition Government of Democratic
Chad, 207
Chapultapec Accord/Agreements, 266, 270
chemical weapons, 23, 217, 218, 319, 320
 banning of, 212, 214
 and Iraq, 85, 94-5, 321, 322, 323
Chemical Weapons Convention (CWC), 213, 214, 214-15, 218, 323, 324
 Iran-Iraq War and, 217
Cheney, Richard, 70, 77
Childers, Erskine, 21, 184
Chile, 295
China
 and Cambodia, 29, 30, 33, 43
 and Khmer Rouge, 11, 27, 30, 41, 42
 and the DPRK, 220
 and UN resolutions on Iraq, 84, 88
 and South China Sea, 17, 18, 222, 223, 224, 225, 226
 and sovereignty, 186
 and Soviet Union, 30
 and Vietnam, 29, 30
civilian police, 45-6, 257
 in El Salvador, 264, 265, 267, 269, 270, 271
Clark, Jeffrey, 173
Clerides, President Glafcos, 278
Clinton, President Bill, 134, 305
Cochran, Merle, 245
Cold War, 94, 107-8, 110, 111, 120, 144, 248

collective security, 319
Colombia, 266
Commonwealth of Nations, 275
Comprehensive Test Ban Treaty, 215
Conference on Disarmament, 213
Conference on Security and Cooperation in Europe (CSCE)
 and Kosovo, 160
 and Macedonia, 158, 159
 and NATO, 148
 and Yugoslavia, 147, 152, 153
confidence building, 23, 213, 223, 226, 277
conflict management, 6, 7, 19, 144, 278, 279
conflict resolution, 4, 5, 6, 24, 38, 191, 192, 326
 in Somalia, 121
 in South America, 268
 and UN, 53, 54, 279
Congress Party, 298
conventional weapons, 212, 214, 215
Cooperating for Peace: The Global Agenda for the 1990s, 1, 4, 7, 325
cooperative security, 2, 214, 327
Cordovez, Diego, 252
Costa Méndez, Nicanor, 232-8 *passim*
crisis management, 4, 5, 143-8
Cristiani, President Alfredo, 262, 264, 267
Cristiani Government, 262
Critchley-duBois Plan, 245, 247, 249
Croatia, 3, 140, 141, 142, 145, 160
 and Europe, 144
 nationalism in, 141
 recognition of, 144, 145, 146
 and sanctions, 144, 315, 316
 Serbian minority in, 140, 145
 and UN, 148-54, 157

see also United Nations Security Council, Resolutions
Cuba, 108, 258, 262
  in Angola, 255, 302
  and Iraq, 83, 84, 87, 88, 323
Cypriot National Guard, 276
Cyprus, 273, 274, 276, 277, 328
  and international community, 277, 278
  and UN, 19, 273
  and UNFICYP, 277, 278, 279
  see also United Nations Peacekeeping Force in Cyprus (UNFICYP); United Nations Security Council, Resolutions

D'Aubuisson, Roberto, 266
Daoud, President Muhammad, 250
Darod clan, 105
Davidoff, Constantino, 232-3, 240
de Klerk, F.W., 313
del Castillo, Graciana, 270
Delors, Jacques, 144
de Soto, Alvaro, 263, 267, 268, 269, 270
de Waal, Alex, 109, 116
de Weert, Sebald, 229
Denktash, 278
Denmark, 278, 295
Desert Shield, 76, 77, 78, 85, 86, 87, 89, 90, 92
Desert Storm, 76, 85, 86, 88, 89, 90, 321
developing countries, 185, 194, 195
di Chamorra, Violetta Barrios, 183
Diego Garcia, 108
Digil clan, 105
Dir clan, 105
disarmament, 23, 211, 213, 214, 216, 220, 319, 324
  in Angola, 306, 310
  on Cyprus, 274
  and Iraq, 324
  in Somalia, 130, 131, 132, 133, 135
  and UN, 22, 23, 24, 212, 215
displaced persons *see* refugees
Dixon, Sir Owen, 288, 292, 296, 300
Djibouti, Republic of, 106
Djibouti agreement, 115, 117
Dolbahante clan, 107
Dole, Bob, 134
Dos Santos, Jose Eduardo, 303
Dozo, Lieutenant-General Lami, 237
DPRK *see* Korea, People's Democratic Republic of
Duarte, José, 261, 262
Dumas, Roland, 80

Eastern Europe, 147
Egmont, Lord, 229
Egypt, 10, 317
  and Gulf War, 66, 74, 96
  and Israel, 280, 281, 285
  and MFO, 283, 284
  and Somali crisis, 14, 112, 115, 116
Egypt-Israeli Peace Treaty, 1979, 283, 287
Ekeus, Rolf, 322
El Salvador, 183, 188, 261, 262, 264
  Commission of Truth of, 266, 271
  economic and social issues in, 266, 270
  elections in, 261, 262, 265, 270, 271, 327
  human rights in, 262, 264, 266, 267, 269
  and international community, 262, 270
  land reform in, 266, 270
  and National Civil Police, 264, 265, 267, 269, 270, 271

and Peace Accords, 262, 263, 264, 265, 271, 272
terrorism in, 262, 271
and UN, 19, 183, 184, 263-5, 270
see also United Nations Security Council, Resolutions
elections
 in Angola, 302, 303, 307
 in Cambodia, 42, 43, 46-9, 53, 54, 57
 proposed for, 27, 29, 32, 34, 36, 41
 in El Salvador, 261, 262, 270, 271, 272, 327
 in Namibia, 256, 257
 and UN operations, 310
Eliasson, Jan, 185
embargoes, 121, 184, 305, 308
Emir of Kuwait, 59, 65, 67, 69, 99
Enders, Thomas, 239
Environmental Modification Treaty, 213
Eritrea, 117, 122, 166
Ermacora, Felix, 251
Esquipulas Agreement, 1985, 262, 268
Ethiopia, 106, 137
 and displaced persons, 169
 food aid to, 166
 relief problems of, 164
 and Somalia, 107-8, 108, 110, 111, 115
ethnic cleansing, 142, 153, 181, 188
Europe, 62, 140, 152, 157
European Community, 17, 181
 and Bosnia, 155, 157
 and Croatia, 157
 and Gulf War, 72, 80
 and Macedonia, 158
 and Somalia, 111, 112, 115
 and Yugoslavia, 143-6, 150, 152
European Parliament, 144, 145
Evans, Senator Gareth, 1, 3

and Cambodian peace initiative, 31
and cooperative security, 2, 327
and preventive diplomacy, 24, 26

Fahd, King, 64, 67, 68, 69, 96
Falkland Islands, 19, 239
 early history of, 229-32
 Haig mediation for, 233-8
 see also Argentina; United Nations General Assembly, Resolutions of; United Nations Security Council, Resolutions
FAO *see* Food and Agricultural Organisation
Finland, 278, 295
FMLN *see* Frente Faribundo Marti Para La Liberacion Nacional
Food and Agricultural Organisation (FAO), 173, 195
food, 187, 198, 200
 and Mozambique, 182
 in Somalia, 173, 176, 177, 178
Ford Foundation Report on Financing an Effective United Nations, 198
France, 143, 146, 148, 156, 208, 229
 and Iraq, 79, 80, 82
 and Somalia, 107, 115
Franks Review, 231fn2, 241
French Somaliland, 106
Frente Faribundo Marti Para La Liberacion Nacional (FMLN), 183, 261-7 *passim*, 271
 and elections, 271, 272
 and ONUSAL, 264, 267, 269
Friends, Society of (Quakers), 10
FUNCINPEC *see* United Front for an Independent, Neutral,

Peaceful and Cooperative Cambodia

Gadabursi clan, 112
Galtieri, General Leopoldo, 235, 236, 237, 239
Gedir, Habr, 115fn16
General Belgrano, 241
Geneva Accords on Afghanistan, 20, 250, 252-3
Geneva Convention, and Additional Protocols (1977), 164, 169, 170, 202
Geneva Peace Conference on the Middle East, 286
Geneva Protocol (1925), 212, 214, 217, 319
genocide, 2, 5, 10, 11, 34, 35, 36
Genocide Convention, 209
Germany, 43, 80, 86, 115, 144, 146, 157, 284
Glaspie, April, 70-1, 95, 98
GOC *see* United Nations Good Offices Committee on the Indonesian Question
Golan Heights, 281, 282, 285
Gorbachev, Mikhail S., 30, 78, 94, 252
Goulding, Marrack, 303
Greece
  and Cyprus, 273, 274, 275, 277
  and Macedonia, 158, 159, 160
Greek Cypriot National Guard, 273, 274
Grytviken, 233
Gulf conflict *see* Gulf War
Gulf Cooperation Council, 12, 13
Gulf Cooperation Countries, 62-9 *passim*, 101, 102
Gulf of Tonkin, 223
Gulf War, 11, 12fn30, 13, 84-6, 91, 118, 217, 220
  background of, 59-63
  and humanitarian intervention, 167-8, 179
  and preventive diplomacy, 58, 65, 65-72, 93-100
  and UN, 12, 13, 58, 72, 86-93
  see also Iraq; preventive diplomacy

Haig, Alexander, 239-42 *passim*
Haiti, 18, 181, 182, 311, 317, 328
  see also United Nations Security Council, Resolutions
Hammadi, Sa'adoun, 66, 74
Hare, Paul J., 305
Hargeisa, 110
Harte clan, 176
Hasan al-Bakr, President Ahmad, 61
Hasan al-Majid, Ali, 66
Hassan, King, 75
Hatta, 243
Hawiye clan, 105, 111, 113, 114
Hindus, 296
Honduras, 261, 271
Horn of Africa, 108, 112, 137
Howe, Admiral Jonathan, 133
human rights, 4, 5, 24, 25, 37, 171, 185, 192
  in Afghanistan, 251
  and Argentina, 239
  and Bosnia, 155-6, 157
  in Cambodia, 35, 37, 49, 53
  and Croatia, 153
  in El Salvador, 262, 263, 264, 266, 267, 269
  in Haiti, 182
  in Iraq, 97, 327
  in Kashmir, 289, 294, 297
  in Kuwait, 91, 102
  in Namibia, 257
  and NGOs, 178, 188
  and Somalia, 110, 111
  and Yugoslavia, 16
Human Rights Commission of the Economic and Social Council, 251

Human Rights, Agreement on, 264
Humanitarian Affairs, Under-Secretary for, 171, 173, 194, 200 *see also* United Nations Department of Humanitarian Affairs
humanitarian conflicts *see* humanitarian emergencies
humanitarian crises *see* humanitarian emergencies
humanitarian disasters *see* humanitarian emergencies
humanitarian emergencies, 9, 25, 104, 166, 181-5, 199, 326
and UN, 26, 138, 139, 195, 197
see also media; and individual countries
humanitarian intervention, 164
benefits of, 183
and Bosnia, 3, 181
and causes of conflict, 199-201
and coercive measures, 201-3
financing of, 180, 202-3
Kurds and, 181
reform of, 198-9
and Red Cross, 189-90
right of, 129, 168-9
in Somalia, 119-20, 121, 137
and sovereignty, 185-7
and UN, 164, 171-85, 187, 202
and US, 127-8, 179
humanitarian law *see* international humanitarian law
humanitarian relief, 183, 184, 194-9
Hun Sen, 31, 42
Hunt, Leamon, 284
Hussein, King, 64, 68, 69, 73, 75, 76
Hussein, Saddam *see* Saddam Hussein

Ibrahim, Izzat, 66, 73
ICJ *see* International Court of Justice

ICORC *see* International Committee on the Reconstruction of Cambodia
India, 10, 43, 301
and Kashmir dispute, 288, 296
domestic considerations and, 288, 298, 299
origins of, 288-90
and sovereignty, 186, 296
and UN, 20, 290, 294
and UNMOGIP, 294, 297
see also United Nations Security Council, Resolutions
Indo-Pakistan war, 1965, 292-3, 300
Indo-Pakistan war, 1971, 293, 300
Indonesia, 19, 222
and Cambodia, 11, 43, 53
and the Netherlands, 243-9 *passim*
and South China Sea, 18, 223, 224
see also United Nations Security Council, Resolutions
Indonesia, United States of (USI), 243, 244, 245
Inhumane Weapons Convention, 213
Intergovernmental Authority on Drought and Development (IGADD), 112, 137
International Atomic Energy Agency (IAEA), 218, 219, 323
and Iraq, 217, 319, 320, 321, 322
safeguards and, 214, 218, 220
International Committee of Red Cross (ICRC), 9, 170, 181, 188, 192, 193
and Cyprus, 274
and early warning of emergencies, 197-8
and humanitarian intervention, 183, 189-90, 202

and Mozambique, 182
and Rwanda, 189
and Somalia, 112, 116, 119, 127, 172, 173, 174, 175, 176, 189
and Sudan, 165
International Committee on the Reconstruction of Cambodia (ICORC), 37, 50, 51
International Conference for the Protection of War Victims, 170
International Convention on State Immunities, 210
International Court of Justice
and ad hoc Chambers procedure, 209-10
and displaced persons, 170
effectiveness of, 22
and Gulf crisis, 91-2, 102
and peacekeeping expenses, 282
and preventive diplomacy, 103
role of, 207, 208-10
and South Africa in Namibia, 255
and South China Sea, 18, 227
International Fact Finding Commission, 171
International Monetary Fund (IMF), 270
International Parliamentary Union, 303
international humanitarian law, 155, 156, 164, 189
enforcement of, 169-71, 202
evolution of, 168-9
and Red Cross, 193
and sovereignty, 185
structure of, 192-4
see also international law
international law, 164, 185, 189, 193, 207, 227
and Iraqi invasion of Kuwait, 59, 86

intervention, 2, 5, 9, 12fn30, 17, 24, 147, 326
and Bosnia, 155, 157
in Somalia, 128-9
intervention, humanitarian *see* humanitarian intervention
Iran, 61, 75, 251, 314
Iran-Iraq War, 33, 77, 94, 96-7, 217
Iraq, 61, 64, 78, 85, 91, 93, 94, 167, 217, 280, 311, 319
and Arab States, 73-6, 99
arms in, 217, 324
economy of, 62-3
hostages in, 78, 81, 82, 88
human rights in, 97, 327
and international community, 58, 61, 72, 77, 82-8 *passim*, 92, 97-100
intervention in, 121, 171, 181, 183, 185
and Iran, 62, 63, 75
and Kuwait, 12, 13, 59-7 *passim*, 327
invasion and annexation of, 11, 58, 74, 75, 76, 81, 86, 97, 100
perceptions of leadership in, 93-7
and preventive diplomacy
by Arab States, 73-6
by UN, 100-2
Western, 76-82
sanctions against, 71-4 *passim*, 77, 82, 87, 92, 92-3, 97, 167, 311, 314, 317, 321-4 *passim*
and UN, 66, 81-6 *passim*, 89, 100-2, 167, 187, 218, 314, 319, 320
and UNHCR, 193
and US, 69-72, 79, 97-8, 179
see also United Nations Security Council, Resolutions; United Nations Special

Commission in Iraq (UNSCOM)
Iraqi Revolutionary Command Council, 61, 76, 97
Isaaq clan, 105, 108, 109, 110, 113, 114
Islamic fundamentalism, 299
Israel, 10, 96, 280, 281
  and Egypt, 281, 285
  and Lebanon, 282, 286
  and MFO, 283, 284
  and Syria, 281, 286
  see also United Nations Security Council, Resolutions
Israel-Egypt Agreement, 281
Israel-Egypt Peace Treaty (1979), 283, 287
Italy, 14, 112, 115, 116, 134, 295
Izetbegovic, Alija, 154, 155

Jammu and Kashmir, State of *see* Kashmir
Jammu, 299
Japan, 41, 43, 62, 86, 284, 303
Jess, Colonel Ahmed Omar, 130
Johnson, General Robert, 175
Jonah, James, 118, 120, 122
Jordan
  and Iraq, 66, 73, 74, 314, 317
  and Israel, 280, 281

Kampuchea, Coalition Government of Democratic (CGDK), 29, 31, 32
Kampuchea, People's Republic of (PRK), 29
Karachi Agreement, 1949, 292, 293
Karmal, President Babrak, 251, 252
Kashmir
  elections in, 289
  and human rights, 294, 297
  and international community, 290, 297-8, 301
  Line of Control in, 293, 294, 295, 297, 300
  origins of dispute over, 288-90
  plebiscite suggestion for, 296, 297, 298
  political stasis in, 295, 299, 300
  and UN, 19, 20, 288, 289, 290-6 *passim*, 299, 300, 301
  UN resolutions on, 290-2, 294, 297-8, 300
  see also India; Pakistan; United Nations Security Council, Resolutions
Kelly, John, 71, 98
Kenya, 14, 106, 107, 108, 112, 137
Khadima, 75
Khalq group, 250, 251
Khmer People's National Liberation Front (KPNLF), 27, 29, 37, 44
Khmer Rouge, 27, 28, 29, 30, 31, 40, 41
  and elections, 47
  and China, 11, 30
  and comprehensive settlement, 35
  and democratisation, 267
  during UNTAC administration, 37
  non-compliance with Paris Agreements, 40-6 *passim*, 53, 54
  see also genocide
Khor Abd Allah estuary, 62
Khor Zubair, 62
Kirkpatrick, Jeane, 234, 240
Kismayu, 113, 123, 128, 130, 175
Kittani, Ismat, 126, 128
Klibi, Chedli, 64, 69, 102
Korea, Democratic People's Republic of (DPRK) (North Korea), 24, 219-20, 220
  see also United Nations

INDEX

Security Council, Resolutions
Korea, Republic of (South Korea), 220
Kosovo, 141, 158, 159-60
Krajina, Republic of Serbian, 149, 150, 151, 315
Kurds, 96, 97, 118, 167, 168, 171, 181
Kuwait, 60, 64, 85
  annexation of, 74, 75, 81
  and Arab states, 66, 74, 102
  human rights in, 91, 102
  and ICJ, 91
  and Iran, 65
  and Iraq, 11, 12, 13, 58-67 passim, 72-6 passim, 86, 99-100, 314, 327
  and sovereignty, 67, 74, 85
  and UN, 91, 100, 101
  and UNSR 678, 89
  and US, 70, 71, 76
  see also Provisional Government of Free Kuwait (PGFK); United Nations Security Council, Resolutions

Ladakh, 299
Laitin, D., 109
Laos, 51, 224
Law of the Sea, Convention on (1982), 18, 22, 227
League of Nations, 195, 212, 311
Lebanon, 280, 281, 282, 286
Leith, 233
Lewis, I.M., 108
Liberia, 168, 181, 182
Libya v Chad, 207
Libya, 207, 311
  and Iraq, 73, 74, 75
  sanctions against, 315, 328
Linggadjati Agreement, 243
Lon Nol, Marshal, 28
Lusaka Peace talks, 327

Maastricht Summit, 146
Macedonia, 3, 141, 158-9, 160, 316 *see also* Yugoslavia, Macedonians in
Madiun, 245
Majerteyn clan, 109, 113, 114
Malaysia, 18, 223, 225, 226
Maley, Michael, 47
Malvinas *see* Falkland Islands
Marehan clan, 105, 107, 112, 113
Marine Scientific Research Working Group, 224
Mauritania, 74, 75
McNaughton, General Andrew, 292
Médecins sans Frontières (MSF), 127, 176, 177, 190-1
media, 14fn32, 166, 189
  and Somalia crisis, 14, 117, 127, 134, 135, 137, 174
Mengistu, President, 109, 111
MFO *see* Multinational Force and Observers in the Sinai
Middle East, 283, 285, 287
Milosevic, Slobodan, 141, 146, 159, 316
minorities, 15, 140, 141, 142, 146, 147
Missile Technology Control Regime (MTCR), 217
missiles, 217, 218, 320, 321, 322
Mitchell, C.R., 6, 9
Mitterand, President François, 79, 80
Mogadishu, 111, 113, 114, 123, 124, 125, 130, 175, 177
  ceasefire in, 191
  Djibouti agreement, 115
  evacuation of UN staff, 117, 118
  fighting in, 112, 119, 122, 123, 134, 137, 138
  food for, 116, 125
Moi, President, 137
Montenegro, 311, 315, 316

Morgan, General Siyad (Mohamed) Hersi, 130, 176
Morocco, 120
Mousouris, Sotirios, 254
Mozambique, 164, 169, 182-3, 312
Mubarak, President Hosni, 64, 68, 69, 96
Mugabe, President Robert, 303, 312
Mujahideen, 251, 252, 253, 254
Multinational Force and Observers in the Sinai (MFO), 280-7 *passim*
Muslims, 141, 154, 156, 157, 160, 296

Najibullah, 252, 253, 254
Namibia, 165, 255, 256, 257, 313
  peacekeeping in, 38, 259
  refugees, 256, 257
  and UN, 20, 21, 32, 179, 255, 256-8, 259
  see also United Nations Security Council, Resolutions; United Nations Transition Assistance Group (UNTAG)
Nasser, President, 10
nationalism, 106, 141, 142, 147, 159, 247
Natsios, Andrew, 120
Nauru v Australia, 208, 209
Nehru, Jawaharlal, 246, 289
Netherlands East Indies, 243, 245
Netherlands 245, 248
  and independence of Indonesia, 243, 244, 245, 246
  'police actions' in Indonesia, 243, 245, 248, 249
Nicaragua, 183, 262, 271
Nicosia International Airport, 276, 277
Nigeria, 9, 10, 124

non-government agencies *see* non-governmental organisations
non-governmental organisations (NGOs), 16, 20, 165, 183, 193-4, 198
  definition of 'humanitarian', 171, 189
  and humanitarian relief, 165, 173, 178
  and human rights, 188
  and intervention, 139, 166, 191
  and preventive diplomacy, 10, 26
  and Somalia, 112, 119, 127, 130, 173, 174
  and UN, 134, 195
non-proliferation, 215, 216, 220
  see also proliferation
North Atlantic Treaty Organisation (NATO), 3, 17, 147, 148, 152
North Korea *see* Korea, Democratic People's Republic of
Norway, 295
Nuclear Non-Proliferation Treaty (NPT), 213, 214, 218
  and the DPRK, 24, 219-20
  and Iraq, 217, 320
nuclear weapons, 23, 212, 214, 218, 301
  and Iraq, 217, 321, 322, 323
Nujoma, Sam, 256

Office of Research and the Collection of Information (ORCI), 101-2
Office of the Secretary-General in Afghanistan and Pakistan (OSGAP) (previously UNGOMAP), 252, 253
Office of the United Nations Coordinator for Humanitarian and Economic Assistance Program

Relating to Afghanistan (UNOCA) (later UNOCHA), 253
Ogaden, 107
Ogaden clan, 105, 106, 107, 110, 113
Ogaden War, 108
Ogata, Sadako, 188
oil, 85, 311, 312
 and Iraq, 93, 321
 over-production of, 65, 66
 price of, 62, 63, 64, 65, 85
 in South China Sea, 222, 224, 226
Oman, 108
ONUSAL see United Nations Observer Mission in El Salvador
Operation Lifeline Sudan, 165-6, 178, 180
Operation Provide Comfort, 168, 180
Operation Provide Relief, 175
Operation Restore Hope, 174, 175, 178
Organisation for the Prohibition of Chemical Weapons (OPCW), 323, 324
Organisation of African Unity (OAU)
 and Angola, 303, 309
 and Republic of Somaliland, 114
 and Somalia, 14, 115, 117, 119, 136, 137
Organisation of Petroleum Exporting Countries (OPEC), 63, 64, 66
Organisation of the Islamic Conference (OIC), 136
Otero, Admiral, 233
Ottoman Empire, 59
Outer Space Treaty, 213
Owen, David, 151, 156, 159

Pakistan, 10, 301
 and Afghanistan, 251, 252
 and Kashmir dispute, 288, 296
 domestic considerations, 288, 298-9
 origins of dispute, 288-90
 and UN, 20, 290, 293, 297-8
 and UNMOGIP, 294, 297
 see also United Nations India Pakistan Observation Mission (UNIPOM); United Nations Security Council, Resolutions
 in Somalia, 125, 133
Palestine, 280 see also United Nations Security Council, Resolutions
Palestine Liberation Organisation (PLO), 73, 74, 75
Panama, 183
Panic, Milan, 316
Papua New Guinea, 188
Paracel Islands, 17, 226
Parcham group, 250
Paris Agreements, 44, 46, 53, 54
Paris Charter, 147
Paris International Conference on Cambodia (PICC), 1989, 11, 31, 35, 36, 37, 41
Partial Test Ban Treaty, 213
Party of Democratic Kampuchea (PDK), see Khmer Rouge
peacekeeping, 21, 38, 51, 279
 administration of, 55, 57
 in Angola, 310
 Cambodia, 36, 52, 54
 and CSCE, 147
 on Cyprus, 273, 274, 275, 276, 277, 278
 in El Salvador, 263, 268, 270
 financing of, 186, 198, 202, 282
 and ICJ, 207, 208
 in Kashmir, 290-4, 295, 299, 300
 and MFO, 285, 286
 and Namibia, 256, 259

and NATO, 148
in Somalia, 122, 132
in Sudan, 165
and UN, 1, 149-52, 170, 201, 260, 295
and UNEF I, 281
and UN Secretary-General, 184
and US, 179
in former Yugoslavia, 3, 17, 149-52, 156, 158
peacemaking, 145-7, 156, 210, 256
and Gulf War, 58, 72-82, 97
Perez de Cuellar, Javier
and Afghanistan, 252
and El Salvador, 183, 264, 269
and Falkland Islands dispute, 241, 242
and Iraq, 81, 101
and Somalia, 120
and Yugoslavia, 146
see also United Nations Secretary-General
Permanent Five see United Nations Security Council, Permanent Five
Persian Gulf, 61
Philippines, 18, 223, 226
PICC see Paris International Conference on Cambodia
Pickering, Thomas, 268, 269
Plattner, Denise, 169
plutonium, 219
Pol Pot, 28, 36
Political Risk Services Ltd, 15
Popular Movement for the Liberation of Angola (MPLA), 303, 307, 309
Port Egmont, 230
Port Stanley, 233
Portugal v Australia, 208
Portugal, 304, 306, 312 see also United Nations Security Council, Resolutions
Powell, General Colin, 178, 179-80

preventive diplomacy, 1, 4, 7, 25, 103, 211
effectiveness, 10, 24
and Gulf War, 13, 58, 65-72, 76, 93-100
and humanitarian emergencies, 199
and Iraq, 65, 72-82, 97, 99, 100
and Kashmir, 301
and South China Sea, 17, 18, 19, 222, 223, 225, 228
and treaties, 216
and the UN, 91, 100
and UN Secretary-General, 184
and former Yugoslavia, 144, 159
Primakov, Evgeny 78, 94, 97
proliferation, 214, 217 see also non-proliferation
Provisional Government of Free Kuwait (PGFK), 59
Pym, Francis, 236, 238

Quakers see Friends, Society of

Rahanweyn clan, 105, 112
Rarotonga, Treaty of, 23, 213
Reagan, President Ronald, 97, 233, 312
Reagan administration, 108, 233, 308
Red Cross see International Committee of the Red Cross
refugees, 52, 163, 164, 199
Afghanistan, 251, 252, 253, 254
and Cambodian civil war, 28, 29, 36, 49-50
in Croatia, 153
and El Salvador, 183, 262
and human rights, 188
and international law, 169, 193
and Liberia, 182
and Mozambique, 182, 183
in Namibia, 256, 257

in Rwanda, 189
in Somalia, 111, 116
and UN, 182
and UNHCR, 193
Renamo, 182, 183
Renville Truce Agreement, 244, 245, 247, 249
Rhodesia, 311-12 *see also* United Nations Security Council, Resolutions
Ridley, Nicholas, 232
Romania, 317
Royal Government of the National Union of Cambodia (GRUNC), 28
Rumaila oil field, 62, 63, 64, 66, 75, 99
Russia, 277, 304, 306
Rwanda, 3, 14, 15, 189, 327

Sadat, Anwar, 286
Saddam Hussein, 58, 63, 85
 foreign relations, 58, 68, 73, 75, 78
 and hostages, 81, 82, 88
 and Kuwait, 59, 73, 74, 75
 perceptions of, 93, 94-7
 and preventive diplomacy, 75, 80, 93
 and sanctions, 92, 314
 speeches of, 63, 64
 and UN, 81, 88, 89
 and US, 69-72
safeguards, 214, 217, 218, 219, 220
Sahnoun, Mohammed, 125, 126, 178
Salim Salim, 117
Samatar, S., 109
sanctions, 24, 25, 147, 148, 310
 against Argentina, 236, 238
 in Cambodia, 42
 and DPRK, 220
 against Haiti, 317, 328
 and humanitarian intervention, 181
 impact of, 317-18
 against Iraq, 71, 72, 74, 77, 82, 87, 92-3, 97, 167, 314, 321, 323-4
 against Libya, 315, 328
 and Rhodesia, 311, 312
 and Serbia, 145
 unintended effects of, 317
 and Yugoslavia, 144, 315-16, 328
Sanderson, Lt-Gen. John, 38, 39, 40, 43, 51
Sarajevo, 155, 172
Saudi Arabia, 66, 80
 and Iraq, 63, 74, 85, 96, 99
 and UN, 85, 101
 and US, 75, 76
Save the Children Fund, 174
Savimibi, Dr Jonas, 303, 306, 307, 308, 309, 310
sea lines of communications (SLOCs), 223
Seabed Treaty, 213
Serbia, 3, 311, 141-5 *passim*, 154, 158, 159
 and sanctions, 144, 145, 315, 316
 see also Bosnia, Serbs in; Croatia, Serbian minority in; Yugoslavia, Serbs in
Sevan, Benon, 253, 254
Shackleton, Lord, 231
Shatt al'Arab waterway, 75
Sheffield, 241
Shermarke, President Abdirashid Ali, 106
Shevardnadze, Eduard, 77, 78
Siad Barre, President Mohamed, 107, 111, 116, 172
 and Aideed, 114, 123
 reliance on clans, 109
 fall of, 110-11, 112, 119
 rebellion against, 109-10
 and US, 108
Sica, Mario, 114fn14
Sierra Leone, 182

Sihanouk, Prince/King Norodom, 27, 28, 32, 36, 37, 49
Sikhs, 296
Simla Agreement, 293-4, 295, 298, 300
Sinai, 282, 283, 284, 285
Singapore, 224
Six-Day War, 281
Slovenia, 141, 144, 145, 146
Smith, Ian, 312
Soekarno, 243
Solarz, Stephen, 32
Solomon Islands, 188
Somali Democratic Association, 112
Somali Democratic Movement, 112, 175
Somali National Army (SNA), 131, 133, 134, 176
Somali National Front (SNF), 116, 176
Somali National Movement (SNM), 108-15 *passim*
Somali National Security Service (NSS), 107, 111
Somali Patriotic Movement (SPM), 110, 112, 113, 114, 116, 123
Somali Salvation Democratic Front (SSDF), 108, 112, 113, 114, 123
Somalia, 3, 106, 107, 116, 122, 174, 311
  African Rights report, 175-7, 178
  aid to, 107, 108, 109, 110, 111, 123, 177
  casualties in, 176
  ceasefire in, 123, 124
  clans in, 104-11 *passim*, 113, 123, 130
    Abgal, 114, 115fn16
    Darod, 105
    Digil, 105
    Dir, 105
    Dolbahante, 107
    Gadabursi, 112
    Harte, 176
    Hawiye, 105, 111, 113, 114
    Isaaq, 105, 108, 109, 110, 113, 114
    Majerteyn, 109, 113, 114
    Marehan, 105, 107, 112, 113
    Ogaden, 105, 106, 107, 110, 113
    Rahanweyn, 105, 112
  and the Cold War, 107-8, 110
  collapse of, 14, 139, 181
  constitution of, 106, 107, 111, 113-16, 115
  Councils of, 131, 132, 133, 134
  disarmament in, 128, 132, 133, 135
  elections in, 110, 111, 115, 133
  and Ethiopia, 107, 107-8
  famine in, 119, 123, 127, 134, 137
  food shortages in, 116, 173, 176, 177, 178
  foreign relations of, 111, 112
  as humanitarian emergency, 104, 116
  humanitarian intervention in, 119-20, 183, 184, 185, 186, 190, 201
  and human rights, 110, 111
  and international community, 116, 118-19, 124
  intervention in, 128-9, 130-1, 139, 171
  irredentism, 106, 108
  and mediation efforts, 112-13, 115, 117, 123
  rehabilitation and political reconciliation attempts, 131-6
  and Soviet Union, 107
  and the West, 107, 113, 137

and the UN, 13, 14, 15, 111-12,
    117-28 *passim*, 137-9,
    170, 173, 187, 201
  and UN intervention, 172-9,
    191
  and UNSCR 794, 168-9
  and US, 110, 139, 178, 179
  warlords in, 122-3, 127
  see also United Nations Interim
    Task Force; United Nations
    Security Council,
    Resolutions; United
    Somali Congress (USC)
Somaliland, Republic of, 114
SOS Kinderdorf, 112
South Africa
  and Angola, 308, 309
  and sanctions against, 311,
    312-14
  and Mozambique, 182
  and Namibia, 255-6, 257, 258,
    259
  see also United Nations Security
    Council, Resolutions
South African Defence Forces, 256
South China Sea
  Declaration on, 1992, 225, 226
  and preventive diplomacy, 17,
    18, 19
  territorial claims to, 222, 223,
    226, 227
  workshops on, 223-5, 225,
    226, 228
South Georgia, 232, 240
South Korea *see* Korea, Republic
  of
South Pacific Nuclear Weapon Free
  Zone, 23
South Sandwich Islands, 231
South Thule, 231, 232
South West Africa Territory Force
  (SWATF), 256
South West African Peoples'
  Organisation (SWAPO),
  255, 256, 257, 258
Southeast Asia, 222

Southern Africa, 309
sovereignty, 17, 25
  and Cambodia, 33, 35, 37
  and Falkland Islands, 231-8
    passim
  and humanitarian intervention,
    121, 184, 185-7, 202
  and India and Pakistan, 299
  and international law, 164
  and Iraq, 321
  in Kashmir, 296
  and Kuwait, 67, 74, 85
  and Macedonia, 158
  in South China Sea, 18, 225,
    226
  Sudan, 165
  and Yugoslavia, 143
Soviet bloc, 282, 284
Soviet Union, 94, 140, 255, 283
  in Afghanistan, 250, 251, 252,
    253
  and Cambodia, 27, 33
  and El Salvador, 262
  support for Ethiopia, 107, 108
  and Gulf War, 72
  and Indochina, 30
  and Iraq, 77, 78, 94
  in Namibia, 258
  and Netherlands/Indonesia
    conflict, 248
  and Somalia, 107, 112, 115
  and South Africa, 313
  and US, 33, 77
  and Yugoslavia, 143
  see also Russia
Soweto massacre, 312
Spain, 229, 230
Spratly Islands, 17, 223, 225,
  226, 227
State of Cambodia (SOC) *see*
  Cambodia, State of
Strait of Tiran, 284
Sudan, 139, 164, 165, 169, 181
  and Iraq, 73, 74, 75
  Operation Lifeline Sudan, 165-6
  and Somalia, 115

Suez War, 281
Sultan, Prince, 77
Supreme Revolutionary Council, Somalia, 107
Swallow Reef, 226
Sweden, 278, 295
Swiss Government, 192, 193
Syria, 74, 96, 280, 281, 286

Tabun nerve agent, 322
Taiwan, 18, 223, 224, 225
Tashkent Agreement, 292
technology transfer, 211
terrorism
  in El Salvador, 261, 262, 271
  in Kashmir, 289, 294, 297
Thailand
  and Cambodia, 31, 41, 43, 51, 53
  and Vietnam, 29
  and South China Sea workshops, 224
Thatcher, Margaret, 234, 236, 238, 239, 242, 240
Third World, 14, 92, 120, 157
Timor Gap Treaty, 227
Tito, President, 141, 154, 158, 159
Tlatelolco, Treaty of, 213
Tokyo Declaration, 50
transparency, 23, 213, 216
Treaty of Amity and Cooperation in Southeast Asia (the Bali Treaty), 18, 225, 226
Treaty of Lausanne, 60
Tudjman, Franjo, 146, 150
Tunisia, 75
Turkey, 160
Turkey, 273, 274, 275, 277, 314
Turkish Cypriots, 273, 275
'Turkish Republic of Northern Cyprus' ('TRNC'), 275, 277, 278
Tutwiler, Margaret, 70

Umm Qasr, 62, 64

UNCI *see* United Nations Commission for Indonesia
UNFICYP *see* United Nations Peacekeeping Force in Cyprus
UNICEF *see* United Nations Childrens Fund
Union Nacional Opositora (UNO), 261
Union of Soviet Socialist Republics (USSR) *see* Soviet Union
UNITA *see* Angola, National Union for the Total Independence of
UNITAF *see* United Nations Interim Task Force
United Arab Emirates, 64, 70, 74, 80, 102
United Front for an Independent, Neutral, Peaceful and Cooperative Cambodia (FUNCINPEC), 27, 29, 37, 44, 48
United Kingdom
  and Argentina, 233, 234, 240
  and Bosnia, 156
  and Cyprus, 273, 274, 275, 276, 277
  and Falkland Islands disute, 229-33 *passim*, 238-9, 241
  and Gulf War, 59, 60, 72, 80, 90, 100
  and Kashmir, 289
  and Namibia, 257
  and Somalia, 107, 125
  sanctions against South Africa, 312
  and UNFICYP, 278
  and US, 240
  and Yugoslavia, 144, 146
United Nations
  and arms control, 22, 23, 24, 215

and conflict management/
  resolution, 163, 178, 326, 327
credibility of, 21, 22
and developing role, 164-5, 200
and disarmament, 22, 23, 24, 212, 213, 215
and displaced persons, 182, 200
and humanitarian intervention, 174, 180, 183, 184, 192, 197-8
and ICJ, 22, 207, 210
inefficiencies in, 15
integrity of, 24, 25
and international humanitarian law, 170
and intervention, 5, 165, 171-85
necessity for, 8, 328
and non-international conflict, 187-92
and peacekeeping, 2, 3, 4, 170, 207, 259-60, 283, 284, 285, 287
  costs of, 202
  administration of, 55, 57
  operations of, 54
  role of, 154
and peacemaking, 210
and preventive diplomacy, 81, 100-2, 103
reform of, 9fn27, 26
relief efforts of, 195-7, 197-8, 198-9
resources of, 21, 154
and sanctions, 25, 311 *see also* sanctions
security and humanitarian functions, 164
as Western power, 167
see also individual countries
United Nations Advance Mission to Cambodia (UNAMIC), 38

United Nations Angola Verification Mission (UNAVEM I), 302
United Nations Angola Verification Mission (UNAVEM II), 21, 303-10 *passim*, 327
United Nations Arms Transfer Register, 216
United Nations Charter, 325, 326, 327
  Chapter VII of, 15, 154
  and Cambodia, 43
  and humanitarian relief, 174
  and Indonesia, 243
  and Iraq, 72, 82, 321
  and invasion of Kuwait, 85
  and Middle East, 283
  and sanctions, 25, 311
  and Somalia, 121, 128, 130, 132
  and Pakistan, 294
  and sanctions, 317
  disarmament, 212
  and the DPRK, 220
  and internal conflicts, 2
  and international law, 164
  and regional arrangements, 228
  and weapons possession, 216
United Nations Childrens Fund (UNICEF), 178, 183, 193, 199
  functions of, 195, 196, 197
  in Somalia, 126, 177
United Nations Commission for India and Pakistan (UNCIP), 291, 292, 299
United Nations Commission for Indonesia (UNCI) (previously GOC), 246, 246-7, 248
United Nations Commission for the Unification and Rehabilitation of Korea (UNCURK), 282

INDEX 349

United Nations Commission on Human Rights (UNCHR), 269
United Nations Council for Namibia, 255
United Nations Department of Humanitarian Affairs, 185, 192, 197, 198, 202 *see also* Humanitarian Affairs, Under-Secretary for
United Nations Development Program (UNDP), 50, 173, 199, 263
  functions of, 195, 196, 197
United Nations Disarmament Commission, 23
United Nations Disengagement Observer Force (UNDOF), 281, 286
United Nations Economic and Social Council (ECOSOC), 199
United Nations Emergency Force (UNEF I), 281
United Nations Emergency Force (UNEF II), 281
United Nations Fund for Population Activities (UNFPA), 199
United Nations General Assembly, 91, 102, 212, 217, 219
  and Afghanistan, 253, 254
  Ali Mahdi appeal to, 118, 119
  Resolutions of
    45/3, Cambodia, 15 October 1990, 35
    46/182, December 1991, 185, 194, 198
    47, 228
    1514 (XV), Falkland Islands, 1960, 230, 236
    2065 (XX), Falkland Islands, 16 December 1965, 231
    2816 (XXVI), 195
United Nations Good Offices Committee on the Indonesian Question (GOC) (later UNCI), 243-9 *passim*
United Nations Good Offices Mission in Afghanistan and Pakistan (UNGOMAP) (later OSGAP), 252
United Nations High Commission for Refugees (UNHCR), 168, 181, 188, 197, 199
  and Afghanistan, 250, 251, 254
  and Bosnia, 188
  and Cambodia, 50
  and Cyprus, 274
  and displaced persons, 193, 194
  in relief structure, 195, 196
  and Somalia, 111, 117
United Nations India Pakistan Observation Mission (UNIPOM), 292, 293, 299
United Nations Interim Force in Lebanon (UNIFIL), 281, 286
United Nations Interim Task Force (UNITAF)(Somalia)
  in Somalia, 131, 132, 133, 135, 138
  evaluation of, 174-5
  formation of 128-9
  mandate, 129-31, 178
United Nations Mediator in Palestine, 280
United Nations Military Observers Group in India and Pakistan (UNMOGIP), 20, 292, 293, 295, 296, 299, 300
  achievements of, 297
  aims of, 292
  costs of, 294-5
United Nations Observer Mission in El Salvador (ONUSAL), 263-5, 271, 327
  achievements of, 267-9
United Nations Office for the Co-ordination of Humanitarian

Assistance to Afghanistan (UNOCHA) (previously UNOCA), 250, 253
United Nations Operation in Mozambique (ONUMOZ), 183
United Nations Operation in Somalia (UNOSOM I), 124, 172, 173
  failure of, 125-7, 137
  mandate, 125, 130
United Nations Operation in Somalia (UNOSOM II), 170, 174
  mandate and operation, 131-6
  and US, 131, 134, 135, 139
United Nations Operation in the Congo (ONUC), 281
United Nations Peacekeeping Force in Cyprus (UNFICYP), 273, 274, 275, 276
  financing of, 276, 277, 279
  mandate, 274, 275, 278
  and peacekeeping, 275, 276, 277, 278
United Nations Protected Areas (UNPAs), 149, 150
United Nations Protection Force (UNPROFOR), 17, 148, 150, 151
  in Bosnia, 155, 156
  in Croatia, 153
  options in Yugoslavia, 152
United Nations Secretariat, 54, 101, 195, 216
United Nations Secretary-General, 15, 26, 103, 138, 169, 178, 185
  and Cambodia, 35, 43, 44, 48, 54
  and Croatia, 154
  and Cyprus, 274, 275
  and Iraq, 91, 101-2
  and El Salvador, 184, 262, 268, 269
  and relief work, 193, 194
  and Somali crisis, 14, 174
  and treaties, 23, 212
  see also Boutros-Ghali, Boutros; Perez de Cuellar, Javier; Waldheim, Dr Kurt
United Nations Security Council
  and armed force, 163
  and conflict resolution, 325
  decision making, 188
  disarmament and arms control, 212, 215
  and humanitarian impact of decisions, 171
  and IAEA, 218
  and intervention, 12, 179-81, 185, 185-7, 201
  Permanent Five, members of, 8fn26, 23fn41, 326
  meetings on Cambodia, 34-5, 43, 53
  Resolutions
  and Kuwait, 86-90
  UNSCR, Indonesia, 1 August 1947, 244, 245
  UNSCR 39, India and Pakistan, 20 January 1948, 291
  UNSCR 47, Kashmir, 21 April 1948, 290, 291
  UNSCR 50, Palestine, 29 May 1948, 281
  UNSCR 54, Palestine, 1948, 281
  UNSCR 73, Palestine, 281
  UNSCR 180, Portugal, 1963, 312
  UNSCR 181, South Africa, 1963, 312
  UNSCR 186, Cyprus, March 1964, 274
  UNSCR 217, Rhodesia, 1965, 312
  UNSCR 232, Rhodesia, 1966, 311

INDEX

UNSCR 244, Cyprus, 1967, 274
UNSCR 307, Kashmir, 1971, 290
UNSCR 355, Cyprus, 1974, 274, 277
UNSCR 359, Cyprus, 1974, 275
UNSCR 418, South Africa, 1977, 312
UNSCR 425, Israel, 19 March 1978, 286
UNSCR 435, Namibia, 1978, 20, 255, 256, 257
UNSCR 502, Falkland Islands, 3 July 1982, 233, 235
UNSCR 622, Afghanistan, 31 October 1988, 252
UNSCR 626, Angola, 1988, 302
UNSCR 660, Iraq, 2 August 1990, 79, 83, 86
UNSCR 661, Iraq, 6 August 1990, 82, 83, 87, 314
UNSCR 662, Iraq, 9 August 1990, 82, 83, 87
UNSCR 664, Iraq, 18 August 1990, 83, 88
UNSCR 665, Iraq, 25 August 1990, 83, 89, 90
UNSCR 666, Iraq, 13 September 1990, 83
UNSCR 667, Iraq, 16 September 1990, 83, 88
UNSCR 668, Cambodia, 20 September 1990, 35
UNSCR 669, Iraq, 24 September 1990, 84
UNSCR 670, Iraq, 25 September 1990, 84, 87, 314
UNSCR 674, Iraq, 29 October 1990, 84, 88, 91, 93
UNSCR 677, Iraq, 28 November 1990, 84
UNSCR 678, Iraq, 29 November 1990, 79, 82, 83, 84, 88-93 *passim*
UNSCR 687, Iraq, 3 April 1991, 167, 319, 319-21, 322
UNSCR 688, Iraq, 5 April 1991, 167, 168, 192
UNSCR 693, El Salvador, 1991, 263
UNSCR 696, Angola, 1991, 302
UNSCR 707, Iraq, August 1991, 322
UNSCR 713, Croatia, 25 September 1991, 148n7, 315
UNSCR 715, Iraq, October 1991, 321
UNSCR 733, Somalia, 23 January 1992, 120-2, 168, 169, 172
UNSCR 746, Somalia, 17 March 1992, 123, 124, 168
UNSCR 747, Angola, 1992, 303
UNSCR 751, Somalia, 24 April 1992, 124, 125, 168, 172
UNSCR 757, Yugoslavia, 30 May 1992, 315
UNSCR 766, Cambodia, 21 July 1992, 41
UNSCR 767, Somalia, 27 July 1992, 127, 168
UNSCR 775, Somalia, 28 August 1992, 127, 168
UNSCR 780, Yugoslavia, 169, 170, 202
UNSCR 783, Cambodia, 13 October 1992, 41
UNSCR 787, Yugoslavia, 16 November 1992, 315
UNSCR 792, Cambodia, 30 November 1992, 42

UNSCR 794, Somalia, 3 December 1992, 129, 131, 168, 169, 174, 194
UNSCR 804, Angola, 29 January 1993, 304, 305
UNSCR 810, Cambodia, 8 March 1993, 43
UNSCR 814, Somalia, 26 March 1993, 131, 169
UNSCR 820, Yugoslavia, 17 April 1993, 315, 316
UNSCR 823, Angola, 30 April 1993, 304
UNSCR 825, North Korea, 11 May 1993, 220
UNSCR 831, Cyprus, 27 May 1993, 277
UNSCR 834, Angola, 1 June 1993, 304
UNSCR 837, Somalia, 6 June 1993, 133
UNSCR 841, Haiti, 16 June 1993, 317
UNSCR 864, Angola, 1993, 305
UNSCR 865, Somalia, 22 September 1993, 134
UNSCR 878, Somalia, 30 October 1993, 135
UNSCR 885, Somalia, 16 November 1993, 136
UNSCR 886, Somalia, 18 November 1993, 136
UNSCR 889, Cyprus, 1993, 279
Sanctions Committee, 189
and sovereignty, 187
strengthening of, 33
and UNDOF, 286
and UNSCOM, 323, 324
and UNTAC, 38
see also individual countries
United Nations Special Commission in Iraq (UNSCOM), 24, 214, 217, 218, 220, 314, 319-24 *passim*
United Nations Transition Assistance Group (UNTAG), 57, 256, 257, 258, 259
United Nations Transitional Authority in Cambodia (UNTAC), 11, 36, 41, 42, 50, 55
casualties in, 54
and Cambodian elections, 43-4, 46-9
and civil administration, 44-6
economic and social effects of, 51-2
financing of, 52, 53, 186
and human rights, 49
mandate in, 36, 37, 43, 54
problems of, 38-9
staffing of, 45, 52, 56-7
United Nations Truce Supervision Organisation (UNTSO)
evaluation of, 282-3
financing of, 282, 284
historical overview of, 280-2
mandate and operations of, 282, 286
as peacekeeping operation, 280
success of, 287
United Nations' Field Operations Division, 38
United Provinces of the River Plate *see* Argentina
United Somali Congress (USC), 111, 112, 113, 114, 116, 123
United States
and Angola, 303, 304, 306, 308
and Argentina, 236, 238
and Berbera, 108
and Bosnia, 156, 157
and Cambodia, 27, 29, 31
and Cyprus, 276, 277
and the DPRK, 220
and El Salvador, 183, 262, 266, 268

INDEX 353

and Europe, 148
and Falkland Islands, 230, 233, 234, 235, 240, 241
and GOC, 247
and Gulf War, 63, 101, 168
  and Iraq, 65, 74, 76, 79, 80, 167
  confused signals to Iraq, 13, 97, 98
  domestic politics and, 94-5

  as leader of multinational force against Iraq, 90, 96
  and preventive diplomacy in, 69-72
  and Saddam Hussein, 58, 94-6, 97
and Haiti, 181
and Iraq, 62, 314 *see also* and Gulf War
and Kurds, 168
and MFO, 283, 284
and military support for humanitarian intervention, 179
and Namibia, 258
and Netherlands/Indonesia conflict, 243, 244, 245, 248
and Panama, 183
and Quakers, 10
and refugees, 188
and sanctions against Rhodesia, 312
rules of engagement, 179, 180
and Saudi Arabia, 75, 77
and Somalia, 108-21 *passim*, 124-9 *passim*, 139, 174, 175, 178 *see also* and UNITAF; and UNOSOM
and South Africa, 312
South China Sea, 226
and UNITAF, 130, 178
and UNOSOM II, 131, 134
and Soviet Union, 77, 33
and UN, 101, 184

and Yugoslavia, 146
United States Aid for International Development (USAID), 197
United States Congress, 312
UNMOGIP *see* United Nations Military Observers Group in India and Pakistan
UNOSOM *see* United Nations Operation in Somalia
UNPROFOR *see* United Nations Protection Force
UNSC *see* United Nations Security Council
UNSCOM *see* United Nations Special Commission in Iraq
UNTAC *see* United Nations Transitional Authority in Cambodia
Urquhart, Brian, 21, 22, 26, 184
Uruguay, 231, 295

Vale of Kashmir, 292, 298
Vance, Cyrus, 145, 146, 148, 151, 153, 155, 156, 159
Vance-Owen plan, 155, 156, 157, 316
Varosha, 277
Venezuela, 266
verification, 213, 214, 215, 216, 219, 220
Vespucci, Amerigo, 229
Vietnam war, 28
Vietnam, 10, 53, 223
  and Cambodia, 11, 27, 28, 29, 33, 53
  withdrawal from, 27, 29, 30, 31, 40
  and Paracel Islands, 223
  and South China Sea, 17, 18, 222, 224, 226
  and Spratly Islands, 223, 226
  and UN 29
  and UNTAC, 51
Vietnamese army, 29

Waldheim, Dr Kurt, 252
Walters, General Vernon, 239
war crimes, 16
Warba island, 12, 62, 65, 66, 75
weapons of mass destruction, 212, 215, 216
 Iraqi, 24, 85, 93, 217, 220, 319, 321, 322, 323
Weinberger, Caspar, 240
Western European Union (WEU), 147, 147-8
Western Somali Liberation Front (WSLF), 107
West New Guinea, 32
World Bank, 200, 270
World Food Program, 166, 168, 193, 198, 199, 251
 and Africa Rights, 178
 in Angola, 304
 functions of, 195, 196, 197
 and Liberia, 182
 and Somalia, 126, 128, 170
World Health Organisation (WHO), 173, 195
World Vision, 175
World War I, 141, 163, 212
World War II, 141, 142, 163

Yemen
 and Iraq, 73, 74, 323
  and UN resolutions on Iraq, 83, 84, 87, 88
 and Somalia, 115
Yongbyon, 219
Yugoslav National Army (JNA), 141, 145, 149, 153, 154
Yugoslavia, 3, 16, 17, 118, 140, 169, 311
 collapse of, 140, 141, 181
 conferences on, 151, 159
 and Europe, 143-6, 146-8
 intervention in, 121, 171, 190
 Macedonians in, 141
 sanctions against, 315-16, 328
 Serbs in, 141
 and UNHCR, 193
 UNSC, 148
 war in, 140-1
 see also United Nations Security Council, Resolutions
Yugoslavia, Federal Republic of (FRY), 315, 316, 317

Zaire, 309
Zimbabwe, 120, 124
Zurich-London Accords, 1959, 273, 275